NINTH EDITION

SEXUALITY TODAY

Gary F. Kelly
Clarkson University

McGraw-Hill
Higher Education

Boston   Burr Ridge, IL   Dubuque, IA   New York   San Francisco   St. Louis
Bangkok   Bogotá   Caracas   Kuala Lumpur   Lisbon   London   Madrid   Mexico City
Milan   Montreal   New Delhi   Santiago   Seoul   Singapore   Sydney   Taipei   Toronto

McGraw-Hill
Higher Education

Published by McGraw-Hill, an imprint of The McGraw-Hill Companies, Inc., 1221 Avenue of the Americas, New York, NY 10020. Copyright © 2008, 2006, 2004, 2001, 1998, 1996 by The McGraw-Hill Companies. All rights reserved. No part of this publication may be reproduced or distributed in any form or by any means, or stored in a database or retrieval system, without the prior written consent of The McGraw-Hill Companies, Inc., including, but not limited to, in any network or other electronic storage or transmission, or broadcast for distance learning.

This book is printed on acid-free paper.

3 4 5 6 7 8 9 0 BAN/BAN 0 9

ISBN 978-0-07-338266-1
MHID 0-07-338266-3

Editor in Chief: *Michael Ryan*
Publisher: *Beth Mejia*
Sponsoring Editor: *Suzanna Z. Ellison*
Marketing Manager: *James Headley*
Director of Development: *Dawn Groundwater*
Developmental Editor: *Trish Nealon*
Supplements Editor: *Emily Pecora*
Text Permissions Coordinator: *Martha Moga*
Production Editor: *Leslie LaDow*
Manuscript Editor: *Mary Roybal*
Art Director: *Jeanne M. Schreiber*

Designer: *Cassandra Chu*
Interior Designer: *Glenda King*
Cover Designer: *Linda Beaupré*
Art Editor: *Ayelet Arbel*
Illustrator: *Patrick Lane*
Photo Research Coordinator: *Nora Agbayani*
Production Supervisor: *Randy Hurst*
Media Project Manager: *Ron Nelms, Jr.*
Composition: *10/12 Garamond by Aptara*
Printing: *45# Pub Thin Bulk by RR Donnelley, Menasha, WI*

Cover: © Keate/Masterfile

Credits: The credits section for this book begins on page C-1 and is considered an extension of the copyright page.

Library of Congress Cataloging-in-Publication Data
Kelly, Gary F.
  Sexuality today/Gary F. Kelly.—9th ed.
    p. cm.
  Includes bibliographical references and index.
  ISBN-13: 978-0-07-338266-1 (alk. paper)
  ISBN-10: 0-07-338266-3
  1. Sex. 2. Sex instruction. 3. Hygiene, Sexual. 4. Sex customs—United States. I. Title.
HQ21. K259 2008   2007036783

The Internet addresses listed in the text were accurate at the time of publication. The inclusion of a Web site does not indicate an endorsement by the authors or McGraw-Hill, and McGraw-Hill does not guarantee the accuracy of the information presented at these sites.

www.mhhe.com

For my family—Betsy, Casey and Sean, and Chelsea and Joey—my companions in learning about life and love. There is nothing more wonderful in my life than being with you.

Gary F. Kelly has been a sexuality educator for 35 years, publishing several popular books in the field. After a 30-year career as Counselor and Vice President for Student Affairs at Clarkson University and as Headmaster of The Clarkson School, he retired from administrative work to devote more time to writing, teaching, and counseling. He continues to teach the undergraduate courses in human sexuality and psycho-active substances in the Psychology Department at Clarkson University. Kelly was an innovator in developing graduate training in human sexuality for counselors and for over 20 years taught graduate courses in the counseling and human development program at St. Lawrence University. He maintains a practice as a licensed mental health counselor.

As a person who strongly believes that young people must have solid basic information about sex and their own sexuality in order to make rational and responsible decisions, Kelly presents here a balanced approach to the physical as well as the psychological and sociological aspects of human sexuality. His work with students received national recognition with his election to the board of directors of the Sexuality Information and Education Council of the United States (SIECUS). Kelly served for eight years as editor of the *Journal of Sex Education and Therapy* and presently serves as a member of the editorial board of the *American Journal of Sexuality Education*. He is a member of the American Association of Sexuality Educators, Counselors, and Therapists and of the Society for the Scientific Study of Human Sexuality. He is also a diplomat of the American Board of Sexology and a clinical fellow of the American Academy of Clinical Sexologists. He believes that his work with people in teaching, counseling, and therapy over the years has broadened his personal and professional perspective on how people integrate their sexuality into their lives.

The real people stories and real student voices in this book reflect that perspective.

Gary F. Kelly is available as a consultant and speaker in the field of human sexuality and sexuality education. For further information, e-mail gary.kelly@clarkson.edu or call (315) 265-2772.

Brief Contents

Contents

PART 2

Understanding Sexuality in Ourselves and in Our Relationships   138

PART 3

Human Reproduction, Contraception, and Abortion: Sexuality Confronts Social Policy   256

Chapter 10   Reproduction, Reproductive Technology, and Birthing   258

Chapter 11   Decision Making about Pregnancy and Parenthood   292

PART 4

Sexual Behavior and Contemporary Society   328

Chapter 12   Solitary Sex and Shared Sex   330

Preface

Approach of the Text

Robert C. Solomon, in *Love, Emotion, Myth, and Metaphor,* states that "love can be understood only 'from the inside,' as a language can be understood only by someone who speaks it, as a world can be understood only by someone who lives in it." I have spent a great deal of time working to understand the nature of my own sexuality and its place in my life. Although my sexual values have shifted and changed through the years, the core of those values has remained stable and forms the basis of my goals for this book.

- Sexual natures are essentially healthy and good. Decisions about sexual behaviors, however, must be made with careful thought, because the potential for negative consequences also exists.
- Each individual must spend time understanding the place and importance of sexuality in his or her life.
- Each of us has a responsibility to show concern for other people who come into our lives in a romantic or sexual encounter. Sex ceases to become healthy and positive when it is exploitative or hurtful.
- People differ greatly in their sexual and gender orientations and behaviors, and it is important for all persons to find the sexual lifestyles that will yield the most happiness, satisfaction, peacefulness, and fulfillment for them.
- People almost inevitably will experience some sort of sexual problem at various points in their lives, and it usually takes some work to overcome those problems and their effects on a person's sense of self. Nonetheless, the responsibility for seeking appropriate help with such problems rests with each individual. Nobody can do it for us.

The Field of Human Sexuality

The field of human sexuality is filled with controversy, even among the sexologists who conduct research, construct models, and develop theories. Scientific findings are not always comfortably aligned with prevailing social opinion. I believe that it is the job of a textbook author to document the various primary bodies of thought as accurately as possible, and I have attempted to stay true to that aim with each revision of the text. Each time, I carefully weigh and consider the prevailing evidence on issues of sexuality and try to do justice to those issues. Although some disagree, I do not feel it is my task to shape the attitudes and belief systems of others beyond what our cultural imperatives demand. My task, I believe, is to inform and enlighten with as much open-mindedness, honesty, and accuracy as possible. The controversies surrounding sexuality fascinate me. For readers of this text, they should become fodder for discussion, debate, and self-appraisal. As I can surely testify, it is reasonable to change your mind after having weighed all the evidence on an issue conscientiously.

With each revision, I am continually reminded of the growth of the field of sexuality in terms of both acceptability and scholarly focus over the past 35 years, as more and more outstanding young academics are attracted to its ranks. As I have watched sexology grow and develop over the course of my career, it has been especially exciting to be able to document the constant progress toward understanding the nuances of sexual physiology, psychology, and relational interaction. It is gratifying to have increasing numbers of students inquire about how they might enter sexology as a profession. I am also very pleased with the positive reactions to past and current editions of the text I have received from both faculty members and students. Their feedback and good suggestions help form the new template for each edition.

Goals of the Text

The charge of the ninth edition was to reinforce and strengthen the four underlying goals that have been in place throughout all editions. Those goals are to provide a text that is

- informative and as up-to-date as possible
- readable, engaging, and interesting for the reader
- colorful, with a relevant illustration and photo program that is scientifically accurate
- personally challenging as it poses ethical and values-related questions to readers

The extensive improvements to the text in this edition are outlined in detail below. I am grateful to all those instructors and students who have provided feedback on their experiences using *Sexuality Today*. Their comments have again served as the cornerstone for this revision.

Overview of Key Changes in the Ninth Edition

The many instructors and students who have used *Sexuality Today* in previous editions have been a valued source of information about changes of topical focus, new areas of interest, and effective strategies for using the book. In this edition, we have focused our revision on three major areas: a streamlined format, updated and reorganized content, and a fresh look at the pedagogical program within the book.

Because an appeal of this book has always been its manageable format, a primary goal of this edition was to streamline extraneous or outdated material where possible to allow inclusion of new topics and illustrations without increasing the size of the book.

This effort has enabled us to add several new photographs and figures, which convey information succinctly and engagingly. In addition, nearly 700 new references, providing the most up-to-date facts and research available from 2004 to 2007, are included in the ninth edition.

Content has been considerably updated and reorganized, designed to better reflect trends in the course and to make the book easier to teach and learn from. For example:

- Chapter 1 is condensed and updated to reflect the current "culture wars" in the United States as reflected in attitudes and policies related to human sexuality.
- The former chapter on the life span is divided into two chapters, based on the advice of several reviewers. This enables us to take a closer look at "Sexuality in Infancy, Childhood, and Adolescence" (Chapter 6) and at "Adult Sexuality and Relationships" (Chapter 7).
- The material on sexuality education is integrated into the new Chapter 6, and the material on sexually debilitating illness has been moved to Chapter 7. These placements are consistent with the developmental focus in these chapters.
- The former chapters on sexually transmitted diseases and HIV/AIDS are combined into a single chapter (Chapter 17) in this edition. This change again was based on reviewer suggestions and represents a positive step in offering more integrated coverage of the material.
- The material on sex and disability groups was moved to Chapter 8, "Sexual Individuality and Sexual Values," where it is a better fit with the themes of the chapter.
- Some new illustrations of same-sex sexual activity are added to Chapter 12, "Solitary Sex and Shared Sex," as recommended by several reviewers.

- The coverage of Chapter 13 is broadened to include identity formation for both heterosexual and homosexual people, based on the latest concepts.
- The opening chapter on sexual problems, Chapter 16, is expanded to include issues of sexual consent, a concept fundamental to understanding sexual coercion.
- In keeping with a growing emphasis on ethical thinking about sexuality, questions and dilemmas of an ethical nature are dispersed throughout the chapters.

Case studies and special sections on high-interest topics help apply concepts in the chapters to everyday life and extend topics into new dimensions. In *Sexuality Today*, these sections serve the overall theme of the book by focusing on topics of current interest, often with an individual voice. For example:

- The Case Studies that previously had a clinical focus have been modified and renamed to reflect stories of "Real People." Each of these stories is accompanied by questions for the student reader to consider.
- A new feature called "Real Student Voices" has been added to each chapter, reflecting engaging and fascinating comments about human sexuality made by actual students.
- The cross-cultural boxes formerly found in each chapter have been omitted in this edition, with cultural material being more fully integrated into the narrative itself. This has reduced the rather limited focus of the "boxes" and promotes better contextual understanding of the crucial role culture plays in establishing attitudes and values related to human sexuality.
- The support program for students and instructors has been streamlined and improved as well.
- With the material formerly found in the SexSource CD now available on SexSource Online, I have been able to add references to even more film clips that students will find helpful to the learning process, and these should be even more easily accessed.

A Word about Accuracy and Research

One of my major concerns has been to document sex-related controversies as objectively as possible. When I served as editor of the *Journal of Sex Education and Therapy,* and currently as a member of the editorial board of the *American Journal of Sexuality Education,* I often have found it disconcerting to note how many authors cite statements from other authors as fact, when they are only hypotheses or generalizations based on limited personal observations. I have taken this into account in preparing this text. It seems that controversy surrounds every sex-related issue. Ideas such as the nature-versus-nurture views on gender identity and sexual orientation, the various points of view about assistive reproductive technologies, the differences and similarities between genders, and the issue of sexually explicit materials on the Internet are examples of topics for which there really is not enough empirical evidence currently to justify definitive conclusions. In this edition, I have used the context of the culture wars in the United States as a way of conceptualizing some of these controversies.

Throughout the book, I have followed the American Psychological Association style, so that authors are cited and enclosed within parentheses; full bibliographical details can be found in the reference list. I have also attempted to follow the guidelines established by the Committee on Lesbian and Gay Concerns of the American Psychological Association in discussing issues related to sexual orientation. Some readers surely will take exception to what they perceive as another attempt at political correctness. I firmly believe that when it comes to the use of words describing various groups of people, we all have a responsibility to choose terms that have been reasonably determined by members of those groups to be fair and inoffensive.

I would welcome comments or suggestions for future editions from readers. I enjoy making contact with those who have connected with my words. If the spirit moves you, let me hear from you.

Supplements

The supplements listed here may accompany Kelly, *Sexuality Today,* Ninth Edition. Contact your McGraw-Hill representative for details concerning policies, prices, and availability, as some restrictions may apply.

Instructional Resources
at www.mhhe.com/kelly9

The instructor's resource site contains the following excellent resources for instructors using the book: Instructor's Manual, Test Bank, and PowerPoint presentations. New features in this comprehensively revised **Instructor's Manual,** by Layton Seth Curl of Metropolitan State College of Denver, include classroom activities, demonstrations, and the new Total Teaching Reference Package. Building on a traditional chapter outline, all the McGraw-Hill resources available to you have been correlated to the main concepts in each chapter. Suggested activities take particular

account of class size and offer a useful timeline estimate for completion. The final section offers tips on study skills and how to use the Internet in teaching, as well as a list of transparencies.

The thoroughly expanded and revised **Test Bank,** by Mike Kelly of Henderson State University, includes a wide range of multiple-choice, fill-in-the-blank, and critical thinking questions, as well as five short essay questions per chapter. Each item is designated as factual, conceptual, or applied as defined by Benjamin Bloom's Taxonomy of Educational Objectives. The **PowerPoint presentations** by Kim Foreman cover the key points of each chapter and include charts and graphs from the text where relevant. They can be used as is or modified to meet your personal needs. The instructor's materials are available on the Instructor's Online Learning Center at www.mhhe.com/kelly9. Ask your McGraw-Hill representative for access information.

SexSource Online

SexSource Online is a website for students and instructors featuring a collection of over 60 educational video clips on core concepts of human sexuality. Icons appear throughout the text to indicate clips that correspond to specific topics. Each video is accompanied by pre- and post-viewing questions. **SexSource Online** content and assessment items are also included in the course cartridge and may be used in an online course. Access **SexSource Online** from the student or instructor Online Learning Center at www.mhhe.com/kelly9. The site is password-protected at the request of many of the video rightsholders, but access is free to all users of this book. Use the following code to register: G8JR-Y9P7-TTEH-9487-THW4.

Online Learning Center for Students

The official website for the text (www.mhhe.com/kelly9), authored by Gary Krolikowski of SUNY Empire State College, contains chapter outlines, practice quizzes that can be e-mailed to the professor, links to relevant Internet sites, and a glossary of key terms.

From McGraw-Hill's Contemporary Learning Series
Annual Editions: Human Sexuality

This annually updated reader is a compilation of carefully selected articles from magazines, newspapers, and journals. An online **Instructor's Resource Guide** with testing materials and **Using *Annual Editions* in the Classroom** are available as support material for instructors.

Taking Sides: Clashing Views in Human Sexuality

This debate-style reader is designed to introduce students to opposing positions on the field's most crucial issues. Each issue is carefully framed for the student, and the pro and con essays represent the arguments of leading scholars and commentators in their fields. An **Instructor's Resource Guide** with testing materials and **Using *Taking Sides* in the Classroom** are also available online for instructors.

Acknowledgments

More people than I can properly recall have given me encouragement and suggestions for writing this book and revising it through its various editions. A number of them have offered specific help toward its improvement. These professionals and colleagues deserve thanks and acknowledgment. Before I began to write an earlier version, helpful suggestions were given to me by the late Mary S. Calderone, founder and former president of the Sexuality Information and Education Council of the United States (SIECUS); Michael Carrera, then at Hunter College, CUNY; and Patricia Schiller, founder of the American Association of Sex Educators, Counselors, and Therapists (AASECT).

I am greatly indebted to a number of my distinguished colleagues who gave their professional advice and helpful comments in reviewing the various editions of this book:

Ninth Edition

Robert D. Boroff, *Mount Jacinto College*
Elizabeth G. Calamidas, *The Richard Stockton College of New Jersey*
Susan Frantz, *Highline Community College*
Lois Laynor Goldblatt, *Arizona State University*
Ethel G. Jones, *South Carolina State University*
Kris Koehne, *University of Tennessee—Knoxville*
Ann Kolodji, *Ithaca College*
Natasha Otto, *Morgan State University*
Jane Vecchio, *Holyoke Community College*

Previous Editions

Connie C. Alexander, *Tarrant County Junior College–Northwest*
Srijana M. Bajracharya, *University of Maine at Presque Isle*
Janice and John Baldwin, *University of California, Santa Barbara*
C. Peter Bankart, *Wabash College*
Karen R. Blaisure, *Virginia Polytechnic Institute and State University*
Marilyn Blumenthal, *SUNY College of Technology at Farmingdale*
Sheila D. Brandick, *University of Regina*

Peggy Brick, *Planned Parenthood, Inc., of Bergen County*
Vern L. Bullough, *State University College of Buffalo*
T. Jean Byrne, *Kent State University*
Sandra L. Caron, *University of Maine, Orono*
Glenn Carter, *Austin Peay State University*
Carol Cassell, *Institute for Sexuality Education and Equity*
Caroline Clements, *University of North Carolina, Wilmington*
Edward E. Coates, *Judge Ely Family Healthcare*
William Collins, *West Virginia University*
Dennis Dailey, *University of Kansas*
Donald R. Devers, *Northern Virginia Community College*
John P. Elia, *San Francisco State University*
Geri Falconer-Ferneau, *Arizona State University*
Richelle Frabotta, *Social Health Education*
Suzanne Frayser, *Colorado College*
Gere B. Fulton, *The University of Toledo*
David A. Gershaw, *Arizona Western College*
Jane F. Gilgun, *University of Minnesota*
Keith Graber-Miller, *Goshen College*
Cynthia Grace, *City College, CUNY*
Maylou Hacker, *Modesto Junior College*
Susan E. Hetherington, *University of Maryland*
Karen M. Hicks, *Lehigh University*
Janet I. Hirsch, *University of Rhode Island*
India Hosch, *Virginia Polytechnic and State University*
Bobby Hutchinson, *Modesto Community College*
Kimberly Hyatt, *Weber State University*
Shulamith Kane, *Nassau Community College*
Peter T. Knoepfler, *sex therapist in private practice*
Jennifer Krumm, *Chabot/Las Positas Community College*
Kelly Kyes, *Wake Forest University*
Molly Laflin, *Bowling Green State University*
Phillip Lau, *DeAnza College*
Bruce D. LeBlanc, *Black Hawk College*
Stuart Lisbe, *William Paterson College of New Jersey*
Teresa L. Mattson, *Keene State College*
Brian R. McNaught, *consultant to corporations and universities on the effects of homophobia; trainer; author*
Amy G. Miron, *Catonsville Community College*
Charles D. Miron, *Catonsville Community College*
Owen Morgan, *Arizona State University*
Lin Myers, *California State University, Stanislaus*
Marilyn Myerson, *University of South Florida*
Christopher Ousley, *North Carolina State University*
Nancy Parsons, *Western Illinois University*
Robert Pollack, *University of Georgia*
James Ponzetti, *Central Washington University*
Barry Poris, *Long Island University*
James H. Price, *University of Toledo*
Laurna Rubison, *University of Illinois*
Robin Sawyer, *University of Maryland*
Kay F. Schepp, *University of Vermont*
Sharon P. Shriver, *Penn State University*
Dick Skeen, *Northern Arizona University*
Stephen Southern, *The Sexual Medicine Institute of Southeast Louisiana*

Sherman Sowby, *California State University, Fresno*

Kandy J. Stahl, *Stephen F. Austin State University*

Ruth Stoltzfus, *Goshen College*

Marilyn Story, *University of Northern Iowa*

Edward R. Sunshine, *Barry University*

Karen S. Tee, *Vanier College*

James E. Tucker, *Minneapolis, Minnesota*

Karen Vail-Smith, *East Carolina University*

Robert F. Valois, *University of Texas at Austin*

Paul Villas, *New Mexico State University, Main Campus*

Michael G. Walraven, *Jackson Community College*

Mary Ann Watson, *Metropolitan State College of Denver*

Marti M. Weaver, *Collin County Community College, Central Park Campus*

Burton A. Weiss, *Drexel University*

Patricia Whelehan, *State University of New York, Potsdam*

Jan Widdell, *Auburn University*

Elva Winter, *York College*

William L. Yarber, *Indiana University*

My wife, Betsy, has been a constant source of good ideas for this text. She read each chapter and offered many suggestions for making the book more readable and interesting. My student assistant, Michael Moses, did a fine job of organizing the many new references for this edition and coordinating the new Reference list.

I want to acknowledge the help of the many people within the McGraw-Hill staff who have played such an essential role in preparing the manuscript and producing the book. They include Suzanna Ellison, Executive Editor; Dawn Groundwater, Director of Development; Trish Nealon, Developmental Editor; Leslie LaDow, Production Editor; Cassandra Chu, Designer; Nora Agbayani, Photo Research Coordinator; Ayelet Arbel, Art Editor; Randy Hurst, Production Supervisor; and Ron Nelms, Media Project Manager. I feel privileged to be able to keep this book available to students through the efforts of this highly motivated and professional group, and I thank them for the high quality that has been maintained in this updated edition.

Gary F. Kelly
Clarkson University
P.O. Box 5825
Potsdam, NY 13699-5825
E-mail: gary.kelly@clarkson.edu

Student Walkthrough

The chapters in this book are carefully organized to help you study efficiently and effectively. Each element has been reviewed and tested by instructors and students using the book in previous editions.

CHAPTER OUTLINE

Each chapter begins with a brief outline of the main headings to preview the topics covered. Use the Chapter Outline along with the Chapter Summary to review the chapter content more effectively.

RELEVANT QUOTATIONS

Each chapter also begins with a brief quotation, some of which come directly from my own counseling sessions or classes. These carefully selected statements, opinions, and ideas provide a personalized perspective on some major concept discussed in the chapter.

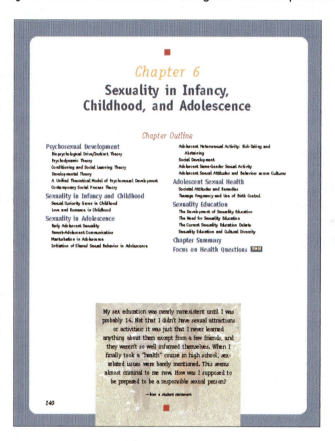

SEXSOURCE ONLINE

This exclusive site contains dozens of video clips related to chapter topics and is available from the Online Learning Center. See p. xiv for the access code.

REAL PEOPLE STORIES

These stories illustrate in some detail a sexual problem or dilemma related to the issues discussed in the chapter. For the most part, I have drawn these anecdotes from my own experience as a sexuality educator and counselor. "Real People" presents statements about specific persons rather than research studies on groups of people.

REAL STUDENT VOICES

These are excerpts from student responses to various written assignments I have given to my own classes. Thanks to my contributors for their permission to use the (anonymous) statements.

CROSS-CULTURAL MATERIAL

This material is now more thoroughly integrated within the text, reflecting the broad diversity of sexual attitudes in today's world.

Real People

Mike: Struggling with a Long-Distance Relationship

Let's return to Mike, the first-year college student intending to be faithful to his long-distance girlfriend, as described on page 208. During his second month away at college, his circumstances become more complicated.

Mike has become friends with other members of the intramural soccer team on which he plays. On a weekend evening in mid-October, the team has a party at an off-campus apartment of some of the upperclass students. A women's intramural team has been invited. Mike is happy to attend the party, because he has been feeling down after a phone conversation with his girlfriend earlier in the week. She hinted that maybe they ought to rethink their relationship and even begin seeing others. Mike expressed his anger and hurt over that option, communicating that he wanted to work hard at maintaining their commitment. Eventually, she agreed that she would abide by their original plan, and she apologized for upsetting him.

The beer at the party is plentiful, the music is loud, and everyone is having a good time. A young woman sits down beside Mike, and they strike up a conversation. He knows her from one of his biology classes and has found her attractive. Eventually, they become engrossed in conversation and with each other. They have a lot in common, and both are having some struggles with long-distance relationships.

As the evening progresses, the girl leans over and kisses Mike on the lips. He is surprised at first but reciprocates, and they continue making out. As others begin to disperse, Mike suggests that she come back to his dorm room with him. He explains that he is lonely but also does not want to do anything either one of them will regret. She kisses him and says that she doesn't believe in regrets.

On their walk back to campus, Mike realizes that he has had a lot to drink and that he probably isn't making the clearest decisions. He also is very curious about what might develop once they get back to his room. Once there, the young woman lies down on his bed and motions for him to join her. He obliges, and before long they are heavily involved in making out again. Eventually, she reaches down and unzips the fly on his pants, indicating that she is willing to perform oral sex on him.

Should Mike continue with this sexual encounter? What is the right thing for him to do? What are the points of ethical conflict raised by this situation? Besides Mike and the young woman he met at the party, who else could be affected by the decisions made and the actions taken? What are the potential consequences of the various actions that could be taken now or have already been taken? What duties and obligations does Mike have?

Think of some behaviors that might ultimately be helpful to someone else but still wouldn't be considered right. Explain your answer.

Another aspect of morality is the expectation that behavior will conform with certain social norms. Every society establishes certain rules and expectations in order to accomplish shared goals. Certainly, social nonconformity sometimes is used as a form of protest against social rules that are considered unfair, but if it is simply a self-serving action to avoid social responsibility, such nonconformity would be considered ethically questionable. Theories of moral development suggest that while parental influences are critical in the early stages, individuals gradually internalize ethical standards without the need for external enforcement; coerced acts cannot really be considered as moral (Hennig, 2003; Pratt, 2003).

Psychologists see empathy, or identifying with the feelings of others, as a strong motivator for ethical behavior. Empathy for another can be very powerful, and it follows that we feel guilt if we act in opposition to the well-being of others. Such reactions are what help make up the human *conscience*.

Ethical dilemmas must also be subject to the reasoning of rational thought processes, as we think through issues concerning justice and fairness. Perhaps one of the most dramatic aspects of a well-developed sense of morality is the willingness to put the needs and interests of someone else ahead of our own needs and interests, especially if some human cost is incurred through the action (Rest, Narvaez, Thoma, & Bebeau, 2000).

Sorting through ethical issues, therefore, involves thoughts, emotions, and eventually behavior. Over the years, I have found it useful to use an ap-

---

Real Student Voices

■ I really love my girlfriend, and we are sexually involved. However, she doesn't talk much about what she enjoys during sex, and I often feel as though she doesn't enjoy it all that much. I'm confused as to whether this is because of something going on with her, or something wrong with my technique.

■ I can't seem to get J to talk about his feelings, and that is very frustrating to me. He says I want to talk about feelings too much, and sometimes he just wants to be quiet and enjoy being together. He also thinks I worry too much about the relationship. Maybe I do, but it's important to me.

■ The two of us are able to talk about everything and anything, which is a lot different than my former relationships. I never thought I could have this kind of relationship, but it is great. We have no secrets.

up games to which only one person knows the rules. Sometimes they work, but when they do a relationship has been established on the basis of manipulation or even dishonesty. Usually the best "strategy" is to work at being yourself.

Myth 4: Using the right line will convince a partner to have sex. Rarely are relationships that simple. While one partner is rehearsing the line to carry out a seduction, the other partner may well be rehearsing the best way to turn down the proposition. Sexual relationships that grow out of invented lines rarely are effective or lasting, and enticing someone into sex in this manner is ethically objectionable.

Myth 5: The rational mind is the only basis for effective communication. People often make the mistake of assuming that logical, rational thought processes constitute the only basis of good communication. There is a common misconception that "feelings only get in the way." In fact, emotional reactions are a legitimate part of what human beings need to communicate, especially in close relationships. To work with only one aspect of human nature during communication is to ignore crucial parts of yourself that need to be shared.

These myths can form the basis of a surefire prescription for how to stifle good communication. They stimulate the development of games, phony conversation, manipulative sexual seduction, and shallow relationships. When effective communication is lacking, even minor sexual problems are more likely to turn into major ones.

See "Communicating about Sex" on SexSource Online.

The Sexual Games We Play

Romantic and sexual relationships can involve a dynamic tension between two people that results in posturing and attempts at "reverse psychology" to achieve certain ends. Whether it is playing hard to get in order to win over the heart of Mr. or Ms. Right or deciding not to return a call until a certain amount of time has passed, people try to develop a strategy that will help them feel they can control an outcome. We live with the illusion that if we always do X and Y, we automatically will get Z as the result. Human relationships are more complicated than mathematical equations or generalized scientific predictions. They must be approached in very individualized ways. Nevertheless, people are forever playing games with one another when it comes to sex and relationships. Following are descriptions of some of the most common sexual games.

---

attitudes and values of Christian missionaries who taught in their boarding schools. Native Americans were originally a more gender-equitable people whose men and women shared the responsibilities of child rearing. European males tended to see themselves as superior to females, however, and the sense of equality between men and women gradually was subsumed by Eurocentric attitudes (Herdt, 2000).

Colleges are working to enhance the understanding and acceptance of cultural diversity, including customs related to gender and sexuality. On many campuses, it is not unusual to see orthodox Muslim women wearing clothing and veils that cover most of their bodies and faces. A *burqua* is a garment that covers the woman's body from head to toe, with only a slot for sight (see Figure 1.2). Islam has very specific religious laws concerning the behaviors of women and men, and male supremacy is a fundamental tenet. Nevertheless, Islam recognizes the complementarity of male and female and celebrates sexual pleasure within marriage.

Around the world, efforts are under way to equalize the availability of sexual health resources cross-culturally. At an international conference in 1994, representatives from 179 nations around the globe agreed to make reproductive health accessible to all by the year 2015. Sexual health services are an integral part of the plan. After this goal slipped out of

favor for a few years, it was reaffirmed at the 2005 World Summit. Progress toward the goal has been uneven; issues of sexual and reproductive health are often paid good lip service but lose out when it comes to the allocation of resources. Nevertheless, in the poorest areas of the world, unsafe sex is the second most important risk factor for disease, disability, or death (Fathalla, Sinding, Rosenfield, & Fathalla, 2006; Glasier et al., 2006).

When it comes to judging the sexual beliefs and practices of people from other cultures, would you consider yourself more of a relativist or an absolutist?

From Sexual Revolution to Culture Wars

Have you heard about the "**sexual revolution**"? What have you imagined to be true of this vaguely defined period in recent history? Unbridled sex? Hippies romping in the nude at Woodstock? What the term really indicates is simply the change that has occurred over time. Ideals and values about sex and love in Western cultures have seen dramatic shifts in the past two centuries. The Puritan ideal was for love between men and women to evolve within marriage, as two people began to know each other better. During the Victorian era (1837–1901), love and sex were considered to be separate human experiences, with love being the romantic and spiritual union that ideally preceded and precipitated marriage. Although sex was recognized as a part of marriage in cautious moderation, lustful passions were not to be let out of control lest people become slaves to their sexual emotions. Love and sex between people of the same gender were not openly discussed. Sex was not linked to love, because to link the two would in fact have been considered a threat to the love that was assumed to undergird marital stability. With sex being given such a conflicted place within marriage, prostitution and pornography flourished in Victorian society (Allyn, 2000).

Following World War II, the United States experienced significant and relatively abrupt changes in sexual attitudes, values, and behaviors. Eventually that period was dubbed the sexual revolution. The sexual revolution encompassed a variety of complex changes in values and behaviors. We will look at some significant examples.

FIGURE 1.2 *Cultural Standards for Appropriate Dress*
People's attitudes about their sexuality and their bodies are strongly influenced by their cultures. These Afghan women wear the traditional burqua that reveals nothing of their bodies or faces. Not all Muslim women accept such strict standards of dress, while others consider them appropriate for their beliefs.
Source: AP Photo/Sergei Grits.

sexual revolution the changes in thinking about sexuality and sexual behavior in society that occurred in the 1960s and 1970s.

CRITICAL THINKING QUESTIONS

Placed strategically throughout the text, these questions can help you look more deeply at the issues, tapping your intellectual and analytical skills to challenge yourself more effectively.

VISUAL ART PROGRAM

Figures were selected to clarify and extend the material in the text. Charts, graphs, and tables reflect the most recent research available. Many new illustrations and four-color photos have been included in this edition. All photographs and drawings were chosen to illustrate the concepts of human sexuality in a practical yet sensitive manner.

SELECTING SPERM

1. Sperm are dosed with a DNA-staining chemical. The X chromosome in a female-producing sperm has slightly more DNA than the Y chromosome in a male-producing sperm, so it takes up more dye.

2. A laser, shining on one sperm at a time, makes the stain glow.

3. The extra stain makes female-producing sperm glow more brightly.

4. A machine automatically sorts brighter sperm from dimmer ones.

FIGURE 10.15 *Selecting the Sex of Sperm*

Source: From Frederic Golden, !Boy? Girl? Up to You," *Time*, 21 September 1998, pp. 82–83. Copyright © 1998 Time, Inc. Reprinted with permission.

What are your opinions about being able to choose the sex of your child? Would you use technology to help you make such a choice?

A few approaches to selecting an infant's sex have emerged in modern technology. There are techniques by which either the X-bearing or the Y-bearing sperm may be sorted out before artificial insemination or IVF to increase the chances of the baby's being a girl or a boy. Though complicated and expensive, these techniques may increase the chances of having a girl to about 80 percent and the chances of having a boy to about 65 percent (see Figure 10.15). Other techniques have been suggested, including changing the diet prior to conception, timing intercourse to be slightly before or slightly after ovulation in the menstrual cycle, and modifying the pH of the vagina. Research has tended to indicate that such procedures do not produce statistically valid results and probably are worthless.

Source: Tribune Media Services, Inc. All rights reserved. Reprinted with permission.

The ability to choose the sex of a child raises some troublesome ethical issues both for the parents and for society. Studies in the United States consistently demonstrate that couples tend to have a preference for sons, especially as their first child. Also, when parents have had two children of the same sex, either female or male, there is a greater likelihood that they will have another child. The preference for male children is found in many cultures and can translate into prejudice and sexism (Belanger, 2002). This has raised fears among some that predetermination of gender could create a population overweighted with males, while others feel couples should be free to use available technology for choosing the sex of their children and that the genders ultimately will balance out (Layne, 1999).

Techniques such as chorionic villi sampling or amniocentesis (see p. 278) can identify the sex of a fetus within a few weeks of conception by identifying the sex chromosomes in fetal cells. Newer, noninvasive techniques are able to detect the sex of fetal cells that may be found in small numbers in the mother's blood, but these techniques are not believed to be entirely reliable (Kaiser, 2005). Beyond simply discovering the sex of their expected child, parents then have the option of early abortion if the sex of the child is not what they have hoped for. This has become a common, though illegal, practice in China, where couples generally are allowed only one child. The ratio of males to females among live births in China has increased in some rural areas to as high as 140 males to 100 females. There is growing concern about the imbalance of males and females in China, and the government has decided to provide financial incentives to parents of daughters in an attempt to offset the trend. Similar trends are developing in India, Bangladesh, Pakistan, and South Korea. Such an imbalance may have profound social implications and eventually may require some new partnering patterns for first marriages (Glenn, 2004).

Ethical questions have also been raised about the use of costly medical resources and procedures for what might be seen as frivolous, nonmedical reasons, when

SELF-EVALUATIONS

Sexuality is not a topic to be considered apart from the self or separate from the nuances of human relationships. I believe that we should take the time to understand our own sexuality and its place in our personality. To this end, I have included—in selected chapters—questionnaires, self-awareness exercises, and values clarification tools, under the heading "Self-Evaluation." By completing these activities, you may discover some things you did not know about yourself.

---

relationship, and the relationship helps shape the scripts and choices of its members. This complex interaction of factors constitutes the *social process* of psychosexual development.

Which of the six theories that attempt to explain psychosexual development seem most convincing to you? Why? Are there any aspects of different theories that you would combine to create a more viable theory?

■ Sexuality in Infancy and Childhood

Infancy and childhood are periods of human development that include a continuing emergence of sexuality that began prior to birth (see Figure 6.4). There is insufficient cross-cultural data to determine whether the patterns of sexual development observed in Western societies apply universally. Most of the anthropological information on childhood sexuality that we do have has been a by-product of broader studies, and anthropologists in general have been reluctant to focus on the sexual development of infants and children. The result is that we really do not have an entirely reliable picture of what constitutes "normal" childhood sexuality (Bancroft, 2003a; Graaf & Rademakers, 2006).

Ultrasound images of fetuses still in the uterus show that a male fetus can experience erection of the penis even before birth. Very soon after birth, infants seem to show interest in exploring their own bodies and in seeking whatever pleasure they can gain from that exploration. There is ample evidence to suggest that baby boys experience genital responses. Erection

FIGURE 6.4 *Infant Sexuality*

Infants develop an awareness of their bodies and their sexuality first through a bonding with their parents and the sensuous contact involved in cuddling and holding and second by exploring their own bodies, including their genitals.

has even been observed within the first few minutes after birth. A number of male infants seem to have orgasms, as evidenced by sequences of tension-building, rhythmic muscular contractions, and pelvic thrusting that culminate in what appear to be pleasurable sensations and relaxation. In baby girls, the labia may be quite prominent and the vaginal lining pinkish in color for several weeks after birth, the result of maternal hormones still present in the bloodstream. There is also evidence of vaginal lubrication that occurs spontaneously in regular cycles from the time a female is born (DeLamater & Friedrich, 2002; Singer, 2002).

Although these early patterns of physical arousal and sensual enjoyment do not represent the socialized patterns of eroticism that form later in human development, they do demonstrate the extreme sensitivity of infants. It has been suggested that the entire surface of the skin in a newborn infant is a single **erogenous zone**, meaning that it is sensitive to sensual stimulation that can contribute to a healthy skin eroticism (Singer, 2002).

The foundations for sensuality, intimacy, and relationship to other people are established during infancy. Bonding between infants and their parents is an important part of this process. Infancy may also be a time when small children begin to notice how they are treated by their fathers and mothers and to form early concepts of their relationships with others.

Several significant developmental tasks are accomplished during infancy. Immediately after birth, there is a period when babies seem very alert, and bonding occurs between them and their parent(s). The holding, touching, and cuddling given to an infant are part of the evolution of its ability to relate to and be intimate with others. Between 6 months and 1 year of age, babies begin to touch their genitals, if they are not prohibited from doing so. Our culture exhibits a fair amount of anxiety on the part of adults about recognizing and legitimizing the concept that for children to experience sexual and sensual *pleasure* might be perfectly healthy and normal. Yet this is a time of life when the very foundations for adult sexual pleasure are established, and this may be accomplished best within the context of a loving and pleasure-affirming environment (Jackson & Scott, 2004; Levine, 2002a). As we have seen in the preceding chapter, infancy is also the time when the baby begins to be socialized with regard to the cultural expectations of gender roles (Muehlenhard et al., 2003).

Sexual Curiosity Grows in Childhood

Children's sexual development proceeds along two parallel routes that sometimes cross. One stream is the

erogenous zone (a-RAJ-a-nus) any area of the body that is sensitive to sexual arousal.

Self-Evaluation

Examining Your Attitudes toward Sexually Transmitted Diseases

The following scale will give you an opportunity to explore some of your own beliefs, feelings, and intentions with regard to STDs. The scale was developed by Yarber, Torabi, and Veenker (1989) and has been tested with hundreds of college and secondary school students. The evaluation is for your own use only.

Directions: Please read each statement carefully. Record your first reaction by marking an "X" through the letter that best describes how much you agree with or disagree with the idea.

USE THIS KEY: SA = strongly agree
A = agree
U = undecided
D = disagree
SD = strongly disagree

Example: Doing things to prevent getting an STD is the job of each person.   SA   A   U   D   SD

REMEMBER: STD means sexually transmitted disease, such as gonorrhea, syphilis, genital herpes, or HIV disease.

(Mark "X" through letter)

1. How one uses his/her sexuality has nothing to do with STD.	SA A U D SD
2. It is easy to use the prevention methods that reduce one's chances of getting an STD.	SA A U D SD
3. Responsible sex is one of the best ways of reducing the risk of STD.	SA A U D SD
4. Getting early medical care is the main key to preventing harmful effects of STD.	SA A U D SD
5. Choosing the right sex partner is important in reducing the risk of getting an STD.	SA A U D SD
6. A high rate of STD should be a concern for all people.	SA A U D SD
7. People with an STD have a duty to get their sex partners to medical care.	SA A U D SD
8. The best way to get a sex partner to STD treatment is to take him/her to the doctor with you.	SA A U D SD
9. Changing one's sex habits is necessary once the presence of an STD is known.	SA A U D SD
10. I would dislike having to follow the medical steps for treating an STD.	SA A U D SD
11. If I were sexually active, I would feel uneasy doing things before and after sex to prevent getting an STD.	SA A U D SD
12. If I were sexually active, it would be insulting if a sex partner suggested we use a condom to avoid infection.	SA A U D SD
13. I dislike talking about STD with my peers.	SA A U D SD

FOCUS ON HEALTH

This feature appears at the end of each chapter and provides a list of questions pertaining to your personal health. Page numbers are provided for each question, and within each chapter the Focus on Health icon appears next to each related section in the text.

CHAPTER SUMMARY

Each chapter ends with a Chapter Summary, which highlights the main ideas of each chapter and has been expanded in this edition. As a study aid, you can coordinate the summary with the Chapter Outline at the beginning of the chapter in order to review the material effectively.

---

26. Scientific research on child and adolescent sexual abuse often has been inadequate, and there is controversy over the possibility that some sex between adolescents and someone older might be perceived positively by the adolescent.

27. Adult sexual abusers may have experienced neurological problems during development. Psychologically, they may view children as sexually motivated, have a history of being abused themselves, and exhibit symptoms of denial and depression. More often than not, the adult abuser is known by the child victim.

28. A child who is sexually abused may have a sense of guilt, shame, and betrayal, and the abuse may lead to an unhealthy sexualization of the child's life. As adults, survivors of sexual abuse are likely to experience depression, anxiety, and other physical and psychological problems, although cause-and-effect relationships have not been fully supported scientifically.

29. Victims of sexual abuse may be helped by immediate crisis intervention as well as longer-term supportive and counseling services.

30. Treatment programs are available for child sexual abuse offenders; the most effective of these programs emphasize ways to control their sexual im-

pulses and reduce their sexual desire for children. Some medications may have some effect in controlling sexual desire.

31. The term *incest* applies to sexual activity between closely related family members. It usually stems from unhealthy family patterns and creates serious confusion for the developing child or adolescent.

32. There is controversy over adult memories of childhood sexual abuse that are recovered in therapy. These recovered memories have been used in lawsuits. Some accused parents have fought such cases, and some professionals argue that these phenomena may represent false memories.

33. The best ways to prevent and deal with sexual problems are to be knowledgeable about human sexuality, develop communication skills based on qualities that facilitate good relationships, have realistic expectations about sex, and exercise caution and responsibility.

34. Sometimes it makes sense to seek professional help for dealing with sexual problems. Check out such professionals with great care and be suspicious about behavior that makes you uncomfortable or seems unethical.

Focus on Health Questions

In this section you will find the kinds of questions that you may have concerning your own health and sexuality. The page references indicate where in the text the answer is located; the exact place is marked with this logo: **F&H**

1. Are there any types of sexual behavior that are in themselves dangerous? **445–446**
2. What is a paraphilia? **446**
3. Is it true that people can become addicted to sex? **446–447**
4. What can I do if I am being sexually harassed? **450**
5. What should I look out for in a partner that might warn of potential sexual abusiveness? **456**
6. Can males be raped? **462**
7. What are the typical psychological reactions to being a victim of forced sex? **462**
8. How may victims of forced sex best be helped to recover? **463**
9. How does sexual abuse affect children during childhood and then later in adulthood? **467–468**
10. What should be done for a child after it has been discovered that the child has been sexually abused? **468–470**
11. Can child sexual abusers be treated? **470**
12. What are the effects of incestuous relationships on children? **470–471**
13. Are there any ways to head off sexual problems before they occur? **472**
14. If I have a sexual problem, how can I find a qualified professional to help me? **473–474**

Institutions and Sexual Issues

Some people with disabilities and chronic illnesses require long-term institutional care, in which case sexual problems may multiply. Where the sexes are segregated, institutional residents may be limited to same-gender sexual contact. They may have little privacy for masturbation or shared sex. The keys to preventing desexualization in institutions are the attitude of the staff and their understanding of the different levels of need that different people might have. Some institutions have provided condoms for patient use, along with educational efforts, and have found that these

actions do not cause an increase in patient sexual activity. Often, in-service training on sex-related issues and the establishment of humane administrative policies regarding sex can help. The first step in preventing sexual problems among the disabled, ill, or institutionalized is admitting that all human beings are sexual and have a right to find the best ways for them, as individuals, to express their sexuality. Steps then may be taken to categorize people according to the types of help they may require in order to realize and take charge of their own sexual identities and needs (Perry & Wright, 2006).

Chapter Summary

1. Human beings have the potential for participating in a range of sexual activities.
2. Definitions of normalcy and abnormality are influenced by prevailing social norms.
3. General labels such as deviation, variation, and paraphilia have been applied to sexual activities and preferences that fall outside the accepted norm.
4. In present-day Western culture, sex is still judged by several fundamental standards: two-person heterosexuality, a focus on coitus, expectation of orgasm and romantic feelings, and degree of safety.
5. The World Association for Sexology has adopted and promulgated a Universal Declaration of Sexual Right that affirms a wide range of freedoms regarding sexuality.
6. The ethnocentric attitude that one's own culture has the right standards in relation to sexuality can be called erotocentricity.
7. The concept of normalcy can be determined by statistical norms, by prevailing expert opinion (such as the *DSM-IV*), by moral standards perpetuated by religion and law, or as part of a more flexible continuum. Normalcy is a relative concept.
8. Labels represent generalities and are an inadequate aid to a full understanding of a particular person's sexuality.
9. The term *homosexual* often has negative connotations. The terms *gay* and *lesbian* are used in reference to people when describing same-gender orientation. The term *bisexual* is used to

describe some level of attraction to, or activity with, members of both sexes.

10. The factors that lead to the development of sexual individuality are highly complex. Patterns seem to be established by adolescence and probably develop through a combination of learning experiences, superimposed on some biological predispositions.
11. Social networks rather than relationships with parents seem to be important in shaping sexual attitudes and behaviors.
12. The Klein Sexual Orientation Grid demonstrates seven different variables that play a role in determining sexual orientation or identity. Sexual individuality includes many different life dimensions.
13. Sexual choices are affected by sexual attitudes. The National Health and Social Life Survey has identified three broad categories of sex-related attitudes in the United States: traditional, relational, and recreational. There is no single system of "American values" regarding sex.
14. Clear links have been observed between sexual attitudes and sexual practices, number of partners, and how often a person thinks about sex. Frequency of sex does not seem to be related to attitudinal group.
15. Large portions of people in the United States have negative feelings and discriminatory attitudes about gay, lesbian, bisexual, and transgender people. These fears and discomforts are called homophobia, biphobia, or transphobia. Professional organizations no longer view

---

GLOSSARY

Important terms and concepts appear in boldface within the text, and their definitions are highlighted in a separate area of the page for quick and easy reference. Other important terms and concepts are italicized within the text. A pronunciation guide is included in the glossary for those terms that are difficult for most students. The accent is indicated in capital letters. A complete alphabetized glossary appears at the end of the book.

Human sexuality and reproduction obviously are linked closely, both biologically and socially. The combining of genetic material in a way that produces another human being with characteristics of both parents is nothing short of a miracle. New understandings of reproduction, coupled with new biomedical technologies, have permitted these processes to be manipulated and transformed in ways that not long ago were considered science fiction.

Although reproduction of the human species once could not have taken place without sexual contact, reproductive technology now can intervene to bring sperm and egg together in a variety of ways. It is no longer even necessary for the sexual mother—the contributor of the egg—to be pregnant with the child that is eventually born. Indeed, reproduction and the prevention of reproduction have gone far beyond the realms of human sexuality and biology. Social policy, politics, legislation, court precedents, and ethical debate are now as much a part of understanding reproduction as is the age-old question "Where do babies come from?" This chapter addresses all these issues.

■ Fertilization and Fetal Development

During the menstrual cycle, an ovum matures and is released from one of the female's ovaries. Research indicates that fertilization of the ovum is most likely to occur when sperm are present during any of the six consecutive days of the cycle that end with the day of ovulation. The old assumption was that the most likely time for fertilization was during the two days following ovulation. However, there is also evidence that substantial numbers of women may ovulate more than once in a single menstrual cycle (Baerwald, Adams, & Pierson, 2003). As soon as semen is ejaculated from the penis into the vagina, the sperm begin their journey into the uterus, and they may remain viable for up to five days. A few thousand usually reach the fallopian tubes. The more sperm that are present, the greater the probability that fertilization, or conception, will occur. Sperm apparently have receptor molecules that are attracted to a sperm-attracting chemical released by the egg, and the membrane of the sperm cell contains a chemical called **fertilin** that seems to play a role in helping the sperm adhere to the egg and eventually penetrate its outer layer.

FIGURE 10.1 *Sperm Penetrating the Egg*

A sperm, with its oval head and long tail, approaches the egg, or ovum. Having been capacitated during its journey through the female reproductive tract, the sperm will secrete an enzyme that will help it penetrate the outer membrane of the ovum.

When a sperm cell comes into contact with the ovum, a very specific cell recognition process is triggered that binds the sperm tightly to the outer membrane of the ovum, or **zona pellucida**. The sperm then secretes enzymes that help it pass through the zona and its underlying membranes to penetrate into the ovum; the proteins on the surface of the ovum change rapidly, making the "lock-and-key" approach of fertilization a constantly evolving process. Usually, only one sperm manages to burrow its way into the interior of the ovum (see Figure 10.1), because a hard protein surface develops that prevents further sperm from entering. The actual mechanisms of sperm penetration and exclusion of other sperm are still only partially understood. If an extra sperm enters an ovum, it may well destroy the ovum, or its own genetic material may be destroyed. As the sperm passes through the outer layers of the ovum, it probably is primed by the hormone progesterone for the actual fertilization process. Contact with the zona pellucida seems to be essential to causing **exocytosis**, in which

fertilin (fer-TILL-in) a chemical in the outer membrane of a sperm that assists in attachment to the egg cell and penetration of the egg's outer membrane.

zona pellucida (ZO-nah pe-LOO-sa-da) the transparent, outer membrane of an ovum.

exocytosis (ex-oh-sye-TOH-sis) the release of genetic material by the sperm cell, permitting fertilization to occur.

SEXUALITY
TODAY

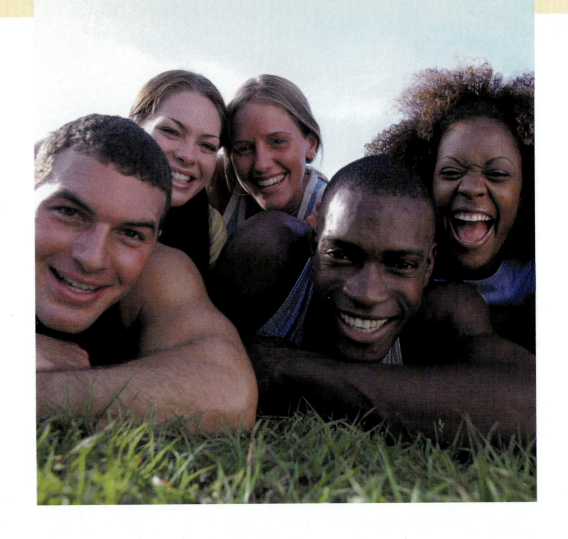

Part 1

Social and Biological Foundations of Human Sexuality

Studying sexuality is one avenue to a more complete understanding of human nature and human societies. In its broadest sense, sexuality is interwoven with all aspects of being human. It has been only during the last few generations that reliable information about human sexual arousal and response has emerged. As we venture further into the twenty-first century, much remains to be understood regarding all aspects of human sexuality.

To study sexuality is to dissolve disciplinary boundaries. The psychology of sex includes sexual orientations, behaviors, emotions, and interpersonal connections. The sociology and anthropology of sex mirror the many social, legal, political, and cultural patterns that play a role in human interactions. It has been said that sex is a biological function and love is a psychological function, but things are not that simple. Our sexuality is related to our attitudes and feelings, our social relationships, our cultural expectations, and our history. In terms of recorded human history, scientific inquiry and the scientific way of thinking represent relatively recent approaches to perceiving the world and human nature. Much work remains if we are to understand fully the interactions of body, mind, emotion, and spirit in human sexuality.

These opening chapters set the stage for the broader perspective of sex and sexuality that will emerge as you progress through this text.

Chapter 1

Cultural, Historical, and Research Perspectives on Sexuality

Chapter Outline

Note: A selection of Focus on Health questions appears at the end of each chapter. Answers to these questions are indicated within the chapter by the symbol in the margin. **FoH**

We must understand that sexuality encompasses more than sexual behavior, that the many aspects of sexuality include not only the physical, but the mental and spiritual as well, and that sexuality is a core component of personality. Sexuality is a fundamental part of human life.

—from Surgeon General David Satcher's introductory letter to *The Surgeon General's Call to Action to Promote Sexual Health and Responsible Sexual Behavior 2001* by the Office of the Surgeon General, 2001, U.S. Government Printing Office

You're beginning the first chapter of a text on human sexuality. What is most important for *you* to learn in this and subsequent chapters? What personal issues are you facing or hoping to explore? Throughout the text you'll find words written by my students as they studied sexuality. What words would *you* write if I asked you to describe yourself as a sexual person?

Perhaps it's because the physical side of sex reminds us that we are animals in the biological scheme of things, or that sexual reproduction is associated with organisms that ultimately die. Perhaps it's because the intensity of sexual passion can lead people to make silly short-term decisions or because romance can leave us feeling vulnerable. Whatever the reasons, sexuality is something about which human beings are startlingly ambivalent (Goldenberg et al., 2002). On one hand, we're drawn to it by curiosity and lust; on the other, we're repelled because of embarrassment, modesty, or guilt. This inner struggle of wills and fears is reflected in the sexual themes that are so much a part of our culture (see Figure 1.1).

Sexual ambivalence becomes particularly evident in sexuality education. Even as parents call for schools to educate their children about sex, they typically feel the need to call for limits on the subject matter so the children will not know "too much." Federal and state governments support educational programs that promote sexual abstinence and balk at the distribution of free condoms, even though evidence shows that many adolescents are sexually active. There is a continuing fear, though refuted by research, that too much education will lead kids to engage in sex. It is not education but ignorance that leads to the riskiest sexual decision making.

It is sometimes difficult to separate myth and exaggeration from truth. Pop singer Sting received widespread media attention for his assertion that, using what he had learned from the sexual practices of tantric yoga, he could make love to his wife for eight hours. While his assertion of sexual endurance spurred plenty of interest in yoga, he eventually admitted to a British television interviewer that he might have left out some details. "What I didn't say," he admitted, was that the eight hours "included four hours of begging and then dinner and a movie."

■ Educating about Sex

Human sexuality is a realm of contrasts and contradictions, social trends and cultural imperatives. The values that surround sexuality are always in flux, moved by the agendas and whims of governments, economic realities, and cultural traditions. Western cultures continue to perpetuate ambivalent and conflicting messages about sex. On one hand, there are suggestions that sex is somehow "dirty." On the other hand, we are encouraged to save it for someone we really love. We are given the impression that sex is sacred and beautiful but that the less young people know about it, the better. It is no wonder that people have been anxious to pursue the study of human sexuality in as well-balanced and scientific a manner as possible. Effective sexuality education offers factual information based on research studies, as well as opportunities for people to sort through their own values and behaviors relating to their sexuality.

Everyone has some strong opinions and feelings about certain sex-related topics. The classroom should be one venue in which these topics can be debated and discussed, without fear of experiencing discomfort or being branded in any way. Instructors have an obligation to be sensitive to the wide range of values their students may have; students have an obligation to confront their own feelings and reactions and to tolerate the feelings and reactions of others even as difficult topics are

■ FIGURE 1.1 *Ambivalence about Sexuality*
Young women are asked to take a survey regarding their preferences for boxers, briefs, or thongs on men. Even with the blatant use of sexuality in marketing, there can be awkward moments.

opened for consideration. Real learning is about growth, and growth sometimes involves a bit of turmoil.

What do you think about the limits or boundaries of sexuality education? In a college course, should some topics be "out of bounds"?

■ Culture and Sexuality

When Margaret Mead conducted her ground-breaking field studies of South Seas island cultures in the 1920s and 1930s, she became one of the first anthropologists to examine sexual customs and attitudes. Mead concluded that the sexual attitudes and behaviors of individual human beings are shaped tremendously by the surrounding cultural imperatives (Mead, 1930). For example, it has often been assumed that passionate love and sexual desire are experienced and expressed universally. Evidence suggests, however, that culture profoundly affects how people perceive love; how susceptible they are to falling in love, and with whom; and why they feel sexual desire (Pertot, 2006; Philaretou, 2005).

Anthropologists usually classify cultures on the basis of their subsistence patterns, that is, on how the people produce and distribute food and other goods. Anything that affects a society's subsistence pattern can influence reproduction and thus sexual behavior. Shortages of food, for example, may lead to decreased reproductive rates. Gender roles are closely tied to both reproductive patterns and other social structures. Sexuality therefore has a place at the center of any culture (Plante, 2006).

In smaller, homogenous cultures—in which the people are expected to be very much alike in their belief patterns and values—a great deal of effort often is spent on maintaining conformity. In such homogenous cultures, individuals tend to conduct their sexual lives in accordance with accepted social roles. Larger, heterogenous cultures—in which there is a good deal of human diversity—do not work as deliberately toward producing or stabilizing behavioral conformity. These cultures tend to have many different patterns of sexual conduct, including not only sexual subcultures based on sexual orientation or behavioral preferences, but also more highly individualistic patterns of behavior within particular groups of people. North America is an example of a heterogenous culture. It has many ethnic and immigrant groups, each with its own viable sexual culture.

Individuals from homogenous cultures who immigrate to places with heterogenous cultures often must undergo a process of reevaluating traditional values brought from their homelands and selecting what sexual norms and options from the new surroundings will be comfortable. For example, immigrant Iranians in Sweden, one of the most sexually liberal nations in

the world, have shifted their views of sexuality from the traditional, authoritarian, and masculine-dominated beliefs of Iran to a greater emphasis on the sexual equality and individuality in relationships more typical of Sweden (Ahmadi, 2003).

When such cultural differences are at work, some uphold a perspective of **cultural relativism** with regard to immigrants, believing that the value systems of their original culture should be honored and allowed. Others advocate **cultural absolutism**, expecting instead that people from other cultures must be held to the sexual standards and beliefs of the culture in which they now live. The direction taken can have a significant impact on the futures of the people involved and on how welcome they feel in their new location (Apodaca, Schultz, Anderson, & McLennan, 2005).

North American culture for a long time was dominated by heritages rooted in Caucasian European ethnic groups whose people migrated to the Americas and reestablished their traditions there. The religions of these people were largely Judeo-Christian in origin. In many ways, the attitudes about human sexuality that have prevailed in North America were influenced by this backdrop of cultural and religious values. In anthropological terms, this perspective has sometimes been called **Eurocentric,** meaning that it grows mainly out of its European roots. The Eurocentric view of the world tends to be dualistic in nature. In other words, it tends to see things in an either-or, black-and-white way. Sexually speaking, this perspective may be expressed in beliefs that people must be either masculine or feminine, heterosexual or homosexual. Also, sexual behaviors tend to be judged as either good or bad. Naturally such worldviews influence the ethical belief systems people hold (Plante, 2006).

The population of North America has become increasingly diverse, with more people of color and people whose heritages are African, Far Eastern, Asian, and Latino. Native Americans and the Inuit or Eskimo cultures of the North are beginning to reclaim the sexual identities that were largely replaced by the

cultural relativism the view that one's culture determines what is normal and acceptable and that judgments about those standards should take into consideration their cultural origins.

cultural absolutism the view that behaviors and values from one's culture of origin should be disregarded once the individual is living in a new culture. The expectation is that immigrants must abide by the cultural standards of their new country.

Eurocentric (ur-oh-SEN-trick) a cultural attitudinal framework typical of people with western European heritages.

attitudes and values of Christian missionaries who taught in their boarding schools. Native Americans were originally a more gender-equitable people whose men and women shared the responsibilities of child rearing. European males tended to see themselves as superior to females, however, and the sense of equality between men and women gradually was subsumed by Eurocentric attitudes (Herdt, 2000).

Colleges are working to enhance the understanding and acceptance of cultural diversity, including customs related to gender and sexuality. On many campuses, it is not unusual to see orthodox Muslim women wearing clothing and veils that cover most of their bodies and faces. A *burqua* is a garment that covers the woman's body from head to toe, with only a slot for sight (see Figure 1.2). Islam has very specific religious laws concerning the behaviors of women and men, and male supremacy is a fundamental tenet. Nevertheless, Islam recognizes the complementarity of male and female and celebrates sexual pleasure within marriage.

Around the world, efforts are under way to equalize the availability of sexual health resources cross-culturally. At an international conference in 1994, representatives from 179 nations around the globe agreed to make reproductive health accessible to all by the year 2015. Sexual health services are an integral part of the plan. After this goal slipped out of

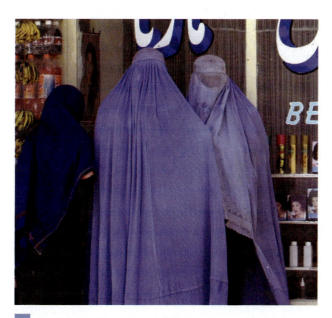

FIGURE 1.2 *Cultural Standards for Appropriate Dress*
People's attitudes about their sexuality and their bodies are strongly influenced by their cultures. These Afghan women wear the traditional burqua that reveals nothing of their bodies or faces. Not all Muslim women accept such strict standards of dress, while others consider them appropriate for their beliefs.
Source: AP Photo/Sergei Grits.

favor for a few years, it was reaffirmed at the 2005 World Summit. Progress toward the goal has been uneven; issues of sexual and reproductive health are often paid good lip service but lose out when it comes to the allocation of resources. Nevertheless, in the poorest areas of the world, unsafe sex is the second most important risk factor for disease, disability, or death (Fathalla, Sinding, Rosenfield, & Fathalla, 2006; Glasier et al., 2006).

When it comes to judging the sexual beliefs and practices of people from other cultures, would you consider yourself more of a relativist or an absolutist?

From Sexual Revolution to Culture Wars

Have you heard about the "**sexual revolution**"? What have you imagined to be true of this vaguely defined period in recent history? Unbridled sex? Hippies romping in the nude at Woodstock? What the term really indicates is simply the change that has occurred over time. Ideals and values about sex and love in Western cultures have seen dramatic shifts in the past two centuries. The Puritan ideal was for love between men and women to evolve within marriage, as two people began to know each other better. During the Victorian era (1837–1901), love and sex were considered to be separate human experiences, with love being the romantic and spiritual union that ideally preceded and precipitated marriage. Although sex was recognized as a part of marriage in cautious moderation, lustful passions were not to be let out of control lest people become slaves to their sexual emotions. Love and sex between people of the same gender were not openly discussed. Sex was not linked to love, because to link the two would in fact have been considered a threat to the love that was assumed to undergird marital stability. With sex being given such a conflicted place within marriage, prostitution and pornography flourished in Victorian society (Allyn, 2000).

Following World War II, the United States experienced significant and relatively abrupt changes in sexual attitudes, values, and behaviors. Eventually that period was dubbed the sexual revolution. The sexual revolution encompassed a variety of complex changes in values and behaviors. We will look at some significant examples.

sexual revolution the changes in thinking about sexuality and sexual behavior in society that occurred in the 1960s and 1970s.

Real People

Anil: Confronting a Faulty Cultural Assumption

Anil was a graduate student from India who came to my office because he had heard that I did counseling regarding sexual matters. He explained that he was to be married in a few months and was anxious to become better prepared to be a loving and sexually adequate husband. Upon questioning him, I learned that he had had very little sexual experience other than masturbation. We went on to discuss other aspects of marriage, including the need for good communication and being considerate of each other's needs.

Eventually, Anil began discussing his fiancée and indicated that she was studying in China. Trying to be sensitive to what I knew of the complications of long-distance relationships, I said to Anil, "You must miss her very much." He looked at me for a moment and laughed. "Actually," he responded, "I've never met her." After recovering from having my preconceived notions disrupted, we talked about how Anil's

marriage had been arranged by his and the woman's parents when Anil and the woman were quite young. Anil had no objections to the arrangement and in fact thought it quite acceptable and appropriate. His only hope was to prepare himself to be the best possible husband in every way.

Anil and I met several times to discuss marriage, and I loaned him several books on sexuality and relationships. By the time our counseling relationship was terminated, both of us felt that he was well prepared for his upcoming marriage. I realized that the ways of relationships in other cultures had just as much validity as those in my own culture.

Have you ever encountered cultural differences that surprised you? How did you react?

Can you think of some potential advantages of arranged marriage?

New Approaches to Morality and Personal Autonomy

One of the most striking trends of Western society during this period was increased resistance to centralized, institutionalized authority. A counterculture movement questioned rules, regulations, and decisions that were set forth without thorough explanation or rationale. The mobility of Western society, along with the decreasing stability of the nuclear family, created conditions that demanded more independence and self-reliance. As values changed, former legal restrictions on sexual activity between consenting adults gradually began to give way. Established religious restraints on sex began to shift. Academic institutions responded to the pressure by giving up their *in loco parentis* positions and liberalizing their residence hall policies on curfews, visits by members of the opposite sex, and privacy. This movement was integrated into a consumption-oriented economy, and advertising picked up on the themes of sex appeal and sexual freedom. Enjoyment of oneself and of one's own body was no longer condemned as immoral. New attitudes about sexuality moved into the mainstream of American life, marked by a trend toward support of the individual right to sexual freedom and expression.

Changing Roles of Women and Men

Another significant outcome of the sexual revolution was a new set of attitudes toward the roles of men and women. The traditional, heterosexual roles of the man as aggressive protector and provider and the woman as passive homemaker were gradually superseded by roles individualized to each person's needs. These changes granted both women and men more freedom to adopt ways of life that fit them more appropriately. It became legitimate for women to express strong sexual feelings and to consider sex important to their lives, even as the initiators of sexual activity. It also became acceptable for women to pursue their careers aggressively. Likewise, men were freed to enjoy the more gentle and emotional aspects of their personalities, to function as homemakers in their own right, and to be the more passive partner in sexual interactions.

Support from Science and Technology

Right after World War II, a time when people were anxious to return to some sense of "normalcy" and to establish new lives and families, Alfred Kinsey published the results of his ground-breaking surveys concerning male and female sexual behavior. The media were filled with stories about the findings, and individuals began to realize that their own needs and behaviors were shared by many others. Awareness of some fundamental truths about sexuality in human life had been revealed and confirmed through scientific study.

As we will see later in this chapter, the work of several researchers has fostered a broader acceptance of what is considered normal and of our sexual individuality, thereby removing much of the element of mystery from sexuality. The sexual revolution helped people grasp the fact that *sex* does not refer only to actions involving the reproductive organs. Many other forms of sensual and sexual sharing may enhance physical pleasure and the expression of caring between people. That is why we tend to use the more inclusive term *sexuality* in our discussion.

Technological advances also helped change the terrain of human sexuality. With new advances in birth control and the legalization of abortion came reduced concerns about the risks of pregnancy, the condition that through the ages has truly shaped the lives of women. These advances were accompanied by hotly debated ethical issues. Reproductive technology made it possible for people who once would not have been able to have children to become pregnant and give birth. Medical advances have improved treatment of some sexually transmitted diseases and resulted in the restoration of sexual functioning for some people who once would have had to give up sexual activity altogether. We have emerged from the sexual revolution, however, with a new realization that it is never enough simply to rely on scientific or technological advances to solve immediate problems; rather, we must also work to understand how these advances affect human lives and decision making (Coleman, 2002a; Melby, 2006a).

Emergence of Sexuality Education

Sexuality education was first introduced into a few public schools over a century ago, but it eventually lost favor. In the early 1960s, more publicity began to appear about sexuality education in public schools and colleges. Organizations were formed that encouraged and supported sexuality education programs. The most influential group, chartered in 1964, was the Sex (now Sexuality) Information and Education Council of the United States (SIECUS). Dr. Mary S. Calderone (1904–1998), one of the cofounders of SIECUS and its first executive director, became a leading advocate of sexuality education. Another professional organization formed in the late 1960s was the American Association of Sex Educators, Counselors

and Therapists (AASECT). It has worked to establish standards for these fields and now certifies individuals who meet training criteria in the three different sexology fields of sexuality education, counseling, and therapy.

Controversies over sexuality education quickly erupted, often leading to polarization of factions of people within communities. Although some groups stood in complete opposition to any form of sexuality education outside the home environment, the majority of people in North America seemed to favor some sort of institutionalized effort, especially within school settings. While sexuality education is now far more common, we will see that controversies regarding its approaches remain commonplace.

New Perspectives on Sexual Orientations and Gender Identities

A great deal of diversity exists in human sexual orientations, behaviors, and expressions of gender. Medical and mental health professionals have at times classified certain differing forms as sick; laws have made them criminal; religions have branded them as sinful; and the general populace has variously feared, hated, pitied, or accepted people who are open about them. As the sexual revolution encouraged a broader perspective on such matters, the American Psychiatric Association removed "homosexuality" from its official list of mental disorders in 1973 (Vellani, 2006).

Attitudes concerning the diversity of gender identities began to change as well. As later chapters of this text will show, not all people fit neatly into female or male, masculine or feminine categories. Transgender identities have received increasing attention and acceptance even as they challenge our traditional assumptions about gender. As social attitudes have changed over time, other sexual interests and behaviors have gained greater social acceptance.

The Changing Interplay of Romance and Commitment

Philosophers since the time of the ancient Greeks have suggested that sexual desire is one type of loving and that love itself is fundamentally a desire for wholeness, the need to unify with the parts of ourselves we find in others. In different cultures and historical periods, infatuation and romantic love have been viewed as something quite separate from, and even unrelated to, sexual longing. In our cultural tradition, marriage has been seen as a social institution based on both romance and sexual desire (Plante, 2006), specifically heterosexual desire. Today we take it to another level: Is marriage always to be between a man and a woman? Could people of the same sex be married?

Many people strongly believe that an enlightened society makes room for all people to share in its customs and benefits.

Also, while it surely is true that people have attempted to keep sex and love separate in certain situations, many people realize that things are not really that simple. Instant sex has had complicated consequences. Casual sexual encounters have not been all they were cracked up to be. A great deal of discussion about a return to intimacy, love, and romance is taking place today. We are reexamining the many faces of love, the intricacies of human commitment and spirituality, and the complications of intimacy.

Times of Transition

Revolutions rarely maintain their momentum for long before forces of moderation begin to temper their power. Some theorists believe that there never was an actual sexual revolution. Call it what you will, but just after the middle of the twentieth century there were a great many changes in perceptions about human sexuality. There were also a number of subsequent developments that influenced the direction of society.

HIV and AIDS

By the mid-1980s, human immunodeficiency virus (HIV) and the terminal disease to which it often leads—acquired immunodeficiency syndrome (AIDS)—changed some of the fundamental ways people viewed sexual behavior. As awareness and fear about HIV and AIDS increased, awareness about the need to make sexual decisions with care and to protect oneself during sexual interactions also increased. In the United States, HIV was first identified among gay males, which led to new forms of negative attitudes about same-sex orientation and raised new fears about interaction with gay or bisexual men. Casual sex became scarier for everyone, and a new emphasis on safer sex emerged. Nevertheless, the consistent use of condoms and avoidance of casual sex were not quick to catch on. As AIDS became the fourth leading cause of death worldwide by the beginning of the new millennium, sexual pleasure consistently was cited as a more important consideration for individuals than was protection against disease or unintended pregnancy (Durex, 2001).

HIV and AIDS also provided more ammunition for those who advocate abstinence from sexual activity outside of marriage. This approach not only continued to ignore or marginalize gay relationships, but also tended to focus blame on the gay community. Fear and anger about same-gender sex increased for a time. While some of the antigay bias eventually subsided, the debate about condom use and safer sex versus abstinence still rages (Melby, 2006b).

Media and Internet Attention to Sexuality

As increasing openness about sexuality emerged in society, it became nearly impossible to avoid sex, nudity, provocative language, and complex sexual themes in public media. Researchers who have generated what they feel are accurate data concerning the types and frequencies of human sexual behaviors believe that the media have played a substantial role in perpetuating myths and exaggerations about the levels of sexual activity among people (Brown, 2002; Farrar et al., 2003).

The 2004 Super Bowl was heftily supported by television commercials for medications that help men achieve erections for sexual activity, yet the real headlines were generated by the fact that one of Janet Jackson's breasts was bared for a couple of seconds (see Figure 1.3). The incident led to hearings in Washington

FIGURE 1.3 *Janet Jackson and Justin Timberlake*

The Super Bowl half-time "wardrobe malfunction."

Real Student Voices

■ In life as a nonsexual woman, I am very conservative. I can be open in conversation, although when people ask me questions about sex, I blush and then answer. I have been thinking about having sex with a guy who has told me that he wants a future with me. Of course, that doesn't justify having sex with him.

■ I used to have the belief that I would not have sexual intercourse until I got married. Since then, I continue to be involved in a six-year loving relationship. After dating for a while, I felt that I was with the right person and my views changed a bit.

■ Growing up, my parents never mentioned sex except to say, "Don't do it!" I gave them the sex talk instead of the other way around. While my friends talked about the horrifying moment when they caught their parents in the act, my parents slept in beds on opposite sides of the house. Then there is me. I initiated sex with my first real boyfriend, and I've been told I give amazing blowjobs. The boys I've had sex with say I'm the best they've ever had. . . . I must have gotten my sexual prowess from the milkman.

■ My parents believed that sex topics were better left swept under the carpet. During adolescence, anything I learned about sexuality came either from health class or television. When I began dating a girl at age 15, I began to explore my sexuality a lot more. I've become quite liberal, I think. I don't have a problem with things such as premarital sex, oral sex, pornography, or masturbation. I had good friends in high school who were homosexual or bisexual, so I'm pretty accepting of other orientations. Whatever floats your boat, so be it.

about the content of television programming and caused the Federal Communications Commission to steeply increase fines for any violation. This is an example of the transition toward greater controls over the sexual imagery of the media and the efforts of government to intervene in what is perceived as out-of-control permissiveness. The pendulum is swinging in the other direction.

Nevertheless, production of hard-core sex videos and DVDs has soared, with millions spent annually in ordering pay-per-view adult movies in homes and in hotels. It is estimated that the U.S. hard-core pornography business grosses up to $10 billion a year. Access to this material has been expanded even more by Internet technology. Not only are explicit sexual pictures just a couple of clicks away, but the ability to observe and verbally interact with live sex performers for a fee is also available. A largely unregulated medium has brought an entirely new and graphic dimension of human sexuality into homes and institutions. Online connections also have helped those with less typical sexual interests and orientations find one another, share their stories, and perhaps not feel quite so alone or out-of-step (Kelly, 2005; Ross, 2005).

Source: Copyright © North American Syndicate.

Sexuality, Politics, and "Family Values"

One of the most interesting responses to increasing sexual freedom is the fact that politicians are adopting sex-related issues as major planks in their political platforms. Similarly, perceptions of their personal lives can vastly influence voters. Elections are won and lost on candidates' positions on abortion rights or access to contraception. An illicit sexual affair can sink a political career practically overnight. Political conservatives are anxious to make known their views about the ethics, morality, and legality of sexual behaviors and orientations. Liberals are equally intent on supporting the rights of gay males and lesbians, the freedom to use sexual words and display graphic representations of sex, and the right to make individual choices.

Because sex-related topics become sensationalized by the media and because they stimulate strong opinions, they are inevitably intertwined with politics. Human sexuality thus is in itself highly politicized, and political trends ultimately affect legislative mandates and court decisions related to sexual and reproductive behaviors.

One term that has been bandied about in political contests is "family values," which has been used to signify a belief in traditional approaches to sexuality and the family. These include upholding abstinence from sex until marriage, the assumption that heterosexual is the proper way to be, the model of a family as consisting of a man and a woman and their children, no availability of abortion, and any number of other ideas that might be considered on the conservative side of politics. Parties and politicians stake a claim to their devotion to religion and family values to this day (Harris, 2005). The problem is that current statistics about our society continue to confirm that the traditional ways of approaching these issues no longer necessarily define the norm in the ways people live their lives. So we are left with more ambivalence, more incongruity between people's hopes and the realities that surround them—prime factors in the development of culture wars.

Where do you stand on "family values"? If reality is not particularly congruent with what these values support, should we work to change society so that it better fits such values? Or should we accept that times change and values must change with them?

And Now: In the Midst of the Culture Wars

Do you ever feel confused about sex? Have you sometimes wondered how sexuality ought to fit into your own life? Have you worried that you've made some sexual mistakes? If you answered yes to any of these questions, it is no wonder! We live in confusing times, and our social ambivalence has never been so obvious.

We have seen that as sex-related issues received more media exposure and as research demonstrated the diversity of human sexual behavior, many hostilities and taboos gradually seemed to slip away. Yet research is beginning to suggest that although there have been some distinct changes along the way, our perceptions about sexual permissiveness may well have been exaggerated, and the rates of sexual experimentation may have leveled off (Kantrowitz, 2006).

To study human beings' attitudes with a great degree of objectivity is no simple matter, especially regarding issues as complex as sexuality. Human attitudes about sex cannot be easily classified, because many different factors are involved in their creation and expression. Likewise, no single set of beliefs easily describes the prevailing North American attitudes toward sex. Researchers have found that there are some clusters of similarity in the way groups of people view various sexual issues and behaviors. These have allowed sociologists to group people into three main categories based on what seem to be their fundamental assumptions about the purposes of sex. The *procreational* or *traditional* category includes those people who see the primary purpose of sexual activity as reproductive. They tend to disapprove of any sex outside marriage as well as sexual activity between members of the same gender. Beyond these attitudes, the group seems somewhat split on other issues, such as pornography and abortion.

A second category of attitudes has been termed *relational.* People in this group tend to view sexual activity as a natural component of intimate and loving relationships. As might be expected, this group generally is accepting of sex within the context of a loving and committed relationship—marriage or otherwise—but has strongly negative attitudes toward extramarital sex or "cheating" on a partner. The final attitudinal category, called *recreational,* consists of people who consider the primary purpose of sex to be pleasure. They tend to believe that any sexual activity between consenting adults would be acceptable and tend to have mixed views on issues such as abortion and same-gender sexual activity (Laumann, Gagnon, et al., 1994).

We may conclude, therefore, that we live in a time when no single set of social attitudes relating to human sexuality predominates. In fact, several different and often quite contradictory attitudinal patterns exist alongside one another. Even more important, we are beginning to see that the sexual attitudes people hold, which are strongly influenced by the social groups to which they belong, also influence the sexual behaviors in which they engage.

In which of the three main attitudinal categories regarding sexual issues and behavior would you place yourself: procreational/traditional, relational, or recreational? Explain your choice.

We have seen that we remain ambivalent about human sexuality. We have also discussed how easily sexual issues become politicized. The combination of these two realities makes for a confusing brew. It has become obvious in the most recent U.S. elections that there is an ongoing struggle between what are called "conservative" and "liberal" ideals in this country. From a political perspective, the conservatives are loosely identified as Republicans and the liberals as Democrats, although these dividing lines do not necessarily hold up well under closer examination. The 2004 election

Real Student Voices

■ I feel that sex is what you make of it, and it works differently for different people. A secondary reason I signed up for this course was because my brother recently informed me and our parents that he is gay. I personally have had no trouble accepting this, but my parents are having problems coming to terms with it. I'd like to learn as much as I can so maybe I can be of help.

■ As a religious person, my views toward sex are strict. I don't care what others do, because sex is natural and good as long as you're being true to yourself and your beliefs, and not everyone has the

same beliefs. I do have a problem with "posers"—those who despite defying the teachings of their religion, continue on as if they were an exception to the rules, lying to themselves.

■ I would say that I am quite experienced in masturbation and have tried several different techniques. I'm very open about this experimentation with my close friends and we often share ideas and techniques. I also watch pornography for sexual arousal and education. You can learn a lot about different positions, and then try to initiate them with your partner.

platforms were influenced by the judgment of the Massachusetts Supreme Judicial Court that it would be discriminatory not to allow gay couples to have all the rights and privileges of marriage. This left presidential candidates and other politicians scrambling to take a position on the matter and state legislators hustling to pass laws to limit marriage to heterosexual couples. It was also the election that popularized the concept of "red states" and "blue states," depending on their apparent political leanings.

In the 2006 elections, when control of Congress hung in the balance, a central issue was the Iraq war. However, just prior to election day an important subtext developed around the scandal of Republican Representative Mark Foley of Florida, who resigned after it was reported that he had sent sexually explicit e-mails to young male congressional pages. An investigation ensued to find out who in the Republican leadership knew what and when they knew it. The sexual nature of the situation clearly made it all the more powerful. A Newsweek poll indicated that it had influenced nearly 30 percent of voters not to support Republican candidates. Ultimately, the sexual scandal may well have helped tip the balance enough to allow the Democrats to regain the majority in both the House of Representatives and the Senate.

It seems that we are a nation and a culture divided and that sexual topics are often where the divisions become most obvious. However, it is dangerous to assume that individual human beings fall so neatly into such categories. They simply do not. In the rest of this chapter, we explore the history of the field of human sexuality and look at the research methods underlying scientific

validity. This text aims to provide the information and background to help you, as an individual, sort through who you are as a sexual person and what you believe.

■ Milestones in Sex Research: A Brief Historical Survey

Many students find studying the history of a field to be rather boring, maybe even irrelevant. I must admit, I used to have the same reaction. Gradually I've come to appreciate how interesting and helpful understanding historical information can be. Can you think of some good reasons why taking a look at historical foundations could be important to your understanding of human sexuality?

Until the mid-twentieth century, serious attempts at studying sexual behavior were seldom made. A few workers cautiously ventured into the realm of sexuality, sometimes risking their personal and professional reputations to do so. Some have wanted their work to fall within the protocols of "pure" science, and others have seen themselves as agents of social change. This section presents a brief historical summary of some of the major advances in sex research. A summary timeline can be found in Table 1.1.

Also see "Timeline" on SexSource Online.

Table 1.1   *A Timeline: Milestones for Western Culture in the Study of Sex*

1880	1890	1900	1910	1920	1930	1940
Richard von Krafft-Ebing publishes *Psychopathia Sexualis*.	Sigmund Freud publishes psychoanalytic interpretations of sexuality in the human personality.			Theodoor van de Velde publishes *Ideal Marriage*.	Helena Wright publishes *The Sex Factor in Marriage*.	Robert L. Dickinson publishes *A Thousand Marriages*.
		Henry Havelock Ellis publishes seven volumes of *Studies in the Psychology of Sex*.				

Early studies slowly bring human sexuality into focus.

Sexual feelings and behaviors are feared to be physically and mentally debilitating, as well as morally questionable. Sex is considered separate from love and romance.			Sexuality begins to find a more legitimate, though still quite negative, place in human experience and early psychology.		Sexual activity is established as a potentially positive aspect of the marital relationship. Sex and love begin to be integrated.	

1950	1960	1970	1980	1990	2000	2010
Alfred C. Kinsey studies at Indiana University on sexual behavior in the human male and female.	Mary J. Sherfey's study on the evolution of female sexuality. John Money's study of gender identity at Johns Hopkins Hospital. First Presidential Commission on Obscenity and Pornography. William H. Masters and Virginia E. Johnson publish *Human Sexual Response* and *Human Sexual Inadequacy*.	Hunt Report. Hite Report. Robert C. Sorenson publishes *Adolescent Sexuality in Contemporary America*. *Redbook* magazine's survey.	Studies on sexual preference and sex in male–female and same-gender relationships. Studies on childhood sexuality and sex in the older years.	Out of concern for the increase in HIV infection and AIDS, several studies on human sexual behavior are undertaken: World Health Organization National AIDS Behavioral Survey Major studies in France and Great Britain Studies of male sexual behavior	National Longitudinal Study of Adolescent Health. National AIDS Behavioral Methodology Survey.	Studies on adolescent sexual behaviors will increase our understanding of this age group. There will be more pressure to understand HIV transmission and prevention. Greater awareness of the need to research female sexual response and behavior.

Janus Report on Sexual Behavior.

National Health and Social Life Survey.

Increased interest in cross-cultural studies of sexual behavior.

Sex research achieves legitimacy as a scientific pursuit as sociosexual values shift.

Sex research becomes a tool for understanding changing sociosexual attitudes and for controlling the spread of HIV/AIDS, and theory in sex research gains a multidisciplinary perspective.

The first statistical sexual behavior studies enlighten the general population about the extent and range of sexual behavior, within and outside of marriage.	Investigations of female sexuality and gender identity broaden our views of femininity and masculinity. The first studies emerge on how the body actually responds during sexual arousal and stimulation to orgasm.	Sex therapy for the treatment of sexual dysfunctions emerges as an interdisciplinary professional field. The "sexual revolution" legitimizes the right to pursue and enhance personal sexual enjoyment.	Surveys clarify the range of human sexual experience across the life span. Gay and lesbian orientation and behavior receive more attention in research.	Controversies develop over sexual values; abortion rights; gay, lesbian, and bisexual rights; and the role of sexuality education. Sex research focuses more on understanding sexual behaviors so that the worldwide spread of HIV infection may be brought under control. The government wrestles with issues of funding for sex research that some officials claim may violate personal privacy.	Sexual behavior is seen more clearly within its social contexts. More accurate data emerge to help us understand human sexual behaviors, painting a less adventurous picture of sexual frequency and activity than had previously been portrayed. Attention is given to bringing greater sophistication to theory in sexual science and to using outcomes for promoting sexual health.	The new millennium will see more broad surveys of sexual behaviors, especially during adolescence. The Internet will become a stronger tool for gathering data in sex research, and research will attempt to clarify the influences of biology and social construction in the determination of variable human traits. Studies emerge with a global focus on sexual behavior and sexual health.

Emerging from the Nineteenth Century

Much as we saw in the discussion of contemporary culture wars, European academics and physicians were immersed in a time of conflicting values and philosophies during the last quarter of the nineteenth century. Some supported an intensely repressive moral code concerning sexual behavior and attitudes, along with the concept that sex was a major factor in the onset of emotional and mental disturbances. When sexual feelings or behaviors inevitably produced guilt, fear, and self-loathing, they might logically be expected to be at the root of many disorders.

Richard von Krafft-Ebing (1840–1902)

Typifying repressive sexual codes, this German-born neurologist and psychiatrist's book *Psychopathia Sexualis* became a widely circulated medical text that portrayed various forms of sexual behavior and arousal as disgusting and pathological. Krafft-Ebing grouped sexual deviations into four classifications of pathology: sadism, masochism, fetishism, and homosexuality. For the first time, awareness was raised of what was then considered to be sexually atypical, and this awareness likely made some people feel that at least they were not alone (Bancroft, 2001). Krafft-Ebing believed that hereditary "weakness" or "taintedness" was the cause of sexual behaviors other than intercourse for the purpose of reproduction, a belief reflective of the moral codes of his time (Money, 2003).

Of special significance was Krafft-Ebing's declaration that masturbation was the cause of all sexual deviations. This is one example of how opinion and speculation, in the absence of the kind of sound research we would expect today, can lead to questionable and misleading conclusions. He illustrated his theories with case studies demonstrating the dire effects of masturbation. His case studies were highly sensational for the times, and they did call attention to the variety of human sexual orientations and activities. His biased conclusions, however, labeled much sexual behavior sick and unnatural. Even though Krafft-Ebing was not viewed as a mainstream sex researcher by his professional contemporaries, his perspective pervaded the medical and psychiatric professions well into the twentieth century (Oosterhuis, 2001).

Sigmund Freud (1856–1939)

This Viennese physician (see Figure 1.4) focused much of his work on the study of the psychosexual

■ **FIGURE 1.4**   *Sigmund Freud*

Freud (1856–1939) was an Austrian neurologist who first theorized that sexuality existed throughout the life cycle and was the basic motivating factor in human behavior. He identified the basic stages of sexual-emotional development as the oral, the anal, and the genital.

development of children and how it affected adult life and mental condition. Freud's contributions have had far more influence on psychology than have those of Krafft-Ebing, although they also perpetuated a decidedly negative attitude toward most aspects of human sexuality. In 1895, Freud published the epochal *Studies in Hysteria,* written in collaboration with Josef Breuer. The book contained discussions of the unconscious mind, repression, and free association, concepts that became the foundation of psychoanalysis. Freud also had become convinced that neuroses were produced by unconscious conflicts of a sexual nature, an idea that alienated most scientists of his time. In 1905, his *Three Essays on the Theory of Sexuality* precipitated a storm of protest. It was in this work that Freud developed his theory of infantile sexuality and attempted to demonstrate how adult sexual perversions were distortions of childhood sexual expressions.

Many of Freud's European contemporaries considered his ideas marginal. His work was highly influential in the United States, however, where for a time publishing in the area of human sexuality was dominated by psychoanalysts who espoused Freudian theories of psychosexual development. Today there is much disagreement as to the value of psychoanalysis and Freud's theories of sexuality, particularly his views about female sexuality. His work, nonetheless, led to an increased interest in sex and a willingness to think and talk about sexuality. Freud did not brand sexual behaviors as immoral, criminal, or pathological. Through his work, sexuality became a legitimate concern of medicine and psychology.

Fresh Perspectives as the Twentieth Century Begins

At the turn of the twentieth century, some liberal intellectuals in Vienna began to develop new perspectives on sexuality that would set the stage for the future. Otto Weininger wrote *Sex and Character,* a controversial book that questioned prevailing views about gender and sexuality. Author Robert Musil explored gender issues, homosexuality, and sadism in the Europe of his time, while refocusing attention on the cultural meanings of gender (Luft, 2003; Ortiz, 2006).

A major shift in methodology, however, occurred in 1906 when a German physician, Iwan Bloch (1872–1922), coined the term "sexual science" and began studying the history of prostitution and what he called "strange" sexual practices. Bloch's work was the first to conceive of history as an important foundation for understanding human sexuality. More recently, historians have accepted sexuality as a legitimate area for historical study, although caution must be taken not to interpret historical studies and beliefs solely in the context of the present (Bancroft, 2001). Bloch might well have been the first **sexologist,** the term given to professionals who study human sexuality from a scientific perspective and with some objectivity.

German psychiatrist Magnus Hirschfeld (1868–1935) was one of the first professionals to take a stand on rights for people who were gay or lesbian. He risked personal persecution and anti-Semitic repercussions for saying that people with same-sex sexual orientation constituted an intermediate third sex that deserved the same rights and privileges as heterosexuals. He also argued against the prevailing claims about the negative effects of masturbation, believing them to be exaggerated and unfounded (Bullough, 2003b).

FIGURE 1.5 *Henry Havelock Ellis*

Ellis (1859–1939), an English physician, invented the term "autoeroticism" to indicate the practice of masturbation in both sexes and all ages. He was farsighted in his views, particularly of the way sexuality affects women and the way mental attitude affects physical behavior.

Henry Havelock Ellis (1859–1939)

This English sex researcher brought a new perspective to sexual science (see Figure 1.5). Ellis spent several decades studying all available information on human sexuality in the Western world and on the sexual mores of other cultures. He also studied the sex lives of his contemporaries and carefully recorded what he learned. Eventually he began writing about his findings, publishing them in six volumes between 1896 and 1910 as *Studies in the Psychology of Sex.* A seventh volume was added in 1928 (Ellis, 1936).

Ellis played a major role in effecting the gradual changes in sexual attitudes that followed Victorian times. His *Studies* recognized that human beings exhibit great variety in their sexual inclinations and behaviors and that sexual mores are determined by cultural and social influences. His conclusions were

sexologist person who studies human sexuality from a scientific perspective.

radical by Victorian standards and amazingly farsighted by present-day standards. Ellis noted that masturbation was a common practice in males and females of all ages. He suggested that sexual orientation toward one gender or the other existed in degrees rather than as an absolute. He legitimized the idea that women could have as great a sexual desire as men, and he pointed out that the orgasms of men and women were remarkably similar. Foreshadowing later trends in sex therapy, Ellis recognized that difficulties in achieving erection or orgasm often were psychological problems rather than physical. He emphasized what most professionals today accept, that "the range of variation within fairly normal limits is immense" when considering the sexual needs and behaviors of humans.

Sexual Studies in the Early Twentieth Century

In 1926, a Dutch physician by the name of Theodoor van de Velde (1873–1937) published the first edition of his book *Ideal Marriage.* Although it was not the only sex manual available at the time, it was significant because van de Velde conveyed the validity of sexual responsiveness to a reading audience that still had Victorian inhibitions. Although van de Velde's suggestions for a more fulfilling sexual relationship were described in a heterosexual, marriage-oriented framework with some moralistic boundaries and an almost obsessive attention to cleanliness, he put forth a generally positive outlook that people by this time were ready to receive. His book described a variety of coital positions, discussed the use of oral sex in foreplay, and offered suggestions for dealing with some sexual problems. Because of the popularity of *Ideal Marriage,* van de Velde's ideas played an important role in helping thousands of couples achieve more sexual enjoyment (Melody & Peterson, 1999).

One outstanding sex research effort of the early twentieth century was a study published in 1932 by Robert Latou Dickinson called *A Thousand Marriages.* Dickinson gathered 5,200 case studies of women he treated between 1882 and 1924 while he was a gynecologist in New York City. He documented how the repressive sexual attitudes of childhood led to disastrous effects on adult sexual functioning—one of the earliest attempts at a better understanding of female sexuality. He also studied the physiological responses of the clitoris, vagina, and cervix during sexual stimulation and orgasm. Realizing that once a woman has been able to experience the pleasure of a self-induced orgasm she is more likely to have orgasm during intercourse, he introduced the use of electric vibrators for women.

Another pioneer in the sexual liberation of women was Helena Wright, who began her gynecological medical practice in London in the 1920s. She discov-

ered that most women found no enjoyment in sex and instead considered it a marital duty. Unlike other women writers, who had discussed sexuality in mostly negative terms, Wright began publishing books that instructed women on how to achieve orgasm, through both intercourse and masturbation. The first of her books, *The Sex Factor in Marriage,* was published in 1930. Subsequent editions of the book and Wright's other publications continued for decades to give explicit instructions to women on becoming fully acquainted with their sex organs and sexual responses.

Mid-Twentieth-Century Sex Research

The preeminent sex researcher at mid-century was Alfred C. Kinsey (1894–1956), a successful zoologist who gradually moved into research on human sexual behavior (see Figure 1.6). It was through his work that sex research became a more legitimate scientific pursuit than it had been, because he applied statistical analysis to sexual behavior instead of drawing conclusions solely from personal observations. In 1937, as a conservative and highly respected biology professor at Indiana University, Kinsey had been selected to teach a new course in sexuality and marriage. In preparing lectures and attempting to answer his students' questions,

■ **FIGURE 1.6** *Alfred C. Kinsey*

Kinsey (1894–1956) was a zoologist, later a biology professor, who was instrumental in compiling face-to-face interviews with thousands of people about their sexual behavior. His work, not highly regarded in his lifetime, has come to be regarded as comprehensive, systematic, and the model on which other studies are based.

Kinsey began to realize that little reliable information about sexuality was available. He began gathering information by interviewing people about their sex lives, eventually involving associates in the interviews. By the end of 1949, he had gathered detailed histories on the sexual lives of more than 16,000 people.

Kinsey founded and directed Indiana University's Institute for Sex Research. Now called the Kinsey Institute for Research in Sex, Gender, and Reproduction (commonly known as the Kinsey Institute), it remains an important center for sex research. Paul Gebhard and Wardell Pomeroy became Kinsey's principal collaborators and helped design the statistical approaches and skillful interview techniques that rendered the Kinsey studies so unique. The two studies that brought Kinsey wide recognition and notoriety were *Sexual Behavior in the Human Male,* published in 1948, and *Sexual Behavior in the Human Female,* published in 1953. Both were considered milestones in the field, and the movie *Kinsey* about his life and career appeared in 2004 (see Figure 1.7).

Although Kinsey's findings were long considered representative of the general population, we now know that his research had some inherent design flaws that probably skewed the statistical results. When Kinsey embarked on his research, he believed—probably rightfully so—that getting a standard, representative sample of the general population was a practical impossibility. He had already decided that face-to-face interviewing would be the best way to obtain information from people, and it took him six months to persuade the first 62 people to participate. He therefore compromised in finding subjects to interview, knowing that the outcome would be less than satisfactory but believing that it was the best that could be done at the time (Bancroft, 2005).

Because Kinsey believed that getting people to discuss their sexual behaviors would be challenging and because he lacked the funding for extensive travel, he settled for what is known as a "sample of convenience." In other words, he and his staff interviewed groups of people who expressed a willingness to respond to their questions. These volunteers included members of college fraternities, sororities, and college classes; other student groups; and inhabitants of rooming houses, prisons, and mental hospitals. Kinsey even interviewed hitchhikers who came through town. To achieve the increased reliability of larger numbers, he would attempt to interview all members of a particular group.

See "Alfred Kinsey Research" on SexSource Online.

This approach had two essential flaws. First, because the interviewees were willing volunteers, the information they offered about their sexual lives could not justifiably be generalized to the larger, national population. Second, it can be assumed that willing volunteers—especially for something such as a sex survey—may well have very different sex-related attitudes, life experiences, and sexual behaviors from those who are reluctant to participate. The data gathered from this group of less hesitant volunteers may well represent an accurate portrayal of the volunteer group, but they are not as likely to reflect broader patterns within the general population.

There can be no argument that Kinsey's work fostered a new level of awareness about the diversity of human sexual behaviors. Until the 1990s, his statistics were about the most accurate and comprehensive available. The surprising thing is that it took 50 years to gather more accurate information about a subject that has been so much in the public eye (Bullough, 2004).

Two researchers who contributed more to our knowledge of sexual functioning than any predecessor were William H. Masters and Virginia E. Johnson (see Figure 1.8). Their work focused on two major areas: the physiology of human sexual response and the treatment of sexual dysfunction. Between 1855 and 1955, several studies were published that described measurements of various human physiological responses during intercourse and masturbation. During the 1940s, Kinsey and his associates had observed intercourse and recorded the physiological responses of the participants. Yet many questions

FIGURE 1.7 *Laura Linney and Liam Neeson*
The actors play Alfred Kinsey and his wife in the 2004 film *Kinsey*.

FIGURE 1.8 *Virginia E. Johnson and William H. Masters*

Masters and Johnson were the first researchers to actually observe, monitor, and film the physiological responses of people engaged in coitus or masturbation. This initial research led them to develop techniques for effectively treating sexual dysfunction.

remained unanswered. William Masters launched his research study in 1954 and hired Virginia Johnson as an interviewer soon after. In the decade that followed, Masters and Johnson used sophisticated instrumentation to measure the physiological responses of 694 individuals during masturbation and coitus. In total, they studied more than 10,000 orgasms in these laboratory conditions. The detailed account of their work is given in *Human Sexual Response* (Masters & Johnson, 1966).

Their second major research effort began in 1959, proceeding simultaneously with the studies on sexual response. For five years, Masters and Johnson developed and perfected clinical techniques for the treatment of male and female sexual dysfunctions. In 1970, their revolutionary treatment format was described in *Human Sexual Inadequacy,* a book that inaugurated the age of sex therapy. Numerous other workers have since modified and enlarged upon the Masters and Johnson work, and sex therapy has become a distinct discipline of medicine and psychology.

Popular Surveys: A Source of Attention but Also Flaws

FOH The seventies became the decade of the sex survey, and books and magazines were filled with new peeks at the most private details of sex lives in the United States. The methodologies of these casual surveys were highly questionable, yet their results generated a great deal of attention and solidified some myths and misconceptions about the variety and frequency of sexual behaviors.

The largest survey on sexual behavior following the Kinsey studies was commissioned in the early 1970s by the Playboy Foundation. A private research foundation selected people from telephone books in 24 U.S. cities at random. Twenty percent of these individuals then agreed to complete a 1,000-item questionnaire, and data were gathered from 982 men and 1,044 women, not a particularly convincing sample. The study was cited frequently in discussions of human sexual behavior, even though the data were not very reliable.

In 1977, *Redbook* magazine published a questionnaire about female sexuality to which more than 100,000 women responded. Again, the results could not be considered representative of the general female population because only about 2 percent of the magazine's readers actually returned the survey. At the time, the study constituted one of the largest surveys of women's attitudes and behaviors ever attempted. The *Redbook* study conveyed a picture of U.S. women as having active sex lives and often initiating sexual activities with their partners.

Although surveys may seem impressive because of their sheer numbers of responses, the number of people who participate in a research study is not its most significant component. Far more important is *how the researcher actually gets the participants.* For example, the percentage of people responding to a widely distributed questionnaire is more important than the raw numbers. A response rate of 2 or 3 percent would yield very questionable data. Social scientists would consider a response rate of about 30 percent to be in the minimum range of acceptability in terms of accuracy. The higher the response rate, the more representative the results are of the total population originally approached. Therein lies the other major flaw of these popular surveys. Who has actually been invited to participate? Readers of a particular magazine, such as *Redbook* or *Playboy,* may be considered to have certain characteristics in common and therefore not be representative of anything more than readers of those magazines. Readers of *The New Republic* or *Christian Century* might be expected to have other, different characteristics as groups.

Another difficulty with survey questionnaires that are distributed en masse is that there is no way of really knowing who has responded. Some respondents might have filled out the survey as a joke or deliberately exaggerated their answers to bias the results. Some men might have pretended to be women, and vice versa, or some might have completed more than one questionnaire. Although surveys of this sort may generate results that capture our attention, we have no way of knowing what their findings really mean.

More Reliable Surveys

Other surveys have made use of more reliable methodologies. Robert Sorensen (1973) published *Adolescent Sexuality in Contemporary America,* based on responses from several hundred adolescents. Melvin Zelnik and John Kantner (1980) used sophisticated research designs and methods of statistical analysis to study the sexual and contraceptive behaviors of teenagers. For years their surveys represented some of the most reliable data available on teenage sexual behavior.

Alan Bell, Martin Weinberg, and Sue Kiefer Hammersmith (1981) of the Kinsey Institute published the results of a unique study of sexual orientation called *Sexual Preference: Its Development in Men and Women.* From a pool of 4,639 gay males and lesbians, they conducted extensive interviews with 979 individuals, obtaining the most in-depth data of any study on same-gender sexual orientation ever conducted. Although the research focused on gay males and lesbians in only one area of the country, the San Francisco Bay Area, it was considered crucial to our evolving understanding of sexual orientation and its development.

Philip Blumstein and Pepper Schwartz (1983), sociologists at the University of Washington, studied completed questionnaires from 4,314 heterosexual couples, 969 gay male couples, and 788 lesbian couples who responded to questions on various aspects of their relationships. Their report, *American Couples,* was considered to be a strong and important sociological study because of its large, diverse sample and its thorough research design. It provided a fresh perspective on the ways modern couples were approaching their sexual and loving relationships.

Sex Research in the Nineties

In 1992, the French government completed a survey of 20,055 people ages 18 to 69. The British also studied the sexual behavior of 18,876 individuals ages 16 to 59 (Johnson et al., 1994). Evidence from these two studies suggested two things that startled a number of sexologists. One was that people were not using condoms during their sexual activities to the extent that would be advisable to protect them against HIV infection. The other controversial finding, which has since been supported in U.S. research (Billy et al., 1993; Michael et al., 1994), was that same-gender (homosexual) sexual activity may not be as prevalent as earlier studies, such as Kinsey's, had suggested.

Puzzled by the many variations in the way HIV may be spread, the World Health Organization (WHO) conducted a major study on sexual behavior in 15 countries. One major methodological difficulty of the international project was designing a questionnaire that could be translated into many different languages so anyone might understand the sexual issues being addressed. Different research packages were designed for Africa, Europe, and the Americas (Cleland & Ferry, 1997). Cross-cultural and regional differences needed to be considered. For example, in some regions of Nigeria, polygamy (marriage to more than one spouse) is accepted for men as part of the culture. If a man there reports having had sex with several different women during a certain time period, it should not be assumed that the man has been "promiscuous" in a Western sense. It might instead mean that he has several wives. The WHO study gathered information on religious attitudes, educational levels, condom use, knowledge about AIDS, and premarital and extramarital sex. It represented the first coordinated international research on sexual behavior ever conducted on a major scale.

A general survey of sexual attitudes and behaviors in the United States was completed by Samuel and Cynthia Janus (1993), who published *The Janus Report on Sexual Behavior.* More than 4,500 people were pretested with a survey instrument, followed by data collection from a cross section of the U.S. adult population. Written questionnaires were completed by all respondents, and these were supplemented by 125 in-depth interviews conducted by carefully trained professionals. Data from 1,347 men and 1,418 women were analyzed to obtain the results of the survey. Although the researchers had responses from every region of the 48 contiguous states and tried to match the proportions of the population in various age groups with a comparable percentage in the survey sample, they also recruited volunteers. Just because their sample reflected some characteristics of the general population does not mean that volunteers who completed their questionnaire produced results that can be generalized to that population. The Janus research did, however, provide some interesting perspectives on the current sexual attitudes and activities of Americans.

Under what conditions would you respond truthfully to a survey about your sexual behavior?

The National Health and Social Life Survey

The most comprehensive study on sexual behavior in the United States to emerge since the Kinsey work was the National Health and Social Life Survey (NHSLS), conducted by highly respected researchers (see Figure 1.9). Even after the proposed research had received federal approval in 1991, conservative members of Congress introduced legislation that effectively eliminated the funding for such research. The researchers managed

FIGURE 1.9   *Robert T. Michael, John H. Gagnon, Stuart Michaels, and Edward O. Laumann*

Laumann, Gagnon, Michael, and Michaels conducted the National Health and Social Life Survey, the most comprehensive study on sexual behavior in the United States to emerge since the Kinsey work. Using scientific methodology, the study determined that most Americans are fairly content with their sexual lives.

to secure funding from eight private foundations and were able to proceed with their study. Their eventual funding supported a sample size of about 3,500 adults ages 18 to 59. Their random sampling techniques were among several characteristics that rendered this research particularly reliable and valuable. Working through the National Opinion Research Center at the University of Chicago to generate randomly selected areas of the country, they identified 4,369 households who had someone eligible to participate in the study and then randomly selected the individual in each household to be interviewed. This is the protocol that social scientists generally have established as valid methodology (Laumann, Gagnon, et al., 1994).

The questionnaire that the researchers employed was carefully designed to avoid confusing people with technical language and to flow naturally from topic to topic without predicting responses. This design is crucial in ensuring valid results. They decided on face-to-face interviews as the best technique to ensure that respondents understood the questions and to assure the respondents' identity. The research team selected 220 professional interviewers who were veterans of other surveys and carefully trained them. The interviewers were then dispersed to various parts of the

United States and encouraged to persuade all eligible individuals to participate in the survey. They sometimes returned several times in attempts to garner participant cooperation, conducting interviews over a seven-month period. This research ultimately demonstrated that people will indeed participate in sex surveys when they are convinced that the research serves legitimate social purposes, that their answers will be considered without judgment, and that their anonymity and confidentiality will be protected (Michael et al., 1994).

Eventually, 3,432 individuals were interviewed, a response rate of nearly 80 percent—one reason why the results of this study are considered to be so accurate. Another is that the sample population was randomly selected and almost exactly mirrored many characteristics of the general American population according to numerous measures. The questionnaire itself had a number of checks and cross-checks that helped validate the responses. Although the work had its detractors, social scientists generally accept the NHSLS data as among the best currently available, resulting from state-of-the-art survey techniques that yielded a high degree of validity to the data. The findings were, in a sense, counterrevolutionary because they reflected a nation that was indeed involved in a wide spectrum of sexual activities but in general was much less sexually active than previously believed. The study also suggested that Americans were, for the most part, more content with their sexual lives than had been assumed.

Long-Term Studies of Adolescent Sexuality

By the mid-1990s, plans were unveiled for a long-term federal study of teenage health, which included questioning some 20,000 teens about their sexual behavior. The study, to be completed in stages over several years, was called the National Longitudinal Study of Adolescent Health. Five hundred trained interviewers visited more than 20,000 adolescents in grades 7 to 12 at their homes, gathering information from them in a confidential manner. Their personal identities were not connected with any of the data. Although political controversies made it difficult for this study to get off the ground, data from the research are still being analyzed and continue to appear in a number of publications, offering a clearer perspective on sexual behavior among teens (Cubbin, Santelli, Brindis, & Braveman, 2005; Shafii et al., 2004).

The long-standing National Survey of Family Growth added questions on sexual behavior in 2002, and the survey reaches young people down to age 15. The Centers for Disease Control and Prevention also include sex-related questions in their ongoing Youth Risk Behavior Surveillance System (YRBS). This study has been closely coordinated with the questions on adolescent sexual health now included in a survey used by 35 areas across the world called Health Behaviors in School-aged Children (HBSC). The attention now being given to understanding adolescent sexuality bodes well for our future understanding of sexual trends and problems (National Center for Health Statistics, 2006; Ross et al., 2004).

Even in a time when adolescents clearly are sexually active, a great deal of controversy surrounds the right of researchers to question adolescents about sexual matters in order to obtain data. What are your feelings on this issue?

Sex Research in the Twenty-First Century

Several trends in sex research seem to be sorting themselves out. As shown in the previous section, we have begun the new century with the most accurate data on adolescent sexual behavior ever available. Also, information likely will continue to emerge from general surveys that more thoroughly examine the relationship of sexual behavior to HIV transmission. There is an expanding focus on multinational studies. The Global Study of Sexual Attitudes and Behaviors (GSSAB) surveyed several aspects of sexuality and relationships among people ages 40 to 80 in 29 countries, and it will take some time to analyze all the data. A total of 13,882 women and 13,618 men were surveyed (Laumann et al., 2005; Laumann et al., 2006). The focus on middle-aged and older adults was likely the result of the fact that the study was funded by a pharmaceutical company that manufactures a drug to help overcome erectile dysfunction in men and lack of sexual desire in women.

Another study reanalyzed data on sexual behavior generated from research conducted in 59 different countries, providing one of the most expansive looks at sexual behavior ever attempted (Wellings et al., 2006). This work highlights the fact that in many areas of the world our understanding of sexual behaviors and their impact on human health is poor.

Of special significance will be the evaluation of data on sexual behaviors and attitudes by ethnic group. Defining the groups by which ethnic factors can legitimately be defined is a matter still to be determined. Research often sorts out data for Hispanics, yet the U.S. Bureau of the Census has decided that data on race and Hispanic origin should be collected separately from other data. Some researchers have suggested that sex research should indeed focus on particular groups, such as African-American males, because of incorrect assumptions that have formed the foundation for past research (Lewis & Kertzner, 2003). On the other hand, Spanish-speaking people do not represent a homogenous race and in fact include whites, indigenous Native Americans, blacks, and even some Asians. Another complicating factor is that increasing numbers of young people are reporting that they have sexual partners who represent ethnicities different from their own (Ford et al., 2002). Adapting to population diversity is a challenge for researchers.

There is growing awareness among sex researchers that understanding the social context of a population being studied can be vitally important. The places people live are filled with meanings, as are the places people choose to make sexual contact. Socioeconomic status often is taken into account in research, yet no clear guidelines exist for defining and measuring this status. Many sex-related issues become reflected in social policies that affect particular groups of people. Good research will need to become better at understanding social contexts and their meanings (Braveman et al., 2005; Kelly & Muñoz-Laboy, 2005).

Sex researchers face some challenges regarding sex-related theory. Theories in sexual science often are oversimplified and fail to take into consideration the multidisciplinary nature of human sexuality. There is a great deal of confusion between **sexology,** the objective scientific study of sexuality, and **sexosophy,** the ideology or philosophy of sex. Much of what is passed off without question as scientific information regarding human sexuality is actually ideological pronouncement with no real scientific merit. As a society, we need to learn how to become more astute at separating the results of valid sex research from sensationalized hype (Reiss, 2000). Sexology needs to strive for greater congruence in theory and a closer fit between theory and practice, as well as a stronger connection to related sciences (Bancroft, 2000).

■ The Methods of Sexological Research

Research into the interdisciplinary realm of sexology has been increasing, and numerous professional journals are devoted exclusively to new concepts, controversies, and information relating to human sexuality (Zucker & Cantor, 2006). Sexuality is a part of human life that has many implications and stimulates many human reactions. Researchers who choose to study various aspects of human sexuality can become subject to questions about their personal and professional motivations, and the effects sometimes can be quite negative. While sex research can be intriguing, it may also carry some liabilities for the researcher (Poole, Giles, & Moore, 2004).

Although scientists are influenced to a degree by their own social and cultural circumstances (Wiederman & Whitley, 2002), sex researchers have a special obligation to approach their subjects without preconceived notions of what the data will show and without an agenda as to what sexual behaviors ought to be. With controversies raging in the culture wars, some people have been tempted to ignore scientific evidence or distort it for their own purposes. Theories about human sexuality represent a consensus among researchers in the field about the best ways to observe and explain things relating to sex, but researchers have a long way to go in creating solid theories about sexuality (Bancroft, 2000).

Perhaps reflective of increased scientific skepticism among the voting public, one battleground on which the culture wars are played out politically is funding for sex-related research. In order to investigate ways to control the spread of HIV and sexually transmitted diseases, it is sometimes necessary to conduct research on human sexual behavior. Conservative groups such as the Traditional Values Coalition have lobbied Congress to prevent the National Institutes of Health and other agencies from funding such studies, claiming that they

have no value in protecting public health. Agencies such as the Centers for Disease Control and Prevention have been forced to remove sex-related scientific data from their websites until they have modified them to reflect the Administration's moral stances. Worldwide, human beings bear a tremendous burden of ill health from sex-related causes, yet political sensitivities continue to hinder adequate funding of sex research. Whether we like it or not, it will be through political pressure and persuasion that this global problem begins to be addressed (Thomas, 2006).

Collecting Research Data on Human Sexuality

One goal of scientific research is to find information that can then be generalized to the "real world" outside the study. Science offers hope of being able to understand, predict, and perhaps control various phenomena. Obviously, using human beings as research subjects creates many problems, because we are not as easily categorized or experimentally controlled as mice or molecules. Sex researchers have the difficult responsibility of ensuring that their own methods and assumptions do not distort the outcome of their work. There is evidence, for example, that researchers' assumptions about sexuality can influence how questions are asked, as can the methods by which the answers are gathered (Graham et al., 2003; Meyer et al., 2002).

Quantitative research gathers information, or *data,* in a form that allows organization of the information into numerical form. Quantification also allows the data to be subjected to various forms of statistical analysis to help summarize the findings and test their reliability and validity. The term *data* is plural, referring to more than one *datum,* a single bit of information. There has been a growing willingness to gather and analyze qualitative data from people, which offer a somewhat more subjective view than do quantitative numbers and statistics (Morse, Swanson, & Kuzel, 2001). An example of qualitative research is interviewing a group of people about some sexual topic in order to solicit their values and beliefs. A rather nonstructured approach might be used, with the researcher then trying to organize all the information into useful categories. Even though such findings might not be easily organized into numerical form, they still could be informative and add value to the field. The particular methodological strategies that follow are used in conducting sex research and can be adapted for both quantitative and qualitative studies.

sexology the scientific study of human sexuality.

sexosophy the philosophies and ideologies relating to human sexuality.

Selecting Population Samples

When we attempt to answer some questions about human sexuality, we obviously would find it impossible to get information about all human beings. Therefore, it is necessary to select a **sample** of the human population from which the results can be generalized to the larger population. The more people included in the sample and the more proportionally representative they are of the various characteristics in the total population, the more statistically reliable the study may be considered to be. The best population sample is a **random sample,** in which individuals are selected at random from the whole population. If the number of persons selected is significant, the sample can be assumed to be highly representative of the whole. It is particularly crucial that population samples be reflective of the proportions of ethnic diversity in a particular population, because ethnicity may influence sexual attitudes and behaviors to at least some degree (Lewis & Kertzner, 2003). However, such studies must also be large and therefore expensive, so very little research of this sort has been conducted for groups as large as the population of an entire country.

Various forms of bias can enter human research studies and influence the results and conclusions. Not everyone may be willing to participate in a study on sexuality or answer honestly even if he or she agrees to participate. This creates volunteer bias, which is bound to affect the outcome of the research (Alexander & Fisher, 2003). Studies have shown that people who volunteer to participate in sexuality studies tend to be more sexually experienced than nonvolunteers, more interested in sexual variety, and generally more interested in sex (Plaud et al., 1999). Beyond this volunteer bias is actual response bias, which means that people may not always be accurate or truthful in self-reporting their sexual behaviors. Response bias can work in one of two ways. Some respondents may underreport or conceal their sexual behaviors out of personal embarrassment, fear that their anonymity will not be guaranteed, or concerns about reprisals. Others may exaggerate or embellish their reports because it is self-enhancing for them to imagine having been more adventurous than they actually have been.

Men seem to report higher levels of permissive sexual attitudes and behaviors than do women and are more likely to revise their reporting downward during later follow-up (Alexander & Fisher, 2003). Women seem to be initially more willing to participate in sex research but also more likely to refuse to continue if the study seems too personal or invasive (Boynton, 2003). In an analysis of studies from 59 countries, it was clear that men have a tendency to exaggerate their sexual activities and women tend to underreport them (Wellings et al., 2006). There is also concern that the results of sexuality studies may be affected by the sex of the experimenter involved in gathering results and by the amount of prior information provided to respondents. In one anonymous survey, if men were administered the survey by a woman and given written information that women are more sexually permissive than men, they tended to report having had more sexual partners than if the survey was administered by a man. This result calls into question the reliability of some previous studies (Fisher, 2007).

Even respondents anxious to be accurate may have distorted or inaccurate memories about sexual experience (Gillmore et al., 2001). There is also evidence that some people may be resistant to participating in certain types of sex research, especially if they perceive that their responses might be viewed in a negative light (Senn & Desmarais, 2001). For all these reasons, research studies on human sexuality must be carefully designed and tested to yield the most reliable data possible.

Taking Surveys

Asking people questions about their sexual attitudes or behaviors is one of the most common methods employed by sex researchers. It may be accomplished in face-to-face interviews, in telephone interviews, on the Internet, or through completion of paper questionnaires or daily diaries in which behaviors are recorded (Bowen, 2005; Yarber et al., 2005). The most surveyed group in the United States has been college students, who are often asked to complete questionnaires on sexuality because they represent a population accessible to faculty working on research—a sample of convenience. Care must be taken in generalizing such data to other populations. Daily telephone calls (touch-tone data entry) and written diaries have both been shown to have their strengths and weaknesses, and the problem of respondents being more reluctant to report certain behaviors than others is always present (Blumberg et al., 2003; Graham et al., 2003; Meyer et al., 2002).

The Kinsey researchers and those who conducted the NHSLS used carefully structured face-to-face interviewing procedures in which researchers were trained in techniques designed to establish an accepting attitude and avoid "leading" people into answers. These techniques may help minimize dishonesty and other forms of questionnaire bias. Printed questionnaires are an efficient and economical way of gathering information from

sample a representative group of a population that is the focus of a scientific poll or study.

random sample a representative group of the larger population that is the focus of a scientific poll or study in which care is taken to select participants without a pattern that might bias research results.

large numbers of people but make it much more difficult to detect dishonest answers, misunderstandings, exaggeration, or frivolity than do face-to-face interviews. Nevertheless, the interviewing mode used and the training and personal characteristics of the interviewer can affect the data that are collected. In any survey technique, it is crucial that the vocabulary used in the questions be understandable to the population being tested and that suitable statistical adjustments be made to account for individuals who have refused to participate or to answer particular questions.

The Internet is increasingly used to recruit research volunteers and to gather sexuality data. The initial studies have relied on samples of convenience, but as researchers become more sophisticated with the use of this medium, they may be able to randomize responses as they are submitted. Some evidence suggests that participants respond more honestly to computers than to human interviewers (Kurth et al., 2004). Internet sex research is a developing field (Bowen, 2005; Ross et al., 2003).

Explaining Gender Discrepancies in Sex Surveys

Surveys of sexual behavior have shown a consistent pattern in the data that has puzzled researchers and the general public alike: Men tend to report having had more female sexual partners than the numbers of male partners women say they have had. Intuitively, this does not make sense unless many men were having sex with a much smaller cohort of women. But this does not seem to be a particularly satisfactory answer. Studies have explored the reasons for this gender discrepancy and have developed a clearer picture of what is happening. The discrepancy seems to rest with the ways men and women tend to report their sexual histories. Men who report having had high numbers of sexual partners (i.e., more than 20) tend to round up their figures by 5s, 10s, and even 25s. This may be because they have a poorer memory as to the exact number of partners, or because men are more comfortable exaggerating the numbers. When the data generated by people who report large numbers of partners are eliminated, the ratio of the number of sex partners reported by males and females falls much closer to a one-to-one ratio—actually, about 1.2 to 1.

It has been suggested that women are more accurate and conservative in their reporting of numbers of partners and also prone to undercounting. The bottom line, then, is that gender discrepancies probably are not very pronounced at all and that sex researchers must find better investigative techniques for eliminating the problem with the data (Wiederman, 1999). It might be advisable to ask questions about shorter time frames and to use questions that help people remember more accurately.

Case Studies and Clinical Research

Professional counselors, physicians, psychologists, and other clinicians often work with individuals who are experiencing some sexual concern or problem. These professionals employ various treatment strategies to help the individual and may devise new methods. They might discover that these strategies and methods are effective for several clients or patients. **Case studies** then may be published, giving an in-depth look at particular individual circumstances. Although it is risky to overgeneralize from case studies, they do offer the professional community new ideas and useful insights.

When some sort of treatment strategy is tested with larger numbers of people, it is called **clinical research.** The study may consider the cause, treatment, and prevention of a disease or condition. For example, Masters and Johnson (1970) conducted clinical studies for several years on nearly 800 individuals who complained of various forms of sexual dysfunction. They categorized and labeled the problems, looked for possible causes, and tried out a variety of treatment methods. They then did follow-up studies on some of the individuals over a five-year period. Although making generalizations to the entire population must be done with caution in such a study, clinical studies of this sort provide a foundation on which further research can build.

Observational Research

Some researchers have chosen to observe an aspect of human sexual behavior directly, thereby eliminating the biases characteristic of research in which people report on themselves. Observational studies may take place in laboratory settings or in the field. The Masters and Johnson (1966) research on human sexual response, discussed earlier in this chapter, is an example of a classic laboratory-based observational study. Various types of instrumentation were used to measure the physiological reactions of 694 people when they were aroused sexually. It was the first large-scale research in which observations of the body's sexual responses were made in a systematic manner.

Masters and Johnson were always careful to point out that their findings might not apply to the responses of all human beings. However, physiologists typically have assumed when dealing with the processes of the

case study an in-depth look at a particular individual and how he or she might be helped to solve a sexual or other problem. Case studies may offer new and useful ideas for counselors to use with other patients.

clinical research the study of the cause, treatment, or prevention of a disease or condition by testing large numbers of people.

human body that such activities really are very similar among different people. It may be difficult to determine how much—if at all—the laboratory setting might affect people's functioning. In subsequent studies that have recruited volunteers to measure physiological responses, significant numbers of people have refused to participate because they do not feel comfortable with the research conditions. Naturally, this biases the population sample (Gaither, Sellbom, & Meier, 2003). Nevertheless, most sexologists have accepted the findings of Masters and Johnson, and many other observational researchers, as fundamental to our understanding of human sexuality.

Ethnosexual Field Studies

Anthropologists often conduct observational field studies of other cultures, living among the people they are studying, observing their customs and behaviors, and attempting to collect data through communications with the members of that society. Collecting information that describes a particular culture is called **ethnography.** When the information pertains specifically to sexual practices and beliefs, the data are sometimes called **ethnosexual.** Anthropologist Margaret Mead was one of the first scientists to openly discuss the sexual mores of other cultures in her writings, including her famous work *Growing Up in New Guinea* (Mead, 1930). One of the earliest detailed cross-cultural surveys to appear in the field of human sexuality was a collection of field studies called *Patterns of Sexual Behavior* published by two ethnographers, Clellan Ford and Frank Beach (1951). It focused on sexual techniques, rules for mating, and the prevalence of various forms of sexual behavior in several different societies.

Cultural values can affect the gathering of sex-related data in several ways. Certain behaviors may be stigmatized in some cultures, leading to reluctance and embarrassment when it comes to discussing or reporting those behaviors. The meaning of terms may get confused when researchers from one culture attempt to discuss sexuality in another culture with which they are relatively unfamiliar. Some sexual terms simply cannot be translated from one language into another. Finally, there are always subcultures within larger cultures, making it difficult to generalize about the entire population. Cross-cultural studies about sexuality therefore demand a great deal of precision, sensitivity, and care in their design (Herdt, 2000).

Experimental Research

A keystone of science is the use of the **controlled experiment.** In this type of research, the investigator examines what happens to a particular **variable** being studied and manipulated while an attempt is made to control all other variables and keep them constant.

The researcher then may draw inferences about cause-and-effect relationships that are difficult or impossible to draw from other kinds of research.

Well-controlled experiments, however, are difficult to design for human subjects, whose complexity makes it nearly impossible to control all possible variables. Additionally, there is always the chance that the artificiality of a controlled experimental setting may influence the outcome of research with humans. For these reasons, experimental research evidence in human sexuality is sparse and ultimately open to the same shortcomings and criticisms found in other methods of study.

Ethical Issues in Sex Research

How willing would you be to be a subject in sex research if you weren't entirely clear about what the researchers were trying to find out? Do you think there could be times when some deception might be all right in sex research, if this were the best way to get accurate data and the test subjects were told the truth after they had taken part in the study?

Four fundamental moral principles must be considered when doing research with human subjects: (1) respect for an individual's autonomy and independent decision making; (2) the importance of doing no harm; (3) the pursuit of benefit for people, balanced with risks and costs; and (4) the pursuit of "distributive justice," that is, ensuring the greatest benefit for the largest number of persons (Cwikel & Hoban, 2005). A great deal of attention is focused on the need to protect and respect those people who participate as subjects in any form of human research. Because sexuality is viewed as such a private aspect of life, the ethical issues involved in sex research are particularly evident and crucial. Unpleasant anecdotes are told about human research subjects being exposed to inappropriate touching and violations of their privacy (Bartlett, 2003).

Human research subjects have the right of **informed consent,** meaning that they must be

ethnography (eth-NAH-gruffy) the anthropological study of other cultures.

ethnosexual referring to data concerning the sexual beliefs and customs of other cultures.

controlled experiment research in which the investigator examines what is happening to one variable while all other variables are kept constant.

variable an aspect of a scientific study that is subject to change.

informed consent the consent given by research subjects, indicating their willingness to participate in a study, after they are informed about the purpose of the study and how they will be asked to participate.

given complete prior information about the purpose of the study and the manner in which they will participate. It has generally been agreed that researchers do not have the right to coerce people into participation or to be dishonest in presenting information about the research. Similarly, scientists have the obligation to protect the confidentiality of their participants by making certain that personal, private facts can never be connected with a particular individual. They must also protect subjects from physical and psychological harm.

Researchers use a variety of methods to provide for anonymity in collecting data and to prevent the inappropriate release of confidential information at some later time. Universities and government agencies usually have institutional review boards that must approve any research design involving human participation. These committees carefully attempt to weigh the potential value of the research to society against any inherent stresses, risks, or dangers for the participants. The decision to allow an investigator to proceed with such research is not always an easy one.

In the course of gathering data from human research subjects, researchers sometimes may be given information that identifies the subject as either the victim or the perpetrator of a sexual crime. This can create an ethical dilemma for the researcher if the subject has been promised anonymity or confidentiality, yet the laws of the state require reporting. For

example, some states mandate the reporting of incidents in which adolescents have been subjected to sexual activity by someone older than themselves, although the adolescent may not have intended to accuse anyone as part of offering the information in a research setting. This ethical issue points up the importance of researchers' understanding laws that could affect their work and modifying their methods and informed consent procedures accordingly (Findholt & Robrecht, 2002).

Ethical dilemmas also have emerged in the study of sexual trafficking, which involves the transport of women across national borders where they are forced to participate in sexual activity for money. These women sometimes have been kidnapped or abducted into prostitution or have been deceived into entering into an unfavorable contractual arrangement with promises of a better life. Because sex trafficking has become a serious global problem, good research is important to understand it more fully. However, researchers face complications in securing valid informed consent, because the women are fearful of punishment. Gaining access to the women in the first place can be both difficult and risky. Of special concern to researchers is their own need to maintain objectivity even though they may be aware of illegal acts being committed during the course of their studies. Debate over appropriate responses to such ethical dilemmas continues (Cwikel & Hoban, 2005).

Attitude Questionnaire

Rate each attitude with one of the following numbers:
0 = uncertain   **3** = relatively neutral
1 = strongly disagree   **4** = somewhat agree
2 = somewhat disagree **5** = strongly agree

Attitude Statement	Rating for Your Parent(s)	Rating for Yourself 4–6 Years Ago	Your Present Rating
1. Masturbation is a healthy, normal mode of sexual expression.	_____	_____	_____
2. Young people should be encouraged to use masturbation as a way of exploring their sexual feelings.	_____	_____	_____
3. Sexual activity without marriage or long-term commitment is all right for a couple who share a loving relationship.	_____	_____	_____
4. Sexual activity solely for physical pleasure is all right if both partners agree to it.	_____	_____	_____
5. In a loving partnership, having sex with others outside the primary relationship is all right if both partners agree.	_____	_____	_____

Attitude Statement	Rating for Your Parent(s)	Rating for Yourself 4–6 Years Ago	Your Present Rating
6. Gay, lesbian, and bisexual lifestyles are acceptable.	_____	_____	_____
7. Lesbians, gay men, and bisexual women or men should not be discriminated against because of their sexual orientation.	_____	_____	_____
8. Pornography depicting sexual activity between adults should be available for adults who wish to purchase and view it.	_____	_____	_____
9. Any sexual behavior is acceptable between consenting adults.	_____	_____	_____
10. At a beach, I would not be offended or made uncomfortable by having others around me in the nude.	_____	_____	_____
11. I would not be uncomfortable being nude myself with other nude people at the beach.	_____	_____	_____
12. The naked human body should be considered a source of beauty and pleasure, and not a source of shame.	_____	_____	_____
13. Women should have the same access and rights to sexual experience that men have.	_____	_____	_____
14. Women can enjoy sex and get as much pleasure from it as men do.	_____	_____	_____
15. Women should be as sexually assertive as men in initiating sexual activity.	_____	_____	_____
16. Accurate sex information should be available to all young people and adults.	_____	_____	_____
17. Birth control information and devices should be available to minors without parental consent.	_____	_____	_____
18. Physicians should be able to treat minors for sexually transmitted diseases without notification of parents.	_____	_____	_____
19. I support abortion as an alternative in cases of unplanned pregnancy.	_____	_____	_____
20. Women should have free choice about and access to abortion.	_____	_____	_____
TOTALS:	_____	_____	_____

Self-Evaluation

You and Your Sexuality

The questionnaires in this section are designed to help you take stock of your own sexual attitudes and their possible changes throughout your lifetime. They will also help you evaluate some of your sexual background and its meaning for your life today as a sexual human being. I hope that taking a closer look at your sexuality now will provide a more personal context for exploring the remainder of this book. Although there may be a variety of ways to use these questionnaires for classroom and group awareness activities, I have intended them for your own personal use.

Sexual Attitudes in Your Life

In the questionnaire on pages 28–29, you are asked to compare your present sexual attitudes with those of your parent(s) (or the primary people who raised you) and with your own values of four to six years ago. It might be interesting to ask your parent(s) to complete the questionnaire. Otherwise, complete the column for your parent(s) with the responses you feel accurately represent their attitudes.

Analysis: The final totals give a rough standard for comparison of your present attitudes with your attitudes of a few years ago and with those of the parent(s) (or others) who gave you your earliest attitudes. Generally speaking, the higher the total score, the more liberal the attitudes (highest possible score is 100). There are no right or wrong responses or good or bad scores. Examine the individual responses and totals to get a clearer picture of how your sexual attitudes compare with those of your parent(s) and how your own attitudes have or have not changed over the past few years.

Your Sexual History

The following questions are intended to provide further means of exploring where you have been as a sexual person and where you are now. It may help you to write the answers down or to talk about the answers with someone you trust.

1. **Nudity**
   a. How often, when you were young, did you see your parent(s) in the nude? What was your family's attitude toward nudity?
   b. If you ever have children (or if you have children now), do you hope to be (or are you now) more accepting of nudity in your family than your parent(s), less accepting, or about the same?

2. **Masturbation**
   a. How did you first learn about or discover masturbation, and how did you feel about it at first?
   b. If you masturbated when you were younger, did you ever let anyone else know about it?
   c. If you masturbate now, how do you feel about the practice?

3. **Sex Slang—"Dirty Words"**
   a. Make a list of the sex-related slang terms (such as "screwing," "fuck," "cock," "cunt," and so forth) that you feel comfortable using, if any.
   b. Which of the words on the list would your parent(s) have been comfortable using?
   c. Which of the words on the list would be offensive to you if you heard them being spoken by a friend of the other gender? Of the same gender?

4. **First Sexual Experience (if applicable)**
   a. What is the first explicit sexual experience with another person that you can remember?
   b. What were your reactions to that first erotic experience?
   c. Has that initial experience affected your feelings about yourself as a sexual person or about sex in general even until today? If so, how?

5. **Male-Female Intercourse**
   a. How did you first learn about sexual intercourse between a woman and a man, and what were your reactions and feelings when you did learn about it?
   b. If you have experienced sexual intercourse with someone of the other gender, what were your feelings following the first experience?
   c. Are your attitudes toward sexuality different now from what they were when you first had intercourse? If so, in what ways?

6. **Same-Gender Activities and Transgender Attitudes**
   a. How did you first learn about attractions and sex between members of the same gender, and what were your reactions and feelings when you did learn about it?
   b. If you have ever participated in a sexual experience (even as a youngster) with someone of the same gender, what are your feelings about the experience?
   c. Do you feel comfortable with the gender roles that are expected of you because of the sex organs with which you were born?
   d. What is your reaction to people who prefer to adopt gender roles or change their bodies so they appear to be of the other gender?

7. **Sexual Behavior**
   a. For you, what kinds of behavior constitute "hooking up"? How about "having sex"?
   b. In thinking about sexual contact, or during sexual involvement with another person, which of the following are exciting for you and which are turnoffs?
      1. *Undressing each other*
      2. *Oral sex performed on you*
      3. *Oral sex performed on partner (by you)*
      4. *Anal sex*
      5. *Kissing and being together nude*
      6. *Intercourse*
      7. *Touching and caressing*
      8. *Using some painful stimulation*
      9. *Acting out a sexual fantasy*
      10. *Mutual masturbation*
   c. If you have had intense shared sexual experiences, what things about the experience(s) have pleased and satisfied you most? Which have displeased or frustrated you most?
   d. What qualities do you desire in your ideal sexual partner?

8. **Your Cultural Heritage**
   a. What do you see as your primary cultural heritage, and how do you think that heritage has been a basis for your sexual values, beliefs, and decisions?
   b. Have you ever felt that your attitudes about sexuality were different from those of others around you because of your cultural differences? If so, how has that made you feel?
   c. Has your race, religion, or ethnic background ever caused others to react to you sexually in a way that you found surprising or uncomfortable?

Chapter Summary

1. Human sexuality is an area of contradictions and complexities that crosses disciplinary boundaries. To study sexuality is a significant way of understanding many different aspects of human cultures, behaviors, and social interactions. To teach about sexuality can be controversial.

2. North America has tended to be Eurocentric in its sexual values, even though it has a very diverse population representing many different ethnic and cultural backgrounds. It is important to recognize that there are many cultural differences in sexual beliefs and customs globally. Understanding the cultural bases for these differences can provide a clearer perspective on the diversity within human sexuality.

3. Small, homogenous cultures are more conformist in their sexual practices than are large, heterogenous cultures. Attitudes and openness about sexuality are changing throughout the world.

4. Just after World War II and for three decades after, dramatic shifts occurred in attitudes concerning various aspects of human sexuality, sometimes referred to as the sexual revolution. There was a new emphasis on personal autonomy, equality between women and men, technological development, the need for sexuality education, openness about different sexual orientations and gender identities, and the relationship between love and sex.

5. Following the changes of the sexual revolution, several factors influenced sexual values and behaviors, including the appearance of HIV/AIDS, greater attention to sex in the media and on the Internet, and use of sex-related issues by politicians.

6. We are presently seeing ongoing "culture wars," based loosely on conservative and liberal ideologies. These become reflected in sex-related debates.

7. North American attitudes regarding sexuality seem to fall roughly into three main categories: traditional or procreational, relational, and recreational. These often contradictory attitudinal systems exist side by side in our society and greatly influence people's sexual choices and behaviors.

8. Attitudes toward particular aspects of sexuality have changed, and there is greater openness about sexual orientations, alternative behaviors, and gender identities.

9. Many areas of human sexuality remain controversial, and studies continue to help clarify different sides of the debates.

10. Three significant pioneers in nineteenth-century studies of human sexuality were Richard von Krafft-Ebing, Sigmund Freud, and Henry Havelock Ellis. Their work established fundamental perspectives on sexuality that persisted well into the twentieth century.

11. The early twentieth century was heavily influenced by Victorian values about sex and romance. The Kinsey studies opened new vistas concerning the spectrum of sexual behavior, and Masters and Johnson pioneered work in understanding sexual physiology and the treatment of sexual dysfunctions.

12. Much early research on sexual behavior did not represent accurate generalizations for the entire population because only population samples of convenience were used in the studies.

13. Several surveys about sex conducted in the 1970s, 1980s, and 1990s gained worldwide attention and offered new perspectives on sexuality. However, they suffered from methodological flaws in how participants were recruited and a lack of control over the completion of questionnaires.

14. Several surveys on sexual behavior have emerged in the United States and Europe, and their results are providing a new picture of sexual attitudes and behaviors.

15. The random sampling and interview techniques employed by the National Health and Social Life Survey have yielded the most statistically reliable results on sexual behaviors and attitudes in the United States. This survey has caused us to reassess many of our assumptions about the spectrum and frequency of sexual activity.

16. Studies on adolescent sexual behavior are providing valuable information and, along with research on global sexual health, represent one of the themes of sex research in the twenty-first century.

17. The scientific study of sex may be quantitative or qualitative and can involve various methods: population samples, surveys, case studies and clinical research, direct observation of behavior, ethnosexual field studies, and controlled experiments.

18. Scientific research raises numerous ethical issues, and researchers sometimes face ethical dilemmas in their work. Informed consent is considered essential to participation in any such research.

19. Understanding ourselves as sexual human beings requires some introspection and self-questioning.

Focus on Health Questions

In this section you will find the kinds of questions that you may have concerning your own health and sexuality. The page references indicate where in the text the answer is located; the exact place is marked with this logo: **FOH**

1. It seems that I am always getting mixed messages about sex. Is it just because of my family, or what? **5–6**

2. My parents came of age during the sexual revolution. Was that a time of greater sexual freedom? **7–10**

3. Is homosexuality sick? **9**

4. Am I the only one that thinks sex just for fun is okay? **12**

5. I was surprised by the results of a survey I saw in a women's magazine. Are these things reliable? **20**

Chapter 2
Female Sexual Anatomy and Physiology

Chapter Outline

Only two times during my childhood did my mother ever have to refer to my genitals, and both times all she could say was "down there." After I grew up, I guess she must have decided there was no need to refer to that region at all. It wasn't until I took this course that I said the word "vagina" out loud myself. It feels as though I had to take 19 years to legitimize the entire sexual part of my body enough to make it part of me.

—from a student essay

The basic anatomy of the sex organs, also called genitals, has been known for centuries, but reliable information on how these organs function and interact was not available until the latter part of the twentieth century. The genital organs have various functions in procreation, in sexual pleasure, and as one route to intimate sharing and communication within a relationship. Some preliminary research indicates that how an individual feels about her or his own genitals may affect general self-image and levels of sexual desire (Berman et al., 2003).

When the female sex organs are studied in sexuality education, the emphasis clearly has tended toward the reproductive functions of the uterus, ovaries, and fallopian tubes. Female sexuality once was represented through a screen of male beliefs and assumptions rather than having a clearly articulated female form of expression (Bean, 2002). The important roles of the vagina, clitoris, and other external structures in sexual pleasure were too often neglected (Miller & Ellis, 2006). Some young men indicate that they find women's bodies to be complex puzzles that are difficult to understand (Koch, 2006). This chapter and subsequent chapters of this text recognize the sex organs of both women and men as potential sources of sexual pleasure and interpersonal intimacy.

The Vulva

Many externally located female sexual structures play an important role in sexual arousal (see Figure 2.1). Internal organs tend to be more important in regulating hormonal cycles and the reproductive processes. The external female sex organs, located between the legs, below and in front of the pubic symphysis (the part of

FIGURE 2.1   *External Female Anatomy*

The human sex organs are important for both procreation and recreation. Historically, sex educators focused on the internal sex organs and reproduction, especially in women. In recent years, they have also focused on the pleasurable aspects of sexual behavior and the external sex organs.

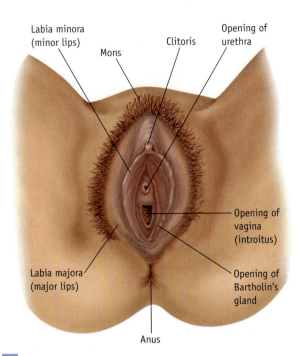

Labia minora (minor lips)   Mons   Clitoris   Opening of urethra

Labia majora (major lips)   Opening of vagina (introitus)   Opening of Bartholin's gland

Anus

FIGURE 2.2   *Vulva*

The external female sex organs consist of the mons, labia, and clitoris. They have numerous nerve endings and therefore are sensitive to stimulation. In shape, size, and color, the external sex organs vary greatly from woman to woman.

the pelvic bone directly above the genitals), are known collectively as the **vulva** (see Figure 2.2). There is a great deal of variation in the sizes and shapes of the various external female genitalia, all perfectly normal. Especially visible on the vulva are the **mons** and the **labia majora** (major or outer lips). The mons, sometimes termed the mons pubis or mons veneris, is a rounded pad of fatty tissue just above the other sex organs on the pubic bone. Pubic hair begins to grow on the mons during puberty, usually arranged in a roughly triangular pattern. The mons is well endowed with nerve endings, and most women find that rubbing or exerting pressure on this area may lead to sexual arousal. The entire area of the vulva is considered a major female erogenous zone because it generally is very sensitive to sexual stimulation.

vulva external sex organs of the female, including the mons, major and minor lips, clitoris, and opening of the vagina.

mons cushion of fatty tissue located over the female's pubic bone.

labia majora (LAY-bee-uh mah-JOR-uh) two outer folds of skin covering the minor lips, clitoris, urinary meatus, and vaginal opening.

Labia majora

Prepuce or foreskin ("hood")

Urinary meatus (opening)

Clitoral shaft (covered by prepuce)

Clitoral glans

Labia minora

FIGURE 2.3 *Clitoris*

The clitoris, the most sensitive area of a female's genitals, is located just beneath the point where the tops of the minor lips meet. It is unique in that it is the only organ of either sex whose sole function is to provide sexual sensation and pleasure.

The labia majora are two folds of skin that extend from the mons down between the legs. They are relatively flat and indistinct in some women and thick and prominent in others. With the advent of cosmetic surgery, some women who have been dissatisfied with the shape or size of the labia have resorted to operations that change their appearance (Berman et al., 2003). During puberty, the skin of the major lips darkens slightly, and hair grows on their outer surfaces. These external labia cover and protect the inner, more sensitive sex organs. The inner structures cannot be seen unless the labia majora are parted, so women may find it useful to position a mirror in such a way that they are able to see the other structures.

When the major lips are separated, another pair of smaller folds of skin becomes visible, the **labia minora** (minor or inner lips). These are observed as pink, hairless, irregular, asymmetrical ridges; they meet at the top to form a sheath of skin covering the clitoris called the **prepuce** or clitoral hood (see Figure 2.3). Both the major and minor lips are sensitive to stimulation and are important in sexual arousal. Just inside the minor lips are openings to ducts connected to **Bartholin's glands,** sometimes called the vulvovaginal glands. These glands produce a small amount of secretion during sexual arousal, which may help moisten the entrance to the vagina and to some extent the labia. This secretion does not play a major role in lubrication of the vagina during arousal, however, and any other functions these glands may have are not known. Bartholin's glands can occasionally become

infected with bacteria (from feces or other sources) and may require medical treatment.

Often the labia minora must be separated before the two openings between them can be seen. Just below the clitoris, a small hole is visible—the **urinary meatus,** or urethral opening. It is through this opening that urine leaves the body. Below the urethra is a larger orifice—the vaginal opening or **introitus**—that leads into the vagina. The opening of the vagina does not usually seem to be a hole and in fact may only be recognized as an opening when something is inserted into it. In some women, particularly in younger age groups, the vaginal opening is partly covered by membranous tissue called the **hymen** (discussed later in the section on the vagina).

Clitoris

The **clitoris** is the most sexually sensitive female sex organ. Appropriate stimulation of the clitoris is usually necessary for women to reach orgasm, although the manner in which that stimulation is best applied varies from woman to woman. The most visible part of the clitoris is usually observed as a rounded tip protruding from the hood or front commissure created by the merging of the labia minora. This external, sensitive head of the clitoris is called the **glans.** For many years, it has been compared to the penis because of its sensitivity to sexual stimulation and capability of erection. It also has been inaccurately viewed as a poorly developed, nonfunctional penis. On the contrary, the clitoris and the entire internal clitoral system of blood

labia minora (LAY-bee-uh mih-NOR-uh) two inner folds of skin that join above the clitoris and extend along the sides of the vaginal and urethral openings.

prepuce (PREE-peus) in the female, tissue of the upper vulva that covers the clitoral shaft.

Bartholin's glands (BAR-tha-lenz) small glands located in the opening through the minor lips that produce some secretion during sexual arousal.

urinary meatus (mee-AY-tuss) opening through which urine passes from the urethra to the outside of the body.

introitus (in-TROID-us) the outer opening of the vagina.

hymen membranous tissue that can cover part of the vaginal opening.

clitoris (KLIT-a-rus) sexually sensitive organ found in the female vulva; it becomes engorged with blood during arousal.

glans sensitive head of the female clitoris, visible between the upper folds of the minor lips.

Real Student Voices

■ The first time I had sex with a woman, I felt intimidated because I knew so little about the female body. She was helpful, but I felt like a complete idiot. I'm glad I know more of the details now; who wants to take a trip without a map?

■ After you suggested in class that everyone should take time to get acquainted with their bodies, I decided to give it a try. I actually got a mirror and a flashlight so I could see better. I was really embarrassed at first—even though I was completely

alone—but I eventually became more comfortable. It's good to know how all the pieces of the puzzle fit together.

■ It was good to learn that I'm not the only woman who has a lot of pain in the vaginal area. It really interferes with intimacy. My family doctor didn't seem to take it very seriously, and I almost felt he thought it was all in my head. I'm going to see a woman gynecologist now, and try some new things.

---

vessels, nerves, and erectile tissue constitute a very functional and important sex organ.

The **shaft** of the clitoris extends back under the clitoral hood, or prepuce. The glans is the only clitoral structure that hangs free, although it is usually not particularly movable (see Figure 2.3). The clitoral shaft is attached to the body along its entire underside. The clitoris contains two columns and two bulbs of spongy tissue, which become engorged with blood during sexual excitement, causing the entire structure to become hardened or erect. When it is not erect, the clitoris is rarely more than an inch in length, with only the tip (glans) external and visible, but during erection it enlarges considerably, especially in diameter (Khalife et al., 2000). Typically, in earlier stages of arousal, the clitoris protrudes more than it does in an unaroused state. As arousal proceeds, it retracts again.

Tiny glands lining the prepuce produce oil that may mix with other secretions to form a substance called **smegma.** If this material collects around the shaft, mild infections may result. An infection could cause some pain or discomfort, especially during sexual activity. If smegma accumulations become a problem, they may be removed by a physician who inserts a small probe under the hood or prepuce. A surgical procedure is sometimes used to cut the prepuce slightly, further exposing the clitoral glans and shaft. The procedure, called **circumcision** in Western culture, is not common in females, and the medical profession has found little legitimacy for it.

Female Genital Cutting

In other cultures and other historical periods, the clitoris and labia have been subjected to various types of

surgery and removal mutilation. With fears of masturbation rife from the mid-nineteenth century to about 1935, it was not unusual for physicians in Europe and the United States to perform female circumcision or to remove part or all of the clitoris, a surgical procedure called **clitoridectomy.** These measures were thought to "cure" masturbation and prevent the insanity that was thought to result.

In several sub-Saharan African and Eastern Asian cultures and religions, clitoridectomy—often inaccurately called "female circumcision"—is still practiced as a rite of passage into adulthood. Millions of women each year worldwide undergo some form of genital cutting, sometimes called female genital mutilation (FGM). Those who advocate such practices object to the mutilation label, saying it is culturally biased. Although such cutting may take the form of a traditional circumcision, in which the hood of tissue covering the clitoris is removed, more often the clitoral glans is removed as well. Sometimes a more extensive clitoridectomy is performed, involving removal of the entire clitoris and much of the labial

shaft in the female, the longer body of the clitoris, containing erectile tissue.

smegma thick, oily substance that may accumulate under the prepuce of the clitoris or penis.

circumcision (SIR-cum-sizh-uhn) of clitoris: surgical procedure that cuts the prepuce, exposing the clitoral shaft.

clitoridectomy (clih-torr-ih-DECK-tah-mee) surgical removal of the clitoris; practiced routinely in some cultures.

tissue surrounding it (James & Robertson, 2002, 2004; Leonard, 2001).

As a rite marking a girl's passage to adulthood, clitoridectomy is meant to remove any vestiges of "maleness," because the clitoris typically is viewed as a miniature penis in these cultures. Thus, to have it removed is viewed as the ultimate symbol of womanhood. Clitoridectomy, however, reduces sexual pleasure, an important aspect in cultures where men are expected to control female sexuality (El-Defrawi et al., 2001). The practice seems to be perpetuated in conditions of poverty and domestic violence toward women (Jackson et al., 2003; Refaat et al., 2001). Taboos have developed in support of the practice. In Nigeria, for example, some women believe that if the head of a newborn touches the clitoris during the birth process, the baby will become insane.

Some cultures also practice **infibulation,** in which the labia minora and sometimes the labia majora are removed and the sides of the external portion of the vagina are sewn together or fastened with thorns or natural glues, ensuring that the woman will not have intercourse prior to marriage. The fastening materials are removed at the time of marriage, although the procedure may be repeated if the husband is going to be absent for long periods of time. Tough scar tissue often forms that can make urination, menstruation, sexual intercourse, and childbirth extremely difficult and painful. Infibulation is meant to protect the virginity of the woman in those cultures that place a high premium on it as a condition of marriage. Infibulated women bring high rewards for their families when they are chosen as brides, in the form of money, goods, and livestock (Leonard, 2001).

These rites may be carried out with crude instruments, without sterile conditions or anesthetic, although often they are performed by physicians (Dandash, Refaat, & Eyada, 2001). Girls and women subjected to such procedures often get serious infections, and the unsterilized instruments have been associated with the spread of HIV. Girls sometimes die from bleeding or infection following genital cutting. There is also a growing body of evidence that ritualized surgical practices can create psychological trauma. Intuitively, we would expect this to be true, but recent research also supports the fact that such procedures can have far-reaching effects on women's sexuality and marriages. It has been believed to disrupt the childbirth process as well, but this does not seem to be documented except in deeper and more extreme forms of cutting (Slanger, Snow, & Okonofua, 2002). Cultural changes have brought some modernization of traditional procedures, and in some places aseptic methods are now used, lowering the risk of infection. For a brief time, Egyptian health authorities encouraged their hospitals to do the procedures in order to

prevent the medical complications common with amateur practices while providing counseling to families to discourage the practice. The Egyptian Health Ministry then decided to bar all health care workers from performing any female genital cutting, but a judge struck down the ban, apparently again out of concern for how the procedures were being carried out by nonmedical practitioners.

There has been growing worldwide condemnation toward these practices as barbaric and sexist. The United States has begun to examine the surrounding issues more closely, because it is becoming clear that some girls in immigrant families from 40 countries may have undergone the procedure in the United States. An African woman named Fauziya Kassindja fled the country of Togo rather than submit to genital cutting, and she eventually entered the United States illegally. After she had spent over a year in jail, the Board of Immigration Appeals ruled that FGM is indeed an act of persecution and constituted legitimate grounds for offering the woman asylum. Although others maintain that such practices represent cultural imperatives and should be respected, this ruling and other movements in the more developed countries are reinforcing the notion that genital cutting constitutes a violation of human rights that should be condemned and halted (James & Robertson, 2002, 2004).

Female genital cutting typically is deeply embedded in a particular culture's way of life, and is reflective of historical patriarchal traditions in which women have been considered the possessions of men and women's sexuality has been subjugated to men. They may be seen as fundamental rites of passage to adulthood and even looked upon with pride by the adult woman. Yet increasing emphasis on women's rights even in developing countries has led to growing worldwide opposition to these procedures. Debates rage within the countries where the practices still exist. Younger, more Westernized women, often with the support of their husbands, are calling for new symbolic rites of passage that can preserve the positive cultural meanings and traditions without subjecting girls to the painful and dangerous surgeries. Feminists in Western cultures have been particularly outspoken on this issue, insisting that such procedures not only are physically dangerous but also represent attempts to emphasize the inferior status of women. The controversy is a classic example of a clash between cultural mores and shifting values about sexuality and gender on a global level (James & Robertson, 2002, 2004).

infibulation (in-fib-you-LAY-shun) surgical procedure, performed in some cultures, that seals the opening of the vagina.

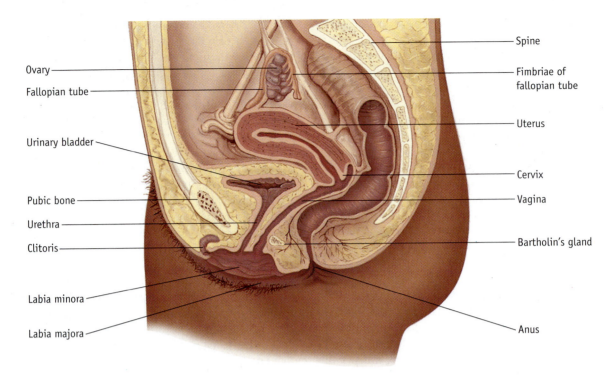

Spine

Fimbriae of
fallopian tube

Uterus

Cervix

Vagina

Bartholin's gland

Anus

Ovary

Fallopian tube

Urinary bladder

Pubic bone

Urethra

Clitoris

Labia minora

Labia majora

FIGURE 2.4 *Female Sexual and Reproductive Organs*

*What do you think about female genital cutting as
practiced in other cultures and historical periods?
How has it been justified in these cultures? Can you
think of any similar North American practices? To
what degree do you think people outside a particular
culture have the right to play an activist role in
calling for an end to such practices?*

■ The Vagina

The **vagina** is a muscular tube that is important as a female organ of reproduction and sexual pleasure (see
Figure 2.4). It has been celebrated as an organ of mystery and power throughout human history (Blackledge,
2004). The muscular walls of the vagina, which are very
elastic, sit together except when something is inserted
into the cavity, so the inner cavity is best described
as a "potential" space. The vagina is usually about
4 inches deep, although during sexual arousal it deepens. The inner lining of the vagina is fleshy and soft and
is corrugated by thin ridges of tissue. The area near the
opening of the vagina, along with the outer third of
the vagina itself, has many nerve endings, and stimulation easily leads to sexual arousal; the inner part of the
vagina, however, is not particularly sensitive.

Two sets of muscles surround the vaginal opening: the *sphincter vaginae* and *levator ani* muscles.
Women can exert some degree of control over these
muscles, but tension, pain, or fear can lead to involun-

tary contraction of the outer vaginal muscles such that
insertion of anything becomes difficult or painful for
the woman. This condition, called **vaginismus,** is discussed in more detail in Chapter 18, "Sexual Dysfunctions and Their Treatment." Women can also exert
some control over the inner **pubococcygeus (PC)
muscle,** which much like the anal sphincter may be
contracted or relaxed (Levin, 2003). This muscle may
play a role in orgasmic response, and its tone can be
improved by exercises, as is true of all voluntary muscles (see Kegel exercises in Chapter 4, "Human Sexual
Arousal and Response").

It is important to note that the vagina cannot contract to the extent that it might trap the penis inside
(penis captivus), even though some people have
heard rumors to the contrary. Africa has many myths
about people becoming stuck together during sex and

vagina (vu-JI-na) muscular canal in the female that is
responsive to sexual arousal; it receives semen during
heterosexual intercourse for reproduction.

vaginismus (vaj-uh-NIZ-mus) involuntary spasm of the
outer vaginal musculature, making penetration of the
vagina difficult or impossible.

pubococcygeus (PC) muscle (pyub-o-kox-a-JEE-us) part
of the supporting musculature of the vagina that is
involved in orgasmic response and over which a woman
can exert some control.

| Cribriform | Annular | Septate | Imperforate |

■ FIGURE 2.5 *Hymen*

A thin, delicate membrane, the hymen partially covers the vaginal opening in a variety of ways. It may bridge the vagina, surround it, or have several different shapes and sizes in the opening to the outside of the body. It has no known physiological function but historically has had psychological and cultural significance as a sign of virginity.

having to be sent to the hospital for separation. Such myths seem to serve a social function in discouraging marital infidelity. When dogs mate, the penis erects in such a way that it is caught inside the vagina until erection subsides, but while this is important to successful mating in canines, nothing similar occurs in humans. During sexual arousal in a woman, a lubricating substance is secreted through the inner lining of the vagina. This is discussed further in Chapter 4, "Human Sexual Arousal and Response."

FOH Douching

Over the years, women have developed various techniques for washing out the vagina, sometimes called douching. Some women believe that menstrual blood is dirty and therefore needs to be washed out. In fact the vagina has its own cleansing mechanisms and a rather delicate balance of naturally occurring microorganisms that are important to its health (Ness, Hillier, & Richter, 2002). Studies continue to demonstrate that, contrary to popular notions, douching is actually dangerous. It can force disease organisms up into the uterus, increasing the risks for uterine and vaginal infection. Women who douche regularly are more likely to get pelvic inflammatory disease than women who douche little or not at all. They also have a fourfold increase in risk for an ectopic pregnancy, in which the embryo becomes dangerously implanted outside the uterus (see Chapter 10, "Reproduction, Reproductive Technology, and Birthing"). The vagina's natural cleansing mechanisms may be disrupted by douching. Unless prescribed for a specific medical condition, douching should be avoided (Wingwood & DiClemente, 2002).

Hymen

The hymen, present in the vaginal opening from birth, is a tissue that usually has one or more openings. There are many different shapes of hymens that cover varying portions of the introitus (see Figure 2.5). The most common type of hymen is annular, meaning that the hymenal tissue surrounds the entire opening of the vagina, with an opening in the middle. Some hymens have tissue that extends into the introitus. The cribriform hymen has a web of tissue over the introitus, in which there may be several small openings; the septate hymen has a single band of tissue that divides the introitus into two distinct apertures. In a very few girls, the hymen has no openings. In this case, the menstrual flow builds up in the vagina and uterus, causing pain and swelling until a physician makes an incision in this **imperforate hymen,** quickly relieving the condition. Occasionally, the hymen is especially thick and tough, a condition called **fibrous hymen.** This condition will interfere with sexual activity and must be treated surgically. Many women who experience pain during sexual activity known as dyspareunia, may have problems with the hymen. Such difficulties often are not diagnosed by physicians, and the pain may be dismissed as psychosomatic. Surgical techniques can relieve dyspareunia caused by problems with the hymen (Stewart & Spencer, 2002).

Most hymens have a large enough opening to admit a finger or tampon. Attempting to insert anything

imperforate hymen condition in which the hymen has no natural openings.

fibrous hymen condition in which the hymen is composed of unnaturally thick, tough tissue.

Real People

Karina: Confronting a New Sexual Way of Life

Karina came to college from a small town and had always maintained relatively conservative values on matters related to sex. She had a serious boyfriend during her junior and senior years of high school. While they had participated in some kissing and mutual touching, they did not share sexual intercourse or oral sex until the summer after their first year together. Karina had been relatively happy with their relationship, and it was difficult for both of them to make the decision to end it when they chose to attend colleges about 2,000 miles apart.

With her committed relationship behind her, Karina has decided that her first year of college will be a time of exploration and experimentation for her. She feels it is important to find out more about the kind of men she enjoys being with. During her first semester, she also drinks alcohol more frequently, another activity she generally avoided in high school. She meets male students easily and several times has hooked up with them sexually. Two of the men are interested in pursuing a more

serious relationship with Karina, but she prefers to keep things casual with these two because she does not find them interesting enough for a long-term relationship. She has talked with two of her friends quite easily about the relationships, and one of them has cautioned her that she is going overboard with casual sex. She replies that she always makes sure a condom is used and also takes birth control pills. She feels that she has been responsible, but sometimes she also feels somewhat guilty that others are perceiving her as irresponsible or "easy." She wonders if alcohol has interfered with her judgment.

If Karina were to ask for your opinion about the choices she has made, what would you say to her? On what information or personal values do you base your response? Do you feel as though Karina is judging herself too harshly, or not harshly enough? Why? What are your feelings regarding drinking and making sexual decisions?

larger, such as the erect penis, usually results in some tearing of the hymen. There are many ways other than sexual activity in which a hymen may be ruptured. The absence of a hymen at birth is an unlikely occurrence, if it occurs at all.

Some hymens apparently are flexible enough to withstand coitus, or sexual intercourse. Consequently, the presence or absence of a hymen is an unreliable indicator of a woman's virginity or nonvirginity. Some societies place special significance on the presence of the hymen and hold rituals for the rupturing of the hymen before a girl's first intercourse.

In the United States, between 1920 and 1950, some gynecologists performed a surgical procedure on women who were about to marry but did not want their husbands to know they were not virgins. The procedure, called the "lover's knot," involved placing several stitches in the labia so that when intercourse happened the stitches would be torn out and some pain and bleeding would follow. Many people in Western societies even today believe that the presence of a hymen proves a female's virginity—a naive outlook at best.

If the hymen is present the first time penetration of the vagina occurs, discomfort or pain and possibly some bleeding may occur when the hymen is torn. The

degree of pain varies in different women from slight to severe. If a woman is concerned about this, she may spend some time prior to the first penetration inserting fingers into the opening of the hymen, gradually widening it. A physician may cut the hymen or stretch its opening with dilators of gradually increasing size. During sexual intercourse, there is usually little trouble inserting the penis through the hymen if the male partner persists with careful and gentle prodding with the erect penis and uses adequate lubrication. The woman also may take responsibility for guiding her partner in controlling the timing and depth of penetration.

See "Self-Awareness" on SexSource Online.

Genital Self-Examination for Women

After they acquaint themselves with their basic external anatomy, it is a good idea for women to examine their genitals monthly, checking for any unusual signs or symptoms. Using a mirror and adequate light, look through pubic hairs to the underlying skin, and pull back the clitoral prepuce or hood. Then part the inner lips, exposing the area around the urethral and vaginal openings more fully. These areas generally should be free of any unusual bumps, sores, or blisters. If such lesions are present, they may be red or light-colored or may be more easily felt than seen. Be sure to look on the inside of each major and minor lip for similar signs. It is a good idea to become aware of what your normal vaginal discharge looks like so you will notice any changes in its color, odor, or consistency. Although such changes may occur normally over the course of the monthly menstrual cycle, some diseases cause distinct changes in vaginal discharge.

Anytime you notice unusual bumps or discharges from the genitals, you should consult a physician or other clinician specializing in women's health concerns. Often these symptoms do not need treatment, but they may signal the beginnings of an infection requiring medical attention. It is important to report any pain or burning upon urination, bleeding between menstrual periods, pain in the pelvic region, or an itchy rash around the vagina (Stewart & Spencer, 2002; Wingwood & DiClemente, 2002).

Disorders of the Female Sex Organs

The female sex and urinary organs may be the sites of infection not transmitted through sexual behavior. **Acute urethral syndrome,** an infection of the urethra, and **cystitis,** a bladder infection, are common complaints and may represent recurrent problems for some women. Urinary tract infections in younger women are associated with frequent sexual intercourse and recent use of diaphragms and spermicides. The symptoms include a frequent urge to urinate, burning or pain on urination, and possibly severe pain during sexual intercourse or when the urethra and bladder are placed under pressure.

Interstitial cystitis (IC) is a relatively rare, chronic bladder condition that can be quite debilitating in some women and interfere with their sex lives. Medical professionals frequently fail to recognize these diseases as the cause of such symptoms and may assume that the woman is imagining the problem. Antibiotics and other medications can be used for treatment. Because one of the most common bacteria to cause cystitis is **E. coli** (short for *Escherichia coli*), the organism that lives in the colon and is found in feces, good personal hygiene is the best preventative measure. Wiping from front to back after a bowel movement is always advisable, as is frequent washing of the vaginal and anal areas. Another good precaution is drinking plenty of liquids and urinating frequently. Washing and urinating after sexual activity are important in cleansing the urethral area of any bacteria that might cause cystitis. Of particular concern is the possibility of a bladder infection spreading to the kidneys, where the condition can be far more serious.

The vagina can be subject to several disorders. One of the more common problems is associated with pain in the vulvovaginal area that may interfere with sexual activity and pleasure. Chronic vulvar pain, called **vulvodynia,** may be of a general nature, spontaneously affecting the entire vulvar area. More commonly, the pain is localized in the entrance, or vestibule, of the vagina and results from physical contact. This type of vulvodynia, called **vulvar vestibulitis,** is a frequent cause of pain during sexual activity. Causes of vulvodynia are multiple and are not easily diagnosed, but it constitutes a clearly defined medical condition. A variety of treatment techniques that are being tried, including psychotherapy and pain control, often lead to improved sexual function (Granot & Lavee, 2005; Kuile & Weijenborg, 2006; Pukall, 2005).

The vagina can undergo **vaginal atrophy,** a condition in which the inner surfaces of the vagina shrink and narrow. This occurs more often in older women as the result of lowered estrogen levels. Sometimes during pregnancy **varicose veins** can develop in the vulva, surrounding the vagina; this leads to an aching, heavy sensation in the pelvis. Several congenital abnormalities may affect female sex organs. **Vaginal atresia,** the absence or closure of the vagina, often is not discovered until puberty. In such rare cases, a surgical construction of a vaginal passageway can be done to permit sexual intercourse or other sexual activity, although

acute urethral syndrome infection or irritation of the urethra.

cystitis (sis-TITE-us) a nonsexually transmitted infection of the urinary bladder.

interstitial cystitis (IC) a chronic bladder inflammation that can cause debilitating discomfort and interfere with sexual enjoyment.

E. coli bacteria naturally living in the human colon that often cause urinary tract infection.

vulvodynia a medical condition characterized by pain and burning in the vulva and outer vagina.

vulvar vestibulitis one form of vulvodynia associated with pain in the entrance of the vagina upon physical contact, often interfering with sexual penetration of the vagina.

vaginal atrophy shrinking and deterioration of the vaginal lining, usually the result of low estrogen levels during aging.

varicose veins overexpanded blood vessels; can occur in veins surrounding the vagina.

vaginal atresia (a-TREE-zha) birth defect in which the vagina is absent or closed.

FIGURE 2.6 *Female Reproductive Organs*

The uterus is a hollow, muscular organ in which an embryo can grow and be nourished until it is a fully developed fetus. The walls of the uterus are of varying thickness and consist of three layers: the perimetrium, the myometrium, and the endometrium. On each side of the uterus are the almond-shaped ovaries. They have two functions: manufacturing the hormones estrogen and progesterone, and producing and releasing eggs.

the constructed passageway usually does not permit vaginal delivery when giving birth. Also rarely, two vaginas may be present at birth. There are also a number of conditions that involve a malformation or absence of the uterus, fallopian tubes, or ovaries, all variably treatable by surgery or hormone therapy. Sometimes **vaginal fistulae,** or abnormal openings, connect the bladder, urethra, or rectum with the vagina; all of these usually require surgical treatment. Incomplete closure of the urethra and urinary tract during fetal development can occur in females, but it usually does not require surgical correction unless it is associated with an inability to retain urine or feces.

■ The Uterus and Ovaries

The neck of the **uterus** (or womb) protrudes into the deepest part of the vagina. The uterus is a thick-walled, muscular organ that provides a nourishing environment for the developing fetus during pregnancy. It is usually about 3 inches long and pear shaped, roughly 2 to 3 inches in diameter at the top and narrowing to a 1-inch diameter at the end that extends into the vagina. During pregnancy, it gradually expands to a much larger size. When a woman is standing, her uterus is almost horizontal and at a right angle to the vagina (see Figure 2.4).

The two main parts of the uterus are the body and the **cervix** or neck, connected by the narrower **isthmus.** The top of the uterus is called the **fundus.** Although the cervix is not especially sensitive to superficial touch, it is sensitive to pressure. The opening in the cervix is called the **os.** The inner cavity of the uterus has varying widths in different sections (see Figure 2.6). The walls of the uterus are composed of three layers: the thin outer cover, or **perimetrium;** the

vaginal fistulae (FISH-cha-lee *or*-lie) abnormal channels that can develop between the vagina and other internal organs.

uterus (YUTE-a-rus) muscular organ of the female reproductive system; a fertilized egg implants itself within the uterus.

cervix (SERV-ix) lower "neck" of the uterus that extends into the back part of the vagina.

isthmus narrowed portion of the uterus just above the cervix.

fundus the broad top portion of the uterus.

os opening in the cervix that leads into the hollow interior of the uterus.

perimetrium outer covering of the uterus.

thick middle layer of muscular tissue, called the **myometrium;** and the inner layer, rich in blood vessels and glands, called the **endometrium.** It is the endometrium that plays a vital role in the menstrual cycle (discussed later in this chapter) and in the nourishment of a developing embryo or fetus (discussed in Chapter 10, "Reproduction, Reproductive Technology, and Birthing").

FOH Pelvic Examination

The uterus, particularly the cervix, is a common site of cancer in women. Because cancer of the uterus may present no symptoms for many years, it is especially dangerous. Women should have an internal, or pelvic, examination periodically, along with a **Pap smear** test (named for its developer, Dr. Papanicolaou), by a qualified gynecologist or other clinician. Four sex-related factors are associated with a higher risk of cervical cancer: (1) very early initiation of sexual intercourse, (2) 10 or more sex partners, (3) a history of pelvic inflammatory disease or a sexually transmitted disease, and (4) having a partner who has recently had multiple sex partners (Hewitt, Devesa, & Breen, 2002).

The latest guidelines from the American Cancer Society recommend that women begin having Pap test screening about three years after becoming sexually active, or by age 21. Annual screening is often recommended up to age 30. Depending on how many risk factors are present and the results of previous tests, the frequency of screening may be reduced to every two to three years after that. Pap smears have been responsible for a steep decline in the incidence of invasive cervical cancer, especially among younger women (Chan, Sung, & Sawaya, 2003). Unfortunately, some misconceptions about the Pap test are prevalent, and many women believe that it screens for other disorders and sexually transmitted diseases, which is not the case. Women who live in poor neighborhoods are more likely to be overdue for Pap screening, and women who have had abnormal tests tend not to return in a timely manner for follow-up (Breitkopf, Pearson, & Breitkopf, 2005; Datta et al., 2006). It is advised that a woman prepare for the pelvic examination by avoiding sexual intercourse and the use of vaginal contraceptives for one or two days prior to having the Pap smear taken.

For a pelvic examination, a speculum is first carefully inserted into the vagina to hold open its walls and permit a visual inspection of the cervix. For the Pap test, a thin spatula or a cotton swab is used while the speculum is in place to remove some cells painlessly from the area of the cervix. A smear is made from the material and is fixed, stained, and examined under a microscope for any indications of abnormal cellular changes that might warn of cancer or precancerous conditions. A newer, liquid-based technique for preparing Pap smears is also used that eliminates some of the excess mucus and blood that sometimes can make detection of abnormal cells on the slide more difficult. This test is therefore more effective and reliable. Another available device, which can be attached to the speculum, projects a chemical light that produces different colors from normal and abnormal cells. It provides an extra measure of help in targeting suspicious areas of the cervix that should be carefully tested.

After the speculum has been removed, a manual examination is performed. Using a rubber glove and lubricant, the clinician inserts two fingers into the vagina and presses on the cervix. The other hand is placed on the abdomen, enabling the clinician to feel the basic shape and size of the uterus and associated structures (Wingwood & DiClemente, 2002).

If suspicious cells are detected in a Pap smear, more aggressive diagnostic procedures may be recommended. First there may be a biopsy to determine whether a malignancy is present. If growth of abnormal cells proves to be advanced, another procedure can be performed, called a dilation and curettage, or D&C. The opening of the cervix is dilated or widened so that an instrument called a curette can be inserted into the inner cavity of the uterus. Some of the uterine lining is gently scraped away and then examined for malignant cells. The D&C occasionally is used to terminate a pregnancy, as an induced abortion, and typically is used to cleanse the uterus of dead tissue following a miscarriage (spontaneous abortion).

Ovaries and Fallopian Tubes

On either side of the uterus, and attached to it, are two almond-shaped glands called the **ovaries** (see Figure 2.6). *Ovarian ligaments* attach the ovaries to the uterus. The ovaries have two primary functions: secretion of two female sex hormones, estrogen and progesterone; and the maturation of the egg cells, or **ova,** necessary for reproduction. Each ovary is about an inch long and weighs about one-fourth ounce. Inside each ovary at a female's birth are tens of thousands of

---

myometrium middle, muscular layer of the uterine wall.

endometrium interior lining of the uterus; the innermost of three layers.

Pap smear medical test that examines a smear of cervical cells to detect any cellular abnormalities.

ovaries pair of female gonads, located in the abdominal cavity, that mature ova and produce female hormones.

ova egg cells produced in the ovary. A single cell is called an ovum; in reproduction, it is fertilized by a sperm cell.

microscopic chambers called **follicles,** each of which contains a cell that has the potential to develop into an ovum. These cells are called **oocytes.** It has been thought that the ovaries do not produce more oocytes after a girl is born. Recent research, however, has shown that mammalian ovaries may indeed continue to produce new oocytes and follicles even into young adulthood, although this has yet to be confirmed in humans (Johnson, Canning, et al., 2004). By the time of puberty, it is believed that only a few thousand follicles remain in each ovary, only a relatively small number of which (400 to 500) will ever mature into ova.

In a mature woman, the surface of the ovaries is irregular and pitted, evidence of the many ova that have pushed their way through the ovary walls in the process of ovulation, described on page 50. When the internal structure of an ovary is observed, follicles are seen in various stages of development. Two distinct parts of the ovary are also visible: the central *medulla* and its thick outer layer, the *cortex* (see Figure 2.7).

Extending from one end of the ovaries to the upper portion of the uterus are the two **fallopian tubes.** The end of each fallopian tube nearest the ovary has a number of fingerlike projections called *fimbriae,* which are not attached to the ovary but rather lie loosely around it. The fimbriae lead into the thickest end of the fallopian tube, the *infundibulum.* A narrow, irregular cavity extends throughout each fallopian tube. The inner cavity gets progressively smaller in the sections of the tube closest to the uterus.

The inner lining of the fallopian tubes is covered by microscopic, hairlike projections called **cilia.** It is by movements of these cilia that an ovum is carried through the tube from the ovary to the uterus (see Figure 2.8). If fertilization is to occur, the sperm must

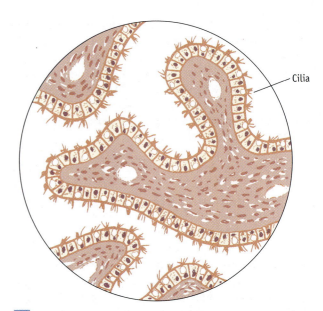

■ **FIGURE 2.8** *Cilia of the Fallopian Tubes*
This is a microscopic view of the cilia, the hairlike filaments that line the fallopian tubes. Their movement helps propel the ovum through the fallopian tube to the uterus.

meet and enter the ovum while the ovum is in the fallopian tubes. The cilia in the tubes must then transport the tiny fertilized ovum to the uterus, where it will implant itself and grow into a fetus (see the section on reproduction in Chapter 10).

When women experience prolonged sexual arousal without having an orgasm, their ovaries may become swollen and congested, leading to pain and feelings of fullness; this problem is not particularly common. The vulva may also become congested and painful following such activity. In former times, this discomfort was often called "engagement ovaries."

See "The Ovaries" on SexSource Online.

Uterine Cancer and Other Disorders

Cancer of the cervix is a common type of malignancy in women, second in frequency only to cancer of the

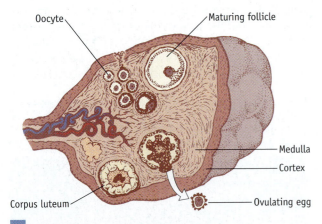

■ **FIGURE 2.7** *Internal Structure of an Ovary*
This cross section of an ovary shows its cortex, or thick outer layer, and its central medulla, as well as the various stages of ovum development. The first cell in the process of maturation is an oocyte, which with its surrounding cells is called the follicle.

follicles capsules of cells in which an ovum matures.

oocytes (OH-a-sites) cells that mature to become ova.

fallopian tubes structures that are connected to the uterus and lead the ovum from an ovary to the inner cavity of the uterus.

cilia microscopic, hairlike projections that help move the ovum through the fallopian tube.

breast. Uterine cancer occurs with about half the frequency of cervical malignancies. The Pap smear test can detect cancerous or precancerous cells, indicating that the condition should be surgically treated or kept under observation.

Two stages of cancer may be detected in a Pap smear. One is **cervical intraepithelial neoplasia (CIN),** in which precancerous or early cancer cells are found. In this case, the cells are still confined to the cervix and can be treated easily. The more advanced and dangerous malignancy is **invasive cancer of the cervix (ICC),** which must be treated promptly with whatever techniques are necessary to reduce the risk of its spreading to other organs. Early treatment of uterine and cervical cancer is highly successful, but if the cancer is allowed to invade other surrounding tissues, it can be far more dangerous. Some strains of the human papillomavirus (HPV) are known to cause cervical cancer. An effective vaccine is now available to prevent HPV infection, and it is recommended for girls and women prior to their becoming sexually active (we will discuss this more in Chapter 17).

The uterus also can be the site of nonmalignant growths and numerous other disorders. Hormonal imbalances may lead to abnormal and profuse bleeding from the uterus. Often such conditions are accompanied by excessive growth of the inner uterine lining (endometrium), a condition called **endometrial hyperplasia.** This may have a variety of causes. A similar disorder, **endometriosis,** occurs in 10 to 15 percent of premenopausal women. In this disorder the uterine lining grows outward into the organs surrounding the uterus, typically causing pain, abnormal menstrual bleeding, and sometimes sterility. The cervix may also become irritated or infected, leading to a gradual erosion of cervical tissues. A history of endometriosis is associated with an elevated risk of ovarian cancer (Berkley, Rapkin, & Papka, 2005; Modugno et al., 2004).

Fibroid tumors that grow on the uterus are benign, but they can interfere with uterine function and cause bleeding. They represent one of the major reasons why some women undergo surgical removal of all or part of the uterus, a procedure called a **hysterectomy.** About 23 percent of white women over the age of 25 in the United States have hysterectomies, compared to only 12 percent of Hispanic women; while the reasons for the difference have not been fully explained, it has been suggested that the surgery may be overused. Some impairment of sexual arousal may follow hysterectomy (Brett & Higgins, 2003; Meston, 2004; Walker & Stewart, 2005).

The uterus is sometimes displaced from its usual position in the abdomen, a condition often called "tipped uterus." Unless pain is connected with the displacement, there is no particular need for surgical intervention. Uterine displacement apparently has no effect on a woman's ability to become pregnant or give birth naturally. Occasionally, the ligaments that support the uterus become weakened to the extent that the uterus drops down and protrudes too far into the vagina. This **prolapse of the uterus** may cause serious discomfort and require surgery.

Tumors of the ovaries—both malignant and benign—are also common in women. If the ovaries must be surgically removed, the procedure is called oophorectomy. Increasing attention is being given to a condition termed **polycystic ovary syndrome (PCOS).** It has been estimated to affect about 6 percent of women, making it the most common female endocrine disorder and a leading cause of infertility. Although symptoms of PCOS vary a great deal among women, it can lead to abnormal production of male hormones, which in turn interfere with the menstrual cycle and can lead to diabetes, heart disease, and other long-term health problems. Surgery is sometimes required, but new medical treatments for PCOS are being developed and have been found to be quite effective in controlling symptoms.

■ Female Breasts

The female breast is not a sex organ, but it has taken on sexual meanings in our society. Women's breasts are often perceived as sources of sexual arousal, and

cervical intraepithelial neoplasia (CIN) (ep-a-THEE-lee-al nee-a-PLAY-zhee-a) abnormal, precancerous cells sometimes identified in a Pap smear.

invasive cancer of the cervix (ICC) advanced and dangerous malignancy requiring prompt treatment.

endometrial hyperplasia (hy-per-PLAY-zhee-a) excessive growth of the inner lining of the uterus (endometrium).

endometriosis (en-doe-mee-tree-O-sus) growth of the endometrium out of the uterus into surrounding organs.

fibroid tumors nonmalignant growths that commonly grow in uterine tissues, often interfering with uterine function.

hysterectomy surgical removal of all or part of the uterus.

prolapse of the uterus weakening of the supportive ligaments of the uterus, causing it to protrude into the vagina.

polycystic ovary syndrome (PCOS) (PAH-lee-SIS-tick) a disorder of the ovaries that can produce a variety of unpleasant physical symptoms, often because of elevated testosterone levels.

many women find stimulation of their breasts, especially the nipples, sexually arousing. There are many individual differences in this respect. There may also be varying degrees of sensitivity depending on the woman's stage in her menstrual cycle.

Each breast (see Figure 2.9) is composed of from 15 to 20 clusters of *milk glands,* with each cluster having a *milk duct* that leads to the nipple. Deposits of *fatty tissue* lie just under the skin of the breast. The darkened circular area of skin surrounding the nipple, called the **areola,** often has a few smaller nubs of skin.

During pregnancy, the breasts go through distinct changes as they prepare for nourishing a newborn infant. Within two or three days after a woman gives birth, her breasts begin to produce milk, the process known as **lactation.** The pituitary hormone **prolactin** stimulates milk production. When the baby sucks at the nipple, the pituitary is stimulated to produce another hormone, **oxytocin,** which leads to the ejection of milk from the breast.

Concern about breast size and shape seems to be one of the most common bodily worries of women. Our culture has created an exaggerated impression that large breasts are sexy and desirable, and advertisers have capitalized on the anxieties of women by offering a wide variety of questionable breast-enlargement techniques and devices. These not only are ineffective in enlarging the breasts but also may be unsafe. Of course, there are a great many different sizes, shapes, and positions of the female breasts. It is typical for one of a woman's breasts to be slightly different in size or shape from the other. Larger breasts can be uncomfortable, and some women may even feel that they are unattractive. Smaller breasts may indeed be more sensitive to sexual stimulation, because the nerve endings in the skin are less dispersed.

See "Breasts" on SexSource Online.

Breast Cancer

Cancer of the breast is one of the more common types of malignancy, although the risks of getting breast cancer are also often misinterpreted. It is commonly stated that women have a one in nine chance of getting breast cancer, but that figure refers to the cumulative lifetime risk for a woman who lives past the age of 85. The chances of getting breast cancer at younger ages are much lower. About 46,000 women die of the disease and its complications each year in the United States. As with any form of cancer, early detection greatly increases the chances of a complete cure.

Researchers have been attempting to find out why breast cancer seems to be on the increase, although the statistical upswing may be partly the result of techniques that allow for earlier detection of the disease. There is now evidence that some breast cancers, especially cases identified prior to age 30, result from a susceptibility caused by gene mutations that some women inherit. Breast cancer in later life is much less likely to result from genetic susceptibility. The faulty genes can occur on human chromosomes 17 and 13 and have been labeled BRCA1 and BRCA2 by researchers. The genes have also been linked to a greater susceptibility to ovarian cancer (King, Marks, & Mandell, 2003; Poole

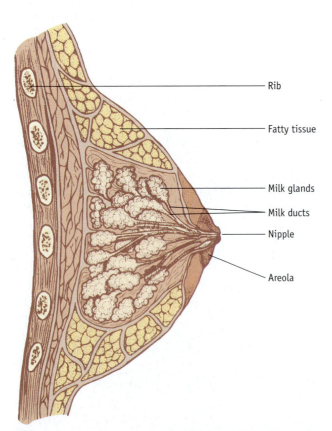

Rib

Fatty tissue

Milk glands

Milk ducts

Nipple

Areola

FIGURE 2.9 *Cross Section of a Female Breast*

The female breast has erotic and reproductive significance. The mammary or milk gland produces nourishment, which flows through the ducts to the nipple. The nipple is highly sensitive to stimulation and thus plays a part in sexual arousal.

areola (a-REE-a-la) darkened, circular area of skin surrounding the nipple of the breast.

lactation production of milk by the milk glands of the breasts.

prolactin pituitary hormone that stimulates the process of lactation.

oxytocin pituitary hormone that plays a role in lactation and in uterine contractions.

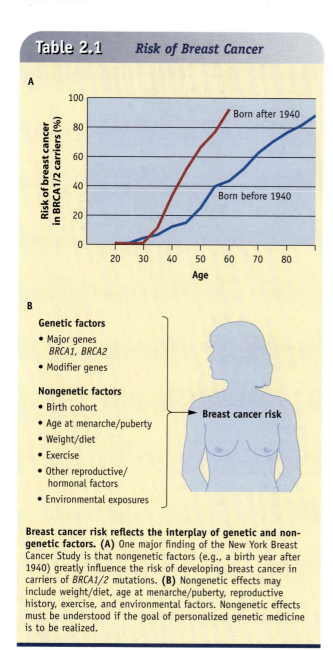

Table 2.1 *Risk of Breast Cancer*

A

(Graph: x-axis "Age" from 20 to 80; y-axis "Risk of breast cancer in BRCA1/2 carriers (%)" from 0 to 100. Two curves labeled "Born after 1940" and "Born before 1940")

B

Genetic factors
- Major genes
  BRCA1, BRCA2
- Modifier genes

Nongenetic factors
- Birth cohort
- Age at menarche/puberty
- Weight/diet
- Exercise
- Other reproductive/hormonal factors
- Environmental exposures

Breast cancer risk

Breast cancer risk reflects the interplay of genetic and nongenetic factors. (A) One major finding of the New York Breast Cancer Study is that nongenetic factors (e.g., a birth year after 1940) greatly influence the risk of developing breast cancer in carriers of *BRCA1/2* mutations. **(B)** Nongenetic effects may include weight/diet, age at menarche/puberty, reproductive history, exercise, and environmental factors. Nongenetic effects must be understood if the goal of personalized genetic medicine is to be realized.

Source: Reprinted with permission from "A Risky Business—Assessing Breast Cancer Risk" by Ephart Levy-Lahad and Sharon E. Plon, *Science, 302,* 574. Copyright © 2003 American Association for the Advancement of Science.

et al., 2006). Women with the mutation face about a 60 percent chance of developing breast cancer by age 50 and an 82 percent chance by age 80. There are several nongenetic risk factors as well, including a woman's weight and diet, the age at which she reached puberty, and whether she has given birth to children (Levy-Lahad & Plon, 2003). See Table 2.1. It has also been found that women who have high breast density, large amounts of connective tissue, and relatively little fat have a higher risk of breast cancer (Balter, 2005).

Another possibility is that replacement hormones, which have been widely used among women during and after menopause (see p. 57), may have been producing an increased risk of breast cancer. A recent study found that when millions of women stopped using hormones following some initial reports of this risk, a sharp decline in the incidence of breast cancer occurred during the following year. These data will require further verification (M. D. Anderson Cancer Center, 2006).

Women identified as having a very high risk of breast cancer sometimes choose to have their breasts surgically removed before they develop cancer. Although it was once believed that fat in the diet led to increased risk, it now appears that an increased exposure to female hormones, particularly estrogen and synthetic hormones used in contraception or other medical treatments, may play a more significant role. New drugs that counteract the effects of hormones are being developed to reduce breast cancer risks (Couzin, 2003).

Breast Self-Examination

A woman can easily examine her breasts in order to detect changes that are large enough to be felt, and the American Cancer Society recommends that breast self-examination be done once each month. Women who regularly examine their breasts become familiar with the natural contours of their breast tissue and therefore are likely to notice any unfamiliar lump that might develop there.

Breast self-examination should include both a visual inspection in a mirror and careful exploration of each breast by hand. It is not a good idea to do this examination just before or during menstruation, because more natural lumps tend to be present during these phases. The best time for self-exam is midway through the menstrual cycle, around the time of ovulation—approximately 12 to 16 days after the first day of the woman's last period. A systematic approach should be followed, as described in the sections that follow.

Visual Examination

Stand before a mirror with your arms at your sides and examine the appearance of both breasts. Then raise your arms high above your head and look for any changes in the contour or skin of either breast. Look for any swelling or dimpling of the skin or for any unusual signs in either nipple. Next place your hands on your hips and flex the chest muscles, again looking for any unusual signs.

Manual Examination

The breasts may be easily examined during a bath or shower because the hands can glide easily over wet skin. Another option is to examine them while lying down. Place a pillow under the shoulder on the same

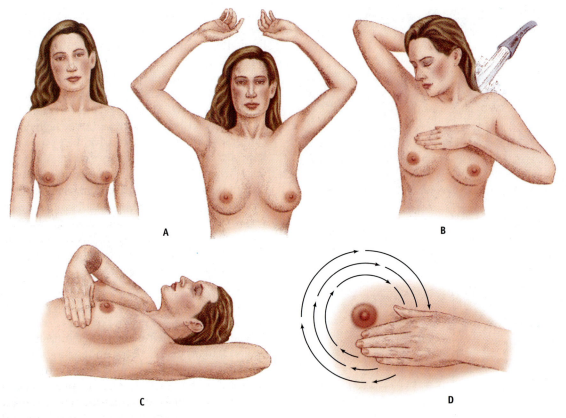

A   **B**   **C**   **D**

■ **FIGURE 2.10**   *Breast Self-Examination*

It is important for a woman to examine her breasts regularly. She should look at her breasts in the mirror, first with her arms at her sides and then with them raised over her head **(A).** In the shower, her hands can easily move over her wet skin **(B).** When she is lying down, a woman can easily examine her breast tissue **(C),** and she should repeat the procedure when in an upright position. The fingers should be held flat and move in complete clockwise circles around the outer portion of the breast, then move progressively inward toward the nipple **(D).**

side as the breast to be examined and place that hand under your head. Use the opposite hand for the actual examination. The fingers should be held together, forming a flat surface. Begin on the outer part of the breast, and move in complete clockwise circles around the outer regions, checking for lumps, hard knots, or any unusual thickening. Then move inward toward the nipple about an inch and circle the breast again. Usually you will need to make at least four concentric circles to examine every part of the breast. It is a good idea to repeat this procedure while sitting or standing, because the upright position redistributes breast tissue. Finally, squeeze each nipple to see if there is any discharge from either breast (see Figure 2.10).

If you find any unusual features in a breast, *do not panic.* Many nonmalignant conditions can cause lumps, swelling, and discharge, but you should not take any chances. Always consult a physician, who can then prescribe further testing to determine whether the abnormality represents a malignancy.

For reasons that are not completely understood, lesbians are less likely than heterosexual women to practice breast self-examination monthly, and some clinicians believe that this places them at higher risk for mortality from breast cancer.

Breast Screening Techniques

A test that is recommended on a regular basis for women over the age of 40 or 50 is **mammography.** A special X-ray picture is taken of the breast and can detect even small lumps. Only low-level radiation is used to produce the image, called a mammogram. Some women are averse to or fearful of the test because it is uncomfortable, but it poses no hazards. There has been some controversy over the age at which women should begin having mammography on a regular basis. Some research studies have reinforced the recommendations of the American Medical Association and the American Cancer Society that a baseline mammogram be taken at

mammography sensitive X-ray technique used to discover small breast tumors.

around age 35 and that annual mammograms then be taken beginning at age 40. About 15 percent of breast cancers detected by mammography were in women under age 50. Other research has found that malignancies in younger age groups tend to grow faster, making early detection and treatment even more crucial. Some research has shown that use of mammograms does not necessarily reduce the overall number of deaths from breast cancer. However, the Department of Health and Human Services still takes the position that, individually, mammograms yield earlier detection and treatment and therefore should be considered a routine part of women's health care (Marshall, 2002).

Modern medicine has made great strides in treatment and cure of malignant tumors. A woman who develops breast cancer has a 50 percent chance of being diagnosed after the age of 65 and now has a 65 percent chance of surviving the illness and ultimately dying from another cause. Various combinations of radiation therapy, chemotherapy, and administration of hormone-inhibiting medications can be used. Sometimes it is necessary to remove the entire breast in a surgical procedure called a **mastectomy,** but current research indicates that a **lumpectomy,** removal of only the lump itself and some surrounding tissue, is often sufficient. Breast cancer and surgeries to remove it represent traumatic events in a woman's life and often affect her feelings of attractiveness and her sexual feelings. These aspects of the disease might not be addressed sufficiently during the treatment process (Anllo, 2000). Again, early discovery of unusual growths in the breast is a woman's best protection.

■ The Menstrual Cycle

Of special importance to the female's role in reproduction is the **menstrual cycle.** From the time of first menstruation, called **menarche,** to the period of life when her menstruation ceases, called **menopause** (or climacteric), a woman's body goes through a periodic cycle that involves hormonal, psychological, and physical changes. This menstrual cycle involves the maturation of an ovum and the periodic preparation of the uterus for pregnancy, followed by a gradual return to the "unprepared" state if pregnancy does not occur.

Today, menarche usually occurs sometime between the ages of 9 and 16, although variations from this range are normal. The onset of menopause typically is between the ages of 45 and 55. The years between menarche and menopause constitute a woman's potential childbearing years, although she is actually able to conceive only for a day or two usually once a month. Women in their teenage years who bear children have a greater risk of experiencing physical complications and having children with birth defects. Likewise, the older a

couple is when having children—especially beyond age 35—the greater the possibility of the offspring having birth defects. In mature women, an average entire menstrual cycle lasts about 28 days, although it may fluctuate a great deal in individuals. In teenage girls, the length of the cycle tends to be more irregular and slightly longer, averaging closer to 31 days.

It is important for girls to be prepared for menarche through appropriate educational efforts. In the past, girls have been frightened by their first menstruation because they had not been educated about what to expect. Mothers have usually been the most significant source of information about menstruation, although today many girls are learning about menarche through school health education programs. When effective education about the menstrual cycle is provided prior to menarche, girls tend to have much more positive attitudes toward the experience and toward their bodies.

The menstrual cycle is regulated by a complex interaction of hormones secreted by the *pituitary gland,* located at the base of the brain; a portion of the brain itself called the *hypothalamus;* and the ovaries. The pituitary gland acts as a sort of relay station between the hypothalamus and ovaries. The hypothalamus produces **gonadotropin-releasing hormone (GnRH),** which stimulates the pituitary gland to produce two hormones, follicle-stimulating hormone and luteinizing hormone, which in turn regulate hormonal secretion by the ovaries. How these hormones control the reproductive organs is described in the following sections. Although the menstrual cycle is continuous, we divide it into four stages, or phases, for ease of explanation: the follicular phase, ovulation, luteal secretion, and menstruation. There is some research to indicate that levels of sexual interest vary through the different phases of the cycle, possibly related to evolutionary adaptation; however, the studies are controversial and not consistent.

---

mastectomy surgical removal of all or part of a breast.

lumpectomy surgical removal of a breast lump, along with a small amount of surrounding tissue.

menstrual cycle the hormonal interactions that prepare a woman's body for possible pregnancy at roughly monthly intervals.

menarche (MEN-are-kee) onset of menstruation at puberty.

menopause (MEN-a-pawz) time in midlife when menstruation ceases.

gonadotropin-releasing hormone (GnRH) (go-nad-a-TRO-pen) hormone from the hypothalamus that stimulates the release of FSH and LH by the pituitary.

FIGURE 2.11 *Preovulatory Preparation*

In the first stage of the menstrual cycle, the maturity of the ovum begins. Follicle-stimulating hormone (FSH) from the pituitary gland influences the production of estrogen by the ovaries that causes the lining of the uterus to thicken in preparation for a fertilized ovum.

Preovulatory Preparation or Follicular Phase

During the first stage of the menstrual cycle (see Figure 2.11), two important things must take place: the maturation of an ovum in one of the ovarian follicles and the beginning preparation of the uterus for the nourishment of an embryo, in case the ovum is fertilized. These developments are initiated by the secretion of **follicle-stimulating hormone (FSH)** from the pituitary gland into the bloodstream. The FSH influences the ovaries to "ripen" one or more of the ova in a follicle and also to increase their production of **estrogen.** The estrogen works directly on the inner lining of the uterus (endometrium), causing it to thicken gradually with enlargement of its many small glands and blood vessels. The estrogen also exerts a "feedback" effect on the pituitary gland, so that as the estrogen level in the blood increases, the production of FSH by the pituitary decreases. In the later days of this phase, and just prior to the surge of another hormone, many women seem to develop stronger sexual desire and more sexual fantasies (Bullivant et al., 2004).

Ovulation

When a high concentration of estrogen is reached (see Figure 2.12), the hypothalamus triggers the release of **luteinizing hormone (LH)** from the pituitary. This hormone causes development of the egg to stop and triggers a chain of chemical and physical events responsible for the rupturing of the mature ovum

through the outer wall of one ovary—the process of **ovulation** (Park et al., 2004). After the ovum has left the ovary, the follicle remains as a tiny mass of cells called the **corpus luteum.** Under the influence of LH, the corpus luteum becomes a small gland. Studies of women's experience of the menstrual cycle have suggested that women tend to have higher levels of sexual arousability around the time of ovulation, possibly the result of the increased levels of a particular biochemical in the bloodstream at that time in the cycle. Also, some research suggests that the increase in sexual desire and initiation of sexual activity in women during this part of the menstrual cycle is particularly evident in women in committed relationships (Nappi et al., 2003; Pillsworth, Haselton, & Buss, 2004).

follicle-stimulating hormone (FSH) pituitary hormone that stimulates the ovaries or testes.

estrogen (ES-tro-jen) hormone produced abundantly by the ovaries; it plays an important role in the menstrual cycle.

luteinizing hormone (LH) (LEW-tee-in-ize-ing) pituitary hormone that triggers ovulation in the ovaries and stimulates sperm production in the testes.

ovulation release of a mature ovum through the wall of an ovary.

corpus luteum cell cluster of the follicle that remains after the ovum is released; secretes hormones that help regulate the menstrual cycle.

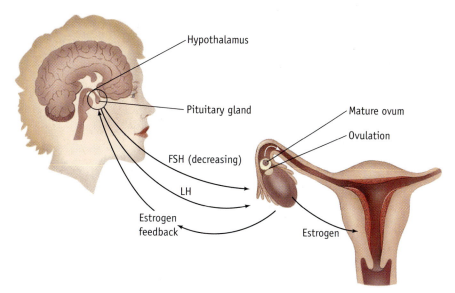

■ FIGURE 2.12 *Ovulation*

The pituitary gland is stimulated to release the luteinizing hormone by the presence of estrogen. This in turn causes the mature ovum to rupture through the outer wall of one ovary (the process of ovulation). The follicle that remains becomes an active gland called the corpus luteum.

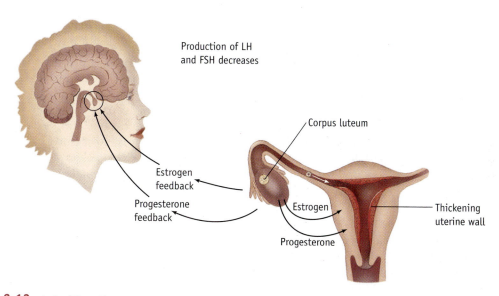

■ FIGURE 2.13 *Luteal Secretion*

The corpus luteum begins secreting progesterone as well as more estrogen, which further thickens the uterine lining in preparation for the possibility that the ovum will be fertilized as it moves through the fallopian tube.

Luteal Secretion

With stimulation by LH, the corpus luteum begins secreting another essential hormone, **progesterone,** along with more estrogen (see Figure 2.13). These hormones further thicken the uterine lining and cause it to begin secreting its own nutrient fluids that can nourish an embryo if pregnancy occurs. The progesterone also has a "feedback" effect on the hypothalamus, causing it to shut off the production of GnRH. This in turn decreases the production of LH and FSH. While these developments are happening, the ovum is slowly being moved through one of the fallopian tubes toward the uterus, a journey of three or four days. If the ovum is fertilized by a sperm, the fertilization will occur in the fallopian tube. If the ovum is not fertilized, it disintegrates.

progesterone (pro-JES-ter-one) ovarian hormone that causes the uterine lining to thicken.

FIGURE 2.14   *Menstruation*

If the ovum is not fertilized, the corpus luteum degenerates, and the progesterone and estrogen levels begin to fall. The portion of the uterus that had begun to thicken now begins to slough off and is lost through the vagina over a period of days.

Menstruation

If the ovum is not fertilized, the corpus luteum degenerates and the production of progesterone ceases. The estrogen level in the bloodstream begins to fall, and the thickened lining of the uterus begins to degenerate. Uterine cellular material, fluids, and a small amount of blood (usually about 2 to 5 ounces) are then lost through the vagina over a period of from three to seven days. This is called **menstruation** or the menstrual period (see Figure 2.14). The estrogen level continues to fall and eventually becomes low enough that the pituitary again begins to produce FSH, initiating the menstrual cycle all over again (see Table 2.2).

Unless a woman experiences pain during menstruation (called **dysmenorrhea**) or some other medical problem, there is no need to curtail any activities during menstruation. There are a number of products that can be used to absorb the menstrual flow. These include various sizes of absorbent pads that are held over the vaginal opening by adhesive that sticks to the underpants. Tampons, cylinders of absorbent material, can be inserted directly into the vagina. Tampons do not stretch the vagina and usually cause no damage to an intact hymen. They are favored by many women who prefer not to wear a pad externally. Because highly absorbent tampons may become breeding areas for bacteria, eventually causing toxic shock syndrome, it is best to use low-absorbency tampons and to change them every four to eight hours (Kelley, 2005).

In some Native American and Eastern cultures, the menstruating female is considered (primarily by the male hierarchy) to be unclean, and sexual intercourse is prohibited during the menstrual period. Even though men and women in these cultures may subscribe to these social imperatives publicly, they do not necessarily do so in private. Research indicates that college-educated, heterosexual women in the United States are less likely to engage in all sexual activities during menstruation, perhaps because of lowered physical interest but also because of social and psychological factors. Women who are more comfortable with their own sexuality tend also to be more comfortable with menstruation and with having sex during their periods (Rempel & Baumgartner, 2003). No particular medical risks are associated with sexual activity during the period per se, although if a woman is infected with HIV, the presence of blood in the vagina may increase the risk that a sexual partner could become infected. Use of a condom would reduce that risk. Some women experience variations in their sex drive during various stages of the menstrual cycle and may also show preferences for different types of men during the different phases (Gangestad & Cousins, 2002). Although there is less chance of pregnancy resulting from intercourse during menstruation, it should not be assumed that it is a totally "safe" time.

menstruation (men-stru-AY-shun) phase of the menstrual cycle in which the inner uterine lining breaks down and sloughs off; the tissue, along with some blood, flows out through the vagina; also called the period.

dysmenorrhea (dis-men-a-REE-a) painful menstruation.

Table 2.2	Summary of the Menstrual Cycle		

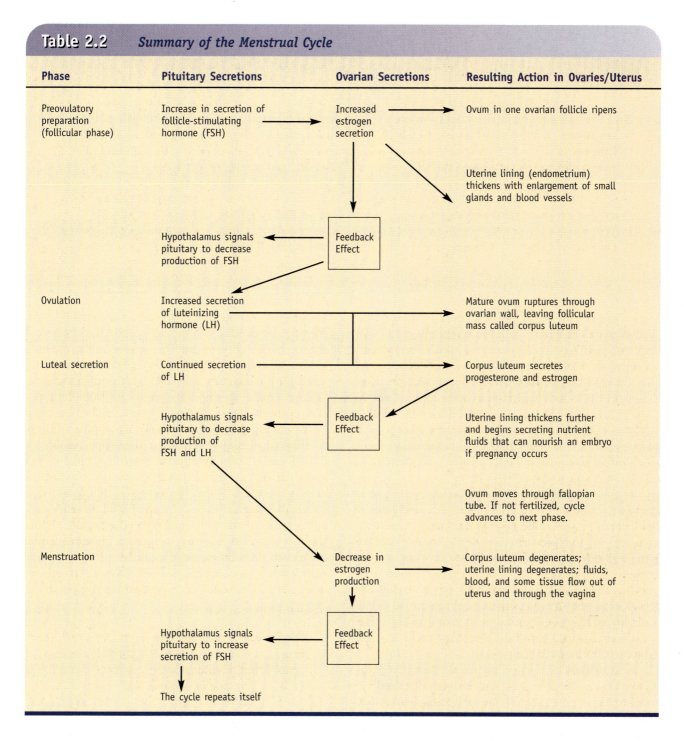

Phase	Pituitary Secretions	Ovarian Secretions	Resulting Action in Ovaries/Uterus
Preovulatory preparation (follicular phase)	Increase in secretion of follicle-stimulating hormone (FSH)	Increased estrogen secretion	Ovum in one ovarian follicle ripens
			Uterine lining (endometrium) thickens with enlargement of small glands and blood vessels
	Hypothalamus signals pituitary to decrease production of FSH	Feedback Effect	
Ovulation	Increased secretion of luteinizing hormone (LH)		Mature ovum ruptures through ovarian wall, leaving follicular mass called corpus luteum
Luteal secretion	Continued secretion of LH		Corpus luteum secretes progesterone and estrogen
	Hypothalamus signals pituitary to decrease production of FSH and LH	Feedback Effect	Uterine lining thickens further and begins secreting nutrient fluids that can nourish an embryo if pregnancy occurs
			Ovum moves through fallopian tube. If not fertilized, cycle advances to next phase.
Menstruation		Decrease in estrogen production	Corpus luteum degenerates; uterine lining degenerates; fluids, blood, and some tissue flow out of uterus and through the vagina
	Hypothalamus signals pituitary to increase secretion of FSH	Feedback Effect	
	The cycle repeats itself		

Menstrual Discomfort and Control

Many women experience some physical discomfort and psychological shifts just prior to or during menstruation. Symptoms include headaches, backaches, fatigue, fluid retention, uterine cramping, breast tenderness, anxiety, depression, and irritability. In 5 to 10 percent of women, these symptoms may become severe enough to interfere with daily activities, and up to 30 percent have enough discomfort to seek treatment for what has come to be known as **premenstrual** **syndrome (PMS),** although PMS is not considered a true medical diagnosis. A small number of these women have a good deal of emotional distress as part of their PMS, including depression, anxiety, and restlessness. These more severe psychological symptoms have been classified as **premenstrual dysphoric disorder (PMDD),** which has been considered a specific medical and psychiatric category (Chrisler & Caplan, 2003). However, there are many individual differences in how women experience and react to these discomforts, and the degree of their severity seems to be related

FOH

Real Student Voices

■ The first time I got my period, I was excited to tell my mother. She told my father, and they both took me out to dinner to celebrate my "womanhood." It made me feel very grown-up and special.

■ I was brought up by my grandmother, and she never said very much about periods and such. I knew from one of my friends that I would get a period eventually, but when it happened, I found it

scary and unsettling. The idea of blood coming out of my body made me feel sick. Actually, the school nurse was good about explaining the whole thing to me and making me feel better.

■ I find periods to be annoying. I've always had a lot of PMS symptoms, and I don't like having to put my sex life on pause. I've been thinking of going on one of the pills that stops you from having periods.

to factors such as the degree of stress in their lives, their own expectations about the symptoms, and how they learned to think about menstrual symptoms (Wingwood & DiClemente, 2002). Sexual interest may vary during the menstrual cycle as well. Women who experience PMS have been found to be more likely to have higher levels of sexual interest during the ovulatory phase of the cycle, whereas women who do not have premenstrual complaints tend to be most interested in sexual activity just prior to menstruation (Gangestad & Cousins, 2002).

Two hormones are believed to be involved in producing the discomfort of PMS. There is a decrease in the level of progesterone prior to menstruation and an increase in the amount of the substance called **prostaglandin,** a hormonelike chemical whose source in the body is as yet unidentified. These changes may lead to physiological and resulting psychological effects. Some research has in fact confirmed that mood shifts, social frustration, and some thinking and creative skills seem to change over the menstrual cycle in some women (Chrisler & Caplan, 2003).

A great deal of controversy exists over how PMS should be treated. Over-the-counter drugs advertised for menstrual cramping generally are antiprostaglandins that interfere with that hormone's contracting effects on the uterus. Research has shown that antidepressant medications that maintain levels of the chemical serotonin in the brain may help relieve PMS symptoms in many women. Some authorities have recommended changes in diet to help alleviate PMS. The most common suggestions are to reduce the intake of salt, refined sugar, and caffeinated foods such as coffee, colas, and chocolate. Eating more frequently during the day, taking high dosages of certain vitamins, increasing fiber intake, and drinking herbal teas have been recommended. In general, however, physicians remain skeptical over the efficacy of many remedies suggested for PMS.

One of the newest approaches to dealing with menstrual cycle discomforts has been to use a different dosage of birth control pills to reprogram the monthly menstrual cycle. For birth control, hormonal pills are taken for three weeks, followed by seven days of nonhormonal pills. This regimen results in a menstrual period every 28 days. However, one variation has been for women to take 84 hormonally active pills in a row so they can actually skip their menstrual period for three months. Another approach involves taking a pill every day of the year so that menstrual periods are entirely eliminated. There can be some unpleasant side effects of pill use, but many women find these less uncomfortable than their menstrual discomfort. While some women do not care to regulate their menstrual cycle with pills, others have been happy and satisfied with fewer periods a year, or even none, if it means reducing the occurrence of menstrual discomfort (Kalb, 2003).

What do you think about using birth control pills to reduce the frequency of menstrual periods a woman has? Is this a reasonable step, or is it too much fiddling with nature?

premenstrual syndrome (PMS) symptoms of physical discomfort, moodiness, and emotional tension that occur in some women for a few days prior to menstruation.

premenstrual dysphoric disorder (PMDD) severe emotional symptoms such as anxiety or depression around the time of menstruation.

prostaglandin hormonelike chemical whose concentrations increase in a woman's body just prior to menstruation.

Changes before "The Change"

There is no typical perimenopause. Some women experience few or no symptoms. Others are not so lucky; they suffer from a wide range. Some of the most common:

Memory lapses and loss of concentration. Some women who take estrogen report an improvement in cognitive function.

Headaches. May be caused by fluctuating hormone levels. Some women begin to suffer migraines.

Mood swings. Changes in hormone levels may interfere with the production of the body's mood-regulator serotonin. Some women feel anxious or weepy.

Dry skin. A decrease in the protein collagen —which may be linked to a decline in estrogen —means less elasticity and more wrinkles.

Bone loss. Declining reproductive hormones translate to less protection for bones. The problem is at its worst after menopause.

Hot flashes. Many perimenopausal women experience them, mostly around the head and upper body. They usually last several minutes. Nocturnal hot flashes, which are known as night sweats, can lead to insomnia.

Erratic menstrual cycles. A classic symptom of perimenopause. Cycles vary widely from 18 days to missed periods. Excessive bleeding is common.

Vaginal dryness. As estrogen levels decline, the vaginal wall thins and becomes less elastic. Intercourse may become painful.

Urinary incontinence. As the vaginal wall weakens, the bladder loses support and urination is harder to control.

FIGURE 2.15 *Perimenopause*

Source: From Sharon Begley, "Understanding Perimenopause," *Newsweek*, Special Issue, Spring/Summer 1999, p. 33. Copyright © 1999 Newsweek, Inc. All rights reserved. Reprinted by permission.

FOH ■ Menopause

Aging is a natural process among living things, with predictable physiological changes occurring over time at all levels, from cells to entire organ systems. For humans, it apparently is a process that is largely genetically controlled. Various degenerative physiological aspects of aging are triggered by genes, although our bodies also experience other effects of normal wear and tear. There are wide individual differences, but each of us experiences a gradual process of slowing down and becoming physically less pliable. Although its rate may be affected by heredity, the environment, and personal health habits, the aging process is inevitable and irreversible. The sexual implications of

aging stem from both psychological and biological changes (Connell et al., 2005). Aging bodies may be perceived as having beauty and strength if they are approached with a positive psychological attitude.

The female body is genetically programmed to cease menstruating sometime in middle age, usually between the ages of 45 and 55. This is called menopause, and the years surrounding menopause are usually termed **perimenopause** (see Figure 2.15). In popular usage, it is sometimes called the "change of life," simply

perimenopause the time of a woman's life surrounding menopause, characterized by symptoms resulting from reduced estrogen levels.

"the change," or a more recently suggested term, "the pause." Modifications in ovarian function usually begin prior to age 30, marked by a gradual decline in the hormonal output of these glands. Structures in the brain contribute to the changes. Eventually there is increased irregularity in ovulation and menstrual periods. Usually there are unpredictable sequences of scanty menstrual flow or increased flow, but a few women simply stop menstruating quite abruptly, never having another period. Although the pituitary gland continues to produce FSH and LH that help control the woman's menstrual cycle, the ovaries apparently become increasingly insensitive to their stimulation. The hormone-producing tissues of the ovaries atrophy until their output of estrogen and progesterone becomes minimal (Chrisler & Caplan, 2003; Dennerstein, Alexander, & Kotz, 2004).

As the woman's hormonal levels drop, the most noticeable result usually is the gradual cessation of menstruation, resulting from the lack of hormonal stimulation to the inner lining of the uterus, or endometrium. This means, of course, that the woman is no longer able to conceive, although most physicians recommend using birth control for a full year after the last menstrual period. However, there are other effects on the body as well. Very gradually, the uterus and breasts decrease somewhat in size. The inner walls of the vagina become thinner, and a reduction in the number of small blood vessels in the pelvic region may result in reduced vaginal lubrication. There also may be changes in the texture and color of the skin and hair and an increased tendency to gain weight, especially on the hips. Women sometimes experience noticeable changes in the quality of the voice (Dennerstein, Alexander, & Kotz, 2004). For reasons that are not entirely understood, women who smoke tend to reach menopause earlier than other women (Palmer et al., 2003).

Another consequence of decreased estrogen production in some women is a weakening of bones, called **osteoporosis.** This condition most frequently strikes postmenopausal women who are slender and slight and who have led sedentary lives. Women suffering from osteoporosis are predisposed to fractures of the hip and arm, and they often suffer chronic back pain because of vertebral collapse. Although this condition cannot be completely cured, it can be treated to reduce the amount of bone weakness. The usual treatments involve the prescription of vitamin D, calcium supplements, estrogen replacement, and/or exercise (see Table 2.3).

> **osteoporosis** (ah-stee-o-po-ROW-sus) disease caused by loss of calcium from the bones in postmenopausal women, leading to brittle bones and stooped posture.

Table 2.3   *The Facts about Menopause*

Factors Affecting Onset
- Smoking. It can bring on menopause as much as two years earlier.
- Left-handedness. Onset is about one year earlier.
- Number of pregnancies. The more pregnancies you've had, the later menopause may arrive.
- Onset of menstruation. If you began menstruating at an early age, menopause will likely be later.
- Mother's age at menopause. Although other factors come into play, heredity makes the age your mother's menopause began a good guidepost.

What Happens to Your Body?
- As early as age 35, estrogen production slows, signaling perimenopause—the beginning of the change of life.
- Premenstrual syndrome may increase or appear for the first time.
- Menstrual cycles may become erratic.
- You still can become pregnant.
- Night sweats and hot flashes may occur.
- Vaginal dryness may develop.
- Sleep may be disrupted.
- Mood swings or difficulty with concentration may occur.
- After you have had no periods for a year, you are postmenopausal. You become susceptible to osteoporosis and have an increased risk of cardiovascular disease.

Demographics
- Menopause commonly occurs between ages 45 and 55. Average age is 51.
- 40 million American women already have reached menopause.
- Most women will live one-third of their life after menopause.
- For every 2,000 postmenopausal women, 20 will develop severe bone loss, 6 will develop breast cancer; and 3 will develop endometrial cancer.

Estrogen Pros
- Can help prevent osteoporosis (the loss of bone mass).
- May help prevent the onset of cardiovascular disease.

Estrogen Cons
- Can increase the risk of endometrial cancer.
- May increase the risk of breast cancer.

What Men Should Know about Menopause
- Everything women should know.
- Passage through menopause can take from one to three years.
- Some drying of the vagina occurs, so lubricants will be necessary during intercourse, and lengthened foreplay is in order.
- Lack of sleep can contribute to irritability and fatigue, making your partner more difficult to live with. She may cry easily.
- Be understanding, and do your share around the house.

Source: From Nancy McVicar, "The Facts about Menopause" in *Sun-Sentinel,* December 12, 1991. Reprinted with permission from the South Florida Sun-Sentinel.

Menopausal changes in the body's hormonal balances may also cause mood alterations and other psychological effects. Some women complain of depression, irritability, or other emotional symptoms. Some experience unpredictable dilation of the blood vessels in the skin, causing a flushed, sweaty feeling called a **hot flash;** its exact cause is unknown. We should not lose sight of the fact that life's major transitions are often and understandably accompanied by some degree of sadness and sense of loss, and these feelings do not have to be perceived as signs of pathology or psychological problems. A loss of some level of sexual interest and function sometimes occurs after menopause (Derogatis et al., 2004; Dennerstein, Alexander, & Kotz, 2004). It should also be emphasized that many women find very positive and liberating aspects in menopause as well. Aging, and the physiological changes it brings, need not be viewed negatively—there is still much about life to be discovered and celebrated (Koch, Mansfield, Thurau, & Carey, 2005).

See "Menopause" on SexSource Online.

FOH Hormone Replacement Therapy

Menopausal women who are treated with dosages of the progesterone and estrogen hormones experience a reversal of the physical changes that accompany menopause. However, such **hormone replacement therapy (HRT)** is a controversial form of medical treatment. First popularized as a way of staying youthful and "feminine" for life, use of estrogen treatment alone eventually came under attack as a risky procedure. A number of studies in the 1970s began to demonstrate a statistical relationship between treatment with estrogen and several medical conditions, including uterine and breast cancer. A link between estrogen replacement therapy and breast cancer was demonstrated, particularly in women who had used estrogen for five years or longer (Chen et al., 2002; London, 2004). Estrogen-only replacement therapy also increases the risk of ovarian cancer (Lacey et al., 2002).

One study examined questionnaires and medical records of 8,881 women, finding that those who received HRT actually tended to live longer than those who did not and to experience lower occurrence of heart disease, stroke, and broken bones. Combining estrogen and progesterone over a long period of time seemed to have the most positive effects, although it also was shown to increase women's risk of breast cancer (Schairer et al., 2000). Other studies have demonstrated that postmenopausal hormone replacement can help make the mind keener and memory sharper, but it was also discovered that the treatment

may actually increase a woman's risk of developing dementia in her later years (Wickelgren, 2003).

For the most part, these research studies passively monitored women who had made their own choices about HRT, so it could not really be determined whether the hormones made women healthier or healthy women simply were more likely to take the hormones. A more scientific study, begun in 1997, recruited nearly 17,000 healthy women across the country and randomly assigned them to take either an estrogen-progestin combination pill or a placebo. Because of the new results that emerged, the study was called off in 2002, three years before it was scheduled to end. Researchers found that while HRT reduced the rate of hip fractures and colon cancer, the risks of other problems increased the longer women took the hormones. The chances of suffering a heart attack or a blood clot in the lungs were higher throughout the study, and the risk of stroke seemed to increase after the second year. Five years into the study, the women on HRT also were developing invasive breast cancer at a higher rate (Grady, Herrington, et al., 2002). All of these risks resulted in the study being halted. Many women ceased the use of replacement hormones after the results were publicized, and a substantial decrease in the incidence of breast cancer occurred soon after (M. D. Anderson Cancer Center, 2006).

Evidence about the benefits and risks of HRT has created some confusion for women and their doctors. However, HRT has not been shown to have a great deal of effect on a woman's health or quality of life, implying that the risks outweigh any potential benefits (Hays et al., 2003). Some physicians still believe that women with particularly severe symptoms may benefit from HRT, especially in the short term, and that other medications could be used to control the risks; others advise their patients not to take replacement hormones. Women often are left with a difficult balancing act in making a decision or the option of exploring other medical remedies or natural treatments for the unpleasant symptoms of menopause (Stewart, 2005).

Implications for Women's Sexuality

Females typically are raised to think of menstruation as a sign of being a woman, with its additional symbolic implications of fertility, femininity, and sexual

> **hot flash** a flushed, sweaty feeling in the skin caused by dilated blood vessels; often associated with menopause.
>
> **hormone replacement therapy (HRT)** treatment of the physical changes of menopause by administering dosages of the hormones estrogen and progesterone.

readiness. Menarche often is heralded as the beginning of womanhood. Consequently, for many women menopause represents a loss of an important facet of womanhood and femininity. They fall prey to some of the menopause-related myths: that it is the beginning of the end of life, that sexual attractiveness and arousal deteriorate after menopause, and that one's purpose as a woman (that is, reproduction) has been lost (Koch, Mansfield, Thurau, & Carey, 2005).

Research studies generally confirm that menopause need not markedly affect a woman's sexual functioning, although there is research to indicate that some women experience a decrease in sexual desire during middle life (Deeks & McCabe, 2001; Dennerstein, Alexander, & Kotz, 2004). A woman facing the physical and psychological changes of menopause may experience a temporary shift in sexual desire. While desire may increase or decrease, usually there are no major, long-lasting changes. Some women perceive menopause as a release from concern about intercourse resulting in an unwanted pregnancy, thus freeing them to be more relaxed sexually. As women approach menopause, they sometimes assume that they are no longer at risk for pregnancy. However, about 25 percent of women ages 40 to 44 are at risk of unwanted pregnancy, and one in five of the at-risk group uses no birth control.

Much of how a woman's sexual life is affected by menopause depends on how she views herself and menopause. This in turn is influenced by the woman's cultural background, values about sex, social environment, overall health, and fantasies and expectations regarding menopause. Nonetheless, even for women who expect menopause to bring a decrease in sexual well-being, that is not necessarily the outcome. It is therefore crucial that women get accurate information and emotional support throughout their menopausal experiences. Counselors, women's centers, and trained social workers can provide such help. Women need to be able to communicate their fears, doubts, and insecurities while being reassured that menopause is simply a natural stage of human development. It is important for the woman's partner to receive information and counseling about her menopausal experience as well (Stewart, 2005).

Self-Evaluation

You and Your Body

When you have sufficient privacy, remove all your clothing and stand before the largest mirror available, preferably a full-length one. Try to relax and take some time to look over your body carefully. Consider the following questions as you look at your body with as much objectivity as you can muster.

1. Do you enjoy looking at and touching your body? Why or why not?

2. What aspects of your body do you like most? Least?

3. If you are a male, how do you feel about your general body shape, your penis, and your testicles, compared with other male bodies you have seen?

4. If you are a female, how do you feel about your general body shape, your breasts, and your external genitals, compared with other female bodies you have seen?

5. Does your body conform to your ideas of what a (feminine or masculine) body should look like?

6. Do you think your nude body is (or would be) sexually attractive to members of the other gender? Of the same gender?

Chapter Summary

1. The female sex organs have always been recognized for their procreative (reproductive) functions, but their potentials for pleasure and intimate communication have become increasingly recognized.

2. The female vulva consists of the external sex organs known as the mons, the labia majora and minora, the clitoris, and the openings to the urethra and vagina.

3. The clitoris has a sensitive tip, or glans, and a shaft that extends back under a covering of tissue called the hood or prepuce.

4. Some cultures, religions, or social customs require surgical procedures such as clitoridectomy

or infibulation to be performed as rites of passage. These forms of female genital cutting have created worldwide controversy.

5. The vagina is a muscular-walled organ of sexual pleasure and reproduction that extends into the woman's body. Its opening may be partially covered by tissue called a hymen.

6. Douching of the vagina is still a common practice, but it increases the risk of internal infections. The vagina has natural cleansing mechanisms.

7. The hymen may be present in the opening of the vagina and may be one of several types.

8. The hymen may cause sexual difficulties if it is imperforate (having no openings) or tough and fibrous.

9. Regular genital self-examination for women ensures early detection of infections or irritations.

10. Acute urethral syndrome and cystitis, or bladder infection, are common in women and may be caused by the *E. coli* bacterium. Interstitial cystitis is chronic and may cause problems with sexual functioning.

11. Vulvodynia refers to pain in the vulval region. If it is limited to the entrance to the vagina and caused by physical contact, it is called vulvar vestibulitis.

12. The vagina is subject to several medical conditions, including atrophy because of lowered estrogen levels, varicose veins, and fistulae (openings between the vagina and other organs).

13. The uterus is the organ in which fetal development takes place. Its cervix extends into the posterior part of the vagina.

14. The ovaries mature eggs (ova) and produce female hormones. The fallopian tubes transport ova down toward the uterus, and it is in these tubes that fertilization of an egg by a sperm can take place.

15. Pap tests offer the possibility of early detection of cervical cancer or precancerous cells in the cervix, called cervical intraepithelial neoplasia

(CIN). Untreated cervical cancer may become invasive cervical cancer (ICC).

16. The uterus may be affected by hormonal imbalances, leading to abnormal bleeding, overgrowth of its lining in the form of either endometrial hyperplasia or endometriosis, or prolapse into the vagina.

17. The female breasts are strongly connected with sexuality in our culture, and women often worry about breast size. Milk glands in the breasts produce milk after a woman gives birth.

18. Breast cancer is one of the more common types of malignancy. Regular breast self-examination is essential to the detection of potentially malignant lumps. Mammography is a form of X ray that can detect breast cancer in very early stages.

19. Between menarche and menopause, a woman's fertility is regulated by the menstrual cycle. At roughly four-week intervals, an ovum ripens in one ovary as the result of increased levels of follicle-stimulating hormone (FSH). Estrogen thickens the uterine wall, producing a suitable location for fetal growth. The ovum breaks through the ovary wall at ovulation. If the ovum is not fertilized, extra blood and tissue are shed from the uterus in menstruation. Hormones from the pituitary, hypothalamus, and ovaries regulate the menstrual cycle.

20. Premenstrual syndrome (PMS) consists of uncomfortable physical and emotional symptoms. Severe symptoms may be classified as premenstrual dysphoria disorder (PMDD).

21. Menopause is the time of life when menstruation ceases. The perimenopausal years may have unpleasant symptoms as hormone production decreases.

22. Hormone replacement therapy (HRT) has been found to carry more risks than benefits and generally is no longer recommended for menopausal women.

Focus on Health Questions

In this section you will find the kinds of questions that you may have concerning your own health and sexuality. The page references indicate where in the text the answer is located; the exact place is marked with this logo: **FOH**

1. Should I douche to keep my vagina clean and odor-free? **39**

2. If my hymen is missing, will my partner be convinced that I have previously had sex? **40**

3. Why is it that the hymen may bleed during first sexual intercourse, and can it cause pain during sex? **40**

4. What are the signs of infection or abnormality in the vulval and vaginal ares? **40–41**

Chapter 3

Male Sexual Anatomy and Physiology

Chapter Outline

I first came to this country as a 12-year-old boy, and in the gym showers I was almost the only boy who was not circumcised. In my country circumcision was never done, and I had never even seen a circumcised penis before. And there I was, with my penis looking different from everybody else's. . . . Of all my cultural adjustments here, that was the most difficult.

—from a student essay

In sexuality education, male sex organs have traditionally been given recognition for their capability of generating pleasant sexual feelings, while their role in reproduction has often been seen as a by-product of that pleasure. As in the female, the external sex organs of the male (see Figure 3.1) are associated more with sexual arousal, and the internal structures are associated more with reproduction (Sonfield, 2002). Men often are not well informed about their bodies or about significant issues that can affect their sexual and reproductive health. Educational efforts are beginning to pay more attention to male sexuality, particularly the needs of younger men (Sherrow et al., 2003).

■ The Testes and Scrotum

The two male sex glands, the **testes** (or testicles), develop within the abdominal cavity during fetal life. A few weeks before birth, the testes gradually move downward through the *inguinal canal* into an external pouch of skin called the **scrotum.** In a small percentage of male infants, the testes do not descend into the scrotum properly, and a few of these cases require medical treatment. The testes have two major functions after puberty. One is the production of the male sex hormone **testosterone,** which plays a significant role in the development of male secondary sex characteristics and also may affect behavior to some degree. The testes also form hundreds of millions of **sperm,** the sex cells necessary for human reproduction.

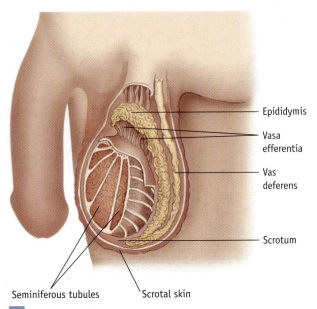

Epididymis

Vasa efferentia

Vas deferens

Scrotum

Seminiferous tubules   Scrotal skin

■ FIGURE 3.2   *Testes*

The testes are the male gonads or reproductive glands. They are paired structures located in the scrotum, and their purpose is to produce sperm and the hormone testosterone that controls male sexual development. The word *testis* is based on the root word for "witness"; the ancient custom in taking an oath was to place a hand on the genitals—to "testify."

Each testis is subdivided internally into several lobes (see Figure 3.2). The lobes are filled with a tangled mass of tiny **seminiferous tubules,** inside of which the sperm cells are formed. Each threadlike tubule is 1 to 3 feet long if extended. Between the tubules are **interstitial cells** (or Leydig cells) that produce testosterone. These cells are close to blood vessels so that the hormone is secreted efficiently into

■ FIGURE 3.1   *External Male Anatomy*

The external male sex organs are more visible and accessible than the female's. As with the female, the external organs are the primary source of sexual pleasure while the internal organs are the source of reproduction, but the distinction is not as clearly defined in males.

testes (TEST-ees) pair of male gonads that produce sperm and male hormones.

scrotum (SKROTE-um) pouch of skin in which the testes are contained.

testosterone (tes-TAHS-ter-one) major male hormone produced by the testes; it helps produce male secondary sex characteristics.

sperm reproductive cells produced in the testes; in fertilization, one sperm unites with an ovum.

seminiferous tubules (sem-a-NIF-a-rus) tightly coiled tubules in the testes in which sperm cells are formed.

interstitial cells (in-ter-STIH-shul) cells between the seminiferous tubules that secrete testosterone and other male hormones.

the bloodstream. The seminiferous tubules combine at their ends to form larger ducts, which empty into a series of even larger tubes, the **vasa efferentia.** Immature sperm from the seminiferous tubules are moved by wavelike contractions into the vasa efferentia and then into a coiled tubing network folded against the back and part of the top of each testis, the **epididymis.** It is in this area that the sperm mature and become ready to leave the body. The epididymis opens into a large duct that leads up into the abdominal cavity from each testis. This duct, the **vas deferens,** transports the sperm up to the *seminal vesicle* during sexual activity.

Learn more about "The Testes" on SexSource Online.

The scrotum of a prepubescent male is quite smooth and light in color. At puberty, the testes and scrotum grow, and hormonal influences cause the outer skin to darken and become somewhat wrinkled. The location of the testes in this external pouch is essential, because sperm production can occur only at temperatures slightly below inner body temperature. The *cremasteric muscles* suspend the testes in the scrotum and help regulate their temperature. In cold surroundings (such as swimming in cold water) or stressful situations, these muscles and the scrotal tissue itself contract, pulling the testes up close to the body to keep them warmer and protected. In warmer surroundings (such as a hot bath), the muscles and scrotal tissue relax so the testes are lowered away from the body to keep them cooler. The adult male testes are about 1.5 inches in length and 1 inch in diameter. They are slightly movable within the scrotum. One testis usually hangs slightly lower than the other—in the majority of men, the left testis is lower, while in left-handed men the right testis tends to hang lower. There seems to be no particular significance either way. The scrotal area is well supplied with nerves, and the testes are very sensitive to pressure or sharp blows. Most men find gentle stimulation of the testes and scrotum sexually arousing.

Tradition once held that during exercise an athletic supporter or jockstrap should be worn by males to hold the testicles up closer to the body, providing support and a measure of protection. However, historians know that athletes in ancient times often competed in the nude. There is now some evidence that during exercise the cremasteric muscles actually contract, providing their own natural support. As body temperature rises, however, they tend to relax, causing the testes to lower away from the body and making them more vulnerable to injury. Younger male athletes are not wearing the traditional jockstrap as much anymore, opting instead for spandex shorts or compression pants that provide a more natural feeling of support. Some are even choosing to wear boxer shorts, which do not provide much support at all. Evidence suggests that severe testicular injury, causing pain and swelling for a day or more, may be associated with later infertility. This has caused some sports health experts to recommend that a hard plastic protective cup be worn over the male genitals during contact sports.

In various times in history, males have had their testicles removed in a surgical procedure called castration. It was believed that castrated males, sometimes called *eunuchs,* were reliable guards for harems of women and also tended to be more level-headed managers and leaders. Some men today fantasize about being castrated for various reasons, and some actually go through with the procedure. These men may be motivated by sexual feelings, a preference to be female, or a desire to have less powerful sexual urges. It can be very dangerous to attempt castration by oneself or to allow someone who is not medically qualified to attempt the procedure, because it can lead to permanent disability or even death (Wassersug, Zelenietz, & Squire, 2004).

Male Genital and Testicular Self-Examination

Men should take time at least monthly to examine their genital organs. Adequate lighting, and sometimes a mirror, can help with the self-examination process. Look through the pubic hair to the skin underneath, and carefully examine the head and shaft of the penis. If you are not circumcised, this will require pulling back the foreskin to expose the penile glans. Check for any bumps, sores, or blisters anywhere in the region. These may be reddish or light in color. It is important to lift up the penis and look underneath, because this area is often overlooked. Also be alert to any soreness in the genitals or to any itching or burning sensations during urination or around the urethral opening. Although many of these symptoms do not indicate serious conditions, you should have them checked by a physician or other clinician who specializes in men's health concerns.

vasa efferentia larger tubes within the testes, into which sperm move after being produced in the seminiferous tubules.

epididymis (ep-a-DID-a-mus) tubular structure on each testis in which sperm cells mature.

vas deferens tube that leads sperm upward from each testis to the seminal vesicles.

FOH Cancer of the testes is a relatively rare disease, with fewer than 5,000 new cases diagnosed each year in the United States. It is primarily a disease of younger men, especially men between the ages of 20 and 35. When it is detected and treated early, the chances of survival are excellent. However, if it is not treated within the first three months, the survival rate falls dramatically, to only about 25 percent. Therefore it is crucial for men to get into the habit of checking their testes regularly for any lumps or other unusual symptoms.

FOH Here is the best way to proceed with testicular self-examination. Choose a time after a hot shower or bath, so that the testes are lowered away from the body. Roll each testicle gently between the thumb and fingers, looking especially for any small hard lumps that might be found directly on the front or side surface of a testis (see Figure 3.3). Such a lump is usually painless. Do not be alarmed at feeling the epididymis toward the top and back of each testis. Although not all lumps are malignant, any growth should be reported to a physician immediately for further investigation. Other symptoms that a man should consider suspicious and worth reporting include any "heavy" feeling in a testicle, accumulation of fluid in the scrotum, swelling of lymph nodes or other discomfort in the groin area, and any swelling or tenderness in the breasts.

If testicular cancer is diagnosed, the usual treatment involves surgical removal of the entire testis. The other testis is left in place and can easily produce enough male hormones on its own. An artificial, gel-filled testis can be placed in the scrotum for cosmetic

reasons. Sexual functioning may change for a time in a proportion of males following treatment for testicular cancer. The most common complaints are a decrease in sexual desire and difficulty reaching orgasm, although many men actually report an increase in sexual satisfaction. Functional problems often improve with time and further treatment (Jonker-Pool et al., 2001). Men should become comfortable with this self-examination procedure as a potentially lifesaving measure.

Disorders of the Testes

There are also several disorders of the testes. In very rare cases, both testes are completely lacking at birth, a disorder known as **anorchism.** A more common problem is **cryptorchidism,** in which the testes have not descended into the scrotum before birth. This condition usually corrects itself within a few years; if it does not, it must be corrected by the time of puberty through hormonal or surgical treatment. If only one testis is present in the scrotum, the condition is termed **monorchidism.** However, one testis can easily handle the work of two, producing sufficient quantities of male hormones and sperm. Occasionally a male suffers from **testicular failure,** in which the testes do not produce male hormones or sperm. This condition usually responds to some form of hormonal therapy. **FOH**

Several organic problems can affect the internal organs of the sexual and urinary systems. In men, the bladder may become infected, and various parts of the testes may occasionally become inflamed. **Epididymitis,** or inflammation of the epididymis at the top of each testis, is relatively common and is treated with antibiotics. It can be caused by many different types of bacteria that make their way into the urethra and eventually back through the vas deferens to the epididymis. In severe cases, surgical intervention may be necessary.

If a man experiences prolonged sexual arousal without having an orgasm, the testes may become

FIGURE 3.3 *Testicular Self-Examination*
The best time for a man to examine his testes is right after a hot bath or shower, because the testicles descend and the scrotal skin relaxes in the heat. He should place his index and middle fingers on the underside of each testicle and his thumbs on top. He should gently roll the testicle between his fingers and thumb. Any abnormal lump would be most likely to be found at the front or the side of the testicle.

anorchism (a-NOR-kiz-um) rare birth defect in which both testes are lacking.

cryptorchidism (krip-TOR-ka-diz-um) condition in which the testes have not descended into the scrotum prior to birth.

monorchidism (ma-NOR-ka-dizm) presence of only one testis in the scrotum.

testicular failure lack of sperm and/or hormone production by the testes.

epididymitis (ep-a-did-a-MITE-us) inflammation of the epididymis of the testis.

Real People

Roland: Confronting an Embarrassing Situation

Roland is a university sophomore. He has not had any serious relationships but considers himself a very sexual person. He thinks and fantasizes about sexual things frequently and has masturbated regularly since he was 11 years old. Residence-hall living during his first year reduced the frequency with which he masturbated, mostly because of the lack of privacy. He appreciates the greater amount of alone time he now has in a suite shared with two others.

He often enjoys accessing free pornographic pictures on the Internet and frequently views these sites during his masturbatory activity. One night recently when he was engrossed in stimulating himself with his boxers pulled down, one of his suitemates returned unexpectedly and found him at the computer. The suitemate was obviously embarrassed, as was Roland, and the other man turned and left the suite without saying a word.

The next day, Roland made a point of apologizing to his suitemate, saying that he had not expected anyone to enter the room. The suitemate told him that he was really upset by what he had witnessed and was thinking of asking for a room change. He added that as far as he was concerned, both masturbation and pornography were immoral and disgusting. He told Roland that he understood every male had difficulty resisting these temptations, but he didn't want to risk walking in on the behavior again. Roland was now even more embarrassed, and while he didn't really think masturbation was wrong, he was not anxious to have university officials find out about what had happened. He assured his suitemate that he wouldn't have to worry about seeing the behavior again, and they agreed not to talk about the incident further. Roland has come away from the situation feeling negative about himself and wondering what he should do about cutting down on masturbation or eliminating the behavior completely.

Do you think Roland was wrong for behaving as he did? What do you think of his suitemate's reaction? Was he overreacting? Was he right to be concerned? If you were in the suitemate's shoes, what would you do? Would you want to change rooms? Would you tell other people what had happened? Is there any obligation to protect Roland's privacy?

swollen, tender, and painful due to their long-term congestion with blood. The vas deferens also may become irritated, causing pain that extends up through the pubic area and lower abdomen. In slang, this condition is often called "lover's nuts," "blue balls," or "stone ache." It is not dangerous or permanently damaging—merely uncomfortable. It is also much less common than usually believed.

■ The Penis

Just above the scrotal sac is the male sex organ called the **penis.** The sensitive, smooth, rounded head of the penis is called the **glans.** The glans is filled with nerve endings and is particularly sensitive to sexual stimulation. The two most sensitive areas of the glans are the **frenulum,** a thin, tightly stretched band of skin on its underside connecting the glans with the shaft (body) of the penis; and the **corona,** the ridge around the edge of the glans. The urinary meatus or urethral opening is found at the tip of the glans. When a male is born, the head of the penis is partly covered by a fold of skin called the prepuce or **foreskin.**

The longer body of the penis is called the **shaft.** The skin on the shaft is quite loose, allowing erection to occur. Inside the penile shaft are three cylinders of

penis male sexual organ that can become erect when stimulated; it leads urine and sperm to the outside of the body.

glans in the male, the sensitive head of the penis.

frenulum (FREN-yu-lum) thin, tightly drawn fold of skin on the underside of the penile glans; it is highly sensitive.

corona the ridge around the penile glans.

foreskin fold of skin covering the penile glans; also called the prepuce.

shaft in the male, the cylindrical base of the penis that contains three columns of spongy tissue: two corpora cavernosa and a corpus spongiosum.

Corpora cavernosa

Urethra

Corpus spongiosum

■ FIGURE 3.4 *Cross Section of a Penis*

The penis is the male organ of urination and copulation. This cross section shows the three internal structures of the penis, all cylindrical in shape. The corpus spongiosum contains the urethra, through which pass semen and urine. All three have spongelike tissue dotted with small blood vessels.

erectile tissue, each full of nerves and blood vessels (see Figure 3.4). The two cylinders of tissues lying parallel along the top and sides of the penis are called the *corpora cavernosa.* The third, slightly narrower cylinder that extends along the underside of the penis is called the *corpus spongiosum.*

The penis not only is important as the male organ for sexual activity and reproduction, but also is the organ through which urine is passed from the body. The tube that carries both sperm and urine in the penis is the **urethra.** It is located in the corpus spongiosum, which extends back to the urinary bladder and connects with the sperm-carrying ducts.

Erection

During sexual arousal, the three cylinders inside the penis become engorged with blood so that the penis expands in circumference, becomes longer and harder, and stands out from the body. This **erection** is usually necessary for successful sexual intercourse. It is possible at times, however, for some men to have an orgasm without erection. During erection, the three cylinders of erectile tissue may be felt distinctly. Penile erection occurs in several phases, involving increased blood flow into the erectile tissue and decreased flow out of the tissue. The penis elongates and expands to its maximum capacity, eventually becoming highly rigid as stimulation continues. Sometimes there is a slight curvature in the erect penis—upward, downward, or to one side. Unless the curvature is caused by some injury or disease (which is quite rare), it will not interfere with sexual performance. The angle at which the penis stands out from the body varies a great deal

as well, most typically ranging from 30 to 90 degrees from the upright vertical.

Erection of the penis is controlled by a spinal reflex and is mostly an involuntary reaction (see Figure 3.5). However, the cerebral cortex and other portions of the brain also have input and are intricately connected to the "erection center" of the spinal cord. Therefore, both reflexive and thought processes can work together to stimulate or inhibit an erection (McKenna, 2000). It should be noted that while erections can be generated solely by medical or mechanical means (such as use of a specially designed pumping device), there is a subjective difference between a man's experience of that type of erection and his experience of one generated by a sexually arousing stimulus (Delizonna et al., 2001). In men whose spinal cords have been severed, which breaks the connection between the erection center and the brain, physical stimulation of the penis still generates erection, although the brain has no awareness of feeling in the penis.

The actual mechanism of erection has only recently begun to be more fully understood. Two muscles in the perineal area (below the scrotum), the *bulbocavernosus muscle* and *ischiocavernosus muscle,* show bursts of activity just prior to erection. This activity apparently is closely related to increases in arterial blood flow into the penis, and the muscles and circulatory vessels then work together to maintain erection. It is now known that during sexual arousal the nervous system stimulates the linings of the penile blood vessels and the nerve endings to produce a chemical called **cyclic GMP,** short for guanosine monophosphate, a biochemical derived from nitric oxide. The smooth muscles that surround the arteries inside the penis normally are contracted when the penis is nonerect. Cyclic GMP causes the muscle cells to relax, allowing the arteries to open so that blood flows into the open spaces in the erectile tissues. The rise in blood pressure within the penis squeezes the veins so that they do not drain blood out of the organ, and the penis becomes engorged with blood and erect. It is common for men to experience some loss of erection if their mind wanders during sexual arousal. This happens because nerve signals from the brain are no longer reaching the penis, and the production of cyclic GMP decreases. The smooth muscle cells then begin contracting again, and arterial blood flow is reduced.

urethra (yu-REE-thrah) tube that passes from the urinary bladder to the outside of the body.

erection enlargement and stiffening of the penis as internal muscles relax and blood engorges the columns of spongy tissue.

cyclic GMP a secretion within the spongy erectile tissues of the penis that facilitates erection.

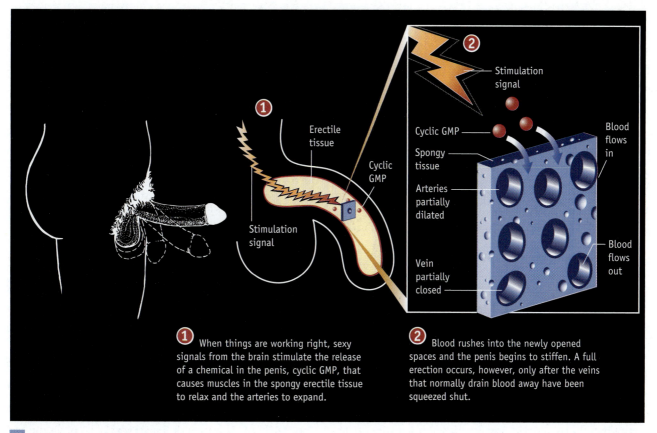

■ FIGURE 3.5 *Penile Erection*

Penile erection is achieved primarily by the increase in blood flow through the corpus spongiosum and the corpora cavernosa during sexual arousal. Other factors, such as spinal reflex and emotion, enter into the physical act of erection.

Source: #1 and #2 from Bruce Handy, "The Viagra Craze," *Time,* May 4, 1998, p. 52. Copyright © 1998 Time, Inc. Reprinted by permission.

Erection clearly is a complex phenomenon involving a carefully balanced interaction of the nervous system, cyclic GMP production, muscle tissue, and blood vessels (McKenna, 2000).

See "Penile Plethysmography" on SexSource Online.

FOH Penis Size

Penis size is a nearly universal concern of men, yet it has not been the subject of very extensive research. Some evidence shows that men are far more likely to rate the size of their penis as average or below average than they are other bodily characteristics, and highly unlikely to rate their penis as much larger than average. This underestimation of the comparative size of genitals may be a response to social pressures and expectations.

Penises clearly vary in length, width, and shape, all perfectly functional and normal. Although some men and women prefer larger penises for sexual activity, there is no basis for believing that any factors of penile size affect a man's ability to be a fully satis-

factory sexual partner. Nevertheless, in a study of 556 women in Croatia, well over half indicated that penis length and/or girth was somewhat important to their sexual pleasure, while around 20 percent said these characteristics were very important. Only one-fourth of the women responded that penis size was unimportant. The more male partners the women in the study had had, the more important penis size was to them. To add more fuel to the insecurities such studies generate for men, over 70 percent of the women in this study said that the overall aesthetic appearance of men's penises (undefined beyond that generality) was also important to their own sexual pleasure (Stulhofer, 2006). Practically speaking, men can do little to alter the characteristics of their genitals. Therefore, learning to become comfortable with one's body and learning from sexual partners how to most effectively engage in sexual activities are the most reasonable goals to pursue.

There is no demonstrated relationship between height, general body size or the size of other particular organs, and penis size (Awwad et al., 2005). Although the research samples have been quite small and the usefulness of the conclusions is doubtful, some evidence

Real People

Jake: Concerns about the Male Body

Jake was a senior in college, and his current relationship seemed to be faltering. He felt depressed and told his best friend how shy he had always been with women. He did not talk about the concerns he had with his body. He had been born with an undescended testicle, and efforts to move the testis into his scrotum during childhood had failed. Prior to entering college, he had had a plastic prosthetic testis surgically implanted in his scrotum because he was concerned that his lacking testis would be noticed in shower rooms. However, he had been dissatisfied with the prosthesis because in his opinion it did not look or feel genuine.

Jake was also concerned about the size of his penis and had written for information on penile enlargement surgery, which he had seen advertised in a men's magazine. After investigating this option further, he gave up the idea of pursuing expensive—and risky—surgery. He decided his penis was within normal size ranges. Nonetheless, he continued to be reluctant in his relationships with women and was troubled by his insecurities.

What do you think Jake ought to do? With whom would you recommend he speak about his personal concerns? Is Jake just being silly in worrying about the size of his penis, or do you think size really matters to men's sexual partners?

exists that there may be significant differences in erect penis lengths among different ethnic groups (Harding & Golombok, 2002).

Penis size continues to be an object of curiosity and comparison, and some research has attempted to document information. Studies on penis size have sometimes been conducted to gather information about how likely it is for a condom to slip off the penis or break during sexual activity. As might be anticipated, researchers face the daunting task of either being allowed by men to measure their penises or asking men to measure their own penises and then report the dimensions. The former technique makes people uncomfortable and may actually affect penis size, and the latter method could be prone to exaggeration (Harding & Golombok, 2002). One study asked gay male couples to measure each other and report back on two different occasions. The researchers believed that the reported inconsistencies rendered the measurements unreliable, while other analysts considered them explainable as random rather than intentional errors (Hershberger, 2003).

A medical text from 1949 offered some measurements but little description of how they were made. The work of Kinsey and of Masters and Johnson did not give definitive results either. Two urologists who performed standardized penile measurements on a group of men at San Francisco General Hospital found that the average nonerect penis was 3.5 inches in length and 3.9 inches in circumference. The average erect penis was 5.1 inches long and 4.9 inches in circumference. Using

the statistical measures of a standard bell curve, the researchers concluded that the range in length for average erect penises would be between 2.8 and 7.2 inches. The 2 percent of men whose erect penises are smaller than 2.8 inches and the 2 percent whose penises are larger than 7.2 inches would be considered smaller or larger than average (Wessels, Lue, & McAninch, 1996).

It has been suggested that measurements of the nonerect penis do not have great meaning because the flaccid penis length of any particular man may vary a great deal depending on emotional and environmental conditions. It is assumed that the erect length would be more consistent from situation to situation, although no reliable data are available support this assumption. Studies generally show that erect penises tend to be somewhat shorter than often believed or as reported in studies relying on self-measurements. A rough grouping of sizes would put about 40 percent of erections between 4.5 and 5.75 inches in length, and about 50 percent of erections between 6 and 7.5 inches long. Probably only about 15 percent of men have erect penises longer than 6.75 inches.

Masters and Johnson found that erection seems to have an equalizing effect: Smaller penises gain proportionately more size than larger penises upon erection. This equalizing effect was confirmed by later researchers (Jamison & Gebhard, 1988) who divided flaccid penises into two categories: short (averaging 3.1 inches) and long (averaging 4.4 inches). They found that shorter penises tended to gain about 85 percent in size during erection, to an average of 5.8 inches, whereas longer penises grew by only 47 percent, to an average of 6.5 inches. Likewise, narrower penises gain more in circumference than wider penises during erection.

Capitalizing on men's concerns about penile size, a variety of "penis enlargement" techniques have been marketed. Most involve using some sort of suction device, with the penis being inserted into a plastic chamber and a plunger-type device then being used to remove some air from the chamber. This stimulation typically creates an erection for men, therefore providing "enlargement." Such devices have been known to cause injury to the penis, if too much suction is used. Some cosmetic surgeons offer surgical techniques to enlarge the penis. One procedure, in which some of the internal ligaments at the base of the penis are cut away so some of the penile structure inside the body can be extended outside, has been found to be too risky. In fact, scarring may result in poor erections or in pulling the penis back, making it appear even shorter. Clinical evidence indicates that many men who have had penis enlargement procedures are unhappy with the results. Experts recommend that surgical interventions not be considered unless the man's *erect* penis falls in the "below average" length category of less than 2.8 inches and he is experiencing significant functional problems with sex because of his penis size (Wessels, Lue, & McAninch, 1996). Also, men born with *micropenis,* an unusually small organ, are known to be able to have happy and pleasurable sex lives (Bankhead, 2005).

Breast size and penis size seem to preoccupy North Americans. How have the media and other factors influenced these concerns? What are your feelings about these issues?

See "Male Anatomy" on SexSource Online.

Male Circumcision: The Debate

When a male is born, his parents may decide to have the foreskin of the baby's penis removed in a surgical procedure called **circumcision,** leaving the glans fully exposed (see Figure 3.6). Until the mid-1970s, most males in the United States were circumcised. The procedure, however, has been much less commonly performed in Europe and Canada. Circumcision has sometimes been a part of religious custom, as for example in the Jewish faith. The other most frequently stated reason for circumcision involves hygiene. It has been assumed that young males will find it troublesome to learn how to pull back the foreskin and wash the glans. Such inattention may

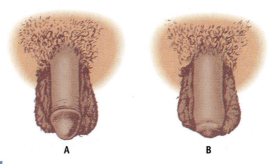

FIGURE 3.6 *Circumcision*

The circumcised penis **(A)** leaves the glans exposed, supposedly making it easier to keep the penis clean and prevent the possibility of cancer. The uncircumcised penis **(B)** in a very few instances may have a condition called *phimosis,* in which the foreskin cannot be retracted over the glans.

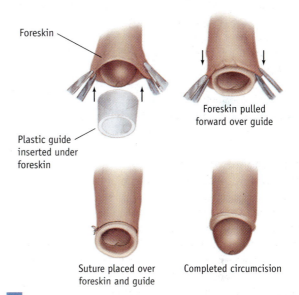

FIGURE 3.7 *Circumcision of an Infant*

The surgical removal of the penile foreskin has a history that goes back as far as 4000 B.C.E. in Egypt. Its justification has been ritualistic, religious, and medical. The surgical procedure illustrated here is usually performed on infant males, but it is sometimes used for adult circumcision.

permit the buildup of a material called smegma that can lead to infection.

There has been continuing controversy over the widespread practice of circumcising male infants (see Figure 3.7). Some have complained that no legitimate reasons justify circumcision or the potential pain and discomfort it might cause to infants. Current standard procedure is to use a form of anesthesia called the dorsal penile nerve block, permitting pain-free surgery. Anticircumcision groups, however, believe that the procedure may be traumatic as well as unnecessary.

circumcision (SIR-cum-sizh-uhn) in the male, surgical removal of the foreskin from the penis.

One medical problem that has been cited as a good reason for circumcision is **phimosis,** or an unusually long and tight foreskin that makes it difficult to retract. Yet opponents of circumcision insist that spontaneous erections begin even before birth and gradually stretch the foreskin, so that by 6 years of age it can be retracted without difficulty in almost 100 percent of cases. If a real problem exists at some later stage in life, circumcision can then be performed. Opponents also believe that in infants the foreskin should be tight and nonretractable to protect the urethral opening from exposure to fecal material or other possible irritants.

In the 1960s, 95 percent of boys in the United States were circumcised. The 1980s saw a distinct decline in the procedure. Later in that decade, mounting evidence seemed to show that this trend was leading to an increase in urinary tract infections in infant boys, a condition that can cause kidney complications. However, even among infants who keep their foreskins, the rate of such infection is only about 1 percent (Springen, 2000). The American Academy of Pediatrics, the American Medical Association, and the American Association of Family Physicians have taken positions opposing routine circumcision, citing evidence that the benefits of circumcising newborns are not significant enough to recommend it as a routine procedure. When circumcision is done, it is recommended that anesthesia be used. A study of 130,475 newborn circumcisions, examining the trade-offs, concluded that the procedure offers practically no medical benefit but also causes virtually no harm. It is believed that today about 60 percent of boys in the United States are circumcised, but the incidence of the procedure seems to be decreasing (Christakis et al., 2000).

Growing evidence from studies in other parts of the globe indicates that circumcision can reduce the likelihood of HIV and HPV infection, and perhaps some other sexually transmitted diseases. Partners of circumcised men are therefore less likely to contract the viruses from them. The HPV virus is associated with the development of cervical cancer in women (Baldwin et al., 2004; Castellsague et al., 2002; Cohen, 2005). The World Health Organization, the U.N. Population Fund, and UNICEF have pointed out that these findings are dramatic enough to warrant reconsideration of circumcision guidelines, at least in the developing world. They also are concerned that people will grow overconfident about the preventative value of circumcision, which clearly does not provide complete protection from disease (World Health Organization, 2006).

Given the available information concerning male circumcision, if you were a physician, would you recommend to parents that they have their newborn baby boy circumcised? Justify your recommendation.

Disorders of the Penis

Disorders of the penis are relatively uncommon, but a few are worth mentioning here. Two disorders relate to the erection of the penis. **Priapism,** a condition that involves continual, painful, undesired erection of the penis, can be caused by circulatory disorders or abuse of certain drugs, including cocaine. If the erection is not medically relieved within a few hours, there can be eventual destruction of the corpora cavernosa, making future erection impossible (Kuefer et al., 2005). **Peyronie's disease** occurs primarily in older males and involves the development of tough, fibrous tissue around the corpora cavernosa within the penis. Eventual calcification of this tissue may result. The disease causes curvature of the penis and painful erection, both of which can make intercourse difficult or impossible. Drug therapy or surgical procedures often can help correct the curvature (Bokarica et al., 2005).

Particularly vigorous stimulation of the penis during sexual activity can sometimes inflame lymphatic vessels, creating a swollen band around the penile shaft just behind the glans. Although this condition may be alarming to men, it is not dangerous, and generally the swelling gradually subsides over a few weeks. Use of ringlike devices to maintain erection can damage penile tissues and blood vessels, especially if they are left on too long. If damage occurs, extensive surgical treatment may be required. If the erect penis is suddenly bent or hit, the tough sheath that encloses the columns of spongy tissue may tear, possibly causing permanent damage to the penis that interferes with erection and sexual function.

Cancer of the penis is quite rare. It may be even less common in circumcised males. Although the hypothesis is open to debate, it has been suggested that the accumulation of secretions and impurities under the foreskin of uncircumcised males may predispose them to malignant growth on their penises. Careful attention to cleanliness and personal hygiene is therefore particularly important for uncircumcised males.

There are a number of congenital conditions of the penis. Occasionally, a male child is born with **agenesis (absence) of the penis,** in which the phallus is very

phimosis (fye-MOE-sus) a condition in which the penile foreskin is too long and tight to retract easily.

priapism (pry-AE-pizm) continual, undesired, and painful erection of the penis that lasts longer than four hours.

Peyronie's disease (pay-ra-NEEZ) development of fibrous tissue in the spongy erectile columns within the penis.

agenesis (absence) of the penis (ae-JEN-a-sis) a congenital condition in which the penis is undersized and nonfunctional.

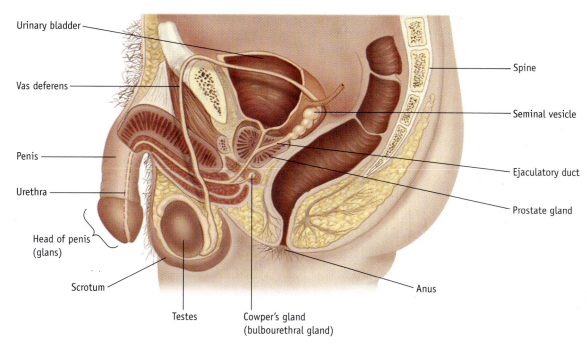

Urinary bladder

Vas deferens

Penis

Urethra

Head of penis
(glans)

Scrotum

Testes

Cowper's gland
(bulbourethral gland)

Spine

Seminal vesicle

Ejaculatory duct

Prostate gland

Anus

■ **FIGURE 3.8** *Male Sexual and Reproductive Organs*

The external and internal sexual and reproductive organs of the male are shown here in longitudinal section. Although men are familiar with their more obvious external sex organs, they often are less well informed about their internal reproductive and sexual anatomy.

tiny and nonfunctional. Surgical intervention and eventual counseling may be necessary to offer help with the sexual adjustments of adolescence and adulthood. In Chapter 5, the gender implications of such conditions are discussed in further detail. Two congenital conditions result from difficulties in fetal development of the penis: **hypospadias** and **epispadias.** Hypospadias is an incompletely fused penis, with an open "gutter" extending along the underside of the penis instead of an internal urethra. In the United States and some European nations, a sharp increase in the incidence of hypospadias has been noted since 1970, although the cause for the increase is not understood. There has been some suspicion that the hormone progestin, found in some birth control pills, might be playing a role. Hypospadias occurs in about 79 of every 10,000 births of males. In epispadias, the urinary bladder empties through a large opening in the abdomen, and the penis is split open along its upper length. Both hypospadias and epispadias require surgical repair, and the penis may not be fully functional for intercourse following the surgery.

■ Internal Male Organs

The vas deferens of each testis carries sperm up into the body cavity, around to the back of the bladder, and back down to the prostate. Near the junction of the two vasa deferentia into a single ejaculatory duct, each vas deferens joins with a saclike structure called the **seminal vesicle.** Both seminal vesicles are about 2 inches long. The seminal vesicles produce secretions that help activate the sperm and make them motile. Secretions from the vesicles, which constitute about 70 percent of the seminal fluid, join with the sperm and empty into the ejaculatory duct, which then joins the urethra inside the prostate gland.

Located at the underside of the urinary bladder, and surrounding the urethra where it enters the bladder, is the **prostate** (see Figure 3.8). This gland, a little larger than a walnut, has three lobes of muscular and glandular tissue. Along with the seminal vesicles,

hypospadias (hye-pa-SPADE-ee-as) birth defect caused by incomplete closure of the urethra during fetal development.

epispadias (ep-a-SPADE-ee-as) birth defect in which the urinary bladder empties through an abdominal opening and the urethra is malformed.

seminal vesicle (SEM-un-al) gland at the end of each vas deferens that secretes a chemical that helps sperm become motile.

prostate gland located beneath the urinary bladder in the male; it produces some of the secretions in semen.

Clearing the way for blessed relief
Some 14 million American men suffer from benign swelling of the prostate.
A new procedure called TUNA could make treatment easier than ever before.

Bladder

Prostate

Urethra

Sphincter

Healthy prostate:
The gland fits around
the urethra like a
well-tailored collar.

Enlarged prostate:
The swelling that comes
with age often blocks
the free flow of urine.

New procedure:
Urologists can now kill
excess tissue by heating it
with tiny needles.

Result:
Within six weeks
to three months, patients
regain normal flow.

FIGURE 3.9 *Prostate Enlargement Using Transurethral Needle Ablation (TUNA)*

Source: From Geoffrey Cowley, "Good News for Boomers," *Newsweek,* 30 December 1996/6 January 1997, p. 74. Copyright © 1997 Newsweek, Inc. All rights reserved. Reprinted by permission.

it produces secretions that help transport the sperm through the penis. This fluid, called **semen** or seminal fluid, is a milky, sticky alkaline substance composed of proteins, citric acid, calcium, fats, and some enzymes. Semen may be quite thick and gelatinous when it leaves the penis, or it may be thin and watery. It usually becomes thicker soon after ejaculation but then liquefies in 15 to 25 minutes.

Below the prostate gland, at the base of the penis and on each side of the urethra, are two pea-size glands called **Cowper's glands** or **bulbourethral glands.** When a male is sexually aroused, these two glands secrete a clear, sticky alkaline substance, or pre-ejaculatory fluid, that coats the inner lining of the urethra. Some of it may appear as droplets at the tip of the penis during arousal. The secretion has often been called a lubricant, and indeed, if present in sufficient amounts, it can serve as a lubricant for sexual activity. However, it is not always produced in such copious amounts and is believed instead to primarily help neutralize acids in the urethra and thus permit safe passage of sperm. Although the primary function of Cowper's gland secretion is not to carry sperm, it often does; therefore, it can be responsible for pregnancy even if ejaculation does not occur within the vagina.

Prostate Problems

A large proportion of men at one time or another suffer from **prostatitis,** or inflammation of the prostate gland (see Figure 3.9). Prostatitis may be of the *acute* form, caused by bacterial infection. Acute symptoms include sudden onset of fever, chills, and urinary discomfort. It may also be *chronic,* typically caused by changes in the prostate other than bacterial infection. Chronic symptoms can include some thin discharge from the penis, pain in the lower abdomen and scrotum, or painful ejaculation. Antibiotics are used for acute prostatitis, but prostatitis in its more chronic forms can be difficult to cure completely.

In older men, enlargement of the prostate gland is common and sometimes is the result of malignant tumors. More than 200,000 new cases of prostatic cancer are detected each year; if found early, the chances of complete cure are good (see Figure 3.10). The number of deaths from prostatic cancer continues to decline because of more refined techniques for detection and treatment (Springen & Adler, 2003). **Benign prostatic hyperplasia (BPH)** refers to nonmalignant prostatic enlargement. Medications are now available to shrink prostate tissues. If the prostate enlarges too much, uri-

semen (SEE-men) mixture of fluids and sperm cells that is ejaculated through the penis.

Cowper's glands two small glands in the male that secrete an alkaline fluid into the urethra during sexual arousal.

bulbourethral glands another term for Cowper's glands.

prostatitis (pras-tuh-TITE-us) inflammation of the prostate gland.

benign prostatic hyperplasia (BPH) enlargement of the prostate gland that is not caused by malignancy.

Rising prostate cancer rates over time
Probability of developing invasive prostate cancer
between the following ages:

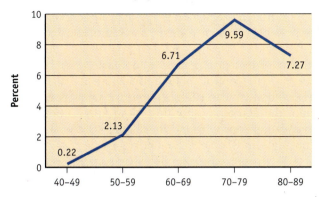

Survival rates, then and now
Percentage of men who are still alive five years after being
diagnosed:

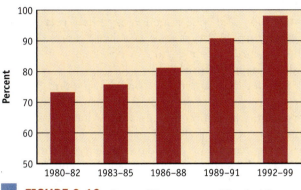

FIGURE 3.10 *Rates of Occurrence and Survival for Prostate Cancer*

Source: From Karen Springen and Jerry Adler, "Prostate Cancer's Difficult Choices," *Newsweek*, 16 June 2003, p. 57. Copyright © 2003 Newsweek, Inc. All rights reserved. Reprinted by permission.

nation may become difficult or eventually even impossible, because the urethral passageway may be pinched by the swollen prostate. This leads to increased susceptibility to bladder and prostate infections. Various surgical treatments are available, ranging from removal of the prostate (prostatectomy), or parts of it, to less invasive treatments that can widen the urethral canal through the prostate and require only a local anesthetic. If a malignancy is present, surgery is often followed by radiation or chemical therapy. Newer surgical techniques reduce the risks of interfering with erectile function or ejaculation, but there are often side effects that decrease sexual satisfaction at least for a time (Arrington, 2003; Quek et al., 2003). One study has suggested that African-American men have a higher risk than white men of being distressed and upset when the treatment for prostate cancer causes problems with sexual functioning (Jenkins et al., 2004).

It is generally recommended that men over age 35 have regular prostate examinations to detect any possi-

ble enlargement or tumors. The physician, using a rubber glove and lubricant, inserts a finger into the rectum, where the surface of the prostate can be felt through the rectal wall. Although such an examination is not particularly pleasant, it represents an important health care measure. A blood test that can help detect prostatic cancer, the prostate-specific antigen (PSA) test, is recommended on a regular basis for men over age 50. The test has led to a dramatic increase in the number of prostate surgeries, yet there is no evidence to prove that the mortality rate from the disease has been lowered. Although research has confirmed the accuracy of the PSA test and most physicians support its use, more research is needed to determine whether such testing significantly reduces the number of deaths from prostate cancer. New tests are being developed to measure other indicators of prostate cancer presence or the risk of developing the malignancy. There is also evidence that a healthy lifestyle, including a diet low in fat and high in vegetables and fruits, may slow the progress of prostate cancer and perhaps prevent its development in the first place (Noonan & Springen, 2002; Springen & Adler, 2003).

Sperm Production and Ejaculation

From puberty to old age, the male testes produce large amounts of sperm cells. The testes are partially controlled by two pituitary hormones, which are also found in females: luteinizing hormone (LH), called **interstitial-cell-stimulating hormone (ICSH)** in males; and follicle-stimulating hormone (FSH). The ICSH begins to be produced at puberty and stimulates the interstitial cells of the testes to produce the male hormone testosterone. The FSH helps stimulate the sperm-producing cells—called **spermatocytes**—in the linings of the seminiferous tubules to produce sperm.

Each mature sperm consists of a head and a tail, separated by a short thickened area (see Figure 3.11). The head contains the male's genetic material, and the thickened middle area contains an energy-releasing mechanism that helps move the tail. Sperm are usually about 55 microns long (0.0021 inch or 0.055 millimeter) and can be seen only through a microscope. An adult male is believed to produce about 15 to 30 billion sperm each month.

During sexual excitement and activity, the sperm are moved from the epididymis in the testes up to the

interstitial-cell-stimulating hormone (ICSH) pituitary hormone that stimulates the testes to secrete testosterone; known as luteinizing hormone (LH) in females.

spermatocytes (sper-MAT-o-sites) cells lining the seminiferous tubules from which sperm cells are produced.

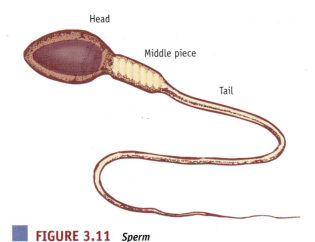

Head

Middle piece

Tail

■ FIGURE 3.11   *Sperm*

A mature sperm consists of a head, middle piece, and tail. The head contains the chromosomes and is the part involved in fertilization. The tail moves the sperm from the ejaculatory duct into the urethra prior to ejaculation. If all the ova needed to repopulate the world would fit into a 2-gallon container, the sperm needed for the same purpose would fit into an aspirin tablet.

ejaculatory duct through each vas deferens. Their tails are activated to make a lashing movement by the secretions of the seminal vesicles. Stimulation of the erect penis sends nerve impulses to the ejaculatory center of the spinal cord. When these impulses have built to a certain threshold, the ejaculatory response is triggered. Sperm from the ejaculatory duct are moved into the urethra, along with fluids from both the seminal vesicles and the prostate that form the semen. Contractions in the muscles surrounding the ejaculatory duct and urethra follow, forcing the semen to be ejaculated through the end of the penis. This usually is accompanied by the pleasurable sensations of **orgasm,** or sexual climax, although the two phenomena— **ejaculation** and orgasm—can occur separately (see Chapter 4, "Human Sexual Arousal and Response").

Studies seem to indicate that average sperm counts in the male population dropped by one-third from the mid-1970s to the mid-1990s. To what has this drop been attributed? What concerns might this trend raise for the future?

The amount of semen ejaculated depends on many factors, including age, amount of sexual stimulation, general health, and interval of time since the last ejaculation, but typically there are 3 to 5 cubic centimeters of semen—about a teaspoonful or less. As much as 11 cubic centimeters of semen can be ejaculated. The typical ejaculate contains 150 million to 600 million sperm. Many men subjectively report that the more intense the sensation of orgasm, the more semen ejaculated and the more force with which it is pro-

pelled out of the penis. Most often the semen oozes out of the penis under some pressure, but it sometimes can spurt several inches.

Although ejaculation is a reflexive phenomenon, it is possible for men to learn to control the length of time it takes to reach orgasm and ejaculation. This usually involves learning how to modulate sexual excitement or to control inner musculature so that when ejaculation is near, stimulation to the penis is reduced until the sensation subsides. More about controlling ejaculation can be found in Chapter 18, "Sexual Dysfunctions and Their Treatment."

As a result of certain illnesses, some prostate surgeries, or the effects of certain tranquilizing drugs, the semen may be ejaculated into the urinary bladder. The muscles at the base of the bladder that normally close off the bladder during ejaculation apparently do not contract, so semen is permitted to enter the bladder. Despite the full sensation of orgasm, no semen leaves the penis. This phenomenon is called **retrograde ejaculation.** Some organic problems simply lead to the absence of semen and a resultant dry orgasm called **anejaculation.**

Under ideal laboratory conditions, sperm may be kept alive for up to two weeks after ejaculation. However, after ejaculation into the vagina during sexual intercourse, it is unlikely that many sperm remain motile for more than two or three days. Older sperm are more likely to have deformities, so it is not considered a good idea to abstain from sexual activity before trying to get pregnant because the newest sperm are the healthiest. Once semen has been deposited in the vagina, some of it begins to seep into the uterus, and the sperm swim against mucous currents and gravitational pull. Healthy sperm can swim about 3 to 7 inches in an hour, and following ejaculation some sperm can be expected to reach the female's fallopian tubes in one to two hours. Despite the many millions of sperm deposited in the vagina, only a few thousand actually reach the fallopian tubes, where fertilization of the ovum can take place.

Concern has been growing that sperm counts in otherwise healthy human males have been dropping in recent years and that the quality of human sperm is

orgasm pleasurable sensations and series of contractions that release sexual tension, usually accompanied by ejaculation in men.

ejaculation muscular expulsion of semen from the penis.

retrograde ejaculation abnormal passage of semen into the urinary bladder at the time of ejaculation.

anejaculation lack of ejaculation at the time of orgasm.

gradually deteriorating as well. Although men continue to produce sperm throughout their lives, studies show that the DNA in sperm tends to undergo more mutational changes as men age. This is of concern, because men are tending to postpone fatherhood until later in life. Aging leads to an increase in DNA damage, which can decrease the chances of conception or produce certain birth defects in offspring. One study has also shown that men who consume substantial amounts of caffeine every day have increased levels of sperm DNA damage that might cause chromosomal aberrations after fertilization (Schmid et al., 2007; Wyrobek et al., 2006).

Men who have fewer than 20 million sperm per milliliter are considered infertile, because the chances of their conceiving a child are slim with that low a sperm count. It has been proposed that chemical pollutants in the environment resembling the female hormone estrogen, fetal exposure to estrogen in the uterus, or possible changes in diet and lifestyle might be responsible for low sperm counts, but no clear link has been established. Several research studies give evidence that cigarette smoking can reduce sperm production significantly, but probably not enough to impair fertility unless a man already had a low sperm count caused by other factors. There is no evidence at this point that fluctuations in sperm count have had any profound effect on male fertility (Schmid et al., 2007).

Male Hormones and the Male Climacteric

Men do not seem to undergo predictable cyclical changes in hormonal levels, such as the female menstrual cycle, that affect their fertility. Some medical conditions, such as epileptic seizures, seem to worsen on roughly monthly cycles, which might be traced to subtle shifts in hormonal concentrations. Studies have shown that testosterone levels tend to be lower in the spring, when literary tradition would have it that men's sex drive is strong. About the only thing psychological tests have correlated with lower hormonal levels is an increase in men's spatial aptitude. There have also been suggestions that men experience periodic emotional ups and downs that seem to follow cyclical patterns, but this has been difficult to substantiate in research.

Although men do not seem to have a well-defined hormonal cycle, they experience changes in their bodies as they age. The concentrations of male hormones found in the body gradually decline through the mid-40s, and by age 75 testosterone levels often drop by up to 90 percent compared with levels before age 30. More significantly, biochemical changes in the body cause more testosterone to become chemically bound

to blood proteins, or plasma, as a man ages, resulting in a lower free testosterone index (FTI). It is the free, unbound testosterone that seems to have the most important influence on the body. For some men over the age of 60 who have lower-than-normal levels of testosterone, there seems to be some correlation with the presence of depression (Seidman, 2006).

Because there usually is no loss of reproductive capacity, nothing in males is completely equivalent to female menopause. Nevertheless, popular media have promoted the idea of a "male menopause." Although it is less predictable and its symptoms are more variable, men often do experience a period of stress as they age. Often called mid-life crisis, the **male climacteric,** aging male syndrome, or "andropause," this period is characterized by increased anxiety, depression, insomnia, hypochondria, loss of appetite, and/or chronic fatigue. These may also be the symptoms of untreated depression. However, there also is usually a reduction in testosterone levels and a decrease in sexual desire and capability as men age. Because of this, the male climacteric has more recently been called ADAM, which stands for androgen decline in the aging male (Barqawi & Crawford, 2006; Seidman & Roose, 2006).

This time in a man's life is often characterized by major changes and realizations. Most professionals believe that these psychological stresses play a role in the male climacteric. In a youth-oriented culture, men must face the fact that they are aging. Men with wives and families are sharing the menopausal changes of their spouses and watching their children leave home. In more traditional family structures, in which the man has been a primary breadwinner, he may begin to feel weary from the years of responsibility for his family. Middle age may be a time when a career plateau has been reached and further vocational opportunities become more limited. Physical changes and stress-generated tension may produce alterations in sexual interest and behavior, resulting in even more worry and discouragement. The male climacteric seems largely to be a vicious cycle of middle-age stresses and gradual physiological changes that feed on one another.

Testosterone Replacement Therapy

Optimal sexual functioning in males may be dependent on the presence of a minimum amount of free testosterone in the body, as stated earlier. For some men in whom the FTI is low, administration of extra testosterone

male climacteric one of the terms applied to a vaguely defined period in male mid-life characterized by hormonal, psychological, and sexual changes.

How Age Can Change a Man's Body

The term "male menopause" drives medical experts crazy. In women, "menopause is a clearly defined biological event," says Dr. Abraham Morgenthaler of Boston's Beth Israel Hospital. "There is no equivalent for men." True enough, but middle age does bring changes, and few of them would qualify as improvements. Here's a rundown of the main ones:

Hair loss. The number of hair follicles on the scalp decreases as men age, and the hair that is left grows at a slower rate.

Vision. By age 50, lifelong thickening of the lens causes a noticeable loss of night vision and close-in focus.

Lung power. Chest wall stiffens, increasing the workload of respiratory muscles. More residual air is left in lungs after each breath.

Aerobic endurance. As the body's ability to deliver oxygen declines, the capacity for physical work falls. The work capacity of a 70-year-old is only half that of a 20-year-old.

Body fat. Between the ages of 25 and 75 the amount of fat in proportion to the body's composition doubles. Much of that growth occurs in muscles and organs.

Muscle and bone. Eventually muscles get smaller and weaker, but those changes can be offset by exercise. Bone loss, a universal aging trait, occurs at individual rates.

Brain function. Concentration and language skills don't change much with age. The ability to store and retrieve information declines slightly but steadily from the 20s on.

Hearing. Eardrums thicken and the ear canal atrophies, making pure tones and high frequencies harder to hear, especially in the late 50s.

Heart response. After 20, the heart becomes less adept at accelerating in response to exertion. Bars show maximum rate in beats per minute:

Age	20	30	40	50	60	70
	200	190	180	170	160	150

Angle of erection. Many men experience a slight loss of upward mobility from 30 to 50, and a major loss from 50 to 70. Preventable vascular disease is largely to blame.

Age 20: 20°
Age 30: 10°
Age 40: 1°
Age 50: −1°
Age 70: −25°

ERECTION DEGREES ABOVE HORIZONTAL

Frequency of sex. Decline in sex drive varies from man to man, but some reduction is inevitable due to lower levels of sex hormones and loss of vitality. Orgasms per year:

Age	20	30	40	50	60	70
	104	121	84	52	35	22

Source: From Geoffrey Cowley, "How Age Can Change a Man's Body," *Newsweek,* 16 September 1996, p. 73. Copyright © 1996 Newsweek, Inc. All rights reserved. Reprinted by permission.

seems to improve sexual interest and potency and may decrease the risks of depression (Seidman & Roose, 2006). **Testosterone replacement therapy (TRT)** carries some increased risks of prostate difficulties and cardiovascular disease, so it must be prescribed with caution. TRT has been touted as a miracle treatment by some patients and clinicians, and branded as risky and dangerous by others. It is generally agreed that administration of testosterone should be done cautiously, and generally only for men who have lower-than-normal levels of testosterone for their age as shown by appropriate medical tests. The Institute of Medicine has recommended further research on the effects of TRT on several hundred older men, and everyone remains mindful of the controversial history of HRT for women.

Surviving the Male Climacteric

Because menopause has been more clearly identified, women may tend to receive more support and understanding for their difficult physical and psychological symptoms. Men may need the same supportive help through their mid-life crises as well. Counseling can help a man express his concerns and deal with his confusing emotions, but men may be reluctant to seek this sort of help. They may need guidance to help them realize that finding appropriate support during life's various crises is a strength, not a weakness. It is important that men be cautioned about making major life changes during the throes of such a crisis. They might be better advised to try sticking with their present careers and relationships as they work to resolve any conflicts or tensions within those important areas of life. Then, as things are brought into a more rational perspective, sensible changes in lifestyle and goals can be considered.

Both medical and psychological sciences are making great progress in understanding the changes within men's bodies and psyches as they age. Just as Viagra and other erection-enhancing medications have offered hope to men with erection problems, treatments likely will become available to help men cope with the various other symptoms associated with sex and aging. Ultimately, the best help will come from within, as men draw on their own resources to accept the natural processes of aging and also the positive outcomes that these processes can yield along with the less positive.

> **testosterone replacement therapy (TRT)** administering testosterone injections to increase sexual interest or potency in older men; not considered safe for routine use.

Self-Evaluation

Learning about Sexuality: Past, Present, and Future

Sexuality education is far more than learning about the body's reproductive system. It is also an exercise in self-awareness—becoming acquainted with one's own sexual feelings, needs, and values. Learning about sexuality is a lifelong process that must constantly integrate new information and changing personal situations. The exercises that follow ask you to examine the process of sexuality education as it relates to your life.

1. **Looking back. Spend some time thinking about your answers to the following questions. They will help clarify some of the background of your learning about sexuality. You may want to discuss your answers with another trusted person.**
   a. Can you recall your first discussions about sexuality when you were a child with another child, a parent, or another adult? If so, can you remember any feelings or attitudes that you developed in relationship to that time and the topic of sex?
   b. How and when did you first learn what you consider to be the important information about the sex organs, reproduction, and other aspects of human sexuality? Was the information conveyed to you in a relatively positive, negative, or neutral atmosphere emotionally?
   c. Do you remember the first book or magazine you read, or the first television program or movie you saw, that had factual information about sex or graphically depicted sexual behaviors? How did you react?
   d. In what ways have you increased your level of information and awareness about human sexuality more recently in your life?

2. **Following these exercises is a list of topics related to human sexuality. You may be better informed on some of them than on others. Using the rating standards shown, rate each topic as to your level of competence, using appropriate check marks.**

3. **As you reexamine the check marks you made in exercise 2, pay attention to those topics you need to know more about. For each of these, indicate what your course of action, if any, will be.**
   a. Will you seek further information on the topic? Why or why not?
   b. Where will you begin your search for the information?
   c. Are any personal implications involved in your wanting to understand the topic better?

4. **Do you expect to have children (or do you have children) for whom you will bear some responsibility to provide effective education about sexuality? If so, consider the following questions.**
   a. Have you already made some attempts at educating children about sexuality? If so, how successful do you think you were, and on what criteria do you base that evaluation?
   b. Make a list of goals that you believe are important to the sexuality education of children at different age levels; choose those goals in whose achievement you may play an active part. What areas would you not want to be a part of your children's sexuality education?

   c. What resources can you have available to assist with the sexuality education process? Consider books, films, television programs, computer software or accessible networks, other people (including professionals), and your own skills and competencies.
   d. Now, either alone or with another adult, try explaining aloud some of the things you would want your child to know about human sexuality, considering the child's age and level of maturity. You might want to tape-record your talk so you can evaluate its effectiveness later, or you might have the other adult make comments and suggestions. This is an exercise to see how clearly and accurately you can express concepts about sexuality. Are you aware of institutional sexuality education programs that might be available in your local schools, churches, or other agencies? If none exist, you might consider becoming instrumental in working for effective sexuality education. If programs already exist, you might want to help evaluate their effectiveness. First of all, you should clarify how you feel about sexuality education and get as much information about various programs as you can.

	I know very little about this and could use further information.	*I understand this reasonably well but could use more information.*	*I feel comfortable with this and do not need further information.*
Male genital anatomy and physiology	____	____	____
Female genital anatomy and physiology	____	____	____
Sexual intercourse	____	____	____
The physiology of reproduction and birth	____	____	____
Advances in reproductive technology	____	____	____
Same-gender orientation and bisexuality	____	____	____
Masturbation	____	____	____
Psychosexual development of children and adolescents	____	____	____
Sex therapy and counseling	____	____	____
Gender identity, masculinity, and femininity	____	____	____
Sexually transmitted diseases	____	____	____
Transmission of HIV	____	____	____
Sexual dysfunctions	____	____	____
Human sexual response	____	____	____
Improving communication in sexual relationships	____	____	____
Sexual variations	____	____	____

Chapter Summary

1. The male testes, located in the scrotum, produce male hormones and sperm. Sperm cells develop best at a temperature slightly lower than inner body temperature, mature in tubes called the epididymis, and will travel upward through the vas deferens.

2. Regular self-examination of the penis and testes is an effective way to detect infections or growths that indicate the presence of testicular cancer.

3. Both testes may not descend into the scrotum before birth.

4. Epididymitis is an inflammation of the epididymis in the testes.

5. The penis has a sensitive, rounded head called the glans and a longer shaft. Three columns of spongy tissue compose the interior of the penile shaft and become filled with blood during erection. Sperm and urine move through the penis via the urethra.

6. Penis size is quite variable among males and includes a wide range of "normal" sizes.

7. Circumcision is a surgical procedure in which the penile foreskin, or prepuce, is removed. Its advisability has been the subject of controversy, although it has been shown to reduce the likelihood of HIV and HPV infection.

8. Some diseases that can affect the penis are priapism (painful, continuous erection), Peyronie's disease (calcification of erectile tissue), phimosis (too-tight foreskin), and cancer.

9. The prostate gland and seminal vesicles of the male produce secretions that mix with sperm to produce the semen that is ejaculated through the penis. Cowper's glands produce a clear secretion that lines the urethra during sexual arousal.

10. Prostatitis, or prostate infection, can be either acute or chronic. A common problem in older men is prostate enlargement, which may be caused by benign prostatic hyperplasia or by malignant tumors. It must be corrected, usually by surgery. The PSA test has proved useful in detection of prostatic cancer.

11. Sperm production is controlled by the secretion of FSH. Interstitial-cell-stimulating hormone (ICSH) stimulates the testes to produce testosterone. Up to 30 billion sperm are produced by the testes each month.

12. Sexual stimulation of the penis can lead to ejaculation of semen. The ejaculate can contain between 150 million and 600 million sperm.

13. The sperm counts of human males may have been decreasing over the past few decades, although fertility has not yet been affected. As men age, the chance for DNA changes in their sperm increases.

14. Men do not seem to have predictable hormonal cycles, although their emotions may follow cyclical patterns.

15. Men experience a less well-defined climacteric than women, involving mood changes that may be associated with reduced production of testosterone.

16. Testosterone replacement therapy may improve sexual desire and other symptoms of male mid-life, but it also carries health risks and needs further research.

Focus on Health Questions

In this section you will find the kinds of questions that you may have concerning your own health and sexuality. The page references indicate where in the text the answer is located; the exact place is marked with this logo: **FOH**

Chapter 4

Human Sexual Arousal and Response

Chapter Outline

My first year in high school I was having erections all the time, always unpredictable and usually without good reason. I could get a hard-on from putting a notebook in my locker or riding on the bus. Worst of all were the ones I would get during oral reports up in front of the class. Fortunately, the thing is a lot more under control now—most of the time.

—from a student essay

Over the centuries, the human body's sexual responses have been explained and interpreted in many different ways. They have been assigned religious significance in some cultures and shunned as unclean in others. Sexual arousal and responsiveness, and how they are perceived and expressed, cannot be understood outside the context of the culture in which a person lives. When Margaret Mead studied the Mundugumor of New Guinea, she remarked that lovemaking was conducted "like the first round of a prizefight," with scratching and biting part of the foreplay. She later found that in Samoa men preceded sexual activity by singing romantic songs and reciting poetry for their women, first preparing their minds with sensual thoughts and then preparing their bodies with sensual touching.

Sexuality has often become intertwined with the spiritual beliefs within cultures as well. In the Jewish tradition, for example, sexuality is intimately associated with concepts of creativity and unity. In Eastern Tantric traditions of yoga, Buddhism, Hinduism, and Taoism, sexual response is perceived as an expression of spiritual energies. It is believed that the energy of life and the spirit may be focused in different ways in the body and that, properly used, sexual energy can help convey people to the highest levels of spiritual consciousness. Various breathing exercises and physical preparations are done to enhance awareness of sexual experiences. The emphasis is on savoring all the sensual and spiritual aspects of sex rather than looking toward the goal of immediate gratification (Richard, 2002).

Western cultural imperatives often place sex in a more goal-oriented context, with orgasm and sensual gratification as primary objectives. A view of sexual arousal and response as holistic experiences involving mind, body, emotions, and spirit might be neglected in cultures that approach such issues from a more scientific perspective (Timmerman, 2001).

■ Models of Sexual Arousal: Activating the Mind and the Body

The early models of an innate human "sex drive" presumed that the body had a preprogrammed sexual mechanism that could be activated by sufficient "sexual stimulation." However, the concept of sex drive has been elusive in the sense that some identifiable biological need is generated during times of sexual abstinence or that the body is physiologically

harmed by lack of sex. Evolutionary theorists suggest that sexual motivation may reflect an innate drive for reproduction to ensure survival of the species, but the evidence to support such a theory remains only suggestive (Kauth, 2006b; Wallen & Zehr, 2004). Scientists are just beginning to piece together the apparently complex puzzle of what activates sexual response and what motivations turn us on and turn us off—the processes of **sexual arousal** (Janssen et al., 2000).

Components of Sexual Arousal

Although various theorists have conceptualized the details in different ways, all models of sexual arousal seem to include stimuli that are both *internal,* referring to phenomena of the mind such as fantasizing about or remembering sexual activity, and *external,* such as direct touching of the sex organs or actually seeing someone who is considered sexy. These two aspects of activating sexual response have been divided into distinct categories: the **central arousal system,** referring to internal factors, and the **peripheral arousal system,** referring to the external. The central arousal system seems to be located largely in the emotional and pleasure centers of the brain; the stimuli generated there form the central, fundamental template for a person's sexual response (Janssen et al., 2002a, 2002b).

The peripheral arousal system is related more to those aspects of stimulation that stem from the spinal cord and its voluntary and involuntary nervous control mechanisms. This system picks up cues directly from the skin, genitals, and sense organs. Sexual arousal from both the central and peripheral systems can be measured by physiological responses, verbal reports, and behavior, although studies continue to show a sometimes very real discordance among various systems and reporting mechanisms (Basson et al., 2003; Janssen et al., 2000; Pfaus, 2000).

We do know that some people have a greater propensity toward activation of sexual response than

sexual arousal the psychological and physiological mechanisms that activate sexual response.

central arousal system internal components of sexual arousal that come from the cognitive and emotional centers of the brain, forming the foundations for sexual response.

peripheral arousal system external components of sexual arousal that reach the brain and spinal cord from the skin, genitals, and sense organs.

others, a quality that might be described as *sexual arousability*. This may vary depending on external conditions as well. The tendency to become sexually aroused is mediated by both excitation factors and inhibition factors, and individuals vary in their propensities for excitation or inhibition. For arousal to occur, these two factors must be in a suitable balance (Graham, Sanders, & Milhausen, 2006). An individual's degree of arousability seems to be influenced by the sensitivity of the entire sexual response system, including not only the genitals and other body systems but also the ways in which the mind and emotions become involved. All human responses tend to be activated by stimuli, and high arousability probably reflects a high sensitivity to both external and internal excitation stimuli that the individual has learned to interpret as sexual.

There is evidence that when a person's nervous system has been excited by some nonsexual stimulus, such as a roller-coaster ride, that individual will react in a way that may make him or her somewhat more susceptible to sexual arousal as well (Meston & Frohlich, 2003). Arousability also may be inhibited or "turned off" by certain negative stimuli. In men, for example, sexual arousal may be inhibited, or interfered with, by concerns over sexual performance, sexual dissatisfaction, or the threat of negative consequences. Some males are more sensitive to such inhibition than others (Janssen et al., 2002a, 2002b; Spiering, Everaerd, & Elzinga. 2002). In women, arousal may be inhibited by concerns about one's body or reputation, unwanted pregnancy, and how the partner is relating. People's level of sexual interest and desire influences the ways they process and interpret sexual words and information, although the relationship between desire and arousal is complex, especially in women (Conaglen, 2004; Graham, Sanders, Milhausen, & McBride, 2004; Meana & Nunnink, 2006; Purdon & Holdaway, 2006).

Research has demonstrated that people's perceptions of their own degree of sexual arousal do not always coincide with the ways their sex organs are actually responding, especially in women. Physiological sexual arousal may be detected by measuring changes in the vagina or the penis. Such measurement can be helpful in comparing bodily reactions to more subjective, psychological experiences associated with arousal. In women, a probe can be placed within the vagina to detect increases or decreases in blood flow to that organ. In men, a **penile strain gauge,** in the form of a cuff or wire, can be placed around the penis and attached to a **plethysmograph,** which will chart changes in the girth of the penis as it responds to sexual arousal or loss of arousal by gaining or losing various degrees of erection (Basson, 2001; Janssen et al., 2000).

Using these techniques, researchers have found that women are less likely than men to pick up on the physiological cues of their own sexual arousal. When shown sexually explicit films, for example, women seem to have genital responses just as quickly as do men, but they are much less likely to identify themselves as being sexually aroused. This may be due partly to socialization that discourages females from paying attention to their genital responses or from feeling comfortable reporting arousal, and partly to the fact that erection of the penis is anatomically more easily noticed than the internal vaginal changes associated with arousal. What is happening within the body's sexual response system might not always be recognized by the information-processing systems of the person's mind or be interpreted in the same way by different people (Janssen, Carpenter, & Graham, 2003; Nobre et al., 2004; Youn, 2006).

Contemporary theorists hold that genital response **FOH** alone does not constitute sexual arousal because the genitals may respond to stimuli not typically thought to be sexually stimulating. In other words, sexual arousal includes both physiological response and some inner, subjective experience that defines the response, and perhaps the surrounding situation, as sexual for a particular individual (Janssen et al., 2002a, 2002b). All models of sexual arousal seem to recognize psychological processes as an essential component. Emotions and the ways the brain processes information play a major role in activating—*or deactivating*—a person's sexual response. The various stimuli that come to the attention of the human mind must be cognitively transformed if they are to result in emotional or sexual responses. This obviously is a very complex process that is profoundly influenced by the learning processes and environments experienced by different people (Nobre & Pinto-Gouveia, 2003; Purdon & Holdaway, 2006).

Things that may seem intrinsically sexual to one individual may be a turnoff for someone else. Then again, a stimulus that is not even perceived by the individual to be pleasurable or sexual can cause a physical response of the genitals (as happened to our student friend when he was putting a notebook in his locker). Also, emotions that have nothing to do with sex per se—such as depression, anxiety, or the thrill of a roller-coaster ride—may still exert a strong influence on sexual arousal mechanisms, both positively and negatively (Basson, 2002a, 2002b).

penile strain gauge a device placed on the penis to measure even subtle changes in its size due to sexual arousal.

plethysmograph (pleh-THIZ-ma-graff) a laboratory measuring device that charts physiological changes over time. Attached to a penile strain gauge, it can chart changes in penis size. This is called penile plethysmography.

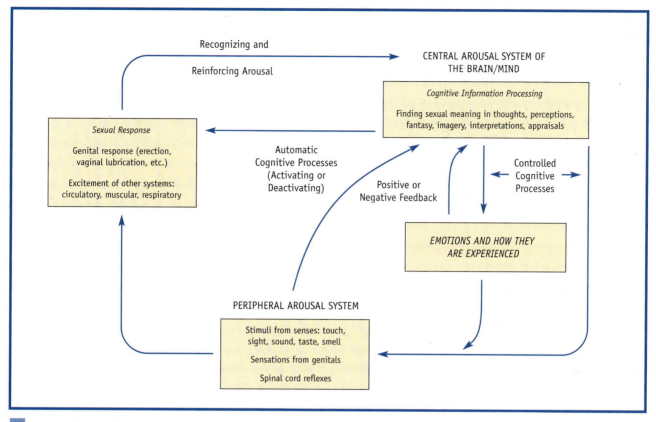

■ **FIGURE 4.1** *Mind–Body Interactions in Sexual Arousal*

This diagram summarizes the models that explain how human sexual response is activated. The initiating mechanism is the central arousal system, mediated by the brain and its ways of processing information. The peripheral arousal system is influenced partly by input from the brain, but it also processes cues that come directly from sensory stimulation. The brain continues to participate in activation, or deactivation, of sexual response, depending on complex positive and negative feedback loops influenced by the individual's learned ways of processing potential sex cues.

Although theories of sexual arousal are still in the earlier stages of development, Figure 4.1 summarizes what is presently believed regarding the activation of sexual response. It is generally agreed that there is a sequence of events leading to sexual arousal involving the combination of central and peripheral mechanisms, with the mind and body interacting in many different ways. If the mind ascribes sexual meaning to a particular stimulus, sexual arousal can be the result. In some cases, this processing seems to be relatively *automatic,* leading to rapid physiological response such as erection or vaginal lubrication. However, the sexual system has to be "primed" in such a way that its conditions match the stimulus coming from the environment. Beyond the automatic response, the brain's responses are more *controlled* in regulating whether sexual response will continue to be facilitated or be inhibited (Spiering, Everaerd, & Janssen, 2003). When human sexual response is easily activated, it is probably the result of the automatic arousal mechanisms. When people are sexually dysfunctional for psychological reasons, these automatic mechanisms are disrupted by controlling factors such as emotions and negative interpretations.

The physiological responses of the genitals and other organ systems provide the physical template on which subjective interpretations and experiences are socially constructed. We know that social standards have been generally less permissive toward female sexual activity than toward that of males. In many laboratory settings, it has been found that men are more attuned to their bodily responses and more likely to interpret them accurately. It seems likely, then, that women's genital responses are less involved in the determination of their subjective experience of sexual arousal than are external factors such as a relationship (Basson, 2001; Basson et al., 2003; Levin, 2002).

People's methods of processing information and attaching sexual meanings to experiences and emotions seem to influence their arousal patterns. Even though an individual's automatic responses may cause some thought or fantasy to generate a genital response, that same person's controlled responses may prevent him or her from experiencing or enjoying the

Real Student Voices

■ My father was always very open with me about what to expect sexually, so I never felt self-conscious or scared about the changes going on in my body. I remember that the first time I actually produced semen, he was the first person I told, and he seemed to be glad too. I realize now that most boys don't have that kind of relationship with their dads. I'm glad I did.

■ The first time I actually saw my friend's erect penis, it kind of scared me. It looked huge, and I couldn't imagine how it would ever fit inside of any girl, let alone me!

■ It takes a lot to turn me on, but once I'm turned on I'm ready to go. It seems that my judgment gets tossed to the wind at that point.

response as sexual. Learning probably plays an essential role in determining how sexual arousal mechanisms actually function in each individual to generate a sexual response. Some differences may be particularly common to males or to females, but it would be impossible to generalize them to all members of either gender (Graham, Sanders, Milhausen, & McBride, 2004; Youn, 2006).

Women, Men, and Sexual Arousal

Of the many purported differences between men and women, the differences in sexual arousability are among the most rigidly believed. From as far back as nineteenth-century psychology, it was believed that males spontaneously get in touch with their potentials for sexual arousal, whereas females become initiated into their sexual potentials within the context of a romantic relationship and the loving touch of a man. These generalizations persist today in the form of the assumptions that women become sexually aroused less often and less rapidly than men. Men and women also are said to become sexually aroused by different stimuli—men by physical stimulation, pictures of nude people, and pictures of sexual acts, and women more by the romantic aspects of loving relationships.

Although these concepts represent stereotypes that cannot be applied to all individuals, research studies do continue to confirm that women tend to "romanticize" the goals of sexual desire, seeing them as love, emotional intimacy, and commitment more than do men. Men, on the other hand, are more likely to "sexualize" these phenomena, seeing the goal of desire and arousal to be sexual activity (Janssen, Carpenter, & Graham, 2003). When asked to identify the *objects* of sexual desire, women are more likely than men to indicate a loved one or a romantic partner, whereas men are more likely to specify that the object

of sexual desire should be physically and sexually attractive (Nobre et al., 2004; Nobre & Pinto-Gouveia, 2003). There seems to be no measurable difference in the ways men and women cognitively process sexual information, but there are distinct differences in the emotional processing of such information (Spiering, Everaerd, & Laan, 2004).

Research on sexual arousal has sometimes been confusing and contradictory. Older evidence suggesting that males are far more easily and quickly sexually aroused than women has not been fully supported, perhaps indicating some important changes in social influences on women concerning their sexual feelings. Women's self-reported feelings about sexual arousal and their evaluations of their own sexual responses tend to be consistently more self-critical and negative than the self-reported feelings and evaluations of men. Men also apparently dream to the point of orgasm more frequently than do women.

What are your feelings about the importance or unimportance of orgasm during sexual activity?

■ Models of Human Sexual Response

It is clear that human response to sexual arousal is not confined to reactions of the sex organs but involves marked changes throughout the body, especially in the muscular and circulatory systems. There are various psychological responses as well. It was in 1966, in their pioneering book *Human Sexual Response,* that William Masters and Virginia Johnson provided the most thoroughly researched information on how the human body responds to sexual stimulation. Their study concentrated on careful observation

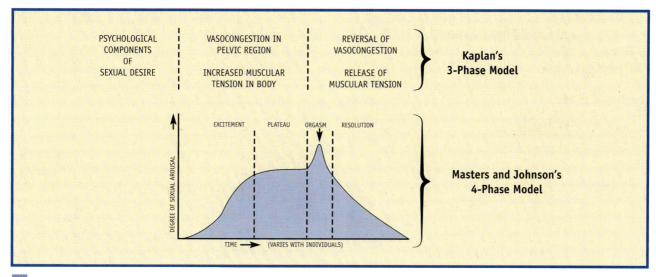

FIGURE 4.2 *Human Sexual Response*

Both Masters and Johnson and Helen Kaplan divided the human physical responses of sexual arousal into different phases. This chart compares their divisions.

and instrumental monitoring of men and women who were engaging in sexual activity. The 694 people who participated in the study were carefully interviewed and screened to obtain as "average" a sample as possible. These individuals were helped to feel comfortable with sexual activity alone in the laboratory setting before they were observed by the research team. Although Masters and Johnson saw their work as an incomplete, preliminary step to understanding human sexual response—and despite the fact that some controversies have grown out of their study—the findings quickly gained general acceptance among professionals. For easier understanding, the body's sexual responses have often been divided into separate phases.

See "Masters and Johnson's Sexual Response Research" on SexSource Online.

The Masters and Johnson Four-Phase Model

As Masters and Johnson observed the sexual responses of men and women in their laboratory, they noticed many similarities in responses between the two sexes. After gathering a great deal of data, they described the sexual response process as a four-phase cycle (see Figure 4.2). It has been argued that the Masters and Johnson model may not represent a fair view of human sexual responsiveness because they only accepted people into their research who indicated that they reached orgasm. They built their cyclical view of sexual responsiveness on the assumptions that orgasm is a natural built-in response and that the response

cycle is programmed to repeat itself over and over during one's lifetime, given the proper stimuli. Some sexologists believe that this may be a narrow, incomplete perspective on human sexual response. It has also been posited that our present models of sexual response are overly male-centered and still tend to create the impression that the male sex organs are more extensive, active, and explosive than are those of females. Because the subjective, or "mind," aspects of arousal and satisfaction are often ignored, our present models may misunderstand female sexual response (Basson, 2001; Basson et al., 2003). Nevertheless, the phases that Masters and Johnson invented to describe sexual responsiveness constitute one way to understand some fundamental aspects of human sexuality.

Masters and Johnson labeled their first phase **excitement,** during which the body begins to show signs of arousal. Blood is routed to the pelvic region, resulting in the earliest signs of arousal, such as erection of the penis and clitoris and vaginal lubrication. A wide range of physical and psychological stimuli can initiate this excitement phase. The intensity of the body's reactions to sexual arousal gradually builds to a higher level and is maintained at that level for varying lengths of time. Masters and Johnson labeled this the **plateau phase** because of its stable, or level, state of arousal.

> **excitement** the first phase of Masters and Johnson's four-phase model of the sexual response cycle, involving genital vasocongestion.
>
> **plateau phase** the stable, leveled-off phase of Masters and Johnson's four-phase model of the sexual response cycle.

The plateau phase, if held for sufficient periods of time, can be a major highlight of sexual response. The intensity of plateau may ebb and flow somewhat during sustained sexual activity and thereby provide some special "highs" of sensual enjoyment. In any case, the buildup of tension may eventually lead to the triggering of a pleasurable sexual release called **orgasm,** or **climax.** This third phase is brief, lasting a few seconds to slightly less than a minute, but it is one in which thought is momentarily suspended and the mind becomes focused inward on a rush of pleasurable physical sensations. Almost immediately after orgasm, the body relaxes and begins to return to its unexcited state, although some people may experience more than one orgasm relatively soon. Masters and Johnson called the time of relaxation the **resolution phase.**

Although it remains only one model for describing human sexual response, the Masters and Johnson four-phase model is used in this chapter to explain the various components of responsiveness. Other researchers have raised legitimate criticisms and have offered alternative models that remain open for consideration and further study. For example, research has not shown a clear demarcation between the excitement and plateau phases in males. Instead, there tends to be a steady and continuous buildup of sexual tension that is not readily divided into stages. Some researchers have maintained that they have been unable to distinguish a measurable plateau phase at all in either men or women. It has been proposed both that the Masters and Johnson approach attempts to impose a model on male sexual response that is far more applicable to women and, conversely, that the model may actually be more applicable to men than it is to women (Basson, 2001; Basson et al., 2003).

Kaplan's Three-Phase Model

Another sex researcher and therapist, Helen Singer Kaplan (1974), initially proposed that it makes more sense, from the standpoint of the body's actual neurophysiological mechanisms, to view sexual response as occurring in two phases. The first phase is characterized by vasocongestion, or buildup of blood in the pelvic area, and an accumulation of muscular tension throughout the body, causing increases in heart rate, breathing, blood pressure, and other involuntary functions. Orgasm acts as the trigger for the second phase, **orgasmic release,** in which the vasocongestion and muscular tension are released first through the sudden orgasmic bursts and then more gradually as the body returns to less excited levels of functioning.

As Kaplan worked with people's problems with sexual arousal, referred to generally as **sexual dysfunctions,** she realized that some people simply did not seem to have much desire to become sexually aroused. This led her to suggest that a **desire phase** precedes the body's physiological responses to arousal (Kaplan, 1979). The desire phase represents a psychological component that can lead to a physical response. It was a modification of the Masters and Johnson model, focusing on the subjective, emotional aspects of sexual arousal.

Sexual desire has been one of the more elusive and interesting areas of sexuality research and has been closely tied to psychological studies of the human motivations behind behavior. It clearly involves an interplay among body, mind, and emotions (Conaglen & Evans, 2006; Tolman & Diamond, 2002). For centuries, the assumption was that the longing for sexual interaction was innate, and an inner drive model was used to explain this longing. This model has been likened to a steam boiler. Internal sexual "steam" would build up until the pressure became so great that the drive to release it was very strong. This view also assumed that some adverse physical consequence would result from not releasing the pressure, an assumption that eventually was shown not to be the case. Human motivation theory eventually began to focus more on the external incentives behind sexual and other forms of motivation (Levine, 2002, 2003). Although sexual desire remains a very complex phenomenon still under study, the incentive motivation model appears to be more accurate model.

Rather than assuming that sexual desire emanates from the physical sexual response system, this model suggests that a complex interaction of external stimuli triggers certain responses: interpretations of reactions, sensations, and memories; and social rules that regulate sexual activity (Conaglen & Evans, 2006). The motivation for sexual activity seems to be rooted not only in seeking pleasurable sensations but also in experiencing social and emotional rewards, such as feeling valued by others and by oneself (Pfaus, 2000; Tolman & Diamond, 2002). For many women, desire may depend to a great extent on feelings of emotional intimacy with a partner, even when the physical signs of sexual arousal are present (Basson et al., 2003).

orgasm (OR-gaz-em) a rush of pleasurable physical sensations associated with the release of sexual tension.

climax another term for orgasm.

resolution phase the term for the return of a body to its unexcited state following orgasm.

orgasmic release reversal of the vasocongestion and muscular tension of sexual arousal, triggered by orgasm.

sexual dysfunctions difficulties people have in achieving sexual arousal and in other stages of sexual response.

desire phase Kaplan's term for the psychological interest in sex that precedes physiological sexual arousal.

Sexual desire has been described with many different verbs and nouns, ranging from *long* to *ache* and from *horny* to *lust*. It is a state of being that encompasses many shades of meaning. It seems to consist of three main factors: a biological component or *drive* that is connected to the body's anatomy and physiology, and perhaps to evolutionary imperatives of reproduction; the psychological component of *motivation,* which can be influenced by moods and relationships; and a cultural component or *wish* that stems from the social meanings and rules in which a person is immersed. Desire is further influenced by gender, age, relationship status, social surroundings, and state of health (Levine, 2003).

What has become known as Kaplan's three-phase model (see Figure 4.2) has special validity when considering the various dysfunctions that can interfere with sexual responsiveness. These problems may involve inhibited sexual desire, sexual aversion, erectile dysfunction, vaginismus, or painful intercourse and usually are centered in the desire phase, the vasocongestive phase, or the orgasmic-release phase of the sexual response cycle (see Chapter 18, "Sexual Dysfunctions and Their Treatment").

Individual Differences in Sexual Response

Clearly there are more physiological similarities than differences in the sexual responses of males and females. Both males and females experience pelvic vasocongestion and a general buildup of muscular tension. Orgasm is very similar in both sexes, although it may not always be experienced. Table 4.1 summarizes the sexual response cycles of females and males. Evidently, within certain bounds, there can be great variation in sexual response among individuals. On average, males tend to reach orgasm more rapidly than females during intercourse, but this phenomenon may well be influenced by the kind of stimulation and by the individual's past learning. Many women respond with orgasm more quickly during masturbation than in intercourse. In fact, it is not unusual for women to respond almost as quickly as men during masturbation. The amount of time for completion of the entire cycle varies with learning, the sexual situation, the kind and intensity of stimulation, and age. An entire cycle from excitement through resolution may take only a few minutes or last several hours (Tolman & Diamond, 2002).

There seem to be subjective differences in the orgasms of males and females. Although male orgasms may vary in intensity and degree of pleasure, the experience is relatively standard among all males. Women often report experiencing different physical and psychological reactions during different orgasms.

Some women even appear to have a very pleasurable feeling of sexual satisfaction even though they do not exhibit the usual physiological responses associated with orgasm (Basson, 2001; Basson et al., 2003).

Women can fake orgasm, and some women feel that faking it is necessary to please their sexual partners. Research has shown that with the new emphasis on female sexual pleasure, some women experience guilt if they do not reach orgasm during sexual intercourse. Even though faking orgasm is less easy for men because of ejaculation, some men do fake orgasm from time to time. When such deception enters a relationship, it can establish conditions for eventual problems. Openness and honesty about sex are a crucial part of a healthy relationship (see Chapter 9, "Sexuality, Communication, and Relationships"). Individual differences in sexual response patterns make it all the more important for sexual partners to take time to learn about each other's responsiveness. This also requires developing effective lines of communication about emotions, needs, and sex.

See "Studying Female Sexual Response" on SexSource Online.

Why was the Kaplan model so important to understanding sexual response? Do you believe men or women have a greater interest in sex? On what do you base your belief?

■ Female Sexual Response

Excitement Phase

When the female body begins to respond sexually, changes are often noticed first in the vagina. As blood begins to build up (vasocongestion) in the blood vessels of the genital region, the vaginal walls darken in color, a change that is not visible externally. This vasocongestion causes a slippery, alkaline fluid to seep through the lining of the vagina. This substance functions as a lubricant for sexual activity and may also help create alkaline conditions in the vagina that are beneficial to sperm. The amount of lubrication in the vagina, however, is not necessarily a sign of how sexually aroused the woman is or how ready she might be for sexual activity. Particularly for females, genital responses must be supported by environmental cues and stimuli in order to create a sexual context (Graham, Sanders, Milhausen, & McBride, 2004; Levin, 2002; Traish, Kim, Munarriz, Morcland, & Goldstein, 2002).

Another change during the excitement phase is the lengthening and distention of the inner one-third of the vagina. The uterus is also pulled upward from

Table 4.1	Female and Male Sexual Response	
Phase	**Female Responses**	**Male Responses**
EXCITEMENT	Clitoris swells in diameter and length.	Penis becomes erect; urethral diameter begins to widen.
	Vagina lubricates, becomes expanded and lengthened and darker in color.	Scrotal skin tenses and thickens.
	Major and minor labia thicken and may open slightly.	Testes elevate slightly within scrotum.
	Breasts increase in size, and nipples become erect.	Nipples become erect in some males.
	Sex flush appears in some females.	
	Muscular tension increases.	Muscular tension increases.
	Heart rate begins to increase.	Heart rate begins to increase.
	Blood pressure begins to rise.	Blood pressure begins to rise.
PLATEAU	Clitoris retracts under prepuce.	Penis increases in diameter and becomes fully erect.
	Vagina expands and lengthens more; orgasmic platform develops.	Scrotum has no changes.
	Uterus is completely elevated.	Testes enlarge and elevate toward body.
	Labia swell more; labia minora have deeper red coloration.	Cowper's glands secrete a few drops of fluid.
	Breasts increase further in size, and nipples become turgid.	Nipples become erect and more turgid.
	Sex flush has appeared in most females and spreads.	Sex flush appears in some males and may spread.
	Muscular tension increases further.	Muscular tension increases further.
	Respiration and heart rates increase.	Respiration and heart rates increase.
	Marked elevation in blood pressure occurs.	Marked elevation in blood pressure occurs.
ORGASM	There are no changes in the clitoris.	Penis and urethra undergo contractions that expel semen.
	Uterus undergoes wavelike contractions.	There are no changes in the scrotum or testes.
	There are no changes in the labia.	
	Breasts and nipples show no changes during orgasm.	Nipples remain erect.
	Sex flush deepens.	Sex flush deepens.
	There is loss of voluntary muscle control, and spasms of some muscles.	There is loss of voluntary muscle control, and spasms of some muscles.
	Respiration and heart rates reach peak intensity.	Respiration and heart rates reach peak intensity.
	Blood pressure reaches its peak.	Blood pressure reaches its peak.
RESOLUTION	Clitoris returns to nonaroused position and loses its erection.	Penis erection is lost, rapidly at first, then more slowly.
	Vaginal walls relax and return to nonaroused coloration.	Scrotal skin relaxes and returns to nonaroused thickness.
	Uterus lowers to usual position, and cervical opening widens for 20 to 30 minutes.	Testes return to nonaroused size and position in scrotum.
	Labia return to nonaroused size, position, and color.	There is a period (refractory period) during which the male cannot be restimulated to orgasm.
	Breasts and nipples return to nonaroused size, position, and color.	Nipples return to nonaroused size.
	Sex flush disappears.	Sex flush disappears.
	Muscles relax rapidly.	Muscles relax rapidly.
	Respiration, heart rate, and blood pressure return to normal.	Respiration, heart rate, and blood pressure return to normal.
	Film of perspiration may appear on skin.	Film of perspiration may appear on skin, usually confined to soles of feet and palms of hands.

Source: From W. Masters and V. E. Johnson, *Human Sexual Response,* Boston, MA: Little, Brown & Company, 1966. Reprinted by permission of Lippencott, Williams & Wilkins.

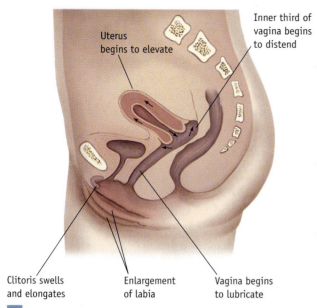

Uterus begins to elevate

Inner third of vagina begins to distend

Clitoris swells and elongates

Enlargement of labia

Vagina begins to lubricate

FIGURE 4.3   *Female Excitement Phase*

In the female, the first sign of sexual arousal is often the lubrication of the vagina. This is accompanied by enlargement of the vaginal area, including the clitoris and the major and minor labia, and a darkening of the color of the vaginal walls.

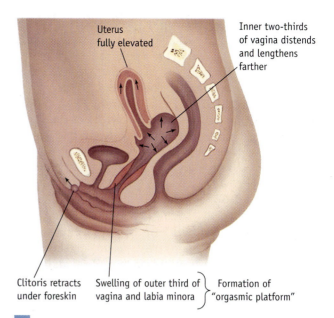

Uterus fully elevated

Inner two-thirds of vagina distends and lengthens farther

Clitoris retracts under foreskin

Swelling of outer third of vagina and labia minora

Formation of "orgasmic platform"

FIGURE 4.4   *Female Plateau Phase*

In the plateau phase of sexual response, high levels of arousal are maintained. In the female, the orgasmic platform is caused by swelling of tissues in the outer third of the vagina, which causes the entrance to it to narrow. The clitoris retracts under its foreskin.

its usual position (see Figure 4.3). The vasocongestion causes changes in the labia majora and minora as they begin to enlarge and sometimes to open slightly. The clitoris begins to swell somewhat, and its shaft may elongate slightly. Some of the vaginal lubrication may flow out onto the labia and clitoris, depending on its copiousness and on whether the particular sexual activity is apt to bring internal secretions to the exterior.

Other areas of the body respond to sexual excitement as well. Often the nipples become harder and erect, although this response also may result from nonsexual stimuli. Many women show a darkening of the skin through the neck, breasts, and upper abdomen during sexual excitement, termed the "sex flush." General muscular tension begins to build throughout the body as heart rate and blood pressure increase.

Plateau Phase

The second stage of the female sexual response cycle leads to further changes in the vagina. The outer third of the vaginal wall becomes swollen with blood, narrowing the space within the vagina slightly. The inner two-thirds of the vagina shows slightly more lengthening and expansion (Min et al., 2001). The labia minora also become engorged with blood, causing thickening and a flaring outward. The swelling of the outer third of the vagina and of the minor lips seems to create the tension that is an important precursor of orgasm, so together they are termed the "orgasmic platform" (see

Figure 4.4). During the plateau phase, the clitoral glans retracts back under its hood or foreskin so that it no longer receives any direct stimulation.

The breasts have usually become somewhat engorged with blood by this time, and nipple erection may be maintained. Increase in breast size is not as pronounced in women who have breast-fed a baby. The sex flush, if present, sometimes spreads to the shoulders, back, buttocks, and thighs during the plateau phase. Muscular tension continues to increase, along with heart rate, respiration rate, and blood pressure. The heart rate usually increases to between 110 and 175 beats per minute.

Orgasm

The pleasurable release of sexual tension occurs during the sexual climax, or orgasm. The subjective experience of orgasm, or the degree of pleasure described, seems to be affected by the sexual situation in which it occurs (Mah & Binik, 2002; Meston et al., 2005). It is an intense experience, both physically and emotionally, and in females it is immediately preceded by a sensation of "suspension," at which time the pulse rate reaches its peak. Then there is a feeling of increased sexual awareness in the area of the clitoris, which spreads upward, and a "suffusion" of warmth that spreads from the pelvis throughout the body. Many women also experience a sensation of throbbing in the lower pelvic area.

The pleasurable feelings of the orgasmic phase are accompanied by muscular contractions in the outer third of the vagina and in the anal area. Following the initial contraction, which may last from 2 to 4 seconds, are three or four rhythmic contractions at intervals of about 0.8 second. There may be up to 15 such contractions, with the interval between them gradually lengthening and their intensity gradually decreasing. Two to 4 seconds after orgasm begins, the uterus has some mild wavelike contractions that move from its top to the cervix (see Figure 4.5).

During orgasm, muscles throughout the body may contract involuntarily, causing pelvic thrusting and spastic movements of the neck, hands, arms, feet, and legs. The woman may scream, gasp, moan, or shout out words during the orgasmic experience. Heart and respiratory rates and blood pressure have all reached their peaks. The pulse rate may be twice as high as normal.

Resolution Phase

Following the release of sexual tension through orgasm, the body gradually returns to its unexcited state. As blood leaves the pelvic region, the vagina returns to its usual size and color, and the labia return to their prearoused state. Within 10 seconds the glans of the clitoris emerges from the foreskin to its typical position, and within 15 to 30 minutes it has returned to its usual size. The uterus also lowers to its prearoused position.

During resolution, the other signs of sexual arousal also gradually disappear. The breasts decrease in size

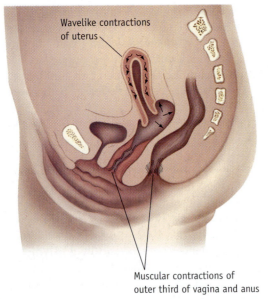

Wavelike contractions
of uterus

Muscular contractions of
outer third of vagina and anus

FIGURE 4.5   *Female Orgasmic Phase*

Orgasm is the release of sexual tension involving a total body response. The female physical response is marked by simultaneous rhythmic muscular contractions of the uterus, the outer third of the vagina, and the anal sphincter.

as blood flow to their tissue decreases, and the nipples lose their erection. The sex flush leaves the body in the reverse order from which it developed, and respiration, pulse, and blood pressure soon return to their normal levels. It is quite common for the body to become wet with perspiration during resolution. As the muscles throughout the body relax, there is often a feeling of drowsiness that may lead to sleep.

Multiple Orgasms in Women

During the resolution phase of sexual response, many females may be restimulated to orgasm. Unlike males, who go through a period when they cannot be restimulated to climax, some females are capable of experiencing numerous orgasms during a single sexual experience. Kinsey and his coworkers (1953) reported that 14 percent of the women surveyed regularly experienced sequential (or multiple) orgasms during sexual encounters, and Masters and Johnson (1966) proposed that most, if not all, women have the potential to experience more than one orgasm.

Research since that time has suggested that the multiorgasmic experience for women may depend a great deal on the type of sexual stimulation involved in their sexual responsiveness, and not all women report having been multiorgasmic. In one study of 720 women, about 47 percent indicated that they usually had single orgasms, and 43 percent reported that they had experienced multiple orgasms. It would appear that women tend to be multiorgasmic through particular means of stimulation. In this study, for example, 26 percent of the women had experienced multiple orgasms through masturbation, 18.3 percent through stimulation by a partner, and 24.7 percent by sexual intercourse. Only 7 percent had experienced more than one orgasm by all three types of stimulation. Of those women who tended to have only single orgasms, 27 percent were interested in being able to experience multiple orgasms (Darling, Davidson, & Jennings, 1991). It has been suggested both that we should stop assuming that female sexual satisfaction rests solely on whether one or more orgasms are experienced and that we should stop undervaluing women's capacity for multiple orgasms by giving precedence to a male-centered, single orgasm norm (Basson, 2001; Basson et al., 2003).

Controversies about Female Sexual Response

Orgasms

For many years, there has been controversy over the existence of two types of female orgasm: clitoral and vaginal. Masters and Johnson (1966) concluded that, regardless of how it is produced, female orgasm

Real People

Angelina: Questioning Orgasmic Abilities

Angelina had been involved in a sexual relationship with her boyfriend for nearly a year when she became concerned about her sexual responsiveness. Although she regularly experienced orgasm during her sexual encounters with her partner, she had come to believe that she should be capable of having more than one orgasm when she had sex.

She had read articles about female sexuality implying that all women had the potential for multiple orgasms during sex, and she felt as though she might have something wrong with hers. Her boyfriend also seemed to want her to try to have more orgasms and sometimes would persist in attempting to offer stimulation that might produce that result. In fact, it was extremely uncomfortable for her to receive further stimulation in the clitoral area following orgasm. Physically and emotionally, she felt quite satisfied with a single orgasm.

Angelina eventually consulted a therapist, who explained to her that many women seem to be sexu-ally satiated with one orgasm and that some apparently find sexual satisfaction without any orgasm at all. She urged Angelina to invite her boyfriend to join her at their next session so that they could talk about their sexual relationship. Although the boyfriend declined to enter counseling, Angelina was able to explain to him that she did not wish to pursue orgasms beyond the one she typically experienced. She realized that this pattern apparently fit her best and that it was a perfectly normal one. Her boyfriend continued to seem skeptical, because his only previous partner had experienced more than one orgasm, but he seemed willing to stop pressuring Angelina.

What is your reaction to Angelina's concerns? How do you feel about her boyfriend, and his skepticism? How would you talk with him, if you were Angelina? Do you believe that women should attempt to have more than a single orgasm during a sexual encounter?

proceeds physiologically in basically the same manner as previously described. They believed that, at least from a biological viewpoint, the clitoral-vaginal dichotomy was unfounded. However, the controversy continues as researchers report distinct differences in how women experience orgasm produced by clitoral or vulval stimulation and that produced by deeper vaginal stimulation. Some women experience orgasm as the result of stimulation of the cervix, called a "uterine orgasm." It has also been suggested that some women experience a "blended orgasm," a combination of the clitoral-vulval experience and the uterine orgasm. The difference in orgasmic responses could be due to the two different nerve pathways that serve the sex organs: the *pudendal nerves* and the *pelvic nerves*. The pudendal nerve system connects with the clitoris, and the *pelvic system* innervates the vagina, cervix, and uterus. It is hypothesized that there may might be two different neurological routes to producing orgasm (Janssen et al., 2000; Levin, 2002; Meston et al., 2005).

This controversy may well represent one of those cases in which it is difficult to reconcile the objective measures of science and the subjective reports of people's experiences. It does seem clear that orgasm has both physiological and psychological components, meaning that each person will have individualized perceptions and interpretations of the experience (Mah & Binik, 2002). Regardless of what sort of orgasm a woman might experience, the most important issue is that she be able to feel that a sexual activity has been fulfilling to her personally.

The G Spot

It is possible that there is an area on the inner front wall of the vagina that may become particularly sexually sensitive. The existence of such an area was proposed years ago by a German physician named Gräfenberg (1950). The idea was revived in the 1980s by other researchers who claimed that there is indeed a mass of tissue in the anterior vagina that swells during sexual arousal and can lead to intense orgasmic experiences. They named it the **G spot,** after Gräfenberg (Ladas, Whipple, & Perry, 1983). Some scientists have objected, feeling that the sensitive "spot" is not found in a large percentage of women and that, when it is present, it is not in a clearly defined location. Evidence does seem

G spot a vaginal area that some researchers feel is particularly sensitive to sexual stimulation when its underlying spongy tissues are engorged with blood.

to suggest that stimulation of the anterior wall of the vagina usually results in more sexual arousal than stimulation of the back wall. It has been suggested that this should be referred to as an "area" rather than a spot because it seems to vary in size (Ladas, 1997).

The confusion might result from the fact that the spongy tissue in this area may not become fully engorged with blood and sensitized until the clitoris is fully engorged. This can take up to 25 minutes in some women, so they may never experience the sensitivity of the G spot. There has also been speculation that this vaginal region may be activated by a different set of nerves (pelvic) than is the clitoris (pudendal) and so it has been difficult to separate the different types of orgasm that may result from their stimulation. As the media created the impression that the G spot was some sort of magic button that could be pushed to enhance female sexual enjoyment, the picture became confusing for both women and their partners. The one thing this controversy has confirmed is that many women are sensitive to vaginal stimulation, thus laying to rest an earlier view of the vagina as a rather insensitive organ (Basson, 2001; Meston et al., 2005). It also reminds us that there are individual differences in sexual response, highlighting the need for good patterns of communication between sexual partners.

Ejaculation

Gräfenberg also suggested in his 1950 article that some women might ejaculate a semenlike substance from their urethra at the time of orgasm. This contention has also seen a recent revival. It has been hypothesized that **Skene's glands,** located inside the urethra, might be similar to the male prostate (Sevely, 1987). During particularly intense orgasms, some women report that a liquid is expelled from their urethra that does not seem to be urine. A survey of 1,230 women in North America found that 40 percent of them had experienced such an ejaculation. Those who had ejaculated were more likely to report their sexual responsiveness as above average in intensity (Darling, Davidson, & Conway-Welch, 1990). Some women seem to assume that the fluid is urine and are therefore reluctant to pursue the matter. Some of those women may even try to prevent themselves from experiencing intense orgasms in an effort to reduce the chances of emitting this fluid. Only further research will finally resolve these issues.

Social factors play an important role in how female orgasm, the G spot, and female ejaculation are perceived in our culture. There may be male power issues involved. If the sexual focus in our society has traditionally been on what pleases men and glorifies their sexual organs, it may be difficult to shift that focus toward those places in women that are associated with intense sexual pleasure (Basson, 2001).

Kegel Exercises and Sexual Response

In the early 1950s, surgeon Arnold Kegel developed exercises for the pubococcygeal (PC) muscle that surrounds the vagina. He originally intended the exercises for girls and women who had difficulty preventing urine from leaking from their bladders. Eventually, Kegel found that in some of his subjects a well-toned PC muscle increased the ability to experience orgasmic satisfaction. Kegel exercises have also been recommended for pregnant women and seem to help the vagina and uterus return to their normal shape and tone more quickly after the delivery of a baby. It has been suggested that men should keep their PC muscles in good shape to ensure good orgasms as well. Although whether the PC muscle actually affects orgasmic capacity is controversial, keeping it in good shape is at least a healthy thing and may also enhance general sexual sensitivity.

Kegel exercises are accomplished by first locating the PC muscle. This is best done by stopping and starting the flow of urine during urination, because the same muscle is involved. Once the individual is familiar with its location, it is usually suggested that the muscle be contracted firmly for 2 or 3 seconds and then released. Although it has been recommended that these contractions be done in sets of tens, building up to several sets each day, some experts now believe that it is unnecessary, and even unwise, to exercise the PC muscle too much.

■ Male Sexual Response

Excitement Phase

Vasocongestion in the pelvic area during early sexual arousal contributes to erection of the penis, the first sign of the excitement phase in males. The degree of erection during this phase depends on the intensity of sexual stimuli. Eventually the inner diameter of the urethra doubles. Vasocongestion also causes thickening of the scrotal tissue, and the scrotum pulls upward toward the body. The testes become elevated within the scrotum, although if the excitement phase continues for more than 5 or 10 minutes, the testes return to their original position for a time (see Figure 4.6).

Nipple erection and appearance of the sex flush are less common in males than in females, but both phenomena usually are first observed during the excitement phase if they occur at all. Muscular tension

Skene's glands secretory cells located inside the female urethra.

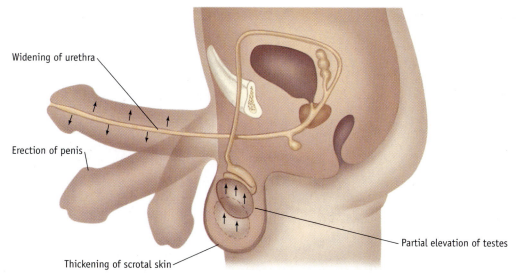

Widening of urethra

Erection of penis

Thickening of scrotal skin

Partial elevation of testes

■ **FIGURE 4.6** *Male Excitement Phase*

Vasocongestion in the male leads to erection of the penis, the first physical sign of sexual arousal. The testes are lifted up in the scrotum as a result of the shortening of the spermatic cords and contraction of the scrotal sac. The scrotal tissue itself thickens.

Full engorgement and darkening in color of glans penis

Appearance of secretion from Cowper's glands

Testes increase in size and elevate farther

Scrotum is pulled upward

Cowper's gland becomes active

■ **FIGURE 4.7** *Male Plateau Phase*

A generalized increase in neuromuscular tension is experienced in both males and females in the plateau phase. In the male, the head of the penis increases slightly in size and deepens in color. The testes swell by 50 to 100 percent. The testes continue to elevate. A secretion from Cowper's glands may appear at the tip of the penis and may carry live sperm.

increases throughout the body during the late excitement phase, and heart rate and blood pressure both increase. Sometimes secretion from Cowper's (bulbourethral) glands appears during this stage or can even precede erection.

Plateau Phase

The penis does not change markedly during the second stage of sexual response, although a man is less likely to lose his erection if he is distracted during the

plateau phase than during excitement. As orgasm nears, the corona of the glans of the penis becomes more swollen, and the glans itself may take on a deeper, often reddish purple color. There are no further changes in the scrotum, but the testes increase in size by 50 percent or more and become elevated toward the body. During plateau, Cowper's glands often secrete a few drops of fluid, some of which may appear at the tip of the penis. The longer plateau stimulation is maintained, the greater the amount of fluid produced (see Figure 4.7).

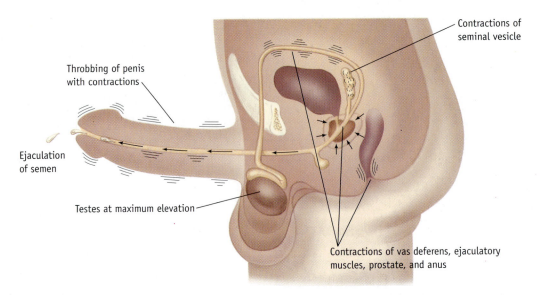

FIGURE 4.8   *Male Orgasmic Phase*

Male orgasm and ejaculation occur in two distinct phases but are perceived as occurring simultaneously. The vas deferens, prostate, and seminal vesicle begin a series of contractions that force semen into the urethra. The contractions continue until the semen is ejaculated.

Muscular tension heightens considerably during the plateau phase, and involuntary body movements increase as orgasm approaches. The nipples may become erect. Males often have clutching or grasping movements of the hands in late plateau. Heart rate increases to between 100 and 175 beats per minute, and blood pressure increases. Respiratory rate also increases, especially in the later plateau phase. If the sex flush is present, it may spread to the neck, back, and buttocks.

Orgasm

In males, actual orgasm and ejaculation are preceded by a distinct inner sensation that orgasm is imminent—a phenomenon called **ejaculatory inevitability.** Almost immediately after that feeling is reached, the male senses that ejaculation cannot be stopped. The most noticeable response in the penis during orgasm is the ejaculation of semen. The muscles at the base of the penis and around the anus contract rhythmically, with intervals of about 0.8 second between the first three or four contractions. This varies in different individuals. The intensity of the contractions then diminishes, and the interval between contractions lengthens. The first few contractions expel the largest amount of semen. The testes are held at their maximum elevation throughout orgasm (see Figure 4.8).

Males often have strong involuntary muscle contractions throughout the body during orgasm and usually exhibit involuntary pelvic thrusting. The hands and feet show spastic contractions, and the entire body may arch backward or contract in a clutching manner. Many men moan or yell during orgasm and have a grimacing

facial expression. Breathing, heart rate, and blood pressure all reach a peak during orgasm, and some men begin perspiring during this stage.

Like women, men have two different nerve pathways to different parts of their sex organs. The pudendal nerve system connects with the penile glans, whereas the pelvic nerve system serves the base of the penis and the prostate gland. This could explain why orgasm is not necessarily always accompanied by ejaculation of semen. Orgasm produced from localized stimulation of the glans may be somewhat less likely to be accompanied by ejaculation. It is also known that different sets of nerves are involved depending on whether erection is generated by direct touching of the genitals or by psychological stimuli such as erotic thoughts and fantasies, although the two systems are somewhat interactive (Janssen et al., 2000). In any case, male orgasm and ejaculation should be viewed as two essentially separate sexual responses that most often happen at the same time.

Resolution

Immediately following ejaculation, the male body begins to return to its unexcited state. About 50 percent of the penile erection is lost right away, and the remainder is lost over a longer period of time, depending on the degree of stimulation and nonsexual activity. Urination, walking, and other distracting activities

ejaculatory inevitability the sensation in the male that ejaculation is imminent.

Real Student Voices

■ I have had two sexual partners prior to the relationship with my present boyfriend. While I didn't know this at the time, I never actually had an orgasm with either of those first two. My boyfriend now took a lot more time with me, and was very romantic, and the second time we had sex, I did have an orgasm. It was great, and I'll always be grateful to him.

■ I always feel like I don't last long enough for my girlfriend. She usually has an orgasm before I ejaculate, but she doesn't really seem to be finished either. She has told me she wishes I could last longer, but nothing I have tried has worked so far.

usually lead to a more rapid return of the penis to its fully flaccid state. The diameter of the urethra returns to its usual width. The scrotum begins to relax as vasocongestion decreases, and the testes return to their nonaroused size and position. Resolution in the scrotum and testes takes varying lengths of time, depending on the individual.

If nipple erection and sex flush have appeared, they gradually diminish. Muscular tension usually is fully dissipated within 5 minutes after orgasm, and the male feels relaxed and drowsy. Many men fall asleep quickly during the resolution phase. About one-third of men begin to perspire during this stage. Heart rate, respiration rate, and blood pressure rapidly return to normal. Resolution is a gradual process that may take as long as 2 hours.

Refractory Period

During resolution, most males experience a period of time during which they cannot be restimulated to ejaculation; known as the **refractory period.** The duration of the refractory period depends on a variety of factors, including the amount of available sexual stimulation, the man's mood, and his age. On average, men in their late thirties cannot be restimulated to orgasm for 30 minutes or more. The period gradually increases with age. Very few men beyond their teenage years are capable of more than one orgasm during sexual encounters, except occasionally. Most men feel sexually satiated with one orgasm.

Multiple Orgasms in Men

There have always been tales of men who are capable of experiencing more than one orgasm during a single sexual experience, presumably without experiencing a refractory period. Some studies have reported on small numbers of men who claim to be able to experience multiple orgasms, and some laboratory measures of

their responses have been taken. These studies suggest that some men seem able to delay ejaculation but still experience some internal contractions and pleasurable sensations associated with orgasm. It has been suggested that men can learn to develop the muscle control necessary to separate orgasm from ejaculation. However, in at least one case study, the man was able to ejaculate each time while reaching six separate orgasms in 36 minutes. Evidence suggests that this pattern is unusual, although this particular male had experienced multiple ejaculations since the age of 15. Some men, especially at younger ages, may have a brief refractory period and may experience a second ejaculation quite rapidly, sometimes without losing their erections (Whipple, Myers, & Komisaruk, 1998). The best current evidence indicates that once ejaculation has occurred, a refractory period follows for most men. A few men (5 percent or less) do seem to be able to experience pleasurable orgasmic reactions two or more times prior to ejaculation. When ejaculation does not occur, the refractory period tends not to occur, so further orgasmic response is possible.

How might our general views of sexual responsiveness be unfair to women or men?

■ Hormones and Sexual Arousal

Do sex hormones control our level of interest in sexual activity? This assumption would have us believe that the more hormones people produce in their bodies, the stronger their sex drives. The picture of how hormones affect sexual behavior is complicated, and it is still uncertain whether the popular assumptions

> **refractory period** time following orgasm during which a man cannot be restimulated to orgasm.

about a direct correlation between hormone levels and sexual activity are at all accurate.

Organizing and Activating Effects

The secretions of the endocrine glands, called hormones, can have many different effects on an individual. Hormones exert their influence in one of two ways. The first, called an **organizing effect,** refers to ways in which hormones control patterns of early development in the body, playing a crucial role in the structure and function of particular organs. Chapter 5, "Developmental and Social Perspectives on Gender," for example, describes how certain hormones control the development of sex glands and external genitals in the fetus and how they may lead to some differences in how the nervous systems of males and females develop (Keefe, 2002). There is growing evidence that once hormones have done their organizing, the same or other hormones may continue to alter later processes of development and patterns of behavior.

The second effect that hormones seem to exert is referred to as an **activating effect.** This describes the potential of some hormones to directly affect an actual behavior, by either activating or deactivating it. In the matter of sexual response, it has been tempting to assume that levels of particular sex hormones in the bloodstream might increase or decrease a person's immediate level of sexual desire or activity, but the evidence in support of such a model has been mixed. Studies demonstrate that the central arousal system, in which internal stimuli are processed by the brain, probably is more dependent on the presence of hormones for activation than is the peripheral arousal system, which is far more susceptible to localized stimuli such as touch or viewing erotic material (Basson, 2003; Janssen et al., 2000).

The hormone that has been shown to have the most effect on sexual desire and behavior in humans is testosterone. Although this is an **androgen,** or "male" hormone, it is produced by both males and females in the sex glands (testes or ovaries) and the adrenal glands. Men's bodies tend to produce 10 to 15 times more testosterone than do women's bodies. However, the hormone also plays a vital role in enabling women to become sexually aroused (Apperloo et al., 2003; Guay & Jacobson, 2002; Traish, Kim, Min, Munarriz, & Goldstein, 2002).

FOH Hormonal Activation of Sexual Arousal

For both men and women, testosterone apparently has an activating effect on sexual interest. It might be viewed as a "switch" for sexual desire, and human beings

seem to require some minimal level of androgen in order to have any potential for sexual desire. What that minimum must be seems to vary among individuals. Increased levels of testosterone beyond this minimal activating level may result in increased interest in sex or higher amounts of sexual activity in some individuals, but probably not in all. To conclude that because women produce generally lower levels of testosterone they have a naturally lower interest in sex would be a mistake. It appears instead that women have a greater degree of sensitivity to testosterone and that their bodies therefore respond to smaller quantities of the hormone (Bancroft, 2002a, 2002b; Bolour & Braunstein, 2005). The effect of "female" hormones, or estrogens, on sexual desire or activity in females is still not entirely understood, although it may be minimal. If males are given doses of estrogen, their interest in sex tends to decrease.

Research on women has yielded a relationship between the levels of androgens such as testosterone (remember that the female body produces some androgens too) and levels of sexual desire (Davis & Tran, 2001). It was once assumed that women who were not particularly interested in sex probably were depressed or tired. Studies of their androgen levels have shown instead that hormone deficiencies are at least associated with such problems. Replacing those hormones often seems to increase both sexual desire and feelings of general physical and psychological well-being. At this point, the actual biochemical pathways by which androgens are produced are only poorly understood, as are the mechanisms that may impair their production (Anders et al., 2005; Guay & Jacobson, 2002; Traish et al., 2002)

Women's levels of sexual activity vary over the menstrual cycle and therefore could be associated with hormonal changes (Bullivant et al., 2004; Pillsworth, Haselton, & Buss, 2004). Early research studies concluded that there did not seem to be any direct or immediate correlation between sexual arousal and the concentration of sex hormones in the blood of either men or women, but newer studies are beginning to indicate at least some correlation. Part of the problem in understanding this picture is that women seem to initi-

organizing effect manner in which hormones control patterns of early development in the body.

activating effect the direct influence some hormones can have on activating or deactivating sexual behavior.

androgen (ANN-dra-gin) a male hormone, such as testosterone, that affects physical development, sexual desire, and behavior. Testosterone is produced by both male and female sex glands and influences each sex in varying degrees.

ate sexual activity at times for reasons other than sexual desire alone; those motivations complicate the analysis of the situation (Basson, 2003). A study of women who sought treatment to reduce hairiness on their faces and bodies showed that when the women were given antiandrogen medications to reduce the effects of androgens in their bodies, their sexual desire seemed to decrease progressively during the treatment (Conaglen & Conaglen, 2003). Researchers who measured hormone levels in women attending dance clubs found that higher androgen levels were associated with those women who wore clothing that was more revealing of their bodies, suggesting higher interest in attracting a sexual partner (Grammer, Renninger, & Fischer, 2004).

Less hormone research has been conducted with males in recent years. One study found a direct correlation between levels of testosterone (tested in saliva) in adolescent males and their levels of sexual activities. However, testosterone has the indirect effect of creating physical changes in adolescent boys that are signs of sexual maturity, which may have the psychological outcome of increasing sexual activity. In certain males—but not all—in whom low testosterone levels have been associated with difficulty achieving erections, administering testosterone as a treatment is sometimes effective in reestablishing sexual function. However, this is not generally recommended as a treatment unless it has been established that the man has levels of testosterone that are clinically below normal. All of this indicates some sort of interaction between sexual behavior and levels of testosterone in the body, but there may be a chicken-and-egg issue here that remains unresolved.

One study measured the amounts of testosterone in the saliva of four male-female couples on nights when they had sexual intercourse and nights when they did not. Saliva samples were taken both before and after the sexual activity. In both the men and the women, the amount of testosterone present in the saliva was greater after the couples had had intercourse. There was no increase in hormone levels prior to intercourse, leading the researchers to conclude that the sexual activity seemed to affect the testosterone concentration more than the hormone affected sexual activity. This is consistent with another finding that testosterone levels rise in men when they become involved in watching sporting events, especially when their team is winning, presumably demonstrating a correlation between hormone levels and general bodily and psychological arousal.

Before reading the section "Effects of Aging on Sexual Response," list your own perceptions of sexual activity after age 60. Include both the positive and the negative aspects.

■ Effects of Aging on Sexual Response

Does aging bring any sort of end to responding sexually? Aging people who accept this myth may allow their beliefs to become a self-fulfilling prophecy. There is evidence of a gradual decrease in both sexual desire and frequency of sexual activity as people age, but aging does not have to signal the loss of sexual responsiveness or pleasure altogether. In fact, sexual satisfaction for women does not diminish appreciably with age (Kingsberg, 2002). Attitudes toward one's own sexual functioning can play an important role in maintaining sexual functioning into old age.

In the original Masters and Johnson (1966) study, 212 men beyond 50 years of age were interviewed concerning their sexual lives. Thirty-nine of these men, the oldest of whom was 89, agreed to have their sexual responses observed by the research team. Thirty-four women over the age of 50 were also observed, and another 118 interviews were conducted with women between 51 and 80 years of age. The following discussion is based partly on these interviews and observations. A summary of the information is given in Table 4.2.

Aging and Female Sexual Response

Two manifestations of postmenopausal hormonal imbalance can cause unpleasant sensations during sexual activity in some older women. First, because the vaginal lining has thinned and vaginal lubrication possibly has lessened, intercourse may produce irritation that persists as burning or itching afterward. Water-soluble lubricants can relieve such problems, and estrogen-based creams may also help by increasing natural vaginal secretions. Second, some women experience uterine cramping during and after orgasm. Masters and Johnson reported that some women beyond age 60 were so distressed by these sensations that they began to avoid coitus and orgasm. We know now that these unpleasant symptoms can be relieved by proper medical treatment (Kingsberg, 2002).

As women age, there seems to be some decrease in orgasmic ability and a general tempering of the usual physiological responses to sexual arousal. This is a very gradual process of change and is somewhat dependent on how sexually active a particular woman remains. For heterosexual women over the age of 70 who have been involved in long-term relationships, their degree of sexual involvement may have a great deal to do with the availability and capability of their male partner. Their partners generally are older and thus more susceptible to medical conditions that interfere with sex. Older people of either gender whose bodies undergo regular sexual stimulation seem to

Table 4.2   Effects of Aging on Female and Male Sexual Response

Changes in the Aging Female	Changes in the Aging Male
Thinning of vaginal lining	Some atrophy of testicular tissue
Reduction in vaginal lubrication	Reduction in secretion of preejaculatory fluid and amount of semen produced
Increase in uterine cramping associated with orgasm	Testes not elevated as much during sexual arousal
Increase in amount of time needed to experience sexual arousal and vaginal lubrication	Increase in amount of time needed to achieve full penile erection
Increase in time of stimulation required to reach orgasm, and fewer muscular contractions associated with orgasm	Increase in time of stimulation required to reach orgasm, and reduced strength of orgasmic muscular contractions
Resolution to unexcited state about the same	Quicker resolution to unexcited state
Women who have been multiorgasmic seem to retain the capability	Lengthened refractory period, so the time before a man may be restimulated to orgasm tends to increase

Source: From W. Masters and V. E. Johnson, *Human Sexual Response,* Boston, MA: Little, Brown & Company, 1966. Reprinted by permission of Lippencott, Williams & Wilkins.

maintain more intense levels of sexual response than those who seldom participate in sex (Kalb, 2000).

One effect of aging on female sexual response is a lengthening of the time for vaginal lubrication and other early signs of sexual arousal to take place. There is also less enlargement of the clitoris, labia, uterus, and breasts during sexual arousal. Orgasm takes a bit longer to occur in older women, and there are usually fewer orgasmic contractions of the vagina, uterus, and pelvic floor. However, women who have a history of multiple orgasms apparently retain this capability even into very old age. The resolution phase of female sexual response, during which the body returns to its unexcited state, appears to be relatively unaffected by the aging process (Kingsberg, 2002).

It is important to emphasize that the degree of decline in sexual response patterns an older woman experiences seems to depend on how sexually involved she remains. This, in turn, depends on factors such as the woman's health, the availability of a partner, the amount of privacy she is afforded, her attitudes and values about sexuality, and the degree of priority she has always placed on her sexual feelings and behaviors. For these reasons, some women remain sexually vital until the end of their lives, whereas others forgo sexual pleasures long before that time and gradually lose their ability to respond sexually. Put in simple and direct language, this concept is often summarized by the phrase "use it or lose it."

Aging and Male Sexual Response

How responsive men remain in their older years seems to depend on a variety of physical, social, and psychological factors. Socially, men may lose their long-standing sexual partner or live in a setting that provides little privacy for sexual expression. Because there is a natural "slowing down" process, some men begin to feel insecure about their sexual capabilities. They may fear sexual "failure," usually meaning erection problems of various sorts, and may eventually withdraw from sexual activities. They may assume that aging is rendering them incapable of sexual performance. As a result, the amount of sexual stimulation they seek is drastically reduced, and the priority they assign to sex is lowered. This can lead eventually to at least a temporary loss of the ability to respond. Men who are in good general physical health may restimulate their sexual interests and response patterns if a change in their life situation makes this appropriate, for example, the availability of a new sexual partner, a renewed sense of self-worth, or sexuality education that makes the man aware of how his responses can be expected to change (Kalb, 2000).

Three aspects of male sexual response undergo predictable changes as men age. The first is erection. It takes a man in his seventies two to three times longer to achieve full penile erection than it did in the man's younger years, and he usually requires direct penile stimulation. Although it is perfectly normal for men of any age to experience waxing and waning of erection during prolonged sexual arousal, it is more difficult for older men to reestablish full rigidity once erection has been partially lost. The angle of the erect penis up from the body also decreases with age.

The second change relates to male orgasm and ejaculation. Older men take longer to reach orgasm than they did earlier in their lives. The strength of the orgasmic contractions is reduced, so semen is ejaculated with less force, sometimes just seeping out of the urethra. The frequency with which men desire orgasm also seems to decline somewhat as they age. Except in rare instances, men over 60 are completely satisfied by one or, at the most, two orgasms in the span of a week. They may enjoy participating in sexual behavior more frequently than that, experiencing full erection but no orgasm. The urge to achieve orgasm seems to be reduced with age. The third change is a lengthening of the male refractory period; by their late fifties or early sixties, most men cannot achieve an erection again for 12 to 24 hours after ejaculation.

Other aspects of the aging male's sexual response also show a decrease. There is a reduction both in the amount of preejaculatory secretion from the Cowper's glands and in the amount of semen produced. The testes and scrotum do not enlarge as much during sexual arousal, nor do the testes elevate as much within the scrotum. The resolution phase of men tends to occur more rapidly with age, and the penis may lose its erection after ejaculation much more quickly.

These changes in female and male sexual response are not necessarily negative developments for people's sexual lives. In fact, many men and women find increased enjoyment in the moderating responses brought about by aging. There is more about sexuality and aging in Chapter 7, "Adult Sexuality and Relationships."

Self-Evaluation

Sexual Arousal and Response in Your Life

This is a highly personal assessment meant for your individual use only. It can help you evaluate and understand some of your reactions to and feelings about your own sexual arousability and responsiveness. As this chapter has emphasized, different people seem to have different levels of arousability and different cues or sensitivities that can activate or deactivate (turn on or turn off) sexual response. There is no single "right" or "normal" way to be.

Complete the questionnaire first and then continue reading to understand what you can learn from it. This evaluation is not in any way meant to be a scientific test; it is only a simple instrument to help you further clarify some of your own reactions.
Use this scale:

5 = strongly agree

4 = somewhat agree

3 = neutral/uncertain

2 = somewhat disagree

1 = strongly disagree

Rate the following statements for yourself. (You might not want to write your responses in the book for others to see.)

1. I find myself thinking about sexual things frequently.
2. I think about sex more than the average person.
3. My thoughts about sex often lead to sexual arousal.
4. I experience sexual arousal several times a week.
5. I can reach orgasm during a sexual experience anytime I wish.
6. In general, I have positive feelings about my own sexual responsiveness.
7. I enjoy the sensations of sexual excitement in my sex organs and in the rest of my body.
8. I like experiencing orgasm (or do not mind at all if I do not reach orgasm) during sexual activity.
9. I know very clearly what turns me on sexually.
10. I am very comfortable with the place that sexual arousal and responsiveness have in my life.
11. Sometimes I get sexually aroused at inappropriate or embarrassing times.
12. I wish I could get sexually aroused more easily than I do.
13. I never/rarely reach orgasm, and this concerns me.
14. (If applicable now or in the past) My partner sometimes seems dissatisfied with my sexual responses.
15. (If applicable) My partner wishes I would get sexually aroused more easily and/or more often.

Evaluating Your Responses

As you examine your responses to the various items, it will be helpful to evaluate them in three different blocks:

Items 1–5: These items relate to the frequency with which you experience sexual thoughts and arousal. The higher your numbers, the more frequently you think about sexuality and experience arousal and response. As you look at the numbers, do you see any trend? What do they say to you about your sexuality?

Items 6–10: These items can help you examine your reactions to your sexual responsiveness. The higher the numbers, the greater degree of relative satisfaction you are indicating for your patterns of sexual arousal and response. The lower the numbers, the greater the likelihood that you are not particularly happy or satisfied with the ways you respond to sexual stimuli.

Items 11–15: These items focus on the dissatisfactions you may be experiencing with regard to your sexual responsiveness and, if applicable, with how your responsiveness fits into a relationship. Higher numbers would suggest that you have a fair amount of discomfort and negative reaction to various aspects of your sexual arousal and response.

What Does It All Mean for You?

Keep in mind that this assessment is a very rough measure of some of your own perceptions. It should help you clarify some of your own thoughts and reactions regarding your sexual responses. As you survey your responses, does any picture seem to emerge? Do you seem to be an individual who is quite comfortable and satisfied with his or her patterns of sexual arousal and response? Are you unsure of yourself and unable to get a very clear look at how sexual responsiveness fits into your life? Have your responses to the items suggested that you have a great deal of dissatisfaction about your sexuality?

Being able to get some general sense of how you react to your own sexual arousal and response may be valuable to you as you read further chapters in this text. It may also alert you to the fact that you have some issues worth considering, some of which may be positive and some negative. If you feel that your profile is reflective of some sexual concerns and problems, you may want to seek professional help or consultation. You might want to move ahead to the section "Preventing and Dealing with Problematic Sex" found in Chapter 16 and complete the Self-Evaluation on pages 474–475. This evaluation can focus your attention on what steps you might want to take.

Chapter Summary

1. Different cultures and spiritual traditions treat human sexual response in different ways.

2. Sexual response must be activated by some mechanism of sexual arousal. Several models of arousal have been proposed.

3. Penile and vaginal plethysmographs have been used in research to measure and compare the degree of sexual arousal in women and men. These studies show that people's perceptions of their own sexual response do not always match physiological measures.

4. Arousal stimuli may be internal or external, roughly corresponding to a central arousal system located in the brain and a peripheral arousal system that picks up cues from the genitals, senses, and spinal reflexes.

5. Emotions and other psychological processes play a significant role in activating or deactivating sexual response.

6. When the mind ascribes sexual meaning to some stimulus, the genital physiological response may be quite automatic.

7. Studies reveal more similarities than differences in arousal patterns of males and females.

8. Masters and Johnson were among the first researchers to study scientifically the body's physiological changes during sexual response. They developed a four-phase model involving excitement, plateau, orgasm, and resolution.

9. A three-phase model proposed by Kaplan views sexual response as beginning with psychological desire, with a subsequent buildup of blood and muscular tension followed by reversal of these states as triggered by orgasm.

10. The term "desire phase" refers to the level of interest in sexual activity an individual may experience.

11. There are many individual differences in human sexual response, and good communication is essential to developing mutual understanding in a sexual relationship.

12. In females, the vagina becomes lubricated during sexual excitement, and an orgasmic platform develops with the swelling of the clitoris and labia. The clitoral glans eventually retracts under its foreskin. Resolution refers to the return of the body to its unexcited state.

13. Some women have the potential for more than one orgasm during a single sexual experience. Women report clitoral, vaginal, uterine, and "blended" orgasms.

14. Some researchers claim that there is a particularly sensitive spot on the inner front part of the

vagina that swells during female arousal. This has been called the G spot.

15. It has been proposed that some women ejaculate a substance from the urethra during intense orgasms.

16. Kegel exercises can keep the urogenital musculature in good tone and may increase the intensity or pleasure of orgasm.

17. In males, penile erection is a major sign of excitement. There are also increases in the size of the testes and scrotum. The testes move upward in the scrotum.

18. In both women and men, sexual response involves increases in respiration, heart rate, blood pressure, and general muscular tension. A reddish "sex flush" appears on the skin of the upper body in some individuals, and nipple erection may also occur.

19. Orgasm is the pleasurable release of sexual tension, involving a series of muscular contractions in both sexes. Ejaculation usually accompanies orgasm in men.

20. During resolution, at the end of sexual response in men there is generally a refractory period during which there can be no restimulation to orgasm.

21. Hormones have both organizing and activating effects in the body. Testosterone, an androgen present in both men and women, acts as an activator for sexual arousal.

22. Androgens may act more directly on the central arousal system than on the peripheral arousal system.

23. In humans, sexual arousal and responsiveness seem to be controlled by both hormonal and social factors.

24. Both men and women may experience slower arousal and somewhat less intensity of response as they age. People who have been more sexually active during their younger years tend to maintain a higher level of sexual activity.

Focus on Health Questions

In this section you will find the kinds of questions that you may have concerning your own health and sexuality. The page references indicate where in the text the answer is located; the exact place is marked with this logo: **FOH**

1. I do not seem to get sexually aroused as quickly as my partner. Does that mean there is something wrong? **82–84**

2. Why is it that when I am turned on, the skin on my neck and shoulders gets all red? **89, 94**

3. Do all women have more than one orgasm during sex? **90**

4. How can I do the exercises that help strengthen the muscles involved with orgasm? **92**

5. Are men's orgasms different from women's? **89–90, 94**

6. Do hormones control my sex drive? **96–97**

7. When I get old, will I still be able to function sexually? **97–99**

Chapter 5

Developmental and Social Perspectives on Gender

Chapter Outline

I consider myself to be a fairly sensitive guy, and I want to treat women with respect and a sense of equality, but I'm never sure what the rules are. Do I open doors for her, or should we take turns? Am I supposed to pay for dinner every time, or do we share the cost? Who is supposed to give the first signals about being interested in having sex?

—statement from a male student

Being a sexual human being amounts to far more than the sexual organs with which we were born and the ways these organs are activated by sexual arousal. There are many other dimensions of sexuality as it relates to individuals. Why is it that humans come in two sexes? Or perhaps the question should be, Are there really just two sexes? What factors influence the development of male and female genitals before birth? What leads to our awareness of ourselves as girl or boy, feminine or masculine, or some combination of the two? Are gender roles determined by biology, socialization, or a combination of the two? How does gender fit into contemporary social and political trends? These are some of the questions we will explore in this chapter.

One unavoidable observation stares us in the face when we explore these topics. It is that the people around us generally are recognizable as male or female. There are surely many shades of overlap in physical structure and social behavior, and at first glance the gender classification of some people seems more ambiguous than that of others. Ultimately, we tend to see people in terms of the two sexes. But is that really fair?

Do you think gender roles are inborn or learned? Explain your answer.

■ How Many Sexes Are There?

Female and male are the two categories from which we are allowed to choose when filling out forms. Our legal systems also require that everyone be categorized as either male or female, and newborns must be identified on birth certificates as one or the other. But are things really that simple? The New York City Board of Health proposed in 2006 that people be allowed to change the sex noted on their birth certificates, even without undergoing sex-change procedures. It was believed that the policy would reduce discrimination against those who choose to live as members of the other sex. The proposal eventually was withdrawn because of unforeseen problems, but it was decided that individuals who had undergone sex-change surgery would be allowed to change the sex indicated on their certificates instead of deleting the designation, as had formerly been the case (Cave, 2006).

There are also documented cases of individuals who have the physical characteristics of both the male

and the female. In sixteenth-century England, because succession of wealth and title often depended on an individual's gender, the courts decided that succession would be based on "the kind of sex that doth prevail," meaning which sex seemed dominant in the individual by the time of adulthood. In 1843, an election for the town board of Salisbury, Connecticut, was tied, and its outcome hinged on the vote of a person named Levi Suydam, whom the local citizens considered to be more woman than man. Women were not allowed to vote. A physician examined Suydam, found a penislike structure, and declared him a male. He thus was eligible to cast a ballot and helped elect a member of the Whig party by a single vote. However, word quickly spread that, penis or not, Suydam also had a vaginal opening and menstruated regularly.

The concept of genders or sexes obviously has biological roots, but even biological facts become interpreted through the screen of cultural assumptions. From the time of the ancient Greeks until the end of the seventeenth century, Western culture embraced an essentially one-sex model; the one sex was male, and the structures of the female anatomy were seen as inverted or underdeveloped forms of the male sex organs. In other words, "both" sexes were actually just different forms of a single sex, one more fully developed than the other. During the early eighteenth century, a clearer distinction began to emerge that recognized female and male as two different sexes (Fausto-Sterling, 2000).

Intersexuality: Disorders of Sex Development

On the larger anatomical level, some human beings do not fit the standardized male-female categories. Medical investigators have long recognized the existence of **intersexuality,** a term that refers to some mixture of male and female anatomical characteristics, often reflected in the presence of ambiguous genitalia. The term is considered disrespectful and unscientific by some, and experts have recently agreed to use the term **disorders of sex development,** or **DSD,** instead

intersexuality a combination of female and male anatomical structures, so that the individual cannot be clearly defined as male or female.

disorders of sex development (DSD) a more scientific term now being applied to those with combinations or ambiguities of female and male anatomical structures.

(Berenbaum, 2007). At least three major subgroups of intersexes exist: **true hermaphrodites,** who have one testis and one ovary; male **pseudohermaphrodites,** who have testes and some female genitals but no ovaries; and female pseudohermaphrodites, who have ovaries and some male genitals but no testes (Zucker, 2000, 2005). The birth of a child with DSD is relatively rare, occurring in about 2 out of every 10,000 births (Sax, 2002).

If your child were born intersexed, what course of action would you consider?

In some historical periods, individuals with DSD were accepted as a "third sex," distinct from male and female. In many societies, alternative social statuses or gender roles are available for intersexed individuals. The American Plains Indians once assigned the social status of *berdache* to men who did not have the skill for or interest in typically masculine, aggressive pursuits. The berdache was considered to hold special powers and sometimes served as a shaman for healing practices or in sacred ceremonies. In India, a third gender called the *hijra* includes elements of both female and male roles, and such people are considered sacred. A genetic mutation within the Sambia tribe of Papua New Guinea has led to the birth of hermaphrodites who are assigned the role of *kwolu-aatmwol,* meaning an individual whose genitals appear to be female but who eventually will develop male secondary sex characteristics. Such individuals are not expected to take either male or female roles in their society but are allowed to become shamans or spirit doctors. All these are examples of alternative gender categories that have become socially institutionalized (Vilain, 2001; Zucker, 2000). The Intersex Society of North America, which was recently established in the United States, was founded to offer support and information for people with DSD and their families.

In modern Western cultures, such combinations of the sexes have been viewed as biological accidents or diseases. Babies who are born with ambiguous genitalia are usually subjected to hormonal and surgical treatment to make them either male or female. Some workers in this field have suggested that this practice represents a narrow-minded perspective and that DSD should be accepted as a legitimate position on the spectrum between female and male (Preves, 2003). Others believe that children typically need to be raised as male or female to conform to the social imperative but that care should be taken in determining the child's inner feelings of gender and their surgical alteration sometimes should be postponed until they can take part in the decision making (Berenbaum, 2007; Colapinto, 2000; Meyer-Bahlburg, 2005a; Zucker, 2002b, 2005).

There are case histories of people with DSD who adjusted to their sexuality quite comfortably. However, once such cases began to be viewed as mistakes of nature, the only alternative was believed to be medical treatment. The stigma of being so very different anatomically was thought to prevent people with DSD from being well adjusted. There is evidence that children with DSD ultimately tend to have later emotional and psychological problems (Berenbaum, 2007; McKenna, Tiefer, & Schober, 2002; Preves, 2003). From this perspective, people with anatomical variations are seen as incomplete males or females and not as persons constituting a separate sex. It also leads to their being subjected to medical intervention as infants, which some resent later in their lives (Diamond, 1998; Vilain, 2001).

These various perspectives represent salient reminders that even though our culture often attempts to define us in polarized ways as female or male, femaleness and maleness are better understood as differing sets of traits with many variations. This chapter explores how these variations occur and how they are defined.

Gender Identity and Role

The term *gender* was popularized in the 1970s as a way of distinguishing the physical aspects of *sex* from what were believed to be the more socially determined and culturally influenced aspects of male-female differences. The term has become more widely used and now is often substituted for what we once would have considered biological qualities (Haig, 2004). Along the way, we have also recognized that distinguishing between nature and nurture when it comes to differentiating between males and females is not a simple task.

Although most people do tend to fit a female or male category anatomically, the picture becomes more confusing when we examine their behaviors and their sense of themselves as men or women or as masculine or feminine. Human beings have a persistent inner sense of themselves as female, male, or some transgendered position between the two. This private, inner experience of one's gender has been termed **gender identity.** People also outwardly demonstrate

true hermaphrodite a person who has one testis and one ovary. External appearance may vary among individuals.

pseudohermaphrodite a person who possesses either testes or ovaries in combination with some external genitals of the other sex.

gender identity a person's inner experience of gender: feelings of maleness, femaleness, or some ambivalent position between the two.

to others the degree to which they are male, female, or transgendered in relationship to their society through what they say, their attempts at sexual attractiveness, and their behavior. This public, outward expression of gender is called **gender role.** The qualities individuals use to assess and understand their own gender are partly physical (such as body shape and sex organs) and partly sociocultural (such as hair length, clothing, and accepted standards of masculine and feminine behavior in a particular society).

What might be some of the effects on a person who experiences gender identity/gender role conflict?

■ Sexual Differentiation

One of the most enduring debates of the human sciences is waged in the arena of human sexuality: the controversy over the relative roles played by biological and social factors in determining human traits and behaviors, including those characteristics associated with being male or female.

Nature or Nurture?

The two camps in this great debate have traditionally been **biological essentialism** and **social constructionism.** The biological essentialists hold that inborn genetic and physiological factors are the determinants not only of such things as physical sex, body form, and temperament but also of the way human beings are programmed to behave in their gender roles—in other words, that physical, sexual, and personality characteristics are established by nature (Laland, 2003; Ridley, 2003).

On the opposite side of the debate are the social constructionists, who believe that human personality traits and behaviors are shaped mostly by social influences, or "nurture." They argue against the idea that gender and sexual behaviors and orientations are natural or inborn. Instead, they believe that these are shaped by learning experiences over the years of human development. Social constructionists do not completely dismiss the role of biology in determining fundamental physical characteristics, but they hold that even biological facts become interpreted through the screen of cultural assumptions (Bancroft, 2002a; Tucker & Keil, 2001).

The process by which organisms develop into the different sexes or genders is called **sexual differentiation.** Here the rubber meets the road with regard to controversies about nature and nurture. Debate has raged for centuries about the relative importance of genetics versus the environment in shaping sex-related characteristics of the body and mind. Ironically, through this debate, both biological essentialists and social constructionists have been forced to confront the inadequacies of either perspective on its own (Fausto-Sterling, 2000).

An Interactive View of Sexual Differentiation

The most reasonable current approach would not be to reduce the debate to a decision about whether some trait is innate or learned. That is too simplistic. Rather, the issue revolves around how variable a trait is and the degree to which its variability is shaped by an *interaction* of biological and environmental factors. Genes do not act on their own; instead their expression may be influenced to a degree by a variety of environmental factors ranging from the chemical composition of cells to cultural and social learning. The environment of the gene itself, as well as the organism's environment, seems to play a role in determining whether the gene is activated or deactivated (Nelson & Gottesman, 2005). Genes, as they are influenced by their environment, guide nerve cells to build brains and nervous systems in particular ways. This, in turn, may shape certain qualities that the individual expresses externally.

Learning operates in various ways through the expression of genes. The social experiences individuals have most likely change the ways their nervous systems function, the hormones they secrete, and the genes that are operating (Ridley, 2003). So the most reasonable conclusion we can reach is that the body is molded by experience and that learning and personality are dependent on the biological mechanisms of the body. The culture in which we live crafts the sex of our bodies and the social nature of our gender in constantly interactive ways.

It is likely that some traits are more susceptible to environmental influence than are others. Likewise, society surely does not shape the characteristics of an

gender role the outward expression and demonstration of gender identity, through behaviors, attire, and culturally determined characteristics of femininity and masculinity.

biological essentialism a theory that holds that human traits and behaviors are formed primarily by inborn biological determinants such as genes and hormonal secretions, rather than by environmental influences.

social constructionism a theory that holds that human traits and behaviors are shaped more by environmental social forces than by innate biological factors.

sexual differentiation the developmental processes—biological, social, and psychological—that lead to different sexes or genders.

individual human being in the absence of a genetic template that determines some degree of variability in traits. The real question to be asked in the debate over the variability of sexual traits in humans is the degree to which that variability is influenced by an interaction of biology and environment (Laland, 2003; Nelson & Gottesman, 2005).

The biological underpinnings of sex may be seen on four major levels (Dennis, 2004; Vilain, 2001):

1. *Genetic sex.* This begins with the genetic combination that is created when the sperm enters the egg at the moment of fertilization. A genetic map is established that will lead to the development of further expressions of maleness, femaleness, or perhaps a disorder of sex development.

2. *Gonadal sex.* The genetic map leads to the development of **gonads** that eventually will produce hormones within the individual's body. Gonads will be either testes or ovaries, and the hormones they produce—or do not produce—have profound effects on sexual development. It has been thought that these hormones are the agents that actually form those structures of body and brain that determine sex and gender, but more recent research suggests that the brain actually "knows" the sex of the individual prior to hormonal influences (Dennis, 2004).

3. *Body sex.* The genes and hormones present, or lacking, during development will partly determine what sorts of internal and external sex organs become apparent in the individual. The anatomical structures with which a person is born will then play a major role in how the person is categorized and how the individual feels about himself, herself, or him-herself (Zucker, 2002b, 2005). Social and other environmental factors become especially interactive at this level.

4. *Brain sex.* How the brain may be sexually differentiated is one of the most intriguing questions facing sexologists today. There is considerable evidence that hormonal influences exerted by the gonads on the brain before and after birth play some role in determining certain "male-type" or "female-type" behaviors. It seems increasingly likely that the brain itself is directly differentiated by genetic influences that work independently from or in cooperation with the hormones (Check, 2005; Dennis, 2004; Hines, 2004).

These biological levels of sex interact with environmental influences ranging from the hormonal concentrations in the bloodstream to the cultural imperatives that shape a person's social environment. As a human being develops from a fertilized egg through the various stages to adulthood, all these different aspects of being a sexual person begin to merge and play a role. Researchers are now examining the dynamic relationships between biology and environment that seem to interact across cultures and historical periods to form sexual anatomy and gender roles (Marshall, 2003).

Social psychologists, who study individuals within the context of their societies, generally accept the fact that biological factors may predispose females and males to certain behavioral variations. However, they also tend to believe that an elaborate system of human thought processes, fueled by social and cultural factors, heavily influences the innate variabilities and may even override them (Cohen, 2002).

The complexities of sexual differentiation demonstrate that human beings are not simply passive recipients of social rules and expectations concerning gender. Instead, they are seen as active participants in the continuing process of creating a particular perspective and personal meaning for the particular characteristics associated with gender. Individuals build the information from their own socialization into particular sets of beliefs, feelings, attitudes, and expectations; these then become the screens through which people perceive their worlds. Psychologists have long known that our internal cognitive systems can influence all our thought processes, tending to confirm only that which we believe (Marshall, 2003). From an interactive perspective, it is also likely that these thought processes influence the body and its functioning, including genes and hormones (Ridley, 2003).

Gender roles may therefore become self-fulfilling prophecies. We all have learned assumptions about differences between boys and girls, men and women, that affect our self-concepts and our views of others. This, in turn, affects how we behave, including how we treat other people as females or males. The entire system becomes self-perpetuating because people usually want to fit into what their society expects of them and because we become more comfortable with what is familiar and predictable (Stephens & Phillips, 2003). There is always the danger that gender roles in any society may create an imbalance of status and power between women and men, giving those who hold the greater status and power a personal and political stake in perpetuating an inequitable system.

Developmental Factors of Sexual Differentiation

Sexual differentiation begins with the genetic level at the moment of fertilization, when a sperm enters an ovum. At that moment, a program is set into motion

gonads sex and reproductive glands, either testes or ovaries, that produce hormones and, eventually, reproductive cells (sperm or eggs).

Real Student Voices

■ I've always assumed that parents can shape their children into being boys or girls. I figure if I have a son someday, I will teach him to play sports and not be a sissy. The information in this chapter is making me nervous. What if I don't have that much control over his development as a real boy?

■ I was always considered a tomboy, and thought it was because I had older brothers who let me play

with them and their friends. Maybe I was born that way. I'm attracted to boys as boyfriends.

■ My brother was born with some kind of problem with his penis that required several surgeries. It still doesn't really look right, and he's very self-conscious about it. We've never really talked about how it functions, but he also has not pursued any sexual relationships that I know of.

---

that eventually will combine with all the hormonal, social, and psychological factors that ultimately result in an adult gender identity. The factors that can exert influence along the way are incredibly varied, complex, and interactive. The model that follows continues to take shape and is always being clarified by new research (Dennis, 2004; Vilain, 2001). We can group the determinants of human sexual differentiation into three categories: prenatal factors, factors of infancy and childhood, and factors at puberty.

1. *Prenatal factors.* Before an infant is born, a variety of genetic, gonadal, and developmental factors interact with one another to set the stage for later identification as female or male. Even before a baby is born and assigned a sex, much of the groundwork for her or his gender identity has been established.

2. *Factors of infancy and childhood.* As soon as a baby is born, its body sex is assigned by the outward appearance of its genitals, and social influences become strong. Although assigning a sex may seem to be a simple enough task, sometimes anomalies of fetal development make it impossible to assign the baby's sex as clearly female or male. Ambiguous genitalia create situations in which decisions must be made about what sort of medical interventions, if any, the parents want to make so that the child fits into a particular category. Once these decisions and interventions are made, the infant is raised as a girl or a boy, regardless of what the individual's genetic sex might be (Zucker, 2005). As we learned earlier, Western cultural imperatives make it less likely that a child will be left in an intersexed state. Eventually, every child begins to develop distinct impressions and perceptions of her or his own body and sex organs. All these factors, in

conjunction with the structure and function of the brain, determine the "core" gender identity of the child.

3. *Factors at puberty.* Every day, children continue to receive confirmation or disconfirmation of their gender identity from other people. At puberty, new hormonal changes occur in the body that lead to further growth of the genitals and the appearance of secondary sex characteristics. There is also an increase in sexual interests around the time of puberty. These developments—if they proceed in the usual way—further confirm the individual's gender identity in the move toward adulthood. If the pubertal changes do not occur as expected—that is, if the gender identity program has some built-in inconsistencies—and the child's gender identity is not confirmed, the result is often confusion and emotional crisis.

We will take a closer look at some of the details in each of these categories in the sections that follow.

Prenatal Factors

Chromosomes

The earliest factor that determines a human being's sex and initiates the program for determining gender identity happens at **conception,** when chromosomes from both parents are combined. Typically, human gametes—the ovum (egg) and sperm—each contain 23 chromosomes, one of which is a sex chromosome.

> **conception** the process by which a sperm unites with an egg, normally joining 23 pairs of chromosomes to establish the genetic "blueprint" for a new individual. The sex chromosomes establish its sex: XX for female, and XY for male.

The sex chromosome carried by the sperm may be either an X chromosome or a Y chromosome. The egg contains only an X chromosome. If an X-bearing sperm fertilizes an egg, the resulting XX combination of sex chromosomes establishes a genetic program to produce a female. If the egg is fertilized by a Y-bearing sperm, the resultant XY combination is destined to become a male. If the genetic mechanisms function normally, the program toward producing a female or male child is well under way (see Figure 5.1). The X and Y chromosomes have some very complex characteristics in themselves, and geneticists are beginning to unravel their secrets (Emerson et al., 2004; Graves, 2005; Segal, 2003; Skaletsky et al., 2003).

A gene that seems to play a major role in the development of male organs has been pinpointed on the Y chromosome, a chromosome that has little other genetic activity. This gene has been labeled **SRY,** for sex-determining region of Y, because its presence or absence is significant in determining whether testes or ovaries will develop in the fetus (Willard, 2003). Because the more genetically active X chromosome contains many genes that are needed by both females and males, it has been suspected for decades that nature must provide some sort of regulating mechanism to prevent females, with their double-X combination, from getting an excess of gene products and also to prevent single-X males from having a deficiency of these same products (Check, 2005; Ross et al., 2005). It has now been demonstrated that a compensation mechanism seems to equalize genetic expression from the X chromosomes for females and males. In every cell of the female's body, there is a permanent deactivation of one of the X chromosomes (Hajkova & Surani, 2004).

Research involving a genetic error in this compensation mechanism led to the possible discovery of a gene on the X chromosome that also may be a sex-determining gene, playing some role in the development of females. Four people were identified who had an XY chromosomal pattern and yet developed some female genitalia and had been raised as girls. Researchers believed that these individuals had an abnormal, double set of the female-producing genes on the X chromosome and that this double dose apparently had overridden the influence of the SRY gene on the Y chromosome that would typically have taken precedence over the X chromosome to produce a male. This suggested that such "sex reversal" is dosage-sensitive, depending on the dosage (number) of female-determining genes present. The gene that likely determines sex on the X chromosome has been identified as a region called **DAX-1** (Vilain, 2001). At least one other gene seems to play a crucial role in sexual differentiation, and there may well be others (Bishop et al., 2000; Segal, 2003).

The actual mechanisms by which any of these genes may operate to develop male or female charac-

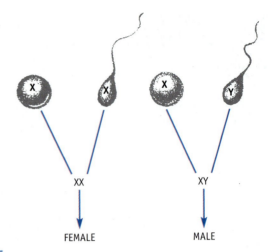

FIGURE 5.1 *Chromosomes*

Chromosomes are the genetic material in the nucleus of every cell. The sex of the offspring is determined at fertilization by the type of chromosome in the sperm. All egg cells and half the sperm cells contain an X sex chromosome; the remaining sperm contain a Y sex chromosome. A zygote with two X chromosomes will become a female, and a zygote with one X and one Y chromosome will become a male.

teristics are not yet fully understood. In rare cases, a fertilized egg has only one X chromosome, or the other X chromosome is somehow damaged. The individual produced develops a female body, but the ovaries do not develop normally, and the adult woman is unable to produce children (Turner syndrome). A fertilized egg left with only a Y sex chromosome and no X apparently cannot survive. No human being has ever been found with only a Y sex chromosome.

Other erroneous sex chromosome combinations in humans are XXX (triple-X syndrome), XXY (Klinefelter syndrome), and XYY (supernumerary Y syndrome). In some cases, there may be a normal pairing of sex chromosomes but some defect in a gene on one of the chromosomes (Zucker, 2002b). Individuals born with these conditions usually show variant development of the sex organs, unusual body shape, behavioral disorders, or intellectual and emotional disabilities. Table 5.1 summarizes this information.

Fetal Gonads

Up until the eighth week of development, it is impossible to determine the sex of a human embryo by the appearance of external genitalia (sex organs). Yet the

SRY the sex-determining region of the Y chromosome.

DAX-1 the region on the X chromosome that seems to play a role in sexual differentiation.

Table 5.1	Human Sex Chromosome Disorders that Affect Gender	
Abnormal Chromosome Combination	**Medical Name**	**Characteristics of Individual**
XXY	Klinefelter syndrome	Male genitals, but with female secondary sex characteristics. Penis, scrotum, and testes are small; enlarged breasts. Sometimes timid and withdrawn; possible learning disabilities; sterile.
XO (no Y present; only one X)	Turner syndrome	Female external genitals; ovaries lacking; lack of menstruation, pubic hair, and breast development. Stunted growth, with several body abnormalities. Sense of direction and spatial relationships may be abnormal.
XO/XY	Mixed gonadal dysgenesis	May have female or male genitals, or a combination of the two. Usually no other bodily abnormalities, except may not mature sexually without treatment, and tend toward short body stature.
XYY	Supernumerary Y syndrome	Appearance of normal male. Tend to be tall in stature. May show some lack of control over impulsive behaviors. Usually average intelligence levels.
XXX	Triple-X syndrome	Appearance of normal female. Sometimes infertile. Occasional impairment of intelligence.
XX/XY	May be a true hermaphrodite	Variable. Have some combination of both ovarian and testicular tissues. Usually have uterus. External genitals may be distinctly masculine or feminine, or may be an ambiguous combination of both. At puberty, most experience breast enlargement, and the majority menstruate.

genetic plan contained within the sex chromosomes carries the necessary information to produce gonads and genital organs. At first, a pair of tiny, sexless gonads form internally, having the potential to become testes or ovaries. Two pairs of duct systems also are present in the embryo: the **Müllerian ducts,** which represent potential female reproductive organs, and the **Wolffian ducts,** which represent potential male reproductive structures. Research has shown that it is the presence or absence of the Y chromosome, with its SRY gene, that determines whether the gonads differentiate into testes or ovaries (Dennis, 2004). As long as at least one Y and one X chromosome are present, testes normally are produced. Any combination of sex chromosomes lacking a Y chromosome produces ovaries. The DAX-1 gene may well play some sort of role in this process, but its role is not yet understood (Vilain, 2001). If testes are to be formed from the fetal gonads, they appear during the sixth week of development. Ovaries develop at a later stage but appear by the twelfth week. Variations in these patterns are rare (see Figure 5.2 on page 110).

Fetal Hormones

Fetal gonads that are programmed by the chromosomes to produce a female will automatically develop into ovaries. However, if the gonads are programmed to produce a male, another process is required, controlled by the SRY normally carried on the Y chromosome. A substance called **H-Y antigen** has been identified as the chemical agent that helps transform the fetal gonads into testes. When testes are produced, they begin secreting two hormones. Testosterone promotes development of the Wolffian ducts into internal male sexual and reproductive structures. The SRY gene also activates the fetal testes to produce **anti-Müllerian hormone (AMH),** which suppresses the development of the Müllerian ducts into the female organs (Zucker, 2000).

It has been suggested that the complicated genetic and biochemical interactions that must be initiated to form a male may well make males somewhat more vulnerable to developmental problems and variations. It is known, for example, that the incidence of mental

Müllerian ducts (myul-EAR-ee-an) embryonic structures that develop into female sexual and reproductive organs unless inhibited by male hormones.

Wolffian ducts (WOOL-fee-an) embryonic structures that develop into male sexual and reproductive organs if male hormones are present.

H-Y antigen a biochemical produced in an embryo when the Y chromosome is present; it plays a role in the development of fetal gonads into testes.

anti-Müllerian hormone (AMH) secretion of the fetal testes that prevents further development of female structures from the Müllerian ducts.

Developing head and brain region

Developing heart

Developing arm

Fetal gonad

Genital tubercle

Developing leg

FIGURE 5.2 *Fetal Gonads in a Developing Fetus*

During the first weeks of development, male and female embryos are anatomically identical. Two primitive gonads form during the fifth and sixth weeks of pregnancy. An H-Y antigen is necessary if the gonads are to develop into testes. Without an H-Y antigen, the gonads develop into ovaries.

retardation, learning disabilities, certain speech pathologies, and variant sexual behaviors is higher among males than among females (Check, 2005; Sanders, Sjodin, & Chastelaine, 2002). Development of female sex and reproductive organs in the fetus may not depend on the production of any hormones. If the SRY gene is not present, and thus male hormones are not produced, the fetal gonads become ovaries and the Müllerian ducts develop into the uterus, fallopian tubes, and part of the vagina. Without testosterone to stimulate their development, the Wolffian ducts simply disintegrate. It was once assumed that developing as a female was in a sense the "default" gender of the fetus when the SRY gene was not present. However, research on the DAX-1 gene segment on the X chromosome has called that assumption into question. In fact, there may be an entirely different mechanism, as yet undiscovered, by which the DAX-1 gene leads to an interruption of male genital formation and causes female genitals to form (Dennis, 2004). Future research may help clarify these mechanisms.

Some other rare problems can arise at these early stages of sexual differentiation. For example, if a male (XY) fetus's new testes produce testosterone but lack AMH, the external male sex organs may develop normally, but the boy will also be born with a uterus and fallopian tubes as well as internal male organs. Other developmental discrepancies may lead to hermaphroditism, in which the individual is born with both testicular and ovarian tissue. In another condition, the male fetus lacks an enzyme necessary for normal syn-

thesis of male hormones. Affected babies usually die, but those who live have very small penises and may at birth be mistakenly identified as females. If testosterone or related androgenic hormones somehow enter the bloodstream of a developing female (XX) fetus—usually because of some medical condition such as a testosterone-producing tumor in the pregnant mother—the baby girl is born with either an enlarged clitoris or a normal-appearing penis and empty scrotum. These and related conditions can lead to the erroneous assignment of the girl as a male at birth (Robinson et al., 2002; Zucker, 2000).

Development of Body Sex: Male or Female Genitals

Until the eighth week of fetal life, the external genitals are indistinguishable as male or female. There is a tiny, sexless genital tubercle on the lower part of the fetus. By the twelfth week of development, the male or female sex organs are clearly distinguishable. Development of the testes, scrotum, and penis require the presence of **dihydrotestosterone (DHT),** which is derived from testosterone. Without DHT, the fetal genital tissue develops into the clitoris and vulval lips (see Figure 5.3). Chromosomal and hormonal variations on this theme can cause the external genitals and their inner ducts to develop in a way that is inconsistent with more typical XX or XY status, as we have already seen in the section on fetal hormones.

See "Hormones and Sexual Differentiation" on SexSource Online.

Brain Sex and Fetal Hormones

One of the most exciting advances in animal sex research has been the discovery that fetal hormones not only control the development of the fetus's sex organs but also may affect development of parts of the brain and pituitary gland. Research with human brains is beginning to demonstrate differences between the number and location of nerve synapses in the hypothalamuses of male and female brains. Some research evidence supports the contention that such differences could lead to different behavior patterns later in life. In many lower mammals, predictably different behavior is observed in the male and female of the species. It was originally assumed that hormones had little to do

dihydrotestosterone (DHT) a chemical produced by the fetal testes that promotes further development of the testes, scrotum, and penis in the fetus.

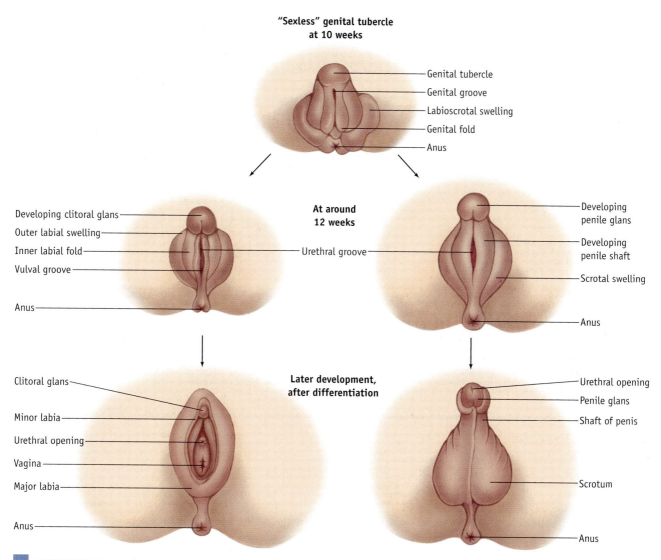

"Sexless" genital tubercle
at 10 weeks

Genital tubercle
Genital groove
Labioscrotal swelling
Genital fold
Anus

At around
12 weeks

Developing clitoral glans
Outer labial swelling
Inner labial fold
Vulval groove
Anus

Urethral groove

Developing penile glans
Developing penile shaft
Scrotal swelling
Anus

Later development,
after differentiation

Clitoral glans
Minor labia
Urethral opening
Vagina
Major labia
Anus

Urethral opening
Penile glans
Shaft of penis
Scrotum
Anus

FIGURE 5.3 *Differentiation of Male and Female Genitals*

From the tenth week of fetal development, sexual differentiation occurs at three different levels: internal sex organs, external sex structures, and the brain. These drawings illustrate the common fetal tissues from which various external genital structures differentiate in both females and males. Genetic and hormonal factors direct this process.

with the determination of differing behavior in the sexes. Subsequent research led to the hypothesis that the presence of testosterone in the fetus of many mammals affects the structures and pathways of the central nervous system, particularly the brain, in such a way as to produce masculine behavior in the adult mammal. If testosterone is not present, the adult behavior becomes feminine. In many mammals, there seems to be a critical period at some point in development and sexual differentiation when the presence of male hormones has this "masculinizing" effect. At the same time, there is a concurrent but independent process of defeminization. The absence of androgens from the testes results in reverse processes: demasculinization and feminization (McFadden, 2002, Zucker, 2000, 2005). Research also suggests that while hormones

may well play a role in the masculinizing or feminizing of the brain, the brain itself may already have "known" its gender from genetic messages before the hormones even come into play (Baron-Cohen, Knickmeyer, & Belmonte, 2005; Dennis, 2004; Hines, 2004).

What Variations in Sexual Differentiation Can Tell Us

The actual chemical mechanisms that control the processes of sexual differentiation are slowly being pieced together, sometimes through animal studies. Because the human brain is structurally different from and more highly developed than animal brains, it is risky to extrapolate the findings of animal research to human beings. As we better understand the interactive

Table 5.2	Summary of Abnormal Forms of Sexual Differentiation		
Condition	**Cause**	**Typical Characteristics**	**Predominant Gender Identity**
Fetally androgenized females	Hormones administered during pregnancy	Genetic females (XX) with enlarged, penislike clitoris. Usually surgically corrected and raised as girls.	Masculine
Exposure to DES	Administration of DES to prevent miscarriage	In boys, less separateness of brain hemisphere functioning; lowered spatial abilities; less assertiveness.	Masculine in boys, with potential for more feminine traits
		In girls, there may be some masculinizing effects, but this is controversial.	Unknown for girls
Congenital adrenal hyperplasia (CAH)	Genital disorder in which androgens accumulate in the body	Masculinization of genitals in genetic females (XX). Even after surgical correction and being raised as female, these girls tend to prefer boys' toys and behavioral patterns, and have higher spatial abilities.	Either, with a tendency toward some masculine traits
Androgen insensitivity syndrome (AIS)	Inability of body cells of genetic males to respond normally to testosterone	Genetic males (XY) are born with normal-appearing female genitals, and are usually raised as girls. At puberty, they develop breasts but cannot menstruate. Tend to behave in feminine ways.	Feminine
DHT-deficiency syndrome	Lack of enzyme necessary for normal development of male sex organs	Genetic males (XY) are born with genitals that tend to appear male. At puberty, they begin to develop masculine secondary characteristics and may then live as males.	Masculine

perspective, it seems likely that there are critical periods in human development during which the interaction of biological (e.g., hormonal) and environmental (e.g., learning behavior from others) factors establishes some permanent characteristics of the individual. Early genetic and hormonal influences probably play a significant role in permanently modifying the ability of tissues to react to later hormonal stimulation and may form the brain template on which patterns of behavior are then formed (Dennis, 2004; Hines, 2004; Sanders, Sjodin, & Chastelaine, 2002). Study of some of the genetic abnormalities of sexual differentiation in humans, as well as some medical treatments that have exposed fetuses to hormonal chemicals, has provided fascinating insights into this issue. Some examples follow and are summarized in Table 5.2.

A Groundbreaking Case

In 1963, one of a set of infant twin boys had his penis damaged beyond repair during a botched circumcision procedure. Experts advised the parents to have his testes removed, his genitalia surgically modified, and estrogen administered so that he could be raised as a girl. For years, the case was cited as proof that gender identity could be largely constructed by social influences, because it was reported that the former anatomical boy had adjusted well to being raised as a girl. However, when the patient was tracked down by other researchers in the mid-1990s, a very different

story emerged. In fact, he reported that during his childhood he had always felt like a boy despite constant assurances that he was a girl. By junior high school, still being forced to dress as a girl, he was standing to urinate, and girls at his school finally forced her/him to use the boys' rest room. A physician and his father told him the truth about his background when he was 14, and he actively began to pursue reidentification as a male. By the age of 25, he had had a penis reconstructed, his breasts had been removed, and he had married a woman and adopted children. He lived and worked entirely as a man. This case is a reminder of the potential innate influences on the formation of gender identity and the complications the medical profession faces when making decisions about infants with ambiguous or damaged genitalia (Colapinto, 2000; Meyer-Bahlburg, 2005b; Zucker, 2005).

Other studies have indicated that when XY males have been raised as females because of some external abnormality although their hormonal environment has been typical during fetal development, they are more likely to want to be reassigned as males later in life (Meyer-Bahlburg, 2005a).

Fetally Androgenized Females

A medical decision made in the 1950s led to one of the first studies to propose the idea of biological and environmental factors interacting at a critical period in human development to influence gender-related behavior. Several pregnant women were given hormones to prevent miscarriages. Later it was discovered that the hormones had a masculinizing effect on the developing fetuses, resulting in the birth of several **fetally androgenized females** with enlarged clitorises and a few genetic females with penises. Most of the girls considered themselves to be tomboys and showed significantly more traditionally boyish traits than did a control group, including a high level of energy expenditure during play, a preference for practical clothing, lack of interest in dolls and infants, and a preference for a future career outside the home rather than homemaking.

Although some researchers who studied these girls believed that the most likely explanation was that the male hormones present during their fetal development had created a masculinizing effect on their brains, others countered that confusion on the part of their parents might instead have affected their socialization. More recently, other studies have confirmed that fetal androgen exposure during the second three months of pregnancy is indeed associated with a masculinizing of behavior that cannot be completely explained by social influences (Zucker, 2000, 2005).

Exposure to Synthetic Hormones

Other evidence demonstrates that exposure of a fetus to certain synthetic hormones that are similar to male or female hormones can lead to eventual behavioral characteristics that could be considered masculine or feminine. Large doses of certain synthetic progestins used to treat other medical conditions during pregnancy seem to affect fetuses in much the same way that testosterone does. Some females exposed to these hormones have been born with genitals that have appeared to be more malelike, for example, with enlarged clitorises. Both females and males exposed to testosterone-like hormones have been studied for later characteristics and compared with controls. On several psychological scales, these individuals tend to score higher on various "masculinity" indexes (Zucker, 2002b).

Some anticonvulsant drugs are known to alter hormone levels in animals, leading to disturbed sexual differentiation. A study of humans whose mothers had taken these drugs during pregnancy found that a higher proportion of them had experienced cross-gender behavior and confusion about their gender identity than had those in a matched controlled group (Dessens et al., 1999).

Congenital Adrenal Hyperplasia

Sometimes called androgenital syndrome, **congenital adrenal hyperplasia (CAH)** is a genetic disorder that causes a buildup of androgenic hormones in the fetus or infant. Genetic females born with this condition often have masculinized genitals, and they may be surgically treated to create genitals that appear more female. There is evidence that girls with CAH tend to prefer toys and activities more typically considered for boys, see themselves as tomboys, and demonstrate more typically masculine traits than do their sisters. They are also more likely to have lower levels of sexual arousal and eventually to develop a gay or bisexual orientation. However, they do not seem to have much confusion in their gender identity (Dessens, Slijper, & Drop, 2005; Hines, Brook, & Conway, 2004; Meyer-Bahlburg et al., 2004; Zucker et al., 2004). Conversely, boys who experience low levels of androgens during development seem to exhibit reduced visual-spatial abilities in comparison with other males. Research on the behavioral outcomes of such disorders has sometimes demonstrated conflicting evidence, and much work remains to be done (Hines, Fane, et al., 2003; Zucker, 2000).

Androgen Insensitivity Syndrome

As explained earlier in this chapter, hormonal secretions from fetal gonads are necessary for the development of male genitals and the possible suppression of female structures. In a rare genetic condition called **androgen insensitivity syndrome (AIS),** the developing body cells of genetic males (XY) are unable to respond normally to the testosterone secreted by the fetal testes. As a result, these males develop normal-appearing female genitals instead of male organs, but the internal female structures develop only incompletely. Breasts develop at puberty and there may be a short vaginal canal, but because there is no uterus, menstruation never occurs. These children are raised from birth as girls because they appear anatomically female; it may not be until the lack of menstruation is noted that the abnormal condition is diagnosed.

Studies of some genetic males with AIS who have been raised and treated as "girls" and "women" have determined that they tend to exhibit traditional feminine traits, including a preference for being homemakers

fetally androgenized females a condition in which hormones administered during pregnancy cause chromosomally female (XX) fetuses to have masculinization of the genitals and perhaps of later behavioral patterns, even though they were raised as girls.

congenital adrenal hyperplasia (CAH) a genetic disorder that masculinizes chromosomal females and seems to lead to a masculinization of behavior as well.

androgen insensitivity syndrome (AIS) a developmental condition in which cells do not respond to fetal androgen, so that chromosomally male (XY) fetuses develop external female genitals; there is also a feminization of later behavioral patterns.

rather than having a career, and having played with dolls in their younger years. They typically report desiring male sexual partners and having dreamed of raising a family. They generally are not confused about their female gender identity and typically do not seek a sex change (Mazur, 2005). Researchers have suggested that in cases of AIS, the ineffectiveness of androgens during these genetic males' fetal development not only has led to feminization of their genitals but also has prevented any masculinization of their brains. This in turn may produce conditions that lead to distinctly feminine behavior in later life (Hines, Ahmed, & Hughes, 2003). Of course, it could also be argued that the socialization process of being raised as girls led to development of traditionally "feminine" characteristics in these genetic males. There is clinical evidence that AIS girls have difficulty adjusting to their infertility and that surgical procedures to increase vaginal size may lead to feelings of inferiority. Effective counseling for children with such disorders, and for their parents, is extremely important (Zucker, 2002b).

DHT-Deficiency Syndromes

There are two genetic variations that can cause genetic males to lack dihydrotestosterone (DHT), a precursor of testosterone necessary for the normal development of external male sex organs in the fetus. Although his internal organs are normal, a boy with **DHT-deficiency syndrome** is born with undescended testes and an underdeveloped penis that may easily be mistaken for a clitoris. Sometimes there is also a partially formed vagina, and the scrotum may be folded in such a way that it resembles labia, but no internal female organs are present. Researchers identified 18 genetic males in the Dominican Republic who had been misassigned as females at birth and then raised as girls (Imperato-McGinley et al., 1982; Sobel & Imperato-McGinley, 2004). At puberty, these children suddenly began to develop male secondary sex characteristics, including an increase in muscle mass, deepening of the voice, and growth of the penis. They did not develop breasts or other female characteristics.

These girls-becoming-boys were subjected to a great deal of ridicule and name-calling in their communities. Sixteen of them eventually adopted male gender patterns and seemed to be sexually interested in women. It has been hypothesized that because these boys apparently had had testosterone secreted by their fetal gonads during prenatal life and only the development of their external genitals had been affected by the disorder, they were able to make the transition to a masculine gender identity and gender role more easily. In other words, whatever masculinizing effects fetal testosterone might have on brain pathways would still have taken place. Others have suggested instead

that social pressures may well have led to the more culturally acceptable choice of behaving as men.

There are two causes of DHT deficiency, both involving deficiencies of enzymes needed to synthesize DHT: 5α-reductase-2 (5α-RD-2) deficiency, in which the brain is still exposed to normal testosterone levels prenatally even though the male genitals do not develop properly, and 17β-hydroxysteroid dehydrogenase-3 (17β-HSD-3) deficiency, in which testosterone production is deficient even during fetal life. It is known that the children identified with DHT deficiency in the Dominican Republic were affected by the former deficiency, which could explain why they made the transition to masculine behavior so easily. By the prenatal brain-masculinization theory, their brains would have been exposed to testosterone during fetal life.

In the United States, children with DHT deficiency typically have been surgically transformed into girls and raised as such. One analysis of cases over time has shown that those who had the latter (17β-HSD-3) deficiency were somewhat less likely to want to change their sex back to male later in life. Again, this could be explained theoretically by the fact that their brains would not have been exposed to as much testosterone during fetal life (Cohen-Kettenis, 2005; Jurgensen, Hampel, Hiort, & Thyen, 2006).

Hormones and Behavior

The effects of fetal hormones on the human brain are only beginning to be understood. No doubt learning after birth is a crucial factor in determining much of what we define as masculine or feminine behavior, and society likely largely determines what is thought to be appropriate behavior for girls and boys. There may well be a **multiplier effect** in which biological and social-environmental factors build on one another more and more as a person grows and matures. At birth, the sexes demonstrate relatively few detectable behavioral differences. As individuals interact more with the environment, they learn certain roles; at puberty, hormonal factors again cause significant changes in sexual differentiation, magnifying female-male differences even more. It is becoming increasingly clear that the interaction of prenatal chromosomal and hormonal influences

DHT-deficiency syndrome a condition in which chromosomally male fetuses have underdeveloped male genitals and may be identified as girls at birth. However, at puberty they begin to develop masculine secondary sex characteristics and seem to maintain masculine patterns of behavior.

multiplier effect the combining of biological and socioenvironmental factors more and more with one another over time in the process of human development.

with environmental and social influences predisposes an infant to a particular type of behavior (Hines, 2004; Sanders, Sjodin, & Chastelaine, 2002).

Recent attention has focused on the significance of the hypothalamus, pituitary gland, and gonads and their interaction during various stages of development. Secretions from these organs may also influence sexual orientation and behavior. Except for reproductive behavior, no behaviors are either absolutely male or absolutely female. Although all behaviors are found in some proportion in all humans, however, the threshold for eliciting a particular behavior may be lower in either females or males. In this case, a combination of prenatal hormonal influences and environmental factors might elicit the behavior in a higher proportion of one sex than of the other.

It can be seen that prenatal factors set the stage for the development of later gender identity and gender behavior. The relationship of these prenatal factors is summarized in Figure 5.4. Let us now consider the role of social and environmental factors in determining how humans become mature women or men.

Factors of Infancy and Childhood

Sex Assignment at Birth

Except for the occasional baby born with ambiguous genitalia, there is usually no question about an infant's sex when it is born. A quick glance at the genitals determines whether the child is classified as female or male, and this is now typically known prior to the child's birth from ultrasound pictures. As soon as someone announces "It's a girl!" or "It's a boy!" the social mechanism that will help shape the individual's adult gender identity has been set into motion.

Rearing a Child as a Girl or a Boy

Most professionals believe that boys and girls are treated differently as they are raised, a phenomenon called **differential socialization.** Every society has its prescribed roles into which females and males are expected to fit, and men and women in every society tend to have fairly consistent views of what those expectations are, whether they like them or not. For example, immediately after sex assignment may follow the distinctive use of pink or blue colors, the choosing of an appropriately sexed name, and reference to the child as "he" or "she." It has also been suggested that girls tend to be treated more gently and with greater protectiveness, whereas boys are treated more roughly and encouraged to be more independent (see Figure 5.5). However, reviews of the scientific literature on differential socialization have reached different conclusions about the degree to which parents treat their daughters

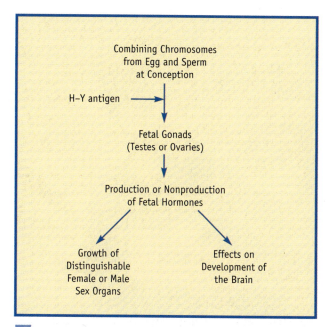

■ **FIGURE 5.4** *Gender Identity—Prenatal Factors*

This portion of a larger figure (see Figure 5.9) details the factors in the development of adult gender identity. Here are shown the prenatal biological factors involved in determining male and female sex organs.

and sons differently. Some analyses point to significant differences, while others have found only minimal evidence that parents treat boys and girls differently.

The continuing interactive influences of biology cannot be dismissed. There is evidence that the previous effects of genetics and hormones actually may predispose boys and girls toward preferences for particular kinds of toys and even colors. Interestingly, a study of nonhuman primates, vervet monkeys, found that the males preferred to play with toy cars and balls, while the females preferred picture books, stuffed animal toys, and pots and pans. This suggested to the researchers that the brain differences between males and females may have been established early in evolutionary patterns (Alexander, 2003; Alexander & Hines, 2002).

The Child's Own Body Image

As children grow older, they become further socialized into the patterns of response and behavior considered appropriate to their gender. As the child's self-awareness increases, he or she begins to respond to the influences of other people and to have a distinct self-concept that includes a sense of being a girl or a boy. The child gradually becomes aware of its body sex—its male or female sex organs—and identifies them as part of her or his

differential socialization the process of treating boys and girls differently as they are growing up.

FIGURE 5.5 *Gender Characteristics*

Although some effort has been made in recent years to change society's stereotypical view of gender roles, Western culture still tends to reinforce in children the traditional differences between boys and girls.

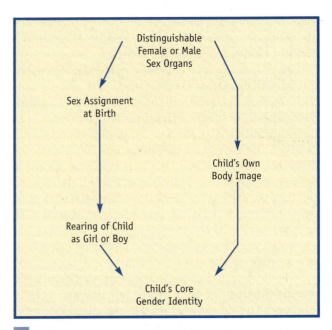

FIGURE 5.6 *Gender Identity—Factors of Infancy and Childhood*

This portion of a larger figure (see Figure 5.9) details the environmental and cultural factors that influence the development of a child's gender identity.

Hormones at Puberty

Following their secreting activities during fetal life, the testes largely cease their production of testosterone just before or just after birth. In both males and females, the onset of puberty is characterized by marked increases in various hormonal secretions once a critical level of body weight and skeletal maturation has been reached. Pubertal development involves two distinct processes. The first stage is *adrenarche,* or the secretion of androgenic hormones by the adrenal glands. This usually happens between the ages of 6 and 8. The exact role of this stage is uncertain, and the only identifiable physical result is some early growth of a small amount of pubic hair.

Adrenarche may well set the stage for the more profound stage of puberty, characterized by *gonadarche,* occurring between the ages of 9 and 13. This stage is accompanied by a series of changes affecting the hypothalamus, the pituitary gland, and the gonads. First, the hypothalamus secretes more gonadotropin-releasing hormone (GnRH). The GnRH then stimulates an increase in gonadotropin hormone from the pituitary gland, which stimulates the gonads (testes or ovaries) to secrete sex hormones (Robinson et al., 2002; Vilain, 2001). It is

sexual nature. All these factors (summarized in Figure 5.6) lead to the evolution of a child's **core gender identity.** In fact, gender identity becomes established so early that, with few exceptions, any attempt at sex reassignment (as in the case of a child erroneously assigned at birth) can be very difficult psychologically beyond the age of 18 or 20 months.

Factors at Puberty

A good deal of evidence supports the contention that even young children have romantic, sensual, and sexual feelings (see Chapter 6, "Sexuality in Infancy, Childhood, and Adolescence"). The individual's core gender identity is established during childhood. Puberty is the time when the gonads (testes or ovaries) begin producing large amounts of hormones, causing that gender identity to declare itself in bodily changes, deepened sexual feelings, and gender-related behaviors.

> **core gender identity** a child's early inner sense of its maleness, femaleness, or ambivalence, established prior to puberty.

these hormones that result in the development of secondary sex characteristics. The renewed secretion of testosterone and DHT from the testes masculinizes boys' bodies, and the ovaries begin their secretion of estrogens that feminize girls' bodies.

FOH Physical Changes during Puberty and Adolescence

After the important differentiation of male or female genitals in the fetus, relatively little further physical differentiation between the sexes occurs until puberty. Except for their genitals, the bodies of young girls and boys are quite similar. The pubertal hormones begin to generate the distinct physical characteristics of a man or a woman, called the **secondary sex characteristics.** Preliminary research has indicated that the hormonal influences of puberty may exert a clear effect on personalities, including some tendencies toward differences in females and males.

In boys, the onset of puberty typically occurs around age 13. The penis begins to enlarge, pubic hair starts to grow, and the growth spurt in height is initiated. The testes and scrotum usually have begun to enlarge about a year earlier. Eventually the voice becomes lower as the larynx grows, ejaculation of semen occurs, and pubic hair and body hair spread to some degree. A moustache and beard usually appear three to five years later. In girls, puberty typically begins around age 11 or 12. The first signs are usually the budding of the breasts, the growth of pubic hair, and the beginning of growth spurts. The first menstruation generally does not occur until after these initial signs have appeared.

Beginning at puberty, the sex glands of girls and boys actually produce the same hormones, with androgens such as testosterone being secreted in higher concentrations in males and estrogen in higher concentrations in females. In the normal male, the higher concentration of androgens and their resulting influences tend to override the effects of the estrogens. This effect is reversed in the normal female. These hormone balances can be temporarily disrupted during puberty and adolescence, producing conditions such as slight breast enlargement in males (gynecomastia) or a deepened voice and an unusually enlarged clitoris in the female. The onset of hormonal puberty can sometimes be either premature or delayed. Any of these conditions can shake the stability of a young person's gender identity and lead to confusion and unhappiness.

Changes in Sexual Drive and Behavior at Puberty

Of particular significance during puberty and adolescence is an increase in interest in sexual behavior. One important way gender identity is confirmed during this

FIGURE 5.7 *Sex Drive in Adolescents*
Adolescents experience the sex drive in different degrees depending on physical as well as emotional factors. Their families, religious background, peers, and the media all influence how adolescents learn to deal with love and the sex drive.

period is through imagery and fantasy. Boys and girls begin to imagine sexual acts and to fantasize about desirable romantic or sexual partners. Adolescents are sometimes upset to find themselves imagining or dreaming about sexual encounters with members of their own gender, sadistic behavior, or other behaviors they may have learned to consider "abnormal" or inconsistent with their assumed sexual orientation. Yet such fantasies may signal some of the final alterations that will be made in their achievement of an adult gender identity and sexual orientation.

Think back to when you went through puberty. Can you remember how you felt about yourself? About the other gender? Explain.

There is great variation in the strength of sexual interest that develops during adolescence (see Figure 5.7). Some youngsters experience frequent fantasies about sex and a strong drive that demands to be put into action. Other adolescents display little interest in sex. In either case, the level of strength of sexual interest may be subject to change in later life. The factors that determine the strength of the sex drive are not known. The levels of sex hormones, particularly testosterone, in the blood may exert some effect, but research into that possibility is incomplete.

The amount of experience with sex and romance gained during adolescence is affected by factors such as social class, degree of interest in sex, peer group

secondary sex characteristics the physical characteristics of mature women and men that begin to develop at puberty.

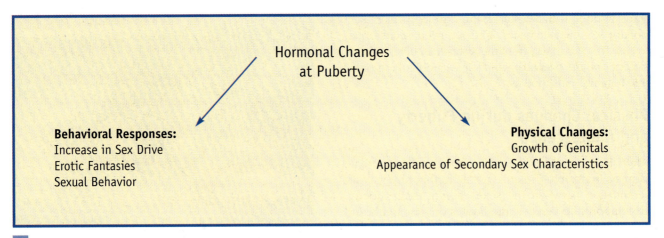

■ **FIGURE 5.8** *Gender Identity—Factors of Puberty*

This diagram details the elements that confirm gender identity in the adolescent. The increase in hormone production produces mature male and female physical characteristics as well as heightened interest in sexual fantasies and sexual behavior.

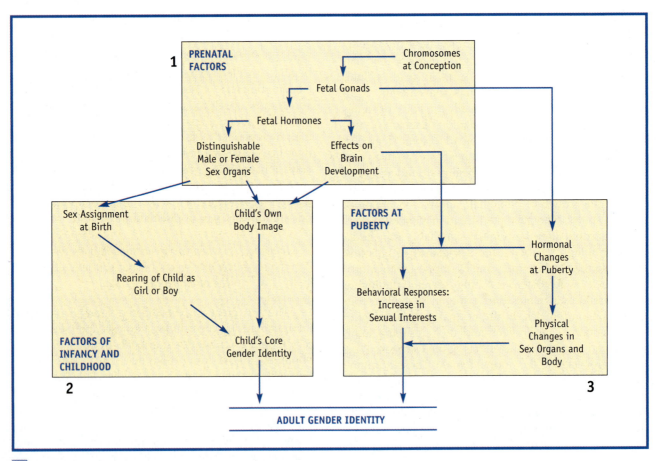

■ **FIGURE 5.9** *Gender Identity—Adult*

This figure integrates the three stages of gender identity and summarizes the prenatal factors (1), factors of infancy and childhood (2), and factors at puberty (3) that influence the development of a mature adult gender identity.

attitudes, religious background, parental influences, and exposure to the media. The newly experienced factors of puberty interact to reestablish firmly the core gender identity established in childhood (see Figure 5.8). There may be a few alterations as time goes on, but the fundamental patterns apparently are unalterable.

Adult Gender Identity and Role

At this point, we can give a general outline of sequences believed to be involved in the establishment of gender identity from conception to adulthood. An overall summary is presented in Figure 5.9. Adult gender identity and gender role usually become distinguishable as more masculine for males and more feminine for females. There may be elements of the masculine and elements of the feminine in all of us, even though our predominant identity leans more toward one or the other. Differences in behavior between males and females therefore are largely quantitative, meaning that they differ mostly in the frequency with which a particular individual exhibits particular behaviors (Hines, 2004; Sanders, Sjodin, & Chastelaine, 2002). It should also be understood that many of what are considered to be appropriate masculine and feminine traits are determined by society and culture.

■ Interpretations of Gender

As we move from the complexities of biology to other factors involved in developing gender identity, we begin to see how many different interactions come into play. At the social and cultural levels, dividing people into two distinct groups based on their gender be-

comes far more complicated. Individuals must sort through the standards and scripts for behavior that their society has identified as "feminine" or "masculine," struggling to live up to the expectations of others while feeling comfortable with themselves. Masculinity and femininity are expressed in clothing styles, ways of walking and talking, mannerisms, hobbies, and all sorts of behaviors. Subsequent parts of this chapter will examine the complex shades of gender roles and the implications they have for individual human beings and the societies in which they live.

Models of Masculinity and Femininity

The simplest model used to conceptualize gender roles is to see "totally masculine" and "totally feminine" as two extremes at opposite poles of a continuum. See Figure 5.10 for a way to visualize this two-pole, or bipolar, model. The assumption implied by this model is that the more frequent or strong a person's masculine behaviors are, the less frequent and strong that individual's feminine behaviors will be, and vice versa.

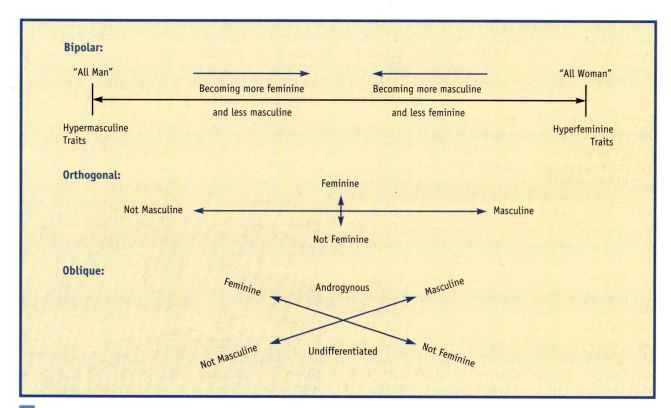

FIGURE 5.10 *Models of Masculinity and Femininity*

The definition of masculine or feminine behavior is based primarily on environmental influences and cultural expectations. The bipolar model assumes a continuum, with increased frequency of traits toward one pole resulting in a decreased frequency of traits from the other pole. The orthogonal model assumes masculinity and femininity to be completely independent traits. The oblique model assumes them to be semi-independent. In the orthogonal and oblique models, human beings are assumed to be able to have varying levels of both masculine and feminine traits (modified after Reinisch & Sanders, 1992).

In other words, the more feminine a person is, the less masculine the person will be.

Other conceptualizations of femininity and masculinity suggest, instead, that the two qualities actually are more independent of each other than the bipolar model suggests. These models propose that some people show high frequencies of both masculine and feminine behaviors. The presence of these high levels in a single individual is called **androgyny,** from the Greek roots *andro,* meaning "male," and *gyn,* meaning "female." Conversely, some people could demonstrate low levels of both behaviors, therefore being relatively undifferentiated in terms of gender. Finally, what would be more typical of human beings is a higher level of one set of behaviors and a lower level of the other, so that the individual would be considered either more masculine or more feminine. The *orthogonal model* assumes complete independence of masculinity and femininity. The *oblique model* assumes that, at least to some degree, the more masculine people are, the less feminine they tend to be, and the more feminine, the less masculine (see Figure 5.10). The models that conceptualize femininity and masculinity in this way differ only in the degree of independence they ascribe between the two factors (Reinisch & Sanders, 1992).

The research literature has included descriptions of people who exaggerate the culturally accepted characteristics of masculinity or femininity. **Hypermasculinity,** sometimes called *machismo,* is a tendency to exaggerate those behaviors perceived to be manly. It takes the form of characteristics such as aggressiveness, unemotional sexual involvement, and an emphasis on defending one's honor if it seems to have been threatened. **Hyperfemininity** is characterized by greater deference to others, particularly men, more acceptance of aggressive sexual behavior from others, and traditional attitudes about the rights and roles of women in society. People who exaggerate the traits of masculinity or femininity probably are acting out some role that they have found to be important to them in the context of their society (Muehlenhard et al., 2003; Zalewski & Lloyd, 2003).

Psychologist Sandra Bem (1993) was one of the first researchers to develop a paper-and-pencil inventory to measure the degree to which people might be androgynous. She considered anyone who had both a high femininity score and a high masculinity score to be androgynous. Her study and others since have indicated that the term can be applied to about one-third of teenagers and college students. Research has suggested that androgynous people may be more adaptable and flexible and may have higher levels of ego development than those who are more polarized in their feminine or masculine traits. For example, people who behave in traditionally masculine ways are more adept at aggressive behavior and less able to share feelings and be gentle. Those who behave in a traditionally feminine manner are more comfortable with showing warmth, concern, and gentleness but less willing or able to demonstrate assertiveness or independence. Androgynous people may feel more at ease being independent and forceful—or warm, nurturing, and kind—depending on the situation and thus are more flexible in adapting to a range of situations. Bem (1993) emphasized that she believed that there are biologically based differences in behavior between males and females, and she did not recommend that societies change in an attempt to eliminate such differences. She believed that cultural restrictions on behavior should be minimal so that men and women can be free to express the full range of individual differences biology allows for both sexes.

Lessons from Transgenderism

Some individuals cross the usual boundaries that delineate "expected" gender roles for women and men and demonstrate some level of discomfort and/or nonconformity with a traditional male or female identity. **Transgenderism** may occur in varying degrees. Psychology traditionally has viewed transgenderism as a pathological state, and the professional literature continues to employ terms to identify it such as **gender identity disorder** and **gender dysphoria.** However, a sentiment is growing even in professional circles that assumptions of pathology or lack of psychological health may not be fair with regard to transgendered individuals. In fact, transgendered identities may well be shaped by the same interacting biological and environmental factors as all other gender identities (Hill, Rozanski, Carfagnini, & Willoughby, 2005; Lev, 2005).

---

androgyny (an-DROJ-a-nee) the presence of high frequencies of both masculine and feminine behaviors and traits in the same individual.

hypermasculinity a tendency to exaggerate manly behaviors; sometimes called machismo.

hyperfemininity a tendency to exaggerate characteristics typically associated with femininity.

transgenderism a crossing of traditional gender lines because of discomfort and nonconformity with gender roles generally accepted by society.

gender identity disorder the expression of gender identity in a way that is socially inconsistent with one's anatomical sex.

gender dysphoria (dis-FOR-ee-a) another term sometimes used to describe a gender identity disorder.

Although nearly everyone has elements of personality that do not quite fit into the stereotyped roles considered appropriate to their sex, some people devote substantial amounts of their time and energy to transgendered pursuits that seem to fit them more comfortably than do the more traditional gender roles. The degree of transgenderism may range from the occasional hour or vacation period during which the individual dresses and acts as a member of the "other" gender all the way to individuals who do so consistently for long periods of time, even establishing an identity to friends and coworkers as a member of that gender (Bloom, 2002). Transgender people provide us with some important lessons as they transcend our notions of the "two" sexes. We are reminded, for example, that an individual's genital organs no longer exclusively define gender. We also find a complex and not fully understood association among gender identity, social sex roles, and sexual orientation (Herman-Jeglinska, Grabowska, & Dulko, 2002; Sandfort, 2005).

People are often reluctant to accept roles that do not fit neatly into their polarized assumptions about what is behaviorally appropriate for females and males. Unfortunately, as transgendered people are identified in real life, they may be met with harsh judgment and prejudice rather than with good-humored acceptance. People often are not willing to understand those who cross the socially determined barriers related to gender. Several organizations have been formed to address the many issues relating to people who fall into sexual or gender minorities. Transgenderism may be expressed in a variety of behaviors, ranging from the "sissy" or "tomboy" behaviors of children (Bailey, Bechtold, & Berenbaum, 2002; Bockting & Ehrbar, 2005) to occasional cross-dressing to surgical and hormonal reassignment to the other sex; the latter two behaviors are explored further in Chapter 14, "The Spectrum of Human Sexual Behavior."

See "Denise Talks about Her Transsexual Experience" on SexSource Online.

Transsexualism

Transsexualism is the most extreme form of transgenderism. Transsexuals (sometimes spelled "transexuals") are anatomically normal males or females who express a strong conviction that they actually have what would collectively or culturally be considered the mind and personality of a member of the other sex. They usually are aware of these feelings at a very young age and often feel as if they have been born into the wrongly sexed body. Procedures have been developed that can be used to transform such individuals surgically and

hormonally to appear as though they are the other sex (see Chapter 14). Low-intensity transsexuals often do not have a high enough level of motivation to pursue such sex reassignment. High-intensity transsexuals, however, are quite likely to decide to change their sex both legally and anatomically.

One of the earliest instances of sex change through surgery was the case of Sophia Hedwig in Germany, who, with the help of physicians in 1882, was transformed into Herman Karl. Occasional attempts at surgically changing sex organs were made over the next 70 years, but the case that attracted the most attention was that of Christine Jorgensen, who in 1952 became a woman after having lived until that time as George Jorgensen. As a result of the ensuing publicity, her doctor was deluged with requests for sex changes, and the science of sex reassignment was off and running (Jorgensen, 2000).

At this time, the origins of transsexualism are unknown, and debate continues about the roles of nature and nurture. Some recent research has shown some anatomical brain differences in male transsexuals, suggesting that biology may play a role (Bancroft, 2002a; Schrock & Reid, 2006). There is agreement that transgender identity tends to be sensed by most individuals at a young age. It has been estimated that as many as 11,000 postoperative transsexuals reside in the United States, although the figures are uncertain and would not include those transsexuals who have not undergone sex reassignment, who certainly outnumber those who have. The total number of transsexuals in the United States and some European countries has been estimated to be 1 per 20,000 to 50,000 people over age 15. The estimates for female-to-male transsexuals have consistently been lower than those for male-to-female, at about a one to three ratio, but that may represent cultural values more than actual numbers. In Poland, for example, the ratios are reversed by almost exact proportions (Herman-Jeglinska, Grabowska, & Dulko, 2002).

Many subtleties of transgenderism have never been categorized or labeled. The most obvious conclusion is that the development of feminine and masculine traits and roles is no less complicated and no better understood than the development of other aspects of our sexuality. Figure 5.11 shows a continuum of various forms of transgenderism as they relate to masculine and feminine traits. It should be noted that a person's gender identity or gender role is not necessarily related to sexual orientation. Many male cross-dressers, sometimes called transvestites, dress in women's clothing but are heterosexual in orientation and prefer female

transsexualism a strong degree of discomfort with one's identity as male or female, characterized by feelings of being in the wrongly sexed body.

■ **FIGURE 5.11** *Gender Identity Disorders and the Masculine-Feminine Continuum*

Transgenderism is not necessarily related to sexual orientation but rather refers to an emotional or psychological attitude that both men and women may have about their own sexual nature.

sexual partners. Some transsexuals have chosen to be surgically changed to the other sex so they can be gay or lesbian and thus interact sexually with members of the sex to which they have been reassigned (Schrock & Reid, 2006).

Biological and Evolutionary Foundations of Gender Roles

Social psychologists and anthropologists have suggested that social behavior, including gender roles, is shaped largely by social and cultural influences. Evolutionary psychologists, who bring genetic and biological perspectives to the debate, believe that there actually may be some discernible behavioral differences between males and females. They cite the research that suggests that across cultures of the world men tend to be more aggressive and competitive, whereas women tend to be less aggressive and less concerned with establishing dominant positions in the social hierarchy. They also have theorized that the human animal has an innate drive to reproduce the species and that males therefore are more prone to seek sexual activity with many different partners, whereas females are more inclined to find stable partners who will provide a comfortable environment for raising children. This view hypothesizes that gender roles are part of the broad evolutionary scheme designed to promote survival of the human species (Alexander, 2003; Marshall, 2003; Okami & Shackelford, 2002).

Naturally, the views of evolutionary psychologists are not particularly popular with those who think the theories are being used to perpetuate unfair gender stereotypes that create negative consequences for a segment of the population. It has been suggested, for example, that gender differences in aggression do not exist in actuality but rather reflect the assumptions under which researchers design their studies. However, evolutionary psychologists claim that if their theories are accurate, they simply represent confirmation of the fact that biology and culture interact in complex ways

to influence gender roles. They point out that the theories do not necessarily place females at a disadvantage, because a major driving force behind gender differences is that men are trying to attract women to fulfill their evolutionary imperatives. Evolutionary theory should be seen as one approach to understanding how gender differences might have come about and not as a mandate for how things ought to be (Okami & Shackelford, 2002).

Differences and Similarities between Females and Males

There are few qualitative differences between females and males that represent the exclusive domain of one sex or the other. A few physiological male-female characteristics or functions, however, cannot be changed on any large scale by culture: Females menstruate, bear children, and produce milk from their mammary glands; males ejaculate semen. The differences in sex organs, their roles in reproduction, and—to a lesser degree—differences in secondary sex characteristics usually are easily distinguishable. Beyond these basic qualitative differences, there is little evidence to suggest that many inborn characteristics can be identified as distinctly female or male.

In 1898, Charlotte Williams wrote, "There is no female mind. The brain is not an organ of sex. As well speak of the female liver." Nearly a hundred years later, psychiatrist and researcher Ellen Leibenluft (1996) reminded us that there are indeed differences in the ways male and female livers metabolize substances as well as differences in the frequencies and effects of various mental illnesses in women and men. Until recently, women often were not included in medical research. Because they have now been studied in greater numbers, it is becoming clear that the female body, its reactions to disease, and the ways in which those diseases should be treated really are quite different from the situation for males. Gender differences should never be used to justify gender inequalities, but to deny that those differences exist or to fail to study them entails risks for everyone. There is evidence that at least some measurable differences exist between the sexes.

There has been a degree of fascination among psychologists regarding the differences between males and females with respect to behaviors, personality, and abilities, sometimes called the *gender differences hypothesis.* A recent meta-analysis of 46 studies led the researcher to conclude that the emphasis on differences may well reside in the context of former research and unjustified assumptions. She concluded from her work that we might better think in terms of a *gender similarities hypothesis,* because she found far more similarities than differences between the sexes (Hyde, 2005).

Research has found evidence of small average differences between human males and females in a few cognitive and motor functions. It is crucial to note that any differences that have been identified are true only as statistical generalizations; they do not apply to *all* women or *all* men. Females, on average, tend to perform at higher levels on tests of verbal fluency, spelling, writing, reading speed and comprehension, understanding of social interactions and emotional information, identification of matching items (perceptual speed), fine-motor skills such as placing pegs in holes on a board, arithmetic calculation, and associative memory. Males perform at higher average levels on tests of field independence (being able to perceive underlying spatial relations in an otherwise confusing context), mathematical reasoning, science, comprehension of spatial relations, target-directed motor skills (referring to the guiding or intercepting of projectiles), and stereotypically male vocational aptitudes such as mechanical

reasoning, electronics information, and auto and shop information (Hyde, 2005; Kimura, 1999). This information is summarized in Table 5.3.

It has been generally accepted that the two cerebral hemispheres of the human brain may be responsible for different functions. There is evidence that the cerebral hemispheres of females and males may be specialized in differing ways for cognitive processing. Males apparently are more lateralized, meaning that they tend to localize particular brain functions in one cerebral hemisphere over the other. This might help explain their greater focus on mechanical aptitudes and understanding of spatial relationships and mathematical reasoning, for example. Females seem to have more interaction between their cerebral hemispheres rather than having functions confined to one hemisphere or the other. This might well allow them a wider range of experience in their mental tasks and may help explain their greater ability to understand and process emotional content and to write well.

■ Theories of Gender Role Development

A substantial part of establishing masculine and feminine gender roles probably results from a learning process—socialization as girls and boys, women and men. As children grow up, they learn to label themselves in various ways and to recognize the attributes, attitudes, and behaviors considered socially appropriate for each sex. Boys and girls tend to indicate a preference for toys that are typical for their genders, but

Table 5.3 *Comparison of Average Performance of Females and Males in Tests of Various Abilities*

Tests Exhibiting Higher Average Female Performance	Tests Exhibiting Equal Average Performance	Tests Exhibiting Higher Average Male Performance
Verbal fluency	Vocabulary	Field independence
Spelling and writing	Ability to reorganize an object from parts	Mathematical reasoning
Reading speed and comprehension	Verbal reasoning	Science
Social comprehension; understanding emotional information	Verbal IQ	Comprehension of spatial reasoning
Identifying matched items (perceptual speed)	Performance IQ	Target-directed motor skills (guiding or intercepting projectiles)
Fine-motor skills		Mechanical reasoning
Arithmetic calculation		Electronics information
Associative memory		Auto and shop information

Sources: From J. Levy and W. Heller, "Gender Differences in Human Neuropsychological Functions," in A. A. Gerall, H. Moltz, and I. L. Ward (Eds.), *Handbook of Behavioral Neurobiology,* Vol. 11, *Sexual Differentiation,* New York: Plenum Press, 1992; D. Kimura, "Sex Differences in the Brain," *Scientific American,* Vol. 267 (3), pp. 119–25; and L. V. Hedges and A. Nowell, "Sex Differences in Mental Test Scores, Variability, and Numbers of High Scoring Individuals" in *Science,* Vol. 269, 1995, pp. 41–45.

some built-in tendencies in addition to learned behaviors might cause this to happen (Alexander, 2003). The learning of gender roles takes place early in life at home, in school, and in play activities. Again, there are differing theoretical positions on how gender roles develop. A summary of these theories follows.

Psychodynamic Perspectives

Psychoanalytic tradition, founded by Sigmund Freud, has gradually evolved into what is now known as the psychodynamic approach. Largely a theoretical perspective on how the human mind works, it has not been subjected to rigorous scientific verification. Modern psychodynamic theory, modeled after earlier Freudian thought, holds that there are three phases of early gender development. Children are first unaware of differences between the sexes. Then, around the age of 2 years, they begin to realize that girls and boys are different. Freud suggested that children tend to attribute superior power and value to the male genitals. He also believed that girls then feel inadequate and experience "penis envy," whereas boys fear that they will lose their genitals and therefore have to cope with castration anxieties (Harding, 2001). In the third phase of gender differentiation in this model, children must work out the implications of their gender in their relationships with the significant men and women in their lives. The contemporary psychodynamic model holds that in this stage children see their parents in terms of gender and tend to relate more with their fathers. For a time, boys are thought to be in a competitive relationship for the affection of their mothers—the Freudian concept of Oedipal wishes—but then give up and take their place as males in their society. Girls are said to have the secret hope that their fathers will give them a penis—the Freudian concept of Electra complexes—but then let go of this hope and become more passive. It is by working through these dilemmas that children eventually find their pathways to masculinity and femininity, with both parents providing support and encouragement throughout the differentiation process (Bornstein & Masling, 2002).

Modern psychodynamic theorists are struggling to come up with a more balanced and workable view of gender development and tend to hold that boys and girls have relatively similar tasks to perform in learning the roles that fit their gender (Harding, 2001). Today, the psychodynamic model of gender role development does not receive wide acceptance.

Social Learning Theory

This popular model was one of the first to propose that gender roles are perpetuated by each culture, learned by children as they are socialized by their parents, peers, and others through observation, imitation, and instruction. It is assumed that this process is continuous and lifelong and that it can be affected by many particular circumstances of an individual's family and personal history. Early proponents of social learning theory tended to portray children as passive recipients of their culture's assumptions concerning gender, imitating or "modeling" the behavior of those around them of the same sex. Modern theorists, however, have emphasized that children themselves play active roles in this dynamic process, helping to shape it in part themselves (Boyle, Marshall, & Robeson, 2003). Research demonstrates as well that children do not simply model their gender behaviors after any one individual but instead respond differently to different people in their lives. Gender is recognized as not being a particularly reliable predictor of behavior because the process is so individualized for each child.

The gender role orientation of parents seems to have some effect on their children's perceptions of themselves, and early interactions with parents probably reinforce social expectations about feminine or masculine behavior. Social learning theory was a precursor to the social constructionist model of gender, which maintains that gender identity is at least partly the result of social and environmental factors. It also provides ammunition to those who feel that expectations of traditional gender roles have been detrimental to women because it demonstrates how prejudice, stereotypes, and discriminatory behavior originate and are passed along in the socialization process (Coy & Kovacs-Long, 2005). This model has largely ignored potential biological influences on gender role except to suggest that the behaviors and values promoted by a culture for a particular gender might in fact be those that are most easily established from a biological standpoint. Subsequent theories have become increasingly comprehensive.

Cognitive-Developmental Theory

Cognitive-developmental theory expanded the fundamental understanding of social learning theory. This theory holds that human thought processes serve to support and reinforce the beliefs about gender that are created by society. It recognizes gender as a basic characteristic used to understand one's social environment and interact with it. The child categorizes itself as girl or boy relatively early in its life through comparison and develops masculine or feminine values out of the need to value those things that are consistent with or like itself. Then the child tends to identify with the same-sex parent and deepens its attachment to the feminine or masculine model. The child also identifies gender roles by interacting with other children. A unique feature of this model is the idea that the child acquires basic male or female values on its own and then, because of its acquired desire to be feminine or masculine, identifies with a woman or a man and other girls or boys as models.

Research shows that children do tend to engage in behavior considered appropriate for their gender at relatively young ages and that by the time they are about 4 years old they tend to regulate their own behaviors, knowing they will feel a sense of self-approval by behaving in a manner consistent with their gender and will feel self-disapproval if they do not. In a sense, children seem to develop a self-sanctioning system about their gender-linked behavior (Bussey & Bandura, 1992).

Critics of the cognitive-developmental model argue that the behavior observed in children as they interact with their peers is merely a reflection of social learning from families and the larger culture. Proponents of the theory counter that it is in the peer group that attitudes toward the opposite gender and one's own gender are forged and that these behavioral styles then carry over into adolescence and adulthood.

Gender Schema Theory

This concept of how people come to define themselves as masculine or feminine represents a more sophisticated variant of social learning theory and cognitive-developmental theory. It emphasizes the pressures inherent in social attitudes that assume the need for differences between females and males, even in situations where sex has no particular relevance (Bem, 1987, 1993). In most cultures, maleness and femaleness are defined by a complex network or pattern of associations, ranging from anatomical differences to the sorts of work people engage in to religious symbolism. This complicated set of associations is called a **gender schema.** As people, including children, encounter their world, all new information and perceptions are filtered through the gender schema, and internal decisions are made concerning gender, self-concept, and behavior toward others. In time, everything becomes interpreted through this dualistic, male-female schema, and the individual models his or her behaviors and life choices according to those interpretations (Signorella, 1999).

Some children and adults are very "gender schematic," meaning that they rely heavily on their gender role associations, whereas others are more "gender aschematic," meaning that they pay less attention to these socially determined associations. Sandra Bem feels that many characteristics of what we have come to classify as femininity or masculinity exist only in the mind of the perceiver: "Look through the lens of gender and you perceive the world as falling into masculine and feminine categories. Put on a different pair of lenses, however, and you perceive the world as falling into other categories" (Bem, 1987, p. 309).

It has been suggested that, among children, behavioral differences between the sexes may be influenced by the ways the children are observed or tested in psychological studies. It has also been argued that so-called scientific pronouncements about gender are nothing more than biased statements about social and political roles. It is certainly true that as science examines questions of gender, political and cultural implications cannot be ignored.

Behavioral Genetics

Another body of research eventually emerged that added a biological dimension to the understanding of gender role development. Behavioral genetics emphasizes the interactive nature of both heredity and environment on childhood socialization. A fundamental assumption of behavioral genetics is that members of the same family are similar because of the genes and environmental factors they have in common. Conversely, family members are different because of the genes and environment they do not share. Studies of twins tend to conclude that personality similarities within a family are probably influenced more by genetics than by environment. The same seems to hold true for behaviors associated with gender. People's attitudes, however, seem to be shaped more by shared genetic and environmental factors (Hamer, 2002; Rogers, 2001).

Only too often, the biological models are used to justify social prejudice and inequity. We must be careful to weigh what research evidence means and to avoid misinterpreting or misusing it. There seems to be ample evidence that, in Western culture, gender roles often are sources of power and status and females have been disproportionately limited by their gender roles. Careful evaluation of all the knowledge we have about gender roles and how these roles develop can help correct such inequities.

Multifactorial "Web"

Some of the newest theories related to gender role continue to deemphasize the divide separating biological, social, and learning components and instead bring these factors together in a multifactorial approach. One of the best-known gender theorists of recent years, Eleanor Maccoby (1998), believes along with others that boys and girls grow up in what might be considered

gender schema a complex cognitive network of associations and ideas through which the individual perceives and interprets information about gender.

two distinct subcultures, each characterized by different sets of expectations and behaviors. Boys' playgroups much more resemble rough-and-tumble hierarchies, whereas girls' groups focus more on maintaining relationships and mutuality. These groups become the foundation of gender identity and role. However, Maccoby believes that it is the biological component, built in at birth, that predisposes boys and girls to different rates of maturation and particular kinds of behavior.

Girls seem to regulate their own behavior much earlier than do boys, and this self-regulation leads to all sorts of activities that please parents and other adults. Boys' greater lack of self-control leads to more disciplinary commands and directions from others. This is where the biological predispositions become influenced by socialization components. This complex "explanatory web" that lies at the root of gender roles is molded by the interactions of many different factors (Lippa, 2002b).

Although some social psychologists once believed that we should work toward a gender-aschematic world in which there would be no differentiation between male and female roles, this goal no longer seems as plausible or desirable as it once did to some. Instead, there is now more emphasis on the celebration of gender differences and efforts toward increased understanding between the sexes (see Figure 5.12).

■ Gender in Society and Culture

As a basic organizing principle of human culture, maleness and femaleness, femininity and masculinity, are central themes in all social structures. Viewed against a backdrop of variations in many aspects of human personality, gender differences may not be as dramatic or significant as often thought. Nevertheless, they influence how people think, believe, and behave.

Growing Up Female and Male

The prevailing opinion in North America has been that social attitudes put females at a disadvantage in many different ways. There is evidence to support this perception. One contention has been that our society permits a wider range of behaviors for girls, from the very frilly to the tomboy, while for boys neither the extreme of the sissy nor the too aggressive bully is acceptable. This has been substantiated by studies indicating that, among younger children, boys tend to see their gender roles and future occupational options much more narrowly than do girls (Sellers, Satcher, & Comas, 1999). For these reasons, parents and other adults typically are less disturbed by the behavior of girls than by that of boys, with the result that more demands are placed on boys to behave appropriately. This may well result in boys being pressured to become more independent and self-controlled, and in fact some studies show males' self-esteem arising from recognition of their individual distinguishing achievements (Major et al., 1999). Early in their lives, boys develop a sense of self-worth that is relatively independent of others' responses. At the same time, female roles are devalued, and boys are criticized for stepping out of their role boundaries by being called "girls" or "sissies" in a derogatory way. As boys grow into adolescence and adulthood, they face harsher consequences for stepping outside the gender-appropriate roles established for them than do girls and women (Carlock, 1999; Sommers, 2000).

Girls, on the other hand, are not as pressured to become independent and self-controlling and therefore remain more dependent on others for physical comfort and a sense of self-worth, often experiencing no strong pressures until puberty. As children, girls are rewarded for their compliant good behavior by receiving good grades, parental love, teacher acceptance, and acceptance into peer groups, leaving them generally more passive and conformist. During adolescence, boys tend to turn their aggressions outward, whereas girls tend to turn these impulses inward—often against themselves—resulting in lowered self-esteem.

Much of the groundwork for whatever gender discrepancies exist later in life is probably laid in the educational institutions that prepare young people for the future, as well as on their playgrounds (Boyle, Marshall, & Robeson, 2003). Schools often seem to provide a different environment for girls than they do for boys. There is evidence that even among young children, boys interrupt teachers in their activities much more than do girls, whereas teachers tend to interrupt girls more than they do boys. Later on, girls in general, and especially black girls, receive significantly

FIGURE 5.12 Many people enjoy pursuing interests that cross over traditional boundaries of gender-stereotypical behaviors.

less attention from and interaction with their teachers than do boys. This manifests itself in the fact that in the early grades girls tend to be equal to, or ahead of, boys on nearly every standardized test, but by high school they tend to fall behind boys on college entrance exams, particularly in mathematics and science (Major et al., 1999; Wilson, R., 2004a). Girls who are athletic and want to pursue sports often have to contend with stereotypes about their being "masculine" or gay, whereas boys are encouraged toward athleticism (Bolin & Granskog, 2003; Malcom, 2003; Shakib, 2003).

Even well-meaning teachers often seem susceptible to gender stereotypes, such as that girls should be quiet listeners in the classroom. Boys tend to be given more esteem-building encouragement than girls. Also, girls are subject to many more forms of sexual harassment in schools that are apt to make school seem a hostile environment for them. Clearly, work remains to be done to ensure that young women and men have an equal chance to get a wide-ranging education in a supportive environment, which in turn will offer them the levels of skill, self-esteem, and confidence necessary to be happy and successful in the work force (AAUW, 1992; Hamson, 2004; Timreck, 2004).

In the mid-1980s, Carol Gilligan and her research team began to study girls ages 6 through 18 over a five-year period. They found that young girls seem to feel very good about themselves and to care deeply for others. Up until about age 11, girls are assertive, speak about their feelings, and accept conflict as a natural part of healthy relationships. During adolescence, however, they are much more hesitant to express their feelings, fearing that they will anger others. These researchers concluded that adolescence tends to be a time of repression for girls. Some girls resist the repression by becoming rebels, whereas others become extremely cautious about what they will say publicly. Often, they resort to "I don't know" as a safe response. They typically do not want to be perceived as "brains" (Carlock, 1999).

A study sponsored by the American Association of University Women (AAUW, 1992, 1993) seemed to reinforce this perception of how girls and boys grow up. Three thousand students in grades 4 through 10 were surveyed in 12 locations throughout the United States. Up to 70 percent of both the boys and the girls at age 9 tended to reflect positive attitudes toward themselves and a willingness to be assertive as needed. The researchers developed a self-esteem index from the questions they asked the children. By age 16, only 29 percent of high school girls indicated that they were happy with themselves, whereas 46 percent of boys retained a sense of self-confidence. Interestingly, the drop in self-esteem was particularly prevalent among white and Hispanic girls. Black girls tended to be better able to maintain their self-esteem during adoles-

cence. In the study, girls who had difficulty with particular academic subjects tended to blame themselves and to assume that they were not competent to do the work. Boys, on the other hand, were more likely to blame the course's subject matter than themselves. During adolescence, girls exhibited a greater concern about appearance and body image than did boys.

Did you ever fall prey to or observe gender stereotyping in the classroom? Explain the circumstance and how you reacted to it.

Gender in the Workplace

Masculinity once was the societal yardstick against which everything was measured. The characteristics traditionally attributed to men were seen as more desirable than those attributed to women. Therefore, women sometimes internalized self-destructive, demoralizing values about their own worth in comparison to that of men. Female employees who exhibited more traditionally masculine characteristics were once considered more promotable than those who showed more feminine traits, depending on cultural contexts. There is growing evidence that women, and "feminine" qualities, are being perceived more positively. Organizational theory is moving away from the devaluation of women's work and the emphasis on masculine organizational structure toward less gender-segregated models (Martin & Collinson, 1999).

Although many institutions and employers are trying to create equal employment opportunities for women, there are still some discrepancies in how women and men fare in their jobs. The possibilities for promotion sometimes are greater for men than for women. Parenting and household responsibilities still often fall to women and may limit the time and energy available for their careers. There are also signs of change, however. Among married couples who both work, over 30 percent of the wives earn more money than their husbands. Also, in increasing numbers of families the woman is the primary breadwinner, while the man stays home to take care of household responsibilities and children (Tyre & McGinn, 2003).

Linguistic researcher Deborah Tannen (1994) believes that the communication styles of women sometimes put them at a disadvantage in more traditional work environments. Women tend to be consensus builders, wanting to solicit the opinions of many others. Male supervisors, who tend toward more aggressive, opinionated styles, may see this as indecisiveness. However, there is evidence that the power and influence of women in the workplace have been increasing dramatically. Many businesses seem to be recognizing the talents of women as communicators, negotiators, and networkers.

Academia is often assumed to be a more open environment for female success, but in fact women faculty often have felt marginalized in colleges and universities (Lawler, 2006). Women tend to be underrepresented on the science and mathematics faculties of major research institutions (see Figure 5.13). While women are not being attracted to the quantitative science and engineering fields to the extent that men are, the proportion of women in those fields has increased by as much as 100 percent over the past two decades. The reasons why girls and women pursue the quantitative fields in fewer numbers than do boys and men seem to be very complex and are not explainable by any single factor (Xie & Shauman, 2003). The biological and social sciences, however, continue to attract women (Handelsman et al., 2005). The social science fields have seen a reduction in the numbers of males, a phenomenon sometimes called "male flight." Since the 1970s, the percentage of women receiving law degrees has been steadily increasing, and the number of businesses owned by women has skyrocketed from less than half a million to about 8 million. The year 2002 represented the first time in history that American women earned more doctoral degrees than American men at U.S. universities (Smallwood, 2003) (see Figure 5.13).

Evidence also shows that women scientists in more advanced, industrialized countries have found it difficult to overcome entrenched systems that seem to favor men (Lawler, 2006). In developing countries, however, science and technology have emerged more

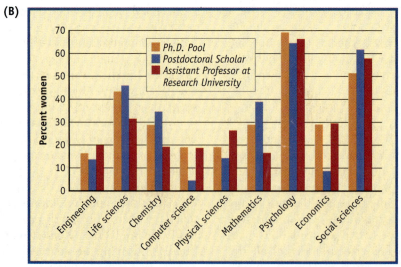

FIGURE 5.13   *Women in Higher Education*

(A) In 2002, for the first time, more American women than men earned doctorates at U.S. universities. The number of American men receiving doctorates has fallen by nearly 15 percent in the past five years. **(B)** As of 2006, women scientists in entry-level academic jobs were still fewer than those in the humanities and social sciences.

Sources: (a) From *The Chronicle of Higher Education*, 12 December 2003, p. A10. Copyright © 2003, The Chronicle of Higher Education. Reprinted with permission. (b) *Science*, Vol. 312, 22 September 2006, p. 1712.

FIGURE 5.14 *U.S. Women Making Progress*

Ruth J. Simmons (left) has been president of both Smith College and Brown University. Carly Fiorina (right), former CEO of Hewlett-Packard Co., rings a bell to open the New York Stock Exchange from her company's headquarters in California.

recently as fields of employment, concurrent with the furthering of women's rights. Scientific research and development typically have not been as connected to industrial economies in these countries, so science is often a low-status, low-paying career. These conditions have made scientific careers more open to women in developing countries (Xie & Shauman, 2003).

Feminism

Within both developing and industrialized societies, there continues to be oppression of women and a marked inequality between women and men that fosters the subservience and secondary status of women. Women themselves often recognize the existence of inequality but choose not to try to correct it because they have learned to be less confrontational and more conciliatory. Instead, they often attempt to compete as individuals, playing by rules that often have been established by and for men (see Figure 5.14).

Feminists are women and men who reject prejudices that imply any inferiority of either gender and are working together to achieve equality. In using the word *equality,* they are not implying that women and men are the same, but rather are stating that women and men deserve equal opportunities and rights. The media have made much of some younger women who

have been dubbed "do me feminists." These are women who do not have as much interest in social or political action and do not particularly admire strong, career-woman role models but are in control of their own desires, know what they want, and go after it. Sexually, they want to feel free to make their own choices. Some commentators insist that such women are not feminists but simply have been caught in stereotyped roles and want to justify them. Others contend that feminists want to avoid compartmentalizing people by narrowly defined characteristics and instead seek to encourage members of both sexes to be comfortable in whatever roles they choose (Chung, 2005).

There have been several waves of feminist activity throughout American history (see Figure 5.15). The first major public outcry for women's rights came in 1848 when Elizabeth Cady Stanton, Susan B. Anthony, and several other women wrote their "Declaration of Sentiments" and presented it at the first U.S. women's rights convention, held in Seneca Falls, New York. As the move to abolish slavery grew in the nineteenth century, women likened their position to that of slaves and began to fight for their own rights. After women gained the right to vote in 1920, the movement subsided somewhat until the mid-1960s. Then, due partly to the atmosphere of protest occasioned by the Vietnam War and partly to a new awareness of inequality in society

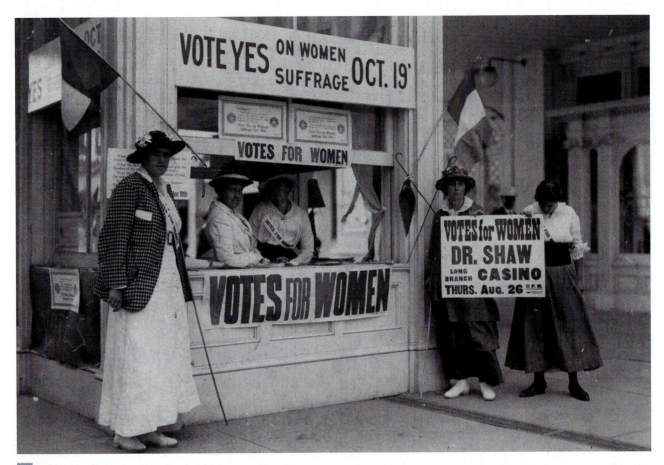

■ FIGURE 5.15 *Active Feminists*

Early feminists campaigning for suffrage were in for a hard fight, but in 1920 they won the right to vote with passage of the Nineteenth Amendment. The size of the eligible voting population nearly doubled, but not until the latter half of the 1900s did the turnout of women at the polls reach the level of male turnout.

that was fueled by mass-media communication, the modern feminist movement gained momentum (Kees, 2005). Terms such as "women's liberation" and "sexism" became part of everyone's vocabulary.

Some people developed an inaccurate image of feminists as bra-burning women who picketed against sexist issues and hated men. In fact, feminists are working to reduce inequality between the sexes. The proportion of women willing to call themselves "feminists" has declined significantly, and the proportion of women who do not consider themselves feminists has risen. Yet it also seems clear that most women recognize and appreciate the many opportunities for greater equality that the most recent feminist movement has created for them (Kees, 2005).

Contemporary feminist thought has led to a renewed awareness that women can be equal participants in sexual activity as well as in other aspects of human life. Traditional stereotypes held that women were less interested in sex and less easily aroused than men. Thus, men were expected to be the primary initiators of sex, wooing and seducing their female partners until they finally gave in. Modern feminism has raised our consciousness about female sexuality, showing that women want to enjoy and be full participants in sex. It has become clear that women can desire sexual intimacy in all its dimensions, and it has become more socially permissible for them to initiate sexual encounters. Sex is no longer something to which women are expected to submit to fulfill their obligation to a male partner (see Figure 5.16). Instead, it is seen as part of the human experience that can be negotiated, discussed, and actively enjoyed by both women and men if and when they so choose.

Do you consider yourself a feminist? Are you uncomfortable with the term? Explain.

Asserting Masculinity

The women's movement raised our consciousness about the ways women in our society often have been victims of injustice and discrimination. Yet it also

Real Student Voices

■ I was brought up in a very feminist household, and encouraged to make my way in the world as an equal of men. I've succeeded for the most part, but I still find it frustrating that there are so few women in my field. It gets lonely.

■ I can't stand women who call themselves feminists. They seem to think they're above other people, and don't have any sense of humor. I just want to tell them to loosen up and have some fun. Men aren't so bad—they ought to give us a try.

brought into focus the fact that men too have been trapped in certain roles and stereotypes. Boys and men often are caught in a vicious circle of proving their strength, invulnerability, and effectiveness as providers yet because of social attitudes are also taught to be dependent on women—first their mothers, then often their romantic partners (Pascoe, 2003; Sommers, 2000). Although women have felt resentment about being treated as sex objects, men sometimes have suffered from being treated as success objects expected to provide status and security for their partners. Many male providers end up feeling powerless, meaningless, and isolated in their jobs, working under constant fear and tension as they strive for promotion and success. Three main aspects of the traditional male role seem especially to make men uncomfortable: (1) the male as competent worker and provider, (2) the male as emotionally controlled and stoic, and (3) the male as sexual aggressor and sexual educator of the female (Marsiglio, 2003).

There has been a growing men's movement in North America, although it has taken multiple and sometimes contrasting directions. Men's groups have sprung up around the country, and men are being encouraged to confront and share their feelings more openly. Many men feel able to celebrate their own masculinity in ways that once would have been considered unmanly. Having

opportunities to talk about gender roles and reassess individual needs and goals continues to prove valuable for men in different age groups (Marsiglio, 2003). Some men have taken pride in their softer sides and have enjoyed dressing well as "metrosexuals," while others have rejected this direction, instead reaffirming the "retrosexual" male stereotype of dressing and eating as they please and being preoccupied with sports (Neal, 2004).

What do you see as some of the positive and negative features of the men's movement? Explain.

There has been some finger pointing between members of the women's movement and members of the men's movement. Increasingly, men are resisting being blamed individually for the inequities between the genders and are calling for a more balanced view of the social picture. They are tired of being the scapegoats for social constructs that they too were born into and that they often have felt little control over. They do not believe that it is fair to brand all men as potential rapists or abusers, insisting instead that most men are decent individuals who want to treat women with respect and care. Many men have participated actively in efforts to create a more gender-equitable and safe society for everyone (Boyd, 2004).

■ **FIGURE 5.16** *Feminism Then and Now*

Some observers believe that feminist influence on popular culture has evolved in the past 30 years from being intellectually provocative, as personified by Gloria Steinem's activism of the 1970s (left), to today's emphasis on stylish fluff and sexy game playing, as typified by the cast of television's *Desperate Housewives* (right).

Most men experience some turmoil and problems as they come to grips with what manhood will mean for them. Men share in the constant struggle to learn how to communicate thoughts, feelings, and the degree of exclusivity they want to maintain in relationships. Emerging out of what once seemed more like a battle between women and men is a new spirit of cooperation. Members of both sexes have called for opportunities to communicate more openly about differences and to make recommendations for more equitable partnerships between men and women.

Gender across Cultures

Gender roles are an integral part of any society. These roles tend to be incorporated by the children of the society into their own formation of ideas and behaviors concerning gender (Aydt & Corsaro, 2003). They reflect the population's attitudes and values toward women and men and often affect individual behaviors and relationships. Ethnographic data from 93 nonindustrial societies show that the gender roles associated with raising children and control of property are closely associated with the degree to which men display dominance in each society. In societies in which men maintain close relationships with children and in which women have a significant amount of control over property, the men are much less likely to affirm their masculinity through boastfulness, aggressiveness, or high levels of sexual activity. The women in such societies tend to be less deferential to the men, and husbands are less likely to dominate their wives. Conversely, in those societies in which men are less involved with children and have more control over property, demonstrations of strength, aggression, sexual prowess, and male dominance in relationships are more likely (Chung, 2005; Yakushko & Chronister, 2005).

In reviewing the literature on perceptions of gender across various cultures, it becomes clear that gender roles can be heavily influenced by cultural values. In the early 1980s, a study was published that compared how various countries valued traditional masculine qualities in the workplace (Hofstede, 1998). This research used various scales of work-related values to assign a masculinity index (MAS) to 40 countries that were being studied. This index measured the degree to which people of both sexes tended to endorse goals that were usually more popular among males. Some countries emerged with a high MAS, including Japan, Austria, Venezuela, Italy, and Switzerland. Others had a low MAS, such as Sweden, Norway, the Netherlands, Denmark, and Finland. When these results were compared with other research findings concerning attitudes, beliefs, and social roles, some interesting findings emerged about work-related values. As Table 5.4 shows, in countries with a low MAS, work had a less central and stress-

Table 5.4	*Summary of Connotations of Masculinity Index (MAS) Differences across Cultures*
Countries with Low MAS	**Countries with High MAS**
Managers relatively less interested in leadership, independence, and self-realization.	Managers have leadership, independence, and self-realization ideal.
Belief in group decisions.	Belief in the independent decision maker.
Weaker achievement motivation.	Stronger achievement motivation.
Achievement defined in terms of human contacts and living environment.	Achievement defined in terms of recognition and wealth.
Work less central in people's lives.	Greater work centrality.
People prefer shorter working hours to higher salary.	People prefer higher salary to shorter working hours.
Company's interference in private life rejected.	Company's interference in private life accepted.
Greater social role attributed to institutions other than corporation.	Greater social role attributed to corporation.
Lower job stress.	Higher job stress.
Less skepticism as to factors leading to getting ahead.	Skepticism as to factors leading to getting ahead.
Managers have more of a service ideal.	Managers relatively less attracted by service role.
Smaller or no value differences between men and women in the same jobs.	Greater value differences between men and women in the same jobs.
Sex-role equity in children's books.	More sex-role differentiation in children's books.

Real People

Ricardo Expresses His Attitudes about "Male Bashing"

During a discussion group following a lecture on male-female relationships on campus, Ricardo voiced his sentiments concerning what he had perceived as antimale attitudes on the part of women. "Men today could never get away with the way some women are treating men, if the situation were reversed. I resent it that men are not supposed to say or do anything that might seem like a put-down to women, but women get away with male bashing all the time. I don't like it when I see one of those shirts that says 'A woman without a man is like a fish without a bicycle.' I'm not saying that women are incomplete without men; it's just that things like that are deliberately mean. And when that woman cut off her husband's penis because she was pissed at him, a lot of women seemed to think it was just a big joke, instead of an act of violence and mutilation. Maybe she was justified to take action against him, but the result wasn't any funnier than violence toward women. I think it's time we tried to get our priorities straight."

Ricardo's remarks generated many comments and some heated exchanges among the group members. Some of the women present said that men were only getting back what they had been dishing out

for years and that they should not complain. Some women and men in the group felt Ricardo was overreacting and should try to lighten up and learn how to take a joke. Others—mostly males—agreed with his point of view and said they were tired of any trend toward antimale messages. They emphasized that it was another example of bigotry based on stereotypes. Many men made a point of saying that they themselves did not treat women in negative or inappropriate ways and resented being lumped together with those who did.

The debate went on for nearly two hours and ended with little resolution between the various factions that were represented. Ricardo left the group feeling that he had at least been able to express his opinions openly, and he hoped that some people who had heard them would try to be more sensitive to the issues that had been raised.

How do you personally react to this story? To what extent do you agree or disagree with Ricardo? Do you believe that it is more acceptable to make disparaging comments about men than it is about women? Was Ricardo being too sensitive?

ful place in people's lives. In those countries with a high MAS, work held a much higher place than family and seemed more directly connected to perceptions of personal success and power.

Cross-cultural studies have demonstrated a fair amount of agreement across cultures as to what characteristics are preferable in selecting a mate. In order of descending importance, these qualities are being kind, understanding, and intelligent; having an exciting personality; being healthy; and being religious. When it comes to issues such as virginity, however, culture plays a central role. In Eastern Europe and Southeast Asia, selecting a virgin as a wife is of great importance. In Northern European countries, virginity is seen as irrelevant or unimportant. There is also a fair amount of agreement in various cultures about those traits associated with women and with men. In a study examining gender stereotypes across 25 countries, men generally were seen as more active, strong, aggressive, and dominating, whereas women were seen as more passive,

weak, nurturing, and self-abasing (Williams & Best, 1990). Newer studies have shown these attitudes to exist in both Egypt and Turkey today (Mensch, Ibrahim, et al., 2003; Sakalh-Ugurlu & Glick, 2003).

A small island society near Papua New Guinea is sometimes cited as one of the only gender-egalitarian cultures in the world. A study of the 2,300 inhabitants of Sudest Island found truly equal participation by women and men in decision making, ritual practices, and property ownership. Both women and men seem to have the same degree of sexual freedom, and both sexes care for younger children. Their language contains no words for masculine or feminine pronouns, reflecting a much less genderized perception of the world than most other languages traditionally demonstrate. Kinship lines are traced through the mother's family. It has been suggested that Sudest Island, known by its inhabitants as "the motherland," may well represent a model of a gender-egalitarian culture (Lepowsky, 1994).

Self-Evaluation

Masculinity and Femininity in Your Life

Attitudes toward masculinity and femininity are in a state of flux. While some people are attempting to blur the stereotyped differences between men and women, others are trying harder than ever to establish definite, identifiable standards of masculinity and femininity. The exercises that follow may help you clarify your present attitudes toward men and women and your view of your own gender role.

1. **On a sheet of paper, list two men, by name, who for you exemplify ideal manhood; list two women, by name, who for you exemplify ideal womanhood. Then proceed with the following.**
   a. Under the men's names and under the women's names, list the characteristics of these people that have made them your choices as representative of the ideal.
   b. Note which of the characteristics, if any, are listed for both the men and the women.
   c. Check those characteristics from either list that you believe you exhibit.

2. **Would you ever consider dressing up in clothing generally identified as being appropriate for members of the opposite sex? If not, why not? If so, consider the following.**
   a. Under what circumstances would you wear clothing of the opposite sex: Only in private? In front of one other highly trusted person? In front of a small group of friends? At a masquerade party? In public places?
   b. If possible and if you are willing, dress up in some clothes of the opposite sex and look yourself over in a full-length mirror. (*Note:* In some areas, it is illegal to cross-dress and be seen in public.) As you look at yourself, how do you feel? Do you feel silly? Sexy? Curious? Happy? Sad? Why do you feel that way?

3. **Examine the following list of qualities and check those that you feel are most important for you to have as a person. (Add other words of your own if you wish.)**

honest	physically strong	responsible
brave	dominating	emotional
athletic	delicate	persuasive
caring	intelligent	protective
competitive	successful	shy
gentle	submissive	reliable
sensitive	manipulative	flighty
aggressive	thoughtful	sincere
considerate	confident	sexy

   a. Now read through the list of qualities again and pick out those that have traditionally been considered masculine and those that have traditionally been considered feminine. Make two separate lists on a sheet of paper. Some words may appear on both lists or on neither. Include any words you have added to the list.
   b. Finally, note where those qualities you checked for yourself fall in your two lists. Think about them. This should help you see how your goals for your own femininity or masculinity relate to traditional ideas about men and women, as you view them.

4. **This exercise should be done with a member of the other gender or with a group of people of both sexes. The men should make two lists on a sheet of paper: the advantages of being female, and the disadvantages of being female. Likewise, the women should make two lists: the advantages of being male, and the disadvantages of being male. When the lists are complete, everyone should compare them and discuss the characteristics.**

5. **As you are watching television or leafing through the pages of a magazine, note how men and women are portrayed in advertisements. Note which of the men and women appeal the most to you and which are unappealing to you, asking yourself "Why?" in each case. Especially note how women and men in the advertisements are shown in traditional or in nontraditional roles.**

6. **Think about each of the following, and attempt to get in touch with your gut reactions about how you feel. Try not to intellectualize and react in the manner in which you think you should. Instead, look carefully at how you are reacting and at what your reactions mean in terms of your attitudes toward gender roles.**
   a. An unmarried woman who wishes to be referred to as Ms.
   b. A married woman who insists on being referred to as Ms.
   c. An all-male organization that refuses to consider admitting women as members.
   d. An all-female organization that refuses to consider admitting men as members.
   e. A board of education that passes a school policy requiring that in all courses "traditional family values

are to be upheld, with the feminine role of wife, mother, and homemaker, and the masculine role of guide, protector, and provider."

f. In considering an equally qualified married man and unmarried woman for a position, a company personnel director hires the woman because the company needs to fulfill its affirmative action goals.

g. After a couple has a new baby, the mother wants to continue working, so the father decides to quit his job and stay home with the child.

Chapter Summary

1. Western culture emphasizes the existence of two sexes, while forms of intersexuality such as hermaphroditism or pseudohermaphroditism also exist. In other cultures and times of history, intersexuality (or disorders of sex development) has been accepted.

2. There has long been debate over the determination of sexual and gender traits by nature or nurture. It now seems most reasonable that gender roles are shaped by the interaction of biological and sociocultural forces.

3. Biological sex is expressed in genetics, the gonads, the body, and the brain and is modified by environmental factors.

4. The development of our gender identity and gender role is determined by a complex interaction of genetic, physiological, and sociocultural factors.

5. During prenatal life (before birth), the combining of chromosomes sets in motion a genetic program for producing a male, a female, or some ambivalent anatomical structure. Although the pairing of sex chromosomes normally is XX for females and XY for males, there can be abnormal combinations (e.g., XXX, XXY, XYY) that produce unusual characteristics.

6. After about a month of embryonic development, an undifferentiated set of fetal gonads appears, along with Müllerian ducts (potential female organs) and Wolffian ducts (potential male organs).

7. If the Y chromosome is present, with its SRY gene, H-Y antigen is produced, transforming the gonads into testes, which in turn produce testosterone and anti-Müllerian hormone. These promote development of male organs from the Wolffian ducts and suppress further development of Müllerian ducts.

8. If the Y chromosome is absent, the fetal gonads become ovaries, and the Wolffian ducts disintegrate. The DAX-1 gene on the X chromosome may control a mechanism by which this gene inhibits the development of male genitals and promotes development of female structures.

9. Male and female genitals and inner reproductive structures then develop. The presence or absence of the male hormones affects development of the nervous system. These hormones have a masculinizing effect, while an independent process of defeminization is going on. The absence of androgens results in processes of demasculinization and feminization.

10. Variant forms of sexual differentiation patterns offer clues about the effects of hormones on fetal development and later behavior.

11. There may be a multiplier effect whereby biological and social factors combine to lead eventually to masculine and feminine behaviors.

12. During infancy and childhood, boys and girls are treated in particular ways, and social influences along with the biological begin to help the child form a core gender identity.

13. At puberty, the testes or ovaries begin secreting male or female hormones, triggering the development of secondary sex characteristics. The first stage of puberty is adrenarche, and the second, more profound stage is gonadarche. Sexual feelings and fantasies also become more pronounced.

14. Adult gender roles can be conceptualized by bipolar, orthogonal, and oblique models, each offering a different view of the relationship between femininity and masculinity.

15. People who exaggerate culturally accepted gender roles are called hypermasculine or hyperfeminine. Androgyny reflects high frequencies of both masculine and feminine traits in the same individual.

16. Transgenderism has often been interpreted as pathological and considered a gender identity disorder, but transgender individuals have been asking for increased recognition in their roles.

17. Transsexualism involves a distinct nonconformity of gender identity with physical attributes

of sex. High-intensity transsexuals are more likely to desire surgical and hormonal sex reassignment.

18. Evolutionary psychologists believe that there may be biological and species-survival bases for some broad categories of gender-related behaviors.

19. Masculinity and femininity are defined by the behaviors found in average men and women. There are some average differences between females and males in a few cognitive and motor functions, but there are more similarities than differences.

20. There are several theoretical positions concerning gender role development. The psychodynamic approach focuses on complex unconscious interactions between children and their parents.

21. Social learning theory emphasizes socialization and the modeling of gender behaviors by children.

22. Cognitive-developmental theory emphasizes the way human thought processes reinforce and perpetuate the gender roles learned from socialization.

23. Gender schema theory highlights the complex network of associations that people hold with regard to gender.

24. Behavioral genetics emphasizes an interaction of nature and nurture in the development of gender roles.

25. Different genders are treated differently within Western society. Girls seem to be more prone to losing self-esteem as they reach adolescence.

26. Representation of women in scientific and technical fields has been lower in industrialized nations than in some developing countries because of the different status science holds in these cultures.

27. The feminist movement in American history began with an outcry for women's rights in 1848 by Elizabeth Cady Stanton and Susan B. Anthony and others.

28. Feminists want to see men and women treated—and compensated—equally and without discrimination.

29. Men have examined the limiting and unhealthy effects of the roles expected of them in our culture.

Focus on Health Questions

In this section you will find the kinds of questions that you may have concerning your own health and sexuality. The page references indicate where in the text the answer is located; the exact place is marked with this logo: **FOH**

1. If a woman takes hormones during pregnancy, can they affect the development of the fetus? **113**

2. What kinds of changes occurred in my body at puberty? **117**

3. Is it possible to be confused about my gender? **120–122**

4. Are boys really more intelligent than girls? **123**

5. Even though I am a male, I agree with the values of my female feminist friends. Can I call myself a feminist too? **129**

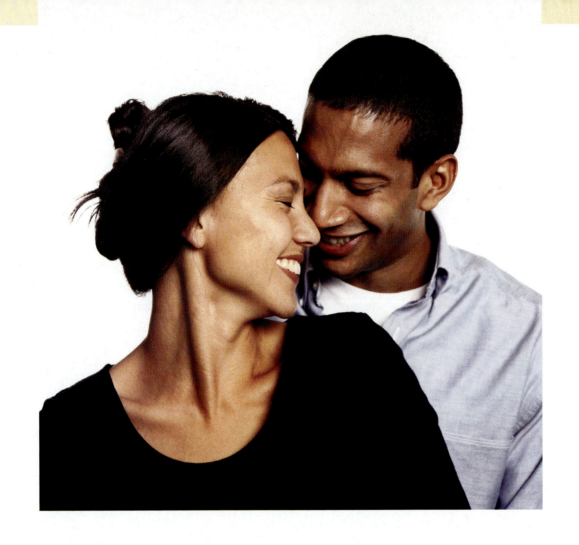

Part 2

Understanding Sexuality in Ourselves and in Our Relationships

■

Our development as sexual human beings begins at the moment of conception and continues throughout our life. During the stages of the life cycle, we move from a generalized awareness of sexuality to more specific awarenesses and experiences. Various aspects of human sexual nature unfold as we pass through these life stages, each with its own particular hurdles.

Adult sexuality typically involves selecting a partner, relating to the other person intimately, and establishing a long-term bond. Relating sexually within the context of a lasting relationship carries its own set of complications and needs, but research shows that people who are married seem to be relatively satisfied with their sexual lives. Aging affects sexuality, as does chronic disease, but neither means that a person is no longer a sexual being.

How human beings either are programmed or taught to behave sexually is a matter of conjecture and debate. The choices we make are based partly on our sexual attitudes and values. In developing an individualized set of sexual needs, orientations, fantasies, turn-ons, turnoffs, and behaviors, we are influenced by social networks and other factors. Developing sexual values is a crucial part of our growth as people. Persons with disabilities are sexual beings, too, and need to be helped to understand the place of sexuality in their lives.

Love is a quality that we continue to struggle to understand. Experts agree that intimacy between people is based on the ability to communicate about a whole range of feelings and issues. There is no such thing as *not* communicating, because the avoidance of talking or sharing is a message in itself. What is most important is the quality of the communication and whether it fosters a more positive interaction and a lessening of tension or instead creates new impasses and stresses that drive people farther apart.

Chapter 6

Sexuality in Infancy, Childhood, and Adolescence

Chapter Outline

Psychosexual Development
Biopsychological Drive/Instinct Theory
Psychodynamic Theory
Conditioning and Social Learning Theory
Developmental Theory
A Unified Theoretical Model of Psychosexual Development
Contemporary Social Process Theory

Sexuality in Infancy and Childhood
Sexual Curiosity Grows in Childhood
Love and Romance in Childhood

Sexuality in Adolescence
Early Adolescent Sexuality
Parent–Adolescent Communication
Masturbation in Adolescence
Initiation of Shared Sexual Behavior in Adolescence

Adolescent Heterosexual Activity: Risk-Taking and
  Abstaining
Social Development
Adolescent Same-Gender Sexual Activity
Adolescent Sexual Attitudes and Behaviors across Cultures

Adolescent Sexual Health
Societal Attitudes and Remedies
Teenage Pregnancy and Use of Birth Control

Sexuality Education
The Development of Sexuality Education
The Need for Sexuality Education
The Current Sexuality Education Debate
Sexuality Education and Cultural Diversity

Chapter Summary
Focus on Health Questions FOH

My sex education was nearly nonexistent until I was probably 14. Not that I didn't have sexual attractions or activities; it was just that I never learned anything about them except from a few friends, and they weren't so well informed themselves. When I finally took a "health" course in high school, sex-related issues were barely mentioned. This seems almost criminal to me now. How was I supposed to be prepared to be a responsible sexual person?

—from a student statement

In the previous chapter, we saw that sexual differentiation is a complex process, involving an interaction between biological and social forces. This chapter focuses on the ways we develop sexually from birth and express our sexual natures in the earlier stages of the life span. How do our sexual feelings and behaviors become part of our personalities and social interactions? In what important ways do children and adolescents become acquainted with their sexual needs and make decisions about acting on them? How does sexuality fit into their social relationships? As we look at some answers to these questions, you will see again that there are many unanswered questions and areas of controversy.

The chapter concludes with a section on sexuality education, one arena in which the battles of the culture wars are being fought. If we want children and adolescents to grow up knowing how to manage their sexual natures in responsible and respectful ways, and to make decisions that will protect their health and well-being, what is the best way to accomplish our goals? Herein lies ammunition for one of the longest-lasting and most bitterly contended battles of human sexuality. Before reading that section of the chapter, what do you personally think about the issue of sexuality education?

■ Psychosexual Development

We all gradually develop our own individualized ways of thinking and feeling about sexuality, along with our own patterns of sexual orientation and behavior. This complex process, called **psychosexual development,** seems to entail interactions of biological factors and learning from the social environment. For the most part, experts seem to agree that human infants essentially are sexually nonspecific. In other words, although they have the capacity to experience physiological sexual response, the specifics of how they will exercise that capacity—or even *if* they will exercise it—probably are heavily influenced by a whole range of factors. As infants grow into children and then develop into adolescents, profound changes happen within their bodies, emotions, and intellects. The processes of psychosexual development begin to form the very individualized sexual natures they will take with them to adulthood.

There may well be critical periods in human development during which a person's stage of biological development interacts with the various processes of socialization present in the environment to establish particular characteristics of the individual's sexuality. Such critical periods would mean that the necessary growth has occurred for learning to be optimal, all capacities are at a maximum, and conditions are ideal for a particular kind of learning to take place. These periods in human development most likely come into play during the younger years of childhood and adolescence.

Various theories of psychosexual development have evolved over the last century. These theories have gradually led to a more comprehensive understanding of how we become sexual human beings, although much still remains to be learned.

Biopsychological Drive/ Instinct Theory

Among the earlier attempts to explain psychosexual development was the idea that humans have an inborn "sexual instinct." Human beings are born with sex organs that become increasingly functional during their early years, and these organs are necessary for the propagation of the species. A logical presumption would be that nature has also built into each of us instincts for putting those sex organs into operation. Evolutionary psychology, which we will study in more detail in the next chapter, is based on the assumption that a fundamental human instinct aims toward reproducing the species. These instinct-based viewpoints assume that a sexual "drive" causes people to experience a buildup of sexual "tension" or "need" over time. When sexual activity is experienced, the drive is believed to be temporarily satisfied and reduced, eventually to build up again so that the cycle continues. Because instinct theory squared intuitively with what many people seemed to experience in their own lives, it received much support.

Sex researchers have begun to believe, however, that the concept of a biopsychological sex drive probably is simplistic and inaccurate. Although genetic and hormonal factors obviously give us potentials for sexual arousal and response, they do not go very far in explaining how individual human beings learn to perceive—or *not* perceive—various stimuli as sexually arousing. There is a growing consensus that social and

> **psychosexual development** factors that form a person's sexual feelings, orientation, and patterns of behavior.

cultural factors are extremely important in shaping sexual behavior, including the encouragements and constraints that social sanctions offer as well as interaction with actual sex partners (Bancroft, 2002a).

Theories about inborn sexual drives or instincts have led to other assumptions about the "naturalness" or "unnaturalness" of particular sexual behaviors. For example, whatever sexual behavior leads to potential propagation of the species (male-female intercourse) could easily be classified as *natural*, whereas other forms of behavior (such as masturbation or same-gender interactions) could be considered *unnatural* by default. This concept has been carried even further into value judgments of good and bad or healthy and sick. Behind it all is the idea that as children grow and develop, their sexual instincts gradually emerge and unfold according to nature's plan. As sexual drive theory has been called into question, we have had to look to other explanations for psychosexual development.

Psychodynamic Theory

Psychodynamic theory, as the name implies, focuses on the working dynamics of the mind. The background of this theory was discussed on page 124. Relying heavily on the concept of instincts, Sigmund Freud postulated the existence of the **libido,** a word he used to describe the sexual longing or sex drive that he believed was built into the human psyche. Freud realized that in addition to this psychological aspect of the sexual instinct there was a physical aspect involving bodily responses and behaviors. He also introduced the concept of the unconscious mind, purported to control much of human development and behavior even though its thought processes are outside conscious awareness. The libido and unconscious thought processes are essential elements in the psychodynamic theory of psychosexual development, although modifications have been made to the theory since Freud's early formulations (Harding, 2001).

The major assumption of this theory is that infants are born with a store of sexual energy in the form of the libido. At first, the energy is completely undifferentiated and indiscriminate. It can be directed at anything. For this reason, Freud said that infants were "polymorphously perverse." This energy gradually becomes associated with different pleasurable areas of the body until it finally localizes in the sex organs. Freud believed that it was variations in this process that molded not only the individual's sexual nature but the entire personality.

Psychodynamic theory sees the libido as becoming invested in bodily parts that are important in a child's physical development. During infancy, when the child has no particular awareness of differences between the sexes, the sexual energies of the infant

FIGURE 6.1 *Freud's Oral Stage*

The Freudian theory of sexual development states that in the first year of life the libido, or sex drive, is located in the mouth. According to Freud, this is the reason why infants enjoy sucking and putting things into their mouth.

become centered in the mouth, an important area of gratification for the young child. This is referred to as the oral stage (see Figure 6.1). As a child begins to be toilet trained and learns how to control pleasurably the retention and elimination of the bowels, her or his libido moves to the anus—a transition to the anal stage. It is believed that by the age of about 3 years, children begin to be aware of their genitals, and the libido becomes centered in the penis or clitoris. By this time, children have begun to become aware of the anatomical differences between the sexes.

Freud believed that a **latency period** follows, during which the sexual energies are said to lie dormant while intellectual and social growth continues.

libido (la-BEED-o or LIB-a-do) a term first used by Freud to define human sexual longing, or sex drive.

latency period Freudian concept that during middle childhood sexual energies are dormant; recent research tends to suggest that latency does not exist.

Not all proponents of psychodynamic theory accept the existence of the latency period because there is evidence that children remain in touch with their sexual and romantic feelings throughout childhood. Freud's perceptions may well have been influenced by the society in which he lived and worked, a society that was reluctant to perceive children as sexual beings. The final stage of his model, the stage when the libido becomes focused in the sex organs, begins at puberty and is called the genital stage.

Psychodynamic theory includes the idea that many things can go wrong as the libido gradually moves to various parts of the body. It holds that adult emotional and mental problems are the result of difficulties during some stage of psychosexual development. Ideally, according to this theory, young women and men should integrate genital orgasm with loving heterosexual relationships, leading toward healthy lifestyles of satisfying sex, reproduction, and work. Needless to say, the emphasis on orgasm in this theory often created undue concern for many people. Others have taken issue with psychodynamic theory because they perceive it to be male-centered, discriminatory toward females, and irrelevant to contemporary knowledge of human sexuality (Harding, 2001).

Conditioning and Social Learning Theory

Early psychology concerned itself with the mechanisms by which animals learned patterns of behavior. Simple conditioning mechanisms were thought to be applicable to some human behaviors as well, including human sexual arousal. It was assumed, for example, that if particular erotic words were heard repeatedly during sexual arousal, eventually the words themselves could become a conditional stimulus that could elicit some degree of sexual arousal—the conditioned response. Later work in psychology clarified more complex principles of operant conditioning. According to these principles, **reinforcement** of behavior—through pleasure, reward, or removal of some unpleasant stimulus—makes the behavior likely to be repeated. Negative consequences of a behavior through unpleasant results, pain, or the loss of rewarding stimuli tend to decrease the frequency of the behavior. Hypothetically applied to sexual development in humans, this perspective emphasizes the influences of positive and negative consequences on sexual behaviors.

Conditioning theorists emphasized that the development of modes of sexual functioning is a complex phenomenon influenced by many different sources. They also used the concept of **generalization** to explain how specific, learned sexual responses might be generalized to other, similar circumstances. For example, an individual who was conditioned to become sexually aroused by seeing female breasts might generalize that experience to other things associated with breasts (bras, other underwear, blouses, other parts of a woman's body, perfume, and so on). The generalization process would be kept in check by **discrimination,** which would enable the individual to avoid responding to one stimulus while responding to similar stimuli.

Conditioning theory, then, held that we learn our sexual preferences and behaviors through observational learning, a complex pattern of reinforcement, and the pairing of stimuli with sexual response. As human beings grew up, social cues would be picked up that helped determine what would be considered "acceptable" sexual behavior. Gradually the set of stimuli to which the individual responded sexually would be narrowed. If sexual behaviors or needs that the person did not consider socially acceptable remained, then conflicts and emotional disturbances might develop.

An extension of conditioning theory emerged in the 1960s with the model called social learning theory. This model suggested that the learning process was influenced by cumulative observation of and identification with other people. This cumulative learning process was seen as crucial, because people's perceptions were seen as being shaped by the impressions and attitudes they formed in their early development. For example, children and adolescents would be prone to imitating (modeling) and adopting the behaviors they see in other people whom they admire and identify with (see Figure 6.2). This theory emphasized the potential power of television and movies, as well as of parents, friends, and others, in the modeling of sexual behaviors.

Although there is ample scientific literature devoted to the roles of conditioning and social learning in establishing patterns of sexual arousal, there really is very little evidence that these represent particularly valid explanations. Their value in helping us understand psychosexual development lies more in their having opened the possibility that sexual behaviors are influenced by environmental factors.

Developmental Theory

Other theorists began to focus more clearly on the influence of social forces on child development that

reinforcement in conditioning theory, any influence that helps shape future behavior as a punishment or reward stimulus.
generalization application of specific learned responses to other, similar situations or experiences.
discrimination the process by which an individual extinguishes a response to one stimulus while preserving it for other stimuli.

FIGURE 6.2 *Social Learning Theory*

According to this theory, children learn attitudes and values by observing and imitating the behavior of others. What they learn depends partly on the power and prestige of the person observed. Television, movies, and music can be powerful influences on the sexual values and behavior of children and adolescents.

FIGURE 6.3 *Erikson's Psychosocial Development*

In Erikson's life-span theory of psychosocial development, young children learn skills as well as identity and values from those around them. Positive values about themselves and their sexuality will aid children in developing intimacy with others as they grow older.

could be applied to psychosexual development. Jean Piaget (1932) had already considered the importance of cognition, intellect, and reasoning in children, and Lawrence Kohlberg (1981) eventually examined the many facets of moral development. Erik Erikson (1968) made significant strides toward devising a model of *developmental psychology* that clearly showed those tasks that had to be accomplished at various stages of human growth and development (see Figure 6.3). He considered the tasks so crucial that he called them crises. Erikson conceptualized an eight-stage life span of **psychosocial development** that extended from birth to old age. Because of his psychoanalytic training, Erikson believed that a powerful libido was built into all of us, but he also realized that cultural and social influences help shape our sexual identities, including our sexual behaviors. He maintained that each of the eight stages of life includes a crisis of psychosocial development that must be resolved (see Table 6.1). Each crisis can take the individual either in a direction of adjustment, health, and positive self-concept or in a direction of maladaptation, unrest, and low self-esteem.

According to Erikson, during adolescence and young adulthood each individual has the task of achieving a clear understanding of herself or himself as a sexual person and of achieving a sense of intimacy with other human beings. Failure to reach these goals may result in role confusion and isolation that can generate unhealthy perceptions of sexuality and relationships for a lifetime. Success in achieving a healthy sexual identity hinges partially on how

successfully the tasks of earlier stages of the life span have been resolved. Erikson also emphasized the importance of other people and their response to the individual—social factors—in this model of psychosexual development.

A Unified Theoretical Model of Psychosexual Development

Researcher John Bancroft (2002a) has proposed a unified theory of how sexual development takes place. It considers the various stages of physical and psychological development through which human beings pass, and it identifies three principal "strands" that are part of each person's developmental framework. These three strands tend to develop in parallel during the childhood years but relatively independently of one another. Then, during adolescence, the strands come together and become more integrated to form the foundations of a sexually mature adult. These strands have been identified as the following:

1. *Gender identity.* The inner experience of one's gender plays a crucial role in sexual development. During childhood the basic identity is established, and during adolescence sexual behaviors serve an important function in reorganizing the specifics of one's gender identity. This begins to establish the sense of oneself as man, woman, or transgendered.
2. *Sexual response and understanding one's sexual orientation.* Puberty triggers a variety of physical and emotional changes within the individual and

psychosocial development the cultural and social influences that help shape human sexual identity.

Table 6.1	The Crises to Be Resolved During Erikson's Stages of Psychosocial Development
Stage in Life Cycle	**Crisis**
Infancy	Gaining trust in self and environment vs. Feeling mistrust and wariness of others
Ages $1\frac{1}{2}$ to 3	Achieving a sense of autonomy vs. Shame and doubt over one's ability to be independent
Ages 3 to $5\frac{1}{2}$	Learning how to take initiative comfortably vs. Feeling guilty over motivations and needs
Ages $5\frac{1}{2}$ to 12 (The time when school and other external influences gain more significance)	Gaining a sense of industry and competence vs. Feeling inferior and inept
Adolescence	Forming a sense of one's own identity vs. Role confusion and self-questioning
Young adulthood	Achieving intimacy and connection with others vs. Feeling alone and isolated
Adulthood	Realizing generativity and positive interpersonal relationships vs. Feeling stagnant and unfulfilled
Maturity	Achieving ego integrity and relative peace with one's life vs. A sense of despair and wastedness

Source: Data from E. Erikson, *Identity: Youth and Crisis,* New York: W. W. Norton, 1968.

usually leads to a greater awareness of and urge toward sexual arousal. Coming to terms with these needs and responses plays an important part in figuring out who one really is sexually.

3. *Capacity for intimate dyadic relationships.* In later adolescence and early adulthood, people begin exploring their sexuality within the context of partnerships or dyads (pairs). How effective the individual is in handling the complexities of dyadic relationships is significant in later sexual development.

Part of sexual development is gaining a deeper understanding of one's own sexual orientation, a process that unfolds as people negotiate the various stages of their physical and psychological development (Bancroft, 2002a; Sanders, 1999). Children first go through a *prelabeling* process, as they begin to identify what is expected of them sexually. Adolescents then begin to categorize their own sexual orientations according to the labels their social groups provide—the *self-labeling* stage of identifying sexual orientation. The adolescent privately compares her or his own feelings and responses to those that are prescribed in the prevailing society. If self-labels are out of step with what the adolescent has learned is expected and desired by the society and culture, a great deal of personal conflict and confusion may result. Finally, sexual orientation is defined through *social labeling,* in which the person's perceptions of self are subject to validation by what is known about the society's labels for various sexual orientations and preferences.

Contemporary Social Process Theory

When the researchers who conducted the National Health and Social Life Survey (NHSLS) designed their comprehensive study of sexual behavior, they realized that research would have to go beyond the study of individual human beings because we do not develop sexually in a social vacuum. To help them interpret the meaning of their statistics on sexual behavior, researchers drew on some of the most respected theories of social psychology, sociology, and economics. The following three theoretical perspectives proved to be the most useful to this work (Laumann, Gagnon, et al., 1994).

Sexual Script Theory: Social Foundations

John Gagnon and William Simon were among the first sociologists to take issue with theories that relied on the presumption of an intense, biologically generated sex drive. They believed that internal sexual energy might not be very intense at all, at least in many individuals. They also proposed that too much emphasis had been placed on the effects of childhood sexual patterns on later development. Many novel factors come into play at the beginning of adolescence that can exert significant influence on sexual development, quite independent of childhood experience. They developed what came to be known as *scripting theory*. This theoretical stance was one of the first attempts to explain how sexual behavior was socially constructed. In addition to minimizing the effects of sex drive, it holds that patterns of sexual conduct are derived from social and cultural contexts that are filled with messages, or **social scripts,** that regulate most human behavior. Through a lifelong acculturation process, people acquire the sexual scripts—or patterns of sexual conduct—that suit

social scripts a complex set of learned responses to a particular situation that is formed by social influences.

their own needs. This sometimes means that people adopt sexual scripts that deviate from cultural norms (Gagnon, 1999; Simon, 1999).

In terms of sexual behavior, this would mean that, although particular social situations are not in themselves sexually oriented, we organize the elements of a situation—for example, an available partner, privacy, sexual desire—in such a way that they become sexual. Because sexual scripts are learned, new learning experiences during each emergent stage of an individual's physical development contribute to that individual's sexual development.

There are three different types of sexual scripts, reflective of different levels of functioning for individuals as they grow up. In the broadest context, scripts have *cultural scenarios,* referring to the messages and instructional guidance about sexual behavior offered by one's culture. It is almost as if every possible message about sex within a culture is part of the picture. One reason the process is so complex and individualized is that there are so many combinations and permutations. The social constructionist view holds that social and cultural imperatives play a significant role in determining what sexual choices people will make within their society or culture.

On an intermediate level are the *interpersonal scripts* determined by the expectations of other people about conduct within interpersonal relationships. At the level of the individual's own mind are the *intrapsychic scripts.* The person takes all the information from the cultural and interpersonal contexts and then processes it internally. As individual men and women make sense of what the surrounding sexual messages mean for them, they begin to develop their own sets of sexual scripts. The three levels of scripting are constantly interacting with one another, and they may be modified over the course of a person's life span.

Choice Theory: Sexual Decision Making

Although sexual scripts provide people with codes of sexual conduct from their cultures, they do not fully explain how individuals choose among the varieties of sexual behavior available to them. *Choice theory,* borrowed from economics, assumes that human beings make choices out of the need to apportion their "resources"—in this case, sexual and relational—in order to reach certain goals. Some typical goals of sexual behavior are experiencing sexual pleasure, deriving emotional satisfaction from intimacy, having children, and building a positive reputation among one's peers. In order to reach these goals, various human resources must be managed, because there is a "cost" involved in securing a sexual partner. It takes time, emotional energy, social skills, and sometimes money. Thus, as with economic outcomes, there is a limit to the number

of sexual partners an individual can "afford" to choose. For most people, that number is really quite small (Laumann, Gagnon, et al., 1994).

Two other components of choice theory have been applied to the sexual arena: risk management and the market. Sexual choices usually are made with a degree of uncertainty, and they involve weighing a degree of risk. There are both positive and negative consequences to be considered, and these can markedly affect people's sexual choices. Some people are better than others at assessing and managing sexual and relational risks. Adolescents typically become aware of these various factors as they begin testing the social waters. All these elements affect how individuals approach the "market" for sex partners. How well a person fares in the social marketplace depends on many variables, including physical attributes, attractiveness, personality, intelligence, and age. It is the components of this social-sexual economy that influence the choices of sexual behavior individual human beings make (Sprecher, 1998).

Social Network Theory: Sexual Relationships

Although scripting and choice theories can help us comprehend how patterns of sexual conduct are determined by the individual's experiences, circumstances, and decisions, they have less to say about the actual social connections that can influence sexual activities. *Social network theory* recognizes that most sexual activity is negotiated within the context of social relationships and that it is the characteristics of those relationships that become significant in determining what sexual activities, if any, will occur. Two-person partnerships, or sexual dyads, that begin forming in childhood and adolescence do not exist in a vacuum; rather, they are part of a larger network of social relationships that also influence the sexual activities of the individuals who are part of them (Sprecher, 1998).

The social composition of a sexual relationship affects the type of sexual behavior that will be experienced in the relationship. For example, whether people share oral sex is clearly affected by their age, educational level, and race (Michael et al., 1994). We also label partnerships in different ways: "lovers," "girlfriend–boyfriend," "one-night stand," "married couple." The way a relationship has been labeled and socially defined affects how the individuals within that relationship view it and also how the larger social network defines what is appropriate sexual conduct for it. Social network theory looks at the principles of relationships, but it must rely on scripting theory and choice theory to explain what happens within specific relationships. At the same time, sexual scripts and choices are influenced by the qualities of the relationship, and the relationship helps shape the scripts and choices of its members. This complex inter-action of factors constitutes the *social process* of psy-chosexual development.

Which of the six theories that attempt to explain psychosexual development seem most convincing to you? Why? Are there any aspects of different theories that you would combine to create a more viable theory?

■ Sexuality in Infancy and Childhood

Infancy and childhood are periods of human develop-ment that include a continuing emergence of sexuality that began prior to birth (see Figure 6.4). There is in-sufficient cross-cultural data to determine whether the patterns of sexual development observed in Western societies apply universally. Most of the anthropological information on childhood sexuality that we do have has been a by-product of broader studies, and anthro-pologists in general have been reluctant to focus on the sexual development of infants and children. The result is that we really do not have an entirely reliable picture of what constitutes "normal" childhood sexual-ity (Bancroft, 2003a; Graaf & Rademakers, 2006).

Ultrasound images of fetuses still in the uterus show that a male fetus can experience erection of the penis even before birth. Very soon after birth, infants seem to show interest in exploring their own bodies and in seeking whatever pleasure they can gain from that exploration. There is ample evidence to suggest that baby boys experience genital responses. Erection

FIGURE 6.4 *Infant Sexuality*

Infants develop an awareness of their bodies and their sexuality first through a bonding with their parents and the sensuous con-tact involved in cuddling and holding and second by exploring their own bodies, including their genitals.

has even been observed within the first few minutes after birth. A number of male infants seem to have or-gasms, as evidenced by sequences of tension-building, rhythmic muscular contractions, and pelvic thrusting that culminate in what appear to be pleasurable sensa-tions and relaxation. In baby girls, the labia may be quite prominent and the vaginal lining pinkish in color for several weeks after birth, the result of maternal hormones still present in the bloodstream. There is also evidence of vaginal lubrication that occurs spon-taneously in regular cycles from the time a female is born (DeLamater & Friedrich, 2002; Singer, 2002).

Although these early patterns of physical arousal and sensual enjoyment do not represent the socialized patterns of eroticism that form later in human develop-ment, they do demonstrate the extreme sensitivity of in-fants. It has been suggested that the entire surface of the skin in a newborn infant is a single **erogenous zone,** meaning that it is sensitive to sensual stimulation that can contribute to a healthy skin eroticism (Singer, 2002).

The foundations for sensuality, intimacy, and rela-tionship to other people are established during in-fancy. Bonding between infants and their parents is an important part of this process. Infancy may also be a time when small children begin to notice how they are treated by their fathers and mothers and to form early concepts of their relationships with others.

Several significant developmental tasks are accom-plished during infancy. Immediately after birth, there is a period when babies seem very alert, and bonding oc-curs between them and their parent(s). The holding, touching, and cuddling given to an infant are part of the evolution of its ability to relate to and be intimate with others. Between 6 months and 1 year of age, babies be-gin to touch their genitals, if they are not prohibited from doing so. Our culture exhibits a fair amount of anxiety on the part of adults about recognizing and le-gitimizing the concept that for children to experience sexual and sensual *pleasure* might be perfectly healthy and normal. Yet this is a time of life when the very foun-dations for adult sexual pleasure are established, and this may be accomplished best within the context of a loving and pleasure-affirming environment (Jackson & Scott, 2004; Levine, 2002a). As we have seen in the pre-ceding chapter, infancy is also the time when the baby begins to be socialized with regard to the cultural ex-pectations of gender roles (Muehlenhard et al., 2003).

Sexual Curiosity Grows in Childhood

Children's sexual development proceeds along two parallel routes that sometimes cross. One stream is the

erogenous zone (a-RAJ-a-nus) any area of the body that is sensitive to sexual arousal.

autoerotic, referring to the sensual and sexual exploration of their own bodies; the other involves interaction with other people, most typically beginning with their caregivers or parents (Graaf & Rademakers, 2006; Singer, 2002). Very young children are often observed fondling their genitals, sometimes seeming to produce sexual excitement and orgasm. Children begin to gain a sense of what their bodies are and of the capacities for pleasure their bodies have. This can be seen as a period of potentiation, when vague awareness of sexual feelings and early ranges of sexual responsiveness are established. Only a few children seem to have particularly specific sexual preferences. Most apparently are "multisexual," able to respond to many different forms of sexual stimulation (Larsson & Svedin, 2002). Children also learn more and more about sex and reproduction as they progress through childhood and as their verbal capabilities grow, with a spurt of knowledge and understanding occurring around age 10 (Herdt & McClintock, 2000).

Two studies have provided new insights into what might be considered "normative" patterns of sexual development during childhood. For the most part, these studies have relied on the reports of parents, especially mothers, concerning the behaviors of their children. The UCLA Family Lifestyles Project (FLS), which followed more than 200 children from birth until adulthood, has been the source of a wealth of longitudinal data (Okami, Olmstead, & Abramson, 1997). An even more comprehensive examination of childhood sexual behavior was conducted by a group of psychologists at the Mayo Clinic, using questionnaires that were administered to the primary female caregivers of 1,114 children ages 2 to 12 (Friedrich et al., 1998). This research confirmed that children exhibit a broad range of sexual behaviors, many of which are common enough to be considered "normal" for various developmental stages. When young adults recall their own sexual behaviors as children, they almost always judge them to have been "normal" (Larsson & Svedin, 2002).

The UCLA study found 77 percent of parents reporting that their children had engaged in sex play prior to age 6, including masturbation. Nearly 47 percent of those parents indicated that their children had engaged in some sort of interactive sex play with another child during the same period of life. By the age of 2 or 3, many children begin to explore the bodies of their playmates, in activities ranging from simple embraces to stroking, caressing, kissing, and touching the genitals. They also continue to have an interest in their own genitals (see Figure 6.5). Some become involved in games that permit mutual body exploration, such as "doctor" or "nurse." From the ages of 3 to 5, awareness of being a boy or a girl seems to appear, although many children cannot really explain how they know they are a girl or a boy. They most often make their

FIGURE 6.5 *Sexual Curiosity*

Most children around the age of 2 or 3 are curious about their own bodies as well as the bodies of others. Any sexual activity usually involves a fondling of the genitals. Because children tend to respond to each other affectionately at these ages, touching, hugging, and kissing may extend to the genital area.

identification based on social markers such as clothing, rather than by anatomical differences such as genitals (Okami, Olmstead, & Abramson, 1997). Knowledge about where babies come from and how they are born seems to become more refined as children grow and develop, and this knowledge may be enhanced by parents who make a point of providing the information to their children (DeLamater & Friedrich, 2002).

The Mayo Clinic research found that the most frequently observed behaviors among children ages 2 to 12 were self-stimulation, exposing body parts to another child, and behaviors relating to the personal boundaries of others, such as rubbing against another person. Other research has confirmed that along with normative behaviors, young school-children are often observed behaving toward others in ways that would be considered inappropriate or problematic (Kaeser, DiSalvo, & Moglia, 2000). More intrusive behaviors, such as oral-genital contact or insertion of things into the vagina or rectum, were less frequently observed. Although the amount of sexual behavior observed among children declines steadily during the childhood years (see Figure 6.6), the researchers have cautioned that this does not mean that the behaviors are decreasing, but only that as children become older they become more private with their sexual behaviors (Friedrich et al., 1998).

Based on their study and the findings of other research, a tentative outline of sexual behaviors was

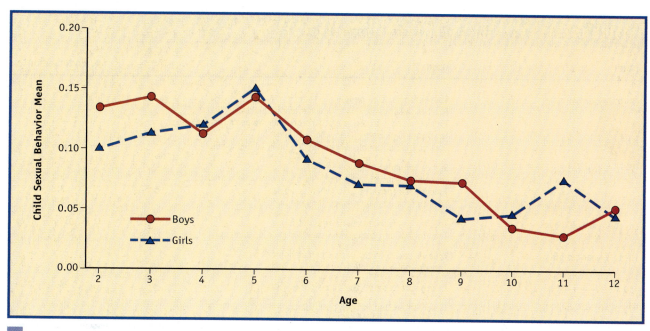

■ **FIGURE 6.6** *Observed Sexual Behavior in Children*

The sexual behaviors of children between the ages of 2 and 12, as observed and reported by their primary caregivers, tend to decrease with age. It is believed that this does not represent a decrease in actual sexual behavior but rather a greater awareness of social appropriateness and a desire for more privacy.

Source: From W. N. Friedrich et al., "Normative Sexual Behavior in Children: A Contemporary Sample." Reproduced with permission from *Pediatrics,* Vol. 101, p. e9. Copyright © 1998.

formulated for boys and girls at various stages in their development (see Table 6.2 on page 150). Although the results confirm much of what has always been assumed about children, they also reflect the greater level of privacy children achieve as they reach adolescence (Friedrich et al., 1998). Exposure to sex play in childhood does not seem to be associated with a person's level of adjustment in the late teen years (Okami, Olmstead, & Abramson, 1997). However, there is evidence that children who are exposed to adverse sexual experiences may well underestimate the risks involved in attempts to achieve intimacy with others during adulthood (Hillis et al., 2001). Even though parents often warn their children to be wary of "strangers," the National Center for Missing and Exploited Children has confirmed that 80 percent of the time an abductor or molester is known to a child. If children become overly fearful of strangers, their fear may prevent them from asking for help if they become separated from a parent.

Masturbating and exhibiting genitals to other children are common forms of childhood sex play. In later childhood, some youngsters experiment with other forms of behavior, including oral-genital contact and attempts at anal or vaginal intercourse (Graaf & Rademakers, 2006). These activities may be engaged in with a same-gender partner or with someone of the other gender. Repeated aggressive sexual behavior in younger children toward other children, such as coer-

cive oral sex, insertion of objects into the rectum, or attempted rape, may represent signs of previous sexual abuse of the child. This is discussed in greater detail in Chapter 16, "Sexual Consent, Coercion, Rape, and Abuse." However, a study of identical twins during childhood suggested that problematic behavior involving excessive masturbation or public sex play might be influenced by genetic factors as well (Langstrom, Grann, & Lichtenstein, 2002).

Parental attitudes and lifestyles seem to play a role in determining how children will behave sexually—or at least how observable their sex play will be. More "relaxed" or liberal approaches to things such as family nudity, co-bathing, and co-sleeping were correlated with higher levels of observed sexual behaviors among children, although this might again be related more to the degree of privacy a child will seek. Ethnicity did not seem to be related to reported sexual behaviors in childhood (Friedrich et al., 1998; Graaf & Rademakers, 2006; Okami, Olmstead, & Abramson, 1997).

How parents and others respond to sex play in children begins to set the stage for later sex-related values. If a parent constantly punishes a child's attempts at genital exploration or sex play, the child may rapidly learn that her or his sex organs and exploratory behaviors are bad. At times, the reactions of anxious adults can transform an innocent, natural phase of sexual exploration and development into a traumatic

Table 6.2	Developmentally Related Sexual Behaviors	
Age	Item	% Endorsement
2- to 5-year-old boys	Stands too close to people	29.3
	Touches sex (private) parts when in public places	26.5
	Touches or tries to touch mother's or other women's breasts	42.4
	Touches sex (private) parts when at home	60.2
	Tries to look at people when they are nude or undressing	26.8
2- to 5-year-old girls	Stands too close to people	25.8
	Touches or tries to touch mother's or other women's breasts	43.7
	Touches sex (private) parts when at home	43.8
	Tries to look at people when they are nude or undressing	26.9
6- to 9-year-old boys	Touches sex (private) parts when at home	39.8
	Tries to look at people when they are nude or undressing	20.2
6- to 9-year-old girls	Touches sex (private) parts when at home	20.7
	Tries to look at people when they are nude or undressing	20.5
10- to 12-year-old boys	Is very interested in the opposite sex	24.1
10- to 12-year-old girls	Is very interested in the opposite sex	28.7

Source: From W. N. Friedrich et al., "Normative Sexual Behavior in Children: A Contemporary Sample." Reproduced with permission from *Pediatrics*, Vol. 101, p. e9. Copyright © 1998.

event (Levine, 2002a). Parents who accept sexual exploration as a natural, positive part of growing up and help their children understand what will be socially acceptable in later life, may contribute enormously to the development of a healthy sexuality in their children. Professionals often recommend that parents be involved in teaching their children the names of their sex organs, as part of a broader sexuality education effort that will include awareness of sexual abuse and personal safety (Kaeser, DiSalvo, & Moglia, 2000).

One of the concerns parents sometimes have is the degree to which nudity should be allowed or encouraged within the family setting. Most professionals agree that when nudity within the home is permitted and there is no sexual abuse, there do not seem to be negative consequences. The same is true of situations in which children have accidentally viewed their parents engaging in sexual behavior. Allowing younger children to sleep at times in the parental bed also does not seem to have any adverse consequences. Children themselves may well reach stages in their development when they signal some discomfort with being seen naked by other family members or with seeing their parents nude. It is important for parents to respect these needs by making as little fuss as possible and avoiding inflicting any embarrassment on the child. Nonetheless, studies confirm that childhood exposure to nudity in the home does not adversely affect an individual's adult sexual adjustment or functioning; in fact, boys with such backgrounds actually may have more positive developmental outcomes, such as increased comfort with physical contact and expressions of affection in adult life and a lower risk of contracting a sexually transmitted disease (Heins, 2001; Okami et al., 1998).

Love and Romance in Childhood

Largely because of the Freudian concept of latency, it was once assumed that children between the ages of roughly 6 and 12 have little interest in sexual feelings or relationships with the opposite gender. Instead, it was believed that their sexual energies lay dormant and that children tended to reject members of the other sex in favor of same-gender friends. Researchers who have studied children and their sexual development have generally expressed skepticism about the existence of a latency phase. They have found evidence that children can develop romantic and even sexual attractions to others as their brains become more fully grown and their bodies begin to reach reproductive maturity (DeLamater & Friedrich, 2002). These romantic and sexual attachments eventually become defined as "love." Around the ages of 10 to 12, girls and boys begin to show a distinct increase in their levels of interest in and attraction toward others, and they begin to develop more intimate relationships when the opportunity becomes available (Hearn, O'Sullivan, & Dudley, 2002; Herdt & McClintock, 2000). Children at this age appear to take their love very seriously and begin to move toward more concrete wishing and planning. A final step is arranging a "date" with the loved one, at least among those 10- to 12-year-olds who have the courage to do so (Graaf & Rademakers, 2006).

In some cases, the preadolescent romantic attachments are with a member of the child's own gender, but because of social pressures children are less inclined to label these attachments "love" and instead describe them as friendships. Some same-gender attachments in earlier years may represent a preliminary awareness of later same-gender orientations and sexual attractions. Other times, even very intense same-gender relationships in childhood appear to have no particular bearing on an individual's future romantic and sexual proclivities.

■ Sexuality in Adolescence

Adolescence is that period of social, emotional, and cognitive development that moves young people toward adulthood. It is a time during which individuals become biologically mature and develop a greater sense of independence, autonomy, and personal identity. The capacity for abstract thinking increases, and planning for the future is balanced with a recognition of the potential impacts of current actions. During adolescence, young people strengthen their gender identities and begin clarifying their sexual orientations and identities as they experience more adultlike erotic feelings and experiment further with sexual behaviors (DeLamater & Friedrich, 2002).

As the culture that invented the term *adolescence,* we in the United States have attempted to prolong the youthful period of the life span, often to provide time for advanced education. The lifestyles, expectations, and responsibilities of adult life tend to be approached very gradually in North America. As a result, our society often asks sexually mature adolescents to fit their sexual interests and behaviors into a lifestyle more appropriate for much younger people.

The boundaries of adolescence are poorly defined in Western societies. In many cultures other than our own, a youthful individual participates in a rite of passage, declaring that she or he is no longer a child. Along with that passage into young adulthood come carefully prescribed (and proscribed) modes of sexual behavior. Youngsters in Western culture usually must deal with their growth into adulthood in a much more vague and gradual way. In their sexual development, as in many other aspects of their growth, adolescents often experience confusion, fear, and misunderstandings about their bodies and emotions.

Early Adolescent Sexuality

Girls typically experience puberty sooner than boys, so there is often an awkward period around ages 11 to 13 when boys' physical maturation lags behind that of girls. Although most adolescents experience some increased interest in sex, this occurs in varying degrees. Some early adolescents experience an insistent

sexual interest and the need [...] fication, while others experie[...] of sexual needs.

As the physical changes of p[...] lescent must begin to integrate ne[...] or his core gender identity. Boys e[...] ejaculations of semen, and girls be[...] calling new attention to their sex org[...] time, parents and others begin to attach [...]eanings to behaviors and emotions. The adolescent must build these developments into an awareness of being a young man or woman.

It is during early adolescence that some very basic attitudes about one's body and bodily functions are established, and these attitudes may significantly affect further development. There is evidence that girls who feel a sense of shame about menstruation and their bodies have lower levels of sexual activity but eventually may become prone to riskier sexual decision making. Girls who grow up feeling more comfortable about their bodies and menstruation are more sexually assertive in their decision making and have higher levels of sexual activity but take fewer sexual risks (Schooler, Ward, Merriwether, & Caruthers, 2005).

Most boys experience their first ejaculation during masturbation, although they may previously have experienced orgasm without emission of semen. The first ejaculation usually occurs between ages 11 and 15. Sometimes first ejaculation happens as a nocturnal emission or "wet dream." Some boys, after puberty, report having "spontaneous" ejaculations from time to time, produced by nonsexual physical activity or psychological influences (e.g., viewing pictures or watching an attractive person). By late adolescence, the capacity to have "spontaneous" orgasms apparently is lost in nearly all males. The capacity for "spontaneous" orgasm, without physical stimulation, apparently exists in some girls and even persists in a few women; they can experience orgasm by viewing sexually arousing material or by just thinking about sex.

Research suggests that boys become sexually active somewhat earlier than girls do. As adolescence progresses, girls clearly become more involved in sexual activity and better acquainted with their sexual responsiveness, a trend that often continues for another 10 to 20 years, when involvement in sexual activity tends to level off. Throughout adolescence, females exhibit a somewhat lower incidence of masturbation, same-gender sexual activity, and heterosexual experimentation (Kontula & Haavio-Mannila, 2002; SIECUS, 2003). Studies suggest that adolescent girls who have older boyfriends are more likely to begin having

adolescence period of emotional, social, and physical transition from childhood to adulthood.

earlier than others. Early-adolescent girls
particularly prone to having intercourse if the
boyfriend is substantially older, such as in his late
teens or early twenties (Lieberman, 2006; Liehmann-
Smith, 2001).

The early adolescent also may experience an increase in erotic fantasies and dreams. As the body matures and new sexual feelings emerge, awareness of the
social significance of sex develops, and young people
begin to daydream about sex. Adolescents may fantasize about loving relationships that involve sexual activity with a particular person or about a wide array of
sexual practices with nonspecific partners (Herdt &
McClintock, 2000). The fantasies that accompany masturbation often are quite vivid and add to the pleasure
of the masturbatory experience, also helping young
people become more fully acquainted with their sexual
preferences. Many adolescents use their fantasy experiences to plan for real sexual and relational encounters
later in life (Kontula & Haavio-Mannila, 2002).

Although the majority of adolescents under age 15
have not engaged in sexual intercourse, the proportion
of those who have is increasing. Two factors have
been shown to be part of this timing. One is the age at
which puberty takes place. Boys who experience puberty at the earlier ages on the scale tend to experience their first sexual arousal earlier and to report a
stronger sex drive and greater acceptance of casual sex
in adulthood. This pattern does not seem typical for
girls. In both sexes, the earlier the first sexual arousal
is experienced, the higher the adult sex drive seems to
be and the more sexual partners the person seems to
have as he or she grows up (Ostovich & Sabini, 2005).

The other factor that seems to be correlated with
the age at which adolescents begin having intercourse
is **cognitive susceptibility,** or their state of mind that
could predispose them to initiating sexual activity or
not. Understanding this concept is critical, because the
younger adolescents are when they begin having intercourse, the less likely they are to use contraceptives
and the higher their risk of contracting diseases or becoming pregnant. Studies indicate that those young
adolescents who are more cognitively susceptible to
initiating intercourse tend to be more physically mature
and to have more feelings of sexual desire than their
peers, as well as more social confidence and a greater
perception that their peers are sexually active. They
also tend to have fewer positive connections with
parents, school, and religious institutions (L'Engle,
Jackson, & Brown, 2006). Younger adolescents seem to
be quite susceptible to belief systems about sex. If they
or their friends believe that a person should refrain
from sexual intercourse, early adolescents are more
likely to abstain, at least for the short term (Santelli et al.,
2004). How these mechanisms might be valuable in
sexuality education settings is not yet clear.

Parent-Adolescent Communication

The primary sources of sex information for the majority of young persons are friends of the same sex and
their independent reading or Internet browsing. Yet
young people indicate that they wish they could hear
from their parents about issues such as dating, relationships, having sex and how to say no to it, sexually
transmitted infections, and preventing pregnancy. In a
survey of more than 7,000 children and adolescents,
the majority of fifth- and sixth-graders (72 percent of
girls and 54 percent of boys) indicated that their
mother would be the first person they would consult
about health- and sex-related questions. Health
providers and fathers were next on their list. As might
be anticipated, older adolescents were less likely to
indicate that they would seek out parents for information, but those in grades 10 through 12 still showed
substantial proportions (46 percent of girls and 35 percent of boys) who would prefer to have their mothers
be their primary source of information. In the older
age groups, friends also became a popular source of
information (Ackard & Neumark-Stainer, 2001).

An increasing body of research data indicates that
mothers' attitudes about dating and sexuality have a
significant effect on the attitudes and behaviors of
their children. When parents, particularly mothers,
disapprove of premarital sex yet are willing to discuss
sexuality and birth control and have clear rules about
dating, adolescents tend to postpone sexual activity
longer and to have sex less frequently (Blake et al.,
2001; Miller, 2002). The mass media and the Internet
are becoming increasingly important to adolescents in
learning about issues such as sexual biology, sexually
transmitted diseases, abortion, and same-gender orientation, but there is less evidence to suggest that this
information actually leads to attitudinal or behavioral
change (SIECUS, 2003).

Sexuality education professionals generally agree
that communication about human sexuality between
parents and their children can be very powerful and
can help shape healthy and responsible values about
sexuality. The sooner such patterns of communication
are established in a child's life, the better. Fathers have
traditionally been assumed to be more reluctant to
engage in such communication, although there is
evidence that their communications with sons can be
very important. Fathers are influenced by the level of
their sons' pubertal development, the kind of communication they had with their own fathers, the outcomes

cognitive susceptibility state of mind, identified by
psychological and situational factors, that suggests a
readiness for or predisposition toward initiating sexual
activity.

Real Student Voices

■ I think most parents are very clueless, and they would rather not think about what is going on with their kids sexually. When I'm a parent, I definitely would prefer an open and truthful relationship.

■ I don't believe parents are yet aware of how young high schoolers—and even middle schoolers—are when they first engage in sexual activity. I hope my generation will be better prepared at these things.

■ My parents are well aware of what is going on with sexuality in teenagers. They were always very honest with me, and never tried to get me to believe things just to keep me from having sex. I hope I will be that way with my own kids someday.

■ I hope most parents educate their kids on how to be safe and trust them to make good decisions, but I know some parents who think their kids aren't doing it. This is naive on their part.

they expect to have, their own sexual values, and the quality of their general father–son communication patterns (Lehr, Demi, DiIorio, & Facteau, 2005).

A study of adolescent girls who received services at birth control clinics found that many of them had talked with their parents about sexual issues and that over two-thirds felt closely connected with their parents. In the case of younger girls, the parents of most of them knew about their clinic visits and had played an active role in helping them make sexual and contraceptive decisions. The majority of the girls believed that their parents had positive attitudes about sexuality and birth control (Jones, Singh, & Purcell, 2005).

Masturbation in Adolescence

The most prevalent form of sexual activity in adolescence is masturbation, or sexually stimulating oneself. Most boys and many girls begin to learn about their bodies' sexual responses through masturbation. In a sample of college students, about 40 percent of the women and 38 percent of the men recalled masturbating prior to reaching puberty (DeLamater & Friedrich, 2002). Adolescent boys have tended to discuss masturbation among themselves—often in a joking way—more than have adolescent girls. Consequently, more slang terms have evolved to describe male masturbation (jerk off, jack off, whack off, beat off, beat the meat) than female masturbation (rubbing off, rolling the pill, fingering). Although we do not have reliable statistics on adolescent masturbation, what data we do have indicate that, at all age levels, masturbation is more common among males than among females. Retrospective studies, in which adults offer information about their behaviors as adolescents, suggest that the majority of adolescent boys masturbate at least

occasionally but that less than half of adolescent girls do so. It has also been found that adults generally are more willing to admit to having masturbated during adolescence than are adolescents themselves (Halpern et al., 2000).

The data indicate that of those adolescents who do masturbate, boys do so about three times more frequently than girls. Studies suggest that about three-fourths of male adolescents masturbate at least two times per week, compared to about one-quarter of female adolescents. Another 12 percent of the boys and 23 percent of the girls admitted to masturbating at least once, up to as often as once per month. A smaller percentage of the boys (11 percent) and the majority of girls (60 percent) said they had never masturbated. There may be a slight decline in frequency of masturbation during the years when young people are in college. A study of more than 300 college students found that 85 percent of the males indicated they masturbated, 70 percent of them with moderate to high frequency. The women in the study were far more likely to indicate that they had never masturbated (63 percent), with 24 percent reporting moderate to high frequency (Halpern et al., 2000).

The masturbation habits practiced in adolescence generally carry through the rest of a person's life, without decreasing much either with age or with partnership status. This is one indication that masturbation does not appear to be a compensation for lack of partnered sex; its frequency continues to be about the same even when a sexual partner is available (Kontula & Haavio-Mannila, 2002). Among adults, frequency of masturbation is affected by factors such as education, religion, and ethnicity, and we can probably assume that these same factors influence masturbatory behavior during adolescence (Halpern et al., 2000; Laumann, Gagnon, et al., 1994). More information on masturbation is given in Chapter 12, "Solitary Sex and Shared Sex."

FOH Initiation of Shared Sexual Behavior in Adolescence

What decisions and conflicts about sexuality did you face as an adolescent? Do you think anything has changed for teens since then? Adolescents today experiment with shared sexual activities at younger ages than was once the case (Forehand et al., 2005). An increase in sexual activity among teens began in the 1970s and continued through the 1980s. During the 1990s, however, the number of high school students who experienced sexual intercourse declined. In 2001, the percentage of high school students indicating that they had experienced intercourse dropped to 45.6 percent, compared to 54.1 percent in 1991. Across high school classes, the average ranges from 34.4 percent of ninth-graders who have had intercourse to 60.5 percent of twelfth-graders (SIECUS, 2003). Since the 1980s, differences in teen sexual behavior patterns across socioeconomic, racial, and ethnic groups have narrowed considerably. The initiation of sexual intercourse has now been established as a typical pattern of behavior in the United States for about half of adolescents ages 15 to 17 and a significant characteristic of the transition to adulthood (see Figure 6.7). Rates have been quite stable during the 2000s, although reported use of condoms during the last intercourse has increased from 58 percent in 2001 to 63 percent in 2003 (Centers for Disease Control, 2004a).

Among those teenagers who refrain from engaging in sexual intercourse, the most common reasons once cited related to fears of pregnancy, disease, or parental disapproval. The least common reasons for abstaining from sex revolved around embarrassment or concern about peer or partner disapproval. In recent studies, fewer adolescents are citing reasons such as not being ready for sex, waiting until they are older, or waiting until marriage (Blinn-Pike et al., 2004).

Adolescents who abstain from intercourse seem to fall into two distinct categories: *Delayers* say they are unlikely to initiate intercourse within the next year and tend to have limited sexual experience of any kind; *anticipators* report that they either are unsure about initiating sex in the near future or are likely to do so and tend to have more sexual experience already. Among boys who desire and anticipate sexual intercourse, the main reason for sexual inexperience is the lack of opportunity to initiate intercourse. That group of boys was more likely to have intercourse within the following year and also more likely to report having engaged in risky sexual behaviors (Forste

FIGURE 6.7 *Adolescent Sexuality*

Adolescents in contemporary industrial societies acquire adult status much later than they acquire biological maturity. This accounts for some of the confusion in adolescent sexual behavior. Adolescence is a time of awkward experimentation in sexual behavior and the acquisition of adult sexual attitudes toward commitment, intimacy, and fidelity.

& Haas, 2002; L'Engle et al., 2006). Adolescent girls who have older siblings, especially brothers, are more likely to delay sexual involvement and to have more traditional values about romance and parenthood (Kornreich et al., 2003).

The reasons surrounding the initiation of sexual intercourse typically are conceptualized in negative terms, with an emphasis on those consequences considered to be unfortunate. This is also true in programs that emphasize abstinence as the best option. Increasing evidence suggests that adolescents pay attention to what they perceive as the positive outcomes of sharing sex, including increased intimacy and pleasure in relationships. Many teenagers see sexual experience as a way to gain greater social status among their peers. In a pattern that continues into adulthood, male adolescents seem to value sexual pleasure more than do their female counterparts, who place a higher value on relational intimacy (Ott, Millstein, Ofner, & Halpern-Felsher, 2006).

There has been speculation that adolescents are engaging more frequently in oral sex, although only limited data are available on the topic. Among adolescents ages 15 to 17 in one study, 40 percent of the males and 32 percent of the females reported having had oral sex, and about half of them did so in order to avoid having sexual intercourse. Studies have also shown that about a quarter of adolescents believe that oral sex tends to be part of both casual and dating relationships and that a somewhat larger proportion of adolescents view oral sex as not "as big a deal as sexual intercourse" (SIECUS, 2003). One study of ninth-graders with an average age of 14.5 years found that 20 percent reported having had oral sex, with a smaller percentage indicating that they had shared intercourse. About a third of these students indicated that they intended to have oral sex in the next six months, while only a quarter expected to have intercourse (Halpern-Felsher et al., 2005). Many adolescents do not consider oral sex to be "having sex," and some young people assume that a range of sexual behaviors other than intercourse can fall under the the label of "abstinence."

There have been persistent claims that sexual activity during the adolescent years leads to negative self-concepts, when in fact the evidence would suggest that sexually experienced adolescents over the age of 15 actually tend to have higher levels of self-esteem than do those who are inexperienced. NHSLS data showed that 71 percent of women and 92 percent of men who experienced heterosexual intercourse during their teen years reported that they wanted it to happen and were not pressured into it (Laumann, Gagnon, et al., 1994). Significant numbers of teenagers who had experienced their first sexual intercourse actually felt better about themselves after their most recent sexual encounter. It seems clear that the context of the early sexual experiences is crucial in determining how teenagers feel about them. More negative outcomes were typical of sexual experiences that took place prior to puberty, were forced, or were the result of peer pressure, drugs, or alcohol. In general, other contexts did not seem associated with much guilt about sex or with other psychological or physical problems (Else-Quest, Hyde, & DeLamater, 2005).

Our society continues to send very powerful and contradictory messages to young people regarding sexuality. Although the media are saturated with messages encouraging sex, educational efforts directed at teenagers emphasize the ideal of refraining from sexual activity. For some time, experts have focused on the dangers and risks of adolescent sexual activity, often overlooking the fact that many adolescents feel a desire for sexual pleasure and are planning to act on that desire when circumstances allow (Levine, 2002b).

Adolescent Heterosexual Activity: Risk-Taking and Abstaining

Sexual experimentation is an important step in the development of many adolescents. Heterosexual contact usually proceeds through stages of progressive intimacy. There is evidence that young people today progress through the stages more rapidly, and perhaps in a different order, than in former years. The first level

of intimacy is kissing and tongue ("French") kissing. Bodily contact below the neck usually begins with hand-holding, breast touching, and touching each other's genitals first through the clothing and then directly. It is quite common during this level of intimacy for the two individuals to bring their genitals close together while clothed. It is not uncommon for adolescent males to experience ejaculation with their clothes on at some time in this process (Woody et al., 2000).

These latter stages of sexual exploration can lead to oral sex or intercourse, although many factors seem to play a role in determining when first intercourse will actually occur. Interestingly, boys with high self-esteem are more likely than their male peers with low self-esteem to have initiated intercourse, while girls with higher self-esteem are less likely than their peers to be sexually experienced (Spencer et al., 2002). Boys who are less able to inhibit their sexual arousal, even in the face of sexual risk, and those who experience increased sexual interest when they are emotionally upset or depressed are more likely to initiate sexual intercourse (Bancroft et al., 2004). Teenagers who are religious, have fewer personal problems, and have talked with their parents about sexuality tend not to initiate sexual intercourse as early as their peers (Clawson & Reese-Weber, 2003; Lehr et al., 2005; Pedersen, Samuelsen, & Wichstrom, 2003).

As adolescents age, the likelihood of their having heterosexual intercourse gradually rises. There are clear trends demonstrating that the percentages of teenagers who have engaged in intercourse, been pregnant, or had an abortion have been decreasing. There is also evidence that condom use among those who are sexually active has been increasing (Santelli et al., 2000; SIECUS, 2003). Figure 6.8 summarizes some of the data on sexual experience among adolescents. Some adolescents seem very comfortable with their decision to remain virgins. Research indicates that once adolescents have had intercourse, it is relatively likely that they will participate more than once, although comparatively few have multiple sexual partners within a year's time (SIECUS, 2003).

Ultimately, adolescents face the decision of whether to get involved in shared sexual activity and how far they should go when doing so. Research on adolescent sexual behavior has often focused on what is termed *risky* sexual behavior, broadly defined as having unprotected sexual intercourse or engaging in any sexual behavior that later was regretted (Coleman & Cater, 2005). Factors involved in the risk-taking decisions are relatively predictable. Adolescents who are more sociable, have strong friendships, and enjoy greater peer acceptance in early adolescence and who have a more mature and attractive appearance at age 13 are more likely to initiate sex earlier and have more sexual partners by age 19 (Zimmer-Gembeck, Siebenbruner, &

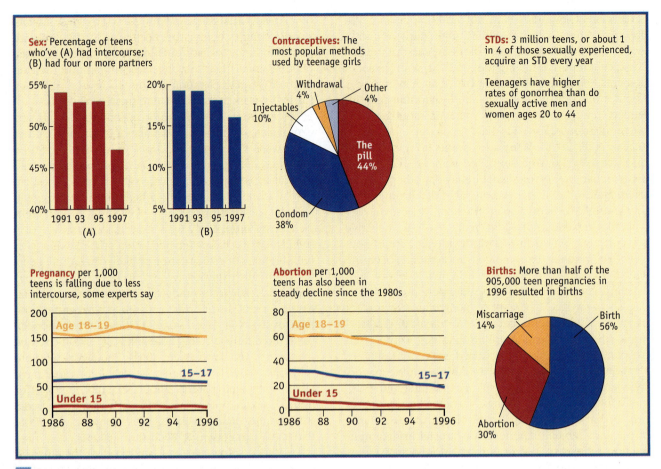

FIGURE 6.8

Data from a variety of sources indicate that teenagers have become more attentive to safety during sex but that some risks remain for them.

Collins, 2004). Peer pressure clearly plays a role, and the social networks with which an adolescent is associated can play a significant role in how prone they will be to initiating intercourse. Adolescents whose friends are sexually experienced or who believe that having sex will gain their friends' respect are more likely to have sexual intercourse (Sieving, Eisenberg, Pettingell, & Skay, 2006; South, Haynie, & Bose, 2005).

Numerous studies have suggested that alcohol use increases the likelihood of having risky sex in adolescence, for several different reasons. It apparently affects young people's assessments of a potential partner's attractiveness while increasing confidence levels and lowering social inhibitions. Sometimes it is used as an excuse for socially unacceptable sexual behavior. The more serious effects of alcohol, associated with higher levels of sexual risk taking, are impaired judgment about what may be sexually risky and loss of control or memory blackouts (Coleman & Cater, 2005). Teenagers who have already had sex in a previous relationship and believe sex to be important will wait less time before initiating sex in a new relationship (Rosengard et al., 2004).

Choosing to use a condom during intercourse is typically assumed to reduce some of the riskiness of the sexual encounter and also to represent a level of responsibility in the decision making. Condom use seems to be associated with a variety of different personal characteristics (Beadnell et al., 2005). Adolescents who used a condom the first time they had intercourse have been found to be more likely to report having used one during their last intercourse. Being drunk during a sexual experience is associated with lower condom use (Shafii et al., 2004). Planning to use a condom seems to work better for young people who are less concerned with expressing love during sex and more concerned with possible negative consequences, such as disease or pregnancy. Adolescents who are trying to express love or are having sex to enhance their mood are less likely to be reliable condom users (Gebhardt, Kuyper, & Dusseldorp, 2006).

Among those adolescents who choose to abstain from sexual intercourse even after they may have tried it (secondary abstinence), the reasons for doing so generally are practical. They tend to fear getting a disease or experiencing an unplanned pregnancy, but they also may have doubts about the appropriateness of having sex at their age. Adolescents who do not think their friends are having sex or fear their parents' disapproval also are more likely to abstain. Males who practice secondary abstinence are more likely to have already caused a pregnancy or to already have a child (Loewenson, Ireland, & Resnick, 2004). Also linked to sexual abstinence are characteristics such as strong aspirations for the future, community involvement, interest in exercise and good nutrition, strong peer role models, and good family communication (Oman, Vesely, & Aspy, 2005).

Recall some of your earliest sexual thoughts and feelings. Describe your reaction to them.

Social Development

Most adolescents become involved in social relationships with members of both sexes. Self-concept can play a major role in how comfortable the person is with these relationships as the individual's identity takes form. In a survey of suburban teenagers, those who indicated that they had experienced oral sex or sexual intercourse tended to be rated by their peers as being perceived as popular, but they did not tend to be seen as best friends or the most desirable people to spend time with (Prinstein, Meade, & Cohen, 2003). Developing the skills needed to be emotionally intimate is important, because the long-term consequences of emotional intimacy are as great as the consequences of sexual intimacy.

Different adolescents place differing degrees of emphasis on identity-formation goals and intimacy goals, a situation that can affect their likelihood of engaging in various forms of sexual behavior (DeLamater & Friedrich, 2002). In their early relationships, adolescents begin to learn about the ground rules for relating to other people and about the commitments and expectations that are part of those relationships from their friends in their social networks (Harper, G., et al., 2004). They gain experience with how relationships can cause emotional hurt and with the limits of one's responsibility toward another person in a relationship. Despite familiar assumptions that boys want sex and girls want love, many boys resist that stand and claim that they too are looking for loving relationships (Allen, 2003).

Important steps in personal development occur within the context of teenage romances and relationships. One phase in the formation of affectionate partnerships is what social psychologists call **dyadic withdrawal,** a period of time during which the couple pulls away from other social responsibilities to parents, peers, and other significant persons in their lives. The potential for sexual involvement increases during this time. Sexual partners are most often chosen from among people of similar characteristics, but there is an increasing trend among adolescents to develop sexual relationships with people of different races and ethnicities. This trend varies with geographic location and the social structure of the area (Ford, Sohn, & Lepkowski, 2003). Given the privacy available to most adolescents, a close relationship can easily progress to sexual exploration if they want it to. Learning how to deal with the new intimacy is essential to becoming comfortable with sharing one's sexuality.

How far sexual intimacy proceeds can be important in defining the boundaries of adolescent relationships. Many sexual activities can be viewed as part of sex play behavior. Some areas have seen an openness to what has been called "buddysex," that is, having nonintercourse sexual activities with friends, with no strings attached. There is no expectation of a continued relationship or any particular commitment beyond friendship. While little research has been done into these casual relationships, anecdotal information would suggest that, at least sometimes, they can become more complicated emotionally than was intended (Stepp, 2003).

Intense sexual sharing takes on extra meaning for most individuals, however. For one thing, to manage such activity successfully, the two people usually have to cooperate in a number of ways. For another, the two individuals are opening themselves to each other more fully—and with more vulnerability—than ever before. These factors, along with the emotional reactions of intense physical intimacy, often lead to a deepening of the relationship. If this is desired and expected, things may go well, but if it is a surprise or undesirable, conflicts may develop between the partners. Whatever the consequences of intense sex, after their initial experiences many adolescents begin to clarify the place sex will have in their adult relationships (Allen, 2003; DeLamater & Friedrich, 2002).

Adolescent Same-Gender Sexual Activity

Adolescence is a period when girls and boys tend to associate more with members of their own gender. Sexual preferences may also be relatively nonspecific at these ages. Consequently, it is not surprising that as youngsters experience pronounced physical changes in their sex organs and begin to become more aware of their sexual feelings, they may experiment with sex through encounters with same-gender peers. Again, the

dyadic withdrawal (die-ADD-ik) the tendency of two people involved in an intimate relationship to withdraw socially for a time from other significant people in their lives.

Real Student Voices

■ As teens get a little older, they respect themselves more. In high school, everyone was having sex with everyone else. Now in college, I feel that people are more responsible and more involved in serious relationships.

■ Some of my friends who are having sex with multiple partners without protection need to start using protection for themselves and their partners.

■ I see my peers engaging in a lot of risky behavior, like intercourse without any protection. This has made me much more cautious in my own sexual experiences. I think alcohol increases the risk of potentially harmful behavior.

■ I have friends who don't use protection the majority of the time, which is absurd to me. Why would anyone take a chance of getting pregnant or getting a disease? Cheating is another thing I can't explain, especially when the girls probably know each other!

statistics on same-gender sexual activity are inconclusive and have not been based on random samples of the population. The incidence of adolescent same-gender sexual behavior has ranged from 5 percent of 13- to 18-year-olds in one study to 11 to 14 percent of adolescent boys and 6 to 11 percent of adolescent girls in another study. In still another study of 3,267 male students ages 12 to 18 who reported having had any "sexual contact," 3 percent indicated that the contact had been with both males and females, and 3 percent indicated that it had been only with males (Goodenow, Netherland, & Szalacha, 2002). Boys tend to report more frequent same-gender experiences in later adolescence (ages 16 to 19), whereas girls reported less frequent experiences at this later age level (Ryan & Futterman, 2001). The reasons for the disparity are not well understood.

Some adolescents begin to get in touch with their same-gender sexual orientations during adolescence, although some may take months or years to clarify their sexual orientation as gay, lesbian, or bisexual (Rosario, Schrimshaw, Hunter, & Braun, 2006). Adult gay men report that their first same-gender experience generally occurred by age 14, whereas adult lesbians report that their first experiences tended to occur in the late teenage years. In a questionnaire administered to 89 gay males and 31 lesbians ages 14 to 21, about one-third indicated that they were aware of their sexual orientation between the ages of 4 and 10. Most of the rest were aware of it by age 17 (Russell, 2001). Biological development and timing of puberty seem to be the same for gay adolescents as they are for those who are heterosexual (Savin-Williams & Ream, 2006).

Cite several reasons why some lesbian and gay adolescents and young adults might refuse to acknowledge their same-gender attractions.

Adolescents who have clearly identified themselves as having a primarily same-gender orientation may experience some conflict with their social environment, especially in school, but there are indications that youthful gay people are coming out earlier and with less conflict than was once the case (Savin-Williams, 2005). Gay, lesbian, and bisexual adolescents seem to have higher risks of psychological distress, running away, dropping out of school, and suicide (Kimmel & Mahler, 2003). Nevertheless, attitudes in recent years toward differing sexual orientations have been changing, and more information and support are available for people with same-gender orientations. Some lesbian, gay, and bisexual teenagers surmount the extra measure of social difficulty with resilience and self-acceptance, whereas others continue to wrestle with their sexual identity issues into adulthood (Savin-Williams, 2005). (See also Chapter 13, "Same-Gender Orientation and Behavior.")

Adolescent Sexual Attitudes and Behaviors across Cultures

Adolescents develop their sexual identities, attitudes, and behaviors within their cultural contexts, which differ markedly from society to society. Distinct changes in the sexual values of adolescents have been occurring in most areas of the globe in recent decades, a reflection of increased urbanization, industrialization, and influence by Western media. As global pressures have caused economic markets to open up, a greater emphasis on competition, personal choice, and individuality has developed. It appears that all over the world, young people are starting to have sex earlier and are placing sexual pleasure ahead of safer sexual practices (Wellings et al., 2006).

When researchers studied trends in five developed countries in the West (Canada, France, Great Britain, Sweden, and the United States), they found sexual attitudes and behaviors to be quite similar. Oral sex has become a common behavior. Attitudes toward sex in these countries and in Australia are relatively casual, and risky behaviors (e.g., nonuse of condoms) have not decreased (Johnson et al., 2001; Maticka-Tyndale, Herold, & Oppermann, 2003; Stone et al., 2006). Adolescent childbearing is far more common among young women in lower socioeconomic groups, but in the United States contraception is used less frequently in all economic groups and teen pregnancy is even more common.

In Mexico and Latin America, adolescents have been caught up in the ambivalence of traditional religious values that seem to conflict with changing patterns of sexual behavior. The *machismo* tradition often creates conflicts surrounding power imbalances in relationships and the degree of comfort males have with their gender identities. Adolescents in Latin America receive information about contraception too late, and they tend to receive sexuality education that emphasizes biological facts over decision-making skills. Despite a high rate of adolescent pregnancy, both information about and access to contraception are very limited (Juarez & Martin, 2006).

Asian cultures have been experiencing marked contrasts between traditional sexual values and the more permissive sexual attitudes among adolescents today. In Eastern nations such as South Korea, sex is a far more private topic, and the rates of sexual activity and pregnancy are considerably lower. In Hong Kong, gay youth are finding it easier to come out about their identities to friends and families (Singh, Darroch, Frost, et al., 2001; Wong & Tang, 2004; Youn, 2001). In Japan, sexuality has been minimized and regulated as being tangential to the performance of responsible duty. Japanese youth consider chastity very important. There is less teenage sexual activity and far less single motherhood than in the United States, although abortion is quite accessible. Japanese youth often rush into sexual activity during late adolescence, as if making up for their more chaste earlier years. As the age of marriage becomes even later, the rate of premarital pregnancies and "shotgun" weddings has been increasing (Kashiwase, 2002).

China has been seeing a marked increase in adolescent sexual activity even in the face of official government condemnation; this may well reflect fundamental cultural shifts in China (Wong & Tang, 2004). Chinese culture still tries to moderate the sexual behaviors of youth, because early sexual activity is considered a sign of psychological distress (Lam et al., 2002). Journalists have reported that in Vietnam, sex before marriage—sometimes referred to as "eating rice before the bell"—is now the norm for adolescents (Mensch, Clark, & Anh, 2003).

African adolescents face mixed signals regarding their sexual behaviors. Some societies encourage youth to postpone sexual activity. Others do not see virginity as a virtue, and in fact may regard it as a sign of unsociableness or ill health. Among the Zulu, girls are supposed to be sexually available to a partner—coy and resistant to his sexual advances, but sexually faithful. Boys have more latitude in terms of what is considered sexually acceptable and are expected to make the sexual decisions, initiate sex, and even be sexually coercive. For a boy to allow a girl to resist his sexual advances would be considered weak (Kaufman et al., 2004; Varga, 2003). In sub-Saharan Africa, where the incidence of HIV infection is extremely high, the situation is made worse by the fact that adolescent girls frequently have sexual relationships with older men, who ultimately decide whether they will wear a condom (Smith, 2004).

■ Adolescent Sexual Health

Societal Attitudes and Remedies

Our culture's ambivalence toward sexuality is particularly evident with regard to sexual activity among the young. We tend to confuse sex-related public health issues with issues of morality and punishment, even as we see the negative consequences of not dealing with these problems head-on. When it comes to the risks of adolescent sex, it is crucial to remember that many adolescents assume an attitude of invulnerability, which makes them believe that the potential negative consequences won't happen to them.

Surveys demonstrate that 88 percent of people ages 15 to 24 believe that their peers are somewhat or very concerned about sexual health issues, including HIV and other diseases and pregnancy. About 70 percent have these concerns for themselves. Worldwide, it is believed that about 42 percent of the estimated 5 million new HIV infections occurred in young people ages 15 to 24, and 16 percent in children and adolescents under age 15 (Kaiser Foundation, 2002a, 2002b). Countries that have been more effective in reducing the numbers of teen pregnancies and sexually transmitted infections have taken the approach that sexual interaction is a normal, anticipated, and potentially healthy part of adolescent development (Lottes, 2002).

If our society is to help adolescents develop into sexually healthy adults, several steps must be taken. We must understand that the sexual health issues and ways of approaching them differ between males and females. Therefore, models of adolescent sexual health must accept and build in these differences (Tolman, Striepe, & Harmon, 2003). At the same time, girls must be helped to understand how femininity can be supportive of sexual health, and boys must be helped to reaffirm the range of behaviors and emotions that are part of being a man (Impett, Schooler, & Tolman, 2006; Sanchez-Flores, 2004). We must begin educating children openly and honestly about their sexuality from the time they are born and promote in them a healthy and positive self-concept. The American Academy of Pediatrics recommends that when health care professionals see adolescents, even for well-care visits, they use the opportunity to discuss issues relevant to sexual health and provide necessary services (Klein et al., 2005). Young people need to be prepared for the realistic work that must go into maintaining long-term relationships. In addition to getting information, they need to learn skills that will help them in practical ways, such as how to put on a condom properly, how to negotiate the use of protection with a partner, or how to say no effectively (Jemmott et al., 2005). Parents can play a significant role in this preparation, although they may need some help and training to do so effectively (Eastman et al., 2005). We must also provide better training to professionals who work with young people so they can be proactive in their sexual health interventions and make certain that funding for teen health care is available (Cozzens, 2006).

It is also necessary to address issues of poverty and political obstacles that prevent some of the population from having an equal opportunity for education and a hopeful future. These issues affect self-esteem and therefore the sex-related decisions that young people make. As a society, we must identify those adolescents who are at high risk of negative sexual consequences. High-risk youth include those who are pregnant or are already parents; have a history of substance abuse; get low grades in school; have been emotionally or physically abused; are homeless or have run away from home; are gay, lesbian, or bisexual; or are institutionalized for any reason. These youth tend to have a greater likelihood of participating in high-risk sexual activities without protections such as condoms. Some turn to prostitution. These young people have special needs for sexuality education, support services, and counseling interventions (Lemoire & Chen, 2005; Rickert et al., 2004; Whitbeck et al., 2004).

At a time when the incidence of shared sexual activity among teenagers is on the rise, evidence continues to mount that their age group is at greater risk for contracting sexually transmitted diseases, including HIV. Even though reports show increased use of condoms, studies also continue to show that many teenagers do not adequately assess the risks of HIV infection and, in fact, participate in high-risk sexual activities. Teenage risk-takers, however, can learn how to reduce their risk of sexual infections as they grow older (Kaestle et al., 2005)

Because our society often treats adolescent sexuality in negative and unrealistic ways, some American teenagers are not being helped to develop sexual attitudes and behaviors that can produce sexually happy and healthy adults. Teenagers need to be able to make decisions about their sexual behavior that will help them set personal limits, understand alternatives to penetrative sex, say no and mean it when they do not wish to participate in any form of sexual involvement, and have convenient access to condoms and contraception. Table 6.3 summarizes the characteristics of sexually healthy adolescents as outlined by the National Commission on Adolescent Sexual Health.

Teenage Pregnancy and Use of Birth Control

Teenage pregnancy continues to be a public health problem, and its rate in the United States is higher than in most other developed countries (Jossi, 2005). It is encouraging that teen birthrates have declined markedly since 1991. Among all 15- to 19-year-olds, birthrates dropped by 33 percent, to 41.7 per 1,000 teens in that age bracket, the lowest rate recorded by the National Center for Health Statistics since they began tracking the numbers in 1940 (Hamilton, Martin, & Ventura, 2006) (see Figure 6.9). During the same time period, birthrates for black 15- to 17-year-olds fell by more than half, from 86 to 39 per 1,000. Evidence suggests that these trends have been the result of two factors among adolescents: delaying the initiation of intercourse and improved use of contraception when they do have sex (Santelli, Morrow, Anderson, & Lindberg, 2006). As shown in Figure 6.10, the rates of pregnancy and abortion have decreased along with the rates of live births among teenagers.

Over the past three decades, use of contraceptives by adolescents has changed in significant ways, including increased use of long-lasting hormonal methods and condoms. Data from the Youth Risk Behavior Survey show that between 1991 and 2003 the number of teen women reporting condom use during their last sexual intercourse increased

Table 6.3 — Characteristics of a Sexually Healthy Adolescent as Established by the National Commission on Adolescent Sexual Health

Self

Appreciates own body
- Understands pubertal change
- Views pubertal changes as normal
- Practices health-promoting behaviors, such as abstaining from alcohol and other drugs and having regular checkups

Takes responsibility for own behaviors
- Identifies own values
- Decides what is personally "right" and acts on these values
- Understands consequences of actions
- Understands that media messages can create unrealistic expectations related to sexuality and intimate relationships
- Is able to distinguish personal desires from the desires of the peer group
- Recognizes behavior that may be self-destructive, and can seek help

Is knowledgeable about sexuality issues
- Enjoys sexual feelings without necessarily acting on them
- Understands the consequences of sexual behaviors
- Makes personal decisions about masturbation consistent with personal values
- Makes personal decisions about sexual behaviors with a partner consistent with personal values
- Understands own gender identity
- Understands effect of gender-role stereotypes and makes choices about appropriate roles for oneself
- Understands own sexual orientation
- Seeks further information about sexuality as needed
- Understands peer and cultural pressure to become sexually active
- Accepts people with different values and experiences

Relationships with Parents and Family Members

Communicates effectively with family about issues, including sexuality
- Maintains appropriate balance between family roles and responsibilities and growing need for independence
- Is able to negotiate with family on boundaries
- Respects rights of others
- Demonstrates respect for adults

Understands and seeks information about parents' and family's values, and considers them in developing own values
- Asks questions of parents and other trusted adults about sexual issues
- Can accept trusted adults' guidance about sexuality issues
- Tries to understand parental point of view

Peers

Interacts with both genders in appropriate and respectful ways
- Communicates effectively with friends
- Has friendships with males and females
- Is able to form empathetic relationships
- Is able to identify and avoid exploitative relationships
- Understands and rejects sexual-harassing behaviors
- Understands pressures to be popular and accepted, and makes decisions consistent with own values

Romantic Partners

Expresses love and intimacy in developmentally appropriate ways
- Believes that boys and girls have equal rights and responsibilities with regard to love and sexual relationships
- Communicates desire not to engage in sexual behaviors and accepts refusals to engage in sexual behaviors
- Is able to distinguish between love and sexual attraction
- Seeks to understand and empathize with partner

Has the skills to evaluate readiness for mature sexual relationships
- Talks with a partner about sexual behaviors before they occur
- Is able to communicate and negotiate sexual limits
- Differentiates between low- and high-risk sexual behaviors
- If having intercourse, protects self and partner from unintended pregnancy and diseases through effective use of contraception and condoms and other safer-sex practices
- Knows how to use and access the health care system, community agencies, religious institutions, and schools; seeks advice, information, and services as needed

Source: From Debra W. Haffner, M. P. H., "Facing Facts: Sexual Health for America's Adolescents," in *SIECUS Report*, Vol. 23 (6), August/September 1995. Used with permission.

from 38 percent to 58 percent, and the proportions relying on withdrawal decreased from 19 percent to 11 percent. Those reporting not using any birth control method dropped from 18 percent to 12 percent. Similar trends were found among teen males (Santelli et al., 2006).

The consistency of contraceptive use among adolescents depends on the kind of relationship they have. Couples who discuss birth control are more likely to use it consistently, and couples who see their relationship as romantic are somewhat less likely to be consistent. Girls who are ambivalent about getting pregnant are less likely to use contraceptives reliably than are those who feel either positive or negative about pregnancy (Bruckner, Martin, & Bearman, 2004; Manlove, Ryan, & Franzetta, 2004). Boys who think they know the most about condoms, even though their knowledge often is inaccurate, are less likely to use condoms than

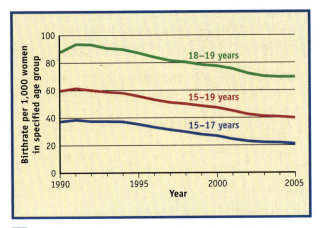

FIGURE 6.9   *Teen Birthrates in the United States, 1990–2005*

Continuing a trend that has been obvious since the 1950s, births to teen mothers fell by one-third between 1990 and 2005, to the lowest rate ever recorded.

Note: Data for 2005 are preliminary.

Source: National Center for Health Statistics, "Births: Preliminary Data for 2005," *National Vital Statistics Report,* 2006, Vol. 55 (11).

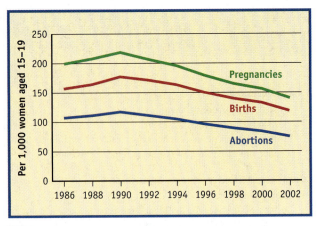

FIGURE 6.10   *Rates of Pregnancy, Birth, and Abortion per 1,000 Women Ages 15 to 19*

This graph shows that the rates among all women ages 15 to 19, including those who were not sexually active, have been declining since the early 1990s.

Source: U.S. Teenage Pregnancy Statistics, Guttmacher Institute, updated September 2006. Reproduced with permission of The Alan Guttmacher Institute.

those who are less confident about their knowledge. In the United States, physicians are less prone to prescribe emergency contraception for teenagers who have had unprotected sex than is the case in other countries. Both of these factors play a role in preventing teen birthrates from falling even further (Rock et al., 2005; Sable et al., 2006).

It is clear that young women who are exposed to abuse, violence, and family strife during childhood are at greater risk for teenage pregnancy, and the greater the number of adverse childhood experiences, the higher the risk (Hillis et al., 2004). Young women who have had one baby are also at special risk of a second pregnancy. Three-quarters of teen mothers in one study reported using contraception no more than half of the times they had intercourse (Koniak-Griffin et al., 2003). While teen mothers may be more conscientious about using contraception in the few months immediately following giving birth, the risks of pregnancy then begin to increase (Kershaw et al., 2003).

Assessments of programs designed to prevent teenage pregnancy have found that those providing access to contraception are most effective in significantly decreasing the proportion of adolescents who become pregnant (Kirby, 2002a; Saunders, 2005). A study of teen pregnancy prevention programs in New York City found that only one program could successfully document a true decline in the pregnancy rates of its participants. This program emphasizes long-term relationships for teenagers, postponing of intercourse, and consistent use of contraception (Philliber et al., 2002). Similar objectives, along with encouraging educational achievement and career goal-setting, have been recommended by professionals attempting to improve the effectiveness of pregnancy-prevention programs among Hispanic adolescents (Russell, Lee, et al., 2004).

Professionals who provide contraceptive health services for adolescents express great concern about efforts to pass legislation that would require parental consent for such services. Most teenagers who make use of pregnancy-prevention services already have talked with their parents about it and therefore would not be affected by such laws. Of those who have not involved their parents, however, only 7 percent indicate they would stop having sex if the services were not available to them. Most would seek clinic services anyway, but 13 perecent would try using withdrawal or the rhythm method, the least reliable contraceptive methods, and 6 percent say they would simply have sex without using any contraception at all. Experts in family planning believe that mandated parental involvement ultimately would result in increased rates of teen pregnancy (Jones & Boonstra, 2004; Jones, Singh, & Purcell, 2005).

Teen pregnancy and childbearing have substantiated social consequences. Adolescent girls who give birth to a child are much less likely than other girls to complete high school or to go on to higher educational attainment (Hofferth, Reid, & Mott, 2001). Youthful unwed fathers are more likely to have prob-

Real People

Amanda Confronts an Ethical Dilemma within Her Family

While Amanda is home for spring break during her junior year of college, her 15-year-old sister confides to her that she has started having sex with her 16-year-old boyfriend. She proudly explains to Amanda that the two of them discussed the decision carefully and went to the family planning clinic together. They decided to use the hormonal patch, which provides contraceptive protection for a week. They also use condoms as a backup measure because both of them are fearful of an unintended pregnancy. Neither had ever had sexual intercourse before.

Amanda is shocked by her little sister's news, and she tells her so. She believes her sister is too young for sexual intercourse, and she knows her parents would feel the same way. Her sister admits that her parents would disapprove but maintains that she has been mature and responsible in her decision making. She is surprised and resentful about Amanda's reaction, telling her that she is being an overconservative prude and warning her not to tell their parents or she will never speak to her again.

The two sisters have always had a close relationship and have shared many secrets over the years, but Amanda feels very torn this time. She believes that her sister has made a mistake that may be significant enough for her parents to become involved. Amanda and her boyfriend have been talking about intercourse as well, although they have not yet taken that step, and Amanda believes that the age difference would justify such a decision in her case. She is reluctant to hurt the relationship with her sister, which she has always enjoyed and valued.

Should Amanda tell her parents about her sister's sexual relationship, or should she keep quiet and continue a dialogue with the younger girl about her concerns?

How do you feel personally about Amanda's concerns? Is she overreacting? Should she be grateful that her sister and the boyfriend have taken responsibility for birth control?

lems with delinquency and economic hardship (Marcell, Raine, & Eyre, 2003). These scenarios create longer-term social and health problems for the entire society, including strains on the social welfare and health care systems because of poor socioeconomic conditions. Analysis of the data also demonstrates that there is no single effect of teenage childbearing and that it is not necessarily the catastrophe it has been portrayed as. Some conditions surrounding teen parents may well have been part of their lives *before* the pregnancy and therefore may have played a role as a cause rather than an effect. Although it has generally been assumed that the children born to teens tend to be at higher risk of poor health, social, and economic outcomes, the research does not necessarily support such assumptions. Further studies need to compare these trends more carefully (Hofferth & Reid, 2002). Teen parents are, however, at risk for depression and social isolation, which in turn may affect the well-being of children (Felix et al., 2003).

What social forces could be playing a role in the dramatic shifts in adolescent sexual behavior that have been observed since the 1970s?

■ Sexuality Education

What kind of sexuality education efforts have you experienced during your development? If you were exposed to programs in school, do you feel they were scientifically objective and accurate? Were they aimed at trying to convince you that a particular decision would be best? One of the long-standing debates in the culture wars surrounds the education of young people about human sexuality. The controversies do not focus so much on whether sexuality education should be offered in schools, because studies continue to confirm that over 90 percent of parents believe students should receive such information. Rather, the central debate is about the fundamental philosophies and content of sexuality education, and this is where things can get very heated.

On one side of the debate are those who feel that adolescents should have all the information they need to make informed and responsible decisions for their lives. They advocate giving teens age-appropriate instruction concerning birth control methods, safe sex, and differing sexual orientations and lifestyles. They believe young people should clarify their own values, while learning negotiating and communication skills that will help them delay sex if they choose to do so. This approach has been called **comprehensive sexuality education.**

On the other side of the debate are those who believe adolescents should be more protected from the details about sex and strongly urged to abstain from sexual activity until they are married. They think it is confusing for young people to learn about contraception, and in fact they fear that it may encourage adolescents to engage in sex. They also tend to be nonsupportive of alternative sexual lifestyles and prefer not to legitimize them through educational information or discussion. This approach is called **abstinence-only-until-marriage sexuality education.** The Bush administration favored this approach and supported such programs with over $1 billion in federal funds to states (Ciardullo, 2005). A few states have refused the aid because of the narrow focus required of the sponsored programs.

The American Public Health Association (APHA) has endorsed the right of children and youth to receive broad-based sexuality education. The group recommended that facts, information, and data be taught within a context that appreciates racial, ethnic, and cultural diversity. In addition, they advocated the teaching of skills that would help young people communicate effectively with others and make responsible decisions about sex (see Figure 6.11). The APHA urged schools to develop kindergarten through twelfth-grade curricula that would not impose religious, ethical, or moral values on students. Most often, the battles over which kind of sexuality education a school will offer are waged at the local level, with elections to local Boards of Education sometimes deeply influenced by advocates from both sides of the debate (Batchelder, 2004).

The Development of Sexuality Education

Only limited and sporadic attention was given to formalized sexuality education until the 1960s, when attention began to focus on the sexual behavior of youth. It was during that decade that two professional groups—the Sex (now Sexuality) Information and Education Council of the United States (SIECUS) and the American Association of Sex Educators, Counselors, and Therapists (AASECT)—began to highlight the need for improved sexuality education efforts and to work toward the establishment of sexuality education programs.

The first generation of sexuality education efforts arose out of a "prevention model," aimed at reducing rates of unwanted pregnancy and the incidence of sexually transmitted disease among the young. These efforts were built on the assumption that if young people

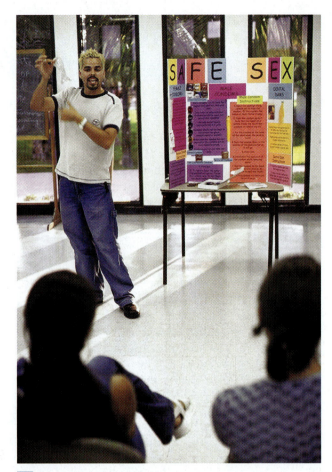

FIGURE 6.11 *Comprehensive Sexuality Education*
The comprehensive approach to sexuality education emphasizes scientific information about sexuality and helps prepare students to make responsible decisions while knowing how to protect themselves against unintended pregnancy and disease.

had more knowledge about sexuality, pregnancy, and birth control, they would avoid unprotected sexual intercourse or perhaps even avoid sex altogether. As it eventually became clear that knowledge in itself was insufficient to prevent unprotected intercourse or pregnancy, a second generation of curricula emerged. These placed increased emphasis on the need for young people to understand and clarify their own values and to learn the decision-making and communication skills that would lead toward more responsible

comprehensive sexuality education an approach to educating young people about human sexuality that includes information about sexuality but also encourages clarifying values and developing decision-making skills.

abstinence-only-until-marriage sexuality education an approach to educating young people that emphasizes the need to abstain from sexual relations until marriage, essentially the "just say no" philosophy.

sexual behavior and relationships. These comprehensive approaches do not seem to lead to an increase in sexual behavior, and they do produce reductions in sexual risk-taking behaviors (Kirby, 2002b).

The abstinence-only programs that emerged in the late 1980s constituted a reaction to what was perceived as a lack of success on the part of the earlier attempts. Some conservative religious and political groups believed that openness about sexuality had gone too far, and they developed programs that emphasized sexual abstinence until marriage. They represented what became known as the "just say no" or "just don't do it" approach to sexuality education. Although evaluative research concerning these programs suggests that they may result in students having more conservative attitudes toward premarital sex in the short term, there is no particular evidence that the students participate in sexual activity any less frequently (Kirby, 2002a). Some emerging evidence suggests that adolescents are delaying the initiation of sexual intercourse at least somewhat, possibly as a result of the abstinence-only approach (Santelli et al., 2006).

Another generation of sexuality education curricula, often referred to as **integrated sexuality education programs,** emerged in reaction to the HIV/AIDS crisis and other health-related issues surrounding sexuality. Often without examining what had worked and not worked in the past, these programs at first urgently tried to alert young people to the very real dangers of unprotected sex in an effort to persuade them to avoid such behaviors. Like earlier sexuality education efforts, these programs were based largely on the apparently faulty assumption that knowledge about consequences translates to immediate changes in behavior. Officials of the Centers for Disease Control and Prevention recognized that careful study must be given to what approaches actually led to behavioral change and that "quick-fix" approaches seemed to have little value (Office of the Surgeon General, 2001). It is now becoming clear that when they are carefully designed, integrated approaches to education and prevention can be effective in reaching young people and helping them make safer decisions (Taverner, 2003).

The Need for Sexuality Education

Studies continue to show that teens often lack the knowledge they need to protect themselves against unintended pregnancy or disease (Kempner, 2003). Nearly all states either mandate or encourage sexuality education and teaching about HIV/AIDS and other sexually transmitted diseases. Most sexuality education instructors are teaching their students about intercourse and abstinence, condom use, sexual decision making, and transmission of HIV. Many other topics are often neglected (Landry et al., 2003). The fact remains, however, that young people still report that they learn the most about sexuality from their peers or from entertainment media. There is a strong likelihood that much of this peer and media education is laden with misinformation and exaggeration.

Many sexuality educators lack professional training in the field. Experts are concerned that many teachers not only are underprepared, but also are being forced to teach material with which they do not feel personally comfortable (Goldfarb, 2003). It has been suggested that compulsory teacher training be part of any legislation mandating sexuality education. There is also a need for some specialization in sexuality education efforts. Special groups in society—for example, the developmentally disabled, the aged, adolescents, and young people living out of their homes—need sexuality education that addresses their special concerns. The trend is toward helping each individual live the most comfortable, problem-free sexual life possible.

To expect all parents to be able to handle the long and complicated job of sexuality education by themselves is simply unrealistic today. There may be times when involving other people in a child's life can be the most valuable direction to take. Parents can participate in parallel programs that will better prepare them for discussing the sex-related topics their children are considering (O'Donnell et al., 2005). We also know that more than a half million young people in the United States live in foster care, group care, or residential living settings. The best sexuality education involves a concerted effort on the part of many different people—parents or other primary caregivers, teachers, religious leaders, counselors, youth organizations, and the media. Young people then receive messages and skills from a variety of individuals and are helped to integrate sexual feelings and decisions into their lives more realistically.

The Current Sexuality Education Debate

Comprehensive sexuality education has usually emphasized a positive view of human sexual behavior, balanced with factual information about its potential risks and consequences. Sexuality educators who espouse the comprehensive model believe that in order for young people to make responsible sexual decisions, they must have a health-promoting and positive view of themselves as sexual human beings (Goldfarb, 2005; Schaalma, Abraham, Gillmore, & Kok, 2004).

integrated sexuality education programs this concept emphasizes the possibility of combining education to prevent pregnancy and the transmission of diseases with realistic approaches to educating young people about sexuality and about how to make safer decisions about sex.

Real Student Voices

■ I don't believe my sex ed was very informative. My teacher never went into much detail, and he never discussed contraception or homosexuality. It was mostly about abstinence.

■ The only time I got any sexuality education was in the 6th grade. I don't remember much about it because that was 10 years ago.

■ I learned more about sex on the bus ride to school than I did in high school sex ed class.

■ During my junior year of high school, we had to get special permission from our parents to be enrolled in the racy sex ed class. As it turned out we rarely talked about sex, and spent most of the time on drugs and eating disorders.

■ My previous sexuality education seemed quite accurate. I still haven't had intercourse, although most of my peers have.

■ My teacher told us she "had to teach" abstinence, but that she didn't believe that was the best way to go, so she also taught all the birth control methods.

Comprehensive Sexuality Education

Comprehensive sexuality educators do not assume that all teenagers are sexually active, but they see in the statistics the prediction that many teens likely will be eventually. Although they may encourage abstinence or postponement of sexual activity, they also want young people to be prepared to protect themselves as much as possible if they choose to engage in sex with others.

The sex-positive view and the emphasis on being prepared for sexual activity have offended and concerned many who oppose comprehensive sexuality education, because they fear it has led to—or at the very least not countered—sexual permissiveness. They feel that permissiveness is exactly what sexuality education should be combating. Proponents of the comprehensive approach cite figures that show how rates of pregnancy among sexually active teenagers have actually declined even as the actual numbers of adolescents having sex have increased. Studies of comprehensive sexuality education indicate that it can have lasting effects on adolescents (Kirby, 2002a). Nevertheless, it is the frequency of sexual activity among the young that has many people concerned, and they believe it is the place of sexuality education to strongly encourage young people not to have sex.

Abstinence-Only Sexuality Education

Aside from fears of promiscuity, pregnancy, or disease, proponents of the abstinence approach believe that chastity is a value to be promoted. Numerous sex-uality education curricula now teach the abstinence-only-until-marriage philosophy. The central theme behind these curricula is that if we can persuade young people to practice sexual abstinence until they marry, many social problems would be solved. Opponents of this approach maintain that it is not a realistic approach, given how prevalent adolescent sexual activity has become in recent years. Opponents point out that even when chastity was taught as the highest virtue, many sexual problems still existed. People simply suffered them in private.

Some abstinence-based curricula seem to have yielded positive results, at least in preliminary studies (Laflin, Sommers, & Chibucos, 2005). Other programs have disturbed observers with their reliance on scare tactics, fear, and shame as ways to discourage students from engaging in sexual activity. Review of numerous such curricula has revealed the following educational and philosophical strategies employed by many of them (Kempner, 2004; Kenny & Sternberg, 2003):

1. The use of simplified slogans and scare tactics to encourage abstinence.
2. Omission of information about contraception, or an emphasis on the unreliability of birth control.
3. Strong emphasis on the negative consequences of sex, and the substitution of biased opinion for fact, while presenting only one side of controversial issues such as abortion, condom use, and the teaching of contraception.
4. Misinformation and inaccuracies concerning the medical aspects of abortion, sexually transmitted diseases, and human sexual response.

5. Lack of discussion about same-gender sexual orientation, or the judgment that such orientations represent an unhealthy "choice."
6. An emphasis on and a reinforcement of traditional stereotypes of male and female gender roles.
7. Lack of recognition of the sexual nature of people with disabilities, and lack of respect for cultural and economic differences among people.
8. Religious bias that advocates only one set of values concerning sexual behavior.
9. A limitation on the number of family structures presented, with nontraditional families depicted as troubled.
10. Failure to adequately involve parents, and marketing the programs with inadequate evaluative data to back up their effectiveness.

Because most of the popular abstinence-based programs are produced by organizations or individuals that represent particular religious moral frameworks, state departments of education and the courts have begun to restrict their use in public school settings (Kenny & Sternberg, 2003). This is not to say that consideration of abstinence or the postponement of sex should not have a place in sexuality education. On the contrary, given the current risks of sexual behavior, they represent very reasonable and rational choices. However, the research evidence suggests that the abstinence message may not be particularly effective. In a study of three middle schools in Minnesota, twice as many students in an abstinence-only sexuality education course said they were sexually active as had indicated being so prior to taking the class (Pierre, 2004). In programs where adolescents take a pledge not to have sex until marriage, the majority do not stick to the pledge, and the rates for developing sexually transmitted diseases are about the same as among young people who do not take such a pledge (Brody, 2004). A recent thorough study of abstinence programs found that participating students were just as likely to have sex as students who were not part of the programs, started having sex at about the same age, and tended to have the same numbers of sexual partners (Trenholm et al., 2007).

Room for Compromise

The middle ground in the sexuality education controversy is represented by programs that place an emphasis on abstinence without relying on scare tactics, misrepresentation of medical facts, or the teachings of any one particular religious doctrine. They share the goal that most sexuality educators feel is legitimate: that young people should indeed postpone sexual sharing until they are ready for mature, well-informed, and safe sexual relationships (Boonstra, 2002).

Some programs have become proactive in teaching young people skills for avoiding peer pressures and

Source: John Branch, *San Antonio Express-News*.

being assertive about postponing sex until they are ready. At the same time, they teach young people how to protect themselves against unwanted pregnancy and disease should they ultimately choose to engage in sexual activities. For many observers of the sexuality education debate, these approaches may ultimately represent the compromising ground (Kempner, 2003).

Which approach to sexuality education do you support: comprehensive sexuality education, sexuality education that focuses on abstinence, or something in between?

Again, some particular approaches to sexuality education have been successful in changing sexual behaviors. These provide accurate information in a variety of ways that students are able to personalize and retain, often using interactive methods rather than lecturing to students. They also address the social pressures to have sex and help young people know how to respond to those pressures. They model ways for young people to decline sexual activity or unprotected sex. They encourage younger, inexperienced youth to wait until they are older, and they advise experienced, high-risk youth always to use a condom. The programs that have been most successful in increasing the use of contraceptives and reducing teenage pregnancy are those that provide access to contraception (Blake et al., 2003; Johnson et al., 2003).

Sexuality Education and Cultural Diversity

One of the greatest challenges for sexuality education programs is the need to develop approaches that will be sensitive to cultural differences. This applies not only to North America, where the population continues to become increasingly diverse, but also to countries around the world that are attempting to develop their own forms of sexuality education (Stockdale, 2003). Although countries often model their approaches after programs developed in the United States, it is crucial that they remain aware of the differences in attitudes, behaviors, expectations, and needs created by differences in social and cultural environments. The perspectives of a Eurocentric, heterosexual culture in sexuality education settings often fail to address the needs of youth of color and youth who are gay, lesbian, or bisexual (Mutchler et al., 2004).

Sexuality educators have to sort through the impact of demographics on people's attitudes and behaviors and move beyond cultural awareness or sensitivity to what has been termed "cultural competence." This is a long-term process by which educators expand their horizons, think critically about issues of power and oppression in societies with diverse populations, and then act appropriately. Educators need to learn the attitudes, knowledge, and skills that will help them develop positive communication and trust with people of varying cultural backgrounds. This is one way to minimize barriers of culture, language, and attitude so that sexuality education can become available for and relevant to a wider spectrum of the population within a democratic format (SIECUS, 2004).

Other countries of the world are also struggling with issues relating to sexuality education as global media become increasingly saturated with sex-related material. The Sexuality Information and Education Council of the United States has been working with organizations in Russia, Brazil, India, and Nigeria to develop components of effective comprehensive sexuality education programs that will reach the youth of these countries. In Belize and Peru, a strategy has been employed that trains peer educators to offer programs combining drama and dance with useful information about human sexuality and decision-making skills. The program has proved to be effective in reaching youth who have already left school (Kohn, 2002).

Taiwanese culture is somewhat reflective of Chinese culture in general, and there has been a good deal of ambivalence in Taiwan about sexuality education. Josephine Cheun-Jue Ho, an English professor at Taiwan's National Central University, had founded the Center for the Study of Sexualities. As part of her work, she had spent seven years developing a data-bank of information about human sexual behaviors. A censorship organization in the country brought a complaint against Professor Ho, charging her with violation of obscenity laws. Other academics on the island have supported her, but there has been a fair amount of opposition to her cause as well. Some say that while sexuality education is all right for the classroom, it should not make its way to the general public. Professor Ho continues to be an outspoken advocate for open and honest discussion of sexuality in Taiwan (Lin-Liu, 2003).

Chapter Summary

1. Individual patterns of sexual orientation and behavior probably develop through the interaction of biological, social, cultural, and psychological factors. The process is called psychosexual development.

2. Biopsychological drive or instinct theories of psychosexual development state that there is a natural, instinctual drive toward sexual behavior.

3. Psychodynamic theory has taught that the sexual instinct, or libido, becomes invested in different bodily areas through four stages in human development: oral, anal, latency, and genital. It is believed that boys and girls must resolve unconscious sexual issues with their parents during their development. This theory has seen much revision in recent years.

4. Conditioning theorists believe that positive and negative reinforcement play a role in how people learn to behave sexually. Social learning theory is an extension of conditioning theory that emphasizes the importance of identifying with other people and of modeling behavior after them.

5. Developmental theory expresses the importance of stages in the emergence of behavior patterns, including those related to sexuality. Erik Erikson described eight stages, each of which has particular tasks to be completed and crises to be resolved.

6. A unified model of psychosexual development considers three crucial strands that eventually integrate to form adult sexuality: gender identity, sexual response and orientation, and the capacity for dyadic intimacy.

7. In shaping sexuality, contemporary social process theory focuses less on individual persons as the unit of analysis and more on the social processes in which the individual is immersed.

8. Social script theory teaches that human behavior is controlled by complex social scripts. Sexual scripts have cultural, interpersonal, and intrapsychic dimensions that shape people's patterns of sexual behavior.

9. Choice theory explains how individuals decide which sexual behaviors to participate in, factoring in resources, risk management, and the "market" of accessible partners.

10. Social network theory focuses on how sexual connections and relationships are negotiated within a social context.

11. In infancy and childhood, the sex organs respond to many stimuli. Babies are sensitive over the entire surface of their bodies. Children become more curious about their bodies and sex-related matters.

12. Children's sexual preferences are at first vague or multisexual. Sex play with other children, masturbatory behavior, and educational efforts by parents can play a significant role in how children feel about sexuality and their own bodies.

13. Children are capable of strong romantic attachments and varying levels of sexual interaction.

14. Adolescence is the period of life between childhood and adulthood. At puberty, the body becomes capable of reproduction and develops its secondary sex characteristics. It is a time for exploring masturbation and relationships.

15. Adolescents learn more about sex and develop their sexual values and attitudes through interaction with peers, by contact with the media, and in their sexual experimentation. There have been social pressures for adolescents to become sexually active at earlier ages.

16. Masturbation is particularly prevalent among adolescents, more so among males than among females. The frequency of masturbation varies a great deal among individuals.

17. Understanding and coping with emotional intimacy are important during the adolescent years and crucial to the establishment of effective social relationships.

18. Same-gender sexual activity among adolescents may be experimental, or it may reflect later sexual orientation. A significant proportion of adolescents have at least one same-gender sexual experience.

19. Heterosexual contact among adolescents often proceeds through levels of increased intimacy, with the likelihood of sexual intercourse increasing with age.

20. Many different factors seem to influence the likelihood of intercourse and the use of condoms, including social dominance, appearance, and testosterone levels in males.

21. Adolescent sexual health has become a more pressing concern with emergence of the risk of HIV infection, increases in sexually transmitted diseases, and the high rate of unintended pregnancy. The National Commission on Adolescent Sexual Health has established clearer guidelines on the subject.

22. Teenage pregnancy continues to be a problem in the United States, creating consequences for teen parents and for the larger society, although rates of teen pregnancy have been decreasing.

23. Age, length of time a male has been sexually active, and social factors influence the likelihood of condom use during sex.

24. Sexuality education has evolved since the early 1960s, when its aims were largely to prevent unwanted pregnancy and disease by giving young people knowledge. The next stage emphasized the need for values clarification and communication skills. The role of the Internet now needs to be considered.

25. The attitude among the general public has tended to be favorable toward sexuality education in schools, although studies show that young people still get most of their sex information from peers or the media. Parents usually cannot provide all the education young people need.

26. There is a debate between groups who advocate comprehensive sexuality education, emphasizing sex-positive concepts and preparing young people for possible sexual activity, and groups who want abstinence-only sexuality education, often based on fear tactics or particular religious biases. Other programs focus on postponing sex but still being prepared with information on contraception, protection, and the need to prevent transmission of HIV.

27. To be successful, sexuality education must recognize cultural differences. Cultural competence on the part of sexuality educators can help them communicate effectively with people from cultural traditions that differ from their own. Other countries of the world are attempting to shape sexuality education programs.

28. Sexuality education can change attitudes, but there is less research on behavioral change. Programs that devote adequate time to issues, are frank, make their goals clear, and discuss contraception and safer sex do seem to change sexual behaviors and to prevent pregnancies and disease transmission. There is no evidence that sexuality education hastens the onset of intercourse.

Focus on Health Questions

In this section you will find the kinds of questions that you may have concerning your own health and sexuality. The page references indicate where in the text the answer is located; the exact place is marked with this logo: **FOH**

1. Does everybody start having sex when they are in high school? **154–157**

2. My parents and my church tell me it is safer to avoid sexual intercourse until I get married. But most of my friends think that attitude is ridiculous. Whom should I believe? **165–167**

Chapter 7

Adult Sexuality and Relationships

Chapter Outline

The thing that scared me the most about getting older was the thought of my sexual powers declining. While I have noticed some degree of moderation in my sexual needs, the frequencies of my sexual activities are really not that much different from when I was in my twenties. I guess the "use it or lose it" principle may be operative here, since I've always believed in using it.

—from a letter to the author

Young adulthood, encompassing roughly the ages of 18 to 24 years, represents an extension of adolescence for many, especially those who attend college and then spend time beginning to build a career. Young adults who go directly into the work force may experience the economic and social pressures of adult life even sooner. Like all other stages of human life, young adulthood is a dynamic time filled with transitions, new decisions, inner journeys to be undertaken, and problems to be resolved. Young adults must further develop means of communication with intimate partners as well as their ability to make responsible, informed decisions about sexuality and reproduction (DeLamater & Friedrich, 2002). One's sexuality weaves its way through all the twists and turns of adult life. Fifty-year-olds may sometimes be just as confused about sex and relationships as fifteen-year-olds (Kantrowitz, 2006).

■ Hurdles of Young Adulthood

There is evidence that the current generation of young people entering college as traditional-age students are members of what has been termed the *millennial generation,* those born since 1982. They generally are a well-adjusted and happy group, much different from the stereotypes of troubled youth left over from previous generations (Howe & Strauss, 2003). They have been quite close to their parents and are grateful for the relatively affluent lives they have led. Sexuality educators and commentators on sexual culture have begun to drop outdated stereotypes of young adults as people who constantly put themselves at risk with irresponsible sexual behavior. Members of the millennial generation are far more likely to be respectful of adults, open to fair-minded explanations about sexuality, and anxious to make our world a better place (Kelly, 2005; Melby, 2006a).

The College Experience

Colleges where most students are commuters allow for a good deal of continuing contact between students and their families. Residential colleges create social networks of their own, around which individualized campus cultures develop and a means for meeting others and building relationships is established. College students often experience the pressures of peer expectations regarding their social and sexual choices (Lefkowitz, Gillen, Shearer, & Boone, 2004). There is evidence that college students, when they leave this somewhat protected world, experience a good deal of anxiety about facing the adult world in a period some authors have dubbed the "quarterlife crisis." Some sixty-five percent of these young adults will live with their parents for a time after graduating, and they are likely to go through several jobs in rapid succession. Their lives may be unsettled and disappointing and may not be conducive to committed relationships (Robbins & Wilner, 2004).

In one study of young adults, 93 percent reported having had vaginal intercourse; 57 percent said they had performed oral sex, and 78 percent said they had received oral sex; and 10 percent reported having engaged in receptive anal sex. Twenty-seven percent of the men said they had had insertive anal sex. For both women and men, having a relationship with an older partner seemed to increase the likelihood of sexual activity at earlier ages (Ompad et al., 2006). Another study found that nearly 30 percent of the 1,114 young adults interviewed indicated they had used some sort of sex toy within a typical four-week period, and more than 10 percent reported having used some drug to enhance sexual pleasure, including alcohol, marijuana, ecstasy, or Viagra (Foxman, Aral, & Holmes, 2006). These behaviors can lead to increased risk of contracting a disease. In one clinic, a sample of young adults found that 74 percent of those whose partners had had another sexual partner during their relationship were not aware of that fact, placing them at much higher risk of contracting a sexually transmitted disease (Drumright, Gorbach, & Holmes, 2004).

As mentioned in Chapter 1, college students are among the most studied of populations when it comes to human sexuality, largely because they are so accessible to researchers in the field. Therefore, we know a little about sex-related issues and trends among college students, although generalizing across particular campuses or regions of the country can be difficult. Some findings that may well be quite generalizable based on previous data include the fact that students who are strongly religious make their sexual decisions while giving consideration to their religious beliefs. Students who consider themselves attractive tend to be somewhat more sexually active than those who do not (Visser, Smith, Richters, & Rissel, 2007; Weeden & Sabini, 2007). We also know that male students who are under the influence of alcohol are more likely to engage in risky sexual behaviors and to not use condoms. In one study of college students, slightly more than 70 percent expressed regrets about at least one previous sexual experience. These negative feelings resulted from doing things that were inconsistent with their morals, the realization that their partner wanted something different from the relationship, not using condoms, or feeling pressured into sex—a regret more commonly expressed by college women than by men (Lefkowitz et al., 2004; Maisto et al., 2004; Oswalt, Cameron, & Koob, 2005).

It is also probably safe to say that women become more assertive sexually during the college years, sometimes taking the initiative to have sex with a partner or even pursuing it somewhat aggressively. Women with body piercings were found to be somewhat less constrained sexually and more likely to have more sexual partners (Skegg, Nada-Raja, Paul, & Skegg, 2007). In a study that examined the sexual strategies of women in southern urban campuses and rural midwestern campuses, the use of persuasion, coercion, and physical force to initiate sex did not differ between the two populations. The study did find that women who had experienced a greater level of sexual activity in the past were more likely to be aggressive in their pursuit of sex (Anderson, Kontos, Tanigoshi, & Struckman-Johnson, 2005).

Depression is relatively common among college students, and there is a great deal of medical evidence that depression tends to lower sexual interest and arousal in both men and women. A study of several hundred students found that about 10 percent of women and a slightly higher percentage of men actually had increased sexual interest and levels of arousal during depressive periods (Lykins, Janssen, & Graham, 2006). Further study is needed to clarify how much this may predispose depressed students to risky sexual behavior.

Another reasonable assumption would be that college students tend to do a fair amount of checking out of potentially available partners (see Figure 7.1). During

FIGURE 7.1 *College Students Survey the Social Scene*
The bar and club scene offers many young adults a place to socialize and meet potential sexual partners.

the sexually exploratory period of young adulthood, many sexual health concerns are raised, because the chances of multiple sexual encounters and risky sexual behavior tend to be higher. This makes it all the more important that consideration be given to the use of condoms during sex. Researchers have confirmed that men tend to feel more confident than women about using condoms and perceive fewer problems with doing so. This may be because women have to negotiate the use of condoms with a male partner and might be perceived as sexually permissive if they carry condoms with them. Other factors also determine whether college students will be likely to use condoms, but planning ahead to do so seems to be quite important (Farmer & Meston, 2006; Reece & Dodge, 2004).

How does the information about college students given above support your own observations about sexuality and relationships on campus?

 See "Men Talk Sex" and "What Women Want" on SexSource Online.

"Hooking Up" and the Double Standard

How do you define "hooking up"? When my own children were in college during the past ten years, they began to use the term, which was entirely new to me. I asked them—and then several hundred of my students—how they defined the term. As far as I can tell, there is no general agreement about exactly what it means to hook up, except that it represents a casual encounter in which some sort of sexual activity may or may not be involved. Sexual intercourse is less typical during a hookup; oral sex seems more common. While it is difficult to compare hooking up with earlier studies of "casual sex," researchers believe that one main difference is the lower likelihood of intercourse during hooking up (McGinn, 2004). A central understanding seems to be the absence of any particular future commitment. Interestingly, while men express somewhat more comfort with hooking up than do women, both sexes tend to overestimate the rates with which the other sex actually is participating in such behavior (Lambert, Kahn, & Apple, 2003).

Evidence from around the world suggests that women and men globally are starting to have sex at earlier ages and with greater frequency than in the recent past. There still exists a double standard that legitimizes sexual permissiveness more for men than for women, but women have also been adopting harsher attitudes toward men's sexual behaviors (Crawford & Popp, 2003; Milhausen & Herold, 2001).

Students entering college in recent years who complete the attitude questionnaire from the Cooperative Institutional Review Program have been showing lower approval rates for casual sexual encounters compared to the responses to the survey when it was first administered in 1966. The approval rate today hovers around 40 percent, considerably lower than the high of 51.9 percent in 1987. This suggests that the current college generation may be becoming somewhat more conservative in its attitudes toward sex without marriage and sex between people who have known each other only for a short time.

Research consistently supports the perception that men tend to be more sexually permissive than women. Although it is no longer assumed within some attitudinal groups that it is crucial for women to remain virgins until they marry, the attitude that it is more acceptable for men to be sexually active with a variety of partners than it is for women persists (Traeen, Holmen, & Stigum, 2007). There still seems to be a double standard regarding males' and females' involvement in sexual activities (Muehlenhard et al., 2003). College students continue to be in touch with a "conditional" double standard that limits the acceptable number of sexual partners for women to a very few, and then only within the context of a meaningful loving relationship.

■ Intimacy, Sexuality, and Coupling

One of the major tasks of early adulthood is to achieve intimacy with others. Intimacy is the ability to open oneself to others in a way that permits mutual sharing and caring; it represents an essential quality in deeper human relationships. Most people long for intimacy and look for opportunities to build the sort of trust with another human being that allows for openness and sharing. The desire for intimacy is also a primary basis for relating to another person sexually.

When people have difficulty establishing intimate relationships, they may well display behaviors that make it difficult for others to relate to them on more than a superficial level, such as shyness, hostility, self-centeredness, or insensitivity. Sexual sharing in a nonintimate context may be physically satisfying, but over time it often loses the deeper feelings of fulfillment and commitment that help a relationship flourish and endure. There is evidence that women and men sometimes view intimacy in different contexts. Men often interpret intimacy within the context of genital sexual activity, while women may perceive it in more romantic terms. Such differences may mean that couples will need to negotiate levels of intimacy that are acceptable to each

partner. There is more about intimacy and the role of effective communication in Chapter 9, "Sexuality, Communication, and Relationships."

Coupling

At some point in their lives, most individuals build an intimate relationship with someone else. Although how partners negotiate their particular partnership shows much variety, cultural expectations and social scripts exist that guide the process of human coupling. In surveys of attitudes toward relationship priorities, sexual satisfaction often rates lower than factors such as family relationships, financial security, and religious or spiritual life. Nevertheless, sexual satisfaction and compatibility are considered to be important to the general satisfaction levels that couples share (Byers, 2005).

Coupling seems to be a process that does not progress in a straight line but instead continues through endless cycles of advancing and retreating, of increasing and decreasing intimacy. The beginning *expansive stage* of coupling is characterized by a burst of romance, sexual attraction, and exploration. It is in this stage that the individual identities of the partners become secondary to the characteristics of the couple. The two "I"s become "we." The relationship seems full of promise. Eventually, this stage is followed by a stage of *contraction and betrayal,* during which old fears, insecurities, and personal realities of the individuals surface. This is a time of bewilderment, as things no longer seem as they were and the partners pull back into themselves in disillusionment. Not all couples survive this stage, and many partnerships end at this point. However, if the partners are able to find ways to confront their differences openly, facing conflicts and working out compromises and accommodations for each other, they can move to the next stage, *resolution*. As much as couples like to believe they can stabilize their relationships indefinitely, coupling really is a continuing process, which may cycle through these stages again and again. Yet it is exactly the process that can keep relationships healthy, growing, and filled with a sense of renewal (Brehm et al., 2002).

Mate Selection

What are the qualities that actually attract two people to one another? Are they mostly physical? Are personality factors crucial? How important are practical considerations like finances? So far, research on mate selection has focused mostly on opposite-sex, or heterosexual, partnerships, although there is some research indicating that people with same-gender sexual orientations seem to be motivated by very similar mate-selection criteria. Theories of mate selection have fallen into three main categories, which we will discuss in the following sections.

Psychological Theory

Pyschological theories of mate selection assume that the process is essentially the same for both women and men and that people search for mates who remind them of their opposite-sexed parent or who at some deeper psychological level represent qualities they long to attain within themselves. It is sometimes assumed that people want mates who have qualities and characteristics similar to their own or, conversely, that opposites attract. Unfortunately, such hypotheses have not lent themselves particularly well to testing and verification.

Social Network Theory

Some aspects of social network theory, as described on page 146, have been supported by research. For example, there seems to be a tendency toward what social psychologists call *equal status contact,* meaning that people initiate and maintain relationships with others who have similar social characteristics. These include factors such as age bracket, race, education, religion, and the way one perceives oneself in terms of social class. These factors seem to be especially influential in more committed, longer-term relationships. People do indeed tend to meet their partners through their most immediate social networks, which involve friends, families, classmates, and coworkers, offering plenty of time to evaluate whether a potential partner will fit in well with family and friends (Michael et al., 1994). In general, sexual relationships also tend to occur between partners who share similar characteristics. There are exceptions, of course, and some sexual contacts—such as extramarital sex or sex with a prostitute—are actually more likely to occur among those of dissimilar social status. These forms of sex, however, tend to take place with little commitment and little likelihood that the two partners will be living together (Laumann, Gagnon, et al., 1994).

People who ultimately enter into long-term commitments such as marriage tend to know their partners longer before having sex with them than do couples who have short-term relationships. Therefore, they are really choosing a mate from a relatively limited group of potential partners within their social networks. Well before adolescents become sexually active, they tend to associate with one another in social circles in which the members are quite similar to one another. An individual who chooses a potential sexual partner from within that social network tends to be more cautious about moving too quickly toward sexual activity,

because there may well be a social price to pay for making a mistake (Michael et al., 1994).

See *"Evolutionary Psychology"* on *SexSource Online.*

Evolutionary or Sociobiological Theory

This theoretical stance assumes that human beings use sexual *strategies* in selecting a mate that are advantageous from an evolutionary perspective because they contribute to the survival and perpetuation of the human species. Evolutionary theory has been applied to sexuality in a variety of ways, and the news media have popularized research findings claiming to have found evidence that evolutionary forces have yielded genetic templates to explain things such as mating preferences in women and men, why men tend to be more prone to sexual relationships outside of primary relationships, and gender role differences between the sexes (Buss, 2003; Okami, 2004).

It has been hypothesized that evolution has yielded three primary emotional systems that lead to mating, reproduction, and parenting: the craving for sexual gratification, or lust; attraction focusing on a particular potential mate; and attachment to that mate, an experience that feels very comfortable (Fisher, 2000). Two other assumptions in evolutionary mate-selection theory are that actual selection behavior will differ in short-term and long-term couplings and that males and females have different mating goals (Buss, 2003). A team of scientists surveyed the mating preferences of more than 10,000 women and men in 37 countries over a six-year period. The data from this extensive cross-cultural survey have shown that there do seem to be some common sexual strategies that supersede cultural influences. One interesting pattern shows that men and women generally differ in their willingness to have sexual intercourse, depending on the length of the relationship. After a couple has been together for five years, both partners are almost equally willing to have sex. Prior to that time, men tend to be more willing than women (Sefcek, Brumbach, Vasquez, & Miller, 2006).

This is one of the cross-cultural findings in support of the evolutionary assumption that male and female sexual strategies differ. Several hypotheses about these strategies have been suggested that the studies of David Buss (2002, 2003) and his colleagues have given some validity. All of them require further support from continued research, and all of them may well be judged as controversial.

Evolutionary theory has been accused of attempting to find a basis for legitimizing behaviors that many deem to be sexist and inappropriate. This is not the intent of sociobiologists, who see their role as clarifying

Real Student Voices

■ In college most people lack good decision-making skills about sex. It's mostly the pressure of being in college and feeling you need to act crazy and do things you would have never done in high school.

■ I just separated myself from a four-year relationship that was mostly sexually inactive. I have always practiced abstinence and felt I would wait for marriage. After exiting this relationship, I'm not sure I will remain abstinent until I marry. I am glad I didn't have sex with my ex-girlfriend. It was hard

enough on her without the added stress of an active sexual life.

■ I'm just glad that different expressions of sexuality are acceptable today. I want my children to grow up being allowed to freely, and without shame, be able to enjoy sex.

■ It bothers me when people don't use condoms or another form of protection because it is unsafe. I also think that for most women, a lot of random hookups is a sign of low self-esteem, which is worrisome.

patterns of behavior in choosing a sexual partner that may indeed differ between men and women (Okami, 2004). Following are four hypotheses to which studies in numerous countries have lent credibility (Buss, 2003; Geary, Vigil, & Byrd-Craven, 2004):

1. Short-term sex partners are more important to men than to women, and men will identify sexually accessible women. This may well be one reason why men tend to have more sex partners than women and tend to find sexual promiscuity more desirable in a short-term partner than do women (Schackelford et al., 2004).
2. When seeking a short-term partner, men tend to want to minimize commitment and therefore find it undesirable when a short-term mate tries to extract signs of commitment (see Table 7.1).
3. In terms of evolutionary success, which translates into success in reproducing, men want to find mates who will likely bear children, and women have more interest in male partners who will be able to provide adequate resources for their offspring, as identified by social status. Studies continue to show that men place a higher value on attractiveness and on a younger partner, whereas women place a higher value on partners who are older and therefore likely to have more resources (Singh, 2004). Figures 7.2 and 7.3 show some of the cross-cultural variations on this theme.
4. Women are more selective than men in choosing a short-term mate because they are more likely to be evaluating a partner as a potential long-term mate. Therefore, even in short-term

Table 7.1   Examples of Costs and Benefits of Short-Term and Long-Term Sexual Relationships

Costs	Benefits
Women's Short-Term Mating	
Risk of STD	Some resources from mate
Risk of pregnancy	Good genes from mate
Reduced value as a long-term mate	
Women's Long-Term Mating	
Restricted sexual opportunity	Significant resources from mate
Sexual obligation to mate	Paternal investment
Men's Short-Term Mating	
Risk of STD	Potential to reproduce
Some resource investment	No paternal investment*
Men's Long-Term Mating	
Restricted sexual opportunity	Increased reproductive certainty
Heavy parental investment	Higher-quality children
Heavy relationship investment	Sexual and social companionship

Note: STD = sexually transmitted disease
*Low paternal investment may result in lower-quality children, but this is not a cost to the man because it does not lower his ability to invest in other relationships.
Source: From David C. Geary, Jacob Virgil, and Jennifer Byrd-Craven, "Evolution of Human Mate Choice." *The Journal of Sex Research,* Vol. 41, No. 1, February 2004, p. 29. Used by permission.

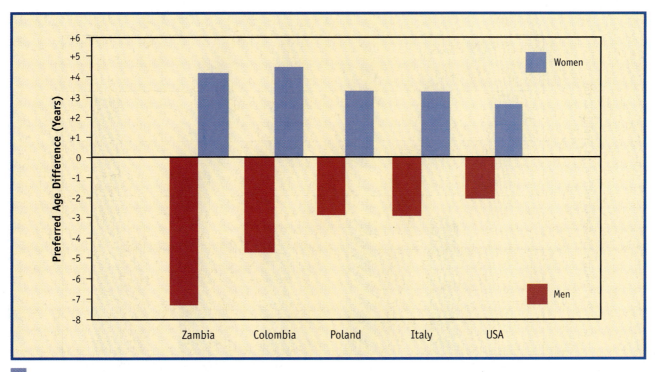

■ FIGURE 7.2 *Age Preferences for Males and Females*

Preferences for an age difference between oneself and one's spouse differ for men and women. Men in each of the 37 cultures examined prefer to mate with younger women, whereas women generally prefer to mate with older men. The disparities between the mating preferences of men and women in the five countries here show some of the cultural variation across the sample.

Source: David M. Buss, "The Strategies of Human Mating," *American Scientist* 82: 238–239, May/June 1994. Reprinted with permission by American Scientist.

couplings, women seek mates who are willing to impart immediate resources. Women appreciate qualities in males such as their likelihood of succeeding in a profession and having a reliable career. When successful men are less available, competition for them among women intensifies (Campbell, 2004).

Evolutionary psychology theorists, then, believe that traditional assumptions about mate selection being an arbitrary or culture-bound pursuit are incorrect. They maintain that cross-cultural evidence suggests that the complex decision-making processes involved in choosing a mate are patterned, universal themes built into human psyches and societies by evolutionary imperatives. This does not mean that men look on women solely as sex objects, or that women view men only as success objects. They also look for personality characteristics suggesting that the other person will be cooperative and make a good parent. Also, both sexes clearly place tremendous importance on factors such as mutual love and kindness when seeking a long-term mate (Buss, 2003; Geary, Vigil, & Byrd-Craven, 2004).

Which factors of the various theories of mate selection seem most plausible to you? Why?

■ Patterns in Adult Partnerships

Everything discussed in this chapter to this point supports the societal and developmental expectation that adults will—and should—pair up as couples, and that one way or another this coupling will formalize and legitimize their sexual relationships. It is important to point out, however, that the concept of formalizing the context for a sexual relationship between two people, traditionally assumed to be a man and a woman, came to this continent with European colonists. Europeans had long seen marriage as one way of maintaining the social order by placing some formal controls on human sexual desire and assuring more predictable care and support for offspring and the dependent. The practice of monogamous marriage became incorporated into the identity of our nation as a politically institutionalized way of doing things for our culture, even though it was not the most widely practiced form of coupling in the world during colonial times (Cott, 2005).

The U.S. Census Bureau and the National Center for Health Statistics are constantly gathering and analyzing data about marriage and other partnerships in

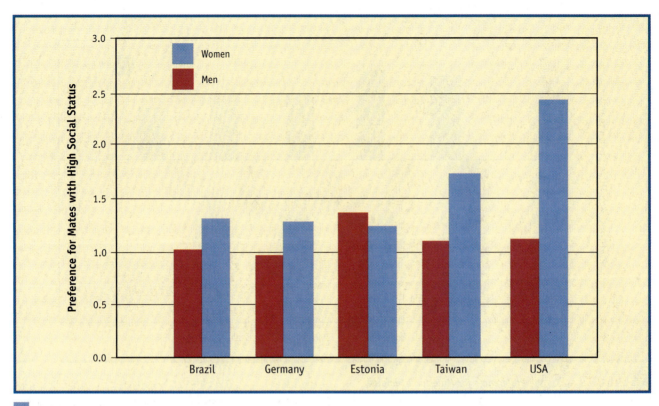

FIGURE 7.3   *Social Status and Human Mating*

Preference for mates with high social status (ranging from 3, *indispensable,* to 0, *unimportant*) typically is greater for women than for men. Of the 37 cultures examined, only males in Estonia valued the social status of their spouses more than did their female counterparts. (A sample of only five countries is shown here.) Women generally prefer men with a high social standing because a man's ability to provide resources for their offspring is related to his social status.

Source: David M. Buss, "The Strategies of Human Mating," *American Scientist* 82: 238–239, May/June 1994. Reprinted with permission by American Scientist.

the United States, although analysis of the data takes several years. Our views of the numbers and trends therefore are always a bit behind the current year. We know that by the late 1990s, 95 percent of men and women in the country had been married at least once by age 55. Up until that age, slightly more women than men had been married (Bramlett & Mosher, 2002).

At any given time, about a quarter of adults in the United States are unmarried, but ultimately only about 5 percent remain single, either by choice or for some reason that has prevented them from being led in that direction. Sometimes, this may be explained by a person's having a nonheterosexual orientation, because marriage traditionally has been assumed to be a male-female institution. It is known that many gay men and lesbian women do enter into heterosexual marriage at some point in their lives. The new social movement toward the legitimization of marriage between members of the same gender may well change the entire picture in years to come. However, it is also recognized that some people simply choose never to be married, for a

variety of reasons. Being single is recognized as a lifestyle in itself, with certain social advantages and disadvantages. Having an adventurous sex life may be one motive for remaining single, especially during younger adulthood, but some evidence supports the fact that people who are married or living with a partner actually have more sex than do singles.

The culture wars' battle over what is typically called "gay marriage" has called attention to the institution of marriage in a broader sense. Some have always questioned the need for legislatures to dictate the terms of legal coupling, as well as the passage of laws that reward people for being married with tax breaks and other advantages. Proponents of same-gender marriage claim that this is simply another civil rights matter and that the benefits of marriage should be extended to all citizens, regardless of sexual orientation. Some individuals and opposite-sex couples, as a gesture of political activism and support, have chosen to refuse marriage until it is permitted for everyone (Gaboury, 2005; Levin-Epstein, 2005).

"WHAT REALLY GETS ME IS THAT OPPOSITE-SEX MARRIAGES HAVE ALWAYS BEEN LEGAL AND, STILL, STAN WON'T PROPOSE."

Source: Copyright © North American Syndicate.

Cohabitation

More than ever before, couples are choosing to live together in loving and sexual relationships without marrying, a pattern called **cohabitation.** More than 5 million people in the United States are estimated to be cohabiting presently, and over 50 percent of couples who are cohabiting for the first time will eventually marry. Cohabitation is now the norm in our society, and a majority of women and men of marriageable age today will spend some time in such a relationship (see Figure 7.4).

The majority of young adults believe that living together prior to marriage is a good idea, although those who do cohabit do not necessarily see the relationship as a long-term commitment. About half of cohabitations end within the first year, and the younger the male partner, the more likely the relationship will terminate. Research shows that cohabitation is certainly no guarantee of a successful marriage. Evidence from a 23-year study suggests that couples who lived together prior to marriage have a substantially higher divorce rate (50 to 100 percent higher) than those who did not live together and have a lower level of marital satisfaction in general (Axinn & Thornton, 1992). This has been called the "cohabitation effect." However, there are some mitigating factors. If the partners have cohabited only with each other, if they have participated in premarital counseling, or if their marriage lasts through seven years, they have no elevated risk of divorce. Cohabiting couples do not seem to develop as effective communication and problem-solving skills as do married couples, perhaps because they have not considered the relationship as a committed one. Unfortunately, this may carry over into their marriage and may help explain the cohabitation effect (Cohan & Kleinbaum, 2002; Teachman, 2002).

See "Mike on Marriage" on SexSource Online.

FIGURE 7.4 *Cohabitation*

Cohabitation can give a couple a chance to try out all aspects of being partners.

cohabitation living together and sharing sex without marrying.

Real People

Ira and Patricia: Making Decisions about Living Together

At the end of their third year in college and their fifteenth month of being a couple, Patricia suggests to Ira that they consider sharing an apartment during their final year of college. They spend most nights together as it is, but both pay for rooms in separate residence halls on the campus. Patricia thinks that the new arrangement would make sense both financially and in terms of what she sees as their growing commitment to each other. She is not entirely certain how her parents will feel about it, but they know about the relationship and she thinks she can reason with them. They will be saving some money on room-and-board costs that they share with her.

Patricia is surprised when Ira expresses some hesitancy about the plan. He reminds her that it will be their senior year and that their plans for after college have not been finalized. He suggests that it might be difficult for them if they end up going their separate ways. Patricia is hurt by this and tells Ira she has been assuming they would make decisions that would allow them to remain together after college. He responds that while this might end up being the case, he thinks they should be cautious about how great a commitment they make at this point. He also says that he is quite sure his parents would not approve.

For Patricia, Ira's reluctance begins to call into question just how solid the relationship really is, and she tells him how disappointed and hurt she is. Ira reassures her of his strong feelings about her but repeats that he wants to be cautious about making any decisions that might jeopardize future planning. He explains that he thinks they are too young to be forming a partnership that is designed to last forever, even though he hopes at this point that it will. Patricia is bewildered and uncertain about how to proceed.

What are your opinions about their situation? Should Patricia persist in trying to convince Ira to cohabit? Is Ira right that they should be cautious and not push things too fast? How much should their parents' possible reactions factor into any decision?

Love and the Marriage Bed

In Western culture, romantic love and sexual attraction have become bases for marriage, along with the expectation that they will be continuing parts of any marriage. This is not as true for other cultures and other periods of the world's history in which marriage has been seen as too serious a step to be left to individual decision making and passions. In some cultures, marriages are arranged by the parents on the basis of age and social status. The partners are expected to build their relationships and learn how to love and care for each other after they are married. One study compared the marital satisfaction of couples whose marriages had been arranged with that of couples who married by choice and found no significant differences in long-term levels of satisfaction (Myers, Madathil, & Tingle, 2005).

However the original connection may have been made, maintaining any loving relationship over a long period of time takes attention, work, and commitment. Married couples must invest their relationships with sharing, energy, and communication if a healthy and growing marriage is to continue. As with any sort of coupling, marital intimacy is maintained best when it involves a sense of equality between the partners, an attempt to understand the other's point of view, and a willingness to work on the relationship through effective communication (Byers, 2005).

Sexual activity is an expected part of a marital relationship in Western cultures. In cultures where marriages are arranged by family members, sex often does not have such a prominent place in the partners' expectations. Research studies on marriage in North America indicate that many different sexual behaviors are shared by married people. The majority of couples apparently include oral-genital sexual activity in their sexual repertoires, and about one-quarter have at least tried anal intercourse. Couples also seem relatively adventurous with regard to the positions they use for sexual intercourse (Laumann, Gagnon, et al., 1994). Women seem to have more positive perceptions of sexual behavior in marriage than do their husbands, who seem to have a more positive perception of marital life in general (Trudel, 2002). It is believed that approximately 20 percent of married couples may have sex infrequently enough to essentially be considered nonsexual (McCarthy, 1999). The level of sexual desire in married couples is strongly correlated with the level of marital satisfaction they experience (Brezsnyak & Whisman, 2004).

Sexual Satisfaction in Partnerships

The frequency of sexual activity tends to be higher in the first two years of a relationship, as partners explore each other sexually, and to gradually decrease with the length of the relationship and the age of the partners. Sexual desire decreases over time as well, but many different patterns are seen in couples (Ridley et al., 2006). Popular myths have led us to believe that people are far more sexually active than studies tend to show. The most recent data show that people in the United States fall into three groups with regard to their frequency of sex with a partner. About one-third have sex with a partner a few times a year or do not have a partner at all. Another third have partnered sex a few times a month, and a final third have sex with a partner two times per week or more. Younger and older people have sex the least often, with people in their twenties having sex most frequently. Married and cohabiting partners have the most sex. Forty percent of married people and over half of cohabiting people have sex two or more times per week. Single people have less sex than other groups. Table 7.2 summarizes the data on frequency of sex with a partner by various

Table 7.2	*Frequency of Sex in the Past 12 Months by Age, Marital Status, and Gender*				
Social Characteristics	**Not at All**	**A Few Times per Year**	**A Few Times per Month**	**2 or 3 Times a Week**	**4 or More Times a Week**
Gender					
Men	14%	16%	37%	26%	8%
Women	10	18	36	30	7
Age					
Men					
18–24	15	21	24	28	12
25–29	7	15	31	36	11
30–39	8	15	37	33	6
40–49	9	18	40	27	6
50–59	11	22	43	20	3
Women					
18–24	11	16	32	29	12
25–29	5	10	38	37	10
30–39	9	16	36	33	6
40–49	15	16	44	20	5
50–59	30	22	35	12	2
Marital/Residential Status					
Men					
Noncohabiting	23	25	26	19	7
Cohabiting	0	8	36	40	16
Married	1	13	43	36	7
Women					
Noncohabiting	32	23	24	15	5
Cohabiting	1	8	35	42	14
Married	3	12	47	32	7

Source: From *Sex in America* by Robert T. Michael et al. Copyright © 1994 by CSG Enterprises, Inc., Edward O. Laumann, Robert T. Michael, and Gina Kolata. By permission of Little, Brown and Company, Inc. and Brockman, Inc.

characteristics. Race, religion, and education do not seem to particularly influence frequency of sex (Laumann, Gagnon, et al., 1994).

Frequency of intercourse, however, should not be construed as a measure of happiness in marriage or cohabitation. Different couples find different levels of sexual interaction appropriate and pleasing for them. Some older research that did not study random samples of the population suggested that sexual satisfaction was directly correlated with sexual frequency, but the newest data paint a different picture. Even people whose frequency of sexual interaction is relatively low often report a high degree of satisfaction with their sexual lives. As people age and the frequency of sexual activity decreases, they still tend to be quite satisfied. Even though popular opinion might imply that swinging singles are the happiest with their sex lives, married couples are, in fact, the most physically satisfied. Eighty-eight percent of married people report that they receive great physical pleasure from their sexual lives, and 85 percent say they receive great emotional satisfaction. People who have more than one sexual partner available report less sexual satisfaction than do those with only one partner (Michael et al., 1994; Trudel, 2002).

Research has confirmed that satisfaction with both a relationship and its sexual component is very closely connected to the emotional ties of the couple and the effectiveness of their communication. This is true for marriages and nonmarital relationships alike. Simply stated, the nicer partners are to each other, the more likely they are to be happy and satisfied and the more likely they will be to feel sexual desire for each other. Good communication seems to lead to a better sexual life and greater relational satisfaction. It seems clear that couples who have difficulty communicating well tend to have lower levels of satisfaction with sex and with the relationship (Byers, 2005; Litzinger & Gordon, 2005; Ridley et al., 2006).

Monogamy versus Nonmonogamy

Not all married or cohabiting individuals remain **monogamous,** sharing sexual relations only with their primary partner. The prevailing social attitude in the United States is that couples, particularly those who are married, should maintain sexual exclusivity. Ninety percent of adults believe that extramarital sexual activity is always or almost always wrong. Less than 2 percent believe that having sex with someone other than a spouse is "not wrong at all" (Laumann, Gagnon, et al., 1994). In social network theory, third parties may be stakeholders in preserving exclusivity within sexual partnerships. For example, friends and family members may want the relationship to remain stable because they want to maintain and legitimize

their own relationships. If they do not stray, they do not want others to do so either. This may be one reason why extramarital activity often occurs outside the social network.

Regardless of how sexually active with different partners people may be prior to marriage or between marriages, the vast majority tend to be sexually faithful to their spouses while the marriage is intact. Statistics from the General Social Survey and from the NHSLS indicate that about 90 percent of married women and more than 75 percent of married men have been sexually exclusive during their marriages. Unmarried, cohabiting couples have a higher rate of extrarelational sex, but not dramatically so. Men are more likely to engage in sex outside of a relationship than are women, as are individuals of either gender who are unhappy in their relationships (Banfield & McCabe, 2001; Cann, Mangum, & Wells, 2001). Of people who had never married but were living together, 75 percent had had only one partner in the previous year. Ninety-four percent of married adults indicate having had only one sex partner during the previous year (Laumann, Gagnon, et al., 1994; Treas & Giesen, 2000).

A study of extradyadic (outside the partnership) sexual relationships in Norway found that 29 percent of the men and 23 percent of the women reported having experienced sex with someone other than their partner at some point in their lives. Sixteen percent of the men and 11 percent of the women said they had experienced extradyadic sex during their current relationship. Men mostly reported having had casual encounters with others, while the women tended to have been involved with someone they knew and to have had a more emotional attachment (Traeen, Holmen, & Stigum, 2007).

There has been almost no research to suggest why people turn to extradyadic or extramarital sex. Sometimes the activity represents a search for sexual variety, excitement, and a need to feel attractive and desirable. More often it seems to be motivated by a need for stronger emotional involvement and intimacy than what is being achieved with one's spouse (Treas & Giesen, 2000).

What are some reasons why sexual fidelity could or could not be important in a relationship?

During the sexual revolution, when attitudes toward human sexuality were seeing some major shifts, there was a fair amount of debate about the viability of monogamous relationships. There was talk then of

monogamous sharing sexual relations with only one person.

Real Student Voices

■ I've always assumed I would get married, although my relationships so far have all been relatively brief. I keep hoping that the right person will come along and we'll fall in love so that it can all happen.

■ The idea of marriage makes me very nervous. My parents got divorced when I was ten, and it was very hard on my brother and me. I don't want to go through that kind of hurting again, or put anyone

else through it. I'd like to think love lasts forever, but I'm skeptical.

■ Because I am gay, I've never really thought very seriously about getting married. Given the way things are going, maybe I should. The idea of having a long-term, settled relationship is appealing to me. Maybe the house and picket fence aren't so far fetched after all.

consensual adultery, in which couples would allow their partners greater sexual freedom. However, these trends were never translated into behavioral change for the majority of married or cohabiting couples. The general maintenance of monogamy has also been shown in major European studies of sexual behavior. While there may be some "swinging" or mate-swapping couples who indulge in recreational sex consensually, they apparently are a very tiny part of the population.

Men have a somewhat greater likelihood of having sexual affairs outside of committed relationships, and evolutionary psychologists have attempted to offer explanations for this trend. Making the assumption that one evolutionary imperative is reproductive success, evolutionary theory holds that males have a built-in need to distribute their sperm among as many different females as possible because females have far fewer eggs available than males have sperm (Cann, Mangum, & Wells, 2001). Some evidence from human mating patterns supports these differences. There are far more cultures in the world that permit **polygamy,** the practice that permits men to have more than one wife, than there are examples of systematic **polyandry,** in which women take more than one husband. Nevertheless, evolutionary psychology presents mostly hypothetical explanations for a phenomenon that is reflected in statistics but has not yet been adequately explained.

We do know that extramarital affairs can take an emotional toll on all who are involved. Secrecy and dishonesty create tension within the various relationships. When one partner suspects the other of infidelity, the unfaithfulness may not be confronted for a time because of uncertainty or fear of the outcome. Once the truth is known, it may lead to intense feelings of betrayal and loss. If the extramarital affair is still going on, decisions must be made by all parties as to how they plan to proceed. Sometimes the marriage ends and the other relationship goes on. The tensions

and bad feelings that develop may instead destroy both relationships. There also may be fears about what risks may be present if the affair involved unprotected sexual activity. If the affair ends and both partners want to preserve the marriage, confronting all feelings with honesty and appropriate counseling can sometimes lead to an even stronger relationship. However, the limited data available suggest that affairs lead to the termination or worsening of the marital relationship in the majority of cases (Brezsnyak & Whisman, 2004; Cann, Mangum, & Wells, 2001).

Trends in Marriage

There has been a trend toward delaying marriage until somewhat later in life than in the past, and younger professional women and men sometimes want to establish themselves in a career before they pursue a committed relationship. Census Bureau statistics show the extent of this trend. Nearly 35 percent of 25- to 34-year-olds have never married. Among people ages 30 to 44, the proportion of never-married individuals has more than doubled since 1970. People are getting married later now than at any time in the past century. The median age for women at first marriage is 25 years, and the median age

consensual adultery permission given to at least one partner within the marital relationship to participate in extramarital sexual activity.

polygamy (pah-LIG-a-mee) practice, in some cultures, of being married to more than one spouse, usually referring to a man having more than one wife.

polyandry (PAH-lee-ann-dree) referring to being married to more than one spouse, usually to a woman having more than one husband; cross-culturally, less common than polygamy.

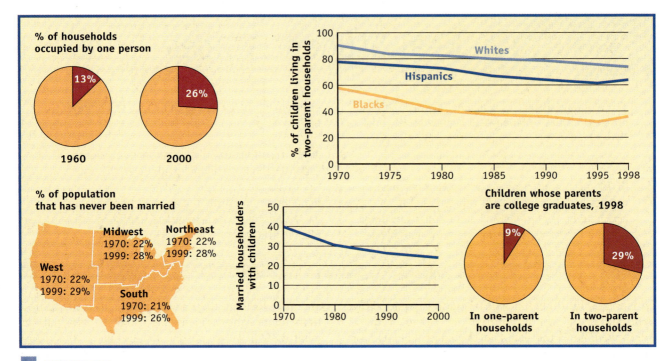

FIGURE 7.5   *Some Trends in American Households*

Sources: U.S. Census Bureau, American Association for Single People, Ameristat, public agenda. Research by Josh Ulick and Newsweek Research Center.

for men marrying for the first time is 27 years—the highest these figures have ever been. Having a child before marriage reduces the likelihood that women will marry. There may also be increased apprehension about divorce rates and economic pressures.

The availability of sexual relations outside of marriage may be contributing somewhat to the trend. Figure 7.5 shows the emerging trends of the American family. Both family structure and family values are moving in congruence away from traditional families with two married parents, an employed father and a stay-at-home mother, and toward modern family types either with only one parent or with two parents both of whom are employed outside the home. The family situation of children has changed over the last quarter-century. In 1973, 72 percent of children under age 18 were living in an intact family with two parents. The percentage fell to about 50 percent by the mid-1990s. According to the 2000 census, 31 percent of children under age 18 are living with either a single parent or no parents at all, up from 12 percent in 1960.

Although no official statistics are kept on the topic, there are indications of an increase in what have been termed "starter marriages." These are marriages between relatively young people who do not have children and amass very little joint property. After a few years, and usually prior to age 30, they divorce. Their uncoupling process is less complicated than in marriages of longer standing. In many ways, these brief marriages are similar to cohabiting relationships, except that the couple

has taken the step of legalizing the commitment. Starter marriages are reminiscent of anthropologist Margaret Mead's suggestion in the 1960s that young couples should have the opportunity to join in legally sanctioned, childless trial marriages (Copeland, 2002).

Divorce

Based on recent statistics, it has been predicted that 20 percent of couples who marry today will be divorced within five years, one-third may be divorced within 10 years, and nearly 50 percent will be divorced before they might have celebrated their 15th anniversary. Ultimately, nearly half of U.S. marriages end in divorce. The number of annual divorces per 1,000 population rose significantly during the twentieth century, although by 1990 there was a leveling off in the national divorce rate. Apparently there is an underreporting of divorce and a lack of statistics about marriages that end in separation without a legal divorce. It is possible that close to two-thirds of first marriages eventually break up. About 70 percent of divorced people try marriage again, hoping that things will be better the second time around. However, close to half of these second marriages also end in divorce, 37 percent of them within the first 10 years.

Some research has been conducted on predicting the likelihood of divorce. The husband's dissatisfaction with the relationship has been found to be one of the most potent predictors of the likelihood of divorce.

Premarital counselors eventually may be able to use tests to make predictions about the long-term stability of a couple's relationship. Because divorce rates continue to be so high, many religious groups and social agencies are placing greater emphasis on divorce prevention. Premarital counseling, coupled with compatibility-rating tests, is becoming more popular. There has also been an increase in the availability of couples' workshops and therapy opportunities designed to teach conflict-resolution techniques that could head off divorce, and couples who have had premarital counseling are more likely to avail themselves of such services. While premarital counseling may help some marriages last longer, there is no evidence to suggest that it ultimately prevents divorce (Schumm, Silliman, & Bell, 2000; Valiente, Belanger, & Estrada, 2002).

To what extent sexual incompatibility and dissatisfaction with sex are factors in divorce is unclear. Couples who are having marital difficulties often experience sexual problems, yet these problems are just as frequently the effect as they are the cause. Most divorced people remarry, typically after about three years. An even higher percentage, about 60 percent, of second marriages also end in divorce. Second marriages tend to be a bit shorter than first ones. There is some evidence that sexual problems present in a first marriage reappear in a second marriage. Adjusting to divorce can be a traumatic experience, and it involves the grieving stages typical of any major loss. Divorced people often experience upheavals in their lifestyles that create new stresses and pressures. They may feel depressed or anxious and experience loss of self-esteem. Children whose parents have divorced often experience stresses that affect their lives into their college years, but it is also true that divorced people and their children can have very positive outcomes (Hetherington & Kelly, 2001).

■ Sexuality and Aging

The sharing of sex is usually portrayed as something for lustful and passionate youth and for the earlier years of marriage, with old age finding people politely asexual. There are anecdotes and jokes about the occasional "dirty old man," an object of ridicule and disgust. Being old is equated with giving up sex. Yet studies have revealed that the elderly are indeed sexual beings. Older people not only retain sexual desires but enjoy the pleasures of the same sexual activities they participated in as younger people. In fact, sometimes they apparently even enjoy them more (Lacy, 2002.)

Cross-cultural studies demonstrate that in the majority of societies, continuation of sexual activity is expected among the aging. Men are not expected to have much, if any, loss of their sexual capabilities until they are quite old, and women also are expected to maintain their sexual interests and activities as they

age. In fact, women frequently report signs of stronger sexual interests and fewer inhibitions about discussing sex after passing their childbearing years. Data from the Study of Women Across the Nation (SWAN) showed that 77 percent of women ages 42 to 52 said that sex was moderately to extremely important to middle-age women's lives (Cain et al., 2003). Whether expressions of sexuality among the aged are encouraged or discouraged seems to depend on the cultural attitudes of a particular society (Lacy, 2002).

Larger proportions of our population than ever before are now in middle and older age groups, as post–World War II baby boomers grow older (see Figure 7.6). Census Bureau statistics show that the number of elderly people in the United States doubled between 1960 and 2000, growing from nearly 17 million to 35 million. In this sense, we are becoming an older society. People also are retiring earlier, extending the amount of time between retirement and old age. Improved medical care and increased emphasis on good health habits are helping many of us enjoy a longer life span than we might once have expected. All these factors have created a considerable interest in and awareness about aging. Nonetheless, many misconceptions about sexuality and the older population persist (Floyd & Weiss, 2001).

Myths and Attitudes about Sex and Aging

Chapter 4, "Human Sexual Arousal and Response," mentioned some of the physiological effects of aging on sexual functions. Here we will discuss some myths and attitudes that lead to misunderstandings about the sexuality of older people.

FIGURE 7.6 *Mid-life Transitions and Commitments*

Middle age is often a period of transition and reevaluation. As couples commit and recommit themeselves to relationships, their sense of shared intimacy and sexual enjoyment may be deepened. This mature couple is entering into marriage.

Loving and Sexual Feelings Are Experienced Only during Youth

In fact, human beings retain a full range of emotions—including romantic and sexual ones—throughout the life span (see Figure 7.7). A major reason behind the suppression of these feelings in many older people is the societal attitude that such reactions are indeed lost with age. To the contrary, a survey of 1,604 people ages 65 to 97 found that 52 percent of the males and 30 percent of the females indicated they were still sexually active. They engaged in sexual activity an average of 2.5 times per month, although they would have preferred to have sex about twice as frequently. During their previous 10 sexual experiences, the men reached orgasm an average of 80 percent of the times, and the women about 50 percent (Mark Clements Research, 1996). Another study of women ages 42 to 52 found that more than 60 percent reported having regular sexual intercourse and 24 percent reported having oral sex fairly regularly (Cain et al., 2003). A survey con-ducted with 1,292 people in their sixties, seventies, and eighties by the National Council on Aging (1998) found that about half had sexual activity at least once a month, and 70 percent of those who were sexually active indicated that their sex lives were at least as satisfying as when they were in their forties.

Sex Is Primarily for Reproduction

This attitude negates a spectrum of nonprocreative sexual experiences and obviously dismisses those who are past the age of reproductive capability or interest. Yet older people who have held to this value during their lifetimes may find it a factor in discouraging sexual expression. Nevertheless, an analysis of national poll data from 6,000 people in the United States has shown that 37 percent of married people over 60 have sexual intercourse once a week, whereas another 16 percent do so even more frequently. Nine out of 10 couples who had sex at least once a week found their spouses "very attractive," and 55 percent said their spouses were skilled lovers. Two-thirds of the sexually active older couples indicated that they still experimented sexually (Calamidas, 1997).

Older Men Remain More Sexually Interesting to Younger Partners Than Do Older Women

There is a distinct double standard when it comes to the sexual desirability and attractiveness of older people. Although the graying hair and bodily changes of an aging man are often perceived as being distinguished, women are more likely to be viewed as becoming less attractive as they age. Such attitudes only foster further negative attitudes in aging women about their own sexuality. The pairing of older men with younger women happens relatively frequently; the reverse situation is still not as common, but it seems to be gaining increased acceptance (Brown, H. G., 2000).

Institutional Prohibitions on Sexual Expression

All these sex-negative myths and attitudes add up to policies or attitudes that prohibit sexual expression among the aged. Nowhere is this more evident than in nursing homes and other institutions that provide care for older men and women. Not only are outward expressions of sexual interest seen as inappropriate and therefore discouraged, but there is often a lack of privacy for any sort of personal or shared sexual activity. Studies have shown, however, that many elderly nursing-home residents remain sexually active and interested in sex. Even when nursing-home personnel are aware of the facts about the sexuality of the aged, their own attitudes may be negative, and appropriate

■ **FIGURE 7.7**   *Old Age and Sexuality*

Patterns of sexual activity vary greatly among the elderly. Cultural and social expectations of sexual behavior as well as the state of health of both partners may play a part in the frequency and type of sexual activity engaged in by elderly couples.

policy changes may be hindered by lack of support from administrative personnel, physicians, and the families of older patients (Hillman, 2000; Lacy, 2002).

Changing such conditions can have positive results. Increased opportunity for physical and emotional interaction often results in a healthier and more cheerful atmosphere and leads to significant improvements in the social behavior of the residents. Only too often, institutional staffs forget that their clients are adults with rights to privacy and social interaction. Providing older people with opportunities for choice and a sense of personal autonomy can enhance their sexual identity and adjustment (Shaw, 2001).

Special Sexual Problems and Patterns of Aging

Because of the hormonal and other physiological changes of older age, many men and women report decreased interest in sexual activity and orgasm as they get older. Although levels of sexual interest and behavior show a distinct decline as people age, many elderly people remain sexually active—or at least capable of sexual activity—until very old age. The following sections describe several life factors that influence sexual potentials in old age.

The Individual's or Couple's Sexual History

A very significant factor is the degree of importance and priority that the individual or couple has placed on sex throughout the life cycle. There is a high correlation between the amount of sexual interest shown in the young adult years and that shown in the older adult years. Those who have tended to see sex as an important part of their lives and who have sought frequent sexual outlets tend to continue these patterns into old age. Likewise, letting sex become a low priority of life may well lead to an absence of sexual interest as a person ages (DeLamater & Sill, 2005).

Partner Availability

How much shared sexual activity is pursued by an older individual depends a great deal on the availability of a sexual partner. Evidence shows that as women age, they become far less likely to have a sexual partner than are men, so this is a more critical factor in women's maintenance of sexual desire and activity (see Figure 7.8). By age 50 to 59, 30 percent of women report having had no partnered sexual activity within the previous year, and by ages 55 to 59

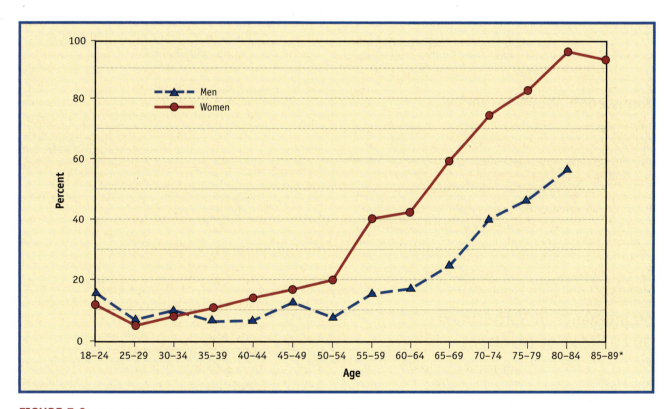

FIGURE 7.8 *U.S. Adults with No Sexual Partner in the Past 12 Months*

As women age, they become far less likely than men to have a sexual partner.

*Insufficient data available for men ages 85 to 89.

Source: From *Sex in America* by Robert T. Michael et al. Copyright © 1994 by CSG Enterprises, Inc., Edward O. Laumann, Robert T. Michael, and Gina Kolata. By permission of Little, Brown and Company, (Inc).

that figure rises to more than 40 percent. Figures from the General Social Survey indicate that 70 percent of women in their seventies no longer have partnered sex and that by the time they are over 80 years old, 90 percent no longer do. This contrasts with figures for men over 80, which indicate that fewer than 60 percent report having no partnered sex. Researchers believe that these figures reflect a disproportionate availability of partners rather than different levels of sexual interest. Men in their forties begin to die in higher numbers than do women of the same age. In the 60 to 64 age bracket, there are 88 men per 100 women. Above age 75, there are only 55 men per 100 women. Clearly, it is more difficult for older women to find potential sexual partners than it is for older men (DeLamater & Sill, 2005; Lacy, 2002; Laumann, Gagnon, et al., 1994).

Sexual Values and Attitudes

Throughout the life span, sexual behaviors are influenced by attitudes and values. People who are old today grew up in times when negative and repressive sexual codes were taught, and many have carried these values with them into old age. They may become self-fulfilling prophecies for many. Research confirms that among older people, negative attitudes toward sex correlate with relative sexual inactivity. Unfortunately, opportunities for older people to discuss, explore, or even change their value systems are often neglected, because it is assumed that their values are too entrenched (DeLamater & Friedrich, 2002).

Knowledge about Sexuality

Ignorance about sex is rampant; this is no less true among seniors than it is among the young. Older people often labor with myths and misinformation about sex and sexual behaviors, leading them to have conflicting attitudes and values about their own sexual lives. At the same time, later people often want more information about sexuality. Men who have attained higher levels of education are more likely to remain sexually active in their later years, perhaps because they are more aware of the inaccuracies of the negative stereotypes (DeLamater & Sill, 2005).

Maintenance of Self-Esteem and a Sense of Identity

Seniors must adapt to many physical, emotional, social, and economic changes in their lives. They may experience loss of companionship, loss of role status after retirement, and some losses of physical and cognitive functioning. The individual's perception of her or his sexuality is a crucial part of adjustment to a new stage of life. Dissatisfaction with sexual activity is related to depression and feelings of worthlessness, which in turn can discourage further activity (Calamidas, 1997).

Masturbation and Heterosexual Intercourse in Old Age

For many older people who have lost their sexual partners, masturbation becomes their sole means of sexual gratification. There are few statistical data concerning masturbation among the aged, although there are indications from the NHSLS that the frequency of masturbation declines in the 54- to 59-year-old age bracket (Laumann, Gagnon, et al., 1994). In their first study on human sexual response, Masters and Johnson (1966) reported that most of the older people in their study had tended to continue masturbating into old age if they had masturbated previously. The frequency of reported masturbation among seniors is determined largely by sexual attitudes and knowledge. In one study, older people over age 65 reported masturbating an average of once per month, and those under age 65 reported doing so about four times per month (Mark Clements Research, 1996).

Research on the sexual behavior of older people has usually concentrated on heterosexual intercourse. Every study suggests that the frequency of intercourse steadily declines with age and that availability of a healthy partner plays a major role in determining the frequency (Laumann, Gagnon, et al., 1994). However, our preoccupation with intercourse as a standard of measurement does not do justice to the sexuality of the aging. When we broaden our definition of "sexually active" to mean a spectrum of sexual and sensual behaviors, older people fare quite well. This may signal the maturation of older people away from the narrow, limiting genital focus of intercourse toward a fuller and more complete sense of what it means to be a sexual human being. In this sense, younger generations may well have lessons to learn from older generations (Calamidas, 1997; Lacy, 2002).

Stereotypes about Aging and Same-Sex Orientation

The research on gay men, lesbians, and bisexuals in mid-life and older age is very limited. For the most part, it is expected that they face the same sorts of passages and adjustments as do heterosexuals. However, it is also true that of those lesbians and gay males who presently are in their older years, few were exposed to very much information or many positive attitudes about same-gender sexual orientation when they were young. This may have made some of their life adjustments more difficult; many older gay, lesbian, or bisexual adults have never disclosed their sexual orientation (Altman, 1999). As in society at large, it has often been believed that the gay and lesbian culture values youth, rendering aging particularly difficult for gay men and lesbians. In actuality, lesbians, gays, and bisexuals do not exhibit any significant decrease in self-acceptance or increase in depression or loneliness as they get older. There is evidence to suggest that gays and lesbians who are in mid-life are beginning to become more open about their sexual orientations and to want medical, legal, and social services appropriate to their needs. In general, studies of aging in lesbians and gay males have focused on urban populations with relative affluence. A great deal more research needs to be done to understand thoroughly any special needs and concerns that aging presents for individuals with same-gender sexual orientation.

FOH Maximizing Sexual Expression during the Later Years

While the aging process makes an indelible mark on the ways the human body responds sexually, older people clearly can remain in touch with the sexual part of their lives if they wish. Table 7.3 summarizes some of the ways to maximize sexual pleasure as one

ages. Some nursing homes and health care clinics have offered sexual education and enhancement programs for the elderly that have helped them understand their own sexuality more completely. Appropriate counseling services for elderly people can also lead to greater sexual satisfaction, and given the increased proportion of older adults in the population, the availability of these services is more crucial than ever (Hillman, 2000).

As human beings age and become less genitally oriented, they have the potential to rediscover the sensuousness of their entire bodies. Older people consistently report the sexual satisfaction they gain from kissing, caressing, holding, cuddling, and other types of lovemaking that involve both spiritual and physical intimacy. In a sense, elderly people can be freed from many of the concerns that interfere with sexual intimacy in younger age groups: risk of pregnancy, the need to "prove" oneself with sex, obsessions with performance and orgasms, balancing work and personal time, and having children to care for. We all could stand to learn from those older people who have come to value sexual intimacy in its holistic sense and have come to realize that sex is far more than what genitals do together. They know the meaning of a cherished touch and the sense of intimacy that shared bodies can enjoy (Brown, H. G., 2000; Lacy, 2002).

Table 7.3	Coping with Sexual Changes That May Accompany Aging
Common Changes	**Solutions to be Considered**
Decreased sexual interest/desire	Evaluation/treatment for depression Medically supervised treatment with estrogen or testosterone Use of mutually agreeable erotic stimuli Evaluation of the role of chronic medical conditions Become more intentional about planning times for sex
Thinning of vaginal walls; less natural vaginal lubrication; lessened orgasmic response	Exploration of possible role medications may play Evaluation of alcohol/drug use Use a personal lubricant Try pelvic exercises that can be prescribed by a clinician Exercise regularly
Softer erections; more difficulty maintaining erection and ejaculating	Evaluation and treatment for high blood pressure, diabetes, heart disease, or other chronic illnesses Exploration of possible role medications may play Evaluation of alcohol/drug use Try using one of the prescription medications that aid in erections Use of vacuum device, self-injected drugs, or surgical implants, as medically advised Try using positions that make vaginal penetration easier Exercise regularly

Sources: Adapted from National Institute on Aging, *Age Page: Sexuality in Later Life,* http://niapublications.org/agepages/PDFs/Sexuality-in-Later-Life.pdf; *Aging Well, Living Well,* http://womenshealth.gov/ow/sexuality/index.cfm; *Non-Surgical Management of Erectile Dysfunction (ED),* http://www.urologyhealth.org/print/index.cfm?topic=174.

■ Sexual Effects of Health and Illness

A long list of medical problems can directly or indirectly affect a person's sex organs and sexual functioning. Debilitating illnesses are more likely to be experienced during the later years of life, but some may appear at earlier stages of the life span as well. The particular diseases and disorders of the female and male sexual organs were discussed briefly in Chapters 2 and 3. Because sexuality is a part of the whole person, anything that affects physical or psychological health and well-being can have implications for sexual functioning as well. Unfortunately, health professionals often fail to assess the sexual implications of various illnesses and do not discuss these aspects with their patients. They may feel personally uncomfortable talking about sex with patients or may be concerned about creating undue embarrassment for them. Especially in long-standing chronic illnesses or in acute illnesses that create serious debilitation, careful sexual assessment should be an integral part of total health care. The partners of patients are often dealing with difficult emotional issues as well, which may affect their sexual attitudes and functioning. Partners should be included in sexual assessment and counseling whenever a serious illness is being treated.

> *What do you foresee as some possible effects of medication and debilitating illness on sexual behavior?*

Treatments for some illnesses, such as medication for blood pressure or chemotherapy for cancer, can have direct effects on sexual functioning. Antidepressant and antipsychotic medications often affect both desire and physiological responsiveness. Chronically ill people may begin to question their identities as women and men and the role their sexual functioning now plays in their identities (DeLamater & Sill, 2005).

Chronic pain accompanies some disorders, and some women experience pelvic pain that remains resistant to traditional pain-relieving treatments. This can be a complex issue, involving many psychological dimensions as well as the physical ones. Pain over time is wearing on any individual and may interfere with sexual desire and pleasure (Randolph & Reddy, 2006).

Among those diseases most frequently found to have adverse effects on sexual functioning are neurological disorders such as multiple sclerosis or stroke, diabetes, cardiovascular disease and heart attacks, chronic lung disease, cancer and its treatments, and arthritis. These illnesses and their treatments may weaken the body, interfere with the control of bodily functions, threaten self-esteem and body image, and inhibit interpersonal intimacy. Because of the potential sexual problems resulting from such diseases, patients should be given thorough information about what to expect and access to therapy designed to help them reestablish whatever degree of sexual functioning might realistically be expected.

Cardiac and stroke patients, for example, are often concerned about the amount of physical exertion that is safe for them during sexual activity. This concern can lead to psychological pressures that can, in turn, produce sexual dysfunctions. Erection problems are particularly common in men who have heart disease. Health workers can gradually encourage post-heart-attack patients to get back in touch with their sexual feelings, even suggesting masturbation when the individual is physically ready for any exertion. Later, specific suggestions can be given for shared sexual activity, at first using positions that require a lesser degree of physical strain and energy. With reassurance and education, most cardiac patients can reestablish full sexual lives.

Diabetes is known to cause some physical complications that can directly interfere with sexual activity. Two of the most commonly reported problems are difficulty having an erection in men and some degree of vaginal dryness and its associated discomfort in women. Physically based complaints of this sort have their psychological spin-offs as well. People begin to feel sexually inadequate and fear failure during their sexual interactions. In turn, new pressures are created on communication within their relationships. Often, these difficulties can be alleviated by intervention by health professionals who are sensitive to the sex-related implications of diabetes.

Likewise, certain surgeries can have effects on sexual behavior and satisfaction that should be thoroughly explained to the older patient. Prostate surgery, for example, is very common in older men and may in a few cases inhibit the capability to have an erection and ejaculate. However, with reassurance, encouragement, and education, many men who have had prostate surgery can resume satisfactory sexual activity (Lacy, 2002). Hysterectomy (removal of the uterus and cervix) need not adversely affect the sex lives of women. Some women face many psychological stresses following hysterectomy, but with appropriate education and adjustment counseling, the majority of women can emerge feeling healthier, sexier, and more self-confident than before.

Mental illness may also adversely affect a person's sexual activities. Its emotional disruption often leads to lack of interest in sex and loss of the ability to be sexually responsive. However, it has also been noted that many mentally ill people still have sexual needs and the desire to pursue sexual activity. In institutional settings, mentally ill persons who seem especially pre-occupied with sex may simply be searching for human warmth and closeness. Activities such as masturbation may become ways for mental patients to control anxiety, affirm the existence of their bodies, or safely act out their sexual fantasies.

Increasingly, health professionals are realizing the importance of exploring sex-related issues with their patients. It is to be hoped that assessment of the potential sexual effects of various illnesses will soon become a standard and accepted part of medical evaluation and treatment.

Self-Evaluation

Looking Ahead: Sex in Later Years

Some of the strongest misconceptions and prejudices about older people relate to their sexuality. It is assumed that older people lose their sexual feelings, needs, and behaviors. Actually, as this chapter has demonstrated, many elderly people are still aware of sexual feelings and still seek physical sexual gratification. This questionnaire is designed with two primary goals: to evaluate your attitudes about sex and aging, and to clarify what you hope your sexual life will be when you are older.

1. **Read each of the following statements and rate your level of approval or disapproval for each, using the following scale:**

   5 = **strongly approve**

   4 = **approve somewhat**

   3 = **neutral**

   2 = **disapprove somewhat**

   1 = **strongly disapprove**

   a. A widowed man age 73 confided to his physician that he enjoyed masturbating occasionally but wondered if this practice might cause any ill effects. The physician encouraged him to masturbate as frequently as he wished—the more the better. _____

   b. A man and a woman, both in their late seventies, whose spouses have died have decided to live and sleep together. For reasons of finances and distribution of estates, they have decided against marrying. _____

   c. A 67-year-old woman announces that she is in love with a 40-year-old man and that they are planning to marry. _____

   d. A 70-year-old widower announces that he is planning to marry a 37-year-old woman. They have been dating for several months, and he has bragged about how the relationship has restored his sexual potency. _____

   e. An elderly man and woman meet in the recreation room of the nursing home where they both reside. The staff at the home will not allow them to spend time together in privacy, even though the older couple has asked for this privilege. _____

2. **Now go back to all the situations in 1a–e and imagine how you would feel if the older person in each instance were your father or mother. Also consider how you would feel if the older person were you.**

3. **Are you frightened about how aging will affect your sex life? Or do you believe it doesn't really matter how sexually active you remain in your later years?**

4. **Ideally, how would you like to see yourself functioning as a sexual human being at age 60? Age 70? Age 80? Age 90? Do you have any plan in mind for working toward these ideals?**

Chapter Summary

1. Adult sexuality involves establishing intimacy with others and the exploration of the place of sex in intimate relationships.

2. Young adulthood (ages 19 to 25) encompasses the college years for some. It is a time during which a great deal of sexual exploration takes place, and young adults may engage in risky behavior.

3. When people form couples today, they face the conflicts of high expectations versus reality, individual fulfillment versus maintenance of the partnership, and the hope of a lifetime relationship

versus the awareness of how frequently relationships break up.

4. Coupling goes through continuing cycles of three stages: the expansive stage, contraction and betrayal, and resolution.

5. There are three main theoretical approaches to understanding how people select a mate or sexual partner. Psychological theory assumes some inner mechanism of attraction; social network theory demonstrates the significance of social groups in finding a partner; evolutionary or sociobiological theory holds that there are certain innate tendencies of males and females that shape their mate selection processes.

6. Most people eventually marry, although some choose to remain single. The issue of same-gender marriage has led to renewed examination of the institution of marriage and its meaning.

7. Some 5 million people are cohabiting, and this is becoming the norm for courtship behaviors leading to marriage. Cohabiting couples often assume that it will help them have a better marriage, but this depends on several factors and does not represent an assurance against eventual divorce.

8. Sexual activity tends to be most frequent in the earlier years of a relationship and then gradually decreases in frequency. Sexual satisfaction does not seem to be correlated with frequency, and married couples express more satisfaction than other groups. Good communication is important to relational and sexual satisfaction.

9. Although monogamy is still accepted as the most socially appropriate type of relationship, some level of extramarital sexual activity has been reported. Sexual infidelity seems to occur with less frequency than was once thought.

10. At least half of marriages in the United States end in divorce, with 70 percent of divorced people going on to subsequent marriages, more than half of which also end in divorce.

11. Even though older people retain their interests in and physical capacities for sexual expression, our youth-oriented culture often fails to recognize this fact. Attitudes about sex and availability of a partner are significant to the continuation of sexual desire.

12. In nursing homes and institutions for the elderly, lack of privacy and policies of sex segregation may prevent expression of sexual needs.

13. The concerns of gay, lesbian, and bisexual persons as they age seem to be essentially the same as those of heterosexuals. Gays do not face a greater likelihood of lowered self-esteem or depression as they age.

14. How sexually active an older person is depends on past activity, partner availability, physical health, and knowledge of sexuality.

15. Debilitating illness, chronic pain, certain medications, and the aftermath of some surgeries can affect people's sexual identities and sexual desires.

Focus on Health Questions

In this section you will find the kinds of questions that you may have concerning your own health and sexuality. The page references indicate where in the text the answer is located; this exact place is marked with this logo: **FOH**

1. I feel extremely awkward when I attempt to have sexual intercourse. Is there anything I can do to make myself more comfortable? **174**

2. If we live together for a while, won't that give us an edge on having a happier marriage? **179**

3. How can I prepare for remaining sexually interested and active when I am older? **189**

4. Is it all right to have sex after one has recovered from a heart attack? **190**

5. What sex-related problems are associated with diabetes? **190**

Chapter 8
Sexual Individuality and Sexual Values

Chapter Outline

> Until I came to college, I thought of myself as a very normal person sexually—a little on the conservative side, maybe, but normal. As I watch my peers' sexual exploits, I'm not so sure anymore. I am doing a lot of questioning about who I really am, or ought to be, sexually.
>
> —from a student essay

Humans have the potential to participate in, and find pleasurable, a wide spectrum of sexual activities. As we have begun to see, there seems to be a complex interaction of innate and social factors that determines which of these activities ultimately are chosen by a particular individual. Cultural and social mores and values also determine the extent and types of sexual behaviors to be found in any human society at any particular time in history. With increased attention being given to the concept of sexual rights across cultures, discussions relating to sexual acceptability also are becoming more globally focused. Political forces within national governments also play a role in establishing certain trends and expectations, as demonstrated by the culture wars in the United States.

We have already discussed the enduring ambivalence people seem to have regarding sex. It holds tremendous potential for pleasure and is vital to the propagation of the human species, yet it is also a source of anxiety, shame, and disgust. Societies attach great symbolic meaning to sex and seek to regulate its expressions. It has been proposed that human ambivalence about things sexual could be rooted in two ideas of which we are reminded when it comes to sexuality. One is the inescapable but uncomfortable fact that we are indeed animals, even though the human animal certainly has many distinguishing characteristics that set it apart. The other reminder is that one of the prices that sexual reproduction incurs is death. Organisms that produce offspring through sexual means ultimately die, a fact that seems to be universally troubling (Goldenberg et al., 2002).

List several sexual activities you believe are considered normal in our society. List several sexual activities you believe are considered abnormal.

■ Labeling Sex: Establishing Standards

For a long time, the predominant assumption in Western culture regarding human sexuality was this: To be **normal** was to be attracted sexually to members of the opposite sex and to desire penis-in-vagina intercourse as the ultimate expression of that attraction; everything else, in varying degrees and at various times, was considered **abnormal.** Yet there is ample historical, anthropological, and psychological evidence to indicate that human beings are—and always

FIGURE 8.1 *Erotic Scene from Attic Cup, Pompeii, Italy, Fifth Century B.C.E.*

For centuries, depictions of human sexual behaviors have reflected various standards of acceptability.

have been—extremely diverse and variable in their sexual attractions and behaviors (see Figure 8.1).

Literature and art have portrayed all sexual activities through the ages, but the extent to which they have been expressed and permitted in various societies and times in history is known only in bits and pieces (see Figure 8.2). For some past cultures, we know what sexual behaviors were considered unlawful or in violation of the codes of sexual activity established by their religion (Gaca, 2003). However, the extent to which information about a sexual activity was recorded in a society may have depended on the extent to which the activity was tolerated and accepted. Consider the examples of prostitution and same-gender sexual behavior. Because prostitution has generally been more accepted over the span of human history than has same-gender behavior, we have far more historical records about it than we do about sexual activity between members of the same sex.

normal a highly subjective term used to describe sexual behaviors and orientations. Standards of normalcy are determined by social, cultural, and historical standards.

abnormal anything considered not to be normal (that is, not conforming to the subjective standards a social group has established as the norm).

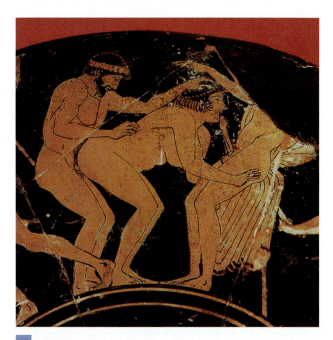

FIGURE 8.2 *A Variety of Sexual Activities as Portrayed by the Painter of This Red-Figured Attic Kylix*

One job of science is to categorize, classify, and label. To organize and to name things and phenomena are the only ways for us to continue being able to communicate about them intelligently. This has been true for human sexuality, as science has attempted to explain, understand, and classify sexual attractions and activities. We must also keep in mind that categories are created by people who have their own particular definitions of meaning, drawn from time, place, and political persuasion. Differences among categories often are exaggerated and therefore have real power to impact those individuals who have been classified either within a category or outside the category. Ultimately, categories are artificial and ever-changing (Muehlenhard, 2000). Recently, there has not even been much agreement as to which genital behaviors actually constitute "having sex" (Pitts & Rahman, 2001).

It is important to remember that scientists, too, are products of their sociocultural environments. Their conclusions and labels may reflect the agendas of their society. Labels can have great power, both positive and negative. You might recall that, during the latter part of the nineteenth century, Richard von Krafft-Ebing condemned masturbation as depraved and identified it as a source of mental contamination, weakened sexual desire, and all manner of physical and sexual problems. His attitudes were promulgated throughout the medical profession, thereby promoting the view that masturbation was one of the most damaging of sexual acts. It was given labels such as secret sin, self-abuse, and self-pollution. Generations of young

people grew up viewing masturbation with fear and frustration.

Krafft-Ebing reflected, reinforced, and perpetuated the values of his place, time, and social network. It was not a time when science could see the description of behavior as being unrelated to moral implications and teachings. The twentieth century, as we have seen, saw a shift in attitudes toward masturbation. Medical science has yielded objective data regarding its effects and its frequency. Although some religious prohibitions against masturbation remain, the general opinion in the professions of medicine and psychology is that the practice is a widespread and generally harmless form of sexual expression. It is interesting that discussions about sex have now shifted to the use of labels such as **self-gratification** and **self-pleasuring** to describe masturbation, which has become one of the norms against which other behaviors are compared and standardized.

For years, sexologists have struggled to come up with general, inclusive terms to describe and classify more atypical behaviors such as sadomasochism or cross-dressing. They continue to face the issue of how to judge whether some sexual activity truly is atypical or socially inappropriate. Psychoanalysis first gave us the term **deviation,** which, of course, implies that a person has strayed from some defined, normal pathway. If the pathway is determined by statistics, the deviant is someone who is located on one of the tails of a bell curve. Or it may be established simply by prevailing values. In any case, the label "deviation" has taken on so much emotional content and vagueness that it no longer is widely used to describe sexual behaviors.

A more recent label has been **variation** or variance, which also implies that an individual is somehow different or aberrant sexually. The question remains of how the standard for determining the norm is established. We might ask, "A variation on what?" or "Different from what?" These terms have come to have negative connotations, even though originally they were not meant to carry any particular value implications.

self-gratification giving oneself pleasure, as in masturbation; a term typically used today instead of more negative descriptors.

self-pleasuring self-gratification; masturbation.

deviation term applied to behaviors or orientations that do not conform to a society's accepted norms; often has negative connotations.

variation a less pejorative term used to describe nonconformity to accepted norms.

The term **paraphilia,** loosely meaning "a love beside," is used to describe sexual attachment or dependency on some unusual or typically unacceptable stimulus. A paraphilia is presently considered to be somewhat pathological and to interfere in some way with an individual's life, and the term is used in psychiatry to label a variety of sexual diagnoses. Some professionals have accepted that some forms of sexual expression seem obviously and categorically disordered and should be treated as such. Other professionals argue that the logic and factual information used to diagnose the paraphilias are flawed and inaccurate enough that the entire classification should be eliminated as a category of mental disorder. The debate rages on (Karasic & Drescher, 2005; Moser & Kleinplatz, 2005).

Sociocultural Standards for Sexual Arousal and Behavior

It is easy to see that labels such as deviation, variation, and paraphilia all imply some degree of aberration from an accepted sexual standard. Several standards permeate the values of Western culture today. In informal—and sometimes quite formalized—ways, they tell us how we are "supposed" to feel and act sexually. These standards are reinforced by prevailing cultural values and mores and by the social networks in which we live. That is not to imply that they are inconsequential or should not be respected, because we are all both products of and integral parts of our society and culture. Yet, at the same time, we cannot ignore the fact that standards shift and alter with time, nor can we deny the fact that significant proportions of the human population simply do not live their sexual lives according to these standards. The standards are described in the sections that follow.

The Heterosexual Standard

We are supposed to be sexually attracted to members of the other gender and therefore to desire to be sexually involved with them (see Figure 8.3). Even though other sexual orientations have achieved increasing levels of acceptance, we have not yet moved beyond the widely accepted notion that to be heterosexual is preferable. This cultural **heterosexism** fosters antigay and antilesbian attitudes by providing a system of values and stereotypes that seem to justify prejudice and discrimination (Brickell, 2001).

The Coital Standard

We are supposed to view sexual intercourse between a woman and a man, or **coitus,** as the ultimate sexual act. Most other forms of shared male-female sexual

■ **FIGURE 8.3** *Heterosexual Standard*

The form and meaning of behavior are influenced by the culture and the time in which a person lives. In North American society at the beginning of the twenty-first century, heterosexuality is the standard form of sexual behavior. The cultural standard, however, should not be confused with a moral and ethical standard that is individualistic and flexible.

activity have traditionally been labeled **foreplay,** with the implication that rather than being enjoyed for their own sake or as sexual goals and ends in their own right, they represent steps toward intercourse. They prepare the couple for coitus. This standard has weakened in recent years as oral sex and other forms of noncoital interaction have become increasingly accepted.

The Orgasmic Standard

We are supposed to experience orgasm as the climax of any sexual interaction. This standard has been particularly prevalent among males in Western culture, although in recent years it has become predominant among women as well.

paraphilia (pair-a-FIL-ee-a) a newer term used to describe sexual orientations and behaviors that vary from the norm in pathological or antisocial ways; it means "a love beside."

heterosexism the biased and discriminatory assumption that people are or should be attracted to members of the other gender.

coitus (KO-at-us or ko-EET-us) heterosexual, penis-in-vagina intercourse.

foreplay sexual activities shared in early stages of sexual arousal, with the term implying that they are leading to a more intense, orgasm-oriented form of activity such as intercourse.

The Two-Person Standard

We are supposed to view sex as an activity for two. Although masturbation has for the most part gained legitimacy as an acceptable behavior, it still is typically viewed as a substitute for shared sexual activity, especially intercourse. According to the standard, it is still better to experience sex as a duo, and any sexual activity involving more than two is considered distinctly kinky.

The Romantic Standard

We are supposed to relate sex to love. Romance and sex have become inseparably intertwined, and it certainly is true that the intimacy generated by one may enhance the other. But it is also true that love and sex can be subject to very different interpretations and values. In Victorian times, healthy and positive loving relationships were supposed to be unspoiled by the desires of the flesh. Today it often seems that romantic love without sex is considered incomplete and that sex without love is considered emotionally shallow and exploitative.

The Safe Sex Standard

The most recently developed standard for our culture, the safe sex standard holds that when people make the choice to share sex, they are supposed to take appropriate precautions to prevent unwanted consequences such as unintended pregnancy or transmission of disease. It evolved out of an increased awareness of the threat of HIV and AIDS and has expressed itself in a new level of emphasis on abstinence from risky sexual behaviors and on the use of condoms during shared sexual activity.

Which sociocultural standards for sexual arousal and behavior do you believe are most commonly held within your social network: the heterosexual standard, the coital standard, the orgasmic standard, the two-person standard, the romantic standard, the safe sex standard? Explain your choices.

Global Sexual Rights

In 1999, the World Association for Sexology (WAS) adopted the Universal Declaration of Sexual Rights. The WAS is a coalition of activists, researchers, academics, medical professionals, and health care providers who work to further the understanding and development of sexology throughout the world. The association has over a hundred member organizations representing over 30 countries. While the Declaration of Sexual Rights is not enforceable, it does represent a set of guidelines that are increasingly being used in policy-making. Here are its components:

- Sexuality is an integral part of the personality of every human being. Its full development depends on the satisfaction of basic human needs such as the desire for contact, intimacy, emotional expression, pleasure, tenderness, and love.
- Sexuality is constructed through the interaction between the individual and social structures. Full development of sexuality is essential for individual, interpersonal, and societal well-being.
- Sexual rights are universal human rights based on the inherent freedom, dignity, and equality of all human beings. Because health is a fundamental human right, so must sexual health be a basic human right. In order to assure that human beings and societies develop healthy sexuality, the following sexual rights must be recognized, promoted, respected, and defended by all societies through all means. Sexual health is the result of an environment that recognizes, respects, and exercises these sexual rights.

1. *The right to sexual freedom.* Sexual freedom encompasses the possibility for individuals to express their full sexual potential. However, this excludes all forms of sexual coercion, exploitation, and abuse at any time and situation in life.
2. *The right to sexual autonomy, sexual integrity, and safety of the sexual body.* This right involves the ability to make autonomous decisions about one's sexual life within a context of one's own personal and social ethics. It also encompasses control and enjoyment of our own bodies free from torture, mutilation, and violence of any sort.
3. *The right to sexual privacy.* This involves the right to make individual decisions and behaviors about intimacy as long as they do not intrude on the sexual rights of others.
4. *The right to sexual equity.* This refers to freedom from all forms of discrimination regardless of sex, gender, sexual orientation, age, race, social class, religion, or physical and emotional disability.
5. *The right to sexual pleasure.* Sexual pleasure, including autoeroticism, is a source of physical, psychological, intellectual, and spiritual well-being.
6. *The right to emotional sexual expression.* Sexual expression is more than erotic pleasure or sexual acts. Individuals have a right to express their sexuality through communication, touch, emotional expression, and love.
7. *The right to sexually associate freely.* This means the possibility to marry or not, to

divorce, and to establish other types of responsible sexual associations.

8. *The right to make free and responsible reproductive choices.* This encompasses the right to decide whether to have children, the number and spacing of children, and the right to full access to the means of fertility regulation.

9. *The right to sexual information based upon scientific inquiry.* This right implies that sexual information should be generated through the process of unencumbered yet scientifically ethical inquiry, and disseminated in appropriate ways at all societal levels.

10. *The right to comprehensive sexuality education.* This is a lifelong process from birth throughout the life cycle and should involve all social institutions.

11. *The right to sexual health care.* Sexual health care should be available for prevention and treatment of all sexual concerns, problems, and disorders.

See "Sex, Sin, and Sickness" on SexSource Online.

Who Is Normal?

Anthropologists speak of **ethnocentricity,** the quality of assuming that one's own culture is the right one and is superior to all others. Our ethnocentricity finds us surprised, amused, and shocked by the beliefs and customs of others, who of course are just as taken aback by ours. In their classic anthropological study *Patterns of Sexual Behavior,* Ford and Beach (1951) concluded that there is such a wide variation in sexual behaviors across cultures that no one society can even be regarded as representative. Yet a type of ethnocentricity that might be called **erotocentricity** leads us to assume that our own—either cultural or individual—sexual values, standards, and activities are right and best.

Ours is a culture of dichotomies and categories. Everything must fit into some classification, and if something is not right, it must be wrong. Likewise, if some behavior is not bad, it must be good (Muehlenhard, 2000). The normal/not-normal dichotomy often is strongly held, and people constantly worry about whether their feelings and behaviors are indeed normal. Every society sets sexual standards and regulates sexual behaviors. These standards are adopted by social networks in varying degrees and then are passed from one generation to the next, sometimes being modified as they are passed on. Boundaries therefore arise, distinguishing the good from the bad, the acceptable from the unacceptable. These boundaries

become the criteria used to establish the concepts of normal and not normal. The most widely accepted methods of defining normalcy in Western culture today are described in the following sections.

Statistical Normalcy

One of the most common ways to decide the relative normalcy of some sexual behavior is based on how widespread and frequent it is in a particular population. If most people do it, then it is considered normal. If it is practiced by only a small minority, it is not considered normal. Some behaviors, such as masturbation and oral sex, began to be considered more "normal" when major sex surveys showed how widespread they were.

Normalcy by Expert Opinion

Every society has its experts, either by choice or by default. Our society venerates educational and professional status and listens to the opinions of those who possess what are perceived to be expert credentials. For example, members of the psychiatric profession's associations may decide, by vote, to consider a certain sexual orientation healthy or unhealthy, normal or abnormal. In 1974, the American Psychiatric Association decided, by polling their members, that same-gender sexual orientation and behavior would no longer be considered an illness (see Figure 8.4). For the purposes of diagnosing and classifying various mental illnesses, including certain sexual behaviors, professionals often refer to a major psychiatric handbook called the *Diagnostic and Statistical Manual of Mental Disorders* (*DSM-IV*). Now in its fourth edition, this manual usually is referred to as the *DSM-IV*. Professional meetings are now under way to make decisions about the contents of the *DSM-IV*. Questions have been raised about the basis for deciding what is considered abnormal and therefore listed in the *DSM-IV* as such. It has been claimed that the process for making such decisions is sometimes arbitrary and scientifically inadequate. Yet often it is expert opinion that will determine what is normal or abnormal, and expert opinion may vary depending on available input (Beutler & Malik, 2002; Karasic & Drescher, 2005).

ethnocentricity (eth-no-sen-TRIS-ih-tee) the tendency of the members of one culture to assume that their values and norms of behavior are the "right" ones in comparison to those of other cultures.

erotocentricity (ee-ROT-oh-sen-TRIS-ih-tee) the application of ethnocentric-like judgments to sexual values and behaviors, creating the assumption that our own ways of approaching sexuality are the only "right" ways.

FIGURE 8.4 *What Is Normal?*

Labels such as "homosexual" are sometimes employed to construct rigid boundaries between "normal" and "not-normal" behavior. In fact, same-gender orientation and behavior are part of a continuum of sexual behavior that encompasses numerous individual factors.

Moral Normalcy

Religions usually have standards regarding sexual morality. The predominant religions in a particular society therefore often establish the norms for morality. These standards may then be perpetuated in laws and social sanctions. In most societies, behaviors and values that are seen as morally acceptable are also defined as normal.

A Continuum of Normalcy

In Western societies, there has been increased acceptance of concepts such as situational morality, reality as a matter of perception, and being nonjudgmental. A result has been an increased willingness to view sexual attraction and activities in relative terms, by asking questions such as these: Is a behavior healthy and fulfilling for a particular person? Is it safe? Does it lead to exploitation of others? Does it take place between responsible, consenting adults? In this outlook, *normal* and *abnormal* are seen as part of a continuum that considers numerous individual and situa-

tional factors. Nevertheless, societies establish sexual norms and make decisions about what is to be done with those people who violate them. They may be treated by healing practitioners with anything from a shaman's spells to modern drugs, depending on the culture. They may be banished from the society or forced to live in a kind of sexual exile. Or they may be subject to legal sanctions and even face imprisonment. They may also be ignored or tolerated. In Western culture, where a male-female double standard clearly still exists, women who experience strong or frequent sexual desire report that they often feel ignored or stigmatized because of their sexual interests (Blumberg, 2003).

Limits and Misuses of Labels: The Language of Sexual Orientation

Labels for various forms of sexual behavior can provide only a very general category of definition. The *DSM-IV* provides diagnostic categories to facilitate communication among clinicians in the psychological and psychiatric professions and to conform with insurance regulations. However, whatever defines groups of people can also separate them. Consider, for example, the term **homosexual.** Most people believe that they understand what is meant by the term. Closer examination might call the use of this label into question (Muehlenhard, 2000). Here are some of the issues to be clarified in deciding who might once have been labeled a homosexual:

1. Must the person participate in actual sexual activity with another of the same gender, or is it enough to just want to do so?
2. If a person has had just one sexual experience with a same-gender partner, should he or she be considered homosexual? If not, how many same-gender sexual acts should lead to such classification?
3. Should only those who have been sexually involved exclusively with members of their own gender be called homosexual? If not, what percentage of same-gender experience is required?
4. Should people who have been attracted sexually to members of their gender all their lives but have married and engaged exclusively in heterosexual activity be considered homosexual?

Because heterosexual orientation and behavior clearly are considered the norm in contemporary society, we would not expect heterosexuals as a group to be particularly noticed. Surely it is true that the term *heterosexual* is not likely to be used to define a person, behavior, or lifestyle, because a great deal of diversity is accepted among those people considered to be heterosexual. The term *homosexual,* on the other hand, is quite a different story. It usually has represented a distinct and permanent category, a defining characteristic of the person who has been labeled that implies a great deal beyond some occasional sexual behavior. As a consequence, people who have any degree of same-gender sexual orientation may be marginalized as a separate minority, often provoking disapproval by their perceived "abnormalcy" or "unhealthiness."

There is a tendency to categorize sexual activities by the gender of the people involved and then draw inferences about those who fit into the categories. Knowing about a person's same-gender sexual behaviors actually reveals nothing about her or his psychological adjustment, hormone balances, masculinity or femininity, childhood development, or any other characteristic that would distinguish the person from one whose sexual behaviors have been exclusively heterosexual. Research data continue to indicate that people who have sex with members of their own gender are remarkably similar to people who do not. Perhaps

science has been trying to invent categories and commonalities where none exist (Muehlenhard, 2000).

Definitions of the term *homosexual* have tended to focus only on sexual activity and thus have sometimes ignored the individual's **affectional** preferences. A person's sexual behavior does not necessarily reflect inner orientations and inclinations. It is quite possible that individuals who find themselves sexually attracted to members of their own gender never participate in sexual acts with them. Instead these individuals may function effectively in relationships with the other gender. It is also possible for those with a primarily heterosexual orientation to participate in same-gender sexual behavior.

Current models of sexual orientation take into consideration many different variables, including behavior, attraction, self-identification, lifestyle, frequency of sex with different partners, and changes over time. The present state of knowledge about human sexuality no longer allows us to identify the term *homosexual* as anything very specific. For these reasons, some psychologists have recommended that the term *homosexual* no longer be applied to people. It is laden with negative stereotypes, often is applied only to males, and generally is ambiguous.

A group from the American Psychological Association has developed guidelines for the use of terms that are considered more precise and less pejorative. "Gay male" and "lesbian" are used primarily to describe people's sexual and affectional identities and the communities of individuals that have developed among people who share those identities. Although the term **gay** is sometimes used to describe either men or women, it will be used in this book mostly in reference to males; the word **lesbian** is used in reference to females. Although there is growing use of the term *queer* by professionals who are gay, bisexual, or transgendered themselves, the term often describes a particular set of political values relating to sexual orientation (Humphrey, 1999). The word has not been widely embraced by those in the gay and lesbian community, and it is not used in this book because it is still

homosexual term traditionally applied to affectional and sexual attractions and activities between members of the same gender.

affectional relating to feelings or emotions, such as romantic attachments.

gay refers to persons who have a predominantly same-gender sexual orientation and identity. More often applied to males.

lesbian (LEZ-bee-un) refers to females who have a predominantly same-gender sexual orientation and identity.

so often employed by others in a negative way. The term **heterosexual** can be used to refer to opposite-gender (male-female) orientation, identity, or behavior. The slang term **straight** is often applied to primarily heterosexual persons, although it also carries the negative connotation that nonheterosexuals are somehow "crooked," perpetuating a stereotype of deviance from the norm.

The term **bisexual** is used in reference to people who relate sexually and affectionally to both females and males. It can be used to describe both sexual identity and behavior. One complex aspect of bisexuality is that it may be manifested in so many different ways. Some bisexual people are simultaneously attracted to both men and women, whereas others have sequential relationships with members of both genders. In other words, some bisexual persons spend some time in a gay male or lesbian relationship, followed by involvement in a heterosexual relationship, or vice versa. Bisexual people often feel as though they do not have a clear place in society that their identity fits into. Heterosexual people, lesbians, and gay males may not be accepting of bisexual orientations and behaviors, assuming that the bisexual person should make a decision to go one way or the other—choosing sides as it were. On one hand, bisexuals may be accused by gay males or lesbians of trying to preserve heterosexual privileges; on the other hand, they often are perceived by both heterosexual people and gay males and lesbians as being gay or lesbian but afraid to admit it (Steffens & Wagner, 2004).

Confusing questions may also arise with other sex-related labels. A man who dresses in women's clothing is often labeled a **transvestite,** yet such behavior has all sorts of different motivations. Terms such as *sadism* and *masochism* are so general and ill-defined that they have little meaning in talking about the behavior of individuals (see Chapter 14, "The Spectrum of Human Sexual Behavior"). Of special concern is the use of specific sexual labels to define the entire person. Only too often an individual's entire identity seems to be summarized in a single descriptor of his or her sexual orientation. We say "Isn't she a lesbian?" or "There goes a transvestite" instead of recognizing these orientations and behaviors as only one small part of an individual's personality. Yet we never label anyone heterosexual or some other term for what we consider normal behavior. Such misuses of terminology are a disservice to the individuality of human beings.

■ Sexual Individuality

Personal sexuality is far more complex than are gender roles and sexual attraction to a particular gender. We may find certain characteristics about other people sexually attracting and arousing: facial features, body types and builds, hairstyles, age, certain parts of their body (for example, legs, buttocks, genitals, breasts), styles of clothing, or lack of clothing. When we interact with others sexually, we usually have specific sexual acts that we prefer. We may have our own particular frequencies and techniques for masturbation, and some people find some activities and things sexually exciting that have little to do with other people.

Most people have a sexual life of the mind as well, consisting of sexual fantasies and dreams along with sensations of sexual need, desire, and attraction (see Figure 8.5 on page 202). Only sometimes are these inner experiences expressed in physical responses or overt sexual behaviors. Because performing sexual acts involves a degree of decision making, our inner sexual reactions and needs are not always consistent with our outward expressions of sexual behavior.

All these aspects of a person's sexuality are intimately intertwined with all other aspects of the personality. As with classifying fingerprints by loops, whorls, and other configurations, it is possible to find general categories for some parts of everyone's sexual nature. Taken together, however, the aspects of our personal sexualities are as individualized and specific as our fingerprints. They constitute our **sexual individuality.**

How Does Sexual Individuality Develop?

Sex research into the origins of sexual attractions, orientations, preferences, and behaviors is still in a preliminary stage. At this point, the most honest assessment would be that we really do not know how human beings take on the specific characteristics of their sexuality. Research has provided us with a few generalizations about sexual orientation and sexual activity that form the underpinnings for further work:

1. The importance of the relationship with parents and of identifying with a parent in determining a

heterosexual refers to attractions or activities between males and females.

straight slang term for "heterosexual."

bisexual refers to some degree of sexual activity with or attraction to members of both sexes.

transvestite an individual who dresses in clothing and adopts mannerisms considered appropriate for the opposite sex.

sexual individuality the unique set of sexual needs, orientations, fantasies, feelings, and activities that develops in each human being.

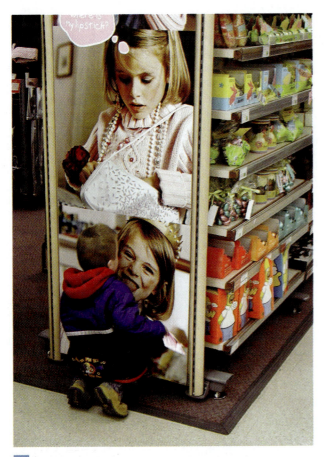

■ **FIGURE 8.5** *Sexual Curiosity and Fantasy*

People are curious about the human body and sexuality most of their lives. Our inner sexual lives often help us develop and explore our sexual needs and interests. Sexual fantasy gives people the opportunity to experience sexual interests in a safe environment and to release inner tensions. Sexual fantasies may mirror developing sexual desires, or in some cases may promote sexual desires.

child's sexual orientation probably has been overestimated in former theories. While parents may influence the development of sexual attractions to some extent, these influences likely are not very profound.

2. An individual's basic sexual orientation is largely determined by adolescence, even though the person may not have been particularly sexually active. Adult expressions of sexual orientation and preference tend to be a continuation and confirmation of earlier sexual feelings, although some of those expressions may not actually be realized behaviorally until later in life.

3. Developing patterns of sexual feelings and responses within children and young people cannot be traced to a single social or psychological root. They are instead the result of many

factors that are a part of any human being's life and are too numerous, complex, and poorly understood at this time to be predictable or controllable.

4. There seem to be some biological bases for the development of sexual orientation and a preference for certain sexual activities. These inborn factors most likely establish sexual predispositions that may then be influenced in various ways by psychological and social factors. Thus, it is likely that the *interaction* between nature and experience, rather than one or the other alone, influences our sexual development, along with most other facets of human development.

5. Social networks, those groups of people with whom we associate on a regular basis, are extremely significant in shaping and perpetuating our individual sexual attitudes and behaviors.

6. There does not seem to be a "natural" sexual way for human beings to be or an inborn sexual instinct to guide sexual behaviors. The diversity of sexual individuality provides ample evidence that there is no single, representative human sexuality.

Fritz Klein (1990) was one of the first researchers to develop a model showing many different components of sexual identity, all related to one another but having a degree of independence at the same time. He initially developed a list of seven variables that needed to be considered when describing a person's sexual orientation or identity: sexual attraction, sexual behavior, sexual fantasies, emotional preference, social preference, self-identification, and actual lifestyle. He soon realized, however, that these dimensions of a person's life often change over time. Where people are today in terms of their sexual identities is not necessarily where they were in the past or where they will be—or would like to be—in the future. Therefore, he developed a matrix, called the Klein Sexual Orientation Grid (KSOG), that considers this time factor along with each of the seven variables (see Figure 8.6).

Other researchers have reinforced the concept that sexual individuality is a combination of many life dimensions and includes many facets of the personality and patterns of behavior. It reflects an evolution of an individual's own perception of self through the development of a sexual identity (Garcia & Hoskins, 2001). To define a person's sexual orientation on the basis of any one activity or fantasy would be too narrow. Labeling a whole person with the name of a single sexual category cannot do justice to the complexity of human sexual identity or orientation. The development of sexual individuality takes place over a lifetime and includes many different components.

Real Student Voices

■ I believe that love and sex are somewhat independent of each other. A couple doesn't need to be in love to have sex, and they don't need to have sex to be in love. Sex without love is great and love without sex is great, but when they are combined, it makes both even better.

■ When people are single, sex mostly has no relation to love. I think I sometimes place too low of a value on sex because I treat it as something to do because I am horny.

■ With me and most college students, all good decision-making skills go down the drain after the first five or six beers.

Variable	Past	Present	Ideal
Sexual attraction			
Sexual behavior			
Sexual fantasies			
Emotional preference			
Social preference			
Self-identification			
Lifestyle			

■ **FIGURE 8.6** *Klein Sexual Orientation Grid (KSOG)*

Where people are today in terms of their sexual identities is not necessarily where they were in the past or where they will be or would like to be in the future. Klein developed this chart, which, when filled out, helps the researcher determine a person's sexual identity.

Source: From Fritz Klein, *Journal of Homosexuality* Volume 11, Issue 1/2, p. 39, 1985. Copyright © The Haworth Press Inc., Binghamton, NY. Used with permission.

Sexual Attitudes and Sexual Choices

Regardless of how we develop sexually—and regardless of the sexual fantasies, needs, attractions, and orientations that become part of every human being—each of us must make choices about his or her sexual behaviors. Through these choices we are able to fulfill some of the other expectations of being civilized human beings: to be responsible, to develop self-respect, and to be nonexploitative toward others. It has been shown that when discrepancies exist between people's actual feelings about their sexuality and what they believe they *should* be about sexually, they have lowered self-esteem and are more prone to depression (Garcia & Hoskins, 2001).

National Health and Social Life Survey (NHSLS) - researchers assessed attitudes on premarital sex, teenage sex, extramarital sex, same-gender sex, pornography, sex and love, religious beliefs, and abortion. They then examined the data using cluster analysis, a statistical technique used when social scientists are searching for patterns in masses of data but do not have a strong theory to guide them or a clearly defined hypothesis to be tested. As discussed in Chapter 1,

Table 8.1 *Description of Seven Normative Attitudinal Orientations toward Sexuality*

	Traditional		Relational			Recreational		
	Conservative	Pro-Choice	Religious	Conventional	Contemporary Religious	Pro-Life	Libertarian	Total Sample
1. Premarital sex is always wrong.	100.0%*	23.6%	0.0%	0.4%	0.8%	6.5%	0.0%	19.7%
2. Premarital sex among teenagers is always wrong.	99.5	90.3	78.6	29.1	33.6	65.7	19.7	60.8
3. Extramarital sex is always wrong.	98.2	91.0	92.1	94.2	52.1	59.3	32.0	76.7
4. Same-gender sex is always wrong.	96.4	94.4	81.9	65.4	6.4	85.9	9.0	64.8
5. There should be laws against the sale of pornography to adults.	70.6	47.2	53.1	12.2	11.7	14.9	6.4	33.6
6. I would not have sex with someone unless I was in love with them.	87.5	66.0	98.0	83.8	65.3	10.1	19.5	65.7
7. My religious beliefs have guided my sexual behavior.	91.3	72.9	74.7	8.7	100.0	25.0	0.0	52.3
8. A woman should be able to obtain a legal abortion if she was raped.	56.3	98.6	82.3	99.1	99.3	84.3	99.8	88.0
9. A woman should be able to obtain a legal abortion if she wants it for any reason.	0.5	100.0	0.0	87.4	84.9	9.3	88.6	52.4
N = 2,843	15.4%	15.2%	19.1%	15.9%	9.3%	8.7%	16.4%	100.0%

*Indicates the percentage of persons in the "Conservative Traditional" cluster who believe that premarital sex is always wrong.

Source: From *Sex in America* by Robert T. Michael et al. Copyright © 1994 by CSG Enterprises, Inc., Edward O. Laumann, Robert T. Michael, and Gina Kolata. By permission of Little, Brown and Company, Inc., and Brockman, Inc.

three broad categories of attitudes emerged, but evidence of some clear differences among groups within each category led to the formation of a few subcategories as well (Laumann, Gagnon, et al., 1994). Table 8.1 summarizes these findings.

About one-third of the population indicated that their religious beliefs always guide their sexual behaviors; this group was called *traditional.* People in this group tended to believe that premarital sex, teenage sex, extramarital sex, and same-gender sex are wrong and that legal abortion should be restricted to some degree. They were divided in their opinions about the availability of abortion, so the group was subdivided into *conservative* and *pro-choice.* The conservative traditionalists were more conservative in all of their sexual attitudes than were the pro-choice traditionalists.

The largest attitudinal group was the *relational* category, consisting of close to half the population. Members of this group believed that sex should be part of a loving relationship but not necessarily reserved exclusively for marriage. Therefore, they did not see premarital sex as wrong but did tend to rate extramari-

tal sex or casual sex as wrong. These people were then divided into three subgroups. The *religious* subgroup, whose religious beliefs shaped their sexual behaviors, was the most conservative, opposing same-gender sex, teenage sex, and abortion. The *conventional* subgroup was less influenced by religious beliefs and tended to be more tolerant than the religious group toward teenage sex, pornography, and abortion, but this group was still opposed to same-gender sex. A third subgroup, *contemporary religious,* was guided in their own behaviors by their religious beliefs but was more tolerant of same-gender sex than were the other subgroups.

About one-fourth of the population fit into a category that was labeled *recreational* because they did not feel that sex and love needed to be connected. Most people in this category also opposed laws that would prohibit the sale of pornography to adults. They were subdivided into a *pro-life* group, which opposed both same-gender sex and abortion but was more accepting of teenage sex and premarital sex, and the most liberal of all groups, the *libertarians,* who were not guided by any religious

Table 8.2 *Distribution of Attitudinal Orientations within Certain Demographic Groups*

Social Characteristics	Traditional	Relational	Recreational
Gender			
Men	26.9%	40.1%	33.0%
Women	33.7	47.6	18.7
Age			
Men			
18–24	17.4	46.9	35.7
25–29	21.0	46.2	32.9
30–39	26.2	38.6	35.2
40–49	31.2	38.2	30.5
50–59	40.1	31.3	28.6
Women			
18–24	23.0	51.8	25.3
25–29	27.5	54.6	17.9
30–39	34.6	46.6	18.8
40–49	34.5	44.9	20.6
50–59	47.0	43.4	9.6
Education			
Men			
Less than high school	31.6	39.5	28.8
High school graduate or equivalent	28.3	40.9	30.8
Any college	25.0	39.8	35.2
Women			
Less than high school	36.6	47.6	15.9
High school graduate or equivalent	38.3	46.0	15.7
Any college	30.4	48.7	20.9
Religion			
Men			
None	11.7	39.1	49.2
Mainline Protestant	24.2	43.8	32.0
Conservative Protestant	44.5	30.1	25.3
Catholic	17.8	49.6	32.6
Women			
None	10.4	44.4	45.2
Mainline Protestant	30.9	51.4	17.7
Conservative Protestant	50.5	38.4	11.2
Catholic	22.2	58.0	19.8

beliefs and were assessed as most accepting on all the attitudinal items.

Which group or subgroup do your sexual attitudes and beliefs most closely align with? Defend your choice.

These findings showed that there is no clear-cut system of "American attitudes" when it comes to human sexuality. There is instead a wide distribution of beliefs across the population. The researchers were able to draw some other interesting conclusions, summarized in Table 8.2. For example, women were somewhat more likely than men to fit into the traditional category and less likely to fit into the recreational group. Older people also were more likely to be traditional. More women than men indicated that

they believed strongly in love and commitment as a part of sexual relationships. Educational level did not seem to be associated with any clear attitudinal pattern, although an increase in educational attainment was associated with a slight trend away from conservative sexual attitudes and toward liberal attitudes. Religious affiliation, on the other hand, did show some correlation with attitudes. Nonreligious people were unlikely to fall into the traditional category and more likely to be in the recreational group. Conservative Protestants were much more likely to be in the traditional category (Michael et al., 1994).

One of the more salient findings of the NHSLS research was the clear link between people's attitudes and their sexual behaviors. Although it is beyond the scope of this text to analyze the correlations in detail, it was shown that an attitudinal group was closely

Real Student Voices

■ Sometimes I know that I allow my sexual needs to take precedence over my better judgment. It really is a choice, I guess, but I think it makes me feel less guilty if I imagine it to be out of my control. It feels that way too.

■ I'm a very religious person, and so it's pretty easy for me to make ethical sexual choices. My church is real clear about what to do, and I follow that.

■ While I believe we are intelligent beings who are completely capable of resisting our innate biological programming for the good of society, I'm a firm believer that love has evolved as a means for us to keep a sense of attachment to our mates, just like the mating habits of other mammals. Basically, it's all about sex for propagating the species.

associated with particular sexual practices and frequency of sexual thoughts. Traditional people tended to have fewer sexual partners and thought less about sex than did the other two groups. Those with recreational attitudes had more sexual partners and thought more frequently about sex. Masturbation, oral sex, anal sex, and same-gender sex all were more common among the recreational group than among the traditional group. Frequency of sexual activity did not seem to be linked to an attitudinal group (Laumann, Gagnon, et al., 1994).

Sexual attitudes are very firmly held in most people. Family members, friends, and other members of our social networks tend to be like-minded in their attitudes and therefore provide constant reinforcement of shared beliefs. This is one reason why people's behaviors tend to be consistent with their belief systems. It may also account for why people find it difficult to understand and accept other attitudinal viewpoints and have no desire to change their own. This realization provides us with some understanding of why so many conflicts arise in our society regarding sexual matters and why discrimination can be one unfortunate result.

Sexual Attitudes and Discrimination: Homophobia, Biphobia, and Transphobia

FOH Irrational fears of lesbians and gay men and strongly held negative attitudes about them have been labeled **homophobia,** although it has been argued that this term is not accurate because a true "phobia" is not usually involved. More accurately it is a form of sexual discrimination (Herek & Gonzalez-Rivera, 2006). Public

attitudes toward people with same-gender sexual orientations have tended to become somewhat less negative in recent years. A TIME/CNN poll of 1,036 adults, slightly over 40 percent of whom had a close friend or family member who was gay or lesbian (see Table 8.3), showed that 64 percent considered same-gender sexual relationships acceptable, compared to 41 percent a decade earlier. Nonetheless, close to half of those surveyed believed that such relationships between consenting adults are morally wrong. Slightly more than half believed that gay and lesbian people could change their sexual orientation if they chose to do so.

There is evidence that college athletics represents an area that still exhibits a high level of homophobia and that gay and lesbian athletes generally have to keep a relatively low profile about their orientation (Wolf-Wendel, Toma, & Morphew, 2001). However, other college students also perceive some barriers to friendships with lesbians and gay men (Mohr & Sedlacek, 2001). Studies across several nations show that men tend on average to be more homophobic than women (Davies, 2004; Lingiardi, Falanga, & D'Augelli, 2005; Negy & Eisenman, 2005).

Some negative attitudes about gay and lesbian people in some specific occupations were evident. Only about half the respondents in the poll wanted openly gay people to be allowed to teach in their community's schools. Apparently there is a common misconception that gay or lesbian teachers might somehow be inappropriate role models for students

> **homophobia** (ho-mo-FO-bee-a) strongly held negative attitudes about and irrational fears of gay men and/or lesbians and their lifestyles.

Table 8.3 *Attitudes toward Same-Gender Sexual Orientation*

How do you feel about homosexual relationships?

	1998	1978
Acceptable for others, but not self	52%	35%
Acceptable for others and self	12%	6%
Not acceptable at all	33%	59%

Are homosexual relationships between consenting adults morally wrong or not a moral issue?

	1998	1978
Yes, morally wrong	48%	53%
Not a moral issue	45%	38%

Do you have a family member or close friend who is gay or lesbian?

	1998	1994
Yes	41%	32%
No	57%	66%

Is homosexuality something that some people are born with, or is it due to factors such as how they were raised or their environment?

Born with	33%
How raised or environment	40%
Both	11%

Can people who are homosexual change their sexual orientation if they choose to do so?

Yes	51%	No	36%

Do you favor or oppose permitting people who are openly gay or lesbian to serve in the military?

Favor	52%	Oppose	39%

Do you favor or oppose permitting people who are openly gay or lesbian to teach in schools in your community?

Favor	51%	Oppose	42%

Source: From Richard Lacayo, "The New Gay Struggle," *Time*, October 26, 1998. Copyright © 1998 Time Inc. Reprinted by permission.

(see Figure 8.7 on page 208). This attitude may also be based on the common misconception that gay men and lesbians are more likely to molest children, a belief that is not supported by statistics (Dunne et al., 2000).

Gay and lesbian students frequently are subjected to harassment, misunderstanding, and discrimination (Brown et al., 2004). Attitudes toward gay men tend to be more negative among other students than are attitudes toward lesbians. Faculty members tend to be more homophobic than those who work with students as student affairs administrators (Schlesinger, 2001).

Sexuality education classes and textbooks often have employed an underlying set of assumed heterosexual norms, leading to the claim that they are unfairly biased in heterosexist directions. Homophobic attitudes found on college campuses may be one reason why gay men and lesbians sometimes find their college environments less emotionally supportive and less tolerant of change and innovation than the environment they would find in the larger society. Campus diversity efforts have begun to challenge heterosexism and to offer active acceptance and nurturance of those with differing sexual orientations. Students with same-gender sexual orientations thus have become increasingly visible. Those institutions that have been successful in creating a supportive environment for gay males, lesbians, and bisexuals have found that

these students can feel comfortable and safe on campus and are less prone to self-destructive attitudes and behaviors than are those in less supportive environments (Brown et al., 2004; Shaffer & Augustine, 2002).

Misunderstanding of and prejudice toward bisexual people, sometimes called **biphobia,** has been on the rise, as has **transphobia,** a term applied to negative feelings toward transgender individuals. Probably the most blatant form of biphobia is the common belief that bisexuality does not exist. The assumption is made that people must fit naturally into either a heterosexual identity or a gay or lesbian identity and that all others simply have not been able to make up their minds where they fit. In one study, heterosexual students had the most strongly negative feelings toward bisexual people, rather than gay men or lesbians (Herek & Gonzalez-Rivera, 2006). Both homophobia and biphobia may be *externalized* or *internalized*. When externalized, they manifest themselves in name-calling, discrimination, or prejudice toward others. It

biphobia prejudice, negative attitudes, and misconceptions toward bisexual people and their lifestyles.

transphobia negative attitudes, prejudice, and misconceptions toward transgender individuals and lifestyles.

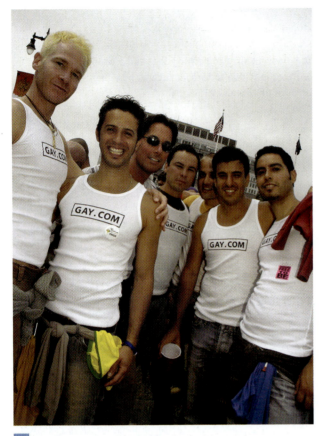

FIGURE 8.7 *Coming Out*

Gay, lesbian, and bisexual people sometimes fear that being open about their sexual orientations will have negative consequences. National Coming Out Day provides an opportunity for some individuals to challenge negative stereotypes and find acceptance.

has frequently been suggested that the homophobic or biphobic reactions of some individuals may arise from confusion or uncertainty about their own sexual identity, although empirical evidence to support such a contention is lacking. When people are uncomfortable about their own same-gender attractions, feelings, desires, or behaviors, their homophobia or biphobia is said to be internalized and may lead to high-risk sexual behaviors, depression, or other personal problems.

Sex and Values

Consider your reactions to the following situations:

- Susan, a sophomore in college, goes with some friends to a favorite bar just off campus. She meets Alan for the first time and they spend two hours together, sharing drinks and conversation. He invites her back to his dorm room, and after some kissing and mutual fondling, he asks her to have intercourse. Susan agrees, with the understanding that they will use a condom, and she spends the night in Alan's room. The next morning, they agree that neither is looking for a heavy relationship, although both would enjoy remaining friends.

- Mike has just entered college and has agreed to maintain an exclusive relationship with his girlfriend at home, some 600 miles away. He feels strongly about their commitment and is determined to make it last. He decides that he will not date at all and that his only sexual outlet will be masturbation.

- Worried about his grades in English, Derek pays a visit to the office of his instructor, a woman in her late twenties. They discuss his recent papers and examinations, with Derek admitting that English has never been his strongest subject. To Derek's surprise, the professor hints that one sure way to earn an A would be to spend some time alone with her at her apartment. At first he thinks she is joking, but she touches his hand and makes it clear that she is being very serious.

- Lucy returns to her dorm room following a shower and begins to dress. Her roommate Karen seems to be watching her rather intently, and Lucy tries to hide her discomfort. Karen asks her to sit down for a moment and is soon telling her about how attracted she has been to her. She expresses fear of Lucy's rejection but explains that she just could not hide her feelings any longer. Lucy is somewhat surprised but not at all angry. In fact, she finds the idea of sex with Karen a bit intriguing.

Now try to think about why you had the reactions and thoughts you did in relation to these sex-related situations. What specific aspects made you feel positively or negatively about the people? Would your reaction be any different if Susan and Alan had been dating for several months before having sex? If they were engaged? If they had failed to use a condom? What if Mike had decided that what his girlfriend does not know will not hurt her? What if he had decided not to masturbate either? What if Derek's instructor had been a man? What if the instructor were a man and the student a woman? What if Lucy and Karen had been two men? What if Lucy had been disgusted by Karen's admission and had immediately sought to change rooms?

How you as an individual view these and other sex-related situations is determined by your **values.** Your reaction is based not simply on your sexual values but also on your values about relationships, coercion, responsibility, and a long list of other issues.

values system of beliefs through which people view life and make decisions, including their sexual decisions.

We weigh our sexual values in our sexual decision making, along with other related values. When people decide to participate in sexual activities that are inconsistent with their values, they may experience some conflict and guilt.

Sexuality as a Moral and Ethical Issue

Moral values deal with the ethics, or rights and wrongs, of life situations. Theories of morality assume that humans are capable of making choices based on rational thought and other internal processes, making them responsible for their decisions and actions. The nature–nurture debate has been represented in two schools of thought regarding the origins of moral values. The *essentialist* perspective holds that there may well be some intrinsic or built-in meanings relating to sexuality in human life. Some believe that energy for sexual connection may be divinely given. The *social constructionist* view is that moral values relating to sexuality are formed by social forces and thus are subject to change as societies go through various transitions.

Because sexuality is such a pervasive and powerful aspect of human nature, all societies have sought to control and regulate it. Religion is the social institution usually concerned with ethics, so moral values related to sex have often been rooted in religious teachings. Sexual morality today tends to be grounded in one of the following ethical traditions.

Legalistic Ethics: Adherence to Divinely Established Laws

Those with an essentialist view of sexual ethics believe that sexual meanings are divinely ordained and establish clear and unwavering boundaries between right and wrong. They may assert further that there is a singular interpretation of holy books such as the Bible or Koran and that there are clearly defined prescriptions and proscriptions for sexual behavior, although many who have studied religious texts claim that such messages are not nearly so clear as they sometimes are purported to be (Haffner, 2004). This legalistic approach to sexual ethics is found in many orthodox or fundamentalist religious traditions, whose teachings tend to fall into traditionalist categories.

Jesus, Moses, Mohammed, and some other prophets spoke of a covenant of love and hope between human beings and their God. Some religious people have interpreted this to mean that moral principles can change as societies and human behavior patterns change (Jakobsen & Pellegrini, 2003). Within this more social constructionist approach to sexual ethics, there is a belief that social values may change over time, rather than being bound to rigid traditional standards. New information from science, medicine, psychology, and sociology may be incorporated into new moral perspectives.

This more flexible approach to morality still calls for the establishment of moral codes of behavior, often by delegations of people in the governing body of some religious group. These people may still decide that adultery or sexual activity between members of the same gender is unacceptable, but they allow the issues to be discussed, debated, and then decided upon.

Situation Ethics

This ethical system sees every situation as a unique collection of considerations and conditions. Therefore, moral decisions are made in the context of a particular situation, with a view toward all the people involved. Situation ethics does not attach moral judgments to any sexual orientations or acts per se. The key to whether some form of sex is right or wrong lies in the human motivations behind it and the foreseeable consequences it might have. From this ethical perspective, a particular sexual behavior might be considered wrong in one context but acceptable in another. Obviously, it gives much more responsibility to the individual for making such judgments in arriving at sexual decisions.

Hedonistic and Ascetic Traditions

These moral perspectives represent opposite ends of an ethical spectrum. **Hedonists** have recreational attitudes, holding that pleasure is the highest good and outweighs religious dogma or situational context. This point of view can be crystallized by the phrase "If it feels good, do it." The sex drive is viewed as an appetite to be satisfied with a maximum amount of physical and emotional pleasure. To manage a purely hedonistic lifestyle is not any easy matter, because the complicated realities of relationships can easily get in the way.

Asceticism, which has been a part of some religious and spiritual traditions, is characterized by celibacy. The goal is to rise above base physical

moral values beliefs associated with ethical issues, or rights and wrongs; often a part of sexual decision making.

hedonists (HEE-don-ists) people who believe that pleasure is the highest good.

asceticism (a-SET-a-siz-um) usually characterized by celibacy, this philosophy emphasizes spiritual purity through self-denial and self-discipline.

pleasures and instead emphasize self-denial, self-discipline, and the life of the mind or spirit. Asceticism often is characterized by the teaching that denial of sexual pleasure helps one be closer to spiritual needs and to God, and it is part of the celibate lifestyle expected of some priests, nuns, and monks.

Holistic Belief Systems

Some contemporary philosophers have suggested that we are coming into a time of human social evolution when we no longer have to view the ascetic and hedonistic pursuits as mutually exclusive. Holistic perspectives propose that we place sexuality in a broader context that considers many different levels of the human experience: physical, emotional, rational, social, and spiritual. It has been suggested that we need both the lofty side of things that at times asks us to rise above self-centered bodily pleasure *and* the earthier, fleshy side that offers sensual delights. Rather than advocating for choosing one direction or the other, the holistic perspective proposes that we seek a more united and whole pursuit of balancing these different but valuable parts of our sexuality in healthful, responsible ways and that we can find this balance in ethically appropriate ways. Many contemporary writers suggest that it is time to reclaim sexual pleasure as part of living comfortably in one's body and of finding one's playful side (Resnick, 2002).

Spirituality, Religion, and Sex

Understanding and developing spirituality are important to many people, and fitting sexuality into the picture is often a significant part of that search. Organized religions are the social institutions that attempt to help people find a place for the spiritual in their lives, although many also seek spiritual development outside this context.

In the earliest religious traditions that archaeologists have been able to trace, the emphasis was on feminine power, fertility, and earth-centeredness as expressed through various great goddesses. It is believed that sexuality and fertility were intimately connected to the practices of these traditions. Sometime between 1800 and 1500 B.C.E., there was a significant transformation in human conceptualizations of God(s), and throughout China, India, the Middle East, and Greece, the female goddess principle gave way to the more phallic (penis-centered) power of male God figures.

Judeo-Christian-Muslim religious values traditionally have constituted the moral backbone for various prohibitions against sexual behaviors in Western culture. In ancient Israel, for example, sexual intercourse was tantamount to marriage, and there was no such thing as a casual, obligation-free sexual relationship. In Christian theology, Augustine (354–430 C.E.) decided that sexual desire represented the ultimate clash between desire and reason, thereby establishing sex as the culprit that passed sin from one generation to the next. Not until the Middle Ages did marriage become a religious event in Christianity and therefore a religious sanctioning of sexual activity (see Figure 8.8). Western religious traditions typically have taken a rather sex-negative position in which the emphasis is on the repression of sexual desire (Beck, 1999). Some Muslim traditions have placed a great deal of importance on the separation of male and female roles, sometimes expressed in the sexual mores that have called for women to keep much of their body covered. Behaviors that might encourage sexual attraction or arousal also are sometimes forbidden (Stayton, 2002).

In contrast to this perspective, the Eastern traditions—Hindu, Buddhist, Tantric, and Taoist—have tended to view sexuality in terms of its creative potential and its power in spiritual development. Eastern thought places more emphasis on the harmony of body and spirit than on the opposition of the two. The combination of desire and a sense of duty has made both ascetic, celibate lifestyles and the religious celebration of sexual pleasure possible in Hinduism. In the Buddhist, Tantric, and Taoist religions, sexual union often is viewed as a mystical and spiritually uplifting experience.

Within all major religious traditions, there are two basic ways in which the world tends to be perceived. One is a fixed worldview, in which it is assumed that the universe was created by a deity and is now completely finished. This is the fundamentalist perspective, which finds followers within every tradition. The other point of view is more process-oriented, seeing the world and human nature as constantly changing and evolving. These two viewpoints usually are associated with differing attitudes toward sexuality as well. The fundamentalist view is that a constant battle is being waged between good and evil and that sex is a major source of temptation and sin. Those with a more evolutionary worldview tend to see the essential goodness of the human body and sexual desire, and they place the emphasis on people choosing sexual behaviors that are healthy, responsible, and considerate of others (Haffner, 2004; Timmerman, 2001).

Several studies have demonstrated correlations between people's religious belief systems and their sexual attitudes and behaviors (see Table 8.4 on page 212). The more religious people consider themselves to be, the more likely they are to feel that it is important to have sexual practices that are in harmony with their religious beliefs and the less likely they are to have sex prior to marriage (Laumann, Gagnon, et al., 1994). Within some religious denominations, attitudes toward

■ **FIGURE 8.8**　*Religious Attitudes toward Sexuality*

Religion may play an important role in establishing the sexual standards of a culture. People may face conflicts if their personal values contradict the established standards. This Hindu couple is shown in traditional wedding dress, standing near a decorated marriage bed.

sex have undergone significant transitions in recent decades. Many religious groups have been debating and changing their official positions regarding sexual activity. One of the most significant areas of impact on religion in recent years has been feminism. There has been a reshaping of some religious symbolism to recognize the feminine images of God that are a part of religious history. Some religious groups have attempted to eliminate what they have come to see as sexist language within their texts—including the Bible—and hymns. Women are taking stronger leadership roles in many religious groups, moving away from the patriarchal structures that have dominated Western religious traditions for centuries (Timmerman, 2001).

Aligning Yourself with Social and Cultural Values

There is now a fair amount of evidence that moral and ethical development proceeds in predictable stages as a child grows and develops. The two primary theorists on the moral development of children have been Jean Piaget and Lawrence Kohlberg (Carpendale, 2000). Their theories have enough similarities to allow us to summarize some of their major points together.

They both believed that children essentially lack any sense of right or wrong when they are born. In their first few years of life, children gradually pick up the rules of behavior expected of them, learning to some degree that they must obey parents or other adult authorities or else risk disapproval and punishment. Their basic approach to life, however, is to satisfy their own needs. They react to their environment reflexively. By the time children are 8 to 10 years old, they are beginning to adapt to the moral codes required of them by their environment. They realize that they are expected to behave in particular ways and often conform in order to be seen as good boys and girls. As adolescence and young adulthood progress, they become increasingly aware of the attitudes and values espoused by their social networks and gradually define the standards of morality and the ethical principles they want to guide their own lives.

Table 8.4	*Influence of Religion on Attitudes toward Sexual Behavior*			
	Very Religious	**Religious**	**Slightly Religious**	**Not Religious**
That My Sex Practices Are in Harmony with My Religion Is:				
Very important	45%	18%	2%	3%
Important	36	38	24	8
Not sure	7	24	26	15
Unimportant	5	17	37	37
Very unimportant	7	3	11	37
Very important + Important	81%	56%	26%	11%
Unimportant + Very unimportant	12%	20%	48%	74%
N =	262	857	976	611

Source: From S. S. Janus and C. L. Janus, *The Janus Report on Sexual Behavior.* Copyright ©1993 by Samuel S. Janus and Cynthia L. Janus. Reprinted with permission.

In a pluralistic society such as our own, it is impossible to find general agreement with any particular approach to sexual morality and values. However, several widely accepted moral principles seem to be in effect today, and they would be supported by most religious teachings as well (Reiss, 2002):

1. *The principle of noncoercion.* People should not be forced to engage in sexual expression. Sexual expression should occur only when there is voluntary consent.
2. *The principle of nondeceit.* People are not to be enticed into sexual expression based on fraud or deception.
3. *The principle of treatment of people as ends.* People are not to be treated as a means only; they must be treated as ends. In the sexual realm, this means that another person should never be viewed solely as a means to one's own sexual satisfaction.
4. *The principle of respect for beliefs.* People must show respect for the sexual values and beliefs of others. This means that one person should not pressure another to act in a way not in accord with the other's sexual values and beliefs. However, this does not preclude someone from attempting to persuade others rationally that they are mistaken in their beliefs.

For people in their late teens, the transition from home to college or some other environment away from home can be filled with new stimuli and new choices. There is often greater freedom to experiment with sexual activities and values, with the possibility of making mistakes. But even mistakes can provide a useful purpose by further clarifying the individual's personal code of sexual morality. However, the balancing act between satisfying one's own sexual needs and living up to the moral principles demanded by one's social networks and oneself may actually last a lifetime. Every stage of life offers new sets of sexual decisions and questions to be resolved, and society's values are always shifting.

Facing Ethical Dilemmas

Sexuality can be a confusing part of life, and most of us eventually face some dilemma in which the most ethical choice to make is not clear. Sometimes it may even seem as though there is no entirely "right" choice. As a student in an ethics course once said to me, "You can make any choice into the right one with some mental gymnastics." While analyzing ethical dilemmas may indeed yield more than one way to proceed and people may sometimes do their best to make a poor choice seem like a good one, it is also true that some answers really are better than others.

Psychologists have been studying moral decision making for many years, and they have developed several indicators for understanding personal morality. It is generally agreed that moral behavior, or ethically proper behavior, will be helpful to another person and will be motivated by this knowledge. Dilemmas arise with the realization that the behavior has broader implications, given that not every "helpful" behavior would necessarily be considered right.

Real People

Mike: Struggling with a Long-Distance Relationship

Let's return to Mike, the first-year college student intending to be faithful to his long-distance girlfriend, as described on page 208. During his second month away at college, his circumstances become more complicated.

Mike has become friends with other members of the intramural soccer team on which he plays. On a weekend evening in mid-October, the team has a party at an off-campus apartment of some of the upperclass students. A women's intramural team has been invited. Mike is happy to attend the party, because he has been feeling down after a phone conversation with his girlfriend earlier in the week. She hinted that maybe they ought to rethink their relationship and even begin seeing others. Mike expressed his anger and hurt over that option, communicating that he wanted to work hard at maintaining their commitment. Eventually, she agreed that she would abide by their original plan, and she apologized for upsetting him.

The beer at the party is plentiful, the music is loud, and everyone is having a good time. A young woman sits down beside Mike, and they strike up a conversation. He knows her from one of his biology classes and has found her attractive. Eventually, they become engrossed in conversation and with each other. They have a lot in common, and both are having some struggles with long-distance relationships.

As the evening progresses, the girl leans over and kisses Mike on the lips. He is surprised at first but reciprocates, and they continue making out. As others begin to disperse, Mike suggests that she come back to his dorm room with him. He explains that he is lonely but also does not want to do anything either one of them will regret. She kisses him and says that she doesn't believe in regrets.

On their walk back to campus, Mike realizes that he has had a lot to drink and that he probably isn't making the clearest decisions. He also is very curious about what might develop once they get back to his room. Once there, the young woman lies down on his bed and motions for him to join her. He obliges, and before long they are heavily involved in making out again. Eventually, she reaches down and unzips the fly on his pants, indicating that she is willing to perform oral sex on him.

Should Mike continue with this sexual encounter? What is the right thing for him to do? What are the points of ethical conflict raised by this situation? Besides Mike and the young woman he met at the party, who else could be affected by the decisions made and the actions taken? What are the potential consequences of the various actions that could be taken now or have already been taken? What duties and obligations does Mike have?

Think of some behaviors that might ultimately be helpful to someone else but still wouldn't be considered right. Explain your answer.

Another aspect of morality is the expectation that behavior will conform with certain social norms. Every society establishes certain rules and expectations in order to accomplish shared goals. Certainly, social nonconformity sometimes is used as a form of protest against social rules that are considered unfair, but if it is simply a self-serving action to avoid social responsibility, such nonconformity would be considered ethically questionable. Theories of moral development suggest that while parental influences are critical in the early stages, individuals gradually internalize ethical standards without the need for external enforcement; coerced acts cannot really be considered as moral (Hennig, 2003; Pratt, 2003).

Psychologists see empathy, or identifying with the feelings of others, as a strong motivator for ethical behavior. Empathy for another can be very powerful, and it follows that we feel guilt if we act in opposition to the well-being of others. Such reactions are what help make up the human *conscience*.

Ethical dilemmas must also be subject to the reasoning of rational thought processes, as we think through issues concerning justice and balance. Perhaps one of the most dramatic aspects of a well-developed sense of morality is the willingness to put the needs and interests of someone else ahead of our own needs and interests, especially if some human cost is incurred through the action (Rest, Narvaez, Thoma, & Bebeau, 2000).

Sorting through ethical issues, therefore, involves thoughts, emotions, and eventually behavior. Over the years, I have found it useful to use an approach that was developed to help students cultivate well-reasoned responses to ethical problems presented by scientific research. There is evidence that practicing the application of the principles of this approach to ethical dilemmas can make people become better at identifying all the issues and reaching a suitable conclusion (Bebeau et al., 1995; Rizzo & Swisher, 2004).

There are five basic guidelines for analyzing an ethical dilemma:

1. *Describe the nature of the ethical conflicts involved.* Look for how the interests, rights, or obligations of the people involved seem to apply. Choices in life sometimes require looking at equally unfavorable alternatives and trying to decide between them. Finding all the points of ethical conflict in a dilemma can be difficult, but the deeper you look, the more issues you may find.

2. *Identify all the interested parties.* Beyond the individuals involved firsthand in the ethical dilemma, there may be others who could be impacted by the choices made or by potential consequences of those choices. Paying attention to all these interests may clarify even more issues that are in conflict.

3. *Think about possible consequences.* While there is no point in identifying every conceivable consequence, anticipating those that are most likely to occur can be reasonably easy. As you examine various reasonable consequences of different ethical choices, you will also want to consider the effects on all the interested parties.

4. *Examine the obligations of the main players in the dilemma.* We all have certain obligations to behave in ethical ways, as specified in our belief systems, societal or institutional expectations, and the legal system. Sorting through these obligations is essential to making a well-reasoned choice in an ethical dilemma.

5. *To the extent possible, discuss the dilemma with others.* Although sex-related situations may demand confidentiality and the protection of others' privacy, it is often helpful to seek input from trusted others who can give you new insights and points to be weighed in the decision making. We can sometimes miss things that other people will see more clearly. Give the process a chance whenever you can.

Now consider Mike's sexual situation, in the "Real People" box, involving a very real ethical dilemma, and use the guidelines above to sort through all the points mentioned. Explore whether the approach can help make you more comfortable with recommending how the situation should be resolved.

Finding Healthy Sexual Values

Achieving a healthy sexuality requires a level of consistency between a person's behaviors and values (see Figure 8.9). In recent years, several different social factions and political groups have claimed to have values that represent the moral high ground. Someone trying to arrive at a personal set of values might find these divergent positions quite confusing. One unfortunate consequence of this confusion for many people is their simply choosing not to choose. Instead of thinking through their values and deciding in advance how they will want to behave in certain sexual situations, they wait until they are swept away by passion or by a persuasive partner. This then may become an excuse for denying responsibility for sex or its consequences.

There are several steps you can take to establish your own set of values regarding sex:

1. Know yourself and work toward acceptance of your sexual needs and orientation. Basic to the

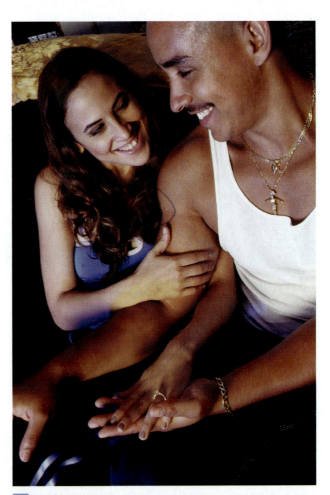

FIGURE 8.9 *Loving Relationships*

An important part of finding healthy sexual values is determining the place of loving relationships in your life. Although loving and sex are often linked within relationships, they do not necessarily need to be.

success of any code of values is feeling good about yourself. Even if you find that there are some aspects of your sexuality you would not feel comfortable acting on, it is important that you accept them as part of you. Whether you ever act on them is up to you. That is what choice and personal decision making are all about.

2. Try not to let yourself be bound by popular sexual standards with which you are personally uncomfortable. Popular songs, television programs, advertising, and the Internet often promulgate specific values about sex and sexual attractiveness. You may at times receive pressure from peers about what is currently in vogue sexually. Weigh all this information carefully, decide how much you want and need to fit in with a particular group, and then choose how you want to proceed sexually. Be cautious about going along with any aspects of sex that do not seem quite right to you. Give yourself as much time as you need to think; after all, your goal is to feel good about yourself.

3. Examine your feelings about religion and find out what your religion has to say about sexual matters. You may be surprised. Many religious groups have given careful consideration to human sexuality and have devised written guidelines to help with personal decision making. You will need to consider just how important your religious background and your current feelings about religion are to you. Even if you do not consider yourself "religious," you may want to explore your spiritual dimensions and how they relate to your sexuality. Agnostics and atheists develop their own codes of moral behavior that emphasize responsibility to others.

4. Think ahead. It is a good idea to think carefully about various sexual situations and issues and to anticipate how you might react to them. This is an excellent way to clarify your personal values about sex. For example, when do you think it is all right for two people to share a sexual relationship? If heterosexual intercourse will be involved, how should decisions about contraception be made? What are some of the possible consequences of various sexual activities, and how would you deal with those consequences? How will you ensure that anyone involved in a sexual encounter will be protected against disease?

5. Consider what level of responsibility you have toward other people. Most forms of sex involve interaction between people. Whenever interpersonal relationships are involved, the issue of responsibility to others comes up. How do you think you should treat others? What degree of responsibility

do you have to not put others in exploitative or potentially hurtful situations?

6. Remember that you are not a mind reader. This is where good communication comes in. Part of sexual values must be knowing how a potential sexual partner thinks and feels about sex before you get involved. It is dangerous to make assumptions about the values and feelings of others. You will need to spend time and energy communicating in order to find out what these are.

7. Decide what role you want loving relationships to play in your life. Loving and sex often are intertwined in relationships, though not necessarily. An important part of establishing your own sex-related values is knowing how you feel about the place of loving relationships in your life.

8. Take opportunities to clarify your sexual values on an ongoing basis. Sexuality education books, classes, and discussion groups provide opportunities for understanding your own sexual values more fully. The Internet has fine websites with good information about sexuality, along with its more explicit sites. Making use of opportunities to clarify values can keep your personal code of moral behavior clear and workable for everyday life.

■ Sexuality and Disability Groups

Physical and mental disabilities may influence a person's sexuality in many different ways. They can affect self-perception and social relationships. Only too often, persons with disabilities are assumed to be asexual or too impaired to have functional sexual responses. These assumptions rarely have any basis in fact. Public consciousness about the needs and rights of individuals with disabilities is leading to greater levels of understanding and acceptance, but many barriers and complications still hamper such people in their attempt to find a fulfilling and meaningful place for their sexuality in their lives.

Adults with disabilities are likely to find acceptance in their roles as fellow employees or casual friends but are much less likely to find themselves perceived as potential dating or sexual partners. Myths and misconceptions about the needs of children with disabilities may lead to impediments in their development as healthy sexual individuals. Parents, educators, counselors, and caregivers for people with disabilities have a special responsibility to not ignore or deny the sexual natures of these individuals. Sexuality needs to be part of a holistic approach in dealing with the special needs and concerns of people with particular disabilities (Ballan, 2004).

Most conditions that are called disabilities do not directly affect the sex organs or their ability to function, nor do they affect the individual's sexual feelings, need for sex, or desire to be physically and emotionally intimate with others (see Figure 8.10). They may, however have a great effect on how people with disabilities view their own attractiveness and the degree to which they seek sexual relationships. Consider a man with a serious skin disease that causes unsightly blotches all over his body, or a woman born with cerebral palsy who has difficulty controlling her arm movements and speech. Although these individuals have the same sexual interests and attractions as anyone else, they may find themselves limited by their own perceptions and by the prejudice and misunderstanding of others. Today we have a wider acceptance of the notion that sexual pleasuring need not be viewed solely as an act of sex organs but rather as an intimate emotional and physical connection between two human beings that may involve a variety of behaviors. This perspective on sexual interaction is particularly valuable in people with disabilities, who may have to make special accommodations in their sexual practices (Tepper, 2001).

Intellectual or Developmental Disability

One of the most sexually oppressed groups of people with disabilities are those with an intellectual or developmental disability. The historical roots of this problem include the fear that sexual activity among those who are intellectually disabled would lead to pregnancies and the risk of passing on genetic defects to children. The trend has been toward integrating individuals with intellectual disabilities into the community as much as

FIGURE 8.10 *Sexuality and People with Disabilities*

People with physical and mental disabilities have as much right to intimacy and sexual pleasure as anyone else. The quality of the sexual relationship will depend, as in any relationship, on the quality of the total care and respect each partner has for the other.

possible, training them in the kinds of skills that will help them interact in socially acceptable ways. There is evidence that people with such disabilities often lack crucial knowledge about their sexuality. Teenagers with mental disabilities often are having sexual intercourse with inadequate knowledge about contraception or disease prevention (Cheng & Udry, 2003). People with attention deficit disorder may experience difficulty achieving intimacy with partners unless they receive appropriate skills training (Betchen, 2003). A cooperative program of education and socialization involving both the school and parents can often be effective in helping those with developmental disabilities adapt to their sexual needs (Littner, Littner, & Shah, 2001).

Educational efforts have been shown to foster both cognitive and behavioral change that will help the developmentally disabled understand and manage their sexual needs. Gradually, those with mental disabilities have been helped to articulate their sexual rights, and educational efforts have been improving. The principle of **normalization** came to the United States in the 1960s from Scandinavia and has led to the development of simplified programs in social skills and sexuality education for use with those who have intellectual disabilities. Such programs are designed to help the intellectually disabled adapt to the norms and patterns of mainstream social life (see Figure 8.11). Some couples with developmental disabilities have been able to marry and have learned how to manage their social and sexual lives effectively as the result of these new efforts.

What guidelines do you think should be in place regarding sexual activity between intellectually impaired people?

Issues related to reproduction by people with intellectual disabilities continue to be debated. In the early 1900s, when a strong eugenics movement advocated careful genetic selection in human reproduction, people with developmental disabilities usually were considered unfit to reproduce and often were involuntarily sterilized in institutions. Now it is clear that many such individuals are able to learn enough about birth control methods to choose and use them effectively. The issue of informed consent for sterilization continues to be a difficult one, because developmentally disabled individuals may not fully understand the procedure and its outcome. Under the influence of authority figures, they may too easily give their consent to sterilization.

normalization integration of mentally retarded persons into the social mainstream as much as possible.

FIGURE 8.11 *Sexuality and Developmental Disability*
With the proper instruction in meeting their own sexual needs and in following the rules and ethics of a given society's sexual behavior, some people with developmental disabilities can lead fulfilling lives in a mutually supportive relationship.

Visual and Auditory Disabilities

Individuals with visual or hearing impairments face two major challenges in developing sexual awareness. The first is gaining an understanding of sex and sexuality. People with impaired sight cannot see diagrams that could help them understand anatomy and physiology. People who are hearing impaired are limited in how information can be presented to them. Both groups may experience delays in the total education process, including learning to read, because of their respective disabilities. The second major difficulty lies in the socialization process. Those who are visually or hearing impaired often are hindered in their social contacts because others are uncomfortable with their disabilities and may feel afraid or embarrassed about their own attempts to communicate. In addition, some of the usual routes for interpersonal communication are blocked. People who are severely visually impaired cannot read the subtleties of facial expressions and body language. People with hearing impairments may miss words in lipreading or might risk being misunderstood when they use sign language with someone who is unfamiliar with it (Getch, 2001).

Sexuality educators for the sensorially impaired have met some of these challenges. Life-size plastic models of human sexual anatomy are now available, as are visual materials such as models, charts, photographs, slides, and transparencies. Captioning services for much of television programming and for visual sexuality education aids provide another op-

portunity for the hearing impaired to understand the material.

See "Mark Discusses Sex after Spinal Cord Injury" on SexSource Online.

Spinal Cord Injuries

The spinal cord, running through the vertebrae that make up the backbone, is the nervous system's major link between the brain and the body's various organs. Injuries to the back or neck can cause damage—or even complete severing—of the spinal cord. If an injury does not prove fatal, there may still be interruption of nerve messages to the parts of the body below the injury, resulting in partial or total paralysis of those organs and muscles. There is little or no sensation, and the muscles can no longer be directed by the brain to contract. Typically, the spinal cord does not heal and repair itself, so the paralysis is permanent. If only the legs are paralyzed, the person is said to be **paraplegic;** if the arms are involved as well, the term used is **quadriplegic.**

It is often assumed that paraplegics and quadriplegics are incapable of sexual sensations or response, but this is not necessarily the case. In a study of 140 males and 46 females with spinal cord injury (SCI), about 25 percent of the males and up to 50 percent of the females reported having sensations in the genital area. By the third year after their injuries, nearly all the females and 90 percent of the males had resumed sexual intercourse and other sexual activities. The degree of interference with sexual functions depends on the exact location and extent of the SCI. When paralysis of the pelvic region exists, thinking sexy thoughts or having sexual needs no longer has any effect on the genitals, because the connection with the brain has been lost. However, erection of the penis and lubrication of the vagina are also partially controlled by a localized spinal reflex (Phelps et al., 2001). Many paralyzed men and women can experience arousal of their sex organs, and sometimes even orgasm, through direct stimulation. Feeling may also remain intact in small areas of skin in the pelvic area. Up to 40 percent of quadriplegic males are able to have an orgasm accompanied by ejaculation. Brain responses as recorded

paraplegic a person paralyzed in the legs, and sometimes pelvic area, as the result of injury to the spinal cord.

quadriplegic a person paralyzed in the upper body, including the arms, and the lower body as the result of spinal cord injury.

by scanning images in women with SCI suggest that genital stimulation may convey input directly to the brain, somehow bypassing the spinal injury (Sipski, Rosen, Alexander, & Gómez-Marín, 2004; Whipple & Komisaruk, 2002).

Each case of SCI is unique, but any patient and his or her partner can learn new forms of sexual expression. Often, intercourse is still possible by making adjustments in position. Some paraplegics and quadriplegics have a bladder catheter (tube) in place to carry urine out of the body to a storage bag. Although the catheter may be an inconvenience during sex, a couple committed to maintaining their sexual relationship can learn how to accommodate it. Some success has also been achieved with the implantation of electrodes on localized nerves that can be stimulated by the individual to increase bladder control or even produce increased blood flow to the genitals (Phelps et al., 2001).

Often, the partners of people with SCI are left out of the adjustment and rehabilitation process. They, too, have many emotional issues to resolve as they face a very stressful time adjusting to the changes that occur in the relationship, including its sexual dimensions. When one partner in a couple suffers injury, the relational difficulties frequently lead to disharmony or a breakup of the relationship. The majority of couples facing SCI experience relational difficulties, but fewer than a quarter of them receive counseling. With appropriate and skilled professional help, couples can learn how to recapture a viable emotional and physical relationship following the devastating effects of SCI. Increasingly, institutions involved in the rehabilitation of SCI patients are dealing with their sexual concerns and providing techniques to assist with their sexual readjustments (Tepper et al., 2001).

Other Physical and Mental Disabilities

Many chronic physical conditions or injuries and mental illnesses can affect sexual functioning and the place of sexuality in relationships. There may be diseased or damaged sex organs, general physical debilitation that lowers interest and energy for sex, difficulty in socializing, or lowered self-worth.

Cerebral palsy, for example, can cause spastic conditions in various parts of the body. People recovering from heart surgery, heart attacks, or strokes may be physically debilitated and might worry about how much physical exertion they can withstand during and after their recovery (Van der Poel & Greeff, 2003). Traumatic brain injury may necessitate the relearning of roles and appropriate sexual behaviors within the

context of a family and other social contexts. A variety of neuromuscular conditions, such as multiple sclerosis and muscular dystrophy, can result in gradual loss of bodily control and can change sexual relationships (McCabe et al., 2003). Chronic lung disease makes exertion during sex difficult and uncomfortable. Cancer can affect sexual organs and/or general body fitness, leading to changes in intimacy within relationships.

Mental and emotional illnesses, ranging from depression to schizophrenia, can rob patients of the sense of security and well-being basic to fulfilling sex. The medications used to treat these conditions may also have sexual side effects, and only too often patients are not informed about these possibilities (Bobes et al., 2003; Rosenberg et al., 2003). People with serious mental illnesses may also have difficulty establishing intimacy and commitment. Although they tend to report consistent condom use, they do tend to have sex with new partners quite frequently, which may help account for a higher rate of HIV infection among the mentally ill (Perry & Wright, 2006).

Terminally ill patients often experience sexual disruption because of internal stress, which in turn affects relationships. They may feel guilty about experiencing sexual arousal, and their lovers may find it difficult to desire intimacy amid the anticipatory grief or fear of their partner's fatal illness. However, open communication and, when available, counseling and the opportunity for privacy in hospital settings can all help with the sexual adjustments of long-term illness.

When people approach the special sexual problems associated with their disabilities and illnesses honestly, they can find new adaptive approaches to sex. It is important to recognize that sexual needs remain even during a health crisis or a disability or in the aftermath of a serious injury or illness. Maintaining involvement in sexual activities can help maintain a person's sense of integrity and personal self-worth. For people whose physical disabilities may interfere with the coordination of masturbation or shared sex, some assistance from a health aide may be necessary. This **facilitated sex** obviously requires special sensitivity and training on the part of the aides or facilitators. It is important to guard the individual's privacy and dignity as much as possible while establishing the conditions necessary for sexual pleasure. This is a relatively new—and controversial—aspect of health care, yet it surely is a sensible extension of the other quality-of-life services provided to persons with disabilities (Melby, 2003).

---

facilitated sex assistance provided to a person with severe physical disabilities in order to enable them to achieve sexual pleasure through masturbation or with a partner.

Institutions and Sexual Issues

Some people with disabilities and chronic illnesses require long-term institutional care, in which case sexual problems may multiply. Where the sexes are segregated, institutional residents may be limited to same-gender sexual contact. They may have little privacy for masturbation or shared sex. The keys to preventing desexualization in institutions are the attitude of the staff and their understanding of the different levels of need that different people might have. Some institutions have provided condoms for patient use, along with educational efforts, and have found that these actions do not cause an increase in patient sexual activity. Often, in-service training on sex-related issues and the establishment of humane administrative policies regarding sex can help. The first step in preventing sexual problems among the disabled, ill, or institutionalized is admitting that all human beings are sexual and have a right to find the best ways for them, as individuals, to express their sexuality. Steps then may be taken to categorize people according to the types of help they may require in order to realize and take charge of their own sexual identities and needs (Perry & Wright, 2006).

Chapter Summary

1. Human beings have the potential for participating in a range of sexual activities.

2. Definitions of normalcy and abnormalcy are influenced by prevailing social norms.

3. General labels such as deviation, variation, and paraphilia have been applied to sexual activities and preferences that fall outside the accepted norm.

4. In present-day Western culture, sex is still judged by several fundamental standards: two-person heterosexuality, a focus on coitus, expectation of orgasm and romantic feelings, and degree of safety.

5. The World Association for Sexology has adopted and promulgated a Universal Declaration of Sexual Right that affirms a wide range of freedoms regarding sexuality.

6. The ethnocentric attitude that one's own culture has the right standards in relation to sexuality can be called erotocentricity.

7. The concept of normalcy can be determined by statistical norms, by prevailing expert opinion (such as the *DSM-IV*), by moral standards perpetuated by religion and law, or as part of a more flexible continuum. Normalcy is a relative concept.

8. Labels represent generalities and are an inadequate aid to a full understanding of a particular person's sexuality.

9. The term *homosexual* often has negative connotations. The terms *gay* and *lesbian* are used in reference to people when describing same-gender orientation. The term *bisexual* is used to describe some level of attraction to, or activity with, members of both sexes.

10. The factors that lead to the development of sexual individuality are highly complex. Patterns seem to be established by adolescence and probably develop through a combination of learning experiences, superimposed on some biological predispositions.

11. Social networks rather than relationships with parents seem to be important in shaping sexual attitudes and behaviors.

12. The Klein Sexual Orientation Grid demonstrates seven different variables that play a role in determining sexual orientation or identity. Sexual individuality includes many different life dimensions.

13. Sexual choices are affected by sexual attitudes. The National Health and Social Life Survey has identified three broad categories of sex-related attitudes in the United States: traditional, relational, and recreational. There is no single system of "American values" regarding sex.

14. Clear links have been observed between sexual attitudes and sexual practices, number of partners, and how often a person thinks about sex. Frequency of sex does not seem to be related to attitudinal group.

15. Large portions of people in the United States have negative feelings and discriminatory attitudes about gay, lesbian, bisexual, and transgender people. These fears and misconceptions are called homophobia, biphobia, or transphobia. Professional organizations no longer view

same-gender orientation within the framework of pathology.

16. Decisions about sexuality often are made after weighing moral values, religious teachings, and ethical beliefs. Some believe that moral values are built-in, whereas others believe that they are socially constructed.

17. Different ethical traditions influence sexual morality: legalistic ethics, situation ethics, the extremes of the hedonistic and ascetic traditions, and holistic belief systems.

18. Many believe that spirituality is connected to sexuality. In recent years, religions have been debating and changing their positions with regard to sexuality.

19. Research has demonstrated several ways in which religious belief systems influence sexual behavior.

20. Noncoercion, nondeceit, treating people as ends rather than means, and respect for the beliefs of others are moral principles that guide sexual decisions today.

21. Some answers to moral dilemmas are better than others, and by considering many dimensions of a dilemma, well-reasoned ethical responses may be found.

22. In developing sexual values that are right for you, it is necessary to see how you will align yourself with the values of your society and culture. Self-examination and introspection are necessary to making decisions that will be healthy and nonhurtful for yourself and others.

23. People with disabilities have the right to recognition and expression of their sexuality.

24. Intellectually or developmentally disabled people need special approaches to sexuality education, including learning how to express their sexuality in private and how to employ appropriate methods of birth control. They are particularly vulnerable to sexual abuse. There is still no ethical consensus about how sterilization of the developmentally disabled should be handled.

25. Spinal cord injuries may affect physical aspects of sexual response. Most paraplegics and quadriplegics can find levels of sexual functioning that will be satisfying to themselves and their partners. Many couples experience relational problems after one partner has had such an injury.

26. Facilitated sex may be an option for people with severe physical disabilities.

Focus on Health Questions

In this section you will find the kinds of questions that you may have concerning your own health and sexuality. The page references indicate where in the text the answer is located; the exact place is marked with this logo: **FOH**

1. How do I know if my sexual feelings and behaviors are normal? **198–199**

2. If I had sexual feelings for both men and women when I was a teenager but have had intercourse only with my opposite gender so far, does that mean I have a same-gender orientation? **199–200**

3. Where do people get their values and moral standards about sex? **201–203**

4. Is homophobia all that bad? What negative effects does it actually produce? **206–207**

5. If I am facing an ethically difficult decision about sex, is there any helpful way I could approach thinking it through? **212–214**

6. If a person becomes paralyzed below the waist, can he or she still engage in and enjoy sex? **217–218**

Chapter 9
Sexuality, Communication, and Relationships

Chapter Outline

He was my first real love, and my first sexual partner. I honestly thought it would last forever. We certainly made each other enough promises that it would. Obviously we were wrong. For about a week, I thought I would never get over it, but I did. I think we're both pretty happy now, and I really wish only the best for him.

—by a student following the breakup of a relationship

Have you ever had a relationship in which it seemed as though you would never want to be apart from the one you loved, and then experienced "falling out of love"? Have you ever been involved in a relationship in which your partner was more attached than you were and you couldn't find an easy way to extricate yourself? Do you think you could explain what it means to be "lovesick"? One way or another, most of us get our hearts broken eventually. Yet, even in the face of this reality, most people long for close relationships with others.

Research shows that nearly all men and women indicate that love is important in their lives. They long for the intimacy, companionship, sharing, and contentment that we associate with friendship and loving relationships. Sometimes, a relationship also brings sexual sharing, although the majority of both men and women see sex and intimacy as two different aspects of relationships. Data from the National Health and Social Life Survey (NHSLS) indicated that of those individuals who freely wanted their first sexual intercourse, women were nearly twice as likely as men to say they loved their first sex partner. Among those who said that their first intercourse was not particularly wanted but they went along with it anyway, 10 percent of the men and 38 percent of the women said they loved the partner (Michael et al., 1994). These statistics would indicate that, at least in their initial heterosexual experiences, females are more likely than males to feel romantically involved with a partner.

Men sometimes wonder if "nice guys finish last" in the sexual arena, and the question has actually been researched. Although definitions of "nice guy" characteristics certainly vary, the majority of women report a preference for nice guys, whom they assume to have had fewer sexual partners. In fact, nice guys who respect women and are sensitive communicators are preferred for friendships and committed, intimate relationships (Herold & Milhausen, 1999).

See "Mike on Dating, Sex, and the Bar Scene" on SexSource Online.

Keeping any relationship on an even keel can be complicated enough; bringing sexual feelings or activities into the picture often only adds complexity and confusion. One major foundation for a healthy, lasting relationship is effective communication between people who feel relatively comfortable and confident with themselves. Couples who have communication difficulties are more likely to experience sexual problems.

As any counselor can testify, relationships typically suffer tension and crisis when the communication process has become blocked or muddled (Brehm et al., 2002; Kelly, Strassberg, & Turner, 2006). This chapter deals with that process, its role in relationships, and how to keep lines of communication open.

■ Communicating about Sex

Communication is an ongoing, dynamic process. It has been said that "one cannot *not* communicate." Even silence and avoiding another person convey certain messages, often very powerful ones. Unfortunately, many people do not realize the importance of communication in building a healthy sexual relationship. As a male student once stated to me, "Sex is something you *do* with each other; you shouldn't have to *talk* about it." That philosophy might work fine if people were simply walking sex organs who slipped in and out of sexual encounters. Instead, human beings have a range of thoughts, feelings, fantasies, and needs that must be shared if we are to maintain relationships within and beyond the bedroom. A great many sexual problems could be prevented or resolved through open, honest communication, yet people often seem reluctant to pursue such communication.

Although information about sexuality certainly has increased in the media, individuals still are insecure about discussing their private concerns regarding their own sexual lives and relationships with others. They may be afraid of seeming inappropriately bold or of betraying some ignorance about sexual matters. Joking about sex is easier for many people than asking about a potential partner's sexual history or explaining to a partner how they feel or what they might like to do sexually. Using a slang term may seem less intimidating than using a scientifically correct word. Our culture delivers a great many mixed messages about sexuality, on one hand saturating our senses with sexy messages and on the other hinting that sex is a dangerous and dirty thing. In a society where the political climate tends to see sexuality in terms of problems to be controlled, it is easy to lose sight of the fact that attaining sexual pleasure is a legitimate human goal and that effective communication is fundamental to achieving that goal (Fay, 2002).

The Communication Process

Just about anything can be communicated—ideas, feelings, attitudes and values, needs and desires. From

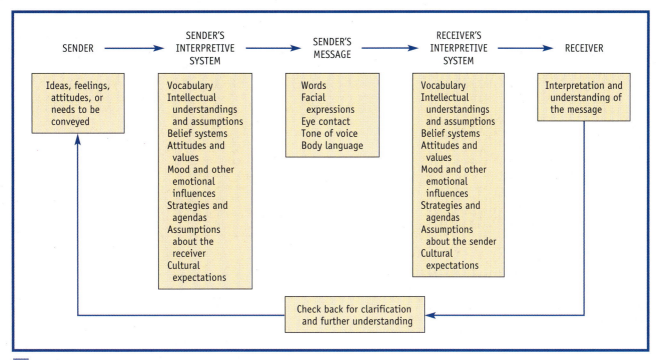

■ **FIGURE 9.1**   *The Process of Communication*

Whatever is to be conveyed from one person to another is filtered through each person's individualized interpretive system. Therefore, the message intended by the sender may be quite different from the message picked up and understood by the receiver. An active feedback system is one of the best ways to keep communication on track.

culture to culture, there is great diversity in the way people communicate, especially about sex-related matters (Smith, 2002). What might seem friendly and intimate in one society might be perceived as overly aggressive and offensive in another. Our eyes, facial expressions, and body language convey a great many messages. The tone and intonation of voice we use in speaking are crucial in communicating subtle aspects of our message. And, of course, words are an important ingredient in any communicative interaction between people. However, words also are imperfect and often imprecise. In our society, when we talk about sex we tend to be caught between terms that are either too scientific or too vulgar to be appropriate in all circumstances. Their meanings may be interpreted differently by different people. One party to the communication process may not be paying as close attention as the other or may be swayed by internal moods or mind-sets.

The process of communication is filled with subtleties and opportunities for misinterpretation. It is not surprising, then, that human communication sometimes is fraught with complications and misunderstandings. Figure 9.1 illustrates the basics of any process of communication. Someone, the sender, has some thought that she or he wishes to convey to someone else, who will become the receiver. However, many factors influence the way the sender's message is formed. It is made up of specific understandings of cer-

tain words and also is filled with beliefs, attitudes and values, cultural expectations, and emotions.

The sender might well hope to fulfill a particular agenda or accomplish some objective. As the thought to be conveyed is filtered through this interpretive system, the message takes shape and is "sent" to the receiver. At this point, it must be filtered through the receiver's own very individualized interpretive system, from which that person then draws his or her own understanding of the message. Obviously, the process is complicated enough that the message intended by the sender may not be at all the message understood by the receiver. Figure 9.2 shows how misunderstandings can take place. Communication works best when there is a well-developed feedback system in place through which the receiver can ask for clarification and check out the assumptions that have been made in understanding the message. As with most shared human processes, good communication takes a committed effort from everyone involved so that misinterpretations and misunderstandings are kept to a minimum.

The Words We Use to Talk about Sex

The sex-related words people use reflect to a great extent the concerns and preoccupations of their society and their time in history (Plaud, Gaither, & Weller, 1998). The appropriateness of particular words can

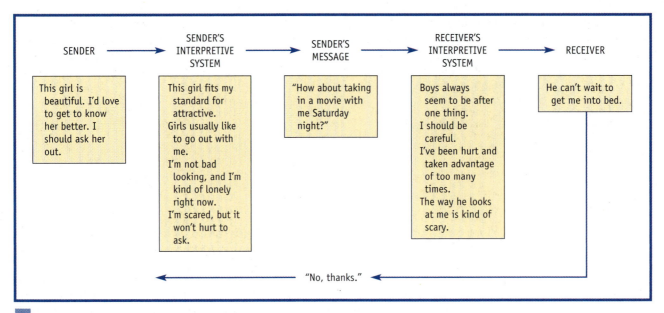

SENDER → SENDER'S INTERPRETIVE SYSTEM → SENDER'S MESSAGE → RECEIVER'S INTERPRETIVE SYSTEM → RECEIVER

This girl is beautiful. I'd love to get to know her better. I should ask her out.

This girl fits my standard for attractive. Girls usually like to go out with me. I'm not bad looking, and I'm kind of lonely right now. I'm scared, but it won't hurt to ask.

"How about taking in a movie with me Saturday night?"

Boys always seem to be after one thing. I should be careful. I've been hurt and taken advantage of too many times. The way he looks at me is kind of scary.

He can't wait to get me into bed.

"No, thanks."

FIGURE 9.2 *Misunderstood Communication*

The process of communication may yield a misunderstanding between sender and receiver.

change over time, sometimes relatively rapidly. In early-twentieth-century America, the words *leg, bull,* and *pregnant* were considered taboo for mixed company because of their presumed sexual connotations. Even in reference to fowl, the terms *drumstick* and *dark meat* were substituted for *leg.* Bulls were referred to as "he-animals," and pregnant women were said to be "expecting" or "in confinement." A generation ago, the term *suck* had clearly sexual connotations not expressed in public, and the slang word *dork* meant penis. Today suck has become a commonplace term used to describe almost anything in a negative way, and *dork* is used like the word *jerk*. These and many other terms have gradually found their way into common usage, reflecting changing social values.

For some people and in some contexts, the "proper" scientific terminology about sex may seem more inappropriate or embarrassing than slang terms. This is probably one reason why so many slang terms exist for the description of sex-related body parts and sexual activities. I have asked students to make lists of slang terms for sexual words. When it comes to some things, such as masturbation, there are far more slang terms used to describe the male practice than the female practice. When it comes to talking about sex in private, there seem to be rather predictable norms for the terms women and men use with each other. For college students, these norms are shaped by the students' social networks.

Some research demonstrates the changing nature of sexual slang among college students. Three decades ago, a study (Sanders, 1978) showed that when talking with a lover men were most likely to refer to their own sex organ as a "dick" (26 percent) or "penis" (25 percent) or to avoid using any term at all (17 percent). In contrast, only 8 percent of women used the term *dick*. Nearly half the women would say "penis," and 18.5 percent used no term for the male organ. In data gathered a decade later with another sample of college students, these trends again became clear, but a significantly greater number of men and women reported that they would use no term at all in reference to the penis (Fischer, 1989).

In 1978, women were even less likely than men to name their own sex organs in intimate conversations, with nearly 25 percent avoiding the use of any term. Those who did use some term were most likely to say "vagina" (32 percent). Men were somewhat more likely to use the term *pussy* (22 percent) to describe the partner's genitals than they were the term *vagina* (19.4 percent). The term *cunt* was more frequently used by men (14 percent) than by women (1 percent), who are more apt to find the term offensive.

In the follow-up study, women were still much less likely to use slang terms to describe the vagina than were men. Again, both sexes showed a much higher number of individuals who would use no term at all to describe the female genitals. The expression "sexual intercourse" was used by over 10 percent of both men and women in 1978, although "make love" was far more popular among both women (56 percent) and men (32 percent). Men used the term *fuck* in their intimate conversations more than women did, although men were more likely to use this word in the presence of other men than in the presence of women. The term *having sex* became more popular, with *intercourse* being used much less frequently. Students in the more recent study were less likely to use terms such as *fuck* or *screw* and again more likely to use no term at all to describe sexual intercourse (Fischer, 1989).

A more recent study found that the slang terms applied to female genitals tend to be vaguer than those applied to men's genitals and that men tend to use more negative terms about female organs than about their own (Braun & Kitzinger, 2001).

When describing the penis, men are more likely to use what has been called "power slang," with labels such as *rod, womp,* and *pistol.* Women tend toward "cute" euphemisms such as *penie, oscar,* or *babymaker.* Whereas males tend to use very specific terms to describe their own genitals, women tend toward more nonspecific personal terms such as *me, mine, she,* or *my body* (Braun & Kitzinger, 2001). Women have been shown to be somewhat more reluctant to use sexual terms than are men (Geer & Melton, 1997; Plaud, Gaither, & Weller, 1998). Men tend to be more comfortable than women today using terms such as *fucking, cunt,* or *cock,* although words such as *lovemaking, vagina,* and *penis* are generally more acceptable to both genders.

What makes communicating about relationships and sexual issues difficult?

Every relationship will evolve its own vocabulary for intimate discussions of sex. Fifty-seven percent of the women and 58 percent of the men in one study considered "talking dirty" to be acceptable within their relationships. Using playful terms to name their genitals has been found to be therapeutic for couples experiencing sexual problems (Godow, 1999). The important thing is that both partners feel comfortable with the terms they use. Neither should employ words that seem offensive, insensitive, or insulting to the other. Working out the details of acceptable terminology may itself require some careful communication and negotiation.

Contemporary Myths about Communication

Different societies and different times in history have always had their mythology surrounding communication within relationships. Unwritten rules evolve from that mythology and make their way into most human interactions. Our society is no exception. Several myths have governed how we communicate in our society. Consider the ways they have played a role in your own interactions with others.

Myth 1: You should have a confident opinion on every issue. We live in opinionated times. Media news focuses its attention on gathering people's opinions. If you listen carefully to the disagreements that people have with one another in everyday life, you will notice that many individuals argue their points without much solid information to back them up. Even when it comes to sex, many people behave as if they must have all the answers, and they never appear uncertain or insecure. The truth of the matter is that nearly everyone feels somewhat shy and scared in new situations, in meeting new people, and in forming new relationships. Whenever we come face-to-face with a stranger and need to communicate, there is usually an initial, tense period during which we begin evaluating what we will have to offer each other. When we find ourselves in a position where we think we have to offer an opinion about some subject about which we know very little, it can be perfectly acceptable to say, "I'd really have to think that through and learn more about it before I could have much of an opinion about it."

Myth 2: An impressive conversationalist never permits any dead air. The most uncomfortable part of any conversation can be silence. People's eyes search around trying to avoid the other person's gaze. They begin to fidget or shift their weight from one foot to the other. They vainly hunt in their minds for some fresh topic to talk about.

This fear of silence can force people to fill the air with words. Silence imposes a kind of intimacy when two people have to look at each other momentarily, simply and quietly sharing each other. That intimacy can often make us feel vulnerable, so we search for topics that will help us keep each other at "words' length." However, when we want to become closer to someone and develop a deeper relationship, being able to be quiet—and to listen carefully—can be important elements of communication.

Myth 3: Mapping out strategies ahead of time makes for better communication. A young man who was once a counseling client of mine told me about the advice a friend had given him before a date at a fraternity party. It went something like this: "Stay loose. Keep three or four things in mind to talk about, but only use them when the conversation lags. Don't look too interested. Smile a lot to yourself and look a little bored. When you look hard to get, women chase even harder. When you're ready to get things really moving, tell her you're sick of the party but she's welcome to come back to your room with you. But don't look too anxious." My client tried to carry out this strategy at the party, only to end up feeling foolish and having his date indicate that she preferred to stay at the party and go home alone. As popular and common as they may be, planned communication strategies set

Real Student Voices

■ I really love my girlfriend, and we are sexually involved. However, she doesn't talk much about what she enjoys during sex, and I often feel as though she doesn't enjoy it all that much. I'm confused as to whether this is because of something going on with her, or something wrong with my technique.

■ I can't seem to get J to talk about his feelings, and that is very frustrating to me. He says I want to talk about feelings too much, and sometimes he just wants to be quiet and enjoy being together. He also thinks I worry too much about the relationship. Maybe I do, but it's important to me.

■ The two of us are able to talk about everything and anything, which is a lot different than my former relationships. I never thought I could have this kind of relationship, but it is great. We have no secrets.

up games to which only one person knows the rules. Sometimes they work, but when they do a relationship has been established on the basis of manipulation or even dishonesty. Usually the best "strategy" is to work at being yourself.

Myth 4: Using the right line will convince a partner to have sex. Rarely are relationships that simple. While one partner is rehearsing the line to carry out a seduction, the other partner may well be rehearsing the best way to turn down the proposition. Sexual relationships that grow out of invented lines rarely are effective or lasting, and enticing someone into sex in this manner is ethically objectionable.

Myth 5: The rational mind is the only basis for effective communication. People often make the mistake of assuming that logical, rational thought processes constitute the only basis of good communication. There is a common misconception that "feelings only get in the way." In fact, emotional reactions are a legitimate part of what human beings need to communicate, especially in close relationships. To work with only one aspect of human nature during communication is to ignore crucial parts of yourself that need to be shared.

These myths can form the basis of a surefire prescription for how to stifle good communication. They stimulate the development of games, phony conversation, manipulative sexual seduction, and shallow relationships. When effective communication is lacking, even minor sexual problems are more likely to turn into major ones.

See "Communicating about Sex" on SexSource Online.

The Sexual Games We Play

Romantic and sexual relationships can involve a dynamic tension between two people that results in posturing and attempts at "reverse psychology" to achieve certain ends. Whether it is playing hard to get in order to win over the heart of Mr. or Ms. Right or deciding not to return a call until a certain amount of time has passed, people try to develop a strategy that will help them feel they can control an outcome. We live with the illusion that if we always do X and Y, we automatically will get Z as the result. Human relationships are more complicated than mathematical equations or generalized scientific predictions. They must be approached in very individualized ways. Nevertheless, people are forever playing games with one another when it comes to sex and relationships. Following are descriptions of some of the most common sexual games.

Power Games

Sex is a common arena for people to express their struggles for power over each other. Most relationships have their share of such struggles. An individual who is fearful of appearing vulnerable may always want to be in a dominant position during sexual activity, quite literally needing always to be "on top." Someone who resents something about a partner might show little interest in sex to punish the other person through the withholding of sexual activity. Men are more likely than women to be deceptive in relationships as one way to maintain power (Blair, Nelson, & Coleman, 2001).

Some men and women use power games to spoil sex by being unavailable at the "right" time. Being drunk sometimes may be a handy way either to avoid sex or to justify a sexual failure. Some people play "hard to get" by being too busy, too tired, or emotionally detached. Power games can turn into a sort of sexual sabotage in which one partner manages to ruin a sexual encounter without looking like the "guilty party." Dropping some subtle criticisms about the other person's sexual performance may sometimes lower that individual's level of sexual interest considerably. As long as these power struggles proceed, sexual sharing will have its difficulties.

Relationship Games

There are many different ways partners play games within their relationships. Some men and women, for example, bring unresolved conflicts and emotional problems with them to their sexual relationships. A stormy relationship with a parent that has resulted in certain patterns of reaction may affect a person's present relationship if some of the old feelings are lingering inside. Mutual trust is a crucial factor in building intimacy and a satisfying sex life. When trust is lacking, the inner barriers stay up, holding a partner at a distance. People who feel as though significant others in their lives have always left them may test how much a partner will put up with. The partner is, in a sense, being called on to prove his or her love and devotion by sticking by the other person no matter what. Such games can create great strain in a relationship and often are the cause of its destruction.

Communication Games

One of the most common communication games is to push for the resolution of a conflict as quickly as possible. One partner, wanting the problem to be over, comes up with what seems the most logical solution to her or him and then tries to impose the solution on the other. The partner might make statements such as

"You shouldn't feel that way" or "Come on, cheer up" or "You're blowing this all out of proportion." In the face of such seemingly logical suggestions, the other person may end up feeling guilty for having the particular reaction and may pretend that all is resolved. Many communication games are designed to avoid confronting potentially hurtful feelings or situations. Yet when truly effective communication happens, both partners perceive that they have permission to feel and express whatever they need to. Sexual and relational difficulties often grow out of situations in which two people fool themselves into thinking that some rough spots have been logically resolved when in actuality their differences are still simmering under the surface.

One key to a full and satisfying sexual relationship is knowing how to communicate effectively with a partner. That does not mean that you have to be an extrovert or be well versed in the social graces. Nor does it mean that you have to be a great conversationalist or even talk a great deal. What it does mean is that you must care enough about yourself, your partner, and the relationship you share to put some effort and energy into communicating with each other.

Before reading the section "Effective Communication," assume the role of counselor and list several strategies that you might suggest to a client seeking to improve her or his communication with a partner.

■ Effective Communication

For the most part, people do not find it easy to communicate about the more intimate aspects of their lives, such as their sexuality. People might discuss the opinion or "idea" topics with some ease—issues such as how society should deal with gay marriage, values concerning casual sex, or which form of birth control is most effective. But when it comes down to talking about one's own sexual orientation, a preferred sexual activity, or the form of birth control one wants to use, the conversation may not flow quite so smoothly. In this section we present some basic guidelines for facilitating good lines of communication.

The Ground Rules

Some preliminary steps must be taken to open up channels for effective communication between two people about sex or any other sensitive topic. Here are some ground rules for getting started:

1. *Think about the degree of commitment you hold for each other and the relationship.* Not much will happen with two-way communication unless

both partners really want it to happen. This may well depend on the quality of the relationship you are sharing. Communicating honestly about sex takes energy. You might begin to feel tired, frustrated, or hopeless at times, and it will take a solid commitment from both of you to see you through the more difficult steps. Relationships in which sex is discussed may exist on many different levels. On one end of the scale is the casual encounter in which two people barely know each other. On the other end is the long-term loving involvement in which discussing sex is continually necessary in order to ensure mutual satisfaction.

2. *Know your own values.* Before you try communicating about sex, it is a good idea to have thought through where you stand on some of the value issues that may be involved. Know your own beliefs while letting yourself be open to the attitudes and values of the other individual.

3. *Understand your cultural differences.* If you are building a relationship with someone who has a cultural heritage different from your own, it will be important first to develop some fundamental understanding of how you may differ in the words or expressions you use or in your levels of comfort in dealing with sexual issues. It is a good idea to spend some time discussing potential areas of conflict or misunderstanding before they turn into problems (Edwards, 2002b).

4. *Keep yourselves on equal ground.* A sense of equality between two people is usually essential to their communicating well. If someone always feels in the "one down" inferior position, he or she is unlikely to be able to communicate very openly or confidently. Power inequalities are dangerous to relationships (Blair, Nelson, & Coleman, 2001; Gottman, 2000).

5. *Build trust for each other.* When there is a lack of trust between two partners, there is likely to be not only a strain in their sexual interactions but also a tendency toward reserved and uncomfortable communication. A sense of trust is fundamental to honest, genuine dialogue. Lack of trust can lead to "stonewalling" the other person during communication, a practice that can create serious obstacles in relationships (Kantrowitz & Wingert, 1999; Williams & Payne, 2002).

6. *Pick the right location and time for talking.* Where and when you talk may be very important. You will both want to feel as relaxed and comfortable as possible and have adequate privacy. Sometimes bed is the ideal place to talk, but it also may produce an emotionally charged situation for some kinds of communication. Beware of atmospheres that encourage

superficial conversations and games. Ask your partner where she or he would feel most comfortable talking, and be certain you feel comfortable there as well.

Making It Happen

A central message of this chapter is that the process of making good communication happen takes some deliberate effort. Sex is deeply personal to most of us, and to discuss it with someone else incurs a certain degree of vulnerability. Yet in a partnership in which sex is shared, words and feelings must also be shared. There are always decisions to be made, signals to be checked, worries to be resolved, and feelings to be discussed. Several qualities have repeatedly been shown through research to facilitate open and honest communication between people.

Demonstrate an Attitude of Warmth, Caring, and Respect

Feeling enough trust to open up to another person and share on more than a superficial level requires some sense of mutual positive regard. However, it is not enough to feel a sense of caring for another person; the feelings need to be demonstrated or communicated in some way (see Figure 9.3). Sometimes it may

■ **FIGURE 9.3**   *Communicating Warmth, Caring, Respect*

Loving relationships depend on attitudes of warmth, caring, and genuine respect for each other.

be a simple willingness to be quiet and listen attentively; other times it will require overt expressions of love or kindness. Patterns of criticism and contempt are extremely harmful to building positive communication (Gottman, 2000).

Avoid Making Snap Judgments and "All-ness" Statements

One of the greatest problems in human communication is the tendency of some to jump to premature conclusions and to make snap judgments about others. Most people open up best to those who are not judgmental. Because sex is one area of life about which people have strong opinions, intimate communication would be improved if we set assumptions aside and allowed other points of view to be expressed openly. In a more specific sense, it is also valuable to avoid using "all-ness" words such as *always* or *never*. When referring to another person, the use of statements including these words is rarely fair or accurate.

Listen Carefully and Really Hear

Often when people appear to be listening, they are actually thinking ahead, formulating their response to what the other person is saying. It is all too easy for ideas and concepts to become garbled and misunderstood unless we listen carefully. Let yourself hear the other person out, and then think through your reactions and responses. Listening is not merely a passive state of resting the senses; it is an active process of being attuned to the words and nonverbal messages someone else is conveying.

Empathize and Understand That Feelings Need to Be Felt

Empathy is the ability to identify with what another person is feeling and to experience, in a sense, "walking a mile in his or her shoes." All of us have experienced a full range of emotions, though for different reasons. When listening to others, also listen for their feelings, and try to recall the experience of your own emotions so you can better understand where they are coming from. Two people who want to communicate about personal things must be willing to share emotions, even hurtful ones, and to empathize with each other. Empathy can help ward off our natural tendency to become defensive when we face disagreements. Constant defensiveness in a relationship can be a source of very real problems.

It is also important for partners to allow each other to express feelings. Sensing that feelings are being heard and understood is one of the most crucial aspects of good communication.

Be Genuine

Hidden agendas make communication more difficult and make problems harder to resolve. Most people can sense superficiality and deceptiveness and respond much more positively to genuineness and honesty. Effective communication about sexual matters must be based on openness. However, sometimes the issues are subtle and difficult, and shades of meaning may cloud the truth. No lasting relationship can escape the need to communicate about difficulties and misunderstandings. Otherwise, they will accumulate under the surface and create problems later. For these reasons, you must work at being honest and being yourself in personal communications. Some level of self-disclosure about sexual feelings and needs seems to enhance the sexual satisfaction experienced within relationships (Byers & Demmons, 1999).

Make Sense and Ask for Clarification

It is all too easy for words or mannerisms to be misunderstood in the communication process. We often make assumptions about what the other person means, without ever bothering to check out those assumptions with that individual. It takes work to listen carefully, understand what is being said, and then clarify whether your understanding is correct.

It is a good idea occasionally to feed back your understanding to your partner by saying "So what I hear you saying is . . ." or "Do you mean . . . ?" When you have clarified your interpretation of his or her words, your partner is then able to correct any misconceptions. In formulating a reply to any message, take the time you need to think it through, choose your words carefully, and give a focused response. The response may not always be verbal but may sometimes be made through expressions of the face, eyes, or body.

Do Not Let Silence Scare You

As pointed out earlier in this chapter, gaps in conversation often make people feel uneasy and vulnerable. You may feel the need to fill such gaps with words. Instead, it is more important to take your time, allowing silence to be a part of communication at times. Silence also can be intimate and calming.

Beware of the "I Don't Want to Hurt You" Trap

In relationships, hurtful things must be shared. That sort of confrontation is not always easy, but in the long run it will help resolve tension-producing conflicts. It is not unusual for counselors to hear partners explain that they avoided dealing with painful topics because they were afraid of hurting someone's feelings. Of course, they also were avoiding their own discomfort that comes from talking about hurtful issues.

Use Self-Talk Effectively

How we talk to ourselves can have a profound effect on how we relate to other people. The things we say inside our own mind can color our emotions and our reactions both positively and negatively. For example, if during sex you are worrying about how you look or sound or are thinking negatively about your own body, sex is not likely to be a very positive experience. However, if you work at positive self-talk, emphasizing how good the experience seems and how much you are enjoying being with your partner, you are much more likely to find the experience enjoyable and fulfilling.

Communication Differences among Different Personality Types

Two things remain clear as we study personality: (1) It may be demonstrated that people really are different in the ways they perceive and approach life, and (2) most people tend to view their own perceptions and approaches as the "right" ones. It is no wonder, then, that when people attempt to establish an intimate partnership, their differences sometimes create tensions, disagreements, and arguments. Having a clearer picture of your own personality and its characteristics can help.

One of the most popular tests used for evaluating personality traits has been the Myers-Briggs Type Indicator (MBTI) (Myers & McCaulley, 1985) and its modified version, the Kiersey Temperament Sorter (Kiersey & Bates, 1984). These tests are based on a model that portrays the human personality as a combination of varying balances among four main pairs of traits. Although any such model is bound to oversimplify the complexities of being human, tests can offer some general insights into an individual's personality. Most counseling centers have such tests available and are willing to interpret and explain their results.

Everyone is familiar with the pair of personality traits known as extroversion and introversion, although these terms are frequently misused and misunderstood. Extroverted individuals tend to be energized by other people and by the external environment. They connect with others easily and enjoy group situations. Introverted people prefer their own company, but being introverted does not necessarily imply being shy or antisocial. Introverts simply tend to draw their energy more from inside themselves. They need more time and privacy for processing their inner experience and often prefer one-to-one interactions with others.

The Myers-Briggs typology also makes a distinction between people who are specific and concrete in their approach to life and those who rely on their abstract, intuitive natures. It suggests, too, that whereas some individuals make their judgments through logical, step-by-step analysis and reasoning, others are influenced more by their feelings and the desire to maintain harmonious relationships. In the final pair of MBTI characteristics, people are viewed either as punctual, decisive, scheduled, and orderly or as unstructured, open-ended, and spontaneous.

These various combinations of personality traits must come together in any relationship between two people, which sometimes creates difficulty in understanding each other (Kiersey & Bates, 1984). The extrovert may be miffed that an introverted friend is more content to stay home and avoid large parties. The individual who pays attention to feelings and wants to preserve harmony between people may be frustrated by a partner who prefers approaching problems in a highly rational manner, wanting only to arrive at the most logical conclusion.

Personality differences in relationships underscore the need for good communication skills and a commitment to using them. The differences may also be expressed through an individual's sexual preferences and styles. Although it is certainly not always true that opposites attract or that it is easy for them to get along well, human differences—sexual and otherwise—can be managed and even enjoyed. They sometimes provide the spice of a loving relationship.

Communication Differences between Women and Men

Women and men sometimes express frustration with their shared communications. Sociolinguist Deborah Tannen (1990, 1994) and speech pathologist Lillian Glass (1992) studied intricacies of communication patterns in males and females. Their work revealed some fascinating differences in the ways the two sexes are taught to communicate. Tannen began by studying videotapes of people in different age groups having conversations with best friends of the same gender. She noticed that girls tended to face each other squarely, look directly at each other, and enjoy talking together. Boys seem to grow up in a much more hierarchical social order than do girls, and their groups usually have a leader who tells others what to do. An elaborate system of rules filters down through the group, and there is a struggle to maintain status within the group. Boys often must vie for attention and deflect the challenges of other boys in order to retain "center stage."

Girls are more apt to play in small groups or in pairs, and they focus on maintaining intimacy and a sense of community. They want to get along with their friends so that everyone can have a turn, and often there are no "winners" or "losers." When they encounter conflict, both boys and girls want to get their own way, but they will try to achieve that in different ways. Boys tend to resort to insistence and threats of physical violence, whereas girls usually try to mediate the situation and preserve harmony through compromise and avoidance of confrontation.

Differences in communication style between adult men and women are rooted in the fact that they have practically grown up in different cultures when it comes to communicating (Maccoby, 1998). Women place a premium on being agreeable and congenial. Men react much more personally to verbal rejection and have a tendency to resist doing what they are told because they do not want to feel dominated or be in a one-down position in their social interactions. These differences may cause confusion and turmoil in male-female relationships. Keep in mind that the patterns discussed are generalizations and certainly do not apply to every individual woman or man. At their roots, women and men are far more similar than they are different (Hyde, 2005).

Talking Over Problems

A man is much less likely to tell a woman about his difficult feelings or life problems because he does not want to worry her or seem helpless. Men also feel more obligated to offer solutions when someone tells them about a problem, even if the other person is just looking for an empathetic ear. They tend to be more brusque, forceful, loud, and demanding in their communications. For women, not being told about something such as personal feelings or troubles seems like rejection from a partner. Women are gentler, softer, and more emotional in their communications. They value the intimacy involved in sharing secrets and worries, whereas men are more likely to feel vulnerable in doing so. Men live in a social milieu in which other men may indeed be trying to put them down, and they therefore have to be somewhat self-protective. The social atmosphere for women is very different, so misunderstandings develop in communicating about problems.

Asking for Directions

Men also are more resistant to asking for directions when they are trying to find or do something, feeling that to do so is putting yourself one down with someone else. Women welcome the chance to connect with another person and are not bothered by seeming to need help.

Expressing Needs

One area of communication that often causes trouble for women and men is expressing various needs. For example, Tannen (1990) cites a typical situation in which a woman asks her husband if he would like to stop in somewhere for a drink. He truthfully answers no, and nothing more is said for the moment. Eventually it becomes evident that the wife was hurt and angered by his response. Although he saw the interaction as a simple statement of fact—he did not want to stop for a drink—she felt that her wishes had not been considered. The wife didn't realize that he would have been open to further negotiation and, in fact, could have been easily persuaded to follow her lead if she had made it clear that the issue was important for her. Tannen theorizes that because of how men learn to communicate, they are more likely to start any sort of negotiation with a clear statement of where they stand, with the understanding that there will be further discussion. Women, on the other hand, are likely to accept any such statement as a clear indication of a man's position and see it as immovable unless they press the communication into some form of unpleasantness.

Another variation on this theme is that when women are trying to focus on intimacy and connection by expressing needs, men tend to view such expression as a demand and feel obligated to resist it. Male socialization causes them to be cautious about one-down positions. So when a woman suggests to her male partner that she would like to know when he is going to be late because otherwise she gets upset, he may see it as a challenge to his freedom and rebel against the suggestion.

Talking and Listening

Research shows that, contrary to popular opinion, men tend to talk more than women in public situations such as meetings, group discussions, or classrooms. When questions are asked in a group meeting, men tend to ask the first question, more questions, and longer questions. They tend to speak in lengthy monologues and to interrupt people more than do women (Moore & Davidson, 2000). Not unexpectedly, in the listening process women tend to show frequently that they are listening to another person, whereas men focus more on the literal content and react only when they agree or disagree.

At home, however, the talking roles seem reversed. Women see talking as a way to foster intimacy with their partners at home. Men, on the other hand, view talking as a way to negotiate status and therefore do not fit it into the private home context as much as do women. When women talk about their feelings and problems and see discussion as a way to work on them, men tend to perceive the communication as wallowing in complaints. They tend to be more solution-oriented and to want to resolve the difficulty with definitive action.

Real People

Jennifer and Ted: Failed Communication

Imagine that you are a peer counselor for the Counseling Center. You have been pretty effective at helping couples with their relationships. The first time you talk with Jennifer and Ted, you can see that their relationship has become precarious. They have already discussed going their separate ways, and they both view counseling as a last-ditch effort to make things work again. Jennifer explains that Ted has become increasingly detached and that she can never get him to talk about what he's feeling. Expressing his frustration, Ted counters that Jennifer always seems to be wanting something from him, but he's never quite sure what. "No matter what I do," he says, "I can't seem to please her. After a while, it doesn't seem worth bothering anymore." Jennifer responds by saying "A relationship has to be more than sleeping together, or going out for a drink, or talking about what happened that day. I want to know more about what's going on inside you."

Ted maintains that Jennifer is looking for something in him that he doesn't think is there. "I just don't have that many deep feelings, and I don't want to make them up for you. I was satisfied with the way things were." Jennifer feels there is a missing dimension in their relationship because Ted seems unwilling or unable to deal with things on an emotional level. Their personality test results suggest that Ted and Jennifer really do have very different approaches to dealing with their reactions to

life. Ted is a very practical and decisive person, dependable in his pursuits and thorough in paying attention to details. He gets along well with other males and doesn't like "fanciness" in speech or manner. He places a high value on loyalty and faithfulness, but he doesn't deal very much with the affective levels of his personality.

In contrast, Jennifer's tests confirm that she is an outgoing and emotionally passionate individual who tends to form her views of the world impulsively. She likes romance and frivolity and has little patience for sorting through all the rational and practical aspects of situations. She observes other people carefully, and she often speculates about their hidden motivations. Ted and Jennifer both agree that these profiles are quite accurate. You explain that when people's personalities differ to such a degree, it takes an extra measure of effort to make mutual communication work. Ted and Jennifer concede that they are hoping to find ways to preserve and improve their relationship.

What do you think about the hopes for this couple? What sort of advice might you offer Ted and Jennifer to help them improve their bond and avoid unnecessary anger or confrontation? Do you think you would be capable of offering the kind of help this couple needs to keep their relationship intact? Would you feel it was your responsibility to keep them together, or would you be okay with their deciding to break up?

Communicating in the Workplace

Differences in communication patterns may also create misunderstandings and differing perceptions of women and men in the workplace. In their interactions with other employees, even those subordinate to them, women often are deferential in their communications, seeming more tentative and polite than their male colleagues when asking to have tasks completed or offering suggestions and new ideas. Men tend to be more assertive and direct than women in their workplace communications. Because they are more used to vying for attention, men also may be less threatened by public-speaking occasions, an essential skill of the

business culture. In occupational settings that are still male-oriented in their power structure, these differences may lead to women being perceived as less decisive or competent than their male counterparts, possibly putting them at a disadvantage for career advancement (Tannen, 1994).

Even though men have more difficulty with it, intimate talking seems to be a healthier mode of communication. The sooner people talk out problems, the sooner they tend to get over them and feel better. Talking in the manner described earlier in this chapter is a learnable skill, even for men. What the work of researchers such as Tannen and Glass has demonstrated, however, is that communication behavior that frustrates a partner of the other sex may represent a normal expression of gender rather than some individual failing. To understand the gender differences in communication is the first step toward changing one's behavior or learning how to live with some of the differences. It is possible to learn, recognize, and celebrate differences for what they truly are—opportunities to find openings into new levels of mutuality.

Quarreling and Relational Impasses

Even the happiest of couples are bound to have disagreements, some of which will become arguments. These conflicts may be complicated by differences in communication styles resulting from personality factors or gender. Conventional wisdom has held that quarreling is a sign of dissatisfaction and unhappiness in the relationship and that it ultimately is destructive for the partnership. Recent research, however, has shown that things are not that clear-cut. In fact, certain kinds of quarreling actually can improve relationships (Greeff & DeBruyne, 2000). Even couples who describe themselves as unhappy but who are able to express their anger and resentment in constructive ways have been shown to be much happier three years later than they had been previously (Gottman, 2000).

The key is whether the mode of arguing is constructive or destructive (see Figure 9.4). In the most destructive kinds of fights, anger is expressed in vicious and attacking ways, marked by blaming and character assassination. The two people are defensive, accusatory, and stubborn, resorting to insults, contemptuous remarks, and whining complaints. A more constructive and hopeful pattern is found in couples who feel free to express their anger to each other but do not allow the anger to escalate until it gets out of control. Such couples make a concerted effort to acknowledge their differences, to be open to each other's points of view, and to listen to each other. Eventually, they work toward arriving at some resolution to their differences, which often involves negotiation and compromise (Greeff & DeBruyne, 2000).

Women and men who are involved in relationships typically play different roles in fights. Males more commonly want to avoid conflict with their partners and may at first withdraw or become defensive. Women, on the other hand, are often the "emotional managers" of relationships. They are more likely to bring up some issue about which there is disagreement, wanting to confront the problem with their partners. However, their anger may be presented in such a way as to lead to positive outcomes. Likewise, men can work at listening to the other point of view and recognizing that there is a problem in need of resolution (Gottman, 2000).

Couples sometimes reach a *relational impasse,* meaning that the process of two people relating has become stuck and unmoving. This is a frustrating predicament, because nothing seems to be happening between the partners, and both have retreated into themselves. Research with groups of women and men has identified three general types of impasse that can shut down relational processes at least for a time. It seems likely that these impasses occur in individual male-female relationships as well (Bergman & Surrey, 1992).

1. *Dread/anger impasse* results when men begin to feel that they are being criticized or that difficult emotional issues are being raised. They get a sense of dread about what is developing and become uncomfortable about dealing with the emotions; they then withdraw into themselves and become silent. Women react to this withdrawal by getting angry and feeling abandoned or misunderstood. Men then either withdraw even further or begin to become angry. It is at this point that impasse can easily occur.

2. *Product/process impasse* reflects some other typical differences in the way men and women approach tasks. When there is a problem to be resolved or a task to be done, women tend to be process-oriented. They want to keep the process open by examining it and understanding all the feelings associated with it. Men, on the other hand, tend to be much more product-oriented, with the clearly defined goal of getting the job done and over with. They get impatient with feeling stalled in the process, whereas women feel hurried along by men toward a goal that has

■ **FIGURE 9.4** *Quarreling*

Quarreling in a relationship can be constructive or destructive. Anger expressed in a violent or accusatory manner is destructive. Couples instead should make an effort to express their views openly, listen to the other person, and learn to compromise.

Table 9.1   *Internal/External Consistency in Communication*

Using assertive communication skills can reduce misunderstandings and conflicts in relationships. The more consistency there is between the thoughts and feelings going on internally and what is expressed externally, the more likely minor concerns may be resolved before they become major problems. Note these hypothetical interactions between a couple: how things were said, and how they could have been expressed more effectively.

As these examples show, effective and assertive communication may not always change the ultimate outcome of people's behavior. It can, however, change how people end up feeling about the interaction, themselves, and each other.

The Setting: Afterplay

	What Was Said:	**What Was Being Thought and Felt:**	**What Could Have Been Said:**
Man	"You haven't seemed very into sex lately. Is there something wrong?"	Something is wrong. She just lies there. I guess I'm not much of a lover.	"I'm embarrassed to bring this up, but I've been worried lately that I'm not pleasing you much during sex."
Woman	"No, I'm fine."	Oh my God, he doesn't think I'm much good in bed.	"I've been worrying that you would think I'm not much good in bed."
Man	"Was it good for you this time?"	Maybe she doesn't love me anymore. Or maybe I'm just not doing something right.	"I really love you a lot, and I've been scared that either you don't feel the same about me or that my sex techniques just aren't working for you."
Woman	"Yes, it was fine, I said."	He must know that I'm not reaching orgasm. This is so embarrassing.	"It's not you. I love you so much. I haven't wanted to admit this to anybody, but I've never been able to have an orgasm. I'm really embarrassed."
Man	"Come on, are you sure? You just don't seem very turned on."	She just doesn't want to admit that she doesn't feel the same about me anymore. I've never been able to hold onto a relationship.	"I was afraid that things were falling apart between us. It must be a real letdown not to be able to come. Maybe we can work on it together."
Woman	"Do we really need to talk about this? I don't really like analyzing our sex life. I've told you everything is okay. Okay?"	I'm going to lose him if I don't find a way to fake having an orgasm. I love him so much.	"It's not easy for me to talk about this, but I would sure like to do something about it."

much less importance for them. Again, they may end up feeling misunderstood and stymied. Many couples get stuck here.

3. *Power-over/power-with impasse* typically emerges when some sort of conflict is being faced. Men tend to see conflict as a competitive contest in which the other person is attempting to gain control of, or power over, them. Women tend to be more concerned that everyone's voice be heard, and they favor the distribution of power between people so that power is shared. Women are put off by definitive stands and may make the mistaken assumption that any room for negotiation or compromise has been lost.

Resolving Impasses Effectively

Impasses signify a difficult place for any relationship to be, because things simply are not going anywhere. Both partners are nursing negative feelings and have withdrawn from relating. However, these problems are not insurmountable. Knowing how to carry on effective relationships involves knowing how to move beyond relational impasses. Table 9.1 details some communication skills that can be used in managing conflicts in relationships.

People have different responses to interpersonal conflict (Greeff & DeBruyne, 2000). Some prefer the obliging style: giving in quickly to satisfy the other,

	What Was Said:	What Was Being Thought and Felt:	What Could Have Been Said:
		The Setting: After Class	
Chris	"How about joining me at the snack bar so we could go over these notes? I'm getting confused."	I'm really attracted to him/her. If there was only a way to strike up a relationship.	"I've been noticing you in class, and I was wondering if you might be interested in going to the snack bar to talk."
Jan	"I'm pretty busy right now. Maybe another time."	What's going on here? S/He has been watching me in class for weeks.	"I've noticed you watching me. You just want to talk?"
Chris	"How about this afternoon? We could meet around 4:30 and then catch a bite to eat."	If I let him/her get away now, there'll never be another chance. Maybe if I press it a little further.	"I'd like a chance to get to know you better. How about it?"
Jan	"I've got another commitment for dinnertime, okay?"	This person doesn't know when to give up. I wish I knew what he/she was really looking for. I've got enough problems.	"I don't know. I'm feeling a little uncomfortable. My life is kind of complicated right now, and I'm hesitant to make any new commitments."
Chris	"Well, how about Friday after class?"	I think I'm making a jerk of myself. S/He thinks s/he's pretty hot stuff, apparently. What's so wrong with me?	"I don't want to look like a jerk, but I really hope you'll consider it. We'll just talk; I'm not so bad."
Jan	"Look, I may not be here Friday. Maybe you could find someone else to go over the notes with you."	I just want to get out of here. Won't this person take no for an answer?	"I appreciate the invitation, but this just isn't a good time for me. I don't mean to hurt your feelings."
Chris	[sarcastically] "Sorry I asked. I won't trouble you again. See you around."	I really blew it. I always have to push too hard.	"Well, if you ever change your mind, I'll be sitting in the same seat in this class. Keep me in mind."
Jan	"Fine."	Maybe I was too hard on him/her. But he/she wouldn't let up. I feel like a heel.	"Look, it was really nice of you to ask. I just don't want any more complications right now. But I will keep you in mind. Thanks for understanding."

avoiding unpleasant encounters altogether by withdrawing from the situation or the relationship, or ignoring the conflict. Those with a dominating style jump in with full force, ignoring the needs of the other and using coercion or power to get their own way. A greater sense of mutuality may be achieved through the integrating style, which involves discussion of differences and collaboration to find a solution acceptable to both people. Similarly, compromising involves a give-and-take approach in which both people sacrifice some of their own needs in order to have other needs met. Although some people place more significance on principles, others place more value on maintaining relationships. One person might want to confront conflicts, while another might want to smooth over ruffled feelings as quickly as possible.

The best way to resolve relational impasses is to enter into the conflict with a sense of mutuality and face the problem as a "we" instead of as a "you" and "me." An important beginning step to working out solutions to conflicts is realizing and admitting that people and their points of view are indeed different. We each have our own perceptions of any situation, and all of us tend to see ourselves as more correct than others in our perspectives. Once couples begin to approach a conflict with a greater sense of mutuality, it is crucial for each partner to explain in clear terms what her or his perception of the problem is. One of the most

Table 9.2   *Useful Strategies for Improving Communication in a Loving Relationship*

Here are some ways to keep your relationship open, honest, and caring:

1. If you must criticize, focus on specific behavior rather than criticizing the person. For example, say something like *"That irritates me"* rather than *"You irritate me."* Your partner will feel less attacked.
2. Don't make assumptions and judgments about your partner, such that you end up telling him or her what he or she is thinking or feeling. We cannot be mind readers.
3. Avoid using "all-ness" words such as *always* and *never*. They typically represent unfair generalizations. Again, try to be more specific.
4. Try to see gray areas in issues rather than strictly black-and-white, good-bad dichotomies. Remember that our own "truths" often depend on our individual perceptions.

5. Use "I feel . . ." messages rather than "You are . . ." statements. No one can dispute what you feel. However, your partner may well be offended by judgments about his or her character that are perceived as unfair or untrue.
6. Be direct and honest, avoiding games, power plays, and attempts at reverse psychology.
7. Work toward a sense of equality. An "I'm OK—You're OK" feeling is fundamental to good communication.
8. Positive reinforcement is preferable to negative reinforcement. Compliment and thank the other person when she or he pleases you. When she or he does something that displeases you, try making a positive suggestion for a change ("Could you try doing . . .") rather than a negative prohibition ("Stop doing that . . .").

And remember:
Whether the issue is pleasant or hurtful, don't put it off. Communicate about it as soon as possible.

effective ways of doing this is to work at formulating "I" messages. This means taking responsibility for communicating about the problem to a partner. For example:

Instead of attacking: "You are such a bastard for doing that."

Use an "I" message: "I feel really hurt whenever this happens."

Instead of making assumptions about another's motives: "You deliberately set out to make a fool of me."

Use an "I" message: "I am really angry and embarrassed about how this situation makes me look."

Instead of dwelling on past offenses: "This is another example of how you show no consideration for me. Last week, you...."

Use an "I" message: "I often feel demoralized and frustrated by the way you treat me."

Typically, when couples struggle with an impasse for a while, there comes a point at which they begin to feel that they are really working together, a *shift to mutuality.* Even though the conflict is not fully resolved, there is at least the sense that progress is being made and all is not lost. Women and men may come to this shift to mutuality in different ways. These days, many women feel tired of doing what they perceive to be much of the work in male-female relationships. They no longer want to be the emotional caretakers and therefore often need to feel that men have some willingness to work on an impasse. Often, women are also looking for new models for their relationships and desire a better balance between the partners in working at communication.

Men may reach the shift to mutuality in somewhat different ways, one of which involves becoming aware of the relationship as an entity and an experience in itself. Labeling relational experience with names such as "our conflict" or "our misunderstanding" is important if men are to understand this experience in a context of mutuality. It is also important for men to learn about the differences in how relationships work for them and for women. They often perceive different communication styles as types of conflict rather than simply as *differences* in how people respond, so they often react initially with defensiveness. Finally, it is crucial for men to learn how to empathize with the feelings of others so that they can begin to understand the feelings that are being experienced.

The communication strategies discussed in this chapter can assist in the resolution of many conflicts. A fundamental principle is to be assertive, stating clearly and in a personalized way how *you* feel. This is different from aggressive behavior, in which you attack, blame, and accuse others and make assumptions and judgments about their motives. Some suggestions for improving communication are given in Table 9.2.

■ Maintaining Loving Relationships

When they enter into a loving relationship, couples want that relationship to last. Researcher John Gottman (2000) of the Relationship Research Institute in Seattle was one of the first scientists to study systematically the qualities that might make or break relationships. In his labora-tories, psychologists conducted extensive interviews with couples and took an array of physiological measurements. They developed an emotion-identification coding system that helped them analyze masses of data about relationships. Although their conclusions have been limited largely to heterosexual marriages, their findings may well hold worthwhile advice for all couples of any gender who want to maintain their loving relationships. Here are some of the main findings:

1. *Couples who have more positive moments than negative moments have a better chance of lasting together.* In fact, the ratio of positive behaviors needed to offset negative behaviors with some weight in order to create a strong bond is about five to one.

2. *Volatile relationships, with heated arguments and passionate reconciliations, can be very lasting.* It seems that such relationships may be as happy as those that are more reserved, as long as conflicts really get resolved.

3. *Emotionally inexpressive relationships can be very successful,* if the five-to-one ratio of positive to negative things couples do share with each other is maintained.

4. *Confronting complaints and differences early in the relationship seems to help.* Avoiding tensions and fights early on leads to a greater likelihood of trouble later. Expressing anger openly also seems to be a continuing factor in keeping relationships vital.

5. *In happy relationships, there is no discernible difference between how women and men express themselves emotionally.* Men may even be more likely than women to reveal intimate information about themselves in a happy relationship.

6. *Positive feelings about the beginning of the relationship are correlated with a higher likelihood of remaining together.* When partners have warm memories about the unfolding of their relationship, psychologists have been able to predict with great accuracy the likelihood that the couple will still be together in three years.

More recently, Gottman began to apply mathematical models to his relationship data, and with the help of colleagues he began to find some predictive value in those models (Gottman et al., 2003). The models show, for example, that in "volatile" relationships, in which couples routinely express anger at one another, they can offset the negative effects of the anger with large doses of warmth and affection. This helps them remain stable in the longer run. Couples who tend to be "validating" or "conflict-avoiding" (see Figure 9.5)

Quantifying Conversations

John M. Gottman and his colleagues have developed "influence functions" to illustrate how the partners in various types of couples influence each other's moods over the course of a difficult conversation. The horizontal axis represents a range of verbal and facial expressions—from highly critical and contemptuous (on the left) to highly supportive and affectionate (on the right). The vertical axis represents the degree to which a person is influenced positively (up) or negatively (down) by his or her spouse's behavior. For example, the husband in a "validating" couple tends to be strongly influenced (in a negative direction) by his wife's negative behavior: That line has a slope of 0.31. The husband in a "conflict-avoiding" couple, on the other hand, actually tends to behave slightly more positively when his wife is negative: That line has a slope of −0.05.

Both "validating" couples and "conflict-avoiding" couples tend to have marriages that are stable and long lasting. Couples are in trouble, though, when they have mismatched influence functions. Consider the "hostile-detached" couple, where the slopes for the husband's and the wife's influences look very different. When the husband behaves positively, he has almost no impact (slope of 0.02) on his detached wife.

FIGURE 9.5 *Quantifying Conversations*

The work of John Gottman and his associates has been used to create mathematical models to describe relationships.

Source: Text from David Glenn, "Every Unhappy Family Has Its Own Bilinear Influence Function," *The Chronicle of Higher Education,* 25 April 2003. Copyright © 2003, The Chronicle of Higher Education. Reprinted with permission. Figures from John M. Gottman, James D. Murray, Catherine Swanson, Rebecca Tyson, and Kristin R. Swanson, *The Mathematics of Marriage: Dynamic Nonlinear Models,* Figures 10.1 and 10.2. Copyright © 2002 Massachusetts Institute of Technology. Reprinted by permission of The MIT Press.

seem to have stabler relationships than couples who are "hostile-detached." The mathematical models eventually incorporated factors that introduced more reality into their predictions. The researchers found, for example, that couples employ both "damping" and "repair" influences during difficult conversations. Damping comes in the form of making hurtful comments when the partner is trying to pull the discussion in a more positive direction. Repair attempts include changing the subject, making a joke, and offering soothing statements that attempt to turn the dialogue in a more positive direction. Without these moderating effects, the mathematical models tend to predict relationship catastrophe that in reality couples tend to prevent and mediate.

Have you ever experienced a communication problem with someone of the other sex based on what might be considered typical communication differences between men and women? Describe this personal experience.

Building any worthwhile relationship takes effort and commitment. When sexual sharing is part of the relationship, it becomes that much more sensitive and complicated. To share sex is to share a deep level of intimacy and the strong feelings that usually accompany such intimacy. Although sex may be important in many relationships, the closeness of another person who is willing to listen, understand, and talk is often just as significant (Bozon, 2002; Brehm et al., 2002). Positive sexual relationships do not just fall into place from one encounter in bed; they evolve from a deliberate process of communicating together and working to be responsive to each other.

The "Other" Risks of Sex

There have always been highly publicized risks of indiscriminate sexual activity, such as unplanned pregnancy or sexually transmitted infection. However, there are other risks of sex too, risks associated with the relational aspects of human interaction. Following are some examples.

Risk: Modeling Your Sexuality after External Standards Rather Than Your Own

Each of us must find ways to bring our own unique blend of sexual needs, orientations, fantasies, attractions, and behaviors into some sort of balance and harmony with our society, which is always circumscribed by its cultural, political, and historical boundaries. Not to achieve that harmony is to be

alienated from ourselves, perhaps playing some sexual role inconsistent with the core of our being. This can create a remarkable degree of personal pain and confusion.

Risk: Confusing Romantic Attachment and Sexual Attraction

Many people find it difficult to distinguish between romantic attachment and sexual attraction. There may be a tendency to rush toward saying "I love you" in order to justify sex. Or sexual interaction may mistakenly be construed as evidence of love. Many cultures other than our own, especially in Eastern countries, have had far less confusion over these matters. In these cultures, love is not allowed to become an excuse for sex, and sexual passion and infatuation are not considered legitimate bases from which to embark on a major life adventure such as marriage.

Risk: Not Allowing Yourself to Be Vulnerable Enough to Accept the Risks Inherent in Loving Relationships

Eventually, every relationship has some pain. Fear of dealing with hurt—in oneself or in a partner—is one of the leading causes of broken relationships. People must be willing to be vulnerable to the fears of being hurt or of hurting someone else. Without vulnerability, relationships and their sexual components eventually become sterile, brittle, and empty. Before we can deal with vulnerability in a healthy, positive manner, we must also know and accept ourselves. We have to develop a level of self-esteem and self-confidence that will help us feel worthwhile and validated as individuals. When we depend too heavily on others to make us feel good, we give up a great deal of personal power in the relationship. This can exaggerate the risks of vulnerability as well as rob us of the right to accept ourselves as we are and to feel good about who we are.

Risk: Being in a Situation in Which You Feel Bound to Do Something Sexual That Just Does Not Feel Quite Right to You

Our society does not encourage much sense of "ownership" over our genitals until we reach some arbitrary age of passage when we suddenly are expected to become sexually responsible. This results in a good deal of confusion about sexual values and behaviors and often leads us to engage in sexual activities out of a sense of obligation rather than a conviction that they are right for us. We need to be open to our sexuality so that we can think and plan ahead. We never have to be at the mercy of whims or urges, whether our own or those of others. It takes introspection, time, and even some experimentation to know where we stand with regard to sexual values and what we want for our lives sexually.

What's Love Got to Do with It?

Love, intimacy, and sex seem to be parts of a singular, confusing package that writers, poets, and scientists have been trying to understand and explain for centuries. Love is a quality and an experience that until recently has seemed more comfortable in the hands of artists than in the hands of scientists, but there is evidence that the experience of passionate love is found in all cultures (Brehm et al., 2002; Collins, R. L., et al., 2003).

Studies on romantic love and sexual desire worldwide have shown three global transformations that seem to be occurring, all of which are affecting loving relationships. First, an increasing belief in the equality of genders and ethnic groups is eroding long-standing double standards and prejudices, freeing people to love without so many social constrictions. The second transformation is that the pursuit of happiness has been becoming a more acceptable and worthwhile goal, leading to a more positive view of passionate love and sexual desire. Finally, there is a growing belief that life can be changed for the better, with the pleasures of love and sex being seen as a legitimate part of life improvement. Love and sex seem to be primary ingredients in bringing people together in intimate relationships. Every loving partnership has its own unique history and configuration. Each relationship has its own identity, just as do the two individuals who comprise it (Bozon, 2002; Levine, 2005).

Love poses a challenge to go beyond the single-minded pursuit of personal gratification and to break down some of the habitual patterns of behavior that have been a part of nonpartnered life. It has been said that love and relationship have a transformative power; they bring together two people who then have to sort through the many complications of being together. We live in a mobile, increasingly disconnected culture and in a time in history when the rules about love and relating are sometimes vague and confusing. In many ways, love is an ideal toward which people strive, often with some level of internal conflict. The external pressures and reasons for people to come together and form a partnership are far less convincing than they once were. It is now internal reactions and the intrinsic qualities of two individuals' personal

connection that keep a relationship going (Bozon, 2002). Creating and sustaining a relationship constitute a whole new frontier in the human journey. Whenever we enter into a loving connection with another person, we enter largely unexplored territory, with all sorts of new things to discover—both within ourselves and within the dynamics of what we share as a couple.

Theories of Love

Love is not something that just happens; rather, it is something to be practiced, perfected, and worked at from the foundation of a person's cultural imperatives and belief systems. Researchers have begun to clarify three primary human emotion-motivation systems associated with what we generally call "love." These systems clearly are interrelated but may also function independently of one another (Aron et al., 2005; Fisher, Aron, Mashek, Li, & Brown, 2002).

1. *Lust* manifests itself as a craving for sexual gratification. From the standpoint of evolutionary theory, this motivation system ensures reproduction of the species.
2. *Attraction* is characterized by heightened energy and attention for a particular partner, often called romantic love, and is accompanied by feelings of exhilaration, "intrusive thinking" about the loved one, and a craving for emotional connection with the other person. From an evolutionary and survival point of view, it saves energy by focusing attention on a particular mate.
3. *Attachment* is characterized by the calm, contented feelings that accompany being close to the loved one and, in a sense, "making the nest" together. From an evolutionary perspective, this system facilitates coupling and parenting.

Close relationships often begin with the attraction process, with feelings of "falling in love" or *infatuation*. This kind of loving involves an intense desire to be close to another person, and strong emotions may surface as well as intense sexual attraction based on certain physical characteristics (see Figure 9.6). Infatuation can be exciting and exhilarating, but it can have its difficult side. Because such strong emotions are involved, it may be particularly painful when the other person is unable to feel mutually attracted and loving. On the other hand, when two people fall in love, they typically seek to spend a great deal of time together, gradually let down their usual barriers, and become more and more vulnerable to each other. Their sense of shared intimacy deepens, and they may eventually progress to sexual sharing. Often they experience a sense of never wanting things to change, of never wanting to be apart. It is typical at this point for partners to make promises to each other such as

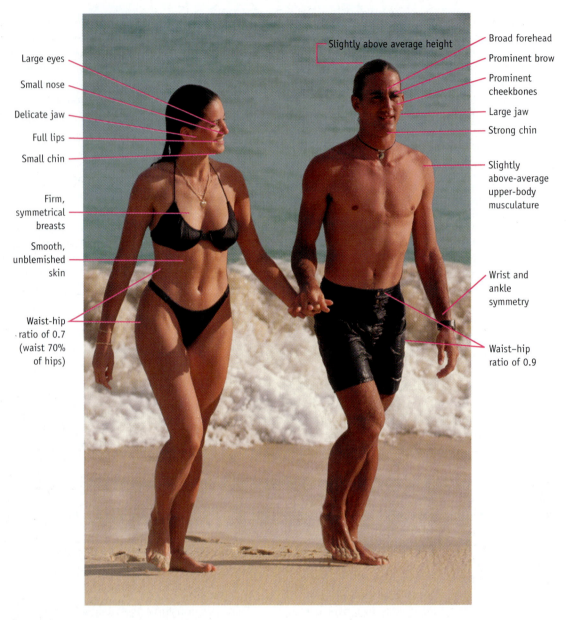

Large eyes

Small nose

Delicate jaw

Full lips

Small chin

Firm, symmetrical breasts

Smooth, unblemished skin

Waist–hip ratio of 0.7 (waist 70% of hips)

Slightly above average height

Broad forehead

Prominent brow

Prominent cheekbones

Large jaw

Strong chin

Slightly above-average upper-body musculature

Wrist and ankle symmetry

Waist–hip ratio of 0.9

■ **FIGURE 9.6** *What Goes into Sex Appeal?*

Studies suggest that male attractiveness hinges on outward signs of maturity, robust health, and, above all, dominance. Most of the features associated with feminine beauty signal youthfulness and an abundance of female reproductive hormones.

"I'll always love you" or "I'll never leave you" or "I'll never hurt you."

See *"Waist-to-Hip Ratio"* on *SexSource Online.*

However, the process of falling in love must always come to an end. At this point relationships often end too, largely because people in our society have been led to believe that infatuation is the only kind of loving worth having. This intense phase may also evolve into the stabler, more deeply committed attachment stage, which might be called *being in love*. This stage involves a conscious choice on the part of both partners to be together, although they certainly may be motivated by the feelings of security, comfort, and contentment that their togetherness produces. They care about and trust each other enough to commit themselves to working at the relationship. They recognize that their love is more than just lust. They see it as a process of communicating, negotiating, compromising when differences get in the way, and agreeing to struggle through the more difficult times together. Being in love also means that two people are struggling to accept and love each other, even in the face of their individual differences and idiosyncrasies. They may eventually find ways to celebrate their mutual differences instead of finding them to be obstacles (Brehm et al., 2002).

Concepts of love gradually have taken shape, although there has been very little research on the topic in recent years. Some scientists insist that love is not so much a built-in tendency as it is a socialized response, whereas others believe it to be a basic human emotion. Comparisons of ethnographic data have shown a good deal of similarity among cross-cultural views of love, sex, and intimacy. Yet they have also suggested that individual differences may well be more powerful than cultural influences in shaping particular people's attitudes and behaviors that constitute their styles of loving. In a survey of 166 societies, evidence of romantic attraction and love was found in 147 of them. Further analysis of data has demonstrated that several predictable characteristics are associated with romantic attraction; these tend to occur in stages and typically are associated with what we call love (Aron et al., 2005; Fisher, Aron, Mashek, Li, & Brown, 2002):

- The initial falling-in-love experience causes the loved one to take on special meaning, usually to the exclusion of anyone else. The lover has a tendency to view the loved one as unique, quite different from everyone else. At least for a time, this causes the lover to see only the positive in the other person, overlooking more negative traits. Little things the loved one says or does are noticed in great detail.
- Individuals who report feelings of romantic love also may experience a great variety of psychological and physical responses, ranging from exhilaration and euphoria to sleeplessness, loss of appetite, and a rapid heartbeat. When the loved one is not present, they may feel a sense of loss, anxiety, or depression.
- In the midst of romantic love, people report thinking obsessively about their loved one. This is sometimes called "intrusive thinking," because it often seems to push its way into other thoughts. This characteristic is also associated with emotional dependency on the relationship and fear of rejection.
- A person in love longs for emotional closeness with the beloved and often experiences a willingness to sacrifice for him or her.
- Lovers may reorder their daily priorities or make changes in their lifestyles in order to spend time with the loved one or to seem more compatible.

- Sexual desire usually accompanies romantic attraction, along with a feeling of possessiveness and a desire for sexual exclusivity. There is a desire to persuade the partner not to have sex with others. However, the desire for emotional intimacy seems to take precedence over a desire for sexual intimacy in the majority of women and men. While sexual union may be very important in romantic love, emotional union is even more important.
- People generally report that their feelings of romantic attraction are not within their control and in fact are involuntary. They can, at times, even seem unwanted.
- Unless some sorts of barriers prevent partners from seeing each other on a regular basis, romantic attraction is impermanent. It eventually ends.

Sternberg's Triangular Theory of Love

Yale researcher Robert Sternberg (1986, 1998) studied the dynamics of loving relationships for several years and developed an interesting model that accounts for three distinct components of love. These components can be viewed as the three sides of a triangle, with the area of the triangle representing the amount and style of loving.

1. *Intimacy,* the emotional component, involves closeness, mutual support, and sharing. It corresponds to the attachment motivation system. In relationships, intimacy tends to increase gradually but steadily at first, naturally leveling off as two persons become more comfortably knowledgeable about each other. In well-established, healthy relationships, intimacy may not even be particularly noticeable on the surface, but it will quickly become evident during some crisis that the couple must face together (see Figure 9.7).

2. *Passion* provides a motivational component to love and corresponds partly with the lust motivation system and partly with the attachment motivation system. It is manifested in a desire to be united with the loved one, leading to sexual arousal and sharing. It is the aspect of some loving that tends to increase most rapidly at first. Sternberg has likened passion to an addictive substance, because people are so drawn to its stimulation and pleasure. If one person abruptly ends the relationship, suddenly withdrawing the outlet for passion, the other person may suffer all the depression, irritability, and emotional pain of the withdrawal process. In time, even in a lasting relationship, passion levels off and does not

provide the stimulation and arousal it did at first. That does not mean that passion necessarily becomes unimportant or lacking. It simply loses some of its importance as a motivating force in the relationship (see Figure 9.7).

3. *Commitment* represents the cognitive side of love, in both its short- and long-term senses, and is at least partially consistent with the attachment motivation. The development of commitment in a relationship is easy to understand, as Figure 9.7 demonstrates. When you first meet another person, there is no particular commitment to the loving process. As you get to know each other better, however, commitment begins to grow and develop. As with all other components of love, commitment eventually levels off; if the relationship fails, it declines even further.

Sternberg's research has also shown that the best predictor of happiness in a loving relationship is the degree of similarity between how an individual wants the other person to feel about him or her and how the individual thinks the partner actually feels. If one person believes that the other does not feel enough love, disappointment and conflict can follow.

The Brain Circuitry and Chemistry of Love

Everyone recognizes that love is one of the more complex human emotions and that it cannot be adequately explained by any single model. It has even been suggested that love has powerful disease-prevention and healing influences within the body. Researchers are just beginning to piece together the even greater puzzle of structures and biochemicals in the brain that are associated with human loving emotions. Various chemical stimuli may activate a romantic reaction toward others. There is increasing evidence that the scents of chemical sex attractants, or **pheromones,** may play an influential role in this process (Cutler, 1999; Sako & Friebely, 2004). A chemical called androstenol is found in male sweat, and its dry, musky smell is appealing to women. When it oxidizes to form androstenone, women tend to react more negatively to its odor *unless they are ovulating.* Copulines are chemicals found in women's vaginal secretions. Controlled experiments in which males inhaled these substances found that the exposure tended to upgrade men's attractions to women and assessments of their beauty. We are beginning to find empirical evidence about the effects of human pheromones demonstrating that pheromones can increase the tendency of both men and women to have shared sexual activity (Cutler, Friedmann, & McCoy, 1998; Sako & Friebely, 2004).

During *attraction,* or the phase of loving that corresponds to infatuation or falling in love, the brain is stim-ulated centrally by phenylethylamine (PEA), dopamine, and norepinephrine. These are close chemical relatives to the stimulant drugs called amphetamines, and they tend to produce elation, increased energy, and euphoria. Attraction makes people feel swept away and energized. At the same time, there may be a decrease in serotonin levels in what are called the "reward pathways" of the brain. Reduced levels of serotonin may be associated with the obsessive and intrusive thinking, anxiety, depression, and moodiness associated with romantic attraction (Aron et al., 2005; Fisher, Aron, Mashek, Li, Strong, & Brown, 2002).

There are also chemical reasons why infatuation cannot last forever. Eventually, the body builds up a certain tolerance to these biochemicals so that their profound effects begin to wear off. Some people seem to become "attraction junkies," constantly craving the intoxicating highs of falling in love. They move from one relationship to the next as the attraction high in the brain begins to run down each time.

Those relationships that endure beyond attraction settle into a longer period of *attachment.* In this phase of loving, being around a loved one stimulates the production of **endorphins** in the brain. These natural painkillers produce a sense of security, tranquility, and calm. The chemical **oxytocin** is produced during cuddling and physical intimacy and is associated with the powerful feelings of orgasm and sexual satisfaction. The *lust* motivation system seems to be mediated in part by the estrogens and the androgens. There is evidence that when orgasm occurs, the pituitary gland produces prolactin, a hormone that tends to suppress sexual desire for a time. This hormone may bring sexual interest to an end following a satisfying sexual experience. The brain chemistry of love is illustrated in Figure 9.8.

Establishing Sensual and Sexual Intimacy

We hear a great deal about intimacy in relationships, and the term seems to mean different things to different people. Intimacy usually describes a special kind of closeness between people, a deep connection that

---

pheromones (FAIR-oh-moans) human chemicals, the scent of which may cause an attraction or behavioral change in other individuals.

endorphins (en-DORE-fins) brain secretions that act as natural tranquilizers and pain relievers.

oxytocin (ox-ee-TOH-sin) a chemical produced by the brain in response to physical intimacy and sexual satisfaction.

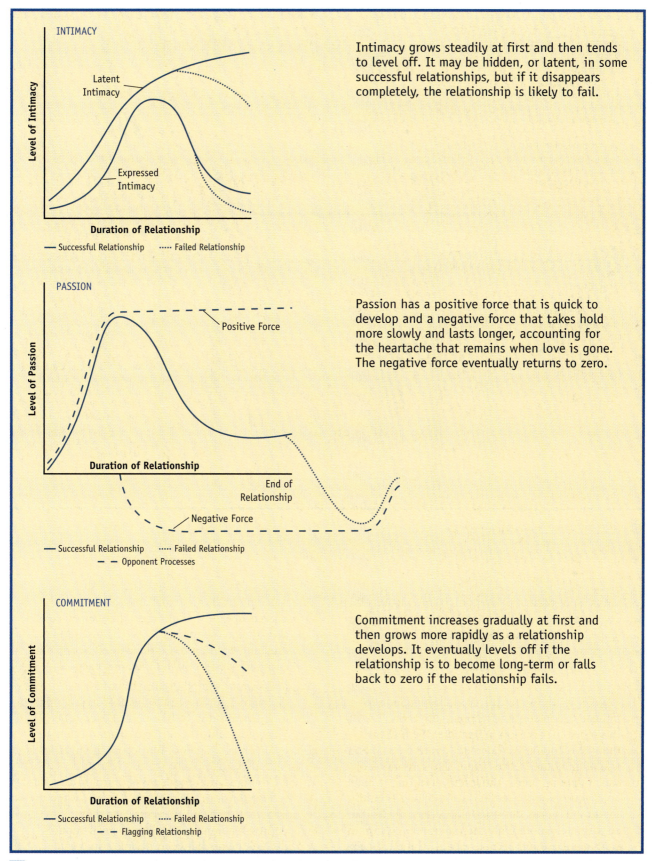

Intimacy grows steadily at first and then tends to level off. It may be hidden, or latent, in some successful relationships, but if it disappears completely, the relationship is likely to fail.

Passion has a positive force that is quick to develop and a negative force that takes hold more slowly and lasts longer, accounting for the heartache that remains when love is gone. The negative force eventually returns to zero.

Commitment increases gradually at first and then grows more rapidly as a relationship develops. It eventually levels off if the relationship is to become long-term or falls back to zero if the relationship fails.

FIGURE 9.7 *Sternberg's Triangular Theory of Love*

Yale researcher Robert Sternberg has developed one model to explain the complicated emotion of love. In the model, he describes intimacy, passion, and commitment as love's basic components.

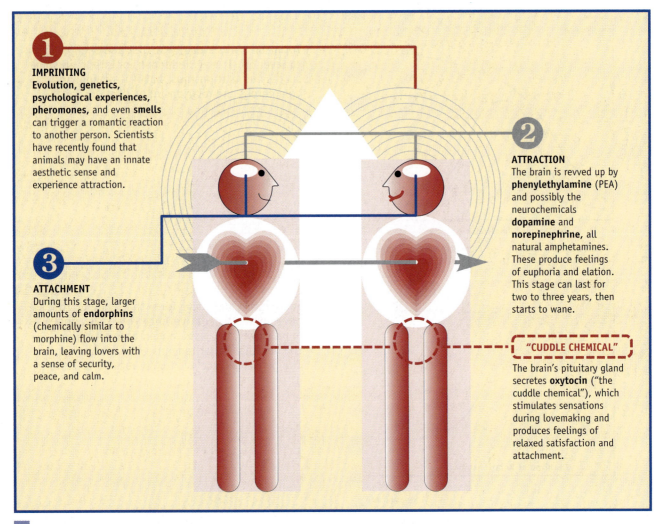

① IMPRINTING
Evolution, genetics, psychological experiences, pheromones, and even **smells** can trigger a romantic reaction to another person. Scientists have recently found that animals may have an innate aesthetic sense and experience attraction.

② ATTRACTION
The brain is revved up by **phenylethylamine** (PEA) and possibly the neurochemicals **dopamine** and **norepinephrine,** all natural amphetamines. These produce feelings of euphoria and elation. This stage can last for two to three years, then starts to wane.

③ ATTACHMENT
During this stage, larger amounts of **endorphins** (chemically similar to morphine) flow into the brain, leaving lovers with a sense of security, peace, and calm.

"CUDDLE CHEMICAL"
The brain's pituitary gland secretes **oxytocin** ("the cuddle chemical"), which stimulates sensations during lovemaking and produces feelings of relaxed satisfaction and attachment.

■ FIGURE 9.8   *The Chemistry of Love*
The various stages of loving correspond to chemical changes in the brain.

feels more special than the superficial interactions that tend to dominate our lives (see Figure 9.9). But how do people go about building the kind of intimacy they seem to crave at some deeper level within themselves? Following are some factors important to established intimacy:

1. *Touching* can establish a crucial foundation for intimacy. Skin sensitivity apparently is the first of the senses to develop in fetal life. We feel with the nerve endings of our skin before we make use of any other sense organ. The sensations of touch then remain at the forefront of our conscious experience. Sensual touching is gratifying to the senses but does not necessarily lead to sexual interaction. Only too often, people's sensual needs are ignored or starved. The need to be touched in caring, loving ways—to be taken care of through touching—is an important need for both women and men. Only too often, if such

touching leads to sexual arousal, the sensual aspects are hurried along so that genital sexual activity may be initiated. Like being in love, touching is an art to be developed, worked at, and perfected through time and practice.

2. *Relaxation* is another important factor in intimacy. People need to be able to feel relaxed together in order to be open to each other. Physiologically, the term *relaxation* refers to a relatively low level of tension in the muscles. Although it is possible to use relaxation techniques and other stress-control methods to reduce tension, psychological factors often are an important part of the picture. Anxiety, depression, anger, hostility, or even subtle disagreements between people can create tension. Even subtle tension can block intimacy and interfere with sexual enjoyment. Although sexual arousal involves a buildup of body

FIGURE 9.9 *Intimacy*

Developing intimacy in a relationship involves touching in a caring, loving manner; learning to reduce tension by physically and psychologically relaxing; and being fully aware of the need to communicate.

tensions, paradoxically it is most effective within the context of a relaxed atmosphere between the partners. The more people have to work at sex, the more likely it is that tension will destroy the sense of intimacy (Klusmann, 2002).

3. *Being a participant* in a relationship is necessary to intimacy. Only too often, people allow themselves to become spectators, in a sense standing outside themselves and watching what is going on. Or they may escape into the withdrawal of daydreams and inattention. It is far better to be fully in touch with your own inner reactions and with your partner at the moment. To be preoccupied with future goals or with how sex is going to go distracts from experiencing and dealing with how things actually are going *right now*. What participating in an intimate relationship is all about is being fully aware of what is going on and taking responsibility for communicating or acting as necessary (Bagarozzi, 2001).

Confusion about Love and Sex in Relationships

Issues of love and sex have become blurred in our culture. In fact, romantic love is a fairly recent development historically, and a century ago it was not necessarily associated with sexual feelings. Love was meant to be a pure feeling expressed through the idealization of the loved one. In the modern period, romantic love has been associated with sex (Brehm et al., 2002), but this change in attitude has not occurred without confusion. One complication of this perspective is that we have come to expect the intense feelings of love and the passion of sex to be a continuing part of lasting relationships such as marriage, when in fact these emotions change with time. Individuals sometimes use sex to hold onto their partners or pretend that having sex must mean that you are in love.

People may assume that if they have chosen a partner well, the love and the relationship should last forever and the love will never change. But loving feelings and levels of interest in sex change over time. The important thing is how well the couple keeps up with the process of change. It is also assumed that when people love each other, sex will just happen. However, most couples have busy lives, and as they spend time together their priorities may change. Sometimes they will have to create the opportunity for sex to happen while not making it seem too contrived (Bozon, 2002).

Love may be abused in relationships as well. It may be used as a justification for controlling others: "I only did it because I love you." Or it may be cited as the reason for imposing some imperative on a partner: "If you really loved me, you would. . . ." This imperative could be completed in any number of ways, including the following:

. . . want sex as often as I do

. . . have eyes for no one else but me

. . . trust me without question

. . . have sex with me now

. . . know how to turn me on

. . . never hurt me

Such imperatives can place the receiver in a situation sometimes called the "double bind." In other words, you are "damned if you do and damned if you don't." The sender of the message has created a no-win situation. If you resist the entreaty, you are demonstrating your lack of caring, but if you follow through as dictated by the imperative, you may be accused of merely trying to please the person and not really meaning it.

Have you ever been "head over heels" in love with someone? Describe the experience.

Confusion over love and sex is best resolved through effective communication methods, based on a real commitment to work together on maintaining a dynamic and caring relationship. In many relationships, partners care as much about their partners' sexual satisfaction as about their own. It seems clear that sexual satisfaction is closely associated with the levels of relationship satisfaction, love, and commitment shown between the partners in the relationship (Levine, 2005; Sprecher, 2002).

Same-Gender Intimate Relationships

In conceptualizing same-gender intimate relationships, it has been typical to single out shared sexual activity between the partners as the primary distinguishing factor. However, nonsexual loving relationships exist between members of the same sex as well. Sometimes two individuals of the same gender share a lengthy sexual affair but do not consider themselves lesbian or gay; they simply have chosen to have sex with this one particular partner. Therefore, in examining some relationships, we must take into consideration how the partners identify themselves (Heaphy, Weeks, & Donovan, 1998).

Theorists have suggested that same-sex partners sometimes are attracted to each other because of differences other than gender. Many lesbian couples seem to form a bond because one woman is exclusively attracted to women and the other has had a more bisexual orientation. Several studies have pointed to the possibility that males are drawn into romantic attachments because of their long-standing sense of being different from other males as they were growing up. The hypothesis suggests that this leads them to an interest in forming a relationship with other males as a way of achieving a sense of self-completion and mergence. Often there is an element of competition in male-male relationships that can interfere with intimacy (George, 1997).

Three primary patterns of intimate relationships can develop between gay men and between lesbians. One pattern employs the heterosexual model for dating and marriage as the prototype for determining roles within the relationship, with one partner adopting more of the traditional masculine functions and the other adopting more of the traditional feminine roles. Another common pattern involves a marked age difference between the partners, with an older individual paired with a younger person of the same gender. A third pattern, which seems to be modeled after friendships, emphasizes sharing and equality between partners who are similar in age and social status. Surveys have found that lesbian partners are more likely to share household tasks. Gay male partners and married heterosexual partners were found to be more likely to have a division of labor in which one partner does more household work than the other (usually the woman of a heterosexual couple).

Connecting: For Better or for Worse

Changes in social norms and available communication technologies change the nature of human connections. The "rules of engagement" become unclear, and new trails need to be blazed. The partnerships that emerge from the new opportunities may leave people feeling frustrated and vulnerable. As this section demonstrates, the personality characteristics that each partner brings to a relationship can determine whether it will remain a healthy and stable partnership. People in loving relationships also risk being hurt if the relationship comes to an end.

Friendship and Sexuality

Many people would say they love their friends, but they would not be referring to a romantic or sexual attachment. Studies on friendship show that, in general, people tend to prefer friendships with members of their own sex and that individuals who have close friendships tend to be less anxious and depressed than those who do not.

Friendships sometimes can become confusing sexually. Single men and women are far more likely than married people to have friends of the other gender. People in a committed relationship may be threatened by knowing that a partner has a close friendship with someone else. There may be a fear that the friendship will lead to deeper intimacy or sexual sharing. Therefore, friendships outside the primary relationship are often considered acceptable only to a point that clearly distinguishes them as auxiliary and secondary to that primary relationship.

Close, intimate friendships are a domain with few clear social rules. The sexual aspect of friendships may well exist and need to be sorted out. To deny sexual attraction within the relationship may prove unhealthy and an obstacle to open communication. Another largely unexplored territory is the friendship that does include sex. An obvious risk here is that one partner's expectations and emotions will shift and more will be wanted than what is being called friendship. To make clear distinctions between friendship and love is sometimes difficult. It may be that "friendship" is simply a safer word that allows couples to remain comfortable with a relationship that has actually become loving but calling it "love" will present a dilemma for their lives (Neuman, 2002).

Relating via the Internet

The ability to communicate over the Internet has created an entirely new virtual community in which people can interact. People are falling in love and sharing online sexual activity through this medium. Computer-mediated communication (CMC) and computer-mediated relating (CMR) have been feared as enemies to human intimacy, yet some studies indicate that they often lead to very positive interpersonal relationships. Online interaction may help people whose sexual interests and orientations are less socially acceptable feel less marginalized (Cooper, 2002; McKenna, Green, & Smith, 2001).

Online dating sites that ask customers to complete questionnaires about themselves are attempting to use scientific methods of matching couples who are believed to be compatible for various reasons. These sites seem to be having at least some success, even though there also seems to be some lessening of interest in registering for such sites (Gottlieb, 2006).

Typically, an individual is drawn to Internet sites by some indication of a common interest with others at the site. Sometimes these expressions of interest may be romantic or overtly sexual. The motivations behind seeking out such contact generally seem to fit into five basic categories: anonymity, time constraints that interfere with the pursuit of face-to-face (FTF) relationships, the desire to share sexual fantasies, the opportunity to share online sexual behavior (often accompanied by masturbation), and the hope of eventually meeting the person with whom a meaningful connection has been made (Benotsch, Kalichman, & Cage, 2002).

Some 40 million Americans visit online sites regularly (Mulrine, 2003). In a study of more than 4,000 people who indicated that they had met a partner through the Internet, those ages 18 to 24 reported having met an average of nearly 10 partners in this manner, including 7 in the past year. Older men and women said they had met an average of 14 partners online, 6 in the past year. Half of the entire research sample indicated that they had had sex with a partner they had met online (McFarlane, Bull, & Rietmeijer, 2002). In sites on which people post personal ads in order to attract partners, women are more likely to emphasize their physical attractiveness and youth, while men tend to advertise their education, employment, and income. Interestingly, in one study that looked at what ads attracted the most responses, the personal posting by a woman who described herself as "financially independent, successful, and ambitious" actually received the most responses from interested men (Strassberg & Holty, 2003).

Some findings are beginning to suggest that romantic relationships in cyberspace may actually enhance FTF relationships rather than completely replacing them. We know, for example, that attraction is fostered through the proximity and familiarity that two people share. Electronic communication can actu-

ally create greater feelings of closeness and familiarity because of the frequency of contact that is possible. The vast network that is available also makes it more likely that people will find others who share similar characteristics and attitudes. CMC surely provides opportunities for self-disclosure and interpersonal intimacy relatively quickly because of the degree of anonymity present at the beginning of the relationship. Finally, the significance of the erotic connection that can develop between people through the Internet should not be underestimated. All these characteristics have the potential for moving relationships into intimate territory quite rapidly (Benotsch, Kalichman, & Cage, 2002).

This is not to say that CMR does not have its share of risks. Certainly there are frightening tales of cyber-relationships ending in harassment, abuse, or violence. One risk of online relating lies in its advantages: the tendency for the relationship to develop very rapidly into an intimate connection (Brown, Maycock, & Burns, 2005). The intensity can also mean that the relationship quickly becomes eroticized but then cannot be sustained because there is insufficient underlying trust and knowledge to support it. If an individual is having an online relationship at the same time as an FTF relationship, the same stresses and strains can develop whenever the boundaries of the relationships are crossed. Among 18- to 24-year-olds who pursue sex with an online partner, the first meeting tends to take place in the partner's home, a park or other outdoor place, or a rest room. They also are less likely to say that condoms were available at the meeting place, making the chances of a risky sexual encounter quite high (McFarlane, Bull, & Rietmeijer, 2002).

All in all, romance and sex via the Internet represent a phenomenon that is rapidly changing the partnering scene and will require further careful study. The pervasive impression created by the media is that the Internet promotes superficial, destructive relationships, but the realities are far more complex—and more positive—than this. The virtual community into which the Internet can lead us is simply a new and evolving kind of community that must develop clearer ethical guidelines for its users. Like any human community, it has its share of untrustworthy, abusive, and even dangerous individuals. It also has many people who are genuinely interested in good relationships founded on courtesy, honesty, integrity, and respect (Cooper et al., 2002).

Attachment Theory: Jealousy and Possessiveness

When we become highly attached to something—whether a material object we have paid dearly to own or another person whom we dearly love—we often fear that we could end up losing what we long to possess. Attachment theory has clarified three main styles of emotional bonding with another person. The *secure* attachment style is characterized by increased self-confidence and self-esteem and a growing sense of satisfaction with the loving relationship. Those who have a *preoccupied* style of attachment are anxious and ambivalent about their relationship, tend to have a negative view of themselves and a positive view of their partner, and are quite dependent on their partners for nurturance. Other people fall into *avoidant* patterns of attachment, meaning that at some level they are managing to hold themselves back from effective emotional attachment with their partner. This last style may well represent a way of avoiding the vulnerability that eventually could open the individual to hurt. There are two subsets of the avoidant style. Some people are *dismissing avoidant,* they view themselves more positively and as more worthwhile than the partner, tending to ignore and diminish their partner. *Fearful avoidant* people hold negative views of both themselves and their partner and seem fearful of intimacy. They often worry that their partner does not care about them as much as they care about their partner (Pistole & Arricale, 2003).

When couples face conflict, as they always do eventually, their attachment style plays a role in how the conflict may be approached. Those who have a secure style feel less threatened by arguments and are less concerned about feelings of closeness during conflict than are those who have preoccupied or fearful styles. Those with dismissive styles are more likely to avoid conflict than are those who are securely attached (Pistole & Arricale, 2003).

Loving relationships can have elements of territoriality and fear. We want the object of our affection to love us in return and, frequently, to love only us.

We fear rejection by that person and especially fear the loss of his or her love to someone else. If we have some inkling, even an imagined one, that a partner's interests might be straying, it is quite natural to feel jealous. A reasonable amount of jealousy can be expected in any relationship. It is an issue about which couples need to communicate openly. It is important to remember that even those individuals who are happy and comfortable in a loving and sexual relationship will still occasionally find themselves attracted to others. This does not have to threaten the relationship, nor does it signal some sort of difficulty between the partners (Buss, 2000; Nannini & Meyers, 2000).

Sometimes jealousy gets out of control and becomes possessiveness, a particularly common occurrence among people who have a preoccupied style of attachment. Such individuals seem always worried about losing their partner and might even imagine that something more is going on in other relationships. There may be an unreasonable degree of anger over the partner's casual and innocent social interactions. Such possessiveness can have many roots. Feelings of inferiority often play a role and may be accompanied by some basic insecurity and immaturity in the individual (Brehm et al., 2002). Some people who become overly possessive expect complete and utter devotion from a partner and have difficulty seeing that individuals always need room for personal growth, even within a committed relationship. Possessiveness usually signals some fundamental insecurities in the person's personality that may well deserve some attention. Professional counseling can be a viable option for consideration (Brown, 2005; Pistole & Arricale, 2003).

Overly jealous people often are not willing to take much responsibility for changing their behavior. They may even consider their obsession with their partner

He loved her more than words could say. She left him because he didn't talk.

Source: Copyright © 1993 by Andrew Lehman.

Real Student Voices

■ My boyfriend has been really upset lately because I have a close friend in my dorm who happens to be male. I would never do anything with this guy—he's just really easy to talk to. I keep telling my boyfriend there is no need to be jealous, but it doesn't seem to help. I wish he could trust me more.

■ I think about sex most of the time but don't ever have sex. That's because I broke up with my girlfriend 10 months ago, and I still can't get her out of my head. When I think about sex, I think about her.

---

perfectly justified. Both men and women who are so obsessed may stalk the person to whom they are attracted (Brownstein, 2000). Lack of assertiveness on the part of young women sometimes plays a role in making them more vulnerable to possessiveness and abusiveness from a partner (Rickert, Sanghvi, & Wiemann, 2002). There are several ways for dealing with a situation in which your partner is being unreasonably jealous:

1. *Do not fall into the trap of trying to answer unreasonable questions.* A jealous lover may be convinced of your unfaithfulness and grill you with questions. As the rules for good communication suggest, focus on how the questions are making you feel, and stick with the truth.

2. *Encourage your partner to work on the jealousy with you.* You may want to suggest seeking out a counselor together. In any case, act with assertiveness. Do not simply give in to keep the peace for the time being. The jealousy may be a sign of trouble in the relationship that should not be ignored.

3. *Do not be ruled by pity for the other person.* Even if you think you understand the unfortunate reasons why your partner is so desperately jealous, do not feel that he or she should justify unfair accusations or suspicions. It is your partner's responsibility to find a way to work on his or her problems. Threats of suicide or violence are the most extreme form of relational coercion and manipulation. They represent serious problems for which you should seek professional advice.

4. *Take a close look at whether this is a relationship that is healthy for you.* If the jealousy and possessiveness begin to seem hopeless, you may simply be unable to find much relaxed fulfillment in the relationship. Even if you love the other person, it

might be important to sort through whether it is wise to remain in the relationship (Brown, 2005). Again, talking the situation over with a trained counselor can be a significant step toward maintaining your own psychological balance.

Dealing with the Loss of a Loving Relationship

FOH

As you look around at loving relationships, it becomes clear that many of them ultimately fail. Does that mean that people are picking out the wrong partners for loving? Not necessarily. Relationships typically begin with attention being given to what matters to the partners in the short form. Like all things, people and their relationships change. The long-range issues may be quite different. Therefore, as relationships grow, it becomes increasingly important for partners to be willing to change their response patterns toward each other. What first seemed a charming idiosyncrasy may in time become a grating nuisance. What once was a sexual turn-on may become boring and humdrum. Couples must be open to these changing patterns in their relationships and learn how to tolerate the changes (Bozon, 2002).

Have you ever had to recover from a broken heart? Describe the process. What suggestions might you offer to others going through a similar experience?

With time and change, it may also become evident that there are too many differences between two people to allow for a comfortable and fulfilling loving relationship and it no longer makes sense for them to remain together. The uncoupling process is almost always painful, but it may also represent a viable choice for a failing relationship in which one or both partners lack the desire and motivation to move to a new level of commitment (Gottman, 2000).

The bottom line is that love holds no guarantees. No matter how much lovers promise to be true to each other forever, there really are no guarantees against the possibility of one or both eventually choosing to end the relationship. Loving leaves a person vulnerable, so to choose to enter a loving relationship is to choose the risk of being hurt. This is one reason why knowing, understanding, and feeling good about yourself can be so crucial before you enter into a relationship.

The initial reactions that follow the breakup of a relationship may be quite varied. If the final days of the relationship have been troubled and full of turmoil, there may even be a sense of relief. Often there are intense feelings of loneliness and grief, accompanied by the sense of having been rejected or by guilt at having initiated the breakup. Anger is also a common emotional reaction and can represent a very healthy response. Anger that is expressed in ways that are not harmful is prevented from turning inward, where it can become depression and self-deprecation. Crying can also be a healthy release of emotion. Studies with college students have found that those whose attach-

ment style has been secure experience a less negative grief experience than do those who have preoccupied or fearful avoidant styles. This may well reflect their more positive feelings about themselves and the relationship. Dismissing avoidant types also do not have as much difficulty with separation, probably because they have not held their partners in particularly high esteem (Brehm et al., 2002).

Some people rush to put the pain of their loss behind them. They may even hurry into a "rebound" relationship to soothe their wounds. However, like any grieving process, the aftermath of a broken relationship must be given its time, and the painful reactions are best resolved by allowing them to be experienced. If you hurry them or try to escape from them, so that the breaking-up process remains incomplete, the reactions eventually will find new outlets in your life. They may make it difficult for you to be trusting and intimate in new relationships that eventually develop for you.

You need to recognize that losing a love is as much a part of life and loving as the joyful experience of falling in love. If you allow yourself to experience that process fully and seek whatever help and support you may need to get through it, you will eventually be able to put the painful aspects behind you and get on with your life and with new relationships.

Self-Evaluation

Communicating about Sex

One of the most necessary human processes, and yet one of the most complex and difficult, is communication. Many difficulties in relationships—including many sexual problems—are at least partly the result of lacking or misunderstood communications.

Thoughts, ideas, feelings, values, attitudes, opinions, needs, and desires are communicated not only verbally but also through eye contact, facial expressions, and body language. The questions and exercises in this section are designed to help you evaluate and facilitate your communication about sex with someone who is important to your life and therefore worth the effort. You might find some of the suggestions difficult to carry out, but good communication takes work.

Working on Communication: An Exercise for Two

The following exercise can help you and your partner improve your patterns of communication. Start by

rating each other, using the rating scale of 1–4, on the qualities listed below. Write your answers on separate sheets of paper without first discussing the rating scale or the qualities with each other.

Rating Scale:

4 = tops. He/she does a great job of showing this quality to me.

3 = okay. Most of the time I feel this from him/her.

2 = fair. I could really stand to have more of this quality from her/him.

1 = poor. I rarely, if ever, feel this from her/him.

*Rating of
Your Partner*   Qualities in Your Partner

_____   Is caring and considerate toward me.

_____   Is able to show warmth and love.

_____ Is sensitive and understanding toward my emotions.

_____ Lets me feel whatever I need to feel, without trying to talk me out of it.

_____ Seems to listen and really hear what I mean.

_____ Acts real and honest with me so that I can feel that he/she is being genuine.

_____ Treats me as an equal.

_____ Does not jump to conclusions or make snap judgments about me or others.

_____ Treats me with respect.

_____ Is trustworthy.

_____ Seems to trust me and shares inner feelings and thoughts with me.

When you have both finished your ratings, exchange them so that you each can take a look at how you were rated by the other. However, you both should agree to the following conditions.

1. **Do not talk about your reactions to the ratings for 15 minutes, during which time you should:**
   a. Think about why your partner might have rated you as he or she did. Assume that the ratings represent honest reactions.
   b. Think about which ratings made you feel best and which made you feel worst.
   c. Ask yourself if you were surprised by any of the ratings. Why or why not?
   d. Look beneath any anger you might feel or any need to "defend" yourself against a rating. If you are hurt, be ready to admit it. Keep in mind that your partner had a right to rate you in any manner that seemed honest to her or him. It can lead to a deeper understanding.

2. **When you are ready to start talking together about your mutual ratings:**
   a. You should agree on the most comfortable location.
   b. Share only your own feelings and reactions, being careful not to make assumptions and judgments about your partner's feelings or motivations. Use "I" messages.
   c. After one of you has had a chance to make a point, the other should spend some time summarizing what was heard so you can be sure you are hearing each other accurately. Clear up any misunderstandings that your partner has about anything you have said. Give each other time to do this. Now where do you go from here? If this exercise has shown you ways to improve your ability to communicate, are you ready to work toward this goal? Decide whether you think the two of you could work on particular areas.

Working on the Fundamentals

Certain basic qualities underscore good communication. Here are some ways to evaluate them.

1. *Lack of manipulation.* In healthy, two-way communication, there is no need for games or manipulation. Before proceeding any further, answer the following questions. Write down your answers.
   a. Why are you working on this section concerning communication?
   b. What are your short-term and long-term goals for improving communication with your partner?
   c. Do you have any ulterior or exploitative motives in pursuing communication about sex? If so, what are they?
   d. Do you really think you can face the vulnerability that comes with honest, two-way communication? Before answering, you might want to look through the remainder of this section. When you answer in the affirmative, proceed.

2. *A desire to involve your partner in communication.* There is no point in waiting. Communication takes at least two people. Now allow your partner to read this section, and share with him or her your answers to the previous questions. If your partner is willing, have him or her answer those same questions and share the answers with you. If you are both willing, proceed with the remainder of this section. It is designed for use by two people who together want to improve their communication about sex.

3. *Sense of equality.* Both of you should write your own answers to the following questions on separate sheets of paper. Do not compare any answers until both of you are finished answering all questions.
   a. Do you feel there is any difference in the general common sense possessed by you and by your partner? If so, which of you do you think has more of this quality?
   b. Does one of you tend to give in more to the other when there are disagreements? If so, who?
   c. Generally in your relationship, does one of you seem to emerge as the dominant partner and the other as the submissive partner? If so, which of you is which?
   d. Which one of you tends to initiate sexual contact most often?
   e. Are there any other factors that seem to lead to continuing feelings of inequality between the two of you?

   After each of you has written answers to all the questions, exchange papers and read them. Agree to the following: Do not make any comments for 10 minutes. Read each other's answers and silently think about them and about how you feel about them.

   Both of you should also read the following two paragraphs:

   As you are thinking about your partner's responses and comparing them to your own, can you detect that one or both of you see certain inequalities in your common sense, willingness to stick by points of view, degree of dominance, and/or willingness to initiate sex?

Two-way communication seems to work best when there is a sense of equality between both partners. Otherwise, there is the danger of one person feeling inadequate to deal with conflicts and disagreements in communication. With this in mind, proceed to part 4.

4. *Working at it.* Your answers to the questions in part 3 can provide some beginning topics for discussion.
   a. If both of you answered questions in a way that reflects nearly complete equality, you might want to move on to the next section of this communication questionnaire. If not, do part b.
   b. Go through the answers to your questions one by one, following these rules:
      1. *State only what you feel or think, without making any judgments or assumptions about what the other person is feeling or thinking or about the other person's accuracy.*
      2. *After one of you has made "I feel ..." and "I think ..." statements about the answers to one question, the other person should take time to summarize what has been heard. Then the first partner should clarify any misunderstandings. Do this with each of the questions. If anger or hostility develops, proceed with rule 3.*
      3. *If you are feeling angry or resentful, try to pause, look beneath your negative feelings, and see what is at their root. Perhaps you are really feeling some hurt or sense of threat. Look honestly at what you are feeling and share it with your partner.*
      4. *Persist with this process until you both feel some real sense of resolution about the differences of opinion that have arisen. If you feel stumped by this, you might want to consider consulting an outside person to talk over some of these issues with you.*
      5. *When you both feel ready, continue with the remaining parts of this communication exercise.*

Sharing Sexual Attitudes and Values

An important part of communication is letting your partner know your personal attitudes and values about sex. The following exercises can help you get started.

1. **Turn back to the sexual attitude questionnaire in Chapter 1, page 28.** If you have not already done so, both of you should complete your ratings for each attitude statement on separate sheets of paper. Go through the questionnaire item by item and compare your present ratings. For those items where you show a difference of opinion, talk about those differences. If either of you

begins to feel anger or tension during the discussion, you might want to try using the approaches in exercise 4b. Remember, it is perfectly all right to have different attitudes. The essential thing is to be able to accept these differences in each other. The key to acceptance is full understanding between partners.

2. **Now continue going through the sexual history section of the questionnaire in Chapter 1.** Share as many of your answers with your partner as you feel comfortable with. If both of you already feel very well acquainted with each other's backgrounds, you might try going through the questions one at a time, answering for your partner in the ways you think are most accurate. Your partner then can clear up any inaccuracies or misconceptions you seem to have concerning his or her sexual history. When you are finished with this process, summarize any new understandings you have gained about your partner.

3. **Here are some other issues that might be worth discussing with each other. You can skip any questions you prefer not to answer. Again, you may either share your answers with each other or try answering each question in the way you think your partner would answer it.**
   a. What is your opinion on abortion? Should it be legal and available to those women who wish to have an abortion? To what degree should the man be allowed to participate in the decision making about abortion?
   b. What sexual activities do you like best? Why?
   c. What are some of your wildest sexual fantasies? How do you feel about them?
   d. How do you feel about your partner's nude body? What parts of his or her body do you like most? Least?
   e. Have you ever participated in sexual activity that was in some way risky or that you have regretted? How do you feel about that now?
   f. What precautions do you consider essential to reducing the risk of contracting sexually transmitted diseases?

Nonverbal Communication

Very often, more can be communicated without words than with them. Following are some activities for nonverbal communication between you and your partner, with each activity becoming progressively more intimate. At any step, some verbal communication may be necessary to sort through difficult feelings that may surface. Before proceeding with each new stage of intimacy, there should be complete mutual agreement and willingness between the two of you. Each activity should continue until one of you feels ready to stop. Even if you both feel that your relationship has already reached deep levels of intimacy, it would be best to spend at least some time with even the earliest steps of the nonverbal communication process.

Activity 1. In comfortable positions, sit facing each other and look at each other's faces. Spend plenty of time looking into each other's eyes and attempting to express positive feelings. You might feel a little foolish and even feel like laughing; go ahead and get it out of your system.

Activity 2. Take turns touching and caressing each other's faces. The person being touched should close his or her eyes and fully enjoy the sensations. The person doing the touching should make an effort to convey warm, caring messages with the touches.

Activity 3. Take turns feeding each other a piece of fruit or some other food.

Chapter Summary

1. Women are more likely than men to have loved their first sexual partners.

2. Communication is key to healthy sexual relationships.

3. Any communicated message is filtered through the interpretive systems of both the sender and the receiver. There is a strong likelihood of misinterpretation and misunderstanding unless a feedback system is part of the process.

4. People often use slang terms, or no words at all, when making sexual references.

5. Communication can be hindered by the myths people believe and the sexual "games" they have learned to play in relationships.

6. Effective communication grows out of mutual commitment, shared understanding, mutual regard, avoidance of snap judgments, careful listening, empathy, genuineness, clear expression, viewing oneself positively, and appropriate confrontation.

7. As the Myers-Briggs Type Indicator demonstrates, there are very real personality differences among people that can have important implications for how they get along with another.

8. Males and females are taught different patterns for communicating as they grow up, and these differences show up in adult communication.

9. There are three main types of relational impasses: dread/anger, product/process, and power-over/power-with.

10. Effective conflict resolution involves approaching it as a couple, having clear ownership of the problem, and using "I" messages to communicate about it.

11. Research has elucidated some of the main characteristics correlated with lasting relationships; one factor is having five times as many positive behaviors toward each other as negative behaviors.

12. Healthy sexual sharing in a relationship involves being comfortable with one's own sexual needs, not confusing romance and sex, knowing how to risk vulnerability, and avoiding sexual coercion.

13. Cross-cultural studies suggest that love attitudes and behaviors may be affected more by individual differences than by genetics or social imperatives.

14. Infatuation or "falling in love" eventually ends; being in love involves a choice and a commitment to the process of being together.

15. There are three primary human emotion-motivation systems associated with love: lust, attraction, and attachment.

16. Sternberg's theory holds that love is a dynamic interaction of three components: intimacy, passion, and commitment.

17. Pheromones are chemicals that give off odors that may act as subliminal attractants to potential sexual partners.

18. Brain chemicals are related to the emotional experience of love following initial imprinting in earlier life. PEA, dopamine, and norepinephrine produce the high of attraction; endorphins produce the peacefulness of attachment; and oxytocin is associated with physical intimacy.

19. Sexual intimacy involves touching, relaxation, involved participation, and a realistic view of how romantic love and sex fit into relationships.

20. Same-gender relationships do not necessarily follow the heterosexual model. Most gay men and lesbians want long-term close relationships and exhibit three main patterns of relating.

21. Sometimes, friends must work out the place sexual attraction will have in their friendship.

22. The Internet is providing a new medium for intimate, and sometimes sexual, relationships to develop. Although some of these relationships seem

very positive, risks are associated with this form of connection.

23. Three main styles of attachment to others have been identified: secure, preoccupied, and avoidant, the last of which may be either dismissing or fearful.

24. Although a degree of jealousy and possessiveness is to be expected in any loving relationship, these qualities may become destructive if they are rooted in serious insecurities.

25. Loss of a loving relationship can be painful and often needs to be followed by a process of grieving.

Focus on Health Questions

In this section you will find the kinds of questions that you may have concerning your own health and sexuality. The page references indicate where in the text the answer is located; the exact place is marked with this logo: **FOH**

1. Most of the time I simply avoid telling my partner something I think will be hurtful. Isn't that better than causing emotional pain? **229**

2. My boyfriend never wants to tell me what's bothering him./My girlfriend just bores me with all that talk about intimacy. I just want to get on with it. How can we learn to understand each other better? **230**

3. Are sex and love the same thing? **245**

4. My partner seems unnecessarily jealous most of the time. What can I do to change the situation? **247–249**

5. How can I get over the end of my most important loving relationship ever? **249–250**

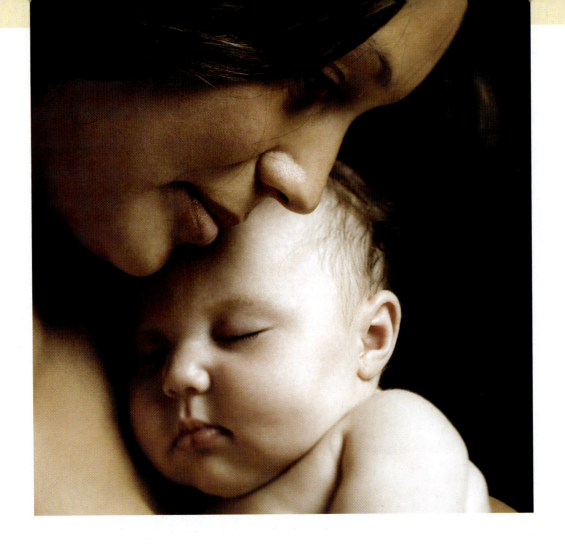

Part 3

*Human Reproduction,
Contraception, and Abortion:
Sexuality Confronts Social Policy*

Sexuality clearly is linked to the process of reproduction. Human biology gives most of us the capability of producing offspring. However, reproductive technology has made reproduction a far more complex issue than mere propagation of the species. For individuals who choose to have children but experience difficulty doing so, medical specialists now offer many forms of technological assistance, some of which have raised serious and complicated ethical questions. We live in an age of assisted reproductive technology.

Society continues to weigh and debate the complicated ethical and legal issues surrounding reproductive technologies, contraception, and abortion. Heterosexual intercourse typically carries the risks and choices relating to pregnancy. There are many ways in which the probability of pregnancy may be reduced, yet we are hardly living in the golden age of contraception. Development of new, more effective, and safer methods of birth control has lagged markedly in recent years, largely because research funding has been scarce. There is still a high rate of unintended pregnancy in our society. Couples fail to use contraception or they use it incorrectly, or it fails, leaving them with some difficult choices.

Reproduction is an important part of human sexuality's complex role in society and should not be taken lightly. The issues surrounding reproduction, contraception, and termination of pregnancy have become highly politicized as social policy evolves. Abortion is the cause of much polarization and political struggle. Human sexual reproduction is far more than a biological phenomenon; it has become a social and cultural controversy closely associated with cutting-edge biotechnology.

![Chapter 10 marker]

Chapter 10

Reproduction, Reproductive Technology, and Birthing

Chapter Outline

It looks as though our only chance to have a baby of our own will be by using in vitro methods. I feel like I am going to end up spending the kid's college education funds before he or she is even conceived. Sometimes the "investment" of time, emotion, and money seems strange, and rather scary.

—from a personal essay given to the author

Human sexuality and reproduction obviously are linked closely, both biologically and socially. The combining of genetic material in a way that produces another human being with characteristics of both parents is nothing short of a miracle. New understandings of reproduction, coupled with new biomedical technologies, have permitted these processes to be manipulated and transformed in ways that not long ago were considered science fiction.

Although reproduction of the human species once could not have taken place without sexual contact, reproductive technology now can intervene to bring sperm and egg together in a variety of ways. It is no longer even necessary for the genetic mother—the contributor of the egg—to be pregnant with the child that is eventually born. Indeed, reproduction and the prevention of reproduction have gone far beyond the realms of human sexuality and biology. Social policy, politics, legislation, court precedents, and ethical debate are now as much a part of understanding reproduction as is the age-old question "Where do babies come from?" This chapter addresses all these issues.

Fertilization and Fetal Development

During the menstrual cycle, an ovum matures and is released from one of the female's ovaries. Research indicates that fertilization of the ovum is most likely to occur when sperm are present during any of the six consecutive days of the cycle that end with the day of ovulation. The old assumption was that the most likely time for fertilization was during the two days following ovulation. However, there is also evidence that substantial numbers of women may ovulate more than once in a single menstrual cycle (Baerwald, Adams, & Pierson, 2003). As soon as semen is ejaculated from the penis into the vagina, the sperm begin their journey into the uterus, and they may remain viable for up to five days. A few thousand usually reach the fallopian tubes. The more sperm that are present, the greater the probability that fertilization, or conception, will occur. Sperm apparently have receptor molecules that are attracted to a sperm-attracting chemical released by the egg, and the membrane of the sperm cell contains a chemical called **fertilin** that seems to play a role in helping the sperm adhere to the egg and eventually penetrate its outer layer.

FIGURE 10.1 *Sperm Penetrating the Egg*

A sperm, with its oval head and long tail, approaches the egg, or ovum. Having been capacitated during its journey through the female reproductive tract, the sperm will secrete an enzyme that will help it penetrate the outer membrane of the ovum.

When a sperm cell comes into contact with the ovum, a very specific cell recognition process is triggered that binds the sperm tightly to the outer membrane of the ovum, or **zona pellucida.** The sperm then secretes enzymes that help it pass through the zona and its underlying membranes to penetrate into the ovum; the proteins on the surface of the ovum change rapidly, making the "lock-and-key" approach of fertilization a constantly evolving process. Usually, only one sperm manages to burrow its way into the interior of the ovum (see Figure 10.1), because a hard protein surface develops that prevents further sperm from entering. The actual mechanisms of sperm penetration and exclusion of other sperm are still only partially understood. If an extra sperm enters an ovum, it may well destroy the ovum, or its own genetic material may be destroyed. As the sperm passes through the outer layers of the ovum, it probably is primed by the hormone progesterone for the actual fertilization process. Contact with the zona pellucida seems to be essential to causing **exocytosis,** in which

fertilin (fer-TILL-in) a chemical in the outer membrane of a sperm that assists in attachment to the egg cell and penetration of the egg's outer membrane.

zona pellucida (ZO-nah pe-LOO-sa-da) the transparent, outer membrane of an ovum.

exocytosis (ex-oh-sye-TOH-sis) the release of genetic material by the sperm cell, permitting fertilization to occur.

the sperm cell opens to allow its chromosomes to be released into the ovum. The combining and pairing of chromosomes from both the sperm and the egg allow fertilization, or conception, to occur. A fertilized ovum is called a **zygote.**

Not only does fertilization initiate the growth of a new human being, but inherited traits are determined at the moment of conception as well. Both the ovum and the sperm contain 23 chromosomes, each bearing genes that contain hereditary information stored in the form of **deoxyribonucleic acid (DNA)** (see Figure 10.2). In the combining and pairing of these 46 chromosomes, essential programs for the individual's heredity are initiated. It is the pairing of sex chromosomes at fertilization that determines the sex of the developing embryo—XX for female, XY for male. The process of sexual differentiation and its implications for later development are discussed in more detail in Chapter 5, "Developmental and Social Perspectives on Gender."

Twinning and Other Multiples

Giving birth to twins, triplets, and other multiples always creates attention and excitement: The more babies born, the more excitement. In the last two decades of the twentieth century, the number of twin births rose by about half, and the number of higher-order multiple births almost quadrupled. Twins now occur in about 30 out of every 1,000 births in the United States, and triplets occur about once in 1,341 births. As Figure 10.3 demonstrates, the rates of multiple births have been increasing markedly in recent years, in small part because children are being born to older mothers, who are more prone to multiple births, but largely because of increased use of fertility drugs (Martin & Park, 1999). These drugs stimulate the ovaries to release more than one ovum in order to enhance the chances of conception taking place and have been shown to be highly successful in yielding pregnancy for infertile couples (Guzick et al., 1999). However, because the risks to both the babies and the mother increase with the number of fetuses, physicians are using fertility drugs with greater care, and there is evidence that lower dosages of the drugs may reduce the incidence of multiple pregnancies (Gleicher et al., 2000). Nevertheless, the number of births of quadruplets (four babies) or more increased from 269 in the United States in 1989 to 361 in 1994. Septuplets (seven babies) have also been born to a couple in the United States who used a fertility drug.

Twins may be either **fraternal twins,** formed from two separate ova fertilized by two separate sperm, or **identical twins,** formed by a single ovum and sperm. Fraternal twins may also be called *dizygotic* because they are produced from two zygotes, whereas identical twins are sometimes called *monozygotic* because they have come from a single zygote. In the case of fraternal twins, the two zygotes develop separately, and the

■ FIGURE 10.2 *DNA*

This model of a molecule of deoxyribonucleic acid (DNA) clearly shows its double helix shape. DNA is the building block of heredity, containing within it the genetic code that produces a specific type of offspring. Scientists hope that by learning more about DNA they will be able to prevent genetic diseases and control some aspects of the reproductive process. Skeptics point to some of the risks involved in manipulating the structure of genes.

---

zygote an ovum that has been fertilized by a sperm.

deoxyribonucleic acid (DNA) (dee-AK-see-rye-bow-new-KLEE-ik) the chemical in each cell that carries the genetic code.

fraternal (dizygotic) twins twins formed from two separate ova that were fertilized by two separate sperm.

identical (monozygotic) twins twins formed by a single ovum that was fertilized by a single sperm before the cell divided in two.

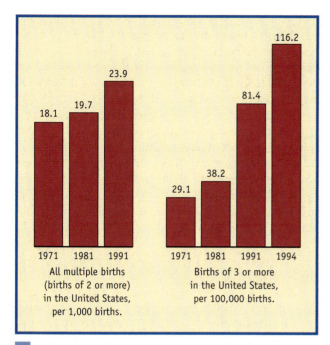

■ FIGURE 10.3   *Multiple Births in the United States*

As statistics from the National Center for Health Statistics demonstrate, the number of multiple births in the United States has been increasing over recent decades. The use of fertility drugs probably constitutes the most significant reason for the increase, although the older ages of mothers may also be a factor because older women are more likely to have multiple births.

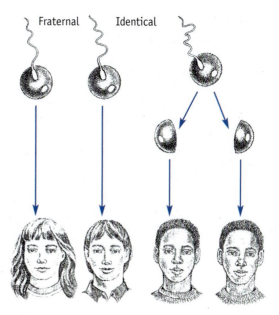

FIGURE 10.4   *Twins*

Fraternal, or dizygotic, twins are formed from the fertilization of two separate ova by two separate sperm. Identical, or monozygotic, twins are formed from the same fertilized ovum that divides before implantation in the uterus.

twins look no more alike than any other siblings in the family. They may be of the same or different sexes. In the case of identical twins, when the first division of the zygote occurs, the two cells separate and develop as two individuals. Because they have exactly the same chromosomes, they are of the same sex and are identical in appearance (see Figure 10.4). Triplets, quadruplets, and other multiple fetuses may all be fraternal or may include one or more sets of identical twins. Identical triplets and higher-order multiples are extremely rare, except when fertility drugs are being used (Gleicher et al., 2000).

The development of multiple fetuses increases the risk of premature birth and birth defects for the baby and may cause other problems for the pregnant woman. The higher the number of fetuses, the greater the likelihood of premature birth, low birth weight, birth defects, or death of an infant before birth or within the first year after birth. When one of the fetuses has some sort of defect, the likelihood of problems in the pregnancy increases even more. The rate of premature birth for twins is nearly 50 percent, compared to 10 percent for single births, and is about 90 percent for multiple births of more than two. The mother faces an increased risk of serious bleeding, high blood pressure, and metabolic disturbances.

To counteract the tendency of fertility drugs to increase the rate of multiple births, a controversial new procedure became available in medical practice. **Selective reduction** involves selectively aborting one or more fetuses in large-multiple pregnancies so that a lower-risk number of two or three remains. In the past, when multiple fetuses were discovered, the couple had the option of either doing nothing and taking their chances on a successful outcome or terminating the entire pregnancy. They now have this third option available, although it may represent a difficult choice. Nonetheless, the selective reduction technique has succeeded in reducing the number of premature multiple births and their accompanying complications.

Implantation of the Embryo

After fertilization has occurred, the zygote begins a process of cell division as it continues to move through the fallopian tube toward the uterus (see Figure 10.5). The first division produces two cells, these both divide to form four, and so on. With each cell division, the chromosomes are replicated so that every new cell has

selective reduction   the use of abortion techniques to reduce the number of fetuses when there are more than three in a pregnancy, thereby increasing the chances of survival for the remaining fetuses.

FIGURE 10.5 *Cell Division*

Four new cells of the forming embryo. Following fertilization of the ovum by the sperm, their chromosomes join, and the genetic plan to produce an embryo is set into motion. The zygote, or fertilized ovum, begins to undergo cell division, first producing two cells, then four, and so on. Each new cell receives a complete set of 46 human chromosomes, programmed to produce an entirely new human being.

a full complement of hereditary material. Within three days, a spherical, solid mass of cells has formed, called the **morula.** By the end of the fifth day after fertilization, the sphere has developed a fluid-filled cavity in its interior and is called the **blastocyst.** By this time, the mass of dividing cells has left the fallopian tube and entered the uterine cavity. Because there is no rich source of nourishment, the cells are not growing, and the blastocyst is not appreciably larger than the original ovum.

About a week after fertilization, the blastocyst comes into contact with the uterine lining, or endometrium. By this time the blastocyst has developed specialized cells that secrete a chemical called L-selectin, which in turn binds to structures that have been formed by the endometrium. Further chemical changes cause the blastocyst to adhere to the uterine lining more tightly and then to burrow into it (Fazleabas & Kim, 2003). The specialized cells of the blastocyst also form blood vessels that grow toward the blood vessels of the uterus. The blastocyst becomes implanted in the uterine wall and is now considered an **embryo,** poised to undergo a series of dramatic changes in growth and development (see Figure 10.6). Occasionally, a blastocyst becomes implanted in a fallopian tube or strays into the abdominal cavity and attaches itself to some other tissue, where it continues to develop as an embryo. This is called an **ectopic pregnancy,** and the embryo must be surgically removed to prevent rupture of the tube and bleeding. Complica-

tions of ectopic pregnancy constitute the seventh leading cause of death during pregnancy. The rate of ectopic pregnancies has risen dramatically, and researchers have speculated that this may be due to the use of fertility drugs or to increases in societal stress and sexually transmitted disease.

Typically, a baby is born after about 266 days (approximately nine months) of development in the uterus. There are wide variations in the length of pregnancy, however. During that period, the fertilized ovum develops into an infant capable of living outside the uterus and weighing about 6 billion times more at birth than at the time of fertilization.

Extraembryonic Membranes and the Placenta

Early in embryonic development, several extraembryonic membranes essential to the embryo's survival are formed from some of its specialized cells. The membrane that creates a sac to enclose the embryo is called the **amnion.** The sac is filled with fluid, which keeps the embryonic tissues moist and protectively cushions the embryo. The amniotic sac, also called the bag of waters, breaks just before birth, releasing its clear watery fluid through the vagina. Two membranes, the *yolk sac* and the *allantois,* seem to function only in early embryonic development and gradually become partly incorporated into the **umbilical cord.** The outermost extraembryonic

---

morula (MOR-yuh-la) a spherical, solid mass of cells formed after three days of embryonic cell division.

blastocyst the ball of cells, after five days of cell division, that has developed a fluid-filled cavity in its interior and has entered the uterine cavity.

embryo (EM-bree-o) the term applied to the developing cells when, about a week after fertilization, the blastocyst implants itself in the uterine wall.

ectopic pregnancy (ek-TOP-ik) the implantation of a blastocyst somewhere other than in the uterus, usually in the fallopian tube.

amnion (AM-nee-on) a thin membrane that forms a closed sac around the embryo; the sac is filled with amniotic fluid, which protects and cushions the embryo.

umbilical cord the tubelike tissues and blood vessels originating at the embryo's navel that connect it to the placenta.

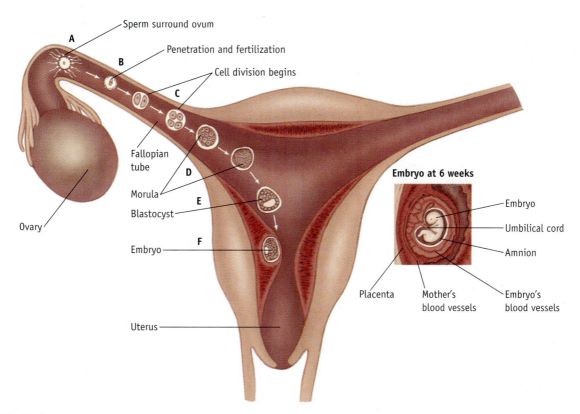

Sperm surround ovum

A

Penetration and fertilization

B

Cell division begins

C

Fallopian
tube

D

Morula

E

Blastocyst

F

Embryo

Ovary

Uterus

Embryo at 6 weeks

Embryo

Umbilical cord

Amnion

Placenta   Mother's
blood vessels

Embryo's
blood vessels

FIGURE 10.6   *Blastocyst Implantation and Placement Function within the Uterus*

After hundreds of sperm surround the ovum **(A)**, one penetrates and fertilizes it **(B).** Cell division begins **(C)** and after three days produces a spherical mass called a morula **(D).** The fifth day after fertilization, the mass develops into a hollow sphere of cells called a blastocyst **(E)** and within a week implants in the uterine lining; it is now considered an embryo **(F). (Insert)** The developing embryo receives nourishment and oxygen from the mother's blood through the placenta and returns embryonic waste products back through it. This exchange takes place through the umbilical cord, which connects the fetal and maternal circulatory systems.

membrane is the **chorion.** It plays an essential role in the formation of the **placenta,** the structure that provides nourishment for the embryo. The chorion produces small fingerlike projections, called **villi,** that grow into the uterine tissue and form a major part of the placenta. It is within the placenta that blood vessels from the embryo come into close contact with blood vessels from the mother, although there is no actual intermingling of the two bloodstreams. When the blood vessels are in close proximity, however, food molecules and oxygen from the maternal blood diffuse into the embryo's blood. Carbon dioxide and other metabolic wastes diffuse from the embryo's blood into the mother's blood, and her body then disposes of them through the lungs and kidneys. The embryo is connected to the placenta by the umbilical cord, which forms during the fifth week of pregnancy. It is through the umbilical cord that the embryo's blood vessels pass into and out of the placenta (see Figure 10.6, insert).

Usually, after two months of development the embryo is called the **fetus.** It is beyond the scope of this book to detail embryonic and fetal development. However, from the moment of conception to the time a baby is born, remarkable changes occur. An entire human body develops, with internal systems that can

chorion (KOR-ee-on) the outermost extraembryonic membrane, essential in the formation of the placenta.

placenta (pla-SEN-ta) the organ that unites the fetus to the mother by bringing their blood vessels close together; it provides nourishment and removes waste for the developing baby.

villi fingerlike projections of the chorion that form a major part of the placenta.

fetus the term given to the embryo after two months of development in the womb.

function to support life and enable the fetus to move and react to stimuli (see Figures 10.7 to 10.10). Figure 10.11 summarizes some of the important stages of fetal development.

Reproductive and Fetal Technology

In recent years, many important social, legal, religious, personal, and ethical questions have been raised by biotechnological advances in the areas of genetic manipulation, gamete retrieval and storage, fertilization, implantation, and medical manipulation of the embryo and fetus. These developments sometimes are collectively called **assisted reproductive technology (ART).** The first "test-tube baby" was born in England in 1978. In the United States today, more than 80,000 babies are born each year as the result of fertility drugs and various other assisted reproductive technology techniques. These techniques have called into question some fundamental assumptions about sex, reproduction, and family structure. In cases where one woman contributes an egg and another woman carries the baby, which is the biological mother? It is even possible for a woman to give birth to her own grandchild. The new ability to become pregnant following menopause challenges age-old concepts of human development. Reproductively, it is already a brave new world. Yet social policies have been slow to adjust to the many ethical and moral issues and decisions that have emerged (Djerassi, 1999; Van der Ploeg, 2002).

We have moved beyond the time when we have to rely exclusively on chance in reproductive sex. Scientists are developing the means to manipulate genes and reproductive processes so that many options are available. Yet the new technologies are controversial because of their medical and ethical implications. There are often risks as well as advantages for both the mother and the fetus (Schieve et al., 2002). There is also the continuing concern that women are being viewed as reproductive vessels to be manipulated by science rather than as human beings. The bypassing of the natural processes of reproduction raises new doubts and concerns about the roles men and women will play in the future of human procreation.

See "Designer Babies" on SexSource Online.

Genetic Engineering and Gene Therapy

Research has yielded significant information on how genes function. The types of offspring produced by sexual reproduction depend on the gene combinations formed during the fertilization of a random sperm and egg. Genes convey chemical messages to cells, causing them to carry out particular functions for which the cells are responsible. The genetic code that determines the traits of the offspring is contained in strands of DNA. The heritable traits of human beings are essentially the result of that random combination and indeed have been at the mercy of the process. Molecular geneticists, however, are continuing to learn more about how genes work and how they can be modified. Scientists are perfecting techniques for removing genetic material from one cell, combining it with genes from another, and implanting the recombinant DNA into a host cell. This results in cells that have a new genetic makeup and therefore new characteristics. Whole new species of microorganisms have sometimes been produced in this manner.

Controlling cellular functioning through the manipulation of genetic material, called **genetic engineering,** has the potential for producing tremendous benefits. It has already been put to a number of agricultural uses. Research is also under way to develop **gene therapy** techniques for treatment of the more than 4,000 human disorders that have genetic causes, such as hemophilia, sickle-cell anemia, some disorders of the immune system, certain types of diabetes and heritable developmental disabilities, diseases of the liver and lung, cystic fibrosis, and Alzheimer's disease. Gene therapy is still too inefficient to be helpful in most cases today, but improved techniques are expected to create a medical revolution within the next three or four decades. Amid growing concerns about lack of monitoring in gene therapy research, the National Institutes of Health are calling for closer regulation of the work (Couzin & Kaiser, 2005).

What are some moral and ethical implications of genetic engineering?

Scientists have completed work on the Human Genome Project, creating a complete map of the human genome, the DNA structure that makes a human being.

assisted reproductive technology (ART) a collection of laboratory techniques that have been developed to help couples overcome infertility problems and have children, usually through bypassing one of the usual biological pathways to pregnancy or gestation.

genetic engineering the modification of the gene structure of cells to change cellular functioning.

gene therapy treatment of genetically caused disorders by substitution of healthy genes.

■ **FIGURE 10.7** *Spine of Embryo at Six Weeks*

At six weeks of development, the embryo floats in the fluid of its amnion. In this rear view of the embryo, its developing spinal cord may be seen clearly, flanked by its two red vertebral arteries. The yolk sac, seen at the lower left of the photograph, eventually will become incorporated into the umbilical cord.

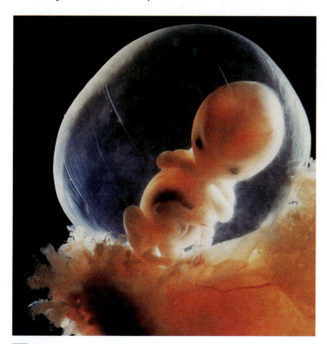

■ **FIGURE 10.8** *Embryo at Seven Weeks*

At seven weeks, the embryo is nearly an inch long, and both its internal and external organs are rapidly forming. Facial features are beginning to take shape, and the skeleton is developing internally. The fontanel, or soft area in the center of the developing skull, is clearly visible in this picture.

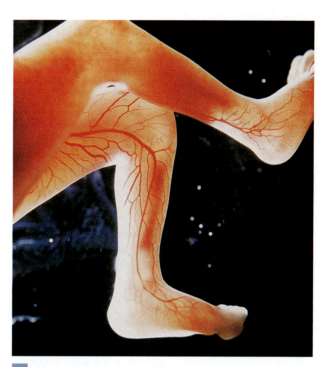

■ **FIGURE 10.9** *Legs of Fetus at Four Months*

The blood vessels and developing bones are visible in the legs of this four-month (6.4-inch) fetus. The skeleton is first formed from cartilage. Bone tissue then begins to grow out from the middle of the cartilage toward both ends. Bone development is not fully completed until an individual reaches about age 25 years.

■ **FIGURE 10.10** *Fetus Sucking Thumb at $4\frac{1}{2}$ Months*

At 4½ months, the fetus has formed its human features and proportions. Survival reflexes, such as the sucking reflex, are already able to function. This photograph provides a startling demonstration of the potential for thumb-sucking in a fetus that is only halfway to full-term.

		Prenatal Development	Changes in Mother
1 Month		Fertilization occurs. Zygote implants itself in the lining of the uterus. Rapid cell division occurs. Embryonic state lasts from 2 weeks to 8 weeks. Cells differentiate into 3 distinct layers: the ectoderm, the mesoderm, and the endoderm. Nervous system begins to develop. Embryo is ½ inch long.	Possible morning sickness, or nausea, and fatigue. Breasts may begin to feel tender. No weight gain.
2 Months		Heart and blood vessels form. Head area develops rapidly. Eyes begin to form detail. Internal organs grow, especially the digestive system. Sex organs develop and gender can be distinguished. Arms and legs form and grow. Heart begins to beat faintly. Embryo is 1 inch long and weighs ¹⁄₁₀ ounce.	Increased frequency of urination. Possible nausea and tiredness. Constipation, heartburn, and indigestion may begin in the second month and last throughout the pregnancy. Breast tenderness. No noticeable weight gain.
3 Months		Head growth occurs rapidly. Bone formation begins. The digestive organs begin to function. Arms, legs, and fingers make spontaneous movements. Fetus is 3 inches long and weighs 1 ounce.	Perspiration may be increased. Possible nausea. Continued need to urinate more frequently than usual. Breast heaviness and tenderness. Small weight gain (2–3 pounds).
4 Months		Lower parts of the body show rapid growth. Bones are distinct in X rays. Reflex movement becomes more active. Heartbeat can be detected. Sex organs are fully formed. Fetus is 7 inches long and weighs 5 ounces.	Belly begins to show. Faint movement of the fetus may be felt. Fatigue. Decrease in frequency of urination. Increase in appetite. Morning sickness may diminish or end. Weight gain in month 4: 3–4 pounds.
5 Months		A fine, downy fuzz covers the entire body. Vernix (a waxy coating) collects over the body. Ears and nose begin to develop cartilage. Fingernails and toenails begin to appear. Fetus may suck thumb, hiccup, and kick. Fetus is 12 inches long and weighs 14 ounces.	Possible shortness of breath. Possible fluttering movements as fetus stretches. Possible food cravings. Pelvic joints begin to relax. Weight gain in month 5: 3–4 pounds.

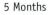

FIGURE 10.11   *Embryonic and Fetal Development and Changes in the Mother's Body*

Source: From Terry F. Pettijohn, *Psychology: A Concise Introduction,* 3d ed. 1992, Guilford, CT: Dushkin Publishing Company, The March of Dimes, and Earth Surface Graphics.

	Prenatal Development	Changes in Mother
6 Months	Eyes and eyelids fully formed. Fat is developing under the skin. Fetus is 14 inches long and weighs 2 pounds.	Possible backache. Fetus's movements now usually felt. Weight gain in month 6: 3–4 pounds.
7 Months	Cerebral cortex of brain develops rapidly. Fetus is 16 inches long and weighs 3 pounds.	Fetus is very active. Possible blotchy skin, which will clear up after the baby is born. Ankles may swell from standing. Possible backache. Weight gain in month 7: 3–4 pounds.
8 Months	Subcutaneous fat is deposited for later use. Fingernails reach beyond the fingertips. Fetus is 17 inches long and weighs 5 pounds.	Occasional headaches, backache, difficulty sleeping. Weight gain in month 8: 3–5 pounds.
9 Months	Hair covering the entire body is shed. Organ systems function actively. Vernix is present over the entire body. Fetus settles into position for birth. Neonate is 21 inches long and weighs 7 pounds.	Uterus has now moved a few inches lower. Feeling of heaviness in lower abdomen. Ankle swelling. Shortness of breath. Weight gain in month 9: 3–5 pounds. Total weight gain: 20–29 pounds.

In one of the largest-scale research projects ever attempted, international efforts mapped the 3 billion bits of human DNA sequences. This map has already led to further types of genetic testing and therapy to diagnose and treat various genetic conditions, a development with tremendous implications for the future of medical science (Collins, Morgan, & Patrinos, 2003). Countries around the world have been debating the ethical consequences of this work and have reached a degree of consensus in several different areas. It is agreed, for example, that information gained through genetic testing should be utilized with great caution and with the individual's full knowledge. Because this information will make predictions of future medical conditions more accurate, many people may ultimately want to preserve their right *not* to know. Similarly, the need for privacy is clear, because knowledge about an individual's genetic makeup might be used in making decisions about employment, parenthood, and health insurance coverage (Kaiser, 2005; Rosenberg & Schechter, 2000).

Mapping, testing, and treatment of the genetics of complex human traits still have a long way to go, but progress is being made. Various forms of genetic testing already allow early detection of certain genetic disorders. Using technology (described later in this chapter) to obtain fetal cells, scientists can now analyze them for possible chromosomal abnormalities. Couples who are concerned about the possibility of transmitting a genetic disorder to their offspring can be tested to determine the likelihood of such an event. People who fear a genetic disorder common in their families also may want to be tested to see if they carry the gene that might predispose them to the disease. For genetic disorders that do irreversible damage to the fetus before birth, techniques are being developed whereby gene therapy could be administered to the fetus while it is still developing in the uterus (Kaiser, 2005). Gene therapy has been used in France to provide a cure for seventeen infants born with an immune disease, although three of the children subsequently developed a type of leukemia. These kinds of results are considered predictable challenges for this new form of medical treatment (Couzin & Kaiser, 2005; Dave, Jenkins, & Copeland, 2004).

Genetic testing has raised certain ethical and social issues. For example, if a fetus is found to have a defective gene, should it be aborted? Who should be allowed access to information concerning potential risks of inherited diseases? In some cases, insurance companies have refused health insurance to couples who have a greater likelihood of giving birth to a child with some genetic disorder. Some states have passed legislation prohibiting discrimination by employers on the basis of genetic traits; there are no clear guidelines as to who should have access to genetic testing information. Public health policy will need to be reshaped to address the many issues of privacy, protection, and safety created by gene therapy. Although some factions argue that gene manipulation should be prohibited as an undesirable tampering with nature, others counter that, in a sense, all medical science represents a tampering with nature (Merikangas & Risch, 2003).

Artificial Insemination

Artificial insemination, or the placing of donated semen in the woman's vagina or uterus without intercourse, has been available for over 200 years, although it was not considered standard medical practice until the 1930s. During the following decade, it was discovered that human semen could be frozen quickly in liquid nitrogen without damaging sperm cells. The first baby conceived from frozen semen was born in 1954.

This method of impregnation is used most typically with couples in which the man's sperm count is low (fewer than 40 million sperm per milliliter of semen) or, in extreme cases, zero, rendering it difficult or impossible for him to impregnate his partner. Although one approach involves concentrating the sperm count from several of the man's own semen specimens, it has not proved especially successful. A more common method is to use semen contributed by an anonymous donor, chosen for characteristics of good health, intelligence, and physical traits similar to those of the intended "father." The semen may be frozen or used fresh, after the donor has been tested for possible HIV infection. For males who are infected with HIV, techniques are being developed by which the virus may be removed from the semen so it can be used for reproduction (Marina, 1998).

The semen is inserted by a physician into the back of the woman's vagina, near the cervix. The pregnancy rate in artificial insemination ranges from 60 percent to 75 percent. The procedure sometimes is used by couples without medical assistance, carried out by the couples themselves with common kitchen devices such as a basting syringe. Lesbian couples and gay male couples, with the help of a cooperative friend, have used artificial insemination in order to have children.

Reproductive technology of this sort has led to legal clarifications related to the meaning and rights of parenthood, as courts must make decisions about complicated cases. In a California court case, a man fought to keep the children his wife had borne after being impregnated by another man's semen. The wife had sued him for custody when she wanted to leave with the children, but the judge ruled that because the man had raised the children as his own, he had no less right to retain custody than did an actual biological father. There have also been two cases in which the U.S. Social Security Commissioner has awarded benefits to a child whose father has died, even though the child was conceived from the man's frozen semen after his death. The commissioner has indicated that technological developments have necessitated a review of existing Social Security laws.

Tissue Transplants and Production and Storage of Gametes and Embryos

Some women and men are unable to produce eggs or sperm that are viable for reproduction. Scientists have had some success turning the embryonic stem cells of mice into both eggs and sperm that eventually can be used for the fertilization process, but such techniques have not yet been attempted with human cells. In time, it might well be possible to produce "artificial" or

artificial insemination injection of the sperm cells of a male into a woman's vagina, with the intention of conceiving a child.

replacement gametes (sperm and eggs) with the appropriate genetic composition of the man or woman who is trying to overcome some fertility problem (Vogel, 2003). In the meantime, ART must rely on the tissues and cells produced by human beings. In 2005, an infertile woman in Alabama received transplanted ovarian tissue from her identical twin sister. She subsequently was able to conceive a child, which she carried to full term in a normal pregnancy. Transplanting of ovarian tissue, as well as the uterus, may well emerge as a future reproductive technology (Del Priore et al., 2007; Silber et al., 2005).

New techniques have also facilitated the storage and handling of human gametes, allowing the advancement of other reproductive techniques. The preservation of sperm by quick-freezing techniques was a major advance in artificial insemination, because men could donate semen for storage in sperm banks to be used later as needed. This technique added efficiency and convenience to the procedure for all involved. Techniques continue to be developed for the freezing of human eggs, to be fertilized at a later time, and in 1997 the first babies were born from eggs fertilized after being frozen and stored.

In the early 1980s, Australian scientists began experimenting with the freezing of human embryos resulting from in vitro fertilization (IVF) for possible later uterine implantation. Their purpose was not only convenience and efficiency, but also the ability to withdraw several eggs in a single surgical procedure, fertilize them, and save them for future use. If one IVF failed, another embryo could then be tried, bypassing all the earlier stages of the technique. The first baby to result from a previously frozen embryo implant was born in 1987.

Numerous ethical issues have arisen surrounding the storage of gametes and embryos. A few years ago, a man proposed starting a sperm bank intended to "strengthen the human gene pool." He wanted to freeze semen from Nobel Prize winners, to be used in the insemination of particularly bright women. Classified advertisements occasionally appear in college newspapers, offering to pay thousands of dollars for the eggs of women who meet certain physical and intellectual criteria. The question of eugenics, or selecting human traits for improvement of the species, has always created controversy. On the most basic level, it becomes a question of who has the right to determine which characteristics should be preserved and fostered and which should be eliminated.

Couples who participate in ART in order to enhance their chance of having children often have several embryos stored for possible future use. The American Fertility Society has reported that the more than 300 fertility clinics in the United States probably have about 100,000 stored embryos. Couples usually are asked ahead of time what they want done with any leftover frozen embryos, which can be destroyed, offered to infertile couples, or used for research. Many want them donated to other couples, and there is a growing movement to promote embryo adoption (Smalley, 2003). Some ethicists feel they should not be destroyed, and others have suggested that they might even be saved for use by future generations. Although early animal research raised some concern that freezing embryos might increase the risk of later difficulties, most research with infants who developed from frozen embryos has not yet shown any greater risk of birth defects or developmental abnormalities. There are reports of abnormalities in a few cases, but whether the technologies used actually led to the problems is not fully understood (Schieve et al., 2002).

Society continues to grapple with the complex ethical and legal ramifications of storage banks for gametes and embryos. Ethical guidelines are being established to help decision makers of the future. It has been suggested that the biotechnical revolution in reproduction has implications as profound as those of the Industrial Revolution and that we are just as unprepared for them.

In Vitro Fertilization

Two fundamental steps must be taken in technologically assisted fertilization. One is to secure viable sperm and ova in the most efficient manner possible, and the other is to bring them together in a way that will maximize the chances of conception occurring. In the late 1960s, a team of English scientists began working with **in vitro fertilization (IVF),** a technique in which ova are fertilized by sperm in laboratory glassware. The first "test-tube baby" produced by IVF was Louise Brown, born in Oldham, England, in 1978. This is still the simplest and most frequently used procedure. Since then, more than 350,000 babies have been born as the result of IVF.

Many infertile women have blockages in the fallopian tubes that prevent the sperm and egg from meeting. IVF permits a woman who otherwise would be unable to conceive to have her own child. In the original technique, ova are removed, or harvested, from one of the woman's ovaries by a simple microsurgical technique and then are mixed with sperm cells from her partner, usually obtained through masturbation. Fertilization can be confirmed by microscopic examination, and the fertilized egg is then placed in the woman's uterus, which has been appropriately readied by hormonal treatment. If the process is successful, the embryo will implant in the uterine

in vitro fertilization (IVF) a process by which the union of the sperm and egg occurs outside the mother's body.

wall as would happen under natural conditions, and development of the fetus will continue.

In one variation on this theme, zygotes resulting from IVF are inserted directly into the woman's fallopian tubes, where they then move naturally down into the uterus and possibly implant. This procedure, called **zygote intrafallopian transfer (ZIFT),** seems to increase the chances of success from about 20 percent to about 24 percent.

Numerous clinics in the United States now offer IVF to infertile couples. A few thousand babies resulting from the IVF method are now born each year. IVF has generated many controversies, one of which is the use of **preimplantation genetic diagnosis (PGD)** to detect any possible defects. One or more cells may be removed from the blastocyst and then analyzed for chromosomal abnormalities. In the United Kingdom, embryos may be tested for possible genetic cancer risks prior to being used for IVF. If some disorder is detected by PGD, the embryo is destroyed, raising ethical concerns on the part of people who consider an embryo a viable stage of human life that should not be terminated. The medical profession generally considers implantation in the uterus to represent the beginning of actual pregnancy (Blackburn, 2006).

While in the United States the success rate of births from IVF averages about 20 percent, patients who have special risk factors—such as being older or having a history of repeated miscarriages—are less likely to be successful. Actual sperm–ovum fertilization is achieved about 60 percent of the time, but the chances of clinical pregnancy occurring with transplants of a single embryo are only about one in six. Beyond that, there is a one-third chance that the pregnancy will be ectopic or end in miscarriage. Success rates are improved when more than one embryo are transferred to a woman's uterus during a single treatment. The chance of pregnancy increases to 25 percent when four embryos are transferred, and to 26 percent with five or six embryos. However, use of multiple embryos increases the potential for multiple pregnancy, with its subsequent risks of miscarriage, premature delivery, and infant mortality at or soon after the time of birth.

Some fertility clinics have advertised inaccurately high IVF success rates of 25 to 50 percent, apparently referring to the estimated number of pregnancies achieved rather than the number of actual live births. It is therefore crucial that couples investigate any IVF clinic's length of service, success rates, costs, and manner of producing statistics on "success." Couples need to know whether all attempts to achieve IVF are included in the statistics or only those that result in actual fertilization and transfer of the embryo to the uterus. The financial stakes can also be high. Even a single treatment cycle can cost thousands of dollars, and the chances that it will yield a viable pregnancy are not that good. It has been estimated that the average couple seeking to have a child through IVF will spend more than $100,000. Because there is no guarantee of success, IVF may also exact a significant emotional toll in continuing disappointment. See Table 10.1 for a summary of various fertilization procedures and their costs.

Other Fertilization Technologies

One of the more complex and costly technological problems with IVF has been ensuring that enough viable sperm and eggs are available for the fertilization process. Alternative techniques have been developed to optimize the chances of conception, depending on the fertility problem involved. In about half of infertile couples, the man has a low enough sperm count to make conception impossible. In one technique designed to increase the likelihood of fertilization for such couples, eggs are removed from the ovary and injected through a catheter into the woman's fallopian tube. Sperm cells that have been separated from the partner's semen, thereby concentrating them, are then injected directly into the same area, making fertilization more likely. This procedure, called **gamete intrafallopian transfer (GIFT),** increases the chances of success to about 28 percent.

Another technique is **intracytoplasmic sperm injection (ICSI).** A single sperm cell is isolated in a microscopic pipette and then injected directly into an ovum that is being held in place by a slightly larger pipette (see Figures 10.12 and 10.13). Although this technique was originally developed in Belgium, it is being used with a 24 percent success rate in the United States. Research has indicated that infants conceived in this manner are about twice as likely to have major abnormalities compared to infants conceived naturally.

---

zygote intrafallopian transfer (ZIFT) a process by which zygotes resulting from IVF are inserted directly into the fallopian tubes.

preimplantation genetic diagnosis (PGD) examination of the chromosomes of an embryo conceived by IVF prior to its implantation in the uterus.

gamete intrafallopian transfer (GIFT) direct placement of the ovum and concentrated sperm cells into the woman's fallopian tube to increase the chances of fertilization.

intracytoplasmic sperm injection (ICSI) a technique involving the injection of a single sperm cell directly into an ovum; useful in cases where the male has a low sperm count.

Table 10.1 — Scientific Methods for Human Conception

Procedure	Method	First Successful Outcome with Humans	Cost	Success Rate
In vitro fertilization (IVF)	Dosing a woman with hormones to trigger superovulation, harvesting the eggs and then uniting them with the father's sperm in the laboratory. The resulting embryo is implanted in the mother's womb.	1978 (England)	About $7,800 for each attempt	18%
Gamete intrafallopian transfer (GIFT)	Using a laparoscope, a doctor inserts eggs and sperm directly into the woman's fallopian tube. Any resulting embryos travel naturally into her uterus.	1984 (United States)	$6,000 to $10,000 for each attempt	28%
Zygote intrafallopian transfer (ZIFT)	Eggs and sperm are combined in the laboratory. If fertilization occurs, the resulting zygotes are inserted into the woman's fallopian tube.	1989 (Belgium)	$8,000 to $10,000 for each attempt	24%
Intracytoplasmic sperm injection (ICSI)	Injecting a single sperm cell into an egg.	1992 (Belgium)	$10,000 to $12,000	24%
Immature oocyte collection	In a twist on conventional IVF, immature eggs are harvested from the ovaries, cultured in the lab, fertilized and transferred back into the woman's womb.	1991 (South Korea)	Not available	Not available

Source: From Denise Grady, "How to Coax New Life," *Time,* Special Issue, Fall 1996, p. 38. Copyright © 1996 Time, Inc. Reprinted by permission.

1. A micropipette 60 microns wide uses gentle suction to hold the egg.

2. A single healthy sperm is taken up by an even smaller pipette 7 microns wide.

3. The pipette with the sperm is carefully inserted into the egg, and the sperm is pumped out.

4. The pipette is withdrawn, allowing the egg to be fertilized. The fertilized egg is then implanted in the woman's uterus.

FIGURE 10.12   *Intracytoplasmic Sperm Injection*

Intracytoplasmic sperm injection, unlike conventional IVF, involves placing the sperm within the egg using a micropipette. About 60 percent of eggs fertilized this way are carried to term.

Source: From "New Method Aids Infertile Men," *New Haven Connecticut Register,* 14 November 1995.

FIGURE 10.13 *The Moment of Truth*
Injection of the egg with the sperm.

There are two ways in which the most viable sperm can be selected for use in ICSI. **Computerized sperm selection** uses a computerized scanning method that identifies the most motile sperm in a semen sample. These sperm are then individually removed by a microscopically fine pipette. For men who have anatomical abnormalities that interfere with transport of sperm out of the testes or whose sperm tend to have low motility, sperm may be suctioned directly out of the epididymis of the testes through a tiny pipette in a procedure called **microscopic epididymal sperm aspiration (MESA).** The technique has even been used to obtain sperm from men who have just died and whose wives wish to reserve the possibility of having their children. One controversial issue surrounding ICSI and related technologies for infertile men is the finding that males produced by such fertilization technologies are likely to perpetuate the genetic glitches that originally caused their fathers' infertility.

The most common technique presently used to obtain eggs from a woman for IVF involves daily fertility injections for a period of two weeks. The injections cause several ova to mature in the ovaries but may also have uncomfortable physical and emotional side effects such as bloating, pain, and mood swings. The ovaries are carefully monitored through daily blood tests and ultrasound techniques so that the mature eggs can be surgically removed at exactly the right time. IVF researchers in Australia are developing a new approach that may save a great deal of time and money and eliminate the need for fertility drugs. Called **immature oocyte collection,** this technique uses a specially designed needle to enter small, immature follicles in the ovary and remove immature egg cells, or oocytes. Cell-culturing processes are then used to ripen the immature eggs in the laboratory, readying them for IVF. Because much of the cost of IVF is associated with the treatment of the ovaries to produce mature eggs, this new process could trim the costs of IVF by as much as 80 percent.

What sorts of ethical controls do you feel should be exerted over reproductive technologies?

Another procedure allows one woman to donate eggs to another woman, whose mate's sperm may then be used for fertilization. This technique, called **ovum donation,** is used in women who have already reached menopause or have some ovarian condition that prevents them from producing healthy ova. Following IVF, the embryo is implanted into the uterus of the woman unable to produce eggs of her own. Some fertility clinics have established "egg banks," so that eggs can be made available to sterile women. In the procedure called **artificial embryonation,** a developing embryo is flushed from the uterus of the donor woman five days after fertilization and transferred to another woman's uterus. This technique has the potential for allowing otherwise infertile couples to go through a pregnancy and birth, although the child would not be genetically their own (Winter & Daniluk, 2004).

Ovum donation and artificial embryonation have helped some women defy their biological clocks, enabling them to become pregnant even after menopause

computerized sperm selection use of computer scanning to identify the most viable sperm, which then are extracted to be used for fertilization of an ovum in the laboratory.

microscopic epididymal sperm aspiration (MESA) a procedure in which sperm are removed directly from the epididymis of the male testes.

immature oocyte collection extraction of immature eggs from undeveloped follicles in an ovary, after which the oocytes are assisted to maturity by cell-culturing methods in preparation for fertilization.

ovum donation use of an egg from another woman for conception, with the fertilized ovum then being implanted in the uterus of the woman wanting to become pregnant.

artificial embryonation a process in which the developing embryo is flushed from the uterus of the donor woman five days after fertilization and placed in another woman's uterus.

What's Available Now

 Fertility Drugs
A woman usually produces one egg a month. These drugs can cause multiple eggs to ripen.

 In Vitro Fertilization
Eggs are harvested from the ovary and fertilized in a petri dish. After embryos begin to develop, they are placed in the uterus.

 Sperm Injection
Using an ultrafine needle, a single sperm is injected into an egg to achieve fertilization.

 Donor Egg
Eggs are taken from one woman and fertilized in a petri dish. The resulting embryos are implanted in another woman.

 Frozen Embryo
Extra embryos created during the in vitro process can be frozen and stored for future use.

What's on the Horizon

 Frozen Eggs
A woman's eggs are harvested and frozen for thawing and fertilization at a later date. The procedure is still experimental and not widely available.

 Frozen Ovaries
Sections of the ovaries containing immature eggs can be removed and frozen. When the eggs are needed, they may be thawed and matured.

 DNA Transfer
To bypass an older egg's less reliable cellular machinery, the nucleus of the older egg is swapped with that of a younger one.

 Cytoplasmic Donation
Cytoplasm from a younger egg can be added to an older one, improving chances that the receiving egg will develop properly.

 Improved Growth Media
New chemical solutions that mimic those in the female reproductive tract will make it possible to implant hardier, more mature embryos.

 FIGURE 10.14 *Infertility Treatment—Now and in the Future*

Source: From Michael D. Lemonick, "The New Revolution in Making Babies," *Time,* 1 December 1997, pp. 42–43. Copyright © 1997 Time, Inc. Reprinted by permission.

(see Figure 10.14). Although menopause causes a cessation of the production of viable eggs, the uterus of a postmenopausal woman sometimes can still support a pregnancy. Techniques have been developed that actually have enabled a number of post-menopausal women to bear children. In one controversial case, a 63-year-old woman told physicians she was 50 and then was treated over a three-year period before becoming pregnant with an IVF embryo formed from a donated ovum fertilized by her husband's sperm. Typically, such procedures are limited to women no older than 55. This case raised ethical issues about the advisability of defying nature in a way that allows older parents to bear children, because they will be relatively old as the child develops and matures. A few postmenopausal women have given birth to their own grandchildren, produced by IVF from their daughters' ova and sons-in-law's sperm. Some countries have considered legislation banning postmenopausal women from becoming pregnant through such techniques, although social commentators have pointed out that older men have never been prohibited from fathering children as long as their biology permits.

For the time being, these reproductive technologies are expensive, somewhat unreliable, or still in development. It is not likely that the expense and inconvenience would persuade anyone to use the procedures as a substitute for procreative sexual intercourse. Yet as the techniques are perfected and made more affordable, it is conceivable that they could be used by women who want their own genetic babies but are unwilling to become pregnant. Their embryos could be transferred to another woman for gestation. An even more startling step would be the complete in vitro gestation of a fetus in a laboratory until such time as it could be removed and be self-sustaining. Some scientists believe it will be only a matter of time and continued experimentation before someone produces a full-term, living baby outside the human body—a true test-tube baby.

Choosing the Sex of a Fetus

People usually are curious about the sex of a child before it is born. In fact, some couples would like to be able to choose the sex of their child ahead of time. Many folk methods purported to predetermine a child's sex have been described in various cultures, but reproductive technology has not yet been able to offer simple and reliable techniques for ensuring the outcome. There has been some evidence over the years that social and psychological factors might affect the sex determination of human offspring. For example, during and after major wars, more males than females are born, sometimes called the "returning soldier effect." The older the father and the younger the mother, the more likely the baby will be a boy. When the mother is older, it is more likely that the baby will be a girl.

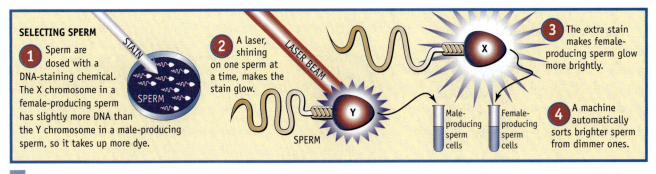

SELECTING SPERM

1 Sperm are dosed with a DNA-staining chemical. The X chromosome in a female-producing sperm has slightly more DNA than the Y chromosome in a male-producing sperm, so it takes up more dye.

STAIN

SPERM

2 A laser, shining on one sperm at a time, makes the stain glow.

LASER BEAM

SPERM

3 The extra stain makes female-producing sperm glow more brightly.

X

Y

Male-producing sperm cells

Female-producing sperm cells

4 A machine automatically sorts brighter sperm from dimmer ones.

FIGURE 10.15 *Selecting the Sex of Sperm*

Source: From Frederic Golden, "Boy? Girl? Up to You," *Time,* 21 September 1998, pp. 82–83. Copyright © 1998 Time, Inc. Reprinted by permission.

What are your opinions about being able to choose the sex of your child? Would you use technology to help you make such a choice?

A few approaches to selecting an infant's sex have emerged in modern technology. There are techniques by which either the X-bearing or the Y-bearing sperm may be sorted out before artificial insemination or IVF to increase the chances of the baby's being a girl or a boy. Though complicated and expensive, these techniques may increase the chances of having a girl to about 80 percent and the chances of having a boy to about 65 percent (see Figure 10.15). Other techniques have been suggested, including changing the diet prior to conception, timing intercourse to be slightly before or slightly after ovulation in the menstrual cycle, and modifying the pH of the vagina. Research has tended to indicate that such procedures do not produce statistically valid results and probably are worthless.

The ability to choose the sex of a child raises some troublesome ethical issues both for the parents and for society. Studies in the United States consistently demonstrate that couples tend to have a preference for sons, especially as their first child. Also, when parents have had two children of the same sex, either female or male, there is a greater likelihood that they will have another child. The preference for male children is found in many cultures and can translate into prejudice and sexism (Belanger, 2002). This has raised fears among some that predetermination of gender could create a population overweighted with males, while others feel couples should be free to use available technology for choosing the sex of their children and that the genders ultimately will balance out (Layne, 1999).

Techniques such as chorionic villi sampling or amniocentesis (see p. 278) can identify the sex of a fetus within a few weeks of conception by identifying the sex chromosomes in fetal cells. Newer, noninvasive techniques are able to detect the sex of fetal cells that may be found in small numbers in the mother's blood, but these techniques are not believed to be entirely reliable (Kaiser, 2005). Beyond simply discovering the sex of their expected child, parents then have the option of early abortion if the sex of the child is not what they have hoped for. This has become a common, though illegal, practice in China, where couples generally are allowed only one child. The ratio of males to females among live births in China has increased in some rural areas to as high as 140 males to 100 females. There is growing concern about the imbalance of males and females in China, and the government has decided to provide financial incentives to parents of daughters in an attempt to offset the trend. Similar trends are developing in India, Bangladesh, Pakistan, and South Korea. Such an inbalance may have profound social implications and eventually may require some new partnering patterns for first marriages (Glenn, 2004).

Ethical questions have also been raised about the use of costly medical resources and procedures for what might be seen as frivolous, nonmedical reasons, when

Source: Copyright © Tribune Media Services, Inc. All rights reserved. Reprinted with permission.

1. A Finn Dorset ewe provides the mammary cell for cloning.
2. A mammary cell contains copies of every gene needed to make a sheep, but only genes for proteins required by mammary cells are active.
3. Cells grow and divide, making carbon copies of themselves. But if the cells are starved of nutrients, they enter a quiescent state. At this point all of their genes can be activated.
4. A Scottish Blackface ewe provides the egg.
5. The egg, or oocyte, is kept alive in a laboratory dish.
6. The nucleus is removed from the egg.
7. The mammary cell and the egg fuse with a spark of electricity. Molecules in the egg then program genes in the mammary cell to produce the lamb embryo.
8. Clusters of embryonic cells are grown.
9. Embryos are implanted into a surrogate mother.
10. The lamb that results is a clone of the donor ewe.

Donor ewe · Isolated mammary cell · Quiescent cell poised for cloning · Fused cells · Multiplied cells · Surrogate mother · Genetic duplicate · Egg provider · Isolated egg · Oocyte

FIGURE 10.16 *Send in the Clones*

Scientists once thought that cloning an animal from an adult cell was impossible. Although every cell contains the complete genetic blueprint for making a new animal, those instructions cannot be read in adult cells because they have become specialists, producing cells only for a single body part. The Scottish team figured out how to turn on all the genes needed to clone a lamb from a single adult sheep cell.

Source: From Sharon Begley, "Little Lamb, Who Made Thee?" *Newsweek,* 10 March 1997, pp. 56–57. Copyright © 1997 Newsweek, Inc. All rights reserved. Reprinted by permission.

some women could not afford the procedures as valid medical treatment. It has been argued that if precedents are set in favor of gender selection, parents may begin selecting for characteristics such as height, weight, skin color, and so on. At this point, the techniques for sex selection are not frequently used in North America because they are unreliable and costly.

Human Cloning

Cloning is a reproductive technology that allows for duplication of genetic material so that the offspring are genetically identical either to the donating "parent" or to the other embryos being produced. The original cloning process bypassed even the fertilization stage. In 1968, Oxford University scientist J. B. Gurdon succeeded in replacing the nucleus of a frog's egg with the nucleus of an intestinal cell from another frog. The egg divided normally and eventually formed a tadpole

that became an adult frog. Because the new frog's cells contained exactly the same set of chromosomes as the frog that donated the intestinal cell, the two frogs were genetically identical. The exact-copy offspring is called a **clone.** A great public stir was created in 1997 when Scottish researcher Ian Wilmut introduced to the world a seven-month-old sheep clone named Dolly. She had been cloned from an udder cell of another sheep and represented the first known successful cloning of a mammal (see Figure 10.16). Subsequently, mice, cows, monkeys, pigs, and mules have also been successfully

cloning a process by which a genetic duplicate of an organism is made either by substituting the chromosomes of a body cell into a donated ovum or by separation of cells early in embryonic development.

clone the genetic-duplicate organism produced by the cloning process.

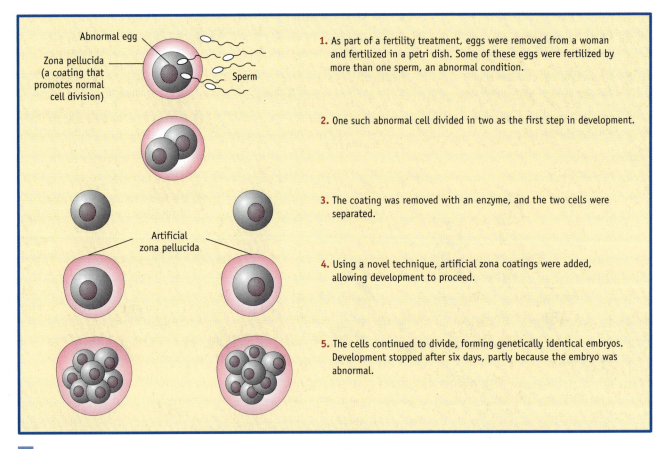

1. As part of a fertility treatment, eggs were removed from a woman and fertilized in a petri dish. Some of these eggs were fertilized by more than one sperm, an abnormal condition.

2. One such abnormal cell divided in two as the first step in development.

3. The coating was removed with an enzyme, and the two cells were separated.

4. Using a novel technique, artificial zona coatings were added, allowing development to proceed.

5. The cells continued to divide, forming genetically identical embryos. Development stopped after six days, partly because the embryo was abnormal.

FIGURE 10.17   *How Human Embryos Can Be Genetically Duplicated*

Duplicate human embryos, "clones" in the sense that their genetic material is exactly the same, were first created in 1993. Although it would be intended primarily to help infertile couples become pregnant, this "cloning" technique has raised serious ethical questions around the world and generally has been considered unethical. The original experiment summarized here used abnormal zygotes, and it was never intended that they be grown for very long.

cloned (Woods et al., 2003). Concerns continue to be raised about the potential for human cloning, and legislatures around the world have proposed laws to ban such work. Given the pace of scientific inquiry, the laws quickly become obsolete. Scientists are equally concerned that haphazard enactment of laws may well interfere with other forms of research that advance the techniques of medicine (Malakoff, 2003).

A variation of the cloning technique has been tried at the human embryonic level; this technique separates embryo cells at a very early stage of development. This "cloning" of embryos is of great interest because of the desire to produce embryos more easily for IVF. Embryonic "stem cells," which have the potential to differentiate into different kinds of cells that could be used to treat certain medical conditions, also could be produced through cloning techniques (Vogel, 2004). Although scientists have been successful in using experimental techniques to clone human embryos in vitro, they have made no attempt to gestate the embryos to maturity. The researchers worked with human ova that had been

fertilized by more than one sperm and thus constituted abnormal embryos. After the fertilized ovum had divided to form two cells, the protective zona pellucida was removed with an enzyme preparation so that the two identical cells could be completely separated. A new artificial protective coating, created from a gel derived from seaweed, was then placed around each cell, and the cells continued to divide for six more days. The development process stopped, apparently because the embryos were genetically abnormal from the time of fertilization (see Figure 10.17).

The purpose of this research was to investigate ways of producing extra embryos to be used for IVF that would avoid the complicated process of removing individual eggs from the ovary and fertilizing each of them with sperm. By using this variant cloning process, multiple embryos could be produced from a single fertilized egg and then stored for possible implantation at a later time. In essence, the researchers created identical twins, or other multiples, that hypothetically could be gestated and born at different times.

Public furor over such research, coupled with ethical doubts within the scientific community, has put much embryonic cloning research on hold (Malakoff, 2003).

Cloning raises fascinating ethical questions concerning the future of reproductive technology. For example, cloning techniques could be used to reproduce a child with exceptional characteristics and achievement for the same or different parents. Or parents might set aside genetic duplicates of each of their children so that if one died they could in theory produce another child who would look exactly the same. Another scenario posits the possibility of using cloned embryos to produce a genetic duplicate if a child needs a bone marrow or kidney transplant, eliminating the problem of immune system rejection. It is even possible that someday a woman could give birth to her own twin. Naturally, these controversial possibilities have raised the ire of many observers. Public opinion polls reflect a predominantly negative stance concerning cloning, although acceptance of a variety of reproductive technologies has been increasing in recent years. Men tend to be more accepting of these technologies than are women (Holden, 2003).

Several mammalian clones either have suffered from serious birth defects or have developed fatal conditions after seeming to be healthy at birth. This suggests that much remains to be learned about the action of genes within cloned animals. Like other reproductive technologies, cloning techniques surely will continue to be developed, and we must begin to prepare for the impact they will have for human sexuality and human life.

Embryo and Stem Cell Research

The complex ethical issues surrounding human embryo and stem cell research have entered the public policy and political arenas. The National Institutes of Health (NIH) have promulgated recommendations from an advisory committee indicating that it would be in the public interest to fund experimentation with human embryos in the early stages of development. Recognizing that moral issues are at stake as well, the NIH also has imposed restrictions on such research. Under pressure from the Bush administration and Congress, the federal agency has temporarily banned new embryo cloning and stem cell research by federally funded researchers, limiting research to cell lines produced previously. Many scientists consider such a tactic to be too conservative and blind to the potential medical value of such research (Kennedy, 2003). Because potentially significant financial gains may eventually emerge from stem cell research, it is likely that private funding will continue to support embryo research in the United States. Some other countries, including France, have banned most forms of embryo research altogether, while the United Kingdom has encouraged it. The controversies are bound to continue and surely will generate heated debate.

New techniques have allowed scientists to extract a single cell from an in vitro embryo without destroying the embryo. The cell then may be used to develop an entire line of stem cells that could be used in research. Such procedures, however, represent some level of risk to the embryo, resulting in continued reluctance to reopen the possibility of federally funded stem cell research in the United States as of the beginning of 2007 (Vogel, 2006).

Surrogate Motherhood

Surrogate motherhood, also called **gestational surrogacy,** has been a feasible reproductive procedure since the 1980s. Typically in these cases, a couple in which the woman is unable to bear children pays another woman several thousand dollars to carry a pregnancy for them. Sometimes the surrogate is inseminated by the infertile woman's husband, and sometimes an embryo formed from IVF of the couple's sperm and egg is implanted in the surrogate's uterus. A legal agreement is drawn up among the parties involved in which the woman who is to be impregnated promises to give the child to the couple when it is born.

The ethical and legal issues surrounding surrogacy were first put to the test in the 1987 "Baby M" case, in which a surrogate mother asked for the return of the child she had borne for another couple. The surrogate mother claimed in court that the intended mother had paid her to have the child because of a desire not to let pregnancy interfere with her own career. The woman and her husband, who had contributed the sperm for the child, argued that they had opted for surrogate motherhood because the woman suffered from multiple sclerosis. Eventually, the court allowed the couple to keep the child but also granted the surrogate mother some visitation rights because she had contributed the egg for conception. In 1993, building on previous state precedents, California's supreme court denied any rights to a surrogate mother who had given birth to a child who was the product of the egg and sperm of the couple who had contracted with her. In this case, the surrogate had no genetic relationship to the child. The court ruled that the surrogacy agreement was as valid as any other voluntary contract and

gestational surrogacy implantation of an embryo created by the sperm and ovum of one set of parents into the uterus of another woman who agrees to gestate the fetus and give birth to the child, which then is given to the original parents.

did not exploit the surrogate mother. Given the complicated issues that have been arising, numerous state legislatures have developed statutes to regulate gestational surrogacy.

Although some have hailed gestational surrogacy as a significant advance for childless couples, others have argued that it is nothing more than reproductive prostitution. It has been suggested that gestational surrogacy, which today can cost well over $25,000 including medical procedures, legal costs, and the fee paid to the surrogate, could represent the first step toward creating a caste of poor female breeders who would bear genetically improved children for upper-class couples. Opponents find little difference between this procedure and the long-prohibited practice of selling babies for private adoption. It has also been claimed that the legal protections for the surrogate mother are slim compared with those for the couple, further advancing the argument that surrogate motherhood represents a form of exploitation of women.

Fetal Technology and Medicine

Problems can occur during fetal development, but great strides are being made in diagnosing and even treating medical difficulties in the fetus. When techniques such as IVF are used, embryos can be genetically tested prior to implantation in the uterus. Beyond that point, several other procedures can be used to monitor the health and genetic makeup of the fetus.

FOH Amniocentesis

One well-known technique is **amniocentesis,** long used to detect certain chromosomal disorders such as Down syndrome. Recently, the American College of Obstetricians and Gynecologists has recommended that all pregnant women be tested to determine whether the fetus has chromosomal abnormalities, using either amniocentesis or one of the less invasive ultrasound procedures now available that can be used earlier in pregnancy (ACOG, 2007). In amniocentesis, a needle is inserted through the abdominal wall into the uterus and the amniotic sac to withdraw amniotic fluid (see Figure 10.18). Cells from the developing fetus may be found in this fluid and their chromosomes studied for possible abnormalities. If some birth defect is identified, the parents can make a decision about whether to continue or terminate the pregnancy. Analysis of chromosomes also can determine whether the fetus is female or male. Because some risks are associated with the procedure, including possible miscarriage, amniocentesis is not used routinely for sex determination. Pregnancy complications are significantly less common when amniocentesis is performed 16 to 19 weeks into pregnancy, compared to 11 to 14 weeks.

FIGURE 10.18   *Amniocentesis*

A woman, 16 weeks pregnant, undergoes the procedure of amniocentesis. Amniotic fluid is extracted from the uterus and analyzed. It will indicate the gender of the child as well as possible birth defects.

Chorionic Villi Sampling

Whereas amniocentesis cannot be used until the end of the fourth month of pregnancy, another diagnostic technique, called **chorionic villi sampling (CVS),** can be used as early as the eighth week. A thin catheter is inserted through the cervix, and a small sample of tissue from the chorionic membrane is withdrawn. The chromosomes in these cells then may be analyzed. Although it was once suspected that CVS was associated with a higher incidence of limb defects in infants, research has now demonstrated that the procedure actually is correlated with a decreased likelihood of such problems.

Ultrasound Images

A technique that has made amniocentesis and other fetal diagnostic methods possible is the use of ultrasound images, or **sonograms.** Ultrasonic waves are used to produce a computer-generated picture of internal

amniocentesis (am-nee-oh-sen-TEE-sis) a process by which medical problems with a fetus can be determined while it is still in the womb; a needle is inserted into the amniotic sac, amniotic fluid is withdrawn, and fetal cells then are examined.

chorionic villi sampling (CVS) a technique for diagnosing medical problems in the fetus as early as the eighth week of pregnancy; a sample of the chorionic membrane is removed through the cervix and studied.

sonograms ultrasonic rays used to project a picture of internal structures such as the fetus; often used in conjunction with amniocentesis or fetal surgery.

Real Student Voices

■ Pregnancy is very scary to me at this point in my life. That's why I always insist that we use a condom every time even though I'm on the pill. I just don't want to take any chances.

■ I am excited about being a father someday, but I'm in no hurry either. It's tough for me to make the connection in my head between having sex and having babies, even though I know that's how it works.

■ I wonder sometimes what I would do if one of us turned out to be infertile. The idea of adopting doesn't excite me, even though I know it's a nice thing to do. But getting involved in a lot of technology doesn't seem very exciting either. Maybe I would just accept not having any children.

structures, assisting in the positioning of the needle for amniocentesis. Sonograms also can be used for finding certain birth defects, determining the position of a fetus, or checking to see if more than one fetus is present. Because ultrasound may produce a slight rise in temperature and jarring vibrations in the surrounding tissues, the Food and Drug Administration (FDA) has recommended that the technique be used as sparingly as possible. Most clinicians now use at least one ultrasound as a routine procedure during pregnancy, even though there is no particular evidence that the outcome for either the fetus or the mother is substantially improved by such use. See Figure 10.19.

As ultrasound technology has improved, now even offering 3D images of the fetus, it has given rise to a burgeoning business in "keepsake" sonograms—lengthy videos and still photos of ultrasound images of the fetus made by nonmedical personnel solely for the enjoyment of the parents and other relatives. One on-line site even includes a kiddie photo contest featuring pictures of the unborn. Despite a recent FDA caution about unnecessary exposure to ultrasound during pregnancy, the relative safety of such nonessential procedures remains controversial. Ultrasound allows many parents to be certain of the sex of their baby well before it is born, and they often choose a name long before birth based on this information.

Embryoscopy, Fetoscopy, and Imaging

Technology now permits visual examination of embryos and fetuses. An endoscope is inserted through a hollow needle used to penetrate the uterus and amnion. The embryoscope or fetoscope may then be used to look for possible developmental abnormalities. Variations on this technique may be used to offer surgery or treatment during the first 12 weeks of pregnancy. Magnetic resonance imaging (MRI) and other noninvasive imaging techniques continue to be developed in ways that might allow them to be used to examine embryos and fetuses.

Fetal Surgery

Ultrasound and other imaging techniques are crucial to one of the newest technological advances, **fetal surgery.** At a few major medical centers, actual surgical procedures can be performed on a fetus while it is still in the uterus. Such surgery has been most successful with urinary tract problems that can be diagnosed during pregnancy. Several successful surgeries have been performed on fetuses that have actually been removed from the uterus, replaced following surgery, and then

■ **FIGURE 10.19** *Ultrasound Image*

This is an actual sonogram of a healthy fetus.

fetal surgery a surgical procedure performed on the fetus while it is still in the uterus or during a temporary period of removal from the uterus.

born normally. This technique has been used to repair diaphragmatic hernia and fetal heart defects. Fetal surgery is one of the frontiers of reproductive and fetal technology that is seeing rapid and dramatic developments on a regular basis, although many fetuses do not survive the surgical procedures.

Even though we have the technology to examine all fetuses for birth defects, should we? Explain your position.

FOH Infertility and Sexuality

Not all couples who want to have children are able to do so. Failure of the occurrence of a successful pregnancy after a year or more of intercourse without contraception may indicate an **infertility** problem. There is evidence that the rate of fertility difficulties is on the rise, and there has been some concern that environmental pollutants may be leading to the increase. About 15 percent of nonsterilized, sexually experienced women, or about 10 percent of all women of reproductive age, report having problems with conceiving or carrying a pregnancy to term. Women with a history of pelvic inflammatory disease, endometriosis, diabetes, or hypertension seem particularly prone to infertility. It may be that half or more of these named infertile women eventually can become pregnant without medical intervention, but for the others the problem may be more persistent.

Male infertility usually is caused by a low sperm count, less than 40 million sperm per cubic centimeter of semen, or by sluggish motility of the sperm. Although low sperm counts do not make conception impossible, they do reduce the chances of its occurring. Several infections and injuries of the testes may damage the sperm-producing tubules and lead to low sperm counts. Certain drugs, alcohol, and tobacco have also been implicated. Although some medical and surgical treatments have been tried with male infertility, the results have been poor. One recommended method has been to avoid ejaculation for 48 hours prior to intercourse in an attempt to raise the number of sperm in the ejaculate, but the usefulness of this method is doubtful. It is also typically suggested that men with low sperm counts avoid lengthy submersion in very warm water, which can temporarily interfere with sperm production. Sperm are produced at a temperature slightly below internal body temperature due to the external location of the testes. An over-the-counter test available from drugstores can evaluate sperm numbers in the privacy of the home. The test, called FertilMARQ, does not offer information about sperm motility or shape, however, both of which can play a role in male fertility.

For couples who have been planning on having children, infertility can be a very real disappointment, accompanied by a sense of deprivation and a range of difficult emotions including guilt, anger, and frustration. The reproductive technologies described previously in this chapter can sometimes help, but they are expensive and may have limited success rates that can actually increase the levels of frustration and disappointment (Bentley & Mascie-Taylor, 2000). However, the effects of infertility may not be as devastating as popular myth has suggested. A survey of the literature on the relational effects of infertility clearly indicated that infertility creates stress and anxiety for both partners, in particular the woman. Males are more distressed when the soruce of the problem is found to be them. Infertility may also create feelings of personal inadequacy and interfere with sexual spontaneity. Nevertheless, it does not seem to have a pervasively negative effect on either marital or sexual satisfaction. In fact, for many couples, working together on infertility often brings a deepened sense of commitment and intimacy to their relationship (Watkins & Baldo, 2004).

■ Pregnancy and Birthing

Prompt diagnosis of pregnancy is crucial so that prenatal care can be sought in a timely manner. Women who are in good health prior to getting pregnant and those who receive more comprehensive prenatal care from the early stages of pregnancy are more likely to avoid birth defects in their babies and to have infants with higher birth weights (Green-Raleigh et al., 2005; Haas et al., 2005). The chances of maternal mortality are lower as well (Harper et al., 2003). Children with low birth weights are at significantly higher risk of developmental disabilities, visual impairments, and cerebral palsy and are less likely to perform well in school (Ricketts, Murray, & Schwalberg, 2005). There is abundant evidence that prenatal care is highly cost effective, eventually reducing the costs associated with delivery, especially in high-risk pregnancies. In poor, rural communities, however, the benefits may not be as great (Alexander, Kogan, & Nabukera, 2002; Guillory et al., 2003). Choosing a clinician with whom the woman can feel comfortable is always helpful. Physicians who provide prenatal care and delivery of babies usually are obstetrician–gynecologists, although many prenatal clinics use nurse practitioners or other health care providers. In addition, nurse-midwives, who can provide care during pregnancy and the birthing process, are in private practice in some areas, with physician backup for complicated cases.

infertility the inability to produce offspring.

Real People

Pregnancy and Birth: A Personal Perspective from the Author's Wife

The distinct moments of giving birth to my two children were the most powerful and profound acts I have ever performed. At no other time in life do the planning, waiting, physical exertion, and time devoted to a task pay off with such magnificent results—the beginning of life for a whole new person. Both times, Gary and I were rendered speechless when our daughters emerged. You always know intellectually that the processes of reproduction and birth are supposed to result in the birth of a child. But not until you see that little body with eyes wide and searching with a powerful intensity are you struck with a miracle that has become reality.

The physical aspects of pregnancy and birth are the most obvious, but the psychological and relational aspects have the most profound effect. During the pregnancies, there were times when I very deeply needed to feel loved and protected by my husband.

There were times before and after the birth that I needed some proof of autonomy from the child that was a physical part of me for nine months. Gary and I both vacillated between periods of wanting to escape the whole thing and feeling certain that this experience would bind us together forever. The most crucial thing about facing all of our conflicting emotions was that each of us allowed the other to feel whatever was surfacing and offered support.

Each time, when I gave that final draining, straining push, and my husband seemed so proud of me and what we had created together, it was a moment like no other in my life. Every rich detail will be forever woven into my memory. To be part of the life-giving forces of the universe is truly an awesome experience.

—Betsy A. Kelly

The cause of the majority of birth defects is not known. However, there is growing evidence that toxins and radiation in the environment may damage sperm cells, resulting in possible damage to the developing fetus. Pregnant women exposed to organic solvents have a sharply elevated risk of having an infant with serious birth defects (Khattak et al., 1999). The chance of birth defects involving development of the brain and spinal cord is increased by exposure to heat during early pregnancy such as through immersion in hot tubs. The likelihood of neurological defects seems to be reduced in women who use supplements of folic acid, one of the B vitamins, before becoming pregnant. Women who become pregnant after age 35 have an increased risk of infant mortality or illness, and these risk factors should be explained carefully to them (Touch et al., 2002). However, it should be noted that women who become pregnant for the first time at age 35 or older seem to adjust emotionally quite well in general. The risks for women who become pregnant at age 50 or older are significantly higher (Salihu et al., 2003).

Both women and men can have a wide range of reactions to pregnancy. Often, periods of elation and excitement alternate with feelings of apprehension and concern. Research has also shown that when the pregnancy has been intended by *both* parents, the outcomes for the infant's health are more positive (Korenman,

Kaestner, & Joyce, 2002). Nonetheless, pregnancy is a stressful time for everyone, bringing many unknowns. Fathers-to-be often have difficulty sorting out their reactions to pregnancy and feel some shifting in their relationship to the woman. Mothers-to-be may feel somewhat trapped in the "pregnant woman" role and resent that their former individual sense of identity seems to slip away at times. Both parents wonder what it will be like to have a new child in the family and worry about potential problems with the pregnancy, the birth, or the baby itself. They may vacillate between being irritable with each other and feeling the special closeness of sharing the pregnancy.

The Biology of Pregnancy

There are many initial signs of pregnancy, although all of them may be caused by other factors. In fact, a study in Germany found that in about one out of every 475 cases, the woman did not realize she was pregnant until after 20 weeks and in some cases not until she went into labor (Wessel & Buscher, 2002). One of the first symptoms is usually the missing of a menstrual period; however, this can have a variety of other causes, including illness, emotional upsets, or changes in living conditions. Also, about 20 percent of women continue having some menstrual flow during the early stages of pregnancy. Other typical early signs of pregnancy are enlargement and tenderness of the breasts, increased frequency of urination, fatigue, and the experiencing of nausea and vomiting, especially upon waking in the morning. If most or all of these symptoms are present, pregnancy should at least be suspected. A clinician can also look for signs such as softening of the lower uterine segment, color changes in the cervical tissues, and enlargement of the uterus.

Pregnancy Tests

Tests for pregnancy involve analysis of the woman's urine or blood to detect the presence of the hormone **human chorionic gonadotropin (HCG),** which is produced by the embryo and the placenta. Many brands of home pregnancy tests are available in stores. Directions should be read and followed very carefully. Research indicates that the accuracy of home-test prediction varies a great deal depending on how carefully the directions have been followed. Women often perform the tests too early in pregnancy, yielding a false positive. Some women may be misled by the results of home-pregnancy testing. Therefore, even if a home test is positive, most clinics or physicians will do a repeat test to confirm the pregnancy. Highly sensitive laboratory diagnostic procedures are considered to be from 95 to 98 percent accurate two weeks after a missed period. Laboratory blood tests for HCG can be almost 100 percent accurate within seven days after conception.

Pregnant women usually are given advice on diet, appropriate vitamin supplements (not self-prescribed megadoses), proper rest, clothing, and moderation of activities. Exercise during pregnancy seems to produce healthful results for both mother and infant. Good nutrition is essential to healthy fetal development, and research indicates that smoking, alcohol, and drugs play a role in causing birth defects and endangering the life of the fetus.

FOH Alcohol, Drugs, and Smoking

Alcohol use during pregnancy increases the chances of having a low-birth-weight baby, especially if the drinking occurs on a regular basis as opposed to very occasional binge drinking (Whitehead & Lipscomb, 2003). Heavy alcohol consumption can lead to **fetal alcohol syndrome (FAS),** characterized by abnormal fetal growth, neurological damage, and facial distortion. FAS is the leading cause of birth defects in the United States and can also cause miscarriage, stillbirth, and premature birth. In infants, FAS can be manifested as brain damage, heart problems, and behavioral difficulties such as hyperactivity. Pregnant women generally are advised to avoid drinking alcohol because of these risks. Smoking has also been associated with compli-

cations in pregnancy, lower birth weights in babies, lowered intellectual abilities, and later behavior disorders in children.

Use of other drugs—whether prescription, over-the-counter, or illegal—is also ill-advised during pregnancy, although many medications are approved for such use. Mothers who use drugs such as cocaine, heroin, amphetamines, or barbiturates give birth to babies who already are addicted themselves and actually can experience dangerous withdrawal symptoms. These babies are also at high risk for cognitive impairments, emotional problems, and a variety of health difficulties (Bauer et al., 2002; Singer et al., 2002).

Sex during and after Pregnancy   FOH

Many clinicians neglect to discuss sexual activity with their patients, and many myths have evolved concerning sex during pregnancy. Research shows that in the absence of a medical problem, there is no particular reason to prohibit sexual intercourse at any time during pregnancy, up until the time the birth process has begun. However, both before and after giving birth, women may experience fatigue and depression that can interfere with sexual desire and satisfaction. A supportive partner who helps stabilize the relationship during such times can help considerably. After the baby is born, the woman's level of satisfaction with her new role as a mother can affect her sexual desire either positively or negatively (De Judicibus & McCabe, 2002).

Clearly, sexual activity that could risk exposure to sexually transmitted diseases should be avoided during pregnancy. In the final months of pregnancy, the woman's abdomen often is distended enough to require modification of the couple's usual intercourse positions. Studies have shown that many pregnant women experience a gradual decline in their sex drive, sexual satisfaction, and frequency of intercourse that becomes even more marked in the final three months. Some women experience some degree of discomfort or pain during intercourse in the third trimester (Aslan et al., 2005; Gokyildiz & Beji, 2005). If coitus is uncomfortable or impossible for either partner, the couple may engage in other forms of sexual activity.

After the baby has been born, there seems to be no medical reason to prohibit intercourse after vaginal bleeding has stopped and any tears in the vaginal opening have healed. Most couples have the lowest

---

human chorionic gonadotropin (HCG) a hormone detectable in the urine of a pregnant woman.

fetal alcohol syndrome (FAS) a condition in a fetus characterized by abnormal growth, neurological damage, and facial distortion caused by the mother's heavy alcohol consumption during pregnancy.

1. Head floating, before engagement.

2. Engagement; flexion, descent.

3. Further descent, internal rotation.

4. Complete rotation, beginning extension.

5. Complete extension.

6. Restitution (external rotation).

7. Delivery of anterior shoulder.

8. Delivery of posterior shoulder.

FIGURE 10.20 *Major Stages in the Birth Process*

The fetus is shown in the uterus as labor contractions begin and the fetus progresses through the stages of birth.

frequency of sexual activity during the four weeks immediately following the birth of a child, although it may remain relatively infrequent for six months or longer. New mothers often simply feel too tired to engage in sex (Ahlborg, Dahlof, & Hallberg, 2005). Research shows that most women resume sexual intercourse within a few weeks, and after 12 months the levels of sexual activity typically have returned to the levels experienced prior to pregnancy. Breast-feeding women tend to have less sexual activity and lower levels of sexual satisfaction, possibly the result of both hormonal and psychological factors (De Judicibus & McCabe, 2002). The responsibilities and activities of parenthood usually absorb much time and energy, which sometimes reduces the opportunities for sex for new parents. Although both partners typically are dissatisfied with their sexual lives during the first few months after giving birth, most are happy with their relationship and with being parents (Ahlborg, Dahlof, & Hallberg, 2005).

Using birth control is crucial to preventing pregnancy too soon after the birth of a baby. The most recent evidence suggests that it is best to space pregnancies at least one to two years apart in order to give the woman's body a chance to build up the nutritional reserves needed to nourish a developing fetus. There is a greater risk of fetal death in pregnancies that occur too soon after a previous pregnancy (Zhu et al., 1999).

FOH The Birth Process

The birth process (see Figures 10.20 and 10.21) is complex, and its controlling mechanisms are not fully understood. The hormone **oxytocin,** manufactured by

the pituitary gland, is believed to play some part in the process. About a month before birth, the fetus shifts to a lower position in the abdomen. By this time, it is normally in its head-down position. The most common signal that the birth process is beginning is the initiation of uterine contractions experienced as **labor.** The mucus plug that blocked the opening of the cervix is usually expelled just before birth begins and sometimes is seen as a small amount of bloody discharge. At some point in the process, the amniotic sac ruptures, and its fluid pours or dribbles out of the vagina.

Labor contractions are relatively mild at first, occurring at intervals of 15 to 20 minutes. Although most couples might find it difficult to relax enough or find the necessary privacy, lovemaking, including intercourse, during the early stages of labor has been shown to facilitate the process of labor and delivery. The uterine contractions gradually increase in strength and frequency as the fetus moves downward in the uterus and the cervix is dilated to a diameter of about 10 centimeters. This process of cervical opening (**dilation**) and thinning (**effacement**) begins before labor and continues until

oxytocin (ox-ee-TOH-sin) a pituitary hormone believed to play a role in initiating the birth process.

labor uterine contractions in a pregnant woman; an indication that the birth process is beginning.

dilation the gradual widening of the cervical opening of the uterus prior to and during labor.

effacement the thinning of cervical tissue of the uterus prior to and during labor.

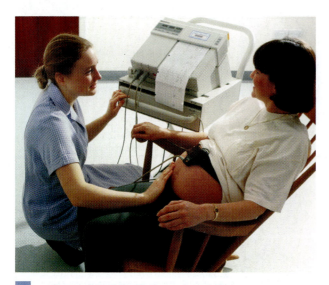

■ **FIGURE 10.21**   *Fetal Heartbeat Monitoring*

As the fetus nears the time for its birth, its heartbeat is monitored.

the cervix is fully open and thinned, permitting delivery of the fetus. This first stage of labor typically takes 10 to 14 hours for a woman experiencing her first delivery. In subsequent deliveries, the time for labor may be somewhat shorter.

The second stage of labor involves the movement of the fetus through the vagina, now called the **birth canal.** This stage takes an hour or two for a first delivery but may proceed more rapidly in subsequent births. The mother can help with this stage of labor by pushing with her abdominal muscles. Eventually, the fetus's head appears at the vaginal opening, followed by one shoulder, then the other shoulder, and finally the rest of the body. The clinician assisting with the birth generally does not pull on the baby but gently guides it out of the birth canal. In the majority of deliveries in North America, it has been typical for a procedure called an **episiotomy** to be performed in order to prevent tearing of the vaginal opening. It involves cutting the outer part of the vaginal tissue. The incision is later sutured and usually heals without problems. Sometimes, however, it becomes infected and may take up to four weeks to heal completely. About one-sixth of women experience pain or discomfort in the episiotomy scar up to a year after giving birth. Some consider episiotomy to be nearly always unnecessary and recommend against its routine use because it may slow the recovery process. The procedure should be used only when the fetus is in distress or when some instrument must be used to assist in delivery.

If serious problems affect the birth process, the fetus seems too large for the woman's pelvis, or the fetus is experiencing some other form of distress, a surgical procedure can be performed in which the fetus is removed through an incision in the abdominal wall and

uterus. Called a **cesarian section,** the method has been used increasingly in recent years to lower the risk of complications for the mother and baby. Progress is being made in predicting which first-time pregnancies may require cesarian delivery (Wilkes et al., 2003). Some authorities believe that a substantial proportion of cesarian births are unnecessary, and there is particular concern about performing the procedure simply because it is requested by the woman. The Department of Health and Human Services has wanted to reduce the rate of cesarian deliveries. In some hospitals this reduction has happened, and in others it has not. However, those hospitals with lower rates of cesarian delivery report higher rates of complications in vaginal delivery (Health Grades, 2003).

Some experts maintain that the availability of cesarian delivery has markedly increased the safety of childbearing and that care should be exercised in reducing its incidence simply to meet an arbitrary goal. It was once standard practice to perform cesarian sections on women who had given birth to an earlier child in this manner, but it has been demonstrated that vaginal delivery can be successful in about 75 percent of women who previously have had a cesarian delivery. Some research also indicates that these women face increased risk of infant death either at the time of delivery or within a few days following (Smith, G. C. S., et al., 2002).

Very soon after the baby has been born, the third stage of the birth process occurs. The placenta, now a disk of tissue about 8 inches in diameter and 2 inches thick, pulls away from the uterine wall. The uterus expels the placenta through the birth canal; along with the remaining section of umbilical cord and the fetal membranes. The expelled tissues are collectively called the **afterbirth.**

Birthing Alternatives

In many cultures, giving birth to a baby is viewed as a natural phenomenon not requiring any particular degree

birth canal term applied to the vagina during the birth process.

episiotomy (ee-piz-ee-OTT-a-mee) a surgical incision in the vaginal opening made by the clinician or obstetrician to prevent the baby from tearing the opening in the process of being born.

cesarian section a surgical method of childbirth in which delivery occurs through an incision in the abdominal wall and uterus.

afterbirth the tissues expelled after childbirth, including the placenta, the remains of the umbilical cord, and fetal membranes.

FOH

Real Student Voices

■ My aunt and her husband used in vitro fertilization to have their child, and it worked the first time they tried it. The baby is beautiful. It's amazing that science has created this opportunity for couples.

■ Being a parent and a student at the same time isn't always easy, but it's nice to have the little guy to go home to after a long day.

of special attention. Over the past century, in more developed countries, medical intervention has increasingly become a part of the birthing process. For a time, the whole process was perceived in an illness context, and physicians emphasized using drugs and anesthetics to reduce pain and prescribed a prolonged period of complete bed rest as "convalescence." Delivery of a baby became a mysterious event, best left to doctors and nurses in a hospital setting. Proponents of several other approaches to giving birth have gradually changed this perspective, restoring more power over birthing to the mother and often to the father as well. Today, women have many more options and may, in fact, design a set of birthing options that seems right to them and gives them better control of the situation (Carmichael, 2004).

Prepared Childbirth

In 1932, British physician Grantly Dick-Read published a book called *Childbirth without Fear.* He believed that the fear of the birthing process generated by medical intervention only created more tension and pain. He educated women thoroughly about labor and delivery and developed relaxation techniques to reduce tension, calling his method **natural childbirth.** He instituted the trend toward returning control of the birth process to women and their partners that continues today.

In the 1950s, a similar approach was introduced by French obstetrician Fernand Lamaze. The **Lamaze method** of "prepared" childbirth and methods patterned after it are popular today and make use of the baby's father or some other willing partner as a coach for the woman. In prenatal classes, the couple is taught how to use different relaxation and breathing techniques through increasing levels of intensity during labor. Although the Lamaze approach does not prohibit the use of pain medication during labor, it usually reduces the need for it. The woman is able to remain an alert and active participant in giving birth to

her baby, a process that her body is well equipped to accomplish.

Pain-Relieving Medication during Birth

As general anesthesia came into common use for surgical procedures, it also became widely used during delivery of babies so that women would not have to endure the pain associated with the latter stages of labor. However, as fetal technology began to demonstrate the potentially harmful effects general anesthetics could have on a newborn baby, alternative methods were explored. In the earlier years, proponents of the natural and prepared childbirth movements discouraged the use of any pain-relieving medications during birthing, arguing that they represented an abdication of control over the process. Some women who eventually resorted to some form of anesthetic when giving birth were left with feelings of guilt and failure. Although the debate over the use of such medications continues, recent statistics indicate that much of the stigma surrounding the use of certain methods of pain control has been lost. More women are now using epidural blocks, anesthetics that are injected at the base of the spinal cord to lessen painful sensations. These medications do not seem to have any effect on the infant being born, and their use does not increase the risk of needing a cesarian procedure, as was once believed (Wong et al., 2005). Others insist that pain can be managed by breathing and positioning techniques that can be learned by women prior to giving birth.

natural childbirth a birthing process that encourages the mother to take control, thus minimizing medical intervention.

Lamaze method (la-MAHZ) a birthing process based on relaxation techniques practiced by the expectant mother; her partner coaches her throughout the birth.

FOH Midwives and Home Birth

Although most professionals still recommend hospital delivery to ensure the availability of appropriate care in case of complications, some couples choose to have a baby born at home. Some research suggests that home births run the risk of compromising the health of both mothers and babies (Pang et al., 2002). Trained and licensed **midwives** or certified nurse-midwives may assist, and it is usually recommended that a cooperative physician at least be on call in case of emergency. Sometimes, other children, family members, and friends are invited to be present for the home birthing event. For low-risk pregnancies, research generally has indicated that planned care and home birth with a nurse-midwife can be as safe as hospital delivery (Jackson, D. J., et al., 2003). Midwives now assist with about 10 percent of vaginal deliveries in the United States.

Birthing Rooms

Responding to the new trend to make birthing a cooperative process, most hospitals have established **birthing rooms.** These usually are decorated and furnished in nonhospital fashion, and sometimes other children or family members are allowed to be present for the birth. When a birthing room is used, the woman remains in the same room and bed for labor and delivery rather than being taken to a separate delivery room for the actual birth.

Additional Birthing Techniques

Some women have given birth in tubs of warm water because the warmth is relaxing. Immersion in water may also speed the delivery along somewhat if labor is progressing slowly. The baby is lifted out of the water immediately after birth and before the umbilical cord is cut. There are also advantages to giving birth in a squatting or kneeling position rather than lying down, because gravity works with the uterine contractions (Carmichael, 2004; Cluett et al., 2004).

French physician Frederick Leboyer advocated several methods for reducing the shock a baby feels when it comes into a bright, noisy delivery area. He recommended that birth take place in a quiet, dimly lit, warm setting and that time be taken for the baby to lie on the mother's abdomen before the umbilical cord is cut. He also suggested giving a newborn baby a gentle, warm bath.

Do you know which method of childbirth your mother used in delivering you? Which method of childbirth do you find most appealing?

FIGURE 10.22 *Birth*

The newborn is placed on its mother's stomach.

The Newborn

After delivery, a baby is checked for any signs of distress, measured, and kept very warm. Drops of dilute silver nitrate or antibiotics are placed in the eyes to prevent infections from bacteria that might have entered the eyes during the birth process. In developing countries, these medications often are too costly, so physicians are now recommending that less expensive antiseptics such as Betadine be used as eyedrops in these areas of the world. This treatment is believed to have the potential to prevent thousands of cases of infant blindness and hundreds of thousands of severe eye infections worldwide each year.

It is widely believed that newborn babies are quite alert for the first hour or two immediately following birth and that time should be given for the parents to form a **bond** with their new infants (see Figures 10.22 to 10.24). This early bonding may well provide more security and comfort for the baby's adjustment and growth processes, although research evidence to confirm this contention is incomplete.

midwives medical professionals, both women and men, trained to assist with the birthing process.

birthing rooms special areas in the hospital, decorated and furnished in a nonhospital way, set aside for giving birth; the woman remains here to give birth rather than being taken to a separate delivery room.

bond the emotional link between parent and child created by cuddling, cooing, and physical and eye contact early in the newborn's life.

FIGURE 10.23   *Identifying the Newborn*

Each newborn is given an identifying bracelet, which the nurse fills in with the names of the baby and the baby's parents.

FIGURE 10.24   *The New Family*

The father, as a part of the natural birthing process, greets his newborn and comforts his wife.

Problems during Pregnancy

About one out of four pregnancies experiences some potentially serious complication. Each year in the United States, more than 31,000 fetuses die prior to delivery, and another 22,000 newborns die within a month of being born. The U.S. infant mortality rate continues to be higher than that of many other industrialized nations. The rates of death of pregnant women and of their fetuses are especially high among black women, and the risks are sharply elevated for women over age 35 (Callagan & Berg, 2003; Chang et al., 2003). Childbearing takes its toll on mothers worldwide as well. The United Nations has reported that about 585,000 women die each year around the globe in pregnancy and childbirth (see Figure 10.25), often due to inadequate medical care. We will not explore all the possible problems of pregnancy in detail here but instead will mention a few common ones.

FIGURE 10.25   *Childbearing's Toll*

A UNICEF study found that 585,000 women worldwide die each year during pregnancy and childbirth, nearly 20 percent more than previously estimated.

Pregnancy-Induced Hypertension

One disorder that occurs in women in fewer than 10 percent of pregnancies is **pregnancy-induced hypertension,** formerly called toxemia or eclampsia. It begins with a rise in blood pressure, swelling in the ankles and other parts of the body, and the appearance of protein in the urine. Usually it can be treated by bed rest, diet, and medication, but sometimes it progresses to serious or life-threatening conditions for the mother such as blindness, convulsions, or coma. Low daily doses of aspirin can be helpful in preventing this condition without harming fetal development. Pregnancy-induced hypertension increases the risk of stroke during the first few weeks following giving birth (Redman & Sargent, 2005).

Premature Birth

Any birth that takes place prior to the 37th week of pregnancy is considered a **premature birth.** In the United States, one out of eight babies is born prematurely. It more commonly occurs in fetuses who are growing more slowly than they should be. About three-quarters of infant deaths in the United States are associated with premature delivery, and preterm births constitute the cause of one-third of infant deaths in the United States (Callaghan et al., 2006). The more prematurely a baby is born, the lower its chances of survival. More than 60 percent of infants born at 22 to 25 weeks of gestation die prior to or during birth or within six months of delivery. Respiratory problems, cranial abnormalities, and their complications are particularly common among these early "preemies." The survival rate steadily rises the later in pregnancy an infant is born.

Often, care in an isolette (formerly called an incubator) is necessary for a time. Although the cause of a premature birth is not always known, it is particularly common among teenage mothers, women who smoke or have a genitourinary tract infection during their pregnancies, and women who have experienced high stress, inadequate nutrition, or lack of proper prenatal medical care. Bacterial infections, allergic reactions, or other health problems that cause inflammation within the mother's body can lead to premature birth, and there is hope that anti-inflammatory drugs may be useful in controlling the problem. New ways are being developed of predicting which women who experience some preterm labor contractions actually will give birth prematurely (Wickelgren, 2004). In some cases, the fetal membranes rupture too soon, leading to premature delivery.

Rh Incompatibility

A major risk for pregnancies in former times was **Rh incompatibility.** The Rh factor is a blood protein; blood may be either Rh positive, if it contains this factor, or Rh negative, if it does not. A baby has its own blood type as the result of a genetic combination from its mother and father and often will not have the same blood type as the mother. If a mother has Rh negative blood and her baby is Rh positive, the mother's body will begin producing antibodies that destroy red blood cells in the fetus, especially in second and subsequent pregnancies. Administering a medication called **RhoGAM** to the mother prevents the formation of these antibodies and has effectively eliminated many of the risks of Rh incompatibility. However, the potential for the problem must be noted in prenatal blood tests, another reason why good prenatal care is so crucial to a pregnant woman and her child-to-be. It is also important for women to take RhoGAM after a miscarriage or an abortion if it is known that there was an Rh incompatibility with the fetus.

Postpartum Care

Following the birth of a baby—the postpartum time—many physical and psychological adjustments must be made by both the mother and the child. Proper medical follow-up for both is essential. As the mother's body returns to its prepregnancy state, the reproductive organs must recover and the internal hormonal balances must be reestablished. It can be a very emotional time, during which support and help from others are extremely important. Many women experience at least a brief period of **postpartum depression,** characterized by low energy levels, feelings of being overwhelmed by new responsibilities, and sleep disturbances. In more severe

---

pregnancy-induced hypertension a disorder that can arise in the latter half of pregnancy, marked by swelling in the ankles and other parts of the body, high blood pressure, and protein in the urine; can progress to coma and death if not treated.

premature birth a birth that takes place prior to the 37th week of pregnancy.

Rh incompatibility condition in which a blood protein of the infant is not the same as the mother's; antibodies formed in the mother can destroy red blood cells in the fetus.

RhoGAM medication administered to a mother to prevent formation of antibodies when the baby is Rh positive and its mother is Rh negative.

postpartum depression a period of low energy and discouragement that is common for mothers following childbearing. Longer-lasting or severe symptoms should receive medical treatment.

cases, prompt medical attention is warranted; antidepressant medications usually are successful.

Breastfeeding

Women must make decisions about whether to breast-feed or bottle-feed their newborns. As the benefits of breastfeeding become increasingly recognized, the number of babies being breast-fed has been steadily increasing (Li et al., 2003). The American Academy of Pediatrics recommends that babies be breast-fed exclusively for the first six months, and then at least partially for the remainder of the first year. In fact, only about a third of mothers are breastfeeding at all at six months (American Academy of Pediatrics, 2005). Those who will soon go back to full-time jobs are less likely to choose breastfeeding as an option, as are women who are fatigued or depressed. Support and encouragement from clinicians seem to help women continue with breastfeeding (Taveras et al., 2003). There is ample evidence to indicate that breast-fed babies tend to have stronger immune systems at first and that over the longer term they may be somewhat more intelligent and less likely to get certain diseases such as diabetes and even breast cancer in later life (Collaborative Group, 2002). Breast-fed babies also are less likely to be overweight in early childhood (Armstrong & Reilly, 2002).

Relational Adjustments

The pressures and responsibilities of parenthood require adjustments on everyone's part. A new baby requires a great deal of care and usually lost hours of sleep. Couples may find themselves tired and irritable at times. Frequency of sexual activity decreases at least for a time. Some fathers become fully engaged in child care, whereas others begin spending less time around the child and the mother. Life passages all have their complications, and becoming a parent is one passage that requires good communication, willingness to adapt and compromise, and mutual emotional support.

Chapter Summary

1. As science has gained new understanding of reproductive processes and has developed new technologies to facilitate them, reproduction has become more closely scrutinized by social policy, legislation, and court actions.

2. A sperm must penetrate the zona pellucida of the ovum for conception to occur. Progesterone and contact with the zona cause exocytosis of the sperm, allowing fertilization.

3. When a sperm fertilizes an ovum to form a zygote within the fallopian tube, 23 chromosomes from both the sperm and the egg combine to form a total of 46 chromosomes. The DNA in these chromosomes establishes the genetic instructions for development of the new organism.

4. The rate of multiple births has been increasing, largely due to increased use of fertility drugs. Multiple births are associated with greater risks of birth defects and premature birth.

5. Fraternal (dizygotic) twins result from the fertilization of two separate ova by two separate sperm. Identical (monozygotic) twins are formed when a single zygote divides into two cells that separate and develop into individual embryos. Because they have exactly the same chromosomes, they are identical in appearance.

6. Selective reduction sometimes is used to reduce the number of fetuses when a multiple pregnancy is diagnosed.

7. The zygote divides into increasing numbers of cells, eventually forming a spherical blastocyst. A few days after fertilization, the blastocyst implants itself in the inner lining (endometrium) of the uterus, where embryonic and fetal development will continue.

8. The embryo forms several extraembryonic membranes for its protection and nourishment. The amnion is a fluid-filled sac that keeps the embryo moist and cushioned. The yolk sac and allantois become partly incorporated into the umbilical cord that connects the fetus with the placenta. The chorion is the outside membrane that helps form the placenta, through which the blood systems of the fetus and the mother come close enough to permit exchange (by diffusion) of nutrients and wastes.

9. Advances in reproductive technology are revolutionizing the processes of conception and gestation. Genetic engineering and gene therapy are

opening the possibility of early diagnosis and treatment of human genetic disorders.

10. The human genome has been mapped, and gene therapy technology raises issues of privacy and consent regarding information about genetic makeup. International guidelines are being developed to regulate genetic engineering.

11. In cases in which one man has a low or nonexistent sperm count, artificial insemination permits sperm from another man to be used for fertilization.

12. Ovarian tissue has been successfully transplanted from one woman to another; there is also a possibility of uterine transplant.

13. Gametes (sperm and eggs) and embryos now may be frozen and stored for long periods for later use in various reproductive technologies. There are growing concerns about the ethics involved with frozen embryos and about possible links of freezing with later problems of pregnancy and birth defects.

14. In vitro fertilization (IVF) allows fertilization outside a woman's body, with the developing embryo then being implanted into the uterus. The success rate of IVF is still limited, and its associated costs are high.

15. Zygote intrafallopian transfer (ZIFT) allows zygotes produced by IVF to be placed directly into fallopian tubes.

16. Gamete intrafallopian transfer (GIFT), in which sperm and eggs are placed directly into the fallopian tube, increases the likelihood of fertilization in the tube.

17. Intracytoplasmic sperm injection (ICSI), computerized sperm selection, and the transplantation of sperm-producing cells to infertile males all offer hope of increasing the likelihood of having viable sperm for reproduction.

18. Immature oocyte collection permits immature eggs to be obtained, after which they are assisted to maturity by cell-culturing methods. This technique could reduce the costs of IVF significantly.

19. Ovum donation and artificial embryonation can be used for women who no longer can produce eggs, and these techniques have enabled postmenopausal women to become pregnant.

20. Choosing the sex of a fetus ahead of time has raised many ethical concerns. Sex selection is causing an imbalance in the number of males born in China and some other countries.

21. Cloning involves the creation of genetically identical organisms. New techniques have allowed the separation of early embryonic cells and thus the creation of genetic duplicates of an early human embryo. The prospect of human cloning raises ethical, social, and legal complications, and clones may be at higher risk for eventual defects.

22. Regulations and guidelines have been developed to control the types of embryonic stem cell research that can be conducted using federal funds.

23. Surrogate motherhood, or gestational surrogacy, is a controversial approach in which one woman agrees, for a fee, to carry a pregnancy and give the baby to another couple. Sometimes the surrogate is impregnated by the sperm of a man whose partner cannot become pregnant, and sometimes IVF is used to transfer an embryo produced from the egg and sperm of one couple into the surrogate's uterus.

24. Several methods are used to diagnose potential medical problems in a fetus. Amniocentesis withdraws fetal cells from the amniotic sac so that possible chromosome abnormalities can be discovered. Chorionic villi sampling (CVS) also examines chromosomes but can be used as early as the eighth week in the pregnancy. Ultrasound pictures, or sonograms, are used to examine the features of the developing fetus. Ultrasound is not recommended for routine use.

25. Embryoscopy and fetoscopy allow visual examination of embryos and fetuses. Fetal surgery is a developing technology that can be used to treat some medical difficulties.

26. Infertility can have many causes and often creates stress for couples who are anxious to have children. New reproductive technologies are offering more hope for infertile couples.

27. Prenatal care is cost-effective and important in preventing problems related to pregnancy and birth defects.

28. Pregnancy may be signaled by many symptoms. Pregnancy tests detect a hormone produced by the embryo and placenta called human chorionic gonadotropin (HCG).

29. Fetal alcohol syndrome (FAS) results from excessive alcohol use during pregnancy.

30. Unless there is a problem with a pregnancy, there is no need to avoid sexual contact during pregnancy. To ensure healthy pregnancies, it is best that they be spaced one to two years apart.

31. The birth process begins with contractions of the uterus, or labor. Gradually, the baby is moved through the birth canal and is born. The placenta, umbilical cord, and fetal membranes follow as the afterbirth.

32. There are many approaches to birthing, including those that emphasize full awareness and participation on the mother's part, such as the Lamaze method. Many women use some pain-relieving medications or anesthesia during labor and delivery.

33. Home delivery and hospital birthing rooms are two options available to pregnant women. Nurse-midwives can assist with deliveries.

34. Dr. Frederick Leboyer advocated a quiet, warm, comfortable area for the baby's delivery.

35. Newborns must be kept very warm, and eyedrops are placed in their eyes to prevent infection by bacteria.

36. Pregnancy-induced hypertension is a possible complication of pregnancy. It involves a rise in the mother's blood pressure and a buildup of fluids in her body, sometimes with life-threatening consequences.

37. Births that occur prior to the 37th week of pregnancy are premature.

38. Prenatal blood tests are crucial so that any dangers of Rh incompatibility can be eliminated with medical treatment. RhoGAM is administered to the mother when Rh incompatibility exists.

39. The postpartum period requires many adjustments and may be characterized by some level of postpartum depression for the new mother.

40. Breastfeeding has many benefits and is increasing in popularity.

Focus on Health Questions

In this section you will find the kinds of questions that you may have concerning your own health and sexuality. The page references indicate where in the text the answer is located; the exact place is marked with this logo: **FOH**

1. Why are identical twins identical? **261**

2. Are there any practical applications of genetic engineering to the cure of human diseases? **264**

3. Members of my family are prone to a certain genetic disorder. Is there any way to determine the risks of my children inheriting the disease? **267–268**

4. What are the chances that artificial insemination will work? **268**

5. My spouse and I are interested in trying in vitro fertilization. What are the chances that it will produce a pregnancy? **270**

6. If a man has a low sperm count, is there any way to increase the chances of fertilization using his own sperm? **270, 272**

7. We're anxious to have a girl. Is there any way to influence the probabilities in that direction? **273–274**

8. Is there a way to tell if a baby has some genetic problem before it is born? **278**

9. We've been trying to get pregnant for two years, without success. What can we do? **280**

10. How can I find out if I'm pregnant? **281–282**

11. Should I avoid smoking and drinking if I am pregnant? What are the risks if I don't? **282**

12. Should we avoid sex during pregnancy? **282**

13. When I go into labor, what is actually happening? **283–284**

14. When I deliver my baby, is it advisable to have an episiotomy? **284**

15. If I use the Lamaze method of childbirth, does that mean I'll have less pain? **285**

16. Can I have my baby at home? **286**

17. What are some of the common physical problems of pregnancy? **287–288**

Chapter 11

Decision Making about Pregnancy and Parenthood

Chapter Outline

We have tried several forms of birth control, and none of them has proven completely satisfactory. I don't think I need to use something like the pill, and I don't like using a diaphragm. He uses condoms sometimes, but we don't seem to be very consistent. That leaves us with withdrawal more often than not, which we both know carries lots of risks.

—from a student essay

Do you plan on having children someday? Would you be prepared to have a child at this point in your life? Is there *any* chance you could? Bringing a child into the world carries important responsibilities—not only to the child but to a planet whose resources are unevenly distributed. There is evidence that social policies involving tax rewards or penalties for having children can help control population growth in either direction. Although family and social pressures to procreate often exist, especially for married couples, there is not a particularly close association between sex and fertility among humans. The primary reason is that, throughout history, people have deliberately sought to weaken that association through the types of sexual activities they choose and the use of birth control. People have tried to avoid pregnancy while continuing to enjoy sexual intercourse.

The terms "birth control" and "contraception" often are used interchangeably, as in this text, but there is a slight distinction between the two from a scientific standpoint. "Birth control" is a general, more encompassing term that refers to any practice, procedure, or device that reduces or eliminates the chances of a birth taking place. "Contraception" applies more to the specific methods of birth control that prevent fertilization or uterine implantation from taking place.

After World War II, the birthrate in the United States rose dramatically. Annual birthrates jumped more than 30 percent between 1945 and 1947 and reached their peak during the 1950s, when women of childbearing age were having an average of 3.7 children each. This period has been called the "baby boom." The birthrate then tapered off to a low point in the mid-1970s, when women were averaging about two children each. Despite some brief increases, the birthrate among U.S. women had fallen to one of its lowest levels ever by the end of the twentieth century. Fertility rates seem to be declining worldwide. Coupled with improvements in health care, this has led to an increase in the proportion of older people in the global population, a trend with many significant social implications that has taken demographers somewhat by surprise.

■ Historical Perspectives

Throughout history, people have found that the practicalities of life sometimes necessitate limiting family size. Various folk methods of contraception, often spiced with liberal doses of superstition, have been developed. Insertion of substances (such as crocodile dung) into the vagina frequently was used in some ancient cultures and may have been the first "barrier" method of contraception. There is evidence that women in antiquity actually may have had significant control over their reproductive lives. As early as the seventh century B.C.E., it is known that sap from the now extinct silphium plant was widely used for its contraceptive effects. The plant was so popular that it was overharvested and apparently disappeared completely by the third or fourth century C.E. Several other botanical preparations were used, with varying degrees of effectiveness. Ingesting the seeds of the Queen Anne's lace plant has long been known to reduce fertility by blocking preparation of the uterus for implantation; this method is still employed in rural areas of India and North Carolina's Appalachians. Folklore also has fostered myths about being able to prevent pregnancy by having intercourse standing up, by jumping up and down following intercourse, or by immersing oneself in a hot bath after intercourse (Tone, 2000).

During ancient and medieval times, people likely engaged in sexual activities that would not result in pregnancy. By the Middle Ages, medical training no longer included information on contraceptive methods, and knowledge about contraceptive preparations and techniques handed down from ancient times gradually disappeared. In the seventeenth century, condoms made from internal sheep membranes had been developed in Europe to contain the ejaculate during intercourse. It is worth noting that condoms originally were designed to protect against syphilis, not to prevent pregnancy. Historically, birth control has sometimes been discouraged by sociocultural values and religious teaching. From such perspectives, sexual intercourse was viewed as a procreative act, and to employ contraception was an indication that sex was being used for the gratification of nonprocreative desires. In many periods of history, the pleasures of the flesh were considered at the very least improper and at the most evil.

As the mores of Victorian England filtered through to the United States in the 1860s, a great deal of attention was focused on sexual vices. A New York grocery clerk by the name of Anthony Comstock was incensed by the distribution of information about birth control methods and set out to suppress it. He became secretary of the New York Society for the Suppression of Vice and lobbied in Washington to have the Federal Mail Act prohibit the mailing of contraceptive information, placing it in the same category as obscene materials. In the 1870s, these federal regulations became known as the **Comstock Laws.** They represented

Comstock Laws federal legislation enacted in the 1870s prohibiting the mailing of information about contraception.

government sanction of the idea that abstinence is the only permissible form of birth control.

The birth control movement in the United States was spurred on by activist Margaret Sanger, a nurse who worked in a section of Brooklyn inhabited by poor people (see Figure 11.1). She saw women who were almost constantly pregnant, often resulting in serious consequences to their health, and women who had so many children they could not effectively raise them. Many of these women resorted to self-induced abortions or abortions performed in unsanitary conditions by illegal abortionists, frequently ending in the women's deaths. Sanger, determined to remedy this problem, in 1914 founded the **National Birth Control League.**

In her protests, Margaret Sanger deliberately violated the Comstock Laws and fought against attitudes that discouraged advertising about the use of contraceptive devices. She eventually opened her own birth control clinic in Brooklyn and was arrested numerous times. After a number of court battles, physicians finally were given the right to offer contraceptive information to women (Katz, 2003). In time, contraception became more socially acceptable, and new methods were developed. In 1965, the last major law forbidding the sale of contraceptives to married people was repealed, following the U.S. Supreme Court's historic *Griswold v. Connecticut* decision. That ruling invalidated a state law that had been used to prosecute a physician for providing contraceptive information to a married couple. It was not until 1972 that the Supreme Court's ruling in *Eisenstadt v. Baird* removed a final state barrier to providing contraceptive information to unmarried individuals.

■ World Population and the Status of Children

It took a million years for the global population to reach 1 billion people, in 1804, and only until 1927 to reach 2 billion. It then took only another 50 years to double that number. By 1970, the global population growth rate had reached an all-time peak of 2.1 percent per year, and concerns arose about overpopulation. As efforts to provide contraception and to make health services more available proved successful, the growth rate fell to just over 1 percent per year. Even at that rate, it is expected that the world's population will increase from the present 6.5 billion people to around 9 billion by 2050. It now takes only 13 to 14 years to add a billion humans to the planet (Cleland et al., 2006; Cohen, 2003a). Proponents of what is called **zero population growth** had hoped that we would reach a steady state, with births equaling deaths by the year 2030, but this will not be possible. There is concern that the earth's ecosystems and resources simply will not support population growth, especially in less-developed regions. With 90 percent of the people added to the global population each year living in economically and ecologically impoverished areas, the situation continues to worsen (Cleland et al., 2006).

The balance of the world population has been changing in such a way that industrialized countries have a decreasing proportion of that population. As Figure 11.2 demonstrates, half the world's nations are now reproducing at below "replacement" levels, including countries in the developing world. This means that they will see declines in their populations over time (Wilson, C., 2004). Some countries have become concerned enough about such declines to create incentives for having babies. Japan recently initiated a "Plus One Plan" that provides social opportunities for people to meet potential marriage mates and encourages married couples to have more than one child (Watts, 2002). Scotland, Spain, and Italy are all

■ **FIGURE 11.1** *Margaret Sanger*

Sanger (1883–1966) was instrumental in increasing the availability of birth control information and contraceptive devices in the United States. She believed that every woman has the right to control her own fertility and was the first president of the International Planned Parenthood Federation.

National Birth Control League an organization founded in 1914 by Margaret Sanger to promote use of contraceptives.

zero population growth the point at which the world's population would stabilize and there would be no further increase in the number of people on earth. Birthrate and death rate become essentially equal.

Real People

Margaret Sanger

In her autobiography, Margaret Sanger told of an incident that took place during her nursing career that convinced her of the direction her life would have to take. In July 1912, she tended a 28-year-old woman who had nearly died from the effects of a self-induced abortion. The woman and her husband, Jake Sachs, already had three children she was barely able to care for on her husband's truck-driver wages. Sanger nursed Mrs. Sachs back to health, although the patient often seemed lost in thought. Finally the woman was able to deal openly with her concerns.

At the end of three weeks, as I was preparing to leave and the fragile patient [preparing] to take up her difficult life once more, she finally voiced her fears, "Another baby will finish me, I suppose?"

"It's too early to talk about that," I temporized.

But when the doctor came to make his last call, I drew him aside. "Mrs. Sachs is worried about having another baby."

"She may well be," replied the doctor, and then he stood before her and said, "Any more such capers, young woman, and there'll be no need to send for me."

"I know, doctor," she replied timidly, "but," and she hesitated as though it took all her courage to say it, "what can I do to prevent it?"

The doctor was a kindly man, and he had worked hard to save her, but such incidents had become so familiar to him that he had long since lost whatever delicacy he might once have had. He laughed good-naturedly, "You want to have your cake and eat it too, do you? Well, it can't be done."

Then picking up his hat to depart, he said, "Tell Jake to sleep on the roof."

I glanced quickly at Mrs. Sachs. Even through my sudden tears I could see stamped on her face an expression of absolute despair. We simply looked at each other, saying no word until the door had closed behind the doctor. Then she lifted her thin, blue-veined hands and clasped them beseechingly, "He can't understand. He's only a man. But you do, don't you? Please tell me the secret, and I'll never breathe it to a soul. *Please!*"

What was I to do? I could not speak the conventionally comforting phrases which would be of no comfort. . . . A little later, when she slept, I tiptoed away.

Night after night the wistful image of Mrs. Sachs appeared before me. I made all sorts of excuses to myself for not going back. I was busy on other cases; I really did not know what to say to her or how to convince her of my own ignorance; I was helpless to avert such monstrous atrocities. Time rolled by and I did nothing.

The telephone rang one evening three months later, and Jake Sachs's agitated voice begged me to come at once; his wife was sick again and from the same cause. . . . I turned into the dingy doorway and climbed the familiar stairs once more. The children were there, young little things.

Mrs. Sachs was in a coma and died within ten minutes. I drew a sheet over her pallid face. Jake was sobbing, running his hands through his hair and pulling it out like an insane person. Over and over again he wailed, "My God! My God! My God!"

I left him pacing desperately back and forth, and for hours I myself walked and walked and walked through the hushed streets. . . . [The city's] pains and griefs crowded in upon me: women writhing in travail to bring forth little babies; the babies themselves naked and hungry, wrapped in newspapers to keep them from the cold; six-year-old children with pinched, pale, wrinkled faces, old in concentrated wretchedness, pushed into gray and fetid cellars, crouching on stone floors, their small scrawny hands scuttling through rags, making lamp shades, artificial flowers; white coffins, black coffins, coffins, coffins interminably passing in never-ending succession. The scenes piled one upon another on another. I could bear it no longer.

As I stood there the darkness faded. It was the dawn of a new day in my life also. The doubt and questioning, the experimenting and trying, were now to be put behind me. I knew I could not go back merely to keeping people alive.

I went to bed, knowing that no matter what it might cost, I was finished with palliatives and superficial cures; I was resolved to seek out the root of evil, to change the destiny of mothers whose miseries were vast as the sky.

Source: Margaret Sanger, Margaret Sanger: An Autobiography, New York: W. W. Norton, 1938. Reprinted with permission.

Imagine what your life might have been like in Margaret Sanger's time. Do you think she would have a difficult time establishing the need for women's health services today? How would people's reactions be different—and the same?

Percentage of population below this level of fertility

FIGURE 11.2 *Cumulative Global Population by Level of Fertility*

Source: From Chris Wilson, "Fertility below Replacement Level" (Letter), *Science*, Vol. 304, 10 April 2004. Reprinted with permission of the author.

concerned about their low birthrates and are considering steps to encourage larger families. As of 2004, the French government has been offering 800 euros to the parents of new babies (Dorozynski, 2003).

Even though populations have been leveling off in countries such as the United States, the status of children has been declining. Nine out of every 1,000 babies in the United States die before their first birthday, one of the highest rates of infant mortality in the industrialized world. Seventeen percent of children in the United States live in poverty. A similar proportion of children between the ages of 19 and 35 months have not received all the necessary immunizations against childhood diseases. Prenatal care for poor pregnant women has become even less available than before, leading to more health and developmental problems for their children. Nearly two-thirds of women with low incomes do not breast-feed, a practice that is believed to bolster immunity and nutrition in children (America's Children, 2006).

There are conflicting views about how we as a world community should address the needs of a burgeoning population. Do you support the promotion of contraception, a redistribution of global wealth, or some other solution? Support your position.

Choosing to Become a Parent

Bringing a child into the world and caring for it through its years of growing up are major life responsibilities. Experts agree that it is best for any couple to choose to become pregnant through a process of discussion and mutual agreement, carefully weighing all the new

obligations parenthood will entail. These are complicated times in which to become parents. Raising a child not only is filled with social requirements, but also is very expensive. It is estimated that the average cost of raising a child to age 18 in the United States—including housing, clothes, food, medical care, public education, and transportation—ranges from $135,000 for lower-income parents to nearly $285,000 for upper-income families, with the average over $200,000. With the number of families requiring child care increasing because of parental occupations, fewer than half of preschoolers are watched by relatives while parents are working. The costs of day care continue to rise, with child-care costs averaging over $100 per week.

There are many *wrong* reasons to become a parent, for example, the desire to give your parents grandchildren or to give your first child a sibling. Nor is it appropriate to have a child in order to save or refresh a shaky relationship. Sometimes a person is anxious to have a baby in order to have something to love or possess, but this desire may reflect other issues in the person's life that need work and resolution; it is not fair to ask a new baby to fill those emotional gaps. Babies who were unwanted or who resulted from mistimed pregnancies tend not to develop skills as quickly as wanted babies; they also tend to be more fearful and more subject to other psychological difficulties (Pulley et al., 2002).

The choice to become a parent should be made after careful consideration of all the positive *and* negative aspects of parenthood (see Figure 11.3). Every stage of child development places demands on parents and requires the exercise of appropriate parenting skills. None of us is born knowing those skills, and they take time to develop. Although it may be a thrill to anticipate the arrival of a baby, any parent can testify that the realities are at times exhausting, nerve-wracking,

FIGURE 11.3 *Pregnancy or Birth Control?*

Deciding to have a child is a complicated issue for most people. Consideration must be given to health, among other issues. Pregnancy itself can have greater risks than any particular method of birth control.

and confusing. To be a parent requires maturity and a commitment to long-term efforts. Having children also changes the relationship between the parents, creating new pressures and complications. Most parents have found, for example, that their sexual lives change markedly with pregnancy and the presence of a child in their lives. It takes real work and communication to maintain a happy and healthy relationship in the face of the pressures of parenthood.

Of course, being a parent carries great satisfaction and rewards as well. Not only can it help individuals become more mature and responsible, but it also may strengthen the bonds between the child's parents—especially couples who make their decision to have children carefully and have thorough information about the implications of parenthood. Choosing if and when to have a child means that contraception must be part of planning for heterosexual intercourse. Any couple that shares intercourse must also give some thought and planning to the possibility that birth control might fail. The information in this chapter is basic to thinking and deciding about these issues.

Birth Control Today

The risk of unintended pregnancy has always been one of the major arguments used by people who wish to discourage premarital sex. Although coitus always carries some risk of pregnancy, modern methods of birth control have at least reduced this risk to the point where many couples pursue their sexual activities with relatively little concern for unintended pregnancy. The World Health Organization estimates that 25 percent of all pregnancies worldwide are unwanted and that about 50 million of them are terminated by abortion each year. Up to 20 million of these abortions are performed by people without needed medical qualifications and/or in unsafe medical conditions (Grimes et al., 2006).

Among developed countries, rates of unintended pregnancy vary widely and often differ among socioeconomic groups. They tend to be especially high in the United States, where the proportion of pregnancies that are unplanned is about 50 percent and nearly one-third of live births are the result of an unintended pregnancy (D'Angelo et al., 2004; Finer & Henshaw, 2006; Hatcher et al., 2004). This is in contrast to countries such as Canada and the Netherlands, where the rates of unintended pregnancy are 39 percent and 6 percent, respectively. Although adults in all three of these countries are relatively well informed about contraceptives, Americans tend to be more skeptical about the effectiveness of birth control methods and more likely to blame the incidence of unwanted pregnancies on societal problems.

Publicly funded family planning agencies continue to face challenges in providing services to all the low-income women who need them, and they sometimes are unable to stock all contraceptive methods because of their costs (Lindberg, Frost, Sten, & Dailard, 2006). Even when birth control techniques are available, people do not necessarily make use of them. Data from various studies indicate that among sexually active individuals, some do not use contraception with any regularity or at all. We can assume that some of these individuals may be attempting to get pregnant, but when data were examined from only those individuals who were unmarried and not cohabiting, it was found that 13 percent of the women and 12 percent of the men reported never using birth control (Kirby, 2002b; Laumann, Gagnon, et al., 1994).

■ Deciding about Contraceptives

Individuals who do not wish to be parents should either avoid intercourse or employ an adequate means of birth control. Different methods of birth control are best suited to different people and situations. It is often wise to consult a gynecologist or family planning specialist to determine which method(s) will be most effective for a particular couple's lifestyle and sexual choices. The information that follows is meant to be a brief guide to various methods of birth control. Making decisions about whether to use a means of birth control, and which method to use, can be very complicated. There are several methods of contraception that, if used consistently and properly, mean that fewer than 5 women in 100 will conceive over the course of a year.

Research has shown that women's attitudes toward sexuality can affect their decision making about contraception. Women who have more positive attitudes about sex tend to use more effective methods of birth control and to do so with greater consistency than women who have negative attitudes (Kirby, 2002b). Women typically select their first method on the basis of its effectiveness, but their second and third selections are more likely to be made on the basis of health concerns and potential effects on the body; for example, it is common for women to choose the birth control pill at first because of its effectiveness. Many different factors must be weighed and considered in making a decision about contraception, but sorting through the complexities is preferable to having sex without first considering the risks of pregnancy or its potential consequences.

Ethical and Religious Influences

For many people, contraception is an ethical issue, rooted in the issue of the "purpose" of sex. Some insist that sexual intercourse is meant to be a biological

Real Student Voices

■ My mom helped me to get on the pill when I was 15. We have always had a good relationship, and I told her that my boyfriend and I were thinking of having sex. We had a good talk about the pros and cons, and then she took me to a clinic. My boyfriend and I didn't actually start having intercourse for a few more months, but I was glad my mom helped me to be prepared.

■ My father gave me a box of condoms when I turned 16, winked, and told me to be careful.

That was the extent of my sex education from him, and I found it embarrassing. In fact, I never used any of those condoms, and didn't need any until I was 22.

■ The first time we had sex, we didn't use any form of protection or birth control. We sweated it out for a month, but fortunately there was no pregnancy! Never again! (Without protection, I mean.)

function, the primary objective of which is reproduction. Others believe that it is their ethical responsibility to prevent unintended pregnancies, or overpopulation, even as they choose to share sex. Those individuals who hold more relational attitudes toward sexual activity perceive sex as an act of shared pleasure and communication within a loving relationship, with procreation an additional aspect to be chosen only when the time is right.

There has been continued recognition of the need for comprehensive reproductive health care and reproductive rights, empowerment of women, and wider access to educational and health services, crucial steps in achieving any decline in fertility (Cleland et al., 2006; Frost et al., 2001). Some of the world's major religious groups, especially Roman Catholic and fundamentalist Muslim groups, are opposed to efforts that encourage birth control or abortion. In general, however, Islamic thought is quite flexible on reproductive matters, and many Muslim countries have active family planning programs (Boonstra, 2001). Any sex-related decision requires examination of the ethical and religious values important in our lives. Sometimes, decisions require an internal balancing act as we sort out how much weight we will give to our various beliefs, opinions, emotions, practical difficulties, and inner drives. Nevertheless, contraception is an issue that can never be ignored.

Political Factors

Political and social forces can play a significant role in determining the availability of various contraceptive methods. In Japan, for example, historical factors led to almost total dependence on condoms, the traditional "rhythm method" (see p. 313), and abortion for fertility control. Concern among those in political power about Japanese sexual morals prevented the approval of birth control pills and other medical contraceptives in that country until just recently (Kihara et al., 2001). In the United States, funding for reproductive health care is always a sensitive political issue prone to influence by whatever political party happens to wield the most power at any particular time. Thousands of family planning clinics in the United States receive funding from federal programs such as Medicaid or Title X, and these—along with managed health care plans—often place restrictions on contraceptive services (Frost, Frohwirth, & Purcell, 2004).

Another volatile area politically has been that of pregnancy and family planning services for teenagers, where issues revolve around two distinct kinds of sexual activity. One takes place in middle or late teenage years among young people who are mature enough to make choices and perhaps use contraception. The other occurs among very young teens, who are unlikely to find the issue of choice very relevant. There continues to be abundant evidence that most adolescent women do not want to bear children. However, there also is continuing debate about how available contraceptives should be for teenagers and whether parental consent should be required before such services are offered (Brocato, 2004). The level of confidentiality teenagers can expect from these services can influence their willingness to seek contraception; in one study, more than half of teenagers said they would discontinue using contraceptive services if their parents were going to be notified (English & Ford, 2004;

Franzini et al., 2004; Jones, 2006; Reddy, Fleming, & Swain, 2002).

Health Considerations

Anytime various methods of birth control are considered, possible effects on health should be an integral part of the decision-making process. Although several methods (such as condoms or diaphragms) have minimal effects, others, such as hormonal methods or the IUD, can have potentially greater effects on a woman's health. Even women who use reliable contraceptive methods may still harbor fears about the health risks they might be incurring.

Sometimes it is difficult to obtain fully accurate information on potential health effects. Pharmaceutical companies anxious to market a particular contraceptive method may popularize research studies that have not fully met rigorous evaluative standards. Myths develop as well that may take time to sort through. Many people, for example, still have misconceptions and fears about the possible dangers of birth control pills. In fact, recent research tends to show that, when properly prescribed, the pill actually is quite safe for non-smokers and may even provide some health advantages. Research on the health implications of the pill and other contraceptive methods is ongoing. Prior to making a decision about birth control, couples should become updated on the most accurate medical knowledge available.

Any potential risks of a method of contraception must be balanced against the risks inherent in pregnancy, which are consistently higher than any method of birth control. The key issue is making sure the chosen contraceptive method is fully understood by the user and properly prescribed if it requires a medical professional's approval. When methods such as the pill, hormonal injections, or the IUD are possibilities, a thorough medical history must be taken and a careful evaluation made of any potential health risks. Women and men should take the responsibility for becoming fully informed about all health considerations so that they can make the most careful and safest decisions possible.

Psychological and Social Factors

How people feel about contraception and how they believe others in their social networks would view their choices are also a part of the decision-making process. We live in a culture that often sends conflicting messages about sexual expression. Although intellectually most people acknowledge that they must practice safe sex, both women and men often are placed in the position of feeling that sexual activity is acceptable only if it is spontaneous and unplanned. Therefore, to plan ahead—to choose and have available a method of contraception "just in case"—can still be a difficult step to take. It can call into question people's views of personal morality, with important implications for how they feel about themselves. Although the majority of men believe that both partners should share equal responsibility for decisions about contraception, some see it as primarily the woman's responsibility (Ford, Sohn, & Lepkowski, 2001; Hogben & Williams, 2001).

Research on the psychological and social factors that determine contraceptive behavior continues to show that negative emotional responses to sex, such as guilt, fear, or anxiety, tend to inhibit sexual intercourse. However, when those same feelings are not sufficiently strong to inhibit a person from having intercourse, they often interfere with the ability to plan for the potential consequences of sex. Therefore, people who have such negative responses tend to have less accurate information about contraception, to select more ineffective contraceptive methods, and to use them much less consistently. Men who are not particularly assertive or good at problem solving are less likely to use contraception, as are those who consume a good deal of alcohol (LaBrie et al., 2005; Nangle & Grover, 2001). To avoid pregnancy requires the successful completion of numerous steps: an acceptance on the part of both partners that their sexual activity places them at risk of pregnancy, obtaining appropriate information about birth control methods and deciding which method to acquire and use, and finally using the contraceptive method consistently and properly. Negative attitudes about the relationship, love, sex, and one's own sexual feelings, or depression, can cause difficulty in negotiating any or all of these steps (Berenson, Breitkopf, & Wu, 2003).

Preparing the Way for Effective Contraception

As the evidence shows, sexual responsibility can entail some personal work on your part to ensure that you are ready to approach sexual intercourse with effective contraception, if you are not ready to be a parent. Here are some of the necessary factors to consider and steps to take in becoming an effective user of birth control:

1. Consider your ethical and moral values about sex, pregnancy, and contraception. What sorts of social, family, and religious influences do you have to take into consideration in your decision making?
2. What health concerns might you have regarding contraception? What resources will you use to

become more fully informed about available facts? How will you check the reliability of your information?

3. Weigh carefully your attitudes about your own sexual feelings and potential sexual activities. If you find a good deal of guilt or anxiety, you might want to rethink the decisions you have made. In particular, consider how you might have been ignoring or neglecting the whole issue of birth control.

4. Can you give yourself permission to be sexual? (This does not have to mean intercourse.) If not, consider how your inner reluctance might interfere with your sexual life.

5. Be prepared to talk with your partner about contraception and the possibility of pregnancy before you engage in sexual intercourse. Sharing mutual concerns, hesitations, and values is the best way to prepare for effective contraception (Harper, C., et al., 2004; Stone & Ingham, 2002). Such discussions need to take place in a comfortable and nonpressured setting *before* sexual activity has begun, not after passionate sexual feelings already are being experienced.

FOH Choosing the "Right" Contraceptive

The goal of people who use some method of birth control is to prevent pregnancy. They have decided they do not want to be parents, at least for the time being. On the surface, then, it might seem most reasonable to look at a chart, find the contraceptive method that shows the lowest rate of failure, and use it. However, choosing a contraceptive is not that simple. Several other issues should be discussed by both partners, preferably with a family planning counselor. Many women do not continue using the contraceptive method they originally chose even though they are relatively satisfied with it, and the rates of switching methods among both married and unmarried women average around 50 percent. Methods most often are changed because of concerns about effectiveness or health risks (Grady, Billy, & Klepinger, 2002; Minnis, Shiboski, & Padian, 2003). The more informed you are in making a choice, the more likely you will be to trust the method and use it consistently.

In choosing a contraceptive method, you should know the risks involved—both the risk that pregnancy may still occur and the risks to your health of any possible side effects. Some methods definitely are more effective or safer than others. Although you should have as much accurate information as possible when choosing a contraceptive, there are many other factors to consider that go beyond statistics:

1. *Age and amount of protection needed.* Age is related to fertility. Younger women may need a higher degree of contraceptive reliability than older women. For example, vaginal barrier methods (diaphragm, cervical cap) are less effective for women under age 25. The progestin-only pill (discussed on p. 306) is particularly effective for older women and women who are breast-feeding (Hatcher et al., 2002). Similarly, a person who has sexual intercourse frequently may want to consider different forms of contraception than someone who has intercourse only occasionally. Also to be weighed are the potential side effects of a particular method versus the complication or crisis a pregnancy would entail.

2. *Safety.* Some birth control methods are not recommended for women with histories of particular medical conditions in themselves or their families. Therefore, suitability for a contraceptive method should be evaluated in cooperation with a trained professional.

3. *Factors that might inhibit use.* In choosing a contraceptive method, you should know yourself and any influences that might hinder regular use of the method. Are there any fears or hesitancies about side effects that create reluctance on your part about its use? Do you find it difficult to remember daily routines, which are necessary in taking birth control pills? Would you be embarrassed to buy supplies in a store or to interrupt sexual activity to put a condom or diaphragm in place? Will your religious values make use uncomfortable for you? Are you reluctant to touch your sex organs or, if you are a woman, to insert something into your vagina? Would you avoid a method for which a visit to a physician or family planning clinic is necessary, possibly with follow-up visits?

4. *Cost.* You will need to choose a method that you know you will be able to afford on a consistent basis. Research indicates that a large percentage of pregnancies are unplanned—and it is safe to extrapolate that a substantial number of unintended pregnancies are unwanted. Sexual intercourse in which the partners do not regularly use some form of contraception runs an extremely high risk (about 90 percent) over a year's time of incurring pregnancy, which can lead to extensive costs of one sort or another. Therefore, birth control typically is very cost-effective considered over time.

The most common methods of birth control are summarized in the section that follows. Their effectiveness, advantages, causes of failure, and potential side effects are listed in Table 11.1. The Self-Evaluation activity on page 324 can help you sort through some of your own personal issues and concerns.

Methods of Birth Control

No method of contraception is foolproof or without both positive and negative aspects (see Figure 11.4). Every method sometimes fails. Over half of unintended pregnancies occur in women who were using some form of birth control, which is why using a method consistently and properly is crucial. This section focuses on the various methods of birth control currently available and evaluates their effectiveness, advantages, and risks.

FOH Understanding Contraceptive Effectiveness

It is important to understand that there is a difference between the **theoretical failure rate** and the **typical use failure rate** of any contraceptive method. The theoretical (sometimes called "perfect" or "lowest observed")

failure rate refers to the percentage of times a method might be expected to fail when used exactly according to directions and without error or technical failure. Typical use failure rate takes into account human error and carelessness as well as technical failure. Contraception can only reduce the risk of pregnancy, not eliminate that risk completely. Clinical trials of contraceptive methods tend to generate lower failure rates, probably because the participants are carefully chosen and are well educated about the method. In real life, methods often are not used correctly or consistently, and couples should be encouraged by clinicians to choose a method that they will be most likely to use properly (Ranjit et al., 2001).

Contraceptive failure rates are measurable, whereas actual rates of *effectiveness* are somewhat more elusive. In other words, it is not so simple to predict how likely it will be that a method of birth control will work, because no studies can ascertain the proportion of women who would have become pregnant had they not used the method. Pregnancy is always a matter of chance, and even when contraception is not used, pregnancy does not necessarily occur. So the best way to express contraceptive "effectiveness" is in terms of how likely it is to fail. Failure rates typically are given as percentages. The failure rates used in this book reflect the percentage of times pregnancy could be expected to occur when 100 couples use the method during a one-year period of average-frequency intercourse; this takes into consideration the total number of times the women were susceptible to pregnancy. The rates given are based on research studies considered to be the best designed and most statistically valid by the widely respected resource *Contraceptive Technology* (Hatcher et al., 2004). The chance of any contraceptive method being effective increases when the method is used correctly and consistently.

Some forms of birth control cause unpleasant or unhealthy side effects in a few individuals. As with any kind of medical treatment, there is even a very small risk of fatal side effects in the use of hormonal contraceptives, intrauterine devices (IUDs), and surgical sterilization of the female. Medical professionals agree, however, that the risks are low enough that these methods should be made fully available to those who wish to use them. Research has also demonstrated repeatedly that the risks inherent in all methods of birth

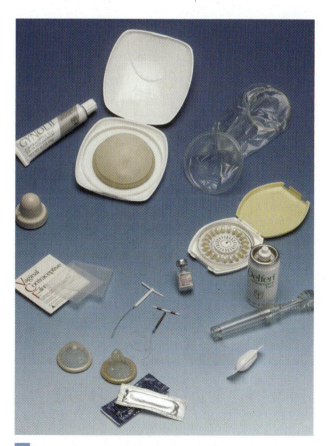

FIGURE 11.4 *Methods of Birth Control*

The goal of people who use some method of birth control is to prevent pregnancy. However, choosing a contraceptive is not that easy. No method is foolproof or without both positive and negative aspects.

theoretical failure rate a measure of how often a birth control method can be expected to fail when used without error or technical problems; sometimes called *perfect use failure rate.*

typical use failure rate a measure of how often a birth control method can be expected to fail when human error and technical failure are considered.

Table 11.1   *Contraceptive Methods: Failure Rates, Advantages, Causes of Failure, and Side Effects*

Method	Theoretical or Perfect Use Failure Rate*	Typical Use Failure Rate in Typical Users*	Potential Advantages to Users	Possible Causes of Failure That Could Result in Pregnancy	Potential Negative Side Effects
Abstinence	0%	—?—	No cost or health risks. Freedom from worry about pregnancy. Prevents infections.	Inability to continue abstaining.	Sexual frustration. Avoiding planning for eventual use of contraception.
Withdrawal (coitus interruptus)	4%	27%	No cost or preparation involved. No risks to health (if sexually transmitted diseases are absent). Available even if no other methods are.	Sperm present in preejaculatory fluid from the penis (even more likely if intercourse is repeated within a few hours). Lack of ejaculatory control, causing ejaculation in vagina. Ejaculating semen too close to vaginal opening after withdrawal.	Inability to fully relax during sexual intercourse and not be on guard. Frustration created by inability to ejaculate in the vagina.
Natural family planning/ fertility awareness	1–9%	20%	Accepted by Roman Catholic Church. May be used to increase chances of pregnancy if that choice is made. No health risks.	Inadequate time devoted to charting female's menstrual cycle or misunderstanding of method. Ovulation at an unexpected time in the cycle. Deciding to have intercourse during the unsafe period of the cycle, without using other contraception.	Sexual frustration during periods of abstinence.
Combined oral contraceptive (birth control pill containing estrogen and progestin)	0.3%	8%	Reliable; offers protection all the time. Brings increased regularity to menstrual cycle. Tends to reduce menstrual cramping, PMS. Associated with lower incidence of breast and ovarian cysts, pelvic inflammatory disease, and ovarian cancer.	Not taking pills as directed or skipping a pill. Improper supervision by clinician. Ceasing taking the pills for any reason.	Nausea, weight gain, fluid retention, breast tenderness, headaches, missed menstrual periods, acne. Mood changes, depression, anxiety, fatigue, decreased sex drive. Circulatory diseases.
Hormonal patch/ vaginal ring	0.3%	8%	Reliable; can be left in place.	Inadvertent removal.	Similar to those of the pill.

control are markedly lower than the risks associated with pregnancy and childbirth.

Sharing the Responsibility for Birth Control

Although women bear children, overpopulation of the world will not be brought under control until men share fully in family planning responsibilities. It is clear that decision making about the type of birth control to be used, and the responsibility for using it, can be shared by the woman and the man. Although choosing and using a method of birth control should always be shared by sexual partners, only a few methods of birth control are available for use exclusively by males: withdrawal, abstinence, the male condom, and vasectomy. The last choice, because it is not always a reversible form of sterilization, is not usually considered

Method	Theoretical or Perfect Use Failure Rate*	Typical Use Failure Rate in Typical Users*	Potential Advantages to Users	Possible Causes of Failure That Could Result in Pregnancy	Potential Negative Side Effects
Minipill (progestin only)	0.3%	8%	Safer for older women. Reliable; offers protection all the time. Brings increased regularity to menstrual cycle. Tends to reduce menstrual cramping, PMS. Associated with lower incidence of breast cysts, pelvic inflammatory disease, and ovarian cancer.	Not taking pills as directed or skipping a pill. Improper supervision by clinician. Ceasing taking the pills for any reason.	Irregular menstrual periods common. Bleeding between menstrual periods. Appearance of ovarian cysts.
Hormonal implants	0.05%	0.05%	Long-term protection. Extremely reliable. Require no attention after initial treatment. Easily reversible. May have same benefits as pills.	Use beyond a five-year period. Gaining a significant amount of weight (less effective in women over 155 lb.).	Slight visibility of implants. Menstrual cycle irregularities, depression. Improper insertion or difficult removal. May have risks similar to pills, but research is incomplete.
Depo-Provera injections	0.3%	3%	Up to three-month protection. Extremely reliable. May protect against endometrial cancer. Convenient, requiring only occasional injection. Easily reversible.	Neglecting to get reinjected after one or three months.	Weight gain. Excessive bleeding. Menstrual cycle irregularities. Increased depression. Decrease in sex drive. May be associated with slight increase in breast cancer risk for younger women, but research is incomplete.
Sponge (contains spermicide)	9–20%	16–32%	Easy to use. Relatively inexpensive. Protection over 24 hours, several acts of intercourse. No odor or taste.	Difficulty in proper insertion and placement. Internal anatomical abnormalities that interfere with placement or retention.	Increased risk of toxic shock syndrome. Allergic reaction to polyurethane or spermicide. Vaginal dryness. Increased risk of vaginal yeast infections.
Cervical cap with spermicide	9–26%	16–32%	Can be left in place for long periods of time.	Improper fitting or insertion/placement. Deterioration by oil-based lubricants or vaginal medications.	Possible risk of toxic shock syndrome. Allergic reaction to rubber or spermicide. Abrasions or irritation to vagina or cervix.

(Continued)

an option until later in life, when a man either has fathered all the children he might want or has decided with certainty that he never will want to have children.

In choosing a contraceptive method, women tend to place the highest priority on pregnancy prevention, whereas men are more likely to consider disease prevention for themselves. Women and men also have differing perceptions about the effectiveness of various methods. Women, for example, are more likely than men to see the pill as a very good method (Eisenberg et al., 2004). Even though most available methods are used by women, there are still many ways couples can share in birth control. For example, male partners can participate in the decision about which method to use, and couples can go together for clinical counseling and care. Clinics must be certain to evaluate males' sexual

Table 11.1   *(Continued)*

Method	Theoretical or Perfect Use Failure Rate*	Typical Use Failure Rate in Typical Users*	Potential Advantages to Users	Possible Causes of Failure That Could Result in Pregnancy	Potential Negative Side Effects
Spermicidal foam, cream, jelly, suppositories, or film	6%	26%	Available without prescription. Minimal health risks. Easy to carry and use. Does not require partner involvement. Provides lubrication for intercourse.	Not using enough spermicide or running out of a supply. Failure to use spermicide out of desire not to interrupt the sexual act. Placing spermicide in vagina too long before intercourse begins. Douching within 6 to 8 hours after intercourse. Failure of suppositories or film to melt or foam properly.	Allergic reactions to the chemical. Unpleasant taste of chemical during oral-genital sex.
Male condom	3%	14%	Available without prescription. Offers protection against sexually transmitted diseases. A method for which the man can take full responsibility. Easy to carry and use.	Breakage of condom. Not leaving space at tip of condom to collect semen. Lubrication with petroleum jelly or presence of some vaginal medications, weakening rubber condom. Seepage of semen around opening of condom or condom slipping off in the vagina after coitus. Storing of condom for more than two years or in extreme temperatures. Not placing condom on penis at beginning of intercourse.	Allergic reactions to latex (natural "skin" condoms and polyurethane condoms are also available). Some reduction in sensation on the penis.
Female condom (vaginal pouch)	5%	21%	Allows woman to choose protection from disease, along with contraception. Easy to carry and use. Polyurethane is strong, conducts body heat easily, and rarely breaks.	Slippage of outer rim into vagina during intercourse. Twisting of pouch during intercourse.	Some reduction in sensations of intercourse. Relatively high rate of contraceptive failure. Sometimes makes noises.

and contraceptive histories if they are to be fully effective in prescribing a useful method (Armstrong, 2003; Ranjit et al., 2001).

Couples can purchase the contraceptives together and share in their actual use. The man can help insert spermicidal foam or a female condom into his partner's vagina, or he can prepare the diaphragm with spermicidal jelly prior to insertion. Men also can play a role in reminding their partners to take a birth control pill each day. A woman can put her partner's condom on him as a part of sexual foreplay. Studies indicate that for this type of shared responsibility to be effective, couples need to develop good communication skills and both genders need to play a role in choosing the contraceptive that will be best for them (Oncale & King, 2001; Stone & Ingham, 2002).

Method	Theoretical or Perfect Use Failure Rate*	Typical Use Failure Rate in Typical Users*	Potential Advantages to Users	Possible Causes of Failure That Could Result in Pregnancy	Potential Negative Side Effects
Diaphragm	6%	16%	Negative side effects are rare. Inexpensive; can be reused.	Improper fitting or insertion of the diaphragm. Removal of diaphragm too soon (within 6 to 8 hours after coitus). Not using sufficient amount of spermicidal jelly with the diaphragm. Leakage in or around diaphragm or slippage of diaphragm. Deterioration by oil-based lubricants or vaginal medications.	Allergic reaction to the rubber (plastic diaphragms are also available) or the spermicide. Increased risk of toxic shock syndrome. Bladder infection or vaginal soreness because of pressure from rim.
Intrauterine device (IUD): Copper T 380A levonorgestrel	0.6% 0.1%	0.8% 0.1%	Reliable. Can be left in place so that nothing must be remembered or prepared immediately prior to intercourse.	Failure to notice that IUD has been expelled by uterus.	Uterine cramping, abnormal bleeding, heavy menstrual flow. Pelvic inflammatory disease following insertion or perforation of the uterus during insertion of the IUD; infection of the ovaries.
Vasectomy	0.1%	0.15%	Permanent; no other preparations. Very reliable. Minimal health risks.	Having unprotected intercourse before reproductive tract is fully cleared of sperm following vasectomy (may be several months). Healing together of the two cut ends of the vas.	Psychological implications of being infertile can sometimes lead to some sexual problems.
Tubal ligation	0.5%	0.5%	Permanent; no other preparations. Very reliable. Minimal health risks.	The procedure not being properly done by the physician.	Rarely, postsurgical infection or other complications. Psychological implications of being infertile.

*See explanation of failure rates in text.

Source: From Robert A. Hutcher et al., *Contraceptive Technology,* 18th ed. Copyright © 2004 by Contraceptive Technology Communications, Inc. Reprinted by permission of Ardent MediaLine.

Good communication between partners should include discussion of what avenues they could pursue should contraception fail. Each partner should be ready to discuss how he or she would want to deal with an unintended pregnancy (Raine et al., 2003). If serious conflicts develop over this issue, the advisability of sharing sexual intercourse at all may be called into question.

Abstinence, Sex without Intercourse, and Withdrawal

One obvious approach to birth control is to avoid the depositing of semen in the vagina. Some couples, especially unmarried teenagers, choose abstinence—usually defined as refraining from sexual intercourse—for this reason. Abstinence is sometimes defined as the avoidance of any form of sexual behavior, but more often it means that intercourse is avoided. There are varieties of sexual behavior that couples may find pleasurable and satisfying without having intercourse. These include massage, mutual masturbation, oral sex, and all sorts of physical intimacy not involving penetration. The alternatives to intercourse, which have been called "outercourse," have been praised as a form of birth control that is simple to use and free of side effects and also may reduce the risks of giving or getting sexually transmitted diseases. College students clearly are engaging in many forms of sexual interaction other than heterosexual intercourse and often do not consider these other behaviors as "having sex."

However it may be defined, the reality of various forms of abstinence is that people do change their minds and may not have an alternative method of birth control prepared for this possibility. While there is no reliable actual use failure rate for abstinence, the method clearly fails quite frequently (Blinn-Pike et al., 2004).

Withdrawal, also known as **coitus interruptus**, is a method that is sometimes used by couples who have not yet obtained some safer method. It is used by about 20 percent of college students in their sexual interactions. The risk of pregnancy with the withdrawal method is high. The penis is withdrawn from the vagina prior to ejaculation, and it is crucial that ejaculation not take place near the opening of the vagina. Withdrawal can prove frustrating for couples who use it frequently. There are a number of reasons why its failure rate is high. One complication is the possibility that sperm may be present in fluids that sometimes are secreted by the penis during intercourse well before ejaculation. There is a greater likelihood of sperm being present in these secretions if the man has experienced ejaculation within the previous few hours. Also, not all men have the ejaculatory control to withdraw in time, and some simply may choose not to do so after all. Nevertheless, when intercourse has been chosen and no other contraceptive method is available, withdrawal is preferable to using no birth control at all.

Oral Contraceptives: The Pill

Birth control pills were introduced in 1960 and rapidly gained in popularity. After concerns developed over potential side effects of some of the earlier types of oral contraception, many women decided to use other methods. However, public opinion about the safety of "the pill" has become markedly more positive, and tens of millions of women around the world now use this method. The pill is available in many countries without prescription, and some believe that its safety and efficacy warrant similar accessibility in North America.

The most widely used birth control pill is the *combined oral contraceptive* that contains a combination of two hormones, estrogen and progestin, taken for 21 days during the menstrual cycle. Most manufacturers provide seven "inert" pills to be taken on the remaining days of the 28-day cycle. There are also *progestin-only pills,* sometimes called *minipills,* which contain only a low dosage of progestin. It is crucial that birth control pills be taken each day at about the same time to avoid compromising their effectiveness. If an entire day goes by without taking the skipped pill, however, it is advisable to use an alternative method of birth control for the remainder of the cycle while continuing to take the rest of the pills. The missed pill should be taken as soon as possible. Indications are that a delay in taking the first three pills of a single cycle does not lead to ovulation during that cycle, provided pill use is resumed. However, taking the pills on schedule during the next cycle is essential; otherwise a backup method should be used (Hatcher et al., 2004). While failure of the pill is uncommon when it is taken on schedule, it is slightly more likely to fail in women who are significantly overweight (Holt, Cushing-Haugen, & Daling, 2002).

It is now possible to obtain a prescription for a three-month regimen that involves taking hormonally active birth control pills for 84 days in a row, followed by seven days of inert pills. These are marketed as Seasonale pills. The woman experiences a menstrual period only every three months, and it is often lighter and briefer than usual (Miller & Notter, 2001). This new approach appears to be proving popular, because it not only reduces the duration of discomfort sometimes associated with menstruation, but also seems to be safe and saves women money on the purchase of female hygiene products (Braunstein et al., 2003).

Oral contraceptives create changes in the menstrual cycle that interrupt normal patterns of ovulation and implantation, thereby preventing pregnancy. Combined oral contraceptives maintain estrogen at artificially high levels, inhibiting the release of FSH and LH, two hormones that control ovulation (see Chapter 2, "Female Sexual Anatomy and Physiology"). Progestin changes the consistency of the cervical mucus so that sperm cannot pass as easily into the uterus and also makes the uterine lining less receptive to implantation by an embryo. Progestin-only pills apparently work in this latter manner, as well as occasionally preventing ovulation. The progestin-only pills are not widely used because they sometimes produce unpleasant side effects, but they are particularly useful for women who are breast-feeding and choose to

coitus interruptus (ko-EET-us *or* KO-ut-us) a method of birth control in which the penis is withdrawn from the vagina prior to ejaculation.

take oral contraceptives. Combined pills sometimes interfere with lactation, whereas the progestin-only pills do not. Neither pill seems to have any negative effects on the babies of women who breast-feed.

The amounts of synthetic hormones contained in oral contraceptives have been markedly reduced since the earlier days of their use, which has reduced the frequency and intensity of their side effects. A number of noncontraceptive benefits of the pill have been identified. It usually makes menstrual periods lighter and more regular, with less cramping. It has reduced the incidence of breast cysts, ovarian cysts, endometriosis, ectopic pregnancy, and pelvic inflammatory disease as well as cancers of the ovary and endometrium (Riman et al., 2002; Greer et al., 2005). Use of the pill has also been associated with increases in bone mass among women in their twenties, perhaps lowering their risk of bone-weakening osteoporosis in later years. Pill use may slightly elevate the risk of heart disease, and the risk of cervical cancer increases the longer the pill is used (Smith, J. S., et al., 2003; Tanis et al., 2001). Oral contraceptives do not seem to increase the risk of breast cancer except among women who have the genetic mutations that make them more susceptible to the disease (Davidson & Helzlsouer, 2002; Narod et al., 2002). It has long been thought that there was a link between the pill and a slight risk of strokes, but as long as women do not smoke or have high blood pressure, that risk now seems negligible (Chan et al., 2004). After discontinuation of the pill for 10 years, all risks are the same as those for women who have never used the pill.

Current research seems to indicate that for healthy women under age 35 who do not smoke, the benefits of the pill outweigh the risks. Although smoking increases the risk of heart attack and stroke for anyone, using the pill seems to compound the risk. Therefore, it usually is inadvisable for a woman who smokes to take birth control pills.

A very important consideration before obtaining oral contraceptives is to get a good physical examination and have a complete health history taken. Certain conditions, such as a history of blood-clotting disorders or high blood pressure, indicate to family planning specialists that the pill should not be prescribed. Follow-up checks that include blood pressure readings and an annual Pap test also should be required of anyone taking birth control pills.

There are a few symptoms a pill user should consider warning signs. Pain in the abdomen or gastrointestinal disorders may signal the development of liver disease, Crohn's disease, or ulcerative colitis, all conditions that occasionally are associated with oral contraceptive use. Chest pain accompanied by coughing or difficulty breathing may be a sign of a blood clot in the lungs or of a heart condition. Pain in the legs may result from blood clots in the veins located there. Severe headaches or marked changes in vision may indicate high blood pressure or other conditions that can increase the risk of stroke and cardiovascular disease. Although these complications are not widespread among women who use oral contraceptives, women need to educate themselves about warning signals and should report symptoms or concerns to a medical clinician immediately (Picardo et al., 2003).

Contraceptive pills can have other troublesome side effects, although they are not usually dangerous. These include depression, acne, fluid retention and associated weight gain, abnormal bleeding, and absence of menstrual periods. Research with the pill has shown mixed results in terms of possible effects on mood or sexual interest (Joffe, Cohen, & Harlow, 2003). Some studies have shown that combined pills may lower the user's sense of well-being and sexual interest, whereas other studies tend to show that combined pill users actually have greater sexual interest than users of the progestin-only pills. The impact of the pill on sexual desire seems to be mixed and unpredictable (Davis & Castano, 2005; Schaffir, 2006). In one study, side effects were reduced by inserting the pill into the vagina, where it may be absorbed into the bloodstream, rather than taking it orally (Ziaei et al., 2002). Certain antibiotics, including ampicillin and tetracycline, interfere with internal absorption of the pill. Tranquilizers, barbiturates, sleeping pills, some anti-inflammatory medications, and some sulfa drugs may also reduce the pill's contraceptive effectiveness. Nevertheless, oral contraceptives continue to be a particularly effective and relatively safe form of birth control for many women.

Hormonal Implants, Patches, and Rings

Contraceptive implants consist of six slender silicone rubber capsules or rods containing a contraceptive steroid called levonorgestrel, a form of progestin. Implants were taken off the market because of a combination of factors, including their cost, unpleasant side effects, and the advent of other effective hormonal methods. They were placed under the skin on the inside of the woman's upper arm, in a fan-shaped configuration, and the drug very slowly diffused through the walls of the capsules into the body. Range of use was up to five years. Like other forms of progestin-only contraception, the implant hormone prevented ovulation and caused cervical mucus to thicken so that sperm could not easily penetrate into the uterus. Research and development continue on new kinds of implants, including single-rod

contraceptive implants contraceptive method in which hormone-releasing rubber cylinders are surgically inserted under the skin of the woman.

FIGURE 11.5   *The Contraceptive Patch*

and two-rod versions, both of which would slowly release progestin into the body (Long, 2003).

Patches that can be placed on the skin and emit hormones into the bloodstream are now available (see Figure 11.5). Currently marketed as Ortho Evra, the patch contains doses of estrogen and progestin, so the side effects are similar to those of the pill. A patch is put in place weekly for three weeks in a row, followed by a week without a patch during which the menstrual period occurs. The patch can be placed on different sites on the body, under the clothing. Care must be taken that it does not fall off (Smallwood et al., 2001).

One of the newest hormonal contraceptives is the **vaginal ring,** marketed as NuvaRing in the United States. It is inserted into the vagina and left there for 21 days, after which it is removed for seven days and menstruation occurs. A new ring is used each month, and women must learn how to insert it properly. It is sometimes felt during intercourse, but in general women seem to like the method, and it has proved to be safe and effective (Dieben, Roumen, & Apter, 2002).

Injectables

Injections of long-acting progestin have also been used for contraception in many countries. One form, **Depo-Provera,** the brand name for depot medroxy-

progesterone acetate (DMPA), acts by creating conditions in the uterus that are inhospitable for embryo implantation. Injections are available that are effective for either one month or three months. Injectables can have a number of side effects, including weight gain, hair loss, heavy menstrual bleeding, disruption of periods, emotional reactions, and fatigue, but the unpleasant side effects are reduced in the once-a-month dosage (Reiss, 2000). Only about 57 percent of women who have received a three-month injection return for a second, and the one-year continuation rate was about 23 percent in one study. Side effects seem to be the main reason why some women discontinue use of the three-month dosage, although the one-month dosage has achieved somewhat better acceptance. Tests on Depo-Provera have generally indicated that it is not associated with an increased risk of liver cancer, and it may protect against cancer of the endometrium, although it might slightly elevate the risk of cervical cancer. It may slightly increase women's risk of becoming infected with certain sexually transmitted diseases, probably because condoms are not used during sexual activity (Guillebaud, 2004; Morrison et al., 2004).

Spermicides, Sponges, and Suppositories

Spermicides, or chemicals that kill sperm, are available without prescription as foams, creams, or jellies or placed in a sponge or suppository. There is also a spermicidal film, a paper-thin sheet that may be placed near the cervix and allowed to melt. The spermicidal chemical usually used is nonoxynol-9 or octoxynol. These generally are not considered a highly effective method of contraception when used alone, but they are very effective when used with other methods such as condoms or diaphragms. Used alone, they must be inserted deeply into the vagina so that they cover the cervical opening. Some spermicides have an unpleasant taste that can limit the pleasure of oral sexual contact with the woman following their insertion, although some companies are marketing flavored and scented brands. Recent research has demonstrated that spermicides can cause vaginal irritation, which may, in fact, increase the risk

vaginal ring a hormonal contraceptive that is inserted into the vagina for three weeks of each monthly cycle.

Depo-Provera an injectable form of progestin that can prevent pregnancy for one or three months.

spermicides chemicals that kill sperm; available as foams, creams, jellies, film, or suppositories.

of HIV infection or other sexually transmitted diseases (Hatcher et al., 2004). The Food and Drug Administration now requires that a warning to this effect be placed on packaging for contraceptives containing spermicides. Some condom makers have ceased using nonoxynol-9 with their products. Research is proceeding with the development of microbicides that would kill sperm as well as disease agents. Such chemicals would represent a major step forward.

The contraceptive **sponge** is a round, thick, polyurethane disk with a dimple that fits over the cervix. Its manufacture was discontinued for a few years in the mid-1990s, but it is now back on the market. The sponge contains nonoxynol-9 and also acts as a barrier to sperm. It may be left in place for up to 24 hours, a significant advantage, although its rate of effectiveness is somewhat lower than that of several other methods.

Contraceptive **suppositories** are designed to melt or foam in the vagina to distribute the spermicide within them. However, this takes between 10 and 30 minutes, necessitating the postponement of intercourse. Some suppositories do not always liquefy completely. Their effectiveness is the same as that of other forms of spermicide. How the new concerns about spermicides and STDs will affect the use of sponges and suppositories remains to be seen.

Barrier Methods

Barrier methods are those contraceptives that block sperm from entering the uterus, thereby preventing conception. Their effectiveness is enhanced when they are used in conjunction with a spermicide, although directions should always be followed carefully to ensure that the proper spermicide is chosen and that it is used correctly with the barrier. Additional use of a condom increases the effectiveness of the other barrier methods and helps prevent the spread of sexually transmitted diseases.

Diaphragms and Cervical Caps

 A **diaphragm** is a latex rubber cup with a flexible rim that is placed in the vagina in such a way as to cover the cervix (see Figure 11.6). **Spermicidal jelly** or cream is placed inside the diaphragm and around its rim to help hold it in place and kill sperm. A clinician must fit the diaphragm to the woman, and the woman must learn how to insert it properly (Hatcher et al., 2004). Once this is learned, insertion of a diaphragm becomes a quick and simple matter. It should not be inserted more than two hours prior to intercourse. After this time period, if intercourse has not yet occurred, a diaphragm should be removed and more spermicide added before intercourse takes place. The diaphragm

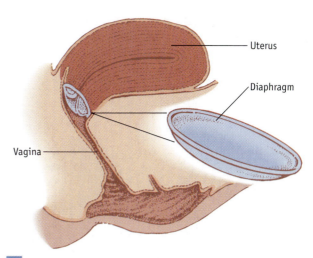

FIGURE 11.6 *Diaphragm*

The diaphragm is a mechanical barrier to sperm that comes in different sizes and must be fitted to a woman by a clinician or physician. Because it may be dislodged during lovemaking, it is best to combine its use with a condom. Its reliability rate is fairly high when used properly and with a spermicide.

is left in place for at least 6 to 8 hours, but not more than 24 hours, following intercourse, after which it is removed and washed. It can be used for many months, although it should be checked by a doctor from time to time to ensure that it still fits over the cervix properly and is not damaged. Because the diaphragm is comparatively inexpensive, can be used for years, and presents few health risks, it has been increasing in popularity in recent years. Also, protecting the cervix may protect against transmission of HIV and other STDs, and new attention is being given to this possible advantage of diaphragm use (Harvey, Bird, & Branch, 2003). Some research is focusing on the development of disposable diaphragms. The diaphragm is not, however, an ideal contraceptive for a woman who might feel uncomfortable touching her own

sponge a thick, polyurethane disk that holds a spermicide and fits over the cervix to prevent conception.

suppositories contraceptive devices designed to distribute their spermicide by melting or foaming in the vagina.

diaphragm (DY-a-fram) a latex rubber cup, filled with spermicide, that is fitted to the cervix by a clinician; the woman must learn to insert it properly for full contraceptive effectiveness.

spermicidal jelly (or cream) sperm-killing chemical in a gel base or cream, used with other contraceptives such as diaphragms.

■ **FIGURE 11.7** *Cervical Caps*

Similar to the diaphragm, the cervical cap must be fitted to the woman by a clinician. It stays in place by suction and can be worn for several weeks at a time. It may be uncomfortable for some males during intercourse and can be easily dislodged.

■ **FIGURE 11.8** *Male Condoms*

A birth control device for men, the condom is made of latex rubber, animal skin, or polyurethane. It is unrolled onto the erect penis before intercourse begins and collects the semen that are ejaculated. Care must be taken that the penis does not lose its erect state while in the vagina. Latex rubber condoms are also important in preventing many sexually transmitted diseases, including protecting against HIV.

genitals or inserting something into her vagina, and concerns about insertion or removal are one drawback of this method for many women (Maher et al., 2004).

The **cervical cap** looks like a large thimble with a tall dome (see Figure 11.7). As its name implies, it is designed to fit over the cervix. Because relatively few companies manufacture them, they are not as easily obtained in the United States as some other methods. Like the diaphragm, caps must be fitted by a clinician, inserted properly, and used with a spermicide. They can dislodge fairly easily during intercourse, and they have been implicated in some scratching of the vagina and cervix. Researchers are working to develop a cervical cap out of a material that will automatically release spermicide when semen is present. A new and more comfortable cervical cap made of silicone rubber is currently available over the counter in several European countries and Canada (Long, 2003).

Diaphragms and cervical caps may increase the risk of a woman's developing **toxic shock syndrome (TSS);** an infection caused by *Staphylococcus aureus* bacteria that are normally present in the body and multiply if something is left in the vagina for a long period of time. TSS has also been associated with tampon use. It is not a common disease, and resulting deaths are rare. Nevertheless, when using a diaphragm or cervical cap, it is advisable not to leave the device in place for more than 48 hours. Use should be avoided during menstruation, for a few months following the birth of a baby, or in the presence of a vaginal infection.

Male Condoms

The **male condom** is a sheath worn over the penis during intercourse that collects the semen when the male ejaculates (see Figure 11.8). Most condoms today are made of latex rubber (hence the name "rubbers") and are available inexpensively in drugstores, supermarkets, convenience stores, vending machines, and some college bookstores. Rubber condoms may be purchased dry or lubricated, and some have a small nipple at the tip, providing a semen-collection area.

cervical cap a device that is shaped like a large thimble and fits over the cervix; not a particularly effective contraceptive because it can dislodge easily during intercourse.

toxic shock syndrome (TSS) an acute disease characterized by fever and sore throat; caused by normal bacteria in the vagina that are activated if tampons or contraceptive devices such as diaphragms are left in for a long period of time.

male condom a sheath worn over the penis during intercourse that collects semen and helps prevent disease transmission.

Some condoms are lubricated with a spermicide that has been shown to be effective in killing sperm within a minute or two after ejaculation, providing more contraceptive effectiveness. Condoms made of animal membrane are also available and cost slightly more than rubber condoms. These skin condoms purportedly allow more sensation on the penis, although they fit more loosely than rubber condoms and should be checked from time to time during intercourse to make certain that slipping has not occurred. Skin condoms are *not* acceptable as a preventive against transmitting HIV, whereas latex rubber condoms offer substantial protection.

Rubber condoms should never be stored in wallets or automobile glove compartments, because warm temperatures deteriorate rubber. Petroleum jelly (such as Vaseline), mineral and vegetable oils, and some moisturizing lotions or creams also will weaken rubber and cause tearing. Polyurethane condoms are also available. Polyurethane is thinner and stronger than latex and is especially beneficial for people who are allergic to latex; these condoms can be used with oil-based lubricants. Polyurethane condoms provide protection against HIV as well as other sexually transmitted diseases, and they receive similar ratings from users as rubber condoms. More specific directions and suggestions for condom use are found in Chapter 17.

Studies of college students have found that for men who use condoms and put them on themselves, problems and errors in use are quite common. Three-fourths of men did not inspect the condoms for damage, and 61 percent failed to check the expiration date on the wrapper. Other common errors included not putting the condom on until after starting sex (43 percent), not leaving a space without air at the tip of the condom (40 percent), and flipping the condom over after putting it on inside out (30 percent) (Crosby et al., 2002). When women put the condoms on their partners, the rate of these mistakes becomes even higher, but counseling in appropriate usage skills can help a great deal (Artz et al., 2005; Sanders et al., 2003). Several studies have placed the rate of latex condom breakage or slippage at under 7 percent, although the more experience the woman or man has with condom use, the less likely breakage or slipping will occur. Although polyurethane condoms are preferred over latex by about half the couples who use them, the frequency with which they break or slip off seems to be somewhat higher, making them somewhat riskier for both pregnancy and disease prevention (Walsh et al., 2003). Young people in the United States often have misinformation about condom use, which may well contribute to its failure (Crosby & Yarber, 2001).

Even though it is widely known that using a condom is one of the best ways to prevent the spread of sexually transmitted diseases, many couples do not use condoms when they have an alternate method of birth control (Nangle & Grover, 2001; Oncale & King, 2001). Condom use increased from a rate of 46 percent at last intercourse in 1991 to a rate of 58 percent in 1999, and use has leveled off at that rate since (Centers for Disease Control, 2002). Although condom use seems to have increased because of awareness of HIV, all studies of condom use tend to suggest that couples are not using them on a consistent basis (Nangle & Grover, 2001). Women tend not to use condoms when they perceive their sexual activity to be at low risk, whereas men are more likely not to use condoms because of a perceived lack of availability or the inconvenience of the method. In a survey administered to 247 college students, 46.7 percent indicated they had participated in sexual activity while not using a condom, when they would have preferred to use one, since the age of 16. Two-thirds of the students had experienced unwanted noncondom use with their current or most recent sexual partner. These findings suggest that partner resistance to condom use may require more assertiveness and support in order for young people to carry out their intentions to protect themselves against pregnancy and disease (Artz et al., 2005; Smith, 2003).

There has been controversy about the distribution of free condoms in school systems or clinics. Research evidence indicates that condom availability in high schools actually does not increase rates of sexual activity but does increase the use of condoms during sex. Such availability particularly increases the likelihood of condom use among people who have multiple sex partners, partly because the cost of condoms is sometimes prohibitive (Sidley, 2003).

Female Condom or Vaginal Pouch   **FOH**

The **female condom** is a lubricated polyurethane pouch that is inserted into the vagina. Sometimes called the *vaginal pouch,* it has been marketed in the United States under the brand name Reality. In Europe, it is called Femidom. The female condom design (see Figure 11.9) consists of a ring at both ends, one of which is sealed. The ring at the closed end is inserted into the back of the vagina and over the cervix, much as a diaphragm would be fitted into place. The open-ended ring then rests outside on the vulva, providing an extra measure of protection

female condom a lubricated polyurethane pouch that is inserted into the vagina before intercourse to collect semen and help prevent disease transmission.

FIGURE 11.9 *Female Condom*

This diagram shows one "female condom" design that is now available. The inner ring is closed and is inserted into the vagina to cover the cervix. The open outer ring covers the vulva.

against skin-to-skin contact. Studies indicate that women often need careful instruction on how to properly insert and place the device and that continued use of the female condom seems to depend on proper instruction in its use (Artz et al., 2005; Hoffman et al., 2003; Van Devanter et al., 2002).

About half of women tend to have initial positive reactions to the female condom, and many eventually prefer it over the male condom. They tend not to be aware of it during intercourse, and in some cases it increases their sexual pleasure. Apparently, using extra lubricant during intercourse is key to reducing each partner's awareness of the presence of the device. Women who have had negative reactions to the vaginal pouch objected to its feel and sound when it was inserted and felt that the lubricant made it messy. Some objected to its appearance on the outside of the vulva. Many women endorse the female condom because it allows them a greater degree of control over maintaining safer sexual practices (Hatcher et al., 2004).

The obvious advantage of the female condom is that women can take full responsibility for its use as a protection against pregnancy and disease. It conducts body heat well, enhancing the sensation for both partners. The device almost never breaks or leaks, although it may slip out of place nearly 10 percent of the time. One study suggested that women using the female condom might have been exposed to semen during 7 to 21 percent of uses of the condom (Lawson et al., 2003; Macaluso et al., 2003). The female condom may be washed and reused up to seven times. It is likely that, in typical use, the failure rate of the female condom is not significantly different from that of the diaphragm and cervical cap. Apparently, the outer edges of the fe-

male condom can get pushed down into the vagina during intercourse, permitting spillage of semen—something that regular checking during intercourse could help detect and avoid. Educating women and their male partners seems to be important in encouraging proper use of female condoms (Witte et al., 2006). As experience with using condoms grows, their failure rates decrease (Valappil et al., 2005).

The barrier methods all must be inserted or put on sometime prior to sex. Although some people find this inconvenient, the possibility exists of integrating the use of a contraceptive into sexual activities. For example, if a couple is using condoms and foam, the man can insert the foam into the woman's vagina, and the woman can unroll the condom onto the man's penis. A man could help insert the female condom into his partner's vagina. Birth control methods, like any other aspect of a responsible sexual relationship, require communication and cooperative effort. The effectiveness of the vaginal barrier methods is heavily influenced by the age of the user. Younger women apparently are more fertile and may have a greater frequency of intercourse. The failure rate of barrier methods for women under age 30 is approximately twice their failure rate for women over age 30 (Hatcher et al., 2004). Because the female condom is the only method women can use by themselves that also helps protect against disease transmission, it is unfortunate that it continues to be less widely accepted than the male condom by both women and men. It is hoped that education about the female device will lead to an increase in its popularity (Hoffman et al., 2004; Kulczycki et al., 2004).

Intrauterine Devices (IUDs)

Intrauterine devices (IUDs) have been used for over a century and were particularly popular in the 1960s and 1970s. Because of concerns about problems with the device and subsequent lawsuits, the IUD was eventually removed from the market but has been gradually reappearing. It is now known that much of the early information was based on faulty data. Myths and misinformation about IUDs continue to cause clinicians to prescribe it infrequently, and then to limit it to certain women. Many experts in contraception believe that this is unfortunate, because the IUD is an extremely effective method that lasts 5 to 10 years, is comparatively inexpensive, requires practically no user maintenance, and is completely reversible (Stanwood, Garrett, & Konrad, 2002).

Two types of IUDs currently are marketed in the United States. One is the TCu380A, which contains

intrauterine devices (IUDs) birth control method involving the insertion of a small plastic device into the uterus.

copper; because of its shape, it is sometimes called the Copper T. Marketed under the brand name Para-Gard, it releases copper ions into the uterus. The other type of IUD, the LNG-IUS, releases the hormone levonorgestrel into the uterus for up to five years. Either type of IUD can produce some side effects. The Copper T can increase menstrual blood loss and cramping, while the LNG-IUS can cause spotting between periods during its first few months of use. Later on, it actually tends to reduce blood loss during menstruation or to cause periods to end in about 20 percent of users (Hubacher, 2002). Its use has not been associated with any increased risk of breast cancer (Backman et al., 2005).

IUDs are made of plastic and have a nylon thread attached to one end. The contraceptive is inserted into the uterus by a clinician, with the thread left protruding into the vagina so that the woman can check regularly to make certain the IUD is still in place (see Figure 11.10). If pregnancy is desired, the device must be removed by a clinician. Threadless IUDs are being tested and may help prevent the uterine infections that sometimes are associated with IUD use.

Contrary to popular belief, IUDs do not cause an embryo to be aborted from the uterus. The most current evidence indicates that the IUD prevents fertilization of the egg through its effects on sperm and on the egg. The chemicals and copper ions present in the uterus and fallopian tubes also alter the transport of sperm. It was once believed that IUDs interfered with

implantation of a fertilized egg in the uterus, but that does not seem to be the case (Guillebaud, 2004). For the first three weeks after insertion of an IUD, the woman has a slightly greater risk of an infection called **pelvic inflammatory disease (PID).** If left untreated for a long enough time, PID can cause damage to the fallopian tubes, resulting in sterility. IUDs once were believed to be associated with a higher risk of ectopic pregnancy, but recent studies have not supported that belief. In fact, the IUD is a very effective form of contraception, and may well become more popular in years to come as some of the myths and misperceptions about its use disappear.

Natural Family Planning/Fertility Awareness

Natural family planning/fertility awareness, once known as the *rhythm method,* relies on awareness of a woman's menstrual/fertility cycle so that intercourse can be avoided when it is likely that the ovum might be available for fertilization. Because it does not require any chemical or manufactured device, it is considered more "natural"; in another sense, it certainly is not natural for a couple to avoid intercourse just when they naturally want to have it. Because it requires a great deal of planning and daily attention, it is associated with a high rate of failure as a contraceptive method. Because fertility awareness allows a couple to know when the ovum is most likely to be present for fertilization, it also can be used by couples who are attempting to get pregnant.

There are three fertility awareness methods. To use each effectively, the woman or couple should receive careful and complete instruction from a specialist trained in any of these methods, which can be used in combination. Various charts must be made for six or more successive months before the method is actually tried as a contraceptive. The *calendar method* charts the beginning and length of the menstrual cycle. The *basal body temperature (BBT) method* charts the resting body temperature of the woman throughout the menstrual cycle (see Figure 11.11). Usually, the temperature drops slightly just before ovulation and rises after. A special oral thermometer is used to take these readings. Finally, the *mucus method* keeps track of the appearance and consistency of the woman's cervical

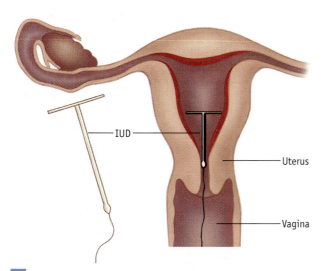

FIGURE 11.10 *IUD*

The IUD, or intrauterine device, is a small plastic object inserted into the uterus by a trained physician or clinician and left in place for long periods of time. It can be a highly effective form of birth control, but serious side effects have been caused by some types of IUDs. Only three types of IUDs remain available in the United States.

pelvic inflammatory disease (PID) a chronic internal infection of the uterus and other organs.

natural family planning/fertility awareness a natural method of birth control that depends on an awareness of the woman's menstrual/fertility cycle.

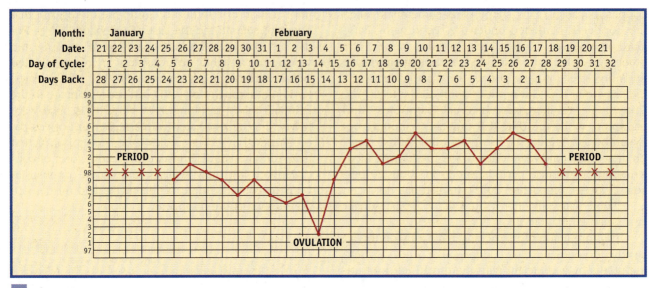

FIGURE 11.11 *Basal Body Temperature Record*

The woman's resting body temperature is taken each morning immediately on waking. Just prior to ovulation, there is a noticeable drop in the temperature. Then, for up to three days after, the temperature rises. It is usually recommended that the basal body temperature be charted for three or four successive months so that any peculiarities in the woman's cycle can be noted. After the time of ovulation has become obviously predictable, the information can be used as part of the natural family planning method of birth control or for determining the best time for conception to occur.

mucus during the menstrual cycle. Women can learn to recognize that cervical mucus becomes clearer and more slippery during ovulation.

By combining the information gained from these methods, the woman should be able to predict with accuracy about when ovulation will take place. During several days prior to ovulation and up to four days after, either intercourse should be avoided or alternative birth control should be used. As a whole, fertility awareness requires a great deal of cooperation and communication between the partners. The most recent research has shown that pregnancy is most likely to occur during the six consecutive days that end in ovulation. This is different from what previously has been believed and may help explain the rather high failure rates associated with this method of birth control (Hatcher et al., 2004).

Some over-the-counter tests are available that can help a woman determine when ovulation is most likely to occur. The tests involve measuring the amount of luteinizing hormone (LH) in the urine once a day for about a week during the middle part of the menstrual cycle. Like other predictive techniques, these tests can be used either to avoid pregnancy or to increase the likelihood of becoming pregnant. When used consistently, these tests can predict ovulation within a 48-hour period. Continued development of accurate, easy-to-use indicators of ovulation may significantly improve the effectiveness of natural family planning.

Voluntary Surgical Contraception (Sterilization)

Voluntary surgical contraception (VSC), or sterilization, usually renders a person permanently infertile and has become the most common method of contraception. Two-fifths of ever-married women or their husbands in the United States ages 15 to 44 have been sterilized. Only a small minority regret the decision (Jamieson et al., 2002). VSC is accomplished either by cutting the vas deferens in the male, the tube through which sperm travel, or by tying or clamping off the fallopian tubes in the woman so an ovum no longer can travel through them. Of course, surgical procedures that remove the uterus or ovaries will also cause sterility.

Male sterilization, called **vasectomy,** is a simple procedure in which a small incision is made in each side of the scrotum and each vas deferens is cut and tied (see Figure 11.12). It is one of the most frequently chosen methods of birth control in the United States

voluntary surgical contraception (VSC) sterilization; rendering a person incapable of conceiving with surgical procedures that interrupt the passage of the egg or sperm.

vasectomy (va-SEK-ta-mee *or* vay-ZEK-ta-mee) a surgical cutting and tying of the vas deferens to induce permanent male sterilization.

Real People

Joanne and Arthur: Settling on a Contraceptive Method

Joanne and Arthur had been involved in a relationship for seven months and had been using male condoms during sexual intercourse. Arthur continued to be dissatisfied with condoms, saying that he found it difficult to maintain his erection while using a condom. They both agreed that they wanted an effective means of preventing pregnancy, and they also realized that the condom was providing protection against possible disease transmission. Both had been sexually active with other partners prior to this relationship. After some discussion, they agreed that because they had both been sexually exclusive with each other, they would get tested for HIV and other sexually transmitted diseases and then make a decision about a contraceptive. Their medical tests were all negative, and they then made an appointment at a local family planning clinic to talk about contraception.

After hearing about the various methods of birth control available to them, Joanne and Arthur decided to consider either the diaphragm or the female condom. Joanne's medical history ruled out hormonal methods such as the pill, the patch, or injections. They wanted to use a method that had as few side effects as possible and could be discontinued with ease. The clinic worker scheduled an appointment for Joanne to be fitted with a diaphragm, but the couple also received some female condoms to try in the meantime. As it turned out, they liked the female pouches because they provided better sexual sensations for both of them. Joanne decided not to proceed with getting a diaphragm because she was not satisfied that it would provide the degree of contraceptive protection she wanted. The couple chose to continue using the female condom because they both found it comfortable and easy to use. The clinician had explained that statistics on the effectiveness of the female device were still incomplete, but Joanne and Arthur felt that they could use it correctly and carefully and would have more control over its effectiveness than they would a diaphragm.

Do you think this couple is making a good decision? Should they be talking about what they would consider if a pregnancy happened to occur? Would you be comfortable with the choice of method they have made? Why or why not?

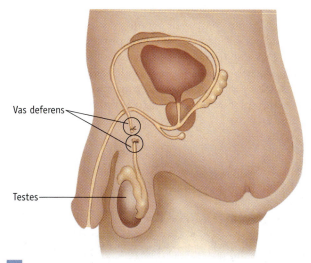

Vas deferens

Testes

■ FIGURE 11.12 *Vasectomy*

A permanent form of male contraception, vasectomy is a surgical procedure in which the vas deferens is cut and tied, blocking the passage of sperm from the testes to the upper part of the vas deferens. It is a simple and safe form of birth control and does not interfere with erection or ejaculation.

(Barone et al., 2004). The operation is usually an office procedure that requires less than 30 minutes. It does not affect sexual functioning or ejaculation. There simply are no more sperm cells in the semen. In a few rare instances, men have again ejaculated sperm and impregnated a partner after an apparently successful vasectomy, so there is a tiny possibility of failure.

See "Vasectomy" on SexSource Online.

Tubal sterilization, the method of sterilization most often used for women, is becoming an even more desirable procedure as the technology improves (Godecker, Thomson, & Bumpass, 2001). It may be performed through an operation called a **laparotomy,**

laparotomy (lap-ar-OTT-uh-mee) operation to perform a tubal ligation, or female sterilization, involving an abdominal incision.

which requires a hospital stay, or by the more simple **laparoscopy,** in which a small fiber-optic scope is inserted into the abdomen through a tiny incision, enabling the physician to see the fallopian tubes clearly. Through either method, the fallopian tubes are located, a small portion of each tube is removed, and then the ends are tied and sealed—a procedure called **tubal ligation** (see Figure 11.13). Although failure of this method is not common, the possibility of failure may persist for many years after the procedure (MacKay et al., 2001). A less invasive sterilization procedure for women has now been approved for use in the United States, but it has been available for a longer time in Canada, Europe, and Australia. The **Essure transcervical sterilization procedure,** as it is called, involves the insertion of a coil through the uterus into each fallopian tube. The coils cause tissue to grow in the tubes over a three-month period, eventually blocking them. During the first three months, an alternative form of birth control must be used. The procedure requires only a local anesthetic (American Health Consultants, 2003; Valle, Carignan, & Wright, 2001).

See "Tubal Ligation" on SexSource Online.

Tubal ligations and vasectomies can sometimes be reversed, restoring fertility. However, attempts at reversal are complicated, expensive, and only 40 to 70 percent

successful. There has been somewhat more success in reversing vasectomies, and a recent study found that in most men who had the procedure reversed within 15 years, sperm could still be produced. Beyond that time, results have been less promising (Boorjian, Lipkin, & Goldstein, 2004). In general, sterilization should be chosen as a contraceptive method only when a decision has been made that a permanent method is desired. Some physicians require the consent of a spouse before performing sterilization or refuse to sterilize individuals who do not have any children, but there are no laws requiring that either condition be met prior to sterilization.

Under what circumstances might you consider having a tubal ligation or vasectomy?

Emergency Contraception: Plan B

Because contraceptive technology is imperfect and people continue to engage in sexual intercourse without birth control, demand continues for "morning-after" or emergency birth control. This has become known as "Plan B." Women who have experienced unprotected intercourse have traditionally used a variety of methods to avoid pregnancy, such as douching (washing out) the vagina, wiping out the vagina with their fingers, or moving their bodies in an attempt to expel the semen. Some folk remedies recommend insertion of objects or special concoctions into the vagina. However, there is no evidence that such techniques in any way reduce the likelihood of conception. Sperm cells will still make their way into the woman's reproductive system, and if an ovum is present, fertilization may well occur.

Current emergency contraceptive methods most often probably delay or prevent ovulation so that the ovum is not available for fertilization. They may sometimes act by causing early menstruation, thereby preventing implantation of a blastocyst in the uterine wall.

FIGURE 11.13 *Tubal Ligation*

A permanent form of female sterilization, this surgical procedure is somewhat more complicated than a vasectomy. The fallopian tubes are cut and tied, usually with a small portion of each tube being removed. This prevents the egg from traveling into the uterus and joining with sperm.

laparoscopy (lap-ar-OSK-uh-pee) simpler procedure for tubal ligation involving the insertion of a small fiber-optic scope into the abdomen, through which the surgeon can see the fallopian tubes and close them off.

tubal ligation (lie-GAY-shun) a surgical cutting and tying of the fallopian tubes to induce permanent female sterilization.

Essure transcervical sterilization procedure a less invasive alternative to tubal ligation in which a small coil is implanted in the fallopian tube through a small abdominal incision. Tissue grows on the coil, eventually blocking the ovum.

For this reason, emergency contraception is controversial. If these methods prevent implantation of the embryo, some would consider them **abortifacients,** substances that cause termination of pregnancy. The American College of Obstetricians and Gynecologists technically defines pregnancy as implantation, and emergency contraception does not allow this to occur. Therefore, proponents of emergency contraception claim that it actually prevents abortions because it eliminates the need to terminate a pregnancy. Unfortunately, press reports about emergency contraception so often are filled with inaccurate information that it is no wonder people are confused about it (Moore & Smith, 2003; Pruitt & Mullen, 2005).

The FDA recently has approved the use of extra doses of birth control pills for emergency contraceptive use, even though many physicians have been prescribing them as such for some time. Typically, a dose of levonorgestrel is given, followed by another dose 12 hours later, although the entire dosage may be given at one time. Both methods have proved quite effective. It is usually recommended that emergency contraception be administered within 72 hours of the unprotected sex, but studies show that it can be effective for up to five days after (Ellertson et al., 2003). In an international study of more than 4,000 women using various methods of emergency contraception, fewer than 2 percent of the women became pregnant, and it was assumed that from 77 to 82 percent of expected pregnancies had been averted (Von Hertzen et al., 2002). Other studies have demonstrated that easy access to emergency contraception does not increase reliance on their use, nor does it lead to riskier sexual behavior (Harper et al., 2005; Marston, Meltzer, & Majeed, 2005; Moreau, Bajos, & Trussell, 2006; Raine et al., 2005).

In recent years, the general public has become increasingly aware of emergency contraceptive availability, and clinicians have been making increased use of these methods. However, there are also indications that women need to be more clearly educated about the method. Most college health centers now have emergency contraception available to students, and several hundred high school–based health centers offer the pills (McCarthy, Telljohann, Coventry, & Price, 2005). Some urban clinics have given at-risk women the emergency contraceptive in advance, to be used if needed. These women were indeed more likely to use the method, although its availability did not seem to affect the consistency with which they used other methods (Gold et al., 2004; Jackson, R. A., et al., 2003). Emergency contraceptive pills are available over the counter in several states, although women often have not been aware of the option, and the FDA may approve such availability throughout the United States (Foster et al., 2006; Weldin et al., 2006).

New Methods of Contraception

Development of new contraceptives has proceeded very slowly. Drug companies often are reluctant to invest in researching new birth control methods because the costs are high, profit potentials often are low, and there are always fears of lawsuits because of possible side effects. There has been continued discussion among family planning specialists about making more methods available for males, and there has been a recent resurgence of interest in developing such methods.

The most promising avenues of research have involved either the suppression of sperm production in males or inhibition of the ability of sperm to fertilize an ovum. For many years, elevated levels of testosterone in men have been known to cause a reversible and pronounced reduction in sperm production. The birth control technique currently being studied involves the use of testosterone implants along with progestin injections, or levonorgestrel implants along with testosterone injections or patches. Each method has been shown to suppress sperm production within a few months. The drugs have had no adverse effects, and sperm production resumes at its normal levels when they are discontinued (Gonzalo, Swerdloff, & Nelson, 2002; Turner et al., 2003). Research and development of such methods for males will continue, and a new product soon may be available to the general public (Anderson & Baird, 2002).

Contraceptive vaccines represent a new possibility for women. One vaccine under development in India involves immunizing women against human chorionic gonadotropin, so that implantation of the blastocyst in the uterus is prevented. These injections would have to be followed by booster shots every few months to offer continued protection. One of the newest avenues for contraceptive research and development involves various ways of blocking the union of sperm and egg. As cellular chemists identify the various protein structures of the outer coverings of the sperm and egg, it may well become possible to develop contraceptive chemicals that could interfere with the sperm's binding to the zona pellucida of the egg or prevent it from burrowing through the zona, preventing fertilization. Such contraceptive methods are not likely to be available for several years, but they provide hope for the future of contraceptive technology.

What method of birth control would you favor and why?

abortifacients any drugs or chemical substances that can trigger the termination of a pregnancy.

Real Student Voices

■ I used one of those home pregnancy tests, and it came out positive (sort of, anyway). My boyfriend and I began to make plans for what we were going to do, although we never really finalized anything. I then had another test at a clinic, and it turned out to be negative. It was a scary time. We've been very careful since that time.

■ I had an abortion during my first year in college. My roommate drove me to the clinic, which was

three hours away. It was a terrible, lonely experience. I never even told the guy, but we didn't have much of a relationship anyway. I don't regret that I had the abortion, but it is not a happy memory either. I've never told my parents about it.

■ My son is the most important thing in my life. I thought of not having him when I first got pregnant, and it hasn't always been easy. But we're making it. He's the light of my life!

 ## ■ Unintended Pregnancy: The Options

There is evidence that the rate of unintended pregnancies among adults in North America has been declining. It has been recognized that "unintendedness" is a complicated concept that must be examined from several different perspectives related to the pregnant woman's life circumstances. A distinction is now made between *unwanted* pregnancies, which occur when no children or no more children are wanted, and *mistimed* pregnancies, which occur earlier than desired or expected. Although the statistics are difficult to analyze and not particularly recent, around half of all pregnancies seem to be unintended, less than the percentage in the 1980s (D'Angelo et al., 2004; Finer & Henshaw, 2006; Santelli et al., 2003).

Worldwide, unwanted pregnancies take an enormous toll. During a recent six-year period, it was estimated that 338 million unwanted pregnancies had occurred, resulting in the deaths of about 700,000 women who had inadequate medical care (Daulaire et al., 2002). In North America, many younger mothers are poor even before they become pregnant. For others, however, pregnancy and young motherhood render them less likely to complete their education and less able to compete in the job market. Some 60 percent continue living with their own parent(s) after giving birth to a child. Regardless of age or circumstances, an unintended pregnancy can lead to emotional anguish and the necessity for careful decision making (Cleland et al., 2006).

Public perceptions about unintended pregnancy also vary among nations. People in the United States tend to see it as a "very big problem" (60 percent), whereas in

Canada about 36 percent of the population rate it in this manner, and in the Netherlands only 6 percent perceive it as such. In the United States, people are likely to blame unintended pregnancy on a decline in moral standards, a lack of education, or barriers to contraceptive use. It should not be forgotten that the fathers involved in unintended pregnancies often experience a great deal of conflict and psychological distress. Contrary to popular belief, most young men do not see impregnating a partner as enhancing their masculinity. Fathers in unintended pregnancies sometimes resent that they have little or no part to play in deciding what to do about the pregnancy yet can be held financially responsible for the baby. They may experience resentment, guilt, and eventual distress if they have little access to their babies or if the woman chooses abortion. Fathers typically are older than mothers, especially when the mothers are teenagers (Boggess & Bradner, 2002).

There are basically three alternatives from which to choose when faced with an unintended pregnancy (see Figure 11.14): keeping the baby, adoption, or termination of the pregnancy (Taverner & Brick, 2006). The choice that ultimately is made apparently depends on several different factors, with attitudes toward childbearing and abortion playing a significant role. Two-thirds of young adults favor women's right to choose abortion, although about the same proportion back the concept of a mandatory waiting period before following through, as well as a requirement that minors obtain parental permission (Kaiser Family Foundation and MTV, 2000). Teenagers tend to have more conservative attitudes toward abortion than adults, yet because of life circumstances they are more likely to decide to have an abortion. It is known that whether a baby is wanted can have long-lasting implications for its health and well-being.

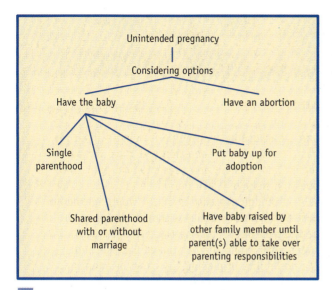

■ **FIGURE 11.14** *The Options Following Unintended Pregnancy*

This chart is a reminder that whenever an unintended pregnancy occurs, some decision must be made. There is no such thing as not making a decision. To avoid considering abortion as an option constitutes a decision to have the baby. The choices might not be comfortable or easy, but one way or another they must be faced and made.

Keeping the Baby

Keeping the baby is a more typical option for married couples or couples who are cohabiting than it is for single individuals. Unmarried young people may face a decision about whether to enter into marriage. Some teenage parents allow their children to be cared for by other relatives until they have completed their education or are otherwise readier to assume parenting responsibility themselves.

In cases of unintended pregnancy, one of the first issues to be considered is whether the mother can accept all the emotional and physical implications of the pregnancy and the birth process. Depending on his degree of involvement, the father's reactions and needs also may need to be considered with care. If other family members will in any way be involved in caring for the child, their feelings about the situation must be weighed. Any individual who is intending to keep a baby should make a clear commitment to and adequate preparations for effective prenatal care, the learning of appropriate parenting skills, and the financial requirements of child rearing.

Adoption

Until about 1970, the majority of young women who had unintended pregnancies placed their babies for adoption. Today the situation is very different, in that fewer than 5 percent of mothers relinquish their babies for adoption. Presently, agencies that handle adoptions are finding it difficult to provide newborn babies for the many childless couples who hope to adopt. This reflects the reality that the availability of abortion has reduced the number of babies available for adoption, as well as a generally negative attitude toward placing children for adoption that is prevalent today (Bitler & Zavodny, 2002). Many young women have learned to think of this option as "giving up your child," the connotations of which are mostly negative. In fact, adoption can be a viable alternative, and in some cases the mother and father are allowed to have contact with the child and the adoptive parents. Young women who place babies for adoption tend to be more affluent, more motivated to pursue education, and more positively disposed toward adoption than are those who keep their babies.

Do you think adopted children/adolescents/adults should be in touch with their birth parents? Defend your position.

Most adoptions are handled through social agencies, but private arrangements involving physicians and/or lawyers sometimes are made. Close to 15,000 children from foreign countries are adopted by American parents each year. It is helpful to talk with adoptive parents and with adults who were adopted as children to get a realistic and complete perspective on the situation. The degree to which adopted children should be allowed to find or contact their birth parents, and vice versa, continues to be a matter of controversy. The most recent studies on children who were adopted as infants have concluded that adopted children and adolescents tend to be happy and well adjusted. Parents of adopted children are more likely than other couples to stay together, and adopted teens are less likely to engage in high-risk health behaviors. It seems that one factor in the positive adjustment of children to the fact of having been adopted is parents who have accepted adoption in a matter-of-fact way and have not dwelled on it.

Adoption is a reasonable option for unintended pregnancy when the mother chooses to continue the pregnancy—or it is too late to do otherwise—yet does not feel ready for the responsibilities of parenthood. Mothers and fathers who choose to have their child adopted often feel that the child will have a chance for a better life with another family. As with any choice that is made in cases of unintended pregnancy, the emotional consequences need to be weighed. Yet most people realize that the option of becoming pregnant will be available again at a later time in life when circumstances lend themselves more fully to acceptance of the responsibility of parenting.

Real People

Max and Millie: Facing a Possible Pregnancy

Max and Millie are seniors in college who have been together for over a year. They often talk about marrying when they have finished school, although Millie is thinking about going to graduate school for a master's degree. They hope to locate near each other after graduation so that the relationship can continue. The two have been sharing a monogamous sexual relationship almost since they began going together, and Millie takes birth control pills for contraception. Last month, Millie missed her period, and they both are concerned that she is pregnant. Millie called the clinic where she had been prescribed the pill, and the nurse told her that if she had mistakenly skipped a pill, she could be pregnant. Millie cannot recall skipping a dose but is not completely certain.

The two of them have been discussing what action they might take if it turns out that Millie is pregnant. Max has said that he would be willing to marry her but admits that such rushed circumstances would not be the scenario he would prefer. Millie has indicated that she probably would want to have an abortion, largely because she does not feel ready to be a good mother and does not want to put her graduate work and career on hold at the moment. Max is uncomfortable with this, partly because he opposes abortion and

partly because he feels Millie is being selfish. He has warned her that abortion will leave her with regrets, depression, and psychological pain. She does not believe it will bother her as much as he says, although she admits that it would not be an easy decision. She believes that it simply would be the best of several unattractive options. A friend with whom she has talked has mentioned the possibility of placing the baby for adoption, but neither Max nor Millie is inclined to do this. Millie indicates that the pregnancy will still be a difficult inconvenience for her life.

Millie has tried a home pregnancy test that came out positive, but the Student Health Center nurse practitioner has told her that she should follow up with a laboratory test to be certain. Max and Millie are feeling tense together and seem to be at a stalemate in terms of agreeing on a course of action if she is in fact pregnant.

If you were asked by either Max or Millie for some objective advice, what would tell them?

How would your own values come into play with regard to the advice?

If you were to find yourself in such a circumstance, what would you do?

Termination of Pregnancy

A pregnancy that terminates naturally is called a **miscarriage** or **spontaneous abortion.** Some women who experience an unintended pregnancy choose to seek ways of terminating it, also known as **induced abortion.** About 1.3 million abortions are performed in the United States each year, representing about a quarter of all pregnancies, although it is believed that abortions are underreported. In recent years, the rate of abortion has decreased by over 10 percent. A number of laws have been passed that restrict access to abortion in numerous ways. In addition, the geographic availability is quite variable, the number of abortion providers has declined, and the costs of abortion procedures have risen, creating barriers to abortion access for many women (Finer & Henshaw, 2003; Henshaw & Finer, 2003; Jones, Darroch, & Henshaw, 2002).

The ratio of abortions to live births has been falling in recent years, primarily because young women under age 15 are opting to have abortions less often than they did a few years ago and because fewer clinics and health care providers are offering abortion. The most common reasons why women seek abortion are the fear that having a baby will interfere with education, work, or caring for dependents (74 percent); the inability to afford a child at the time (73 percent); and not wanting to be a single mother or having relationship problems (48 percent). In one study, about 70 percent

miscarriage a natural termination of pregnancy.

spontaneous abortion another term for miscarriage.

induced abortion a termination of pregnancy by artificial means.

of women in prenatal care and intending to have their babies did not rule out the possibility of terminating a future pregnancy (Finer et al., 2005; Learman et al., 2005).

Support for abortion has been declining in recent years. Polls indicate that about 55 percent of people in the United States believe abortion should be available under certain circumstances and that 23 percent believe abortion should be legally available for any reason. About 21 percent of Americans believe abortion should be illegal under all circumstances (Harris Poll, 2005). There has been a trend toward conditional acceptance of abortion, with the majority of people favoring the procedure in cases of rape, when the health of the mother is endangered, or when there is a strong chance of a defect in the baby.

Only about half of medical residency programs in obstetrics and gynecology offer routine training in abortion procedures, while another 39 percent offer optional training (Eastwood et al., 2006). Some experts believe that training in abortion procedures should be more available in medical schools. There is evidence that physicians who have had thorough training in abortion procedures are more likely to perform abortions (Shotorbani et al., 2004; Steinauer, 2003). Globally, there is evidence that in areas of the world where abortion is not available through medical facilities, up to 20 million unsafe abortions are performed annually, and some 68,000 women die as a result. Millions more women experience complications that compromise their health, sometimes permanently (Grimes et al., 2006).

The many moral and political conflicts regarding abortion hinge on an essential difference in the beliefs of right-to-life antiabortion forces and pro-choice supporters concerning when human life begins. Abortion foes often believe that life begins at the moment of conception and therefore abortion is tantamount to murder because it involves the ending of another human life. Some extremist factions have even felt that the burning or bombing of abortion facilities or the murder of abortionists is justified by these views. Although most proponents of the availability of abortion feel that it should not be a decision made lightly, they see it as a woman's right to choose in a world in which many families cannot adequately care for the children they have. They tend not to hold to the idea that life begins at conception and instead see the potential quality of life for the unborn child and its parents as the primary issue. Advocates insist that women should have the right to determine what happens to their own bodies, including whether to proceed with a pregnancy (Millner & Hanks, 2002).

The Supreme Court has struggled with the continuing debate. The historic *Roe v. Wade* decision in 1973 legalized a woman's right to obtain an abortion from a qualified physician. In subsequent rulings, the Court has upheld the right to abortion established by *Roe v. Wade,* while giving states the right to legislate various restrictions on abortion in order to accommodate the beliefs of their citizens (Hull & Hoffer, 2001). For example, state laws have been enacted that prohibit certain health care personnel from providing information about abortion; require notification of the husband or, in the case of minors, a parent; require a waiting period of up to 24 hours before the abortion can take place; and/or prohibit the use of public facilities for abortions. As might be expected, such laws have placed added burdens of time and cost on women seeking an abortion and on the facilities that serve them (Gold, 2002). In Texas, a law requires parental notification for teenagers under age 18 seeking an abortion. This requirement has resulted in a decline in overall abortions but an increase in riskier, later-term abortions, presumably because teens delay notifying their parents until early abortion is no longer an option (Joyce, Kaestner, & Colman, 2006).

All studies have indicated that legal medical abortions have fewer risks for the woman than carrying a pregnancy to full term and giving birth. Although in both cases the risk of the woman's death is extremely low, the chance of a relatively healthy woman dying from a legal abortion in the United States is about 1 in 100,000 for abortions performed up to 12 weeks of pregnancy. The rate rises somewhat as the length of the pregnancy increases. In comparison, nearly 20 deaths per 100,000 women occur in continued pregnancies and births (Hatcher et al., 2004). Although rumors of an increased risk of breast cancer have circulated with regard to abortion, analysis of data from about 83,000 women has shown that the risk of breast cancer for women who have had an abortion and women who have not is statistically indistinguishable (Collaborative Group, 2004).

First-trimester abortions are simplest and safest and have few complications other than some excessive bleeding or subsequent infection that can be treated with antibiotics. If all of the fetal tissue is not removed, infection can result, requiring further scraping of the uterine wall, usually through a D & C procedure (see page 323). Later abortions have somewhat higher risks of bleeding or infection because labor is induced, but the risk of fatal complications is still minimal. Although having two or more abortions has been linked with a higher incidence of miscarriage in later pregnancies and also increases the likelihood of later ectopic pregnancy, abortion does not reduce fertility or the ability to conceive (Cohen, 2001).

Methods of Abortion

Several procedures can be employed to terminate pregnancy (see Table 11.2). The particular method chosen usually depends on the stage of pregnancy. An abortion

Table 11.2   *Means to an End: Three Abortion Techniques*

Though their results are the same—the termination of a pregnancy—medical and early-stage surgical abortion techniques work in different ways. The benefits and disadvantages of three methods are listed.

Procedure	Side Effects, Risks	Cost, Timing, Status
RU 486 Mifepristone (RU 486) pills block hormone sustaining pregnancy; misoprostol pills two days later induce contractions.	Intense cramping and bleeding can last more than a week. Four percent failure rate.	About $300. Effective until the 9th week of pregnancy. FDA has given provisional approval.
Methotrexate and Misoprostol A shot stops fetal cells from dividing. A vaginal suppository 5 to 7 days later induces contractions.	Nausea and diarrhea in rare cases. Four percent failure rate.	Drugs are $10, M.D. visits bring tab to $300. Effective up to 9th week. Approved in 1998.
Surgery Usually vacuum aspiration of the fetus through the vagina. Performed under a local anesthetic.	Slight chance of perforation of the uterus or injury to the cervix.	About $300. Used from 6th to (in rare cases) 24th week. Legal, but 85% of U.S. counties have no practitioners.

Source: From Debra Rosenberg, Michele Ingrassia, and Sharon Begley, "Blood and Tears," *Newsweek,* 18 September 1995. Copyright © Newsweek, Inc. All rights reserved. Reprinted by permission.

can be performed legally in the United States by a doctor through the 24th week of pregnancy (measured from the first day of the last menstrual period). The earlier it is performed, the simpler the procedure, the lower the risks to the woman, and the lower the cost.

Vacuum Curettage

About 90 percent of abortions in the United States are performed within the first trimester, that is, the first 12 weeks of pregnancy. The method most often used during this stage is **vacuum curettage,** sometimes called vacuum aspiration or the suction method. First, the cervical opening is dilated through the use of graduated metal dilators. Another, gentler approach to cervical dilation involves the earlier insertion of a cylinder made from a dried seaweed called **laminaria.** The laminaria insert slowly absorbs moisture from the cervix, and as it expands the cervical os opens wider. Maximum dilation can take from 12 to 24 hours. This procedure is more comfortable for the woman and reduces the risk of injury to the cervix. After the cervical opening is dilated, a thin plastic tube is inserted into the uterus and connected to a suction pump. The uterine lining, along with fetal and placental tissue, is then suctioned out. This part of the procedure usually takes from 10 to 15 minutes. The complication rate for the procedure is quite low, even for abortions during the first six weeks of pregnancy (Paul et al., 2002).

Medical Induction

FOH

Mifepristone, or **RU 486,** has been widely used in Europe for early abortions and is now used routinely in the United States. The earlier it is used during the pregnancy, the higher its rate of effectiveness. It typically is used within seven weeks of the first day of the woman's last menstrual period. The drug is administered in tablet form under a physician's supervision, and it causes the embryo to break away from the uterine wall. Two days later, misoprostol, a hormonelike chemical, is administered orally or by injection or suppository, causing the uterus to contract and expel the embryo. Studies have shown that use of mifepristone is less painful and carries less danger of infection than surgical methods of abortion. Injection of methotrexate, a drug already on the U.S. market for other purposes, also has proved to be 96 percent effective for inducing abortion when combined with misoprostol. This method requires less medical monitoring than

vacuum curettage (kyur-a-TAZH) a method of induced abortion performed with a suction pump.

laminaria (lam-a-NER-ee-a) a dried seaweed sometimes used in dilating the cervical opening prior to vacuum curettage.

mifepristone (RU 486) a progesterone antagonist used as a postcoital contraceptive.

mifepristone (Fielding, Edmunds, & Schaff, 2002; Jones & Henshaw, 2002).

Aside from the objections of antiabortion groups, concerns have been raised about drug-induced abortion for other reasons. Some fear that if drugs become too readily available, they will be used too often without proper medical supervision, jeopardizing women's health and safety. In reality, medical abortion protocols have been quite slow to catch on, although there has been a gradual expansion of their use (Coeytaux, Moore, & Gelberg, 2003; Hwang et al., 2005). Clinicians need to help women understand the different methods of abortion as the women choose between surgical or medical procedures (Harvey, Beckman, & Satre, 2001).

Dilation and Evacuation, or Dilation, and Curettage

Beyond the first trimester, the uterus has enlarged, and as a result its walls have become thinner. The contents of the uterus cannot be as easily removed by suction or by injections of drugs such as misoprostol. Vacuum curettage is not considered as safe and suitable for abortions in the second trimester of pregnancy.

During the 13- to 16-week period of pregnancy, the usual method employed is **dilation and evacuation (D & E).** After cervical dilation, a suction tube is still used, but this is followed by the scraping of the inner wall of the uterus with a metal curette to ensure that all fetal tissue is removed. This is a variation of **dilation and curettage (D & C),** which omits the initial vacuum aspiration of the uterus and sometimes is used to terminate pregnancy (Autry et al., 2002).

Procedures Used Later in Pregnancy

For abortions later in pregnancy (16 to 24 weeks), procedures usually must be employed that render the fetus nonviable and induce its delivery through the vagina. These approaches are more physically uncomfortable and often more emotionally upsetting for the woman because she experiences uterine contractions for several hours and then expels a lifeless fetus. The two most commonly used procedures at this stage of pregnancy are **prostaglandin-induced abortions** and **saline-induced abortions.**

Prostaglandins are injected directly into the amniotic sac through the abdominal wall, administered intravenously to the woman, or inserted into the vagina in suppository form. Prostaglandins stimulate uterine contractions, leading to delivery. Saline (salt) solution injected into the amniotic fluid has a similar effect. Some clinicians have also substituted a substance called "urea" for saline. Sometimes, various combinations of prostaglandins, saline, and urea are used to terminate later pregnancies (Hatcher et al., 2004). Late-term abortions, sometimes called partial-birth abortions, have cre-

ated a great deal of controversy, but many clinicians feel that it is essential to maintain their availability (Drey et al., 2006). In 2007, the U.S. Supreme Court took a position that makes certain partial-birth procedures illegal.

Use of Embryonic Tissue

An issue related to abortion has surfaced among the other controversies—the use of embryonic human tissue in research and medical treatment. Although "stem cell" tissues are no longer obtained from aborted fetuses, researchers could be working with embryos that have been created by in vitro fertilization in first forming a line of stem cell tissue for further use. Stem cells are particularly valuable because they grow faster, are more adaptable to a variety of environments, and are less likely to be rejected by the recipient's immune system than are tissues transplanted from other adults. Work has been done to investigate the value of stem cell transplants in treating Parkinson's disease, Alzheimer's disease, spinal cord damage, diabetes, epilepsy, and a variety of neuromuscular disorders. The outcomes of the research have been encouraging, but much work remains to be done.

Use of embryonic tissue has, of course, been fraught with controversy, and there have been various governmentally imposed bans on federal funding for any research involving its use. Although the U.S. government approved the use of certain stem cell lines, scientists claim that the limitations are harming exploration of potentially valuable cures (Brivanlou et al., 2003; Zerhouni, 2003).

Do you believe that abortion should continue to be a legal option? If so, under what circumstances?

Psychological Considerations

The psychological effects of abortion on a woman depend a great deal on her beliefs and values and the degree of care with which she has made the decision. She needs to consider her own feelings as well as the reactions of others close to her. Few people see

dilation and evacuation (D & E) a method of induced abortion in the second trimester of pregnancy that combines suction with a scraping of the inner wall of the uterus.

dilation and curettage (D & C) a method of induced abortion in the second trimester of pregnancy that involves a scraping of the uterine wall.

prostaglandin- and saline-induced abortions a method used in the 16th to 24th weeks of pregnancy in which prostaglandins, salt solutions, or urea is injected into the amniotic sac, administered intravenously, or inserted into the vagina in suppository form to induce contractions and fetal delivery.

abortion as an easy option, but many view it as a necessary choice given their personal circumstances. In a study of 97 women who had had early abortions, most indicated substantial improvement in their quality of life soon after having the procedure. They felt better emotionally, could think more clearly, slept better, and had improved appetites (Westhoff, Picardo, & Morrow, 2003). An analysis of data from the National Longitudinal Survey of Youth found that women who terminate an unintended first pregnancy are at no greater risk for depression than are those who carry the pregnancy to term (Schmiege & Russo, 2005).

Although serious emotional complications following abortion are quite rare, some women and their male partners do experience some degree of depression, grieving, regret, or sense of loss. These reactions tend to be even more likely with second or third abortions. Support and counseling from friends, family members, or professionals following an abortion often help lighten this distress, which typically fades within several weeks after the procedure. Counseling often helps in cases where the distress is not alleviated in a reasonable time. A review of the wealth of data gathered in studies conducted for the American Psychological Association suggested that most women will not suffer lasting psychological trauma following an abortion. There does not seem to be any evidence to support the existence of what has been termed a "postabortion syndrome," and severe negative reactions following an abortion apparently are rare.

Self-Evaluation

Contraceptive Comfort and Confidence Scale

Method of birth control you are considering using: _____

Length of time you used this method in the past: _____

Answer YES or NO to the following questions:

	YES	NO
1. Have I had problems using this method before?	❏	❏
2. Have I ever become pregnant while using this method?	❏	❏
3. Am I afraid of using this method?	❏	❏
4. Would I really rather not use this method?	❏	❏
5. Will I have trouble remembering to use this method?	❏	❏
6. Will I have trouble using this method correctly?	❏	❏
7. Do I still have unanswered questions about this method?	❏	❏
8. Does this method make menstrual periods longer or more painful?	❏	❏
9. Does this method cost more than I can afford?	❏	❏
10. Could this method cause me to have serious complications?	❏	❏
11. Am I opposed to this method because of any religious or moral beliefs?	❏	❏
12. Is my partner opposed to this method?	❏	❏
13. Am I using this method without my partner's knowledge?	❏	❏
14. Will using this method embarrass my partner?	❏	❏
15. Will using this method embarrass me?	❏	❏
16. Will I enjoy intercourse less because of this method?	❏	❏
17. If this method interrupts lovemaking, will I avoid using it?	❏	❏
18. Has a nurse or doctor ever told me NOT to use this method?	❏	❏
19. Is there anything about my personality that could lead me to use this method incorrectly?	❏	❏
20. Am I at any risk of being exposed to HIV (the AIDS virus) or other sexually transmitted infections if I use this method?	❏	❏

Total Number of Yes Answers: ___ ___

Most individuals will have a few "yes" answers. "Yes" answers mean that potential problems may arise. If you have more than a few "yes" responses, you may want to talk to your physician, counselor, partner, or friend to help you decide whether to use this method or how to use it so that it will really be effective for you. In general, the more "yes" answers you have, the less likely you are to use this method consistently and correctly at every act of intercourse.

Source: R. A. Hatcher et al., *Contraceptive Technology,* 17th ed. Copyright © 1998 by Contraceptive Technology Communications, Inc. Reprinted by permission of Ardent MediaLine.

Chapter Summary

1. People's sense of well-being contributes to their choices about having children. Human beings have sought to minimize the connections between sex and childbirth.

2. In ancient times, botanical preparations may have provided contraceptive protection.

3. Distribution of information about birth control was limited in the United States by the Comstock Laws, passed in the 1870s. Activist Margaret Sanger was influential in broadening the rights of women to learn about and use contraception in the early part of this century, although laws prohibiting the sale of contraceptives continued to exist until the 1960s.

4. While the world's population continues to grow, the rate of growth has been slowing down. Over half the world's people are now reproducing at below replacement rates. Many children live in substandard conditions.

5. The decision to have children is an important one, involving significant costs and personal responsibilities.

6. It is believed that many pregnancies globally are unwanted. Political and social factors may determine what kinds of birth control are accessible.

7. In making decisions about contraceptive use, people are influenced by several factors, including ethical/moral and religious beliefs, political forces, possible effects on the woman's health, and psychological and social factors. Guilt, fear, or anxiety may not always inhibit sexual behavior but may inhibit preparing for it.

8. Each person must sort through his or her personal values and concerns about birth control, understand his or her personal reactions to sexual feelings and activities, and learn how to communicate with a partner effectively in order to prepare fully for contraceptive decision making.

9. There is no "best" method of birth control for all individuals. Each couple must consider several factors in making a choice: age and amount of protection required, the safety of the method, how long the method will be used, what might hinder the method's use, and cost.

10. The theoretical or perfect use failure rate assumes that the birth control method is being used correctly and without technical failure. The typical use failure rate, the more realistic rating of the method, takes into account human error, carelessness, and technical failure.

11. Even though most methods of contraception are designed for women, there are many ways for the responsibility to be shared by both partners: cooperating in applying the method, communicating openly about birth control, and sharing the cost. Cultural imperatives sometimes interfere with the sharing of this responsibility.

12. Table 11.1 gives summary information on methods of contraception, their rates of effectiveness, potential advantages, possible causes of failure, and possible negative side effects.

13. Couples who choose abstinence from intercourse as a birth control method have many alternatives for sexual and nonsexual intimacy. Although withdrawal is not one of the more reliable forms of contraception, it is better than no method at all.

14. Hormones that prevent ovulation and change the consistency of cervical mucus can be administered in the form of combined oral contraceptive pills or progestin-only minipills. The pill provides protection against ovarian and endometrial cancers but may also have some harmful side effects.

15. Hormonal implants consist of six capsules that are implanted under the skin, releasing a synthetic hormone that prevents ovulation for up to five years. They are no longer on the market, although new versions are in development. Hormonal patches and the vaginal ring also provide reliable contraceptive protection.

16. Hormonal injections create a hostile uterine environment for sperm and for implantation. One-month and three-month dosages are available.

17. Spermicides kill sperm and are available without prescription as foams, film, jellies, creams, and vaginal suppositories and implanted on the contraceptive sponge. Spermicides may increase the risk of infection by HIV or other STDs.

18. Barrier methods of contraception prevent sperm from entering the uterus and are most effective when used with a spermicide. They include the diaphragm, cervical cap, and condom.

19. Condoms provide protection against disease as well as against as pregnancy. Male condoms fit over the penis and are made of latex, natural membranes, or polyurethane. Female condoms consist of a polyurethane pouch that is inserted into the vagina. Female condoms do not have as high a rate of effectiveness as male condoms.

20. The intrauterine device (IUD) is inserted into the uterus and may work by preventing fertilization.

21. Natural family planning/fertility awareness allows the woman to become more aware of her fertile period during the menstrual cycle by charting the length of her cycle, her basal body temperature, and the consistency of cervical mucus.

22. Vasectomy involves cutting and tying the male vas deferens. Tubal ligation and Essure transcervical sterilization seal off the fallopian tubes.

23. Emergency contraception, or Plan B, is available in the form of hormonal pills that are taken in either a single dose or two doses.

24. New forms of contraception are being researched. For males, these include testosterone injections and other chemicals that suppress sperm production. For women, a vaccine that would immunize against gonadotropin could prevent implantation.

25. When an unintended pregnancy occurs, one of several options must be chosen: keeping the baby, placing the baby up for adoption, or terminating the pregnancy.

26. When an unintended pregnancy occurs, couples in established relationships are more likely to keep the baby. Fewer than 5 percent of mothers now place their babies for adoption. Adopted children are as well adjusted, or better adjusted, than other children.

27. Some pregnancies terminate naturally in a miscarriage or spontaneous abortion.

28. Induced abortion has been legal in the United States since 1973, but Supreme Court decisions have gradually allowed states to restrict its availability. There are still conflicts between right-to-life and pro-choice groups about whether abortion should continue to be a legal option.

29. First-trimester abortions usually are done by vacuum curettage. Mifepristone (RU 486) in combination with prostaglandins offers a nonsurgical medical alternative. Later abortions may be done by dilation and evacuation (D & E) or dilation and curettage (D & C) or may be induced by injection of prostaglandins, saline, or urea.

30. The use of fetal tissue transplants in medical research has become part of the abortion controversy. The U.S. federal government currently allows fetal tissue to be used for research.

31. Abortion is statistically safer for the woman than pregnancy and giving birth, and many women experience an improved quality of life following the procedure. Some women experience a degree of guilt, loss, or some other psychological reaction. The availability of supportive counseling before and after an abortion is important.

Focus on Health Questions

In this section you will find the kinds of questions that you may have concerning your own health and sexuality. The page references indicate where in the text the answer is located; the exact place is marked with this logo: **FOH**

1. I'm thinking about getting sexually involved. Should I be thinking about birth control yet? **299**

2. What will be the best contraceptive for me? **300**

3. Are some methods of birth control more effective than others? **301**

4. What are the health risks and benefits of taking the pill? **306–307**

5. Is the vaginal ring effective? How is it used? **308**

6. How long does a Depo-Provera injection last, and what are its side effects? **308**

7. How long after intercourse should I leave my diaphragm in? **309**

8. Is the female condom as effective in preventing pregnancy and disease as the male condom? **311**

9. Are IUDs dangerous? **312–313**

10. How does natural family planning work? **313–314**

11. Can vasectomies and tubal ligations be reversed if a sterilized person changes his or her mind? **316**

12. Is it true that taking extra birth control pills on "the morning after" can prevent pregnancy? **316**

13. Are there any male contraceptives that prevent sperm production? **317**

14. What are my options if I am pregnant but don't want to be? **318–320**

15. Is abortion legal? **321**

16. What are the different types of abortion? **321–323**

17. How safe is it to have an abortion? **321**

18. Is the drug RU 486 safe for preventing or terminating pregnancy? **323–324**

19. Is it legal for embryonic tissue to be used in medical research? **323**

20. How will I feel after I have an abortion? **323–324**

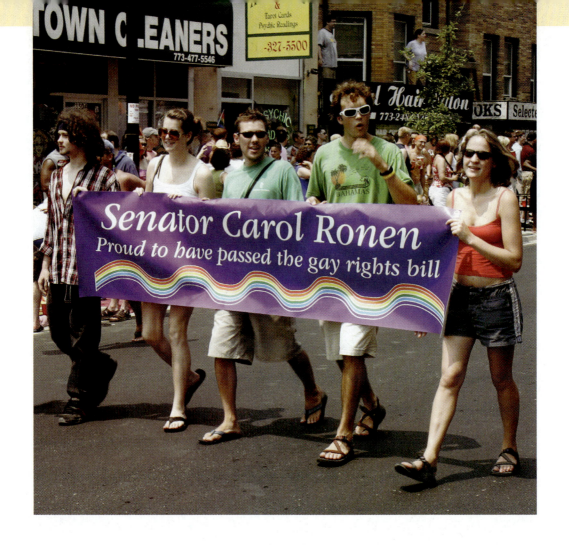

Part 4

Sexual Behavior and Contemporary Society

■

The three most common forms of sexual activity are masturbation, oral-genital sex, and heterosexual intercourse. Although masturbation is usually a solitary activity, there are many other behaviors that constitute shared sexual encounters. The dynamics of the interaction, whether they relate to technique or to how personalities are connecting, become crucial to determining whether a sexual interaction is pleasurable or exploitative.

It seems clear from research that a substantial percentage of human beings are sexually attracted predominantly to member of their own gender. Although many people espouse a live-and-let-live attitude toward gay males, lesbians, and bisexual and transgender persons and their sexual behaviors, our culture continues to be essentially heterosexist.

The kinds of sexual activities in which people choose to participate seem limited only by the imagination. Only in recent years has scientific research begun to give us a clearer picture of human sexual diversity, although social norms and values play a significant role in determining the degree to which that diversity is accepted in any society.

Information technology has created new forms of relationships in cyberspace and has made the distribution of sexual images faster and easier than ever before. What are the effects of sexually explicit materials? How have sexual themes become a part of art, literature, films, television, and computer technology? To what extent should laws regulate erotic themes in the media and the sexual activities of human beings? These are major issues facing society today, and courts and legislative bodies are struggling to grapple with their complicated nature.

Chapter 12
Solitary Sex and Shared Sex

Chapter Outline

I think about sex a lot, and I enjoy experiencing sex, whether by myself or with a partner. I've managed to be careful about the partners I have chosen, and I always am careful to protect both of us. These days, though, sex alone seems much less complicated, but sometimes you just long to be with somebody too.

—from a student essay

This chapter examines some of the most common sexual behaviors in which human beings participate. Although masturbation and heterosexual or vaginal intercourse have primary roles in the discussion, many other forms of sexual experiences that can be shared by partners of the same or different genders are also examined. A fair amount of evidence seems to suggest that, generally speaking, males demonstrate higher levels of sexual interest and activity than do females. Men are more likely to report pleasure as a significant motive for sex, while women are more likely to report love as a motive. This is probably due to an interaction of biological and social factors (Browning, Hatfield, Kessler, & Levine, 2000).

Although Kinsey (1948, 1953) emphasized that the statistics on sexual behavior gained from his sample of about 16,000 individuals could not be generalized to the total population, they did allow us to glimpse the many variations of human sexual experience. The data from the National Health and Social Life Survey (NHSLS) have given us more reliable statistics on the types and frequencies of sexual behaviors among people in the United States; they seem to be relatively consistent with data coming from European research. For the first time, we can make some generalizations from the random population sample surveyed in the NHSLS to the general population. We also can see that sexual behaviors are influenced by factors such as age, race, religious beliefs, and educational background (Laumann, Gagnon, et al., 1994).

List several factors that might influence the acceptability and frequency of various sexual behaviors.

Statistics should be considered approximations of what people are doing, and only that. Although they can give us interesting information and establish certain statistical norms for sexual behavior in particular groups of people, we must not assume that such data necessarily represent standards for behavior. The fact that most males masturbate does not mean that males should masturbate or that nonmasturbating males are abnormal. That the majority of females have not experienced intercourse by age 17 does not mean that 15-year-old females who have had intercourse are immoral.

Each of us possesses his or her own specific sexual interests, values, preferences, needs, and behaviors. These aspects of our sexuality may change many times during our lifetimes because sexual individuality is more a dynamic process than a fixed state of being. The information in the chapters concerning sexual be-

havior is aimed at helping you gain a clearer understanding of your own sexuality as it is now and opening your mind to the spectrum of sexual behaviors that are part of the human experience. New legitimacy is being given to the concept of sexual pleasure, an area about which there has been a good deal of ambivalence since Victorian times (Resnick, 2002). Sexual feelings and behaviors often are still shrouded by embarrassment and guilt that go beyond modesty or the protection of privacy. However, people are slowly beginning to accept that enjoying sexual pleasure in ways that do not exploit others is a positive thing.

There are two distinct worlds of human sexual experience. One is the social world in which sex is shared with others. This world necessitates all sorts of negotiable processes between people and involves expectations, judgments, performances, and consequences that can be both positive and negative. The other is the private world that in many ways may be even more active and consuming than the partnered world. In this domain, personal pleasure is paramount, and social constraints may be less intrusive, although private sex often is not without its guilt or fear of discovery.

■ Solitary Sex: The Private World

The private world of sex involves the solitary pursuit of sexual thoughts and fantasies, erotic materials and toys, and masturbation, often in combination. The NHSLS data showed that men report thinking about sex more frequently than do women. Over half of men (54 percent) said that they think about sex every day or even several times a day, with another 43 percent reporting that they think about sex a few times a month or week. Only 19 percent of women indicated that they think about sex every day, while 33 percent said that they think about sex a few times per week or month. Four percent of men and 14 percent of women reported thinking about sex less than once a month or never. As Table 12.1 shows, men also are considerably more likely than women to purchase and seek out materials and activities associated with private sexual arousal and pleasure.

Conventional wisdom holds that people who engage in solitary sexual pleasures probably do so because of the unavailability of sexual partners. In fact, research has shown that this assumption is incorrect. According to NHSLS data, people who are most likely

Table 12.1 — Percentage Purchasing Autoerotic Materials in the Past 12 Months

Materials	Men	Women
X-rated movies or videos	23%	11%
Visit to a club with nude or seminude dancers	22	4
Sexually explicit books or magazines	16	4
Vibrators or dildos	2	2
Other sex toys	1	2
Sex phone numbers	1	1
Any of the above	41	16

Note: Percentages are independent for each cell.

Source: From *Sex in America* by Robert T. Michael et al. Copyright © 1994 by CSG Enterprises, Inc., Edward O. Laumann, Robert T. Michael, and Gina Kolata. By permission of Little, Brown and Company, Inc.

to think about sex the most, to pursue erotic materials for their own use, and to masturbate also tend to have the most active sexual lives with partners. Other research has confirmed this. The more private sexual experience an individual has, the more shared sexual experience he or she is likely to have (Michael et al., 1994; Pinkerton et al., 2002).

Sexual Pleasure for One

Masturbation is one of the most common ways human beings seek sexual pleasure. I will use the term *masturbation* to refer to deliberate, rhythmic stimulation of the sex organs—often along with other parts of the body—to produce pleasurable sexual sensations and (usually) orgasm. Masturbation is not confined to the human species; it is common among many mammals, especially the primates. This form of sexual behavior has been subject to much misunderstanding, folklore, religious attention, moral analysis, and ignorance.

Because of its decidedly private nature, masturbation as a sexual practice is infrequently discussed. As sexuality was being brought into the domain of medicine during the eighteenth century, negative attitudes about masturbation made their way into the medical profession. A Swiss physician named Tissot published a book in 1741 that perpetuated the popular belief of the time that body fluids needed to be kept in perfect balance for a person to be healthy. It was further believed that expending the body's sexual fluids would deplete it of essential fluids and lead to illness. Physi-

cians of this time also believed that the stimulation of the nervous system that took place during sexual arousal and orgasm was damaging. Tissot's theories were perpetuated by medical writers throughout the nineteenth century, and claims that physical and mental deterioration would result from masturbation became even more extreme. Although the medical perspective on the practice has been almost completely reversed, masturbation still remains cloaked in a somewhat negative, and often inaccurate, shroud of secrecy (Bullough, 2002). In contrast, the topic of masturbation has become more openly discussed in contemporary media and often is the subject of jokes.

Although statistics from previous research samples have not been representative of the total population, it is reasonable to conclude from the data we have that masturbation is a common practice among adolescents and that the vast majority of people masturbate at some time in their lives. Adolescent males are less likely to report their masturbatory activity while still adolescents than they are retrospectively as young adults (Halpern et al., 2000).

In one recent survey of college students, 98 percent of the men and 64 percent of the women indicated that they had masturbated, with the men averaging 12 times per month and the women averaging about 5 times per month. The earlier the students had begun masturbating and the more pleasurable they found it to be, the more likely the women were to have been masturbated by a partner and the more likely the men were to have used condoms with their partners. These findings may reflect some greater level of comfort with their own genitals (Pinkerton et al., 2002). College women are likely to feel negatively about a man's masturbation or use of pornographic materials for self-stimulation, apparently because they see it as a sign of dissatisfaction with his partner. College men are more accepting of solitary sexual behavior on the part of women (Clark & Wiederman, 2000).

Comparison studies done in 1966, 1981, and 1996 concluded that during that 30-year period, men and especially women began to masturbate at earlier ages and the behavior became more accepted as being pleasurable in its own right, coexisting quite naturally with the availability of partnered sex (Dekker & Schmidt, 2002). A cross-cultural analysis of studies conducted in Finland, Sweden, Estonia, and Russia found that rates of masturbation had increased in recent years and that adults tended to maintain the habits and frequencies of masturbation that they developed during adolescence. The study concluded that masturbation did not, in fact, decrease with age when the social norms of the culture during the generation's teenage years were considered as the basis for forming particular masturbatory habits. The study

FIGURE 12.1 *Female Masturbation*

also found that masturbation was not particularly related to the presence of a sex partner or to levels of activity with that partner. Masturbation was seen as an independent way to experience sexual pleasure rather than as compensation for an unavailable partner (Kontula & Haavio-Mannila, 2002).

Do you feel that masturbation is a behavior deserving of moral judgment or prohibition? What is the basis for your answer? If you masturbate, how do you feel about your own behavior?

NHSLS statistics found similar patterns in the United States. Eighty-five percent of men and 45 percent of women who were living with a sexual partner indicated that they had masturbated during the previous year, although frequency of masturbation does not seem to be correlated with how often they have sex with a partner. White, educated liberals apparently are more likely to masturbate. Most people reported that they masturbate in order to "relieve sexual tension." About one-third of men and women said they did so because they did not have a sexual partner. One-third of men and one-fourth of women indicated that they used masturbation to help them relax. Very few of the people surveyed—5 percent of the women and 7 percent of the men—said they masturbated in order to avoid HIV infection or other sexually transmitted diseases (Michael et al., 1994). While there are no valid statistics on group masturbation, anecdotal evidence indicates that at least a small percentage of adolescents participate in various forms of group masturbation, usually with members of their own sex. The phenomenon seems to be more common among boys than among girls, and groups occasionally are composed of both genders. Some groups

of adults, usually males, get together periodically just to masturbate. A few mixed-gender adult masturbation groups exist as well (Cornog, 2001).

How Girls and Women Masturbate

Masturbation is one way many women become acquainted with their own sexual responsiveness and learn how to have an orgasm (see Figure 12.1). This may serve them well as they develop their responsiveness with a partner. Masters and Johnson (1966) reported in a study in which they observed women masturbating that although no two women out of a sample of several hundred masturbated in exactly the same way, very few of them seemed to use direct stimulation of the glans clitoris. The tissues of the clitoral glans, like the glans of the penis, apparently are too sensitive for any prolonged direct stimulation. Women who stimulate the clitoris tend to gently stroke only the shaft. Right-handed women usually manipulate the right side of the shaft, and left-handed women the left side. A more common way for females to masturbate is by manipulating the entire mons area, which exerts less direct stimulation on the clitoris. The minor lips or other areas surrounding the clitoris also are frequently stimulated. It is important to note that immediately following orgasm, the clitoral glans is especially sensitive to touch or pressure, and most women avoid touching it at that time.

Although use of the hands is the most common method of masturbation, many girls and women use other means of stimulating their genitals. Rubbing the mons or other parts of the vulva against a pillow, bed, doorknob, or some other object is typical. It also is not unusual for a female to insert a finger or some suitably shaped long object into the vagina during masturbation. Cylindrical electric vibrators or flexible plastic

FIGURE 12.2   *Male Masturbation*

devices (often called dildos) may be used during masturbation. Some women are able to produce sexual arousal and orgasm by creating muscular tension in the pelvic region through the tightening of leg and abdominal muscles. Others cross their legs and apply rhythmic stimulation to the vulva by contracting and relaxing the thigh muscles. Women sometimes find that running a stream of warm water over the vulva, and especially the clitoris, or sitting in a whirlpool bath can create sexual stimulation. Many women stimulate other parts of their bodies while masturbating. For example, stimulation of the breasts and nipples is common, and some women enjoy stroking the anal region. There are many individual differences in the ways people stimulate themselves for sexual pleasure. No one pattern need be considered the only right way. Common sense dictates that cleanliness should be observed during masturbation and that women should not insert sharp, pointed, or rasping objects into their vagina. It is also important not to introduce bacteria from the anal region into the genital area, because infection may result.

How Boys and Men Masturbate

Masters and Johnson (1966) also found highly individualized methods of masturbating among the hundreds of men they observed. Some type of stimulation of the penis almost always occurs in male masturbation. Typically, the penis is grasped by the hand and stroked until orgasm takes place (see Figure 12.2). How the penis is grasped and stroked varies with different males. The most common method is for the man to stroke the shaft of the penis, just touching the top edge of the corona around the glans and the frenulum on the underside, where the glans and shaft join. The amount of pressure used, the number of fingers employed on the penis, how rapidly the stroking proceeds, and how far up and down the hand moves all vary from man to man. Some men—particularly those with circumcised penises—stimulate just the glans by pulling at it or rubbing its entire surface. As men get closer to orgasm, the stroking or rubbing of the penis tends to become more rapid,

and then usually slows or stops during actual ejaculation. Most women, in contrast, continue stroking the clitoris during orgasm.

During manual masturbation, many men enjoy occasionally using both hands to stroke the penis or using their free hand to fondle the scrotum or anal region. Some men insert a finger or other object into the anus during masturbation. It also is not unusual for a male to use some sort of lubricating jelly or liquid on his hand during masturbation to create intense sexual sensations. It seems safe to assume that most boys and men experiment with a variety of ways of producing orgasm. Many males enjoy rubbing their penis on blankets, pillows, beds, and other suitable objects. Kinsey (1948) reported that a significant proportion of men attempt **autofellatio** at one time or another; that is, they try to put their penis into their own mouth, a feat that very few have the acrobatic dexterity to achieve.

There are also masturbation aids marketed for men, including rubber pouches into which the penis can be inserted, artificial vaginas made of flesh-simulating plastics that often show the external organs of the vulva, and full-size inflatable dolls with built-in pouches at the location of the vagina, mouth, and/or anus. Insertion of the penis into bottles or other openings that may ultimately be too small for the erect penis can result in serious difficulty in removing the penis and can cause penile damage (Voegeli & Effert, 2005). A few boys and men, especially those who find pain sexually arousing, enjoy inserting objects into the urethra at the end of the penis. There are obvious dangers associated with this practice, because injury or infection in the urethra could result. Physicians occasionally see boys or men who have inserted some small object into their urethra, or larger objects into their rectum, only to have it become lodged there.

autofellatio (aw-toh-fe-LAY-she-o) the act of a male providing oral stimulation to his own penis, which most males do not have the physical agility to perform.

Real Student Voices

■ My girlfriend and I often enjoy masturbating with each other. We find it extremely arousing. Sometimes, we end up having intercourse, sometimes not.

■ I started masturbating when I was about five or six, just by rubbing myself. I never told anybody about it until I was a teenager, and I never heard anything about it that would have led me to believe it was bad or wrong. I think it has helped me be a

healthy sexual woman, and I'm glad I was never discouraged from doing it.

■ I would rather not masturbate as much as I do, even though I guess there is really nothing wrong with it. Sometimes I try to skip it or put it off, just to see how much control I can have. Usually, I don't succeed. So you could say I'm still somewhat confused. I just feel as though I shouldn't give in to sexual desire so much (6 to 12 times per week).

Again, it is common sense that masturbation should be done with attention to basic cleanliness and safety so that genitourinary injury or infection will not result.

Fantasy and Pictures in Masturbation

As noted earlier, many people fantasize about sex or employ pornography and sex toys as part of their autoerotic activities, with males doing so more frequently than females. In a survey of college students, more than 60 percent of the males reported that they had used pornographic magazines or videos to enhance masturbation, whereas only about 12 percent of the females reported doing so. Males also were more likely to use nonpornographic magazines or advertisements during masturbation. The most common fantasies seem to involve sexual activity with a loved partner, although fantasies about sexual involvement with acquaintances, celebrities, and strangers also are typical. The majority of men and women admit to having had recent sexual fantasies about people other than their main partner, with men having more such fantasies than women (Hicks & Leitenberg, 2001). It has also been claimed that one reason men watch pornography is to see other men having sex (Strager, 2003). Added to these fantasies is the whole gamut of fantasies about group sex, being forced to have sex, forcing another person to have sex, and every other imaginable form of behavior (Zurbriggen & Yost, 2004). It is probably safe to assume that erotic pictures, videos, and literature help generate fantasies in many individuals during masturbation and that people often project themselves into the subject matter of the erotic material (Friedman & Downey, 2000).

Facts and Fallacies about Masturbation

It is surprising how many myths and misconceptions about masturbation persist. The next few paragraphs attempt to separate the fallacies from the facts. Each of the following italicized statements is a fact.

Fact: Masturbation is not confined to childhood and adolescence or to single persons. Many adult men and women—including married individuals—continue to masturbate throughout their lives. There is solid evidence to indicate that the majority of adult males and close to half of adult females masturbate from time to time. Their frequency of masturbation actually seems to be highest between the ages of 24 and 50. Married people, particularly married men, tend to masturbate somewhat less often than single people. There is a wide range among those who masturbate very seldom (once or twice a year) and those who masturbate more frequently (once a day or more). All these patterns are found in normal, healthy, happy individuals (Coleman, 2002a).

Fact: Masturbation is not necessarily a substitute for sex with a partner. It is certainly true that masturbation sometimes is used as a substitute for sexual activity with a partner; however, masturbation also represents a form of sexual expression in itself, regardless of what other sexual activities are available to the individual. Many people who have very fulfilling sexual lives and have access to shared sexual activity whenever they wish still enjoy masturbating. Research shows that an active masturbatory and private sexual life seems to be one component of a generally active sexual life that also includes shared sex. People who masturbate frequently also are more likely to participate in partnered sex frequently (Dekker & Schmidt, 2002; Michael et al., 1994; Pinkerton et al., 2002). Some people may actually prefer masturbation to other forms of sexual behavior; this should not be considered a sign of immaturity or sexual dissatisfaction.

Fact: Masturbation can be shared. In my counseling and sex therapy practice, I never cease to be surprised by the number of couples who share sex but are reluctant to discuss masturbation. Even though both partners may masturbate regularly, it is often impossible for them to admit that fact to each other. Masturbation apparently is one of the secrets that partners most often keep from each other. Being able to surmount this communication barrier and talk about masturbation can be an important step to better sexual communication. Some couples find that masturbating together or watching each other masturbate can be an enjoyable form of sexual sharing.

Fact: There is no such thing as excessive masturbation. For years, books on sex for young people implied that there is nothing wrong with masturbation as long as it is not practiced to excess. The fact is that no medical definition of excessive masturbation exists. Frequent masturbation does not cause physical harm. For the most part, it seems to be a self-limiting practice: When the individual is sexually satiated, he or she loses interest in being sexually aroused. The number of orgasms necessary to reach satiation will vary among individuals and their circumstances. Of course, if a person has masturbated to satiation, she or he might not be interested in other forms of sex for a while. Masters and Johnson (1966) reported that most of the men they questioned expressed vague concerns over excessive masturbation but consistently stated the frequency they considered excessive to be greater than their own masturbatory frequency. A man who masturbated once a month stated that once or twice a week would be excessive, whereas a man who masturbated two or three times a day thought that five or six times a day might be excessive.

Fact: Masturbation can be as sexually satisfying physically as shared sex. From a purely physical standpoint, masturbation can offer full sexual satisfaction for some people. Of course, if both physical and emotional intimacy with another person are important to an individual's fully experiencing sexual feelings, masturbation will leave some gaps. The degree of orgasmic pleasure may be judged more by the intensity of physical sensations during masturbation or a casual sexual encounter, whereas in sexual encounters with an intimate sex partner emotional aspects of pleasure probably play a larger role (Mah & Binik, 2002). Particularly in women, however, masturbation often provides the opportunity for the kind of self-regulated stimulation that produces a more intense orgasm than can be obtained with coitus. Some of that effective stimulation can be transferred to shared sex when the partners have good communication about sex.

Fact: Masturbation is a good way to learn about sexual feelings and responsiveness. Among sex therapists and sexuality educators, the attitude is quite prevalent that masturbation not only is healthy and normal but also can be a useful learning experience (Coleman, 2002a). In males, patterns of sexual functioning may be influenced by early patterns of masturbation. A boy who learns to masturbate to orgasm in the shortest possible time may carry the pattern into later intercourse as premature ejaculation. Men who have learned to prolong the time it takes to ejaculate during masturbation often can transfer that control to their shared sexual activities. There is one caveat here: A few men develop patterns of masturbation that require unusual amounts of penile pressure or stimulation, and some of these men have difficulty replicating these sensations in shared sexual experiences.

For women, masturbation is recognized as an important way to learn what orgasm feels like and how to produce it. Various masturbation exercises are commonly used as a preliminary step to orgasmic response and full enjoyment in shared sexual activity. Research has shown that, compared to married women who have never experienced an orgasm through masturbation, married women who have masturbated to orgasm have significantly more orgasms in shared sex, greater sexual desire, higher self-esteem, a greater level of marital and sexual satisfaction, and a tendency to require less time to become sexually aroused with a partner (Zamboni & Crawford, 2002).

Fact: Masturbation does not lead to weakness, mental illness, or physical debilitation. As myths of masturbation's connection with mental and physical maladies have faded, it is now clear that masturbation causes no medical conditions, regardless of frequency. Coaches once warned athletes to avoid masturbation or sex, especially the night before the big game, because they saw it as an energy-sapping practice. Although orgasm may indeed release tension and lead to relaxation, many athletes claim that this actually can boost their performance. Masturbation does not drain the body of energy (Bullough, 2002; Coleman, 2002a).

Fact: Males do not eventually run out of semen if they masturbate frequently. A common misconception has been that the male body is granted the potential of producing only a certain amount of semen and that each ejaculation leads a man closer to the bottom of the barrel. In actuality, the glands that produce sperm and semen tend to be active from puberty into old age. They do not cease production after a certain number of orgasms. In fact, there is evidence that the more sexually active an individual is in earlier life, the more active he or she will be in later years. The more semen a male ejaculates, the more his body produces.

Fact: Masturbation does not lead to same-gender orientation and behavior. In many people's minds, masturbation is associated with sexual attraction to one's own gender. Apparently, the idea of a person seeking pleasure from her or his own genitals is interpreted as sexual attraction to same-sexed genitals. This simply is not true. Heterosexual people masturbate, and so do gay, lesbian, and bisexual people. The practice does not change sexual orientation.

Fact: Masturbation is not physically essential. Some people—particularly men—believe that it may be harmful to abstain from having orgasms. They fear that storing sperm and semen or experiencing erection without orgasm eventually may be harmful to the body. Actually, the body adjusts its production of semen to the amount of sexual activity. Although masturbation can be a pleasurable learning experience and may be important to a person's sexual life, it is not essential for physical or mental well-being.

Masturbation, Guilt, and Morality

Perhaps because of the long-standing negative attitudes toward masturbation, it is not always a guilt-free sexual practice. About half of women and men report some degree of guilt in association with their masturbatory activities. Guilt does not seem to affect the frequency of masturbation in males, but it is somewhat associated with less frequent masturbation in females (Laumann, Gagnon, et al., 1994). Women who feel guilty about their self-stimulation are less likely to have positive physical and psychological reactions to masturbation and are less likely to report being sexually adjusted or satisfied (Coleman, 2002a).

Adolescent males seem to talk together more about masturbation than do adolescent females. Why might this be?

As with all other forms of sexual behavior, various cultures and religions have attached many different moral implications to masturbation. The Judeo-Christian-Muslim position was once predominantly antimasturbation, although their attitude, along with that of most religious groups, has largely changed with the new findings of medicine and psychology. The story of Onan has often been cited as evidence of the sinfulness of masturbation. The Old Testament tells that while he was having sexual intercourse with the wife of his deceased brother, Onan withdrew before ejaculation and "spilled his seed on the ground." God was angered and struck him dead. Actually, of course, Onan was not masturbating but instead was practicing what we now call coitus interruptus, or withdrawal, as a means of birth control. In any case, masturbation has also been called **onanism.** Clearly, each individual—giving consideration to his or her religious, parental, and peer values—must decide whether masturbation will be part of an acceptable personal repertoire of sexual behaviors.

See "Mother and Daughter Discussing Sex" on SexSource Online.

■ Shared Sexual Behavior

The kinds of physical contact described in this section are usually sexually arousing, may in themselves lead to orgasm, or may serve as a prelude to other behaviors that may or may not include orgasm. As data from the NHSLS research in Table 12.2 indicate, vaginal intercourse is clearly the most popular of all shared sexual behaviors among all age groups of both women and men. The researchers were somewhat surprised to find that the second most appealing activity was watching a partner undress. This was even more appealing to men than to women (Michael et al., 1994).

Although vaginal intercourse is still often assumed to be the definitive heterosexual act, there is growing evidence that other forms of shared sexual activity have gained in popularity and are practiced for the pleasure they provide in themselves, rather than as a prelude to intercourse. The pursuit of somewhat casual sexual encounters with acquaintances, collectively called "hooking up," seems to have led to an increase in noncoital sexual sharing, often involving oral sex. Intercourse does not seem to be one of the activities that is most typical of hooking up (Lambert, Kahn, & Apple, 2003). Because of the higher risks associated with intercourse, couples seem to be more comfortable with engaging in other forms of sex that also can be highly satisfying.

A continuing sexual relationship involves a gradual learning process between the partners concerning their own individual preferences for various activities. Conflicts may arise when one partner finds a particular activity appealing and desirable but the other partner finds it offensive or unappealing. Such conflicts may have to be accepted as part of the relationship and appropriate compromises may have to be made, but it is also quite typical for people to experiment with new activities as a relationship progresses, sometimes even learning to enjoy them more than they did before.

onanism (O-na-niz-um) a term sometimes used to describe masturbation; the term stems from the biblical story of Onan, who practiced coitus interruptus and "spilled his seed on the ground."

Table 12.2   The Appeal of Selected Sexual Practices

Panel A: Women

Selected Sexual Practices	Ages 18–44				Ages 45–59			
	Very Appealing	Somewhat Appealing	Not Appealing	Not at All Appealing	Very Appealing	Somewhat Appealing	Not Appealing	Not at All Appealing
Vaginal intercourse	78%	18%	1%	3%	74%	19%	2%	6%
Watching partner undress	30	51	11	9	18	49	16	17
Receiving oral sex	33	35	11	21	16	24	14	45
Giving oral sex	19	38	15	28	11	20	17	52
Group sex	1	8	14	78	1	4	9	87
Anus stimulated by partner's fingers	4	14	18	65	6	12	14	68
Stimulate partner's anus with your fingers	2	11	16	70	4	12	12	73
Using dildo/vibrator	3	13	23	61	4	14	17	65
Watching others do sexual things	2	18	15	66	2	11	13	74
Same-gender sex partner	3	3	9	85	2	2	6	90
Sex with stranger	1	9	11	80	1	4	6	89
Passive anal intercourse	1	4	9	87	1	3	8	88
Forcing someone to do something sexual	0	2	7	91	0	0	5	95
Being forced to do something sexual	0	2	6	92	0	1	5	95

Nongenital Oral Stimulation

The lips, tongue, and oral cavity are often associated with intimate, sexually arousing activity (see Figure 12.3). The oral areas are replete with nerve endings, are moist, and are associated with pleasurable sensations of taste and food consumption. The mobility of the tongue and lips affords them versatility and allows them to be voluntarily controlled by the individual. All these factors play a role in the various uses of the mouth in pleasurable sexual sharing.

Although a few small societies exist where kissing is not practiced at all or is frowned upon, it is used to express affection in most parts of the world. Kissing usually carries with it important messages concerning the depth of intimacy in a relationship. The least intimate kiss is the simple peck on the cheek. Lengthy lip contact, gentle rubbing of another person's lips, and insertion of the tongue into the partner's mouth (French kissing or soul kissing) are considered more deeply intimate and sexually arousing. Kissing, licking, or nibbling at other parts of the body—such as the abdomen, breasts, ears, or genitals—is also considered particularly intimate by many.

FIGURE 12.3 *Kissing*

In mort parts of the world, kissing is a sign of affection. This young couple shares a warm and loving moment.

Panel B: Men

Selected Sexual Practices	Ages 18–44				Ages 45–59			
	Very Appealing	Somewhat Appealing	Not Appealing	Not at All Appealing	Very Appealing	Somewhat Appealing	Not Appealing	Not at All Appealing
Vaginal intercourse	83%	12%	1%	4%	85%	10%	1%	4%
Watching partner undress	50	43	3	4	40	47	7	5
Receiving oral sex	50	33	5	12	29	32	11	28
Giving oral sex	37	39	9	15	22	33	13	32
Group sex	14	32	20	33	10	18	22	50
Anus stimulated by partner's fingers	6	16	24	54	4	12	23	60
Stimulate partner's anus with your fingers	7	19	22	52	4	16	20	60
Active anal intercourse	5	9	13	73	1	7	9	83
Using dildo/vibrator	5	18	27	50	3	17	24	57
Watching others do sexual things	6	34	21	39	4	25	21	50
Same-gender sex partner	4	2	5	89	2	1	5	92
Sex with stranger	5	29	25	42	2	23	23	52
Passive anal intercourse	3	8	15	75	2	5	10	84
Forcing someone to do something sexual	0	2	14	84	1	2	12	86
Being forced to do something sexual	0	3	13	84	0	2	10	89

Note: Row percentages total 100 percent.

Source: From *Sex in America* by Robert T. Michael et al. Copyright © 1994 by CSG Enterprises, Inc., Edward O. Laumann, Robert T. Michael, and Gina Kolata. By permission of Little, Brown and Company, Inc.

Stimulation of Erogenous Zones

Certain areas of the body almost always generate sexual arousal when they are touched. The penis and the clitoris are two examples. However, it seems that almost any area of the body can become conditioned to respond erotically to tactile stimulation in particular individuals. If touching a certain part of a person's body leads to sexual arousal, the area is called an erogenous zone for that person. Typical nongenital erogenous zones are the mouth, earlobes, breasts, buttocks, lower abdomen, inner thighs, and anal-perineal area. In a fulfilling sexual relationship, it is important for both partners to learn about the most pleasurable kinds of stimulation to exert on these zones.

In treating sexual dysfunctions (see Chapter 18), sex therapists have long recognized that touch is a vi-tal part of the experience that gives meaning to sexual responsiveness for women and men. Therapy programs typically encourage couples to spend time together in the nude, gently massaging, fondling, and tracing each other's bodies in pleasurable ways. Both partners are encouraged to accept and enjoy being stimulated to the fullest extent possible. Most people in our culture find some degree of sexual arousal in having their bodies close to another naked body and having the opportunity to share touching experiences. The sense of touch usually is an essential part of sexual arousal.

Some people find an element of sexual arousal in more aggressive forms of touch. Sexual contact can have its aggressive, even violent side. Light scratching, pinching, and biting are considered enjoyable by some. It is not unusual for one partner to bite and suck the other during strong sexual passion, even to the

■ **FIGURE 12.4**   *Male-Female Fellatio*

extent of producing a bruise. Such a bruise on the neck, commonly called a hickey, seems to represent a badge of experience for some individuals.

Oral-Genital and Oral-Anal Sex

Many individuals derive intense genital pleasure from being orally stimulated, partly because they can relax and enjoy it and partly because their partner can provide intense, localized stimulation. Although using the mouth to stimulate the genitals of a sexual partner can be highly exciting for some people, it can be disgusting for others. The term **fellatio** refers to kissing, licking, or sucking on the penis or allowing the penis to move in and out of the mouth. Some men particularly enjoy oral stimulation of the frenulum on the underside of the penile head, one of their most sensitive genital areas (see Figures 12.4 and 12.5). **Cunnilingus** involves kissing, licking, or sucking the clitoris, labia, and vaginal opening or inserting the tongue into the vagina. (see Figures 12.6 and 12.7). Partners sometimes perform oral sex on each other simultaneously, in the position called in slang "sixty-nine" due to the relative positions of the bodies.

The NHSLS provided the most reliable statistics on oral sex ever made available. A fair amount of evidence indicates that oral sex became an increasingly acceptable and desirable form of sexual behavior on college campuses during the 1960s and 1970s, and the NHSLS data make it clear that the practice is still espe-

cially popular among young, better-educated white persons. It is much less common among people with less education and among blacks. According to the survey, 68 percent of women and 77 percent of men had performed oral sex on a partner during their lifetime, with 19 percent of women and 27 percent of men having done so in their last sexual interaction. Similar proportions of both genders had been recipients of oral sex—73 percent of women and 79 percent of men during their lifetime; and 20 percent and 28 percent, respectively, during their last sexual experience. A willingness to perform oral sex and/or have it performed on them is twice as common among women who have gone to college compared to women who did not finish high school. People over age 60 and those who have a conservative Protestant religious background are much less likely to engage in oral sexual practices (Laumann, Gagnon, et al., 1994). As Table 12.2 shows, oral sex ranks third on the list of people's favorite shared sexual activities, with almost every other behavior trailing rather distantly behind. There is compelling evidence that oral sex has become quite acceptable among the young and in fact is often the starting point of shared sexual activity. More

fellatio oral stimulation of the penis.

cunnilingus (kun-a-LEAN-gus) oral stimulation of the clitoris, vaginal opening, or other parts of the vulva.

FIGURE 12.5 *Male-Male Fellatio*

FIGURE 12.6 *Male-Female Cunnilingus*

mouths during fellatio because of the mistaken notion that the substance is, in itself, dangerous to ingest. If the male is known to be free of sexually transmitted diseases, HIV, and prostate infection and the partner wishes to do so, there is no particular danger in swallowing semen. It is simply digested.

There are documented cases of HIV being transmitted through oral sex, although the actual degree of risk remains unclear. Therefore, unless there is absolute certainty about a partner's lack of exposure to HIV, the safest practice is for a condom to be worn during fellatio or for a **rubber dam** to be placed over the vulva during cunnilingus. Rubber dams may be of the type used in dental work or may be a nonlubricated latex condom or a rubber surgical glove cut to form a sheet of rubber. As yet, no studies have been done concerning the actual effectiveness of such rubber dams in preventing the transmission of HIV, but experts have reasoned that any barrier to the mixing of body fluids certainly reduces the risk. How practical the rubber dam can be in even acting as a barrier is particularly debatable. Other infections can also be transmitted through oral-genital contact, including throat infections from genital bacteria and urethral or vaginal infections transmitted from the mouth. It is unsafe to blow into the penis during fellatio (even though a common slang term is "blow job") or to blow into the vagina during cunnilingus because bacteria may be forced in or actual injury may result. There are some indications that blowing air into the vagina, particularly during pregnancy, can lead to the formation of air embolisms in a woman's blood vessels that could potentially be fatal.

research is needed to determine how accurate such assessments are (Grunseit et al., 2005; Remez, 2000).

Why do you think oral sex and some other forms of sexual behavior are more common among women who have gone to college than among women who did not finish high school?

FOH With the important proviso that oral-genital sex can be responsible for spreading sexually transmitted diseases, it is generally considered a relatively safe practice as long as the basic rules of hygiene are followed. Some partners fear the ejaculation of semen into their

rubber dam a piece of rubber material, such as that used in dental work, placed over the vulva during cunnilingus.

■ **FIGURE 12.7**   *Female-Female Cunnilingus*

Sometimes the anal region is stimulated orally, but strict hygienic measures are crucial to preventing transmission of bacteria. Even with thorough washing, some rectal bacteria or viruses may be ingested. Again, this practice would be considered dangerous if there were any chance that hepatitis or HIV was present in the person being stimulated anally. A rubber dam can be placed over the anal region to protect against transmission of HIV, other sexually transmitted diseases, and bacteria.

Mutual Manual Stimulation and Masturbation

Most sexually active couples use some form of mutual manual stimulation of the genitals. The clitoris may be manipulated with a finger, although direct stimulation of the glans can be uncomfortable for some. One or more fingers may be inserted into the vagina and moved. The penis may be grasped and stroked and the scrotum fondled. These techniques often are used by sexual partners to stimulate each other to orgasm. Mutual manual stimulation of genitals and the anal region is also one of the most common forms of sexual sharing. See Figure 12.8.

Although some couples find it difficult to discuss their masturbatory practices and even more difficult to masturbate in each other's presence, others report that they find enjoyment in watching their partner masturbate and in being so observed. Slightly more than one-third of college students reported having masturbated while another person watched. Masturbation usually is a private experience, and sharing it often represents a level of intimacy even deeper than some other forms

■ **FIGURE 12.8**   *Males Sharing Masturbation*

of sexual sharing. Many couples at least occasionally incorporate manual stimulation of the partner or masturbation into their shared sexual activities.

Interfemoral and Anal Intercourse

Many sexual partnerships that include at least one male use various forms of nonvaginal penile intercourse. The penis is versatile and can be inserted into

Real People

Sybil and Carl: Trying to Find Sexual Compatibility

Sybil is a graduate student, and her husband Carl is a teacher in the local high school. They have been married for three years, after living together for two years during their undergraduate years. They have decided to postpone having a family for at least another three years, although they both look forward to having children.

Sybil has been more satisfied than Carl with their sexual relationship. Early in their partnership, Sybil had been unable to reach orgasm but gradually became able to do so. She feels especially intimate with Carl when they have intercourse and enjoys their physical closeness. While Carl also enjoys intercourse, he has expressed interest in being more adventurous in their sexual activities. More than once, he has asked Sybil to watch a pornographic video during their sex play. While she finds the videos interesting, and even arousing, she has not felt as though she wanted to participate in the sexual acts that Carl has suggested. He is particularly anxious to have her be more open to oral sex—both fellatio and cunnilingus. They have experimented with these behaviors in the past, but Sybil does not much enjoy either one. Carl also wants to try anal

intercourse, which Sybil does not find acceptable at all. She has said that she believes anal sex would be uncomfortable and even dangerous, and she has no desire even to try it once.

Recently, Carl has been expressing his frustrations more adamantly, and the two have been arguing about sex more frequently. Carl insists that Sybil's lack of responsiveness to his sexual interests signals a lack of sensitivity and caring on her part, while Sybil counters that if he really cared about her, he wouldn't keep trying to pressure her into sexual acts that she finds distasteful. They both have begun to say that perhaps they are incompatible sexually, and they are fearful about what that might mean for their entire relationship.

How would you sum up the difficulties that Sybil and Carl are experiencing? Do you feel that one of them is more "right" than the other? Is there a suitable compromise toward which they should be working? Do you think the sexual differences they are encountering would be a reasonable cause for the couple—or any couple—to end their relationship?

the partner's hand, between female breasts, between the buttocks, or between the thighs (interfemoral intercourse), or it can be rubbed on the partner's abdomen or any other body area. These forms of sexual activity often are accompanied by pelvic thrusting. It is wise for heterosexual couples who practice interfemoral intercourse to know that semen ejaculated near or at the vaginal opening carries some risk of pregnancy. Even a small amount of semen entering the vagina will carry sperm, and although the chances are minimal, it is possible for some of those sperm to travel into the fallopian tubes and fertilize an ovum.

A type of sexual sharing that seems to wax and wane in popularity is **anal intercourse,** or insertion of the penis into the partner's rectum. In most countries, the prevalence of anal intercourse is quite high. NHSLS data showed the activity to be somewhat more prevalent than might be expected, with a slightly greater tendency for white and better-

educated people to have experienced anal sex. For the total study population, 26 percent of men had engaged in anal intercourse during their lifetime, and 10 percent had done so in the previous year. Twenty percent of women had had anal sex during their lifetime, 9 percent during the prior year (Laumann, Gagnon, et al., 1994). About 20 to 25 percent of college students have engaged in anal sex, according to a few studies (Baldwin & Baldwin, 2000). As Table 12.2 shows, anal intercourse is somewhat more appealing to males than to females. It is interesting to note that 11 percent of males indicated that they found being the passive partner in anal intercourse, presumably a male-male activity, to be somewhat or very appealing.

anal intercourse insertion of the penis into the rectum of a partner.

The anal sphincter muscles tend to resist penile entry. It usually takes appropriate lubrication, gentle prodding by the penis, and concentrated relaxation of the anus by the partner to permit penetration. Physicians occasionally see rectal or anal injuries resulting from anal sex, and these can be quite serious. There is a danger that tissue damage related to anal intercourse may increase the chances of transmitting HIV if the inserting male is infected. Again, unless there is absolute certainty that the man is not infected, a condom should be worn to provide substantial—but not absolute—protection. Condoms are somewhat more likely to break during anal intercourse. It is unsafe to insert the penis into the mouth or vagina following anal intercourse, because bacteria are easily transferred and may cause infection. Male-female anal intercourse is a behavior that too often is omitted from college sexuality education, even though it apparently is a reasonably common behavior that carries some risks (Baldwin & Baldwin, 2000).

Vibrators, Pornography, and Fantasies

Any aids used for sexual stimulation by individuals can be shared and probably often are. Electric vibrators typically used in masturbation may be used by couples to provide intense sexual pleasuring for each other. NHSLS data show that 16 percent of women and 23 percent of men find such devices appealing. Some couples enjoy viewing pornographic materials together, such as magazine photographs or movies showing a variety of sexual acts. Others enjoy reading books that describe sexual scenes in explicit language. It has long been recognized that fantasy can be an integral part of sexual experiences and can induce sexual arousal. Some books have dealt with the sexual fantasies of individuals, and many people seem more willing to talk about their own fantasies than once was the case. Some couples enjoy acting out their sexual fantasies together and find them sexually stimulating. Fantasies that involve inflicting pain or humiliation on a partner are stimulating to some people. Such behavior, termed sadomasochism, is discussed in more detail in Chapter 14, "The Spectrum of Human Sexual Behavior."

FOH Aphrodisiacs

Some foods and chemicals have been purported to act as sexual stimulants for those who consume them. Substances that create erotic stimulation are called **aphrodisiacs.** A wide variety of exotic substances have been labeled aphrodisiacs, including powdered rhinoceros horn, powdered stag's horn, dried salamanders, and dried beetles as well as some common foods such as eggs, olives, peanuts, oysters, venison, and bananas. Although most of these substances have not been scientifically studied, expert opinion suggests that they don't actually have any effect. In one study, powdered deer horn or a placebo was given to a group of men who over a period of three months were asked about their sexual experiences. The results showed that the deer horn had absolutely no effect on sexual desire, arousal, performance, frequency, or pleasure (Conaglen, Suttie, & Conaglen, 2003).

Some individuals report increased interest in sex under the influence of alcohol or marijuana. Both of these drugs lead to relaxation and lowered inhibitions and therefore when used in moderation enhance sexual activity. Used in larger amounts, however, they may inhibit sexual desire and arousal. Even though cocaine has been purported to act as an aphrodisiac in women, a study of heavy users of crack cocaine showed, that they actually had lower levels of interest in sex and a greater likelihood of problems with sexual functioning. In some individuals, another group of chemicals—the volatile nitrites—are reported to enhance response to sexual stimulation and orgasm. These chemicals, especially amyl nitrite and isobutyl nitrite, have been marketed as room deodorizers. They are volatile and are absorbed quickly by inhalation, causing immediate dilation of blood vessels, with a resulting rush. They are also highly flammable. Although most users have suffered no ill effects other than headache and a temporary pounding pulse, these chemicals have been implicated in some fatal cerebral hemorrhages. NHSLS data showed that drug use in association with sexual activity actually is quite rare, with only about 1 percent of males and 0.5 percent of females having used drugs before sex in the previous year. Alcohol use was far more common, with 9 percent of males and 6 percent of females saying that they frequently drank alcohol before or during sexual activity.

Sex therapists have been experimenting with various medications that might increase sexual desire or enhance sexual performance. This work has led to the use of some prescribed drugs to improve sexual functioning, including yohimbine, opioid receptor blockers, and dopamines. These drugs seem to act in the brain or central nervous system in ways

> **aphrodisiacs** (af-ro-DEE-zee-aks) foods or chemicals purported to foster sexual arousal; believed to be more myth than fact.

that can stimulate sexual response, but they do not affect sexual desire to any great degree and their effects on sexual responsiveness seem to be unpredictable.

A widely touted aphrodisiac is "Spanish fly," the slang name for **cantharides,** a chemical extracted from a certain species of southern European beetle. Taken internally, the drug produces inflammation of the urinary tract and dilation of blood vessels in the genital area, which can lead to prolonged, often painful erection of the penis. Cantharides is considered a dangerous chemical that can cause serious illness and even death.

Have you ever heard of anyone using an aphrodisiac? If so, describe his or her experience.

Available research would suggest that there are no surefire aphrodisiacs available. So-called aphrodisiacs probably work because their user believes in their effectiveness. Whenever an individual desires sexual stimulation, looks for it, and expects it, it is not surprising that it may be generated.

The Aftermath of Shared Sex

Many couples find that the period during which they are together following shared sexual activity is significant to their relationship. If the sexual experience has been satisfying to both partners and both are feeling relaxed or even drowsy, it may be a time for communicating quiet, gentle, loving feelings. Women in general seem to take longer than men in the resolution phase of the sexual response cycle, although this may be the result of lack of satiation due to an inadequate number of orgasms.

Satisfaction with sexual activity seems to depend on a variety of factors, with orgasm representing only one of them. About 29 percent of women and 75 percent of men report always having an orgasm in their sexual activities, yet the proportion of both sexes who report being extremely emotionally satisfied is about 40 percent. Clearly, there is more to a good sex life than being able to have an orgasm, and not everyone who has an orgasm is necessarily satisfied with sex in other respects. Thirty percent of women and 5 percent of men report having orgasms sometimes or never, although married women are much more likely than unmarried women to reach orgasm more frequently in their shared sexual activities. NHSLS research showed that people who report being happy with their lives in general also are more likely to be happy with their sex lives. The more satisfied people are sexually, the more they tend to stay married and

faithful to their spouses (Guo, Ng, & Chan, 2004; Laumann, Gagnon, et al., 1994).

When sex has been unsuccessful in any way or has generated some negative feelings, the period following sexual contact may be an especially valuable time for two-way communication. Many couples store up fears, resentments, and feelings of inadequacy because of sexual problems, only to find that these tensions eventually catch up with the relationship and place strains on it. Talking out the negative feelings while they are fresh—in an atmosphere of mutual warmth, caring, and reassurance—can strengthen any relationship.

After a suitable length of time (see Chapter 4, "Human Sexual Arousal and Response," on the male's refractory period), some couples proceed to orgasm a second time. Whether a second orgasmic experience takes place depends on many factors, including age, level of sexual arousal, the arousing aspects of the surroundings, the newness of the relationship, and the desire for further sex on the part of both partners.

■ Same-Gender Sexual Sharing

To approach an understanding of different persons' lifestyles solely from the perspective of their sexual orientation is constraining and limiting, because sexuality represents only one aspect of people's sharing. Partners of any gender combination can share a full range of sexual activity and find great joy and satisfaction in this sharing. Some men fondle each other's genitals or masturbate each other. Often they engage in gentle, loving gestures such as kisses, embraces, and body stroking. Oral-genital contact is common, and many gay males practice fellatio, as illustrated in Figure 12.5. Anal intercourse is practiced by some male couples (see Figure 12.9), although not as frequently as fellatio (Kippax & Smith, 2001; Laumann, Gagnon, et al., 1994). Gay men now approach both fellatio and anal intercourse with increased caution and are more likely to wear condoms because of concern about transmission of HIV. Some gay men participate in intentional unprotected anal sex, popularly called "barebacking," but they are most likely to do so with another man who shares the same positive

cantharides (kan-THAR-a-deez) a chemical extracted from a beetle that, when taken internally, creates irritation of blood vessels in the genital region; can cause physical harm.

■ **FIGURE 12.9**   *Male-Male Anal Intercourse*

or negative HIV status (Halkitis, Parsons, & Wilton, 2003). In one sample of gay men, 88 percent were able to label themselves "tops," meaning they preferred to take the insertive role in anal sex; "bottoms," signaling a preference for the receptive role in anal sex; or "versatiles," indicating an openness to either role. These labels did not mean the men would participate only as the preference suggested, but simply that they were more likely to engage in that form of shared sex (Hart et al., 2003).

Men who share sex have definite preferences, and some are not at all interested in oral-genital sex or anal intercourse. Many gay males apparently have a strong preference for manual manipulation of the genitals or lying together in such a way that the genitals may be rubbed together. It is also common for one partner to practice interfemoral intercourse or to rub his penis on the other's abdomen. There have been some reports of fisting or handballing, in which the hand of one partner is inserted into the rectum of the other, producing an intense sexual experience. Such practices risk damaging the anal or rectal tissue.

Lesbians may share a wide range of intimate activities, and research indicates that even though lesbian couples share sex less frequently than do heterosexual

or gay male couples, they tend to be more satisfied with their sexual lives and to feel a greater sense of intimacy. Many women almost exclusively use activities such as kissing and general body contact, especially women who are less experienced with female-female sexual activity (see Figure 12.7). Manual manipulation of each other's genitals with finger penetration is one of the most frequently used forms of stimulation among lesbian couples, with oral-genital contact (cunnilingus) the preferred technique for reaching orgasm. The use of dildos or other objects in vaginal insertion is less common (see Figure 12.10). Women involved in a sexual encounter usually spend a longer period than male couples in gentle and affectionate foreplay, also giving more attention to caressing and nongenital stimulation. Single lesbians have sex less frequently than single gay men, and lesbians involved in a long-term committed relationship have relatively low levels of sexual activity. They often seem to prefer hugging and cuddling to more genitalized forms of sexual sharing (see Figure 12.11).

See "The Dance of Life" on SexSource Online.

FIGURE 12.10 *Women Sharing Sex Toys*

FIGURE 12.11 *Women Sharing Sensual Expression*

■ Heterosexual Intercourse

In most cultures, the act of vaginal sexual intercourse, or coitus, is surrounded by a variety of moral and social values. Most societies and religions have sought to place some restrictions on coital behavior in order to regulate which heterosexual couples have babies, to prevent people from enjoying bodily pleasures that some consider sinful, and to regulate sexual forces be considered too powerful to be indulged in casually. NHSLS statistics indicate that vaginal intercourse is the most prevalent shared sexual activity. Eighty percent of survey respondents said they had vaginal sex every time they shared a sexual experience in the previous year. An additional 15 percent indicated that they usually had vaginal sex during the previous year (Michael et al., 1994).

Sexual intercourse, like all forms of sex, takes on different meanings for different couples and in different circumstances. The personal needs and characteristics each partner brings to coitus help determine the depth and degree of pleasure that results. Factual knowledge about sex, the capacity to accept differences in needs and responses, and personal attitudes all play a part in determining the enjoyment and meaning of coitus for each individual and each couple (Barrientos & Paez, 2006). A study of women's emotional responses to intercourse found that women experience coitus in three distinct ways. The *relationship-centered experience* is characterized by positive feelings about the relationship with the partner and the desirability of sex on both their parts. The *pleasure-centered* experience is characterized by feelings of satisfaction and enjoyment, along with a sense of letting go and focusing on one's own sexual needs and feelings. The *worry-centered* experience, as the name implies, tends to be accompanied by aversive feelings such as anger, emptiness, vulnerability, disappointment, and a sense of inadequacy. As might be predicted, the first two types of experiences were more likely to be accompanied by orgasm and enjoyment (Birnbaum, Glaubman, & Mikulincer, 2001).

Sexual Intercourse and Diseases   **FOH**

Vaginal intercourse is one way in which sexually transmitted diseases and HIV may be transmitted, because bacteria and viruses are carried in semen and vaginal fluids. If a partner has ever had sex with someone else, there is at least some risk that he or she carries a disease-causing organism. It is always safest for a male partner to wear a condom during intercourse or for the female to wear a vaginal pouch (female condom) unless there is absolute certainty that neither person ever could have been exposed to an STD or to HIV. See Chapter 17 for additional information on STDs, HIV, their transmission, and how the risk of infection can be minimized.

Real Student Voices

■ As a gay man, I object that your book doesn't have more drawings of males having sex together. You have a regular Kama Sutra of heterosexual positions, but not much to illustrate how two men or two women could engage in sex. The first few times I had sex with other men, I was pretty ignorant about what we might do. Books like this don't help much. What's up?

■ I don't really understand why people are so interested in having sex in so many different positions. Does it really matter how much of a gymnast you are? It just seems silly to me.

■ I don't know many men who like to see much pubic hair on women. I prefer that women shave most of their genital hair, and likewise I try to keep the hair around my penis and testicles well trimmed.

■ It's important to me that my boyfriend take his time during intercourse and that I have time to reach orgasm a couple of times. Sometimes even after he is finished, he continues to touch and stimulate me so that I can be fully satisfied. Fortunately, he thinks this is a good thing, and doesn't take it personally.

Intromission

Male-female sexual intercourse, by definition, involves the insertion of the penis into the vagina. Comfortable intromission requires a suitable degree of penile erection, lubrication, relaxation of the vaginal opening, and cooperation between the two partners. Erection of the penis is a natural part of male sexual arousal, and the vagina usually produces enough lubricant to permit easy movement of the penis into the vagina. If vaginal lubrication is insufficient, artificial lubricants can be applied to the penis and the vaginal opening. Water-soluble silica-based lubricants, such as K-Y, or saliva generally are satisfactory. Petroleum-based jellies are not recommended, because they are less healthful for tissues and less easily cleansed away.

The vaginal opening is sometimes tense, and gentle patience is necessary to give it time to relax. If the outer vaginal muscles cannot relax to the point where intromission can take place comfortably, the woman may be experiencing vaginismus. If there is some difficulty with intromission, the male may begin to lose some of his erection. Both of these problems are discussed in Chapter 18, "Sexual Dysfuntions and Their Treatment." Actual insertion of the penis can be awkward for both partners, and active cooperation is helpful. Either partner may part the minor lips to expose the vaginal opening and then guide the penis into the vagina. The position of the couple also helps determine the ease of intro-

mission. The first few coital thrusts of the male may be progressively more forceful as the penis is pushed gradually deeper into the vagina. Depth of penetration depends on the size of the penis and the vagina, the coital position, and the relative comfort for both partners.

As discussed in Chapter 2, "Female Sexual Anatomy and Physiology," if the hymen is still present at the opening of the vagina, prodding by the penis may be necessary to rupture it, and the female should expect some discomfort or pain. Cooperation and understanding on the part of both partners can lead to easy, unembarrassing intromission. Some males feel awkward in attempting to find the opening and the best angle for inserting the penis; the female partner may be able to help lessen such difficulties. Frequently, difficulties or discomfort in intromission during early coital experiences generates performance fears in both males and females. These fears can lead to problems in later experiences, such as lack of erection or lack of vaginal lubrication. After several sexual contacts, intromission usually is accomplished with more ease.

Intercourse

Intercourse usually involves movement of the penis into and out of the vagina, resulting from pelvic movements of both partners. A few studies have viewed couples having intercourse with magnetic resonance imaging (MRI) techniques. These studies have demonstrated that the penis, the erection of which extends back into the male's body further than previously realized, tends to become somewhat boomerang-shaped during coitus. The glans penis tends to push forward alongside the uterus (Faix et al., 2001, 2002). Different coital positions afford different amounts of control over these movements to both partners. The rate and vigor of thrusting depend to a large degree on the mood of the couple and how long they wish to prolong coitus. The factor that usually determines duration of intercourse is the length of time required for the male to reach orgasm. Because erection of the penis almost always subsides following orgasm, intercourse can rarely continue after orgasm. Rapid, forceful movements of the penis generally bring males to orgasm quite quickly, and the amount of precoital stimulation also plays an important role. Intercourse itself may not be effective in generating orgasm for women, and additional clitoral stimulation may be necessary.

It is possible for couples to learn how to modulate the amount of stimulation required for both of them to obtain maximum enjoyment. By occasionally slowing his pelvic thrusting, making shallow thrusts of the penis, and even temporarily ceasing coital movements, the male can exert a great deal of control over the amount of time required for him to reach orgasm. Certain positions enhance this control. Data from the NHSLS found that about 70 percent of people said that their last shared sexual event lasted from 15 minutes to an hour. That time typically would include more than just the experience of intercourse. Roughly 15 percent of people indicated that their last shared sex took 15 minutes or less, and another 15 percent said it took an hour or more (Laumann, Gagnon, et al., 1994). It is up to each couple to work on developing the duration of sexual activity most suitable for them, and open and specific communication can be an important help in this process.

The movements made by both partners during intercourse may vary a great deal, and finding the most pleasurable movements can be an exciting learning process in a growing sexual relationship. Alternating shallow and deep thrusts of the penis is often recommended, and the penis may also be rotated or moved from side to side in the vagina. According to most research, including that reported in this text, penis size has no bearing on the amount of sexual pleasure derived by the female during intercourse. Although some women contend that the size of the penis makes a difference to them in terms of physical pleasure, it is more typical for them to report that it is not a crucial factor in their pleasure. Clitoral stimulation by some means is often important for women during intercourse. Many couples caress

each other and use their hands to give added pleasure. Some couples strive for the simultaneous orgasm of both partners. Although some couples enjoy simultaneous orgasm and can accomplish it with relative ease, others find that trying for orgasm at the same time detracts from their sexual pleasure. Some people enjoy experiencing their partner's orgasm without being preoccupied with their own. If one partner has not reached orgasm during coitus and wishes to do so, it is appropriate for the other to employ suitable techniques to help the partner achieve orgasm.

Do you believe orgasm is essential for both partners during shared sexual activity? Why or why not?

Couples usually have intercourse in bed, but many at least occasionally experiment with other locations, including the outdoors. Although some people prefer coitus in the dark or in dim lighting, others enjoy bright light. Finding ways to enhance the pleasure of sexual intercourse is a continual human pursuit.

Positions for Intercourse

There are various body positions in which the penis may be inserted comfortably into the vagina. Many couples enjoy experimenting with different positions and find that sex can be more interesting by changing positions during intercourse, often several times. A good fit of the two bodies is usually important to full sexual pleasure, especially for the woman to reach orgasm (Pierce, 2000). Some changes of position can be accomplished by rolling over or other slight movements, without any interruption of coitus. Other changes require that the penis be withdrawn until the new position is assumed. Which position a couple finds most enjoyable, comfortable, and manageable depends on their own individual characteristics, such as body size and weight, degree of physical fitness, length and diameter of the erect penis, personal attitudes about particular positions, and the couple's moods during the sexual encounter. Different positions may place more physical strain on one or the other partner and afford one of them more ability to control the rate and vigor of coital movements. It should be emphasized that sexual intercourse need not be a series of acrobatics to be pleasurable for both partners. Yet if both partners are willing and able, varying coital position from time to time can lead excitement to an ongoing sexual relationship. Each of the following 10 basic positions has myriad variations.

FIGURE 12.12   *Man on Top, Woman Supine*

Reclining Face-to-Face

Positions in which the two partners face each other are most commonly used because the two are freer to look at each other, kiss, and communicate in these positions. Reclining positions are preferred because they usually require less physical energy than supporting the body in some upright posture. There are several variations of face-to-face reclining positions.

Man on Top, Woman Supine

This position, the most common one used in European and American societies, is erroneously considered by some couples to be the only normal way to have intercourse (see Figure 12.12). Recent studies show that most people now at least experiment with a variety of positions. The position seems particularly compatible from an anatomical standpoint, considering the usual angles of the erect penis and the vagina in a reclining position. The male often supports part of his weight on his arms and knees, although this may place real strain on some men. Women sometimes find it suitable in this position to hold up their legs somewhat or wrap them around the male's waist or even over his shoulders, the latter variation requiring more of a kneeling position for the man. Some couples insert a pillow under the woman's buttocks for greater ease. These positions give the male partner maximum control over coital thrusting, because the female's pelvis is relatively immobile, and also allow deep penetration by the penis. Conversely, they may make it somewhat more difficult for the woman to have the sort of stimulation necessary to achieve orgasm. Women or their partners may want to increase manual stimulation of the clitoris during intercourse to help produce the orgasmic response.

Woman on Top, Man Supine

This is the second most commonly used coital position (see Figure 12.13). It has many variations, because the woman can lie on the man with her legs fully extended or can straddle him in a sitting, crouching, or kneeling position. The position provides the woman more opportunity to control the coital movements and leaves the male's hands freer to caress her body. Some men experience some difficulty keeping the penis in the vagina in this position, and some women experience discomfort with the deep penile penetration it makes possible. However, this position reportedly is more likely to result in orgasm for the female partner, due to the fact that exerting more control over the movements leads to better stimulation for her.

Side-by-Side

There are many advantages to coital positions in which both partners lie on their sides, and this lateral position often is recommended in the treatment of several sexual dysfunctions (see Figure 12.14). Many couples use a side-by-side position more frequently than other positions. Because both partners are lying down and need to worry less about supporting their bodies, there is less strain on both of them. They are

FIGURE 12.13 *Woman on Top, Man Supine*

FIGURE 12.14 *Side-by-Side*

able to share in controlling their thrusting motions, and both are free to use their hands for touching and caressing. Deep penetration by the penis sometimes is more difficult in the side-by-side positions, and some couples find it less comfortable than other positions.

Other Variations on Face-to-Face

Woman on Edge of Bed or Chair

When the woman positions herself on the edge of a bed or chair, with her back reclining and her feet resting on the floor, the man can either stand or kneel on the floor in a manner that enables him to enter her (see Figure 12.15). The male is in control in these positions. The male's position on the floor gives him a good deal of leverage for controlling his movements and giving powerful thrusts. He also is easily able to vary the angle at which the penis enters the vagina.

Both Partners Seated

Seated intercourse with the partners facing each other is easier for some couples to achieve than it is for others. Typically, the male sits, sometimes in a chair or on the edge of the bed (a reasonably solid support usually is more desirable), and the female then lowers herself onto his erect penis, either keeping her feet on the floor or placing her legs around his waist. The woman usually has greater control over the coital movements in this position, although the degree of

control varies with the positioning of her legs and feet. The man's hands are relatively free, and he may help move the female's body up and down on his penis. Deep penile penetration usually is possible in seated positions.

Both Partners Standing

Coital positions in which both partners stand generally are the most difficult to manage and sustain. Attention must be given to maintaining balance and stability, along with keeping the penis comfortably inside the vagina. Although many couples experiment with standing intercourse and some use the position occasionally, it is not a popular position. Deep penile penetration is difficult while standing because the angles of the penis and the vagina are not particularly complementary. For couples who find standing intercourse positions comfortable, this option apparently is exciting for occasional variation.

Rear Vaginal Entry

Most mammals use a rear entry position for copulation. It may be for precisely this reason that many people do not choose such positions. Yet couples who do use these variations often find them comfortable and exciting, and many cultures around the world employ then regularly. Although some intimacy may be lost without face-to-face contact, natural body contours afford especially close body contact with many rear-entry positions.

■ **FIGURE 12.15**   *Woman on Edge of Bed or Chair*

Both Partners Kneeling

In this position, the woman may hold the upper part of her body up on her arms while kneeling or may lower her shoulders and head (see Figure 12.16). The man kneels behind her and inserts his penis into the vagina from behind. He may also assume a higher crouched position. Deep penile penetration usually is achieved in this position. The man's hands generally are free to offer stimulating contact for the woman, including contact with the clitoris. Another variation is

the wheelbarrow position, in which the male stands behind the female and holds her legs while having intercourse.

Man on Top, Woman Lying on Her Abdomen

This position is difficult for some couples to manage, but it can be enjoyable (see Figure 12.17). The man may lie on top of the woman with his legs fully extended or straddle her body in a crouched or seated position. If the woman arches her back somewhat, pushing her vulva backward, penile entry usually is easily accomplished. This can be a relatively comfortable position, although deep penetration may be difficult.

Side-by-Side

In the side-by-side position, intromission is quite easily accomplished, and this position is often recommended during pregnancy. Both, partners are lying down, and neither is placed under any strain. Their hands generally are quite free for touching each other, although because the man is behind, his hands have easier access to his partner (e.g., her breasts and clitoris).

Both Partners Seated or Standing

Rear entry is also possible when both partners are seated or standing (see Figure 12.18). The seated position is the easiest and is a comfortable way for the woman to sit on the man's lap while participating in intercourse. She can exercise a good deal of control

FIGURE 12.16 *Both Partners Kneeling, Rear Entry*

FIGURE 12.17 *Man on Top, Woman on Abdomen, Rear Entry*

and marriage has become less clearly defined than it once was.

In other cultures, sexual relationships fit differently into the varying structures of marriage. In societies in which people are permitted to have more than one spouse or in which married couples are encouraged to forge close working bonds with one another, sexual intercourse may be permitted among many different combinations of persons. There are also nonsexual marriages; these arrangements are based on political or economic benefits to the partners or their relatives and have no expectation of sexual interaction.

There can be no doubt that in North America sex is perceived as a significant part of marriage. Sexual problems can lead to severe marital difficulties and even divorce, and all sorts of publications are available to spice up and renew sex within marriage. It is also true that communication problems in marriage often are reflected in sexual difficulties between the partners. Sex is a potential source of marriage enrichment, reinforcing the interdependence of husband and wife, unifying them through shared enjoyment, symbolizing their shared life, and helping resolve episodes of alienation. Sexual activity can exert these same positive influences on relationships other than those involving marriage.

If and when you received your formal sexuality education, did your source address masturbation, or was sex discussed solely as a penis-in-vagina act? Was intercourse presented merely as a procreative act? Were the emotional aspects as well as the biological aspects discussed? Were other forms of sexual sharing also presented?

For most married individuals, vaginal sexual intercourse with the spouse constitutes the major and preferred—though not only—form of sexual outlet. Oral-genital sex seems to be second in preference as a sexual outlet within marriage (Laumann, Gagnon, et al., 1994). The frequency of shared sexual activity seems to vary a great deal. The average frequency of sex for women is six times per month, and the average frequency for men is seven times per month. Of course, individual couples show wide variation from this average, and many factors can affect the frequency of intercourse.

Our society has a mix of values concerning premarital and extramarital sexual activity. On the basis of present evidence, it seems safe to state that not only have more people been experiencing coitus before marriage and at a younger age, but they also have been doing so more often and with fewer inhibitions than in the past.

FIGURE 12.18 *Both Partners Seated or Standing, Rear Entry*

over coital movements. Standing rear entry is not as easily managed, although it generally is easier than face-to-face standing intercourse.

Intercourse and Marriage

The social mores related to sexual intercourse often are intimately associated with a particular society's marriage customs. In many societies, including most Western societies, marriage represents a social and/or religious legitimation of coitus and childbearing. Hence sex, with its risk of pregnancy, often has been discouraged outside the context of marriage. Social institutions such as religion, school, family, and social networks typically are charged with the enforcement of the rules related to sex and marriage. Premarital and extramarital sex are more permissible in some societies than in others. In Western cultures, definitions of what constitutes a family have changed a great deal, with the result that the relationship between sex

Chapter Summary

1. NHSLS statistics are the most reliable data we have on human sexual behavior in the United States.

2. The social world of sex involves negotiative processes among people and has different consequences than the private world of sex.

3. Solitary sex includes thoughts and fantasies, erotic materials and toys, and masturbation. Males think about sex and seek out erotic materials more frequently than do females.

4. The frequency with which people experience private sexual pleasure seems to be positively correlated with how frequently they seek shared sex. Solitary sex does not seem to be a compensation for lack of availability of a sexual partner.

5. Masturbation, or self-stimulation of the genitals, is a sexual activity in which most people participate at one time or another.

6. People masturbate in a variety of ways, although most commonly women stimulate their clitoral area and men stimulate the penis.

7. Masturbation can be practiced at all stages of life. Medically speaking, there is no such thing as excessive masturbation; it does not produce physical weakness or illness.

8. Some people feel guilty about masturbation. Guilt does not affect frequency of masturbation in males, but it does to some extent in females.

9. Vaginal intercourse is the most popular of all shared sexual behaviors, followed by watching a partner undress and then oral sex. Partners must communicate about their mutual sexual preferences.

10. Many forms of shared nongenital stimulation are considered intimate and arousing. Kissing and massaging of erogenous zones may be highly erotic.

11. Fellatio is oral stimulation of the penis, and cunnilingus is oral stimulation of the clitoris and other areas of the vulva. Oral sex has become more acceptable in recent years, especially among young, better-educated white people.

12. The penis may be inserted between a partner's legs, breasts, or buttocks or into the anus. Anal intercourse is somewhat more appealing to males than to females, and it is one of the high-risk behaviors for transmission of HIV.

13. Vibrators, erotic pictures and films, and personal sexual fantasies may be integrated into shared sex.

14. There are many myths about foods or chemicals as stimulants to sexual arousal. Substances that create erotic stimulation are labeled aphrodisiacs, although they are believed to operate largely on suggestion and imagination.

15. The period following the end of shared sexual activity may be a quiet, warm, and comfortable time for communication between partners, or it may become a time of tension and further misunderstanding.

16. Couples of the same gender share a wide range of sexual activities, depending on individual preferences and tastes. Male-male oral sex is more common than anal sex; female couples often prefer nonpenetrative activities.

17. Heterosexual intercourse is often subject to strict moral, social, and relational codes of behavior. It also carries the risk of spreading sexually transmitted diseases and HIV.

18. The techniques and timing of intercourse vary, as do the positions in which a woman and man can share penile-vaginal penetration.

19. Happier people seem more satisfied with their sexual lives. Satisfaction is not necessarily correlated with having orgasms.

20. Intercourse is closely associated with marriage customs in most cultures. In North America, sex is considered to be a significant part of the marital relationship, with vaginal intercourse the most preferred activity.

Focus on Health Questions

In this section you will find the kinds of questions that you may have concerning your own health and sexuality. The page references indicate where in the text the answer is located; the exact place is marked with this logo: **FOH**

1. Do both males and females masturbate? **332**

2. When do most people stop masturbating during their lives? **335**

3. If people who are involved in a sexual relationship masturbate, does that mean there is something wrong with their sex life? **335**

4. How much is too much masturbation? **336**

5. Are there any dangers to masturbating? **336**

6. Does masturbation interfere with athletic prowess? **336**

7. Are there any health risks associated with oral sex? **341**

8. What are the dangers of anal intercourse? **343–344**

9. Are there any foods or drugs that turn people on sexually? **344**

10. How can the risk of contracting a disease be reduced in heterosexual intercourse? **347** (See also pp. **507–509,** Chapter 17.)

11. How long should intercourse last? **349**

12. How do different positions for intercourse affect sexual pleasure? **350–354**

Chapter 13
Sexual Orientation, Identity, and Behavior

Chapter Outline

I somewhat resent the pressure that I feel to define myself as straight, gay, or bisexual. I am who I am. I have had romantic and sexual involvement with both men and women, and eventually got married. That doesn't mean I have lost my attraction to or interest for others of my sex, or the other sex for that matter. I have simply made a commitment to monogamy.

—from a letter to the author

Do you think you can tell if somebody is gay from appearance and mannerisms? Do you laugh at jokes about "queers"? Have you ever felt attracted to a member of your own gender?

These are controversial questions for many, and in the arena of political correctness you sometimes have to be careful how you respond to them. Of all the sexual topics I have attempted to write about over the years with objectivity and attention to emerging research, more has shifted and changed with regard to sexual orientation than to anything else. The terms used by professionals seem always in flux, new theories wax and wane, and new political agendas continually emerge.

The bottom line is that we assume human beings to have a **sexual orientation,** that is, a set of physical and emotional attractions and interests that draws them both sexually and romantically to other people. If we look at the possibilities simplistically, we might also assume that there are three possible sexual orientations: straight, gay, or bisexual. As we have already learned in previous chapters, human sexuality is rarely that simple, and research and theory on sexual orientation confirm that the picture is quite complex.

Contemporary research has suggested that as part of their psychosexual development, especially during adolescence and young adulthood, human beings go through stages of establishing a **sexual orientation identity** or an inner awareness of what their sexual orientation means for their life in terms of sexual and romantic relationships. It has been assumed that sexual orientation and sexual identity, once they are established and recognized by the individual, remain stable throughout life. However, emerging evidence indicates that this may not be the case at all and that many people report changes in their sexual fantasies, romantic attractions, and sexual behaviors over time that cross the orientation and identity boundaries. These qualities are not as stable as they once were thought to be (Kinnish, Strassberg, & Turner, 2005).

This is not to say that people wake up one morning with a new sexual orientation or that an individual can suddenly "turn" gay or straight. It simply means that the components of what we find attractive, sexually exciting, and romantically enticing may be more fluid and dynamic than they are static or fixed. Some sexual scientists have insisted that it is time to acknowledge that the evidence calls into question the concept of a straight-gay dichotomy and suggests instead that most human beings have some potential for a range of sexual feelings and attractions over time (McConaghy, 2005).

FIGURE 13.1

Heath Ledger and Jake Gyllenhaal starred in *Brokeback Mountain,* a film that captured public attention for its portrayal of a long-time love affair between two cowboys, both of whom eventually married women.

This chapter focuses largely on nonheterosexual orientation and identity, because they have formed the basis for most available research and theory. In a heterosexist society, straight is considered the norm and not really that important for study. It is the *differences* that attract scientific attention: gay, lesbian, bisexual. I will elucidate what research tells us about these sexual orientations and identities, asking only that you keep in mind that although everyone has some sexual orientation and identity, it might not be as clearly defined or predictable as you might assume.

An example of how dramatic the issues of sexual orientation can become in our culture is the tremendous amount of media attention that accompanied the release of the film *Brokeback Mountain* in late 2005 (see Figure 13.1). A love story involving two cowboys and set in the 1960s, the film generated reactions ranging from people who refused to see it to those who thought it deserved an Academy Award. Even though the essential storyline of the movie was not unlike the ordinary lives of many people, we as a culture clearly are not ready to accept the mundane fact that men whom we expect to be icons of masculinity sometimes have sex with one another and even fall in love. Women whom we expect to be icons of femininity do the same but somehow create less fuss among the media. There is, in fact, an International Gay Rodeo

sexual orientation the set of physical and emotional qualities that attracts human beings to one another sexually and romantically.

sexual orientation identity an inner awareness of what one's sexual orientation means for one's life in terms of sexual and romantic relationships and social interaction.

Association to which some 4,000 men and women belong (Cho, 2006).

Do you believe sexual orientation is biologically or socially mandated? On what do you base your opinion?

■ Understanding Sexual Orientation

Concepts of sexual orientation and identity have been evolving much as our views of masculinity and femininity did when these traits came under closer scientific scrutiny. Instead of identifying masculinity and femininity as polarized entities in themselves, we now see them as representing clusters of relatively independent traits that may coexist within the same individual, regardless of whether that individual is male or female. Masculinity and femininity are now viewed as multidimensional sets of characteristics that exist to varying degrees within both men and women. It seems increasingly evident that sexual orientation is also a multidimensional phenomenon rather than an either-or proposition (Kauth, 2002).

The Perspective of the Kinsey Scale

When Alfred Kinsey began his research on sexual behavior in the 1930s and 1940s, he faced the same confusion we face today about what constitutes homosexuality. At that time, sexual acts between women often were ignored altogether, and no consideration was given to the frequency with which same-gender sexual acts took place. One sexual experience with a member of the same gender might be sufficient to define a person as a "homosexual." Social scientists of that day gave little consideration to making distinctions among behaviors, orientations, attractions, and identities. What an individual did sexually was assumed to reflect inner experience as well.

Kinsey recognized early on in his research that substantial numbers of people had experienced both same-gender and other-gender sexual activity. He devised a seven-category sexual behavior rating scale for use in his studies designed to classify individuals based on their behavior (see Figure 13.2). On the scale, he used the numbers 0 to 6, with 0 representing exclusively heterosexual behavior (i.e., no homosexual behavior) and 6 representing exclusively homosexual, or same-gender, behavior. Those individuals who showed some combination of both behaviors were classified somewhere between these two extremes. Categories 1 and 5 were for those who showed predominantly heterosexual or same-gender sexual

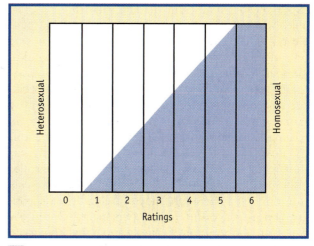

FIGURE 13.2 *Heterosexual-Homosexual Rating Scale*
Based on both psychological reactions and overt experience, individuals rate as follows:
0 = exclusively heterosexual with no homosexual
1 = predominantly heterosexual, only incidentally homosexual
2 = predominantly heterosexual, but more than incidentally homosexual
3 = equally heterosexual and homosexual
4 = predominantly homosexual, but more than incidentally heterosexual
5 = predominantly homosexual, but incidentally heterosexual
6 = exclusively homosexual
Kinsey recognized that for some people the strict dichotomy between same-gender and heterosexual behavior did not exist. In order to classify his clients into appropriate categories for study, Kinsey devised this rating scale.

behavior, respectively, but had experienced at least some of the other type of behavior. Category 2 included people who had experienced more than incidental same-gender behavior but still leaned more toward the heterosexual end of the scale; category 4 was for those who leaned more toward same-gender behavior but had experienced more than incidental heterosexual behavior. Category 3 included people with approximately equal amounts of sexual experience with men and with women (Kinsey et al., 1953).

Kinsey's scale has been called a "stroke of political genius," because it represented a step toward resolving issues that had been troubling researchers for many years and opened up a whole new way of understanding human sexual behavior. Kinsey's scale and the behavioral statistics that accompanied it demonstrated that sexual behavior between people of the same gender was more common in the U.S. population than had been believed—a comforting revelation not only to persons who perceived themselves as gay, lesbian, or bisexual but also to people who considered themselves heterosexual yet had experienced some same-gender activity. Because there was now a continuum of sexual behavior, people no longer had to see themselves as being at one pole of experience or the other. The middle ground of the scale clarified the idea that a range of sexual behavior exists that does not fall neatly into dualistic categories. Kinsey's approach is believed to have played a major role in allowing American society to begin coming to terms with same-gender sexual orientation.

Research since the time of Kinsey's work has shown that the more we know about the complexities of human sexuality, the less valuable his bipolar scale is in offering a thorough understanding of sexual orientation as part of the human personality. One problem with the scale is its implication that the more same-gender-oriented one is, the less heterosexual one can be, and vice versa. It has been proposed instead that these characteristics could in fact be relatively independent. Some people may exhibit high levels of both same-gender eroticism and heteroeroticism, low levels of both, or differing levels of each. Across their life spans, people may experience changes and discontinuities in sexual behavior patterns, sexual fantasies, and romantic attractions and identities (Kinnish, Strassberg, & Turner, 2005).

Incidence of Sexual Orientations, Behaviors, and Attractions

Given the apparently dynamic, changeable nature of sexual orientation and the many different dimensions of the human experience that must be considered, it is indeed a challenge to seek data on the frequencies of sexual orientations and all their complex variations. Researchers must rely primarily on self-reported data, with the additional complication of needing to rely on subjective interpretations and selective memories regarding inner experiences such as desire, fantasy, and attraction. Such measures are always imperfect.

Although Kinsey did state that it was critical to consider affectional, or romantic, factors when considering sexual orientation, his interviews focused largely on reports of sexual behavior. The average figures most frequently cited from his work (Kinsey et al., 1948, 1953), often without much explanation, were that 37 percent of the men and 13 percent of the women surveyed in his research population of more than 16,000 people had had at least one same-gender sexual experience to the point of orgasm since adolescence. The Kinsey data also were cited as evidence that 13.95 percent of males and 4.25 percent of females, or a combined average of 9.13 percent of the total population, had had either extensive same-gender experiences (21 or more partners or 52 or more experiences) or more than incidental same-gender

experiences (5 to 20 partners or 21 to 50 experiences) (Gebhard, 1977). This figure often was rounded up and said to mean that about 10 percent of the population is gay or lesbian. More recent evidence suggests that these figures probably are not representative of the total population, partly due to the fact that Kinsey researchers did not employ a random sample of the population and also partly due to the rather broad definitions they employed in analyzing their data.

Several studies have indicated a lower incidence of same-gender behavior than suggested by the widely quoted Kinsey figures. A Louis Harris poll of 739 men found that 4.4 percent reported having had sex with another man during the previous five years. In one survey of 3,321 men ages 20 to 39, only 2 percent reported having had any same-gender oral or anal sexual activity during the last 10 years, and only 1 percent reported being exclusively gay (Billy et al., 1993). Some research has suggested that to be *exclusively* same-gender-oriented in behavior, attraction, fantasies, and falling in love actually may be relatively rare, although leaning strongly in a same-gender direction is not. People who indicate that they have had sexual partners of both sexes tend to have had more sexual partners in general, to have had a higher frequency of both oral and anal sex, and to have begun experiencing masturbation and orgasm at a younger age (Traeen, Stigum, & Sorensen, 2002).

The researchers who conducted the National Health and Social Life Survey (NHSLS) found many subtleties and gray areas in attempting to identify the incidence of sexual orientations and behaviors (see Figure 13.3). They found that people often change

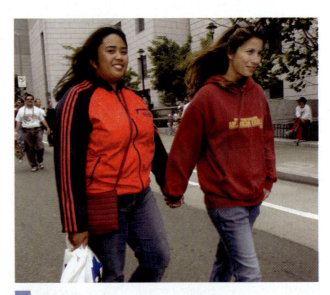

FIGURE 13.3 *Intimate Relationships*

It is erroneous to view gay and lesbian relationships strictly in terms of sexual behavior. Like heterosexual relationships, same-gender intimacy is based primarily on warmth and caring.

their patterns of sexual behavior over their lifetimes, making it difficult to generalize about orientation in any definitive manner (Tolman & Diamond, 2002). They also realized that no single set of desires uniquely defines an individual as lesbian, gay, or bisexual. Does sexual desire for someone of your same gender define you as gay, even if you have never acted on that desire? Does identifying yourself as a lesbian make you so if you have never had sex with another woman? Finally, researchers recognized that because of the stigma and discrimination still associated with same-gender sexual orientation, some people might be reluctant to say much about same-gender attractions or behaviors. The survey was designed to encourage honest answers as much as possible, and it focused on same-gender behaviors and attractions in several different ways, using the term "homosexual" in only one question (Michael et al., 1994).

The NHSLS sought data about three aspects of sexual orientation, recognizing it as a multidimensional aspect of human sexuality (Laumann, Gagnon,

et al., 1994). The researchers asked questions about *desire*, focusing on attractions to others of the same gender and the appeal of various sex acts; sexual *behavior* with same-gender partners; and *self-identification*, or the sexual orientation one associates with oneself. Figure 13.4 summarizes the findings of these aspects of the study. The results of the survey showed that more people find others of their gender sexually attractive than ultimately act on that attraction.

Desire issues were measured by two questions, indicated by the "attraction" and "appeal" scales on the graph. One question asked, "In general are you sexually attracted to . . . ?" and offered five choices as answers: only women, mostly women, both men and women, mostly men, or only men. About 4 percent of the women and over 5 percent of the men in the study responded that they were attracted to others of their own gender. When asked about the degree of appeal they found in the thought of having sex with someone of their own gender, 5.5 percent of the women and slightly more than 4 percent of the men indicated they

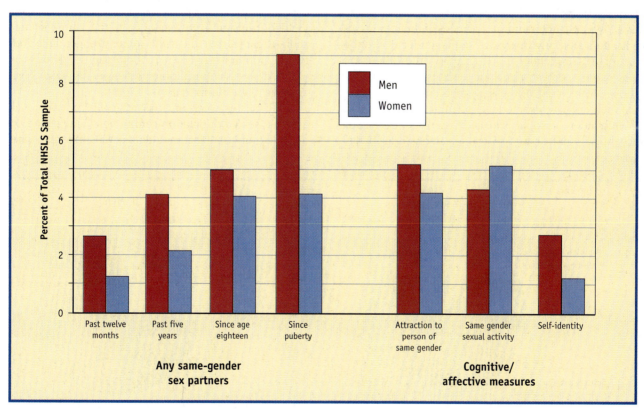

■ **FIGURE 13.4** *Aspects of Same-Gender Sexuality*

The NHSLS revealed that more men and women find others of their own gender sexually attractive or find sex with a same-gender partner appealing than identify themselves as gay, lesbian, or bisexual. In addition, many of those who have not recently had any same-gender sex partners report having had same-gender sex partners at some time in their lives.

Note: Attraction measured by the following question: "In general, are you sexually attracted to . . . only women, mostly women, both men and women, mostly men, only men?" (order of answer categories reversed for women). Appeal measured by the following question: "How would you rate this activity: having sex with someone of the same sex . . . very appealing, somewhat appealing, not appealing, not at all appealing?" Self-identification was derived from the following question: "Do you think of yourself as . . . heterosexual, homosexual, bisexual, something else?"

Source: From *Sex in America* by Robert T. Michael et al. Copyright © 1994 by CSG Enterprises, Inc., Edward O. Laumann, Robert T. Michael, and Gina Kolata. By permission of Little, Brown & Company, Inc.

found the idea very appealing or appealing. When asked about having engaged in same-gender sexual behavior, fewer than 2 percent of women had done so in the previous year, and about 4 percent had done so since age 18. Nine percent the men surveyed indicated having had sex with another male since puberty, but 40 percent of these (5 percent of all the men surveyed) indicated that the behavior had occurred prior to age 18. Somewhat more than 2 percent of all men said they had had sex with another man in the previous year. One clear difference between males and females that emerged in the survey data was that much of the same-gender sexual contact of males happened during the earlier teenage years, whereas women were more likely to have had sex with another woman after age 18.

Regardless of the rates of same-gender sexual activity or attraction, the lowest rates of response were found with the question of self-identification. About 2.8 percent of the men and about 1.4 percent of the women identified themselves as "homosexual" or "bisexual." NHSLS researchers also analyzed all relevant data from the 150 women (8.6 percent of the total 1,749) and 143 men (10.1 percent of the total 1,410) who indicated any degree of same-gender desire, behavior, or self-identification to see how the various factors overlapped or were independent. As Figure 13.5 shows, 59 percent of these women and 44 percent of the men indicated some level of attraction to others of their gender or some appeal of same-gender sexual acts but did not report any actual same-gender behav-

ior or self-identification. Thirteen percent of the women and 22 percent of the men had had some kind of same-gender sexual behavior but did not report any desire or self-identification as "homosexual," lesbian," or "bisexual." All three dimensions of same-gender sexual orientation were reported by only 15 percent of the 150 women and 24 percent of the 143 men who had indicated same-gender desire, behavior, or self-identification (Laumann, Gagnon, et al., 1994).

A sample of about 8,000 college students in the United States and Canada was studied on four different aspects of sexual orientation: behavior, attraction, fantasy, and self-identity. Over 97 percent of the women and men in the study identified themselves as heterosexual, with the proportion of those self-identifying as homosexual or bisexual being about 2 percent of the women and 3 percent of the men. About 10 percent of both genders indicated that at least half of their sexual fantasies involved same-gender partners. When researchers sought to make statistical comparisons among the four measures used in the study, they found an unsettling number of inconsistencies and contradictions. Attempts to refine their measurements yielded no significant change in the numbers described earlier but did find some stronger links between reports of cross-gender play activities as children and identification of same-gender sexual orientation (Ellis, Robb, & Burke, 2005).

All of this work confirms that the prevalence of any one sexual orientation cannot be characterized by a single number. It is a multidimensional phenomenon

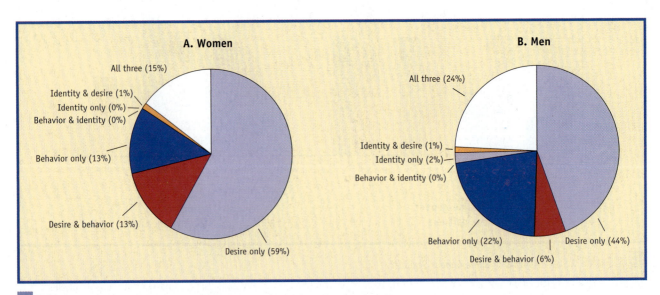

FIGURE 13.5 *Interrelation of Different Aspects of Same-Gender Sexuality*

Same-gender desire, behavior, and identity are separate aspects of same-gender sexuality. The NHSLS analysis confirmed that same-gender sexuality is a multidimensional phenomenon.

Note: A. For 150 women (8.6 percent of the total 1,749) who reported any adult same-gender sexuality. B. For 143 men (10.1 percent of the total 1,410) who reported any adult same-gender sexuality.

Source: From *The Social Organization of Sexuality* by Edward O. Laumann et al. Copyright © 1994 by Edward O. Laumann, Robert T. Michael, CSG Enterprises, Inc., and Stuart Michaels. Used by permission of The University of Chicago Press.

that may be perceived and interpreted in a variety of ways. In the NHSLS, of the people who found same-gender sex desirable in some way, only about half of the men and slightly more than 40 percent of the women ever acted on those desires. Men who desired other men and had sex with them were more likely than women with same-gender desire and behavior to identify themselves as gay ("homosexual" in the survey) or bisexual. The research data also showed that people who identified themselves as lesbian, gay, or bisexual tended to be more highly educated and to have middle- or high-class socioeconomic status. This may indicate, however, only that middle-class, college-educated people are more willing than others to report a same-gender sexual orientation.

The NHSLS research demonstrated that the incidence of same-gender sexuality can be influenced by factors such as age and geographic location. For example, the proportion of people who identified themselves as gay, lesbian, or bisexual was much higher in cities than in suburban or rural locations, although this trend was more pronounced among gay men than among lesbians. As Figure 13.6 indicates, in the 12 largest U.S. cities, more than 9 percent of the men identified themselves as gay or bisexual, and close to 3 percent of the women identified themselves as lesbian or bisexual. One obvious conclusion to be reached from these data would be that city life provides a concentration of people sufficient to allow identifiable sexual cultures and communities to become visible, increasing the likelihood of relationships developing. Although it is true that people with same-gender interests tend to move away from suburban and rural locations to cities, another intriguing finding was that people raised in cities actually were more likely to be gay or lesbian than people raised in the suburbs or in rural areas. We can only speculate as to the reason for this finding, but it may be that it is easier to realize and explore same-gender lifestyles in urban areas, where they are more noticeable.

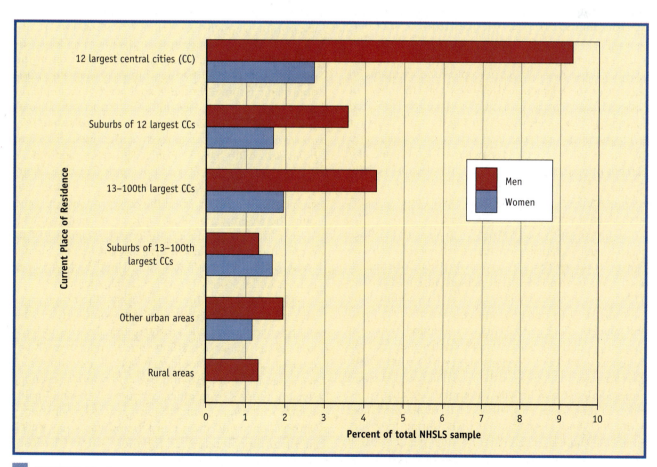

FIGURE 13.6 *Percentage of NHSLS Subjects Identifying Themselves as Homosexual or Bisexual*

NHSLS research demonstrated that the incidence of same-gender sexuality can be influenced by geographic location. We can only speculate as to the reason people raised in cities are more likely to identify as gay or lesbian.

Source: From *Sex in America* by Robert T. Michael et al. Copyright © 1994 by CSG Enterprises, Inc., Edward O. Laumann, Robert T. Michael, and Gina Kolata. By permission of Little, Brown & Company, Inc.

Cross-Cultural Comparisons

Cross-cultural generalizations about sexual behavior between members of the same gender are practically impossible, particularly when we try to interpret or understand the sexual behaviors of other cultures using the psychological, sociological, or biological theories developed within the context of our own culture. Same-gender sex has not been substantially researched in most areas of the world (Wellings et al., 2006). Even applying our terminology to those behaviors makes little sense, because terms carry the assumptions of the time and place in which they were first coined (Knauft, 2004). The Nanshoku culture of Japan has recognized the behavior of men having sex with other men without having a need to devise words for a separate identity, such as "gay." In India, same-gender sexual behaviors are accepted without labels that separate the people who practice them into categories of sexual identity or status.

European studies have found rates of same-gender sexual behavior just slightly lower than those found by the NHSLS. A major study in France surveyed the sexual behaviors of 20,055 people ages 18 to 69. Four percent of the men and 3 percent of the women said they had experienced same-gender sex during their lifetime. Of these persons, 82 percent of the men and 78 percent of the women had had sex with members of both genders. Lower proportions of people reported having had same-gender sex during the previous year (1.1 percent of men and 0.3 percent of women) and the previous five years (1.4 percent of men and 0.4 percent of women). Same-gender and bisexual activity was considerably higher among residents of Paris than among rural residents. (Analyse des Comportements Sexuels en France Investigators, 1992).

A British study of 18,876 people ages 16 to 59 reported similar statistics on male-male sexual activity; female same-gender sexual activity was not studied. Of the male respondents, 6 percent reported having had "some homosexual" experience as defined by themselves. Four percent indicated that they had had oral, anal, or other genital contact with another male at some time, and 1.4 percent reported that they had experienced such contact within the previous five years. Men younger than 35 were the most likely to have had same-gender sexual activity within the past five years, whereas those ages 35 to 44 were most likely to have had same-gender sex at some point during their lifetime. The highest percentage of same-gender sexual activity was reported among men who lived in the greater London area, where 9 percent reported having had a same-gender sexual partner, 5 percent within the previous five years (Johnson et al., 2001).

The similarities in U.S. and European data reflect similarities in the ways these cultures perceive and define sexual orientation. This is not necessarily the case in other cultures. In fact, most research on sexual orientation has been conducted in North America, Western Europe, and Australia, all of which conceptualize the issues in much the same way. As small studies begin to emerge from other cultures, how broader social and political themes are reflected in perceptions of sexual orientation and sexual behavior becomes clearer.

Different rates of same-gender sexual behavior do not seem to bear any particular relationship to a society's climate, racial makeup, affluence, typical family structure, or state of development. Rules and social sanctions, however, seem to have some effect at least on the visibility of such behavior. In societies where it is approved or praised, it tends to be more frequently observed, and in societies where it is condemned, sexual and romantic relationships between members of the same gender tend to be less frequently observed (Traeen, Stigum, & Sorensen, 2002). In nations where sex between members of the same gender is stigmatized or criminalized, the incidence of unsafe, unprotected sexual activity increases, and condoms are used less frequently than in countries that are more accepting of same-gender sex (Wellings et al., 2006)

In Mediterranean regions and some nonindustrialized societies, sexual categories are based not on the gender of the sexual partner, but instead on the position being assumed in the sexual act. For example, in one Brazilian fishing village, three distinct sexual categories were identified among males: the *persistent heterosexuals,* who have sex only with women; *paneleiros,* who have sex only with other men but always in the "bottom," receptive role for anal intercourse; and *paneleiros lovers,* who have sex with women and men but when they are with men assume only the insertive, or "top," role in anal intercourse. Men in this last category are not considered gay or bisexual per se but are in their own category. Such a system of categorization is intertwined with views of gender in the society (Cardoso, 2002, 2005).

Cultures around the globe display their own complex attitudes and mores related to same-gender sexual orientation and relationships. Brazil seems to have ambiguous values regarding same-gender sexual orientation. The long-standing gay subculture in Brazilian cities seems to flourish and be highly public, even attracting tourists from other countries. Yet some males with a machismo mentality have reacted against gays with violence and even murder, and many gay males in Brazil apparently fear for their safety (Cardoso, 2005; Hindley, 2001). Similar conflicts and political struggles are evident in machismo countries such as Mexico (Izasola-Licea et al., 2000). In areas of the world where negative attitudes toward gays and bisexuals are supported by prevailing values, such people may experience more personal problems. In Turkey, for example, a predominantly Muslim nation where homosexuality is strictly forbidden, people with a same-gender sexual orientation are more likely to report sexual abuse during childhood, to report more distance between themselves and their parents, and to be at greater risk for suicide (Eskin, Kaynak-Demir, & Demir, 2005). Likewise, in Hong Kong, Taiwan, and mainland China, studies are beginning to show higher levels of psychological disturbance, less likelihood of condom use during sex, and a struggle for sexual freedom among those who are nonheterosexual in orientation (Kuang, Mathy, Carol, & Nojima, 2003; Shiu-Ki, 2004; Wong & Tang, 2004).

Some preindustrial societies have been known to use same-gender sexual behavior, particularly between males, in their coming-of-age rites. It is sometimes believed that an older male giving semen to a young boy orally or anally strengthens the boy and helps make him into a man. Such age-structured behavior typically would be viewed as a stage of an individual's development. It previously was practiced in some Melanesian societies in the southwest Pacific. In these societies, a male would engage in sexual activity with other males until he married; then he was to adopt heterosexual behavior. Most men made the transition and remained exclusively heterosexual, but a few continued to have sexual relationships with other males. As Melanesian societies have had increased contact with Western ideas and religions, ritualized sexual activity between males as a rite of passage seems to have largely disappeared, and younger generations are shocked to learn of the former practices (Knauft, 2004).

Same-gender sexual behaviors and relationships apparently exist to varying degrees in all cultures and are assigned many different meanings. They are sometimes accepted or tolerated, sometimes condemned or punished. Nevertheless, subcultures of people with same-gender orientations seem to appear in all societies, and social norms apparently have little effect on whether these orientations emerge (Tolman & Diamond, 2002).

FOH The Effects of Homophobia and Biphobia

Homophobia, biphobia, and their resultant prejudices take their toll on people's lives and on their attitudes toward themselves. The murders of college student Matthew Sheppard in 1998 and others focused public attention on the very real dangers of homophobia. For example, even boys who are not attracted to other males fear behaving in any way that might give an appearance of being gay. The Boy Scouts of America have for a number of years explicitly excluded gay youth from membership and gay men from being scoutmasters. The U.S. Supreme Court upheld their right to do so as a private organization. This has caused debate and anger both inside and outside the Boy Scouts. Some have left scouting in protest, and many have ceased giving donations to the group. Others insist that their position is an appropriate one. It is a controversy that will not end soon (France, 2001). In contrast, the Canadian Boy Scouts organization does not believe that sexual orientation should be an issue and has allowed gay members. The founding of the Boy Scouts in Great Britain in 1907 was characterized by Victorian concerns about sexual distractions of any kind, reflecting 1907 values (Pryke, 2001).

Several professional organizations have taken public stands with regard to same-gender sexual orientation and behavior. In 1973, the American Psychiatric Association's board of trustees voted unanimously to remove homosexuality from its list of mental illnesses, declaring that it does not constitute a psychiatric disorder. Individuals who are either disturbed by or in conflict about their same-gender inclinations have since then been considered to have a sexual orientation disturbance. The American Psychological Association has taken a similar stand. Some concerns about gay teachers in the classroom still exist, typically based in stereotypes and misinformation that have no basis in fact. Gay and bisexual educators, fearing criticism, often feel that they must be cautious about how open they are about their lifestyles (Meyer, 2005; Rofes, 2000).

There is a growing recognition among American corporations that homophobia is bad for business. More companies are now advertising their products in publications directed specifically at gay males and, to a lesser degree, lesbians, because they realize that this segment of the population represents a substantial market. Because gay and lesbian workers cannot function optimally if they have to be constantly concerned about the attitudes and behaviors of their colleagues, some businesses have begun to offer workshops to their employees with the aim of reducing homophobic attitudes. In the corporate environment, as well as on college campuses, homophobic attitudes will not change until a serious effort is made to educate people about sexual orientation by dispelling some of the stereotypical beliefs about gays, lesbians, and bisexuals (Brown et al., 2004).

How accepting do you think students on your campus are of same-gender relationships and sexual behavior?

Religious Views FOH

The attitudes and teachings of some religions toward same-gender sexual behavior have traditionally played an important role in the formation of public opinion.

Sex not intended for the purpose of reproduction may be viewed by some as lustful and therefore sinful. Furthermore, sexual behavior that cannot be conducted within the bond of heterosexual marriage is sometimes viewed as sinful. Many Judeo-Christian-Muslim denominations have sought to judge and regulate various forms of sexual behavior, including same-gender sexual behavior (Plugge-Foust & Strickland, 2000).

In the ancient world, no religion other than Judaism categorically prohibited same-gender sexual behavior (the Torah's prohibition applied only to male-male sexual behavior), although some religions did advocate celibacy. Around 400 CE, Christianity began to introduce a new sexual code that focused on maintaining "purity" and equated some sexual behaviors with the "fallen" state of the human soul. Over the centuries, same-gender sexual behavior has been variously accepted and condemned within religious traditions. In recent times, many theologians have called for increased understanding and acceptance of gays, lesbians, and bisexuals, and some have gone further in calling for reform of attitudes that see same-gender orientation as sinful (Jakobsen & Pellegrini, 2003).

All of the major Judeo-Christian-Muslim religious denominations have theologians who argue that the Torah, the Christian Bible, and the Koran do not condemn same-gender behavior as we know it. Scholars have debated the meanings of various passages in religious texts. Some insist that these passages admonish people for same-gender behavior, and others claim that such meanings are misinterpretations. A number of religious groups are studying the moral implications of same-gender orientation and behavior (Plugge-Foust & Strickland, 2000). Gay men and lesbians have called for a new religious and moral ethic that would allow for human diversity, acknowledge variant sexual orientations, honor the concept of mutual sharing by consent, and affirm the freedom to grow and change. Many religiously oriented counselors help people sort out these issues in relation to their own lives.

■ Conceptualizing Same-Gender Sexual Orientation

The origins of sexual orientation have been the subject of much conjecture, research, and debate in recent years. Sexual orientation concerns sometimes are brought to physicians, psychiatrists, psychologists, and counselors. The manner in which professionals deal with these issues may differ according to the theoretical framework within which they work. It is worth noting that same-gender sexual orientation was "medicalized"

and defined as a "disease" between 1880 and 1900, being called at first "sexual inversion" and later "homosexuality." One of the medical assumptions was that people with a same-gender sexual orientation were fundamentally different from those with a heterosexual orientation. This is a classic example of a social construction, in which social beliefs create whole new perceptions of phenomena that have always existed, thereby constructing a concept that then is perpetuated as a scientific or medical truth (Tolman & Diamond, 2002).

Theories and models about the origins of sexual orientation have focused on psychodynamic, biological, and socioenvironmental factors. In weighing the issues, it is crucial to keep in mind that there is a great deal of diversity among individuals who identify themselves as bisexual, lesbian, or gay. It is possible that same-gender behavior and attraction may be about the only thing these individuals have in common. There may be many different pathways to a common sexual orientation—whether same-gender, bisexual, or heterosexual. We will look at several different conceptual models concerning same-gender sexual orientation.

Psychodynamic Models

Freud believed that same-gender sexual inclinations could result from a variety of difficulties in passing through the various stages of development—oral, anal, latent, and genital. Late in his life, Freud stated that he did not consider homosexuality an illness but instead a sexual function produced by arrested sexual development. Nevertheless, many psychoanalysts advanced numerous hypotheses about the psychodynamics behind the development of same-gender sexual orientation, viewing it as a type of neurosis that should receive psychiatric treatment. One traditional psychodynamic perspective, popularized in the 1960s, was that family interactions caused same-gender orientation in males, with the most typical background consisting of a close-binding, overprotective mother and a detached, absent, or openly hostile father. It is now known that this theory has no basis in fact, although a few professionals still espouse it. Many recent psychodynamic theorists have modified classical assumptions by integrating some of the newer findings about possible biological and social influences on sexual orientation. Same-gender sexual orientation now is generally accepted as a normal, mature, developmental state rather than as a pathological condition requiring treatment. Psychoanalysts conceptualize gay males and lesbians from a new, more positive perspective that rejects notions of problematic psychosexual development or "arrested" psychological development. It has been claimed that psychodynamic theory is a significant

Real Student Voices

■ When I joined the Boy Scouts, I didn't really think of myself as gay, although as I look back, it should have been obvious to me. My first sexual relationship took place at a summer Boy Scout camp. Although I knew that scouts weren't supposed to be gay, I had pretty much learned that nobody was supposed to be, so it didn't seem to make much difference. I became an Eagle Scout before I left scouting. It was a good experience for me.

■ Although I might want to settle down with another woman someday, it doesn't really matter much to me if we are able to get married. I think we can have just as good a relationship, and be just as committed, whether we have a marriage license or not. There may be some other advantages of marriage, but that remains to be seen.

tool in understanding sexual orientation because it focuses on the unconscious mind and fantasy (Downing, 2005; Friedman & Downey, 2002).

Normal Variant Model

Beginning in the 1960s, an increasingly large and powerful group of theorists and researchers began to conceptualize same-gender sexual orientation as a normal variation within the continuum of human sexual behavior (see Figure 13.7). They recognized that same-gender sexual behavior was less common than heterosexual behavior, but they did not see any grounds for classifying it as pathological, deviant, perverse, or abnormal. Instead, they viewed same-gender behavior as a natural, though less prevalent, form of sexual expression (DeLamater & Friedrich, 2002; Dunne et al., 2000).

FOH   In the United States, Evelyn Hooker was one of the most influential researchers to propose that same-gender sexual orientation and behavior are normal variants. As a young psychologist in Chicago in the 1950s, she had been taught that homosexuality was a pathological condition. However, she had befriended a group of young gay men, and her real-life observations seemed to suggest that these men were quite healthy and well-adjusted. One of the men said to her one day, "Now, Evelyn, it is your scientific duty to study men like me." She was struck with the realization that very little scientific information was available about same-gender orientation. Hooker received a grant from the National Institute of Mental Health and began to study gay men living in the gay community, eventually expanding her research to include lesbians. Her findings confirmed that in terms of psychological

■ **FIGURE 13.7** *Same-Gender Orientation*

Many researchers believe that same-gender sexual behavior is simply a variant on the continuum of human sexual activity. The psychological health of both heterosexuals and gay men or lesbians appears to be statistically about the same.

health, people with same-gender and heterosexual orientations were indistinguishable. She reported that many gay men and lesbians were living happy, productive lives. She was critical of earlier studies that had focused on people who were either patients in psychoanalysis or prisoners, and she suggested that same-gender orientation could not be defined scientifically as pathological (Hooker, 1993).

More recent studies continue to confirm the absence of significant psychological differences between heterosexuals and people with a same-gender orientation, and few psychologists today would view same-gender sexual orientation within a pathological context. Some recent studies, however, have found a greater incidence of depression and anxiety among gay people, especially gay men. One study found that some gay men had a somewhat lower quality of life than heterosexual controls, seemingly related to lower self-esteem and a lesser sense of personal mastery (Sandfort, de Graff, & Bijl, 2003). The cause-and-effect connections are still unexplained. It could be that the threat of discrimination and violence, along with living in a society that debates the validity of your relationships, leads to some emotional difficulties, or it may be that gay men have a greater biological predisposition to depression and anxiety (Bailey, 2003).

The Bell, Weinberg, and Hammersmith Study on Sexual Orientation

A groundbreaking study on the development of sexual orientation focused on a research population of lesbians and gay men in ways that attempted to identify possible "causes" of same-gender orientation. Representing the Kinsey Institute, Alan Bell, Martin Weinberg, and Sue Kiefer Hammersmith (1981) carried out a controlled study involving interviews with 979 gay men and lesbians and a comparison sample of 477 heterosexual men and women. In examining any difference found between the two population samples, the researchers controlled for the possible effects of age, education, and social status to make sure the difference between the two groups was not due to these factors.

A tremendous amount of data was gathered in the three- to five-hour, face-to-face interviews conducted with each person. The questions asked in the interview were drawn from a variety of theoretical stances concerning the development of same-gender sexual orientations. The data then were subjected to a statistical technique known as path analysis. The researchers drew the following conclusions concerning sexual orientation:

1. Sexual orientation appears to be largely determined prior to adolescence, even when youngsters have not been particularly sexually active.
2. Same-gender attractions typically are experienced for about three years prior to any overt same-gender sexual behavior. Such feelings play more of a role in eventually identifying oneself as gay or lesbian than do any particular activities with others.
3. Lesbians and gay men tend to have a history of heterosexual experiences during childhood and adolescence. Unlike the control-group heterosexuals, however, they report these experiences as being relatively unsatisfying.
4. Identification with a parent of either gender appears to play no significant role in the development of sexual orientation.
5. There is no support for the hypothesis that any particular type of mother produces children with a same-gender orientation. In the study, there was a slightly higher proportion of lesbians and gay men who had poor relationships with their fathers. However, it was impossible to determine if this was a causative factor in their sexual orientation or simply a reflection of the difficulty that sexually different sons or daughters might have in relating to their fathers.

These findings provided little support for the models of same-gender sexual orientation that existed at the time. Although these researchers did not study genetic or hormonal characteristics, they did state that their findings were "not inconsistent with what one would expect to find if, indeed, there were a biological basis for sexual [orientation]." They further speculated that such a biological mechanism probably would account for gender identity as well as sexual orientation and that it might well be operative in varying degrees. That is, it might operate more powerfully in individuals who are exclusively same-gender-oriented or heterosexual than in bisexual people. This crucial study shed new light on the development of sexual orientation.

Biological Determinants Model

In one of the last revisions of his famous work *Three Essays on the Theory of Sexuality,* Freud speculated that the roots of homosexuality might eventually be found in the effects of hormones on mind and body. Since that suggestion was made in 1920, theories emphasizing a biological basis for same-gender orientation—hormonal, genetic, and/or anatomical—have waxed and waned. Research studies have approached the issue from five different angles: (1) examining possible hormonal influences, especially during prenatal development; (2) sorting out the possible influences of birth order in males; (3) attempting to detect genetic factors that might be involved in the determination of later sexual orientations and activities; (4) examining anatomical differences between the brain structures of gay and heterosexual men; and (5) looking at potential correlations among orientation, gender identity, and gender role. It would seem unlikely that any of these aspects of human development would operate completely independently, and in fact they may well be closely interconnected (Bogaert, Friesen, & Klentrou, 2002; Mustanski, Chivers, & Bailey, 2003).

FOH Hormonal Influences

Because research has demonstrated the crucial role hormones can play in regulating the sexual behaviors of nonhuman animals, it is not surprising that endocrinologists have speculated that hormones might well play a role in the development of sexual orientation. It has been found, for example, that from 6 to 10 percent of rams seem to prefer another male as a sexual partner, while the majority of rams prefer females. The rams that approach other rams have been found to have a different testosterone profile and stress response than the "heterosexual" rams (Roselli, Resko, & Stormshak, 2002). Administering testosterone to fetal sheep before they are born seems to interfere with their later ovarian hormone cycles and their responsiveness to other hormones (Robinson et al., 2002). There are, in fact, many examples of animals who seem to be drawn sexually to others of their sex (Vassey, 2003). Extrapolating findings from animal studies to humans can be risky business, but interest is fueled further by findings that prenatal hormonal factors might exert some influence over later human gender identity or gender role, as described in Chapter 5, "Developmental and Social Perspectives on Gender." The evidence suggests that certain brain structures may be masculinized and defeminized by male hormones produced in the fetal testes or otherwise found in the fetal environment.

A potential relationship between such prenatal factors and the development of sexual orientation in humans is beginning to take shape at least theoretically. It is known that genetic females born with congenital adrenal hyperplasia (CAH) exhibit some masculinizing hormonal influences on their central nervous systems (see Chapter 5, p. 113), and there is evidence that close to 40 percent of women with CAH identify themselves as lesbian or bisexual, a much higher percentage than in the general population (Cohen, 2002; Money, 2002). Conversely, those individuals who have androgen insensitivity show no evidence that the lower levels of androgen have any effect on their later sexual orientation.

Several seemingly random characteristics have emerged as being different between some gay persons and heterosexual persons. It has been found, for example, that gay men tend to have reached puberty earlier than heterosexual men and that they may score, on average, toward the typical female end on measures of predictable male-female differences in physical and developmental characteristics. Lesbian and heterosexual women do not seem to have any difference in age of puberty (Bogaert, Friesen, & Klentrou, 2002). Gay men and lesbians have been found to have a shorter sleep cycle than their heterosexual counterparts. While this information in itself may seem inconsequential, researchers suggest that it provides further evidence of some built-in differences between gays and heterosexuals (Rahman & Silber, 2000). The significance of prenatal hormonal influences is becoming clearer all the time, but it should not be forgotten that it is probably the genes that actually instruct the brain, perhaps through hormones, to develop in a particular way (Cohen, 2002).

Fraternal Birth Order

One interesting finding is that males who have older brothers have a greater likelihood of being gay, and the more older brothers there are, the stronger the likelihood. Each additional older brother in the family increases the odds for the youngest brother to be gay by about 33 percent (Cantor et al., 2002). A number of studies seem to support this *fraternal birth order hypothesis,* and it has been suggested that the mechanism could be the basis for as many as 25 percent of gay males (Bogaert, 2000, 2005; Purcell, Blanchard, & Zucker, 2000). Attempts to explain the phenomenon based on the way older brothers might have treated a younger brother have not yielded relevant results (Bogaert, 2003). It would appear that the mother's body may actually "remember" previously carrying male fetuses and that this somehow alters the fetal development of subsequent sons. Again, the fundamental presumption is that prenatal development is involved (Williams et al., 2000; Zucker & Blanchard, 2003).

Genetic Influences FOH

Behavioral geneticists are increasingly coming to the conclusion that several genes may actually be involved in the expression of particular human behaviors (Hamer, 2002). Recent research has begun to suggest some interesting genetic links to sexual orientation. Some data have emerged indicating that same-gender orientation tends to run in families. Gay males have a significantly higher likelihood of having a brother, uncle, or male cousin who is gay. Lesbian women also have a greater likelihood of having a lesbian or bisexual sister, although this tendency is less pronounced than is the trend among males. It is not yet completely clear whether gay males are more likely to have lesbian sisters or whether lesbians are more likely to have gay brothers, but this does not seem to be the case. These findings could indicate some sort of familial connection in the development of sexual orientation, especially in male or female lineages (Mustanski, Chivers, & Bailey, 2003).

It has been speculated that studying twins might provide some clues to the development of sexual orientation. One study compared 56 identical male twins, 54 fraternal male twins, and 57 genetically unrelated adopted brothers. At least one in each pair of brothers was gay or bisexual and had a twin or an adopted brother with whom he had started living at least by age 2. The assumption of the researchers was that if same-gender sexual orientation is at least partly genetic in origin, the more closely related people are, the more likely their sexual orientation will be the same. Their findings tended to support that assumption. Among the pairs of adoptive brothers, only 11 percent were both gay. That rate rose to 22 percent for the fraternal twins and 52 percent for the identical twins. The results suggest that same-gender sexual orientation is highly attributable to genetic influences (Mustanski, Chivers, & Bailey, 2003).

Another study was conducted with 147 lesbians and their sisters. Of the 71 lesbians who had identical twins, 48 percent of the twins also were lesbians. Of those whose sisters were fraternal twins, 16 percent of the sisters were lesbians. Only 6 percent of adopted sisters had a same-gender orientation. These statistics were consistent with lower incidences of same-gender orientation typically reported for women compared to men. Lesbians are four times more likely to have a lesbian sister than are heterosexual women but only slightly more likely to have a gay brother. However, much same-gender-orientation research has focused on males, and more needs to be done in order to better understand lesbian orientation (Mustanski, Chivers, & Bailey, 2003).

Fingerprints and right- or left-handedness have emerged as other characteristics possibly associated with sexual orientation. While the finding has not been confirmed by other studies, one researcher found that in female twins where one is lesbian and the other is heterosexual, the number of ridges in their fingerprints differs in that the lesbian women tend to have fewer ridges than the heterosexual women (Hall, 2000). Both lesbian women and gay males have been found to be left-handed more frequently than are heterosexuals (Lippa, 2003). It has also been found that the ratio between the lengths of the second and fourth fingers is smaller in "butch" or more masculine lesbians than it is in "femme" or more feminine lesbians. Men have a

smaller finger ratio than do women (Brown et al., 2002). A study with identical female twins where one of the individuals was lesbian found that the lesbian twins did indeed have a lower ratio between finger sizes than did their identical sisters. Among control groups in which both twins were lesbians or both were heterosexual, no difference in finger size ratios was found (Hall & Love, 2003).

Analyzing the correlations of such physical traits may seem trivial at first glance, but determining what body differences seem to correlate with sexual orientation might make it possible to draw some conclusions about when these characteristics are formed during fetal development and what this implies about the development of sexual orientation. In the finger-size-ratio study cited, it was suggested that the differences could be explained by hormonal differences that might well occur during the first trimester of fetal development. This might correspond with periods during prenatal development when the brain circuitry is programmed for sexual orientation (Mustanski, Chivers, & Bailey, 2003).

These studies do not mean that same-gender sexual orientation is 100 percent dependent on genetics, as are characteristics such as eye color. Rather, they suggest some degree of *heritability*, meaning that sexual orientation is at least partially dependent on genes passed from generation to generation. For example, a person's height is about 90 percent genetically determined, but it also can be affected slightly by factors such as nutrition. Height is therefore said to be multifactorial, meaning that many factors—including genetics—play a role in its expression. It may be that same-gender sexual orientation is 50 to 70 percent attributable to genetics, but its expression would also be multifactorial and probably quite complex (Hamer, 1999).

One of the biggest supports for proponents of a genetic basis for same-gender sexual orientation came from researchers who traced the family backgrounds of 76 gay men, identifying as many family members as they could who had a same-gender orientation. Confirming the findings of earlier studies, they discovered that gay men were more likely to have a gay brother than were men in the general population. However, they also found a greater likelihood that these men would have gay male relatives on the maternal side of the family, suggesting that sexual orientation might be linked in some way to the X chromosome that males inherit from their mothers. The researchers then took DNA samples from 40 pairs of gay brothers and analyzed them for genetic markers. Of the 40 pairs of brothers, 33 pairs shared a set of five genetic markers on one end of their X chromosomes. This was the first time sexual orientation had ever been linked to a specific part of a chromosome. Debate continues about whether genetic markers for male same-gender sexual orientation actually exist, and nothing that specific has yet been identified (Hamer, 2002; Mustanski, Chivers, & Bailey, 2003).

The Curious Case of Identical Triplets with Different Sexual Orientations

Even though the identical twin studies suggest a much greater chance that monozygotic (identical) twins will have the same sexual orientation, how do we explain the roughly half of cases in which one twin is gay or bisexual and the other is straight? What happened to genetic influences? Aside from the possibility that life experiences might differ subtly between twins, there has been a case published about a set of 21-year-old identical (monozygotic) male triplets in which two were certain they were heterosexual and the third was just as certain he was gay. The three brothers were administered a variety of psychological tests, and all were essentially similar except for measures of sexual orientation, which supported their self-indentities.

The researchers who studied the triplets believed that the case demonstrated how prenatal hormones might have a lasting effect on certain traits, including sexual orientation and behavior (Hershberger & Segal, 2004). But how could this happen when all three boys were born at the same time, from the same mother? Three hypothetical explanations were offered, based on other studies. It is known, for example, that in non-human mammals, the position of a fetus in the uterus is associated with later sex-related behavior. Another possibility has to do with when the zygote split to form three offspring. The first split forms twin cells, but later one of those cells splits again to form the third identical cell that will become the third fetus. It is believed that the two fetuses formed from the second zygotic split might have a more similar developmental course that could be different from that of the original "twin" cell that did not split a second time. *Developmental instability theory* has suggested that such disruptions might cause one fetus to react differently to prenatal hormone exposure than other fetuses sharing the same womb (Gangestad, Bennett, & Thornhill, 2001).

A third explanatory hypothesis stems from the fact that triplets rarely share a single placenta during development. The triplet from the first zygotic split may well have had a placenta separate from the two who were formed from the later, second split. It is known that placental status is associated with the concordance or discordance (similarity or dissimilarity) of certain traits between identical twins and triplets. What we can conclude from all this is that even fetuses with identical genetic makeups may experience subtle environmental differences during their development in the uterus. These conjectures constitute fascinating directions for further research (Hershberger & Segal, 2004).

Anatomical Factors

Anatomical differences have also been found between the brains of gay and heterosexual men. The first such study found that a part of the brain that governs daily rhythms, the suprachiasmatic nucleus, is twice as large in gay men as it is in heterosexual men. Because that part of the brain has not been associated with sexual behavior, brain researchers went on to study the hypothalamus, again finding some measurable differences. The development of the hypothalamus seems to be influenced by hormones, and it is known to play a role in determining sexual behavior in some mammalian groups. It is also known that the anterior part of the human hypothalamus plays some role in human sexuality. Highly compelling research has determined that a particular collection of cells typically found in the anterior hypothalamus is much smaller in gay men and in women than it is in heterosexual men (LeVay, 1996). The finding again suggests that sexual orientation may be part of a larger package of brain characteristics. These findings need further confirmation, and their implications are still being debated.

Studies on certain motor tasks that are determined by the brain's cerebral hemispheres have found that gay males sometimes function more similarly to heterosexual women than to heterosexual men (Sanders & Wright, 1997). It has also been determined that the inner ears of lesbian and bisexual women function more like the inner ears of men than like those of heterosexual women (Loehlin & McFadden, 2003).

Sexual Orientation and Gender

Until recently, the prevailing opinion has been that gender identity and role, and therefore "femininity" or "masculinity," are quite independent of sexual orientation. That view does not necessarily square with anecdotal observations that gay men sometimes are associated with characteristics that might be considered feminine and that lesbians sometimes seem to have some masculine traits. Because this area raises uncomfortable stereotypes related to both gender and sexual orientation, it is controversial and tends to raise people's hackles. There seems to be a growing tendency to pursue this issue, although most of the research so far has focused on the effeminacy of gay men. There is growing evidence that boys who are more "feminine" during childhood and avoid or dislike boy sports probably have a higher probability of becoming gay men. Connecting similar observations of "masculine" traits in young girls with their becoming lesbians has been somewhat more elusive.

One way to examine this factor would be to relate some of the biologically identified traits of gay people with their gender characteristics. In a small study performed at Harvard University, finger-size ratio was correlated with some gender traits. Interestingly, gay males who had a smaller finger-size ratio (as do women) were more likely to report that they had been quite feminine as children and preferred "feminine"-identified occupations (such as costume designer, dance teacher, florist, or interior decorator) over "masculine"-identified occupations (such as computer programmer, engineer, or physicist). They were also slightly more likely to prefer being receptive (bottoms) in anal intercourse. The author believed that, biologically, this phenomenon could be related to lower exposure to testosterone during prenatal life (McIntyre, 2003).

Well-known sex researcher J. Michael Bailey (2003) has begun to pose more questions about the relationship between orientation and gender, generating a good deal of controversy. He has cited some research and called for further study that relates to the ways gay men talk, move their arms, and walk that may sometimes be considered feminine. He concedes that many gay men are not particularly effeminate, but he offers some theories about why masculinity actually is preferred among the gay male community, especially when seeking sexual partners. Much work remains to be done in understanding how gender roles and sexual orientation may be related.

Proponents of the biological model insist that there is now enough evidence from a variety of different researchers, using different methodologies, to make a strong case that sexual orientation is at least partly biologically determined. They also argue that the evidence for a purely social constructionist perspective does not hold up to close scrutiny (Hamer, 2002). The discovery of specific biological differences has increased the danger that homophobic people may react by claiming that these differences clearly are "defects." There is concern that as genetic engineering becomes more closely linked with human reproduction, parents may be able to "select" various characteristics they want in a child. Debate continues about this entire issue, but at times it has focused on the moral desirability of allowing parents to select a child's sexual orientation. There are arguments on both sides of this issue (Greenberg & Bailey, 2001; West, 2001).

If you were planning to have children and had access to genetic engineering technology that would enable you to choose certain traits, would you be concerned about determining the sexual orientation of your children? If so, in what ways and why?

Evolutionary Theory

As described earlier, evolutionary psychologists, or sociobiologists, have theorized that mating behavior and mate selection have evolved based on whatever strate-gies will assure the best chances for survival of the species. This theory implies that heterosexual pairing and sex a fundamental part of the strategy, because they lead to reproduction. For this reason, same-gender orientation and behavior pose somewhat of a problem for evolutionary theorists, because in general gay men produce fewer children than do straight men. From an evolutionary perspective, this calls into question how the "gay trait" would be perpetuated over time in evolution. Several explanatory models have emerged, but there is only sparse empirical evidence to back them up. One proposed model suggests that over the eons females chose as mates less aggressive males, who would be more disposed to helping with child care and other "home" tasks, and that evolution also gradually reduced gender differences between the sexes. The model presupposes that less aggressive and more caring brain structure are associated with same-gender attraction and that these qualities were genetically perpetuated because the offspring of these males, who took more care of their children, had better chances of survival (Berman, 2003). It has also been posited that the male-male alliances that same-gender attraction would have created might have enhanced the chances of male survival and therefore male reproduction (Muscarella, 2006; Vasey, 2006).

Another proposed explanation similarly suggests that in prehistoric times homosexual men helped care for the children of their kin, such as nieces and nephews, thereby assuring that some of the genes associated with their sexual orientation did indeed survive. A contemporary study that attempted to test this "kin selection hypothesis" actually found no difference in general family affinity or in generous or benevolent feelings (including a willingness to babysit) between heterosexual and homosexual men (Rahman & Hull, 2005). Similarly, it has been proposed that the heterosexual relatives (uncles, aunts, siblings, cousins, nephews, and nieces) of gay men might compensate by producing more children, again leading to the perpetuation of whatever genes might be associated with homosexuality. One contemporary study actually did show that the close relatives of gay men tended to have larger families, but further research is needed to confirm this effect (King et al., 2005). Researchers still have a long way to go in rationalizing homosexuality through evolutionary theory (Hellberg, 2006).

Multifactorial Model

Theorists have been broadening the nature-*or*-nurture perspective in favor of a more *multifactorial model* that incorporates a biopsychosocial view, taking into account a range of biological, psychological, and socioenvironmental factors. It seems likely that sexual orientation develops through a complex interaction of innate and external influences. There might be different subpopulations of people with same-gender sexual orientations, representing different combinations of causative factors. Some of the "programming" that results in an individual's sexual orientation may take place during critical periods of development when biology and environment interact, possibly both during prenatal life and after birth (Bancroft, 2002a).

A view is emerging of the brain as a mosaic of different areas that may respond to sex hormones at various stages of fetal and childhood development. This could mean that different regions of the same brain might undergo various kinds of sexual differentiation. Hormone levels and the timing of their exposure to the developing brain could influence a wide range of characteristics, including handedness, finger growth, and sexual orientation. It has also been proposed that these influences could produce different childhood temperaments that then might lead to varying erotic attractions during development (Bem, 2000).

There is a growing realization that biologists and social psychologists might simply be looking at and interpreting the same phenomena from different perspectives. Biologists tend to view things from the standpoint of molecular influences and neurological mechanisms. Social psychologists look at the broader behavioral implications that stem from cultural influences. Theorists now suggest that sexual orientation is, in fact, the result of complex interactions of all these factors: biological processes and predispositions, life experiences in the context of a particular culture, the structure of the nervous system, genetics, and brain development (Kauth, 2002).

Research to date on biological factors associated with sexual orientation suggests that it is not 100 percent genetic and that other factors play a role. When one of the gay men involved in a twin genetic study informed his identical twin brother that he was gay, the brother was surprised. The brother had been living a distinctly heterosexual lifestyle and yet had also been aware of some level of attraction to other men. It had never occurred to him to define his feelings as gay. Following his brother's revelation, he decided to try sex with men and indeed found these experiences more fulfilling than his heterosexual encounters. A year later, both twins told their parents they were gay. This example is a clear reminder that powerful social influences can affect how individuals define themselves sexually, even when some traits may be inborn. Some theorists have suggested that people pick and choose from a wide variety of environmental stimuli, based on their genetic makeup. In doing so, they actually create their own environments in a sense. This perspective sees human beings as dynamic, creative organisms whose learning and experience amplify and modify the effects of genetics (Bem, 2000). It has been

suggested that human beings might be "flavored" by genetics rather than "programmed" by them. Our genes thus may provide the foundation for a range of outcomes.

The multifactorial model suggests the possibility of many shades of sexual orientation, the origins of which are more complex and subtler than the either-or approach can accommodate. Human beings exhibit individual quirks and ambiguities that defy simple classification (Bancroft, 2002a). It has also been recognized that male sexual orientation seems to be relatively stable at early ages, whereas female sexual orientation may be much less quickly or easily defined (Peplau et al., 2000; Tolman & Diamond, 2002). As research into the origins of sexual orientation continues, it seems likely that further support will emerge for a perspective that considers a wide range of factors.

Perspectives on Therapy   FOH

When same-gender orientation was viewed as a disorder, a great deal of attention was given to therapy and cure. The psychodynamic models usually recommended that people with a same-gender orientation face the conflicts and problems left over from childhood, resolve them in some manner, and thereby free themselves to pursue heterosexuality. However, the lack of change in actual practice, along with emerging information about biological determinants of sexual orientation, forced a reexamination of such points of view (Friedman & Downey, 2002).

Some psychotherapists claim to have "cured" gay or lesbian people, changing them into heterosexuals. This is sometimes called "reparative" therapy, a term that makes some people cringe because it clearly implies that there is something to be "fixed," or reorientation therapy. The conventional wisdom today assumes that when people say they have been able to "change" from being gay, it means they have stopped participating in same-gender sexual behavior and have begun functioning sexually with members of the opposite sex. It also is assumed that the people who have made this change have been unhappy with their same-gender activities and have wished very much to give them up. Other professionals assert that a behavioral shift simply represents a conscious choice to act in a way that both the patient and the therapist consider more appropriate and thus does not constitute a real change in sexual orientation (Zucker, 2003b).

Given that gay people have struggled for decades to escape various negative labels, discussion about reorienting or changing their sexual interests is not particularly welcome or popular. Some groups and therapists continue to offer avenues of change for those who might wish to pursue them. A recent study interviewed 143 males and 57 females who reported that they had changed at least somewhat from a same-gender to a heterosexual orientation. The most common reasons they gave for wanting to change were not finding gay life emotionally satisfying and experiencing conflict between their sexual attractions and behaviors and their religious beliefs. Sixty-seven percent of the males and 35 percent of the females indicated that they had wanted either to stay married or to get married. About half of the individuals had consulted a counselor or psychologist, and about a third had participated in an "ex-gays" or religious support group. While many of the people, especially the men, continued to have sexual attractions to others of their gender, most had avoided same-gender contact during the previous year (Spitzer, 2003).

The journal that published this study gave experts an opportunity to respond to the study because its topic was considered so controversial. The responses ranged from support for finding out more about why and how people might change to claims that the ex-gays were simply deceiving themselves and others and to criticisms of the research ethics methodology (Bancroft, 2003b; Byrd, 2003; Cohen & Savin-Williams, 2003; Friedman, 2003; Strassberg, 2003). Given present beliefs, it seems unlikely that reorientation therapies will enjoy much popularity among most lesbian women or gay men in the near future.

Some counselors and therapists have homophobic or biphobic attitudes that may be detrimental to bisexual, lesbian, or gay clients. Of particular concern are professionals who are not aware of their own prejudices but bring their negative sentiments to the counseling process in subtle ways (Perez, DeBord, & Bieschke, 2000). Recent surveys have shown gay men, lesbians, and bisexuals to be quite satisfied with their counseling and psychotherapy experiences, although they sometimes encounter negative messages from professionals (Jones & Gabriel, 1999). They sometimes prefer to select a professional who also has a same-gender sexual orientation, avoiding those who might hold homophobic attitudes. However, many heterosexual counselors have been able to offer effective, unbiased support and counsel. It is worth noting that even a gay, lesbian, or bisexual counselor may have some homophobic or biphobic attitudes of his or her own (Pearson, 2003).

■ Forming a Sexual Orientation Identity

Sometimes people need to apply a label or category to themselves in order to have a greater sense of who they are. This inner sense of personal identity can have important implications for the way we experience our own self. It is also true, however, that we have many different identities to integrate into our sense of self: ethnicity, gender, occupation, marital status, and parenthood, among others. The formalized, theoretical concept of sexual identity emerged in European and North American sociopsychology (Ryan & Futterman, 2001). Again, however, the original focus was on "minority" sexual identities. How, theorists wondered, did gay, lesbian, and bisexual people get a good sense of their individual identities in a society where heterosexuality was considered the norm?

This emphasis surely made sense. Gay, lesbian, and bisexual people in North America and Europe usually had had little more than myths and stereotypes with which to identify. Although some gay males are effeminate and some lesbians are somewhat "mannish," people with a same-gender sexual orientation often are indistinguishable from heterosexual people, and there are no general characteristics that clearly distinguish either group. Some men with effeminate mannerisms and some women with masculine mannerisms are exclusively heterosexual; there are macho gay men and delicate lesbian women. The majority of gay men dislike effeminacy and are not sexually aroused by it, even if they may have feminine mannerisms themselves (Bailey, 2003). As indicated earlier, there is some evidence that children and adolescents who show gender nonconformity in appearance and mannerisms have a somewhat greater likelihood of same-gender attractions and behaviors later in life (Dunne et al., 2000).

It was in the late 1960s and early 1970s that the notion of "homosexual identity" began to emerge. It was an important transition socially, because it began to draw attention away from specific sexual behaviors and toward an understanding of sexual orientation as it becomes integrated into the personality and sense of self. Being able to define oneself as gay or lesbian, personally accepting that definition, and disclosing that orientation to selected others seem important to forming a comfortable sexual identity and promoting one's psychological adjustment (Elizur & Mintzer, 2001).

Heterosexual Identity Development

Quite recently, it has been proposed that in addition to understanding the developmental processes of particular sexual minorities, it is also important to clarify and understand how members of majority populations develop their sexual orientation identities (Worthington & Mohr, 2002). Obviously, the members of the more "privileged" group will not encounter the same kinds of biases or challenges, but their developmental processes can help us understand the broader perspective of how human beings internalize their sexual orientation (Hoffman, 2004).

Heterosexual identity development encompasses six important dimensions to be accomplished over time (Worthington et al., 2002):

1. Identification and awareness of one's sexual needs, as determined by sexual orientation.
2. Adoption of personal values related to sexual behavior and sexuality in general.
3. Awareness of which sexual activities are preferred.
4. Awareness of the specific characteristics that are preferred in sexual partners.
5. Awareness of preferred modes of sexual expression.
6. Recognition of one's sexual orientation and personal identification with that orientation.

These are the components of *individual sexual identity development.* As a person establishes these various qualities of identity, they evolve and interact with two processes of *heterosexual social identity development:* feeling a sense of group identity (fitting in with other heterosexuals) and developing attitudes toward sexual minorities (largely learned from the social group). Fitting in socially is an important quality in sexual identity formation (Mohr, 2002).

Naturally, people with a heterosexual orientation do not face the obstacle of being ostracized or criticized for their preferences, but they do seem to go through some rather predictable developmental stages as they integrate their sexual orientation into their personalities. Early on, they realize their heterosexual orientation but have not yet acted on it sexually. This stage is called *unexplored commitment* to being heterosexual. They may then enter into *active exploration,* during which they intentionally try out various sexual ideas and fantasies, as well as sexual activities with members of the other gender. During this time, they clarify much about what they enjoy and prefer in terms of activities and partners. Some people experience what has been termed *diffusion,* which may involve sexual exploration, but with less intentionality and goal direction than active exploration. After some amount of exploration, accompanied by physical and emotional maturation, heterosexuals enter into the status of *deepening and commitment,* which is characterized by more intimacy and loving feelings in their relationships.

Because ours is a culture that accepts heterosexuality as the norm, some people move directly from unexplored commitment to deepening and commitment, simply because they have matured enough to do so. The final status of heterosexual identity development is *synthesis,* in which all the various elements of identity, group membership, and attitudes toward sexual minorities have achieved congruence and meaning in

the person, although this may be a difficult status to achieve (Hoffman, 2004; Worthington et al., 2002). We now have a model that helps us conceptualize how heterosexual people gradually integrate their sexual orientation into their sense of self.

Same-Gender Sexual Identity Development

Because people who have a same-gender orientation function in a society with mostly heterosexist assumptions, at some point in their lives they begin to perceive themselves as members of a minority. Identity development involves changes in values and redefinitions of acceptable behavior and is largely an internal, psychological process that seems to involve various stages (Dube, 2000). Models of same-gender sexual identity development tend to have several things in common. There is almost always a predictable progression from some sort of first awareness of same-gender attractions and feelings; to a stage of self-labeling as being gay, lesbian, or bisexual; through stages of becoming more accepting of the new identity and sharing it with others; to a final stage of incorporating the identity into the total sense of self (Savin-Williams & Diamond, 2000).

See *"Corey Johnson: An Athlete Comes Out"* on SexSource Online.

Australian psychologist Vivienne Cass (1983–1984, 1990) emphasized the need to pay attention to people's self-perceptions in attempts to understand the experience of same-gender sexual orientation. This perspective assumes that sexual orientation is not so rigidly fixed that it cannot be modified and that people's perceptions of their sexuality may shift with time, even during the adult years, with such shifts potentially resulting in new patterns of sexual behavior or relationships. In other words, sexual identity is not something that is necessarily permanently fixed, even though it may be long-lasting and relatively unswerving for many people. This model of sexual orientation also assumes that individuals may consciously alter their sexual behaviors to a degree depending on how they have come to see themselves (Kinnish, Strassberg, & Turner, 2005).

Stages of Same-Gender Sexual Identity Formation

The concept of navigating through various stages in order to clarify a sexual identity may apply more aptly to dominant North American and European cultures and be much less applicable to other ethnic groups.

Real People

Nancy Considers Coming Out to Her Parents

Nancy is a junior majoring in business. During spring semester of her sophomore year, she began attending meetings of the local Gay, Lesbian, Bisexual, and Transgender student group, primarily because she was feeling lonely and wanted to talk further about her sexual feelings. Since high school, she had been quite certain that she was a lesbian, but she had been reluctant to come out as such or to talk with anyone else about it. She had dated boys in high school, thinking that maybe she would become more interested, but she did not. Since coming to college, she had avoided the social scene for the most part. At one of the meetings in the spring, she met a young woman from the community, and they talked alone a few times. They stayed in touch over the summer, and Nancy looked forward to pursuing the relationship when she returned in the fall.

Nancy and Jill did become more serious during the fall, and they both enjoyed their sexual and social interactions. Jill took Nancy to meet her parents, who seemed very friendly and accepting of their relationship. This was encouraging to Nancy, who had not yet told her own parents about her sexual orientation. She had an older brother who during the Thanksgiving holiday had announced that he was gay, and this had seemed to upset their parents a great deal. She now felt even more reluctant to come out to them herself. At the same time, she wanted to begin building a lifestyle in which she could be as open about her sexuality as she cared to be and not have secrets.

At this point, she has told several friends about her sexuality and has received strong support from them. Some of them have told her that they were not at all surprised and in fact had assumed that she was attracted to women. She is still trying to decide what to do about her parents. She has always felt close enough to them to want their communications to be open and without secrecy. On the other hand, she wants to make certain that their dealing with their son's sexuality would not interfere with their trying to work with her. Jill continues to be a strong source of support for her as she tries to make a decision.

Should Nancy tell her parents about her sexual orientation? Is it important that her parents know? Is she running any risks if she does tell them? Explain.

Sexual identity may be somewhat public and even have political overtones, which may not suit some populations. For example, many African Americans, Latino men and Latina women, and Asian Americans do not seem to want or need a gay, lesbian, or bisexual identity as such and instead tend to integrate their same-gender sexual behaviors into other, nonsexual identities. Asians and Asian Americans often see sexual behavior as a strictly private matter that does not need to fit into any larger social scheme (Chung & Katayama, 1999; Savin-Williams, 2005).

Cass's theory holds that in order for the process of same-gender sexual identity formation to begin, the individual must experience some degree of sexual interest in, or attraction for, someone of the same gender. This does not necessarily have to be expressed through any overt sexual behavior but may instead take the form of fantasies or daydreams. Cass has elucidated six stages in the process of sexual identity formation and maintains that there may be many individ-

ual variations in how different people progress through these stages. The ages at which people experience the stages vary with both maturational and social factors (Floyd & Bakeman, 2006). A summary of Cass's six stages follows (Cass, 1990).

Stage I: Identity Confusion

This stage occurs when people begin to realize that information about same-gender sexual orientation somehow relates to them and to their reactions. As they realize that the personal relevance of this information cannot be ignored, they begin to experience a sense of inconsistency and incongruence in their view of their sexual selves. This period of confusion may go on for some time, during which there may be an attempt to avoid sexual activities with members of the same gender, even in the face of persistent dreams and fantasies about them (Savin-Williams, 2001, 2005). Individuals may attempt to find more information about same-gender orientation as the question "Am I gay/lesbian/bisexual?" is addressed. This moves them toward the second stage of identity formation.

Stage II: Identity Comparison

During this stage, people begin to examine the broader implications of being lesbian, gay, or bisexual as they begin to feel different from family members and peers. Nearly everyone grows up with certain heterosexual expectations and behavioral guidelines. As people's same-gender identities develop, those expectations and guidelines gradually are given up, and a profound sense of loss and grieving may follow. Individuals who experience this sense of social alienation may react in a variety of ways. They may react positively to being different and begin devaluing the importance of heterosexuality in their lives. Or they may still need to "pass," or pretend heterosexuality, in order to avoid negative confrontations over their sexual orientation that they are not prepared to deal with. Many people react by rejecting a same-gender identity at this point, even though they may recognize their behavior and inclination toward members of their own gender. They may define their same-gender behavior as the result of a particular relationship or of having been innocently seduced, or as only a temporary state. They may devalue same-gender identity because of fear of negative reactions from others. Some people at this stage undoubtedly turn their own confusion and "internalized homophobia" into antigay and antilesbian attitudes and exaggerated heterosexual behavior, even though they may be covertly indulging in same-gender activities or fantasies (Dube, 2000). Males are quite likely to pursue sex with other males prior to defining themselves as gay (Floyd & Bakeman, 2006; Schindhelm & Hospers, 2004).

Stage III: Identity Tolerance

When individuals accept their same-gender sexual orientation and begin to recognize the sexual, social, and emotional needs that accompany it, they develop an increased commitment to and tolerance for the identity. Typical behavior includes increased involvement with others in the gay or lesbian community, which offers a support group that understands the person's concerns, a greater opportunity to meet partners and see positive role models, and a forum for feeling more at ease with the identity. This stage may be more difficult for people who are shy and lacking in social skills or who have low self-esteem and fear having their sexual identity known by others. People whose experiences are largely negative during this stage may never progress any further in the development of a same-gender sexual identity. However, those who perceive

their experiences as more positive eventually will develop enough commitment to their identity to be able to say, "I am lesbian/gay/bisexual" (Elizur & Mintzer, 2001; Herman, 2005).

Because many forms of discrimination and homophobic sentiment still exist, decisions must be faced about how open an individual wishes to be about his or her sexual orientation. Being secretive about one's same-gender orientation has been called being in the closet. The process of allowing oneself to acknowledge same-gender attractions and then express them to others has been called **coming out** of the closet. How far a gay man, lesbian, or bisexual will come out, and to whom, depends on a variety of factors. One of the most important is the person's degree of self-acceptance. Some feel that sharing sexual orientation with friends and family members is crucial, whereas others feel that it is a personal matter with no relevance to others. Decisions about coming out must be weighed with care, and the possibility of negative or hurtful consequences needs to be considered. Many people have found, however, that others accept their same-gender sexual orientation comfortably. Teenagers who are gay are coming out at younger ages than was formerly the case, and it is not unusual for high school students to be open and activist about their same-gender sexual orientation (Floyd & Bakeman, 2006; Hall, 2003; Savin-Williams, 2005).

Stage IV: Identity Acceptance

This stage occurs when people accept a self-image as lesbian, gay, or bisexual rather than simply tolerating it and when they have continuing and increased contact with gay and lesbian culture. They share a positive identification with others who have a same-gender orientation. The attitudes and lifestyles of these other people can play a significant role in determining how comfortable individuals are in expressing their own identity. If they associate with others who feel that a same-gender orientation is fully legitimate, then this is the attitude they will most likely adopt. As self-acceptance increases, people move toward stage V (Stevens, 2004).

Stage V: Identity Pride

By this point in their identity formation, people with a same-gender sexual identity are not as likely to use heterosexuality as the standard by which they judge themselves and the behavior of others. As they identify more with the gay and lesbian community, pride in the

coming out acknowledging to oneself and others that one is lesbian, gay, or bisexual.

accomplishments of that community deepens. Sometimes people in this stage become activists in political movements to fight discrimination and homophobia, and they may face more confrontations with the heterosexual establishment. For many, this is an angry stage. Efforts to conceal one's sexual orientation are increasingly abandoned, and selected family members and coworkers may be informed of the orientation (Floyd & Bakeman, 2006).

Because of prevailing social attitudes, people may be alarmed to discover that a spouse, parent, child, sibling, or friend is bisexual, gay, or lesbian. Some people react to such a discovery with fear and loathing, others with blame and guilt, and still others with tolerance, understanding, sensitivity, and acceptance. It is quite typical for parents, on discovering that a son or daughter is gay or lesbian, to blame themselves and wonder "what we did wrong." Yet, as earlier sections of this chapter have demonstrated, there is no solid evidence to support the belief that parental behavioral influences are important in the formation of sexual orientation. Coming out to parents and other family members remains one of the greatest challenges for gay men and lesbian women as they consolidate their personal identity (Savin-Williams, 2001, 2005). Through an organization called Parents and Friends of Lesbians and Gays (PFLAG), parents and others can learn more about same-gender sexual orientation and deal with their feelings. Many parents eventually come to accept the sexual identity of their child. In other unfortunate cases, however, the lesbian daughter or gay son is excluded from the family, a reaction that usually only intensifies feelings of guilt and rejection.

What do you believe are the most powerful determinants of sexual orientation?

Whether individuals move to the final stage of sexual identity formation is often determined by the reaction of significant others to the disclosure of their orientation. If the reactions are mostly negative, the person may only feel more confirmed in her or his belief that heterosexuals represent the opposition and are not to be trusted. Reactions that tend toward the positive and accepting may allow individuals to move on (Stevens, 2004).

Stage VI: Identity Synthesis

In this final stage of identity formation, people realize that the world is not divided into us (gays, lesbians, and bisexuals) and them (heterosexuals). Not all heterosexuals need to be viewed negatively, and not all people with same-gender orientation need to be viewed positively. The anger that so often is experienced in stage V dissipates, and the gay, lesbian, or bisexual aspects of one's identity may be fully integrated with other aspects of the self. The identity formation process is complete.

Male-Female Differences in Same-Gender Sexual Identity Formation

Different patterns of socialization between women and men lead to a few differences in the ways same-gender sexual identity is acquired by the two sexes. For example, the evidence suggests that, on average, more gay males seek contact with a variety of sexual partners than do lesbians or heterosexual males (Laumann, Gagnon, et al., 1994). They may also be more willing to participate in anonymous, casual sexual encounters, a practice that is almost unknown among lesbians. Several research studies have indicated that gay males may tend to become aware of their same-gender orientation earlier than do lesbians, often during childhood or adolescence, and in a somewhat more abrupt manner (Floyd & Bakeman, 2006; Kertzner, 2002)

Because of their earlier awareness of same-gender sexual feelings and attractions, males are more likely to enter the identity formation process earlier than is typical for females. They often fantasize sexually about other males relatively early in their lives. Males also are more likely than females to enter the process of sexual identity formation on the basis of sexual stimulation, while at the same time adjusting to male-stereotypical roles by dressing and acting in the traditional male manner. There may be less incentive for gay men to reject male gender roles because these roles are more highly valued in our culture than are traditional female gender roles, which tend to be granted lower status (Richardson, 2000; Tolman & Diamond, 2002).

Achieving a lesbian identity seems to be a somewhat more ambiguous and fluid process. Most lesbians fully embrace their same-gender identity only after involvement in an intense romantic relationship with another woman. Most have also had previous sexual involvement with men that has proved to be less fulfilling than what they discover with other women (Peplau et al., 2000). A common myth holds that if gay men or lesbians were exposed to a happy heterosexual encounter with a good lover, they would realize "what they are missing." However, same-gender sexual orientation is not caused by traumatic heterosexual experiences, nor is it changed by a positive heterosexual experience (Kerr & Mathy, 2003).

Lesbians are less likely to use sexual stimulation as a route into the same-gender sexual identity formation process. Instead, that process more typically is initiated when a woman falls in love with another woman. Again, because same-gender attraction occurs later in life for women than for men, it is not uncommon for a woman in midlife to experience same-gender love for the first time (Robinson & Parks, 2003). In the earlier stages of sexual identity formation, women are more likely to reject the passive, nurturing aspects of the traditional female sex role (Peplau et al., 2000). Sometimes, women begin adopting a lesbian identity as the result of their association with feminist groups and philosophies, which also may have put them in touch with loving feelings for other women that have previously been unrealized or unexplored (Richardson, 2000). Other times, a woman may first begin to have fantasies about and feelings for other women only after having experienced pleasurable sex with a woman. For these reasons, it may also be that the lesbian experience of sexual orientation does not fit the more sexual behavior–oriented Kinsey scale particularly well. Women generally seem to show less consistency than men over time in their sexual fantasies, emotional attractions, and behaviors. Achieving a lesbian identity may also be more dependent on the social climate in which the woman finds herself than is the case for gay men (Tolman & Diamond, 2002; Tomlinson & Fassinger, 2003).

FOH Bisexual Identity Formation

All studies of human sexual behavior have indicated that substantial numbers of people have had at least some sexual experience with both females and males (Laumann, Gagnon, et al., 1994). Slang terms such as "AC/DC" and "switch-hitter" have been applied to these people. It is likely that such individuals often are identified as gay or lesbian, although data from the NHSLS indicated that among people who had experienced sex with someone of their own gender, many did not consider themselves bisexual, gay, or lesbian.

Even people who have experienced a great deal of same-gender behavior or who have had a fairly even mix of same-gender and opposite-gender sexual activity tend not to define themselves as bisexual. They are more likely to see themselves as either gay or heterosexual, with occasional bisexual behavior due to social expectations or other circumstances. This may reflect the difficulties people face in forming a bisexual identity, which can be exacerbated by being tacitly told by both heterosexuals and gays or lesbians to make up their minds and make a choice (Ryan & Futterman, 2001). Because they often do not conform to a heterosexist culture, many bisexual people align themselves with the gay and lesbian communities for support. However, they may find a level of biphobia there as well, and they sometimes are considered to be political fence-sitters, traitors, and cop-outs. Heterosexual women tend to perceive bisexuals less favorably than do heterosexual men, who tend to view both bisexuals and gay men rather negatively (Herek, 2002).

A study of male arousal patterns has called into question whether bisexuality actually represents a distinct pattern of genital sexual arousal in men or instead one way of interpreting or reporting sexual arousal. The study compared patterns of genital arousal on exposure to sexual pictures of males and females in heterosexual men, gay men, and men who identified themselves as bisexual. One hypothesis would be that bisexuals would have some sexual arousal to both male and female stimuli. Interestingly, this was not the result. About 75 percent of the men who called themselves bisexual became aroused only by the male stimuli, the same percentage as gay males. The rest became aroused only by female stimuli, the same percentage as heterosexuals. The bisexual men in the study reported having been aroused by and sexually involved with people of both genders, yet their arousal patterns during the research seemed distinctly straight or gay. More work needs to be done to clarify this seeming contradiction between self-identification and sexual arousal (Rieger, Chivers, & Bailey, 2005).

Some individuals may go through a period of bisexuality when they are in transition from heterosexual behavior and identity to same-gender sexual behavior and identity. There is evidence that many people define themselves as bisexual before eventually defining themselves as lesbian or gay (Ryan & Futterman, 2001). This may also help explain the apparent disconnect in the study cited above. Arriving at a bisexual identity in this way often is associated with confusion, conflict, and ambivalence about sexual orientation— the *conflict model* of bisexual identity formation. In contrast, the *flexibility model* associates bisexual identity with personal growth, a wider range of possibilities for fulfillment, and flexibility in personal lifestyle (Rust, 2003).

It may be that bisexual people respond emotionally and erotically to particular human qualities not exclusive to either females or males. The identity formation process for bisexuals may not follow a linear, stage-by-stage progression. Bisexual identity may well be more of an ongoing process, emerging from either a formerly heterosexual identity or a gay or lesbian identity. The process may include both self-acknowledgment and disclosure to others (Rust, 2003). However, bisexual identity formation reminds us again of how changeable people may be over time in their sexual inclinations depending on many different factors in their lives. Because our society has been more reluctant to affirm bisexuality than gay or lesbian orientation, either scientifically or socially, taking on a bisexual identity requires a higher tolerance for ambiguity than does accepting a gay or lesbian identity (Rust, 2003; Ryan & Futterman, 2001).

■ Sexual Orientation and Society

Same-gender sexual behavior has always received attention from our social institutions. Some civil laws have prohibited or restricted sexual behavior between people of the same gender. Families frequently face crises when they discover that one of their members is lesbian, gay, or bisexual. Openly gay, lesbian, and bisexual persons have at times not been allowed to hold positions with the CIA, FBI, or U.S. military. Nevertheless, people with a same-gender sexual orientation have achieved a much more visible presence in North American society in recent years. This section deals briefly with the relationship between same-gender orientation and society.

Gay and Lesbian Culture

Data from the NHSLS showed that gay, lesbian, and bisexual persons are not evenly distributed geographically but in fact tend to live in large cities. More than 9 percent of males in the 12 largest cities in the United States identified themselves as gay, compared to between 3 and 4 percent of males in suburban locations and about 1 percent in rural areas. Lesbians also seem to be somewhat more clustered in cities, but not to the same extent as gay males. Researchers believe that cities offer an environment where critical masses of same-gender-oriented individuals are likely to develop, providing more well-developed social networks and greater economic opportunity. It is clear that many lesbians, gays, and bisexuals move to cities in order to find a greater sense of community, although it may also be that people who grow up in cities are somewhat more able to identify same-gender tendencies in themselves and ultimately self-identify as such (Michael et al., 1994). Other researchers have found

"SORRY, WILLIAM, BUT THIS IS JUST TOO OLD-FASHIONED... YOU NEED TO UPDATE THE STORY... AGAINST THEIR FAMILIES WISHES, THE TWO LOVERS GET MARRIED IN SAN FRANCISCO... CALL IT 'ROMEO AND JULIO'..."

Source: Gary Brookins. Copyright © North American Syndicate.

that gay couples are more likely to settle in cities with fewer extremes in weather, fewer people who vote Republican, and lower rates of unemployment (Walther & Poston, 2004).

Wherever the social atmosphere permits—and this is sometimes in suburban or rural areas as well as in cities—it is typical for some lesbians and gay males to group together as a community. The size and structure of such a community vary depending on many circumstances. Colleges and universities often have gay, lesbian, and bisexual organizations or course offerings (Parker, 2004; Tomlinson & Fassinger, 2003); cities and even some smaller communities have gay and lesbian organizations, meeting centers, bookstores, newspapers and magazines, political groups, health and counseling services, housing cooperatives, restaurants, and bars, sometimes located in specific sections or on certain streets. Many people with a same-gender orientation, on the other hand, may never associate themselves with a gay/lesbian community. Even in cities with well-developed lesbian communities, many lesbians do not participate, preferring instead to associate with smaller groups of friends (Laumann, Gagnon, et al., 1994). There has always been controversy about whether certain professions tend to be more populated by gay persons than others. One study indicated that male professional dancers are more likely to be gay, whereas only a small percentage of female dancers were lesbians (Bailey, 2003).

The gay, lesbian, and bisexual community has come to serve several important functions, one of which is bringing people together socially. The community also provides a supportive atmosphere in which people can share mutual concerns and experiences and be met with understanding. Another important function of the community is to provide a culture of language and ideology that accepts same-gender orientations and behaviors as valid lifestyles, identities, and modes of romantic and sexual expression. Various forms of nonverbal communication have developed in the gay community as a means to let others know that one is gay. One researcher studied two different types of eye-gaze that some gay men and lesbians use to send nonverbal messages to others who interest them. "Gaydar," the somewhat facetious term that sometimes has been used to describe the identity recognition mechanisms gay people use to identify one another, seems to be a real part of gay and lesbian culture (Nicholas, 2004; Philipps, 2006).

What are the existing policies on your campus regarding gay and lesbian couples living together in residence halls?

Some college campuses have been the site of controversy about the cohabitation of same-gender

Real Student Voices

■ I have known I was gay since I was quite a little boy. I couldn't attach words to what I was feeling at first, but I knew I was interested in Superman and Batman for different reasons than my friends were. I came out to a few of my friends in high school, and then to my mother just before my graduation party. Needless to say, this wasn't great timing for her, but she didn't fall apart either. I have a great relationship with my parents now, and they accept my boyfriend fully.

■ I told my parents that I was gay two years ago, and they were really upset at first, wondering what they had done wrong. My mother came around, and she and I can talk about it openly. My father is a different story. He has acknowledged it, but prefers not to discuss it or have the topic brought up. Maybe someday.

■ I think my parents expect that I am gay, but I haven't felt any particular need to confirm that. In some ways, I don't feel as though it's any of their business. As a female athlete, a lot of my friends are gay too.

couples in residence halls. Opponents claim that having special living areas for gay or lesbian partners would create a kind of segregation that might aggravate tensions between campus groups, leading to possible harassment of or violence against same-gender couples. On the other side of the debate are those who feel that these residences permit people who have certain commonalities, such as sexual orientation, to share other important aspects of their culture more easily.

There is evidence that gay male relationships have their share of domestic violence, with many gay men in the United States being battered or physically abused by their partners each year. Substantial numbers of gay men report having been subjected to sexual coercion or force as well (Krahè et al., 2000). Power imbalances within male-male relationships ultimately determine which partner is the victim and which the batterer. Domestic violence also is believed to occur in about 25 percent of lesbian relationships (Peterman & Dixon, 2003).

Studies of fundamental quality-of-life issues have found in general that sexual orientation does not seem to have any particular effect, one way or the other, on quality of life, income level, lifestyle, or health indicators (Horowitz, Weis, & Laflin, 2001). One controversy in a society that has an increasing number of same-gender families is whether schools should educate children about various family configurations. Some schools have faced heated debates about the use of books in elementary school that portray households headed by two adults of the same gender. Proponents insist that children should understand the many part-nership arrangements they might encounter, whereas others argue that such materials promote a lifestyle they consider inappropriate or immoral.

HIV/AIDS and the Gay Community

The disease that can result from sexual transmission of HIV, called acquired immunodeficiency syndrome or AIDS (see Chapter 17), was first recognized in the United States among gay males who had shared sex with numerous partners. HIV infection is now clearly a problem for all populations, but because it initially was associated with gay men, the stigma has been difficult to shake (see Figure 13.8). Early education efforts about safer sex were directed at helping gay men change some sexual practices. At first, there was a decline in unsafe sexual encounters among gay males, but there is new concern that the rate of unprotected sexual encounters has been increasing. As is common with all populations, even though gay men are aware of the risks of unprotected sex, they do not always protect themselves adequately. Thirty percent of HIV-positive men in one study reported having had unprotected anal sex in the previous year, either with a steady male partner who was not infected or with someone of unknown HIV status (Denning & Campsmith, 2005). In a six-city study of 4,295 HIV-negative men who had sex with men, 78 percent had had sex with a male partner of unknown HIV status in the previous six months, and 28 percent had had sex with someone they knew to be HIV-positive. About half indicated that their anal sexual encounters had not included the use of a condom (Koblin et al., 2003).

FIGURE 13.8   *HIV/AIDS and the Gay and Lesbian Community*

Although not exclusively a disease of gay men, HIV and AIDS have visibly affected the gay community in the United States. To call attention to the need for more research to combat AIDS, the Names Project sponsored the creation of the AIDS Quilt, a 150- by 450-foot memorial consisting of individual squares of cloth, each one representing someone who has died of AIDS.

Because of the emphasis on HIV in gay male culture, two issues often are part of sexual activity among gay males. One is *sexual negotiation,* which refers to the sharing of preferences and dislikes regarding particular sexual activities, along with associated information about the degree of risk or safety. This sharing can be important in determining the level of HIV risk involved in a sexual encounter. The other issue, *serostatus disclosure,* refers to informing the other partner about HIV status. Obviously, honesty and integrity are essential to determining the degree of risk involved, but there are also concerns about how much these negotiative and disclosure processes may hinder sex and relationships (Carballo-Diéguez et al., 2006; Feldstein et al., 2006).

Men in a continuing relationship often consider this an issue of trust and love and do not feel condoms are necessary. In this they mirror the behavior of couples who know that both partners are HIV-negative. However, men sometimes do not use good judgment because of alcohol or drugs or because of mistaken assumptions that a partner is HIV-negative. Sometimes, risky sexual practices are inadvertent or forced. Some gay men engage voluntarily in "barebacking," even if they are aware that a partner is HIV-positive. They may take precautions that are considered to be forms of "harm reduction," such as avoidance of ejaculation during oral or anal sex. Some research suggests that men who engage in such behavior are tired of using condoms and may even have erectile difficulties when they use them. Some have false optimism about the current risks of HIV or have low levels of self-esteem. There is no evidence, however, that they are deliberately trying to spread HIV or get sick themselves. Educational efforts must be targeted carefully to those who engage in such high-risk behaviors (Adam, Husbands, Murray, & Maxwell, 2005; Huebner, Proescholdbell, & Nemeroff, 2006).

HIV/AIDS education efforts have been burdened with homophobia and biphobia as well as with blaming, hostility, and misinformation about same-gender sexual behavior and AIDS. This may account for the fact that fewer than half of some gay and bisexual youth have been tested for HIV even though they continue to engage in risky sexual activities. An advertising campaign has attempted to reach African-American men who call themselves straight but have sexual intercourse with other men, known as being "on the down low" or simply "D. L." Cultural pressures sometimes push them into a continuing dual identity that enables them to deny their gay orientation (Crawford et al., 2002).

Anal intercourse has been shown to be a primary means of transmitting HIV. Wearing a condom can substantially reduce, but not completely eliminate, the risk. Many gay males are using condoms more consistently or choosing sexual activities that are less risky, such as mutual masturbation. In an apparent search for connectedness and sexual affirmation, others seem to be paying less attention to health and safety issues (Chiasson, et al., 2005; Whittier, St. Lawrence, & Seeley, 2005).

Although the risks of woman-to-woman transfer of the virus are less certain, experts warn about the exchange of vaginal fluids. The likelihood of transmission of HIV between women probably is less than between men, but women too should guard against contact involving internal bodily fluids if any risk might be involved. There is evidence that substantial numbers of lesbian and bisexual women do take risks by having unprotected sex with potentially infected males. Rubber dental dams or sheets of latex cut from condoms or rubber gloves can be used to cover the

Real Student Voices

◼ I was raised by two lesbian women, although that didn't really sink in until just recently. My mother and father got divorced when I was eight, and we moved in with this female friend of hers when I was twelve. I just thought it was more convenient and practical for all of us. Janet, my mother's partner, has always treated us children as her own, and we came to love her. I never thought much about the fact that she and my mother shared a bed. My sister told me they were gay just before I went to college. I think it's funny that I didn't get it until then. But it doesn't really change anything for me.

◼ I want to go into the Air Force, but I am concerned that my sexual orientation will eventually be discovered. I think I can be just as good a pilot and soldier as anyone, but I don't want to be humiliated by being discovered either. I am hoping the military will change their policies.

vulva and vaginal opening during oral sexual contact, and rubber gloves or finger cots can be worn when inserting a finger into the vagina or anus.

HIV and AIDS have taken an emotional toll within the gay community. Some gay men have lost friends to the disease and know others who are infected with HIV. For some, this has led to clinical depression, hypochondria, sexual dysfunction, or a profound sense of personal loss. The realization that there will be more losses to face, along with fears for personal health, creates a great deal of stress. Gay men who are not infected with HIV sometimes feel guilty about being able to enjoy jobs, relationships, and other aspects of life while witnessing the suffering and stresses of other gays who are infected (Springer & Lease, 2000).

Sexual Orientation and the Military

For many years, there was a ban on lesbians and gays serving in the U.S. military, and the enlistment forms asked about sexual orientation. The "Don't ask, don't tell" policy, put in place in 1994, ended the long-standing practice of questioning recruits about their sexual orientation. All forms of sexual behavior on military bases continued to be prohibited, except between married couples in their living quarters. However, people who openly declared themselves to be gay or lesbian could still be discharged from the military because their sexual orientation still was officially considered "incompatible with military service," regardless of whether they were known to be sexually active.

The number of people discharged annually by the U.S. armed forces for reasons of same-gender sexual orientation or behavior increased nearly every year, peaking at 1,227 discharges in 2001. To the dismay of some advocacy groups, the wars in Afghanistan and Iraq led to lower rates of discharge. In 2006, there were 612 such discharges, fewer than half the number in 2001. Even though the policy was challenged in federal court as being discriminatory and was declared unconstitutional for equating sexual orientation with misconduct, a degree of confusion still exists about the relationship between the U.S. military and gay and lesbian individuals. Although new training policies have been initiated to prevent the harassment of individuals in the military who are thought to be gay, the number of reported cases of antigay harassment actually have increased. Some retired top military officers have come out following their retirement and have claimed that, in addition to being discriminatory, the "Don't ask, don't tell" policy simply is not working. The American Society for Adolescent Psychiatry (2002) recently issued a position statement calling for an end to discrimination against gay men and lesbian women in the military. The armed services in numerous other countries allow gay men and lesbians to serve, in spite of the homophobic attitudes and abuse these servicemen and -women have sometimes encountered.

Do you think your attitudes and feelings about same-gender orientation differ from those of your parents? Your grandparents? Explain.

Marriage and Legalized Same-Gender Partnerships

Many people with a bisexual or same-gender sexual orientation marry members of the other gender. In choosing heterosexual marriage, an individual may have decided to live as an exclusive heterosexual or may still expect to maintain some level of sexual activity with members of the same gender.

What are some social pressures exerted on same-gender couples that heterosexual couples do not have to cope with?

Bisexuals, lesbians, and gay men enter into heterosexual marriages for a variety of reasons. It is clear that some do not become fully aware of their sexual inclinations until after they have married. Others see marriage as a way to achieve social respectability, as an escape from their sexual tendencies, or as a way to avoid the loneliness they may stereotypically associate with gay or lesbian lifestyles. Still others want children and feel strong loving feelings toward their spouses. Yet these marriages often face sexual conflicts of various sorts. Some couples can deal with such conflicts honestly and with sensitivity, enriching their marriage. Others cannot handle such conflicts and can no longer continue their marriage.

During the 1990s, the rates of same-gender partnering increased significantly (Butler, 2000). Legalized partnerships between members of the same gender have received increasing attention in recent years; despite the legal hurdles, many couples of the same gender have found ways to formalize their partnerships (see Figure 13.9). Some members of the clergy have sanctioned same-gender partnerships. The Metropolitan Community Church has branches in numerous cities aimed specifically at members of the gay and lesbian community. Unitarian-Universalist ministers, and some other members of the clergy, conduct unions of lesbian and gay male couples. Although holy union ceremonies are performed in these and some other churches, they are not legally binding in the United States. The Vermont Supreme Court issued a ruling that gay and lesbian couples in that state should enjoy all benefits and privileges afforded heterosexual couples who can marry. The Vermont legislature subsequently passed a law confirming these civil rights and allowing legalized "civil unions," while not actually providing for same-gender marriage (Rosenberg, 2000).

In 2003, the U.S. Supreme Court struck down a Texas law that had led to the arrest of a gay male couple who were observed having sex in their own apartment. For the first time, the Court explicitly stated that gay people were "entitled to respect for their private lives" and that the "state cannot demean their existence or control their destiny by making their private sexual conduct a crime." Just a few months later, in 2004, the Massachusetts Supreme Judicial Court ruled that civil unions would not truly provide equal rights to same-gender couples and that such couples should in fact have the right to marry. For a time, same-gender couples were allowed to marry in other parts of the country as a result of the Massachusetts ruling. In mid-May, same-gender couples began marrying in that state. Ultimately, most gay marriages were put on hold

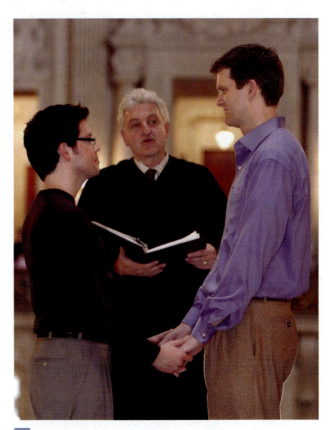

■ **FIGURE 13.9** *Intimate Relationships*

It is erroneous to view gay and lesbian relationships strictly in terms of sexual behavior. A gay couple in Boston is shown here exchanging vows in a union ceremony to symbolize their shared relational commitment to each other.

by various legal maneuvers, and the issue has become a major controversy among politicians. A call for a constitutional amendment that would define marriage as being between a male and a female has not achieved much support (Rosenberg, 2004). It seems likely that same-sex marriage will continue to be debated by state legislatures and that some states ultimately will allow such legalized partnerships. The debates over the issue solidify some clear positions in the culture wars (Rosenberg, 2006).

In many cities, partners in a long-term gay relationship now qualify as a family and therefore may be eligible for the same rights as those afforded a married couple for many purposes. Some cities maintain a registry of "lawfully recognized domestic partners." Couples who register are given a certificate similar to a marriage license. Registration as domestic partners entitles couples to things such as discounts on health club memberships and airline tickets, visitation rights in hospitals or prisons, and rent-control housing. A number of states have passed legislation that allows them not to recognize the legality of marriages between members of the same gender, and the U.S. Congress passed the

Defense of Marriage Act, which permits states to do this. Many major U.S. corporations and colleges have extended employee health and insurance benefits to the partners of gay and lesbian workers, including IBM, Walt Disney Company, American Express, Time Warner, and Apple. Gay rights activists consider these major steps toward recognition of the legal rights of nonheterosexual couples (Wilson, R., 2004b).

Gay and Lesbian Families

Many gay, lesbian, and bisexual persons have children, either from heterosexual marriages or through deliberate efforts to conceive or adopt (see Figure 13.10). Research on lesbian mothers, gay fathers, and their children has taken place only rather recently, and then usually because of legal attempts to decide if lesbians and gay males could be considered fit parents. The available research confirms that lesbian and gay families indeed can provide as healthy an environment as any family structure and that the parenting skills of gays and lesbians are as adequate as those of heterosexuals (Johnson & O'Connor, 2002). Studies have also confirmed that children raised by gay parents are no more likely than children raised by straight parents to have a same-gender sexual orientation themselves. The children also seem to have no greater likelihood of social or emotional difficulties. Legal precedents are still being set with regard to custody of children by gay and lesbian parents.

More and more same-gender couples are intentionally planning their own families. Lesbian couples have the options of artificial insemination and choosing a male partner for reproductive purposes. Gay male couples must depend on either adoption or surrogate motherhood. Because this type of family struc-

FIGURE 13.10   *Parents of the Same Gender Raising Children*

Most children adapt readily to families with parents of same-gender orientation. But not all communities accept their lifestyle, and some families struggle to be accepted. This lesbian couple is shown with their children.

ture is of relatively recent origin, there is less research on children raised in such families. The studies that have been done again suggest that there are no particular differences between the children of lesbian and gay parents and children raised in mixed-gender households. As society increasingly accepts same-gender partnerships, there has been increasing visibility of gay and lesbian families with children who have made their way into the mainstream of social life (Johnson & Piore, 2004).

See "That's a Family" on SexSource Online.

Self-Evaluation

What Is Your Sexual Orientation?

Figuring out your own sexual orientation can sometimes be more confusing and unsettling than might generally be assumed. As you have discovered in this chapter, the literature on sexual orientation tells us that many factors may determine sexual orientation, that sexual attractions and behaviors may change to some extent with time and circumstances, that most people identify themselves as straight, and

that society still can be hard on people who are nonheterosexual. Clearly, there is plenty of pressure to be heterosexual—or at least to say that you are.

The following questions can help you determine a bit more about *your* sexual orientation at this point in your life, *if you are honest with yourself about the answers*. **Note: *You should not be asked to divulge information about your answers to these questions unless*** *you wish to do so, are very clear about how the information is being used, and are assured of your privacy and confidentiality.*

Use this scale in responding to questions 1–4:

1 = completely oriented toward members of the other gender

2 = mostly the other gender, but occasionally involving someone of the same gender

3 = both the other gender and the same gender

4 = mostly the same gender, but occasionally involving someone of the other gender

5 = completely oriented toward members of the same gender

1. As you recall your sexual desires of the past year and the present, how would you rate them according to the scale?

2. As you recall your loving feelings and romantic attractions of the past year and the present, how would you rate them?

3. During the past year and at present, what rating would you use regarding your sexual fantasies when you are sexually aroused?

4. During the past year and at present, what rating would you use regarding the sexual partners you have had (if any)?

5. If you were to identify your sexual orientation using the terms *straight, gay,* or *bisexual*, which one would most accurately describe you right now in your life?

6. When you answered question 5 for yourself, did you feel any internal pressure to define yourself in any particular way? If so, where did that pressure come from?

7. Do you consider yourself homophobic or biphobic? Has anyone ever used one of those terms to describe you? Why or why not?

8. Are you comfortable with the sexual orientation you have indicated you have?

9. How much do you think your sexual orientation matters to various people close to you in your life? Why? How much does it matter to society as a whole?

10. In what ways might you honor your sexual orientation and develop the sense of integrity and appropriateness that can help you be a good person?

Chapter Summary

1. People have an inner set of sexual and romantic attractions called a sexual orientation and eventually develop an inner awareness of how that orientation fits into their lives—their sexual orientation identity.

2. Sexual orientation seems to be more changeable than once believed, but studies have focused more on nonheterosexual orientation because it typically has been perceived as "different."

3. Sexual orientation seems to be a multidimensional phenomenon involving many different aspects of the personality.

4. Kinsey developed a scale demonstrating that there is no single pattern of same-gender sexual behavior but rather different degrees between the heterosexual (opposite-gender) and same-gender orientations. His bipolar scale is less useful today.

5. The incidence of same-gender orientation among humans has been an issue of controversy, and different studies have reached their conclusions in different ways. Some people may identify themselves as gay, lesbian, or bisexual even though their behaviors do not seem consistent with the labels, and vice versa.

6. The NHSLS data examined desire, behavior, and self-identification with regard to same-gender sexuality, finding differences in the incidence of each, with some overlap among the three factors. More people indicated having felt attraction to members of their own gender than had experienced same-gender sex.

7. People in urban areas are more likely to identify themselves as gay, lesbian, or bisexual.

8. Same-gender orientation and behavior are found across all cultures, typically in similar proportions.

9. Homophobia and biphobia can have negative effects on individuals who have same-gender orientations and behaviors. Leading professional organizations no longer view same-gender sexual orientation within the framework of pathology, and many businesses are attempting to reach gay and lesbian markets.

10. Religions take various morally based positions regarding sexual orientation and behavior. Some religious groups take an accepting and positive view of same-gender orientation.

11. About a century ago, same-gender sexual orientation was medicalized as an illness or a pathology,

a conceptualization that determined many perceptions of gay men and lesbians for some time.

12. There continues to be controversy between the biological essentialist point of view, that same-gender orientation is somehow inborn, and the social constructionist perspective, which holds that its origins lie more in socioenvironmental factors. Evidence suggests that it involves interaction between genetics and the environment.

13. Psychodynamic theories focus on the different stages of psychosexual development involved in creating sexual orientation. The normal variant model sees same-gender orientation and behavior as one form of expression within a range of sexual orientations and behaviors.

14. The Bell, Weinberg, and Hammersmith research was one of the most thorough studies on the development of sexual orientation and established a foundation on which more biologically based models could be built.

15. Some researchers believe that hormonal factors during prenatal life may predispose people to particular sexual orientations. The fraternal birth order hypothesis lends some credibility to the belief.

16. Twin studies have suggested that same-gender orientation may be genetically linked and partly heritable. Studies of brain anatomy have demonstrated some measurable differences in brain structure among gay men, heterosexual men, and women.

17. Evolutionary theory has had difficulty explaining same-gender orientation, but several explanations have been presented to explain why the orientation has persisted in evolution.

18. The multifactorial model holds that there are shades of difference in sexual orientation, determined partly by biological factors that interact with socioenvironmental factors.

19. Among professionals who have viewed same-gender orientation and behavior within the framework of a model suggesting illness or abnormalcy, attempts have been made to change people to a more heterosexual orientation. Current professional opinion leans more toward seeing it as one of several orientations that need no particular intervention or cure. Gay and lesbian people do not have any more psychological problems than do heterosexual people.

20. Recent theories have been advanced concerning the development of heterosexual identity from the perspectives of individual identity and social identity.

21. Several theories have been advanced concerning the development of a lesbian, gay, or bisexual identity. Cass's theory proposes that sexual identity formation involves a series of up to six stages. People proceed through these stages differently, and a person's perceptions of his or her sexual orientation may shift over time. This model may apply only to North American and European cultures; other cultures may not need a sense of sexual "identity" per se.

22. There are some differences in the ways gay males and lesbians progress through the stages of sexual identity formation. Gay males tend to enter the process earlier in life than do lesbians. Lesbians are more likely to realize their identity after experiencing an intense same-gender relationship.

23. Most cities have well-developed same-gender communities that are an avenue of communication and support for lesbians, gay men, and bisexuals. This may be one reason why city populations have a higher proportion of people with same-gender sexual orientation.

24. AIDS was first identified in the United States among gay men, and HIV spread rapidly among the gay male population. This led to increased homophobia and biphobia. There are still concerns about how gay men negotiate sexual encounters and disclose their HIV status.

25. The U.S. military continues to judge same-gender sexual orientation incompatible with military service. The "Don't ask, don't tell" policy has not markedly changed the fact that gays and lesbians frequently are discharged from the armed forces.

26. Many bisexuals, gays, and lesbians marry heterosexual partners and raise families. Their same-gender orientation may or may not be known by their partners. Gays and lesbians have been fighting for the right to enter into legal partnerships with members of the same gender because they carry financial and legal implications. Although same-gender marriage is not sanctioned by law, some churches will perform holy union ceremonies, and some cities register domestic partnerships.

27. Children raised by gay or lesbian parents do not seem to differ particularly from children raised by mixed-gender parents, nor are they more likely to develop same-gender sexual orientations themselves.

Focus on Health Questions

In this section you will find the kinds of questions that you may have concerning your own health and sexuality. The page references indicate where in the text the answer is located; the exact place is marked with this logo: **FOH**

1. Do gay and lesbian people actually love members of their own gender? **358**

2. Is homophobia all that bad? What negative effects does it actually produce? **365**

3. If I acknowledge my same-gender orientation, will my church condemn me? **365–366**

4. Do gay males come from families where the mother dominates the father? **366**

5. Isn't same-gender sexual orientation a sign of psychological problems? **367**

6. Is sexual orientation the result of hormones or genes? **369–371**

7. Can therapy help people with a same-gender orientation become heterosexual? **373–374**

8. How can I know if I am gay (or lesbian or bisexual)? **374–378**

9. Are some people really bisexual, or are they just pretending to be so they won't have to think of themselves as lesbian or gay? **379**

10. Will it be easier for me to "come out" as a bisexual than it would be if I were gay? **379**

11. Isn't HIV primarily a gay male infection? (See also Chapter 17.) **381–382**

12. Do scare tactics help gay males change their unsafe sex practices? **382**

Chapter 14

The Spectrum of Human Sexual Behavior

Chapter Outline

I never realized how diverse human beings are in
their sexual interests and needs until I finished
reading this chapter. I can hardly say that very
many of these options interest me, but on the
other hand, I do not necessarily condemn them
either. Human sexuality can be a mysterious thing!

—from a student essay

We are living in a time unmatched for its diversity of sexual values and the openness with which various sexual lifestyles and behaviors can be expressed. Our culture has attempted to reconcile a plurality of value systems and sexual interests within a framework of political culture wars. A fundamental question for such a society is how wide a latitude of sexual values and expressions will be permitted. Never has there been such freedom to accept and live out nearly any aspect of one's sexual individuality. At the same time, debate continues over which behaviors will be accepted and tolerated.

In the earlier days of sex research, Kinsey based his understandings of sexual expression on a concept of *total sexual outlet,* or what has been termed the "hydraulic theory" of sex. Kinsey saw orgasm as the outlet for people's sexual tensions, and he assumed that varying levels of sex drive in different individuals could be expressed through a range of sexual expression. In this way, sexual expression was seen as following the principles of hydraulics, or the movement of liquids. If one sexual outlet was blocked or unavailable, another outlet would simply be used. It usually was assumed, for example, that autoerotic activity, such as masturbation, compensated for a lack of partnered sex, an assumption we now know to be inaccurate (Laumann, Gagnon, et al., 1994).

This concept was closely related to the assumption that the sexual impulse was a biologically driven need that required periodic satisfaction. Although some sexual conditions are innately pleasurable, such as genital stimulation or orgasm, the concept of sex drive is ambiguous. It is used to describe a motivation toward or craving for sexual pleasure, but there has not been much scientific support for the idea that a sex drive is "built-in," or innate (Okami & Shackelford, 2002). The most recent findings in sex research concerning the types of sexual behaviors in which people participate suggest that the specific content of any person's sexual conduct depends a great deal on the cultural meanings that person has attributed to various sexual behaviors as the result of social interactions (Kauth, 2006a).

Cross-cultural studies demonstrate that cultures impose many guidelines for how people should feel and act about sex. There is also increasing evidence that sexuality can be situational and changeable and that people's sexual needs and behaviors may be modified by day-to-day life circumstances, a concept called *erotic plasticity*. Contrary to what might first be imagined, it has been hypothesized that women actually have greater erotic plasticity than men (Baumeister, 2000; Diamond, 2006). Over time, men seem to be more rigid

about maintaining a reasonably constant frequency of sexual outlets, or orgasms, while women can move between high and low outlet frequencies. While males often are found in greater numbers than females in studies of various sexual activities, individual men tend to be more rigid than individual women with regard to the sexual activities they choose to participate in (Okami & Shackelford, 2002). The research so far has not clarified how individualized preferences for seeking sexual arousal and orgasm are formed or how they may be modified over time. As the previous chapter suggested, sexual orientation seems to develop from the interaction of many influences. It has also been suggested that it makes more sense to study individual sexual behaviors rather than trying to categorize these behaviors into "orientations" (Kauth, 2006b).

Sex research has tended to ignore the distinction between *sexual performance,* which might be measured objectively by things such as number of orgasms or types of behavior, and the more *subjective erotic experience* going on in a person's mind and emotions. This latter experience includes *desire,* or the ways a person might be drawn emotionally to people and things. Simply stated, sexual desire refers to interest in sexual activity, and that interest may be for either solitary or shared activity. Studies have shown that desire and behavior are not necessarily connected (Ellis, Robb, & Burke, 2005). Sexual desire does not always lead to sexual activity, and people sometimes engage in sexual behavior even when they are not experiencing a sense of desire. Subjective eroticism also includes what has been termed *sensuosity* or *sensuality,* referring to the inner enjoyment of the whole sensual experience of sex, not just orgasm.

We know that the spectrum of human sexual preferences and behaviors is broad indeed, and the varieties of these activities have been subject to many medical, legal, and moral judgments. Although some professionals still use words such as *aberrant, deviant, abnormal,* and *perverse* to describe some sexual preferences and acts, two other terms have gained acceptance recently. The term *variant* implies that a particular sexual phenomenon varies from what is considered typical or that it exists in addition to more mainstream sexual behaviors. The term *paraphilia* carries with it the same connotations but is used more often to describe sexual preferences and behaviors that are viewed within a framework that considers them pathological or antisocial. There is continuing debate about whether such judgments are fairly applied to sexual behaviors, and some feel that the paraphilias should no longer be considered pathologies (Spitzer, 2005).

This chapter deals with sexual preferences and behaviors that are not as common as masturbation or heterosexual and same-gender sexual activity. We will look at variations that are part of the extensive mix of feelings, expressions, and activities from which components of any person's sexual individuality may be drawn. Studies of sexual behavior continue to demonstrate that even what would be considered "normal" samples of people exhibit a wide range of sexual stimuli and sexual experiences, some of which would even be considered illegal.

■ Varying Degrees of Sexual Interest and Activity

It is evident that different people have different degrees of interest in sex, pursue sexual activity with different amounts of energy, and participate in sex with varying degrees of frequency. Some people report thinking about sex and being interested in sexual matters several times each day, whereas others report that they seldom or never think about sex (Michael et al., 1994). Studies generally have confirmed that, on average, men's motivation for sex tends to be more constant than women's, and women seem to have more negative attitudes toward sexuality, although the level of sexual motivation varies a great deal among individuals. Women's motivation often waxes and wanes during the menstrual cycle, with the highest interest correlating to the time surrounding ovulation (Bullivant et al., 2004; Geer & Robertson, 2005; Okami & Shackelford, 2002). Some women have a more persistent level of interest and arousal (Blumberg, 2003; Leiblum & Nathan, 2001). It is logical to conclude that the more interested a person is in sex, the more he or she becomes sexually aroused and seeks sexual gratification. Yet some individuals feel guilty or anxious about their sexual preferences and interests and therefore tend to engage in sexual activity as seldom as possible. Others are influenced by their social networks to behave in certain ways. Still others have relatively low interest in sex but feel obligated by social or personal pressures to participate in a great deal of sexual behavior. Levels of sexual activity therefore do not necessarily correlate with levels of sexual desire (Levine, S. B., 2002).

Consistently responding positively to sexual cues is called **erotophilia;** responding negatively is termed **erotophobia.** The degree to which any individual is erotophilic or erotophobic obviously depends on a great many factors, including learning during childhood and adolescence. Erotophilia–erotophobia affects many dimensions of a person's sexual response. Erotophobic individuals tend to react negatively to sexual images, to have little interest in sexual activities, to be less likely to use contraceptives during inter-

course, and to experience more guilt about sexual behaviors and fantasies.

Some individuals possess a very high level of sexual desire or **hypersexuality,** whereas others have an abnormally low level of sexual interest, or **hyposexuality.** These might also be considered the extremes on the bipolar scale of erotophilia and erotophobia. And although some physical and emotional factors can cause a drop in sexual interest and activities, some people appear to have been fundamentally asexual throughout their lives. Most people, of course, tend to fall somewhere in the middle of the spectrum. Hypersexuality once seemed to generate more attention than hyposexuality; it was the extremely sexually active person whom society seemed to have the most trouble understanding and accepting. However, media attention recently has focused more on low sexual desire and how it might be overcome. In a society that has placed a high premium on sexual performance and exhibits a high level of interest in sex, such a shift in attitudes is not surprising (Levine, S. B., 2002). Nor is it surprising that women with high levels of sexual interest tend to be seen in a more negative light than are men with such interests, with the result that such women often struggle with a negative self-image (Blumberg, 2003).

Define promiscuity as you perceive it, and then describe any social or personal biases that you might bring to your definition.

Promiscuity is a term that is applied to the behavior of those who have sexual contact with several different partners on a relatively emotionally uninvolved, casual basis. It is a morally loaded label that also has been applied to those who have had more than one sexual partner. Because of the double standard of our society, it is more often applied negatively to women than to men. Although promiscuous men often are praised and admired for their impressive "records," promiscuous women often tend to suffer guilt, self-abasement, and social ostracism. It seems

---

erotophilia (air-aht-oh-FEEL-i-ah) consistent positive responding to sexual cues.

erotophobia (air-aht-oh-FOBE-i-ah) consistent negative responding to sexual cues.

hypersexuality an unusually high level of interest in and drive for sex.

hyposexuality an especially low level of sexual interest and drive.

promiscuity (prah-mis-KIU-i-tee) sharing casual sexual activity with many different partners.

likely from clinical evidence that some people simply enjoy sex with a variety of partners, perhaps for a limited period during their lives, and prefer to avoid emotional involvement for various reasons. If the individual approaches these encounters in a responsible, nonexploitative manner, takes appropriate steps to reduce the risks of transmitting disease, and emerges from them without negative feelings or inner conflict, there is no particular reason to judge the behavior as problematic (Blumberg, 2003).

Sometimes, however, having multiple sex partners may be motivated by unhealthier factors. These include unsatisfactory personal relationships, antagonism toward members of the opposite sex, and lack of self-respect. Some individuals may feel a need to prove themselves—for example, men who must live up to the macho ideal of having a long list of sexual "conquests" and women who use sex to experience a sense of power or control. A high level of sexual activity may become compulsive in some people. Compulsive sexual behavior sometimes is a response to some stressful situation, such as separation from parents upon entering college, the onset of early menopause, the experience of a significant loss, or some other traumatic event. There is evidence that among college students sexual compulsivity is associated with sexual behaviors that carry a higher risk of infection by sexually transmitted diseases and HIV (Dodge, Reece, Cole, & Sandfort, 2004).

The more compulsive form of hypersexuality, purportedly characterized by uncontrollable sexual drives as part of various mental illnesses, is known as **erotomania.** This condition has sometimes been called **nymphomania** in females and **satyriasis** in males. Again, the double standard seems to generate a far greater interest in women's compulsive sexual needs than in men's. "Nymphomaniac" often is used rather lightly and applied mistakenly to women who show any level of interest in sex. Yet "nymphomania" actually is difficult to define and has fallen victim to a great deal of interpretation rooted in prejudice, double standards, and male chauvinism (Groneman, 2000). The term is so vague and outmoded that it should be dropped altogether. Erotomania and other conditions of uncontrollable sexual desire (discussed in Chapter 16, "Sexual Consent, Coercion, Rape, and Abuse") are extremely rare; erotomania most often is probably a misdiagnosed form of compulsive sexual behavior (Montaldi, 2002). Very few people seek help for excessive sexual desire, and even among those who do, it is doubtful that many of the cases could truly be classified as erotomania. High rates of sexual behavior do tend to be correlated with unstable childhoods, relational instability, poor management of sexual risks, and use of tobacco, alcohol, and other drugs (Langstrom & Hanson, 2006; Strong et al., 2005).

People often worry about having too much or too little sexual desire and activity, especially if their degree of interest or activity differs significantly from that of a continuing sexual partner. The individual with low levels of sexual desire and behavior is often made to feel dull and uninteresting or as if there must be something wrong with him or her. Available evidence would suggest that wide variations in sexual desire and activity are part of the normal human sexual continuum. There is nothing inherently dangerous or harmful in thinking about sex and engaging in sexual activity very often, nor is there any harm or danger per se in a lack of sexual interest or activity (Levine, S. B., 2002).

Celibacy as a Choice   FOH

Celibacy, or not engaging in any kind of partnership sex, might be viewed with suspicion and surprise in a culture that places such a high premium on sexual gratification and enjoyment. Celibacy can be the result of life circumstances, such as imprisonment or the death of a partner; it may represent normal **asexuality,** characterized by a very low interest in sex; or it may be a conscious choice (Abbott, 2001). In a study of over 18,000 people, 1 percent indicated that they were asexual, and this response was correlated with a later onset of menarche in women, strong religious beliefs, low levels of education and socioeconomic status, and poor health (Bogaert, 2004).

Erotophobic individuals may be celibate out of guilt or fear about sexual issues. The term *asexuality* sometimes is used in reference to celibate individuals, although it can be misconstrued as suggesting that they have no sexual interest or arousal, which usually is not the case. Many people who report being celibate would rather not be but are unable to establish relationships or are part of a sexless relationship (Donnelly et al., 2001). The National Health and Social Life Survey (NHSLS) did find that 4 percent of men and 14 percent of women reported rarely or never thinking about sex. Fourteen percent of the men and 10 percent

erotomania (air-aht-oh-MAY-nee-ah) a very rare form of mental illness characterized by a highly compulsive need for sex.

nymphomania (nim-fa-MAY-nee-ah) a term sometimes used to describe erotomania in women.

satyriasis (sate-a-RYE-a-sus) a term sometimes used to describe erotomania in men.

celibacy (SELL-a-buh-see) choosing not to share sexual activity with others.

asexuality a condition characterized by a low interest in sex.

of the women in the survey reported that they had not had a sexual partner in the previous year (Laumann, Gagnon, et al., 1994).

Some priests and nuns vow to be celibate because their church requires it. Other people make such a choice because of their personal values. The recent child abuse scandal within the Roman Catholic Church has obscured the fact that many priests struggle with celibacy because of their heterosexual desires, with many eventually leaving to marry (Zoll, 2003). An increasing number of young to middle-aged adults in Western culture are choosing to be celibate. Some of these individuals are reacting to having tried various sexual lifestyles and finding them unfulfilling or destructive, others are looking for alternatives to the pressures brought about by the sexual revolution. They sometimes have found that the intensity of sex created tension in their relationships (Sobo & Bell, 2001). Concern over the spread of HIV also has made celibacy seem to be a less risky, healthier, and more acceptable choice of lifestyle for some individuals (Abbott, 2001). People who are HIV-positive often become celibate in their later years, partly because they do not want to risk infecting others, but also because they harbor anger or mistrust (Siegel & Schrimshaw, 2003).

Celibacy is not necessarily a symptom of a problem or of feelings of inadequacy. Some marriages become sexless eventually, but this is not necessarily a difficulty. Often, deep affection and respect between the partners provide adequate fulfillment for the couple, and sex is not a necessary component of their relationship. It is important to be reminded that sexuality is far more than an interaction of sex organs. Caressing, kissing, and other forms of physical sharing that are not overtly sexual can be deeply satisfying to some couples.

The Variability of Sexual Individuality

Statistical evidence highlights an interesting fact about human sexuality: Men in general seem more prone to participating in atypical sexual activities and straying more from established societal norms and standards than do women. All available statistics on the frequency of various nonstandard forms of sexual orientation and behavior show them to be more common in men than in women. However, men individually are more likely to stick to a rather narrow set of behaviors over time, while women exhibit more erotic plasticity, willing individually to try a broader spectrum of behaviors (Diamond, 2006; Okami & Shackelford, 2002).

Attempts have been made to explain this with both social and biological theories. It has been proposed that our culture traditionally has been more disapproving of female sexual expression and therefore has tended to discourage women from getting in touch

with their sexuality. For whatever social or political reason, a double standard with regard to sexual behavior has persisted in our culture. Men have been permitted, even expected, be more sexually active than women. Such an attitude offers one explanation for less involvement on the part of women in varied sexual practices, but it may not be the only one. Research shows that although women very much believe that a double standard still exists in North American culture, they tend personally not to support this double standard (Milhausen & Herold, 1999).

It is interesting to note that during childhood and adolescence, preferences for specific body types begin to develop and become refined. In one study, 511 children ranging in age from 6 to 17 were shown silhouettes of men and women of various body weights and with varying hip-to-waist ratios. The younger children tended to say that the very thin people looked best; that judgment gradually changed to average weight with the adolescents. It is known that adults tend to prefer female figures with a narrower waist and somewhat wider hips, and male figures with more similarity in the two measurements. The children and adolescents in the study, especially the adolescents, seemed to have the same preference (Connolly, Slaughter, & Mealey, 2004). This suggests strong social influences at relatively young ages on the development of some preferences.

There may also be some inborn biological propensities that cause male sexual behavior to exhibit greater diversity. Biologically based hypotheses have begun to receive higher levels of acceptance and scientific verification. It has been proposed that prenatal developmental differences make males more responsive than females to visual stimuli in learning sexual cues (Fisher, Aron, Mashek, Li, Strong, & Brown, 2002; Levine, 2003). Men may establish images of erotic arousal in response to early life experiences at certain critical periods of development. If the visual image indeed plays a larger role in sexual arousal in males than in females, men would be far more easily influenced by diverse and variable kinds of visual learning than would women. Further research is needed to explain this sexually differentiated characteristic (Okami & Shackelford, 2002).

■ Transgender Identities and Behaviors

Chapter 5 discussed theories concerning the development of gender identity and gender role and introduced transgender—sometimes called cross-gender—identities. Because of gender dualism in our culture—that is, the pressure to be either male or female—there has been a tendency to view transgender phenomena as pathological. More and more transgender individuals are affirming that their identities simply do not fit the dualistic model. Communication technologies such as the Internet have allowed "trans" individuals to develop better connections with other trans, alleviating potential loneliness and creating a stronger sense of community (Hill, 2005). This section presents various transgender behaviors and lifestyles, demonstrating the many ways humans express their transgenderism.

Before reading the section on transvestism, describe what you would consider a "typical" transvestite.

FOH Cross-Dressing: Transvestism

Definitions of cross-dressing behavior vary. The term *transvestite* has been applied to anyone who cross-dresses, or wears clothes of the opposite sex, for any reason. It also has been applied to individuals who feel driven to cross-dress, sometimes in association with sexual arousal. Many cross-dressers gain a greater sense of relaxation in escaping their usual gender roles. Cross-dressing certainly is not a new phenomenon; it has been identified in most cultures, from earliest recorded history through the Greco-Roman, Judeo-Christian-Muslim, and Renaissance periods (Bloom, 2002). Cross-dressing is found among heterosexual people, but also in people with a same-gender sexual orientation, bisexuals, and people with low levels of any sexual attraction or desire. Together these represent a very diverse group. Cross-dressed males sometimes are said to be "in drag."

One form of transvestism represents a fetishism in which a person is sexually attracted to some object of clothing usually worn by the opposite sex. For example, a male may become sexually aroused by viewing and touching various objects of women's underwear. He may find it even more exciting to actually wear the garments, usually as an accompaniment to masturbation or other sexual activity. In one study of 2,450 people drawn from a general population of Swedish adults ages 18 to 60, 2.8 percent of the males and 0.4 percent of the females reported at least one instance of cross-dressing associated with sexual arousal (Langstrom & Zucker, 2005).

The heterosexual male transvestite may become aroused by dressing completely in women's attire and makeup and adopting feminine mannerisms (see Figure 14.1). Sometimes there is only minimal sexual arousal associated with the activity, or the sexual arousal may eventually fade. Individuals often continue to cross-dress because it makes them feel more relaxed and emotionally open. These behaviors usually begin in childhood and become well established by adolescence. Sometimes they disappear by adulthood, but most often they do not.

There are no reliable statistics on the incidence of cross-dressing, but it is probably more common than generally believed. Another survey of sexual behavior

FIGURE 14.1 *Transvestism*

Those who dress in clothes of the opposite sex seem to derive sexual pleasure from doing so. Anthropologist Robert Monroe has noted that transvestism occurs more frequently in cultures in which the male assumes more of the economic burden than does the female.

indicated that 6 percent of men and 3 percent of women had had personal experience with cross-dressing (Janus & Janus, 1993). Although the evidence suggests that cross-dressing is more common in males, there are cases of women who have an erotic attachment to men's garments. At least in the limited number of female examples available, the drive toward cross-dressing seems less demanding than it typically is in

"No! No! No! . . . *You* Tarzan, *me* Jane!"

Source: By permission of Leigh Rubin and © Creators Syndicate, Inc.

Real People

Vincent: Living a Transgender Identity

Vincent was a college student who considered himself transgendered and resented having to be categorized as one sex or the other. He knew that anatomically he was fully male, and he had no intention of changing that. In fact, he said that he was very satisfied with his male body most of the time.

However, Vincent said that since he was quite young, he had come to value what he called his "feminine side." To him, this was made up of the soft, gentle, and sensitive aspects of his personality that felt very comfortable to him. He felt that the masculine and feminine sides that he experienced seemed quite distinct. He sometimes preferred to dress in women's clothes and use a female name. He tried to do this as discreetly as possible, but others on his dorm floor may once have noticed some women's clothes in his closet. Although he was not anxious to incur the wrath of anyone who might consider him somehow odd, he also seemed to have

a rather strong resolve not to hide his transgenderism with undue vigor. As he put it, "It's time for people to wake up to the fact that not everybody fits the same mold."

Vincent remained at the college and would occasionally surprise or shock people by wearing some article of female attire in a public setting. Some people on the campus openly expressed their distaste for these practices, feeling that he was being too flagrant in his propensities. He occasionally heard himself being called names, but he persisted in what he felt were valid educational efforts. He also made many friends and was an active participant in campus activities.

What is your reaction to Vincent's story? How would you have reacted if you lived on his dormitory floor? Would you have been shocked or disturbed by his cross-dressing? Would you be willing to be his friend?

---

male transvestites. Western society permits a wider range of fashion for women than for men. Few, if any, male outfits now would be deemed inappropriate for a woman. Conversely, men are quite specifically restricted from wearing most articles of female attire unless they are willing to risk ostracism and name-calling. This very different social context for male cross-dressing demands privacy and often subterfuge.

Some male transvestites participate in an underground subculture. There are organizations and magazines designed for men who experience a need to wear women's clothing to relieve tension and anxiety. Occasional regional gatherings are held for such individuals, with meetings on fashion and makeup techniques. The majority of the participants are heterosexuals, although there may be a higher proportion of gay and bisexual transvestites than has generally been believed. A study of 1,032 male cross-dressers found that 87 percent described themselves as heterosexual. All but 17 percent had been married, and 60 percent were married at the time of the study. Some hide their transvestism from their wives and cross-dress away from home; others inform their wives of the practice. The limited clinical evidence available indicates that some wives are able to accept their husbands' cross-dressing behaviors and integrate them into their lives (Monro & Warren, 2004; Rupp & Taylor, 2003).

There have been ongoing studies of boys ranging in age from 4 years through adolescence who have shown a preference for dressing in girls' clothing. When denied access to such garments, these boys even will fashion their own dresses from blankets, T-shirts, and other materials (Bailey, 2003). They also have tended to assume female roles during play and to exhibit distinctly feminine mannerisms. It is as yet impossible to predict which of these behaviors represent simple play activity and which are expressions of transgenderism.

Beyond Cross-Dressing: Autogynephilia

In the early 1990s, a particular type of transgender male came to the attention of researchers. Most typically, these were individuals who had had a relatively typical masculine childhood and were primarily heterosexual in terms of sexual attraction. In late childhood or adolescence they may have found themselves sexually aroused by women's undergarments or other clothing, resulting in trying on such garments (or fantasizing about them) and masturbating. (Being aroused by girls' undergarments is not unusual among boys.) For these men, the thoughts and images become quite strong, even obsessive, and they may fantasize frequently about being a woman, having a woman's body, or having a woman's sexual organs. This tendency is called **autogynephilia** (Blanchard, 1991, 2005).

While autogynephilia develops in association with heterosexual attraction and arousal and alongside typical masculine interests, the obsession with being a woman may eventually begin to compete with heterosexual attraction and desire. The sexual arousal accompanying the cross-dressing and fantasy may diminish and even compete with fantasies and desires about having sex as a woman and being sexually penetrated by a man. In this way, autogynephiles may become transsexuals and may want to go even farther by actually changing their bodies to be consistent with their sexual fantasies and desires (Bailey, 2003).

Transgender Lifestyles

An understanding of autogynephilia helps clarify why among males there are "gay transsexuals," or men who have long felt trapped in the body of the wrong sex and who are sexually attracted to men, and also "autogynephilic transsexuals," whose interest in becoming women grew out of strong sexual attractions toward women and then became internalized as a desire to become women themselves. Some people remain in their cross-dressed roles for days or even months at a time, depending on their life situation, often becoming comfortable with sustaining this identity. Transgendered individuals also may maintain separate lives more consistent with their anatomical gender for varying periods of time (Meyerowitz, 2002).

An interesting historical example is English writer William Sharp, who lived from 1855 to 1905. Over a period of some years, he created for himself the person of a woman he called Fiona MacLeod. He spent increasing proportions of time as Fiona, who emerged as a leading writer in the Scottish Celtic literary movement. In his later years, very little of the male William Sharp identity was left.

There is a spectrum of intensities among transgender persons that often reflects the degree of dissatisfaction they may experience with regard to their anatomy. Some transgenderists are very comfortable with their bodies and are content to cross-dress and adopt mannerisms of the other gender. Some transsexuals, however, feel a strong enough level of discomfort or disgust with their bodies, or a sufficient desire to have female genitals, to lead them to prefer not to have the sexual anatomy with which they were born (Mathy, 2002; Schrock & Reid, 2006).

Sex Reassignment for Transsexuals   F●H

Transsexuals may be troubled and unhappy because of feeling trapped in the wrongly sexed body and wishing for a different anatomy. Psychotherapy alone has not proved especially effective with transsexuals, but it does offer opportunities for them to explore their personal conflicts and options for dealing with their gender identity (Rehman et al., 1999). One recognized form of rehabilitative therapy is the hormonal and surgical transformation of the individual's external features into a form resembling the anatomy of the other sex (see Figure 14.2). This typically is part of a series of therapeutic interventions that would include living as a

■ **FIGURE 14.2** *Transsexualism*

Transsexuals are people who are one sex biologically but feel an identity with the opposite sex. Renée Richards faced many legal battles when she attempted to compete as a female tennis player after undergoing male-to-female surgery in the 1970s.

autogynephilia (otto-guy-nuh-FEEL-ee-ah) a tendency found in some males to become sexually aroused by obsessive thoughts and images of being female and having female attributes, or even female sex organs.

member of the desired gender for an extended period of time, both prior to and during the medical treatments. Clearly defined standards for evaluating the broader mental health issues of transgendered patients and proceeding with sex reassignment have been established by specialists in the field. To avoid patient dissatisfaction or regret following surgery, it is essential that these standards be strictly followed (Meyer et al., 2001; Meyerowitz, 2002; Olsson & Moller, 2006).

After being diagnosed as a candidate for sex reassignment, the individual must face the medical expenses of the process, which amount to tens of thousands of dollars. Most health insurance companies consider such processes elective and cosmetic and do not cover them. Sometimes, if a physician such as a psychiatrist is willing to indicate that reassignment is necessary to the person's future well-being, health insurance will cover part of the costs. The city of San Francisco has a health insurance program that will pay up to $50,000 for the sex reassignment procedures of municipal employees.

Anyone who desires advice about these matters should go to a medical center that specializes in such treatments. In North America, most gender clinics are designed to diagnose and treat gender identity disorders, as well as offering sex reassignment procedures. Typically, an individual is given a psychiatric evaluation, a series of psychological tests, and counseling. Then, if sex reassignment emerges as the most reasonable course of treatment, it begins with the trial period, a real-life test lasting up to two years. Usually, it is during this time that the person dresses and lives as a member of the desired sex while receiving adjustment counseling and appropriate legal advice concerning a name change, a new birth certificate, and a new driver's license (Meyer et al., 2001). Changing genders has been likened to migrating to another culture, because the individual must face new adjustments and seek acceptance in a new lifestyle (King, 2003; Schrock & Reid, 2006).

It is also during the real-life test that hormonal treatment usually begins. The changes brought about by hormone therapy, with the exception of a deepened voice in the female-to-male transsexual, are reversible should a decision be made not to continue the reassignment process. Female hormones administered to men cause breast enlargement and a feminine redistribution of fat. Although the growth of facial and body hair may be somewhat slowed, it is necessary to remove permanently unwanted beard and body hairs by electrolysis. Hormonal masculinization of the female, in addition to deepening the voice, suppresses menstruation and promotes growth of some facial and body hair. If the real-life test continues to confirm the individual's resolve to change sex, the surgical procedures are begun. The lowest possible dosages of hormones are recommended due to potential longer-term complications of hormonal therapy.

See "Changing Genders" on SexSource Online.

Although a detailed description of sex-change surgery is beyond the scope of this text, we will give a summary. In male-to-female surgery, the testes are removed, and an artificial vagina, clitoris, and labia are constructed from the sensitive skin of the penis and scrotum (see Figure 14.3). Breasts are fashioned through the use of mammary implants (see Figure 14.4). Following reassignment, male-to-female transsexuals usually report having longer, smoother, and more intense orgasms (DeCuypere et al., 2005; Lawrence, 2005).

FIGURE 14.3 *Postsurgical Male-to-Female Transsexual*
Following surgical procedures to construct a vulva and a vagina from sensitive penile and scrotal tissues, this individual's external genitals are hardly distinguishable from those of woman.

FIGURE 14.4 *Surgically Constructed Breasts*
In male-to-female transsexual surgery, the breasts may respond to hormone treatment; if not, they generally are augmented with implants.

Real People

Marilyn: Exploring Sex Reassignment

At age 17, Marilyn had talked with her high school counselor about wanting to change her sex. The counselor referred her to a therapist who specialized in sexual matters. Marilyn explained to the therapist that she had always felt more like a boy inside than a girl. In fact, she came dressed to the session in a manner that made her appear quite masculine. She wore jeans, a loose-fitting flannel shirt, and an athletic jacket, with a hat covering her short hair. After seeing a television talk show when she was 13 that featured transsexuals, she had begun to believe that this label indeed fitted her too.

The history that she described supported that self-diagnosis. She had always been interested in traditionally male activities and presently had a girlfriend with whom she was sexually involved. However, she also expressed frustration with the assumption that she was a lesbian, because she said she would much prefer to be a male in her sexual interactions. She had adopted her initials, M. J., as her nickname and preferred that her friends call her "Mike." She had negative feelings about her breasts and genitals, and she indicated a preference for having a penis. She had done some reading about the sex reassignment processes and was aware that they would require a large amount of money. She already had a job and was attempting to save funds for the future. Her mother, a single parent, had

been relatively uninvolved in her upbringing and expressed support for whatever direction M. J. wished to take.

The therapist put M. J. in touch with some organizations and clinics that specialized in supportive help for transsexuals and that carried out sex reassignment procedures. It was explained to her that she would have to be carefully tested to confirm that she was a good candidate for reassignment and that the entire process might well take several years. Her resolve to pursue this direction seemed strong, and she continued to see the therapist over a period of months as she began to establish preliminary contacts with the nearest gender identity clinic. About a year after her initial session with the therapist, M. J. was beginning the evaluative process to determine whether this particular clinic would consider initiating the legal and medical procedures that would lead to her reassignment as a male.

How do you react to M. J.'s story? Do you think she should be considering sex reassignment, or do you think she should be older before pursuing it? Do you think M. J. might simply be a "tomboy" and the professionals involved are overreacting? Do you believe M. J.'s feelings should be considered pathological, that is, an illness or disorder? Why or why not?

In female-to-male surgery, the breasts, uterus, and ovaries are first removed. There are two options for genital surgery. *Metoidioplasty,* a simpler and less expensive surgery, is the more typically chosen option today. The clitoris, which has been enlarged somewhat by testosterone therapy, is formed into a small penis, and the labia are formed to look like a small scrotum. Because the penis resulting from metoidioplasty is too small for penetrative sexual activity, most high-intensity female-to-male transsexuals choose the more complex and expensive procedure called *phalloplasty.* An artificial penis is created over several operations from skin taken from other parts of the body. A scrotum is also constructed, using tissue from the labia that is stretched by inserting increasingly larger silicon balls (see Figure 14.5). The clitoris

usually is left intact beneath the new penis and remains sensitive to sexual arousal. Most female-to-male transsexuals report orgasmic capacity following surgery, saying that their orgasms tend to be shorter but more powerful than they had been, although metoidioplasty seems to preserve orgasmic capability better than does the more extensive phalloplasty. Several techniques are being tried to simulate penile erection, ranging from the insertion of a plastic rod into a special canal within the constructed penis to surgical implantation of a special hydraulic system. Sometimes a canal is created through the middle of the penis so it can be used for urination. Patients with the erectile prosthesis tend to be more satisfied with the sexual outcomes (DeCuypere et al., 2005). Postsurgical transsexuals cannot reproduce, ejaculate, or menstruate.

■ **FIGURE 14.5** *Surgically Constructed Penis*

In female-to-male phalloplasty, the penis is constructed from forearm tissue or from labial and perineal tissue. The penis is not capable of erection in response to sexual arousal, but several inflatable devices are available that produce an erection, as shown in this photograph.

The standard medical protocol has been to restrict surgical intervention to transsexuals meeting highly selective criteria (Meyer et al., 2001). Clinical evidence and research suggest that sex reassignment can indeed lead to improved psychological and social adjustment for many individuals (Lippa, 2001; Wolfrandt & Neumann, 2001). Reviews of the world literature on this surgery indicate only a 10 to 15 percent failure rate with patients. In general, people seem subjectively satisfied with their sex reassignments. Dissatisfaction with the results was more common as the age of the patients increased and in cases where the person was not a carefully diagnosed, highly motivated transsexual (Olsson & Moller, 2006; Osborne & Wise, 2002; Rehman et al., 1999). In a study of 232 postoperative male-to-female transsexuals, none of the patients expressed outright regret about having undergone reassignment, and their level of satisfaction seemed to be related largely to how happy they were with their new bodies and how those bodies functioned (Lawrence 2003, 2005; Lawrence et al., 2005).

Transgender Identity and Sexual Orientation

One of the most interesting factors related to transgenderism is the fact that some transsexuals, both before and after changing their anatomical sex, are sexually attracted to members of their "newly" assigned gender. Studies of postsurgical female-to-male transsexuals have found that significant proportions of them are attracted to other men, just as some male-to-female transsexuals are attracted to women (Chivers & Bailey, 2000; Docter & Fleming, 2001). Such data are often confusing because conventional wisdom assumes that

people who would go through the trouble of changing their sex would surely want to be able to have sex with members of what has become the other gender. The fact that at least some men are autogynephilic transsexuals and may have been attracted to women in the first place offers one explanation. In fact, this information serves as a significant reminder that gender identity and sexual orientation may even be somewhat independent aspects of human sexuality (Mathy, 2001). Transsexuals who have changed their sex may be heterosexual, gay, lesbian, or bisexual in their transformed bodies. There are cases in which sexual orientation seems to change following sex reassignment. Some male-to-female transsexuals who considered themselves heterosexual (attracted to women) prior to their reassignments report having become more interested in and sexually active with men after their hormonal and surgical treatments (Daskalos, 1998; Lawrence et al., 2005). This probably is more common among autogynephilic transsexuals (Bailey, 2003).

Nevertheless, studies also suggest that there may be some correlation between childhood gender behavior and eventual sexual orientation. The majority of gay men and lesbians had a history as children of engaging in cross-dressing and cross-gendered games and of preferring playmates of the other gender. It has been estimated that only about one in seven of the gay males and lesbians actually would have been formally diagnosed as having a gender identity disorder as children, but that may be related chiefly to the lack of guidelines for making such diagnoses. Information of this sort suggests some interaction of factors in the formation of gender identity and sexual orientation, although the mechanisms of such interaction are completely unknown. One researcher has even postulated that transsexualism is at the far end of a continuum that includes same-gender sexual orientation (Bailey, 2003). The data also confirm that childhood gender behaviors are not wholly accurate predictors of eventual sexual orientation or identity.

Implications of Treating and Diagnosing Gender Identity Disorders

Using terms such as "treatment" in conjunction with a label such as "gender identity disorder" obviously implies that something is wrong that indeed requires therapy. This is a situation that many transgendered people resent. They believe that because their gender-related expressions and preferences do not harm or exploit others, the decision about whether any kind of treatment is indicated, and what type, should be left to them. Because sex reassignment is a complicated medical process, the medical profession has assumed the right and responsibility of deciding who will receive various treatment alternatives. Our society is only beginning to question this mode of decision making, but transsexuals do not always consider the present system fair to them (Schrock & Reid, 2006).

Another complicated issue involves the diagnosis of gender identity disorder during childhood or adolescence. The current edition of the American Psychiatric Association's *Diagnostic and Statistical Manual,* usually called the *DSM-IV,* has for the first time included some guidelines for determining whether a child has a gender identity disorder. These include a strong, persistent identification with the opposite sex, including the desire to cross-dress; behaving in transgender roles; and preferring playmates of that gender. Other criteria include expressed discomfort and dissatisfaction with their own sex and significant distress, self-hatred, or impairment of their lives because of the condition.

One difficulty in diagnosing children is that there are no clearly defined lines of "appropriate" gender behavior. We must be cautious not to stigmatize children who simply do not fit the gender expectations someone has created for them. There is evidence that boys and girls with gender identity disorders do indeed display behaviors that are less characteristic of their physical sex than do same-sexed controls (Bailey, 2003). These findings, and the diagnosis of gender identity disorders in childhood in general, raise questions about how such children should be treated. There is some evidence that children who are treated prior to the age of about 8 may be helped through therapy to become more comfortable with roles consistent with their anatomy. There is also evidence that adolescents who want to change their sex and then subsequently do so in adulthood tend to have very stable psychological functioning (Fink, 2005; Kleinplatz & Moser, 2005; Meyer et al., 2001; Smith, Cohen, & Cohen-Kettenis, 2002).

Several studies have examined men who as children stated that they wanted to be girls and who acted out their wishes through dress and play activities. Often these men have not carried their desire to be female into adulthood, leading the researchers to conclude that the likelihood of adult transsexualism or transvestism cannot yet be reliably predicted in childhood.

What treatment do you think should be made available to children who have been diagnosed with a gender identity disorder?

Because most parents do not recognize or seek help for gender identity disorders in their children, the issues around treating children and adolescents remain controversial. How early should hormonal or surgical treatment be used, especially given that not all transgendered young people grow up to be high-intensity transsexuals? If transsexualism could be identified prior to puberty, hormonal intervention could take place prior to the development of secondary sex characteristics, making the process far simpler and more effective. While some hormonal treatments create effects that are reversible, certain other treatments must be considered nonreversible (Meyer et al., 2001). The ethical issues and objections surrounding these questions obviously are complicated and are far from being resolved.

■ The Desire to Enhance Sexual Arousal

Being a sexual human being, expressing that sexuality, and experiencing sexual responsiveness involve far more than our sex organs. Human senses, especially sight and touch, play a major role in sexual individuality. Our sensory input, emotions, and thought processes blend in our brains to promote or inhibit sexual desire and arousal in ways that are only poorly understood at this point. We do know that the sensations of sexual stimulation and orgasm are controlled by the pleasure centers in the limbic system of the brain.

Human beings whose personalities are on the erotophilic side of the spectrum may spend a great deal of time and energy perfecting and enhancing their sexual experiences. Just as some people become good cooks and connoisseurs of great food, so do some people take pride in learning the sexual techniques that will provide optimal levels of enjoyment and satisfaction for them and their partners. As men and women learn the very individualized triggers and enhancers for their own sexual arousal, they find many different avenues to explore.

Use of Erotica and Pornography

Nudity and a variety of sexual acts have been depicted in statuary, pottery, and paintings since ancient times. It is estimated that in the United States today the sale of sexually explicit media—magazines, videotapes, and material accessed via the Internet—is a multibillion-dollar-a-year business. Such materials are often associated with sexual arousal. Researchers for the NHSLS reported that 23 percent of the males and 11 percent of the females surveyed had watched an X-rated movie or video within the previous year. Twenty-two percent of the men and 4 percent of the women had visited a club that had nude or seminude dancers within the same time period (Laumann, Gagnon, et al., 1994).

While women sometimes have negative reactions to their male partners' viewing of erotic materials, this does not seem to be representative of women in general. In fact, women on average seem to be relatively neutral or even mildly positive with regard to pornography viewing by their intimate partners (Bridges, Bergner, & Hesson-McInnis, 2003). There is also evidence that, at least in males, continued exposure to the same pornographic material results in habituation, meaning that sexual arousal in response to the same material decreases over time. Therefore, one reason why erotica and pornography are such strong businesses is that customers continually seek new material to view (Attwood, 2005). Sexually explicit media continue to be extremely controversial, as we will explore further in Chapter 15, "Sex, Art, the Media, and the Law."

Sexual Devices and Toys

Although sexual-enhancement toys are nothing new, their availability to the general public has been increasing since the 1960s. Sex shops sell a variety of devices designed to heighten sexual arousal and pleasure. Mail-order catalogs and Internet sites are easily found. The devices vary in their effectiveness, and each has advocates who have found that it satisfies their tastes and needs. Most individuals who give sex toys a try use them only occasionally or as an experiment. A few people come to rely on them as constant aids to sexual satisfaction.

Vibrators probably are the most common sexual aid, providing an intense vibration to the genitals or other sensitive body parts. There are battery-operated and plug-in models. Some are cylindrical or penis-shaped, in a variety of lengths and widths. Others come with several attachments to be used for stimulating different sex organs. Vibrators sometimes are recommended for people who have trouble reaching orgasm, especially women. The rapid, localized vibration is often helpful in triggering the orgasmic reflex. Vibrators can, of course, be used for masturbation or integrated into shared activities.

Cylindrical dildos, made of everything from ivory to clay, have existed for at least 2,500 years. Today they usually are made of soft, flexible plastics. Although they may be used for solitary masturbation, with vaginal or anal insertion, dildos are also used in some partnership sex. Plastic penis extenders are designed to fit over the head of a man's penis, supposedly to make it seem longer during sex. Actually, such devices rarely yield much extra pleasure for either partner and may even reduce sexual sensations for the man. NHSLS data reported that during the previous year 2 percent of both the women and the men had used a vibrator or dildo, and 1 percent of the men and

2 percent of the women had used "other sex toys" (Laumann, Gagnon, et al., 1994). A survey of 7,700 people ages 18 to 90 found that 10.2 percent said they had used sex toys with a partner, although it is believed that even more people tend to use such devices during masturbation. Sex toy use was most common among persons ages 30 to 49 (Catania, 1997).

Some men enjoy wearing various bondage or pressure devices, including metal, leather, or rubber rings that fit around the base of the penis and scrotum. Although these "cock rings" are advertised as being helpful in maintaining erection, there is no particular evidence that they do so, and, in fact, if they are too tight they can cause some damage. A variation on this is the clitoral or French tickler, worn at the base of the penis and having projections on the top surface. The projections are supposed to press on the female's clitoris during vaginal intercourse, providing extra stimulation.

Sexual Fantasy

FOH

The NHSLS found that 19 percent of women and 54 percent of men fantasize about sex at least once a day (Laumann, Gagnon, et al., 1994). Mental images, daydreams, and fantasies seem to be a significant part of most people's sexual individuality. Such imagery may be fleeting and incomplete or lengthy and detailed. Sexual fantasy is not necessarily representative of a person's sexual behavior. For example, most men who fantasize about forcing a partner to have sex with them would never carry out such an action. Studies indicate that human beings fantasize about many sexual practices in which they would never actually participate in real life and sometimes experience these fantasies negatively. Fantasies may also reflect areas of sexual longing and frustration in a person's life (Byers, Purdon, & Clark, 1998).

Studies find some gender differences in the typical fantasy lives of males and females. Sexual fantasies tend to begin between the ages of 11 and 13, with males usually having their first fantasies at earlier ages than females and feeling more positive and guilt-free about them (Byers, Purdon, & Clark, 1998; Hicks & Leitenberg, 2001). Men's fantasies tend to be more active, impersonal, and visually oriented, whereas women's fantasy themes generally are more passive and romantic. Women who have fantasies of forced sex tend to be more erotophilic, interested in a range of sexual activities, and more sexually experienced (Sierra, Ortega, & Zubeidat, 2006; Strassberg & Lockerd, 1998).

Sexual fantasies have been categorized into four main groups: *exploratory,* including themes such as group sex, mate swapping, and same-gender behavior; *intimate,* with themes of passionate kissing, oral sex, making love outdoors, and mutual masturbation; *impersonal,* including sex with strangers, looking at pornography, watching others engage in sex, and fetishism; and *sadomasochistic,* with themes such as whipping, spanking, and forceful sex. Men tend to have more fantasies in all four of these categories, but the greatest proportion for both sexes is in the intimate category. The most common sexual fantasies involve having sex with a past, new, or imaginary partner or having sex in various settings and positions. The fewest number of fantasies among both men and women reflect impersonal or sadomasochistic themes (Friedman & Downey, 2000; Hicks & Leitenberg, 2001; Sierra, Ortega, & Zubeidat, 2006).

The kinds of sexual fantasies people experience— their length and degree of explicitness—seem to be determined to a large degree by the amount of guilt they feel about sex. As might be expected, the less guilt people experience and the more liberal their attitudes about sex, the longer and more explicit their fantasies tend to be. In general, sexual fantasies do not seem to be indications of an inactive sex life or dissatisfaction with sex. Fantasies occur more often in people who have high rates of sexual activity and are relatively happy with their sexual lives. Sexual fantasies do sometimes produce guilt or other unpleasant reactions (Byers, Purdon, and Clark, 1998; Friedman & Downey, 2000).

Why do you think sexual fantasies occur more often in people who have high rates of sexual activity and are relatively happy with their sex lives?

Different people have different levels of imaginative ability and use it in very individualized ways to enhance sexual arousal and gratification. Sexual fantasies can be one of the most powerful avenues to sexual arousal. Sex therapists often encourage people to make use of their "inner erotica."

Fetishism

Fetishism is usually defined as finding sexual excitement in objects, articles of clothing, or the textures of particular materials not usually considered to be sex-related in themselves. Sometimes parts of the body not usually considered sexually arousing are included in the definition. There are many degrees of fetishism, ranging from those mild preferences that accompany most sexual relations to an intense drive and complete substitution of the fetish for any other form of sexual gratification.

Certain things are commonly held as fetishes, including underwear, soft and silky clothing, rubber, and leather. Women's breasts can have an almost fetishistic attachment for some men, and occasionally feet are

found to be sexually arousing. The inner mechanisms by which sexual fetishism develops are unknown, but it is typical for the fetishist to have experienced sexual arousal in association with the object at some point in her or his life. Use of the fetish during masturbation is most typical; in this case, the object is fondled, rubbed on the genitals, viewed, or used for direct stimulation of sex organs. Some males ejaculate in or on the object. Fetishes sometimes are integrated into shared activities, but this may create some emotional discomfort for the fetishist's partner.

Most fetishes are harmless and inoffensive to others. However, they sometimes are carried to extremes that may have negative implications for others. It is not uncommon to read newspaper accounts of an adolescent male who has entered someone's home to touch the feet of a sleeping girl or to steal some of her undergarments. True **kleptomania,** which involves sexual excitement when stealing, and **pyromania,** in which the individual derives sexual arousal from setting fires, are considered forms of fetishism.

Fetishes are a poorly understood facet of sexual individuality. Because they usually are socially innocuous, they have not generated much attention among sex researchers. It is possible that someone who is inordinately sexually attached to a fetish, to the exclusion of other forms of sex, may be exhibiting some signs of emotional insecurity or stress worthy of professional consultation. This level of fetishism would be considered a paraphilia.

Varying the Numbers

Partly because of social standards that place sex within the context of an intimate and romantic one-to-one relationship, sex for more than two has generally been considered inappropriate in Western culture. In other cultures, large orgies are sometimes a part of rites or religious ceremonies. In our culture, sex among more than two people more typically involves experimentation that develops unplanned out of some other social activity. It may be seen as a way to enhance the usual arousal patterns. Of the people interviewed in the NHSLS, 1 percent of the women and 13 percent of the men indicated that they found group sex very appealing, although they had not necessarily participated in it (Laumann, Gagnon, et al., 1994).

fetishism (FEH-tish-i-zum) sexual arousal triggered by objects or materials not usually considered sexual.

kleptomania extreme form of fetishism in which sexual arousal is generated by stealing.

pyromania sexual arousal generated by setting fires.

Real People

Craig: A Harmless Fetish Worries a Young Groom

Following a class in human sexuality, a male graduate student named Craig asked to speak with me in private to talk about a personal sexual concern. In my office, he nervously described his plans for marriage in two months and said that there was an aspect of his sexuality that bothered him. He went on to explain that he became sexually aroused by touching soft blankets and often enjoyed lying on a blanket during masturbation or intercourse. He was also quite certain that his partiality to blankets resulted from his earliest masturbatory experiences, in which he would rub his penis against a blanket.

I told Craig that the fetish did not seem particularly troublesome, and some further questioning elicited other important facts about his preference. Basically he had very open and positive attitudes toward his sexuality and felt concern only about his mild blanket fetish. Of special importance was the fact that he did not feel compelled or driven to become sexually aroused by blankets, instead employing them only when convenient. His fiancée not only had been told about his inclinations but found the situation humorous. She had assured Craig that she would be happy to cooperate in the use of blankets in their sexual experiences whenever he wished. They were both highly satisfied with their present sexual relationship. On the basis of this information, it was concluded that if Craig could come to accept his blanket fetish as a desirable, harmless part of his sexual responsiveness, there was no reason to see it as a problem or a sign of sexual disturbance. Before leaving the counseling session, he sighed with great relief and said that he felt confident he could feel very positively about the fetish as long as he did not have to view it as sick or abnormal.

What is your opinion about Craig's interest in soft blankets? Instead of reassuring him, should I have discouraged the fetish and encouraged him to stop using it? What do you think of this outcome?

I was invited to Craig's wedding, and as a wedding gift I gave the couple a king-size soft blanket. They seemed appreciative. What do you think about this gift?

Group sex can apply to a variety of situations, ranging from threesomes **(troilism** or **ménage à trois)** to large groups. Among college students surveyed, 13 percent of the men and 10 percent of the women reported having participated in a sexual threesome (Elliott & Brantley, 1997). The activity may involve one or more persons simply observing a couple engaging in sex or actual physical interaction among all present. Probably the most common form of group sex occurs when more than one couple engage in sexual activity but each couple remains separate from the other(s). A group in which everyone participates with one another may be called an **orgy,** although this term is somewhat outmoded. The incidence of such behavior is uncertain. Available evidence suggests that it is not commonly a continuing or regular form of sexual behavior and instead usually represents an occasional episode.

There are, of course, other implications to group sex. The elements of exhibitionism, voyeurism, and same-gender sexual interaction that are natural by-products of group activities are sought by some partic-ipants and upsetting to others. There is always the risk of generating discord among participants, because it is difficult to devise shared activities that will help everyone feel involved, cared for, and satisfied. Possessiveness and jealousy may easily arise, or spontaneity may be destroyed by an individual who becomes too autocratic or ritualized. As with any kind of shared intimacy, later nonsexual social contacts between the people involved may feel awkward and strained. Group sex may accompany mate swapping, also called swinging, as well as other variations on extra-relational sex. By the end of the twentieth century, swing clubs had become even more popular, perhaps

troilism (TROY-i-liz-um) sexual activity shared by three people.

ménage à trois (may-NAZH-ah-TRWAH) another name for troilism.

orgy (OR-jee) group sex.

through Internet contacts, and were believed to number about 400 in the United States. However, the swinging phenomenon has not been studied for many years (Jenks, 1998).

■ Atypical and Potentially Problematic Sexual Connections

As earlier sections of this book have indicated, human sexual desire and behavior are extremely variable and may be associated with a wide range of relational circumstances and objects of attraction. Sometimes sexual practices fall enough outside societal norms that they are considered paraphilias, or at the very least atypical. In some cases, they may become problematic because of their potential consequences for the individual participant or for others who may be affected by the behavior. This section deals with some of those sexual interests.

The Sex Worker Industry

Like anything that can provide people with pleasure, sex has in some situations become a commodity. Both male and female prostitutes, or sex workers, participate in sexual activity for money. Often called the world's oldest profession, prostitution has recently been explained by some observers as representing the only way some women in a male-dominated world have been able to survive (Bullough & Bullough, 1997; Parsons, 2005). Prostitution has met with varying degrees of tolerance throughout history and in different societies. A prevalent attitude has been that prostitution represents exploitation and victimization, primarily of women. However, a countering set of opinions suggests that sex workers should have a right to make their living in this manner free from harassment or interference by various authorities (Vanwesenbeeck, 2002). In Canada, exchanging money for sex is not illegal, although many of the actions associated with procuring sex are against the law. Windsor, Ontario, a Canadian city that borders Detroit, Michigan, has been able to manage commercial sex workers in ways that prevent their victimization and keep them from being isolated in any sort of "red light district." The city has at the same time been able to maintain its image as a family-oriented and safe city (Lewis et al., 2005; Maticka-Tyndale, Lewis, & Street, 2005).

Male sex workers who serve women have been known as gigolos or, more recently, as escorts. However, escorts sometimes are just that—companions for some social event. Almost no empirical data have been gathered on gigolos or male companions. More typi-

cally, male sex workers engage in sexual activity with other males. Some young male prostitutes consider themselves heterosexual and view their same-gender involvement purely as a business venture. The longer they work as prostitutes, however, the more likely they are to think of themselves—and be identified by their peers—as gay. Male **hustlers** tend to work full-time as sex workers on the street or in other locations. Some particularly good-looking and well-mannered male prostitutes may eventually become attached to an older, affluent man or become more highly paid **call boys.** Research suggests that male sex workers do not always engage in safe sex practices, but their rate of HIV infection does not seem to be much higher than that of other groups (Disogra, Marino, & Minichiello, 2005; Minichiello et al., 2000; Weinberg, Worth, & Williams, 2001).

Male sex workers usually are expected to have an orgasm during a paid sexual encounter. Given the realities of male sexual response, particularly the refractory period, this limits the numbers of clients a male can serve in one day. Female sex workers, in contrast, are not limited by this physiology and typically do not experience orgasm in their paid encounters. The most commonly requested behavior from female sex workers is fellatio, and the next most common is vaginal intercourse. Both are intended more for the male partner's orgasm than the sexworker's.

Men seem to seek out prostitutes either out of a need for intimacy or out of a desire for more variety in their sex activities (Monto, 2001; Xantidis & McCabe, 2000). A study of 612 men in Australia found that 23.4 percent of them had paid for sex at least once and that the sex-worker clients were more likely than the non-clients to be older, less likely to have an education beyond high school, and less likely to have had a regular sexual partner during the previous six months other than a casual partner. They indicated that the main reasons they had paid for sex were to satisfy sexual needs, the fact that it was easier and less complicated to pay for the encounter, and the fact that it was entertaining (Pitts et al., 2004). Studies of female street sex workers have found that many of them do, in fact, enjoy intercourse and oral sex with their customers and also enjoy sex with their boyfriends or husbands as well. Neither the image of sex workers as "happy hookers" nor their depiction as depressed victims of childhood sexual abuse seems particularly accurate. Although a substantial number of sex workers have a history of drug abuse, and some are clinically depressed, most have voluntarily chosen their work

hustlers male street prostitutes.

call boys highly paid male prostitutes.

(Chudakov et al., 2002; Morrison & Whitehead, 2005). In interviews of female sex workers who were mothers, it was clear that they faced special problems as parents that often were unaddressed by social agencies (Sloss & Harper, 2004).

The most common street name given to female sex workers is **hookers.** Although **brothels,** or houses of prostitution, can still be found, they have largely been replaced by **streetwalkers** who work for **pimps** and by **massage parlor** workers (see Figure 14.6). Much of the sexual servicing of clients now takes place indoors rather than in more public venues (Thukral, 2005). **Call girls** tend to be more highly paid prostitutes who cater to a more exclusive clientele.

There is controversy over whether the sex worker industry actually constitutes a victimless line of business. Research continues to demonstrate that many sex workers have a background of alcohol and drug abuse and of sexual and physical abuse that presumably played a role in leading them to prostitution. Sex work also can be a dangerous job in which women and men may be raped, beaten, robbed, or forced to perform various sexual acts against their will. Another increasingly serious concern is the spread of HIV or other sexually transmitted diseases through prostitution (Hansen, Lopez-Iftikhar, & Alegria, 2002; Reback et al., 2005; Surratt, Kurtz, Weaver, & Inciardi, 2005). Male clients of female sex workers typically prefer not to wear a condom and, in fact, may pay extra to avoid doing so. The sex workers themselves may also prefer not to bother with condoms or may be uninformed about

their importance (Bucardo et al., 2004; Jackson, Sowinski, Bennett, & Ryan, 2005). However, it has also been claimed that a relatively small amount of disease transmission actually results from prostitution and that this amount would be reduced if prostitution were decriminalized and regulated. Although absolute protection cannot be guaranteed for the prostitute or the client, any man seeking sex with a prostitute should wear a condom throughout the sexual activity. Clients of male sex workers should insist that they wear a condom in order to somewhat reduce the risk of HIV transmission.

Of increasing concern among professionals is the number of sex workers who are adolescents, ranging in age from 13 to 18. Girls are particularly susceptible to becoming prostitutes if they have a poor self-image, have run away from home, have friends who are already prostitutes, or are seeking an adult on whom they can depend. Pimps quite often fill this need by showering a girl with attention and gifts, developing a romantic attachment to her, and then using the relationship to entice the girl into prostitution. Most experts in this area believe that one way to reduce or eliminate adolescent female prostitution would be to address social problems, such as poverty and sexual abuse, that sometimes lead girls to the activity in the first place. Worldwide, there is growing concern about girls and women being tricked or sold into sex-trade trafficking. They often are promised the hope of a better life, only to be smuggled into other countries to work as prostitutes and forced to give the money they earn to their "owners." Increasing pressure is being put on nations to enact legislation prohibiting human trafficking and to punish offenders. Sex-trade trafficking has been particularly problematic in Europe and Asia, where laws governing such matters are extremely diverse. When one country passes tough legislation, traffickers may find it easy to move their sex slaves to a neighboring country.

Close Encounters

There are several forms of sexual connection that involve some form of contact with a typically unknown

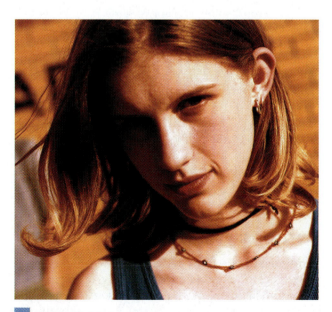

FIGURE 14.6 *Streetwise*

Young girls are particularly vulnerable to becoming prostitutes if they have a poor self-image, have run away from home, have friends who are already prostitutes, or are seeking an adult to care for them.

hookers street name for female prostitutes.

brothels houses of prostitution.

streetwalkers female prostitutes who work on the streets.

pimps men who have female prostitutes working for them.

massage parlors places where women can be hired to perform sexual acts under the guise of giving a massage.

call girls highly paid female prostitutes who work by appointment with an exclusive clientele.

and often unwilling participant. The unknowing person who is sought out for such a sexual connection may be a victim to the degree that she or he has participated unwillingly in someone else's sexual activity. The degree of victimization may range from feeling some petty annoyance to being seriously traumatized by the experience.

Obscene Telephone Calls

Men who have strong feelings of insecurity and inadequacy have a tendency to engage in obscene telephone calls, a condition sometimes called *telephone scatologia*. Their phone calls to women, or occasionally other men, represent a way to anonymously assert their sexuality without having to face a frightening social contact. Because their calls are usually spiced with sexual obscenities designed to shock or surprise women particularly, the behavior may also reflect some negative attitudes toward women. Sometimes such calls merely represent a prank, but they also may become a continuing form of sexual release, often accompanied by masturbation. It is very rare for an obscene telephone caller to follow up the call with any sort of actual contact with the victim. The best way to react to such a call is to hang up immediately, without comment, and then use call-tracing methods while reporting the call to the telephone company or law enforcement.

Consensual Telephone Sex

Another form of sexual encounter, which involves a professional sex worker, is represented by the "900" and sometimes "800" telephone numbers people can call to reach those willing to converse in a sexually provocative way over the phone or to access someone else talking in this manner (see Figure 14.7). Most callers to dial-for-sex services apparently are men who typically masturbate during their phone call. In a survey of college students, 13 percent of the men and 7 percent of the women said they had used phone-sex lines (Elliott & Brantley, 1997). There is very little research on telephone sex at this point, but it may well represent a relatively harmless, and certainly safe, form of sexual encounter.

See "Sharon: Phone Sex" on SexSource Online.

Internet Websites and Chat Lines

The Internet has also provided ways for people to carry on sexually suggestive or explicit communications with relative anonymity. Websites such as My-

■ **FIGURE 14.7** *Consensual Telephone Sex*

Dial-for-sex services allow callers to reach women or men who will talk in a sexually provocative manner. Because of concerns about the easy access of minors to "dial-a-porn," some telephone companies have imposed stricter controls to prevent calls from minors.

Space allow people to post photographs and personal information, much of which is sexually oriented. A great deal of media attention has been paid to the use of such sites by adult sexual predators who attempt to connect with adolescents for sexual purposes. Although it is sometimes suggested that such contact represents a way of replacing face-to-face relationships, it may also enhance relationships. Chat lines are preferred by women over the more explicit erotic sites (Cooper, 2000). For a small proportion of regular chat line visitors, the behavior becomes compulsive and is associated with difficulties within their personal relationships. Many Internet users find it a relatively quick way to make contact with potential partners for dating or sex and may exchange phone numbers for future contact (Carvalheira & Gomes, 2003).

Frotteurism and Toucherism

Frotteurism is a term that applies to gaining sexual enjoyment from pressing or rubbing one's genitals against another, unknown person in some anonymous setting. Crowded places such as elevators, subways, or

frotteurism (frah-TOUR-izm) gaining sexual gratification from anonymously pressing or rubbing one's genitals against others, usually in crowded settings.

theaters are common locations in which the **frotteur** may operate, because the close contact usually will go unnoticed. **Toucherism** refers to the intimate touching of an unknown person's body, typically on the buttocks or breasts. It is sometimes considered a subcategory of frotteurism. Little is known about frotteurism or toucherism, but professionals again assume that these behaviors represent a way for insecure people to seek out minimal physical contact with someone who is sexually appealing to them. The act probably is often followed by masturbation in private.

FOH Exhibitionism

Exposing the genitals to someone else for sexual pleasure is called **exhibitionism.** Usually, the person who commits this act is a man who exposes his penis to children or to an adult woman, although women sometimes gain sexual pleasure from exposing their breasts. The exhibitionist may go to great pains to make it seem as though he was caught undressing or urinating so that the victim will be less prone to report it as a crime. People who are arrested for such behavior are charged with indecent exposure or public lewdness. The repeat male exhibitionist usually gains pleasure from shocking others with the sight of his penis, thereby gaining some sort of confirmation of his male power.

What might motivate a man to expose his penis to others? A woman to expose her breasts?

It is apparent that many people display some degree of exhibitionism in their attempts to appear and

"You don't often see a real silk lining, these days . . ."
Source: Copyright © Punch/Rothko.

feel sexy. Bikinis for women and men, see-through clothing, and tight trousers and blouses all attest to this fact. Some women add extra padding to their bras to emphasize their breasts, and some males admit to adding extra padding to their genital areas occasionally. These are subtle forms of exhibitionism. Nudity is obviously a form of exhibitionism, although it may have few, if any, sexual connotations. People shower together in gym locker rooms, and at least some of them report feeling enjoyment in being nude together with other people. There seem to be few sexual implications of nudity in actual nudist camps or on nude beaches, and in fact attaching sexual meanings to nudism in these settings generally is frowned upon. It can be expected, however, that in a society that typically requires the sex organs to be covered, a sense of liberation and sexual pleasure might sometimes accompany the uncovering of these organs in the presence of other people.

A study of 2,450 Swedish people ages 18 to 60 found that 3.1 percent of the respondents reported at least one incident of sexual arousal because of exposing their genitals to a stranger. Those who had done so were more likely to be male and to have more psychological problems than other respondents (Langstrom & Seto, 2006). Because such behaviors generally are considered antisocial, exhibitionism is one of the more common sexual offenses for which men are arrested in Europe, the United States, and Canada. Various treatment programs are designed to help these individuals channel their sexual energies into more acceptable directions, and some medications have proved successful in treating their compulsive behaviors (Abouesh & Clayton, 1999).

The motivations behind exhibitionism vary among individuals. Although exhibitionism often is found in the criminal and sexual histories of rapists and child abusers, it typically stems from the exhibitionist's feelings of inadequacy and inferiority. In exposing his penis, a man seeks reassurance of his maleness and his masculinity. There are probably some aggressive motives as well, because the victim may react strongly enough to the situation that the exhibitionist creates a degree of emotional distress. If a victim does not react with any particular surprise or fear upon being confronted by an exhibitionist, his primary source of gratification is absent. Public exhibitionism can be

> **frotteur** one who practices frotteurism.
>
> **toucherism** gaining sexual gratification from the touching of an unknown person's body, such as on the buttocks or breasts.
>
> **exhibitionism** exposing the genitals to others for sexual pleasure.

offensive to the individual who, without consenting, is forced to see someone else's sex organs. This is not necessarily a seriously harmful event, but it can be emotionally exploitative. Whenever possible, the best response to an exhibitionist is probably to ignore him. The police or other authorities may also be contacted and asked to take action.

Voyeurism

Gaining sexual pleasure from observing others who are nude or disrobing or engaging in sexual acts is called **voyeurism.** There is certainly an element of voyeurism in most of us, and it is quite natural to be interested in other people's genitals and body form. The NHSLS found that watching a partner undress was the second most appealing of all sexual practices, after vaginal intercourse. The survey also reported that 16 percent of the women interviewed and about 33 percent of the men found the idea of "watching others do sexual things" at least somewhat appealing (Laumann, Gagnon, et al., 1994). In a survey of American college students, 13 percent of both the women and the men said they had taken photographs of nudity or sexual acts, and 5 percent indicated that they had used a video camera during sex (Elliott & Brantley, 1997). In the Swedish study cited previously, 7.7 percent of the respondents indicated that they had experienced at least one incident of sexual arousal while spying on others having sex (Langstrom & Seto, 2006).

The prevalence of sexually explicit media materials and strip clubs provides ample evidence of the voyeuristic needs of the public (Frank, 2005). Voyeuristic behavior becomes more offensive when the voyeur, or "peeper," goes out of his or her way to peer into windows of bedrooms or to spy on people in public bathrooms to satisfy his or her needs. Voyeurs tend to be younger males in their early twenties, usually unmarried or separated; about 25 percent are married. Very few seem to have any serious mental disorders, but most have had unsatisfactory sexual relationships. Voyeurs usually are interested in viewing strangers and normally do not interact physically with their victims. Nonetheless, the act is an obvious violation of another's right to privacy. Again, it may not harm the victim, and in fact the voyeur's presence may never be known, but it is an exploitative act. Because voyeurism is less easily detected than other sexual proclivities, it is not reported to authorities as frequently as behaviors such as exhibitionism.

It is certainly true that men are implicated in these forms of sexual connection far more often than are women, and the scanty statistics available seem to confirm that males do indeed find such behaviors sexually arousing, more so than females. However, social attitudes and values may also be operating here. It has been suggested, for example, that if a man is standing outside an open window watching a woman undress, he will be arrested for being a voyeur. However, if the situation were reversed, with the woman watching the man undress beyond the open window, it would still be the man who would be arrested—for exhibitionism.

Sadomasochism

Sadomasochism (or S & M) is probably the least understood of the relatively common routes to sexual arousal and connection. The sexual activities involved often are popularly described with the acronym BDSM, standing for bondage and discipline, dominance and submission, and sadism and masochism (or "slave" and "master"). Practitioners of BDSM sometimes refer to more conventional sexual interests as "vanilla," although BDSM interests may coexist with vanilla desires and behaviors (Kleinplatz & Moser, 2004). The term includes a whole range of sexual behaviors that seem to fit into four general themes: *hypermasculinity,* involving excretion or excrement and binding of the genitals; *administration or receipt of pain; humiliation,* usually involving dominance and submission with verbal put-downs or the whipping of one person; and *physical restraint* or bondage, involving tying up or restraining all or part of the body (Santilla, Sandnabba, Alison, & Nordling, 2002). Hypermasculinity practices are associated more with males, especially gay men, while humiliation is associated more with females and heterosexual men (Alison et al., 2001).

It has been traditional to define the **sadist** (or "dom") as the partner who derives sexual pleasure from being in the dominant role, perhaps inflicting, or threatening to inflict, some usually negative stimulus on another person, and the **masochist** (or "sub") as the individual who is aroused by being in the submissive, receptive role. These are simplistic definitions, because many people seem to be able to enjoy either role. Sadism and masochism are opposite sides of the same coin and tend to accompany each other, even though one may dominate the other at any given time.

---

voyeurism (VOYE-yur-i-zum)   sexual gratification from viewing others who are nude or who are engaging in sexual activities.

sadomasochism (sade-o-MASS-o-kiz-um) refers to sexual themes or activities involving bondage, pain, domination, or humiliation of one partner by the other.

sadist   the individual in a sadomasochistic sexual relationship who takes the dominant role.

masochist   the individual in a sadomasochistic sexual relationship who takes the submissive role.

Real Student Voices

■ Sometimes I can't believe the sexual stuff some of my friends are involved in. Maybe it interests them, but it turns me off completely.

■ I had a girlfriend that was really into BDSM. I found it arousing to allow her to take charge sometimes, but I wasn't interested in going too far with

the whole thing. There is something exciting about letting a partner take control over you.

■ I'm not going to reveal my fetish in writing, but I will tell you that it has been a relief to realize that I'm not as weird as I thought I was!

Sadomasochism is always a matter of degree, but its more extreme forms have gained interest as the Internet has increased access to the BDSM subculture (Kleinplatz & Moser, 2004). For most people, shared sexual activity has its share of urgency and rapid movements, with tightly gripping hands, hard sucking, and the possibility of mild pinching, scratching, and biting. Between 25 and 30 percent of college students surveyed indicated that they had engaged in spanking or some sort of bondage during sexual activities (Elliott & Brantley, 1997). Such behaviors are part of the intensity of sex for these individuals.

For those interested in BDSM, variants of such stimuli have become an important part of their sexual arousal and gratification. The intensity of the stimulation desired may vary from scratching or biting to spanking, whipping, and severe beating. Occasionally, cutting to draw blood or to mutilate may be involved. People who pair up for sadomasochistic sex usually make careful agreements and may even sign written contracts ahead of time concerning how far the activities should go. There is alway the risk of such contracts being broken, of course. It is also true, ironically, that the person in the submissive or masochistic role often wields more power and control over the interaction because it is his or her reactions that will largely determine the eventual direction of the encounter (Langdridge & Butt, 2004; Santilla et al., 2002; Taylor & Ussher, 2001).

See "Shannon: Private Club Dancer" on SexSource Online.

The acting out of fantasies or rituals in which one individual plays a dominant role is probably the most common sadomasochistic activity. Often the dominant person plays the role of a severe parent, teacher, or police officer who demands compliance from the submissive partner. The scenario often ends with some

mock forced sexual activity. Urination and defecation sometimes are included in the sexual acts, and some individuals find sexual interest and arousal in urine **(urophilia)** or feces **(coprophilia).** In the Janus and Janus (1993) survey of sexual behavior, 4 percent of women and 6 percent of men reported experience with "golden showers," or urophilic behavior, and about the same percentages found the behavior acceptable. In the recent college student survey, nearly 10 percent of respondents indicated that they had been involved with golden showers (Elliott & Brantley, 1997; Wilson, 2005).

Bondage, the tying or restraining of parts of the body, seems to be one form of sadomasochism. Wearing a hood is often part of such shared activities. Adult sex shops sell all sorts of devices for binding the body or genitals. Most common are rings, straps, and other pressure devices used by males to bind the penis and/or testicles to generate or heighten sexual pleasure. Eleven percent of both women and men report having had a sexual experience involving dominance or bondage.

A very dangerous variation on the bondage theme is **hypoxphilia,** which may lead to **autoerotic asphyxiation.** Some people, usually boys or men, have found that wearing a noose around the neck, which

urophilia sexual arousal connected with urine or urination.

coprophilia sexual arousal connected with feces.

bondage tying, restraining, or applying pressure to body parts as part of sexual arousal.

hypoxphilia creating pressure around the neck during sexual activity to enhance sexual pleasure.

autoerotic asphyxiation accidental death from pressure placed around the neck during masturbatory behavior.

induces a state of *hypoxia* (reduced oxygen to the brain), can enhance erotic pleasure and orgasm. They often devise various hanging techniques from which they can cut themselves loose prior to losing consciousness (Johnstone & Huws, 1997). What these individuals do not realize is how easy it is to lose consciousness when pressure is placed on the carotid artery in the neck. The Federal Bureau of Investigation estimates that between 500 and 1,000 people die accidentally each year from this sort of sexual activity. Given these statistics, the practice evidently is more widespread than commonly assumed. Families of victims are often confused about the sexual nature of the death and are embarrassed about reporting it as such. Partly for the same reason, the dangers of this kind of bondage have not been widely publicized to young people.

There are few statistics on the frequency of sadomasochistic preferences and activities. In a survey of more than 2,000 students in the United States, Canada, and Europe, 8 percent of males and 5 percent of females in the United States reported that they had engaged in "whipping or spanking before petting or other intimacy." These percentages were markedly higher among British students (17 percent of males, 33 percent of females), where spanking is a prevalent form of childhood punishment and may well take on sexual meanings (Butt & Hearn, 1998). There is a well-developed network of gay male and lesbian sadomasochists within the gay/lesbian culture as well.

In sex-oriented tabloids and on Internet bulletin boards, sadomasochists advertise for sexual partners, making it clear which role is preferred. Here are some examples of typical advertisements:

DISCRIMINATING MASTER, 32. Caucasian, very controlled but strict, desires applications from obedient, attentive slaves. T. J. M., Box 172.

FEMALES AND FEMININE MALES only. Have you had a good cry lately, or are you too grown up for that? Have you disciplined yourself so much that you mask your real feelings? Well, if you wear that mask in front of me, I'll slap you right out of it! I'm an attractive, imaginative black female, late 20s, and will give you highly private teachings in freeing your emotions. Send phone and fantasies to: Josa, Box 82.

The masochistic behavior may represent an escape from the usual burdens and responsibilities of an individual's normal identity. In a masochistic role, the individual is spared the anxiety of making decisions, asserting control, or maintaining a favorable image. The role may also deter feelings of guilt and insecurity. Practitioners of S&M are generally well-adjusted socially, and these behaviors may simply facilitate their sexual lives. They tend to be flexible in their role-

taking, although those who prefer the dominant role tend to be younger and more sexually active than those who prefer the passive role (Rathbone, 2001; Taylor & Ussher, 2001). A study of men involved in heterosexual dominance found that, contrary to the predictions of researchers, the men did not have low self-esteem or highly sexist attitudes (Damon, 2002).

A survey of research on S&M has suggested that these behaviors constitute a social phenomenon that occurs in cultures with certain characteristics. For example, dominance and submission are usually embedded in the culture, and aggression is socially valued. These cultures also have a clear and unequal distribution of power among social groups, creating a situation in which the temporary illusion of power reversals could become erotically stimulating. Two additional social characteristics are sufficient affluence to provide the leisure and opportunity for such involved sexual practices and the positive valuing of creativity and imagination (Alison et al., 2001). A study of BDSM practitioners found that, in general, they do not seem to have any significant psychological problems surrounding their sexual preferences. This calls into question whether such behavior should be considered a diagnosable pathology, appearing in the *DSM-IV* as it does presently (Connolly, 2006). There is much that we do not understand about sadomasochism, and future research needs to focus on S&M relationships and the role of symbolism in such sexual practices.

Sex with Animals

Since before recorded history, humans have lived in close association with a variety of domesticated animals. Folklore and the literature of mythology contain many examples of humans having sex with animals, often portraying a woman who has become enamored of the large genitals and sexual prowess of some animal. The half-bull, half-human Minotaur of Greek mythology was the offspring of Pasiphae, wife of the King of Crete, and a bull whom she seduced (Falkner, 2004). Throughout history, there is evidence of people having sex with animals. It is known that in North America both Native Americans and early British colonists engaged in the practice (Miletski, 2006).

Cross-cultural studies have reported many cases of humans having sex with animals, such as dogs, cattle, sheep, burros, horses, and chickens. This activity is called **bestiality** or **zoophilia.** There was even the suggestion, still unsubstantiated, that some animals

bestiality (beest-ee-AL-i-tee) sexual contact between a human being and an animal.

zoophilia (zoo-a-FILL-ee-a) another name for bestiality.

may make sexual advances toward humans (Ford & Beach, 1951). The Alfred Kinsey studies reported that 8 percent of the adult males and 3 percent of the adult females in his research sample admitted having had at least some sexual contact with animals. In the Kinsey research, among men raised on farms, 17 percent reported having had at least one orgasm after puberty through contact with an animal. The greater likelihood of zoophilia in rural populations has been confirmed more recently. Internet access has opened opportunities for interaction among zoophiles, although the numbers remain relatively small even for this medium (Miletski, 2006; Williams & Weinberg, 2003).

It appears likely that sex with animals usually represents sexual experimentation and/or arises from the frustration of lacking an available sexual partner. It does not necessarily reflect a serious psychological disturbance and seldom becomes a continuing pattern of sexual activity. The desire for affection seems to form the basis for most initial encounters with animals, and the ease of pleasure and not having to deal with the complications of human relationships are among the reasons the contact sometimes continues (Williams & Weinberg, 2003). What humans actually do with animals is as varied as any other aspect of human sexuality. Kinsey found masturbation of the animal and actual intercourse to be more common among men. General body contact with the animal is more common among women. Oral-genital sex, vaginal intercourse, and anal intercourse with animals have been reported by both women and men (Miletski, 2001, 2006; Williams & Weinberg, 2003).

Sex with animals is a concept usually met with abhorrence and disgust, for several reasons. First, Judeo-Christian-Muslim tradition carries strong prohibitions against humans having sex with animals, which may have grown out of fears that monstrous hybrids might be formed by such unions. In fact, no offspring can be formed by sexual intercourse between humans and animals because of the genetic differences between species. Second, possible injury or pain may be inflicted on the animal, especially if restraints have been used to keep it from moving during the sexual activity. The behavior is illegal in most areas today, covered by various laws concerning sodomy and lewd behavior. Zoophiles have become somewhat more activist in recent times, and some even claim to love their animal partners and to be "married" to them. Their interests have not achieved much approval or support from the general public.

Sex with the Dead

Probably no form of sexual behavior stirs negative reactions in quite the same way as **necrophilia,** or sexual relations with a corpse. It has been said that in ancient Egypt women of high rank and women of particular beauty were not given to embalmers until they had been dead for three or four days, to prevent the embalmers from having intercourse with them.

There are no statistics concerning the incidence of necrophilia, and almost nothing has been written about people who participate in sex with the dead. It is believed to be a rare phenomenon, because few people have access to cadavers. It is likely that necrophilic sex acts are committed primarily by people who work with corpses, as in mortuaries or morgues, and therefore have become desensitized to them. Case studies of necrophiles published decades ago showed that they sought jobs where they would be able to have such contact (Klaf & Brown, 1958). This behavior is prohibited under laws regarding the handling of bodies in most states, although Iowa passed such a law only in 1996 after a man was discovered fondling a woman's body at a funeral home and no law in effect at the time could be invoked against the behavior.

Which, if any, sexual behaviors, as described in this chapter, do you believe should be condemned or regulated by law?

Other Unusual Sexual Variations

For reasons that are as yet not fully understood, the sexual interests and behaviors of some people become associated with atypical stimuli. Some of these sexual variations have received little attention in the literature, suggesting that they may be relatively rare. They may elicit disbelief or jokes when we hear about them, but we should keep in mind that they represent the sexual proclivities of at least some human beings. As has happened with other sexual variations, perhaps we eventually will discover that they are more widespread than has been assumed to date.

One such variation, termed *apotemnophilia,* applies to a sex-related desire to have a normal limb (typically a leg) amputated. Sometimes associated with a sexual preference for partners who are amputees, the phenomenon has come to the attention of a number of professionals over the years. It has been compared to a desire for sex reassignment in that it involves dissatisfaction with certain body parts accompanied by the desire to have them removed. There are documented cases of surgeons fulfilling the wishes such patients (Lawrence, 2006).

Another variation at least sometimes associated with sexual arousal is *adult baby syndrome,* in which an adult is motivated to act like an infant, wearing diapers,

necrophilia (nek-ro-FILL-ee-a) sexual activity with a dead body.

drinking milk from a bottle, eating baby food, and doing other things associated with infants. The syndrome has not yet been classified as a paraphilia or other disorder, but it is being considered for some designation. How closely connected the syndrome is to sexual interests and behaviors is unclear (Evcimen & Gratz, 2006).

Finally, there is continuing concern about certain breathing or strangulation practices sometimes associated with sexual behavior. It is known that some people attempt to enhance their sexual experience by applying pressure to their neck, altering the blood supply to the brain. Adolescents sometimes play the "choking game" to induce altered states of consciousness, although how connected the practice may be to sexual arousal is unknown at this time. In either case, such behavior is known to be dangerous, and each year a number of people die after losing consciousness while attempting to tighten some ligature around their necks. Somewhat related to this is hyperventilation, or fast breathing, during sexual activity, which may also enhance feelings but also can result in an unpleasant *acute hyperventilation syndrome* that may require medical treatment. There are cases where such hyperventilation has occurred during sexual intercourse (Passie et al., 2004).

The human sexual imagination appears to be vast, and other curious sexual proclivities surely will make themselves known in the years to come.

Self-Evaluation

Your Sexual Fantasies

It seems that nearly everyone experiences a rich sexual life in his or her imagination. Yet we react to our sexual fantasies in different ways. We may feel aroused, amused, frightened, ashamed, proud, or guilty, depending on how we have learned to think of our sexual fantasies. They may give us clues to what we like and dislike about sex, help us plan future sexual encounters, put us in touch with the richness of our imaginations, and provide interesting accompaniments to our sexual activities. Sexual fantasies are just that—fantasies. There is no particular need to fight or deny them. In fact, sometimes the more we try not to think about something, the more it plagues us. Keep in mind that it is our sexual actions for which we must accept responsibility; our fantasies need only be accepted as very personal parts of our mind. The following questions and exercises may help you take a closer look at your fantasy life and its meaning.

1. **Take some time to think in some detail about your most common sexual fantasies. It may help to close your eyes and relax. Write down each fantasy if you wish.**
   a. What are the predominant feelings generated in you by each fantasy? Start by deciding whether it gives you mostly positive feelings that make you glad to indulge in it or instead generates negative feelings that make you wish the fantasy would go away.
   b. More specifically, what feelings does each fantasy generate? Write down a list of all the feelings you experience during each fantasy.
   c. Have you ever told another person about any or all of your sexual fantasies? Why or why not? If so, what conditions helped you feel able to share such a personal aspect of your life?

2. **Here is a list of some typical topics of sexual fantasies. They may simply be fleeting thoughts or may be rich in detail. For each fantasy you can remember experiencing, assign it a number, using the following scale as a way of noting the relative intensities of your fantasies.**

   0 = I have not experienced this fantasy.
   1 = This was an appealing, arousing, enjoyable fantasy.
   2 = Most aspects of the fantasy were enjoyable and positive.
   3 = This fantasy had a mixture of positive and negative aspects.
   4 = Most aspects of the fantasy were unenjoyable and negative.
   5 = This was a disgusting, guilt-producing, unenjoyable fantasy.

   a. Having sex with someone to whom you are attracted but who is unavailable to you or uninterested in you. _____
   b. Kissing or hugging someone of your own gender or admiring his or her nude body. _____

c. Having quick, uninvolved sex with a stranger you will never see again. _____

d. Having sex with someone of your own gender. _____

e. Watching a couple you know having sex with each other. _____

f. Forcing another person to have sex with you. _____

g. Being forced to have sex with someone against your will. _____

h. Seeing the nude body and genitals of someone you judge to be attractive. _____

i. Being watched while you masturbate. _____

j. Being watched while engaging in some sexual activity with a partner. _____

k. Inflicting or being subjected to pain or humiliation during sexual activity. _____

l. Paying a female or male prostitute to have sex with you. _____

m. Having sex with someone under the legal age of consent. _____

n. Being tied up during sex or tying up someone else during sex. _____

o. Participating in oral-genital sex with a desirable partner. _____

p. Being part of a group sexual experience or an orgy. _____

3. Are there any sexual fantasies that you enjoy using as an accompaniment to masturbation? If so, try to sort out the unique features of each fantasy that contribute to your sexual enjoyment.

4. Do you sometimes find yourself fantasizing while engaging in masturbation or sexual activity with a partner?

a. If so, how does this make you feel?

b. Do you consider such fantasizing unusual? (It's not.)

c. Have you ever discussed these fantasies with your sexual partner? If so, did your partner share any of his or her sexual fantasies with you?

d. Have you ever acted out a sexual fantasy with a partner or considered doing so? (Some couples find this to be an occasional source of enjoyment and mutual arousal.)

5. Have you been able to give yourself permission to experience, accept, and enjoy your sexual fantasies? If not, is this a goal toward which you would like to work? If your fantasies are giving you problems, perhaps you would like to consider talking with a qualified professional about your concerns.

Chapter Summary

1. The total sexual outlet concept (hydraulic theory) of sexuality has been modified by data from the latest sex research.

2. Contemporary sex research has emphasized the physical, orgasmic aspects of sex. The subjective erotic experience that includes sensuosity and desire is also important.

3. Individuals, preferences for various sexual behaviors and objects of sexual desire may change with circumstances and time. Women seem to have a greater degree of erotic plasticity than men do.

4. Human beings are diverse in their sexual orientations and activities. Behaviors that differ from whatever is considered the norm may be classified by terms such as *deviance, variance,* or *paraphilia.*

5. There is a wide range of levels of interest in sex and amounts of actual sexual activity among people, ranging from the erotophilic to the erotophobic. An unusually high level of sexual interest or drive is called hypersexuality; an especially low level is called hyposexuality. Although either may reflect a normal pattern for a particular person, they also may signal deeper emotional distress.

6. Compulsive sexual behavior can result from traumatic life experiences. Erotomania is an apparently rare form of mental illness characterized by extreme sexual compulsivity. It has been called nymphomania in females and satyriasis in males.

7. Celibacy refers to the choice not to share sexual activity with other people. It can represent a response to ethical or religious values.

8. Diverse sexual behaviors are more common among men than among women.

9. People with transgender identities may sometimes cross-dress or live for periods of time as if they were members of the other sex.

10. There are specific surgical procedures for male-to-female and female-to-male transsexuals. Either metoidioplasty or phalloplasty can be used to surgically form penislike structures.

11. Transgender identity and sexual orientation may be formed by similar developmental mechanisms and may interact to some degree.

12. Now that diagnostic guidelines have been published for gender identity disorder in children, there is controversy over what treatments or counseling should be made available to them.

13. People sometimes enhance sexual experiences through the use of various sexual media and toys and through sexual fantasy.

14. Fetishism is the term used to describe sexual arousal by objects, parts of the body, or materials not usually considered sexually arousing.

15. There are several forms of sexual interaction involving more than two persons.

16. There are both female and male sex workers. Legal debates over prostitution continue, and the HIV/AIDS issue has raised new concerns about this kind of casual sex.

17. Among the sex-related behaviors that have unwilling or unwitting victims are obscene telephone calls, frotteurism, and toucherism.

18. Consensual telephone sex and Internet chat lines offer an opportunity for sex-related communication on a relatively anonymous basis.

19. Frotteurism and toucherism involve sexual arousal through close contact with other people.

20. Exhibitionism refers to exposing the genitals or breasts to others, usually for sexual arousal.

21. Voyeurism refers to finding sexual arousal by viewing others in the nude, disrobing, or engaging in sexual activity.

22. Sadomasochism, sometimes called BDSM, encompasses a range of behavior involving inflicting pain or humiliation, tying parts of the body (bondage), or acting out dominant-submissive fantasies, all for sexual arousal. Hypoxphilia is the dangerous practice of using devices to reduce oxygen to the brain for sexual enhancement.

23. Sex with animals has been reported in a small percentage of humans, and it has been receiving increasing attention from sex researchers.

24. Sex with the dead (necrophilia) is a rare phenomenon and typically is prohibited by law.

25. There are a few other sex-related interests and behaviors that have received little study, including apotemnophilia, the desire for limb amputation; adult baby syndrome; and strangulation or hyperventilation syndrome.

Focus on Health Questions

In this section you will find the kinds of questions that you may have concerning your own health and sexuality. The page references indicate where in the text the answer is located; the exact place is marked with this logo: **FOH**

1. Are some people "oversexed" or "undersexed"? **391**

2. How do I know whether I'm promiscuous or just normally enjoying sex with several partners? **391–392**

3. Isn't there something wrong with someone who doesn't want to have sex? **392–393**

4. Is it abnormal for a man to enjoy dressing in women's clothes? **394**

5. What actually happens when a person gets a sex change? **369–399**

6. Is it normal to fantasize about sex a lot? **401–402**

7. What exactly is a foot fetish? **402**

8. What is wrong with those who expose their genitals to other people? **407**

9. Isn't sadomasochism painful and dangerous? **408–410**

Chapter 15

Sex, Art, the Media, and the Law

Chapter Outline

When I was about 12, my mother found some porno magazines that I had hidden in my bedroom closet. She turned them over to my father, who gave me the biggest lecture of my lifetime about what kinds of material would be permitted in our house. I was really embarrassed, but I also hated losing those magazines.

—from a student essay

What do you think about the availability of pornography online? Have you ever accessed such materials out of curiosity or for sexual arousal? Should it be available, or should it be censored? Should we keep it away from the eyes of children, and, if so, how could that be accomplished? Arguably, one of the most persistent disagreements within the world's cultures revolves around the accessibility and appropriateness of representations of the human body and human sexual behaviors. It has been estimated that the Internet has more than 4 million porn sites, generating some $12 billion annually in the United States. An Internet tracking firm recently reported that about 40 percent of Internet users in the United States access adult sites each month (Crary, 2006). On one side of the contemporary culture wars are those who believe that adults should have the freedom to access such materials; on the other are those who feel that pornography destroys relationships and increases the rate of sexual crimes. No one has figured out exactly how to regulate such material or keep it from young people without interfering with access to educational information as well. The U.S. Supreme Court continues to consider cases brought by both sides in the battle (Melby, 2006c).

Although the almost limitless availability of Internet pornography is unprecedented in history, the essential controversy is not new. Depictions of human sexuality have been abundant in most cultures and most periods of history, from the figures on a Greek urn to the billboards on Times Square, from the couples on a television soap opera to the advertisements for Abercrombie and Fitch clothing, and from frontal nudity on the big screen to the lyrics of the most current rap artist. These images and words, implicitly or explicitly, reflect the attitudinal trends of the society in which they appear. Such gestures sometimes purposely push the envelope of political and religious sensitivities. The more tolerant a society becomes in its representation of sexuality, the more it invites criticisms from certain internal and external factions. It has become clear in recent times that some world cultures have come to view Western openness and tolerance with regard to sexuality and sexual imagery as a threat to their perceptions of the way human beings and human life ought to be.

The terms **pornography** and **obscenity** are often used interchangeably. Both terms are subject to multiple definitions and interpretations, and both have become emotionally charged. Typically, pornography refers to any visual or literary portrayal that may be sexually arousing to some people. Obscenity

Akio Takamori, *Appearance of Kwannon to a Man*, 1995.

usually includes material that may be offensive to public taste and morals. The term "sexually explicit material" sometimes is used to describe pornography.

In erotically realistic art or fiction, sometimes called **erotica,** sex is portrayed as part of the broad spectrum of human emotions present in intimate relationships. The people involved are shown to be complex human beings with a variety of nonsexual feelings in addition to sexual ones. The sex may be depicted in just as graphic a way as in pornography; it is the overall context that differs. It has also been suggested that pornography has aspects of violence, aggression, or the degradation of another human being, whereas erotica balances sexual acts with mutual respect, affection, and pleasure.

■ Nudity and Sex in Art

In recent times in Western culture, art has been a relatively uncensored means of expression in which nudity, at least, has been considered quite permissible. That is not to say, however, that paintings or sculptures of nudes have not incurred the ire of some viewers. Erotic art has a long history, as do the cultural and social reactions to it.

pornography photographs, films, or literature intended to be sexually arousing through explicit depictions of sexual activity.

obscenity depiction of sexual activity in a repulsive or disgusting manner.

erotica artistic representations of nudity or sexual activity.

Historical Foundations of Erotic Art

Prehistoric representations of the human body and sexual activities very likely were fertility symbols with magical and religious significance. Representations of the sex organs themselves probably became objects of worship with great symbolic meaning. Penis-shaped monuments and adornments have been found in the ruins of many ancient cultures. Religious erotic art tended to portray those aspects of sex that were seen as important and necessary to the survival and well-being of the human species (e.g., intercourse for procreation). Other forms of erotic art, mostly three-dimensional, were used to ward off evil spirits or to improve the harvesting of crops.

Every culture has seen its share of erotic art that departs from such religious intent. Artists, sometimes by definition, test the limits of moral values and sexual tolerance. It is this form of erotic art that sometimes is treated with greater secrecy, used for sexual titillation, or strictly limited to a select group of privileged viewers. Many Greek and Etruscan paintings show sexual intercourse, fellatio, orgies, pedophilic behavior, and a variety of other sexual activities. Some examples of pre-Columbian pottery from Mexico and Peru represent male masturbation and fellatio, often with great exaggeration of phallic size (see Figure 15.1). Some-

times, homoerotic themes were represented more symbolically through animal figures engaged in sexual activities (Olsen, 2004).

Some erotic art has been used for special educational functions. Japan had a tradition of "bride scrolls" and "position pictures," or *shunga,* which were passed on from mother to daughter upon the daughter's betrothal. Their dual purpose apparently was to offer instruction and to encourage the daughter's erotic interest in her husband-to-be. This tradition reflects the double purpose of most erotic art—to make us think as well as to encourage us to respond with feeling, including sexual arousal. Erotic art is also of use in fostering an understanding of the sexual values and mores of both historic and present-day cultures other than our own. Japanese culture also produced ceramic sake cups and figurines depicting various forms of sexual activity.

Do you think public funding should be available for the creation of art with sexual themes? Defend your position.

Nudity in art is often directly affected by cultural attitudes. Ancient Greek artists portrayed the nude male and female figures without hesitation. Gradually, however, as their attitude toward nakedness changed, they began to include gestures of modesty, at least partially covering the genitals.

The roots of modern, commercial sexually explicit material probably can be found in the sixteenth century, when engraving, etching, and woodcutting made reproduction of erotic scenes simpler and much less expensive. By the eighteenth century, representations of nudes were quite acceptable, as long as the genital areas were obscured (Stewart, 2004). Eventually, the resurgence of a more puritan attitude discouraged artistic representations of nudity and sex. This repressive movement probably contains the roots of modern censorship and suppression of erotic images. However, there have also been claims that art historians sometimes glorify and eroticize acts that we would today judge in a negative light, such as the rapes portrayed in many Renaissance paintings (see Figure 15.2) (Wolfthal, 1999).

FIGURE 15.1 *Pre-Columbian Pottery*

The ancient Peruvians from the southern coast of Mochica were famous for their stirrup-spout jars. They were molded without the aid of a potter's wheel and featured a large flat bottom with a dominant sculptured form. This jar shows an act of fellatio.

Erotic Art Today

The first two or three decades of the twentieth century saw some new approaches to erotic art (see Figure 15.3). Surrealism, for instance, often relied on sexual fantasy and free association borrowed from psychoanalysis. Although contemporary art has created some fresh erotic themes in Western culture, it seems that photography, video, films, and computer images now

■ FIGURE 15.2   *Renaissance Painting*

Peter Paul Rubens's painting *The Rape of the Daughters of Leucippus* (1617) depicts the abduction of two young mortals by the gods Castor and Pollux, who have fallen in love with them. The content of the painting was less interesting historically than were its composition and the artist's technique of using paint and light. Some accuse art historians of glorifying what most people today would find objectionable subject matter for any type of art.

■ FIGURE 15.3   *Life Model*

One basic area of study for art students continues to be the depiction of the nude human body. Students frequently work with life models, men or women who often pose in the nude.

Controversies of this sort highlight the difficult balance every society must struggle to find between freedom of expression, which might include rather explicit images that may be offensive to some, and the ongoing interest on the part of others to prevent such images from being available. For several months, the George Pompidou Center in Paris exhibited 500 works of twentieth-century art that explored sexual themes ranging from transgenderism to voyeurism to sadomasochism. This exhibit served as a reminder of the many ways eroticism and sexuality make their way into the artwork of all eras and how these themes might well be at the root of artistic creativity.

■ Sex and the Printed Page

Just as erotic themes have universally found their way into visual art, so have they always been a part of literature. The explicitness of sexual descriptions varies with the cultural and sexual mores of the times. In some societies and periods of history, little more than a romantic embrace is described, with the participants fully clothed and the rest left to the reader's imagination. In other societies and times, minute and graphic details of a sexual encounter are discussed, requiring no flight of imaginative fancy on the part of the reader. Like other erotic art forms, sexually explicit literature often has been available only as costly contraband.

The Evolution of Sexuality in Literature

It seems that because sex was viewed as joyous and pleasurable in ancient times, authors were permitted to write about it openly and unashamedly. In most

provide the erotic stimuli that painting, drawing, etching, and sculpture once did. These media have elicited their share of controversy as well. Some observers believe that homosexual themes in art have been suppressed in recent times (Filice, 2005).

It has been the custom of many governments to subsidize artists. However, when the work produced from such support offends the tastes of some individuals, debates erupt over the use of public funds for products that fly in the face of prevailing sexual values. The photographic themes of Robert Mapplethorpe's art, which include homoerotic and sadomasochistic themes, came under fire because of the artist's support from the National Endowment for the Arts (NEA). Galleries that display such works are also subject to criticism. When Rudolph Giuliani was mayor of New York City, he threatened to withhold funds from the Brooklyn Museum of Art when the museum displayed a series of controversial works in its "Sensational" exhibit. Federal courts in the United States have tended to rule that funding of the arts should not be limited by controversy or based on the artist's social or political messages.

languages, including English, some of the oldest writings are the most ribald. Sumerian love songs written about 4,000 years ago contain verses that are more explicit than the love songs of today.

Ancient Greek writers drew much of their eroticism from the fertility rites of Dionysian festivals, dramatic rites in honor of certain Greek gods of pleasure and intoxication. These rites developed into wild orgies in some communities, occasionally to the dismay of Greeks who preferred more staid and formal ceremonies (Hamel, 2003). The plays and songs that emerged, the mass media of the time, often glorified the phallus and retold stories about the sexual activities of the gods. Many of the masters of Greek tragic and comedic writing created plays in which sexual themes were central (Heacox, 2004). The erotic literature of the ancient Romans was more lighthearted than that of the Greeks, although there is evidence that their sexual behaviors surpassed whatever excesses the Greeks may have displayed. One of the most famous Roman "pornographers" was Ovid, whose *Art of Love* and *Heroides* are erotic classics. Another Roman, Caius Petronius, wrote the *Satyricon,* a work filled with sexual themes.

It has been suggested that prior to the early nineteenth century, there was no separate or distinct genre of literature meant to arouse sexual feelings. Sexually explicit materials instead were used as vehicles to criticize political and religious authorities. Sexual literary themes have been associated with freethinkers and political activists and often have proliferated prior to major political revolutions against restrictive or oppressive regimes. Italian journalist Pietro Aretino, born in 1492, is sometimes called the originator of European pornography. In 1527, he published Europe's first "stroke book," titled *I Modi (The Ways),* combining 16 sexually explicit sonnets with engravings of couples having sex in a variety of positions. The Pope declared reprinting of the book punishable by death; soon thereafter a second, embellished version was published.

Shakespeare integrated sexual themes into his plays and sonnets, and their meanings continue to be debated today (Tambling, 2004). Pornography seems to have begun taking on its more distinctively sexually titillating role during the late eighteenth century, as a more materialistic view of the world emerged in philosophy and science (Boone, 1998).

The nineteenth century brought a rise in prudery. During this period, ladies could be offended not only by explicit sexual references but by any sort of indelicate statement made in writing. Sexual feelings were increasingly repressed, and people's sexual attitudes, at least superficially, became models of propriety. Nevertheless, erotic literature flourished; by 1834, 57 pornography shops had opened on one London street.

Themes in Contemporary Literature, Lyrics, and Plays

Although sexuality has never been totally repressed in literature, the kind of exuberance and acceptance of erotic themes prevalent in Greek and Roman literature did not fully manifest itself again until the twentieth century. In the early years of that century, some writers rebelled against the notion that sex must be accompanied by shame and guilt. Undoubtedly, the writings of Sigmund Freud, Havelock Ellis, Kinsey, Masters and Johnson, and others influenced the emergence of new sexual attitudes.

D. H. Lawrence's *Lady Chatterley's Lover* (1929) stirred controversy for decades with its sexual explicitness. Lawrence is now recognized as a literary genius who was a pioneer in the sensitive treatment of erotic themes. James Joyce's *Ulysses* was not allowed into the United States for years after it was published. In 1933, John Woolsey, a district judge for New York, wrote a landmark decision that redefined the limits of pornography and allowed *Ulysses* to be available to readers in the United States. Woolsey's basic principle was that the redeeming artistic value of an entire book needed to be considered before it could be banned as obscene because of any given passage. This decision set a precedent that has persisted to this day, and *Ulysses* became recognized as a modern masterpiece.

All sexual themes have today found their way into literature, song lyrics, and play scripts. Tens of thousands of books have been published, on many different levels of literary quality, that treat sex openly and frankly. Sometimes the erotic themes are interwoven with other themes of literary importance. In other cases, the author's intent seems to be to crowd as many sexually explicit scenes onto the pages as possible. There has also been a resurgence in the popularity of romantic themes, often in combination with eroticism. Nearly half of all mass-market paperbacks are romance novels, read by both women and men. In addition, some experts believe that economic and sexual pressures are making monogamous, romantic relationships more appealing both in real life and in literature. Another recent trend in romance novels has been the portrayal of men who are interested and involved in fatherhood and family life.

The sale of erotic books, collections of short stories, and poetry has been booming. Women dominate the erotic literature scene both as writers and as buyers and readers. This seems to reflect a new trend in eroticism in which sexual themes are intertwined with good literary style and well-developed characters who also have an emotional side. Helen Gurley Brown, long-time editor of *Cosmopolitan* magazine, published a 2003 revised edition of her ground-breaking work from 1962, *Sex and the Single Girl*. The original edition was one of the early manifestos declaring a new level of sexual freedom for women.

The sexual references of song lyrics continue to worry parents and educators with their explicitness, and sometimes their violence, yet this is not a new phenomenon. Music has long been one of the most important means of sexual expression for adolescents. Plays, another variation of the written word, often have sexual themes. The winner of the 2002 Tony award for best play of 2002 was the Broadway production of *The Goat* by Edward Albee. In the play, a man falls in love with a goat and attends a therapy group for people who love animals more than is considered socially acceptable (Williams & Weinberg, 2003).

Although there have been no recent widespread attempts to censor erotic themes in literature, local libraries and school systems frequently are subjected to pressures by special-interest groups to remove books these groups judge to be too sexually suggestive. The number of challenges concerning materials used in public schools escalated during the 1990s, and in close to half these cases books or other materials were removed or given some restricted status. Some of the titles challenged most often included classics and award-winning books such as Judy Blume's *Forever,* Mark Twain's *Huckleberry Finn,* and Maya Angelou's *I Know Why the Caged Bird Sings.*

Can you think of any books that should not be allowed in your college library? In a high school library? In a public library?

Magazines, Journals, Tabloids, and Comics

Magazines with stories and/or articles about sex have been available for more than a century. Only within recent times, however, have they been so readily available and openly displayed. When *Esquire: The Magazine for Men* appeared in 1933, a new precedent was set for sophistication in erotic magazines. Twenty years after *Esquire*'s beginnings, *Playboy* appeared on newsstands. This magazine attempted to strike a balance among offerings on sex information, advice on male attire, an open philosophy toward sex, photographs of nude women, and titillating fiction. The *Playboy* approach was adopted by a large number of other magazines for men. As women began to ask for a more balanced view of sex, magazines such as *Cosmopolitan* and *Playgirl* began printing photographs of nude men and stories with special erotic appeal for women.

By the late 1960s, other magazines appeared that were more blatantly sex-oriented and included hardcore pornography. *Penthouse, Hustler,* and *Oui* were among the first to deal explicitly with sex. In 1968, *Screw* scored a resounding commercial success for a time and was followed by a number of other sex tabloids with provocative titles, including *Smut, Ball, Stud, Hot Stuff,* and *Sex.* Not only did the sex tabloids publish photographs of male and female nudes showing genitals, but they usually also published pictures of people engaged in a variety of sexual activities, as well as fiction, articles related to new developments in the study of sex, and a classified section in which people advertised their sexual services or requested sexual partners for all sorts of activities. The sex magazines now compete with the Internet, and they are not competing particularly well. *Screw* and *Penthouse* went bankrupt after suffering major declines in their circulation rates.

In a typical year, close to 1,000 new magazines appear, about 15 percent of which are sex publications. Only about a third of new magazines survive as long as a few years, but among the more popular ones the trend has been toward more coverage of sex-related articles and news. Popular women's magazines such as *Glamour* and *Cosmopolitan* have generally forsaken feminist themes in favor of articles about sexuality (Kuczynski, 1999). "Lifestyle" magazines are now the most common venues for publishing short articles about improving one's sex life (Tyler, 2004). Several new men's magazines have appeared that seem to emphasize some of the traditional gender stereotypes regarding men's interests in explicit sexual themes and photographs. Magazines such as *Maxim* and *Stuff* are designed to appeal to young male readers in a variety of ways. One analysis of the photographs that appear in these two magazines concluded that they tended to portray women as willing sex objects much more than they did men (Krassas, Blauwkamp, & Wesselink, 2003).

Professional journals that publish papers related to human sexuality have also proliferated. Some journals have a panel of expert reviewers, or "referees," who help editors decide whether particular research or a specific topic is worth publishing, offering suggestions for revision and clarification along the way. Refereed journals are generally considered to offer the best-quality material. In 1971, there were only three scientific journals related to sexuality; today there are more than 75. Various print and online catalogs and archives of published topics are available to make literature searches somewhat easier (Zucker & Cantor, 2003).

Until recently, comic books and comic strips in newspapers did not venture into gender- or sex-related themes, but that has been changing. Women have become superheroes in some comics. A character in Marvel Comics' "Alpha Flight" declared that he was gay, and another gay character appeared in DC Publications' "Flash" series. In the comic book series "Icon," the 15-year-old girl who tells the story becomes pregnant. The newspaper comic strip "For Better or for Worse" featured the character of a gay teenage boy who came out to his parents and his best friend. The issue was carried through several days of the strip but was blended into the story line in such a way as to not appear startlingly unusual. In Japan, comic books, called *manga,* for both men and women are quite popular, and they often feature sexually explicit material, including rape themes or other depictions of forced sexual submission. Those published for younger girls often portray relationships between gay males. It is believed that such themes in women's comics may help women play out the themes of their subconscious mind within the context of a sexually conservative culture (Perper & Cornog, 2002).

■ Sex in the Media

Film, television, video/DVD, and the Internet represent modern mass media. They have undergone—and continue to undergo—an evolutionary process that parallels, reflects, and often stimulates the evolution of social attitudes. The integration of nudity and sex into films and television has been gradual and careful, yet because of their mass audiences, reaction to nudity and sex in these media has been more visible than any responses to erotic art or literature ever were (Brown, 2002). Research studies confirm that sexually explicit films and videos produce higher levels of arousal response in viewers than do still pictures (Bogaert, 2001).

Films

From the earliest days of film, some moviemakers made use of the medium to photograph sexual activity. At first, such films were available only through the underground market. The movies that were offered to the public for the first 50 years were almost totally lacking in anything that today would be judged sexually explicit. There were innuendos and seductive women even in silent films. Greta Garbo's first talking picture, *Anna Christie* (1930), was about a prostitute. But whatever people did together sexually was left strictly to the viewer's imagination. Movie actors were never seen wearing less than a bathing suit considered appropriate at the time; a man and a woman were never shown in bed together; kisses rarely betrayed any sense of real passion. This was due partially to the producers' code established by the movie industry itself as a response to several sexual themes that appeared in a few movies in the 1920s.

The Roman Catholic Church instituted the Legion of Decency in 1934, and its standards were soon adopted by Hollywood producers (Walsh, 1996). Conservative attitudes in the early twentieth century influenced the depiction of alcohol, drug abuse, equality for blacks, women's rights, prostitution, communism, and other themes that did not fit into the prevailing mode of behavior or thought. That is not to say that "sex symbols" did not emerge from among the movie stars. Actors such as Mae West, Jean Harlow, Clark Gable, Humphrey Bogart, James Dean, and Marilyn Monroe undoubtedly drew theatergoers who were romantically attracted to their film images. New media sex symbols emerge every year.

In 1965, *The Pawnbroker* became the first American film to show bare female breasts. Today they are standard in a great many movies, and overtly erotic themes and explicitly sexual scenes are increasingly common in films. *Midnight Cowboy* (1969) dramatized the story of a male prostitute, and *Klute* (1971) dealt with some intimate details of a female prostitute's life. *The Graduate* (1967), one of the most popular films of its day, portrayed a brief sexual encounter between a young man and an older woman. *Myra Breckinridge* (1970) and *The Christine Jorgensen Story* (1970) dealt with sex-change operations.

Every sexual theme has found its way into the movies. The film *Boogie Nights* (1997) followed the life of a physically well-endowed young man into the underworld of pornographic film production. Director Stanley Kubrick's last film, the well-publicized *Eyes Wide Shut* (1999), presented the surrealistic sexual adventures of a married but sexually bored couple. Extramarital sexual temptations and their possible consequences were explored in the steamy *Unfaithful* (2002).

As sexual explicitness and nudity have increased in films, the industry continues to struggle with the question of ratings. The X rating for films, which proved to be a box office liability for movies carrying it, was replaced with the NC-17 classification, meaning no children under the age of 17 were permitted in the theater. However, the new rating seems to carry the same stigma as the old X rating, and many theaters will not show NC-17 movies. Polls have found that R-rated films are the most popular, particularly among the 18- to 34-year-old age group, followed by films with PG-13 ratings, and then by films with a PG rating. Films with NC-17 and G ratings trail far behind the others in their popularity. Producers face decisions about whether to cut explicit sexual scenes from their films in order to win the safer, and more lucrative, R rating. There has been a recent trend toward sexy films that clearly are aimed at teenagers, who often can manage to see R-rated films even if they are under age 17. The films *American Pie* (1999), *Road Trip* (2001), and *American Wedding* (2003) are examples. Sex among middle-aged people is becoming a more popular theme as the population ages. *In the Bedroom* (2002), *Sexy Beast* (2002), and *Something's Gotta Give* (2004) are good examples of this genre.

Educators, philosophers, and psychologists have engaged in a good deal of debate concerning the significance of sex-related themes in films. As a society evolves, does its art reflect its changing values, or do artists and filmmakers form the avant-garde in effecting these changes? As a society becomes more tolerant and breaks down the barriers of its stereotypical attitudes toward groups of people and sexual behaviors, how does the art of that society reflect these changes? There are no definitive answers to these questions, but a discussion of some cinematic themes might provide a clue.

Women in Films

There has been controversy over how women have been depicted in American films. One study that compared male and female roles from 1927 through the late 1980s found that women's roles generally were rather rigidly stereotyped (Geiger, 2001). Women have frequently been portrayed as self-destructive, manipulative, and sexually seductive (see Figure 15.4). A common cinematic scene over the years has involved an aggressive man pulling a woman into his arms and

FIGURE 15.4

Sharon Stone poses provocatively in the film *Basic Instinct*.

Source: Everett Collection, Inc.

forcing kisses on her. At first the woman pushes and fights against him with clenched fists, but eventually her body softens, her hands open and slide around his neck, and she surrenders herself to him passionately. This "rape myth" is believed to be perpetuated by such cinematic themes. The film *Secretary* (2002), which portrayed a sadomasochistic relationship between a troubled woman and her boss involving both verbal and physical domination, troubled some people with its apparent abusiveness toward the female lead, but there was also a level of warmth in their relationship. Nonetheless, some films offer stronger, more positive images of women, often depicting strong bonds of friendship between women.

Name two recent films in which women are portrayed in positive roles. Explain your definition of "positive role."

Same-Gender Relationships in Films

Prior to 1960, gay and lesbian relationships were avoided as a cinematic theme. Some European films were frank about same-gender relationships, but American films tended to obscure even suggestions of same-gender attractions. When plays such as *A Streetcar Named Desire* (1952), *Tea and Sympathy* (1957), and *Cat on a Hot Tin Roof* (1958) were made into movies, their significant allusions to same-gender sexuality were lost. In the early 1960s, however, Hollywood became less hesitant about using gay themes. Tennessee Williams's 1960 film *Suddenly Last Summer* was reasonably straightforward about the topic (Waugh, 1996).

As society has become more tolerant of lesbian and gay relationships, such themes have been depicted in a variety of ways. *The Boys in the Band* emerged in 1972 as the first film to explore the problems of the gay male subculture, although some people have objected to the stereotyped image it presents. In the 1980s, the film *Making Love* (1982) dealt frankly with a married man who eventually left his wife to establish a gay relationship with another man. *Kiss of the Spider Woman* (1985) focused on the touching relationship of two male political prisoners, one openly gay and the other heterosexual. *The Crying Game* (1993) delighted critics and viewers alike with its intriguing story of a man who falls in love with a woman, only to learn later that "she" is actually a man. The film poses complex questions of romantic and sexual attraction. More stereotypical and sometimes comical roles were the focus of films such as *Birdcage* (1996); *To Wong Foo, Thanks for Everything! Julie Newmar* (1996); *In & Out* (1997); and *The Next Best Thing* (2000). These also were very popular movies in which gay characters had the lead roles, however. The movie *Monster* (2003) showed a loving and sexual relationship between two troubled women, one of whom kills a man who raped her.

A recent movie that attracted a great deal of attention for its homoerotic theme was *Brokeback Mountain* (2005), a film about two cowboys who fall in love and continue their relationship for years, even after they both have married. The fact that the cowboys did not fit common stereotypes of gay men may well have added to the film's popularity.

Gender Identity in Films

Questions of romantic sexual attraction are complicated by issues of self-identity and social perceptions of gender in four films from the 1990s. In *The Ballad of Little Jo* (1993), Josephine masquerades as a young male in the American frontier as a means of survival. As a woman she is vulnerable to male violence, but as a male she realizes that she has lost her identity. In *Farewell My Concubine* (1993), a male character prepares to play the female lead in a Chinese opera. Offstage, he sexually desires his male counterpart in the opera, thus confusing his own nature. This film at the same time becomes a metaphor for the identity crisis of China itself from the time of the warlords to the end of Mao's Cultural Revolution. *M. Butterfly* (1993), also set in the world of Chinese opera, tells the true story of a French diplomat who had a long affair with an opera star, while never knowing, by his own account, that "she" was really a man. The diplomat is depicted as being unable to see beyond the artifice of femininity, and thus his perception of his lover becomes his reality. The award-winning U.S. film *Boys Don't Cry* (1999) depicted a woman who lived as a man and eventually was murdered by intolerant men (Willox, 2003). More recently, actress Felicity Huffman was nominated for an Academy Award for her portrayal of a man in the process of becoming a woman who travels cross-country with his/her son in the movie *Transamerica* (2005).

Romantic Themes

As discussed earlier, romantic themes are finding their way back into the media, and cinematic fare has been no exception. From period romances such as *Circle of Friends* (1995), *Sense and Sensibility* (1996), and *Titanic* (1998) to contemporary stories such as *You've Got Mail* (1999), *Love Actually* (2003), and *Music and Lyrics* (2007), romance has overtaken explicit sex. There continues to be evidence that women particularly enjoy romantic themes in movies, tending to see sex as part of an organic whole, whereas men tend to be more focused on sexual behaviors.

Pornographic Films and Videos/DVDs

Films whose main purpose is to show lengthy scenes of genitals and/or persons engaged in any form of sexual activity are considered **hard-core pornography.** The earliest "adult films" were made before 1925, mostly by professionals who had access to 35mm movie camera equipment. As 16mm and 8mm film became available, amateurs began producing hard-core films for private use and sale. Popular from the 1950s through the early 1980s, these movies were 10 to 20 minutes in length and were sold for amounts that far exceeded the costs of production. In Great Britain, they were called blue movies, and in the United States, they were often labeled stag films. The latter term reflects the fact that such films generally were shown at all-male (stag) parties (Waugh, 2001).

As explicit sex began to be permissible in movie theaters, the underground pornographic film industry suffered. The picture quality was often poor, and the films were expensive, so many viewers chose to pay less for what could be seen more clearly. As home videocassette recorders (VCRs) and video cameras proliferated, the adult movie business in theaters was reduced to almost nothing, and the video business boomed. Video shops often have sections devoted exclusively to full-length adult films that show explicit sexual acts. In 1978, about 100 hard-core films were produced. Today, thousands of new hard-core videos and DVDs are released every year, some costing only a few thousand dollars to produce. In the United States alone, there are some 25,000 stores that rent or sell such videos, often deriving as much as a third of their income from them. Online pornography, however, may be cutting into the direct rental and sale business.

Although men are the largest consumers of pornography, evidence suggests that a good share of adult videos are rented by women, who often rent explicit videos to watch with their husbands after their children have watched their PG films and gone to bed. Adult videos/DVDs are rented most frequently on weekend nights. A few companies produce "female porn," depicting sex between lesbian women or with men. Some chains of video stores have asked sexologists for guidelines in choosing sexually explicit materials for their outlets. These experts discourage the distribution of films in which actors who might appear to be minors are portrayed sexually in any way and scenes in which sex is associated with violence or

hard-core pornography pornography that makes use of highly explicit depictions of sexual activity or shows lengthy scenes of genitals.

Real Student Voices

■ I was eleven when I was shown my first porn on-line. My best friend showed me on his computer. I must admit I was turned on, and it has been part of my available "repertoire" ever since. My parents never realized what I was accessing, and I'm grateful for that.

■ About a month ago, I discovered on my boyfriend's laptop that he had been downloading pornography. It really bothers me even though he says it shouldn't. I don't understand why he needs to do that if he's really happy with me and our sexual relationship. It makes me feel that I'm not really enough, and that I can't really trust him.

■ When I was a teenager, my parents installed software on our computers that blocked all adult sites. Eventually, I discovered ways around the blocks. In the meantime, I just used my friends' computers.

■ One night every week, my fraternity shows porno DVDs on the big screen. Even though I find the stuff embarrassing, there is a lot of pressure to watch as a group, so I join in. I haven't come out to them yet, so I can't tell them I'd rather see gay porno.

blood. Some believe that explicit videos are a significant source of sexuality education for many people and therefore should be regulated to provide as positive a sexual message as possible. The viewing public now seems to react more negatively to adult film themes that seem degrading to women, and in fact more recent videos and DVDs portray women in more equal and sex-initiating roles than once was the case.

Research into the content of sexually explicit video material has yielded some interesting findings. Over time, there has been a decrease in the number and proportion of sexually aggressive scenes in such material (Bogaert, 2001). Explicit DVDs/videotapes have a higher proportion of sexual behaviors but a lower proportion of violent behaviors compared to R-rated movies. Four common themes have been noted in sexually explicit video material: high levels of sexual desire, diverse sexual activity, ready availability of many sexual partners, and pleasure as the purpose of sexual activity.

Some sexual-enhancement video materials have been produced by sexologists specifically for use by couples in their homes for educational purposes. These videos and DVDs offer explicit graphic instruction for the improvement of sexual relationships and sometimes for the treatment of particular sexual dysfunctions. Clearly, there is a fine line between the sexual arousal people enjoy from pornography and what they experience watching educational video material.

A newer pornographic video phenomenon is the homemade, amateur sex video, taped by couples in their own homes. Apparently, some people who make

such videos derive sexual excitement from knowing that others will be viewing their sexual acts. Numerous companies will pay modest sums for these videos and then distribute them via mail order to others. It is believed that from one-fifth to one-third of the hard-core videos and DVDs being sold in the United States today are at least partly amateur, and one company offers a selection of 500 such videos to its customers, with new submissions being sent to their offices every week.

Technological Access to Pornography

The technologies people can use to access and view sexually explicit materials have advanced in startling ways over the past quarter-century. The videocassette player overlapped the development of DVD technology, and both overlapped the constantly increasing accessibility of the Internet and other computer-based technologies (Buzzell, 2005). The Internet has been adapted for a variety of sex-related uses, ranging from computer dating services and sexuality education to the transmission of sexually explicit materials. It has opened new vistas for sexual communications and raised new concerns about how cyberspace interactions should be controlled and regulated. Not only can people living some distance apart carry on sensual conversations on their keyboards or play X-rated computer games with each other, but they can also access services that provide the most recent information on a variety of sexual topics.

There are websites and forums for every imaginable sexual interest and fetish, easily accessible to people of all ages from the privacy of their own computers (Fisher & Barak, 2001). In a single year, nearly 10 million people logged on to the 10 most popular cybersex sites (Cooper, 2000). On some sites, scantily clad or nude women and men may be viewed live while participating in an ongoing live chat with viewers. Private time, during which the models perform sexual acts for one or a few viewers, can be purchased, constituting a form of long-distance cyber-prostitution.

Pornographic websites now exceed 4 million (Crary, 2006). The majority of consumers of online computer porn are male (Buzzell, 2005; Leland, 1999a). For those who are predisposed to compulsive behavior, use of the Internet to access sexual material may also become compulsive or addictive (Griffiths, 2001). The combination of easy access, affordability, and anonymity often conspires to cause some individuals to become involved with sexually explicit materials for hours at a time, sometimes interfering with daily life and work (Cooper, 2000). The Internet has also provided links among people who share a common sexual orientation or paraphilia, helping them feel less marginalized by their sexual interests (McKenna, Green, & Smith, 2001). Some people have virtual sexual experiences via the Internet, and the issue of "cheating" on one's real sexual partner has become an area for discussion and counseling (Crary, 2006; Gwinell, 2001).

See "Technology and Sexual Fantasy" on SexSource Online.

Software in the form of CD-ROMs or DVDs offers self-help for understanding and enhancing sexual relationships and for treating sexual dysfunctions and other problems. These media have received high ratings from users in comparison to other modes of seeking help because they are relatively inexpensive, easily available, and very private. There are also games that simulate erotic encounters in CD-ROM form (Stern & Handel, 2001). A new series of DVDs called "Virtual Sex with . . ." features various porn stars, and the viewer can choose particular moods and positions for viewing—a further step toward interactive sex via computer.

Like any medium, computers have the potential for abuse in sex-related matters. Some people have been subjected to sexual harassment or stalking by anonymous participants in computer networks (Foote, 1999). Internet bulletin boards that serve child pornographers by transmitting explicit sexual photos of children have been shut down by the government. Concern still exists about uncontrolled access to cybersex by underage individuals, and some pedophiles have used computer networks to make contact with young people. Even though there are a number of Internet controls that can be used to prevent access by minors to sexual material, these filters may also block legitimate, nonpornographic information as well, including sites on breast cancer and reproductive health. The U.S. Congress has tried to take steps that would essentially eliminate expressions of sexuality from the Internet altogether, but the Supreme Court has tended to block such efforts on constitutional grounds. For example, the Court ruled in 2002 that to exclude virtual images of nude people engaged in sexual activity, even if they are virtual depictions of children, would be unconstitutional. The battle continues between the Justice Department and those who champion the right of people to access sex-related materials (Melby, 2006c).

Television

For several decades, television has represented one of the most powerful forms of mass communication, and it has increasingly emphasized sexual themes. The Telecommunications Reform Act of 1996 required the television industry to develop a ratings system for viewers. The original system was based on motion picture ratings related to sex and violence. The general public and Congress determined that the TV ratings system was not having much of an impact, so additional rating letters were proposed to designate sexual content, violence, and explicit language.

Television soap operas, with more than 35 million viewers, average seven sexual incidents per hour. Two-thirds of prime-time television shows include sexual themes or behaviors but only rarely feature any reference to condoms, unintended pregnancy, or emotional consequences. Twelve percent of prime-time TV shows depict characters involved in sexual intercourse (Farrar et al., 2003). Producers of soap operas have been attempting to become more educative about safe sex and issues such as date rape and unintended pregnancy. At the same time, in their attempts to appeal to youthful audiences, the sexual activity in TV shows is extending to younger characters in the stories. The soaps tend to reflect sexual content that is true to society's current sex-related themes, and although it is not yet known with any real accuracy how these shows affect viewers' attitudes and values, it is generally believed that they do have some effect on their perceptions of sexuality (Greenberg & Woods, 1999; Stern & Handel, 2001).

There is conflicting research evidence about the effects of television on the sexual activities of teenagers. Nearly three out of four teens believe that sexual content on television influences the sexual behaviors of people their age. About a third indicate that such sexual content has caused them to have a conversation with their parents about a sexual issue, and half have found useful information by watching such programs (Brown, 2002; Kaiser Family Foundation, 2002). When an episode of *Friends* demonstrated that condom use does not always prevent pregnancy, that message was understood by a substantial proportion of teenagers who viewed the show (Collins et al., 2003). Talk about sex is extremely frequent on television, as are depictions of flirting and kissing. Intercourse is either depicted or strongly implied in roughly one of every eight shows on television (Kunkel, Cope, & Biely, 1999). Several studies have documented that within any rather brief period of television viewing, a great many suggestive remarks and scenes will be part of the fare (Farrar et al., 2003; Lampman et al., 2002).

A number of television shows featuring teenagers in sexual situations have dealt with sexuality frankly. *Friday Night Lights* has portrayed the developing sexual relationship of a teenage couple. In the former *Boston Public,* a couple was caught during an act of fellatio; *Dawson's Creek* featured the first romantic kiss between two teenage boys; *The OC* depicted a young man's first awkward experiences with intercourse. There is certainly evidence that adolescents are somewhat affected by such content. The more teens are exposed to these themes on TV, the stronger their endorsement of recreational sexual activity and the higher their expectations of the amount of sex their peers are experiencing (Ward & Rivadeneyra, 1999). However, evidence also shows that there is more to the relationship between teenagers and the media than simple "exposure." Teens' own sense of themselves—their identity—determines not only what they will seek out to view in the media, but also how they will interact with and be affected by what they see (Steele, 1999).

Studies have been done on the portrayals of women and men on television. It has been reported that men on TV frequently comment on women's bodies and physical appearance and that masculinity is often equated with being sexual. Feminist issues and themes tend to be trivialized and undervalued. Experts have warned that television needs to offer images of sexuality that emphasize planning, honesty, pleasure, and protection (Stern & Handel, 2001).

It is increasingly common for sexuality to become part of the scripts for TV dramas and situation comedies. The now-syndicated comedy show *Seinfeld* was the first prime-time network television program to deal with masturbation as a theme, and allusions to masturbation now have made their way into most situation comedies, along with frequent references to penises and breasts. The British production *Queer as Folk* has been a hit on Showtime (see Figure 15.5), and the prime-time show *Brothers and Sisters* features an openly gay man who is searching for a strong relationship. The popular *Queer Eye for the Straight Guy,* in which a team of five gay men give a straight man a grooming, fashion, and decorating makeover, has been featured during the morning hours on network TV (Sigesmund, 2003). Television talk shows have a reputation for dealing with every conceivable sexual variation and relationship, even during daytime hours. Today's television viewing public is arguably the most widely sexuality-exposed public in history. How much of an impact that exposure to sexual themes has on the lives of people in all age brackets is yet to be fully understood. It does seem clear that television in the United States has not been used much for the promotion of sexual health or responsible sexual behavior (Keller & Brown, 2002).

Advertising

More than any other medium in American society today, advertising uses and exploits sex, and the evidence suggests that it is a powerful sales tool

FIGURE 15.5

Cast members of *Queer as Folk* on Showtime.

Source: Everett Collection, Inc.

(Reichert, 2003). Advertisements for underwear have been highly popular, although Calvin Klein came under fire for using models who appeared to be underage. Print advertisements for Obsession perfume often use naked bodies in rather subdued romantic lighting. The young, attractive male and the beautiful female predominate in advertisements for alcoholic beverages, perfume, jewelry, cars, and clothing, because the basic idea behind using sex to sell a product is something advertisers call "identification." The message is that if the consumer uses a certain perfume, wears a certain pair of jeans, or drives a certain car, he or she will be as glamorous and attractive as the model and will experience the kind of excitement and romance implied in the advertisement (see Figure 15.6).

If the advertisement is not blatantly sexual, then it may be subliminally sexual. Advertisers may use a technique called embedding, in which they deliberately hide emotionally or sexually charged words or pictures in the background of an advertisement (Reichert, 2003). More frequently, women and men tend to be portrayed in advertising in rather specific and stereotypical ways, generating criticism that their portrayal perpetuates outmoded and unfair images. On the other hand, it has been argued that such images are simply reflections of the prevailing attitudes about gender that seem to help sell products on the basis of sex appeal. It is clear that women are used more frequently than men as sex-related objects in advertising (Reichert & Lambiase, 2003). Precisely because of these facts, such advertising causes consternation among critics, some of whom view these advertising messages as a type of mind control.

The question has been posed concerning why condom ads have not become more mainstream in the media given the prevalence of other sex-related messages. Some publishers and broadcasters claim they are worried that the public will disapprove of such advertising, although surveys have shown that 71 percent of Americans favor condom advertising on television (Pardun & Forde, 2003).

We might also ask why the sexual message is so powerful. Why does everyone want to identify with a symbol of sex? One possible answer is that in our culture sex is synonymous with youth, attractiveness, and desirability, and it implies wealth and power. However, whether the media have created that image identification or simply mirror it is a debatable point.

Child Pornography

One of the most secretive, most lucrative, and most damaging types of pornography is that involving children. Children are emotionally unable to give true consent to sexual behavior and thus are the innocent victims of adult greed. **Kiddie porn,** as it is more popularly known, involves everything from children simply posing in the nude, to suggestive movement, to sexual activity with others their own age and with adults. Although statistics on child pornography can only be estimates, U.S. customs officials believe that thousands of pieces of such material are smuggled into this country each week, primarily from Scandinavia. Although they are often monitored by authorities, child pornography sites are still available through the Internet. "Sting" operations have been directed at arresting people who have downloaded child pornography, but some observers have said that these events may create more hype than actual deterrence (Fulda, 2002).

Courts in the United States continue to support the contention that child pornography lies outside First Amendment protection. The Child Pornography Prevention Act of 1996 supports stiff penalties for those who involve children in sexual exploitation through

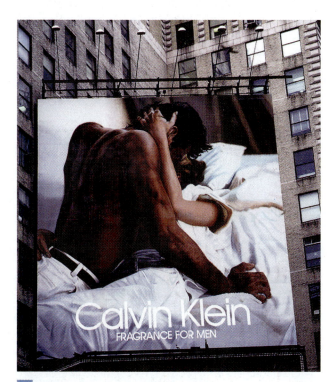

■ **FIGURE 15.6** *Sex in Advertising*
This Calvin Klein billboard in Times Square in New York City provides a graphic reminder that sexual themes play a significant role in advertising. The typical suggestion is that using a certain product will somehow lead to a better sex life.

kiddie porn the distribution and sale of photographs and films of children or younger teenagers engaging in some form of sexual activity.

the making and distribution of pornography. The penalties for causing a child to engage in explicit sexual behavior before a camera or for distributing child pornography have escalated. There are now more than 3,000 new cases opened by the FBI each year for the posting of child pornography and related violations (Nordland & Bartholet, 2001). Rings of people engaged in the transmission of child sex images over the Internet have been prosecuted and given stiff sentences. Some photographers, book distributors, and librarians believe that parts of the law are too restrictive and run counter to constitutional guarantees of freedom of speech (Jenkins, 2001). There has also been controversy over what constitutes child pornography. In one case, a man was convicted because he had videotapes of teenage and preteen girls in bathing suits who were dancing, and he had zoomed in on the clothed genital area; another court overturned the conviction because there was no nudity or discernible "lascivious exhibitions." Virtual computer images of children and adolescents, found to be permissible by the Supreme Court, may well become part of this market. Such controversies certainly will persist, but the message condemning the use of underage individuals in pornography seems clear.

■ Differing Perspectives on the Effects of Sexually Explicit Materials

Many people have conflicting attitudes about sexually explicit material. They may be reluctant to admit that they are aroused by seeing pornographic material, or they may have some degree of guilt about their reactions. There seems to be a greater level of acceptance of pornography among males and younger people, and people under age 25 tend to report higher rates of usage. In one Norwegian study, three basic dimensions of attitudes about pornography were identified. Some people seem to perceive pornography mostly as a way of enhancing sexual pleasure. Others judge it to be a moral issue, seeing it as either right or wrong. A final group places pornography within the social framework of its use; when explicit media are viewed by groups of friends, it may not seem as "dirty" or even as sexual as it would have had it been viewed in private. Attitudes toward the material seem to mediate how individuals may or may not access sexually explicit materials (Traeen, Spitznogle, & Beverfjord, 2004).

Perhaps because pornography makes usually private acts very public, various groups in society have been concerned with the effect pornographic material is likely to have on those who view it. Early

research into the effects of pornography tended to concentrate on the immediate and short-term effects, especially on males. Results were mixed and hardly representative of the general population. However, it has seemed clear that exposure to sexually explicit materials can lead to sexual arousal, to both positive and negative emotional reactions, and to participation in some form of sexual activity that the individual viewer tends to prefer.

Conflicting positions on the positive and negative potentials of sexually explicit material were once based in two major theoretical camps. **Modeling theory** held that people exposed to sexual acts through pornography had a greater likelihood of copying this behavior in their own lives. Another point of view, the **catharsis theory,** maintained that pornography actually prevented violence or unconventional sexual behavior by providing a release of sexual tension for the viewer or reader. More recently, sexually explicit material has been examined from the perspective that it might lead to attitudinal changes (Bogaert, 2001; Davis & Bauserman, 1993; Malamuth, Addison, & Koss, 2001).

National Commissions on Pornography

Dozens of studies have attempted to examine the effects of sexually explicit materials on adults. Some of these studies have been part of national efforts to resolve questions about the regulation of pornography. In the United States during the Nixon and Reagan administrations, groups were established to examine the effects of pornography and its regulation.

Presidential Commission on Obscenity and Pornography, 1970

This commission's majority report recommended the repeal of legislation prohibiting the sale, exhibition, or distribution of sexual materials to consenting adults. The report stated that the recommendation was based on the commission's having found "no evidence to date that exposure to explicit sexual materials plays a significant role in the causation of delinquent or criminal behavior among youth or adults." Additionally, the commission declared that pornography did not cause "social or individual harms such as . . . sexual or

> **modeling theory** a perspective that suggests that people will copy behavior they view in pornography.
>
> **catharsis theory** the suggestion that viewing pornography provides a release for sexual tension, thereby preventing antisocial behavior.

nonsexual deviancy or severe emotional disturbance" (pp. 32, 58). A minority of commission members did not concur with the report, however, and the U.S. Senate and President Richard Nixon rejected the commission's recommendations. Some critics maintained that the commission should have considered more thoroughly evidence about the connections between violence and sex and about how people sometimes imitate the behavior they observe in others. Also, it did not use any studies conducted with young people. Instead, the committee's conclusions about youth were drawn from retrospective reports offered by adult research subjects.

United States Attorney General's Commission on Pornography, 1986

In 1984, a new commission was established to hold hearings on the effects of pornography. From its inception, this commission was charged with making recommendations on how "the spread of pornography could be contained." Its work was governed by the premise that pornography was a "serious national problem." Commission members were chosen for their recognized anti-pornography stances. The commission had neither the funds nor the time to support new research studies, relying instead on the testimony of witnesses. This led to claims that the group's conclusions were simplistic and not justified by scientific data (Mosher, 1986). The majority report concluded that violent pornography caused sexually aggressive behavior toward women and children and fostered accepting attitudes toward rape. There were mixed opinions on the potential effects of pornography deemed "nonviolent and nondegrading" by the commission. The commission made recommendations for the control and elimination of pornography through stricter law enforcement and stiffer penalties for offenders. Others opposed the recommendations as unconstitutional intrusions on various civil liberties.

Governmental commissions clearly serve mainly to fulfill the political agendas of particular administrations. To a degree, however, they may also reflect the prevailing attitudes of a society. Comparing the conclusions of the 1986 commission report to the one from 1970 provides interesting grounds for speculation about how social attitudes and values regarding pornography and individual freedom may have shifted during that period.

Exposure to Sexually Explicit Materials

Fifty years of research have amassed a variety of findings concerning exposure to sexually explicit materials and its effects. Writers of commentaries or opinions about pornography often begin with some ideological assumption and then cite highly selective research to support their assertions (Stires, 1999). Researchers also may bring their own particular attitudes and points of view to their work. Consequently, there has been a great deal of confusion about the results of research on exposure to sexually explicit materials and exactly what those results mean.

Recent researchers have done a more comprehensive job to date of systematically analyzing and integrating research on sexually explicit materials, using contemporary psychological theory on attitude change as a basis of understanding. Their analysis has brought some fundamental principles about the effects of pornography into perspective. These researchers see sexually explicit material as a form of *persuasive communication,* because it clearly has an impact on those who view it. The questions revolve around how much impact, and what kinds of impact, it actually has (Bogaert, 2001; Davis & Bauserman, 1993; Malamuth, Addison, & Koss, 2001).

Arousal and Emotional Reactions

To be commercially successful, pornography must produce sexual arousal and positive emotional reactions as defined by the viewer. These also appear to be the primary motivations for people to seek out and view sexually explicit materials. Almost all such materials do produce arousal, as demonstrated by the self-reporting of research participants and by direct measurement of genital and other physiological changes. Emotional responses have been measured on scales of from 5 to 50 points of variation, on which people rate their intensity of both pleasant and unpleasant reactions. Seventy to 90 percent of both men and women experience measurable physiological arousal in response to sexually explicit material (Slade, 2001). Self-reporting scales have found either no particular differences between men and women or more arousal among men than women when viewing pornography. There is no support in the research literature for the contention that women are not aroused by graphic depictions of sex that lack romantic aspects or that women are more aroused when romance is included in the depictions.

Across various studies, men fairly consistently react with more positive emotions to sexually explicit material, and women with higher levels of negative emotions (Janssen, Carpenter, & Graham, 2003). People who find material sexually arousing are more likely to react positively to it, but sometimes the arousal and emotional reactions are quite independent. Depicted sexual behaviors that the individual considers bizarre or socially deviant are likely to produce a negative emotional response, even if the person has also been sexually aroused by seeing them (Koukounas & McCabe, 2001). Average adult males tend to have the highest levels of arousal in response to sexually explicit materials featuring adults of their preferred sex, but they may also have substantial levels of arousal when postpubescent children or adolescents of the preferred sex are shown. They have minimal, though often measurable, levels of response to children depicted in pornography. One study of adult pedophiles who were attracted to boys found that viewing erotica involving nudity and sexual acts of boys did not seem to cause them to commit sexual acts with boys (Riegel, 2004). The research confirms that for every type of sexually explicit stimulus, at least some people react with arousal and positive emotions. For those same stimuli, other people are not aroused and/or have a negative emotional response (Bogaert, 2001).

Effects on Attitudes

There have been many claims about how viewing sexually explicit materials might change people's attitudes toward sexuality, relationships, or other people (Ciclitira, 2004). Theories of attitude change postulate that there are two paths through which human beings process persuasive communication such as sexually explicit material. The *central* processing route involves careful, thoughtful, and systematic processing of the information, whereas the *peripheral* processing route is more automatic and involves a minimum of cognitive effort. It is theorized that for real attitudinal change to occur, material must be processed thoroughly through the central route and the individual must possess clear motivation and the ability to pursue this path. For most people, sexually explicit material is viewed solely for its arousal value, and psychologists believe that as such viewers tend to be distracted from processing it through any central path. It is not likely that it leads to substantial or long-term attitudinal changes in most people. However, the effects of such materials are the result of complex interactions of the viewer's predispositions, the nature of the pornography being viewed, and the amount of exposure. The research suggests that a single exposure to sexually explicit stories, pictures, or films produces minimal change in sexuality-related attitudes (Slade, 2001). More exposure may result in somewhat more permissive attitudes as viewers experience less anxiety and more positive feelings.

A great deal of research has focused on the effects of pornography on the attitudes of men toward women. The findings show that males who have a history of more exposure to sexually explicit materials do not hold more negative attitudes toward women and,

in fact, may be more gender egalitarian in their attitudes. Research subjects tend to respond more negatively to scenes depicting sexual aggression and more positively to egalitarian scenes, but attitudes seem unaffected (Bauserman, 1998; DeVoss, 2002). On the other hand, exposure to massive amounts of material that depicts callousness or adversarial relationships with women seems to strengthen such attitudes in men who have a predisposition toward them. For the most part, however, exposure to sexually explicit material appears to have little effect on attitudes (Bauserman, 1998; Koukounas & McCabe, 2001). It is often claimed that pornography turns women into sexual objects. A recent analysis of 50 popular sexually explicit films actually found that, based on 12 measures of objectification, women were no more objectified than were the men in the films (McKee, 2005).

Effects on Behavior

The research on the possible behavioral effects of sexually explicit materials has focused primarily on sexual and aggressive behaviors. As might be anticipated, most research has found that at least some, and often the majority of, participants report an increase in sexual behavior within 24 hours following exposure. The behaviors tend to be those in which the person would participate with some frequency anyway, including sexual thoughts and fantasies, daydreams, talking about sex, masturbation, and sexual intercourse. Sexual behaviors that occur with lower frequency for the individual do not seem to increase following exposure to such materials.

It is neither ethical nor practical for researchers to carry out "real-world" studies to determine whether people will behave in a sexually aggressive manner following exposure to pornography. Instead, researchers have created an artificial situation to measure aggression: After a subject has been exposed to pornography, a "confederate" will attempt to provoke aggressive behavior by insulting the subject. Males who are exposed to nonaggressive pornography are no more likely to be aggressive toward females than are controls who have been exposed to neutral, or nonexplicit, material. Exposure to aggressive depictions in pornography sometimes seems to increase nonsexual aggression somewhat, though usually only when the subject is provoked again by a confederate. These effects have been limited to laboratory settings and seem to disappear rapidly (Davis & Bauserman, 1993; Slade, 2001). The intellectual ability of subjects has also been shown to be a variable in such research. Men with lower IQs are more likely to act more sexually suggestive toward women and to stand closer to them following the viewing of sexual violence; no difference was noted in men with higher IQs (Bogaert, Woodard, & Hafer, 1999).

Real People

A T-Shirt Places a Male Residence Hall under Fire

A freshman residence hall that had traditionally been all male had developed a reputation for its macho image on the campus. In fun, the dorm was nicknamed "The Cave," and its residents took pride in their special identity. Although college officials discouraged use of the building's nickname, the staff who lived there often boasted of the camaraderie that its residents seemed to share. They had intramural sports teams, parties, and a variety of annual special events. One of The Cave's traditions was to create a specially designed T-shirt for its residents each fall. One year, the T-shirt pictured a drawing of two cavemen figures dragging a cavewoman by the hair toward a door labeled "The Cave."

Soon after the T-shirt began to appear, there was an outcry from various campus constituencies condemning the shirt and what was perceived as its antiwoman message. Some faculty members banned the wearing of the T-shirts in the classroom, claiming that it constituted harassment of women. Many of the men wearing the shirt took offense at this reaction, saying that there had been no malicious intent in the shirt's design and claiming that the U.S. Constitution protected their right of freedom of expression. They received support from some women on the campus, who agreed that the shirt certainly did not reflect the attitudes of men in the dorm toward women. They argued that opponents were going too far in their assumptions. College officials made certain that institutional funds had not been

used to pay for the T-shirt, and they also issued a statement that they did not support the negative message it conveyed. However, officials declined to prohibit the wearing of the shirt on a general basis. They reminded those individuals who felt that the shirt was in any way personally harassing that they could lodge complaints through the institution's grievance procedures.

The "Cave T-Shirt," as it came to be known, turned out to be a highly educational phenomenon. It generated many open debates and classroom discussions about individual rights of expression versus the rights of individuals to live and work in a non-hostile environment. It provided an excellent real-life situation that tested the complicated issues on all sides of the question. The controversy led men and women to talk more openly about their attitudes toward one another. As things turned out, no one ever brought formal complaints about the T-shirt, and the wearers of the shirt tried to be considerate of those faculty members who explained that they were personally offended by the picture. Although it rather quickly faded from popularity, the T-shirt's impact remained legendary on the campus.

Would you have been offended by the drawing on this T-shirt? If so, would you have been moved to take any formal action against being exposed to it? Are there drawings, pictures, or words on a T-shirt that in your opinion should be banned from being worn in public? Explain.

Pornography, Aggression, and Violence

Although researchers have difficulty designing studies to find whether exposure to pornography will cause sexual aggression or violence, they have conducted studies to see if an association can be found between a history of exposure to pornography and later sexual behaviors. Early studies on longer-term effects of pornography were concerned particularly with how exposure to pornography might relate to antisocial or criminal sexual behavior in males. Institutionalized sex offenders

and pornography users who frequented "adult" bookstores and cinemas were compared to a carefully matched sample of individuals in a control group. It was found that the controls—average, nonoffender heterosexuals—had actually been exposed to more pornography during adolescence than had other groups surveyed, and to more explicit forms of pornography as well. Some interesting findings emerged concerning sex-offender groups. Unlike the controls, they reported responses to pornography typical of people who had a great deal of emotional guilt about sexual thoughts and behaviors; at the same time, they had less frequent exposure to pornographic materials. Sex offenders' reactions to pornography during adulthood also seemed more typical of what one might expect of adolescents—especially because arousal so often led to masturbation. The control groups tended to seek heterosexual outlets after being aroused by erotic materials.

Should pornography be available to the general public? Should there be any restrictions in terms of age of consumer or theme of material?

In studying the use of pornography among a population of child molesters and a control group, it has been found that the child molesters have, in fact, been significantly older when first exposed to pornography than have the controls. Several researchers have concluded that there is no demonstrable evidence to support the contention that use of pornography might be associated with a greater likelihood of committing sexually violent acts such as rape. In a survey of four countries where pornographic materials are widely available—Denmark, Sweden, Germany, and the United States—there did not seem to be any correlation between that availability and the incidence of rape in the society. It has been proposed that the motivation to rape may not be influenced by exposure to pornography, but rather that pornography could reinforce already existing beliefs and values about rape (Wilson et al., 2002). There is support for the existence of an association between sexually aggressive behaviors and frequent use of violent pornography among men of lower intelligence already prone to aggressive and antisocial behaviors. Men also may be more likely to model aggressive behavior after the aggressiveness of other males (Mitchell et al., 2002). Men of higher intelligence who are not prone to aggression tend not to choose violent pornography and do not seem to be moved to antisocial behavior by other types of sexually explicit material (Bogaert, 2001; Malamuth, Addison, & Koss, 2001).

A considerable amount of research has focused on males' responses to depictions of coercive sex or rape. There seems to be a distinct difference in how men respond to portrayals of realistic rape, in which the woman shows pain and revulsion, and to what psychologists call "rape myth" portrayals, in which the woman eventually becomes aroused and participates willingly. The realistic depictions tend not to be as arousing as the rape myths and often produce negative emotional responses (Bauserman, 1998). Greater exposure to sexually explicit material that features violence may cause some men to believe more strongly in the rape myth (Davis & Bauserman, 1993). However, the research conditions themselves may play a significant role in these results. Real-life conditions produced no noticeable changes in the acceptance of rape

myths, whereas more direct experimental conditions did produce some such changes.

■ Legal Aspects of Pornography and Sexual Behavior

Lawmakers and law enforcers seem to fall into two major philosophical camps. Some believe that the law has a responsibility to enforce private morals publicly and to prohibit whatever the community or society deems morally wrong or offensive. Others hold that the purpose of the law is to protect rather than to prohibit. They are not concerned about enforcing laws against pornography or sexual activities that involve consenting adults, and they believe that government should stay out of the bedrooms of private citizens (Graupner, 2000).

Pornography, the Courts, and the Law

The pornography issue is intimately associated with the principles of freedom of speech and freedom of press and with the role of the courts and the law in upholding those principles. Although some people crusade against censorship and for the freedom to read or view whatever sexually oriented matter one wishes, others argue that "trash" can and should be distinguished from "art" and that censorship should be allowed even in a democracy. Two fundamental issues in the censorship argument are the assumptions that sexual images will lead to inappropriate behavior and that these images objectify human beings, in a sense dehumanizing them. There are those who do not feel that the evidence supports such assumptions and that, although censorship may offer the illusion of solving social problems, in reality it leads to the loss of freedoms. Some evidence indicates that enforcement of anti-pornography laws does not significantly change the rate of arrests for rape, prostitution, or other sex offenses (Levesque, 2002; McKee, 2005).

Local governments, state courts, federal legislation, and federal courts have tended to be inconsistent in their treatment of cases related to sexually explicit materials. In 1868, obscenity was legally defined as any material whose tendency was to "deprave and corrupt those whose minds are open to such immoral influences, and into whose hands a publication of this sort may fall." It was illegal to purvey obscenity to the public. In the landmark 1957 Supreme Court case *Roth v. United States,* obscenity was redefined as matter appealing to prurient interest ("a shameful or morbid interest in nudity, sex, or excretion, which goes beyond customary limits of candor"). The Court further ruled, however, that censorship of obscene material would not be allowed if the material had some "socially redeeming significance." In 1969, in *Stanley v. Georgia,* the Court ruled that a person is entitled to possess pornography in the privacy of his or her own home and to use that pornography to satisfy whatever intellectual or emotional needs he or she desires.

In 1973, the Supreme Court took a different position on pornography, deciding that a connection between pornography and antisocial behavior could be neither proved nor disproved. On this basis, the Court ruled that individual state legislatures may adopt their own limits on commerce in pornography, placing more of the responsibility for judgments about pornography on local governments. The Court also dropped the obscenity standard of lack of "redeeming social value" in favor of a new standard specifying that the work, taken as a whole, must lack serious literary, artistic, political, or scientific merit. The Court limited the standard to works that depict or describe sexual conduct. The vagueness of these definitions and the apparent reversals in Supreme Court positions continue to create confusion in other court decisions, leading to widely disparate attitudes toward pornography in different communities around the country. The Court is still hearing cases concerning the Child Online Protection Act, a 1998 law that would penalize pornographers who fail to restrict children's access to their Internet sites. The law has yet to be enforced because of continuing legal challenges to its constitutionality (Melby, 2006c).

The controversy has continued in other arenas. Legislatures have entertained bills that would permit suits by people who felt they had been victims of crimes somehow associated with the use of pornography. Like similar legislative attempts, these are considered to be a radical departure from accepted constitutional principles related to freedom of expression. The Supreme Court of Canada decided that pornographic materials by definition "subordinated or degraded" women and declared it legitimate to suppress such materials. Deciding what constitutes undue sexual exploitation is still left to individual prosecutors and lower courts in Canada, creating a great deal of confusion and leading to ongoing debate. Again, the problems seem to lie in the vague definition of what constitutes pornography, the assumption that it is harmful, and the provision that anyone harmed may bring suit. Clearly, pornography presents very real challenges in defining freedom of expression and setting the boundaries that any society will use in regulating such materials (Levesque, 2002).

What role, if any, should the government take in legislating sexual behavior or access to sexually explicit materials?

Legal Regulation of Sexual Behavior

In the area of sexual behavior, it seems that for every activity some people find disturbing or worthy of moral disapproval, a law has been enacted to prohibit the activity. Laws have attempted to regulate the criteria of consent for sex, the nature of the sexual act, the object to which it may be directed, and where the act may take place. Although the laws concerning sexual behavior differ among the states, it is likely that a great many adults in the United States have performed sexual acts considered at least in some states to be criminal under the law. There are only two types of sexual behavior that are not potentially subject to criminal prosecution as long as they are practiced in private: solitary masturbation and intercourse between husband and wife.

Several states have statutes specifically prohibiting sexual activity between persons of the same gender. Some other states have laws prohibiting forms of behavior that fall into the category of "deviate sexual intercourse," without necessarily specifying the gender of the participants. This means that the behaviors could be considered criminal between heterosexual partners as well. These laws were once called **sodomy laws,** with the term *sodomy* being applied rather freely to many behaviors legally defined as deviate sexual intercourse, including oral-genital, genital-anal, oral-anal, and manual-genital contact. More than half of the 50 states no longer have such laws, essentially permitting consenting adults to engage in private sexual acts of their choosing (Quindlen, 2003).

The U.S. Supreme Court handed down a landmark ruling in 2003 that overturned a Texas sodomy law. The law had been invoked against a gay male couple who had been having sex in private in their own home. The police had broken in because of a false report of a weapon being present, and the men were arrested for their sexual activity. The Court ruled that the law was demeaning to gay people and that the government has no authority to regulate the sexual conduct of "consenting adults acting in private." A similar case in Georgia in 1986 had been decided differently, but the law subsequently was repealed in the state.

The debate over whether sex-related laws should aim at prohibition or protection continues. The American Bar Association has joined the Group for the Advancement of Psychiatry in calling for sex offenders to be confined for appropriate treatment of their sexual disorders rather than simply incarcerated for punishment.

sodomy laws laws in some states that prohibit a variety of sexual behaviors, often described as deviate sexual intercourse. These laws often are enforced discriminatorily against particular groups, such as gay males.

Those in favor of legal reforms argue that laws prohibiting sexual behavior between consenting adults are attempts to impose specific moral and religious standards on citizens.

See "The Right to Privacy" on SexSource Online.

Sex and the Constitution

The legal aspects of sexual behavior cannot be considered fairly without examining some of the constitutional implications. Since the U.S. Constitution was written, there has been a conflict over the extent to which it guarantees personal liberty in cases where other people are not harmed. The debate sometimes has focused on the laws governing, or attempting to govern, sexual behavior. Some experts insist that laws prohibiting consensual sexual activity between adults—particularly gay men or lesbians—are indeed unconstitutional. When these laws have been vaguely worded, courts have sometimes declared them "void for vagueness."

Three other constitutional principles have been used to overturn laws regulating consensual adult sexual behavior. One is the "independent rights" doctrine, which holds that the Constitution imposes certain restrictions on state laws that might interfere with personal liberty. Another is the "right of privacy" doctrine, which, in many courts, has been used to uphold the concept that what people do in private should not be the concern of prohibitive laws unless someone is being harmed. Finally, the "equal protection" clause of the Fourteenth Amendment has been interpreted to require that state laws be nondiscriminatory both in their statutory expression and in their enforcement. Colorado became the first state to pass a state constitutional amendment in the 1990s that denied gays and lesbians legal protection from discrimination. The amendment never took effect because of an initial court ruling against it, and the U.S. Supreme Court struck down the measure on constitutional grounds as discriminatory and hostile toward a particular group of people.

The debate over laws concerning consensual sexual behavior and other seemingly "victimless" crimes will continue. These issues should be of concern to all citizens because they often have implications for our freedom in other areas. In recent years, it has become clear that the makeup of both the Congress and the Supreme Court—the primary branch of government that interprets the Constitution and sets precedents concerning legal interventions—plays a key role in determining whether decisions will lean in more conser-

vative or more liberal directions with regard to sex-related issues (Levesque, 2002).

See "Arthur, An Attorney for First Amendment Issues," on SexSource Online.

Special Issues and the Law

Sexuality Education

Although it has not been subject to much court action, sexuality education has met with controversy that has reached as far as the U.S. Congress. As far back as 1919, federal authorities determined that sexuality education was more properly a task of the schools. Two federal education laws still prohibit the federal government from dictating the content of sexuality education courses. A landmark court case was initiated in 1970 against the board of education of Topeka, Kansas, alleging that the school district's sexuality education program was unconstitutional because it violated the parents' personal liberty to determine what subjects their children are taught. It was alleged further that the authority to instruct children about sexuality is reserved for the parents. At the conclusion of the trial, the judge found for the schools, permitting them to continue their sexuality education program.

Although the teaching of sexuality education topics has been left to the jurisdiction of state laws and local boards of education, there have been continuing waves of anti-sexuality education sentiment. Citizen groups, often affiliated with religious institutions, have attacked sexuality education in public school settings and have pressured, boards of education into reversing previous decisions. Some precedents have already been set, suggesting that religiously based sexuality education values are not to be considered suitable for the public schools. The U.S. Congress continues to fund state grants to be used by states in abstinence-based sexuality education to discourage sexual activity outside of marriage, part of the continuing congressional debate on the content of sexuality education programs. There is a growing likelihood that comprehensive sexuality education will be discouraged in favor of abstinence-based recommendations and mandates at the federal level.

Sexual Assault and Rape

Historically, women were not regarded as equal to men under the law and instead were treated as men's possessions. Therefore, forced sex was viewed not as a crime against the female victim but as a property crime against the man who "owned" her—either her father or her husband. In the United States, laws passed in 1868 required that rape be corroborated by evidence of actual penetration, the use of force, and identification of the rapist. In the 1970s, corroboration laws were generally repealed, lessening the burden of proof for the victim. Nonetheless, conviction has still depended on the prosecution's being able to provide tangible evidence that a sexual assault has occurred. A landmark decision emerged in 1979 when a Massachusetts court found a man guilty of raping his wife. During the previous year, there had been a trial in Oregon involving a case in which a husband was accused of raping his wife, but there was no conviction. In the Massachusetts case, the couple had been separated for several months when the man forced his way into his wife's apartment and threatened to kill her if she did not have intercourse with him. A jury of eight men and four women found him guilty, and he was sentenced to three to five years in prison, along with several years of probation.

Many states have been reevaluating their legislation that applies to the investigation and prosecution of rape cases. Legislative measures have now been adopted in most states that help rape victims and increase the chances of convicting the perpetrators. Symptoms of the rape trauma syndrome are sometimes admissible as evidence in rape trials (see Chapter 16, "Sexual Consent, Coercion, Rape, and Abuse"). Members of police agencies, especially those who deal with rape victims, also have been receiving training with respect to sexual assault. Some local agencies provide counselors who act as advocates and sources of support for the rape victim throughout the judicial process. Some agencies also recommend third-party reporting of rape in case a victim is reluctant to come forward. This at least informs authorities that a rape has occurred, which may be valuable if the victim later decides to proceed with a report. After centuries of neglect and mistreatment by most judicial systems, it would appear that rape victims are finding the prospect of having their attackers prosecuted and convicted more likely than ever before.

The Kobe Bryant rape trial in Colorado tested rape shield laws, which typically do not allow testimony concerning the woman's sexual history. Lawyers on the Bryant defense team argued that particular sexual actions of the woman might be relevant to the case. Others argued that to reveal information about the victim would undo years of progress in prosecuting rapists (Markels, 2003).

Sex Workers, Nude Dancing, and Peep Shows

Legal reforms are difficult in the area of sex workers. Prostitution has often been considered a "victimless"

crime because the sexual activity is seemingly between two consenting adults. Two types of laws attempt to control overt prostitution: those that prohibit loitering with the intent to commit an act of prostitution, and those that prohibit either offering or agreeing to an act of prostitution. Again, the basic philosophy behind such laws is the regulation of private morality. However, many groups insist that it is a social necessity to attempt legal control of sex workers. Police claim that the street environment generated by sex workers breeds crime of other sorts. Public health officials say that prostitutes are responsible for much of the increase in rates of sexually transmitted infections. Moralists attack sex workers on religious grounds.

Some people favor the *decriminalization* of prostitution, which would lead to regulation of the trade. Under such a plan, prostitution would be subject to certain age requirements, taxation rules, and standards of hygiene. Sex workers would be required to obtain a license. Decriminalization would protect the civil rights of both prostitutes and their clients. It would free sex workers from the system of arrests, bail, and release to the street; the abuse of pimps; and the harassment of society.

The Supreme Court has also been called on to decide on the constitutionality of nude dancing and stripping in bars. The owners of a strip club had been convicted of violating an Indiana law prohibiting nude dancing. G-strings and "pasties" over the nipples were considered to be minimum attire for a dancer. A federal court of appeals first overturned the conviction, maintaining that nude dancing is "inherently expressive" and therefore constitutionally protected. However, the Supreme Court ruled that states may ban nude dancing in the interest of "protecting order and morality." The requirement for G-strings and pasties was considered appropriate because it combated what the chief justice called the "evil" of public nudity without suppressing the "erotic message" of the expressive dancing. This continues to be a somewhat ambiguous area, because the dancers are working voluntarily and the men who frequent the places seem to be trying to relax for the most part. There typically are no expectations of actual sex acts. Former stripper Katherine Frank (2003), now a college professor, continues to research the practices and meanings associated with strip clubs.

A controversy emerged in San Diego, California, when the city passed an ordinance restricting the hours during which peep show establishments could operate. These businesses, which have booths in which viewers can watch explicit films by themselves, were not allowed to have the booths open between 2:00 a.m. and 6:00 a.m. because it was claimed that there was increased crime in their vicinity. One group of researchers studied the issue and concluded that there was in fact no greater incidence of crime associated with either the peep show establishments themselves or their general neighborhoods. They saw the governmental regulation as an illegitimate infringement on communication about sex. Others fired back that the group's research was flawed and the results were unreliable, and the controversy continued (Linz, Paul, & Yao, 2006; McCleary & Meeker, 2006).

Reproductive Rights

Among the controversial issues that have found their way into courts and laws are birth control, welfare benefits for teenage and unwed mothers, sterilization, and abortion (see also Chapter 11 "Decision Making about Pregnancy and Parenthood"). The Supreme Court did not declare bans on the use of contraceptives unconstitutional until the mid-1960s. Sterilization has been a more complicated issue. In several cases, black women or people with mental retardation have been sterilized without their consent. Such actions seem to rest on the assumption that judges and physicians know best and have the right, and privilege, to decide whether an individual will be a fit parent and whether the individual's children are apt to be "suitable" for society. This notion has been met by challenges. The Supreme Court refused to hear a case concerning a state law that would have required a minor woman to notify a parent 48 hours prior to obtaining an abortion because the Court previously had required such laws to include provisions to bypass such notification when parents cannot be involved. Some states, however, have parental notification laws regarding abortion for minors.

Several states have attempted to pass laws that would prohibit abortion altogether and even limit the use of certain kinds of contraceptives. On the other hand, a few states have passed laws affirming the right of women to obtain legal abortions. The Supreme Court is expected to continue handing down decisions that will have an impact on reproductive rights, and the U.S. Congress is expected to continue proposing legislation to regulate various aspects of reproduction, contraception, and abortion (Boonstra & Nash, 2000).

The Rights and Responsibilities of Sexual Partners

There are clear dangers involved in sharing sexual activity with someone who is unwilling to be open and honest about his or her sexual history. It is possible to contract a fatal disease or a nonfatal sexually transmitted infection from a partner who does not reveal his or her physical condition or who fails to provide appropriate protection, such as use of a condom.

Most states have passed statutes that make the rights and responsibilities of sexual partners clear. The individual who is aware of carrying genital herpes, hepatitis-B, or HIV but fails to inform a sexual partner and fails to use adequate protection to prevent transmission of the disease will most probably be prosecuted for criminal behavior. States have not been as aggressive in passing laws that protect the confidentiality of persons who test positive for HIV, not only compromising the privacy of these individuals but also creating a disincentive to be tested.

The legal aspects of human sexual behavior will probably always be in conflict with some of the personal, emotional aspects. The public has a right to protection from dangerous behavior, and the individual has a right to behave in any way she or he chooses as long as the behavior does not harm others. In some cases, it is not possible to separate public and private rights. Then a legal interpretation of the situation must be made and a judgment passed on whose right has priority. As historical cycles vacillate between progressivism and conservatism, the judgment will continue to waver between private freedom and what courts and legislatures consider to comprise the public good.

Chapter Summary

1. Graphic depictions of human nudity and sexual behavior have been a part of every society and historical period. Pornography, or sexually explicit material, is generally meant to sexually arouse. Erotica is a name given to sexually realistic art or fiction.

2. In many ancient cultures, erotic art was used for purposes of instructing people in sexual behaviors.

There has been controversy over the use of public funding for the creation of art with sexual themes.

3. The practice of writing about sex can be traced back 4,000 years. There have been cycles of acceptance and repression of erotic writings over the centuries.

4. Even in nineteenth-century Victorian literature, there were frank accounts of sexual behavior.

Contemporary literature has explored all sex-related themes.

5. Adult magazines and tabloids proliferated by the late 1960s, and new sex magazines appear each year. Lifestyle magazines now frequently carry articles about sexuality.

6. Sexuality has become increasingly open in films, television, and other media. Almost all sex-related themes have appeared in movies. The film rating system categorizes films based on sexuality issues. R- and PG-rated films are the most popular at the box office.

7. Portrayals of women in films once were often stereotypical or negative, but positive female roles have become more common in recent years. Romantic themes have made a comeback in the movies and in other media.

8. Hard-core pornography is now almost exclusively found in video/DVD format or on the Internet. Sexually explicit material is widely available today in North American and European countries.

9. The Internet provides up-to-date information on sexuality as well as sexually explicit materials. There are websites and chat rooms through which people anonymously communicate intimate sexual messages. Attempts are being made to regulate sexuality-related communications over computer networks.

10. Advertising frequently uses sexual themes to popularize and sell products, sometimes using subliminal embedding techniques.

11. Child pornography represents a lucrative market and is prohibited in the United States by federal laws.

12. The presumed effects of sexually explicit materials often have been founded in either modeling theory or catharsis theory. Research has begun to examine such effects in the context of psychological attitude change theory.

13. The presidential commission of 1970 found no particular evidence that pornography caused criminal behavior or contributed to emotional problems. The pornography commission established in the 1980s made sweeping recommendations for limiting pornography on the basis of its presumed negative effects.

14. Sexually explicit materials are clearly a form of persuasive communication. Exposure usually results in sexual arousal for both men and women and some sort of emotional reaction. The viewer's emotional reaction is often governed by his or her attitudes toward particular sexual behaviors.

15. When analyzed within the context of contemporary attitude change theory, which assumes both central and peripheral paths for processing persuasive communication, pornography appears to have minimal effects on people's attitudes, including men's attitudes toward women.

16. Exposure to sexually explicit material is likely to increase sexual behavior that the individual considers acceptable very soon after exposure. There is some controversy over whether sexually violent depictions might lead to a slight increase in aggression.

17. Some research claims that pornography can increase already held negative attitudes toward women, especially if it depicts sexual aggression or violence. Research does not support the claim that women are more objectified in pornography than men are.

18. Sex offenders do not seem to have had earlier or more frequent exposure to pornography than control populations.

19. Sexually explicit material has been subject to various laws throughout recent history. Since 1973, individual states have been allowed to develop their own legislation.

20. In the United States, sodomy laws, or laws against deviate sexual intercourse, have prohibited certain sexual behaviors considered to be deviate. Civil rights groups have argued that any sexual behavior between consenting adults should be considered legal, and the Supreme Court has upheld the right of adults to engage in consensual sex in private.

21. Constitutional issues sometimes are raised by the regulation of sexual behavior, centered on vaguely stated laws, the independent rights doctrine, the right of privacy, and discriminatory enforcement of laws.

22. State legislatures sometimes are called on to determine whether sexuality education should be recommended or mandated in public schools. Courts and boards of education sometimes must determine the appropriateness of educational materials for public school use.

23. Rape has been considered illegal in recent history, although victims often have been subjected to humiliating and difficult treatment in prosecuting the rapist. Newer laws have allowed for greater sensitivity toward the victim, increasing the chances of conviction. There are also laws making marital rape a crime.

24. In most states, prostitution is prohibited by law. Nude dancing may be regulated by state laws. Controversy has also developed over peep shows.

25. Birth control was prohibited by law in some states until the mid-1960s. Sterilization of people without their consent has been challenged in the courts. States are increasingly placing restrictions on abortion.

26. Increasingly, statutes are being enacted clarifying that sex partners have certain legal rights and responsibilities.

Focus on Health Questions

In this section you will find the kinds of questions that you may have concerning your own health and sexuality. The page references indicate where in the text the answer is located; the exact place is marked with this logo: **FOH**

1. What is the difference between what people call pornography and erotica? **416**

2. Does pornography that includes violent scenes encourage sexual violence? **431–432**

3. Are there laws that prohibit some kinds of sex? **433–434**

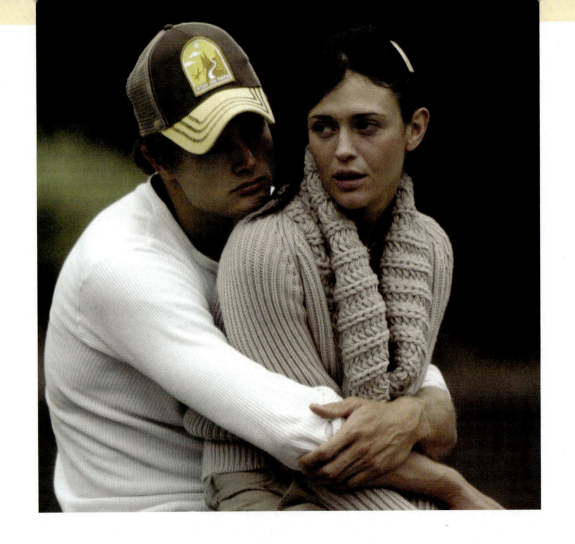

Part 5

Dealing with Sexual Problems

Most people face a sex-related problem sometime during their lives, and when they do they may have to cope with a wide range of emotions, including guilt, anxiety, depression, self-doubt, and feelings of inadequacy. In seeking professional help, it is important to find someone who is well equipped to deal with sex-related matters. There are many different types of sexual problems, different perspectives from which these problems may be viewed, and differing ways in which professionals approach them.

Sexual consent is a fundamental issue in sexual unions, and problems develop when consent is not given. Coercive and exploitative sexual behaviors—including sexual harassment, forced sex, and child sexual abuse—are issues that continue to make headlines and create stress within people's lives.

Sexual interaction has always been associated with the transmission of certain diseases, one reason why many social and religious codes of conduct have been established to regulate sexual behavior. For a time, it seemed that antibiotics would save us from the disease threats that came with sex. However, herpes, HPV, and HIV are cruel reminders that there are many health risks associated with shared sex, and many of the antibiotics that offered early hope have begun to lose their effectiveness.

People's bodies do not always function sexually the way they expect or want, or the way a partner might prefer. There may be lack of sexual desire, difficulty becoming aroused or achieving orgasm, or pain associated with sex. In such cases, the person may be experiencing a sexual dysfunction. Approaches continue to be developed in the field of sex therapy for treating these dysfunctions.

Most sexual problems do not have to remain problems forever. The chapters in this section of the text provide helpful suggestions for preventing and seeking help with problematic sex.

Chapter 16
Sexual Consent, Coercion, Rape, and Abuse

Chapter Outline

I was in total shock when the dean told me the girl had accused me of raping her. I just couldn't believe it. We didn't exactly talk about what we were going to do, but she never said no or tried to get out of bed. She seems to really believe that I forced her into this. It's all like a bad dream.

—from a counseling session

This chapter examines various forms of sexual coercion, abuse, and victimization. Within a wide range of human sexual behaviors, some are seen as problematic in particular social and cultural belief systems. Behaviors and feelings that are troublesome for one person may be pleasurable and enjoyable for another. In one sense, any kind of sexual activity may become a problem if someone is feeling worried, guilty, fearful, or ashamed about it. Are the negative feelings justified in terms of present knowledge and attitudes, or do they simply stem from ignorance and misinformation? The answer often is rooted in complex social issues. To a degree, sexual behaviors and feelings become problems or "offenses" because of the cultural values that surround them and the social judgments that are made about them. Whether someone has given consent for a particular sexual interaction may seem like a simple enough concept, but in fact it sometimes becomes rather muddled. Clearly, any sexual activity that involves lack of consent or the coercion, assault, abuse, or exploitation of someone else is a serious problem. This chapter focuses on those sex-related behaviors, and the reactions to them, that constitute contemporary social problems (Coleman, 2002a).

■ When and How Does Sex Become a Problem?

Consider the following case study of a 34-year-old attorney who consulted a professional sex therapist. She complained of her lack of interest in sex and expressed hope that the therapist could help her become a more sexually active partner for her husband. She explained that her husband, a 36-year-old accountant, had a stronger sex drive than she did. On the surface of things, this might seem to be a relatively straightforward problem of sexual incompatibility—one partner wanting sexual involvement more frequently than the other. Sex counselors and therapists encounter such discrepancies in relationships often and use various techniques that may help resolve the difficulties. Therapists continue to clarify what it actually means to have a sexual problem (Bancroft, Loftus, & Long, 2003).

However, as the therapist gathered a thorough history of the woman's situation, a much more complex picture emerged. The woman reported that her husband desired and expected to have sexual intercourse two or three times every day. He wanted sex at bedtime and frequently upon awakening in the morning. It was not unusual for him to rouse his wife out of

sleep in the middle of the night for sex. If they both came home for lunch during their afternoon breaks, he often wanted to have intercourse. At times she had protested, only to have him coerce her emotionally or even physically into having intercourse. The woman did not question her husband's high level of sexual desire and wanted only to find ways of becoming a more willing and interested partner for him.

The therapist was now in somewhat of a dilemma, finding serious concerns other than the woman's level of sexual interest in the relationship. The therapist thought that the client probably exhibited normal levels of sexual arousal and that the constant "excessive" sexual demands and pressures of her husband had quite predictably led to sexual boredom, depression, and burnout on her part. The therapist was also concerned about the continuing patterns of noncommunication and coercion evident in the couple's relationship.

What should the therapist have done? Should she have attempted to fulfill the woman's request and tried to help her become more interested in sex? Should she have redefined the problem in different terms and tried to help the woman see it that way? Should she instead have told the woman she did not have a problem but her husband did, or encouraged marriage counseling for the couple?

This case study illustrates some fundamental difficulties in considering problematic sex. For example, who is to define whether a problem actually exists at all? And to what degree does a problem exist? What problems are worthy of professional treatment? What are the standards by which problematic and nonproblematic behaviors are to be distinguished from one another (Pertot, 2006)? The following sections describe several causes of sex-related problems.

Negative Self-Attitudes

People often grow up with little information about bodily development or with misconceptions about sexual attractiveness. The young man unprepared for his first ejaculation of semen and the young woman shocked by her first discharge of menstrual blood are bound to experience some fear and worry. Those who have negative feelings about the sex organs and sexual activities are bound to experience guilt over masturbation and sexual fantasies. Research has shown that people who tend not to feel good about their bodies or about themselves after having sex or who report not having been comfortable during sex have an elevated risk of acquiring a sexually transmitted disease or getting involved in other risky behavior, and tend to lack the assertiveness that could help extricate themselves from such situations (Schooler, Ward, Merriwether, & Caruthers, 2005; Whitten et al., 2003).

Society and the media often perpetuate stereotypes about sexual attractiveness and sexual behaviors. List several of these stereotypes as they apply to women and as they apply to men.

Try the "Beautiful" interactivity on SexSource Online.

Society has perpetuated some rather specific stereotypes of sexual attractiveness through popular myths and advertising (see Figure 16.1). Some individ-

■ **FIGURE 16.1** *Stereotypes of Attractiveness*

Both men and women pursue endless hours of aerobics and weight training to make their bodies live up to stereotyped ideals of sexual attractiveness, such as that of the strong, young, muscular male. Those who perceive themselves as not living up to these ideals may experience self-conflict and self-doubt, which affect their ability to understand and fulfill their sexual needs.

uals even become obsessive about the perceived inadequacies of their bodies, developing a psychiatric problem called **body dysmorphic disorder.** Negative body image is associated with lower levels of sexual experience, which probably results from avoidance of certain social experiences. Social phobias lead some people to avoid contact with others whenever possible; in men, this condition is often associated with premature ejaculation during sexual encounters (Corretti, Pierucci, DeScisciolo, & Nisita, 2006).

Boys and men are more prone to concerns about their height, the muscularity of their body, and the size of their penis. Girls and women are more prone to concerns about their weight, their breast size, and the curvaceousness of their body. Eating disorders are particularly common in women who have difficulty perceiving their feminine qualities in positive ways (Cash & Pruzinsky, 2004; Choate, 2005). Those who end up feeling inadequate and do not perceive themselves as living up to the prevailing standards of sex appeal often experience negative feelings, low self-esteem, and even social isolation. When discrepancies exist between what a person perceives as the actual and the ideal in their body and sexual life, he or she is more likely to have lower sexual self-esteem and to be sexually depressed (Garcia & Hoskins, 2001).

Personal conflict is a frequent result of the struggles to understand and fulfill our sexual needs. Most people have experienced their share of remorse, guilt, and self-hatred over sexual mistakes, misconceptions, or intrusive thoughts. In one study of college students, nearly 72 percent had regretted their sexual decisions at least once (Byers, Purdon, & Clark, 1998; Oswalt, Cameron, & Koob, 2005). Guilt seems to be more common in people with lower self-esteem, general discomfort with sexuality, and poor communication with parents. It also seems to set the stage for later dissatisfactions with sex. At times, the negative self-attitudes and guilt feelings become troublesome enough to warrant counseling or other professional help (Berlo & Ensink, 2001). Again, it may be important for a professional to evaluate carefully whether a sexual problem is a reasonable adaptation to some adverse condition in the person's life or relationship or instead represents some treatable malfunction in the person's communication or sexual response system (Bancroft, Loftus, & Long, 2003).

body dysmorphic disorder a preoccupation with imagined or slight defects in one's bodily appearance that may focus on weight, muscularity, skin appearance, the genitals, or other body parts.

Coercion, Abuse, or Assault of Others

When sex is forced on someone against her or his will, there are many negative consequences for the victim. Although most forms of shared sex have elements of mutual seduction, the issue of consent may be confusing and complicated at times. Individuals must have the knowledge base to understand fully what they are consenting to, and the consent must be given freely. At times physical or emotional coercion may be part of persuading a partner to become sexually involved, and in such cases people may be more likely to be acquiescing to sex than consenting (Dreznick, Cronin, Waterman, & Glasheen, 2003). In a relationship, one person may be interested in sex before the other and may begin using various forms of pressure to convince the reluctant partner to get involved. Emotional blackmail, such as saying "You would have sex with me if you really loved me" or hinting that the relationship will end if sex does not improve, certainly constitutes sexual coercion and a relationship problem. About a quarter of college students in one study indicated that they had felt pressured by a partner to have sex (Oswalt, Cameron, & Koob, 2005).

Many forms of sexual coercion and abuse are discussed later in this chapter. Most often, they involve one individual using some imbalance in age, status, or power to take advantage of someone else. The offender often uses various forms of rationalization to justify his or her coercive or abusive behavior. In its more extreme forms, coercive sexual behavior takes the form of sexual assault, in which the offender forces another person into some undesired sexual activity.

Prejudice and Ignorance

The price of being openly different sexually in any society can be high. Although we have made some inroads in alleviating various forms of prejudice in recent decades, prejudice about sexual differences remains deeply ingrained in our society's values. Keep in mind that prejudice consists of holding strong attitudes that are seen as truth even though they have no basis in fact. Prejudice grows out of exaggerated stereotypes and lack of information. Stigmatization of people's sexual identities may easily lead to anger and rage among those being stigmatized, and eventually may even lead to violence (Lemoire & Chen, 2005; Schneider, 2002).

As any sex counselor can confirm, prejudice takes its toll. People with unconventional sexual orientations or lifestyles often feel forced into secret relationships and deception. They may end up feeling as though they live double lives, struggling to exhibit a socially acceptable public image while quietly maintaining a very different lifestyle in private. The stresses of such an existence can have serious consequences in a person's life. There may be a deepening lack of self-respect and self-esteem. Some enter into socially acceptable relationships in hopes that they will be able to pass as acceptable, only to experience instead interpersonal conflict and unhappiness (Hill, 2005; Kalichman et al., 2001).

Failure of the Body to Function as Expected or Desired

Most of us have some expectations and hopes about how our sexual encounters with others should go. We expect that our sex organs will simply go along too, cooperatively and excitedly. It can be quite a shock when that does not happen. Men and women may have difficulty becoming sexually aroused. A man may not achieve erection of his penis; a woman may not produce lubrication in her vagina. There may be difficulty in reaching orgasm, or it may happen too quickly or not quickly enough. There may be pain, tightness, or dryness. For a variety of reasons, our bodies simply may not function sexually the way we want or expect them to (Pertot, 2006).

These are the sexual problems that fall into the category of sexual dysfunctions. They may have physical roots or may be caused by psychological blocks and stresses. Depression has been implicated as a cause of many sexual dysfunctions, and a correlation has also been found between young men who have some functional difficulties with sex and future drug abuse (Frohlich & Meston, 2002; LaPera et al., 2003). Unrealistic beliefs about sexual performance may also play a role (Nobre & Pinto-Gouveia, 2006). These problems are discussed in detail in Chapter 18, "Sexual Dysfunctions and Their Treatment."

Self-Destructive Behaviors and the Paraphilias

People who find themselves participating in some sexual activity they view as unhealthy or immoral certainly can experience self-destructive reactions over time. This includes people who choose sexual acts that involve violence or are viewed as sexual offenses, for which arrest and prosecution are possible. They may also enter into certain situations with a false sense of invulnerability, believing that harm "won't happen to me." In a study of the reports of college students about regrettable sexual experiences, the regrets tended to involve experiencing disappointing first-time sex, having unprotected sex, cheating on a partner, or having a one-night stand. Use of alcohol is often involved in regrettable sexual decision making and is also associated with higher-risk sexual activities (Caron & Moskey, 2002; Kaly, Heesacker, & Frost, 2002; Oswalt, Cameron, & Koob, 2005).

It has been hypothesized that violent and antisocial sexual behaviors could be rooted in a link between stress and sexual arousal at a biological level or to some of the chemical disturbances of the brain associated with other obsessive or compulsive tendencies. Some people resort to self-mutilation of their genitals (Catalano, Catalano, & Carroll, 2002). Whatever their cause, it is the violent and self-destructive sexual behaviors that we have come to view as personal and social problems (Bradford, 2000).

FOH The paraphilias are characterized by sexual arousal from exposure to objects or situations that are not considered part of normative patterns of arousal and activity. They frequently have self-destructive or victimizing aspects. The American Psychiatric Association's *Diagnostic and Statistical Manual of Mental Disorders* (*DSM*) categorizes many forms of behavior under the label paraphilia, including exhibitionism, voyeurism, sexual attraction to children, sadomasochism, fetishism, frotteurism, obscene telephone calls, necrophilia, zoophilia, and several other behaviors (see Chapter 14). An actual diagnosis of pathology with regard to paraphilias is thought to be unnecessary unless the individual acts on the sexual urges, fantasies, and attractions or unless he or she is troubled by them. As discussed in Chapter 14, certain of these behaviors—fetishism, for example—may be relatively harmless as long as they do not involve any sort of victimization of others. Some sexologists feel that it is time for a reevaluation of the paraphilias, and there is controversy over whether they should remain in the *DSM* as disorders (Moser & Kleinplatz, 2005; Spitzer, 2005).

The paraphilias are often the types of behavior that become classified as sexual offenses depending on the culture in which they occur. One dimension of the sexual offense is the mental control mechanism of the offender that leads to the paraphilic behavior (Krueger & Kaplan, 2001). The other dimension is the way a particular culture categorizes a range of sexual behaviors. Much more research is needed to compare paraphilic behaviors across cultures in any meaningful way.

Paraphiles or **paraphilics,** people who are attracted to some form of paraphilia, may repeat the same behavior compulsively over time. Research has suggested that paraphiles lack general controls over their behaviors because of chemical brain disorders or social disadvantage and may be prone to a variety of sexually impulsive behaviors (Aksaray et al., 2001). There has been some success in treating paraphilias with medications that are used in the treatment of depression and obsessive-compulsive disorders or with drugs that interfere with the release and activation of certain hormones (Briken, Nika, & Berner, 2001; Chow & Choy, 2002).

Sex Trafficking as a Global Problem

In some areas of the world, young girls and boys from poverty-stricken families may enter prostitution and may even be sold to sex traffickers for funds that will help support their families. Adult women may also be coerced into the sex worker trade. They may eventually become sex slaves, kept in line with threats and continued poverty. Indonesia, for example, is known as a country to which men sometimes travel to be able to buy sex with a minor, although foreign sex slaves often make their way to North America as well (Melby, 2004).

Human rights organizations around the world are concerned about girls and boys who become ensnared in sex trafficking rings, and a variety of policies and laws have been enacted to prosecute those responsible. However, it seems that as long as people are willing to pay for illicit sex, there will be an underground of sellers ready to meet the need.

The Sex Addiction Controversy   **FOH**

What has come to be called **sex addiction** provides another example of the crucial role expert opinion plays in defining and labeling sexual behavior. It is clear that sexual activity becomes compulsive for some people, for whom regulating sexual behavior is difficult or impossible. On the other hand, there continues to be debate concerning what kinds of repeated sexual behaviors should necessarily be considered pathological or paraphilic (Coleman, 2003). In *Out of the Shadows: Understanding Sexual Addiction* and other publications, Patrick Carnes (1992, 2003) has compared compulsive sexual behavior to alcoholism or other chemical dependencies. He has maintained that sex addiction is characterized by the typical symptoms of other forms of addiction, such as an inability to stop the behavior even in the face of serious consequences. These could include physical consequences, such as self-mutilation, disease, or unwanted pregnancy; occupational consequences, such as losing one's job or being charged with sexual harassment; and/or relational consequences, such as losing one's partner (Griffiths, 2001). As with all compulsions, sexual addiction has been thought to follow a cycle of negative feelings that leads to repetition of the behavior and other sexual

paraphiles (paraphilics) people who are drawn to one or more of the paraphilias, or behaviors characterized by non-normative sexual arousal.
sex addiction inability to regulate sexual behavior.

problems, and treatment programs have been developed that are similar to the 12-step programs used with alcoholics and drug abusers. Attendance at the meetings offered by such programs is considered essential to a real cure (Carnes, 2003).

Many sexologists have taken exception to the sex addiction model, believing it to be misleading and even dangerous because it may prevent people from getting appropriate treatment. They charge that the addiction model does not lend itself well to sexually compulsive behaviors and instead brands some perfectly normal behaviors as signs of addiction. There is concern that it has encouraged people to diagnose themselves as "sex addicts" when they actually may simply be ignorant or misinformed about normal sexual behavior, as well as concern that the treatment approaches have been developed and operated largely by people who are not trained in the field of human sexuality (Klein, 2003). Again, we face the difficulty of defining what is problematic. The sexual addiction movement has been seen as having a missionary zeal, offering a program that might be dangerously oversimplified for some people (Coleman, 2003).

Research confirms that some people seem unable to exercise control over their sexual behaviors even in the face of negative consequences, but little attention has been given to why sex becomes problematic for some. Three patterns have emerged in the study of self-defined sex addicts with regard to their sexual interests and responsiveness. Some are able to retain sexual interest and response even when they are depressed. Others seem to use sexual stimulation as a way to distract themselves from thoughts that might induce a negative mood. A third pattern involves a tendency toward increased sexual arousal when experiencing a state of anxiety or stress. Until we better understand the connections between sexual behavior and negative mood states, some researchers recommend that we refer to *out-of-control* sexual behaviors rather than calling them either addictions or compulsions (Bancroft & Vukadinovic, 2004).

Sexual Harassment

A form of sexual coercion and exploitation that can be very subtle or even confusing to identify and yet be highly upsetting to the victim involves unwanted sexual advances, suggestiveness, sexually motivated physical contact, requests for sexual favors, or coercion of one person by another, particularly in academic settings or the workplace. The term used to describe such behavior is **sexual harassment.** Although the definitions of sexual harassment may vary among people, it would appear to be widespread (see Figure 16.2). It is estimated that about 50 percent of

FIGURE 16.2 *Is It Sexual Harassment?*

Three waitresses at a restaurant in Beverly Hills, California, filed a lawsuit against their employer for allegedly firing them for refusing to wear new uniforms. Kelly Thornton (left) and Christy Tharpe (right) pose in the attire that they formerly wore on the job. A model in the center is wearing the new uniform that the other two refused to wear for work.

women are victims of some form of sexual harassment, mostly the "hands-off" type but occasionally involving physical contact (Sbraga & O'Donohue, 2001). The number of sexual harassment complaints filed with the U.S. Equal Opportunity Employment Commission more than doubled during the 1990s, leveling off at about 15,500 new cases every year. Sexual harassment has not been studied extensively in other cultures. The first study done in China showed the incidence of sexual harassment there to be quite similar to the figures for the United States and other developed countries (Parish, Das, & Laumann, 2006).

Have you ever thought that you were being sexually harassed? Describe the circumstances. Be sure to include how you felt.

Although studies have tended to focus on harassment of women, it certainly is not rare for men to be victims of sexual harassment. However, when faced with situations that are potentially sexually harassing,

sexual harassment unwanted sexual advances or coercion that can occur in the workplace or in academic settings.

men are somewhat more likely to perceive women's behavior as simply being sexy rather than harassing. In general, they tend not to be as offended or uncomfortable with the behavior as women tend to be. The U.S. Supreme Court has ruled that men can take legal action against other men who make unwanted sexual advances, and in fact the harassment of men is often perpetrated by other males (Sbraga & O'Donohue, 2001). Studies of college men and women indicate that the males tend to be more tolerant of sexual harassment and more likely to see heterosexual relationships in adversarial terms, to believe the myths about rape, and to admit that under certain circumstances they might be sexually aggressive.

Sexual harassment may affect people in many different ways, sometimes even indirectly. There are four main bases for complaints about sexual harassment (Sbraga & O'Donohue, 2001):

1. *Coercion and bribery.* This form of harassment is linked to the granting or denial of some benefit or privilege. Legally it is called **quid pro quo** harassment, meaning that something is gained from something else. Most typically it takes the form of an individual who has or is perceived to have more power using sex as a form of coercion or bribery. An example might be a college professor suggesting to a student that complying or not complying with her or his sexual overtures will affect the student's grade one way or the other.

2. *Hostile environment.* If a person's school or work environment is made uncomfortable because of unwanted sexual attention such as sexual innuendos, suggestive remarks or pictures, repeated requests for dates, and uninvited advances, it is considered a form of sexual harassment. Court cases continue to affirm that school authorities and work supervisors have a responsibility to prevent the development or perpetuation of such hostile environments.

3. *Aggressive acts.* Among the more overt forms of sexual harassment are actual physical behaviors, such as unwanted embraces, kissing, touching, fondling, or more assaultive forms of sexual behavior.

4. *Third-party effects.* Sometimes a third person will be affected by the sexual or romantic relationships of others. For example, if one student is getting better grades because of involvement in a sexual relationship with the professor, other students who are legitimately working for their grades are unfairly affected. Or if a supervisor is having an affair with a secretary, making it more likely that the secretary will get pay raises or other benefits, other workers are affected. These are forms of third-party sexual harassment.

Certain risk factors increase the likelihood that sexual harassment will take place, including an unprofessional environment in the workplace, a sexist atmosphere, and lack of knowledge about the organization's grievance policies (O'Hare & O'Donohue, 1998). Victims of sexual harassment often minimize the importance of the event in their own minds, or they may react with shock and disbelief. They may feel ambivalent toward the offender and sometimes even blame themselves for not having prevented the situation from developing. In this sense, the injuries of harassment may be subtle and emotional, calling the victim's own sense of self into question. Only too often, these reactions lead victims to ignore the incident and not report it to anyone in authority. This is particularly unfortunate in cases where the harasser is unaware of how his or her behavior is being perceived. Sometimes, a simple and clear statement to the harasser that the behavior is unwelcome and considered to be sexually harassing will be enough to end it (Sbraga & O'Donohue, 2001). See Table 16.1.

Usually, however, there is an imbalance of power in sexual harassment cases through which the offender tries to take unfair advantage of the victim. The result of such a trap for the individual being harassed is often a sense of helplessness that can lead to depression, other emotional upsets, and even physical illness. Victims often have been known to quit their jobs or leave school as a result of continuing sexual harassment that they feel at a loss to cope with.

Sexual Harassment in Schools and Colleges

A survey of 2,002 readers of *Seventeen* magazine found that 89 percent of girls said they had been targets of unwanted sexual comments, gestures, or looks during their precollege school years. The American Association of University Women sponsored a Louis Harris survey of 1,632 students in grades 8 through 11 in 79 U.S. schools to determine the incidence of sexual harassment (AAUW, 1993). This study found that 85 percent of the girls and 76 percent of the boys said they had been subjected to unwelcome sexual behavior at least once in their school lives. Two-thirds of the girls and a considerably smaller proportion of boys said they had been harassed "often" or "occasionally." Sixty-five percent of the girls and 42 percent of the boys indicated that they had been touched, grabbed, or pinched in a sexual way. Nearly one-fourth of the girls had been forced to kiss someone, and 10 percent of both the boys and the girls reported having

quid pro quo something gained from something given.

Table 16.1 — How Men Can Tell If Their Behavior Is Sexual Harassment

Some men (and women) are confused as to what behaviors constitute sexual harassment. The following questions may be especially helpful in assessing one's own behavior. If the answer to any of these questions is yes, the chances of the behavior being considered sexual harassment are very high. Because such behavior is likely to be high risk, if you have to ask, it is probably better not to do it.

- Would I mind if someone treated my wife, partner, girlfriend, mother, sister, or daughter this way?
- Would I mind if this person told my wife, partner, girlfriend, mother, sister, or daughter about what I was saying or doing?
- Would I do this if my wife, partner, girlfriend, mother, sister, or daughter were present?
- Would I mind if a reporter wanted to write about what I was doing?
- If I ask someone for a date and the answer is "no," do I keep asking?
- If someone asks me to stop a particular behavior, do I get angry and do more of the same instead of apologizing and stopping?
- Do I tell jokes or make "funny" remarks involving women and/or sexuality? (Such jokes may offend many people.)

Source: Bernice R. Sandler, "How Men Can Tell If Their Behavior Is Sexual Harassment," *About Women on Campus,* Vol. 3 (3), Summer 1994. Courtesy of Bernice Sandler. www.bernicesandler.com

been forced against their wills to do something sexual other than kissing. Eighty percent of the unwelcome sexual behavior had come from other students, with the remainder coming from teachers, coaches, or other adults.

These statistics were similar to those found in other surveys. The studies have focused attention on sexually harassing behavior in the adolescent years. Even though many students, especially girls, found the behavior at least somewhat upsetting, there was also pressure on students to dismiss these activities as part of growing up or "no big deal." This may set the stage for misperceiving the significance of sexual harassment later in life. Because college students are adults, there is more likelihood of sexual contact between them and their professors, accompanied by all the potential complications of such relationships (Francis, 2000).

Do you believe colleges and universities have the right to prohibit or regulate consensual relationships between faculty and students? Defend your position.

One of the issues being debated in academia is whether even consensual relationships between faculty and students should be prohibited, because of the power imbalance and the potential for harassment. On one side of the argument are the issues of personal privacy and freedom for legal adults to make choices about their relationships. On the other side of the debate are concerns about how imbalances of power, even when unintended, may lead to exploitation, sexual coercion, a hostile environment, or third-party harassment. Sensitive to the risk of lawsuits, some universities have tried to enact policies that would prohibit all romantic and sexual relationships between faculty and students, but most have opted for less pervasive policies, prohibiting relationships specifically between a professor and a student whom the professor supervises in some way (Lahelma, Palmu, & Gordon, 2000). There is always the risk that one party, usually the student, will be hurt in some way by the relationship and bring some sort of charges against the other party. For these reasons, educational institutions need to develop sexual harassment policies with great care and to educate both students and faculty about the dangers and concerns. Any such policy must provide for grievance procedures so that an individual who feels unfairly charged is offered an opportunity for defense (Francis, 2000).

Sexual Harassment in the Military

Results of one Pentagon survey of armed forces personnel showed that 82 percent of the women and 74 percent of the men had felt sexually harassed by teasing, jokes, remarks, or questions. Sixty percent of the women and 51 percent of the men reported having been victims of physical forms of harassment, including being leaned over, touched, cornered, pinched, or brushed against in a deliberately sexual manner. Fifteen percent of the armed forces women and 2 percent of the men indicated that they actually had been pressured for sexual favors. The General Accounting Office has also reported that well over 90 percent of female students at national military academies experience some form of sexual harassment. Much of this harassment has not been formally reported or investigated, although the sexual abuse scandal at the Air Force Academy led to the issuing of stronger educational guidelines and disciplinary action against offenders and against the academy leaders who had not acted quickly or decisively enough on complaints.

The armed forces represent a somewhat special social situation, because for such a long time they were male-dominated. As women have been gradually integrated into the military services, sexual harassment and abuse have become serious problems. They seem to be one way for military males to attempt to reassert their dominance. The military considers even consensual sex between persons of different rank to be inappropriate, because it can lead to a breakdown of discipline and of the cohesiveness of units; it sometimes is deemed to be rape, especially when a recruit is clearly in a position of being afraid to say no to a superior. The seriousness of sexual harassment and of the issue of consensual sex in the military has come into focus with scandals and court-martials of high-ranking officers at several installations. Experts agree that the living situations and power imbalances in military life create unique problems for both women and men. Sexual incidents on military bases have reminded everyone that even in places of traditional male dominance, sexual harassment and abuse will no longer be ignored (Richard, 2003).

Sexual Harassment in the Workplace

Scenarios in the civilian world are similar to those in schools and the military. They involve, for example, the worker who is subjected to intimate touching or sexual innuendos from a superior. The worker often feels trapped in an uncomfortable situation, resenting the uninvited attention but fearful that reporting it will create embarrassing confrontations or even jeopardize future employment. Some women are afraid of the economic consequences of either reporting the incident or quitting and therefore choose to remain on the job, sometimes being subjected to further sexual harassment. There is evidence that in recent years women have become more willing to report harassment on the job, and complaints have been on the increase.

American companies have realized that they can be held accountable for their workers' actions and that it is their responsibility to prevent the development of hostile work environments. It is critical that training about sexual harassment be given to workers and that harassment policies be publicized regularly. Court cases continue to support these positions. Men have also become more concerned about behaviors that could be seen as sexually harassing, and many men have been modifying their actions to prevent misunderstanding or the possibility that they would be charged with sexual harassment. Experts continue to wrestle with the complex issue of how to affirm positive relationships between coworkers. Although such relationships may have sexual components, appropriate constraints must be established on the degree to which sexuality becomes a part of workplace interactions (Sbraga & O'Donohue, 2001).

FOH Responding to Sexual Harassment

Public and private schools, colleges, military service branches, and corporations now generally have specific policies defining what sort of conduct constitutes sexual harassment and outlining procedures for dealing with cases. Until recently, most legal cases related to harass-

ment in the United States were decided under Title VII of the Civil Rights Act of 1964 and Title IX of the Education Amendments of 1972, both of which clearly prohibit sexual harassment of employees and students. After the U.S. Senate passed the Civil Rights Act of 1991, additional policies were implemented to deter harassment in the workplace. In 1993, the U.S. Supreme Court ruled unanimously that victims need not have suffered severe psychological damage in order to claim that they have been sexually harassed, granting harassment a broader definition than was previously accepted by the Court. However, even with such policies and precedents in place, sexual harassment can be a difficult issue to resolve. People in administrative positions may not agree on how to define the problem and may have a stake in trying to protect the offender. It is also an offense for which little tangible evidence usually is available to substantiate the victim's claims. It then becomes a situation of one person's word against another's.

Recommendations for those who encounter sexual harassment emphasize the need to take as much control over the situation as possible. There are several specific suggestions for steps that can be taken:

1. *Seek sources of personal support.* Find an individual or small support group with whom you can share your fears and frustrations. This can provide support and encouragement through a difficult time, put the incident(s) and your concerns in clearer perspective, and give you guidance in making decisions about how you want to proceed.

2. *Find out which authorities or administrators are designated for the reporting of sexual harassment.* Institutions usually have an affirmative action officer or other administrator who handles reports of sexual harassment. Even if these individuals feel that a lack of substantive evidence may make pursuit of a particular case difficult, they may have helpful suggestions for putting an end to the offensive behavior. Remember, too, that if a person in authority receives more than one complaint about a particular employee, he or she will have more evidence on which to act. In the case of a student who is being harassed by a professor, reporting the incident may be useful in rectifying a situation in which an unfair grade eventually is given by the teacher as retribution. Keeping careful records of classroom performance would, of course, be necessary in arguing such a point. Most forms of harassment can be considered violations of law, and you might consider reporting them to police authorities.

3. *Be clear about your needs.* One common reaction of many victims of sexual harassment is to feel guilty for having somehow precipitated the

sexual advances. Regardless of any ambivalence you may once have felt about the offender, if you now feel certain that you do not appreciate the behavior, be firm in your resolve to end the harassment and be assertive about it.

4. *Write a letter to the offender.* This is considered one of the best approaches to ending sexual harassment. It is a clear and direct statement to the offender made without formal charges and public confrontation. It also may provide the harasser with a new perspective on the behavior. Not all offenders realize how negatively their actions affect others. A copy of the letter should be kept and used as supportive evidence later if the harassment does not cease. Such a letter should clearly and directly state the following: (a) specifically what actions have taken place, giving as many details, dates, and times as possible but without evaluation; (b) the feelings and reactions that have been generated by the actions; and (c) a very short statement that you want the harassment to stop and also want your relationship to return to an appropriate professional, or student–teacher, level. Such letters usually are quite useful in placing a harasser on warning, and they typically lead to a quick cessation of the behavior.

5. *Consider making use of mediation services.* Even in those cases where an individual does not want to take formal action against a harasser, mediation may be helpful. It is a voluntary process in which an impartial mediator allows the two parties, the victim and the harasser, to explain their positions and feelings to each other, eventually developing a plan of resolution to which both parties can agree. This approach is especially useful in subtler harassment situations, in which the offender could benefit from realizing how the actions have been affecting the victim.

Institutional policies and recent court decisions continue to confirm that everyone deserves to work or pursue an education in an environment that is free from inappropriate sexual overtures. If you find yourself subjected to such behavior, take action promptly to avoid escalation in the tensions and consequences that may result.

■ Sexual Boundary Violations by Professionals

Closely related to the sexual harassment issue is a growing concern about professionals—physicians, nurses, therapists, clergy, lawyers, bodywork thera-

pists, social workers—who take advantage of their patients or clients sexually. The crisis over sexual abuse of children and adolescents by priests has shaken the Roman Catholic Church in the United States. A report issued in 2004 by the U.S. Conference of Catholic Bishops reported that between 1950 and 2002 in the United States, nearly 4,500 Roman Catholic priests were accused of sexually molesting a total of 11,000 children. Seventy-eight percent of the alleged victims were between the ages of 11 and 17, 16 percent were 8 to 10 years old, and the remaining 6 percent were 7 or younger at the time of the abuse.

These cases constitute what are called *boundary violations* in situations that usually involves some power differential because one of the individuals is perceived as a helper for the other. It is typically assumed that the person being helped or served should not have to be concerned about the helper crossing sexual boundaries (Lief, 2001; Smith, 1999). Although it is difficult to get accurate data on the frequency with which such behavior occurs, there is evidence that up to 10 percent of male therapists have engaged in intimate contact with patients either during or following the professional relationship and that smaller numbers of female professionals have done so. In a survey of 714 nurses in psychiatric hospitals in Europe, while nearly all the nurses agreed that physical contact of a sexual nature with patients was inappropriate, 17 percent of the male nurses and 11 percent of the female nurses admitted to having had such contact (Bachmann et al., 2000).

Most professions in which one individual acts in a helping role for another have seen their share of reports about sexual boundary violations. Unfortunately, these professions often have been slow to acknowledge the scope of the problem, sort through the complex problem of who was responsible for the actions, and develop mechanisms for handling allegations of sexual abuse (Finger, 2000). For patients, clients, or parishioners who have been subjected to such violations, a typical question is "Why did you keep going back?" Research indicates that confusing feelings of shame, being wanted and cared for, helplessness, and lack of self-confidence seem to interact to create conditions that make it difficult for victims to take charge of the situation (Penfold, 1999).

Dynamics behind Sexual Abuse of Female Clients

There seem to be particular dynamics behind the abuse of female clients by male professionals. Women come to these men in a highly vulnerable state and may perceive the men as being warm, caring, and helpful. At the same time, men who have achieved professional status may sometimes see themselves as being above ordinary rules of ethical conduct. They may also see vulnerable women as potential sources of help for their own stresses, depressions, and relational problems. These perceptions conspire to create a situation in which the patient is vulnerable to sexual abuse (Smith, 1999).

It has become increasingly clear that helper–client sexual exploitation often has disastrous consequences. The client may end up feeling used and angry, and whatever trust had been established with the professional is destroyed. The client may feel dehumanized by the actions. Again, there is a tendency for clients who have been sexually exploited to blame themselves and to assume that they should have prevented the behavior. The professional, too, suffers serious consequences. His career can be jeopardized because of the abuse, and with good reason (Fones et al., 1999). Experts agree that it is up to the professional worker to establish and maintain appropriate boundaries in the helping relationship (Finger, 2000). For these reasons, it is crucial that physicians, lawyers, therapists, priests, and others in such professions be educated to pay attention to their feelings and reactions and work to prevent situations that might lead to unethical, exploitative actions. A number of states have enacted legislation providing civil and criminal penalties for professionals who violate ethical standards and participate in sexual or other inappropriate contact with their clients.

Education for Sexuality Professionals

Boundary violations might be better prevented if professionals received focused training in ways to confront their own feelings and protect their clients. Most sexuality professionals have advanced degrees, but few actually have specialized in the field of human sexuality. Sexuality professionals are found in education, medicine, social work, psychotherapy, counseling, and any other area that deals with the special concerns of people's lives. Unfortunately, the presence of sexuality education in schools has not translated into adequate preparation of those teachers who ultimately may be expected to conduct the classes, and many have never had any formal academic preparation in sexuality. In fact, almost no public school preparation and certification programs require any courses on sexuality (Goldfarb, 2003; Kelly, 2005).

Seminaries and theological schools have begun to prepare their students for working with sexual issues, because it is often suggested that people talk to their religious advisors when they are troubled by problems with their sexuality. This training has little

standardization, however, and experts have recommended a better balance in training between the positive, pleasurable aspects of sexuality and its problematic issues (Conklin, 2001; Stayton, 2002).

Significant headway has been made in training those individuals who are preparing for work within the clinical health and psychology professions. An extensive survey of U.S. and Canadian medical schools revealed that about a third of these schools have gradually increased the number of curriculum hours devoted to studying human sexuality, with 92 percent of medical schools requiring core curriculum preparation in sexuality. However, 61 percent of future physicians were found to receive 10 hours or less of training in human sexuality, and fewer than 30 percent of medical schools offer full courses on human sexuality (Melby, 2000). The goals in sexuality education for professionals are not always clearly defined, and the courses either may not be required or may neglect the broad range of sexual issues that could eventually be encountered in work settings, including the impact of illness and disability on sex. In addition, clinical supervision of professionals as they learn how to offer treatment for sexual problems often is lacking in professional training programs (Ward et al., 2001).

The ability of educators, health and counseling professionals, and clergy to perceive sexual problems in their students, patients, or clients and then to pursue these problems once they have been noticed depends on the degree of comfort the professionals have toward sexuality. The more anxious professionals are about dealing with sexual issues, the less apt they will be to ask about a patient's sexual history. Medical students often have levels of homophobia that interfere with certain aspects of treating gay male and lesbian patients (Klamen, Grossman, & Kopacz, 1999). Some health professionals also avoid discussing sex because they are uncertain of how to alleviate patient anxiety about the topic. Training programs that involve mentoring by professionals who already have experience in dealing with sexual concerns can be of particular value in overcoming such reluctance (Pearson, 2003). Fortunately, a number of sexuality education programs for professionals now help them see and understand their own sexual values, detect sexual concerns in their patients or clients, and develop the skills needed to treat these sex-related problems while maintaining appropriate boundaries.

Do you have confidence that the following professionals would be able to advise you correctly on matters of sexuality: your family physician, your clergyperson, a school counselor, a private therapist, a nurse in your health center?

■ Consent, Coercion, and Forced Sex

The Issue of Consent

A key issue in many problematic sexual situations is that one partner has not given consent for the sexual activity to take place. Whether it is a case of two college students who have sexual intercourse after an evening of excessive drinking and the woman claims she was too drunk to know what she was doing or a case of a 15-year-old who willingly has sex with an 18-year-old who later is arrested for the behavior, the fundamental problem is lack of consent. It can be considered rape to have sex with someone whose judgment is impaired by alcohol, and the law considers minors to be too young to offer legitimate consent even if they say they participated willingly. For such a central issue in sexual matters, consent has received minimal attention by researchers.

The importance of consent and its validity can depend on a variety of factors, and both moral and legal distinctions may be made. The risk of harm may have to be evaluated, along with the experiencing of harm by a "victim" and the potential violation of one's rights. The validity of an individual's sexual consent may be compromised if coercion or deception has been involved or if the competence of one of the individuals is questionable because of age, mental retardation or illness, or intoxication. While societies establish specific guidelines and laws in an attempt to bring greater clarity to such issues, subtleties of interpretation can make analysis of individual cases complicated (Wertheimer, 2003).

A study on the ways people ask for and give sexual consent offers some preliminary clues as to where things can go wrong. Nonverbal behaviors are used significantly more frequently than verbal expressions. People tend to initiate sex with a partner through touch and other nonverbal behaviors (kissing, caressing, undressing) and sometimes through verbalizations ("I want you"; "Is this okay?"). Partners then respond by not resisting the advances or with undressing behaviors, or other nonverbal cues (eye contact, smiling, kissing and touching in return). Women are somewhat more likely than men to use verbal responses (Beres, Herold, & Maitland, 2004). Considering the complexities of filtering all these signals through individual communication processing systems, it is clear why things sometimes go amiss.

Recognizing that many sexual problems develop on college campuses over consent issues, after extensive campus discussions Antioch College instituted a policy requiring students to obtain verbal consent for each level of sexual behavior. The policy received a great deal of press when it first appeared, along with plenty of jokes. Yet the policy was developed by students themselves and makes good sense in many ways. Perhaps one of the most telling anecdotes regarding the value of the policy involved a freshman male student who learned about it at orientation and said that if he had to ask, he wouldn't get what he wanted. After the policy took effect, a newsletter called *About Women on Campus* published the following list of reasons why it makes good sense to seek consent for sexual behaviors (Ten Reasons, 1994):

1. Because many partners find it sexy to be asked, as sex progresses, if it's okay.
2. Because sex is better when each partner enjoys what is happening and no one is being forced to do something he or she doesn't want to do.
3. Because if your partner is having a good time and is not forced to do something against her will, she may be more likely to want to see you again. Mutual respect is the best basis for friendship and intimacy.
4. Because forcing sexual activity on another person can violate state and federal laws and your school's policy. In most instances, unwanted touching and fondling constitute sexual assault.
5. Because it prevents misunderstandings (silence is not a yes).
6. Because you won't be accused of rape.
7. Because you won't go to jail or be expelled.
8. Because it's better to be safe than sorry.
9. Because if you want to impose your sexual will on someone, your behavior has more to do with dominating that person than with enjoying sexuality and an intimate relationship.
10. Why would you want to have sex with someone who doesn't like what you are doing?

The bottom line is that one of the responsibilities we have in our sexual interactions with other people is to make certain that they are fully willing to participate in those activities we would like to share with them. It is not legitimate to avoid confronting the issue out of selfish concerns or because we are too shy to ask. When consent is left open to interpretation or is vague in any way, we may be courting troublesome consequences.

Sexual Coercion and Force

Coercing or forcing other people to have unwanted sexual activity is a behavior found in nearly every culture studied. Usually it is males who force women into sexual activities against their will, but substantial numbers of males also report having engaged in unwanted sexual acts. Social norms, and the types of sexual activities they regulate or prohibit, seem to play a major

Real Student Voices

■ My first serious relationship in high school turned out to be a disaster. I really loved the boy, but he was always very jealous and possessive. He was always pressing me to have sex with him, even though I didn't feel ready. Finally I gave in, mostly because he wore me down rather than really wanting to do it. I realize now how emotionally abusive he was. It took me a while to get beyond it. I found it hard to trust boys.

■ I get really pissed when I hear about guys getting accused of date rape. Why is it that males are always supposed to be sober and in control? How come women seem to have the right to get drunk and go back to guys' rooms, but then claim they didn't want to do anything? I understand that if she says no, we should stop, but if she doesn't say no, how are we supposed to know? I don't think I'm the only one who feels this way.

■ As a woman, I don't think I should always have to be on alert that someone might take advantage of me sexually. What kind of world is it if I can't even go out and have a drink without being scared of getting raped? I always go with a couple of other girls, and we watch out for each other. But it's not right that we have to be that paranoid all the time.

---

role in determining the types of forced sex that are allowed or condoned within a particular culture. These same norms determine how women are perceived within the contexts of sexuality and relationships and also the degree to which their perceptions of the experiences are used in determining what is consensual (Thornhill & Palmer, 2000).

In North America, acts that once might have been tolerated as the girl's fault or bad manners on the boy's part are now more clearly considered transgressions, for example, date rape. In some other cultures, it would not be considered at all inappropriate for a man to force his wife to have sexual intercourse, whereas in North America this is now generally considered to be a crime.

In a study of 275 college men and 381 college women, 78 percent of the women and 58 percent of the men reported having been subjected to persistent efforts to get them sexually involved, even after they had refused. The tactics used seemed to occur on four different levels (Struckman-Johnson, Struckman-Johnson, & Anderson, 2003):

Level 1: Sexual arousal. The perpetrator uses touching, kissing, massage, and genital stimulation to continue to entice the person, and eventually the person may give in. Men experience such tactics relatively frequently, but not as often as women do.

Level 2: Emotional manipulation and lies. The most common manipulation is repeated requests for sex; men tend to do this about twice as frequently as

women do, perhaps because men are more practiced at saying what they want. Various lies may be told as someone tries to convince a partner to have sex, including promising not to insert the penis and then doing so, misrepresenting one's age, and telling someone that he or she is abnormal for not having sex. Women sometimes manipulate men's emotions by saying they love the man or by offering compliments; they are more likely to offer threats of blackmail if the man does not cooperate.

Level 3: Exploitation of the intoxicated. Thirty percent of men and 42 percent of women in this study reported having been sexually exploited when they were intoxicated. They sometimes were plied with drinks and then lured to a private area for sex. Sometimes the victim was so drunk that she or he did not remember much about the situation, and in a very few circumstances the victim was purposely drugged.

Level 4: Physical force and harm. About 20 percent of both women and men reported that someone had attempted to block them from leaving a room, but women were about twice as likely to have been subjected to physical restraint. Women sometimes hit men in an effort to persuade them to have sex or to punish them for not doing so.

The rather upsetting conclusion reached by the authors of the study was that sexual coercion and persistence are relatively common among college students.

FIGURE 16.3 *Rape*

Rape is forced sexual participation, as depicted in this enactment using models. Although sexual assault usually is perpetrated against women, it is not limited to them; men and children are also potential rape victims.

Another study found that students perceive sexually coercive men as aggressive and sexually coercive women as promiscuous but that, in general, coercive behaviors were not seen as particularly problematic (Oswald & Russell, 2006).

In countries in which women tend to have more institutional power and where the levels of violent crime generally are lower, the rates of sexual coercion among university students also are lower. The United States has one of the highest rates of sexual assault among developed countries. Fear of sexual victimization is prevalent among women and affects their lives profoundly. Studies have shown that the fear of sexual assault often makes women feel vulnerable. They grow up learning to limit and restrict their behavior in various ways, such as never walking alone in certain locations or at night, yet at the same time they resent having to live with these fears and limitations. Women who have previously been physically abused are more likely to be abused again. Abuse may begin verbally but then progress to physical and sexual violence (Rickert et al., 2002; Smith, White, & Holland, 2003). Issues of power and control are often fundamental to sexual coercion and violence (Gage & Hutchinson, 2006).

In general usage, the term *rape* refers to any form of sex in which one person forces another person to participate (see Figure 16.3). When used as a verb, it means making an individual engage in a sexual act without that individual's consent or against that individual's will. In many states, rape is legally defined as forced vaginal sexual intercourse between a man and a woman. However, in about one-third of forced sexual encounters, penile-vaginal contact never occurs;

rather, a variety of other forms of forced sex, including oral and anal penetration by the penis or vaginal penetration by fingers or objects, may occur. Recognizing that these acts may be just as physically and psychologically damaging to the victim as intercourse, the American Law Institute has recommended that violent and forced sexual acts all be prosecuted under the more general label of "rape and related offenses"; the term "sexual assault" is also often used. Again, the perception of consent can be a complicating factor in rape cases. Courts have sometimes failed to find men guilty of rape in the absence of clear evidence of resistance on the woman's part, even though that may have been due to her being very frightened or suffering impaired judgment from use of alcohol or some other substance (Lawson, 2003).

Several different typologies have been proposed to describe different types of rape and rapists, but little research ties those types to actual behavioral characteristics. One study has found certain behaviors in males that do indeed seem to correspond to certain motives for sexual assault. Men who rape out of *anger and retaliation* express anger and rage during the rape, often using a weapon and displaying a macho image. Such men may assault women who represent people the offender hates. *Power* motives often play a role in rape as well. Men who feel personally inadequate and hostile toward women may seek to assert their power, control, and dominance over women through forced sex. There are also *sadistic* rapists who have sexually aggressive fantasies and may carry out various forms of mental and physical aggression, domination, and torture during rape for their own sexual pleasure (McCabe & Wauchope, 2005).

Statutory rape is a legal term used in situations in which an adult or adolescent has sexual intercourse with a younger partner who is under the age of consent, even if that partner is willing to have sex. Legal age of consent varies in some states, but it is usually age 17 or 18. There are many cases in which older teens are arrested under these statutes for having consensual sexual contact with a slightly younger partner, and these teens may ultimately be required to register as sex offenders. Concerns have been raised about cultural differences among immigrant populations, for which relationships between a man age 18 or somewhat older and a teenage woman are not considered inappropriate or abusive. Some believe that these men should still be subject to prevailing state laws, while cultural relativists hold that the statutes are not fair to them (Apodaca, Schultz, Anderson, & McLennan, 2005).

Coercive and Abusive Relationships

There seem to be some common characteristics among people who tend toward sexually aggressive behavior. They are likely to have come from environments that yielded poor self-images and underdeveloped social skills. They also may have been subjected to violence or sexual abuse themselves and may tend toward insecure and fearful attachment styles in their relationships (Julian et al., 1999). Abuse of alcohol often plays a role in sexually aggressive and coercive situations. Offenders may show serious personality disturbances, have difficulty maintaining social relationships, and have a propensity for depression, loneliness, and personal rigidity. They seem to have more problems with aggressiveness in general and a lack of impulse control (Giotakos et al., 2003). They tend not to have been particularly successful or competent in their social interactions with the opposite sex (Dreznick, 2003). They may also have participated in prior paraphilic behaviors such as exhibitionism (Freund & Seto, 1998). Men who strongly endorse casual sex tend to have had sex earlier, more frequently, and with more partners than have others and also tend to have more conservative attitudes toward women. Such men may act more adversarially toward women in attempts to assert power over them and can sometimes be more sexually aggressive (Yost & Zurbriggen, 2006).

People who tend to resort to coercion and domination in order to solve conflicts are more likely to become aggressive in their sexual behavior, and higher levels of traditionally masculine or macho traits also are associated with tendencies toward aggressiveness. Men who are able to justify their sexual aggression through rationalization, who lack control of their emotions, and

who seem to have other personality problems apparently are more likely to become sexually coercive or aggressive (Wryobeck & Wiederman, 1999).

Most commonly, sexual coercion takes the form of emotional manipulation, lies or false promises, and taking advantage of people who are intoxicated (Struckman-Johnson, Struckman-Johnson, & Anderson, 2003). The most typical lies include indicating a higher level of caring or commitment than actually is the case and trying to deny that the relationship is a one-night stand. Men's attitudes toward women play at least some role in the likelihood of their telling such lies.

Enough is known about the predictors of aggressive behavior to allow women to pay attention to certain warning signals in their relationships. These signals do not mean that a man definitely will be sexually coercive or aggressive, but they are warnings that a man has a greater likelihood of being sexually aggressive. These predictors are the following:

1. Lack of respect for women, as evidenced by his not listening well or ignoring what you say.
2. A tendency to become more physically involved and invasive than makes you feel comfortable, along with a refusal to respect your discomfort.
3. Expression of generally hostile or angry reactions to women.
4. Disregarding your wishes and doing as he pleases; a tendency to make decisions about dating and other issues without consulting you.
5. A tendency to act jealous and possessive or to make you feel guilty if you resist his sexual overtures.
6. Attitudes and values about women that are negative and domineering (such as "Women are supposed to serve men").
7. A tendency to drink heavily and to become abusive when drunk.

There are a number of programs designed to prevent sexual assault and ward off potential attackers. There is evidence that women who convey attitudes of assertiveness and confidence are somewhat less likely to be sexually victimized. However, it may also be helpful for women to learn some specific physical self-defense skills, because verbal resistance alone is not always sufficient to prevent physical injury. Studies of women who either have been raped or have avoided rape suggest that screaming, fleeing, and forcefully resisting an attacker are more effective than nonresistance in reducing the severity of the sexual abuse.

statutory rape a legal term used to indicate sexual activity when one partner is younger than the age of consent; in most states, that age is 18.

Incidence of Forced Sex

Determining the incidence of forced sex is difficult because it is assumed that reported cases represent only the tip of the iceberg. It is encouraging that, according to the FBI, the incidence of reported rapes has declined from 0.4 rape per 1,000 people in 1992 to 0.3 rape per 1,000 people in 2004. Data from the National Longitudinal Study of Adolescent Health found that 8 percent of girls in grades 7 to 12 indicated that they had been forced to have sex against their will. These women also seemed somewhat more likely to have been revictimized at a later time (Raghavan et al., 2004). The results of a three-year study on forced sex in the United States based on 40,000 interviews indicated that 13 percent of women, or 12.1 million, had been raped, many of them during childhood or adolescence. Several studies have shown that younger women are often subjected to unwanted sexual experiences. A survey of 1,149 teenage girls found that about 21 percent of them had experienced unwanted sexual contact within the previous year, with one-third of the cases involving forced sexual intercourse and a higher proportion among older girls. The most likely perpetrators were boyfriends, other male friends, or first dates. Unwanted sex was more common among girls who had been subjected to earlier sexual abuse by an adult, who drank heavily, or whose parents failed to monitor their whereabouts and behaviors closely (Humphrey & White, 2000). Statistics suggest that in a given year about 3 percent of women on college campuses are victims of rape or attempted rape (Olsen, 2001).

The National Health and Social Life Survey (NHSLS) interspersed questions about forced sex throughout the survey. It asked about times when respondents had participated in sex against their will because they were threatened or felt they had no choice. Twenty-two percent of the women had been forced to do something sexual at some time in their lives, almost always by males. Figure 16.4 summarizes the relationship these women had to the males who forced them into sex. Two percent of the men reported having been forced into some sexual activity, one-third of the time by another male (Laumann, Gagnon, et al., 1994).

NHSLS researchers were struck by the marked difference in the number of women who said they had been forced to do something sexual (22 percent) and the small proportion of men who admitted ever having forced a woman to have sex (2.8 percent of the men surveyed). Even taking into consideration underreporting and not telling the truth, the researchers felt that this result reflected some other phenomenon. In their responses to other questions, it was clear that almost no men found the idea of forced sex at all appealing. It was concluded that the most likely

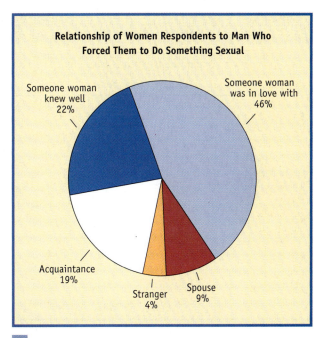

FIGURE 16.4 *Men Who Commit Rape*

NHSLS data suggest that, contrary to stereotypes, few of the men who force women to do something sexual are strangers. For more than three-quarters of the women who had experienced forced sexual contact, the victimizer was a man the woman was in love with (46 percent) or knew well (22 percent) or was her husband (9 percent).

Source: From *Sex in America* by Robert T. Michael et al. Copyright © 1994 by CSG Enterprises, Inc., Edward O. Laumann, Robert T. Michael, and Gina Kolata. By permission of Little, Brown & Company, and Brockman, Inc.

explanation was that most men who had forced women to have sex did not recognize how coercive the women had perceived their behavior to be (Michael et al., 1994). This is yet another reminder that sexual behavior has different meanings to different people and that the issue of consent often has been muddled in our culture. Women and men seem, at least sometimes, to approach these issues from very different perceptual frameworks. See Table 16.2.

*See "Sarah Recalls Being Date Raped"
on SexSource Online.*

Acquaintance Rape

The NHSLS data showed that only 4 percent of the males who had forced women to have sex were strangers to the women (Laumann, Gagnon, et al., 1994). In a more limited sample of data involving rapes reported to authorities, strangers were the perpetrators in only about 22 percent of the rapes. The rest were committed by current or former husbands (9 percent),

Table 16.2   What Constitutes Rape?

Do you believe a woman who is raped is partly to blame if:	Age	Yes	No
She is under the influence of drugs or alcohol	18–34	31%	66%
	35–49	35	58
	50+	57	36
She initially says yes to having sex and then changes her mind	18–34	34	60
	35–49	43	53
	50+	43	46
She dresses provocatively	18–34	28	70
	35–49	31	67
	50+	53	42
She agrees to go to the man's room or home	18–34	20	76
	35–49	29	70
	50+	53	41
		Yes	**No**
Have you ever been in a situation with a man in which you said no but ended up having sex anyway?	Asked of females	18	80

Would you classify the following as rape or not?		Rape	Not Rape
A man has sex with a woman who has passed out after drinking too much	FEMALE	88%	9%
	MALE	77%	17%
A married man has sex with his wife even though she does not want him to	FEMALE	61	30
	MALE	56	38
A man argues with a woman who does not want to have sex until she agrees to have sex	FEMALE	42	53
	MALE	33	59
A man uses emotional pressure, but no physical force, to get a woman to have sex	FEMALE	39	55
	MALE	33	59
		Yes	**No**
Do you believe that some women like to be talked into having sex?	FEMALE	54	33
	MALE	69	20

Note: From a telephone poll of 500 American adults taken for TIME/CNN on May 8 by Yankelovich Clancy Shulman. Sampling error is plus or minus 4.5%. "Not sures" omitted.
Source: From Nancy Gibbs, "When Is It Rape?" *Time,* 3 June 1991. Copyright © 1991 Time, Inc. Reprinted by permission.

fathers or stepfathers (11 percent), other relatives (16 percent), boyfriends (10 percent), and other acquaintances, including friends, neighbors, and coworkers (29 percent). A rape committed by a boyfriend or other acquaintance is called **acquaintance rape** or **date rape.**

Acquaintance rape happens on all college campuses and in many nonacademic settings. Twenty percent of college women in another study indicated that they had been forced to have sexual intercourse, most often by someone known to them (Brener et al., 1999). Use of alcohol or other drugs on the part of both the victim and the perpetrator is common in acquaintance rape situations (Kaly, Heesacker, & Frost, 2002).

On college campuses, sexual victimization often has been associated with male athletes and fraternity members. It has been suggested that the elevated status of these campus constituencies and the sense of power members gain from being identified as a closely bonded group conspire to make them more likely to be sexually coercive toward women (Foubert & LaVoy, 2000). There has been increasing alarm about the use

of powerful drugs to spike drinks, causing women to become unconscious with the aim of sexually assaulting them. Rohypnol has received publicity in recent years, but an even more dangerous and potentially fatal drug called gamma hydroxybutyrate, or GHB, has also received notoriety as a "date rape drug." It can be produced in large quantities by amateurs and is easily disguised because it looks like clear water (Hensley, 2003). Table 16.3 offers suggestions for preventing drug-facilitated rape.

Statistics aside, acquaintance rape clearly continues to affect the lives of many people and deserves careful attention from anyone involved in a relationship in which the possibility of coercion exists. It is one of the most difficult sexual abuse situations to predict or avoid because most women have dated or befriended a man partly because they have assumed they

acquaintance (date) rape a sexual encounter forced by someone who is known to the victim.

Table 16.3   Strategies to Prevent Drug-Facilitated Rape

1. Students should avoid any drink that they didn't receive directly from the bar or that they didn't open themselves.
2. If someone offers a student a drink, students should walk with him or her to the bar, watch it being poured, and carry it themselves.
3. When at a bar or party, students should avoid trying new concoctions that they have never before tasted. Shooters, shots, and drinks with multiple liquors may mask the slightly salty taste of GHB. Concoctions such as margaritas, Long Island Iced Teas, fruity daiquiris, Goldschlager (a cinnamon-flavored liquor), and "fishbowl" drinks have all been used to drug women without their knowledge.
4. Students should not accept a drink poured from a punchbowl. Further, they should avoid sharing drinks that are passed from person to person.
5. Students should not leave their drinks unattended for any reason—they can carry drinks with them when going to the restroom, dancing, talking to someone across the room, and using the phone. If their drinks have been left unattended for any reason, they should discard them immediately.
6. Students should use the buddy system. They should watch friends for signs of sudden intoxication such as slurred speech or having difficulty walking. If a friend is disproportionately intoxicated in relation to the amount of alcohol he or she has consumed, students should assist him or her in leaving the situation immediately.
7. If friends have passed out (particularly if disproportionately intoxicated in relation to the amount of alcohol the student knows they have consumed), students should not allow friends to "sleep it off." GHB-related deaths have occurred from friends deciding to put friends to bed rather than seeking immediate medical assistance. While waiting for medical intervention, students should make sure the victim is on his or her side to prevent aspiration. They should not leave friends unattended for any reason.
8. If students suspect they have ingested GHB, they should go to the emergency room immediately. Students should request a urine sample to screen for the presence of GHB within 12 hours of ingestion. This screen is not routinely done, as many medical professionals are not familiar with GHB symptoms.

Source: From Laura Hensley, "GHB Abuse Trends and Use in Drug-Facilitated Sexual Assault: Implications for Prevention," *NASPA Journal,* Vol. 40, No. 2, Winter 2003, p. 23. Copyright © 2003 National Association of Student Personnel Administrators. Reprinted with permission.

could trust him. Also of concern is that up to one-third of college students indicate that they have consented to unwanted sexual activity in order to satisfy a partner's needs, promote intimacy, or avoid tension in the relationship (O'Sullivan & Allegeier, 1998).

Misunderstandings and lack of communication between partners are crucial issues in acquaintance rape. Mixed signals can confuse both individuals. Although we have seen that consent may involve both verbal and physical signals, it is often given by making no particular response at all—by simply going along with the activity (Bryant et al., 2001). Various studies have shown that some women admit to having said no to sex when they wanted their partners to persist longer and, in a sense, "talk them into it," and there is also evidence that persistence can indeed lead people to "give in" to having sex (Struckman-Johnson, Struckman-Johnson, & Anderson, 2003). Obviously, these confusing nuances of communication make the issue of acquaintance rape even more complicated.

The "rape myth," often given credence by scenarios in movies and other media, implies that even when women say no, they mean yes. Men sometimes think that it is their task to persuade women to have sex until the woman finally realizes how good it is and ceases her protest. Research indicates, for example, that many college students, male and female alike, do not consider a simple "No, I don't want to"

sufficient reason to define subsequent sex as rape. How much physical force was used, how much the woman protested, and when in their interactions the woman's protest began seem to be important factors in making that determination (Bryant et al., 2001; Yost & Zurbriggen, 2006).

Because of social pressures on women concerning their sexual expression, they may be truly confused about what they want and how far they should go. If a woman begins to place limits on a man in the midst of sex play, she may not be prepared to deal with his anger or expressed frustration. All of this can add up to an uncomfortable or even dangerous situation. Although most men are not potential rapists, this ambiguous atmosphere can trigger violence and power issues in those men who are basically insecure, who need to prove their manhood to women, or who simply are used to getting and taking what they want (McCabe & Wauchope, 2005; Sapp et al., 1999).

Do you believe that the focus on acquaintance rape on college campuses has been appropriate and necessary, or overblown? Elaborate.

Acquaintance rape cannot always be prevented. In fact, research indicates that the most frequent acquaintance rapists are men whose victims apparently know them well. However, there are several ways both

Real People

Barbara: Facing Acquaintance Rape

Barbara is a junior at the university and has maintained outstanding grades throughout her academic career. She belongs to a sorority and considers herself to be a very outgoing, friendly person who is fun to be around. She enjoys social functions and socializes almost every weekend with her friends. In November, at a Saturday night party off campus, Barbara enjoyed the attention Charlie was giving her. Charlie is also a junior, and Barbara has been attracted to him since their first year on campus. She had hinted more than once to him that she would like to get to know him better, but for various reasons nothing ever worked out. This time, things seemed different, and he was clearly coming on to her.

As the evening progressed, both of them consumed a fair amount of alcohol. Barbara always stays in reasonable control even with alcohol, although this time she was feeling a bit woozy. When Charlie suggested that they go back to his room, she did not hesitate to agree. Once there, they lay on his bed together, continuing to kiss and touch each other. Charlie put his hand on hers and moved it toward his penis, which he had taken out of his pants. Barbara did not mind stroking it as they continued to kiss and as he massaged her breasts. Eventually, Charlie suggested that they have intercourse, and by this time they had removed most of their clothing. Barbara did not feel ready to go this far with Charlie, so she said that she did not want to do it. He continued to persist gently, and she suddenly realized that he had entered her. She tried

to push him away and told him to stop, but he whispered "It'll be all right. Relax." Before ejaculating, he withdrew, and then he pulled the covers over her. They both fell asleep. Barbara woke up early, feeling hung over and upset. She woke up Charlie and said she wanted to talk. After she said that she felt he had gone too far, Charlie apologized and said that he had thought she wanted him to. He reminded her that he had not ejaculated inside her and that there was nothing to worry about.

Barbara has continued to have mixed feelings about the incident. She knows that she felt attracted to Charlie and had been glad he wanted to be with her. On the other hand, she has felt as though he should not have had intercourse with her. Upon telling a female friend about the incident, the other woman insisted that she had been raped, but Barbara argued that she did not feel this was the case. She was not about to get anyone in trouble. She continues to feel depressed about what happened and has avoided seeing Charlie, even though he has called her more than once to go out. Her concentration has slipped, and she has been finding it difficult to study. Her grades are slipping, too. She doesn't feel like talking about what happened.

Do you believe Barbara was a victim of date rape? Should she have reported the incident to appropriate officials immediately so action could be taken against Charlie? How could she proceed now to help herself deal with her feelings?

women and men can reduce the risks (see Table 16.4). The most important steps involve developing a relationship based on mutual trust, respect, and understanding. Training sessions for men in which they are encouraged to have more empathy for women may have some success (see Figure 16.5), although it is also evident that clearer communication between partners is essential as well (Berg, Lonsway, & Fitzgerald, 1999). Achieving open and honest communication takes work, but it is important that each partner knows about the other's needs and feelings.

If women are subjected to acquaintance rape or other forms of coercive sex, *it is important that they not blame themselves*. Many women feel that they should

have been more forceful in their resistance or that they may have somehow encouraged the sexual abuse. This can be especially confusing if their body responded sexually during the assault. However, that does not automatically mean that they enjoyed the experience, nor does it mean that they really wanted it to happen.

Marital Rape

In former times, it was impossible in the eyes of the law for a woman to be raped by her husband. In many countries, this is still the case. It was once assumed that it was a wife's duty to submit to her husband's sexual desires. In recent years, that assumption has been challenged,

Table 16.4 Acquaintance Rape: What You Can Do

Think
- When is it safe to act on my sexual urges?
- What role do I want sex to play in my life?
- Do I often have sex that I later regret?
- Do I try to work a "Yes" out of a reluctant partner?
- How does alcohol affect my sexual decision making?
- How do I learn someone's desires and limits?
- How do I express my own desires and limits?
- Do I make assumptions about the sexual needs and desires of my dates or sexual partners?

Communicate Effectively
Saying "No" or "Yes" to sexual activities may be difficult, but it's important. Acting sorry or unsure sends mixed messages. The other person can't really know how you feel without hearing it *from you.*

- **Communicate your limits carefully.** If someone starts to offend you, tell them firmly and early. Polite approaches may be misunderstood or ignored.
- **Be assertive.** Often silence or passivity is interpreted as permission. Be direct and firm with someone who is sexually pressuring you. Tell an acquaintance or your partner what you want—or don't want—and stick with your decision.
- **Trust your instincts.** If you feel you are being pressured into unwanted sex, you probably are. If you feel uncomfortable or threatened around an acquaintance or your partner, get out of the situation immediately. If you misread someone's signals, you can always explain later.
- **Listen carefully to what the other person is saying.** Are you getting mixed messages? Do you understand her or him? If not, ask. "Yes" only means "Yes" when said clearly, not when your partner is drunk, high, asleep, or impaired in any way.
- **Ask, rather than assume.** Be aware of the potential for misunderstanding. You and your partner should talk about what would be most enjoyable together.
- **Remember that effective communication may not always work.** Sometimes people simply don't listen. However, no one ever *deserves* to be raped.
- **Respond physically.** If someone is assaulting you and not responding to your objections, push the person away, scream "No," and say that you consider what the person is doing to be rape.
- **Intervene as a bystander.** Challenge your friends who downplay rape or who support definitions of sex and gender roles that allow forcing someone to have sex. Intervene if you see a potential rape or assault. Encourage those around you to express and respect each other's desires and sexual boundaries.

Source: From the brochure *Acquaintance and Date Rape: What Everyone Should Know.* Copyright © 2006 by the American College Health Association. Used with permission.

FIGURE 16.5 *Rape Prevention Training*
Antirape talks are an important part of educating the public about avoiding situations that might lead to rape. Here male students attend a rape-prevention workshop.

and the concept of **marital rape** has gained acceptance. Of women in the NHSLS who reported having been forced to have sex, 9 percent had been forced by their husbands (Michael et al., 1994). In the majority of marital cases that have gone to trial, the husbands have been convicted. The evidence suggests that marital rape is more likely to occur in relationships marked by continued disagreement, alcohol or drug abuse, and nonsexual violence (Melendez et al., 2003).

Increased awareness of marital rape has led nearly all states to reassess their rape laws and to eliminate any preferential treatment for husbands. A few states require extenuating circumstances—such as gross brutality—to be present before a husband can be charged with rape. Wives may be reluctant to report rape by their husbands to authorities because of potential consequences for themselves, their children, or the marriage. They sometimes still believe that it is their duty to submit to their husband's sexual demands. These beliefs often leave women feeling trapped, helpless, and fearful. Their self-worth and self-respect may plummet, resulting in depression and anxiety. In most cities and many rural areas, centers are springing up to help victims of marital violence. They sometimes offer temporary housing for women and children who must leave a potentially violent

marital rape a woman being forced by her husband to have sex.

home situation, along with counseling to help with decision making for the future.

Muslim delegates to the United Nations once mustered enough support to eliminate marital rape from a resolution on violence against women. They argued that marital rape is not considered a crime in many countries. Although not mentioning this act specifically, the final resolution urged nations to take measures "to prevent, prohibit, eliminate and impose effective sanctions against rape or sexual assault."

FOH Men Forced to Have Sex

Rape of men was once considered by some to be a paradoxical concept, especially when rape was narrowly defined as penile-vaginal contact. However, there are increasing reports of men who have been subjected to sexual abuse either by other men or by women, and sex forced on males is gradually becoming recognized as a real phenomenon (Lew, 2004). In various studies of college men, between 34 and 78 percent reported attempts to pressure or force them into sexual activity since age 16. The most typical forms of coercion were employing tactics of persuasion, getting the man intoxicated, and threatening a withdrawal of love. In 12 percent of reported cases, physical intimidation or restraints were used (Struckman-Johnson, Struckman-Johnson, & Anderson, 2003). The number of men who have been forced to have sex by other men is considerably higher in the gay and bisexual male population, probably reaching close to 30 percent (Kalichman et al., 2001). Men rarely report the crime. Among male prison populations, sexual assault of men by men seems to be quite common. In one of the few studies available, of 486 male inmates, 101 had been targets of at least attempted sexual contact.

Women's forcing men to have sex has received little attention in the sexological literature and has never been taken particularly seriously by the general public. The assumption is made that men simply would not be able to respond with erection unless they were willing to participate in sexual activity. In fact, there is clear evidence that males can be quite capable of erection and ejaculation in situations in which they are afraid, unwilling, or anxious. In fact, anxiety may heighten the potential for physical response, even when the man is an unwilling victim. There are case studies of sexual assault in which women threatened, restrained, and stimulated men until they responded sexually against their will. NHSLS data indicated that 1.5 percent of women admitted to having forced a male to have sex (Laumann, Gagnon, et al., 1994). In one study of 400 heterosexual men, more than 25 percent of them indicated that they had been subjected to pressures from women to have nonconsensual sex, and they cited their own "inability to offer resistance"

as having been taken advantage of. For the most part, they rated the experiences as moderately upsetting (Krahè, Scheinberger-Olwig, & Bieneck, 2003). At the very least, pressure and coercion seem to lead many men into sexual experiences they later regret.

Males appear to react to sexual coercion and violence in the same essential ways as women, primarily feeling a tremendous loss of control. Responding to what is viewed as a humiliating assault, males feel demasculinized, embarrassed, traumatized, and depressed. Males are taught that they should not be victims, a mindset that probably often prevents them from ever reporting such abuse to authorities or fully coping with their reactions. Yet males require the same support and counseling as women to deal with the emotions, conflicts, depression, anxiety, self-blame, and loss of self-esteem that follow being forced into sex (Kalichman et al., 2001; Walker, Archer, & Davies, 2005).

The Aftermath of Forced Sex   FOH

Victims of forced sex experience a variety of negative reactions that can disrupt the physical, sexual, social, and psychological aspects of their lives. The majority of victims report feeling permanently changed by the experience. The psychological pain that follows a sexual assault may vary in its intensity depending on a variety of circumstances, although the reactions generally are difficult and unpleasant (Bartoi, Kinder, & Tomianovic, 2000; Lipschitz et al., 1999).

The typical reaction to forced sex, sometimes called the **rape trauma syndrome**, often occurs in two phases. The first (acute or disruptive) phase is characterized by what has been called posttraumatic stress disorder, involving stress and emotional reactions such as anxiety, depression, lowered self-esteem, and social adjustment problems. The victims may be anxious to deny the experience, insisting that they just want to put it all out of their minds. At the same time, they may be agitated, hyperalert, and filled with anxiety (Morgan & Grillon, 1999). The second (recovery) phase may last many months and involves a long-term reorganization to regain a sense of personal security and control over one's environment. Relationships with a partner or family members may be seriously disrupted, and divisions need to be resolved over a period of time (Connop & Petrak, 2004). Typically, the victim is reluctant to participate in usual shared sexual activities. Many victims feel a great deal of anger, which needs to be expressed outwardly rather than be allowed to turn into inner guilt, depression, or self-

rape trauma syndrome the predictable sequence of reactions that a victim experiences following a rape.

hatred (Berlo & Ensink, 2001). Some women eventually feel the need to move residences, change jobs, and change their telephone listings.

FOH Treatment following forced sex also proceeds in two phases. Early crisis intervention aims at helping the individual see herself or himself as a survivor rather than as a victim (see Figure 16.6). She or he needs to accept the consequences of the rape and begin to reestablish a sense of personal competence and control. Often, it takes time to regain a sense of continuity and meaning in life. It is important for the survivor to express her or his feelings and to seek social support and counseling. Over the longer run, treatment focuses on sexual and relational problems that have resulted from the trauma, as well as reactions such as depression or the physical symptoms of coping with stress. With proper follow-up and treatment, survivors of forced sexual experiences can make a complete recovery and live their lives with a comfortable sense of security and self-respect. Many women experience a loss of interest in sex and are subject to specific sexual dysfunctions following an experience of forced sex. These women may wish to abstain from sexual activity for months following the incident. Some are reluctant to talk about such issues, and it has been recommended that counselors who work with rape victims take the time to bring up these sensitive subjects during the counseling process (Berlo & Ensink, 2001).

Professionals who help victims work through the aftermath of forced sex have begun to identify criteria that indicate a successful resolution of the problems (Wuest & Merritt-Gray, 1999):

1. The victim can think about the events of the assault at will, without being troubled by intrusive

memories, nightmares, or frightening flashbacks and associations.
2. Memories of the event are accompanied by appropriately intense emotions, rather than by a false sense of detachment.
3. The feelings associated with the forced sex can be identified and endured without overwhelming the victim.
4. Symptoms of depression, anxiety, and sexual dysfunction either have passed or are at least reasonably tolerable and predictable.
5. The victim is not isolated from relationships and has reestablished the ability to feel a sense of affinity, trust, and attachment for others.
6. Feelings of self-blame have been replaced by self-esteem, and the victim has assigned some meaning to the trauma and sense of loss. Obsessive thoughts about the event have been replaced by a realistic evaluation of it.

Police agencies are becoming better equipped to deal with reports of sexual assault, and the U.S. Department of Justice is promulgating guidelines for responding to victims of sexual assault competently and compassionately (Office on Violence Against Women, 2004). Officers have been trained to interview victims in a sensitive way that minimizes their humiliation and discomfort. Most sexual assault counselors agree that people should report incidents of being forced to have sex, even if they are not yet certain they want to proceed with prosecution of the perpetrator. The victim should receive a medical examination prior to showering or douching, in order to gather important evidence such as semen samples. In an estimated 5 percent of female rapes, pregnancy results, requiring decisions to be made about this consequence. About half of such pregnancies end in abortion.

The courts often have had to wrestle with difficult issues related to rape survivors' privacy. Many states have rape-shield laws that protect a victim from having any details of a former romantic relationship with the rapist—or other information about former sexual behaviors—admitted as evidence during the rapist's trial. There has been general agreement among the media not to release the names of victims. However, some accused offenders have declared this unfair because their names may be released before they have been tried. Decisions about these matters continue to be made in favor of protecting the victim.

Individual therapy and group counseling are the most commonly used approaches for helping victims of sexual assault cope with their trauma. Most cities and larger communities have rape crisis centers that are equipped to help women deal with all aspects of the aftermath of forced sex. The partners of assault victims often become secondary survivors, experiencing a whole

FIGURE 16.6 *Rape Intervention Program*

Victims of rape need help in seeing themselves as survivors rather than victims and in reestablishing a sense of self-worth. Other problems, such as depression and physical or sexual dysfunctions as a result of the rape, need to be confronted and treated as well.

range of emotional reactions and posttraumatic symptoms. They may require support and counseling as well (Connop & Petrak, 2004; Reavey & Gough, 2000).

Sexual Abuse of Children and Adolescents

A substantial percentage of children and adolescents are subjected to sexual abuse by adults or other adolescents, also known as **child molesting** or **pedophilia.** In the *DSM-IV,* pedophilia applies specifically to recurrent sexual interactions with children prior to their reaching puberty, usually around age 13, and in cases where the perpetrator is at least 16 years old and five years older than the child (Green, 2002). A term more frequently being used to describe the sexual abuse of adolescents is **hebephilia,** although it has not yet been recognized as a diagnostic term. Given that adult–child sexual interaction is not considered pathological in all cultures, there is continuing controversy over whether it should be considered a mental illness or disorder (Schmidt, 2002; Zucker, 2002a). Given Western cultural values and a body of evidence indicating that sexual interactions with adults have harmful outcomes for children, such behavior has largely been viewed in terms of pathology and illegality.

However, there is a growing awareness that the science of child and adolescent sexual abuse has been flawed and inadequate. Population samples have been small and nonrepresentative and statistical analysis limited, and because sexual abuse victims often have been subjected to other forms of victimization, the conclusions drawn about cause and effect are often unsupportable. Others insist that, even in the face of scientific weaknesses, there is enough evidence to assume negative consequences for children and adolescents in such relationships (Najman, Dunne, & Boyle, 2007; Rind & Tromovitch, 2007). Experts in the field have called for interdisciplinary cooperation among medical and mental health workers, social scientists, and criminal justice representatives to carry out reliable research on the many issues surrounding sexual abuse of the young so that sensible, realistic social policies and treatment strategies can be enacted (Freyd et al., 2005).

Various models have been proposed that consider several different dimensions and levels of severity of a potentially abusive situation. First, the type of sexual behavior is considered, particularly whether physical contact has occurred (as in fondling, intercourse, or oral sex) or has not (as in exhibitionism). Also, the age of the subject of sexual contact is considered a significant aspect of the ability to consent, as is the age of the perpetrator. Most agree that if the subject is under age 12 and the perpetrator is older by some years, then the situation may be assumed to be abusive. The relationship of the perpetrator to the subject is also considered, as is the rather complex issue of the subject's degree of willingness to participate in the activity. When the victim is between the ages of 13 and 17, the issue becomes somewhat more complicated, and definitions of abuse typically depend on the age of the perpetrator and whether the subject wanted the sexual contact (Bullough, 2003a; Johnson, 2000).

A few professionals point out that among adolescents who have been involved sexually with adults, the outcomes sometimes have been positive rather than harmful. In taking such a stand, these professionals risk being attacked by opponents and having their careers jeopardized. One such researcher reminds us that the field has been filled with hyperbole on the part of "child protectionists" for about 30 years and it is time for a better balance in factual knowledge and level of scientific validity (Bullough, 2003a; Riegel, 2005; Rind, 2003; Rind & Tromovich, 2007).

Incidence of Child Sexual Abuse

Because of the difficulties involved in isolating an appropriate population sample and deciding what ages constitute childhood and adolescence, and inconsistencies in the definitions of various forms of abuse, it has been difficult to come up with reliable statistics on the incidence of sexual abuse in these groups (Goldman & Padayachi, 2000). Analyses of various surveys, in which the incidence of child sexual abuse was reported over a wide range, have concluded that a reasonable summary statistic would be that about 20 percent of females and about 5 to 10 percent of males are sexually abused as children or adolescents. The abuse of members of both sexes is almost always perpetrated by males. Girls are somewhat more likely to be abused by family members, and boys are more likely to be abused by strangers, although stranger abuse accounts for only about 4 percent of cases. There is generally a low rate of reporting of such incidents to authorities.

The NHSLS statistics, believed to be more representative of the U.S. population, indicated that 12 percent of the male respondents and 17 percent of the females reported having been sexually touched as children. The most typical forms of sexual activity reported included genital touching, kissing, oral sex, vaginal intercourse, and male-male anal intercourse. There were no differential statistics across race, ethnicity, or educational level.

---

child molesting sexual abuse of a child by an adult.
pedophilia (pee-da-FIL-ee-a) a pathological desire to sexually abuse children.
hebephilia (HEE-beh-fil-ee-a) a term being used to describe the sexual abuse of adolescents.

Real Student Voices

■ When I was about 10 or 11, my older cousin, who was about 13, showed me how to masturbate. For a while we would sneak off and do it together. In a way, I suppose he could have been considered a sexual abuser, but I've never thought of it that way. I still see him occainally, but we've never talked about it. I guess we'd both be embarrassed.

■ One of my brother's friends fooled around with me when I was about seven years old. He touched and fondled my vulva, and made me touch him. It made me feel really dirty, even though I didn't entirely understand what was going on. I told my mom, and she reported it to the police. I know he got arrested, although I never did find out the whole story. I had to talk with a counselor a few times after it happened. I never really hated the guy, but I knew what he had done was wrong. He and his family moved away.

Girls were touched primarily by males. For 28 percent of these girls, the males were between the ages of 14 and 17 when the touching took place; for 63 percent, the males were over 18. Only 4 percent of females indicated that they had been touched by other females. Boys had been touched more frequently by females (for 45 percent, by females ages 14 to 17, and for 9 percent, by females over 18), but they also had quite frequently been touched by other males (15 percent had been touched by males ages 14 to 17, and 23 percent by males over 18). Smaller groups of boys and girls had been touched by both males and females. It might be concluded from these findings that girls are at greatest risk of sexual abuse from adult men, followed by adolescent males; whereas boys are at greatest risk from abuse by adolescent females, followed by adult men, and then by adolescent males (Laumann, Gagnon, et al., 1994).

The stereotypes would lead us to believe that pedophiles or hebophiles are degenerate men who lurk in trench coats near schools and parks, waiting to accost youngsters. Actually, the majority of sexual abuse victims are molested by a family member or someone known to the child. As Table 16.5 shows, family friends and relatives are among the most common abusers of children. Files released by the Boy Scouts of America for a 20-year period revealed that about 1,800 scoutmasters had been removed from duty because of suspected or actual sexual abuse of boys. The organization has produced videotapes and printed materials informing boys about how to protect themselves from sexual abuse.

There is evidence that abuse of boys is less likely to be reported than is abuse of girls, and the phenomenon also has been researched to a much lesser extent. Both of these facts need to be understood within the context of our culture's views of maleness and mas-

culinity. Our society may at some level feel that boys really do not need or deserve the same protection against sexual abuse as do girls. It may also be that reporting an incident of sexual abuse would be viewed by the boy himself, or by someone close to him, as an admission of having been a powerless victim, a role that is not respected for males (Schmidt, 2002).

Table 16.5 *Relationship to Child Sexual Abuse Victims of Their Abusers (percentages)*

	Female Victims	Male Victims
Stranger	7%	4%
Teacher	3	4
Family friend	29	40
Mother's boyfriend	2	1
Older friend of respondent	1	4
Other relative	29	13
Older brother	9	4
Stepfather	7	1
Father	7	1
Other	19	17
Number of cases	289	166

Note: The table entries add up to more than 100 percent because some respondents were touched by more than one adult.

Source: From *The Social Organization of Sexuality,* by Edward O. Laumann et al. Copyright © 1994 by Edward O. Laumann, Robert T. Michael, CSG Enterprises, Inc., and Stuart Michaels. Reprinted with permission of The University of Chicago Press.

Children in our culture are taught to respect and obey adults and at the same time often are given little direct information about sex and their own sex organs. They therefore are easily manipulated, both physically and psychologically, and often are easily frightened into silent sexual compliance. Child molestation is as much an act of power as it is a sexual act. The victims of abuse often blame themselves for what has happened, concluding that they have somehow been bad or deserving of punishment. Persistent feelings of shame may come to pervade the individual's self-concept (Sgroi, 2000).

Children often are reluctant to report sexual abuse, especially if the perpetrator is a family member or friend, or they may lack the verbal development to explain clearly what happened (Freyd, 2005). Unfortunately, even when children report sexual abuse, they sometimes are not taken seriously. In some instances, adults want to avoid confrontations with relatives or friends who might be accused of molesting their child. Those children who do report abuse sometimes communicate directly to a close adult or professional person, either in language or by demonstrating what happened on an anatomically correct doll (see Figure 16.7). However, information gained from children's use of anatomically correct dolls has not been found to be very reliable in deciding whether a child has been sexually abused (Hewitt, 1999).

■ **FIGURE 16.7** *Anatomically Correct Dolls*

These anatomically correct dolls called "Teach-A-Bodies" are used to educate young children about sex and to assist young victims in explaining what happened to them during an incidence of alleged sexual abuse. However, studies suggest that information gained from children's use of such dolls about incidents of alleged abuse may be unreliable.

Adult Sexual Abusers

We have only an incomplete understanding of the psychological dynamics of adult perpetrators of child sexual abuse. Professionals once believed that such behavior might well be rooted in the perpetrator's own treatment as a child, with at least some evidence suggesting that abusive adults were themselves sometimes sexually abused as children. However, research has also suggested that other factors are crucial in the development of sexually abusive behavior. For example, child abusers tend to have lacked confidants during their own childhoods and tend to have been emotionally isolated. They tend to report high levels of emotional distress and difficulties with thinking clearly and concentrating. Some of these characteristics may be related to neurological abnormalities that may have afflicted some perpetrators during their early development (Miccio-Fonseca, 2001; Seto, 2005). Like research findings regarding sexual orientation, studies are beginning to find correlations between a tendency toward sexual offenses and factors such as left-handedness and birth order, further suggesting the possibility of genetic and neurological factors (Cantor et al., 2005; MacCulloch et al., 2004).

Adult male sexual abusers often come from families that have been rejecting and controlling but not necessarily harsh in discipline. They often have had a disturbed relationship with their own father, are likely to have experienced some prior trauma in their life, and may fantasize about children in sexual ways. Sexual abusers of children seem to have well-developed mechanisms for coping internally with what they have done. They may distort or rationalize their behaviors in their own minds, and they may also be very self-denigrating, making it even more likely that they will feel unable to control their paraphilic sexual urges. Some offenders blame their victims for the sexual abuse or blame third parties, such as a spouse, for not providing sexual satisfaction for them (Blumenthal, Gudjonsson, & Burns, 1999; Wilson, 1999). Some recent studies have suggested that male pedophiles often report having had a serious head injury prior to age 13, and it has been theorized that such injuries could increase the risk of becoming a pedophile (Blanchard et al., 2002; Blanchard et al., 2003).

Little is known about women who sexually abuse children. Studies of convicted female child molesters frequently have shown them to be of marginal intelligence, to have a history of sexual and physical abuse themselves, and to experience dissatisfaction with their adult sexual lives. They tend to have a high incidence of psychiatric disorders (Chow & Choy, 2002). They often act out of anger or in retaliation against a partner or spouse. Frequently, they commit the sexual abuse with another adult present, usually a male offender. It has been proposed that because we traditionally view women as nonviolent and nurturing, professionals and law enforcement personnel fail to ask victims questions that would help reveal the woman's role in abuse cases, and victims themselves may find it difficult to acknowledge or express the role a woman has played. Similarly, female offenders may be particularly reluctant to admit to the abuse because it is seen in our society as a particularly abhorrent and unexpected behavior for a woman (Denov, 2003). It may also be that the sexually abusive behavior of women is more covert than that of men, making it less noticeable to victims and authorities.

Recent attention has focused on priests and other clergy who sexually abuse children. The Roman Catholic Church has come under fire for not acting more swiftly and proactively in some situations where priests have been accused of sexual abuse (Scheper-Hughes & Devine, 2003; Shepard, 2003). As a result, the Council of Bishops has adopted extensive new zero-tolerance guidelines for dealing with such cases. Most church leaders are realizing that it is crucial to take allegations of abuse seriously, remove the offender from service immediately if evidence is sufficient, comply with civil law and any civil investigations, and offer help to victims and their families. Formal procedures are now in place within most denominations for dealing with clergy abuse cases.

Child and Adolescent Sexual Abusers

There has been an increase in reported sex abuse perpetrated by both other children and adolescents. About one in every six sexual abuse incidents is committed by another child, often 6 to 9 years old. These children may have been victims of abuse themselves, and they tend to respond to counseling that helps them understand that the behavior is inappropriate (Hunter & Figueredo, 1999). Adolescents typically abuse younger children or other adolescents. Teenage babysitters, or their friends, are common offenders. Adolescent sex abusers are usually males, although NHSLS data showed that boys are not infrequently abused by adolescent females (Laumann, Gagnon, et al., 1994). Abusive adolescents often come from dysfunctional family backgrounds and have serious developmental and psychological difficulties. It is quite typical for juvenile sex abusers to have been subjected to physical abuse themselves, sometimes sexual abuse. They are likely to have parents who have sexual pathologies, and they often show symptoms of depression (Rasmussen, 1999).

Parents who learn about a son's sexual abusiveness often experience difficulty in dealing with the situation. There may be tensions about communicating with the son about his actions and confusion over is-

sues related to punishment or treatment. Parents may feel overwhelmed by the situation and may be troubled by a sense of helplessness. Gradually, they may begin to engage themselves in reevaluating their relationship with their offending son and may become more actively involved in seeing the situation through to resolution. These are not easy issues for families to face. Ultimately, the treatment of adolescent sex offenders involves helping them learn how to interrupt their sexual fantasies concerning their inappropriate behavior and how to better empathize with the feelings and reactions of their victims (Aylwin, Reddon, & Burke, 2005; Oliver, 2005).

Effects of Child Sexual Abuse

Longitudinal studies on the effects of child sexual abuse suggest that symptoms of stress and trauma in the child gradually decline in the months following the abuse. Some studies have found that a substantial number of sexually abused children do not seem to show any measurable symptoms, nor do they necessarily define the experience in negative terms (Bauserman & Rind, 1997; Rind, 2003). It may be that the degree of coercion and violence involved in sexual abuse is crucial in determining the amount of trauma experienced, but there seems to be general agreement that children cannot truly consent to sexual contact and that being coerced into sexual activity by an adult may well create problems later in the individual's life (Cecil & Matson, 2005; Dennerstein, Guthrie, & Alford, 2004; Zweig et al., 1999).

Among a sample of men who had been sexually involved with older partners when they were children, about 40 percent did not consider the experience to have been abusive. Those that did perceive their experiences to have been abusive were more likely to have been younger when it happened and to have been physically or emotionally threatened. They also were more likely as adults to have problems with alcohol, suggesting that longer-term effects may well be related to how the early sexual experiences were perceived by the individual (Dolezal & Carballo-Dieguez, 2002).

Although it is difficult to generalize about the short- or long-term effects of sexual abuse on children and adolescents, several categories of ill effects have been identified (Leonard & Follette, 2003; Loeb et al., 2003):

1. *Traumatic sexualization* means that the child's feelings, attitudes, and behaviors related to sex may be exhibited in ways that are inappropriate to the child's age and stage of development. Sexually abused children may behave in inappropriate, sexually aggressive ways (Johnson, 2000; Meston, Heiman, & Trapnell, 1999).
2. *A sense of betrayal* may result among children who find that someone they trusted and

depended on has caused them harm. This is particularly true when the perpetrator of the abuse is a family member. This sense of betrayal may be intensified if the child's report of sexual abuse is disbelieved or if the child is blamed for the event. Children often have negative reactions toward the abuser.

3. *Disempowerment* results when a child feels that his or her will or desires have been ignored and deliberately violated. The more physical force or coercion the perpetrator has used in the sexual activity, the greater the child's sense of powerlessness. This outcome may play a role in the susceptibility of victims to sexually abusive situations later in life (Humphrey & White, 2000).

4. *Stigmatization* is particularly problematic when the child is expected to react to the event with feelings of shame and guilt. Such negative connotations may come directly from the abuser, who may want the victim to take the blame for the activity, or they may be reinforced by others in the family or community who hear of the abuse.

We are just beginning to understand the effects sexual abuse may have on later adult life, although a direct cause-and-effect connection sometimes is difficult to support. Child sexual abuse has been found to be a risk factor in depression, anxiety, sexual dysfunction, difficulty maintaining adult relationships, and suicidal feelings in women. Women who suffer from chronic pelvic pain, other gynecological problems, headaches, chronic gastrointestinal problems, phobias, and depression often have a history of sexual abuse, although the cause-and-effect relationship has not been firmly established (Dennerstein, Guthrie, & Alford, 2004; Gladstone et al., 1999; Najman, Dunne, & Boyle, 2007; Najman, Dunne, Purdie, et al., 2005; Reilly et al., 1999). There is certainly evidence to indicate that many adult psychiatric patients, substance abusers, sex workers, and people with eating disorders have a history of sexual abuse at higher rates than in the general population (Abramovich, 2005; Deep et al., 1999; Finlinson et al., 2003; Vaddiparti et al., 2006). Teenagers who have previously experienced sexual abuse have a greater likelihood of participating in unsafe sexual practices that could lead to pregnancy or disease transmission (Johnson & Hellerstedt, 2002; Raj, Silverman, & Amaro, 2000).

Although most studies have assumed a cause-and-effect relationship between child sexual abuse and mental disturbance, it has also been proposed that certain mental disorders might predispose some children to involve themselves in inappropriate sexual activities with adults. Researchers have often assumed that borderline personality disturbance could be caused by childhood sexual abuse. More recently, the alternate cause-and-effect pathway has been proposed (Bailey & Shriver, 1999). It is evident that many subtleties exist in interpreting causes and consequences of sexual abuse.

While it has been widely accepted that adults who were abused as children are likely to become abusive to children as adults, recent reviews of the literature indicate that unqualified acceptance of that belief is unfounded. Other factors are associated with eventual sexually abusive behavior, including the social supports available while growing up, the extent of emotional isolation, and the effects of poverty and stress (Seto, 2005).

There is less empirical evidence about the effects of childhood sexual abuse on boys' later development and adult sexual behavior than on that of girls. The studies that have been done suggest that these men may have confusion about their male identity, poor body image, or some difficulty in maintaining healthy, intimate relationships. Again, male socialization patterns appear to play a role in how men eventually perceive themselves in the aftermath of childhood sexual abuse (Dolezal & Carballo-Dieguez, 2002; Meston, Heimen, & Trapnell, 1999). A study of boys who had had sexual contacts with adults but had not been involved in any kind of clinical treatment found a broad range of reactions from negative to positive. The relationship to the adult, perceptions of consent, and the presence of force were all factors that helped determine boys' reactions to the behaviors (Bauserman & Rind, 1997; Rind, 2003).

It would appear that the effects of sexual abuse can be quite subtle but may also be long-lasting, possibly resulting in more negative attitudes about sex as an adult (Rellini & Meston, 2007). The more serious effects most probably are the result of violence or severe coercion inflicted on the victim by the adult. Professionals agree that an important determinant of these effects is how the child is treated by authorities and how much counseling help the child is given to deal with his or her confusion and fear. Many victims of child sexual abuse do not confront their feelings and reactions until adulthood. There are support groups that can help such adults deal with their experiences (Rollins, 2005).

Treating Victims of Child Sexual Abuse

FOH

Crisis intervention may be the first line of action in treating child sexual abuse cases. A safe environment must be established for the child, and the offender must be removed from any contact with her or him. Legal authorities should be involved in handling any criminal charges and sanctions, and social service agencies should work with the child and family members. A variety of treatment programs have been developed to deal with sexually abused children; some

Real People

Tony: Sexual Abuse as an Adolescent

Tony is a somewhat shy young man who tends to be a loner. He is majoring in mechanical engineering and spends much of his free time in the auto shop, working on his car. He has a circle of good male friends, and they go drinking and skiing together. He is a good snowboarder and has even won some regional competitions in the sport. Shy around women, Tony has mostly avoided relationships with them. He has hooked up with women sexually several times and has enjoyed the experiences, but he does not feel ready for a commitment.

Tony harbors a secret that has interfered with his life considerably. When he was 14, he went on a camping trip with several boys, some of whom were older and not well known by him. He ended up sharing a tent with a 17-year-old. After he had fallen asleep, he felt someone moving on top of him and realized that the other boy was turning him over in the dark. He was told to be quiet and to just do what he was told. Tony was scared and wanted to fight back, but the other boy was much stronger and continued to threaten him. He was penetrated anally, which hurt, but he felt almost paralyzed by the situation. After the older boy had finished, he left Tony alone

and went back to sleep. Tony lay awake until dawn, crept out of the tent, and took a canoe out for a paddle alone. The other boy ignored him the rest of the day on the trip home, and he has not seen him since.

The memories of this incident continue to bother Tony. He has never told anyone about it and in fact feels too embarrassed to discuss it. He believes that most people would think he should have been able to defend himself better. Sometimes even he wonders if he should have fought back more, and he feels sure he would do so if a similar situation happened again. He works out to keep himself strong. He has no doubts about his sexuality, but when he masturbates or gets involved sexually with a girl, the bad feelings sometimes return. He plans on toughing it out and hopes that eventually the negative feelings will diminish.

How do you feel about Tony's secret experience? Do you think he should have resisted the sexual assault more strenuously? Should he have reported the incident immediately to appropriate authorities so that action could have been taken against his attacker? Would you say that Tony was raped?

of these programs involve family therapy, because other family members may be deeply affected by the abuse as well. There is evidence that support from family members is extremely important for children who have been sexually abused. The level of support sometimes is compromised when another family member has been the abuser of the child (Jinich & Litrownik, 1999; Stroud, 1999).

The therapist treating an abused child must anticipate a variety of possible reactions in the child. Many children express anger during the early stages of therapy, and they need to know that limits will be placed on expressing this anger. Later, feelings of guilt, shame, loss, neglect, and depression may emerge. In particularly violent sexual abuse cases, children may experience personality dissociation that can lead to disturbances involving multiple personalities. The therapist may also be called on to deal with the highly sexualized nature that has been stimulated in a young child and to help the child learn more age-appropriate responses (Goozen et al., 2002).

Many victims live with the secret of their sexual abuse well into adulthood. Therapy most often is initiated for other reasons at first, because adult survivors of sexual abuse may experience a range of physical, psychological, relational, and sexual symptoms that interfere with their lives (Berman, L. A., et al., 2001). They sometimes do not volunteer any information about childhood abuse unless directly questioned about it. It is important to work through all the complicated feelings and reactions about the abuse and the offender. The therapist will help the individual express the range of emotions, which often includes anger diverted toward the abuser and toward others perceived as not having provided sufficient protection. Mental imagery techniques are used to help the survivor deal with anger and resentment (Maltz, 2003). Dance therapy has helped women feel more comfortable in their bodies and better able to deal with other emotions (Mills & Daniluk, 2002). The ultimate goal is for adult survivors of child abuse to accept their feelings about the offender, develop a stronger and more positive sense of self, and work on developing a healthy and pleasure-oriented attitude toward adult sexual interactions. Group therapy approaches have proved to be particularly effective with some adults who were sexually abused as children (Morgan & Cummings, 1999; Rollins, 2005).

Treating Offenders

There has been continuing controversy among professionals concerning the effectiveness of treatment for sex offenders. Although standard approaches to psychotherapy that do not focus specifically on the offending behavior tend to be of limited value, some treatment programs have been found to be quite successful with child sexual abusers (Alexander, 1999; Grossman, Martis, & Fichtner, 1999). These usually involve various combinations of group therapy, cognitive-behavioral techniques to help abusers gain better control over their sexual impulses, relapse prevention strategies to head off further occurrences of abuse, and education about sexuality. Abusers need to improve their self-concept, and they may be helped, through enhancement of their abilities, to empathize with the feelings of others (Brown, 2000; Craissati, 1999; Pithers, 1999). They also may be helped to redirect some of the skills they have used to abuse people toward skills for preventing such abuse.

Over a number of years, professionals have agreed on a set of standards for the treatment of adult sex offenders, and a number of advances have been made in treatment strategies (Coleman et al., 2001; Miner & Coleman, 2001). Treating sex offenders with drugs to reduce their sexual drive has gained in popularity during recent years. Some of these drugs interfere with the production of male hormones or with the action of these hormones (Chow & Choy, 2002; Saleh, 2005; Schober et al., 2005). Antidepressant medications have also been used with offenders who seem to have depressive symptoms and may reduce the obsessive-compulsive tendencies that sometimes are part of the abusive behaviors. It has been suggested that when offenders also have a sexual dysfunction, treating the dysfunction may improve the individual's quality of life and deter further abusiveness (Metz & Sawyer, 2004). Although much remains to be done to clarify the effectiveness of medical treatment of child sexual abusers, the preliminary data available suggest that such treatments are of limited value unless they are part of a more comprehensive program of psychotherapy and behavior modification (Briken, Nika, & Berner, 2001; Zonana & Norko, 1999).

Untreated sexual abusers tend to have a recidivism rate of between 35 and 50 percent. Cognitive-behavioral approaches that eliminate or reduce inappropriate sexual arousal seem to reduce recidivism rates somewhat over the short term, although long-term studies are lacking. The goal of all such treatment is to help the offender control future behavior so that sexual abuse is not repeated and the offender is able to establish healthy, age-appropriate sexual relationships (Brown, 2000; Seto, Harris, Rice, & Barbaree, 2004). Therefore, the operative word seems to be *control* rather than *cure*.

Incestuous Sex

Virtually every society has strong prohibitions against sexual relationships within families. This is often called the **incest taboo.** There are many theories about why the incest taboo exists. One of the most common involves the desire to avoid disruption of the family system. The biosocial theory holds that the intimacy among family members in early childhood development triggers innate sexual inhibitions about later sexual contact with family, but the theory remains unproven (Hendrix & Schneider, 1999).

There are exceptions to the taboo, however. In the Trobriand Islands, a girl who has intercourse with her mother's brother is committing incest. If she has intercourse with her father, she is not. Among the Kubeo Indians of South America, boys come of age only after having sexual intercourse with their mothers. Strictly defined, the term **incest** refers to sexual intercourse between close blood relatives. It tends to be used in a broader context these days, referring to any sort of sexual contact between close blood relatives, stepparents, or others who live together in a family-like system. Confusion concerning definitions of incest has created some difficulty in researching the extent of the problem. NHSLS researchers found that 9 percent of girls and 4 percent of boys had been sexually involved with an older brother, 14 percent of girls and 2 percent of boys with their father or stepfather and 29 percent of girls and 13 percent of boys with another relative (Laumann, Gagnon, et al., 1994).

Although there are few other reliable statistics to support contentions about the incidence of various forms of incest, it is believed that father–daughter sexual contact constitutes slightly less than 25 percent of incest cases. Stepfather–daughter incest also accounts for about 25 percent of cases. The remaining 50 percent of cases involve brothers, uncles, in-laws, grandfathers, stepfamily members, and live-in boyfriends of mothers; it is generally believed that brother–sister incest is the most common among these cases. A study of sibling incest showed some dynamics that the fami-

incest taboo cultural prohibitions against incest, typical of most societies.
incest (IN-sest) sexual activity between closely related family members.

lies tended to have in common. The parents often were emotionally distant, inaccessible, and controlling. They tended to stimulate a sexual climate at home, and there were often family secrets, such as one parent having an affair. The incidence of mother–son incest is much less clear, and many researchers believe that although such behavior is not as common as incestual abuse of girls, it also may be reported with much less frequency when it occurs (Lawson, 1993).

Incest often results from unhealthy family interactions, and its discovery causes reverberations throughout the family structure. Families in which the relationship between the father and the mother is weak and in which a daughter takes on many household responsibilities are susceptible to incestuous contact between father and daughter. Abuse of boys by their fathers is known to be more common in households where the father is very domineering, has alcohol and marital problems, and is physically abusive toward other family members. Abuse of boys by their mothers occurs more often when the mother is overreliant on the son for emotional support. Families in which there is a great deal of chaos, role confusion, and blurring of boundaries between generations are also frequently involved in incest (Hamer, M., 2002; Maddock & Larson, 1995).

Like other forms of sexual abuse, incest is usually a confusing interaction for a child. Youngsters may be quite passive during the relationship and may even exhibit a kind of seductive behavior that encourages the sexual activity. As a result of the experiences, they may become highly erotic and more interested in sex than would be expected for their age, or they may exhibit self-destructive and aggressive forms of behavior due to feelings of guilt, resentment, and low self-worth (Courtois, 2000).

A primary goal in helping victims of incest has been to convince them that they are not to blame for the incestuous relationship. However, this approach may have its negative side. Even though such reassurances may be well intentioned, they may intensify the sense of powerlessness and lack of control the child already has felt because of the incident. While providing empathy and support through any traumatic responses the children may have encountered, therapists can empower them to see future situations as at least potentially controllable. Treatment is an issue for the whole family and should be viewed as a healing opportunity for individual family members. Women who have been victims of past incest often must work through barriers to the effective parenting of their own children (Armsworth & Stronck, 1999; Courtois, 2000).

It is not unusual for psychiatric patients, alcoholics, or perpetrators of sexual assault to admit during therapy that they were once victims of incest. Incest survivors are sometimes overachievers at work who tend to suffer from depression and suicide attempts.

They may still be struggling to understand how and why the incest occurred. Research indicates that being able to deal with these unresolved feelings can help people gain a new sense of mastery over their lives. Group psychotherapy is one of the more common therapeutic approaches for incest victims, although one-to-one counseling is often used as well (Marotta & Asner, 1999; Rollins, 2005). Therapists often must help adult survivors of incest deal with years of shame and anger that in many instances have caused difficulties in relationships. These adults need assurances that they are worthwhile and strong human beings.

Recovered or False Memories: The Controversy

As awareness of the extent of childhood sexual abuse has grown in recent years, the controversial issue of remembering childhood sexual abuse through therapy has emerged. Some publications have included lists of psychological and physical symptoms typical of adults who were sexually abused as children. Some counselors and therapists began to explore in greater depth the histories of their adult clients with such symptoms in hopes of finding out whether these individuals indeed had been subjected to sexual abuse earlier in life. Articles based on case studies began to be written about clients' *recovered memories* of past sexual abuse, often by a family member. There were several highly publicized cases in which parents were sued by their adult daughters because of sexual or other abuse that the daughter remembered during therapy. Some of these parents insisted that they were being unjustly accused and claimed that unethical or incompetent therapists had, in effect, planted *false memories* about abuse in their clients.

What are your opinions regarding adult memories of childhood sexual abuse that are recovered in therapy?

Although it has generally been accepted by those in the fields of psychology and psychiatry that traumatic events during childhood may be lost to conscious recall and later recalled, research has not been particularly supportive of that contention. A fair amount of evidence indicates that adult victims of child sexual abuse remember the incidents in varying degrees of detail (Banyard & Williams, 1999; Gold, Hughes, & Swingle, 1999). Controversy also surrounds the reliability of the details of those memories that do exist. Studies demonstrate that fantasies may be constructed out of events or emotions experienced during childhood or through suggestion by an outside person (Beckman, 2003; Freyd et al., 2005). As proponents of recovered memories call for understanding of the victims of past sexual abuse, some family members who feel they have been falsely accused have rallied together within the False Memory Syndrome Foundation. This group has dedicated its efforts to combating the possible effects of inaccurate recovered memories. There may be some people whose memories of sexual abuse during childhood have been repressed and indeed may be reconstructed. On the other hand, there is recognition that some individuals' memories sometimes may be incomplete, inaccurate, or invented out of other thought processes. Either way, the crucial issues revolve around how such memories should be treated in therapeutic situations and how reliable they should be considered when they are used in legal actions against actual or remembered offenders.

■ Preventing and Dealing with Problematic Sex

Sexual problems and concerns need not be devastating or permanently disruptive. Before moving on to the following chapters, which deal with various types of sexual problems, it is important to discuss how each of us can work to prevent sexual problems in our own lives and deal with them should they arise (Kalmuss, 2004). Consider each of the following points with care, and think about how you might apply them in your own life.

Learning about Sex

It is a good idea to learn about your own body, its sexual parts, and what they are called. You should also understand the patterns of sexual response that are part of your body's repertoire. Gradually, with time and experience, you will begin to understand your own sexual orientations and preferences—the things that turn you on. However important sexual self-knowledge is, it is not enough. You also need to take time to understand the many individual sexual differences found in human beings; which range from different sizes of sex organs to different sexual orientations. Accepting the fact that we are all different can be an important step toward preventing sexual difficulties.

Children need to understand the concepts of appropriate and inappropriate touching, and they need to be alert to possible behaviors that could lead to sexual abuse. They should be taught to be alert to behaviors, such as bribery and coercion, that adults might use to entice them into sexual activity (Tabachnick, 2000). Experts at the National Center for Missing and Exploited Children indicate that being able to recognize and avoid certain risky situations is more valuable than following the traditional warning not to talk to strangers. In the vast majority of cases, sexual offenders are not strangers to the child.

Knowing How to Communicate

Communication is fundamental to a continuing, healthy sexual relationship. Counselors who work with couples find that flaws in communication are one of the most common roots of sexual problems. There are many different things that must be communicated between people: thoughts, ideas, feelings, values, opinions, needs, and desires. They are communicated not only verbally but also through eye contact, facial expressions, and body language. It is important for people to have enough sense of personal empowerment to be able to learn about and use assertiveness when it comes to refusing sexual overtures and to be persistent when they do not want to have sex. This can be tricky at times, but it requires a strong sense of self and the skills to stand up to persuasion (East & Adams, 2002; Tolman, 2003). Communication is far more difficult than is often believed, and most people are given very little help in learning how to communicate effectively. See Chapter 9, "Sexuality, Communication, and Relationships," for a more complete discussion of communication and sexuality.

Having Realistic Expectations

People are prone to compare themselves to others sexually. "Am I normal?" is one of the most commonly asked questions when it comes to sex. The media provide models of sexual attractiveness and suggest standards of sexual prowess. All this can create unrealistic expectations that people then struggle to live up to. Sexual problems often stem from setting expectations for attractiveness or level of sexual activity that simply cannot be met. It is important to know yourself sexually and to work toward sexual goals that are comfortable, attainable, and consistent with your personal values. To live with unrealistic goals is to invite sexual problems.

Being Cautious and Responsible

Shared sex always has some consequences, potentially positive or negative. It is important to approach sexual decision making with an awareness of possible consequences, knowledge about sex, and open communication between the partners. Sexual problems such as guilt, unwanted pregnancy, contracting a sexually transmitted disease, and feelings of having been exploited usually can be prevented with a cautious attitude toward sexual choices. It is particularly important to be careful about sex-related interactions on the Internet. Personal identity, location, and contact information should be guarded with care, because there are sexual predators in cyberspace who sometimes use such information to find victims (Cooper, 2002).

Responsible sexual decisions are made by keeping the other person in mind as well as yourself. Only too often, people shirk their sexual responsibility with excuses: "I didn't mean to go so far"; "It just happened"; "I was so drunk I didn't know what I was doing." Responsibility means approaching relationships with an awareness of how powerful sexual emotions can be and how complicated the aftermath of sex can sometimes be, even if sex was desired at the time. Responsible sexual decision making can do more to prevent problematic sex than any other step.

FOH Finding Sex Counseling and Therapy

A part of being a healthy, sexually fulfilled person is knowing when you have exhausted your own resources. Sometimes you can cope with a problem yourself, sometimes not. Often it helps just to talk things out with another person, pulling thoughts and feelings into a more manageable perspective—especially when you know that person will protect your confidentiality (Breslin, 1998). It can be important to have the objectivity that an outsider can bring to a situation. Sometimes specific suggestions and strategies are needed that only someone with professional training can offer. Best friends seldom make the best counselors, regardless of how good their intentions may be.

Usually the best time to seek professional help is when you realize you need it and feel ready to seek it, even if you are nervous about it. Early intervention can prevent further complications. Do not assume that a routine visit to a clinician necessarily means that the professional will uncover any sexual concerns. Many professionals fail to take advantage of routine visits to ask questions about a person's sexual life and problems (Burstein et al., 2003). You will most likely need to share some basic information with the professional. There is another important point to keep in mind, however. No professional counselor or therapist can wave a magic wand and make the problem disappear. No treatment can be successful without a sincere motivation to change. You will have to want to work on the problem and be willing to expend some energy doing so. If it is a problem shared between partners, then both people usually will have to be committed to working together on it (Spitalnick & McNair, 2005).

Here are some specific guidelines to consider when deciding whether to seek professional help and when looking for an appropriate counselor or therapist:

1. *Make a preliminary assessment of the seriousness of the problem.* This has implications for the type of help you may want to seek. Problems with disease or pain generally need to be addressed by medical professionals. Concern over sexual orientation, decision making, and sexual behaviors can be handled by sex counselors. Sexual

dysfunctions (see also Chapter 18) are best dealt with by a specially trained sex therapist or medical professional.

2. *Do not be afraid to seek help.* Professional help often can resolve sexual concerns and problems and help individuals and couples feel better about themselves. To seek such help is not a weakness but instead constitutes a sign of maturity, strength, and personal responsibility.

3. *Locate a qualified professional.* You may want to ask a trusted doctor, teacher, or religious leader to suggest a professional he or she would recommend for dealing with sexual problems. The yellow pages of telephone directories often list people who specialize in treating sex-related concerns. The counseling centers or health centers of larger colleges and universities offer sex counseling and therapy services for students. Large medical centers usually offer a variety of sexual health services, and several organizations listed in the appendix of this text can offer referrals.

4. *Investigate and ask questions.* It is always advisable to be an informed consumer. Do not be hesitant or embarrassed about checking out professionals' qualifications and inquiring about their background preparation. Asking questions during an initial visit, or even prior to a first visit, is a good way to find out what to expect. A true professional will not be offended or insulted by such questions. Here are some areas you might consider finding out more about:
   - What does the service cost, and how frequent are visits?
   - What sort of education, training, and other credentials does the person have?
   - What records are kept, and are they treated in a completely confidential manner? How long are records kept on file?
   - Is the professional appropriately licensed or certified by the state or by any professional society?

5. *Know what you are looking for.* You should be able to feel comfortable and relatively relaxed with a counselor or therapist. Look for the kind of atmosphere in which you are free to discuss sex openly and to express your feelings without being judged, put down, or made to feel embarrassed. You should sense a degree of trust, caring, and respect between yourself and the therapist. Any counseling process has its ups and downs, but you should be able to sense eventual progress as long as you are working on it. If you feel discouraged, you should be able to discuss this with the counselor or therapist.

6. *Know what you are not looking for.* Be skeptical about anyone who promises quick and easy

solutions. If the person seems to have personal values that might interfere with her or his objectivity in assessing your situation, think about changing to another professional. Also watch out for any seductiveness or sexual aggression from the professional. This is considered unethical behavior and may be grounds for taking action against the offender. Be cautious, too, about people who seem overly anxious to persuade you to adopt their sexual values. Finally, unless the professional is a physician or other medical clinician who must conduct a legitimate physical examination, reject any suggestions that you should remove your clothing or submit to some sort of sexual touching. Codes of professional ethics consider such behavior inappropriate.

7. *Check with people who are familiar with the counselor's or therapist's work.* Word-of-mouth recommendations or criticisms are worth taking into consideration. People who have had profes-sional contacts with a counselor or therapist, as either a client or a colleague, may be able to offer especially valuable insights. However, such opinions do not represent the final word. Some people can be impressed by a professional who knows how to sound well informed; some may gripe about a therapist who cannot perform miracles on demand.

Problematic sex need not be allowed to become a sexual catastrophe. Help is now available for any sexual problem and can be obtained confidentially from well-qualified professionals. Preventing and dealing with sexual problems is largely a matter of personal responsibility. You must be ready to accept that any sexual act has a variety of potential consequences, both positive and negative. Most of all, you must be responsible enough to recognize that anyone can experience a sexual problem, and you must then *do something about it.*

Self-Evaluation

Your Sexual Concerns and Problems

Most of us do not feel fully comfortable with or relaxed about all aspects of our sexuality all the time. It is difficult to say when discomfort becomes a concern or when a concern becomes a problem. However, this questionnaire may help you evaluate your particular sex-related worries and what you want to do about them. The chapters that follow may offer more information about your specific concerns. Before proceeding with the questionnaire, take the following two preliminary steps:

Step 1. Ask yourself if you really need to proceed with this questionnaire. If you have had or now have some area of sexuality that has caused you to experience a continuing sense of unrest or worry, it probably will be worth your time to answer the questions. If you feel fully comfortable with your sexual needs, feelings, orientations, and activities all the time, skip this questionnaire.

Step 2. If possible, make certain you have all the facts about those sexual areas that are of special concern to you. Before going on with this questionnaire, read the earlier parts of this book pertaining to those areas. The table of contents and index can help you find appropriate information. You might even want to read some of the articles that are cited in each chapter. Some worries and problems fade with appropriate, accurate sexuality education.

1. **Mentally, or on paper, list the sexual concern(s) or problem(s) that presently are most worrisome for you. Do not list more than three.**

2. **For each concern you have listed, answer the following questions.**
   a. *For how long has this worried you?*
   b. Can you identify the particular incident or time in your life when it started to become a real concern? If so, think it over in as much detail as you can recall.
      1. *What were your feelings at the time?*
      2. *What are your feelings now as you think back?*
      3. *Is there anything you wish you could change about the origins of your concern?*
      4. *If another person was involved in the origins of your concern, how do you feel about that person now?*
   c. Is there another person directly involved in (or affected by) the problem now? If so, how would you summarize your present relationship with that person?

3. Evaluate your concerns.

  a. For each concern you have listed, read through the categories listed in the table and decide which category best describes your concern. Note whether it is labeled I, II, III, or IV.

Category Number	Types of Concerns
I.	*Body appearance* *Size or shape of genitals or breasts* *Sexual things you have done in the past but no longer care about doing*
II.	*Sexually transmitted disease or other infection of sex organs* *Concern about having been infected with HIV* *Pregnancy or difficulty with birth control methods* *Fear of sexual exertion following a heart attack or other illness* *Other medical problems related to sex organs*
III.	*Masturbation* *Sexual fantasies* *Things or people to whom you feel sexually attracted that do not fit the typical socially accepted standards* *Sexual interests and/or activities of your partner or another important person in your life that are upsetting to you in some way* *Lack of information about sex* *Lack of communication with a sexual partner*
IV.	*Deep, long-term guilt, dissatisfaction, or unhappiness with your sexuality* *A feeling that you are being sexually harassed by another person* *A history of sexual abuse as a child that you have not dealt with completely or effectively* *Concern about rape or other forms of sexual assault or coercion* *Worries about your body image to the extent that you avoid eating, or binge on food and then vomit or take laxatives* *Sexual activities in which you now engage that are unusual, illegal, or not generally accepted socially* *Problems with sexual functioning (e.g., erectile problems, premature ejaculation, lack of sexual arousal, difficulty reaching orgasm (in yourself or your partner) or pain during sexual activity*

  b. Do you feel discouraged, depressed, and hopeless about your sexual worries and problems? Do not give up on yourself, because for others to be able to help you, you must be willing to work on your problem. There may be many things that will help. Also, be careful not to blame someone else for your problem. Regardless of the type of problem or who has it, you are responsible for how it affects you and what you do about it. Keep reading.

  c. Now what are you going to do? First go back and note the category of your concern from part 3a. Regardless of the category, it might be worth considering talking with a professional counselor who has a good understanding of human sexuality. Here are some specific comments about each category; note the remarks for the category you have chosen.

    1. Category I for the most part includes problems that you cannot do very much about. One way or another, you probably are going to have to try to become more comfortable with what you have or what you have done. Counseling could help you do that.

    2. Category II consists of medical problems. If you have not already consulted a physician, do so. If you already have but are unsatisfied, try to find another physician who can help. Your city or county medical society might be able to help with this. Most communities also have STD and HIV testing services and family planning clinics.

    3. Category III includes some of the most common types of sexual problems. Although many people learn to live with them, some form of counseling often can do wonders. (See part d.)

    4. Category IV includes problems that might easily fit into category III but that also sometimes require more intensive sex therapy or psychotherapy. In seeking a professional to help you deal with such problems, choose carefully and check credentials.

  d. If you decide to seek professional help, consider the following:

    1. Should your spouse or sexual partner be involved in the counseling? If you are having difficulty communicating, see Chapter 9.

    2. Try to gain a clear idea of what your goals are in dealing with your sexual concern(s), and express them to the person from whom you seek help.

Chapter Summary

1. The determination as to when some sexual orientation, preference, or behavior becomes a problem can be highly subjective. It often needs to be viewed within the contexts of an individual's reactions and lifestyle and the surrounding cultural and social belief systems.

2. Negative attitudes about the self, especially concern about one's body image, or a lack of accurate

information related to sexuality can become a problem.

3. Sexual coercion, abuse, and assault of others represent serious sexual problems. The issue of what constitutes consensual sex, as opposed to acquiescence, can be complicated.

4. Ignorance about human sexuality can generate prejudice toward those who in some way are different sexually.

5. Some sexual behaviors, including some sadomasochistic activities, represent obvious physical dangers to individuals and sometimes reflect self-destructive qualities. There may be a biological link between stress and sexual arousal.

6. There is a range of paraphilias, in which people respond sexually to objects or situations not usually considered sexually arousing. Paraphiles or paraphilics may be compulsive in their sexual behaviors.

7. The trafficking of girls, boys, and women for sexual purposes has become a worldwide problem. These victims are bought out of poverty only to become sex slaves who have few options for change.

8. There has been an ongoing controversy over whether people can become addicted to sex and whether sex "addiction" treatments are adequate. Out-of-control sex seems to be correlated with certain reactions to negative mood states.

9. Sexual harassment refers to unwanted sexual advances. There are four main types: coercion and bribery, hostile environment, aggressive acts, and third-party effects.

10. Awareness of sexual harassment in schools and colleges is increasing. There is controversy over the degree to which faculty–student relationships at colleges should be limited or prohibited.

11. The military has been facing serious difficulties with sexual harassment and the issue of consensual sexual relationships, and it has been developing educational programs to address these issues.

12. Sexual harassment in the workplace has long been a problem, and laws require that workers enjoy freedom from such pressures.

13. Most institutions have policies against sexual harassment, and several federal laws prohibit the behavior.

14. It is best to respond promptly to harassing situations by getting personal support, seeking out appropriate authorities, being clear about your needs, possibly writing a letter to the harasser, and making use of mediation services.

15. Sexual boundary violations by professionals are prohibited by ethical standards, and they often represent coercion based on power imbalances in the relationship.

16. Consent is a fundamental issue in sexual interactions that has not been studied extensively. Many factors can compromise the validity of consent and lead to charges of coercion or force.

17. Women and men report having been coerced into sex by sexual arousal, emotional manipulation and lies, exploitation while intoxicated, or physical force.

18. The term *rape* is used in various ways to refer to forced sex. There are several different motivations behind rape. Statutory rape relates to the legal age of consent.

19. There are some predictors of aggression and violence in relationships. In female-male relationships, early warning signals can suggest that a man has negative or disrespectful attitudes toward women and could potentially be abusive.

20. Forced sex is believed to be far more common than is generally realized or reported. It often represents an attempt to humiliate someone and exercise power over the person. Men and women frequently perceive sexually coercive situations differently.

21. In many cases, the offender in forced sex is known by the victim, and the offense is called acquaintance rape or date rape. Care should be taken to avoid the possibility of being incapacitated by a "date rape" drug.

22. A small percentage of wives admit to having been raped by their present or former husbands. Husbands are now subject to the legal consequences of raping their spouses.

23. Men also can be forced or coerced into having sex, sometimes by women and sometimes by other men. They react with humiliation, depression, and posttraumatic stress, but they may be less likely than women to report such assaults.

24. Victims of forced sex go through various phases of the rape trauma syndrome, a type of posttraumatic stress disorder. They must adjust to the event, cope with a range of emotions, and attempt to reestablish a sense of control and safety in their lives. Counseling and support are necessary during these phases of adjustment.

25. Sexual abuse of children, called pedophilia or child molestation, is a common and serious problem. Sexual attraction to or abuse of adolescents is sometimes called hebephilia.

26. Scientific research on child and adolescent sexual abuse often has been inadequate, and there is controversy over the possibility that some sex between adolescents and someone older might be perceived positively by the adolescent.

27. Adult sexual abusers may have experienced neurological problems during development. Psychologically, they may view children as sexually motivated, have a history of being abused themselves, and exhibit symptoms of denial and depression. More often than not, the adult abuser is known by the child victim.

28. A child who is sexually abused may have a sense of guilt, shame, and betrayal, and the abuse may lead to an unhealthy sexualization of the child's life. As adults, survivors of sexual abuse are likely to experience depression, anxiety, and other physical and psychological problems, although cause-and-effect relationships have not been fully supported scientifically.

29. Victims of sexual abuse may be helped by immediate crisis intervention as well as longer-term supportive and counseling services.

30. Treatment programs are available for child sexual abuse offenders; the most effective of these programs emphasize ways to control their sexual impulses and reduce their sexual desire for children. Some medications may have some effect in controlling sexual desire.

31. The term *incest* applies to sexual activity between closely related family members. It usually stems from unhealthy family patterns and creates serious confusion for the developing child or adolescent.

32. There is controversy over adult memories of childhood sexual abuse that are recovered in therapy. These recovered memories have been used in lawsuits. Some accused parents have fought such cases, and some professionals argue that these phenomena may represent false memories.

33. The best ways to prevent and deal with sexual problems are to be knowledgeable about human sexuality, develop communication skills based on qualities that facilitate good relationships, have realistic expectations about sex, and exercise caution and responsibility.

34. Sometimes it makes sense to seek professional help for dealing with sexual problems. Check out such professionals with great care and be suspicious about behavior that makes you uncomfortable or seems unethical.

Focus on Health Questions

In this section you will find the kinds of questions that you may have concerning your own health and sexuality. The page references indicate where in the text the answer is located; the exact place is marked with this logo: **FOH**

1. Are there any types of sexual behavior that are in themselves dangerous? **445–446**

2. What is a paraphilia? **446**

3. Is it true that people can become addicted to sex? **446–447**

4. What can I do if I am being sexually harassed? **450**

5. What should I look out for in a partner that might warn of potential sexual abusiveness? **456**

6. Can males be raped? **462**

7. What are the typical psychological reactions to being a victim of forced sex? **462**

8. How may victims of forced sex best be helped to recover? **463**

9. How does sexual abuse affect children during childhood and then later in adulthood? **467–468**

10. What should be done for a child after it has been discovered that the child has been sexually abused? **468–470**

11. Can child sexual abusers be treated? **470**

12. What are the effects of incestuous relationships on children? **470–471**

13. Are there any ways to head off sexual problems before they occur? **472**

14. If I have a sexual problem, how can I find a qualified professional to help me? **473–474**

Chapter 17

Sexually Transmitted Diseases, HIV/AIDS, and Sexual Decisions

Chapter Outline

> I couldn't understand why the nurse suggested that I have a test for a disease when I had no symptoms whatsoever. I was really shocked when the results showed that I had chlamydia. Then she said I should get tested for HIV. I never thought I would get any of those diseases. I'm pretty careful.
>
> —based on a counseling session

Sexual interaction involves close body contact and often the mingling of bodily fluids, making it a likely way for certain disease-causing organisms to be passed between people. Many sexually transmitted diseases (STDs) are continuing to spread rapidly among some populations. They also are commonly called sexually transmitted *infections* (STIs), but this term is used internationally more than in the United States. STD is still the official category used by the Centers for Disease Control and Prevention. STDs represent an important global health issue that is too often neglected, and experts have stressed that we cannot allow stigma, prejudice, or moral values concerning sexuality to get in the way of effective control of these diseases (Low et al., 2006). People sometimes take it for granted that their primary physician will know how to manage STDs, but diagnostic and treatment information is being updated constantly. A survey of physicians has shown that not all doctors have the levels of knowledge to diagnose and treat some infections effectively (Wiesenfeld et al., 2005).

The epidemic of HIV infection and AIDS is now well into its third decade. It has garnered more attention than any new disease to appear in recent history, and it continues to spread. **Acquired immunodeficiency syndrome,** better known as **AIDS,** threatens significant portions of the human population. The prevalence of **human immunodeficiency virus (HIV),** the virus that eventually can produce AIDS when it infects humans, has raised political and economic issues. Although HIV and AIDS have garnered a great deal of attention and are discussed in this chapter, some other STDs have reached epidemic proportions and their significance must not be minimized. In fact, persons with an STD infection are two to five times more likely to acquire HIV when exposed to it by an infected individual (CDC, 2006a).

See "STDs: The Silent Epidemic" on SexSource Online.

■ History and Incidence of Sexually Transmitted Diseases and HIV

STDs: The Hidden Epidemic

At various times in history, some sexually transmitted diseases, such as **syphilis,** have represented scourges that attacked large segments of societies. They were feared and often were assumed to represent retribution from the gods. When soldiers of the French army were garrisoned in Naples in the winter of 1495, they suffered syphilitic sores on the genitals, followed by skin eruptions. The Italians called it the "French sickness," although the French blamed it on the Italians. The Turkish people would come to call it the Christian disease, and the Chinese dubbed it the Portuguese disease. Nearly every major nationality, ethnic group, and religion eventually would be blamed for the scourge of syphilis. Gonorrhea and syphilis were significant problems among U.S. troops during World War II, and extensive educational efforts were launched to prevent their spread. However, effective and rapid medical treatments for the venereal diseases (VD), as they were once called, were generally lacking, and their incidence increased at alarming rates. Scientists are beginning to trace the histories of some of these disease organisms through their genetic lines (Zimmer, 2001).

Which STDs do you believe are most common in the United States?

When penicillin and other antibiotics began to appear in the late 1940s, it seemed as though VD had finally been conquered. By 1957, the number of cases of both gonorrhea and syphilis had dropped to an all-time low. However, as public concern began to fade amid assurances of a quick cure, the incidence of STDs began to rise again. It has been suggested that some health policymakers have always had mixed feelings about curing or eradicating STDs, because these diseases have been perceived as one factor that might discourage illicit sexual behavior. It seems likely that gonorrhea and syphilis might well have been completely eradicated if our culture had taken a less moralistic stance on STDs and had made more aggressive use of antibiotics (Michael et al., 1994).

acquired immunodeficiency syndrome (AIDS) a fatal disease caused by a virus that is transmitted through the exchange of bodily fluids, primarily in sexual activity and intravenous drug use.

human immunodeficiency virus (HIV) the virus that initially attacks the human immune system, causing HIV disease and eventually AIDS.

syphilis (SIF-uh-lus) a sexually transmitted disease (STD) characterized by four stages, beginning with the appearance of a chancre.

Real Student Voices

■ I was always a lot more scared of getting pregnant than I was of getting an STD. Even after I went on the pill, I always insisted that my boyfriend wear a condom. After a while, we got pretty comfortable with just using the pill, until I discovered I had chlamydia. So much for trust.

■ Having HPV isn't particularly scary for me as a male, but I do worry about spreading it to the women I have sex with. I always use condoms, but eventually I hope to settle down and get married. The new vaccine is great, because when we want to have a baby I won't have to feel guilty about giving her the virus or cancer.

■ Thinking about STDs just makes sex seem so unappealing! Yuck!

Instead, more antibiotic-resistant strains of these diseases have developed, and new disease-causing microbes—such as chlamydia and a variety of viral diseases—now have been added to the list of more than 25 infectious organisms that can be transmitted by intimate bodily contact. Several new STDs have been identified in recent years, and the problem continues to evolve (CDC, 2006a).

STDs have been called the "hidden epidemic" because they so often escape public attention. For one thing, many STDs lack clear symptoms and may go undetected for some time. Partly for this reason, they may also have serious, longer-term health consequences, including infertility, cancer, and other chronic illnesses. Another reason is that because of the social stigma associated with sex-related diseases, public discussion and education about STDs often are avoided, which may even inhibit health professionals from educating their patients about potential consequences (Cates et al., 2004).

U.S. teenagers often lack basic knowledge about STDs. In one study, nearly all the adolescents surveyed had received sexuality education, and 91 percent identified HIV as a major STD. However, only 2 percent could identify all eight major STDs, and few could distinguish between the curable and the incurable diseases (Clark, Jackson, & Allen-Taylor, 2002). The majority of adolescents do not seem to consider themselves at risk of infection, yet at the same time about half of the sexually experienced teenagers did not use a condom every time they had sex. Also, their knowledge of the risk factors presented by their sexual partners is quite low. Many teenagers have never discussed STDs with their most recent sexual partners (Ethier et al., 2003; Ford et al., 2004; Stoner, 2003). They often assume that they do not have an STD because they have no symptoms. When asked to name the most common STDs, only a small proportion can name human papilloma virus or trichomonas, even though these two diseases are among the most common of the new cases of STDs reported each year (Weinstock, Berman, & Cates, 2004).

Current data indicate that of the approximately 19 million new cases of STDs that occur annually in the United States, nearly 50 percent occur among persons ages 15 to 24. The consequences of these infections on human health continue to be staggering. More than 100,000 women are rendered infertile each year as the result of an STD, and half of the 88,000 annual ectopic pregnancies are due to a preexisting infection. Direct medical costs associated with STDs among people under age 25 alone are more than $7 billion a year (Cates et al., 2004; CDC, 2006a; Chesson et al., 2004).

What is your response to the suggestion that health policymakers have failed to use all of their resources to eradicate STDs?

Estimates vary concerning the incidence of STDs because of deficiencies in how the data are collected. Even though the Centers for Disease Control and Prevention (CDC) consider many STDs to be *reportable diseases* and gather statistics on them, many private physicians do not consistently report their occurrence. Public clinics are more likely to report those diseases that are easily diagnosed, such as the highly recognizable STD gonorrhea. They are less likely to be able to offer the expensive diagnostic techniques necessary to detect some of the viral STDs, such as HPV or hepatitis B. In addition, STDs are reported as "cases" rather than as patients, meaning that if the same individual were to report back to a clinic several times with a reinfection of the same disease, each new infection would be reported as a separate case. It is now believed that nearly

60 million people in the United States, or one out of every five, are infected with some form of viral STD (such as herpes or hepatitis B) that can be controlled but not cured (CDC, 2006b). From a political perspective, it is worth noting that STDs are the only diseases that are categorized specifically by their mode of transmission.

The Appearance of HIV and AIDS

In the early 1980s, articles began to appear in medical journals describing symptoms that had appeared in a number of gay men and users of intravenous drugs who shared needles. One thing all these individuals seemed to have in common was an apparent weakness in their immune system, the collection of mechanisms with which the body wards off disease. The patients experienced long periods of ill health while their bodies struggled to fight various bacteria, protozoa, and viruses. Eventually, the infections, often in rare forms, became more tenacious, finally resulting in death. The CDC labeled the new and puzzling disorder acquired immunodeficiency syndrome. It soon became clear that the disease-causing agent, eventually identified as HIV, could be transmitted between people and that it was frighteningly lethal.

No one knows for certain how long HIV has been around. It may be that in earlier years people who actually died of AIDS were diagnosed as having died of one of the many infections that the disease produces or that medical personnel simply had no way of knowing what they were dealing with. Genetic studies indicate that HIV probably had been infecting animal hosts for a long time and eventually diversified and began to infect humans sometime around 1930 (Korber et al., 2000). Although there have been some puzzling cases from earlier years leading to speculation about when and how HIV actually reached North America, it is generally believed that it arrived sometime during the mid-1970s.

The predominant theory, although it remains only a theory, about the origin of HIV is that a variant of the virus infected chimpanzees, perhaps for thousands of years. The virus eventually mutated into a form that could infect humans and may well have been transmitted to humans in central Africa during the butchering of chimps for food. The virus may have remained isolated in small, remote societies for decades until changing ways of African life brought it to urban centers, from where it was transported to the rest of the world by infected persons. Changing lifestyles, such as increased international travel, have had profound effects on the spread of such epidemics (Hillis, 2000). We will never completely understand the routes by which HIV has spread throughout the world. Once a pool of infected people became established in a population center that interacted with outside areas, it was only a matter of time before the virus would make its way into large segments of the human population.

Incidence of HIV/AIDS

Epidemiological studies continue to survey the extent of HIV infection in North America and worldwide (see Figure 17.1). One method used is gathering surveillance data concerning the number of HIV-positive cases reported by hospitals, clinics, physicians, and medical record systems. It is believed that in the United States at least 90 percent of cases are actually reported, a very high rate compared to the reporting of other diseases. Worldwide, AIDS has become the fourth-largest cause of human death. The rates of infection and death are much greater in the poorer nations of the world (UNAIDS, 2006).

In the United States in 2005, it was believed that between 720,000 and 1.2 million (or an estimated 1 million) people were currently living with HIV or AIDS, with about another 40,000 new diagnoses each year (CDC, 2006a; UNAIDS, 2006). Men continue to represent the majority (73 percent) of HIV diagnoses in the United States, although the proportion of women among newly diagnosed HIV or AIDS cases has been increasing dramatically, from 15 percent prior to 1995 to 27 percent in 2004. Three-quarters of these women are infected during unprotected sex with male partners who were intravenous drug users or who had sex with other men. About 20 percent acquired HIV through their own intravenous drug use, through use of contaminated needles (UNAIDS, 2006).

In the United States, HIV spread most rapidly at first through the gay male population and among intravenous drug abusers who shared needles. Many **hemophiliacs** and some surgical patients who received transfusions prior to the routine checking of donated blood for the virus were infected, and several thousand of these developed the disease. The proportion of reported cases among gays decreased for a time because of effective educational strategies. However, unsafe sex between men is now the most common means of infection in the United States, accounting for about 44 percent of HIV/AIDS cases, followed by unprotected heterosexual intercourse, which accounts for 33 percent of cases (UNAIDS, 2006). Worldwide, males transmit the virus to females much more often

epidemiological (e-pe-dee-mee-a-LAHJ-i-cahl) referring to the branch of medical science that deals with the incidence, distribution, and control of disease in a population.

hemophiliacs (hee-mo-FIL-ee-aks) people with the hereditary blood defect hemophilia, primarily affecting males and characterized by difficulty in clotting.

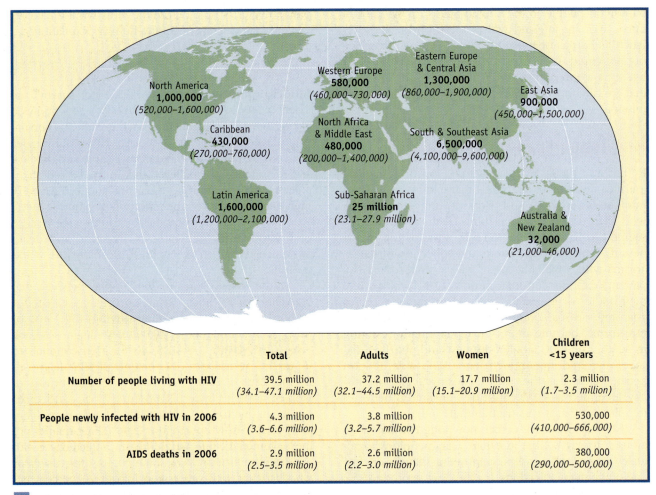

	Total	Adults	Women	Children <15 years
Number of people living with HIV	39.5 million *(34.1–47.1 million)*	37.2 million *(32.1–44.5 million)*	17.7 million *(15.1–20.9 million)*	2.3 million *(1.7–3.5 million)*
People newly infected with HIV in 2006	4.3 million *(3.6–6.6 million)*	3.8 million *(3.2–5.7 million)*		530,000 *(410,000–666,000)*
AIDS deaths in 2006	2.9 million *(2.5–3.5 million)*	2.6 million *(2.2–3.0 million)*		380,000 *(290,000–500,000)*

FIGURE 17.1 *Global Estimates of HIV and AIDS as of the End of 2006*

Source: Reproduced with kind permission from UNAIDS (2006).

than females transmit it to males. It appears that male-to-female transmission of HIV is more efficient than female-to-male transmission.

Children continue to be born infected with HIV. They seem to become infected **perinatally,** or during pregnancy; during the birth process itself; or soon after birth. The use of drugs such as zidovudine alone or in combination with other drugs by HIV-infected women who are pregnant seems to lessen the risk that they will transmit the virus to their babies, and such use has accounted for a marked decline in perinatal infections. These drugs have not been shown to produce serious ill effects for either the infant or the mother, although there is an occasional risk of lower birth weight for the baby (Tuomala et al., 2002).

HIV and AIDS have disproportionately affected people in racial and ethnic minority groups in the United States, a condition situation that probably reflects a number of social and economic issues. About half of HIV/AIDS diagnoses in recent years have been among African Americans, even though they represent only 13 percent of the population. Hispanics account for about 20 percent of new diagnoses, even though they make up only 12 percent of the population. About half of African-American men acquire HIV through sex with other men, and 78 percent of African-American women acquire it from heterosexual intercourse. It is interesting to note that while African-American men seem to have similar, or even lower, rates of risky sexual behavior than other men, their risk of contracting HIV seem to be greater. This may be the result of a higher incidence of other STDs that can increase the risk of getting HIV from an infected partner (CDC, 2006a).

The Global Picture of HIV/AIDS

HIV infection represents a serious global threat. The UNAIDS Organization estimates that between 34.1 and

perinatally related to pregnancy, birth, or the period immediately following birth.

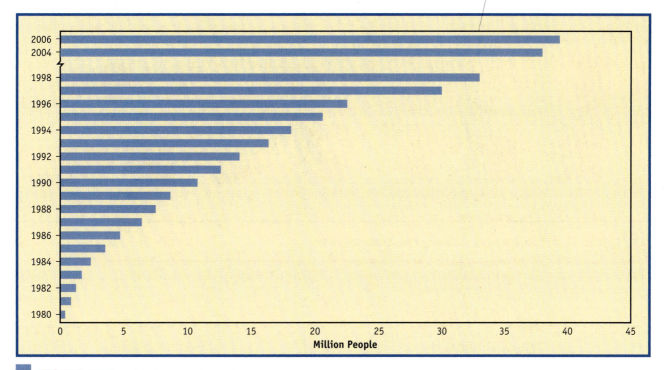

■ **FIGURE 17.2** *Global Increase in HIV/AIDS Cases*

This graph illustrates the startling increase in worldwide numbers of people living with HIV/AIDS since 1980.

47.1 million people are currently infected with HIV worldwide, with some 4.3 million new infections each year (see Figure 17.2). It is thought that about 75 percent of the global infections are acquired through heterosexual contact. The predictions for the future have been equally grim, with an estimate that by the year 2020, the disease could be responsible for the deaths of over 125 million people. Southern and Southeast Asia and sub-Saharan African countries have been hardest hit by HIV infection and AIDS. In sub-Saharan Africa, 25 million people are believed to be living with HIV/AIDS. In some of these countries, it is expected that 35 percent of the boys now age 15 will die of AIDS. The situation is quickly worsening in India, China, and Southeast Asia, where the numbers soon could surpass those of Africa unless decisive preventative actions are taken immediately (Norman, 2004; Piot et al., 2004; UNAIDS, 2006).

We will return to our discussion of HIV and AIDS after examining the other sexually transmitted diseases that are troublesome and dangerous for people.

Risk Factors for STDs

The National Health and Social Life Survey (NHSLS) questioned its research participants about their own histories with regard to several STDs. Eighteen percent of women and 16 percent of men, or about one person in six, had been diagnosed by a physician as having at least one of these diseases at some point in their lives (see Figure 17.3). During the previous year, 1.5 percent

had been diagnosed with an STD, 1 percent of which were bacterial infections and 0.5 percent of which were viral. Women were more likely to have had an STD than were men, reflecting the medical fact that it is about twice as easy for a male to transmit a sexual infection to a woman than it is for a female to transmit a sexual infection to a man (Laumann, Gagnon, et al., 1994).

Many people are mistakenly convinced that they could not contract an STD because of their care in choosing sexual partners or because they maintain high standards of personal hygiene. The NHSLS statistics confirm that STDs are not confined to the ignorant or the uninformed or to those who have poor hygiene. Race, educational level, and socioeconomic group were all shown to be relatively insignificant in predicting the risks of STDs in this study. The high-risk profile that emerged from the research was, in fact, remarkably consistent and predictable. As Figure 17.4 shows, the risk of contracting an STD rises with the number of sexual partners a person has because, according to the data, those partners will have had many sexual partners themselves. When women acquire a new sexual partner, their risk of getting an STD increases. People who have sex with multiple partners generally engage in casual sexual experiences with virtual strangers while under the influence of alcohol or other drugs. And even though they may have used condoms, condom use probably was not consistent

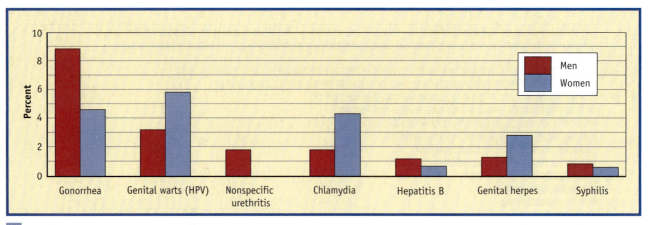

■ **FIGURE 17.3**   *Lifetime Rates of Sexually Transmitted Infections*

Statistics from the NHSLS indicate the percentages of respondents who had been diagnosed with various STDs during their lifetime.

Source: From *Sex in America* by Robert T. Michael et al. Copyright © 1994 by CSG Enterprises, Inc., Edward O. Laumann, Robert T. Michael, and Gina Kolata. By permission of Little, Brown & Company, and Brockman, Inc.

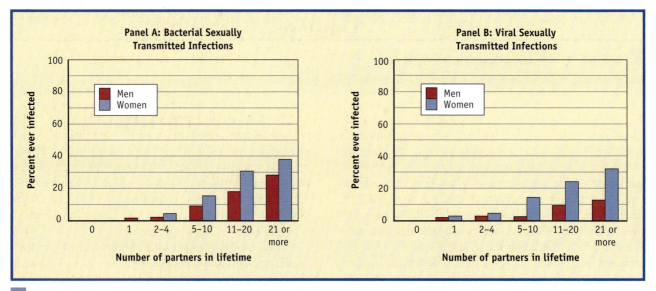

■ **FIGURE 17.4**   *Lifetime Rates of Sexually Transmitted Infections, by Number of Partners and Gender*

These two graphs, based on NHSLS data, show that the likelihood of contracting either bacterial or viral STDs increases proportionately with the number of sexual partners a person has.

Source: From *Sex in America* by Robert T. Michael et al. Copyright © 1994 by CSG Enterprises, Inc., Edward O. Laumann, Robert T. Michael, and Gina Kolata. By permission of Little, Brown & Company, and Brockman, Inc.

enough to offset the risks (Lee, Jennings, & Ellen, 2003; Michael et al., 1994; Niccolai et al., 2004; Rana et al., 2006; Wald et al., 2005). It takes only a single unprotected sexual encounter with an infected partner to become infected with the disease. Unfortunately, those who have negative emotions about having sex in the first place are less likely to use protection than are those who feel positively about it (Whitten et al., 2003).

Some people are embarrassed to seek treatment once they realize their symptoms are suggestive of an STD. One of the difficulties with most STDs is that their symptoms may be relatively mild at first, especially in women. Gonorrhea, syphilis, and chlamydia are particularly known for the inconspicuousness of their symptoms in the early stages. They may progress into full-blown infections with potentially serious consequences before they have been recognized (Fiscus, Ford, & Miller, 2004; Mehta et al., 2003a). Pelvic inflammatory disease (PID) in women often results from untreated STDs (see Chapter 11, "Decision Making about Pregnancy and Parenthood").

The following sections outline basic information on STDs. See Table 17.1 for a summary of the information.

Table 17.1	Common Sexually Transmitted Diseases			
Disease & Estimated Number of New Cases Annually	**Incubation Period**	**Symptoms**	**Treatment**	**Comments**
		Nonviral/Bacterial STDs		
Gonorrhea 650,000	2–6 days (but can take up to 30 days)	Infection of cervix, urethra, rectum, or throat. Symptoms can be mild or absent in women, but include discharge from penis, vagina, or rectum and burning or itching during urination, or sore throat.	Doses of a cephalosporin antibiotic.	Many antibiotic-resistant strains have formed.
Syphilis 70,000	*Stage 1:* 1–12 weeks *Stage 2:* 6 weeks to 6 months after chancre appears	Usually acquired by vaginal, anal, or oral sex with someone who has an active infection. Produces painless sores near the site of infection that disappear within weeks, but without treatment disease may eventually damage heart, brain, eyes, nervous system, bones, and joints.	Single injection of penicillin; tetracycline, erythromycin, or doxycycline may also be used.	HIV testing should be done for anyone infected with syphilis.
Chlamydia (often the cause of urethritis in males) 3 million	7–21 days	Acquired chiefly through vaginal or anal intercourse. Symptoms include genital discharge, burning during urination (nonspecific urethritis in males); women may suffer pain in lower abdomen or pain during intercourse. Up to three-quarters of cases in women are without symptoms.	Weeklong regimen of azithromycin, doxycycline, or erythromycin.	Has reached epidemic proportions among college students.
Trichomoniasis or gardnerella vaginal infection 5 million	2–21 days	Infection most often occurs in female vagina. Symptoms are often absent. May include vaginal discharge, discomfort during intercourse, odor, painful urination.	Penicillin, ampicillin, amoxicillin, tetracycline, or metronidazole (Flagyl).	Partners must be treated too, or reinfection is likely.
		Viral STDs		
Genital herpes 1 million	Up to 3 weeks	Itching or burning and blisters, usually in genital area. May recur. Causes painful, open genital lesions, sometimes accompanied by swollen, tender lymph nodes in the groin.	No cure, but antiviral drugs may suppress outbreaks: acyclovir, famciclovir, valacyclovir.	Antiviral drugs should not be used by pregnant women.
Human papilloma virus (HPV) 5.5 million	6 weeks– 8 months	Spread by anal, oral, or vaginal sex and causes painless, fleshy warts in affected area.	Warts can be suppressed by chemicals, freezing, laser therapy, and surgery.	Some strains are associated with cervical and other cancers.
Hepatitis A (variable)	1–4 months	Loss of appetite, nausea, vomiting, diarrhea, yellowish discoloration of urine, darkening of urine. Fever, general feelings of malaise. There may be liver enlargement, and occasional liver damage. Hepatitis A is more likely to clear up on its own and not recur.	No cure. Medications may relieve some symptoms.	Virus is carried in feces; may be spread when oral-anal sexual contact is involved.
Hepatitis B 120,000	1–4 months	Virus found in semen, saliva, blood, and urine and passed through sexual contact, sharing drug needles, and piercing the skin with contaminated medical instruments. Infection attacks the liver, with similar symptoms to	Same as hepatitis A above.	Vaccine is available that provides immunity after 3 injections.

(continued)

Table 17.1   *Common Sexually Transmitted Diseases (continued)*

Disease & Estimated Number of New Cases Annually	Incubation Period	Symptoms	Treatment	Comments
		hepatitis A. Most infections clear up by themselves within 8 weeks, but some individuals become chronically infected.		
Sexually Transmitted Parasitic Skin Infections				
Pubic lice ("crabs") (unknown)	Eggs hatch in 5–10 days	The lice feed on the skin in the pubic area, causing blue and gray spots. The lice and their eggs (nits) are tiny but can be seen.	Permethrin cream, Lindane shampoo (Kwell)	Clothing and bedding must be thoroughly cleaned too.
Scabies (unknown)	5–10 days	Redness and itching of affected skin areas, with possible secondary skin infections.	Lindane lotion or cream applied to entire body and left for several hours. Oral Ivermectin may be used.	Spreads easily in close quarters.

For quick and accurate answers to any personal questions you might have, or for referral to a local clinic for testing or treatment, call the STD/AIDS National Hotline, available 24 hours per day, 7 days per week, at their toll-free number. The number is 1-800-227-8922 from anywhere in the United States.

■ Nonviral Sexually Transmitted Diseases

Several STIs are caused by bacteria or bacterialike organisms. When diagnosed and treated in the early stages, these diseases are the most likely to be cured.

Gonorrhea

With some 650,000 reported cases of **gonorrhea** (in slang, "clap" or "the drip") each year in the United States, it is also the most commonly reported communicable disease. The CDC estimates that if unreported cases are included, there may be more than a million cases of the disease annually (CDC, 2006a). There has been a gradual decline in the incidence of the disease in recent years. However, the statistics on most STDs tend to show periodic fluctuations whose reasons are difficult to explain.

Caused by the bacterium *Neisseria gonorrhoeae* (named after Dr. Albert Neisser, who discovered the bacterium in 1879), gonorrhea seems to be transmitted almost exclusively through sexual contact. Sexual activity—vaginal intercourse, oral sex, or anal sex—with an infected partner is riskier for women than for men. There is over a 50 percent chance of women contracting the disease on a single exposure during intercourse, whereas for men the risk is about 25 percent. Bacteria migrate less easily into the male urethra than into the female vulva, where they have more moist locations in which to multiply. Of course, the risk increases for both men and women with each repeated exposure. Men have a high rate of reinfection if they engage in sex with partners who have sex with others for either money or drugs (Mehta et al., 2003b).

Babies may pick up the bacteria during the birth process if the mother is infected. Their eyes are particularly vulnerable to gonorrheal infection, and blindness can result. It is a routine precaution in most hospital obstetrical units to put a few drops of an antibacterial agent into the eyes of newborns in order to kill any bacteria.

Symptoms

Probably one of the major reasons why genital gonorrhea is the most commonly reported STD is that its symptoms tend to appear quite quickly and may be decidedly unpleasant for men. However, it is also

gonorrhea (gon-uh-REE-uh) bacterial STD causing urethral pain and discharge in males; often no initial symptoms in females.

possible for the infection to be mild and relatively asymptomatic. In men, within two weeks after infection, burning and itching sensations develop in the urethra, especially during urination. There is also a thick, puslike discharge from the urethra, often showing up on underwear (see Figure 17.5).

Although up to 80 percent of women do not detect gonorrhea in its earlier stages, its most typical early symptom is a green or yellow discharge from the cervical area, where the bacteria tend to strike first. Some vaginal irritation or irregularities in menstruation may follow. Gonorrheal infections in the throat tend to create soreness and some mucus in the throat. Rectal infection causes soreness, itching, rectal discharge, and bowel abnormalities.

If gonorrhea is not treated in its early stages, the initial symptoms usually disappear on their own, but the bacteria often move to other organs, causing more serious infections and complications. In men, the disease may affect the bladder, prostate, kidneys, or epididymis of the testes. Left untreated in either sex, the disease can cause sterility. In women, the infection often moves into the reproductive organs, such as the uterus, fallopian tubes, and ovaries, and may eventually result in pelvic inflammatory disease (PID). Very occasionally, in either sex, the bacteria create systemic infections throughout the body, with generalized symptoms, arthritis, and complications in major organs such as the heart or brain.

Diagnosis

There are three main ways in which gonorrhea bacteria are identified. First, a smear is made of the discharge, taken from the penile urethra, cervix, throat, or rectum, depending on where infection most likely took place. The material is stained and examined microscopically for evidence of the bacteria. A second method involves taking a culture, with bacteria grown on a nutrient medium and then examined for the gonorrhea bacterium. The culture method has been used most widely with women. More recently, an enzyme-sensitive immunoassay test has been developed that can detect the bacteria with great accuracy.

Treatment

Because many new strains of gonorrhea bacteria are resistant to the antibiotics that typically have been used to treat gonorrhea, the CDC changed their recommended treatment in 2007. A whole different class of antibiotics, the cephalosporins, are now considered the only drugs effective in treating gonorrhea. This is a very real public health concern, because these drugs presently are the last resort among available medicines. Some gonorrhea bacteria may not be completely eliminated by typical treatment, so follow-up checks should be made about a week after treatment has ended. Treatment should include antibiotics that destroy chlamydia organisms as well, because that infection often coexists with gonorrhea. It is often a good idea for the sex partners of gonorrhea patients to be treated as quickly as possible to avoid reinfection (Golden et al., 2005). Individuals who are infected with either disease are at high risk for acquiring both syphilis and HIV, so further testing may be indicated. As with any STD, sexual partners of a patient with gonorrhea should be notified of their risk so that they can seek appropriate diagnosis and treatment.

Syphilis

Intermittently throughout history, syphilis has been considered a scourge. Some historians have speculated that some of the "leprosy" present in biblical times actually may have been syphilis. An epidemic of the disease spread through Europe at the end of the fifteenth century, leading to speculation that a virulent form of the disease was brought back to Europe by Christopher Columbus and his crew. In 1905, the spiral-shaped organism, or spirochete, that causes syphilis was identified and named *Treponema pallidum*.

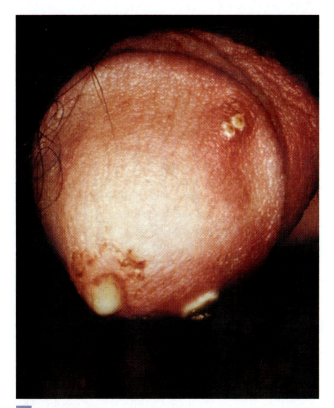

FIGURE 17.5 *Gonorrhea*
Symptoms of gonorrhea in men include a puslike discharge. About 80 percent of women, however, are asymptomatic.

The number of reported syphilis infections in the United States has traditionally been lower than reported cases of gonorrhea, and syphilis now averages slightly more than 20,000 reported cases per year. The incidence of the disease has been cyclic over the years. It dropped to its lowest rate on record in 2000, but has since increased. Many states still require a blood test for syphilis as a prerequisite to obtaining a marriage license, and benefits have been reported from automatically testing people in jail after they have been arrested (Kahn, R. H., et al., 2002).

FOH Symptoms

Syphilis can progress through four major stages, beginning two weeks to a month after infection. The first stage, or *primary syphilis,* is nearly always characterized by the appearance of a painless sore wherever the spirochete entered the body. The painless sore, called a chancre, begins as a reddish bump that develops into a pimple. It then opens and ulcerates, often oozing pus until a scab develops. The chancre sometimes is surrounded by a pink border. This sore is infested with the treponema organism, and the individual is highly infectious at this stage. Usually the chancre appears on the genitals (see Figure 17.6), al-

A

B

FIGURE 17.6   *Primary Syphilis Chancre*

(A) On female genitalia. **(B)** On the penis.

FIGURE 17.7   *Secondary Syphilis*

though it can appear on the mouth, anal area, and fingers or breasts. In women it occurs frequently on the inner vaginal wall or cervix and sometimes in the rectum. In one study conducted in a major city, oral sexual contact was found to be a significant means of transmission, ranging from 6 to 7 percent of cases in heterosexual women and men to 20 percent for men who had sex with men (Ciesielski, Tabidze, & Brown, 2004). Because it tends to be painless in the mouth, it may not be noticed there. Within four to six weeks, the chancre heals even without treatment, and there may be no further symptoms for up to six months (CDC, 2006b).

The next stage, *secondary syphilis,* usually begins with a bumpy skin rash (see Figure 17.7), accompanied by general symptoms of illness such as fever, swollen lymph nodes of the neck, nausea, headache, sore throat, loss of scalp hair, and loss of appetite. Additional moist sores may appear around the genitals or anal region. Again, even without treatment, the symptoms eventually abate within a few weeks, and the disease enters its *latent stage.* It is estimated that slightly more than half of untreated syphilis victims remain in this latent stage for the rest of their lives.

People who progress to the *tertiary syphilis* stage usually face serious complications resulting from the spirochete's infecting inner tissues and organs. It may attack the heart, brain and spinal cord, eyes, joints, and numerous other areas, leading to life-threatening disease, blindness, psychosis, or paralysis. Although modern medical treatment has greatly reduced the number of syphilis cases progressing to the tertiary stage, they still occur. In later tertiary stages, the disease typically cannot be transmitted to others.

Congenital syphilis refers to an unborn fetus being infected by the disease through its mother's bloodstream while in the womb. It can result in significant birth defects, especially of the bones, blood, and kidneys. If a pregnant woman with syphilis is treated prior to the 16th week of pregnancy, congenital syphilis can be averted. It is important, therefore, that a pregnant woman have a blood test for syphilis before the fourth month of pregnancy. Perhaps because of stronger educational and testing efforts, the incidence of congenital syphilis has been declining (Edozien et al., 2004).

Diagnosis and Treatment

The two main ways syphilis can be identified are through one of several blood tests or by microscopic examination of fluid from the chancre, in which the spirochete may be seen. Once diagnosed, it usually is treated in its primary and secondary stages by a single injection of penicillin. Tetracycline, erythromycin, or doxycycline may also be used. Latent and tertiary syphilis require larger doses of antibiotics over a period of several weeks. Because so many people who have been infected with syphilis are also infected with HIV, patients who have a positive test for syphilis should also be tested for HIV (CDC, 2006a).

Eradication of Syphilis

The U.S. Public Health Service has targeted syphilis for national elimination. With rates of infection low enough and treatment methods effective enough virtual eradication of the disease could be a real possibility. To date, this goal has been elusive, and slight increases in the incidence of the disease have been seen. Syphilis has been noted particularly as a disease that seems to increase the risk of HIV infection, so continued work on its eradication will surely continue.

Chlamydia

It has long been known that the organism *Chlamydia trachomatis* is a frequent cause of inflammation in the urinary and genital systems. Only in the mid-1980s, however, was **chlamydia** recognized as a widespread STD with a range of serious complications (see Figure

FIGURE 17.8 *Chlamydia*

17.8). The CDC estimates that there are close to 3 million chlamydial infections each year in the United States, although others believe the actual number to be much higher. Nearly a million cases are officially reported each year. It first became an officially reportable disease in 1995 and has since taken its place

chlamydia (kluh-MID-ee-uh) now known to be a common STD, a major cause of urethritis in males; often presents no symptoms in females.

as one of the most common of the STDs and the most commonly reported infectious disease in the United States. The chlamydia organism invades the cells it attacks and multiplies within those cells. Therefore, it can create a variety of symptoms and can be resistant to some antibiotics. It is a particularly common infection on college campuses. Chlamydia prevention programs, involving education, screening, and aggressive treatment, have been found to lower the rate of infection (Terán, Walsh, & Irwin, 2001).

Like gonorrhea, chlamydia carries special risks for the eyes of newborns. *Conjunctivitis,* an inflammation of the eye, can be contracted at birth as the baby passes through the vagina, or birth canal. If this is not treated thoroughly and promptly, blindness can result. Such transmission may well be the most widespread preventable cause of blindness throughout the world. Babies also may develop chlamydial pneumonia during their first few months of life. Although the disease is spread primarily through sexual contact, once the infection is established it can be spread to other areas of the body or to other people by hand contact, insects, or contact with human excretions. These modes of transmission are particularly prevalent in underdeveloped countries where overpopulation and inadequate sanitation are factors.

Symptoms

The symptoms of chlamydial infection are often vague or nonexistent, and they can masquerade as symptoms of other diseases. This is one reason why many such infections go unnoticed or are inaccurately diagnosed. About 70 percent of all cases have no early symptoms, and it may take more serious later complications to alert the infected individual that something is wrong.

Males who are symptomatic often experience a burning sensation during urination and a discharge of pus from the penis. If the organism moves farther into the body, swelling and discomfort in the testicles may result. Untreated, it can cause infertility in men. In females, the early symptoms are often mild but can involve itching or burning of the vulva, some discharge, and irritation during urination. In its later stages, the disease may cause PID, with fever, nausea, abdominal pain, and abnormal patterns of menstruation. It also can damage the fallopian tubes and is now known to be a common cause of infertility and ectopic pregnancy. There is mounting evidence that long-term infection with chlamydia may be linked to human heart disease (CDC, 2006b).

Diagnosis and Treatment

Until recently, tests for chlamydia were time-consuming and expensive, requiring the growing of the organism in a laboratory culture for identification. Several tests are now available that can render a quick, inexpensive, and relatively accurate diagnosis. A urine test for chlamydia is now available.

Once diagnosed, the disease usually can be cured with a weeklong treatment of azithromycin, doxycycline, or erythromycin. Penicillin is not an effective treatment. As with any antibiotic treatment, it is crucial that the entire dosage of the prescribed medication be taken. Otherwise, the infection may continue in more persistent forms. Ointments containing tetracycline or erythromycin also may be applied to the eyes of newborns to prevent the development of chlamydial conjunctivitis (CDC, 2006b). It is essential that sexual partners be treated as well, because in some regions the number of reinfection cases exceeds the number of new cases (Golden et al., 2005).

Health workers continue to emphasize that chlamydia is a serious infection that has reached epidemic proportions. Thus, people should pay attention to and seek appropriate medical checkups for any unusual sensations or discomforts in the genital or urinary tracts. It is a good idea to request a chlamydia culture test in routine pelvic exams.

Nonspecific Urethritis in Males

Sometimes called *nongonococcal urethritis (NGU),* **nonspecific urethritis (NSU)** refers to any inflammation of the male urethra that is not caused by gonorrhea. NSU is a much more common infection than gonorrhea and has been on the increase. The most common cause of NSU is chlamydial infection, accounting for about half the cases. Another 20 to 25 percent are caused by the mycoplasmic bacterium *Ureaplasma urealyticum.* The remainder of NSU cases apparently are caused by other microorganisms or by local irritation from soap, vaginal secretions, or spermicides, although the exact cause is sometimes impossible to isolate.

Although the symptoms often are less pronounced than those associated with gonorrhea, there is usually some degree of burning and itching during and after urination. There may also be some discharge of pus, often more evident in the morning.

Prompt treatment of NSU is crucial, even though the symptoms typically subside and disappear on their own within a few weeks. The organism causing the inflammation usually will persist somewhere in the body, increasing the likelihood of a repeat infection or of more serious complications at a later time. Again,

nonspecific urethritis (NSU) (yur-i-THRYT-us) infection or irritation in the male urethra caused by bacteria or local irritants.

Real People

Carolyn: Discovering a Sexually Transmitted Infection

Because her menstrual period was over a week late, Carolyn visited her college's health center for a pregnancy test. The test was negative, but the nurse practitioner thought she ought to have some other testing. Following the examination, the practitioner told Carolyn that she had a chlamydia infection. This surprised her because she had not experienced any symptoms that would suggest that she had been infected by an STD. She was told that it would be important for both her and her sexual partner to be treated, or they would simply keep re-infecting each other. Carolyn expressed concern and embarrassment over telling her boyfriend, because when making a decision about having unprotected sexual intercourse, they had both declared that they had not had sex with previous partners. The nurse practitioner explained that if Carolyn truly had not had intercourse with other men, then her boyfriend must have contracted the disease from another female partner. The nurse continued to press the importance of his being treated.

The next day, Carolyn returned to the clinic with her boyfriend. He had admitted that he had had a one-night stand with a woman just prior to his relationship with Carolyn, and he was anxious to receive treatment for the chlamydia. The nurse practitioner reminded both of them that if he had been exposed to one disease, there was a chance that he had been exposed to other diseases as well. She recommended further tests for the couple, including an HIV antibody test. This was alarming to both of them and heightened Carolyn's feelings of betrayal and mistrust. All the other tests turned out to be negative, but the experience created a significant strain in their relationship.

What would you recommend to Carolyn and/or her boyfriend at this point? Do you think their relationship should continue or be ended? What would you say to her boyfriend about his lack of honesty? What would you do in a case like this?

---

antibiotics such as azithromycin, erythromycin, or doxycycline are most frequently used to treat NSU, although they are not always effective. Regardless of the cause, it is advisable for any sexual partner of a man with NSU to be examined to determine the possible presence of infection as well (CDC, 2006b).

Vulvovaginal Infections

Vulvovaginitis, or infection within the vulval region and vagina, is extremely common and often is not caused by an STD. Almost every woman will experience a vulvovaginal infection sometime during her life. The lining of the vagina has a carefully balanced system for cleansing itself. Fluids from the tissues in the vaginal lining and the uterine cervix, along with discarded cells from the uterus, form a discharge that cleanses the vagina and protects it from infection by hostile bacteria. However, the balance of this cleansing mechanism may change during various stages of the menstrual cycle, during pregnancy, or with the use of birth control pills, antibiotics, or other medications. The pH of the vagina, usually slightly acidic, may be-

come more alkaline. Any such upset can make the vagina more vulnerable to infection. Infections of the vagina are not necessarily related to sexual activity, but such activity increases the likelihood of infection (Yen et al., 2003).

Symptoms

All types of vulvovaginitis are usually characterized by some discharge, whose color, thickness, and odor vary with the type of infection. There are often sensations of burning and itching in the vulval region and outer vagina.

Types

There are four main types of vulvovaginitis. The first three may be transmitted by sexual activity, although their microorganisms are found naturally in the environment and in the body and may develop into an

vulvovaginitis (vul-voe-vaj-uh-NITE-us) general term for inflammation of the vulva and/or vagina.

infection without sexual contact if advantageous conditions present themselves.

1. *Bacterial vaginosis* is most often caused by the bacterium *Gardnerella vaginalis*. Men apparently can carry gardnerella, but they often do not experience any symptoms of disease. Occasionally, it causes urethritis, bladder infection, or infection of the penile foreskin in males. Vaginal gardnerella is treated with oral antibiotics such as penicillin, ampicillin, amoxicillin, or tetracycline, and also with a drug called metronidazole, commonly known as Flagyl. Sexual partners usually are treated at the same time to reduce the risk of reinfecting each other. Bacterial vaginosis increases the risk of premature delivery for pregnant women, although this risk may be reduced with administration of the drug clindamycin (CDC, 2006b). There is increasing evidence that bacterial vaginosis can be transmitted sexually, including between women who share sex (Bailey et al., 2004; Bradshaw et al., 2005).

2. **Yeast infection** in the vagina, sometimes called *monilial vaginitis,* occurs when conditions within the vagina permit an overgrowth of a fungus, *Candida albicans,* that normally is found there. Such infections sometimes can mask the presence of other STDs, so it is important to check for other STDs whenever a yeast infection is found. This disease is treated with fungicides, such as miconazole or nystatin, that are used within the vagina in cream or suppository form. Treatments for yeast infections are available without prescription, although studies indicate that women may not be using them appropriately because their self-diagnosis skills are not particularly accurate.*

3. **Trichomoniasis** is an infection caused by a one-celled protozoan organism, *Trichomonas,* that can take up residence within the vulva and vagina and also in the male urethra. It is one of the most common causes of vaginal infection, leading to some 3 million new infections each year. It is becoming increasingly common among younger women (Miller et al., 2005). Frequently there are no noticeable symptoms. Again, it is necessary to treat sexual partners as well as the woman infected in order to prevent reinfection. The drug used is metronidazole (Flagyl), which is not considered safe for use during pregnancy or when a woman is nursing a baby.

4. *Atrophic vaginitis* is caused by low estrogen levels and occurs almost exclusively after menopause. It

*Note: Yeast infections can also affect males, in the form of an itchy rash on the penis and scrotum.

is not an STD, although it can lower a woman's resistance to vulvovaginal infection by other microorganisms.

Prevention of Vulvovaginal Infections

One of the best ways to prevent sexually transmitted vaginosis is for the male to use a condom during sexual intercourse. There are several simple hygienic measures that can at least reduce the risk of vaginal infection through nonsexual contamination. These include daily washing of the vulva with mild soap and water, followed by thorough drying because dampness heightens the risk of infection. For this reason, too, underwear made of nonabsorbent synthetic fibers such as nylon is not recommended. Experts also recommend against the use of vaginal sprays and douches unless they have been specifically prescribed for some medical condition. They often are implicated in upsetting the balance of the vagina's natural cleansing mechanisms, increasing the likelihood of infection. Treating vulvovaginal infections may lower a woman's risk of contracting genital herpes (Cherpes et al., 2003).

■ Viral Sexually Transmitted Diseases

The sexually transmitted viral infections are believed to have already infected at least 20 percent of the population. Although viral infections often can be kept under control and their symptoms relieved, the virus typically continues to reside in the body's cells. This may lead to periodic outbreaks of symptoms or may be associated with cellular abnormalities that have been linked to certain types of cancer. In this sense, viral STIs are controllable but not yet curable.

Genital Herpes

Genital herpes is caused by the *Herpes simplex* virus. There are two strains of the virus: herpes simplex virus

yeast infection a type of vaginitis caused by an overgrowth of a fungus normally found in an inactive state in the vagina.

trichomoniasis (trik-uh-ma-NEE-uh-sis) a vaginal infection caused by the *Trichomonas* organism.

genital herpes (HER-peez) a viral STD characterized by painful sores on the sex organs.

type 1 *(HSV-1)* and type 2 *(HSV-2)*. It has generally been believed that cold sores on the mouth usually are caused by HSV-1, whereas lesions in the genital area most often are caused by HSV-2. It is now known, however, that a high percentage of genital herpes cases are linked to the HSV-1 virus. Although why this is the case is not clearly understood, it has been proposed that an increase in oral-genital sexual activities may play a role. However, cases of genital herpes caused by HSV-1 are less likely to recur than are those caused by HSV-2 (CDC, 2006b).

It is estimated that close to 50 million people in the United States have been infected with the virus, with up to another million contracting the disease each year. Research indicates that people tend to have unreasonable fears and misconceptions about herpes, leading to negative stereotypes regarding herpes sufferers. HSV-2 is transmitted almost exclusively by sexual contact, although the virus can survive externally for several hours in moist, warm conditions. Once the herpes simplex virus has been contracted, it may continue to live in the body, even if no symptoms of the disease are present.

A new vaccine has been developed that can protect people from herpes infection as long as they have not previously been infected or experienced cold sores. As yet there are no medications to eradicate the virus from the body, but it is hoped that a broader-spectrum vaccine will be developed soon (Weibley, 2001). The actual appearance of the painful herpes blisters seems to be associated with periods when disease resistance might be weakened by other illnesses, stress, exhaustion, or inadequate nutrition. It may also be triggered by irritation to the susceptible regions of the skin, such as overexposure to the sun or irritation from clothing.

FOH Symptoms

Genital herpes is characterized by the appearance of what may be painful or itchy clusters of blisters, like cold sores, on the sex organs. During the first outbreak, women usually have blisters on the cervix as well as externally on the vulva (see Figure 17.9). Within a few days, the blisters open and ulcerate, leaving wet, open sores that are highly contagious. Care is especially crucial during these outbreaks to prevent transmission of the virus to other individuals or even to other parts of the infected person's own body. Exposure of the eyes to the virus is particularly dangerous, because a severe eye infection called *herpes keratitis* may develop that can cause serious damage to the cornea. The sores should be touched as little as possible and only when followed by thorough washing of the hands. Sometimes, outbreaks of the blisters

FIGURE 17.9 *Herpes Blisters in the Vulval Area*

are accompanied by other symptoms of illness, such as fever, achiness, or pain in the groin or thighs. It usually takes another two weeks for the sores to crust over and heal.

Up to 70 percent of people who have had a genital herpes infection will experience at least one recurrence of the disease. This usually begins with prickling or burning sensations in the skin where the blisters are about to appear. During such outbreaks, sexual contact—or any direct contact with the infected area—is particularly risky. It is advisable to avoid such contact until at least 10 days after the sores have healed completely. However, the risk of infection remains even when the blisters are not present. Use of a condom reduces the chance of infection. Up to 30 percent of infected people never have a further outbreak of the herpes sores.

Most men do not experience any complications from a herpes infection, although herpes increases the risk of vulnerability to infection by HIV (see Figure 17.10). Though relatively rare, there are possible complications for women and their babies. For one thing, there is a higher incidence of cervical and vulval cancer among women who have had genital herpes, even though the cause-and-effect mechanism behind this phenomenon is not understood. For this reason, women with HSV-2 are advised to have an annual pelvic examination and Pap smear to

FIGURE 17.10 *Herpes Blisters on the Penis*

detect any abnormal cells in the cervix. The second danger is to a baby during the birth process, in which the presence of HSV-2 can lead to seriously damaging infection or even death. This is called *congenital herpes*. In women with a history of genital herpes, cultures are taken from the cervix, vagina, and vulva several times during the final weeks of pregnancy to detect a possible recurrence of the disease. If there is a risk of infection being passed to the baby during birth, the delivery may be accomplished by a cesarean section.

FOH Diagnosis and Treatment

Genital herpes usually is diagnosed by direct observation of the blisters, although a variety of tests are available that use cultures of the virus for positive identification. While there is no cure for the disease, three antiviral drugs have been found to relieve some symptoms and may be used to suppress recurrences. These drugs, acyclovir, famciclovir, and valacyclovir, sometimes can lengthen relapse intervals from a month to nearly a year. Acyclovir can be applied to the blisters in ointment form during the initial outbreak, although it proves less useful with recurrent outbreaks. Orally administered drugs have been shown to reduce recurrent infections in those who are susceptible to frequent outbreaks and also to reduce the duration and severity of the infection. The drugs have not been tested in pregnant or nursing women (CDC, 2006b). Other antiviral drugs are presently being tested for possible use with herpes infections.

Health care professionals offer some suggestions for relieving the painful symptoms of a herpes outbreak, such as keeping the infected area as clean and dry as possible. Baby powder or cornstarch may be used to absorb moisture. Aspirin or other pain re-

lievers can help, as can direct application of an ice pack.

Human Papillomavirus (HPV)

The **human papillomavirus (HPV)** is similar to the virus that causes warts in other bodily regions. There are about a hundred known strains of the virus. The condition is also known as *condylomata acuminata* or *genital warts*. This disease is now the most common sexually transmitted viral disease in the United States, with up to a million new cases occurring annually. It is assumed that about half of sexually active adults ultimately contract the virus. HPV occurs more frequently in people who began sexual activity comparatively early in their lives and have had multiple sexual partners and casual sexual relationships. Women who had their first sexual experiences at an early age are more likely to have HPV (Kahn, J. A., et al., 2002). Women with HPV are likely to have had male sexual partners with warts on the penis or partners who are carrying the virus. With each new sexual partner, the risk of infection increases (Winer et al., 2003).

Symptoms

The warts, or condylomata, usually do not appear on the genitals for about three months after exposure to an infected partner. Their color and texture can vary with location, with soft, pinkish lesions occurring in moist areas and harder, grayish white warts in dry areas. They have irregular surfaces (see Figure 17.11). The warts usually grow on the penis, vulva, anal area, or urethra. They may appear in the anal area even if the individual has not engaged in anal sex. If they grow inside the urethra, they can cause difficulty in urinating and can lead to other infections. For the most part, they are not particularly painful or dangerous in themselves. How- **FOH** ever, some strains of HPV have increasingly been associated with a high incidence of cancerous or precancerous cells in the cervix, a condition called *cervical intraepithelial neoplasia (CIN)*. Well over 90 percent of cervical cancers are also infected with the virus. It is believed that HPV can cause abnormal cell division in cervical tissues. More recent evidence indicates that these viruses also may be implicated in a variety of other cancers, including those on the genitals or other bodily organs. It also appears that they can lead to penile and anal cancers in men.

> **human papillomavirus (HPV)** an infection causing small lesions on genital skin; certain strains of this STD increase later risks of cervical cancer.

FIGURE 17.11 *Condylomata Caused by HPV around the Penile Glans*

Treatment and Prevention

Genital warts can be removed by laser surgery, electrosurgery (using an electrical current), freezing with liquid nitrogen, or surgical excision. For external warts, chemicals such as podophyllin may be applied over a period of three or four weeks, often causing the lesions to heal. However, because the virus remains in the body, the warts can recur until immunity develops over several months or years. In 2006, the U.S. Food and Drug Administration licensed a new vaccine that prevents infection by four of the HPV strains that have been linked to cervical cancer. This is, in fact, the first time a vaccine to prevent a type of cancer has become available. The vaccine, called Gardasil, is intended for females and is to be administered prior to the onset of sexual activity. It is recommended for females ages 13 to 26 and can be used at younger ages as well. The vaccine has been shown to be nearly 100 percent effective in blocking the virus, but it does not work against existing infections. This is why early vaccination, prior to any sexual activity, is highly recommended. There is no similar vaccine for males (CDC, 2006b).

See "HPV" on SexSource Online.

Hepatitis A, B, and C

There are several identified viruses that can cause the liver infection known as hepatitis. The *hepatitis A virus,* contracted through the mouth from food contaminated by fecal material, was for a long time not considered to be associated with an STD. However, hepatitis A virus can be transmitted through oral-anal contact, and about one-quarter of hepatitis A cases are now attributable to either sexual contact or other contact within the household (ASHA, 2004). The **hepatitis B virus (HBV)** is nearly always sexually transmitted and also causes liver infection. Although **hepatitis C virus (HCV)** is most often transmitted by direct contact with tainted blood, it is now clear that it can be transmitted sexually as well (CDC, 2006a). An estimated 1.25 million people in the United States are chronic carriers of HBV, even though most are unaware that they carry it. HCV is now the most common chronic blood-borne infection in the United States, with an estimated 2.7 million persons chronically infected (CDC, 2006a). Men and women who engage in high-risk sexual behavior are at greater risk of contracting hepatitis C. Both HBV and HCV can be transmitted by sharing intravenous needles for illicit drug use, but hepatitis B is more likely to be transmitted sexually because it is found in bodily fluids such as saliva, semen, and vaginal secretions in addition to blood.

HBV has become such a major health problem in **F⊕H** the United States, especially among young adults ages 15 to 25, that it is standard medical practice to recommend that older adolescents and young adults be vaccinated against the disease. The vaccination must be given in three doses, with total cost averaging about $130. There is also a worldwide effort to make HBV vaccination more available to all populations that might be at risk, and some clinicians have suggested combining it with the vaccine for hepatitis A as an extra precaution (Jacobs & Meyerhoff, 2003; Low et al., 2006). There is no vaccine for hepatitis C as yet.

Symptoms

Hepatitis A tends to be a milder disease than the other two. Hepatitis B and C have several degrees of severity. They may have no symptoms at all or may cause complications serious enough to be fatal. About 5,000 people in the United States die each year from chronic liver disease caused by HBV or HCV. Typical early symptoms of both infections include loss of appetite, lethargy, headache, joint achiness, nausea, vomiting, diarrhea, yellowing of the skin (jaundice), darkening of the urine, and some enlargement of the liver.

hepatitis B virus (HBV) a liver infection that frequently is sexually transmitted.

hepatitis C virus (HCV) a liver infection that may occasionally be sexually transmitted.

Hospitalization usually is unnecessary. Infection with hepatitis B or C increases the later risk of developing liver cancer (CDC, 2006b).

Treatment

As with all viral infections, there is no cure for hepatitis at present. Some medications can provide relief of symptoms, and a period of bed rest and heavy fluid intake usually is required. Gradually, the body's immune system conquers the disease, although in more severe cases this process can take several months. Sometimes, the virus develops into chronic conditions that can lead to destruction of the liver or other organs over a period of years.

■ Other Sexually Transmitted Diseases

The list of disease agents that can be transmitted sexually continues to grow. This section contains information about several of those organisms.

FOH Pubic Lice

The STD commonly called "crabs" is caused by a tiny (1- to 4-mm) parasitic louse with the scientific name *Phthirus pubis*. Health workers often refer to an infestation of these lice as *pediculosis pubis*. The lice have claws that allow them to hold tightly to hairs, usually in the pubic, anal, and **perineal area.** Occasionally, they spread to the armpits or even the scalp. The lice found in head hair are usually of a different species, however, and are not spread by sexual contact.

Pubic lice bite into the skin to feed on blood from tiny blood vessels. This creates little papules on the skin that cause intense itching. The lice lay their eggs, or nits, on hairs to which they are tightly attached (see Figure 17.12). These eggs can drop onto sheets or bedclothes and survive for several days. The lice also can live away from the body for about a day in clothing, sheets, towels, and even furniture, making their way to other people if the opportunity presents itself. Both the whitish nits and the adult lice can be seen upon close examination.

Any treatment must be thorough to ensure complete eradication of the lice. Permethrin cream rinse can be applied to the affected area and rinsed off after 10 minutes. Lindane shampoo, applied for only 4 minutes, is available by prescription under the brand name Kwell. It is somewhat toxic to humans and is not recommended for children under age 2 or for women who are pregnant or nursing babies. Other shampoo treatments containing pyrethrins and piperonyl butoxide can be purchased without a prescription. A repeat

■ **FIGURE 17.12**   *Pubic Lice and Nits*
Pubic lice and nits on pubic hairs.

treatment may be recommended after seven days to take care of any eggs that may have been missed the first time. Sexual partners must be treated as well. It is crucial that all potentially exposed bedclothes, underwear, towels, or other materials be thoroughly washed or dry cleaned. An insecticide spray is available to treat furniture. Close physical contact with others should be avoided until treatment is completed.

Sexually Transmitted Diseases of Tropical Climates

Several other STDs more common in tropical climates have recently been on the increase in temperate-zone countries such as the United States.

perineal area (pair-a-NEE-al) the sensitive skin between the genitals and the anus.

pubic lice small insects that can infect skin in the pubic area, causing a rash and severe itching.

FIGURE 17.13   *Scabies Mite*

Lymphogranuloma venereum (LGV) is caused by several strains of *Chlamydia* and produces painless, pimplelike ulcers on the genitals or rectum. It may have other symptoms, such as fever, hives, or swollen lymph nodes in the groin. If left untreated, it can cause blockage of lymph vessels, resulting in swollen limbs or bodily organs. In the tropics, this condition is called *elephantiasis.* LGV is treated with antibiotics such as doxycycline, tetracycline, or erythromycin or with sulfa drugs.

Chancroid is caused by the bacterium *Hemophilus ducreyi.* Within a week after infection, several small sores appear on the genitals. They are filled with pus and may rupture to form painful open sores that bleed easily. Antibiotics and sulfa drugs are effective in curing the disease; if it is left untreated, it can cause swelling, pain, and rupture of lymph tissue at the surface of the skin.

Granuloma inguinale is a rare infection caused by *Calymmatobacterium granulomatis.* It involves the appearance of small blisters and swelling of the lymph nodes. The sores often do not heal easily unless treated, and they can become infected, eventually causing permanent damage and scarring of tissue. The infection can be cured with antibiotics such as tetracycline, streptomycin, and erythromycin.

Because cases of LGV, chancroid, and granuloma inguinale number only in the thousands annually in the

United States, they are less commonly seen by physicians and STD clinics. This makes them harder to diagnose, which may result in dangerously delayed treatment.

Sexually Transmitted Skin Infections

Two skin diseases in the United States are transmitted by direct bodily contact, not necessarily sexual. One is **molluscum contagiosum,** a pox virus that causes small papules to appear on the skin. They often look similar to whiteheads and have a hard, seedlike core. They usually do not create any discomfort or pain. Occasionally, they may become infected by other bacteria and ulcerate. Molluscum blisters often heal by themselves, although they can be removed by scraping, freezing, or chemical treatment. If all the lesions are not removed, they often will recur.

Scabies is caused by a tiny mite that burrows under the skin to lay its eggs (see Figure 17.13). It causes redness and itching and may lead to secondary infections. It is more stubborn to treat than pubic lice, because the scabies mite is under the skin. Epidemics of scabies often spread throughout schools, hospitals, or other institutions where people interact closely. Obviously, sexual contact also provides an easy mode of transmission for the disease. Treatment involves the application of a medicated lotion or cream to the entire body from the neck down, which then is washed off after 8 to 14 hours. Permethrin cream is used most

lymphogranuloma venereum (LGV) (lim-foe-gran-yu-LOW-ma va-NEAR-ee-um) a contagious STD caused by several strains of *Chlamydia* and marked by swelling and ulceration of lymph nodes in the groin.

chancroid (SHAN-kroyd) an STD caused by the bacterium *Hemophilus ducreyi* and characterized by sores on the genitals, which if left untreated, could result in pain and rupture of the sores.

granuloma inguinale (gran-ya-LOW-ma in-gwa-NAL-ee or -*NALE*) an STD characterized by ulcerations and granulations beginning in the groin and spreading to the buttocks and genitals.

molluscum contagiosum (ma-LUS-kum kan-taje-ee-O-sum) a skin disease transmitted by direct bodily contact, not necessarily sexual, and characterized by eruptions on the skin that appear similar to whiteheads, with a hard seedlike core.

scabies (SKAY-beez) a skin disease caused by a mite that burrows under the skin to lay its eggs, causing redness and itching; transmitted by bodily contact that may or may not be sexual.

frequently, but Lindane lotion or cream is also recommended. An oral medication called Ivermectin is sometimes used (CDC, 2006b).

■ HIV: The Virus and the Infection

Viruses are among the tiniest of microorganisms to infect human tissues. Typically, they attach themselves to the outside of a cell and inject their genetic material inside, where it takes over the DNA of its host cell to produce new viruses. These viruses then spread to other cells, disrupting or killing them as new viruses are produced. It is the destruction of tissue that causes the symptoms of the viral infection. HIV belongs to the class of viruses called **retroviruses.** In all living things, the hereditary code stored in the DNA of each cell's genes determines the characteristics of the organism. The complex biochemical processes of life are governed by that code. The DNA passes its messages to another chemical found in all cells, RNA, which then plays many roles in helping the cell manufacture all the products it requires to live and function. Retroviruses are unique in that their genetic code is instead carried in the form of RNA. When a retrovirus attacks a cell, a chemical orders the cell's RNA to translate the genetic blueprint of the virus into the cell's DNA, thereby instructing it to make a whole new crop of virus particles. It is because this mechanism is the reverse of the usual order of things that these viruses are called retroviruses.

HIV manages to make its way into the body's white blood cells, ultimately weakening and destroying the immune system. To reproduce itself and multiply in the body, HIV destroys the very cells that are essential to helping the body produce immunity to all types of disease. These cells are the T-lymphocytes known as CD4s, a type of white blood cell that plays a major role in bringing together the body's immune defenses. HIV is capable of reproducing in staggering numbers, constantly needing to move on to new, uninfected cells in order to survive.

For reasons that still are not fully understood, the numbers of cells infected by HIV tend to remain relatively stable for a time, sometimes years, during which the person tends to be quite symptom-free. One theory is that the immune system finally becomes exhausted by the infection and falters. At this point, the infected individual begins to become more vulnerable to opportunistic diseases. Antibiotics and other known medications are not effective against viral infections, although they may be extremely useful in combating bacterial infections.

It is important to focus on the entire course of infection by HIV and not just the late stage of that process that has become known as AIDS. When HIV disease is diagnosed in its earlier stages, the patient may be able to get treatment that may delay certain aspects of the infection and prevent some complications. HIV infection passes through predictable stages during which the body's immune system is gradually undermined. Although the duration of the infection varies depending on the person's health and behavior, there is a gradual depletion of cells in the body that are crucial to its defense against disease-causing agents.

Soon after contracting HIV, some people develop a fever, swollen glands, fatigue, and perhaps a rash. This is called *primary HIV disease.* These early symptoms usually disappear within a few weeks as the body manages to ward off the infection with its remaining immune defenses. The second stage, *chronic asymptomatic disease,* is characterized by a gradual decline in immune cells even though there are no particular disease symptoms. Eventually, most people infected with HIV begin to experience chronically swollen lymph nodes, although they may have few other symptoms. It is important to note that there are other diseases that can manifest these symptoms as well, most of which are not nearly as serious as HIV disease.

As the infection progresses, there is a continual drop in the number of immune cells in the body. The individual becomes increasingly vulnerable to **opportunistic infection,** in which disease-causing organisms normally present in the environment become able to attack the person by taking advantage of the body's weakened resistance. This third stage is called *chronic symptomatic disease.* One of the most common infections in this stage of HIV disease is a yeast infection of the mouth called **thrush** (this disease in itself is not necessarily a sign of a serious disorder). Infections of the skin and moist inner membranes of the body may also be present. There may be general feelings of discomfort and weakness, accompanied by sustained fevers, drenching night sweats, weight loss, and frequent diarrhea.

The actual incubation period for HIV seems to be variable. The diagnosis of full-blown AIDS is made after one or more of 26 diseases have been manifested in an HIV-infected individual. The term **syndrome** refers to a

retroviruses (RET-ro-vi-rus-es) a class of viruses that integrate their genetic code into that of the host cell, establishing permanent infection.

opportunistic infection a disease resulting from lowered resistance of a weakened immune system.

thrush a disease caused by a fungus and characterized by white patches in the oral cavity.

syndrome (SIN-drome) a group of signs or symptoms that occur together and characterize a given condition.

collection of disease symptoms that tend to cluster together. Unlike most syndromes, AIDS can have a spectrum of symptoms, and the disease can progress in many different ways. Ultimately, there can be months of debilitating illness that lasts until the body can no longer prevail and the victim dies. Medical interventions often are successful in maintaining the immune system for years, but there is no cure for the disease as yet.

FOH How HIV Is Transmitted

It is now clear that HIV is transmitted by the direct transfer of certain bodily fluids from one infected individual to another (see Figure 17.14). Semen, blood, and vaginal secretions are the fluids most often implicated in transmission of HIV. The virus may be transmitted by infected people who have not developed any symptoms. People with AIDS or who are experiencing other symptoms of HIV disease are even more likely to transmit the virus. HIV enters the body through internal linings of organs (such as the vagina, rectum, urethra within the penis, or mouth) or through openings in the skin, such as tiny cuts or open sores.

Researchers have shown that the most typical fluids involved in transmission of the virus are blood, semen, and vaginal secretions. The virus can be transmitted from mother to fetus perinatally (around the time of birth), and there is evidence that it can be transmitted to an infant through breast milk. Additionally, there is documentation of HIV being found in saliva, tears, urine, and feces, but little direct evidence exists that the virus actually has been transmitted by these secretions and excretions.

Several routes of HIV infection have been clearly documented:

1. Anal or vaginal intercourse.
2. Oral-genital sexual activity.
3. Contact with semen or vaginal fluids from an infected person.
4. Organs transplanted from infected persons.
5. Contact with infected blood, through use of contaminated needles and syringes shared by drug users or used for tattooing, ear piercing, or injection of steroids.
6. FOH Transfer from mother to child, the risks of which are increased when invasive procedures such as amniocentesis are used during pregnancy and when certain diseases are present in the mother's body. After the amniotic membranes have ruptured prior to birth, the risk of the fetus contracting the virus from its mother increases hourly until birth (Cohen, 2003b; International Perinatal HIV Group, 2001).

Sharing anal intercourse is especially risky behavior, because the virus from the semen enters the blood-

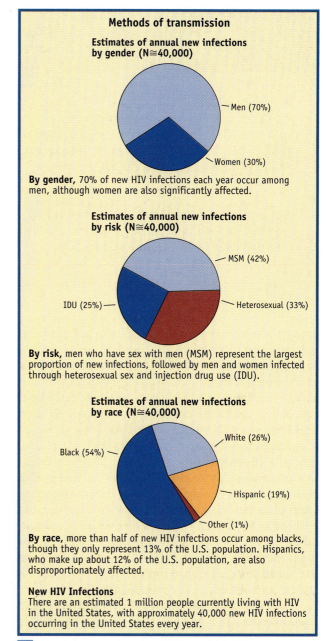

Methods of transmission

Estimates of annual new infections by gender (N≅40,000)

Men (70%)
Women (30%)

By gender, 70% of new HIV infections each year occur among men, although women are also significantly affected.

Estimates of annual new infections by risk (N≅40,000)

MSM (42%)
IDU (25%)
Heterosexual (33%)

By risk, men who have sex with men (MSM) represent the largest proportion of new infections, followed by men and women infected through heterosexual sex and injection drug use (IDU).

Estimates of annual new infections by race (N≅40,000)

White (26%)
Black (54%)
Hispanic (19%)
Other (1%)

By race, more than half of new HIV infections occur among blacks, though they only represent 13% of the U.S. population. Hispanics, who make up about 12% of the U.S. population, are also disproportionately affected.

New HIV Infections
There are an estimated 1 million people currently living with HIV in the United States, with approximately 40,000 new HIV infections occurring in the United States every year.

FIGURE 17.14 *Data on Methods of HIV Infection*
Recent figures on HIV infections help us understand the seriousness of infection trends.
Source: Centers for Disease Control, Atlanta, GA.

stream through the many small tears in the colon. While male-to-male anal intercourse had been on the decline, the rise in the incidence of "barebacking," or unprotected anal sex between men, is alarming. Because a substantial number of women engage in anal intercourse with men, it should be recognized as a potentially risky sexual behavior for them as well (Cubbins & Tanfer, 2000).

The risks associated with oral-genital sex have been difficult to quantify, partly because this behavior

Real Student Voices

■ One of my best friends in high school was gay, and he got in touch with me recently to let me know he is HIV-positive. He seems pretty upbeat about it, but it shocked me. I knew he was gay, but he always was so careful too. I'm not sure how he let it happen.

■ I've been told so many scary things about drugs and sex since I was in elementary school, only to find out that a lot of it wasn't even true, I am always skeptical. When they taught us about AIDS in high school, it was obviously meant to stop us from having sex. I don't think most of us paid much attention. But now I worry I took too many foolish chances.

■ AIDS is one of the reasons I've remained a virgin. I don't see the point of taking the risk. When I find someone I really want to get intimate with, I'll make sure we both get all the tests—just to prove I am clean too.

usually is practiced in conjunction with other sexual activities that may be highly risky. However, there have been cases in which HIV was transmitted from a man's semen during fellatio (oral sex performed on a male). There is less evidence of transmission during cunnilingus (oral sex performed on a female). Women who have sex with other women have been shown to have an elevated risk of contracting HIV (Marrazzo, Coffey, & Bingham, 2005).

Although ordinary kissing appears to pose only a minor threat, the CDC has reported a case of HIV transmission through kissing. Both parties had gum disease, confirming the earlier suspicion that viruses carried in saliva could enter the body through tiny breaks or sores within the mouth or enter the lymphatic cells in the tonsils. Experts therefore continue to caution against prolonged, wet deep kissing (French kissing).

The other group in which HIV has spread rapidly is intravenous (IV) drug abusers, through sharing of needles. Intravenous drug abusers represent the largest heterosexual population in the United States infected with HIV; they also act as a significant vehicle for heterosexual transmission of the virus. In the research on bisexual men in the United States and Canada, four themes have emerged. In general, bisexual men tend to participate in less unsafe sexual behavior than do exclusively gay men. Some groups of bisexual men, however, are at particularly high risk of HIV infection. They also tend to use condoms less often with female partners than with their male partners. Finally, bisexual men may have high rates of injection drug use (CDC, 2006a).

Casual contacts with infected persons—even in crowded households, social settings, schools, or the workplace—are not dangerous. There are no documented cases of HIV being transmitted through food,

water, toilets, swimming pools or hot tubs, shared drinking or eating utensils, telephones, or used clothing. Several research studies have demonstrated that the virus is not transmitted by insects, nor was it spread by the early polio vaccines.

Since the HIV epidemic began, the actual number of infections transmitted by heterosexual contact has been rising steadily. In studies on heterosexual couples in which one partner had already been infected with HIV, it has been clearly shown that the risk of women contracting HIV from men is 10 to 18 times greater than the risk of men getting the virus from women. The risk of transmission is even greater when another sexually transmitted disease (STD) is already present. The inflammation of tissues resulting from STDs may well make it easier for HIV to enter the body.

Several research studies have focused on particular characteristics of certain populations that might make them more vulnerable to HIV infection. There is evidence that people living in small towns and rural areas often assume that they do not need to worry about HIV or AIDS and that they are prone to engaging in high-risk sexual practices such as unprotected penetrative sex. However, HIV continues to spread into rural areas and does not respect urban-rural barriers (Heckman et al., 2003).

The HIV Epidemic in Perspective

As we have seen, the spread of STDs is influenced primarily by the number of sexual partners a person has and how often he or she uses a condom. These factors, along with abuse of alcohol and other drugs, also constitute risk factors in contracting HIV. However, researchers are finding that the picture of the HIV epidemic and where it is heading may be somewhat different from the pattern followed by other STDs.

Urban areas continue to be the epicenter of the epidemic, and it tends to concentrate more in poor neighborhoods where the sale and use of IV drugs constitute an ongoing part of the culture. There continues to be controversy over whether the disease is likely to remain relatively confined to these groups and regions. Many political and public policy issues are impacted by this debate. There is a risk that if HIV is perceived as affecting groups that tend to be socially invisible or ostracized, momentum will be lost for the funding of research to cure and prevent the disease. There is also concern that if education promulgates a "Sex will kill you" message beyond what the data support, information about the very real risks of HIV infection will lose its impact (Race, 2001).

NHSLS researchers proposed a social behavior model regarding the spread of HIV. In order for HIV to become an epidemic in the general population, two specific conditions need to be met: a sustained "bridge" from the infected population to the general population, and frequent sex or needle sharing among the members of the general population to perpetuate epidemic-level proportions of the disease. NHSLS data suggest that these conditions are not being met (Michael et al., 1994). However, such findings should not be misconstrued to mean that we can afford to be complacent about the risk of HIV. Although epidemiologists and sociologists often view risk in terms of broad statistical generalizations, everyone must be concerned about the potential risks of individual behavioral choices.

At least in the United States, some experts believe that the challenge will be to sustain the compassion, research funds, and top-notch treatment necessary for those suffering from the disease, especially individuals who are not perceived as part of the privileged classes. It will be especially crucial for educators to reach those in high-risk areas in order to educate them to make choices that will minimize the risks of spreading HIV. Another challenge will be to convince young people who are not as close to the population centers of the HIV threat to take the risks of unprotected sexual activity or other behaviors as seriously as they must. The incidence of HIV infection has increased in rural areas (Heckman et al., 2003).

■ HIV Testing, Treatment, and Vaccines

When HIV infects people, their bodies begin the natural process of combating the disease. Antibodies begin to form that will attempt to destroy the reproducing viruses. The tests that most frequently are used to confirm the presence of the virus can help detect the antibodies a person's body is producing, although the antibodies may not be detectable for several weeks or even months after the person actually has been infected. It has been generally accepted that such antibodies show up within six weeks following infection, although it can take longer in some people. Continued testing at additional six-month intervals following a potential exposure to HIV has sometimes been recommended. About half of adults in the United States have had an HIV test, but for those whose results are positive, the testing often has occurred late in the course of their infection, hindering the success of potential treatments (Mack & Lansky, 2003).

The blood test currently in greatest use is called an *enzyme-linked immunosorbent assay* (**ELISA.**) It is inexpensive, can be completed within five hours, and is not technically difficult to interpret. However, the ELISA test tends to give a high percentage of false positives, so the results may signal the presence of HIV antibodies when in fact none are present. A positive result is then further tested with the **Western blot** or immunoblot test. More accurate than ELISA, it is lengthy and expensive and must be interpreted by trained and experienced technicians, so it usually is not utilized as a primary test in large-scale screenings.

New generations of HIV tests are extremely sensitive and can distinguish between different strains of HIV. These tests are especially valuable in developing countries because they are one-step procedures, require less sophisticated laboratory facilities, and can detect strains more common in those areas. There are also new tests being used to detect HIV in pregnant women who are in labor and in very young infants. This is especially important, because early detection can lead to earlier treatment and a potentially longer period of survival (Bultyres et al., 2004). Because blood donated in clinics is automatically screened for HIV antibodies, some people are giving blood with the knowledge that they will be notified if they are HIV-positive. Health professionals have a responsibility to prepare patients through pretest counseling and to offer follow-up counseling and support if the results are positive.

A saliva test for HIV is available that offers results in 20 minutes with over 99 percent accuracy. A positive result should still be confirmed with a blood test, but this new, quicker method means that people do not have to wait two weeks to get their results. The saliva test has not been approved for over-the-counter

---

ELISA the primary test used to determine the presence of HIV in humans.

Western blot the test used to verify the presence of HIV antibodies already detected by the ELISA.

sale without a prescription and is used only within medical settings.

Depending on where a person is tested, the results may be considered *confidential,* meaning that the individual's name would be connected to the test results even though the results generally are not shared with others. This is the case in most physicians' offices. Many clinics provide *anonymous* testing, in which the patient is assigned a number for obtaining the test results at a later time. Because the individual's name is never used, privacy is ensured.

FOH HIV Testing Guidelines

Mandatory testing for HIV has already been implemented among those applying for marriage licenses in more than half the states, those seeking immigrant visas, and those wishing to enlist in the U.S. armed forces. In rape cases, alleged rapists have been asked to submit to HIV testing so that the victim can know if the risk of infection exists. Most states now have laws that can force convicted rapists to be tested. It has been suggested, however, that this information may not be as useful as it seems and that there can be a negative side. For example, there is always a chance that the rapist was infected after the rape occurred. In addition, there is only a relatively small chance of becoming infected with HIV after one incident of intercourse—about 1 chance in 300 to 500. Therefore, the rape survivor may be left not knowing for sure if actual infection has taken place. No matter the outcome of the rapist's test, it is still important for the victim to be tested immediately and again several months later.

Studies have shown that routine testing for STDs in hospital patients and in prison settings detects many infections that otherwise would have been missed (Huppert et al., 2005; Robertson et al., 2005). Some states require their family planning and STD clinics to offer free, voluntary testing for HIV. Experts have recommended routine screening for HIV within all medical settings, citing that it would be a cost-effective way of discovering the infection and offering timely medical care (Bozzette, 2005). The CDC has made the following recommendations concerning HIV testing:

1. Couples planning marriage should be provided "ready access" to testing and to information about HIV and AIDS.
2. People should have the "right to choose not to be tested" and be given appropriate counseling prior to testing. They should also give explicit consent, orally or in writing, before being tested.
3. Anyone seeking treatment for other sexually transmitted infections should be encouraged to undergo HIV testing.

4. People with a history of IV drug use who have shared equipment with others should be encouraged to be tested, as should their sexual partners.
5. It is now recommended that all pregnant women be tested.
6. Women seeking family planning services should be routinely counseled about HIV infection and have testing made available to them.
7. Gay and bisexual men should be tested annually for HIV, chlamydia, gonorrhea, and syphilis.

The waiting period of several days before test results can be made available may create high levels of anxiety. For those people whose tests are positive, it is crucial that they receive appropriate counseling to deal with their feelings and to learn about suitable treatment options. If the test results are negative, counseling can be important in providing the person with information about avoiding infection in the future. For this reason, most state health departments require that an individual come in person to find out the results rather than being told over the telephone or by mail. Unfortunately, youth at high risk for contracting HIV often tend not to return to a clinic for the results and are more likely to check the results if they can do so by telephone (Tsu et al., 2002).

Although home testing has traditionally been discouraged by professionals in this field because it does not allow for face-to-face counseling, it is also recognized that many potentially infected persons are avoiding testing because of embarrassment or the lack of anonymity. Home-testing kits, in which a person draws his or her own blood and sends it to a testing center, have been approved by the FDA. The person being tested calls a toll-free number after a few days to receive the result using a code number. If the test is positive, this result is reported to the caller by a trained counselor who discusses the implications of the test with the person. There is still controversy over this approach, because some professionals believe that face-to-face counseling should be required in order to help HIV-positive persons deal more effectively with their diagnoses.

Promise of Microbicides

A new strategy is being developed that may help prevent STDs and HIV infection in the future through the use of topical microbicides. This would involve the use of gels or creams that would be inserted into the vagina (and possibly the rectum) prior to sexual intercourse. Not only would they offer some physical barrier in the lubricant itself, but the microbicide would disrupt the infective potential of the disease-causing agents. Although this approach is not meant to be a substitute for condom use, it would provide an extra measure of protection for women that would not

Real People

Brent: Worrying about Potential HIV Infection

Brent was a gay man and had been active in a college social group for gays. At one of the meetings of the group, he had met a gay male who was a few years younger than himself, and they had begun seeing each other. The younger man had been more sexually active than Brent, who had had only two previous same-gender sexual experiences. After an evening out, Brent and his new partner decided to have sex. One of the activities they shared was anal intercourse. While the other man was having intercourse with Brent, the condom he was wearing broke without his knowledge, and he ejaculated without the protection of the condom. He was apologetic and assured Brent that he did not have any diseases, but Brent was still worried. He did not fully trust the other man and was very aware that he had been active sexually with numerous partners.

This was the first time Brent could potentially have been exposed to STDs, including HIV. He had been vaccinated for hepatitis B before entering college. He contacted an STD clinic and set up an

appointment to be checked for various STDs. All tests proved to be negative. The other reality was that he would have to wait several months before a test for HIV could be considered reliable. This was highly uncomfortable for him. During the waiting period, he also had a flulike illness, which frightened him even more. The health clinic assured him that his symptoms were exactly like those being experienced by many other people at that time of year. After six months, Brent had the blood tests for HIV, which involved another two weeks of tense waiting for the results. He was relieved to learn that the tests were negative, and he had them repeated after another six months for further reassurance.

If Brent were a friend of yours and confided in you about his concerns during the waiting period, how would you have responded to him? If another friend of yours said to you that Brent simply got what he deserved, how would you respond to this other person?

depend on male cooperation (Trager, 2003). The regulatory hurdles for the development and licensing of microbicides continue to increase, even though their research and development can be shown to be cost effective (Coplan, Mitchnick, & Rosenberg, 2004).

FOH Treatment for HIV Disease

Although the final stage of HIV disease, AIDS, is a fatal disease, appropriate medical treatment earlier in the course of the infection can prolong a patient's life and improve its quality. Experienced physicians can monitor progress of the virus and provide appropriate interventions, because the strategy for treatment varies with the stage of the infection. As opportunistic diseases develop, carefully selected medications may be used to relieve symptoms and help the body fight the infections.

If you contracted HIV, would you seek medical treatment to prolong your life, knowing that there is no cure for AIDS? Why or why not?

Since research with HIV treatments began, a remarkable number of new antiretroviral preparations have gone into testing. There are now so many, in fact, that the clinical testing system has been strained (see

Figure 17.15). Treatment is most effective when it is begun as soon as possible after infection, and the regimen must be followed faithfully (Peters et al., 2003).

FIGURE 17.15 *HIV/AIDS Awareness and Education*

Jeff Getty, an AIDS patient who received a baboon bone marrow transplant as an experimental treatment, holds a press conference with other AIDS activists to heighten consciousness about the need for new research on treating HIV-positive individuals.

FOH One of the most widely used drugs has been zidovudine, often in combination with other drugs, although these can have severe side effects. The most hopeful approach to emerge so far in treating HIV is the combination, or cocktail, therapy. It is based on the knowledge that HIV mutates rapidly to different forms and therefore can quickly become resistant to a particular drug. Combination therapy uses two or more drugs at once so that HIV is kept off balance and under control and the body is encouraged to build its number of immune cells. One of the new drugs usually used as part of the therapy is a protease inhibitor, which attacks the virus in one of its reproductive steps (Cohen, 2005b). This approach to treatment is also called *highly active antiretroviral therapy (HAART)*. Unfortunately, these combination therapies do not seem to improve patients' mental health, and they can be so complicated that many patients cease treatment after a short time (Murphy et al., 2005; Samet et al., 2003; Siegel, Karus, & Dean, 2004).

A newer approach to treatment that is raising hopes attempts to deal with the troublesome fact that HIV can hide out in a latent state in various cells and then appear and multiply later on. The technique forces these "resting" cells out of hiding and uses chemical combinations to eradicate them. It will be some time before we can know how effective such treatment will be (Cohen, 2005c)

FOH ## Vaccines and Prophylaxis for HIV

The search for an HIV vaccine has been a top priority since 1984, and experts still rank such a vaccine as the most urgently needed in the world. Several major complications make the search difficult. First, HIV seems to be able to "hide" in cells by installing its genes within the genes of the cell. Second, there is no particularly good animal model for the disease, and this is where testing normally would begin. Third, because HIV infection is so dangerous, experimental trials for a vaccine with humans have had to proceed with the utmost caution. In such trials, a substantial number of at-risk people are given the vaccine, and their rate of infection is compared to a control group of persons who have not received the vaccine. Most vaccine trials so far have yielded disappointing results. Finally, there are concerns that there may be very real ethical problems involved in conducting vaccine trials with people in the less industrialized nations of the world who have not been given the benefit of other forms of medical treatment (Emini & Koff, 2004; Mills & Rennie, 2006).

Because there are different strains of HIV, it is possible that several vaccines will have to be developed to protect people (UK Group, 2005). Some virologists believe that enough weak spots can be found that are common to most of the strains to allow a single vaccine to produce immunity. Animal testing with vaccines has demonstrated enough success that experimental trials with humans are now under way. The first tests were done with *therapeutic vaccines* that are used to expand the immune responses of people already infected with HIV in an effort to delay or prevent the onset of disease symptoms.

As these vaccines prove to be safe, they may well be tested on uninfected people as *preventative vaccines* that would forestall infection with the virus in the first place. Another promising preventative approach is *chemoprophylaxis*. This uses powerful chemicals that stay in the body for an extended period of time and may well disable HIV if it enters the body. This approach differs from the use of a deactivated viral vaccine, but it could ultimately prove more effective. Clinical trials of the technique are under way (Grant et al., 2005).

Ethical Issues and HIV/AIDS

Several ethical issues have arisen concerning HIV and AIDS:

The Issue of Confidentiality

In the field of medicine, patient confidentiality has traditionally been afforded the utmost respect. Yet some information from health records has been subject to disclosure, with the patient's permission, for a variety of purposes. The question remains: Who should be allowed access to information about an individual's sexual lifestyle or infection with HIV? Such information can affect reputation, employment, and insurance coverage. Yet if an individual who is known to be HIV-infected continues to behave in ways that clearly endanger others, how and under what circumstances would it be legitimate for the infection to be revealed? The federal HIPAA (Health Insurance Portability and Accountability Act) regulations require that patients be given thorough information about how their privacy can be protected.

Do you believe doctors should have the right to reveal a patient's HIV status to anyone? For instance, should doctors inform school systems that a student is HIV-positive? Should coaches know an athlete's status? Explain your position.

Among nonmedical professionals such as counselors, social workers, and psychotherapists, the confidentiality dilemmas become more complex. Ethical guidelines require such professionals to violate confidentiality if a third party is facing some immediate threat of danger, but the guidelines about potential HIV infection are less clear. Everyone agrees that the first line of action would be to strongly encourage the client to inform others about the disease and cease any behaviors that could potentially endanger others. If that fails, there is less agreement about how the professional should proceed. In one program that provided voluntary counseling and testing for partners of individuals just diagnosed as HIV-positive, several hundred people came in for testing, and 21 percent tested positive (Foust et al., 2003).

The Costs of Caring for HIV-Infected Patients and Supporting Research

The costs of HIV and AIDS are proving to be staggering. There has been a growing concern that certain other diseases that affect as many or more people as HIV are not getting their fair share of research dollars. Some states in which the rates of infection are particularly high contribute millions of dollars each year to efforts to contain the infection. The increasing number of patients with HIV disease is raising the issue of where the money to care for them will come from (Chen et al., 2006).

HIV-Positive People and Pregnancy

HIV-positive men and women who want to parent children have a number of options for pregnancy. There are techniques for "cleansing" semen of the virus, and pregnant women can take various drugs to reduce the chances of transmitting HIV to their babies without risking negative side effects (Anderson, Ebrahim, & Sansom, 2004; Kirshenbaum et al., 2004).

HIV/AIDS Education

Most states already require their schools to offer HIV/AIDS education. However, there is controversy over the age at which such education should begin and what its content should be. In many ways, these controversial factors are extensions of debates that have been raging in the field of sexuality education for years. Some experts recommend beginning HIV/AIDS education with 9-, 10-, and 11-year-olds; others oppose starting at such early ages. Some groups claim that it is unrealistic to expect all youth to abstain from shared sexual activity because of the HIV scare, and they advocate the teaching of safer sex practices that will at least minimize the risk of contracting HIV (see Figure 17.16). Critics of this approach believe that teaching about preventative measures condones casual sex. Among schools that have mandated HIV/AIDS education, some have also required that the emphasis be placed on sexual abstinence.

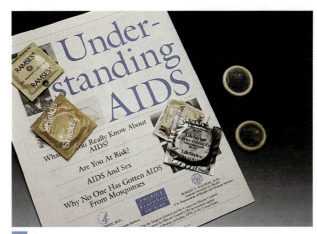

FIGURE 17.16 *Condom Advertisement*

The Centers for Disease Control and Prevention and other agencies hope to educate the public about safe sex and the use of condoms with advertisements like this.

Most experts agree that, in the general population, older teenagers and young adults tend to be the most sexually active and therefore at higher risk of HIV than some other groups. They also tend to have attitudes of invulnerability and a false sense of security, assuming that the negative consequences will not happen to them. Reports from high schools and colleges suggest that some students have been slow to accept the potential risks of HIV and AIDS around them. College students still sometimes neglect to use condoms in their sexual activities, and those who do often encounter problems with their use (Crosby et al., 2002; Sanders et al., 2003).

Unfortunately, too many people are still participating in risky sexual behaviors without the protection of condoms. Lower levels of self-esteem, use of alcohol and other substances, and lack of skill in communicating with sexual partners all play a role in reducing the likelihood that people will use condoms. Experts believe that HIV education must go beyond the presentation of information to help everyone develop the intentions and skills they need to successfully protect themselves from infection. Women may need educational strategies directed specifically at their gender (Exner, Hoffman, Dworkin, & Ehrhardt, 2004; Smith, L. A., 2003).

The issue of HIV/AIDS education is taking sexuality education in new directions and encouraging further debate about curriculum content and philosophy. One thing is certain: No one grows up today without hearing a great deal about HIV and AIDS and their connections to sex.

See "Just Like Me" on SexSource Online.

■ Can Sex Be Safe and Satisfying?

Everyone has to make his or her own decisions about sexual behavior, considering the risks of STD and HIV transmission. Although slightly more individuals than in the recent past may be postponing penetrative sexual contact until they find a lasting, monogamous relationship, others clearly are choosing to share sex now. How seriously they consider the risks of contracting a disease or what sorts of practices they employ to decrease those risks depend on a variety of psychological and social factors, including the following.

1. *Degree of willingness to be prepared for sex.* The fear of condemnation from parents, religious leaders, and society often has made it difficult for young people to plan ahead and prepare for sexual activity. Many therefore prefer to regard sex as accidental or spontaneous in order to bear less responsibility for a bad decision or immoral behavior. Such attitudes only interfere with the kind of mutual questioning and preparation that can render a sexual encounter safe from the risk of disease (Johnson et al., 2003).
2. *Self-esteem and assertiveness.* To protect oneself against infection while remaining sexually active requires enough self-esteem and sense of self-worth to hold one's health in need of protection. It also requires enough self-confidence and assertiveness to make it clear to one's partner that certain rules must govern a sexual encounter. This sort of behavior often is difficult for people who believe that their popularity or attractiveness, or even an entire relationship, may be in question (Silvestre et al., 2002).
3. *Willingness to overcome peer pressures about use of condoms.* As birth control devices, condoms often have been given a bad name. Some people claim they reduce sexual sensations. They may be embarrassing to purchase. For such a simple device, they frequently are not used completely correctly, and they occasionally break or slip off. The fact remains, however, that for now latex condoms are one of the best protections against disease transmission in sexual encounters (Warner et al., 2005). People are learning that sex with condoms not only is safer but can still be pleasurable and satisfying. Although use of condoms has been increasing, rates of consistent condom use still need to improve.
4. *Degree of understanding of personal vulnerability.* At various times in life, people are prone to feeling relatively invincible or may believe that any consequence, even a negative one, is reversible. It is crucial for everyone to realize that STDs and HIV represent a very real threat. At the present time, there is no cure for some viral STDs and HIV.
5. *Willingness to accept the struggles of establishing a sexual identity.* Even people who consider themselves heterosexual sometimes have sexual encounters with members of their same gender. Because such choices may be personally difficult to accept psychologically, there may also be a tendency to not pay attention to proper protection during same-gender sex. Males who share sexual activity with other males, in particular, must give careful consideration to the risks involved, and both partners should take precautions to prevent transmission of HIV and other viral infections. Some young men who identify themselves primarily as gay are also having sex with women and thus need to take the same precautions (Koblin et al., 2003).

Despite the threat of various diseases, couples still can regard sex in a positive way as an integral part of enhancing relationships. Potential sexual partners need to think more carefully about their sexual decisions, open up channels of communication, and protect themselves more deliberately from the spread of disease. These new approaches to sex should prove of real value in reducing a spectrum of negative sexual and social consequences. (see Table 17.2).

SAFE SEX

Source: Copyright © The New Yorker Collection 1987 Peter Steiner, from cartoonbank.com. All rights reserved.

Table 17.2	*Degree of Safety in Types of Sexual Activity*	
Safest	**Possibly Safe**	**Unsafe**
Dry kissing	Vaginal or anal intercourse using a latex or synthetic condom	Fellatio or cunnilingus without a condom or rubber dam
Body-to-body contact and embracing	Wet kissing with no broken skin or damaged mouth tissue	Semen in the mouth
Massage	Cunnilingus using a dam	Vaginal intercourse without a condom
Mutual masturbation (with care in avoiding contact with semen)	Fellatio using a condom	Anal intercourse without a condom
Erotic books, movies, and conversation	Hand-to-genital stimulation without breaks in skin	Other anal contact, orally or manually
		Sharing sex toys

Source: Hatcher et al., *Contraceptive Technology,* 18th ed., New York: Ardent Media, 2004.

 ## Minimizing the Sexual Risks of Contracting STDs and HIV

The occurrence of STDs and HIV in the population has reached epidemic proportions, and there is no particularly effective system in place for the prevention and control of these infections (Low et al., 2006). Parents have shown a willingness to have their children vaccinated against STDs, regardless of their age (Zimet et al., 2005). It is estimated that more than 20 million women in the United States would be interested in using some sort of STD- and HIV-prevention chemical that could be placed in the vagina prior to sex. The pharmaceutical industry has been encouraged to work on the development of such vaginal microbicides, which could reduce the risks of STDs. Microbicides provide a chemical barrier, rather than a physical one, that actually kills or disables disease germs. Testing is showing promising results, although regulatory obstacles to the testing and licensing of these new drugs are becoming increasingly challenging (Coplan, Mitchnick, & Rosenberg, 2004).

As yet there are no easy solutions, so the possibility of contracting or transmitting disease should be weighed as part of the responsibility of engaging in sexual behavior. Here are some specific suggestions for minimizing the chances of getting or transmitting an STD or HIV:

1. *Recognize that abstinence from sex is a rational choice in the face of the risks.* There are plenty of pressures to have sex. Our sexual feelings may be strong and difficult to resist. However, each individual must make his or her own decisions about how involved to get with others sexually. With the increase of persistent and dangerous diseases, abstinence or delaying sexual activity has become a viable alternative and a rational choice. A major risk of this choice is changing your mind with short notice. While it may go against the grain of abstinence thinking, it is wise to have a backup method of protection easily accessible.

2. *Remember that sexual sharing does not have to involve internal penetration.* Most of these diseases are transmitted by penetration involving mingling of bodily secretions (oral-genital, anal-genital, or penile-vaginal). The transmission of these diseases could be sharply reduced by emphasis on forms of sexual sharing that do not require such penetration, including massage, most forms of mutual masturbation, and some degree of external mutual genital contact. Unfortunately, social values often have led us to believe that some form of penetration is necessary to legitimize a sexual experience. Given the prevalence of STDs and HIV, alternative values may well make sense.

3. *If you are contemplating having sex with a new partner, it is crucial to make some agreements and live up to them:*
   - Agree not to share sex with any other partners for the duration of the relationship.
   - Agree to be tested for STDs and HIV regularly after any sexual contact that could have transmitted it. It can take up to six months, or perhaps longer, for HIV antibodies to develop and show up on a blood test.
   - Agree either to wait a few weeks to share sex, after you both have had various tests, or to use protection for that period of time.

4. *Avoid multiple partners and partners who are not well known to you.* The more partners you have and the less well known they are to you, the greater the risk of contracting an STD. This fact has been confirmed by research. Casual sex is simply riskier sex. There is less chance that partners' sexual histories will be known, that their suspicious

symptoms will be noticed, and that you will be notified if a disease is eventually diagnosed.

See "Mike on STDs and Sexual Histories" on SexSource Online.

5. *Know your sexual partners and take responsibility for yourself and your own protection.* You can take several measures to protect yourself and reduce the risk of getting a disease from sex. They may not always be easy steps to take and may require some degree of assertiveness, but they are part of sexual responsibility. First, it is important to talk with a partner about sex and even to ask about possible infections, although there is evidence that such an information exchange between partners is not always particularly accurate (Ciccarone et al., 2003). You might want to ask if your partner has ever had a herpes infection or any recent symptoms of infection. Second, it can be important to observe your partner's genitals, checking for any sores, warts, discharge, lice, or rashes. It is also a good idea to take responsibility for washing your genital area with soap and water before and promptly after sex. Although these suggestions may not be conducive to sexual intimacy, they are worth considering as precautionary measures in preventing STDs. It is also important to avoid the use of alcohol and other drugs that may alter your judgment. Indiscriminate use of such substances is associated with higher rates of STD.

One older but rather disturbing study found that in a sample of 422 sexually active 18- to 25-year-olds, 34 percent of the males and 10 percent of the females admitted to having lied about their sexual histories in order to have sex with a new partner. When asked if they would lie to a partner about having a negative AIDS test when they actually had not had such a test, 20 percent of the men and 4 percent of the women said they would (Cochran & Mays, 1990). More recent research found that about 40 percent of sexually active HIV-positive men and women have had sex without disclosing their status to their sexual partners, and 13 percent of those who did not disclose it also did not use condoms consistently during their sexual contacts (Ciccarone et al., 2003). You should be aware of this sinister type of risk.

6. *Use a condom, vaginal pouch, or diaphragm.* Male condoms or female condoms (vaginal pouches) can reduce the risk of transmission (see Chapter 11, "Decision Making about Pregnancy and Parenthood," for more information). They do not offer total protection, but they certainly reduce the risks substantially (Niccolai et al., 2005). Although the spermicide nonoxynol-9, placed in the vagina, seems to reduce the risks of gonorrheal and chlamydial infection, it does not seem to reduce viral infections and may even increase the risk of contracting them. Many condom manufacturers no longer use the spermicide in their lubricants.

The male condom should be unrolled onto the erect penis before intercourse begins, leaving an empty (not air-filled) space at the tip for semen. This is best accomplished by pinching the tip of the condom while unrolling it onto the penis (see Figure 17.17). After ejaculation has occurred, the man or his partner should hold onto the base of the condom when removing the penis from the vagina so the condom does not slip off and so semen does not seep out of the open end of the condom. Some newly designed condoms have adhesive around the shaft to prevent slippage and leakage. Condoms slip off or break between 2 and 3 percent of the times they are used. The "female condom," or vaginal pouch (see Chapter 11, p. 311), also provides protection, but probably not quite as effectively as male condoms (Hatcher et al., 2004).

Diaphragms have been shown to offer some protection against STDs as well, although more research is needed to clarify their degree of effectiveness (Maher et al., 2004).

7. Avoid direct contact with any bodily fluids or excretions from a partner.

FIGURE 17.17 *How to Use the Condom*

Do not allow the penis to make sexual entry or contact before putting on the condom. Semen and sperm can escape from the penis at any time. The end of the condom should be pinched to eliminate air before it is unrolled fully to cover the erect penis.

8. If you are an uncircumcised HIV-negative male, consider circumcision. The newest evidence about the degree of protection that circumcision offers against HIV infection is quite compelling. Circumcised men may have as much as a 60 percent reduction in their chances of contracting HIV. The inner tissue of the penile foreskin is the same kind of epithelial tissue found in the outer parts of other body cavities, making it more susceptible to infection. New York City health officials are considering a campaign to encourage high-risk males to get circumcised and may even offer the procedure at hospitals without charge.

9. Use a *rubber dam* during oral contact with the vulva or anus. Oral contact with sites where the virus could be harbored is considered risky. Some experts have recommended that small, square latex sheets of the sort dentists sometimes use in the mouth be placed over the vulva, vagina, or anus. This would allow for some oral stimulation without direct contact from the tongue or lips. There is no research to date that can show how effective or necessary such a dam might be in preventing the transmission of diseases, but it may be the best precaution given the present state of our knowledge. Although the latex dams are not widely available, they could be obtained at medical/dental supply stores. Some dentists might be willing to provide them. Rubber dams also may be improvised by cutting a latex condom along its length and then spreading it out, or by cutting out a section of a surgical rubber glove. Rubber gloves or individual rubber fingercots that fit over a single finger might also be considered if a finger is to be inserted into the vagina or anus; this can offer protection from the virus entering through a break in the skin.

10. *Get medical screening periodically, and seek medical treatment promptly if symptoms develop.* If you are sexually active, it is a good idea to occasionally seek screening tests that can determine if you might have one of the STDs that tend to have few symptoms in their beginning stages, including HIV. STD clinics, family planning clinics, and college health centers usually are able to help with such screening. Whenever you have any suspicious or uncomfortable symptoms in the genital area or urinary tract, seek medical advice and treatment right away. Most cities have STD and HIV clinics, staffed by workers who have expertise in this area. Clinical workers are nonjudgmental, and the tests are nearly always painless.

11. *Inform sexual partners, and urge them to seek treatment.* Whenever a disease contracted through sex is diagnosed, it is crucial for sexual partners of the infected person to be notified and to have a physical examination. Remember, many diseases do not have obvious symptoms in the earlier stages but still require prompt treatment to prevent complications. Many clinics have found that it is best to provide a couple-friendly atmosphere in which both partners can be treated and counseled about their disease and its implications (CDC, 2006b).

How comfortable do you feel asking a potential sex partner about her or his history of STDs? Would you inform that partner of your own history? Why or why not?

These practices cannot provide a guarantee of safety against disease transmission, but they can minimize your risks. They also represent the most responsible ways to approach sexual activity.

Legal and Personal Responsibility Aspects of Sexually Transmitted Diseases

Most of us assume that a person would not knowingly or deliberately transmit a disease to another person. For the most part, such assumptions probably are correct. However, sexual behavior is an area of life about which people can be extremely private and secretive. They may feel uncomfortable with certain aspects of their past sexual activities and may worry that to discuss their sexual history will jeopardize present relationships. People also tend to avoid protecting themselves against the riskier aspects of sexual behavior, especially when they are caught up in powerful romantic or sexual feelings.

In recent years, more attention has been focused on the legal responsibilities of sexual partners as they relate to STDs. Individuals who have contracted an STD after being assured that there was no danger of doing so, or without being informed of potential risks, have resorted to legal action. Multimillion-dollar lawsuits have been brought against people who seem to have spread diseases purposely or carelessly. More than half the states have statutes that make it a criminal offense to knowingly transmit an STD, and HIV is increasingly being treated in the same manner. Legal experts warn that the law expects people to be responsible in their sexual behaviors and to protect others from any potential harm that might come from sexual activity. As STDs and HIV have reached epidemic proportions, legal precedents are being established that demand even higher levels of responsibility during sexual encounters.

Self-Evaluation

Examining Your Attitudes toward Sexually Transmitted Diseases

The following scale will give you an opportunity to explore some of your own beliefs, feelings, and intentions with regard to STDs. The scale was developed by Yarber, Torabi, and Veenker (1989) and has been tested with hundreds of college and secondary school students. The evaluation is for your own use only.

Directions: Please read each statement carefully. Record your first reaction by marking an "X" through the letter that best describes how much you agree or disagree with the idea.

USE THIS KEY: SA = strongly agree
A = agree
U = undecided
D = disagree
SD = strongly disagree

Example: Doing things to prevent getting an STD is the job of each person.   SA   A   U̶   D   SD

REMEMBER: STD means sexually transmitted disease, such as gonorrhea, syphilis, genital herpes, or HIV disease.

	(Mark "X" through letter)				
1. How one uses his/her sexuality has nothing to do with STD.	SA	A	U	D	SD
2. It is easy to use the prevention methods that reduce one's chances of getting an STD.	SA	A	U	D	SD
3. Responsible sex is one of the best ways of reducing the risk of STD.	SA	A	U	D	SD
4. Getting early medical care is the main key to preventing harmful effects of STD.	SA	A	U	D	SD
5. Choosing the right sex partner is important in reducing the risk of getting an STD.	SA	A	U	D	SD
6. A high rate of STD should be a concern for all people.	SA	A	U	D	SD
7. People with an STD have a duty to get their sex partners to medical care.	SA	A	U	D	SD
8. The best way to get a sex partner to STD treatment is to take him/her to the doctor with you.	SA	A	U	D	SD
9. Changing one's sex habits is necessary once the presence of an STD is known.	SA	A	U	D	SD
10. I would dislike having to follow the medical steps for treating an STD.	SA	A	U	D	SD
11. If I were sexually active, I would feel uneasy doing things before and after sex to prevent getting an STD.	SA	A	U	D	SD
12. If I were sexually active, it would be insulting if a sex partner suggested we use a condom to avoid STD.	SA	A	U	D	SD
13. I dislike talking about STD with my peers.	SA	A	U	D	SD

14. I would be uncertain about going to the doctor unless I were sure I really had an STD.   SA   A   U   D   SD

15. I would feel that I should take my sex partner with me to a clinic if I thought I had an STD.   SA   A   U   D   SD

16. It would be embarrassing to discuss STD with one's partner if one were sexually active.   SA   A   U   D   SD

17. If I were to have sex, the chance of getting an STD would make me uneasy about having sex with more than one person.   SA   A   U   D   SD

18. I like the idea of sexual abstinence (not having sex) as the best way of avoiding STD.   SA   A   U   D   SD

19. If I had an STD, I would cooperate with public health persons to find the sources of STD.   SA   A   U   D   SD

20. If I had an STD, I would avoid exposing others while I was being treated.   SA   A   U   D   SD

21. I would have regular STD checkups if I were having sex with more than one partner.   SA   A   U   D   SD

22. I intend to look for STD signs before deciding to have sex with anyone.   SA   A   U   D   SD

23. I will limit my sexual activity to just one partner because of the chances I might get an STD.   SA   A   U   D   SD

24. I will avoid sexual contact anytime I think there is even a slight chance of getting an STD.   SA   A   U   D   SD

25. The chance of getting an STD would not stop me from having sex.   SA   A   U   D   SD

26. If I had a chance, I would support community efforts toward controlling STD.   SA   A   U   D   SD

27. I would be willing to work with others to make people aware of STD problems in my town.   SA   A   U   D   SD

Self-Evaluation Scoring: Calculate total points for each subscale and total scale, using the point values below.

For items 1, 10–14, 16, 25

Strongly agree = 5 points
Agree = 4 points
Undecided = 3 points
Disagree = 2 points
Strongly disagree = 1 point

For items 2–9, 15, 17–24, 26, 27

Strongly agree = 1 point
Agree = 2 points
Undecided = 3 points
Disagree = 4 points
Strongly disagree = 5 points

Total scale: items 1–27
Belief subscale: items 1–9
Feeling subscale: items 10–18
Intention to act subscale: items 19–27

Interpretation: The higher your score, the higher your risk of behavior that can spread sexually transmitted diseases.

Source: From *Journal of Sex Education and Therapy,* Vol. 15, No. 1, 1989, pp. 42–43. Reprinted by permission of the American Association of Sex Educators, Counselors & Therapists.

Self-Evaluation

Considering Being Tested for HIV

The percentages of people being tested for HIV have been growing steadily. Seeking testing reflects the likelihood that they have engaged in some sort of risky behavior at some point in their lives, whether they admit it or not. Although it may take up to six months or more for HIV antibodies to show up in the body, testing is one of the best ways to find out your status and protect your sexual partners. Testing usually is reliable after six weeks. If you are involved in a relationship in which you may eventually wish to participate in unprotected, penetrative sex and either of you has had any possibility of HIV exposure, testing is the most sensible route to take. Unless you have participated in frequent high-risk behaviors, it is quite likely that your test results will be negative. Nevertheless, it is best to find out for sure.

Here is a series of questions that can help you think through the process of being tested for HIV and also your reactions to that process. Consider your responses with care, and then *get tested*.

Knowing the Mechanics

Consult your local public health agency or student health center for more information, and try to secure answers to the following questions:

1. Where can you get tested for HIV?
2. Does your state or provincial government require reporting of test results to some central agency?
3. Will your name be associated with your test results, as they are in *confidential* medical records? Or will the results be *anonymous,* identified only by a number you hold?
4. Who will be explaining the results of the test to you?

5. What kind of testing is used (blood or saliva), and how long will it take to get the results?
6. Are you making the decision to be tested without coercion and with full and informed consent?

Knowing Your Motivations and Feelings

7. Why are you considering being tested for HIV?
8. Is peace of mind important to you? Are you tired of wondering about the possibility you could have been infected?
9. Are you ready to cope with some anxiety while awaiting the test results? Will you have sources of support and counseling in the meantime?
10. Are you ready to give honest answers to the health care provider who will interview you prior to testing?
11. Have you discussed HIV testing with your partner?

If the Results Are Positive . . .

12. How do you think you will feel, and whom will you tell first?
13. Who will be your sources of support and counseling?
14. Where will you seek further medical evaluation and treatment, and how will this be paid for?
15. What will be the implications for the various relationships in your life (relatives, friends, lovers)?
16. Do you know that you can still have a satisfying and productive life ahead?

If the Results Are Negative . . .

17. How do you think you will feel, and whom will you tell first?
18. Are you prepared to take appropriate precautions in the future to minimize the risks of HIV infection? What are your plans?

Chapter Summary

1. Sexually transmitted diseases (STDs) have caused much human misery throughout the centuries and continue to be serious health problems today.
2. Human immunodeficiency virus (HIV) has raised many medical, political, economic, and social issues. Acquired immunodeficiency syndrome (AIDS) is the final, eventually terminal, stage of HIV infection.

3. The development of penicillin was a major step in conquering some STDs.
4. It is estimated that there are 19 million new cases of STD in the United States each year, half in people under age 25. About 60 million people in the United States are infected with some viral STD.

5. Although the origins of HIV are uncertain, it may have begun in Africa. HIV has infected millions of people throughout the world.

6. Epidemiological studies show that the incidence of HIV infection varies in different parts of the world. Although HIV spread first among gay males and intravenous (IV) drug abusers in the United States, HIV infection now is found among heterosexual adolescents, heterosexual men, women, and children.

7. The more sexual partners an individual has and the less consistently condoms are used, the more likely infection with an STD becomes.

8. Gonorrhea can be spread through vaginal, anal, and oral sexual contact and infects over a half million people each year. The eyes of babies are vulnerable to infection during birth and are routinely treated to prevent gonorrheal blindness. Many strains of gonorrhea are now penicillin-resistant, so other antibiotics are used for treatment.

9. Syphilis progresses through four major stages. About 20,000 people each year in the United States are infected with syphilis.

10. The large proportion of the population infected with the *Chlamydia* organism was not recognized until the mid-1980s. It is the cause of many different forms of genital and urinary tract infections in both men and women, and it can cause infertility. It is one of the most common STDs and one of the most commonly reported reportable infectious diseases.

11. Nonspecific urethritis (NSU) has been steadily increasing as an STD problem affecting males.

12. Vulvovaginal inflammation may be caused by bacteria, yeast organisms, or trichomonads. Taking proper hygienic measures and keeping the vulval area dry can reduce the risk of contracting vaginitis.

13. Genital herpes is caused by the herpes simplex virus. Once the virus has infected the body, it can cause recurrent outbreaks of the lesions. The disease has been associated with a higher incidence of cervical and vulval cancer in women and can be dangerous to newborn infants.

14. Human papillomavirus (HPV) causes genital warts (condylomata) and also is associated with a higher incidence of cervical and anal cancers.

15. Hepatitis A can be sexually transmitted and causes a liver infection from which most people recover completely. Hepatitis B virus (HBV) can cause serious liver infection, and it has been recommended that college students be vaccinated against the virus. Hepatitis C virus (HCV) is also a serious disease, but it is less likely to be transmitted sexually.

16. Pubic lice must be thoroughly treated to ensure that all insects and their eggs have been eliminated from body hairs.

17. Lymphogranuloma venereum (LGV), chancroid, and granuloma inguinale are STDs that are more common in tropical climates.

18. Two skin diseases that may be transmitted by the intimate bodily contact of sex are molluscum contagiosum and scabies.

19. HIV is a retrovirus that progressively destroys the body's immune system so that opportunistic infections weaken the victim. In its final stages, HIV infection is known as AIDS and eventually is fatal.

20. The documented routes of HIV infection are anal or vaginal sexual intercourse; oral-genital sex; other contacts with semen, transplanted organs, or blood (as through contaminated needles); and transfer from mother to child perinatally or through breast milk.

21. HIV is more prevalent in urban neighborhoods, especially where there is a great deal of IV drug abuse. This could pose a challenge to keeping funding for research to seek a cure for the disease.

22. Tests to detect HIV antibodies in the blood may not show evidence of the virus for six months or more after actual infection. The ELISA test is usually confirmed with the Western blot test. A saliva test is available that gives results in about 20 minutes.

23. There is controversy over whether HIV testing should be required. In the United States, all potential immigrants and armed forces enlistees are required to be tested. Many states now require premarital testing. It is recommended that pregnant women be tested. Home testing raises the problem of finding out results without the assurance of face-to-face counseling.

24. There is no cure for HIV infection. Treatment focuses on prevention and control of opportunistic infections. Use of combinations of drugs (HAART) against the retrovirus has proved to be effective in prolonging life.

25. Many drugs have been developed to treat HIV, and combination drug therapies involving protease inhibitors are proving to be the most effective. HIV can develop drug resistance because it mutates quickly and multiplies in great numbers. Many other drugs are being developed and tested.

26. Vaccines to fool the body into creating antibodies to help slow the rate of HIV infection are being tested. Preventative vaccines are also being tested, as are other chemicals that are part of chemoprophylaxis.

27. Caring for and research on people living with HIV or AIDS raise issues of confidentiality and cost. Legal and ethical conflicts about HIV infection and confidentiality are becoming increasingly common.

28. Sex can still be a pleasurable and safe part of relationships if approached responsibly and with appropriate precautions.

29. Part of responsible sexual decision making is taking appropriate measures to prevent the transmission of STDs. Among the best preventative precautions are considering abstinence, avoiding penetration, avoiding multiple partners, avoiding abuse of alcohol or other drugs that impair judgment, knowing partners, getting screened for disease, and using condoms, vaginal pouches, or diaphragms. If infected, prompt medical treatment is essential, as is telling any potentially infected partners.

30. Spreading STDs or HIV carelessly or knowingly has legal implications.

Focus on Health Questions

In this section you will find the kinds of questions that you may have concerning your own health and sexuality. The page references indicate where in the text the answer is located; the exact place is marked with this logo: **FOH**

1. Haven't most STDs been brought under control? **480**

2. What are the symptoms of gonorrhea? **486–487**

3. How is gonorrhea treated? **487**

4. If a person has syphilis, what does the sore that appears actually look like? **488**

5. What are the other diseases that syphilis can cause? **489**

6. Is it true that chlamydia is a common STD among college students? **490**

7. Does chlamydia have any noticeable symptoms? **490**

8. What are the other types of infection of the penis and vulva or vagina? **490–492**

9. How would I know if I have the virus for genital herpes? **493**

10. Is there any cure or treatment for genital herpes? **494**

11. Is it true that HPV can cause cancer? **494**

12. Can I be vaccinated against the type of hepatitis that is spread by sexual contact? **495**

13. What are crabs? **496**

14. What symptoms would I get if I have been infected with HIV? **498**

15. What are the most common ways people are exposed to HIV? **499–500**

16. Can a pregnant woman give HIV to her baby? **499**

17. What tests are used to determine if I am infected with HIV, and how reliable are they? **501–502**

18. Should I get tested for HIV? **502**

19. Does everybody who is infected with HIV get AIDS and die? **503–504**

20. Is there a vaccination or a chemical I could take so that I won't have to worry about HIV? **504**

21. What medications are used to treat HIV disease? **506**

22. What are the best ways to decrease the risks of infection during sexual activity? **506–508**

Chapter 18

Sexual Dysfunctions and Their Treatment

Chapter Outline

When we first started having sex, he was far more interested in whether I had an orgasm than I was. The fact was, I almost never had an orgasm, but I still thought our sex life was great. As our relationship has grown, I now reach orgasm almost every time and would miss it more than I once did.

—statement written by a college student

Workers in the medical and helping professions—for example, physicians and other medical clinicians, psychologists, counselors, and social workers—have always been presented with the sexual concerns and complaints of their clients. Until the publication of *Human Sexual Inadequacy* by Masters and Johnson in 1970, these professionals rarely received any specialized training in dealing with sexual problems, and there were no clearly defined guidelines for treating such problems. People facing problems with sexual functioning typically were offered a vague blend of reassurance, moralizing, and poorly researched suggestions for living up to the performance standards of the culture.

■ Understanding Sexual Dysfunctions

The field of sex therapy has expanded rapidly, and the systematized treatment of sexual problems has become commonplace. Dysfunctional symptoms have labels that can be used in both professional and popular communication. Sex therapy was originally backed by only rudimentary research studies, which often were flawed in their methodologies. Gradually, more attention was given to the effectiveness of various treatment approaches. A number of new medical treatments were developed, leading to a gap between how physicians approached certain sexual problems and those therapeutic approaches employed by nonmedical sex therapists. It has become apparent that many of the newer medical treatments seem to be most effective when combined with some of the more traditional psychotherapeutic techniques (Tiefer, 2002).

FOH When Is a Dysfunction Really a Dysfunction?

Traditionally, men who experience difficulty controlling their ejaculations are said to have premature ejaculation. Women who never experience orgasm are said to be experiencing orgasmic disorder. However, the situation may be more complex than these handy labels suggest. Who is to define whether some phenomenon of sexual response is actually a dysfunction or a disorder? If the woman enjoys her sexual encounters without feeling any need for orgasm, should she be treated for a dysfunction? If the rapidly ejaculating man and his partner are perfectly comfortable with his pattern of response, should they be told they have a problem (Levin, 2004)?

Some definitions of sexual dysfunction include a statement about the condition causing sufficient "personal distress" for the individual to consider it a problem. However, some sexologists believe it is possible to be suffering from a dysfunction without realizing it or being personally upset by it (Althof, 2001; Basson et al., 2003; Meston, 2001). It has been proposed that individual sexual responsiveness may in part be defined by people's gender roles or by rigid definitions of what constitutes a "normal" sexual response cycle. We therefore must allow for individual differences in actual response and in how that response is interpreted (Bean, 2002; Tiefer, Hall, & Tavris, 2002).

Some statistics are available on the frequency of orgasm in women during shared sexual encounters. The most recent data in the United States from the National Health and Social Life Survey (NHSLS) found that among women ages 18 to 24, 8 percent never experience orgasm. This number decreases among older age groups, with only 2 percent of women ages 40 to 59 reporting complete lack of orgasm (Laumann, Gagnon, et al., 1994). Other studies confirm that there are some women who do not seem to experience orgasmic response in their sexual encounters. However, 20 to 33 percent of these women do not consider lack of orgasm a problem and indeed find their sexual interactions satisfying and happy (Heiman, 2002b). There is less research on lack of orgasm in men, although the NHSLS data indicate that only about 1 percent of men say they rarely or never reach orgasm (Laumann, Gagnon, et al., 1994).

Treatment of sexual problems cannot be reduced to a series of mechanical steps, although there are some specific skills that may help a great deal. Helping people with sexual dysfunctions requires sensitivity, creativity, openness to new directions, and well-honed expertise. An individual cannot attempt to change sexual functioning without also being prepared to examine sexual values, cultural and religious influences, the quality of relationships, and other highly subjective life issues (McCarthy, 2002; Ribner, 2004). However dysfunctions are defined, it is critical that those who treat them be given professional latitude to exercise judgment in helping their clients to not be misled by unrealistic societal standards.

Because we do not yet have reliable and valid norms for human sexual response patterns, we must use whatever statistical and clinical evidence is available in order to establish ranges of sexual responsiveness that we then can use to make practical judgments about sexual dysfunctions. The individual's

Real People

Elizabeth: Working on an Orgasmic Disorder

Since being in college, Elizabeth has had two lasting relationships that involved an active sexual component. For her, however, the sex has been somewhat disappointing because she has been unable to reach orgasm with either partner. With her first boyfriend, Larry, she was happy with their sexual relationship at the outset. Eventually, Larry began questioning her about her responses, and she realized that he thought she should be reaching orgasm, as he did when they had intercourse. Elizabeth was able to reach orgasm during masturbation but somehow could not do so during shared sexual activity. She had enjoyed the physical intimacy but had realized as well that she was not experiencing orgasm. It had not mattered much to her at first, but the more Larry pressed the issue, the more she began to feel as though she should make it a higher priority. The relationship ended before she had a chance to pursue the matter further with Larry.

When Elizabeth's relationship with Robert began, she felt determined to get more from their sexual contact. She even shared with Robert that she had not been able to reach orgasm during intercourse. He assured her that things would be different with him, but as it turned out they were not. This time, Robert seemed frustrated at not being able to bring

Elizabeth to orgasm no matter how hard he tried. She began to feel guilty about not giving him what he wanted, and he began to doubt whether she was really turned on by him. She insisted that she was, but Robert remained unconvinced. Her pattern of responsiveness with him was usually about the same: She would feel sexually aroused and enjoy the building of intensity of her sexual feelings. She would get close to the point of orgasm, but then the feeling seemed simply to dissipate. Sometimes, she would be able to build up the tension again for a while, but it always seemed to get interrupted eventually. Elizabeth and Robert usually would talk after sex, trying to figure out what had gone wrong. They sometimes would try new approaches the next time, but nothing seemed to work. Elizabeth is now feeling depressed about the whole thing, and Robert is thinking that perhaps it is time to end their relationship.

What are your opinions about Larry and Robert and the ways they have responded to Elizabeth's problem? If you could give either one of these men some advice, what would you say to them? What would you recommend to Elizabeth to help her overcome the problem?

own sexual history and feelings are particularly important in arriving at any diagnosis. Sexual health seems to be intimately tied to other levels of physical and mental well-being. There is emerging evidence that for many women sexual dysfunction is closely aligned with difficulties in their relationships, whereas male dysfunctions often are best studied from a medical point of view as well (Althof et al., 2005; Heiman, 2002b; Lloyd, 2005). The vast majority of people feel that enjoyable sexual relations add to a person's sense of well-being and quality of life.

Most cultures through the ages have established certain mythical standards and expectations regarding sexual performance. The performance standards for men have been fairly rigid, whereas those for women have been more vague and mysterious. When people's bodies do not function sexually as expected and desired, people often feel frustrated, inadequate, and unhappy (Nobre & Pinto-Gouveia, 2006). In a society

such as our own, which places a premium on being successful in sex, to "fail" in a sexual encounter is perceived as tantamount to being a failure at manhood or womanhood.

Mythical Performance Standards

Men have always been plagued by the standard that successful sex requires an erect penis. It is even assumed by most males that their partners cannot be expected to find sexual pleasure unless an erection is achieved and maintained. Closely allied to this standard is the standard of postponing ejaculation or orgasm. Because a penis tends to lose its erection following ejaculation, the longer a man can postpone ejaculation, the better a sexual performer he will be considered. A third standard might be stated best as the unquestioned assumption it has always been—that men reach orgasm without difficulty and find in this peak experience the ultimate pleasure of sex. It is now known that men do indeed have difficulty reaching orgasm at times.

Historically, the sexual performance standards for women have focused on issues of sexual attractiveness and availability rather than desire. More recent attitudes have encouraged women to take a more active role in sex. However, women also have become more bound by new standards of sexual performance. Women today are under pressure to become intensely aroused and ready for sexual contact, to reach orgasm without difficulty, and to have more than one orgasm during a single sexual encounter (Shifren & Ferrari, 2004).

These become the standards on which men and women pin their sexual hopes and by which they play out their roles in bed and judge their performances afterward. It is little wonder that so many people end up feeling inadequate, dissatisfied, and disillusioned by what is actually happening in their sex lives. When individuals experience some functional problem during sex or when their bodies fail to perform as expected and desired with some consistency, they are said to be experiencing sexual dysfunction. Today, more than ever before, such problems need not signal a lifetime of unfulfilled sexual needs. As this chapter will demonstrate, most sexual dysfunctions can be eased and corrected.

Cultural Influences

Every culture has its own definitions for what constitutes a "normal" sexual relationship, the meanings of sexual dysfunctions, and how dysfunctions should be treated. Cultural beliefs can have a strong impact on sexual functioning, and strongly held beliefs can make vulnerable individuals particularly susceptible to anxiety about their sexual performance. The roles of men and women in society and expectations about sexuality are crucial to how sexual functioning is perceived. In some Polynesian languages, there is no word for erection problems. It is simply assumed that when a male does not get an erection, he must not have wanted to have sex after all. Removing such performance pressures is what Western modes of sex therapy have struggled to achieve.

Cross-cultural research on sexual dysfunctions and levels of sexual satisfaction is very sparse. The Global Study of Sexual Attitudes and Behaviors is beginning to yield some interesting data, but it has encountered difficulty in persuading some people to participate, potentially causing volunteer bias. Using cluster analysis, the study has identified three distinct areas of the world based on measurements of sexual well-being, as defined by physical and emotional pleasure, satisfaction with sexual function, and the importance given to sex. One cluster is characterized as being relatively

gender-equal, meaning that the people value marriage and sex in which decisions and power are more equally shared. This cluster includes many European countries, Australia, Canada, and the United States. The levels of sexual satisfaction were highest in these countries (Laumann, Paik, et al., 2006).

In male-centered cultures, including many Mediterranean and Islamic nations, (e.g., Algeria, Egypt, Israel, Italy, and Turkey), one South American country (Brazil), and a few Asian countries (e.g., Korea and the Philippines), men tend to take a more dominant, patriarchal role, including initiating and controlling sex. In this cluster, researchers found middle levels of sexual satisfaction. A third cluster was found among East Asian countries such as China, Indonesia, Japan, Taiwan, and Thailand. These countries also were largely male-dominated but were additionally characterized by low levels of sexual satisfaction. The researchers found that despite cross-cultural variations in attitudes and beliefs, the best predictors of sexual well-being across the globe seem to be physical and mental health, sexual practices, and the quality of relationships. The clusters suggested that how sexuality fits within gender balances in a culture is also critical (Laumann, Nicolosi, et al., 2006; Laumann, Paik, et al., 2006; Parish et al., 2007).

Most cultures have their folk remedies to allay men's concerns about sexual adequacy. Women's sexual dysfunctions are rarely addressed by these techniques, further evidence of the performance pressures felt by men in most parts of the world and of the lack of significance assigned to female sexual enjoyment. In some parts of Africa, for example, impotent men drink potions made of bark or resort to ritual ceremonies. Hashish is used in Morocco by dysfunctional males, and nonorgasmic women are encouraged to take a younger lover or have a lesbian relationship. In Thailand, men drink the bile of a cobra and the blood of a monkey, mixed in a local liquor. In India, men apply an herb to the penis that is a potent urinary irritant. However, workshops for people in India have been focusing on the improvement of sexual functioning, and clinics have begun to treat Indian couples who have dysfunctions (Verma, Khaitan, & Singh, 1998). Wives of impotent men in the West Indies may serve them the penis of a turtle marinated in wine or a soup made of ox penis and testes. European men usually treat their dysfunctions with various alterations in their diet. In other parts of the world, seal testes and penises are consumed to cure erectile problems.

Traditional Chinese medicine has long made use of complicated herbal preparations and acupuncture, both of which are believed to bring the body's energies into balance and restore normal sexual functioning. Even with the advent of newer treatment techniques in China, the traditional ways remain very popular. Some

Chinese herbal plants—such as "ox-knee" root, used for several sexual difficulties, and milk vetch seeds, used to treat premature ejaculation—have become endangered because of their widespread use. Asian males are not always comfortable with traditional Western treatment methods, particularly methods that suggest masturbatory activity (Gupta, 1999).

Although treatment approaches may differ significantly among various societies, they seem to be highly effective within the particular population for whom they have been designed (Shokrollahi, Mirmohamadi, Mehrabi, & Babaei, 1999). The key is for therapists to be sensitive to the beliefs and practices of the culture. Sex therapy often involves practicing new behaviors through the use of masturbation. This can be a problem for some ultraorthodox Jewish couples, because ejaculation outside the vagina is considered to be against their beliefs except in very specific circumstances. These couples may require special permission from a rabbi in order to participate in some therapeutic interventions (Levine, 2004; Ribner & Rosenbaum, 2005).

What Labels Tell Us

Scientific communication demands a terminology, and each sexual difficulty has been given a general label. The most commonly accepted source of diagnostic categories is the *Diagnostic and Statistical Manual of Mental Disorders,* or *DSM-IV.* A new system for defining and classifying female sexual dysfunctions emerged from an international conference and subsequent analyses (Basson et al., 2001, 2003). It is important not to lose sight of the fact that such labels may have profound implications for the individual experiencing the dysfunction. Consider the term **impotence,** which conjures up images of failure and powerlessness, hardly reassuring concepts for a man with erectile difficulties. Certain modifying terms are employed in diagnosing and describing sexual dysfunctions. The term **lifelong dysfunction** means that the problem has been present since the onset of the person's sexual functioning. The term **acquired dysfunction** is used to describe a dysfunction that has developed after a period of normal function. (The terms *primary* and *secondary* once were used for *lifelong* and *acquired,* respectively.) Thus, a woman with lifelong orgasmic disorder has never been able to reach orgasm, whereas the woman with acquired orgasmic disorder is no longer able to be orgasmic but once was. Dysfunctions may also be *generalized* when the problem occurs in all of an individual's sexual encounters, or *situational,* meaning that it happens only under specific conditions, with certain types of stimulation, situations, or partners. Various new subtype descriptors have been proposed for female arousal dysfunctions; it appears that women's arousal is strongly influenced by the context within which a sexual interaction takes place (Basson, 2003). These are discussed later in this chapter.

> *What do you think is one of the most common complaints brought to sex therapists? Why do you think this?*

The Sexual Response Cycle

Chapter 4, "Human Sexual Arousal and Response," described various models for understanding the predictable sequence of physiological events that constitute the human sexual response cycle. The Masters and Johnson (1966) model includes four phases: excitement, plateau, orgasm, and resolution. A three-phase model (discussed on pages 85–87) is of greater value in understanding the relationship of sexual dysfunctions to sexual response (Kaplan, 1979). This model suggests that sexual response consists of three distinct components:

1. A *desire phase,* having to do with one's degree of interest in and desire for sexual gratification. Sexual desire is probably controlled by centers of the limbic system in the brain—centers that seem to activate as well as inhibit sexual desire. The desire phase precedes more profound physiological changes in the sex organs and throughout the body. This phase may be influenced by emotion, memory, context, and/or conditioning (Symonds, Boolell, & Quirk, 2005; Utian et al., 2005). Desire has been assumed to be an important component in the triggering of sexual arousal, although recent studies have shown that, in women, arousal often precedes the desire to participate in sex (Basson et al., 2003).

2. *Sexual arousal,* characterized by a buildup of blood in the genital areas that causes the typical signs of sexual arousal, such as penile and clitoral erection and lubrication of the vagina. This phase is accompanied by increased muscular tension and arousal throughout the body. It is controlled primarily by the parasympathetic division of the autonomic nervous system, which may be excited or inhibited in ways that are quite predictable for particular individuals (Janssen et al., 2002a, 2002b).

impotence (IM-puh-tense) difficulty achieving or maintaining erection of the penis.

lifelong dysfunction a difficulty with sexual functioning that has always existed for a particular person.

acquired dysfunction a difficulty with sexual functioning that develops after some period of normal sexual functioning.

Table 18.1   The Sexual Response Cycle and Sexual Dysfunctions

Desire Disorders	Arousal (Vasocongestive) Disorders	Orgasmic (Reversed Vasocongestive) Disorders
Normal asexuality: the individual who naturally has low levels of need for sexual gratification (not necessarily a dysfunction) Hypoactive sexual desire disorder (HSDD) Sexual aversion disorder: caused by anxiety and phobias related to sexual activity	Problems in achieving a suitable level of sexual arousal Male erectile disorder Female sexual arousal disorder: lack of vaginal lubrication, general sexual dysfunction	Problems in triggering orgasm, creating an inordinate orgasmic delay or a complete inability to reach orgasm Male orgasmic disorder Female orgasmic disorder Premature ejaculation: lack of ejaculatory control in men

Sexual Pain Disorders		
Spasm of outer vaginal musculature in women: vaginismus Dyspareunia Postejaculatory pain		

Source: *Diagnostic and Statistical Manual for Mental Disorders*, 4th ed. *(DSM-IV)*. Washington, D.C.: American Psychiatric Association, 1994.

3. *Orgasm,* which triggers the reversal of the genital blood flow and muscular relaxation. This phase is controlled mostly by the sympathetic division of the autonomic nervous system.

Things can go wrong in any of these phases of sexual response. Table 18.1 summarizes the relationship of various sexual dysfunctions to the three-phase model. Each is described in more detail in the sections that follow. Many people seem to experience dysfunctions in more than one phase of sexual response.

Incidence of Sexual Dysfunction

Studies on the incidence of sexual dysfunctions have yielded a wide range of estimates. The Global Study of Sexual Attitudes and Behaviors found that among adults ages 40 to 80 in 29 countries, the highest prevalence of sexual problems was found in East and Southeast Asia. Worldwide, lack of interest in sex and difficulty reaching orgasm were the most commonly reported problems among women, ranging in various countries from 26 to 43 percent and 18 to 41 percent, respectively. The most commonly reported dysfunction among men was early ejaculation, with nearly a third of men in Southeast Asia reporting the difficulty. Arousal problems constituted a common complaint as well, ranging from 13 to 28 percent in men and 16 to 38 percent in women (Laumann et al., 2005). The NHSLS researchers asked study participants in the United States if they had experienced particular sexual problems during the previous year for a period of several months or more. The findings are summarized in Figure 18.1.

The proportions of people reporting sexual disorders in the NHSLS varied from about 5 to 33 percent, with about one-third of women reporting they had lacked interest in sex for several months or more and nearly 30 percent of men reporting they ejaculate too rapidly. In general, women tended to report more sexual problems than men, except with regard to anxiety about performance and reaching orgasm too early. Ten percent of all the men reported having difficulty maintaining an erection, and 19 percent of the women reported having trouble with vaginal lubrication. For both sexes, these problems occurred with higher incidence in the older age groups, although that trend was somewhat more marked for men than it was for women. This has been confirmed by other studies as well, although given the natural slowing of sexual interest and responsiveness in older age, there is controversy over whether it should be considered dysfunctional (Bancroft, Loftus, & Long, 2003). Lack of pleasure during sex and inability to achieve orgasm have been reported by women about three times more often than by men. In correlating these data with other findings, researchers found that people who reported themselves as being unhappy were more likely to report one or more sexual problems than were people who reported being extremely or very happy. There was no way to determine a cause-and-effect relationship between these factors (Heiman, 2002b; Laumann et al., 2005; Rosen & Laumann, 2003).

Sexual Interest/Desire Disorders

Although most people can identify and describe inner feelings of needing or desiring sexual gratification, along with sexual fantasies, it is not yet well understood why the reported levels of interest in sex vary so much among individuals, along with the frequency with which

FIGURE 18.1 ***Sexual Dysfunction, by Gender***

The percentage of people reporting sexual problems they experienced over several months or more during the previous year in the National Health and Social Life Survey.

Source: From *The Social Organization of Sexuality,* by Edward O. Laumann et al., p. 369. Copyright © 1994 by Edward O. Laumann, Robert T. Michael, CSG Enterprises, Inc., and Stuart Michaels. Reprinted by permission of The University of Chicago Press.

they choose to have sex. We do know, however, that these differences in sexual interest and desire, whatever their causes, can become an important concern in people's lives. A discrepancy in level of sexual desire between two partners is a common complaint brought to sex therapists (Weeks & Gambescia, 2002).

It might be that low levels of sexual desire result from lack of activity in the brain centers that control the sexual "appetite," and this may in turn affect the levels of hormones that mitigate sexual desire (Giargiari, Mahaffey, Craighead, & Hutchison, 2005; Janssen et al., 2002a, 2002b). Sexual boredom may play a role. Sexual desire disorders seem to be more common in couples where there is less experimentation with sexual behaviors and a low level of pleasure associated with such experimentation. Diagnosing sexual desire disorders is somewhat difficult, because subjective judgments must be made about what is a "normal" human sexual appetite and how much distress the perceived lack of desire is creating. Although there is no absolute scale of sexual desire, there are measurable discrepancies between people's sexual styles and interests (Bancroft, Graham, & McCord, 2001).

It has become clear that understanding and describing sexual "desire" in women is a complicated task and that women's motivations for sex may differ depending on whether the relationship is new or of longer duration. In newly established relationships, sexual desire may be triggered by the sense of novelty, uncertainty, and even secrecy. In longer-term relationships, the sexual motivations may be extremely varied—and even somewhat nonsexual, including the wish to experience tenderness and appreciation or to have one's desirability confirmed by the partner. Sometimes women participate in sex in order to avoid angering or disappointing a partner. Therefore, it has been suggested that we use the term *interest,* more of a cognitive function, along with the more emotional assumptions of *desire.* It has also been recommended that when clinicians diagnose these problems, they should include a careful description of the contexts and relationship dynamics that accompany them (Basson et al., 2003).

Some people seem to have very infrequent interest in or desire for sex and are not bothered by this. Even in a sex-saturated society, it is possible to maintain feelings of well-being and self-worth with minimal levels of sexual interest. It is also possible for some people to choose a celibate or sexually inactive lifestyle that represents a mature, responsible approach to life and is manifested by a suppressed sexual desire, or at least a suppressed expression of

the desire. This nonpathological way of life has been called **normal asexuality** and need not be considered a problem or dysfunction.

Sometimes, however, low sexual desire is viewed as a problem, and desire phase complaints are being brought to therapy clinics in increasing numbers. As a dysfunction, this so-called **hypoactive sexual desire disorder (HSDD)** may be characterized by a loss of attraction to formerly exciting stimuli and a lack of pleasure even in direct stimulation of the sex organs. It may also result from a failure of sexual desire to develop during those years when it typically takes form. Dysfunctional individuals may not be particularly aroused by seeing attractive people or fantasizing about sex, and they rarely seek sexual activity. They may still function normally when sexual stimulation is permitted, but the physical pleasure they derive from it is limited and fleeting (Basson et al., 2001; Clayton et al., 2006; Heiman, 2002b).

There are some gender differences in the occurrence of hypoactive sexual desire. Men with HSDD tend to be older than women; the average age for men with HSDD is 50, and the average age for women is 33. Women with hypoactive sexual desire are more likely than men to report other forms of psychological distress, such as anxiety, depression, and hostility, and they also complain of higher levels of life stress. Women are more likely to have had another sexual dysfunction (such as arousal disorder) of long-standing duration, whereas men are more likely to have had another sexual dysfunction (such as erectile disorder) for only a short period before experiencing HSDD. For women, especially, HSDD often is rooted in intimacy difficulties within a relationship that need to be resolved before sexual interactions can improve or become more frequent (Basson, 2002b; Nobre, Pinto-Gouveia, & Gomes, 2006).

Sexual aversion disorder, characterized by some level of fear or disgust about sex and avoidance of sexual activity, is generated by anxieties and phobias about sexual contact (see Figure 18.2). Some men and

FIGURE 18.2 *Sexual Aversion Disorder*

An aversion to or fear of sexual intimacy is considered one form of sexual dysfunction. A real or imagined physical problem or psychological stress might cause someone to sabotage an otherwise satisfactory relationship in order to avoid sexual contact.

women develop fearful or avoidant reactions toward sex or its possible consequences and eventually become exaggeratedly aversive toward becoming sexually involved. These reactions can stem from psychological stress resulting from an inhibiting or punitive upbringing, a rigidly religious background, health concerns, or a history of physical and/or sexual abuse. Often such individuals become involved in close relationships and are successful in making themselves attractive to others. As the levels of intimacy and commitment deepen, however, there usually comes a point where they become fearful about sex. They then may find ways to sabotage the relationship or find fault with their partner so that they will not feel obligated to go any further with sex. They may, for example, become increasingly irritable or critical so that arguments constantly develop. Women are somewhat more likely to have aversive reactions to sexual activity than are men, with more reports of sexual distress and avoidance, more fear of sexual intercourse, and greater concerns about infections and unintended pregnancy (Basson et al., 2003; Heiman, 2002b).

It often is difficult for therapists to distinguish HSDD or sexual aversion from problems with arousal because individuals with HSDD and sexual aversions

HOW ABOUT A BAN ON NO-SEX MARRIAGES?

Source: Mike Peters EDTCTN. Copyright © King Features/Syndicate.

normal asexuality an absence or low level of sexual desire, considered normal for a particular person.

hypoactive sexual desire disorder (HSDD) loss of interest and pleasure in what formerly were arousing sexual stimuli.

sexual aversion disorder avoidance of or exaggerated fears toward forms of sexual expression.

may also experience trouble becoming sexually aroused. It is up to the sex therapist to seek specific information about a particular person's level of sexual desire in order to make valid judgments about a proper course of treatment (Heiman, 2002b; Meston, 2003).

Arousal Disorders

Whenever something interferes with blood flow into the sex organs, the human body fails to exhibit the preliminary signs of sexual arousal. In men, the penis fails to become erect or loses some of its erection. This has traditionally been called impotence but is now diagnosed as **male erectile disorder (ED).** In women, lack of arousal is characterized by the vagina remaining dry and tight and by their not experiencing the sensations of tingling or throbbing typical of arousal. The term **female sexual arousal disorder** is now the most widely accepted among professionals for this disorder, although two subtypes have been proposed. One subtype is referred to as *subjective sexual arousal disorder* and is applied to situations in which a woman's genitals seem to be lubricating normally, but the woman fails to realize or appreciate the fact that her genitals are responding. From a subjective viewpoint, she does not experience arousal. The other proposed subtype is called *genital sexual arousal disorder* and refers specifically to a lack of physiological response in the clitoris and vagina, even though the woman may report feeling subjectively aroused. This type of arousal dysfunction seems more typically associated with nerve damage, estrogen deficiency, or bodily changes following menopause. Sometimes, these two subtypes occur together, and any type of sexual stimulation fails to create a sense of sexual desire or interest (Basson et al., 2003). It may be that the nerve endings in women with arousal disorder are not as sensitive as they are in other women (Frohlich & Meston, 2005b).

Because the control mechanisms in the brain and nervous system for the arousal phase of sexual response are different from those that control orgasm, it is possible—though unusual—for people who show few characteristics of arousal to be orgasmic. A man with erectile disorder may achieve orgasm, ejaculating with a flaccid (nonerect) penis. Likewise, some women who do not manifest the usual signs of sexual arousal, such as vaginal lubrication and clitoral erection, may still have an orgasmic response.

FOH Erectile Disorder in Men

Not only can thoughts, fantasies, and sensory stimuli trigger erection of the penis, but they can inhibit it as well. Most men will experience some instances of erectile difficulty during their lifetime, typically as a re-

sult of fatigue, excessive consumption of alcohol, or simply not being in the mood for sex. Aging is a particular risk factor, and ED often begins in the fifties or sixties (Rowland, Incrocci, and Slob, 2005). Depression is often associated with ED (Strand et al., 2002). ED can affect men in any age bracket, but among younger men it tends to be linked more to relational and psychological stress and to smoking tobacco. Heavy smoking has been identified as a significant factor in ED among younger men (Natali et al., 2005, Shiri et al., 2005; Swindle et al., 2004). Younger men and their sexual partners have more difficulty adjusting to the problem than do older men and their partners (Chevret et al., 2004a, 2004b; Moore et al., 2003).

There seem to be some identifiable differences between problems with *achieving* a suitable erection at the beginning of sexual stimulation and problems with *maintaining* an erection during sustained sexual activity. Although psychological stress can interfere with erection at either stage, men who have trouble achieving an erection in the first place are more likely to have an underlying physical, organic disturbance. These include vascular problems, diabetes and metabolic syndrome, and obesity. Men who lose an erection during sexual activity are more likely to have psychological and relational stressors (Corona et al., 2005; Esposito & Giugliano, 2005; Koskimaki et al., 2005, Ponholzer, Temml, Rauchenwald, & Madersbacher, 2006). It is not uncommon for erection to take place easily during masturbation but be lost during shared activities such as intercourse (Chakrabarti, Chopra, & Sinha, 2002).

Several approaches are used to determine whether erectile disorder may have physical causes. One simple and reliable method is measuring *nocturnal penile tumescence (NPT),* the number of times the man experiences erection while he is asleep. Normally, the penis becomes erect numerous times during a typical sleep cycle. If nocturnal erection is continuing normally, there is probably no organic cause for erectile difficulties. The man may be given a device that is attached to the penis at bedtime and records spontaneous erections during the night. However, there are some indications that psychological stress may sometimes disrupt NPT, and there is a small chance that the cause of the erectile disorder might be misdiagnosed as physical when it is actually psychological. Whenever potential organic conditions exist as a cause of erectile disorder, a thorough medical history should be

male erectile disorder (ED) difficulty achieving or maintaining penile erection (impotence).

female sexual arousal disorder difficulty for a woman in achieving sexual arousal.

FIGURE 18.3 *Erectile Disorder*

Men in our society place great emphasis on their penises and a performance standard that may not be realistic for all people. Mental attitude, fatigue, alcohol, or organic problems can all affect a man's ability to have an erection. Failure to have an erection can lead to depression and further erectile problems.

taken and some tests administered that, for example, can determine whether blood flow to the penis has been hampered by damage to the blood vessels (Corona et al., 2005; Heiman, 2002b).

Men in our culture place a great deal of importance on their penis and often consider erection to be one of the trappings of masculinity. They typically have adopted the unwarranted performance standard that good sex requires an erect penis. Therefore, experiencing erectile dysfunction can be devastatingly embarrassing and frightening for most men (see Figure 18.3). They may feel as if they are not whole men.

It is not unusual for men to experience trouble having an erection after having had some other sexual disorder for a period of time. If, for example, a man continually has trouble reaching orgasm or constantly believes he is disappointing a partner by ejaculating too rapidly, he may begin to feel frustrated and discouraged. He may eventually feel anxiety about any sexual involvement, and his body may fail to become aroused (Nobre, Pinto-Gouveia, & Gomes, 2006).

Sexual Arousal Disorders in Women

Women have traditionally experienced less pressure to prove their womanhood by being able to become sexually aroused, primarily because they are at least physically capable of participating in sexual activity even without arousal. With increased attention being given to female sexual response in recent times, some women have felt the need to fake arousal and orgasm in order to meet performance standards. Some women

with sexual arousal disorder report that they still enjoy the physical intimacy of sexual contact. More often, unresponsive women eventually come to think of sex as something to be endured. They become trapped between their lack of physical arousal and their desire to live up to social standards of eroticism. Some experts claim that this negative reaction is caused by the societal assumption that everyone should become sexually aroused; these experts believe that lack of arousal should be considered legitimate and nonpathological (Basson et al., 2003: Everaerd & Both, 2001).

A newly identified dysfunction seems to belong at the other end of the spectrum of arousal disorders. Rather than being frustrated by lack of sexual arousal, these women experience sensations of sexual arousal in the absence of any particular sexual interest or desire. They feel tingling, pulsating, and throbbing in the vulvovaginal area much of the time that does not seem to be relieved by orgasm. Most women find the sensations unpleasant, especially since they may persist for hours or even days. Although almost no research on this condition has been done, Internet communications seem to indicate that it is not as rare as once was assumed. Further study is needed (Basson et al., 2003).

Vaginismus and the Sexual Pain Disorders

A woman suffering from **vaginismus** may occasionally enjoy sexual arousal and be capable of orgasms with clitoral stimulation. However, when an attempt is made to introduce a penis or other object into the vagina, the woman experiences anticipatory anxiety, and some pelvic muscles may contract reflexively (see Figure 18.4). It has traditionally been stated that this is due to a spasm of the outer vaginal musculature, although such a spasm has never been scientifically documented. In any case, the tension of vaginismus makes intromission nearly impossible or painfully difficult. Some women with this dysfunction seem to be fearful about sexual intercourse or other forms of vaginal penetration, and they have misconceptions about the delicacy of the vaginal lining, believing that it can be easily injured. Some women with vaginismus are overly dependent on others or feel personally incompetent, although in general they do not seem to show unusually high levels of psychological distress (Basson et al., 2003; Payne et al., 2005; Reissing et al., 2004).

vaginismus (vadg-ih-NISS-muss) involuntary contraction of the outer vaginal musculature when vaginal penetration is attempted.

A   B

FIGURE 18.4 *Vaginismus*

Vaginismus involves constriction of the outer vaginal muscles, prohibiting intercourse. Vaginismus might be caused by ignorance of bodily functions or might be considered a physical manifestation of a psychological fear. The drawing on the left (**A**) illustrates the relaxed vagina, and the drawing on the right (**B**) illustrates vaginismus.

Vaginismus is the major cause of unconsummated marriages (marriages in which sexual intercourse has not taken place). Because it interferes with sexual intercourse so blatantly, it is one of the sexual dysfunctions for which heterosexual couples are more likely to seek treatment (Jeng et al., 2006; Koehler, 2002). Some heterosexual couples, however, adopt alternative methods of sexual expression that are mutually pleasurable without intercourse. There are even documented cases of pregnancy resulting from semen being deposited near the vagina of women with vaginismus, without coitus actually having taken place. This should serve as a further warning to those who rely on withdrawal as a birth control method.

It is not unusual for women who experience vaginismus to have had an unpleasant or forced early sexual experience. For example, those who have not been told that first intercourse may generate some pain and bleeding if a hymen is present may have a traumatic experience or may assume that it will be more painful than it is in actuality (Koehler, 2002). Vaginismus is now considered to be one of the *sexual pain disorders*. The term used for pain that is experienced persistently during sexual intercourse is **dyspareunia.** Some research suggests that women with dyspareunia may have some level of aversion and anxiety concerning intercourse. They also may have some physiological condition, including dryness of the vagina caused by antihistamines or other drugs, infection of the clitoris or vulval area, injury or irritation in the vagina, or tumors of the internal reproductive organs. Such negative stimuli can easily establish a fear of sex that is expressed through contractions of the vaginal musculature. However, it has also been suggested that these problems should not be considered sexual dysfunctions at all but rather *genital pain disorders* that may interfere with sex. In this model, the source of the pain

would be explored medically before any concerns about sexual function are addressed. There is evidence that women with dyspareunia often can experience genital sexual arousal even though they may not be as aware of it subjectively (Binik, 2005; Binik et al., 2002; Brauer, Laan, & Kuile, 2006; Graziottin & Brotto, 2004).

Gay men who participate in anal intercourse sometimes experience pain that inhibits their sexual enjoyment. It appears that this **anodyspareunia** is associated with the depth of anal penetration and rate of thrusting and with anxiety or embarrassment about the sexual activity. Lack of adequate lubrication often seems to play a role in generating the problem. As with vaginismus, men with anodyspareunia may have experienced the problem all their lives, have significant anxiety about it, and avoid being the receptive partner in sex for long periods of time as a result. As a way of coping, half of the affected men in one study restricted their anal sexual activities to being the insertive partner (Damon & Rosser, 2005).

Orgasmic Disorder

Lifelong orgasmic disorder, in which an individual has never been able to achieve an orgasm, is far more common in females than in males. It has been estimated that from 5 to 20 percent of women are unable to reach orgasm through any form of stimulation (Heiman, 2002b). However, it is essential when diagnosing an orgasmic problem to determine whether the individual actually has become sexually aroused and

dyspareunia recurrent or persistent genital pain related to sexual activity.

anodyspareunia pain associated with anal intercourse.

whether adequate stimulation has been maintained. Some people, particularly women, experience lack of arousal and therefore are not likely to achieve orgasm (Basson et al., 2003). There are very few documented cases of men who have never been able to reach orgasm even through masturbation. On the other hand, NHSLS data showed that between 5 and 14 percent of men reported some level of difficulty in reaching orgasm, at least in particular situations (Heiman, 2002b; Laumann, Gagnon, et al., 1994).

There has been some speculation about why men experience this orgasmic disorder. One theory is that these men are so focused on their partners' pleasure or have so many conflicting feelings about sexual pleasure that they have what might be called a "numb" erection. In other words, even though they have no difficulty with erection, they do not experience many of the subjective sensations of sexual arousal and stimulation associated with orgasm. It surely is true that many of the positive sensations of orgasm have psychological components as well as physical ones (Mah & Binik, 2005).

Women, however, generally have not been given as much social permission as men to develop and enjoy their sexual responsiveness. As a result, more women experience orgasmic disorder, with a far greater range of variability than in men. Orgasmic disorder is among the most common problems women bring to therapists. It has been demonstrated that women with orgasmic disorder tend to have more negative attitudes toward sex, greater discomfort in communicating about sex, and higher levels of guilt over sexual matters. For women, sexual intercourse holds many different and complex meanings, some of which seem to inhibit orgasm (Birnbaum, 2003; Meston et al., 2005). Women in societies with fewer prohibitions on female sexual involvement and where sexual expression is permitted and even encouraged are less likely to experience orgasmic inhibition.

Before reading further, can you think of some reasons why premature ejaculation might occur?

FOH Premature Ejaculation: Lack of Ejaculatory Control

About one-quarter to one-third of men surveyed in various studies have indicated that they have problems with reaching orgasm too quickly (Byers & Grenier, 2003; Laumann et al., 2005). Yet it would not be scientifically acceptable to assume that a substantial number of those men were dysfunctional and were experiencing what is termed **premature ejaculation (PE),** also called rapid ejaculation (RE). As with much sexual behavior, the line between normal function and dysfunction

is not absolute. It may be largely culturally determined. For example, in East Bay, Melanesia, a man who took more than 30 seconds to ejaculate after intromission would assume he had a problem.

Clinical workers in the United States have variously defined premature ejaculation as orgasm occurring within a certain number of minutes following intromission or orgasm occurring prior to the man's accomplishing anywhere from 8 to 15 pelvic thrusts—arbitrary diagnoses, to be sure. Masters and Johnson (1970), acknowledging the arbitrary nature of their statement, chose to label a heterosexual man a premature ejaculator if he reached orgasm prior to his partner in 50 percent or more of their coital experiences. This definition presumes that the partner is orgasmic within a reasonable length of time. More recently, a male has been considered dysfunctional if he persistently and recurrently ejaculates too rapidly for his own or his partner's sexual enjoyment, usually with minimal sexual stimulation, and is so consistently unable to exert ejaculatory control that one or both of them consider it a problem. More complex definitions have been proposed that consider a variety of factors about the man's life and state of health (Rowland, Cooper, & Schneider, 2001).

There has been speculation that men who ejaculate rapidly might have a greater degree of penile sensitivity than other men, but research has not supported that conclusion. It has also been proposed that some men who ejaculate quickly may have a hypersensitivity of the sympathetic nervous system that renders it difficult for them to be aware of the sense of ejaculatory inevitability that typically alerts males that they are about to reach orgasm. Under laboratory conditions involving manual stimulation by a female laboratory worker or by a vibrator affixed to the underside of the penis, most men seem to ejaculate within a relatively brief period of time; men who have previously self-reported premature ejaculation seem to take less time to ejaculate than do males used as controls. Some complaints about premature ejaculation seem to rest in exaggerated expectations about how long a sexual experience should actually last, and affected men are more critical about their performance than their partners tend to be (Byers & Grenier, 2003).

Premature ejaculation may not be related to timing as much as it is to a lack of voluntary control over the ejaculatory reflex. This is not surprising when we consider some typical ways males learn about their sexual responses. Most boys have begun masturbating with

premature ejaculation difficulty that some men experience in controlling the ejaculatory reflex, resulting in rapid ejaculation.

Real People

Rudy: Struggling with Rapid Ejaculation

Rudolph's friends call him Rudy, and he is usually the life of the party. He is also considered to be a real player with women, but not one who is at all ready to settle down. He is an outstanding soccer player and has been thinking of becoming a coach someday.

In fact, Rudy does not believe that he has been very successful with women at all, primarily because during his sexual encounters he finds it very difficult to postpone orgasm for long. It is not unusual for him to ejaculate almost immediately upon penetration. He finds this frustrating and embarrassing. He has tried several remedies in an attempt to slow down his sexual responses. For a while, he tried thinking negative thoughts and conjuring up foul images, hoping it would distract him. He has tried biting the inside of his mouth or pinching his arm to create physical discomfort. Neither of these approaches proved effective. Seeing some anesthetic cream advertised to delay ejaculation, he sent for a

supply. Although the cream made the head of his penis feel somewhat numb, it did nothing to slow down his orgasm.

Recently, Rudy has found himself wanting to avoid sex with women altogether because the result is so discouraging. It almost doesn't seem worth it, and he is afraid that women may be talking about his "poor performance" among themselves. He has heard some of his male friends joke about having similar problems, but they sound more like one-time events rather than continuing difficulties. He is not sure what to do and can't imagine how a marital relationship will ever work for him.

Given what you have learned in this chapter, what would you recommend to Rudy? Does he have to be "stuck" with this sexual dysfunction, or can he do something about it? What would you do if you or your partner were experiencing this problem?

some regularity by age 15, yet they usually have done so with little accurate sex information and a measure of guilt. Therefore, they may develop a pattern of stimulating themselves relatively rapidly, reaching orgasm in a hurry. For some men, this rapid response might become habitual. The intense arousal typical of most males' first shared sexual experiences leads them to ejaculate quickly in these instances.

The end result of this conditioning can be a linear approach to their own sexual responsiveness. Some men progress from the absence of arousal through the stages of sexual excitement and directly to orgasm, with little hesitation or modulation along the way. There is also evidence that anxiety plays a role in initiating rapid ejaculatory response, and physiological propensities may well be involved. Men may feel disappointed and frustrated by their lack of control, but because they are still experiencing the pleasure of orgasm they may not be urgently motivated to seek help with the problem. Often it is their partners, who are just building their own sexual arousal when these men ejaculate, who suffer the most. Continuing problems with premature ejaculation in a sexual partnership can generate conflict and further sexual dysfunction between the two people (Byers & Grenier, 2003; Heiman, 2002b; Symonds et al., 2003). Partners who become

angry and disillusioned due to continuing patterns of premature ejaculation in the other partner may themselves begin to experience loss of interest in and arousal for sex.

Postejaculatory Pain

Postejaculatory pain is a type of male dyspareunia, or recurrent painful sex, that results from a muscle spasm problem that can occur either during ejaculation or immediately after. This is a relatively rare problem, probably not affecting more than 3 percent of men on a consistent basis (Simons & Carey, 2001). The disorder apparently is caused by involuntary contraction of the ejaculatory musculature and some other associated muscles. Occasionally, the cremasteric muscles that help control suspension of the testes in the scrotum are also involved. The result is intense pain following ejaculation. It usually subsides within a few minutes, but it can last longer.

Men who experience postejaculatory pain often develop a pattern of general sexual avoidance. Because their sexual activities end unpleasantly and uncomfortably, they may begin developing problems with erection or orgasm. Although the immediate cause of the pain is muscular spasm, there seem to be deeper psychological roots to the disorder. Many men who experience postejaculatory pain harbor guilt about sexual pleasure, are ambivalent about their relationships, and hold on to repressed anger and resentment. Such inner conflict can add to concerns about experiencing pain and create a continuing cycle of pain associated with ejaculation (Heiman, 2002b).

■ Causes of Sexual Dysfunctions

The causes of any one person's sexual problems may be quite complex and may involve overlapping physical, emotional, and relational components. Our understanding of the causes of functional sexual problems is based far more on clinical observations than on controlled research studies. Nevertheless, some generalizations can be drawn from the information that has been accumulated over the years.

1. Sexual dysfunctions are most often caused by multiple factors. In deciding how to treat a sexual dysfunction, a sex therapist or physician must consider the range of factors that may be involved.
2. Some factors that cause sexual dysfunctions are of a *predisposing nature,* meaning that they are biological characteristics or prior life experiences that establish some fundamental vulnerabilities for eventual sexual disorders. A disease such as diabetes or a history of childhood sexual abuse may predispose an individual to a sexual dysfunction. *Precipitating factors,* such as alcoholism or job stress, may then trigger it. Finally, *maintaining factors,* such as continuing relational problems, perpetuate the sexual dysfunction over time.
3. Causes of sexual dysfunctions may also be classified into several frames of reference. They may be inherently *biological* or *medical,* resulting from organic disturbances of the sexual response cycle. Dysfunctions often are *substance-induced,* precipitated either by the abuse of alcohol or drugs or by the side effects of prescription medications. They may be *psychological,* meaning that the processes of the mind, such as the stresses of performance pressure, generate the disorder, or they may stem from a person's *social context,* growing out of relational tensions and poor communication.

Investigating Medical Causes

Prior to any treatment for a sexual dysfunction, any potential organic cause for the problem, such as an illness or anatomical defect, should be investigated. This may require an examination by a physician, including relevant laboratory testing. In most large clinics where sexual dysfunctions are treated, physical examinations are considered routine procedure. Many nonmedical sex therapists, especially those working in private practice, require a physical examination by a physician only when a client's symptoms raise some suspicion of a possible organic disorder. In such cases, referral should be made to a physician who possesses specialized knowledge.

Although dysfunctions such as premature ejaculation rarely seem to be rooted in illnesses per se, the possibility of organic causes exists. Usually, only if the onset of ejaculatory control problems is abrupt, following a long period of good functioning, are various potential neurological or urological disorders investigated. The same might be said for vaginismus. It rarely has a *direct* organic cause; however, there are many diseases that can cause genital pain during sex, and pain often is the original stimulus that plays a part in the development of vaginismus. In treating vaginismus, it must be determined whether any painful conditions are present that could further aggravate the muscular contractions of the vagina (Graziottin & Brotto, 2004; Pukall, Binik, & Khalife, 2004).

Sexual desire and arousal seem to be more susceptible to interference by physical problems. Any sort of illness characterized by general malaise, fever, or exhaustion can cause desire disorders, male erectile disorder, or female sexual arousal disorder. Because rather complex circulatory and neurological mechanisms are involved in arousal, any medical condition that interferes with these mechanisms will inhibit arousal. Spinal cord injury and blocked or diseased arteries leading to the genitals are common causes of arousal dysfunctions. Diabetes often leads to the development of conditions that affect arousal, including impaired erection of the penis and vaginal dryness (Erol et al., 2002). High blood pressure may be implicated in desire and arousal difficulties in both sexes, although more study is needed to understand the potential mechanisms involved (Barr et al., 2003; Burchardt et al., 2002).

Any painful condition in the body can interfere with the sexual response cycle, including heart conditions, lower back pain, sexually transmitted disease (STD) or other infection, and specific genital conditions such as cysts. Painful adhesions around the clitoris, for example, may make it difficult for a woman to reach orgasm (Munarriz et al., 2002; Quek et al., 2003). Male orgasmic disorder has few organic causes, although general systemic illness can interfere with orgasmic capacity.

In the past few decades, there has been some evidence that the pubococcygeus (PC) muscle, deep in the pelvis, must have good tone to permit a full orgasmic experience, particularly in women. Exercises to strengthen the PC muscle have been developed, often called Kegel exercises after the man who first suggested their use. He and subsequent researchers have claimed that women who strengthen this muscle are more able to build voluntarily the muscular tension that helps trigger orgasm. Some books on male sexuality have suggested that men's orgasmic responses can be heightened by strengthening the PC muscle as well.

Multiple sclerosis, Parkinson's disease and other neurological disorders, endocrine gland diseases, lung disease, kidney disorders, AIDS, and cancer are a few of the other illnesses that can be predisposing factors for sexual dysfunctions (Bronner et al., 2004; Schover et al., 2004; Siegel, Schrimshaw, & Lekas, 2006; Sipski, 2002; Warkentin, Gray, & Wassersug, 2006). Sometimes it is the individual's psychological reaction to a disease that actually precipitates the dysfunction. For example, those who have suffered a heart attack may be fearful of the exertion connected with sexual activity. Some research has gone into the determination of the limits of activity for various types of cardiac diseases so that patients may be given guidelines about exertion during sex. It has also been found that sexual dysfunction often occurs in men with kidney disease who have to undergo regular dialysis treatment. ED traditionally was thought to be rooted mostly in psychological causes. Recent work has shown, however, that many men who have problems with erection may have an underlying physical problem that can be compounded by psychological stress and worry (Baldwin, Ginsberg, & Harkaway, 2003; Barsky, Friedman, & Rosen, 2006). It is simplistic to view psychological and physical causes as mutually exclusive. Often, it is a combination of the two that leads to problems with erection. Table 18.2 summarizes some of the possible sexual consequences of various physical conditions that can lead to sexual dysfunctions.

Table 18.2 — Organic Conditions That Can Cause Sexual Dysfunctions

Sexual Dysfunction	Potential Organic Causes
Hypoactive sexual desire disorder	Diseases, abnormalities, or tumors of the pituitary gland Diseases of the immune system Infections, abnormalities, or tumors of the testes or ovaries Chronic kidney or liver disease, adrenal insufficiency, diabetes, hypothyroidism, Parkinson's disease, certain types of epilepsy, and strokes Diseases associated with chronic pain, debility, anxiety, or depression
Male erectile disorder	Congenital abnormality of or later injury to penis Multiple sclerosis or spinal cord injury Arteriosclerosis or blockage of blood vessels in penis Endocrine gland disease, especially if there is a testosterone deficiency Diabetes (probably impairs circulatory and neurological mechanisms of erection)
Female sexual arousal disorder	Estrogen deficiency, causing lack of vaginal lubrication Injury or disease of the central nervous system Multiple sclerosis, amyotrophic lateral sclerosis, alcoholic neuropathy Endocrine gland insufficiency, especially thyroid, adrenals, or pituitary Diabetes
Vaginismus	Factors that may cause pain or discomfort, such as previous surgery or vulvovaginal infection Endometriosis Rigid hymen or hymenal tags
Premature ejaculation	No documented organic causes, except the anxiety that may accompany various physical complaints
Female orgasmic disorder	Severe malnutrition, vitamin deficiencies Disease or injury of the spinal cord Diabetes Deficiency of thyroid, adrenals, or pituitary
Male orgasmic disorder	Injury to nervous system Parkinson's disease, multiple sclerosis, diabetes, alcoholism, uremia
Postejaculatory pain	Prostate infection or enlargement Infections of the epididymis or vas deferens Urethritis Other diseases of the penis

Sources: Data from H. S. Kaplan, *The Evaluation of Sexual Disorders,* New York: Brunner/Mazel, 1983; J. P. Wincze and M. P. Carey, *Sexual Dysfunction: A Guide for Assessment and Treatment,* New York: Guilford Press, 1991; N. McConaghy, *Sexual Behavior: Problems and Management,* New York: Plenum Press, 1993; and *Diagnostic and Statistical Manual (DSM-IV),* Washington, D.C.: American Psychiatric Association, 1994.

FOH Alcohol, Drugs, and Medications

Many people experience their first sexual arousal problems after having drunk too much alcohol. Like other depressant drugs, such as barbiturates and narcotics, alcohol may at first lower inhibitions and cause people to feel an increased sexual desire. As concentration of the drug builds in the body, however, the physiological responses of sexual arousal are inhibited, leading to poor sexual performance. Some people believe that alcohol relieves sexual dysfunctions and even use it for self-treatment when, in fact, it actually is more likely to cause the dysfunctions or make them worse (George & Stoner, 2001). Men who are heavy smokers are also about 50 percent more likely to experience ED than are nonsmokers (Natali et al., 2005; Shiri et al., 2005).

Many mood-altering or hallucinogenic drugs seem to have unpredictable effects on sexual functioning. Some—such as marijuana, LSD, and cocaine—are often reported to enhance sexual experiences when taken in highly erotic situations with positive expectations. However, the same drugs also are capable of compounding negative moods and may even magnify preexisting sexual disorders (see Figure 18.5). The placebo effect, generation of the drug's perceived effect by the consumer's expectations, undoubtedly plays a major role here. In addition, drugs such as marijuana and cocaine may at first enhance sexual satisfaction but with chronic use begin to interfere with sexual responsiveness and pleasure. Use of anabolic steroids for muscle building has been found

to be associated with increased erectile problems for males (Johnson, Phelps, & Cottler, 2004).

Many chemical substances affect people's sex FOH lives, either by producing changes in the level of interest in sex, by diminishing general erotic pleasure, or by altering the reactions of the genitals. Prescribed medications can exert profound influences over sexual desire and functioning and may be useful in treating serious dysfunctions. Antidepressant medications frequently cause a reduction in sexual desire, arousal, or orgasmic capability, although some new classes of antidepressant drugs may avoid the sexual side effects (Ashton, Mahmood, & Iqbal, 2005; Bolton, Sareen, & Reiss, 2006; Frohlich & Meston, 2005a). Some men who take phenothiazine tranquilizers are alarmed to find that they no longer experience ejaculation of semen at the time of orgasm. Other antipsychotic drugs may interfere with arousal and the triggering of orgasmic responses (Knegtering et al., 2006). The adverse sexual effects are usually reversed with a change in dosage or discontinuation of the drug. Some medications used to treat high blood pressure can cause arousal disorders. Stimulant drugs, such as amphetamines, sometimes enhance sexual awareness in small dosages but interfere with sexual responsiveness when consumed in larger quantities. Anti-ulcer medications and certain drugs for migraine headaches have been associated with disorders of hypoactive sexual desire and arousal.

Describe some emotional/psychological factors that you think might have an influence on sexual functioning. Be sure to include factors that influence male sexual functioning and factors that influence female sexual functioning.

Psychological Factors: The Pressure to Perform FOH

In the mid-1700s, an English physician by the name of Dr. John Hunter wrote this brief description of how he treated a man with erectile disorder:

> I told him that he was to go to bed with this woman but first promise himself that he would not have any connection with her for six nights, let his inclinations and powers be what they would: which he engaged to do. About a fortnight after, he told me that this resolution had produced such a total alteration in the state of his mind that the power soon took place, for instead of going to bed with fear of inability, he went with fears that he should be possessed with too much desire. And when he had once broken the spell, the mind and powers went on together.

FIGURE 18.5 *Marijuana and Sexual Functioning*

Sensations of touch and taste generally are enhanced by smoking marijuana, but any increase in sexual desire may be as much a function of psychological expectation as of the drug. Testosterone and sperm levels may be reduced in some men by smoking marijuana, but the total effect on sexual functioning is not completely known. This youth in the Netherlands can easily buy and smoke marijuana in coffee shops.

Dr. Hunter's approach clearly demonstrates his intuitive understanding of how performance pressures can create enough stress to interfere with sexual function.

Socially imposed standards of sexual performance reach almost mythological proportions for some people. The media add to the myths by suggesting that those who are physically attractive have sex all the time. People become convinced that all normal men get rock-hard erections on demand and have sexual intercourse for hours in every imaginable position without reaching orgasm, while their female partners writhe about in the throes of one orgasm after another. They become convinced that all women must have size 5 bodies and flowing, windblown hair. Both women and men may become so concerned about their body image that they are too preoccupied to experience the pleasure of sexual touch and intimacy, and they may actually avoid sexual encounters. Depression may make such concerns loom even larger for the individual (Frohlich & Meston, 2002a). Even for individuals with less exaggerated sexual expectations, the pressures to perform can be enormous.

Stage fright is not an uncommon reaction to any situation in which a good performance is expected. It is just this kind of anxiety that can generate the typical vicious circle of sexual dysfunction that is depicted in Figure 18.6. This pattern can turn what would have been an isolated sexual failure into a continuing cycle of sexual dysfunction. A term commonly used to describe the "stage fright" associated with sexual performance pressure is **spectatoring.** Instead of being able to relax and lose

themselves in the sensual delights of the sexual experience, individuals may constantly seem to be outside themselves, wondering how they are doing and judging their sexual expertise as if they were spectators at someone else's sexual event. These sorts of reactions may even be more common in people with panic disorder or social phobia. Such individuals also may be especially conscious of their partner's degree of involvement and enjoyment in the sexual encounter. Performance anxieties may also revolve around potential negative consequences of sex, such as being caught while engaged in the act or fear of pregnancy or disease (Figueira et al., 2001; Nobre & Pinto-Gouveia, 2006).

Performance pressure often is rooted in an excessive need to please a partner. It is not unusual for a heterosexual man to assume that he is responsible for bringing pleasure to a woman, whereas heterosexual women are prone to believe that they must serve a man's sexual desires and whims. A person may also have a nagging insecurity that generates continual worry that the partner will become sexually bored or interested in someone else. All of these sources of anxiety are likely to interfere with sexual responsiveness on some level (Bianchi-Demicheli & Zutter, 2005).

Relationships and Sexual Functioning

Many dysfunctions are rooted in problems that have developed in the partners' relationship. Lack of communication and intimacy is one of the most widespread of these problems (Greeff & Malherbe, 2001). Communication difficulties may be relatively uncomplicated at first, such as a failure to let one's partner know what types of stimulation are particularly enjoyed and which might better be avoided. Left to fester, these minor relational irritants may turn into more serious and lasting conflicts. Communication problems also may originate at much deeper levels and be symptomatic of severe disturbances and a lack of compatibility between the two people involved (Clement, 2002).

Loving relationships have complex dynamics, and both the joys and discord in any relationship usually get played out in the sexual arena. When power struggles result in two people trying to wrest control from each other, sex will be affected. If one partner is having trouble trusting the other or if some pattern of outright rejection has emerged, the possibilities of sexual dysfunction are enormous. Sometimes, subtle games of sexual sabotage, which result in turning off one's partner,

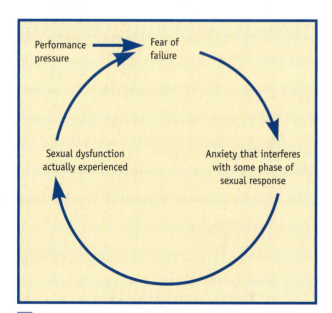

FIGURE 18.6 *Vicious Circle of Sexual Dysfunction*

Some people may be more prone than others to feeling the pressure that society exerts to perform sexually. These real or imagined pressures may result in fear of performing adequately and ultimately may produce sexual dysfunction.

spectatoring term used by Masters and Johnson to describe self-consciousness and self-observation during sex.

Real Student Voices: Men

■ The first time it happened, I made an excuse to my girlfriend that I was just too tired. When it happened again, I really started to get worried and she started to ask questions. I was thinking about taking Viagra, but after talking it over with a counselor, I realized that I just needed to relax and stop worrying. My girlfriend was very helpful and understanding once I told her what was going on. Before long, I was back to normal and very relieved!

■ The first few times I had sex with a partner, I was practically done before we got started. It was embarrassing and disappointing. By consulting a book, I was able to learn some techniques for slowing down, and they worked. It's much better now.

■ This doesn't happen every time, but sometimes no matter how hard I try, I can't seem to come. A few times, I've just given up eventually. My girlfriend doesn't mind. Why should she? It can be very frustrating though.

will mask some deeper relational problems in couples. These factors also may be important in determining the outcome of therapy for sexual problems. It is likely that the happier and stabler a couple's relationship is, the more positive and satisfactory the outcome of therapy will be (Bianchi-Demicheli & Zutter, 2005; Cameron, Rosen, & Swindle, 2005; Metz & Epstein, 2002).

■ Treating Sexual Dysfunctions

Every individual troubled by a sexual dysfunction will have his or her own set of interacting causes. Sometimes treatment can proceed without much time being spent on elucidating all of these causes. Other times, an effective therapeutic outcome depends on the untangling of a complex web of medical, psychological, and relational causes. Likewise, an integrated approach to treatment often is necessary (Metz & McCarthy, 2005). Because some people may be reluctant to seek professional help for such personal problems, home remedies and patent medicines often claim to cure various sexual dysfunctions. In the United States, males who are concerned about their lack of ejaculatory control sometimes purchase sprays or creams to be applied to the penis. These products primarily contain a mild anesthetic that dulls sensation in the head of the penis, and there is some evidence that they can slow down the ejaculatory response in some men (Slob, Berkel, & Bosch, 2000). Men also have invented their own techniques for delaying ejaculation, such as wearing more than one condom or masturbating just prior to shared sex. They may try to distract themselves by thinking about other things, clenching their fists, or biting themselves to produce pain, or they may devise a number of other techniques. Unfortunately, such home remedies may only intensify the problem.

As they worked on developing a model for the effective treatment of sexual dysfunctions, Masters and Johnson (1970) realized that they needed techniques to help patients relax and restructure their behavior. They were faced with the challenge of modifying psychological, relational, and cultural factors that were interfering with the physiological sexual responsiveness of the human body. They also believed that sexual dysfunctions could not be considered the problem of an individual but rather the problem of a couple, so their treatment methods provided ample opportunity for sexually dysfunctional couples to learn more about their shared sexual feelings and responses.

Effective treatment for sexual dysfunction cannot be carried out in a step-by-step, mechanical way. Treatments must be designed and improvised for particular clients. The intricacies of each individual and each relationship must be taken into consideration. It is, in a sense, an art to be practiced with skill and creativity.

Medical Treatments

There has been increased use of various medical regimens in the treatment of sexual dysfunctions. Because it is known that androgenic hormones such as testosterone have some influence on sexual arousal, numerous studies have been done on administering these hormones in order to increase both sexual desire and arousal capabilities. Although more research is needed,

Real Student Voices: Women

■ My boyfriend gets more upset than I do when I can't orgasm. I've never been able to orgasm very often during intercourse, and I'm not sure I ever really have. Lately, I've even been faking it, because it's easier than dealing with him trying to work at giving me one after I feel done.

■ Lack of desire on my part is definitely a problem for us. I really enjoy physical intimacy and cuddling, but not so much for the sexual aspects. I like seeing my partner get sexual pleasure, but it doesn't matter that much if I do. We both wish I enjoyed sex more for sex's sake.

■ I manage to avoid intercourse or even having anybody touch my vagina. The first couple of times I had intercourse were very painful, and I've become scared to even try it. I seem to be able to satisfy boys in other ways, but I wonder when I want to have intercourse if I'll be able to.

it does seem clear that the use of androgens can increase sexual desire in both men and women who have an abnormally low concentration of the hormones, although it is critical that men who are treated in this manner have no underlying prostate cancer (Anders et al., 2005; Barqawi & Crawford, 2006; Kingsberg, 2005; Wylie & Davies-South, 2004). Some herbal preparations, although typically not subjected to rigorous scientific testing, have been used with some success in treating certain sexual dysfunctions, including ED and female arousal disorder (Ferguson et al., 2003; Ito, Polan, Whipple, & Trant, 2006; Rowland & Tai, 2003).

ED has also been treated successfully with muscle relaxants and a chemical called yohimbine. Certain antidepressant drugs have been found to slow down the ejaculatory reflex and thus have been used with some success in treating premature ejaculation. Men who develop inhibited ejaculation because of the use of such medications may be helped by changing to another drug. HSDD sometimes responds to treatment with medications, and, in cases of sexual aversion and phobia, antidepressant medications or anxiety-reducing drugs may prove effective (Rowland & Burnett, 2000).

Two medical treatments for ED have received wide publicity. In one method, the man injects the muscle relaxant papaverine or one of several similar chemicals that act locally within the spongy erectile tissues of the penis to produce erection. A newer variation of this approach involves insertion of a tiny suppository of the chemical into the urethral opening, where it is absorbed into the spongy tissues. The erection may last for an hour or more, even after the man has ejaculated and feels finished with sexual activity (Rowland & Burnett, 2000; Slob et al., 2002). These treatments seem to work best when combined with appropriate sex therapy or psychotherapy. In cases

where ED has psychological roots, the injection and suppository approaches sometimes can generate renewed levels of self-confidence that prove useful in overcoming the performance pressures that conspired to produce the problem in the first place. These treatments are not used as frequently as the medications described in the next paragraph.

See "Viagra and Sexual Pharmacology" on SexSource Online.

One of the most significant medical advances to treat sexual dysfunctions in recent years has been a class of drugs that began with sildenafil, popularly known as Viagra. When it was first approved for use in treating ED in 1998, it caused a media furor, and men rushed to their physicians for prescriptions. Its annual sales continue to top $1 billion, and it has now been joined by two medications whose potential effectiveness lasts for longer time periods: vardenafil, sold as Levitra, and tadalafil, marketed under the name Cialis. These medications work by inhibiting the action of a particular enzyme, which in turn prolongs the effects of cyclic GMP, the substance that relaxes smooth muscles within the erectile tissues of the penis, allowing blood to flow in and cause erection.

Studies with Viagra and the other medications demonstrate that they can be very effective in treating male ED and that, in most cases, side effects are minor and quite tolerable. Men who have heart disease that necessitates taking medications such as nitroglycerin for chest pain generally should not use these medications (Rosen & McKenna, 2003). A proportion of men who begin treatment with some form of ED medication do not continue taking the drug, often because of disappointing results or lack of sexual interest and desire

(DeRose, Gallo, & Carmignani, 2005; Jiann, Yu, Su, & Tsai, 2006; Klotz et al., 2005; Rosen et al., 2006). Although the drug has not yet been extensively tested on women or approved for the treatment of female sexual arousal disorders, some women have reported that it works for them as well (Berman et al., 2001). Other medications and topically applied creams have been tried with women (Meston & Worcel, 2002; Padma-Nathan et al., 2003). However, there is growing evidence that simply enhancing the ability of the female genitals to become engorged with blood will not go far enough in resolving most female arousal problems (Rosen, 2002).

Controversies abound about the dangers of the medicalization of sex therapy, especially for women, but the evidence would suggest that medical treatments can indeed be effective, especially when combined with other modes of therapy (McCarthy & Fucito, 2005). Development of new medications surely will continue, because the pharmaceutical companies are aware of the strong market available for drugs that treat sexual dysfunctions.

Biomedical Engineering Devices

Various sorts of vacuum and constriction devices and splintlike penile supports have been used to help men achieve and maintain erections, but their long-term usefulness has not been proved. They also may hold some potential risk of penile damage. Studies of the vacuum devices, in which the penis is "pumped up" within a vacuum tube and then a band is placed around the base, have shown the technique to be close to 90 percent successful, with a relatively low patient

dropout rate (Raina et al., 2005; Wylie, Jones, & Walters, 2003). A device to produce some level of suction and vacuum effect on the clitoris has proved to help some women with sexual arousal problems enjoy sexual stimulation and orgasm more consistently (Billups et al., 2001).

In cases where some organic damage makes erection impossible, prosthetic devices have been developed that can simulate erection. They fall into two main categories: semirigid rods that are surgically inserted into the penis, leaving the organ in a somewhat permanently erect state that can be held in place by underwear, and inflatable tubular devices that can produce an artificial erection when surgically implanted into the penis (see Figure 18.7). Tens of thousands of these prosthetic devices are now being implanted annually, and they have a relatively high success rate. Repairs need to be made within the first five years in 5 to 10 percent of cases. The ultimate success of the surgery, however, often seems to depend on the quality of the relationship between the man and his partner (Garber, 2003).

Psychotherapeutic Treatments

Although some dysfunctions clearly are rooted in negative emotional states such as anxiety, fear, guilt, or depression, others may be generated by unconscious psychological conflict. *Psychotherapy* is a term that applies to any one of a number of techniques that may help people resolve psychological problems. In recent years, short-term forms of psychotherapy have gained in popularity, and they can be quite effective when they incorporate the specific

Reservoir — Cylinders — Pump

■ **FIGURE 18.7**   *Penile Implant*

If impotence cannot be cured, particularly if it is caused by an organic physical condition such as damage to the spine, intercourse can be made possible by the implantation of a mechanical device. A reservoir filled with fluid is implanted in the abdomen. It is connected by tubes to a pump inserted into the scrotum and in turn connected to two cylinders that are slipped into the penis. To cause an erection, the man pumps the fluid into the cylinders; to reverse the procedure, he releases a valve in the pump, returning the fluid to the reservoir.

treatment exercises developed in behavioral therapy. While medical treatments for sexual dysfunctions have enjoyed increasing success, continued attention needs to be paid to psychotherapeutic approaches, used either alone or in combination with medical regimens (Bianchi-Demicheli & Zutter, 2005; Heiman, 2002a; McCarthy & Fucito, 2005).

Couples Therapy

A basic premise of psychotherapeutic approaches to sex therapy is that a sexual dysfunction represents a shared problem and therefore one to be worked on together as a couple. Sexual symptoms often are the outcome of a mixture of experiences that both partners have had during their lifetimes. Sometimes a dysfunction in one partner actually can act as a relationship or personal stabilizer for the other. For example, a man whose partner has vaginismus does not have to face any anxieties he himself may have about erectile function. Even liberal-minded, well-educated couples may be ignorant about each other's bodies and how best to pleasure them. Couples therapy provides a venue in which the couple can work together to improve their sexual life and focus on the relational dynamics that may play a role in the dysfunction and the therapy process (Gehring, 2003). Couples sometimes decide not to remain together as a result of couples therapy; this may even be viewed as a positive result of the therapy process.

Hypnotherapy

There has always been some interest in hypnosis as a therapeutic approach to sexual problems. Hypnosis may be considered a form of psychotherapy that uses relaxation and suggestion in helping susceptible, or willing, individuals to change. Patients also need to be able to use mental imagery for mentally "rehearsing" situations that formerly have made them tense or anxious. There are case studies dealing with the successful use of hypnosis in treating a variety of sexual problems and dysfunctions. Hypnotherapeutic treatment often is used as an adjunct to other treatment techniques (Kandyba & Binik, 2003). Reports on the outcomes of hypnotherapy for sexual dysfunctions tend to be anecdotal, and larger studies are needed. There are few generalized conclusions to be drawn at this time about the effectiveness of such methods.

Group Therapy

Group therapy has been used successfully with some sexual dysfunctions. Behavioral techniques are usually prescribed for individual patients within the course of treatment, and the group setting provides the information and support for the sharing of feelings necessary to a successful outcome. Group methods have been used successfully with women with orgasmic disorder and also have been successful for men with ED or problems with ejaculatory control (Gehring & Chan, 2001; Kanas, 1999). Even so, most people express a preference for individual treatment over group strategies, perhaps because the issues involved are often deeply personal.

Behavior Therapy

Behavior therapy was the predominant mode of sex therapy for a number of years. Behavioral approaches typically involve the use of **systematic desensitization,** through which the patient gradually unlearns the tension-producing behaviors that are causing problems. More desirable behaviors then are learned to replace the old, dysfunctional patterns. Behavior therapy techniques still provide the basic structure for most psychotherapy-based sex therapy today. When used to treat sexual disorders, behavior therapy entails physical activities that are practiced at home by the couple or, in some cases, as self-help approaches by single clients.

Most counselors and therapists are somewhat eclectic in their treatment of sexual dysfunctions, meaning that they combine therapy techniques in a variety of ways to meet the needs of individual patients as effectively as possible. Although they may draw methods from some primary school of thought, they recognize the need to be flexible and to keep pace with changing techniques and a growing body of research knowledge. Today, this increasingly means consideration of the medical treatments that are emerging for various dysfunctions (McCabe, 2001; Melnik & Abdo, 2005).

Surrogates

Clients in behavioral sex therapy who do not have partners raise the additional issue of using **sexual surrogates,** or paid partners, for the purpose of practicing therapeutic exercises. In the early phases of their work to develop treatment strategies, Masters and Johnson used female surrogates to work with single

behavior therapy therapy that uses techniques to change patterns of behavior; often employed in sex therapy.

systematic desensitization step-by-step approaches to unlearning tension-producing behaviors and developing new behavior patterns.

sexual surrogates paid partners used during sex therapy with clients who lack their own partners; used only rarely today.

men. These women were not prostitutes but instead were well-trained, sexually responsive women who were culturally matched with patients and were able to cooperate in all the behavioral exercises designed to improve sexual functioning. There also have been a few male surrogates who work with female partners. As might be anticipated, ethical difficulties arose with the use of paid surrogate partners because sex for pay usually is considered illegal and/or immoral. Masters and Johnson soon discontinued the use of surrogates, although some other clinics continue to believe they are the only viable option for single patients.

Combination Treatment Approaches

Given the growing consensus that sexual dysfunctions may have many different causes and that treatment strategies must be tailored to the specific needs of individual clients and couples, there is increasing acceptance of combining treatment approaches in sex therapy. Psychotherapeutic approaches usually have been eclectic in nature, borrowing from a variety of strategies to develop a treatment plan (Metz & McCarthy, 2005). With the emergence of apparently effective medical treatments, it is even more crucial to consider these methods in working with sexually dysfunctional people. This requires closer communication among professionals from a variety of disciplines.

Treatment for sexual dysfunction is a rapidly changing field, and its future well-being may depend largely on the degree of flexibility that everyone involved in sex therapy services can achieve in combining many different treatment approaches. Many studies are showing the efficacy of combination treatment approaches. For the good of clients seeking help with sexual dysfunctions, creative linking among the many disciplines that deal with sexual dysfunctions is essential (McCarthy & Fucito, 2005; Metz & McCarthy, 2005).

What Is a Sex Therapist?

The term **sex therapist** entered popular usage in the early 1970s. Defined narrowly, the term refers to professionals who have been trained to treat sexual dysfunctions. Counselors are now being trained to treat sexual problems as well. However, they usually work within a broader context. Sex therapists and counselors attempt to restore sex to its natural context so that it can be a spontaneous human function and also to reestablish the positive pleasurable sensations and attitudes naturally present in childhood. They can help people enrich their sex lives, overcome lack of interest in sex, improve communication about sex between partners, and overcome specific sexual problems.

See "Taking a Sexual History" on SexSource Online.

Because human sexuality is a multidisciplinary field, professionals enter sex therapy from a variety of backgrounds. Some have had medical training as physicians or nurses. Some hold degrees in psychology, counseling, or social work. A few have a background in pastoral counseling and hold degrees in religion. A national organization called the American Association of Sexuality Educators, Counselors and Therapists (AASECT) took the lead in establishing criteria with which to certify individuals who have met appropriate training standards as sex therapists. These criteria include not only a degree in one of the helping professions but also specialized coursework in human sexuality and many hours of practical therapy work under the supervision of an already certified sex therapist. AASECT was also the first organization to formulate specific ethics statements concerning how therapists were to conduct their work (see "Is Sex Therapy Effective and Ethical?" p. 542).

Although the members of the sex therapy profession continue to call for strictly established guidelines to govern their work, state legislatures have been slow to enact regulations concerning the licensing of sex therapists. This increases the risks for the consumer, because in many states anyone, regardless of training or other professional credentials, can lawfully call himself or herself a sex therapist and set up a private practice. Any new profession has its share of quacks and charlatans, and sex therapy has been no exception.

One way to find a good sex therapist is to ask two or more trusted professionals whom they would recommend for help with a sexual problem. Sometimes an individual's name will come up more than once—probably a good sign. It is always appropriate to check out a sex therapist's qualifications directly as well. Consumers may wish to ask about degrees and training, the therapy model used, the kinds of records kept, the costs, and whether the therapist is certified to practice sex therapy by any professional group. More than half of patients do not seem to have a particular preference for the gender of their sex therapists, but others do. This may be one issue to consider in choosing a therapist. It is important to watch out for any sort of unethical behavior, such as a suggestion by a sex therapist that nudity or sexual relations with the therapist might be appropriate. It should be

sex therapist a professional trained in the treatment of sexual dysfunctions.

expected, however, that a therapist will ask rather specific and intimate questions about sexual functioning in evaluating the problem and deciding on a course of treatment.

One issue to be resolved in treating sexual dysfunctions is the number of therapists to participate in the therapy. A few clinics still accept only couples for treatment and provide therapists of both sexes to work with those couples (see Figure 18.8). Most sex counselors or therapists in private practice work alone and work effectively with couples. Other issues arise in specific situations. Lesbian or gay male couples may seek a therapist of the same gender. Some counselors and therapists also will agree to work with clients who do not have a partner available or whose partners are unwilling to participate in therapy. They use audiotapes, videotapes, DVDs, online services, or other techniques designed specifically for clients without sexual partners. Certain types of problems are amenable to self-help approaches and do not necessarily require the cooperation of a partner.

AASECT (P.O. Box 1960, Ashland, VA 23005-1960) can provide listings by mail, for a slight charge, of certified counselors and sex therapists or of clinics that treat sexual dysfunctions. Anyone consulting a sex therapist should expect treatment that is conducted in a respectful, caring, and dignified manner. Potential medical problems should be investigated carefully. It is even appropriate to set some tentative deadlines for meeting certain goals. If the results are not forthcoming, reevaluating the worth of the therapy process is certainly in order.

FIGURE 18.8 *Co-therapist Counseling Session*

In the earlier days of sex therapy, couples often were seen by a co-therapy team consisting of a woman and a man as therapists. This model is still sometimes used today, because it may bring a more balanced approach to couples therapy. Even when there is only a single therapist, it usually is considered most beneficial to involve both partners in counseling sessions. This provides an opportunity for both to cooperate in finding solutions to their relational and sexual difficulties.

Behavioral Approaches to Sex Therapy

As discussed earlier in this chapter, behavior therapy techniques, involving the learning of tension-reduction techniques and more effective approaches to sharing sexual activity, are a mainstay of sex therapy. They may be used in combination with medical or psychotherapeutic techniques. This section provides an overview of how such techniques are employed in therapy.

Basic Goals of Behavioral Sex Therapy

Behavior therapy essentially involves unlearning ineffective, dysfunction-promoting sexual behavior and replacing it with more positive, healthier patterns. Sex therapists attempt to move their clients toward achieving the following major goals.

Gaining a Sense of Permission to Value One's Sexuality

Those suffering from a sexual dysfunction often have long-standing problems with accepting and feeling good about their sexuality. Whether stemming from social pressures, religious training, parental attitudes, or previous negative experiences, sexually dysfunctional individuals may feel guilty and uncomfortable about their sexual feelings, attractions, and behaviors. Therefore, a primary principle of therapy is to impart a sense of permission that it is all right to be sexual and that sexuality is a natural and healthy aspect of the human personality. Sex therapists encourage their clients to place a higher priority on sexual enjoyment, including saving time to work on sexual activities. Many sex therapy exercises are designed to help clients get in touch with their bodies, their sexual sensations, and their emotional reactions in more positive ways than ever before.

Taking More Time to Make Sexual Activity a Priority

We live in busy times, and in many relationships both partners have careers. Sexual activity eventually may take a backseat to other priorities in a couple's life together. In sex therapy, time is put aside specifically for working on sexual problems. Therapists usually assign suggested activities and recommend a time frame for their completion. All of this helps the couple develop a higher priority for improving sexual functioning.

Eliminating Elements That Are Blocking Full Sexual Response

The human sexual response cycle—starting with sexual desire and proceeding through sexual arousal, higher levels of excitement to orgasm, and then resolution—is a normal part of every human being. People seek therapy when some factor has interfered with all or part of that cycle. Sex therapists, then, must work to eliminate whatever elements are hindering full and satisfying sexual functioning. This means tracking down the causes of a dysfunction and then mapping out a realistic plan for correcting them. This can be a simple matter of teaching new relaxation and communication techniques, or it may necessitate in-depth counseling for deep-seated personal or relational conflicts. If alcohol or drugs are part of the problem, they need to be eliminated or reduced. Guilt reactions or other emotional blocks also must be overcome.

Reducing Performance Pressures

Sex therapy clients must learn how to stop focusing on their own sexual performance in order to relax and let sex happen. Behavior therapy provides techniques to distract people from this spectatoring and to keep their body as relaxed as possible. Partners are helped to change their emphasis from feeling responsible for giving each other pleasure to working on their own sexual satisfaction.

Using Specific Sexual Exercises to Develop More Positive Ways of Functioning Sexually

Over the years, sex therapists have devised activities that actually can help a sexually dysfunctional person overcome his or her problem. These exercises are done at home in private and must be prescribed in a very systematic manner, with the opportunity available to talk about reactions after each stage. The sex therapist makes decisions about how quickly to move through increasingly intimate stages of therapy, based on how both partners are progressing and feeling. These sexual exercises constitute the most significant route to behavioral change in this form of treatment.

Self-Help Approaches

Many sex therapists have determined there is enough clinical data to justify prescribing self-help approaches to overcoming sexual dysfunctions, although there is little evidence to demonstrate the long-term effectiveness of such approaches. Although the low cost and complete privacy of self-directed sex therapy are obvious advantages, many sexual dysfunctions can be treated effectively only by professional therapists. Self-help approaches cannot reach some of the more complex personal and relational factors at the root of many dysfunctions. The self-help guides may provide solid information, offer a positive beginning for many who want to improve their sexual functioning, and help people be more relaxed in discussing sexual matters. Rarely can they effect a total cure.

Many therapists do suggest techniques for individuals to try at home on their own and not with a partner. The two most common self-help themes use body exploration and masturbation (Weiss, 2001). Many sexually dysfunctional men and women have never taken the time to become acquainted with their sex organs or even with other parts of their bodies. Body exploration exercises involve viewing one's own body in a mirror and touching oneself to elicit emotions and physical sensitivities. Sometimes, very specific directions are given to discover how various parts of the genitals respond to stimulation.

Masturbation exercises have proved especially useful in treating female orgasmic disorder and premature ejaculation. Once the orgasmic capability is well established through these self-help techniques, the woman gradually integrates her partner into the activities, teaching that partner the best approaches for bringing her to orgasm. Helping women learn how to have orgasm consistently has also proved valuable in the treatment of female HSDD (Zamboni & Crawford, 2002).

As mentioned earlier, long-standing patterns of hurried masturbation may contribute to ejaculatory control difficulties in men. Self-help techniques that encourage men to slow down masturbation have been effective in establishing more modulated forms of male sexual response that can carry over to better orgasmic control with partners (Carufel & Trudel, 2006). Masturbatory self-help techniques may not be as suitable for individuals or cultural groups who have negative feelings or attitudes about masturbation.

Other self-help techniques can be used to reorient negative thought patterns about sex, rehearse fantasized situations with partners ahead of time, or learn patterns of distraction to prevent excessive focusing on one's own sexual functioning. There is general agreement among sex professionals that self-awareness, along with an ability to explain one's own sexual needs and idiosyncrasies to a partner, is an important aspect of healthy sexual adjustment.

Partnership Approaches

Most behavioral techniques used in treating sexual dysfunctions are prescribed for couples to use together. Therapists view the partnership therapeutic experience as important in the couple's growing ability to communicate and function together sexually. Partnership approaches involve graduated steps. Therapists usually need to be satisfied that each of the following stages of treatment has been mastered successfully before moving on to the next:

1. Learning how to enjoy and relax with each other's bodies while providing nonsexual touching and massage.
2. Providing each other with light genital stimulation designed to be pleasurable but without any pressure to respond with arousal or orgasm.
3. Learning how to communicate and physically guide each other toward the most effective forms of sexual stimulation.
4. Using specific exercises to reverse dysfunctional patterns and establish a pattern of sexual interaction that is pleasing and satisfying to both partners.

To accomplish the first three goals outlined, sex therapists prescribe various types of mutual body-pleasuring exercises, often called **sensate focus.** These exercises provide couples with an opportunity to develop and appreciate physical sensations generated by each other, bringing a physically pleasurable dimension into the relationship. An added positive outcome of sensate focus can be the reduction of power imbalances in the sexual relationship that may be making one partner feel pressured, untrusting, coerced, or misunderstood (see Figure 18.9).

The first phase of sensate focus activities involves nongenital touching. The partners are instructed by the therapist to be together nude, in as warm and relaxing a private setting as possible. They take turns giving and receiving gentle physical pleasuring that is not overtly sexual. With a minimum of talking, the giver provides caring touches to the partner in the form of massaging, tracing, and rubbing. The receiver has only to relax and enjoy the pleasant sensations, giving positive verbal suggestions for changing the form of touching if anything is in any way uncomfortable or irritating. After an agreed-upon length of time, the partners switch sensate focus roles. For many couples, these exercises represent the first time they have experienced physical intimacy and pleasure without the tensions and pressures of performing sexually. Obviously, such activities can be an important step in overcoming some dysfunctions.

In the second phase of sensate focus, light genital stimulation and teasing are encouraged, but without the goal of generating sexual arousal. The couple is, in fact, instructed not to allow sensate focus activities to lead to sexual overtures. Instead, they are told simply to enjoy and accept whatever sexual arousal may occur and then let it dissipate. Again, sexual sensations are made a part of a relaxed, nonpressured context that nonetheless is pleasurable.

A final phase of mutual pleasuring typically involves some form of guiding procedure in which one partner carefully shows the other how to give her or him optimum sexual stimulation. This will involve some mutually comfortable position in which one

sensate focus early phase of sex therapy treatment, in which the partners pleasure each other without employing direct stimulation of the sex organs.

FIGURE 18.9 *Mutual Pleasuring or Sensate Focus*

partner can place a hand directly on top of the other partner's hand, carefully guiding it in genital stimulation. Figure 18.10 shows a position that is often used for women who are teaching their partner how to provide clitoral stimulation to produce orgasm.

The number of times a couple participates in the various phases of sensate focus may depend on how well and how rapidly they seem to be proceeding. Therapists watch for potential resistance or other difficulties in the therapy process and try to ensure that positive results have been achieved at each stage before couples move on.

Sex therapists who employ behavioral therapy understand that it is crucial for couples to build a pattern of successful sexual experiences, reversing the series of failures they have been experiencing with the dysfunction. Therefore, during the early stages of treatment, therapists usually ask their clients to avoid sexual intercourse or other forms of sexual interaction that have been beset with problems. Gradually, as confidence and relaxation are achieved with each new goal, a couple will begin to attempt intercourse again.

It is important to have a graduated and realistic strategy for bringing the couple back to sexual intercourse. Based on the assumption that most heterosexual couples in Western cultures use—and perhaps prefer—an intercourse position with the man on top and the woman on the bottom, the typical strategy usually begins with the woman in the top position. This seems to be effective in treating women's dysfunctions, because it affords women a greater sense of control over the sexual experience. It also is useful in dealing with male dysfunctions, because the men are more able to relax while their partners takes more responsibility for controlling the sexual action. This is an interesting commentary on some typical causative factors behind female and male dysfunctions: Women often feel somewhat compromised by male-dominant intercourse positions, whereas men feel threatened by the weight of responsibility for sexual expertise usually assigned to them.

An excellent intermediate step on the way to developing confidence with man-on-top intercourse is a face-to-face, side-by-side position that enables both partners to be more physically relaxed (see Chapter 12, "Solitary Sex and Shared Sex"). Neither is called on to support his or her full weight (see Figure 18.11), resulting in a greater sense of shared responsibility. Sex therapists find that many heterosexual couples enjoy this position so much that they begin to use it on a more regular basis than their former man-on-top intercourse position.

The final therapeutic step, provided it is the desired goal of the couple, is to succeed in their usual

FIGURE 18.10 *A Guiding Position for Clitoral Stimulation*

FIGURE 18.11 *Side-by-Side Position for Relaxation*

intercourse position, with all sexual functioning proceeding as desired. Coital position may play a role in improving sexual functioning in other ways as well. One study showed that both women and men experienced more "complete and satisfying" orgasms when they used a position in which the penis moves higher on the mons and clitoris and presses on this area. Women who experience painful intercourse often are helped by positions in which they are on top. Again, the process of overcoming a couple's sexually dysfunctional patterns involves systematically desensitizing them to the tension-producing difficulties of the past, conditioning them instead to the practice of new, more mutually comfortable and enjoyable behaviors.

Some Specific Behavioral Methods

Aside from the general techniques already described, some specific behavioral exercises are used in treating each sexual dysfunction. An exhaustive survey of these techniques is not appropriate to this text, but we will explore some examples.

Vaginismus involves the involuntary contraction of vaginal muscles, making entry of the penis difficult or impossible for heterosexual intercourse. Because this dysfunction is almost always caused by fears and earlier negative experiences, it is crucial to help the woman learn how to develop a positive pattern of relaxation and pleasure with insertion into her vagina. The behavioral exercises used in therapy therefore are designed to reduce tension and permit relaxation and pleasure. They might begin with the suggestion that the woman privately examine the opening of her vagina with a mirror, using some relaxation technique at the same time. Gradually, over a period of time, she will insert her little finger (or a small dilator made of plastic or rubber) into her vagina, also using a relaxation technique. Eventually, the partner's fingers will be used in the same manner, but under the complete control and direction of the woman. In the final phases of treating vaginismus, the man's penis will be slowly and gently inserted, again with the woman having full control over how deeply and for how long this takes place. The ultimate goal is to achieve relaxed and pleasurable intercourse (Heiman, 2002b; Kabakci & Batur, 2003).

In the past, men tended to try to delay ejaculation by focusing on anything but their pleasurable sexual sensations. In treating premature ejaculation in males today, the emphasis is on helping the man become aware of the inner subjective sensations that signal when his ejaculation is imminent. Men have pelvic sensations just prior to ejaculating that they need to identify so that they may take some action to prevent orgasm before they have passed the "point of no return." There is a simple behavioral technique that many sex therapists suggest. Known as the stop-start method, it asks men to stop any stimulation when they feel the sensation of imminent orgasm. The sensations completely disappear quite rapidly, and stimulation may then be resumed. Most sex therapists recommend that the partner use slow manual stimulation on the man's penis at first, in a convenient position (see Figure 18.12). The man gives a prearranged signal to halt the stimulation when he feels orgasm approaching. Some therapists recommend that the partner add the squeeze technique at this point, giving a firm

FIGURE 18.12 *Manual Stimulation of the Penis*

squeeze to the head of the penis (see Figure 18.13). This further diminishes the sensation of imminent orgasm. Over a period of time, the man gains better control over his ejaculatory reflex and feels increased confidence in his sexual abilities. These behavioral exercises lead to the development of sexual patterns through which the man is able to slow down and modulate his stimulation so that he takes longer to reach orgasm. In the intercourse sequence described earlier for treating vaginismus, he gradually integrates his control into sexual relations with his partner. During intercourse, the squeeze technique may be applied at the base of the penile shaft so that the penis need not be withdrawn from the vagina.

Various specific behavioral methods are used in the treatment of the other sexual dysfunctions. These help couples unlearn the conditions that have led to their sexual dissatisfaction and learn how to function normally and happily. Sometimes sex therapy aids people in saying no to sex when they are not in the mood, or to particular sexual activities they do not enjoy. Sex therapists attempt to meet the specific objectives of their clients as realistically as possible.

■ Is Sex Therapy Effective and Ethical?　FOH

The American Psychological Association has proposed two main categories for what they would consider validated treatments for various disorders, including sexual dysfunctions. One category, *well-established treatments,* consists of those strategies that have been shown to be effective through carefully controlled group studies or a large series of well-designed case studies. These treatments typically have manuals describing their use and clearly specify the types of clients for whom they are most effective. The other category, *probably efficacious treatments,* have—as the name implies—been subjected to less rigorous testing. This group consists of treatments shown to be effective in a very few studies or in studies less well controlled than those in the other category. They usually do not have treatment manuals or clearly established guidelines for client identification (Heiman, 2002a, 2002b).

So far, the psychotherapeutic strategies for treating sexual dysfunctions tend to fall into the "probably efficacious" category. Valid scientific research must always be replicable; that is, the researcher must outline all the experimental and control variables and analyze the results with statistical care so that another researcher could repeat the same procedures and expect similar results. Sex therapy has not been widely studied in this manner, and step-by-step treatment manuals tend not to be available. Many of the medical treatments for sexual dysfunctions are new enough that data continue to emerge concerning their effectiveness, especially with regard to the various criteria of patients for whom these treatments are most likely to lead to success. Because pharmaceutical companies have a greater financial stake in proving the effectiveness of medical treatments, they provide funding for outcome studies that surpasses any resources available for impartial study of the effectiveness of psychological methods (Tiefer, 2001).

Some dysfunctions, such as inhibited female orgasm and male premature ejaculation, seem to lend themselves better to standardized treatments than does HSDD. Those couples who continue their "homework" activities, such as sensate focus, into the late stages of therapy seem to have a better chance of positive outcomes. Therapy also may be more effective with younger couples and those who have a higher level of positive regard for each other at the outset. Current research seems to support the contention

A

B

■ **FIGURE 18.13** *The Squeeze Technique: Base of Penis (A) and Head of Penis (B)*

that sex therapy can be highly effective when it is carried out over a full course of treatment by well-trained professional therapists and when various methods of treatment are combined to meet the needs of particular clients (Daker-White, 2002; Melnik & Abdo, 2006; Metz & McCarthy, 2005).

What are your opinions about sex therapy as one of the helping professions?

Most sexologists would agree that sex therapists should do more than restore desired sexual functioning. They also should provide a foundation for change within the individual and the relationship so that a relapse can be prevented, and they should assist in the correction of any medical condition that may lie behind the problem. To this end, partners also may be helped to establish more realistic sexual expectations of each other (see Figure 18.14). Sex therapists can maximize the continuing value of treatment by encouraging occasional use of the behavioral techniques employed during therapy, continuing medical treatment as appropriate, and suggesting follow-up visits if necessary.

Human sexual conduct is interwoven into our sociocultural values, and sex has become associated with a variety of moral issues. When professionals intervene in the sexual lives and decision making of their clients,

FIGURE 18.14 *Mutual Understanding*
Sex therapists emphasize that communication and understanding are very important factors in solving sexual problems and developing a relationship that is complete and fulfilling for both partners.

many ethical issues need to be confronted. Work in sexology demands the highest standards of professionalism, confidentiality, and informed consent. Yet professionals also bring their own sets of values to their work, and these values often influence the decisions they make about ethical behavior. Sex therapy sometimes has come under fire as being a white, middle-class, heterosexual phenomenon, lacking in multicultural awareness and technical expertise.

Sex therapists face their share of ethical dilemmas. For example, if in the course of treating a married couple for some sexual dysfunction one of the partners privately admits to having contracted an STD during a recent extramarital affair, the therapist must make some decisions. Confidentiality has been promised, yet the other partner may be at risk of catching the disease. The extramarital affair may have implications for the entire treatment process that cannot be explored as long as it is kept secret. The therapist may feel as though she or he has been drawn into a dishonest alliance with the partner who had the affair. Deciding how to proceed is an exercise in professional ethics for the therapist.

Ethical questions in sex therapy are raised daily. Who decides whether there is actually a problem at all? What methods will be used to treat the problem? Should masturbatory exercises be assigned to a client whose religion or culture sees masturbation as unacceptable? Should sexual intercourse be prescribed for an unmarried client?

AASECT has promulgated its own code of ethics. It deals with several basic issues designed to protect clients against exploitation or incompetence. The central points of this code are as follows:

1. Sex therapists must receive adequate training and have a strong sense of integrity.
2. Strict standards of confidentiality must govern a sex therapist's work, and there should be no disclosure of information about a client without the individual's written consent.
3. Because clients are often in a vulnerable position, their welfare is to be protected and respected at all times by the therapist.

In making this final point, the AASECT Code of Ethics places strict limitations on nudity of clients and therapists and on the use of sexual surrogates as partners during therapy. Sexual contact between therapists and their clients has been a major concern in sex therapy ethics and has been the subject of some lawsuits.

All helping professions face their share of ethical dilemmas. Codes of ethics establish general guidelines but can never offer hard and fast advice to be used in a specific complicated case. It is crucial for sex therapists, as well as others in the helping professions, to understand their own value systems regarding sexuality and to sort through the moral and ethical issues involved.

Sex therapy has often been restrictive, available only to heterosexual couples who can afford the luxury of full sexual enjoyment. Only recently have some therapists begun to treat other groups. Some people desire individual treatment for sexual dysfunctions, either because the dysfunction has prevented them from finding a partner or because their partner is unwilling to participate. Some same-gender couples want to improve their sexual interactions, and sex therapy methods have proved to be successful

with lesbian and gay male couples. However, very little is known about the sexual problems of same-gender couples, and more research is needed before appropriate therapeutic protocols can be established (Sandfort & Keizer, 2002).

As professional organizations and state legislatures continue to examine these issues and to clarify standards for the training and licensing of sex therapists, the efficacy, methods, and ethical standards of the therapy process will be further clarified.

Chapter Summary

1. Individual differences in sexual responsiveness should be considered to determine whether a true dysfunction is present.

2. Every culture sets its own sexual performance standards—sometimes unrealistic ones. These may become debilitating pressures and unfair expectations for men and women. Cultures also have their own folk remedies for treating dysfunctions.

3. The labels attached to sexual dysfunctions may carry negative or positive connotations.

4. Scientific terminology indicates that sexual dysfunctions may be lifelong or acquired, generalized or situational.

5. Sexual dysfunctions represent disruption of one or more of the three major phases of the human sexual response cycle: desire, arousal, or orgasm.

6. Individuals who have impaired desire for sexual gratification may be experiencing hypoactive sexual desire disorder (HSDD), which is also characterized by lack of sexual interest.

7. Sexual aversion disorder is characterized by fears about and avoidance of sexual activity.

8. Arousal problems are expressed as male erectile disorder (ED), involving interference with penile erection, or female sexual arousal disorder, characterized by an absence of vaginal lubrication and other signs of sexual excitement. Arousal disorder in women may be subjective and/or genital.

9. Vaginismus is caused by anxiety and avoidance, along with reflexive contractions of the pelvic musculature that result in difficulty with insertion

into the vagina. Pain associated with sexual activity is called dyspareunia.

10. Both men and women can experience orgasmic disorder.

11. Premature or rapid ejaculation in males may well be a conditioned response and is the most common sexual dysfunction in men.

12. Postejaculatory pain is a relatively rare disorder involving involuntary muscular spasms that create pain associated with ejaculation in males.

13. Sexual dysfunctions may have causes at several different levels involving predisposing factors, precipitating factors, and/or maintaining factors. Causes also may be biological or medical (organic), substance-induced, psychological, or social/relational.

14. Performance pressures and difficulties in relationships (such as poor communication) are often at the root of sexual dysfunctions, although possible medical causes must first be investigated.

15. Alcohol, drugs, and medications can play a role in interfering with sexual response.

16. Behavioral techniques are widely used as treatment by sex therapists, although medical treatments are becoming more common.

17. Oral medications such as Viagra, Levitra, or Cialis, or injection and suppository applications directly into the penis, are sometimes used to treat ED. Medications are also used to treat premature ejaculation and HSDD.

18. Prosthetic and vacuum devices have also been used with some cases of ED.

19. Psychotherapeutic treatments including couples therapy, hypnosis, and group therapy have been used to treat sexual dysfunctions. Combining psychotherapy with medication is becoming a more common treatment mode.

20. The ethics, training standards, and certification standards for sex therapists are still being developed by national professional organizations.

21. For sex therapy clients without partners, sexual surrogates sometimes have been available, but this is not common practice today.

22. Behavioral sex therapy helps dysfunctional individuals unlearn ineffective behaviors and replace them with positive, effective patterns of sexual interaction.

23. Specific homework exercises are assigned to those in therapy, using both self-help and partnership approaches.

24. Methods for treating sexual dysfunctions have been classified as either well established or probably efficacious in terms of their effectiveness.

25. Sex therapy raises certain ethical issues and dilemmas, and specific guidelines have been developed for the ethical conduct of therapists.

26. Sex therapy has gradually been made available to multicultural groups and to same-gender couples.

Focus on Health Questions

In this section you will find the kinds of questions that you may have concerning your own health and sexuality. The page references indicate where in the text the answer is located; the exact place is marked with this logo: **FOH**

1. I don't always have an orgasm when I have sex. My partner thinks this is a problem, but I feel perfectly satisfied with things the way they are. Do I have a problem? **516**

2. My partner never seems to be interested in sex anymore. What is going on? **520–522**

3. I have been having difficulty maintaining an erection. Is there any way to find out whether this is a physical problem, or something going on in my mind? **523–524**

4. What could cause sexual intercourse to be painful? **524–525**

5. I think I ejaculate too soon, although my partner doesn't complain. Could I have a problem with premature ejaculation? **526**

6. What could be going on if sometimes after I ejaculate I get a pain inside my genitals? **527**

7. What causes the body not to function sexually the way one would expect it to? **528**

8. Will I perform better, sexually, if I have a few alcoholic drinks first? **530**

9. If I'm taking prescribed medications, will they affect my sexual performance? **530**

10. What is meant by "performance pressure"? **530–531**

11. How do Viagra, Levitra, and Cialis work, and are they always effective for men with erectile disorder? **533**

12. If I go to a sex therapist, will I have to perform sexually with a stranger? **535–536**

13. What is the best way to find a reliable and experienced sex therapist? **537**

14. How can I practice being more relaxed sexually with my partner? **539**

15. Does sex therapy always work? **542**

Glossary

abnormal   anything considered not to be normal (that is, not conforming to the subjective standards a social group has established as the norm). 194

abortifacients   any drugs or chemical substances that can trigger the termination of a pregnancy. 317

abstinence-only-until-marriage sexuality education   an approach to educating young people that emphasizes the need to abstain from sexual relations until marriage, essentially the "just say no" philosophy. 164

acquaintance (date) rape   a sexual encounter forced by someone who is known to the victim. 458

acquired dysfunction   a difficulty with sexual functioning that develops after some period of normal sexual functioning. 519

acquired immunodeficiency syndrome (AIDS)   a fatal disease caused by a virus that is transmitted through the exchange of bodily fluids, primarily in sexual activity and intravenous drug use. 479

activating effect   the direct influence some hormones can have on activating or deactivating sexual behavior. 96

acute urethral syndrome   infection or irritation of the urethra. 41

adolescence   period of emotional, social, and physical transition from childhood to adulthood. 151

affectional   relating to feelings or emotions, such as romantic attachments. 200

afterbirth   the tissues expelled after childbirth, including the placenta, the remains of the umbilical cord, and fetal membranes. 284

agenesis (absence) of the penis (ae-JEN-a-sis)   a congenital condition in which the penis is undersized and nonfunctional. 70

amniocentesis (am-nee-oh-sen-TEE-sis)   a process by which medical problems with a fetus can be determined while it is still in the womb; a needle is inserted into the amniotic sac, amniotic fluid is withdrawn, and fetal cells then are examined. 278

amnion (AM-nee-on)   a thin membrane that forms a closed sac around the embryo; the sac is filled with amniotic fluid, which protects and cushions the embryo. 262

anal intercourse   insertion of the penis into the rectum of a partner. 343

androgen (ANN-dra-gin)   a male hormone, such as testosterone, that affects physical development, sexual desire, and behavior. Testosterone is produced by both male and female sex glands and influences each sex in varying degrees. 96

androgen insensitivity syndrome (AIS)   a developmental condition in which cells do not respond to fetal androgen, so that chromosomally male (XY) fetuses develop external female genitals; there is also a feminization of later behavioral patterns. 113

androgyny (an-DROJ-a-nee)   the presence of high frequencies of both masculine and feminine behaviors and traits in the same individual. 120

anejaculation   lack of ejaculation at the time of orgasm. 74

anodyspareunia   pain associated with anal intercourse. 525

anorchism (a-NOR-kiz-um)   rare birth defect in which both testes are lacking. 64

anti-Müllerian hormone (AMH)   secretion of the fetal testes that prevents further development of female structures from the Müllerian ducts. 110

aphrodisiacs (af-ro-DEE-zee-aks)   foods or chemicals purported to foster sexual arousal; believed to be more myth than fact. 344

areola (a-REE-a-la)   darkened, circular area of skin surrounding the nipple of the breast. 46

artificial embryonation   a process in which the developing embryo is flushed from the uterus of the donor woman five days after fertilization and placed in another woman's uterus. 272

artificial insemination   injection of the sperm cells of a male into a woman's vagina, with the intention of conceiving a child. 268

asceticism (a-SET-a-siz-um)   usually characterized by celibacy, this philosophy emphasizes spiritual purity through self-denial and self-discipline. 209

asexuality   a condition characterized by a low interest in sex. 392

assisted reproductive technology (ART)   a collection of laboratory techniques that have been developed to help couples overcome infertility problems and have children, usually through bypassing one of the usual biological pathways to pregnancy or gestation. 265

autoerotic asphyxiation   accidental death from pressure placed around the neck during masturbatory behavior. 409

autofellatio (aw-toh-fe-LAY-she-o)   the act of a male providing oral stimulation to his own penis, which most males do not have the physical agility to perform. 334

autogynephilia (otto-guy-nuh-FEEL-ee-ah)   a tendency found in some males to become sexually aroused by obsessive thoughts and images of being female and having female attributes, or even female sex organs. 396

Bartholin's glands (BAR-tha-lenz)   small glands located in the opening through the minor lips that produce some secretion during sexual arousal. 35

behavior therapy   therapy that uses techniques to change patterns of behavior; often employed in sex therapy. 535

benign prostatic hyperplasia (BPH)   enlargement of the prostate gland that is not caused by malignancy. 72

bestiality (beest-ee-AL-i-tee)   sexual contact between a human being and an animal. 410

biological essentialism   a theory that holds that human traits and behaviors are formed primarily by inborn biological determinants such as genes and hormonal secretions, rather than by environmental influences. 105

biphobia   prejudice, negative attitudes, and misconceptions toward bisexual people and their lifestyles. 207

birth canal   term applied to the vagina during the birth process. 284

birthing rooms   special areas in the hospital, decorated and furnished in a nonhospital way, set aside for giving birth; the woman remains here to give birth rather than being taken to a separate delivery room. 286

bisexual   refers to some degree of sexual activity with or attraction to members of both sexes. 201

blastocyst   the ball of cells, after five days of cell division, that has developed a fluid-filled cavity in its interior and has entered the uterine cavity. 262

body dysmorphic disorder   a preoccupation with imagined or slight defects in one's bodily appearance that may focus on weight, muscularity, skin appearance, the genitals, or other body parts. 444

bond   the emotional link between parent and child created by cuddling, cooing, and physical and eye contact early in the newborn's life. 286

bondage   tying, restraining, or applying pressure to body parts as part of sexual arousal. 409

brothels   houses of prostitution. 405

bulbourethral glands   another term for Cowper's glands. 72

call boys   highly paid male prostitutes. 404

call girls   highly paid female prostitutes who work by appointment with an exclusive clientele. 405

cantharides (kan-THAR-a-deez)   a chemical extracted from a beetle that, when taken internally, creates irritation of blood vessels in the genital region; can cause physical harm. 345

case study   an in-depth look at a particular individual and how he or she might be helped to solve a sexual or other problem. Case studies may offer new and useful ideas for counselors to use with other patients. 26

catharsis theory   the suggestion that viewing pornography provides a release for sexual tension, thereby preventing antisocial behavior. 428

celibacy (SELL-a-buh-see)   choosing not to share sexual activity with others. 392

central arousal system   internal components of sexual arousal that come from the cognitive and emotional centers of the brain, forming the foundations for sexual response. 81

cervical cap   a device that is shaped like a large thimble and fits over the cervix; not a particularly effective contraceptive because it can dislodge easily during intercourse. 310

cervical intraepithelial neoplasia (CIN) (ep-a-THEE-lee-al nee-a-PLAY-zhee-a)   abnormal, precancerous cells sometimes identified in a Pap smear. 45

cervix (SERV-ix)   lower "neck" of the uterus that extends into the back part of the vagina. 42

cesarian section   a surgical method of childbirth in which delivery occurs through an incision in the abdominal wall and uterus. 284

chancroid (SHAN-kroyd)   an STD caused by the bacterium *Hemophilus ducreyi* and characterized by sores on the genitals, which if left untreated, could result in pain and rupture of the sores. 497

child molesting   sexual abuse of a child by an adult. 464

chlamydia (kluh-MID-ee-uh)   now known to be a common STD, a major cause of urethritis in males; often presents no symptoms in females. 489

chorion (KOR-ee-on)   the outermost extraembryonic membrane, essential in the formation of the placenta. 263

chorionic villi sampling (CVS)   a technique for diagnosing medical problems in the fetus as early as the eighth week of pregnancy; a sample of the chorionic membrane is removed through the cervix and studied. 278

cilia   microscopic, hairlike projections that help move the ovum through the fallopian tube. 44

circumcision (SIR-cum-sizh-uhn)   in the male, surgical removal of the foreskin from the penis; in the female, a surgical procedure that cuts the prepuce, exposing the clitoral shaft. 36, 69

climax   another term for orgasm. 86

clinical research   the study of the cause, treatment, or prevention of a disease or condition by testing large numbers of people. 26

clitoridectomy (clih-torr-ih-DECK-tah-mee)   surgical removal of the clitoris; practiced routinely in some cultures. 36

clitoris (KLIT-a-rus)   sexually sensitive organ found in the female vulva; it becomes engorged with blood during arousal. 35

clone   the genetic-duplicate organism produced by the cloning process. 275

cloning   a process by which a genetic duplicate of an organism is made either by substituting the chromo-somes of a body cell into a donated ovum or by separation of cells early in embryonic development. 275

cognitive susceptibility   state of mind, identified by psychological and situational factors, that suggests a readiness for or predisposition toward initiating sexual activity. 152

cohabitation   living together and sharing sex without marrying. 179

coitus (KO-at-us or ko-EET-us)   heterosexual, penis-in-vagina intercourse. 196

coitus interruptus   a method of birth control in which the penis is withdrawn from the vagina prior to ejaculation. 306

coming out   acknowledging to oneself and others that one is lesbian, gay, or bisexual. 377

comprehensive sexuality education   an approach to educating young people about human sexuality that includes information about sexuality but also encourages clarifying values and developing decision-making skills. 164

computerized sperm selection   use of computer scanning to identify the most viable sperm, which then are extracted to be used for fertilization of an ovum in the laboratory. 272

Comstock Laws   federal legislation enacted in the 1870s prohibiting the mailing of information about contraception. 293

conception   the process by which a sperm unites with an egg, normally joining 23 pairs of chromosomes to establish the genetic "blueprint" for a new individual. The sex chromosomes establish its sex: XX for female, and XY for male. 107

congenital adrenal hyperplasia (CAH)   a genetic disorder that masculinizes chromosomal females and seems to lead to a masculinization of behavior as well. 113

consensual adultery   permission given to at least one partner within the marital relationship to participate in extramarital sexual activity. 183

contraceptive implants   contraceptive method in which hormone-releasing rubber cylinders are surgically inserted under the skin of the woman. 307

controlled experiment   research in which the investigator examines what is happening to one variable while all other variables are kept constant. 27

coprophilia   sexual arousal connected with feces. 409

core gender identity a child's early inner sense of its maleness, femaleness, or ambivalence, established prior to puberty. 116

corona the ridge around the penile glans. 65

corpus luteum cell cluster of the follicle that remains after the ovum is released; secretes hormones that help regulate the menstrual cycle. 50

Cowper's glands two small glands in the male that secrete an alkaline fluid into the urethra during sexual arousal. 72

cryptorchidism (krip-TOR-ka-diz-um) condition in which the testes have not descended into the scrotum prior to birth. 64

cultural absolutism the view that behaviors and values from one's culture of origin should be disregarded once the individual is living in a new culture. The expectation is that immigrants must abide by the cultural standards of their new country. 6

cultural relativism the view that one's culture determines what is normal and acceptable and that judgments about those standards should take into consideration their cultural origins. 6

cunnilingus (kun-a-LEAN-gus) oral stimulation of the clitoris, vaginal opening, or other parts of the vulva. 340

cyclic GMP a secretion within the spongy erectile tissues of the penis that facilitates erection. 66

cystitis (sis-TITE-us) a nonsexually transmitted infection of the urinary bladder. 41

DAX-1 the region on the X chromosome that seems to play a role in sexual differentiation. 108

deoxyribonucleic acid (DNA) (dee-AK-see-rye-bow-new-KLEE-ik) the chemical in each cell that carries the genetic code. 260

Depo-Provera an injectable form of progestin that can prevent pregnancy for one or three months. 308

desire phase Kaplan's term for the psychological interest in sex that precedes physiological sexual arousal. 86

deviation term applied to behaviors or orientations that do not conform to a society's accepted norms; often has negative connotations. 195

DHT-deficiency syndrome a condition in which chromosomally male fetuses have underdeveloped male genitals and may be identified as

girls at birth. However, at puberty they begin to develop masculine secondary sex characteristics and seem to maintain masculine patterns of behavior. 114

diaphragm (DY-a-fram) a latex rubber cup, filled with spermicide, that is fitted to the cervix by a clinician; the woman must learn to insert it properly for full contraceptive effectiveness. 309

differential socialization the process of treating boys and girls differently as they are growing up. 115

dihydrotestosterone (DHT) a chemical produced by the fetal testes that promotes further development of the testes, scrotum, and penis in the fetus. 110

dilation the gradual widening of the cervical opening of the uterus prior to and during labor. 284

dilation and curettage (D & C) a method of induced abortion in the second trimester of pregnancy that involves a scraping of the uterine wall. 323

dilation and evacuation (D & E) a method of induced abortion in the second trimester of pregnancy that combines suction with a scraping of the inner wall of the uterus. 323

discrimination the process by which an individual extinguishes a response to one stimulus while preserving it for other stimuli. 143

disorders of sex development (DSD) a more scientific term now being applied to those with combinations or ambiguities of female and male anatomical structures. 103

dyadic withdrawal (die-ADD-ik) the tendency of two people involved in an intimate relationship to withdraw socially for a time from other significant people in their lives. 157

dysmenorrhea (dis-men-a-REE-a) painful menstruation. 52

dyspareunia recurrent or persistent genital pain related to sexual activity. 525

E. coli bacteria naturally living in the human colon that often cause urinary tract infection. 41

ectopic pregnancy (ek-TOP-ik) the implantation of a blastocyst somewhere other than in the uterus, usually in the fallopian tube. 262

effacement the thinning of cervical tissue of the uterus prior to and during labor. 284

ejaculation muscular expulsion of semen from the penis. 74

ejaculatory inevitability the sensation in the male that ejaculation is imminent. 94

ELISA the primary test used to determine the presence of HIV in humans. 501

embryo (EM-bree-o) the term applied to the developing cells when, about a week after fertilization, the blastocyst implants itself in the uterine wall. 262

endometrial hyperplasia (hy-per-PLAY-zhee-a) excessive growth of the inner lining of the uterus (endometrium). 45

endometriosis (en-doe-mee-tree-O-sus) growth of the endometrium out of the uterus into surrounding organs. 45

endometrium interior lining of the uterus; the innermost of three layers. 43

endorphins (en-DORE-fins) brain secretions that act as natural tranquilizers and pain relievers. 243

epidemiological (e-pe-dee-mee-a-LA-i-cahl) referring to the branch of medical science that deals with the incidence, distribution, and control of disease in a population. 481

epididymis (ep-a-DID-a-mus) tubular structure on each testis in which sperm cells mature. 63

epididymitis (ep-a-did-a-MITE-us) inflammation of the epididymis of the testis. 64

episiotomy (ee-piz-ee-OTT-a-mee) a surgical incision in the vaginal opening made by the clinician or obstetrician to prevent the baby from tearing the opening in the process of being born. 284

epispadias (ep-a-SPADE-ee-as) birth defect in which the urinary bladder empties through an abdominal opening and the urethra is malformed. 71

erection enlargement and stiffening of the penis as internal muscles relax and blood engorges the columns of spongy tissue. 66

erogenous zone (a-RAJ-a-nus) any area of the body that is sensitive to sexual arousal. 147

erotica artistic representations of nudity or sexual activity. 416

erotocentricity (ee-ROT-oh-sen-TRIS-ih-tee) the application of ethnocentric-like judgments to sexual values and behaviors, creating the assumption that our own ways of approaching sexuality are the only "right" ways. 198

erotomania (air-aht-oh-MAY-nee-ah) a very rare form of mental illness characterized by a highly compulsive need for sex. 392

erotophilia (air-aht-oh-FEEL-i-ah) consistent positive responding to sexual cues. 391

erotophobia (air-aht-oh-FOBE-i-ah) consistent negative responding to sexual cues. 391

Essure transcervical sterilization procedure a less invasive alternative to tubal ligation in which a small coil is implanted in the fallopian tube through a small abdominal incision. Tissue grows on the coil, eventually blocking the ovum. 316

estrogen (ES-tro-jen) hormone produced abundantly by the ovaries; it plays an important role in the menstrual cycle. 50

ethnocentricity (eth-no-sen-TRIS-ih-tee) the tendency of the members of one culture to assume that their values and norms of behavior are the "right" ones in comparison to those of other cultures. 198

ethnography (eth-NAH-gruffy) the anthropological study of other cultures. 27

ethnosexual referring to data concerning the sexual beliefs and customs of other cultures. 27

Eurocentric (ur-oh-SEN-trick) a cultural attitudinal framework typical of people with western European heritages. 6

excitement the first phase of Masters and Johnson's four-phase model of the sexual response cycle, involving genital vasocongestion. 85

exhibitionism exposing the genitals to others for sexual pleasure. 407

exocytosis (ex-oh-sye-TOH-sis) the release of genetic material by the sperm cell, permitting fertilization to occur. 259

facilitated sex assistance provided to a person with severe physical disabilities in order to enable them to achieve sexual pleasure through masturbation or with a partner. 218

fallopian tubes structures that are connected to the uterus and lead the ovum from an ovary to the inner cavity of the uterus. 44

fellatio oral stimulation of the penis. 339

female condom a lubricated polyurethane pouch that is inserted into the vagina before intercourse to collect semen and help prevent disease transmission. 311

female sexual arousal disorder difficulty for a woman in achieving sexual arousal. 523

fertilin (fer-TILL-in) a chemical in the outer membrane of a sperm that assists in attachment to the egg cell and penetration of the egg's outer membrane. 259

fetal alcohol syndrome (FAS) a condition in a fetus characterized by abnormal growth, neurological damage, and facial distortion caused by the mother's heavy alcohol consumption during pregnancy. 282

fetal surgery a surgical procedure performed on the fetus while it is still in the uterus or during a temporary period of removal from the uterus. 279

fetally androgenized females a condition in which hormones administered during pregnancy cause chromosomally female (XX) fetuses to have masculinization of the genitals and perhaps of later behavioral patterns, even though they were raised as girls. 113

fetishism (FEH-tish-i-zum) sexual arousal triggered by objects or materials not usually considered sexual. 402

fetus the term given to the embryo after two months of development in the womb. 263

fibroid tumors nonmalignant growths that commonly grow in uterine tissues, often interfering with uterine function. 45

fibrous hymen condition in which the hymen is composed of unnaturally thick, tough tissue. 39

follicle-stimulating hormone (FSH) pituitary hormone that stimulates the ovaries or testes. 50

follicles capsules of cells in which an ovum matures. 44

foreplay sexual activities shared in early stages of sexual arousal, with the term implying that they are leading to a more intense, orgasm-oriented form of activity such as intercourse. 196

foreskin fold of skin covering the penile glans; also called the prepuce. 65

fraternal (dizygotic) twins twins formed from two separate ova that were fertilized by two separate sperm. 261

frenulum (FREN-yu-lum) thin, tightly drawn fold of skin on the underside of the penile glans; it is highly sensitive. 65

frotteur one who practices frotteurism. 407

frotteurism (frah-TOUR-izm) gaining sexual gratification from anonymously pressing or rubbing one's genitals

against others, usually in crowded settings. 406

fundus the broad top portion of the uterus. 42

G spot a vaginal area that some researchers feel is particularly sensitive to sexual stimulation when its underlying spongy tissues are engorged with blood. 91

gamete intrafallopian transfer (GIFT) direct placement of the ovum and concentrated sperm cells into the woman's fallopian tube to increase the chances of fertilization. 270

gay refers to persons who have a predominantly same-gender sexual orientation and identity. More often applied to males. 200

gender dysphoria (dis-FOR-ee-a) another term sometimes used to describe a gender identity disorder. 120

gender identity a person's inner experience of gender: feelings of maleness, femaleness, or some ambivalent position between the two. 104

gender identity disorder the expression of gender identity in a way that is socially inconsistent with one's anatomical sex. 120

gender role the outward expression and demonstration of gender identity, through behaviors, attire, and culturally determined characteristics of femininity and masculinity. 105

gender schema a complex cognitive network of associations and ideas through which the individual perceives and interprets information about gender. 125

gene therapy treatment of genetically caused disorders by substitution of healthy genes. 265

generalization application of specific learned responses to other, similar situations or experiences. 143

genetic engineering the modification of the gene structure of cells to change cellular functioning. 265

genital herpes (HER-peez) a viral STD characterized by painful sores on the sex organs. 492

gestational surrogacy implantation of an embryo created by the sperm and ovum of one set of parents into the uterus of another woman who agrees to gestate the fetus and give birth to the child, which then is given to the original parents. 277

glans in the male, the sensitive head of the penis; in the females, the sensitive head of the clitoris, visible between the upper folds of the minor lips. 35, 65

gonadotropin-releasing hormone (GnRH) (go-nad-a-TRO-pen) hormone from the hypothalamus that stimulates the release of FSH and LH by the pituitary. 49

gonads sex and reproductive glands, either testes or ovaries, that produce hormones and, eventually, reproductive cells (sperm or eggs). 106

gonorrhea (gon-uh-REE-uh) bacterial STD causing urethral pain and discharge in males; often no initial symptoms in females. 486

granuloma inguinale (gran-ya-LOW-ma in-gwa-NAL-ee or -NALE) an STD characterized by ulcerations and granulations beginning in the groin and spreading to the buttocks and genitals. 497

H-Y antigen a biochemical produced in an embryo when the Y chromosome is present; it plays a role in the development of fetal gonads into testes. 110

hard-core pornography pornography that makes use of highly explicit depictions of sexual activity or shows lengthy scenes of genitals. 423

hebephilia (HEE-beh-fil-ee-a) a term being used to describe the sexual abuse of adolescents. 464

hedonists (HEE-don-ists) people who believe that pleasure is the highest good. 209

hemophiliacs (hee-mo-FIL-ee-aks) people with the hereditary blood defect hemophilia, primarily affecting males and characterized by difficulty in clotting. 481

hepatitis B virus (HBV) a liver infection that frequently is sexually transmitted. 495

hepatitis C virus (HCV) a liver infection that may occasionally be sexually transmitted. 495

heterosexism the biased and discriminatory assumption that people are or should be attracted to members of the other gender. 196

heterosexual refers to attractions or activities between males and females. 201

homophobia (ho-mo-FO-bee-a) strongly held negative attitudes about and irrational fears of gay men and/or lesbians and their lifestyles. 206

homosexual term traditionally applied to affectional and sexual attractions and activities between members of the same gender. 200

hookers street name for female prostitutes. 405

hormone replacement therapy (HRT) treatment of the physical changes of menopause by administering dosages of the hormones estrogen and progesterone. 57

hot flash a flushed, sweaty feeling in the skin caused by dilated blood vessels; often associated with menopause. 57

human chorionic gonadotropin (HCG) a hormone detectable in the urine of a pregnant woman. 282

human immunodeficiency virus (HIV) the virus that initially attacks the human immune system, causing HIV disease and eventually AIDS. 479

human papillomavirus (HPV) an infection causing small lesions on genital skin; certain strains of this STD increase later risks of cervical cancer. 494

hustlers male street prostitutes. 404

hymen membranous tissue that can cover part of the vaginal opening. 35

hyperfemininity a tendency to exaggerate characteristics typically associated with femininity. 120

hypermasculinity a tendency to exaggerate manly behaviors; sometimes called machismo. 120

hypersexuality an unusually high level of interest in and drive for sex. 391

hypoactive sexual desire disorder (HSDD) loss of interest and pleasure in what formerly were arousing sexual stimuli. 522

hyposexuality an especially low level of sexual interest and drive. 391

hypospadias (hye-pa-SPADE-ee-as) birth defect caused by incomplete closure of the urethra during fetal development. 71

hypoxphilia creating pressure around the neck during sexual activity to enhance sexual pleasure. 409

hysterectomy surgical removal of all or part of the uterus. 45

identical (monozygotic) twins twins formed by a single ovum that was fertilized by a single sperm before the cell divided in two. 261

immature oocyte collection extraction of immature eggs from undeveloped follicles in an ovary, after which the oocytes are assisted to maturity by cell-culturing methods in preparation for fertilization. 272

imperforate hymen condition in which the hymen has no natural openings. 39

impotence (IM-puh-tense) difficulty achieving or maintaining erection of the penis. 519

in vitro fertilization (IVF) a process by which the union of the sperm and egg occurs outside the mother's body. 269

incest (IN-sest) sexual activity between closely related family members. 470

incest taboo cultural prohibitions against incest, typical of most societies. 470

induced abortion a termination of pregnancy by artificial means. 320

infertility the inability to produce offspring. 280

infibulation (in-fib-you-LAY-shun) surgical procedure, performed in some cultures, that seals the opening of the vagina. 37

informed consent the consent given by research subjects, indicating their willingness to participate in a study, after they are informed about the purpose of the study a and how they will be asked to participate. 27

integrated sexuality education programs this concept emphasizes the possibility of combining education to prevent pregnancy and the transmission of diseases with realistic approaches to educating young people about sexuality and about how to make safer decisions about sex. 165

intersexuality a combination of female and male anatomical structures, so that the individual cannot be clearly defined as male or female. 103

interstitial cells (in-ter-STIH-shul) cells between the seminiferous tubules that secrete testosterone and other male hormones. 62

interstitial-cell-stimulating hormone (ICSH) pituitary hormone that stimulates the testes to secrete testosterone; known as luteinizing hormone (LH) in females. 73

interstitial cystitis (IC) a chronic bladder inflammation that can cause debilitating discomfort and interfere with sexual enjoyment. 41

intracytoplasmic sperm injection (ICSI) a technique involving the injection of a single sperm cell directly into an ovum; useful in cases where the male has a low sperm sperm count. 270

intrauterine devices (IUDs) birth control method involving the insertion of a small plastic device into the uterus. 312

introitus (in-TROID-us) the outer opening of the vagina. 35

invasive cancer of the cervix (ICC) advanced and dangerous malignancy requiring prompt treatment. 45

isthmus narrowed portion of the uterus just above the cervix. 42

kiddie porn the distribution and sale of photographs and films of children or younger teenagers engaging in some form of sexual activity. 427

kleptomania extreme form of fetishism in which sexual arousal is generated by stealing. 402

labia majora (LAY-bee-uh mah-JOR-uh) two outer folds of skin covering the minor lips, clitoris, urinary meatus, and vaginal opening. 34

labia minora (LAY-bee-uh mih-NOR-uh) two inner folds of skin that join above the clitoris and extend along the sides of the vaginal and urethral openings. 35

labor uterine contractions in a pregnant woman; an indication that the birth process is beginning. 283

lactation production of milk by the milk glands of the breasts. 46

Lamaze method (la-MAHZ) a birthing process based on relaxation techniques practiced by the expectant mother; her partner coaches her throughout the birth. 285

laminaria (lam-a-NER-ee-a) a dried seaweed sometimes used in dilating the cervical opening prior to vacuum curettage. 322

laparoscopy (lap-ar-OSK-uh-pee) simpler procedure for tubal ligation involving the insertion of a small fiber-optic scope into the abdomen, through which the surgeon can see the fallopian tubes and close them off. 316

laparotomy (lap-ar-OTT-uh-mee) operation to perform a tubal ligation, or female sterilization, involving an abdominal incision. 315

latency period Freudian concept that during middle childhood sexual energies are dormant; recent research tends to suggest that latency does not exist. 142

lesbian (LEZ-bee-un) refers to females who have a predominantly same-gender sexual orientation and identity. 200

libido (la-BEED-o or LIB-a-do) a term first used by Freud to define human sexual longing, or sex drive. 142

lifelong dysfunction a difficulty with sexual functioning that has always existed for a particular person. 519

lumpectomy surgical removal of a breast lump, along with a small amount of surrounding tissue. 49

luteinizing hormone (LH) (LEW-tee-in-ize-ing) pituitary hormone that triggers ovulation in the ovaries and stimulates sperm production in the testes. 50

lymphogranuloma venereum (LGV) (lim-foe-gran-yu-LOW-ma va-NEAR-ee-um) a contagious STD caused by several strains of *Chlamydia* and marked by swelling and ulceration of lymph nodes in the groin. 497

male climacteric one of the terms applied to a vaguely defined period in male mid-life characterized by hormonal, psychological, and sexual changes. 75

male condom a sheath worn over the penis during intercourse that collects semen and helps prevent disease transmission. 310

male erectile disorder (ED) difficulty achieving or maintaining penile erection (impotence). 523

mammography sensitive X-ray technique used to discover small breast tumors. 48

marital rape a woman being forced by her husband to have sex. 461

masochist the individual in a sado-masochistic sexual relationship who takes the submissive role. 408

massage parlors places where women can be hired to perform sexual acts under the guise of giving a massage. 405

mastectomy surgical removal of all or part of a breast. 49

ménage à trois (may-NAZH-ah-TRWAH) another name for troilism. 403

menarche (MEN-are-kee) onset of menstruation at puberty. 49

menopause (MEN-a-pawz) time in midlife when menstruation ceases. 49

menstrual cycle the hormonal interactions that prepare a woman's body for possible pregnancy at roughly monthly intervals. 49

menstruation (men-stru-AY-shun) phase of the menstrual cycle in which the inner uterine lining breaks down and sloughs off; the tissue, along with some blood, flows out through the vagina; also called the period. 52

microscopic epididymal sperm aspiration (MESA) a procedure in which sperm are removed directly from the epididymis of the male testes. 272

midwives medical professionals, both women and men, trained to assist ith the birthing process. 286

mifepristone (RU 486) a progesterone antagonist used as a post-coital contraceptive. 322

miscarriage a natural termination of pregnancy. 320

modeling theory a perspective that suggests that people will copy behavior they view in pornography. 428

molluscum contagiosum (ma-LUS-kum kan-taje-ee-O-sum) a skin disease transmitted by direct bodily contact, not necessarily sexual, and characterized by eruptions on the skin that appear similar to white-heads, with a hard seedlike core. 497

monogamous sharing sexual relations with only one person. 182

monorchidism (ma-NOR-ka-dizm) presence of only one testis in the scrotum. 64

mons cushion of fatty tissue located over the female's pubic bone. 34

moral values beliefs associated with ethical issues, or rights and wrongs; often a part of sexual decision making. 209

morula (MOR-yuh-la) a spherical, solid mass of cells formed after three days of embryonic cell division. 262

Müllerian ducts (myul-EAR-ee-an) embryonic structures that develop into female sexual and reproductive organs unless inhibited by male hormones. 109

multiplier effect the combining of biological and socioenvironmental factors more and more with one another over time in the process of human development. 114

myometrium middle, muscular layer of the uterine wall. 43

National Birth Control League an organization founded in 1914 by Margaret Sanger to promote use of contraceptives. 294

natural childbirth a birthing process that encourages the mother to take control, thus minimizing medical intervention. 285

natural family planning/fertility awareness a natural method of birth control that depends on an awareness of the woman's menstrual/fertility cycle. 313

necrophilia (nek-ro-FILL-ee-a) sexual activity with a dead body. 411

nonspecific urethritis (NSU) (yur-i-THRYT-us) infection or irritation in the male urethra caused by bacteria or local irritants. 490

normal a highly subjective term used to describe sexual behaviors and orientations. Standards of normalcy are determined by social, cultural, and historical standards. 194

normal asexuality an absence or low level of sexual desire, considered normal for a particular person. 522

normalization integration of mentally retarded persons into the social mainstream as much as possible. 216

nymphomania (nim-fa-MAY-nee-ah) a term sometimes used to describe erotomania in women. 392

obscenity depiction of sexual activity in a repulsive or disgusting manner. 416

onanism (O-na-niz-um) a term sometimes used to describe masturbation; the term stems from the biblical story of Onan, who practiced coitus interruptus and "spilled his seed on the ground." 337

oocytes (OH-a-sites) cells that mature to become ova. 44

opportunistic infection a disease resulting from lowered resistance of a weakened immune system. 498

organizing effect manner in which hormones control patterns of early development in the body. 96

orgasm pleasurable sensations and series of contractions that release sexual tension, usually accompanied by ejaculation in men. 74

orgasmic release reversal of the vasocongestion and muscular tension of sexual arousal, triggered by orgasm. 86

orgy (OR-jee) group sex. 403

os opening in the cervix that leads into the hollow interior of the uterus. 42

osteoporosis (ah-stee-o-po-ROW-sus) disease caused by loss of calcium from the bones in postmenopausal women, leading to brittle bones and stooped posture. 56

ova egg cells produced in the ovary. A single cell is called an ovum; in reproduction, it is fertilized by a sperm cell. 43

ovaries pair of female gonads, located in the abdominal cavity, that mature ova and produce female hormones. 43

ovulation release of a mature ovum through the wall of an ovary. 50

ovum donation use of an egg from another woman for conception, with the fertilized ovum then being implanted in the uterus of the woman wanting to become pregnant. 272

oxytocin pituitary hormone that plays a role in lactation and in uterine contractions response to physical intimacy and sexual satisfaction, and in initiating the birth process. 46, 243, 283

Pap smear medical test that examines a smear of cervical cells to detect any cellular abnormalities. 43

paraphiles (paraphilics) people who are drawn to one or more of the paraphilias, or behaviors characterized by non-normative sexual arousal. 446

paraphilia (pair-a-FIL-ee-a) a newer term used to describe sexual orientations and behaviors that vary from the norm in pathological or antisocial ways; it means "a love beside." 196

paraplegic a person paralyzed in the legs, and sometimes pelvic area, as the result of injury to the spinal cord. 217

pedophilia (pee-da-FIL-ee-a) a pathological desire to sexually abuse children. 464

pelvic inflammatory disease (PID) a chronic internal infection of the uterus and other organs. 313

penile strain gauge a device placed on the penis to measure even subtle changes in its size due to sexual arousal. 82

penis male sexual organ that can become erect when stimulated; it leads urine and sperm to the outside of the body. 65

perimenopause the time of a woman's life surrounding menopause, characterized by symptoms resulting from reduced estrogen levels. 55

perimetrium outer covering of the uterus. 42

perinatally related to pregnancy, birth, or the period immediately following birth. 482

perineal area (pair-a-NEE-al) the sensitive skin between the genitals and the anus. 496

peripheral arousal system external components of sexual arousal that reach the brain and spinal cord from the skin, genitals, and sense organs. 81

Peyronie's disease (pay-ra-NEEZ) development of fibrous tissue in the spongy erectile columns within the penis. 70

pheromones (FAIR-oh-moans) human chemicals, the scent of which may cause an attraction or behavioral change in other individuals. 243

phimosis (fye-MOE-sus) a condition in which the penile foreskin is too long and tight to retract easily. 70

pimps men who have female prostitutes working for them. 405

placenta (pla-SEN-ta) the organ that unites the fetus to the mother by bringing their blood vessels close together; it provides nourishment and removes waste for the developing baby. 263

plateau phase the stable, leveled-off phase of Masters and Johnson's four-phase model of the sexual response cycle. 85

plethysmograph (pleh-THIZ-ma-graff) a laboratory measuring device that charts physiological changes over time. Attached to a penile strain gauge, it can chart changes in penis size. This is called penile plethysmography. 82

polyandry (PAH-lee-ann-dree) referring to being married to more than one spouse, usually to a woman having more than one husband; cross-culturally, less common than polygamy. 183

polycystic ovary syndrome (PCOS) (PAH-lee-SIS-tick) a disorder of the ovaries that can produce a variety of unpleasant physical symptoms, often because of elevated testosterone levels. 45

polygamy (pah-LIG-a-mee) practice, in some cultures, of being married to more than one spouse, usually referring to a man having more than one wife. 183

pornography photographs, films, or literature intended to be sexually arousing through explicit depictions of sexual activity. 416

postpartum depression a period of low energy and discouragement that is common for mothers following childbearing. Longer-lasting or severe symptoms should receive medical treatment. 288

pregnancy-induced hypertension a disorder that can arise in the latter half of pregnancy, marked by swelling in the ankles and other parts of the body, high blood pressure, and protein in the urine; can progress to coma and death if not treated. 288

preimplantation genetic diagnosis (PGD) examination of the chromosomes of an embryo conceived by IVF prior to its implantation in the uterus. 270

premature birth a birth that takes place prior to the 37th week of pregnancy. 288

premature ejaculation difficulty that some men experience in controlling the ejaculatory reflex, resulting in rapid ejaculation. 526

premenstrual dysphoric disorder (PMDD) severe emotional symptoms such as anxiety or depression around the time of menstruation. 54

premenstrual syndrome (PMS) symptoms of physical discomfort, moodiness, and emotional tension that occur in some women for a few days prior to menstruation. 54

prepuce (PREE-peus) in the female, tissue of the upper vulva that covers the clitoral shaft. 35

priapism (pry-AE-pizm) continual, undesired, and painful erection of the penis that lasts longer than four hours. 70

progesterone (pro-JES-ter-one) ovarian hormone that causes the uterine lining to thicken. 51

prolactin pituitary hormone that stimulates the process of lactation. 46

prolapse of the uterus weakening of the supportive ligaments of the uterus, causing it to protrude into the vagina. 45

promiscuity (prah-mis-KIU-i-tee) sharing casual sexual activity with many different partners. 391

prostaglandin hormonelike chemical whose concentrations increase in a woman's body just prior to menstruation. 54

prostaglandin- and saline-induced abortions a method used in the 16th to 24th weeks of pregnancy in which prostaglandins, salt solutions, or urea is injected into the amniotic sac, administered intravenously, or inserted into the vagina in suppository form to induce contractions and fetal delivery. 323

prostate gland located beneath the urinary bladder in the male; it produces some of the secretions in semen. 71

prostatitis (pras-tuh-TITE-us) inflammation of the prostate gland. 72

pseudohermaphrodite a person who possesses either testes or ovaries in combination with some external genitals of the other sex. 104

psychosexual development factors that form a person's sexual feelings, orientation, and patterns of behavior. 141

psychosocial development the cultural and social influences that help shape human sexual identity. 144

pubic lice small insects that can infect skin in the pubic area, causing a rash and severe itching. 496

pubococcygeus (PC) muscle (pyub-o-kox-a-JEE-us) part of the supporting musculature of the vagina that is involved in orgasmic response and over which a woman can exert some control. 38

pyromania sexual arousal generated by setting fires. 402

quadriplegic a person paralyzed in the upper body, including the arms, and the lower body as the result of spinal cord injury. 217

quid pro quo something gained from something given. 448

random sample a representative group of the larger population that is the focus of a scientific poll or study in which care is taken to select participants without a pattern that might bias research results. 25

rape trauma syndrome the predictable sequence of reactions that a victim experiences following a rape. 462

refractory period time following orgasm during which a man cannot be restimulated to orgasm. 95

reinforcement in conditioning theory, any influence that helps shape future behavior as a punishment or reward stimulus. 143

resolution phase the term for the return of a body to its unexcited state following orgasm. 86

retrograde ejaculation abnormal passage of semen into the urinary bladder at the time of ejaculation. 74

retroviruses (RET-ro-vi-rus-es) a class of viruses that integrate their genetic code into that of the host cell, establishing permanent infection. 498

Rh incompatibility condition in which a blood protein of the infant is not the same as the mother's; antibodies formed in the mother can destroy red blood cells in the fetus. 288

RhoGAM medication administered to a mother to prevent formation of antibodies when the baby is Rh positive and its mother is Rh negative. 288

rubber dam a piece of rubber material, such as that used in dental work, placed over the vulva during cunnilingus. 341

sadist the individual in a sado-masochistic sexual relationship who takes the dominant role. 408

sadomasochism (sade-o-MASS-o-kiz-um) refers to sexual themes or activities involving bondage, pain, or domination or humiliation of one partner by the other. 408

sample a representative group of a population that is the focus of a scientific poll or study. 25

satyriasis (sate-a-RYE-a-sus) a term sometimes used to describe erotomania in men. 392

scabies (SKAY-beez) a skin disease caused by a mite that burrows under the skin to lay its eggs, causing redness and itching; transmitted by bodily contact that may or may not be sexual. 497

scrotum (SKROTE-um) pouch of skin in which the testes are contained. 62

secondary sex characteristics the physical characteristics of mature women and men that begin to develop at puberty. 117

selective reduction the use of abortion techniques to reduce the number of fetuses when there are more than three in a pregnancy, thereby increasing the chances of survival for the remaining fetuses. 261

self-gratification giving oneself pleasure, as in masturbation; a term typically used today instead of more negative descriptors. 195

self-pleasuring self-gratification; masturbation. 195

semen (SEE-men) mixture of fluids and sperm cells that is ejaculated through the penis. 72

seminal vesicle (SEM-un-al) gland at the end of each vas deferens that secretes a chemical that helps sperm become motile. 71

seminiferous tubules (sem-a-NIF-a-rus) tightly coiled tubules in the testes in which sperm cells are formed. 62

sensate focus early phase of sex therapy treatment, in which the partners pleasure each other without employing direct stimulation of the sex organs. 539

sex addiction inability to regulate sexual behavior. 447

sex therapist a professional trained in the treatment of sexual dysfunctions. 536

sexologist person who studies human sexuality from a scientific perspective. 17

sexology the scientific study of human sexuality. 24

sexosophy the philosophies and ideologies relating to human sexuality. 24

sexual arousal the psychological and physiological mechanisms that activate sexual response. 81

sexual aversion disorder avoidance of or exaggerated fears toward forms of sexual expression. 522

sexual differentiation the developmental processes—biological, social, and psychological—that lead to different sexes or genders. 105

sexual dysfunctions difficulties people have in achieving sexual arousal and in other stages of sexual response. 86

sexual harassment unwanted sexual advances or coercion that can occur in the workplace or in academic settings. 447

sexual individuality the unique set of sexual needs, orientations, fantasies, feelings, and activities that develops in each human being. 201

sexual orientation the set of physical and emotional qualities that attracts human beings to one another sexually and romantically. 358

sexual orientation identity an inner awareness of what one's sexual orientation means for one's life in terms of sexual and romantic relationships and social interaction. 358

sexual revolution the changes in thinking about sexuality and sexual behavior in society that occurred in the 1960s and 1970s. 7

sexual surrogates paid partners used during sex therapy with clients who lack their own partners; used only rarely today. 535

shaft in the female, the longer body of the clitoris, containing erectile tissue; in the male, the cylindrical base of the penis that contains three columns of spongy tissue: two corpora cavernosa and a corpus spongiosum. 36, 65

Skene's glands secretory cells located inside the female urethra. 92

smegma thick, oily substance that may accumulate under the prepuce of the clitoris or penis. 36

social constructionism a theory that holds that human traits and behaviors are shaped more by environmental social forces than by innate biological factors. 105

social scripts a complex set of learned responses to a particular situation that is formed by social influences. 145

sodomy laws laws in some states that prohibit a variety of sexual behaviors, often described as deviate sexual intercourse. These laws often are enforced discriminatorily against

particular groups, such as gay males. 433

sonograms ultrasonic rays used to project a picture of internal structures such as the fetus; often used in conjunction with amniocentesis or fetal surgery. 278

spectatoring term used by Masters and Johnson to describe self-consciousness and self-observation during sex. 531

sperm reproductive cells produced in the testes; in fertilization, one sperm unites with an ovum. 62

spermatocytes (sper-MAT-o-sites) cells lining the seminiferous tubules from which sperm cells are produced. 73

spermicidal jelly (or cream) sperm-killing chemical in a gel base or cream, used with other contraceptives such as diaphragms. 309

spermicides chemicals that kill sperm; available as foams, creams, jellies, film, or suppositories. 308

sponge a thick, polyurethane disk that holds a spermicide and fits over the cervix to prevent conception. 309

spontaneous abortion another term for miscarriage. 320

SRY the sex-determining region of the Y chromosome. 108

statutory rape a legal term used to indicate sexual activity when one partner is younger than the age of consent; in most states, that age is 18. 455

straight slang term for "heterosexual." 201

streetwalkers female prostitutes who work on the streets. 405

suppositories contraceptive devices designed to distribute their spermicide by melting or foaming in the vagina. 309

syndrome (SIN-drome) a group of signs or symptoms that occur together and characterize a given condition. 498

syphilis (SIF-uh-lus) a sexually transmitted disease (STD) characterized by four stages, beginning with the appearance of a chancre. 479

systematic desensitization step-by-step approaches to unlearning tension-producing behaviors and developing new behavior patterns. 535

testes (TEST-ees) pair of male gonads that produce sperm and male hormones. 62

testicular failure lack of sperm and/or hormone production by the testes. 64

testosterone (tes-TAHS-ter-one) major male hormone produced by the testes; it helps produce male secondary sex characteristics. 62

testosterone replacement therapy (TRT) administering testosterone injections to increase sexual interest or potency in older men; not considered safe for routine use. 77

theoretical failure rate a measure of how often a birth control method can be expected to fail when used without error or technical problems; sometimes called perfect use failure rate. 301

thrush a disease caused by a fungus and characterized by white patches in the oral cavity. 498

toucherism gaining sexual gratification from the touching of an unknown person's body, such as on the buttocks or breasts. 407

toxic shock syndrome (TSS) an acute disease characterized by fever and sore throat; caused by normal bacteria in the vagina that are activated if tampons or contraceptive devices such as diaphragms are left in for a long period of time. 310

transgenderism a crossing of traditional gender lines because of discomfort and nonconformity with gender roles generally accepted by society. 120

transphobia negative attitudes, prejudice, and misconceptions toward transgender individuals and lifestyles. 207

transsexualism a strong degree of discomfort with one's identity as male or female, characterized by feelings of being in the wrongly sexed body. 121

transvestite an individual who dresses in clothing and adopts mannerisms considered appropriate for the opposite sex. 201

trichomoniasis (trik-uh-ma-NEE-uh-sis) a vaginal infection caused by the *Trichomonas* organism. 492

troilism (TROY-i-liz-um) sexual activity shared by three people. 403

true hermaphrodite a person who has one testis and one ovary. External appearance may vary among individuals. 104

tubal ligation (lie-GAY-shun) a surgical cutting and tying of the fallopian tubes to induce permanent female sterilization. 316

typical use failure rate a measure of how often a birth control method can be expected to fail when human error and technical failure are considered. 301

umbilical cord   the tubelike tissues and blood vessels originating at the embryo's navel that connect it to the placenta. 262

urethra (yu-REE-thrah)   tube that passes from the urinary bladder to the outside of the body. 66

urinary meatus (mee-AY-tuss)   opening through which urine passes from the urethra to the outside of the body. 35

urophilia   sexual arousal connected with urine or urination. 409

uterus (YUTE-a-rus)   muscular organ of the female reproductive system; a fertilized egg implants itself within the uterus. 42

vacuum curettage (kyur-a-TAZH)   a method of induced abortion performed with a suction pump. 322

vagina (vu-JI-na)   muscular canal in the female that is responsive to sexual arousal; it receives semen during heterosexual intercourse for reproduction. 38

vaginal atresia (a-TREE-zha)   birth defect in which the vagina is absent or closed. 41

vaginal atrophy   shrinking and deterioration of the vaginal lining, usually the result of low estrogen levels during aging. 41

vaginal fistulae (FISH-cha-lee or-lie)   abnormal channels that can develop between the vagina and other internal organs. 42

vaginal ring   a hormonal contraceptive that is inserted into the vagina for three weeks of each monthly cycle. 308

vaginismus (vaj-uh-NIZ-mus)   involuntary spasm of the outer vaginal musculature, making penetration of the vagina difficult or impossible. 38, 524

values   system of beliefs through which people view life and make decisions, including their sexual decisions. 208

variable   an aspect of a scientific study that is subject to change. 27

variation   a less pejorative term used to describe nonconformity to accepted norms. 195

varicose veins   overexpanded blood vessels; can occur in veins surrounding the vagina. 41

vas deferens   tube that leads sperm upward from each testis to the seminal vesicles. 63

vasa efferentia   larger tubes within the testes, into which sperm move after being produced in the seminiferous tubules. 63

vasectomy (va-SEK-ta-mee or vay-ZEK-ta-mee)   a surgical cutting and tying of the vas deferens to induce permanent male sterilization. 314

villi   fingerlike projections of the chorion that form a major part of the placenta. 263

voluntary surgical contraception (VSC)   sterilization; rendering a person incapable of conceiving with surgical procedures that interrupt the passage of the egg or sperm. 314

voyeurism (VOYE-yur-i-zum)   sexual gratification from viewing others who are nude or who are engaging in sexual activities. 408

vulva   external sex organs of the female, including the mons, major and minor lips, clitoris, and opening of the vagina. 34

vulvar vestibulitis   one form of vulvodynia associated with pain in the entrance of the vagina upon physical contact, often interfering with sexual penetration of the vagina. 41

vulvodynia   a medical condition characterized by pain and burning in the vulva and outer vagina. 41

vulvovaginitis (vul-voe-vaj-uh-NITE-us)   general term for inflammation of the vulva and/or vagina. 491

Western blot   the test used to verify the presence of HIV antibodies already detected by the ELISA. 501

Wolffian ducts (WOOL-fee-an)   embryonic structures that develop into male sexual and reproductive organs if male hormones are present. 109

yeast infection   a type of vaginitis caused by an overgrowth of a fungus normally found in an inactive state in the vagina. 492

zero population growth   the point at which the world's population would stabilize and there would be no further increase in the number of people on earth. Birthrate and death rate become essentially equal. 294

zona pellucida (ZO-nah pe-LOO-sa-da)   the transparent, outer membrane of an ovum. 259

zoophilia (zoo-a-FILL-ee-a)   another name for bestiality. 410

zygote   an ovum that has been fertilized by a sperm. 260

zygote intrafallopian transfer (ZIFT)   a process by which zygotes resulting from IVF are inserted directly into the fallopian tubes. 270

References

AAUW. (1992). *How schools shortchange girls: Executive summary.* Washington, DC: Author.

AAUW. (1993). *Hostile hallways.* Washington, DC: Author.

Abbott, E. (2001). *A history of celibacy.* Toronto: DaCapo Press.

Abouesh, A., & Clayton, A. (1999). Compulsive voyeurism and exhibitionism: A clinical response to paroxetine. *Archives of Sexual Behavior, 28*(1), 23–30.

Abramovich, E. (2005). Childhood sexual abuse as a risk factor for subsequent involvement in sex work: A review of empirical findings. *Journal of Psychology and Human Sexuality, 17*(1/2), 131–146.

Ackard, D. M., & Neumark-Stainer, D. (2001). Health care information sources for adolescents: Age and gender differences on use, concerns, and needs. *Journal of Adolescent Health, 29*(3), 170–176.

ACOG. (2007). ACOG practice bulletin no. 77: Screening for fetal chromosomal abnormalities. *Obstetrics and Gynecology, 109,* 217–228.

Adam, B. D., Husbands, W., Murray, J., & Maxwell, J. (2005). AIDS optimism, condom fatigue, or self-esteem? Explaining unsafe sex among gay and bisexual men. *Journal of Sex Research, 42*(3), 238–248.

Ahlborg, T., Dahlof, L., & Hallberg, L. R. (2005). Quality of the intimate and sexual relationship in first-time parents six months after delivery. *Journal of Sex Research, 42*(2), 167–174.

Ahmadi, N. (2003). Rocking sexualities: Iranian migrants' views on sexuality. *Archives of Sexual Behavior, 32*(4), 317–326.

Aksaray, G., Yelken, B., Kaptanoglu, C., Oflu, S., & Ozaltin, M. (2001). Sexuality in women with obsessive compulsive disorder. *Journal of Sex and Marital Therapy, 27,* 273–277.

Alexander, G. M. (2003). An evolutionary perspective of sex-typed toy preferences: Pink, blue, and the brain. *Archives of Sexual Behavior, 32*(1), 7–14.

Alexander, G. M., & Hines, M. (2002). Sex differences in response to children's toys in nonhuman primates (*Cercopithecus aethiops sabaeus*). *Evolution and Human Behavior, 23*(6), 467–479.

Alexander, G. R., Kogan, M. D., & Nabukera, S. (2002). Racial differences in prenatal care use in the United States: Are disparities decreasing? *American Journal of Public Health, 92*(12), 1970–1975.

Alexander, M. A. (1999). Sexual offender treatment efficacy revisited. *Sexual Abuse: Journal of Research and Treatment, 15,* 36–47.

Alexander, M. G., & Fisher, T. D. (2003). Truth and consequences: Using the bogus pipeline to examine sex differences in self-reported sexuality. *Journal of Sex Research, 40*(1), 27–35.

Alison, L., Santtila, P., Sandnabba, N. K., & Nordling, N. (2001). adomasochistically oriented behavior: Diversity in practice and meaning. *Archives of Sexual Behavior, 30*(1), 1–12.

Allen, L. (2003). Girls want sex, boys want love: Resisting dominant discourses of (hetero)sexuality. *Sexualities, 6*(2), 215–236.

Allyn, D. (2000). *Make love not war: The sexual revolution, an unfettered history.* Boston: Little, Brown.

Althaus, F. (2001). Cesarean section poses fewer risks than vaginal delivery for term infants in breech presentation. *Family Planning Perspectives, 33*(2), 92.

Althof, S. E. (2001). My personal distress over the inclusion of personal distress. *Journal of Sex and Marital Therapy, 27,* 123–125.

Althof, S. E., et al. (2005). Outcome measurement in female sexual dysfunction clinical trials: Review and recommendations. *Journal of Sex and Marital Therapy, 31,* 153–166.

Altman, C. (1999). Gay and lesbian seniors: Unique challenges of coming out in later life. *SIECUS Report, 27* (3), 14–17.

American Academy of Pediatrics. (2005). Breastfeeding and the use of human milk. *Pediatrics, 115*(2), 496–506.

American Health Consultants. (2003). Women who want permanent birth control now have a second option. *Contraceptive Technology Update, 24* (1), 1–4.

American Society for Adolescent Psychiatry. (2002). Gays in the military. *Adolescent Psychiatry, 26*(257), 257–259.

America's Children. (2006). America's children in brief: Key national indicators of well-being. Washington, DC: Forum on Child and Family Statistics.

Analyse des Comportements Sexuels en France Investigators. (1992). AIDS and sexual behavior in France. *Nature, 360,* 407–409.

Anders, S. M., Chernick, A. B., Chernick, B. A., Hampson, E., & Fisher, W. A. (2005). Preliminary clinical experience with androgen administration for pre- and postmenopausal women with hypoactive sexual desire. *Journal of Sex and Marital Therapy, 31,* 173–185.

Anderson, J. E., Ebrahim, S. H., & Sansom, S. (2004). Women's knowledge about treatment to prevent mother-to-child human immunodeficiency virus transmission. *Obstetrics and Gynecology, 103*(1), 165–168.

Anderson, P. B., Kontos, A. P., Tanigoshi, H., & Struckman-Johnson, C. (2005). An examination of sexual strategies used by urban southern and rural midwestern university women. *Journal of Sex Research, 42*(4), 335–341.

Anderson, R. A., & Baird, D. T. (2002). Male contraception. *Endocrinology Review, 23,* 735–762.

Ankomah, A. (1999). Sex, love, money and AIDS: The dynamics of premarital sexual relationships in Ghana. *Sexualities, 2*(3) 291–308.

Anllo, L. M. (2000). Sexual life after breast cancer. *Journal of Sex and Marital Therapy, 26,* 241–248.

Apodaca, R. F., Schultz, J. M., Anderson, A. N., & McLennan, M. D. (2005). Young, unassimilated Hispanic offenders: Absolutist vs. relativist cultural assumptions. *Sexuality and Culture, 9*(3), 3–23.

Apperloo, M. J., Van Der Stege, J. G., Hoek, A., & Weijmar Schultz, W. C. (2003). In the mood for sex: The value of androgens. *Journal of Sex and Marital Therapy, 29*(2), 87–102.

Armstrong, B. (2003). The young men's clinic: Addressing men's reproductive health and responsibilities. *Perspectives on Sexual and Reproductive Health, 35*(5), 220–225.

Armstrong, J., & Reilly, J. J. (2002). Breastfeeding and lowering the risk of childhood obesity. *Lancet, 359* (9322), 2003–2004.

Armsworth, M. W., & Stronck, K. (1999). Intergenerational effects of incest on parenting: Skills, abilities, and attitudes. *Journal of Counseling and Development, 77,* 303–314.

Aron, A., Fisher, H., Mashek, D. J., Strong, G., Haifang, L., & Brown, L. (2005). Reward, motivation, and emotion systems associated with early-stage intense romantic love. *Journal of Neurophysiology, 94,* 327–337.

Arrington, M. I. (2003). "I don't want to be an artificial man": Narrative reconstruction of sexuality among prostate cancer survivors. *Sexuality and Culture, 7*(2), 30–58.

Artz, L., et al. (2005). A randomized trial of clinician-delivered interventions promoting barrier contraception for sexually transmitted disease prevention. *Sexually Transmitted Diseases, 32*(11), 672–679.

ASHA. (2004). The STDs nobody knows. *Perspectives on Sexual and Reproductive Health, 36*(3), 97.

Ashton, A. K., Mahmood, A., & Iqbal, F. (2005). Improvement in SSRI/ SNRI-induced sexual dysfunction by switching to escitalopram. *Journal of Sex and Marital Therapy, 31,* 257–262.

Aslan, G., Aslan, D., Kizilyar, A., Ispahi, C., & Esen, A. (2005). A prospective analysis of sexual functions during pregnancy. *International Journal of Impotence Research, 17*(2), 154–157.

Attwood, F. (2005). What do people do with porn? Qualitative research into the consumption, use, and experience of pornography and other sexually explicit media. *Sexuality & Culture, 9*(2), 65–86.

Autry, A. M., et al. (2002). A comparison of medical induction and D&E for second-trimester abortion. *American Journal of Obstetrics and Gynecology, 187*(2), 393–397.

Awwad, Z., et al. (2005). Penile measurements in normal adult Jordanians and in patients with erectile dysfunction. *International Journal of Impotence Research, 17*(2), 191–195.

Axinn, W. G., & Thornton, A. (1992). The relationship between cohabitation and divorce: Selectivity or causal influence? *Demography, 29,* 357–374.

Aydt, H., & Corsaro, W. A. (2003). Differences in children's construction of gender across culture. *American Behavioral Scientist, 46*(10), 1306–1325.

Aylwin, A. S., Reddon, J. R., & Burke, A. R. (2005). Sexual fantasies of adolescent male sex offenders in residential treatment: A descriptive study. *Archives of Sexual Behavior, 34*(2), 231–239.

Bachmann, K. M., Bossi, J., Moggi, F., Stirnemann-Lewis, F., Sommer, R., & Brenner, H. D. (2000). Nurse–patient sexual contact in psychiatric hospitals. *Archives of Sexual Behavior, 29*(4), 335–347.

Backman, T., et al. (2005). Use of the levonorgestrel-releasing intrauterine system and breast cancer. *Obstetrics and Gynecology, 106*(4), 813–817.

Baerwald, A. R., Adams, G. P., & Pierson, R. A. (2003). A new model for ovarian follicular development during the human menstrual cycle. *Fertility and Sterility, 80*(1), 116–122.

Bagarozzi, D. A. (2001). *Enhancing intimacy in marriage.* New York: Brunner-Routledge.

Bailey, J. M. (2003). *The man who would be queen: The science of gender-bending and transsexualism.* Washington, DC: Joseph Henry Press.

Bailey, J. M., Bechtold, K. T., & Berenbaum, S. A. (2002). Who are tomboys and why should we study them? *Archives of Sexual Behavior, 31*(4), 333–341.

Bailey, J. M., & Shriver, A. (1999). Does childhood sexual abuse cause borderline personality disorder? *Journal of Sex and Marital Therapy, 25,* 45–57.

Bailey, J. V., et al. (2004). Bacterial vaginosis in lesbian and bisexual women. *Sexually Transmitted Diseases, 31*(11), 691–694.

Baldwin, J. I., & Baldwin, J. D. (2000). Heterosexual anal intercourse: An understudied, high-risk sexual behavior. *Archives of Sexual Behavior, 29*(4), 357–373.

Baldwin, K., Ginsberg, P., & Harkaway, R. C. (2003). Under-reporting of erectile dysfunction among men with unrelated urologic conditions. *International Journal of Impotence Research, 15*(2), 87–89.

Baldwin, S. B., et al. (2004). Condom use and other factors affecting penile human papillomavirus detection in men attending a sexually transmitted disease clinic. *Sexually Transmitted Diseases, 31*(10), 601–607.

Ballan, M. (2004). Parents as sexuality educators for their children with developmental disabilities. *SIECUS Report, 32*(2), 29–30.

Balter, M. (2005). Dissecting a hidden breast cancer risk. *Science, 309,* 1664–1666.

Bancroft, J. (2000). *The role of theory in sex research.* Bloomington, IN: Indiana University Press.

Bancroft, J. (2001). Review symposium: Krafft-Ebing, a hundred years on. *Sexualities, 4*(4), 497–509.

Bancroft, J. (2002a). Biological factors in human sexuality. *Journal of Sex Research, 39*(1), 15–21.

Bancroft, J. (2002b). Sexual effects of androgens in women: Some theoretical considerations. *Fertility and Sterility, 77,* 55–59.

Bancroft, J. (Ed.). (2003a). *Sexual development in childhood.* Bloomington, IN: Indiana University Press.

Bancroft, J. (2003b). Can sexual orientation change? A running saga. *Archives of Sexual Behavior, 32*(5), 419–421.

Bancroft, J. (2005). Alfred C. Kinsey and the politics of sex research. *Annual Review of Sex Research, 15,* 1–38.

Bancroft, J., Graham, C. A., & McCord, C. (2001). Conceptualizing women's sexual problems. *Journal of Sex and Marital Therapy, 27,* 95–103.

Bancroft, J., Loftus, J., & Long, J. S. (2003). Distress about sex: A national survey of women in heterosexual relationships. *Archives of Sexual Behavior, 32*(3), 193–208.

Bancroft, J., et al. (2004). Sexual activity and risk taking in young heterosexual men: The relevance of sexual arousability, mood, and sensation seeking. *Journal of Sex Research, 41*(2), 181–192.

Bancroft, J., & Vukadinovic, Z. (2004). Sexual addiction, sexual compulsivity, sexual impulsivity, or what? Toward a theoretical model. *Journal of Sex Research, 41*(3), 225–234.

Banfield, S. M., & McCabe, M. P. (2001). Extra relationship involvement among women: Are they different from men? *Archives of Sexual Behavior, 30*(2), 119–142.

Bankhead, C. (2005). Men with micropenis have well-adjusted outcome. *Urology Times, 33,* 20.

Banyard, V. L., & Williams, L. M. (1999). Memories for child sexual abuse and mental health functioning: Findings on a sample of women and implications for future research. In L. M. Williams & V. L. Banyard (Eds.),

Trauma and Memory (pp. 115–125). Thousand Oaks, CA: Sage.

Bar-Hava, M., Azam, F., Yovel, I., Lessing, J. B., Amit, A., Abramov, L., Militscher, I., & Chen, J. (2001). The interrelationship between coping strategies and sexual functioning in in-vitro fertilization patients. *Journal of Sex and Marital Therapy, 27,* 389–394.

Barbach, L. G. (1988). *Becoming orgasmic.* Englewood Cliffs, NJ: Prentice Hall.

Baron-Cohen, S., Knickmeyer, R. C., & Belmonte, M. K. (2005). Sex differences in the brain: Implications for explaining autism. *Science, 310,* 819–823.

Barone, M. A., Johnson, C. H., Luick, M. A., Teutonico, D. L., & Magnani, R. J. (2004). Characteristics of men receiving vasectomies in the United States, 1998–1999. *Perspectives on Sexual and Reproductive Health, 36*(1), 27–33.

Barqawi, A., & Crawford, E. D. (2006). Testosterone replacement therapy and the risk of prostate cancer. Is there a link? *International Journal of Impotence Research, 18,* 323–328.

Barr, W. B., Lawrence-Cleary, K., Gracia, C. R., & Quinones, J. N. (2003). Letter. *Journal of Sex and Marital Therapy, 29*(4), 247–248.

Barrientos, J. E., & Paez, D. (2006). Psychosocial variables of sexual satisfaction in Chile. *Journal of Sex and Marital Therapy, 32,* 351–368.

Barsky, J. L., Friedman, M. A., & Rosen, R. C. (2006). Sexual dysfunction and chronic illness: The role of flexibility in coping. *Journal of Sex and Marital Therapy, 32,* 235–253.

Bartlett, T. (2003, October 24). Did a university let a sex researcher go too far? *Chronicle of Higher Education,* A10–12.

Bartoi, M. G., Kinder, B. N., & Tomianovic, D. (2000). Interaction effects of emotional status and sexual abuse on adult sexuality. *Journal of Sex and Marital Therapy, 26,* 1–23.

Basson, R. (2001). Human sex-response cycles. *Journal of Sex and Marital Therapy, 27,* 33–43.

Basson, R. (2002a). A model of women's sexual arousal. *Journal of Sex and Marital Therapy, 28,* 1–10.

Basson, R. (2002b). Women's sexual desire—disordered or misunderstood? *Journal of Sex and Marital Therapy, 28*(s), 17–28.

Basson, R. (2003). Commentary on "In the mood for sex—the value of

androgens." *Journal of Sex and Marital Therapy, 29*(2), 177–179.

Basson, R., et al. (2001). Report of the International Consensus Development Conference on female sexual dysfunction: Definitions and classifications. *Journal of Sex and Marital Therapy, 27,* 83–94.

Basson, R., et al. (2003). Definitions of women's sexual dysfunction reconsidered: Advocating expansion and revision. *Journal of Psychosomatic Obstetrics and Gynecology, 24,* 221–229.

Batchelder, M. (2004). Many debates, many players: Controversies over sexuality education during the 2003–2004 school year. *SIECUS Report, 32*(4), 9–21.

Bauer, C. R., et al. (2002). The maternal lifestyle study: Drug exposure during pregnancy and short-term maternal outcomes. *American Journal of Obstetrics and Gynecology, 186*(3), 487–495.

Baumeister, R. F. (2000). Gender differences in erotic plasticity: The female sex drive as socially flexible and responsive. *Psychological Bulletin, 126,* 347–374.

Bauserman, R. (1998). Egalitarian, sexist, and aggressive sexual materials: Attitude effects and viewer responses. *Journal of Sex Research, 35*(3), 244–253.

Bauserman, R., & Rind, B. (1997). Psychological correlates of male child and adolescent sexual experiences with adults: A review of the nonclinical literature. *Archives of Sexual Behavior, 26*(2), 105–141.

Beadnell, B., et al. (2005). Condom use, frequency of sex, and number of partners: Multidimensional characterization of adolescent sexual risk-taking. *Journal of Sex Research, 42*(3), 192–202.

Bean, J. L. (2002). Expression of female sexuality. *Journal of Sex and Marital Therapy, 28*(s), 29–38.

Bebeau, M. J., Pimple, K. D., Muskavitch, K., Borden, S. L., & Smith, D. H. (1995). *Moral reasoning in scientific research: Cases for teaching and assessment.* Bloomington, IN: Poynter Center for the Study of Ethics and American Institutions.

Beck, J. (1999). Should homosexuality be taught as an acceptable alternative lifestyle? A Muslim perspective: A response to Halstead and Lewicka. *Cambridge Journal of Education, 29* (1), 121–230.

Beckman, M. (2003). False memories, true pain. *Science, 299,* 1306.

Beksinska, M. E., et al. (2001). Structural integrity of the female condom after multiple uses, washing, drying, and relubrication. *Contraception, 63*(1), 33–36.

Belanger, D. (2002). Son preference in a rural village in North Vietnam. *Studies in Family Planning, 33*(4), 321–334.

Bell, A., Weinberg, M. S., & Hammersmith, S. K. (1981). *Sexual preference: Its development in men and women.* Bloomington: Indiana University Press.

Bem, D. J. (2000). Exotic becomes erotic: Interpreting the biological correlates of sexual orientation. *Archives of Sexual Behavior, 29*(6), 531–548.

Bem, S. L. (1987). Masculinity and femininity exist only in the mind of the perceiver. In J. H. Reinisch, L. A. Rosenblum, & S. A. Sanders (Eds.), *Masculinity/femininity: Basic perspectives* (pp. 304–311). New York: Oxford University Press.

Bem, S. L. (1993). *The lenses of gender.* New Haven, CT: Yale University Press.

Benotsch, E. G., Kalichman, S., & Cage, M. (2002). Men who have met sex partners via the Internet: Prevalence, predictors, and implications for HIV prevention. *Archives of Sexual Behavior, 31*(2), 177–183.

Bentley, G. R., & Mascie-Taylor, C. G. N. (2000). *Infertility in the modern world: Present and future prospects.* Cambridge, England: Cambridge University Press.

Berenbaum, S. A. (2007). Psychological outcome in children with disorders of sex development: Implications for treatment and understanding typical development. *Annual Review of Sex Research, 7,* 1–38.

Berenson, A. B., Breitkopf, C. R., & Wu, Z. H. (2003). Reproductive correlates of depressive symptoms among low-income minority women. *Obstetrics and Gynecology, 102*(6), 1310–1317.

Beres, M. A., Herold, E., & Maitland, S. B. (2004). Sexual consent behaviors in same-sex relationships. *Archives of Sexual Behavior, 33*(5), 475–486.

Berg, D. R., Lonsway, K. A., & Fitzgerald, L. F. (1999). Rape prevention education for men: The effectiveness of empathy-induction techniques. *Journal of College Student Development, 40*(3), 219–234.

Bergman, S. J., & Surrey, J. (1992). *Work in progress: The woman–man relationship: Impasses and possibilities.* Wellesley, MA: Stone Center, Wellesley College.

Berkley, K. J., Rapkin, A. J., & Papka, R. E. (2005). The pains of endometriosis. *Science, 308,* 1587–1588.

Berlo, W. V., & Ensink, B. (2001). Problems with sexuality after sexual assault. *Annual Review of Sex Research, 11,* 235–257.

Berman, J. R., Berman, L. A., Lin, H., Flaherty, E., Lahey, N., & Goldstein, I. (2001). Effect of sildenafil on subjective and physiologic parameters of the female sexual response in women with sexual arousal disorder. *Journal of Sex and Marital Therapy, 27,* 411–420.

Berman, L. (2003). *The puzzle: Exploring the evolutionary puzzle of male homosexuality.* Wilmette, IL: Godot Press.

Berman, L. A., Berman, J. R., Bruck, D., Pawar, R. V., & Goldstein, I. (2001). Pharmacotherapy and psychotherapy?: Effective treatment for FSD related to unresolved childhood sexual abuse. *Journal of Sex and Marital Therapy, 27,* 421–425.

Berman, L. A., Berman, J. R., Miles, M., Pollets, D., & Powell, J. A. (2003). Genital self-image as a component of sexual health: Relationship between genital self-image, female sexual function, and quality of life measures. *Journal of Sex and Marital Therapy, 29,* 11–21.

Betchen, S. J. (2003). Suggestions for improving intimacy in couples in which one partner has attention deficit/hyperactivity disorder. *Journal of Sex and Marital Therapy, 29*(2), 103–124.

Beutler, L. E., & Malik, M. L. (Eds.). (2002). *Rethinking the DSM: A psychological perspective.* Washington, DC: American Psychological Association.

Bianchi-Demicheli, F., & Zutter, A. (2005). Intensive short-term dynamic sex therapy: A proposal. *Journal of Sex and Marital Therapy, 31,* 57–72.

Billups, K. L., Berman, L., Berman, J., Metz, M. E., Glennon, M. E., & Goldstein, I. (2001). A new non-pharmacological vacuum therapy for female sexual dysfunction. *Journal of Sex and Marital Therapy, 27,* 435–441.

Billy, J., Tanfer, K., Grady, W. R., & Klepinger, D. H. (1993). The sexual behavior of men in the United States. *Family Planning Perspectives, 25*(2), 52–60.

Binik, Y. M. (2005). Should dyspareunia be retained as a sexual dysfunction in *DSM-V?* A painful classification

decision. *Archives of Sexual Behavior, 34*(1), 11–21.

Binik, Y. M., Reissing, E., Pukall, C., Flory, N., Payne, K. A., & Khalifé, S. (2002). The female sexual pain disorders: Genital pain or sexual dysfunction. *Archives of Sexual Behavior, 31*(5), 425–429.

Birnbaum, G. E. (2003). The meaning of heterosexual intercourse among women with female orgasmic disorder. *Archives of Sexual Behavior, 32*(1), 61–71.

Birnbaum, G., Glaubman, H., & Mikulincer, M. (2001). Women's experience of heterosexual intercourse—scale construction, factor structure, and relations to orgasmic disorder. *Journal of Sex Research, 38*(3), 191–204.

Bishop, C. E., Whitworth, Y. Q., Agoulnik, A. I., Agoulnik, I. U., Harrison, W. R., Behringer, R. R., & Overbeek, P. A. (2000). A transgenic insertion upstream of Sox 9 is associated with dominant XX sex reversal in the mouth. *Nature Genetics, 26*(4), 490–494.

Bitler, M., & Zavodny, M. (2002). Did abortion legalization reduce the number of unwanted children? Evidence of adoptions. *Perspectives on Sexual and Reproductive Health, 34*(1), 25–34.

Blackburn, L. (2006). U. K. embryos may be screened for cancer risk. *Science, 312,* 984.

Blackledge, C. (2004). *The story of V: Opening Pandora's box.* London: Weidenfeld and Nicolson.

Blair, T. M., Nelson, E. S., & Coleman, P. K. (2001). Deception, power, and self-differentiation in college students' romantic relationships: An exploratory study. *Journal of Sex and Marital Therapy, 27,* 57–71.

Blake, S. M., Simkin, L., Ledsky, R., Perkins, C., & Calabrese, J. M. (2001). Effects of a parent-child communications intervention on young adolescents' risk for early onset of sexual intercourse. *Family Planning Perspectives, 33*(2), 52–61.

Blake, S. M., et al. (2003). Condom availability programs in Massachusetts high schools: Relationships with condom use and sexual behavior. *American Journal of Public Health, 93*(6), 955–962.

Blanchard, R. (1991). Clinical observations and systematic studies of autogynephilia. *Journal of Sex and Marital Therapy, 17*(4), 235–251.

Blanchard, R. (2005). Early history of the concept of autogynephilia.

Archives of Sexual Behavior, 34(4), 439–446.

Blanchard, R., Christensen, B. K., Strong, S. M., Cantor, J. M., Kuban, M. E., Klassen, P., Dickey, R., & Blak, T. (2002). Retrospective self-reports of childhood accidents causing unconsciousness in phallometrically diagnosed pedophiles. *Archives of Sexual Behavior, 31*(6), 511–526.

Blanchard, R., Kuban, M. E., Klassen, P., Dickey, R., Christensen, B. K., Cantor, J. M., & Blak, T. (2003). Self-reported head injuries before and after age 13 in pedophilic and nonpedophilic men referred for clinical assessment. *Archives of Sexual Behavior, 32*(6), 573–581.

Blinn-Pike, L., et al. (2004). Sexually abstinent adolescents: An 18-month follow-up. *Journal of Adolescent Research, 19*(5), 495–511.

Bloom, A. (2002). *Normal: Transsexual CEOs, cross-dressing cops, and hermaphrodites with attitude.* New York: Random House.

Blumberg, E. S. (2003). The lives and voices of highly sexual women. *Journal of Sex Research, 40*(2), 146–157.

Blumberg, S. J., Cynamon, M. L., Osborn, L., & Olson, L. (2003). *Journal of Sex Research, 40*(2), 121–128.

Blumenthal, S., Gudjonsson, G., & Burns, J. (1999). Cognitive distortions and blame attribution in sex offenders against adults and children. *Child Abuse and Neglect, 23*(2), 129–143.

Blumstein, P. W., & Schwartz, P. (1983). *American couples.* New York: William Morrow.

Bobes, J., Garcia-Portilla, M. P., Rejas, J., Hernandez, G., Garcia-Garcia, M., Rico-Villademoros, F., & Porras, A. (2003). Frequency of sexual dysfunction and mother reproductive side-effects in patients with schizophrenia treated with risperidone, olanzapine, quetiapine, or haloperidol: The results of the ERIE study. *Journal of Sex and Marital Therapy, 29*(2), 125–147.

Bockting, W. O., & Ehrbar, R. D. (2005). Commentary: Gender variance, dissonance, or identity disorder? *Journal of Psychology and Human Sexuality, 17*(3/4), 125–134.

Bogaert, A. F. (2000). Birth order and sexual orientation in a national probability sample. *Journal of Sex Research, 37*(4), 361–368.

Bogaert, A. F. (2001). Personality, individual differences, and preferences for the sexual media. *Archives of Sexual Behavior, 30*(1), 29–53.

Bogaert, A. F. (2003). Interaction of older brothers and sex-typing in the prediction of sexual orientation in men. *Archives of Sexual Behavior, 32*(2), 129–134.

Bogaert, A. F. (2004). Asexuality: Prevalence and associated factors in a national probability sample. *Journal of Sex Research, 41*(3), 279–287.

Bogaert, A. F. (2005). Sibling sex ratio and sexual orientation in men and women: New tests in two national probability samples. *Archives of Sexual Behavior, 34*(1), 111–116.

Bogaert, A. F., Friesen, C., & Klentrou, P. (2002). Age of puberty and sexual orientation in a national probability sample. *Archives of Sexual Behavior, 31*(1), 73–81.

Bogaert, A. F., Woodard, U., & Hafer, C. L. (1999). Intellectual ability and reactions to pornography. *Journal of Sex Research, 36*(3) 283–291.

Boggess, J. E. (2002). How can pharmacies improve access to emergency contraception? *Perspectives on Sexual and Reproductive Health, 34*(3), 162–165.

Boggess, J., & Bradner, C. (2002, May/June). Trends in adolescent males' abortion attitudes, 1988–1995: Difference by race and ethnicity. *Family Planning Perspectives, 32*(3), 118–123.

Bokarica, P., Parazajder, J., Mazuran, B., & Gilja, I. (2005). Surgical treatment of Peyronie's disease based on penile length and degree of curvature. *International Journal of Impotence Research, 17,* 170–174.

Bolin, A., & Granskog, J. (2003). *Athletic intruders: Ethnographic research on women, culture, and exercise.* Albany: State University of New York Press.

Bolour, S., & Braunstein, G. (2005). Testosterone therapy in women: A review. *International Journal of Impotence Research, 17,* 399–408.

Bolton, J. M., Sareen, J., & Reiss, J. P. (2006). Genital anaesthesia persisting six years after sertraline discontinuation. *Journal of Sex and Marital Therapy, 32,* 327–330.

Boone, J. A. (1998). *Libidinal currents: Sexuality and the shaping of modernism.* Chicago: Chicago University Press.

Boonstra, H. (2001). Islam, women and family planning: A primer. *The Guttmacher Report on Public Policy, 4*(6), 4–7.

Boonstra, H. (2002). Legislators craft alternative vision of sex education to counter abstinence-only drive. *The Guttmacher Report, 5*(2), 1–3.

Boonstra, H., & Nash, E. (2000). Minors and the right to consent to health care. *The Guttmacher Report on Public Policy, 3*(4), 4–8.

Boorjian, S., Lipkin, M., & Goldstein, M. (2004). The impact of obstructive interval and sperm granuloma on outcome of vasectomy reversal. *Journal of Urology, 171*(1), 304–306.

Bornstein, R. F., & Masling, J. M. (Eds.). (2002). *The psychodynamics of gender and gender role.* Washington, DC: American Psychological Association.

Both, S., Spiering, M., Everaerd, W., & Laan, E. (2004). Sexual behavior and responsiveness to sexual stimuli following laboratory-induced sexual arousal. *The Journal of Sex Research, 41*(3), 242–258.

Bowen, A. (2005). Internet sexuality research with rural men who have sex with men: Can we recruit and retain them? *Journal of Sex Research, 42*(4), 317–323.

Boyd, N. (2004). *Big sister: How extreme feminism has betrayed the fight for sexual equality.* Vancouver, BC: Greystone Books.

Boyle, D. E., Marshall, N. L., & Robeson, W. W. (2003). Gender at play: Fourth-grade girls and boys on the playground. *American Behavioral Scientist, 46*(10), 1326–1345.

Boynton, P. M. (2003). "I'm just a girl who can't say no": Women, consent, and sex research. *Journal of Sex and Marital Therapy, 29,* 23–32.

Bozon, M. (2002). Sexuality, gender, and the couple: A sociohistorical perspective. *Annual Review of Sex Research, 7,* 1–32.

Bozzette, S. A. (2005). Routine screening for HIV infection—timely and cost-effective. *New England Journal of Medicine, 352*(6), 620–621.

Bradford, J. M. W. (2000). The treatment of sexual deviation using a pharmacological approach. *Journal of Sex Research, 37*(3), 248–257.

Bradshaw, C. S., et al. (2005). Higher-risk behavioral practices associated with bacterial vaginosis compared with vaginal candidiasis. *Obstetrics and Gynecology, 106*(1), 105–114.

Bramlett, M. D., & Mosher, W. D. (2002). Cohabitation, marriage, divorce, and remarriage in the United States. *Vital and Health Statistics, 23*(22), 1–5.

Brauer, M., Laan, E., & Kuile, M. M. (2006). Sexual arousal in women with superficial dyspareunia. *Archives of Sexual Behavior, 35*(2), 191–200.

Braun, V., & Kitzinger, C. (2001). "Snatch," "hole," or "honey-pot"? Semantic categories and the problems of nonspecificity in female genital slang. *Journal of Sex Research, 38*(2), 146–158.

Braunstein, J. B., et al. (2003). Economics of reducing menstruation with trimonthly-cycle oral contraceptive therapy: Comparison with standard-cycle regimens. *Obstetrics and Gynecology, 102*(4): 699–708.

Braveman, P. A., et al. (2005). Socioeconomic status in health research: One size does not fit all. *Journal of the American Medical Association, 294*(22), 2879–2888.

Brehm, S. S., Miller, R. S., Perlman, D., & Campbell, S. M. (2002). *Intimate relationships.* Boston: McGraw-Hill.

Breitkopf, C. R., Pearson, H. C., & Breitkopf, D. M. (2005). Poor knowledge regarding the pap test among low-income women undergoing routine screening. *Perspectives on Sexual and Reproductive Health, 37*(2), 78–84.

Brener, N. D., McMahon, P. M., Warren, C. W., & Douglas, K. A. (1999). Forced sexual intercourse and associated health-risk behaviors among female college students in the United States. *Journal of Consulting and Clinical Psychology, 67*(2), 252–259.

Breslau, E. S., et al. (2003). The hormone therapy dilemma: Women respond. *Journal of the American Medical Women's Association, 58*(1), 33–43.

Breslin, M. (1998). When physicians assure confidentiality, teenagers are willing to talk openly. *Family Planning Perspectives, 30*(1), 52.

Brett, K. M., & Higgins, J. A. (2003). Hysterectomy prevalence by Hispanic ethnicity: Evidence from a national survey. *American Journal of Public Health, 93*(2), 307–312.

Brezsnyak, M., & Whisman, M. A. (2004). Sexual desire and relationship functioning: The effects of marital satisfaction and power. *Journal of Sex and Marital Therapy, 30,* 199–217.

Brickell, C. (2001). Whose "special treatment"? Heterosexism and the problems with liberalism. *Sexualities, 4*(2), 211–235.

Bridges, A. J., Bergner, R. M., & Hesson-McInnis, M. (2003). Romantic partners' use of pornography: Its significance for women. *Journal of Sex and Marital Therapy, 29,* 1–14.

Briken, P., Nika, E., & Berner, W. (2001). Treatment of paraphilia with luteinizing hormone-releasing hormones agonists. *Journal of Sex and Marital Therapy, 27,* 45–55.

Brivanlou, A. H., Gage, F. H., Jaenisch, R., Jessell, T., Melton, D., & Rossant, J. (2003). Setting standards for human embryonic stem cells. *Science, 300,* 913–916.

Brocato, V. (2004). U.S.-based opposition to sexual and reproductive rights goes international. *SIECUS Report, 32* (4), 22–27.

Brochert, A. (2001). IN clinical use, low-dose medical abortion method proves highly successful. *Family Planning Perspectives, 33*(3), 138.

Brody, J. E. (2004, June 9). Relying on abstinence in sex education proves risky. *New York Times,* as reprinted in *Watertown Daily Times,* B1, B8.

Bronner, G., Royter, V., Korczyn, A. D., & Giladi, N. (2004). Sexual dysfunction in Parkinson's disease. *Journal of Sex and Marital Therapy, 30,* 95–105.

Brown, G., Maycock, B., & Burns, S. (2005). Your picture is your bait: Use and meaning of cyberspace among gay men. *Journal of Sex Research, 42*(1), 63–73.

Brown, H. G. (2000, May 29). Don't give up on sex after 60. *Newsweek,* 55.

Brown, J. D. (2002). Mass media influences on sexuality. *Journal of Sex Research, 39*(1), 42–45.

Brown, R. D., Clarke, B., Gortmaker, V., & Robinson-Keilig, R. (2004). Assessing the campus climate for gay, lesbian, bisexual, and transgender (GLBT) students using a multiple perspectives approach. *Journal of College Student Development, 45*(1), 8–26.

Brown, S. M. (2000). Healthy sexuality and the treatment of sexually abusive youth. *SIECUS Report, 29*(1), 40–46.

Brown, W. M., Finn, C. J., Cooke, B. M., & Breedlove, S. M. (2002). Difference in finger length ratios between self-identified "butch" and "femme" lesbians. *Archives of Sexual Behavior, 31*(1), 123–127.

Browning, J. R., Hatfield, E., Kessler, D., & Levine, T. (2000). Sexual motives, gender, and sexual behavior. *Archives of Sexual Behavior, 29*(2), 135–153.

Brownstein, A. (2000, December 8). In the campus shadows, women are stalkers as well as the stalked. *Chronicals of Higher Education,* A40–42.

Bruckner, H., Martin, A., & Bearman, P. (2004). Ambivalence and pregnancy: Adolescents' attitudes, contraceptive use and pregnancy. *Perspectives on Sexual and Reproductive Health, 36* (6), 248–257.

Bryant, J. A., Mealey, L., Herzog, E. A., & Rychwalski, W. L. (2001). Paradoxical effect of surveyor's conservative versus provocative clothing on rape myth acceptance of males and females. *Journal of Psychology and Human Sexuality, 13*(1), 55–66.

Bucardo, J., Semple, S. J., Fraga-Vallejo, M., Davila, W., & Patterson, T. L. (2004). A qualitative exploration of female sex work in Tijuana, Mexico. *Archives of Sexual Behavior, 33*(4), 343–351.

Bullivant, S. B., Sellergren, S. A., Stern, K., Spencer, N. A., Jacob, S., Mennella, J. A., & McClintock, M. K. (2004). Women's sexual experience during the menstrual cycle: Identification of the sexual phase by noninvasive measurement of luteinizing hormone. *Journal of Sex Research, 41*(1), 82–93.

Bullough, B., & Bullough, V. (1997). Female prostitution: Current research and changing interpretations. *Annual Review of Sex Research, 7,* 158–180.

Bullough, V. L. (2002). Masturbation: A historical overview. *Journal of Psychology and Human Sexuality, 14*(2/3), 17–33.

Bullough, V. L. (2003a). Bruce Rind the truth teller. *Journal of Psychology and Human Sexuality, 15*(1), 1–3.

Bullough, V. L. (2003b). Magnus Hirschfeld, an often overlooked pioneer. *Sexuality and Culture, 7*(1), 62–72.

Bullough, V. L. (2004). Sex will never be the same: The contributions of Alfred C. Kinsey. *Archives of Sexual Behavior, 33*(3), 277–286.

Bulterys, M., et al. (2004). Rapid HIV-1 testing during labor: A multicenter study. *Journal of the American Medical Association, 292*(2), 219–223.

Burchardt, M., Burchardt, T., Anasasiadis, A. G., Kiss, A. J., Baer, L., Pawar, A., et al. (2002). Sexual dysfunction is common and overlooked in female patients with hypertension. *Journal of Sex and Marital Therapy, 28,* 17–26.

Burstein, G. R., et al. (2003). Missed opportunities for sexually transmitted diseases, human immunodeficiency virus, and pregnancy prevention services during adolescent health supervision visits. *Pediatrics, 111*(5), 996–1001.

Buss, D. M. (2000). *The dangerous passion: Why jealousy is as necessary as love and sex.* New York: Free Press.

Buss, D. M. (2002). Human mate guarding. *Neuroendocrinology Letters, 23*(4), 23–29.

Buss, D. M. (2003). *The evolution of desire: Strategies of human mating* (Rev. ed.). New York: Basic Books.

Bussey, K., & Bandura, A. (1992). Self-regulatory mechanisms governing gender development. *Child Development, 63*(5), 1236–1250.

Butler, A. C. (2000). Trends in same-gender sexual partnering, 1988–1998. *Journal of Sex Research, 37*(4), 333–343.

Butt, T., & Hearn, J. (1998). The sexualization of corporal punishment: The construction of sexual meaning. *Sexualities, 1*(2), 203–227.

Buzzell, T. (2005). Demographic characteristics of persons using pornography in three technological contexts. *Sexuality and Culture, 9*(1), 28–48.

Byers, E. S. (2005). Relationship satisfaction and sexual satisfaction: A longitudinal study of individuals in long-term relationships. *Journal of Sex Research, 42*(2), 113–118.

Byers, E. S., & Demmons, S. (1999). Sexual satisfaction and sexual self-disclosure within dating relationships. *Journal of Sex Research, 36*(2), 180–189.

Byers, E. S., & Grenier, G. (2003). Premature or rapid ejaculation: Heterosexual couples' perceptions of men's ejaculatory behavior. *Archives of Sexual Behavior, 32*(3), 261–270.

Byers, E. S., Purdon, C., & Clark, D. A. (1998). Sexual intrusive thoughts of college students. *Journal of Sex Research, 35*(4), 359–369.

Byrd, A. D. (2003). The malleability of homosexuality: A debate long overdue. *Archives of Sexual Behavior, 32*(5), 423–425.

Cain, V. S., Johannes, C. B., Avis, N. E., Mohr, B., Schocken, M., Skurnick, J., & Ory, M. (2003). Sexual functioning and practices in a multi-ethnic study of midlife women: Baseline results from SWAN. *Journal of Sex Research, 40*(3), 266–276.

Calamidas, E. G. (1997). Promoting healthy sexuality among older adults: Educational challenges for health professionals. *Journal of Sex Education and Therapy, 22*(2), 45–49.

Callaghan, W. M., & Berg, C. J. (2003). Pregnancy-related mortality among women aged 35 years and older, United States, 1991–1997. *Obstetrics and Gynecology, 102*(5), 1015–1021.

Callaghan, W. M., MacDorman, M. F., Rasmussen, S. A., Qin, C., & Lackritz,

E. M. (2006). The contribution of preterm birth to infant mortality rates in the United States. *Pediatrics, 118,* 1566–1573.

Cameron, A., Rosen, R. C., & Swindle, R. W. (2005). Sexual and relationship characteristics among an Internet-based sample of U.S. men with and without erectile dysfunction. *Journal of Sex and Marital Therapy, 31,* 229–242.

Campbell, A. (2004). Female competition: Causes, constraints, content, and contexts. *Journal of Sex Research, 41*(1), 16–26.

Cann, A., Mangum, J. L., & Wells, M. (2001). Distress in response to relationship infidelity: The roles of gender and attitudes about relationships. *Journal of Sex Research, 38*(3), 185–190.

Cantor, J. M., Blanchard, R., Paterson, A. D., & Bogaert, A. F. (2002). How many gay men owe their sexual orientation to fraternal birth order? *Archives of Sexual Behavior, 31*(1), 63–71.

Cantor, J. M., et al. (2005). Handedness in pedophilia and hebephilia. *Archives of Sexual Behavior, 34*(4), 447–459.

Carballo-Diéguez, A., Miner, M., Dolezal, C., Rosser, B. R. S., & Jacoby, S. (2006). Sexual negotiation, HIV-status disclosure, and sexual risk behavior among Latino men who use the Internet to seek sex with other men. *Archives of Sexual Behavior, 35,* 473–481.

Cardoso, F. L. (2002). "Fishermen": Masculinity and sexuality in a Brazilian fishing community. *Sexuality and Culture, 6*(4), 45–72.

Cardoso, F. L. (2005). Cultural universals and differences in male homosexuality: The case of a Brazilian fishing village. *Archives of Sexual Behavior, 34*(1), 103–109.

Carlock, C. J. (1999). Gender and self-esteem. In C. J. Carlock (Ed.), *Enhancing self-esteem* (pp. 251–285). Philadelphia: Accelerated Development.

Carmichael, M. (2004, May 10). Have it your way: Redesigning birth. *Newsweek,* 70–72.

Carnes, P. (1992). *Out of the shadows: Understanding sexual addiction* (2d ed.). Center City, MN: Hazelden.

Carnes, P. (2003). Understanding sexual addiction. *SIECUS Report, 31*(5), 5–7.

Caron, S. L., & Moskey, E. G. (2002). Regrettable sex: An exploratory analysis of college students' experiences.

Journal of Psychology and Human Sexuality, 14(1), 47–54.

Carpendale, J. J. M. (2000). Kohlberg and Piaget on stages and moral reasoning. *Developmental Review, 20,* 181–205.

Carufel, F., & Trudel, G. (2006). Effects of a new functional-sexological treatment for premature ejaculation. *Journal of Sex and Marital Therapy, 32,* 97–114.

Carvalheira, A., & Gomes, F. A. (2003). Cybersex in Portuguese chatrooms: A study of sexual behaviors related to online sex. *Journal of Sex and Marital Therapy, 29,* 345–360.

Cash, T. F., & Pruzinsky, T. (2004). *Body image: A handbook of theory, research, and clinical practice.* New York: Guilford Press.

Cass, V. C. (1983–1984). Homosexual identity: A concept in need of definition. *Journal of Homosexuality, 9,* 105–126.

Cass, V. C. (1990). The implications of homosexual identity formation for the Kinsey model and scale of sexual preference. In D. P. McWhirter, S. A. Sanders, & J. M Reinisch (Eds.), *Homosexuality/heterosexuality: Concepts of sexual orientation* (pp. 239–266). New York: Oxford University Press.

Castellsague, X., Bosch, F. X., Munoz, N., Meijer, C. J., et al. (2002, April 11). Male circumcision, penile human papillomavirus infection, and cervical cancer in female partners. *New England Journal of Medicine, 346*(15), 1105–1112.

Catalano, G., Catalano, M. C., & Carroll, K. M. (2002). Repetitive male genital self-mutilation: A case report and discussion of possible risk factors. *Journal of Sex and Marital Therapy, 28,* 27–37.

Catania, J. (1997). 10% of sexually active U.S. adults use sex toys in partner sex. *Sexual Science, 38*(4), 1, 8.

Cates, J. R., Herndon, N. L., Schulz, S. L., et al. (2004). *Our voices, our lives, our futures: Youth and sexually transmitted diseases.* Chapel Hill, NC: School of Journalism and Mass Communication, University of North Carolina.

Cave, D. (2006, December 6). City drops plans to change definition of gender. *New York Times,* B1.

Cecil, H., & Matson, S. C. (2005). Differences in psychological health and family dysfunction by sexual victimization type in a clinical sample of African American adolescent women. *Journal of Sex Research, 42*(3), 203–214.

Centers for Disease Control and Prevention (CDC). (2002). Trends in sexual risk behaviors among high school students—United States, 1991–2001. *Morbidity and Mortality Weekly Report, 51*(38), 856–859.

CDC. (2004a). Cases of HIV infection and AIDS in the United States, by race/ethnicity, 1998–2002. *HIV/AIDS Surveillance Supplemental Report, 10*(1).

CDC. (2004b). National Youth Risk Behavior Survey: 1991–2003: Trends in the prevalence of sexual behaviors. *Healthy Youth.* Atlanta: Centers for Disease Control and Prevention.

CDC. (2006a). *STD surveillance 2005.* Atlanta: Dept. of Health and Human Services, Centers for Disease Control and Prevention.

CDC. (2006b). *STD treatment guidelines, 2006.* Atlanta: Dept. of Health and Human Services, Centers for Disease Control and Prevention.

Chakrabarti, N., Chopra, V. K., & Sinha, V. K. (2002). Masturbatory guilt leading to severe depression and erectile dysfunction. *Journal of Sex and Marital Therapy, 28,* 285–287.

Chan, P. G., Sung, H-Y, & Sawaya, G. F. (2003). Changes in cervical cancer incidence after three decades of screening U.S. women less than 30 years old. *Obstetrics and Gynecology, 102*(4), 765–773.

Chan, W. S., et al. (2004). Risk of stroke in women exposed to low-dose oral contraceptives: A critical evaluation of the evidence. *Archives of Internal Medicine, 164*(7), 741–747.

Chang, J., et al. (2003). Pregnancy-related mortality surveillance—United States, 1991–1999. *Morbidity and Mortality Weekly Report, 52* (SS–2).

Check, E. (2005). The X factor. *Nature, 434,* 266–267.

Chen, C-L. et al. (2002). Hormone replacement therapy in relation to breast cancer. *Journal of the American Medical Association, 287*(6), 734–741.

Chen, R. Y., et al. (2006). Distribution of health care expenditures for HIV-infected patients. *Clinical Infectious Diseases, 42*(2), 1003–1010.

Cheng, M. M., & Udry, J. R. (2003). How much do mentally disabled adolescents know about sex and birth control? *Adolescent and Family Health, 3*(1), 28–38.

Cherpes, T. L., et al. (2003). Risk factors for infection with herpes simplex virus type 2: Role of smoking, douching, uncircumcised males, and vaginal flora. *Sexually Transmitted Diseases, 30*(5), 405–410.

Chesson, H. W., Blandford, J. M., Gift, T. L., Tao, G., & Irwin, K. L. (2004). The estimated direct medical cost of sexually transmitted diseases among American youth, 2000. *Perspectives on Sexual and Reproductive Health, 36*(1), 11–19.

Chevret, M., Jaudinot, E., Sullivan, K., Marrel, A., & DeGendre, A. S. (2004a). Impact of erectile dysfunction (ED) on sexual life of female partners: Assessment with the index of sexual life (ISL) questionnaire. *Journal of Sex and Marital Therapy, 30,* 157–172.

Chevret, M., Jaudinot, E., Sullivan, K., Marrel, A., & DeGendre, A. S. (2004b). Quality of sexual life and satisfaction in female partners of men with ED: Psychometric validation of the index of sexual life (ISL) questionnaire. *Journal of Sex and Marital Therapy, 30,* 141–155.

Chiasson, M., et al. (2005). Increased high risk sexual behavior after September 11 in men who have sex with men: An Internet study. *Archives of Sexual Behavior, 34*(5), 527–535.

Chivers, M. L., & Bailey, J. M. (2000). Sexual orientation of female-to-male transsexuals: A comparison of homosexual and nonhomosexual types. *Archives of Sexual Behavior, 29,* 259–278.

Cho, C. H. (2006, March 12). The power of "Brokeback Inc." *Watertown Daily Times Sunday Weekly,* 5.

Choate, L. H. (2005). Toward a theoretical model of women's body image resilience. *Journal of Counseling and Development, 83,* 320–330.

Chow, E. W. C., & Choy, A. L. (2002). Clinical characteristics and treatment response to SSRI in a female pedophile. *Archives of Sexual Behavior, 31*(2), 211–215.

Chrisler, J. C., & Caplan, P. (2003). The strange case of Dr. Jekyll and Ms. Hyde: How PMS became a cultural phenomenon and a psychiatric disorder. *Annual Review of Sex Research, 13,* 274–306.

Christakis, D. A., Harvey, E., Zerr, D. M., Feudtner, C., Wright, J. A., & Connell, F. A. (2000). A trade-off analysis of routine newborn circumcision. *Pediatrics, 105*(1), 246–249.

Chudakov, B., Ilan, K., Belmaker, R. H., & Cwikel, J. (2002). The motivation and mental health of sex workers. *Journal of Sex and Marital Therapy, 28,* 305–315.

Chung, R. C. (2005). Women, human rights, and counseling: Crossing international boundaries. *Journal of Counseling and Development, 83,* 262–268.

Chung, Y. B., & Katayama, M. (1999). Ethnic and sexual identity development of Asian American lesbian and gay adolescents. In K. S. Ng (Ed.), *Counseling Asian families from a systems perspective* (pp. 159–169). Alexandria, VA: American Counseling Association.

Ciardullo, M. (2005). Advocates on both sides are as passionate as ever. *SIECUS Report, 33*(4), 4–19.

Ciccarone, D. H., Kanouse, D. E., Collins, R. L., Miu, A., Chen, J. L., Morton, S. C., & Stall, R. (2003). Sex without disclosure of HIV serostatus in a U.S. probability sample of persons receiving medical care for HIV infection. *American Journal of Public Health, 93*(6), 949–954.

Ciclitira, K. (2004). Pornography, women and feminism: Between pleasure and politics. *Sexualities, 7*(3), 281–301.

Ciesielski, C., Tabidze, I., & Brown, C. (2004). Transmission of primary and secondary syphilis by oral sex— Chicago, Illinois, 1998–2002. *Morbidity and Mortality Weekly Report, 53*(41), 966–968.

Clark, C. A., & Wiederman, M. W. (2000). Gender and reactions to a hypothetical relationship partner's masturbation and use of sexually explicit media. *Journal of Sex Research, 37*(2), 133–141.

Clark, L. R., Jackson, M., & Allen-Taylor, L. (2002). Adolescent knowledge about sexually transmitted diseases. *Sexually Transmitted Diseases, 29*(8), 436–443.

Clawson, C. L., & Reese-Weber, M. (2003). The amount and timing of parent-adolescent sexual communication as predictors of late adolescent sexual risk-taking behaviors. *Journal of Sex Research, 40*(3), 256–265.

Clayton, A. H., et al. (2006). Reliability and validity of the sexual interest and desire inventory—female (SIDI-F), a scale designed to measure severity of female hypoactive sexual desire disorder. *Journal of Sex and Marital Therapy, 32,* 115–135.

Cleland, J., Bernstein, S., Ezeh, A., Faundes, A., Glasier, A., & Innis, J. (2006). Family planning: The unfinished agenda. *The Lancet, Early Online Publication: DOI:* 10.1016/S0140-6736(06)69480-4.

Cleland, J., & Ferry, B. (Eds.). (1997). *Sexual behaviour and knowledge about AIDS in the developing world: Findings from a multisite study.* London: Taylor and Francis.

Clement, U. (2002). Sex in long-term relationships: A systemic approach to sexual desire problems. *Archives of Sexual Behavior, 31*(3), 241–246.

Cluett, E. R., et al. (2004). Randomized controlled trial of laboring in water compared with standard augmentation for management of dystocia in first stage of labor. *British Medical Journal, 328*(7435), 314–319.

Cochran, S. D., & Mays, V. M. (1990). Sex, lies, and HIV. *New England Journal of Medicine, 322*(11), 774–775.

Coeytaux, F., Moore, K., & Gelberg, L. (2003). Convincing new providers to offer medical abortion: What will it take? *Perspectives on Sexual and Reproductive Health, 35*(1), 44–47.

Cohan, C. L., & Kleinbaum, S. (2002). Toward a greater understanding of the cohabitation effect: Premarital cohabitation and marital communication. *Journal of Marriage and Family, 64*(1), 180–192.

Cohen, J. (2003a). Human population: The next half century. *Science, 302,* 1172–1175.

Cohen, J. (2003b). Mothers' malaria appears to enhance spread of AIDS virus. *Science, 302,* 1311.

Cohen, J. (2005a). Male circumcision thwarts HIV infection. *Science, 309,* 860.

Cohen, J. (2005b). Prevention cocktails: Combining tools to stop HIV's spread. *Science, 309,* 1002–1006.

Cohen, J. (2005c). Report of novel treatment aimed at latent HIV raises the "C word". *Science, 309,* 999–1000.

Cohen, K. M. (2002). Relationships among childhood sex-atypical behavior, spatial ability, handedness, and sexual orientation in men. *Archives of Sexual Behavior, 31*(1), 129–143.

Cohen, K. M., & Savin-Williams, R. C. (2003). Are converts to be believed? Assessing sexual orientation "conversions." *Archives of Sexual Behavior, 32*(5), 427–429.

Cohen, S. (2001). A message to the president: Abortion can be safe, legal *and* still rare. *The Guttmacher Report on Public Policy, 4*(1), 1–2.

Cohen-Kettenis, P. T. (2005). Gender change in 46,XY persons with 5α-reductase-2 deficiency and 17β-hydroxysteroid-dehydrogenase-3 deficiency. *Archives of Sexual Behavior, 34*(4), 399–410.

Colapinto, J. (2000). *As nature made him: The boy who was raised as a girl*. New York: HarperCollins.

Coleman, E. (2002a). Promoting sexual health and responsible sexual behavior. *Journal of Sex Research, 39*(1), 3–6.

Coleman, E. (2002b). Masturbation as a means of achieving sexual health. *Journal of Psychology and Human Sexuality, 14*(2/3), 5–16.

Coleman, E. (2003). Compulsive sexual behavior: What to call it, how to treat it. *SIECUS Report, 31*(5), 12–16.

Coleman, E., et al. (2001). Standards of care for the treatment of adult sex offenders. *Journal of Psychology and Human Sexuality, 13*(3/4), 115–121.

Coleman, L. M., & Cater, S. (2005). A qualitative study of the relationship between alcohol consumption and risky sex in adolescents. *Archives of Sexual Behavior, 34*(6), 649–661.

Collaborative Group on Hormonal Factors in Breast Cancer. (2002). Breast cancer and breastfeeding collaborative reanalysis of individual data from 47 epidemiological studies in 30 countries, including 50,302 women with breast cancer and 96,973 women without the disease. *Lancet, 360*(9328), 187–195.

Collaborative Group on Hormonal Factors in Breast Cancer. (2004). Breast cancer and abortion: Collaborative reanalysis of data from 53 epidemiological studies, including 83,000 women with breast cancer from 16 countries. *Lancet, 363*(9414), 1007–1016.

Collins, F. S., Morgan, M., & Patrinos, A. (2003). The human genome project: Lessons from large-scale biology. *Science, 300*, 286–290.

Collins, R. L., et al. (2003). Entertainment television as a healthy sex educator: The impact of condom-efficacy information in an episode of *Friends. Pediatrics, 112*(5), 1115–1121.

Conaglen, H. M. (2004). Sexual content induced delay: A reexamination investigating relation to sexual desire. *Archives of Sexual Behavior, 33*(4), 359–367.

Conaglen, H. M., & Conaglen, J. V. (2003). Sexual desire in women presenting for anti-androgen therapy. *Journal of Sex and Marital Therapy, 29*(4), 255–267.

Conaglen, H. M., & Evans, I. M. (2006). Pictorial clues and sexual desire: An experimental approach. *Archives of Sexual Behavior, 35*(2), 201–216.

Conaglen, H. M., Suttie, J. M., & Conaglen, J. V. (2003). Effect of deer velvet on sexual function in men and their partners: A double-blind, placebo-controlled study. *Archives of Sexual Behavior, 32*(3), 271–278.

Conklin, S. C. (2001). Seminary sexuality education survey: Current efforts, perceived need and readiness in accredited Christian institutions. *Journal of Sex Education and Therapy, 26*(4), 301–309.

Connell, K., et al. (2005). Effects of age, menopause, and comorbidities on neurological function of the female genitalia. *International Journal of Impotence Research, 17*(1), 63–70.

Connolly, J. M., Slaughter, V., & Mealey, L. (2004). The development of preferences for specific body shapes. *Journal of Sex Research, 41*(1), 5–15.

Connolly, P. H. (2006). Psychological functioning of bondage/ domination/sado-masochism (BDSM) practitioners. *Journal of Psychology and Human Sexuality, 18*(1), 79–120.

Connop, V., & Petrak, J. (2004). The impact of sexual assault on heterosexual couples. *Sexual and Relationship Therapy, 19*(1), 29–38.

Cooper, A. (2000). Sexual pathology and the Internet. *Professional Psychology: Research and Practice, 30*(2).

Cooper, A. (2002). *Sex and the Internet: A guidebook for clinicians*. Philadelphia: Brunner-Routledge.

Cooper, A., Morahan-Martin, J., Mathy, R. M., & Maheu, M. (2002). Toward an increased understanding of user demographics in online sexual activities. *Journal of Sex and Marital Therapy, 28*, 105–129.

Copeland, L. (2002, February 10). False hopes lead to "starter marriage" explosion. *Watertown Daily Times*, 7.

Coplan, P. M., Mitchnick, M., & Rosenberg, Z. F. (2004). Regulatory challenges in microbicide development. *Science, 304*, 1911–1912.

Cornog, M. (2001). Group masturbation among young and old(er): A summary with questions. *Journal of Sex Education and Therapy, 26*(4), 340–346.

Corona, G., et al. (2005). Difficulties in achieving vs. maintaining erection: Organic, psychogenic, and relational determinants. *International Journal of Impotence Research, 17*, 252–258.

Corretti, G., Pierucci, S., DeSciscolo, M., & Nisita, C. (2006). Comorbidity between social phobia and premature ejaculation: Study on 242 males affected by sexual disorders. *Journal of Sex and Marital Therapy, 32*, 183–187.

Cott, N. F. (2005). Public vows: A history of marriage and the nation. *SIECUS Report, 33*(1), 5–12.

Courtois, C. A. (2000). The sexual after-effects of incest/child sexual abuse. *SIECUS Report, 29*(1), 11–16.

Couzin, J. (2003). The twists and turns in BRCA's path. *Science, 302*, 591–593.

Couzin, J., & Kaiser, J. (2005). As Gelsinger case ends, gene therapy suffers another blow. *Science, 307*, 1028.

Coy, D. R., & Kovacs-Long, J. (2005). Maslow and Miller: An exploration of gender affiliation in the journey to competence. *Journal of Counseling and Development, 83*, 138–144.

Cozzens, J. (2006). Assessing the awareness of adolescent sexual health among teachers-in-training. *American Journal of Sexuality Education, 1*(3), 25–50.

Craissati, J. (1999). *Child sexual abusers: A community treatment approach*. Philadelphia: Brunner/ Mazel.

Crary, D. (2006, April 9). The porn divide: Home wrecker or harmless fun? *Associated Press/Watertown Daily Times Sunday Weekly*, 6–7.

Crawford, I., Allison, K. W., Zamboni, B. D., & Soto, T. (2002). The influence of dual-identity development on the psychosocial functioning of African-American gay and bisexual men. *Journal of Sex Research, 39*(3), 179–189.

Crawford, M., & Popp, D. (2003). Sexual double standards: A review and methodological critique of two decades of research. *Journal of Sex Research, 40*(1), 13–26.

Creamer, E. G. (1994). Gender and publications in core higher education journals. *Journal of College Student Development, 35*, 35–39.

Crosby, R. A., & Yarber, W. L. (2001). Perceived versus actual knowledge about correct condom use among U.S. adolescents: Results from a national study. *Journal of Adolescent Health, 128*(5), 415–420.

Crosby, R. A., et al. (2002). Condom use errors and problems among college men. *Sexually Transmitted Diseases, 29*(9), 552–557.

Cubbin, C., Santelli, J., Brindis, C. D., & Braveman, P. (2005). Neighborhood context and sexual behaviors among adolescents: Findings from the national longitudinal study of adolescent health. *Perspectives on Sexual and Reproductive Health, 37* (3), 125–134.

Cubbins, L. A., & Tanfer, K. (2000). The influence of gender on sex: A study of men's and women's self-reported high-risk sex behavior. *Archives of Sexual Behavior, 29* (3), 229–257.

Cutler, W. B. (1999). Human sex-attractant hormones: Discovery, research, development, and application in therapy. *Psychiatric Annals, 29* (1), 54–59.

Cutler, W. B., Friedmann, E., & McCoy, N. L. (1998). Pheromonal influences on sociosexual behavior in men. *Archives of Sexual Behavior, 27* (1), 1–13.

Cwikel, J., & Hoban, E. (2005). Contentious issues in research on trafficked women working in the sex industry: Study design, ethics, and methodology. *Journal of Sex Research, 42* (4), 306–316.

Daker-White, G. (2002). Reliable and valid self-report outcome measures in sexual (dys)function: A systematic review. *Archives of Sexual Behavior, 31* (2), 197–209.

Damon, W. (2002). Dominance, sexism, and inadequacy: Testing a compensatory conceptualization in a sample of heterosexual men involved in SM. *Journal of Psychology and Human Sexuality, 14* (4), 15–46.

Damon, W., & Rosser, B. (2005). Anodyspareunia in men who have sex with men: Prevalence, predictors, consequences and the development of DSM diagnostic criteria. *Journal of Sex and Marital Therapy, 31,* 129–141.

Dandash, K. F., Refaat, A. H., & Eyada, M. (2001). Female genital mutilation: A prospective view. *Journal of Sex and Marital Therapy, 27,* 459–464.

D'Angelo, D. V., Gilbert, B. C., Rochat, R. W., Santelli, J. S., & Herold, J. M. (2004). Differences between mistimed and unwanted pregnancies among women who have live births. *Perspectives on Sexual and Reproductive Health, 36* (5), 192–197.

Darling, C. A., Davidson, J. K., & Conway-Welch, C. (1990). Female ejaculation: Perceived origins, the Grafenberg spot/area, and sexual responsiveness. *Archives of Sexual Behavior, 19* (1), 29–47.

Darling, C. A., Davidson, J. K., & Jennings, D. A. (1991). The female sexual response revisited: Understanding the multiorgasmic experience in women. *Archives of Sexual Behavior, 20* (6), 527–540.

Daskalos, C. T. (1998). Changes in the sexual orientation of six male-to-female transsexuals. *Archives of Sexual Behavior, 27* (6), 605–614.

Datta, G., et al. (2006). Individual-, neighborhood-, and state-level socioeconomic predictors of cervical carcinoma screening among U.S. black women: A multilevel analysis. *Cancer, 106* (3), 664–669.

Daulaire, N., et al. (2002). *Promises to keep: The toll of unintended pregnancies on women's lives in the developing world.* Washington: Global Health Council.

Dave, U. P., Jenkins, N. A., & Copeland, N. G. (2004). Gene therapy insertional mutagenesis insights. *Science, 303,* 333.

Davidson, N. E., & Helzlsouer, K. J. (2002). Good news about oral contraceptives. *New England Journal of Medicine, 346* (26), 2078–2079.

Davies, M. (2004). Correlates of negative attitudes toward gay men: Sexism, male role norms, and male sexuality. *Journal of Sex Research, 41* (3), 259–266.

Davis, A. R., & Castano, P. M. (2005). Oral contraceptives and libido in women. *Annual Review of Sex Research, 15,* 297–320.

Davis, C. M., & Bauserman, R. (1993). Exposure to sexually explicit materials: An attitude change perspective. *Annual Review of Sex Research, 4,* 121–209.

Davis, S. R., & Tran, J. (2001). Testosterone influences libido and well-being in women. *Trends in Endocrinology and Metabolism, 12,* 33–37.

DeCuypere, G., et al. (2005). Sexual and physical health after sex reassignment surgery. *Archives of Sexual Behavior, 34* (6), 679–690.

Deeks, A. A., & McCabe, M. P. (2001). Sexual function and the menopausal woman: The importance of age and partner's sexual functioning. *Journal of Sex Research, 38* (3), 219–225.

Deep, A. L., Lilenfeld, L. R., Plotnicov, K. H., Pollice, C., & Kaye, W. H. (1999). Sexual abuse in eating disorder subtypes and control women: The role of comorbid substance dependence in bulimia nervosa. *International Journal of Eating Disorders, 25* (1), 1–10.

De Judicibus, M. A., & McCabe, M. P. (2002). Psychological factors and the sexuality of pregnant and postpartum women. *Journal of Sex Research, 39* (2), 94–103.

Dekker, A., & Schmidt, G. (2002). Patterns of masturbatory behaviour: Changes between the sixties and the nineties. *Journal of Psychology and Human Sexuality, 14* (2/3), 35–48.

DeLamater, J., & Friedrich, W. N. (2002). Human sexual development. *Journal of Sex Research, 39* (1), 10–14.

DeLamater, J. D., & Sill, M. (2005). Sexual desire in later life. *Journal of Sex Research, 42* (2), 138–149.

Delizonna, L. L., Wincze, J. P., Litz, B. T., Brown, T. A., & Barlow, D. H. (2001). A comparison of subjective and physiological measures of mechanically produced and erotically produced erections (or, is an erection an erection?). *Journal of Sex and Marital Therapy, 27,* 21–31.

Del Priore, G., Stega, J., Sieunarine, K., Ungar, L., & Smith, J. R. (2007). Human uterus retrieval from a multi-organ donor. *Obstetrics & Gynecology, 109,* 101–104.

Dennerstein, L., Alexander, J. L., & Kotz, K. (2004). The menopause and sexual functioning: A review of the population-based studies. *Annual Review of Sex Research, 14,* 64–82.

Dennerstein, L., Guthrie, J. R., & Alford, S. (2004). Childhood abuse and its association with mid-aged women's sexual functioning. *Journal of Sex and Marital Therapy, 30,* 225–234.

Denning, P. H., & Campsmith, M. L. (2005). Unprotected anal intercourse among HIV-positive men who have a steady male sex partner with negative or unknown HIV serostatus. *American Journal of Public Health, 95* (1), 152–158.

Dennis, C. (2004). The most important sexual organ. *Nature, 427,* 390–392.

Denov, M. S. (2003). The myth of innocence: Sexual scripts and the recognition of child sexual abuse by female perpetrators. *Journal of Sex Research, 40* (3), 303–314.

Derogatis, L., Rust, J., Golombok, S., et al. (2004). Validation of the profile of female sexual function (PFSF) in surgically and naturally menopausal women. *Journal of Sex and Marital Therapy, 30,* 25–36.

DeRose, A. F., Gallo, F., & Carmignani, G. (2005). Evaluation of sexual activity in patients treated with tadalafil: A randomized prospective placebo-controlled trial. *International Journal of Impotence Research, 17* (1), 76–79.

Dessens, A. B., Cohen-Kettenis, P. T., Mellenbergh, G. J., Poll, N., Koppe, J. G., & Boer, K. (1999). Prenatal exposure to anticonvulsants and psychosexual development. *Archives of Sexual Behavior, 28*(1), 31–44.

Dessens, A. B., Slijper, F. M. E., & Drop, S. L. S. (2005). Gender dysphoria and gender change in chromosomal females with congenital adrenal hyperplasia. *Archives of Sexual Behavior, 34*(4), 389–397.

DeVoss, D. (2002). Women's porn sites—spaces of fissure and eruption or "I'm a little bit of everything." *Sexuality and Culture, 6*(3), 75–94.

Diamond, L. M. (2006). The evolution of plasticity in female-female desire. *Journal of Psychology and Human Sexuality, 18*(4), 245–274.

Diamond, M. (1998). Intersexuality: Recommendations for management. *Archives of Sexual Behavior, 27,* 634–641.

Dieben, T., Roumen, F., & Apter, D. (2002). Efficacy, cycle control, and user acceptability of a novel combined contraceptive vaginal ring. *Obstetrics and Gynecology, 100*(3), 585–593.

Disogra, C. E., Mariño, R., & Minichiello, V. (2005). Self-reported use of health services, contact with police and views about sex work organizations among male sex workers in Cordoba, Argentina. *Journal of Psychology and Human Sexuality, 17*(1/2), 181–195.

Djerassi, C. (1999). Sex in an age of mechanical reproduction. *Science, 285,* 53–55.

Docter, R. F., & Fleming, J. S. (2001). Measures of transgender behavior. *Archives of Sexual Behavior, 30*(3), 255–271.

Dodge, B., Reece, M., Cole, S. L., & Sandfort, T. G. M. (2004). Sexual compulsivity among heterosexual college students. *Journal of Sex Research, 41*(4), 343–350.

Dolezal, C., & Carballo-Dieguez, A. (2002). Childhood sexual experiences and the perception of abuse among Latino men who have sex with men. *Journal of Sex Research, 39*(3), 165–173.

Donnelly, D., Burgess, E., Anderson, S., Davis, R., & Dillard, J. (2001). Involuntary celibacy: A life course analysis. *Journal of Sex Research, 38*(2), 159–169.

Dorozynski, A. (2003). France offers 800 reward for each new baby. *British Medical Journal, 326*(7397), 1002.

Downing, L. (2005). Review of *Beyond Sexuality* by T. Dean. *Archives of Sexual Behavior, 34*(2), 255–263.

Drey, E. A., et al. (2006). Risk factors associated with presenting for abortion in the second trimester. *Obstetrics and Gynecology, 107*(1), 128–135.

Dreznick, M. T. (2003). Heterosocial competence of rapists and child molesters: A meta-analysis. *Journal of Sex Research, 40*(2), 170–178.

Dreznick, M. T., Cronin, J. M., Waterman, C. K., & Glasheen, C. (2003). Saying yes when meaning no: An investigation of gender and individual differences in token seduction. *Journal of Psychology and Human Sexuality, 15*(1), 69–84.

Drumright, L. N., Gorbach, P. M., & Holmes, K. K. (2004). Do people really know their sexual partners? Concurrency, knowledge of partner behavior, and sexually transmitted infections within partnerships. *Sexually Transmitted Diseases, 31*(7), 437–442.

Dube, E. M. (2000). The role of sexual behavior in the identification process of gay and bisexual males. *Journal of Sex Research, 37*(2), 123–132.

Dunne, M. P., Bailey, J. M., Kirk, K. M., & Martin, N. G. (2000). The subtlety of sex-atypicality. *Archives of Sexual Behavior, 29*(6), 549–563.

Durex (2001). *Global survey 2001.* London: Durex.

East, P., & Adams, J. (2002). Sexual assertiveness and adolescents' sexual rights. *Perspectives on Sexual and Reproductive Health, 34*(4), 212–213.

Eastman, K., Corona, R., Ryan, G., Warsofsky, A., & Schuster, M. (2005). Worksite-based parenting programs to promote healthy adolescent sexual development: A qualitative study of feasibility and potential content. *Perspectives on Sexual and Reproductive Health, 37*(2), 62–69.

Eastwood, K. L., et al. (2006). Abortion training in United States obstetrics and gynecology residency programs. *Obstetrics and Gynecology, 108*(2), 303–308.

Ebrahim, S. H., McKenna, M. T., & Marks, J. S. (2005). Sexual behavior: Related adverse health burden in the United States. *Sexually Transmitted Infections, 81*(1), 38–40.

Edozian, A. O., et al. (2004). Congenital syphilis—United States, 2002. *Morbidity and Mortality Weekly Report, 53*(31), 716–719.

Edwards, M. (2002b). Sexual pleasure has central place in the human potential. *SIECUS Report, 30*(4), 3–4.

Eisenberg, M. E., Bearinger, L. H., Sieving, R. E., Swain, C., & Resnick, M. D. (2004). Parents' beliefs about condoms and oral contraceptives: Are they medically accurate? *Perspectives on Sexual and Reproductive Health, 36*(2), 50–57.

El-Defrawi, M. H., Lofty, G., Dandash, K. F., Refaat, A. H., & Eyada, M. (2001). Female genital mutilation and its psychosexual impact. *Journal of Sex and Marital Therapy, 27,* 465–473.

Elizur, Y., & Mintzer, A. (2001). A framework for the formation of gay male identity: Processes associated with adult attachment style and support from family and friends. *Archives of Sexual Behavior, 30*(2), 143–167.

Ellertson, C., et al. (2003). Extending the time limit for starting the Yuzpe regimen of emergency contraception to 120 hours. *Obstetrics and Gynecology, 101*(6), 1168–1171.

Elliott, L., & Brantley, C. (1997). *Sex on campus.* New York: Random House.

Ellis, H. H. (1936). *Studies in the psychology of sex* (7 vols. in 2). New York: Modern Library. (Original edition published 1896–1928).

Ellis, L., Robb, B., & Burke, D. (2005). Sexual orientation in United States and Canadian college students. *Archives of Sexual Behavior, 34*(5), 569–581.

Else-Quest, N., Hyde, J. S., & DeLamater, J. D. (2005). Context counts: Long-term sequelae of premarital intercourse or abstinence. *Journal of Sex Research, 42*(2), 102–112.

Emerson, J. J., Kaessmann, H., Betran, E., & Long, M. (2004). Extensive gene traffic on the mammalian X chromosome. *Science, 303,* 537–540.

Emini, E. A., & Koff, W. C. (2004). Developing an AIDS vaccine: Need, uncertainty, hope. *Science, 304,* 1913–1914.

English, A., & Ford, C. A. (2004). The HIPAA privacy rule and adolescents: Legal questions and clinical challenges. *Perspectives on Sexual and Reproductive Health, 36*(2), 80–86.

Erikson, E. (1968). *Identity: Youth and crisis.* New York: W. W. Norton.

Erol, B., Tefekli, A., Ozbey, I., Salman, F., Dincag, N., et al. (2002). Sexual dysfunction in type II diabetic females: A comparative study. *Journal of Sex and Marital Therapy, 28*(s), 55–62.

Eskin, M., Kaynak-Demir, H., & Demir, S. (2005). Same-sex sexual orientation, childhood sexual abuse, and suicidal behavior in university students in Turkey. *Archives of Sexual Behavior, 34*(2), 185–195.

Esposito, K., & Giugliano, D. (2005). Obesity, the metabolic syndrome, and sexual dysfunction. *International Journal of Impotence Research, 17,* 391–398.

Essig, L., (1999). *Queer in Russia: A story of sex, self, and the other.* Durham and London: Duke University Press.

Evcimen, H., & Gratz, S. (2006). Adult baby syndrome [Letter]. *Archives of Sexual Behavior, 35*(2), 115–116.

Everaerd, W., & Both, S. (2001). Ideal female sexual function. *Journal of Sex and Marital Therapy, 27,* 137–139.

Exner, T. M., Hoffman, S., Dworkin, S. L., & Ehrhardt, A. A. (2004). Beyond the male condom: The evolution of gender-specific HIV interventions for women. *Annual Review of Sex Research, 14,* 114–136.

Faix, A., Lapray, J. F., Callede, O., Maubon, A., & Lanfrey, K. (2002). Magnetic resonance imaging (MRI) of sexual intercourse: Second experience in missionary position and initial experience in posterior position. *Journal of Sex and Marital Therapy, 28* (s), 63–76.

Faix, A., Lapray, J. F., Courtieu, C., Maubon, A., & Lanfrey, K. (2001). Magnetic resonance imaging of sexual intercourse: Initial experience. *Journal of Sex and Marital Therapy, 27,* 475–482.

Falkner, S. R. (2004). "Having it off" with fish, camels, and lads: Sodomitic pleasures in German-language Turcica. *Journal of the History of Sexuality, 13*(4), 401–426.

Farmer, M., & Meston, C. M. (2006). Predictors of condom use self-efficacy in an ethnically diverse university sample. *Archives of Sexual Behavior, 35*(3), 313–326.

Farrar, K., Kunkel, D., Biely, E., Eyal, K., Fandrich, R., & Donnerstein, E. (2003). Sexual messages during prime-time programming. *Sexuality and Culture, 7*(3), 7–37.

Fathalla, M. F., Sinding, S. W., Rosenfield, A., & Fathalla, M. M. F. (2006). Sexual and reproductive health for all: A call for action. *The Lancet DOI:* 10.1016/S0140-6736(06)69483-X.

Fausto-Sterling, A. (2000). *Sexing the body: Gender politics and the construction of sexuality.* New York: Basic Books.

Fay, J. (2002). Teaching teens about sexual pleasure. *SIECUS Report, 30*(4), 12–17.

Fazleabas, A. T., & Kim, J. J. (2003). What makes an embryo stick. *Science, 299,* 355–408.

Feldstein, G. A., Parsons, J. T., Bimbi, D. S., Nanin, J. E., & Gomez, C. A. (2006). Age and judgments of attractiveness as factors of HIV preventive behavior among HIV-positive men who have sex with men. *Journal of Psychology and Human Sexuality, 18*(1), 43–65.

Felix, E. D., et al. (2003). Cross-generational parenting influences on psychosocial functioning of adolescent mothers in substitute care. *Journal of Adolescent Research, 18* (2), 154–168.

Ferguson, D. M., Steidle, C. P., Singh, G. S., Alexander, J. S., Weihmiller, M. K., & Crosby, M. G. (2003). Randomized, placebo-controlled, double blind, crossover design trial of the efficacy and safety of *Zestra for Women* in women with and without female sexual arousal disorder. *Journal of Sex and Marital Therapy, 29,* 33–44.

Fielding, S. L., Edmunds, E., & Schaff, E. A. (2002). Having an abortion using mifepristone and home misoprostol: A qualitative analysis of women's experiences. *Perspectives on Sexual and Reproductive Health, 34* (1), 34–40.

Figueira, I., Possidente, E., Marques, C., & Hayes, K. (2001). Sexual dysfunction: A neglected complication of panic disorder and social phobia. *Archives of Sexual Behavior, 30*(4), 369–377.

Filice, E. (2005). Review of *Outlaw representation: Censorship and homosexuality in twentieth-century American art* by Richard Meyer. *Sexualities, 8*(1), 116–118.

Findholt, N., & Robrecht, L. C. (2002). Legal and ethical considerations in research with sexually active adolescents: The requirement to report statutory rape. *Perspectives on Reproductive and Sexual Health, 34*(5), 259–264.

Finer, L. B., Frohwirth, L. F., Dauphinee, L. A., Singh, S., & Moore, A. M. (2005). Reasons U.S. women have abortions: Quantitative and qualitative perspectives. *Perspectives on Sexual and Reproductive Health, 37*(3), 110–118.

Finer, L. B., & Henshaw, S. K. (2003). Abortion incidence and services in the United States in 2000. *Perspectives on Sexual and Reproductive Health, 35*(1), 6–15.

Finer, L. B., & Henshaw, S. K. (2006). Disparities in rates of unintended pregnancy in the United States, 1994 and 2001. *Perspectives on Sexual and Reproductive Health, 38*(2), 90–96.

Finger, W. W. (2000). Avoiding sexual exploitation: Guidelines for therapists. *SIECUS Report, 28*(3), 12–13.

Fink, P. J. (2005). Sexual and gender identity disorders: Discussion of questions for DSM-V. *Journal of Psychology and Human Sexuality, 17*(3/4), 117–123.

Finlinson, H. A., et al. (2003). Puerto Rican drug users' experiences of physical and sexual abuse: Comparisons based on sexual identities. *Journal of Sex Research, 40*(3), 277–285.

Fischer, G. J. (1989). Sex words used by partners in a relationship. *Journal of Sex Education and Therapy, 15* (1), 50–58.

Fiscus, L. C., Ford, C. A., & Miller, W. C. (2004). Infrequency of sexually transmitted disease screening among sexually experienced U.S. female adolescents. *Perspectives on Sexual and Reproductive Health, 36*(6), 233–238.

Fisher, H. (2000). Lust, attraction, attachment: Biology and evolution of the three primary emotion systems for mating, reproduction, and parenting. *Journal of Sex Education and Therapy, 25* (1), 96–104.

Fisher, H., Aron, A., Mashek, D., Li, H., & Brown, L. L. (2002). Defining the brain systems of lust, romantic attraction, and attachment. *Archives of Sexual Behavior, 31*(5), 413–419.

Fisher, H., Aron, A., Mashek, D., Li, H., Strong, G., & Brown, L. L. (2002). The neural mechanisms of mate choice: A hypothesis. *Neuroendocrinology Letters, 23*(4), 92–97.

Fisher, T. D. (2007). Sex of experimenter and social norm effects on reports of sexual behavior in young men and women. *Archives of Sexual Behavior, 36,* 89–100.

Fisher, W. A., & Barak, A. (2001). Internet pornography: A social psychological perspective on Internet sexuality. *Journal of Sex Research, 38*(4), 312–323.

Floyd, F. J., & Bakeman, R. (2006). Coming-out across the life course: Implications of age and historical context. *Archives of Sexual Behavior, 35*(3), 287–296.

Floyd, M., and Weiss, L. (2001). Sex and aging: A survey of young adults. *Journal of Sex Education and Therapy, 26*(2), 133–139.

Fones, C. S., Levine, S. B., Althof, S. E., & Risen, C. B. (1999). The sexual struggles of 23 clergymen: A follow-up study. *Journal of Sex and Marital Therapy, 25,* 183–195.

Foote, D. (1999, February 8). You could get raped. *Newsweek,* 64–65.

Ford, C. S., & Beach, F. A. (1951). *Patterns of sexual behavior.* New York: Harper.

Ford, K., Sohn, W., & Lepkowski, J. (2001). Characteristics of adolescents' sexual partners and their association with use of condoms and other contraceptive methods. *Family Planning Perspectives, 33*(3), 100–105, 132.

Ford, K., Sohn, W., & Lepkowski, J. (2003). Ethnicity or race, area characteristics, and sexual partner choice among American adolescents. *Journal of Sex Research, 40*(2), 211–218.

Ford, K., et al. (2002). American adolescents: Sexual mixing patterns, bridge partners, and concurrency. *Sexually Transmitted Diseases, 29*(1), 13–19.

Forehand, R., et al. (2005). Sexual intentions of black preadolescents: Associations with risk and adaptive behaviors. *Perspectives on Sexual and Reproductive Health, 37*(1), 13–18.

Forste, R., & Haas, D. W. (2002). The transition of adolescent males to first sexual intercourse: Anticipated or delayed? *Perspectives on Sexual and Reproductive Health, 34*(4), 184–190.

Foster, D. G., et al. (2006). Pharmacy access to emergency contraception in California. *Perspectives on Sexual and Reproductive Health, 38*(1), 46–52.

Foubert, J. D., & LaVoy, S. A. (2000). A qualitative assessment of "the rape program": The impact of a rape prevention program on fraternity men. *NASPA Journal, 38*(1), 18–30.

Foust, E., et al. (2003). Partner counseling and referral services to identify persons with undiagnosed HIV. *Morbidity and Mortality Weekly Report, 52*(48), 1181–1184.

Foxman, B., Aral, S. O., & Holmes, K. K. (2006). Common use in the general population of sexual enrichment aids and drugs to enhance sexual pleasure. *Sexually Transmitted Diseases, 33*(3), 156–162.

France, D. (2001, August 6). Scouts divided. *Newsweek,* 44–51.

Francis, L. P. (2000). *Sexual harassment as an ethical issue in academic life.* Walnut Creek, CA: Rowman and Littlefield.

Frank, K. (2003). "Just trying to relax": Masculinity, masculinizing practices, and strip club regulars. *Journal of Sex Research, 40*(1), 61–75.

Frank, K. (2005). Exploring the motivations and fantasies of strip club customers in relation to legal regulations. *Archives of Sexual Behavior, 34*(5), 487–504.

Franzini, L., et al. (2004). Projected economic costs due to health consequences of teenagers' loss of confidentiality in obtaining reproductive health care services in Texas. *Archives of Pediatrics and Adolescent Medicine, 158*(12), 1140–1146.

Freund, K., & Seto, M. C. (1998). Preferential rape in the theory of courtship disorder. *Archives of Sexual Behavior, 27*(5), 433–443.

Freyd, J. J., et al. (2005). The science of child sexual abuse. *Science, 308,* 501.

Friedman, R. C. (2003). Sexual orientation change: A study of atypical cases. *Archives of Sexual Behavior, 32*(5), 432–434.

Friedman, R. C., & Downey, J. I. (2000). Psychoanalysis and sexual fantasies. *Archives of Sexual Behavior, 29*(3), 567–586.

Friedman, R. C., & Downey, J. I. (2002). *Sexual orientation and psychoanalysis: Sexual science and clinical practice.* New York: Columbia University Press.

Friedrich, W. N., Fisher, J., Broughton, D., Houston, M., & Shafran, C. R. (1998). Normative sexual behavior in children: A contemporary sample. *Pediatrics, 101*(4), e9.

Frohlich, P., & Meston, C. (2002). Sexual functioning and self-reported depressive symptoms among college women. *Journal of Sex Research, 39*(4), 321–325.

Frohlich, P., & Meston, C. M. (2005a). Fluoxetine-induced changes in tactile sensation and sexual functioning among clinically depressed women. *Journal of Sex and Marital Therapy, 31,* 113–128.

Frohlich, P. F., & Meston, C. M. (2005b). Tactile sensitivity in women with sexual arousal disorder. *Archives of Sexual Behavior, 34*(2), 207–217.

Frost, J. J., Frohwirth, L., & Purcell, A. (2004). The availability and use of publicly funded family planning clinics: U.S. trends, 1994–2001. *Perspectives on Sexual and Reproductive Health, 36*(5), 206–215.

Frost, J. J., Ranjit, N., Manzella, K., Darroch, J. E., & Audam, S. (2001). Family planning clinic services in the United States: Patterns and trends in the late 1990s. *Family Planning Perspectives, 33*(3), 113–122.

Fulda, J. S. (2002). Do Internet stings directed at pedophiles capture offenders or create offenders? And allied questions. *Sexuality and Culture, 6*(4), 73–100.

Gaboury, J. (2005). A personal perspective: Saying "I don't". *SIECUS Report, 33*(1), 29–32.

Gaca, K. L. (2003). *The making of fornication: Eros, ethics, and political reform in Greek philosophy and early Christianity.* Berkeley: University of California Press.

Gage, A. J., & Hutchinson, P. L. (2006). Power, control, and intimate partner sexual violence in Haiti. *Archives of Sexual Behavior, 35*(1), 11–24.

Gagnon, J. H. (1999). Sexual conduct: As today's memory serves. *Sexualities, 2*(1), 115–126.

Gaither, G. A., Sellbom, M, & Meier, B. P. (2003). The effect of stimulus content on volunteering for sexual interest research among college students. *Journal of Sex Research, 40*(3), 240–248.

Gangestad, S. W., Bennett, K. L., & Thornhill, R. (2001). A latent model of developmental instability in relation to men's sexual behaviour. *Proceedings of the Royal Society of London, 268,* 1677–1684.

Gangestad, S. W., & Cousins, A. J. (2002). Adaptive design, female mate preferences, and shifts across the menstrual cycle. *Annual Review of Sex Research, 12,* 145–185.

Garber, B. B. (2003). Inflatable penile prosthesis: Site specific malfunction analysis. *International Journal of Impotence Research, 15*(1), 22–25.

Garcia, L. T., & Hoskins, R. (2001). Actual-ideal self discrepancy and sexual esteem and depression. *Journal of Psychology and Human Sexuality, 13*(2), 49–61.

Geary, D. C., Vigil, J., & Byrd-Craven, J. (2004). Evolution of human mate choice. *Journal of Sex Research, 41*(1), 27–42.

Gebhardt, W., Kuyper, L., & Dusseldorp, E. (2006). Condom use at first intercourse with a new partner in female adolescents and young adults: The role of cognitive planning and motives for having sex. *Archives of Sexual Behavior, 35*(2), 217–223.

Geer, J. H., & Melton, J. S. (1997). Sexual content-induced delay with double-entendre words. *Archives of Sexual Behavior, 26*(3), 295–316.

Geer, J. H., & Robertson, G. G. (2005). Implicit attitudes in sexuality: Gender differences. *Archives of Sexual Behavior, 34*(6), 671–677.

Gehring, D. (2003). Couple therapy for low sexual desire: A systemic approach. *Journal of Sex and Marital Therapy, 29,* 25–38.

Gehring, D., & Chan, A. W. C. (2001). Group therapy—a useful treatment modality for women diagnosed with primary and secondary vaginismus. *Journal of Sex Education and Therapy, 26*(1), 59–67.

Geiger, J. (2001). Re-assessing the past and future of feminist film theory. *Sexualities, 4*(2), 246–251.

Geis, F. L. (1993). Self-fulfilling prophecies: A social psychological view of gender. In A. E. Beall & R. J. Steinberg (Eds.), *The psychology of gender* (pp. 9–54). New York: Guilford Press.

George, K. D. (1997). Male couples: The struggle with competition. *SIECUS Report, 25*(5), 11–12.

George, W. H., & Stoner, S. A. (2001). Understanding acute alcohol effects on sexual behavior. *Annual Review of Sex Research, 11,* 92–124.

Getch, Y. (2001). Deaf students lack specially-designed sexuality education curricula (based on an interview). *SIECUS Report, 29*(3), 13.

Giami, A. (2003). Sexual health: The emergence, development, and diversity of a concept. *Annual Review of Sex Research, 13,* 1–35.

Giargiari, T. D., Mahaffey, A. L., Craighead, W. E., & Hutchison, K. E. (2005). Appetitive responses to sexual stimuli are attenuated in individuals with low levels of sexual desire. *Archives of Sexual Behavior, 34*(5), 547–556.

Gillmore, M. R., Gaylord, J., Hartway, J., Hoppe, M. J., Morrison, D. M., Leigh, B. C., & Rainey, D. T. (2001). Daily data collection of sexual and other health-related behaviors. *Journal of Sex Research, 38*(1), 35–42.

Giotakos, O., Markianos, M., Vaidakis, N., & Christodoulou, G. N. (2003). Aggression, impulsivity, plasma sex hormones, and biogenic amine turnover in a forensic population of rapists. *Journal of Sex and Marital Therapy, 29*(3), 215–225.

Gladstone, G., Parker, G., Wilhelm, K., Mitchell, P., & Austin, M. (1999). Characteristics of depressed patients who report childhood sexual abuse. *American Journal of Psychiatry, 156*(3), 431–437.

Glasier, A., Gulmezoglu, A. M., Schmid, G. P., Moreno, C. G., & Van Look, P. F. A. (2006). Sexual and reproductive health: A matter of life and death. *The Lancet DOI:* 10.1016/S0140-6736(06)69478-6.

Glass, L. (1992). *He says, she says.* New York: G. P. Putnam's Sons.

Gleicher, N., Oleske, D. M., Tur-Kaspa, I., Vidali, A., & Karande, V. (2000, June 6). Reducing the risk of high-order multiple pregnancy after ovarian stimulation with gonadotropins. *New England Journal of Medicine, 343*(1), 2–7.

Glenn, D. (2003, April 25). Every unhappy family has its own bilinear influence function. *Chronicle of Higher Education,* A14–15.

Glenn, D. (2004, April 30). A dangerous surplus of sons? *Chronicle of Higher Education,* A14–18.

Godecker, A. L., Thomson, E., & Bumpass, L. L. (2001). Union status, marital history and female contraceptive sterilization in the United States. *Family Planning Perspectives, 33*(1), 35–41, 49.

Godow, A. G. (1999). Playful language. *Contemporary Sexuality, 33* (2), 1–2.

Gokyildiz, S., & Beji, N. K. (2005). The effects of pregnancy on sexual life. *Journal of Sex and Marital Therapy, 31,* 201–215.

Gold, M. A., et al. (2004). The effects of advance provision of emergency contraception on adolescent women's sexual and contraceptive behaviors. *Journal of Pediatric and Adolescent Gynecology, 17*(2), 87–96.

Gold, R. B. (2002). Efforts renew to deny family planning funds to agencies that offer abortions. *The Guttmacher Report on Public Policy, 5*(1), 4–6.

Gold, S. N., Hughes, D. M., & Swingle, J. M. (1999). Degrees of memory of childhood sexual abuse among women survivors in therapy. *Journal of Family Violence, 14*(1), 35–46.

Golden, M. R., et al. (2005). Effect of expedited treatment of sex partners on recurrent or persistent gonorrhea or chlamydial infection. *New England Journal of Medicine, 352*(7), 676–685.

Goldenberg, J. L., Cox, C. R., Pyszczynski, T., Greenberg, J., & Solomon, S. (2002). Understanding human ambivalence about sex: The effects of stripping sex of meaning. *Journal of Sex Research, 39*(4), 310–320.

Goldfarb, E. S. (2003). What teachers want, need, and deserve. *SIECUS Report, 31*(6), 18–19.

Goldfarb, E. S. (2005). What is comprehensive sexuality education really all about? Perceptions of students enrolled in an undergraduate human sexuality course. *American Journal of Sexuality Education, 1* (1), 85–102.

Goldman, J. D., & Padayachi, U. K. (2000). Some methodological problems in estimating incidence and prevalence in child sexual abuse research. *Journal of Sex Research, 37*(4), 305–314.

Gonzalo, I. T., Swerdloff, R. S., & Nelson, A. L. (2002). Levonorgestrel implants (Norplant II) for male contraception clinical trials: Combination with transdermal and injectable testosterone. *Journal of Clinical Endocrinology and Metabolism, 87,* 3562–3572.

Goodenow, C., Netherland, J., & Szalacha, L. (2002). AIDS-related risk among adolescent males who have sex with males, females, or both: Evidence from a statewide survey. *American Journal of Public Health, 92*(2), 203–210.

Goozen, S. H., Cohen-Kettenis, P. T., Matthys, W., & VanEngeland, H. (2002). Preference for aggressive and sexual stimuli in children with disruptive behavior disorder and normal controls. *Archives of Sexual Behavior, 31*(3), 247–253.

Gottlieb, L. (2006, March). How do I love thee? *Atlantic Monthly,* 58–70.

Gottman, J. M. (2000). *Seven principles for making marriages work.* New York: Three Rivers Press.

Gottman, J. M., Murray, J. D., Swanson, C., Tyson, R., & Swanson, K. R. (2003). *The mathematics of marriage: Dynamic linear models.* Cambridge, MA: MIT Press.

Graaf, H. de, & Rademakers, J. (2006). Sexual behavior of prepubertal children. *Journal of Psychology and Human Sexuality, 18*(1), 1–21.

Grady, D., Herrington, D., Bittner, V., Blumenthal, R., et al. (2002). Cardiovascular disease outcomes during 6.8 years of hormone therapy. *Journal of the American Medical Association, 288*(1): 49–57.

Grady, W. R., Billy, J. O. G., & Klepinger, D. H. (2002). Contraceptive method switching in the United States. *Perspectives on Sexual and Reproductive Health, 34*(3), 135–145.

Grafenberg, E. (1950). The role of the urethra. *International Journal of Sexology, 3,* 145–148.

Graham, C. A., Catania, J. A., Brand, R., Duong, T., & Canchola, J. A. (2003).

Recalling sexual behavior: A methodological analysis of memory recall bias via interview using the diary as the gold standard. *Journal of Sex Research, 40*(4), 325–332.

Graham, C. A., Sanders, S. A., Milhausen, R. R., & McBride, K. R. (2004). Turning on and turning off: A focus group study of the factors that affect women's sexual arousal. *Archives of Sexual Behavior, 33*(6), 527–538.

Graham, C. A., Sanders, S. A., & Milhausen, R. R. (2006). The sexual excitation/sexual inhibition inventory for women: Psychometric properties. *Archives of Sexual Behavior, 35,* 397–409.

Grammer, K., Renninger, L. A., & Fischer, B. (2004). Disco clothing, female sexual motivation, and relationship status: Is she dressed to impress? *Journal of Sex Research, 41*(1), 66–74.

Granot, M., & Lavee, Y. (2005). Psychological factors associated with perception of experimental pain in vulvar vestibulitis syndrome. *Journal of Sex and Marital Therapy, 31,* 285–302.

Grant, R. M., et al. (2005). Promote HIV chemoprophylaxis research, don't prevent it. *Science, 309,* 2170–2171.

Graupner, H. (2000). Sexual consent: The criminal law in Europe and overseas. *Archives of Sexual Behavior, 29*(5), 415–461.

Graves, J. A. M. (2005). Recycling the Y chromosome. *Science, 307,* 50–51.

Graziottin, A., & Brotto, L. A. (2004). Vulvar vestibulitis syndrome: A clinical approach. *Journal of Sex and Marital Therapy, 30,* 125–139.

Greeff, A. P., & DeBruyne, T. (2000). Conflict management style and marital satisfaction. *Journal of Sex and Marital Therapy, 26,* 321–334.

Greeff, A. P., & Malherbe, H. L. (2001). Intimacy and marital satisfaction in spouses. *Journal of Sex and Marital Therapy, 27,* 247–257.

Green, R. (2002). Is pedophilia a mental disorder? *Archives of Sexual Behavior, 31*(6), 467–471.

Greenberg, A. S., & Bailey, M. (2001). Parental selection of children's sexual orientation. *Archives of Sexual Behavior, 30*(4), 423–437.

Greenberg, B. S., & Woods, M. G. (1999). The soaps: Their sex, gratifications, and outcomes. *Journal of Sex Research, 36*(3), 250–257.

Green-Raleigh, K., Lawrence, J. M., Chen, H., Devine, O., & Prue, C. (2005). Pregnancy planning status and health behaviors among non-pregnant women in a California managed health care organization. *Perspectives on Sexual and Reproductive Health, 37*(4), 179–183.

Greer, J. B., et al. (2005). Short-term oral contraceptive use and the risk of epithelial ovarian cancer. *American Journal of Epidemiology, 162*(1), 66–72.

Griffiths, M. (2001). Sex on the Internet: Observations and implications for Internet sex addiction. *Journal of Sex Research, 38*(4), 333–342.

Grimes, D. A., et al. (2006). Unsafe abortion: The preventable pandemic. *The Lancet, Early Online Publication,* DOI: 10.1016/S0140-6736(06)69481-6.

Groneman, C. (2000). *Nymphomania: A History.* New York: W. W. Norton.

Grossman, L. S., Martis, B., & Fichtner, C. G. (1999). Are sex offenders treatable? A research overview. *Psychiatric Services, 50*(3), 349–361.

Grunseit, A., Richters, J., Crawford, J., Song, A., & Kippax, S. (2005). Stability and change in sexual practices among first-year Australian university students (1990–1999). *Archives of Sexual Behavior, 34*(5), 557–568.

Guay, A. T., & Jacobson, J. (2002). Decreased free testosterone and dehydroepiandrosterone-sulfate (DHEA-S) levels in women with decreased libido. *Journal of Sex and Marital Therapy, 28*(s), 129–142.

Guillebaud, J. (2004). *Contraception: Your questions answered.* London: Churchill Livingstone.

Guillory, V. J., et al. (2003). Prenatal care and infant birth outcomes among Medicaid recipients. *Journal of Health Care for the Poor and Underserved, 14*(2), 272–289.

Guo, Y. N., Ng, E. M. L., & Chan, K. (2004). Foreplay, orgasm and afterplay among Shanghai couples and its integrative relation with their marital satisfaction. *Sexual and Relationship Therapy, 19*(1), 65–78.

Gupta, M. (1999). An alternative combined approach to the treatment of premature ejaculation in Asian men. *Sexual and Marital Therapy, 14*(1), 71–76.

Guzick, D. S., Carson, S. A., et al. (1999). Efficacy of superovulation and intrauterine insemination in the treatment of infertility. *New England Journal of Medicine, 340*(3), 177–183.

Gwinell, E. (2001). Risk factors for the development of Internet adultery. *Journal of Sex Education and Therapy, 26*(1), 45–49.

Haas, J. S., et al. (2005). Prepregnancy health status and the risk of preterm delivery. *Archives of Pediatrics and Adolescent Medicine, 159*(1), 58–63.

Haffner, D. W. (2004). Sexuality and scripture. *Contemporary Sexuality, 38*(1), 7–14.

Haig, D. (2004). The inexorable rise of gender and the decline of sex: Social change in academic titles, 1945–2001. *Archives of Sexual Behavior, 33*(2), 87–96.

Hajkova, P., & Surani, M. A. (2004). Programming the X chromosome. *Science, 303,* 633–649.

Halkitis, P. N., Parsons, J. T., & Wilton, L. (2003). Barebacking among gay and bisexual men in New York City: Explanations for the emergence of intentional unsafe behavior. *Archives of Sexual Behavior, 32*(4), 351–357.

Hall, D. (2003). Forming a gay straight alliance without controversy. *SIECUS Report, 31*(6), 32.

Hall, L. S. (2000). Dermatoglyphic analysis of total finger ridge count in female monozygotic twins discordant for sexual orientation. *Journal of Sex Research, 37*(4), 315–320.

Hall, L. S., & Love, C. T. (2003). Finger-length ratios in female monozygotic twins discordant for sexual orientation. *Archives of Sexual Behavior, 32*(1), 23–28.

Halpern, C. T., Udry, J. R., Suchindran, C., & Campbell, B. (2000). Adolescent males' willingness to report masturbation. *Journal of Sex Research, 37*(4), 327–332.

Halpern-Felsher, B. L., et al. (2005). Oral versus vaginal sex among adolescents: Perceptions, attitudes, and behavior. *Pediatrics, 115*(4), 845–851.

Hamel, D. (2003). *Trying Neaira: The true story of a courtesan's scandalous life in ancient Greece.* New Haven, CT: Yale University Press.

Hamer, D. (1999). Genetics and male sexual orientation. *Science, 285,* 803a.

Hamer, D. (2002). Rethinking behavior genetics. *Science, 298,* 71–72.

Hamer, M. (2002). *Incest: A new perspective.* Malden, MA.: Blackwell.

Hamilton, B. E., Martin, J. A., & Ventura, S. J. (2006). Birth: Preliminary data for 2005. *National Vital Statistics Reports, 55*(11), 1–19.

Hamson, S. (2004). The passive/active divide: What the village is teaching our children about gender. *SIECUS Report, 32*(3), 14–16.

Handelsman, J., et al. (2005). More women in science. *Science, 309,* 1190–1191.

Hansen, H., Lopez-Iftikhar, M. M., & Alegria, M. (2002). The economy of risk and respect: Accounts by Puerto Rican sex workers of HIV risk taking. *Journal of Sex Research, 39*(4), 292–301.

Harding, C. (Ed.). (2001). *Sexuality: Psychoanalytic perspectives*. Philadelphia: Brunner-Routledge.

Harding, R., & Golombok, S. E. (2002). Test-retest reliability of the measurement of penile dimensions in a sample of gay men. *Archives of Sexual Behavior, 31*(4), 351–357.

Harper, C., Callegari, L., Raine, T., Blum, M., & Darney, P. (2004). Adolescent clinic visits for contraception: Support from mothers, male partners and friends. *Perspectives on Sexual and Reproductive Health, 36*(1), 20–26.

Harper, C. C., et al. (2005). The effect of increased access to emergency contraception among young adolescents. *Obstetrics and Gynecology, 106*(3), 483–491.

Harper, G., Gannon, C., Watson, S., Catania, J., & Dolcini, M. (2004). The role of close friends in African American adolescents' dating and sexual behavior. *Journal of Sex Research, 41*(4), 351–362.

Harper, M. A., et al. (2003). Pregnancy-related death and health care services. *Obstetrics and Gynecology, 102*(2), 273–278.

Harris, A. C. (2005). Review of *Regulating sex*, E. Bernstein & L. Schaffner (eds.). *Journal of Sex Research, 42*(4), 371–372.

Harris Poll. (2005, March 3). Majority back Roe v. Wade, but opposition is rising. *The Wall Street Journal Online*.

Hart, T. A., Wolitski, R. J., Purcell, D. W., Gomez, C., & Halkitis, P. (2003). Sexual behavior among HIV-positive men who have sex with men: What's in a label. *Journal of Sex Research, 40*(2), 179–188.

Harvey, S. M., Beckman, L. J., & Satre, S. J. (2001). Choice of and satisfaction with methods of medical and surgical abortion among U.S. clinical patients. *Family Planning Perspectives, 33*(5), 212–216.

Harvey, S. M., Bird, S. T., & Branch, M. R. (2003). A new look at an old method: The diaphragm. *Perspectives on Sexual and Reproductive Health, 35*(6), 270–271.

Hatcher, R. A., et al. (2002). *A pocket guide to managing contraception*. Dawsonville, GA: Bridging the Gap Communications.

Hatcher, R. A., et al. (2004). *Contraceptive technology* (18th ed.). New York: Ardent, Media.

Hays, J., et al. (2003). Effects of estrogen plus progestin on health-related quality of life. *New England Journal of Medicine, 348*(19), 1839–1854.

Heacox, T. L. (2004). "Idealized through Greece": Hellenism and homoeroticism in works by Wilde, Symonds, Mann, and Forster. *Sexuality and Culture, 8*(2), 52–79.

Health Grades (2003). *First time pre-planned and "patient choice" cesarean section rates in the United States*. Lakewood, CO: Health Grades.

Heaphy, B., Weeks, J., & Donovan, C. (1998). "That's like my life": Researching stories on nonheterosexual relationships. *Sexualities, 1*(4), 453–470.

Hearn, K. D., O'Sullivan, L. F., & Dudley, C. D. (2002). Assessing reliability of early adolescent girls' reports of romantic and sexual behavior. *Archives of Sexual Behavior, 32*(6), 513–521.

Heckman, T. G., et al. (2003). HIV transmission risk practices in rural persons living with HIV disease. *Sexually Transmitted Diseases, 30*(2), 134–136.

Heiman, J. R. (2002a). Psychologic treatments for female sexual dysfunction: Are they effective and do we need them? *Archives of Sexual Behavior, 31*(5), 445–450.

Heiman, J. R. (2002b). Sexual dysfunction: Overview of prevalence, etiological factors, and treatments. *Journal of Sex Research, 39*(1), 73–78.

Heins, M. (2001). *Not in front of the children: "Indecency," censorship, and the innocence of youth*. New York: Hill and Wang.

Hellberg, J. (2006). Review of *The Puzzle* by L. A. Berman. *Archives of Sexual Behavior, 35*(2), 243–244.

Hendrix, L., & Schneider, M. A. (1999). Assumptions on sex and society in the biosocial theory of incest. *Cross-Cultural Research: The Journal of Comparative Social Science, 33*(2), 193–218.

Hennig, K. H. (2003). Parenting style and the development of moral reasoning. *Journal of Moral Education, 28*, 359–374.

Henshaw, S. K., & Finer, L. B. (2003). The accessibility of abortion services in the United States, 2001. *Perspectives on Sexual and Reproductive Health, 35*(1), 16–24.

Hensley, L. (2003). GHB abuse trends and use in drug-facilitated sexual assault: Implications for prevention. *NASPA Journal, 40*(2), 17–42.

Herdt, G. (2000). Clinical ethnography and sexual culture. *Annual Review of Sex Research, 9*, 100–119.

Herdt, G., & McClintock, M. (2000). The magical age of 10. *Archives of Sexual Behavior, 29*(6), 587–606.

Herek, G. M. (2002). Heterosexuals' attitudes toward bisexual men and women in the United States. *Journal of Sex Research, 39*(4), 264–274.

Herek, G. M., & Gonzalez-Rivera, M. (2006). Attitudes toward homosexuality among U.S. residents of Mexican descent. *Journal of Sex Research, 43*(2), 122–135.

Herman, D. (2005). "I'm gay": Declarations, desire, and coming out on prime-time television. *Sexualities, 8*(1), 7–29.

Herman-Jeglinska, A., Grabowska, A., & Dulko, S. (2002). Masculinity, femininity, and transsexualism. *Archives of Sexual Behavior, 31*(6), 527–534.

Herold, E. S., & Milhausen, R. R. (1999). Dating preferences of university women: An analysis of the nice guy stereotype. *Journal of Sex and Marital Therapy, 25*, 333–343.

Hershberger, S. L. (2003). Low test-retest reliability does not diminish the value of penile self-measurement. *Archives of Sexual Behavior, 32*(2), 91–92.

Hershberger, S. L., & Segal, N. (2004). The cognitive, behavioral, and personality profiles of a male monozygotic triplet set discordant for sexual orientation. *Archives of Sexual Behavior, 33*(5), 497–514.

Hetherington, E. M., & Kelly, J. (2001). *For better or for worse*. New York: W. W. Norton.

Hewitt, M., Devesa, S., & Breen, N. (2002). Papanicolaou test use among reproductive-age women at high risk for cervical cancer: Analysis of the 1995 National Survey of Family Growth. *American Journal of Public Health, 92*(4), 666–669.

Hewitt, S. K. (1999). *Assessing allegations of sexual abuse in preschool children: Understanding small voices*. Thousand Oaks, CA: Sage.

Hicks, T. V., & Leitenberg, H. (2001). Sexual fantasies about one's partner versus someone else: Gender differences in incidence and frequency. *Journal of Sex Research, 38*(1), 43–50.

Hill, D. B. (2005). Coming to terms: Using technology to know identity. *Sexuality and Culture, 9*(3), 24–52.

Hill, D. B., Rozanski, C., Carfagnini, J., & Willoughby, B. (2005). Gender identity disorders in childhood and adolescence: A critical inquiry. *Journal of Psychology and Human Sexuality, 17*(3/4), 7–33.

Hillis, D. M. (2000). Origins of HIV. *Science, 288,* 1757–1760.

Hillis, S. D., Anda, R. F., Felitti, V. J., & Marchbanks, P. A. (2001). Adverse childhood experiences and sexual risk behaviors in women: A retrospective cohort study. *Family Planning Perspectives, 33*(5), 206–211.

Hillis, S. D., et al. (2004). The association between adverse childhood experiences and adolescent pregnancy, long-term psychosocial consequences, and fetal death. *Pediatrics, 113*(2), 320–327.

Hillman, J. L. (2000). *Clinical perspectives on elderly sexuality.* New York: Kluwer Academic/Plenum Publishers.

Hindley, J. (2001). Beyond the stereotypes: Transgressive desires and male homosexualities in Latin America. *Sexualities, 4*(1), 116–121.

Hines, M. (2004). *Brain gender.* New York: Oxford University Press.

Hines, M., Ahmed, S. F., & Hughes, I. A. (2003). Psychological outcomes and gender-related development in complete androgen insensitivity syndrome. *Archives of Sexual Behavior, 32*(2), 93–101.

Hines, M., Brook, C., & Conway, G. S. (2004). Androgen and psychosexual development: Core gender identity, sexual orientation, and recalled childhood gender role behavior in women and men with congenital adrenal hyperplasia (CAH). *Journal of Sex Research, 41*(1), 75–81.

Hines, M., Fane, B. A., Pasterski, V. L., Mathews, G. A., Conway, G. S., & Brook, C. (2003). Spatial abilities following prenatal androgen abnormality: Targeting and mental rotations performance in individuals with congenital adrenal hyperplasia (CAH). *Psychoneuroendocrinology, 28,* 1010–1026.

Hite, S. (1977). *The Hite report.* New York: Dell.

Hofferth, S. L., & Reid, L. (2002, January/February). Early childbearing and children's achievement and behavior over time. *Perspectives on Sexual and Reproductive Health, 34*(1), 41–50.

Hofferth, S. L., Reid, L., & Mott, F. L. (2001, November/December). The effects of early childbearing on schooling over time. *Family Planning Perspectives, 33*(6), 259–268.

Hoffman, R. M. (2004). Conceptualizing heterosexual identity development: Issues and challenges. *Journal of Counseling and Development, 82,* 375–380.

Hoffman, S., et al. (2003). Female-condom use in a gender-specific family planning clinic trial. *American Journal of Public Health, 93*(11), 1897–1903.

Hoffman, S., Mantell, J., Exner, T., & Stein, Z. (2004). The future of the female condom. *Perspectives on Sexual and Reproductive Health, 36*(3), 120–126.

Hofstede, G. (1998). *Masculinity and femininity: The taboo of national culture.* Thousand Oaks, CA: Sage.

Hogben, M., & Williams, S. P. (2001). Exploring the context of women's relationship perceptions, sexual behavior, and contraceptive strategies. *Journal of Psychology and Human Sexuality, 13*(2), 1–19.

Holden, C. (2003). More men ready for cloning. *Science, 299,* 41.

Holt, V. L., Cushing-Haugen, K. L., & Daling, J. R. (2002). Body weight and risk of oral contraceptive failure. *Obstetrics and Gynecology, 99*(5), 820–827.

Hooker, E. (1993). Reflections of a 40-year exploration: A scientific view on homosexuality. *American Psychologist, 48*(4), 450–453.

Horowitz, S. M., Weis, D. L., & Laflin, M. T. (2001). Differences between sexual orientation behavior groups and social background, quality of life, and health behaviors. *Journal of Sex Research, 38*(3), 205–218.

Howe, N., & Strauss, W. (2003). *Millennials go to college.* New York: American Association of Collegiate Registrars and Admissions Officers, and LifeCourse Associates.

Hubacher, D. (2002). The checkered history and bright future of intrauterine contraception in the United States. *Perspectives on Sexual and Reproductive Health, 34*(2), 98–103.

Huebner, D. M., Proescholdbell, R. J., & Nemeroff, C. J. (2006). Do gay and bisexual men share researchers' definitions of barebacking? *Journal of Psychology and Human Sexuality, 18*(1), 67–77.

Hull, N. E. H., & Hoffer, P. C. (2001, November 2). Teaching above the fray: A multidisciplinary approach to Roe v. Wade. *Chronicle of Higher Education,* 313–315.

Humphrey, J. A., & White, J. W. (2000). Women's vulnerability to sexual assault from adolescence to young adulthood. *Journal of Adolescent Health, 27*(6), 419–424.

Humphrey, J. C. (1999). To queer or not to queer a lesbian and gay group? Sexual and gendered politics at the turn of the century. *Sexualities, 2*(2), 223–246.

Hunt, M. (1975). *Sexual behavior in the 1970s.* New York: Dell.

Hunter, J. A., & Figueredo, A. J. (1999). Factors associated with treatment compliance in population of juvenile sexual offenders. *Sexual Abuse: Journal of Research and Treatment, 11*(1), 49–67.

Huppert, J. S., et al. (2005). Sexually transmitted infection testing and screening in hospital-based primary care visits by women. *Obstetrics & Gynecology, 105*(2), 390–396.

Huyck, M. H. (1999). Gender roles and gender identity in midlife. In S. L. Willis & J. D. Reid (Eds.), *Life in the middle: Psychological and social development in middle age* (pp. 209–232). San Diego, CA: Academic Press.

Hwang, A. C., Koyama, A., Taylor, D., Henderson, J. T., & Miller, S. (2005). Advanced practice clinicians' interest in providing medical abortion: Results of a California survey. *Perspectives on Sexual and Reproductive Health, 37*(2), 92–97.

Hyde, J. S. (2005). The gender similarities hypothesis. *American Psychologist, 60*(6), 581–592.

Hyde, J. S., & Linn, M. C. (2006) Gender similarities in mathematics and science. *Science, 314,* 599–600.

Imperato-McGinley, J., Peterson, R. E., Gautier, T., Looper, G., Danner, R., Arthur, A., Morris, P. L., Sweeney, W. J., & Schackleton, C. (1982). Hormonal evaluation of a large kindred with complete androgen insensitivity: Evidence for secondary 5-alpha-reductase deficiency. *Journal of Clinical Endocrinology Metabolism, 54,* 15–22.

Impett, E., Schooler, D., & Tolman, D. (2006). To be seen and not heard: Femininity ideology and adolescent girls' sexual health. *Archives of Sexual Behavior, 35*(2), 131–144.

International Perinatal HIV Group. (2001). Duration of ruptured membranes and vertical transmission of HIV-1: A meta-analysis from 15 prospective cohort studies, *AIDS, 15*(3), 357–368.

Ito, T. Y., Polan, M. L., Whipple, B., & Trant, A. S. (2006). The enhancement of female sexual function with argin-max, a nutritional supplement, among women differing in meno-pausal status. *Journal of Sex and Marital Therapy, 32,* 369–378.

Izasola-Licea, J. A., Gortmaker, S. L., Tolbert, K., DeGruttola, V., & Mann, J. (2000). Prevalence of same-gender sexual behavior and HIV in a proba-bility household survey in Mexican men. *Journal of Sex Research, 37*(1), 37–43.

Jackson, D. J., et al. (2003). Outcomes, safety, and resource utilization in a collaborative care birth center pro-gram compared with traditional physician-based perinatal care. *American Journal of Public Health, 93*(6), 999–1006.

Jackson, E. F., Akweongo, P., Sakeah, E., Hodgson, A., Asuru, R., & Phillips, J. F. (2003). Inconsistent reporting of female genital cutting status in North-ern Ghana: Explanatory factors and analytical consequences. *Studies in Family Planning, 34*(3), 200–210.

Jackson, L. A., Sowinski, B., Bennett, C., & Ryan, D. (2005). Female sex trade workers, condoms, and the public-private divide. *Journal of Psychology and Human Sexuality, 17*(1/2), 83–105.

Jackson, R. A., et al. (2003). Advance supply of emergency contraception: Effect on use and usual contraception—a randomized trial. *Obstetrics and Gynecology, 102* (1), 8–16.

Jackson, S., & Scott, S. (2004). Sexual antinomies in late modernity. *Sexua-lities, 7*(2), 233–248.

Jacobs, R. J., & Meyerhoff, A. S. (2003). Cost effectiveness of hepatitis A/B vaccine versus hepatitis B vaccine in public sexually transmitted disease clinics. *Sexually Transmitted Dis-eases, 30*(11), 859–865.

Jakobsen, J. R., & Pellegrini, A. (2003). *Love and sin: Sexual regulation and the limits of religious tolerance.* New York: New York University Press.

James, S. M., & Robertson, C. C. (2002). *Genital cutting and transnational sisterhood: Disputing U.S. polemics.* Urbana, IL: University of Illinois Press.

James, S. M., & Robertson, C. C. (2004). Sorting out misunderstandings: Geni-tal cutting and transnational sister-

hood. *Archives of Sexual Behavior, 33*(1), 2–3.

Jamieson, D. J., et al. (2002). A compari-son of women's regret after vasec-tomy versus tubal sterilization. *Obstetrics and Gynecology, 99*(6), 1073–1079.

Jamison, P. L., & Gebhard, P. H. (1988). Penis size increase between flaccid and erect states: An analysis of the Kinsey data. *Journal of Sex Research, 24*(1), 177–183.

Janssen, E., Carpenter, D., & Graham, C. A. (2003). Selecting films for sex research: Gender differences in erotic film preference. *Archives of Sexual Behavior, 32*(3), 243–251.

Janssen, E., Everaerd, W., Spiering, M., & Janssen, J. (2000). Automatic processes and the appraisal of sexual stimuli: Toward an information processing model of sexual arousal. *Journal of Sex Research, 37*(1), 8–23.

Janssen, E., Vorst, H., Finn, P., Bancroft, J. (2002a). The sexual inhibition (SIS) and sexual excitation (SES) scales: I. Measuring sexual inhibition and excitation proneness in men. *Journal of Sex Research, 39*(2), 114–126.

Janssen, E., Vorst, H., Finn, P., Bancroft, J. (2002b). The sexual inhibition (SIS) and sexual excitation (SES) scales: II. Predicting psychophysiological response patterns. *Journal of Sex Research, 39*(2), 127–132.

Janus, S. S., & Janus, C. L. (1993). *The Janus report on sexual behavior.* New York: John Wiley.

Jemmott, J. B., et al. (2005). HIV/STD risk reduction interventions for African American and Latino adoles-cent girls at an adolescent medicine clinic: A randomized controlled trial. *Archives of Pediatrics and Adolescent Medicine, 159*(5), 440–449.

Jeng, C., Wang, L., Chou, C., Shen, J., & Tzeng, C. (2006). Management and outcome of primary vaginismus. *Journal of Sex and Marital Therapy, 32,* 379–387.

Jenkins, P. (2001). *Beyond tolerance: Child pornography online.* New York: New York University Press.

Jenkins, R., et al. (2004). Sexuality and health-related quality of life after prostate cancer in African-American and white men treated for localized disease. *Journal of Sex and Marital Therapy, 30,* 79–93.

Jenks, R. J. (1998). Swinging: A review of the literature. *Archives of Sexual Behavior, 27*(5), 507–521.

Jiann, B., Yu, C., Su, C., & Tsai, J. (2006). Compliance of sildenafil

treatment for erectile dysfunction and factors affecting it. *International Journal of Impotence Research, 18,* 146–149.

Jinich, S., & Litrownik, A. J. (1999). Coping with sexual abuse: Develop-ment and evaluation of a videotape intervention for nonoffending par-ents. *Child Abuse and Neglect, 23*(2), 175–190.

Joffe, H., Cohen, L. S., & Harlow, B. L. (2003). Impact of oral contraceptive pills on premenstrual mood: Predic-tors of improvement and deteriora-tion. *Obstetrics and Gynecology, 189*(6), 1523–1530.

Johnson, A., Wadsworth, J., Wellings, K., & Field, J. (1994). *Sexual attitudes and lifestyles.* Cambridge, MA: Blackwell Scientific.

Johnson, A. M., et al. (2001). Sexual behaviour in Britain: Partnerships, practices, and HIV risk behaviours. *Lancet, 358,* 1835–1842.

Johnson, B. T., et al. (2003). Interven-tions to reduce sexual risk for the human immunodeficiency virus in adolescents. *Archives of Pediatrics and Adolescent Medicine, 157*(4), 381–388.

Johnson, D., & Piore, A. (2004, October 18). Home in two worlds. *Newsweek,* 52–54.

Johnson, J., Canning, J., Kaneko, T., Pru, J. K., & Tilly, J. L. (2004). Germline stem cells and follicular renewal in the postnatal mammalian ovary. *Nature, 428,* 145–150.

Johnson, P. J., & Hellerstedt, W. L. (2002). Current or past physical or sexual abuse as a risk marker for sexually transmitted disease in preg-nant women. *Perspectives on Sexual and Reproductive Health, 34* (2), 62–67.

Johnson, S. D., Phelps, D. L., & Cottler, L. B. (2004). The association of sexual dysfunction and substance use among a community epidemiological sample. *Archives of Sexual Behavior, 33*(1), 55–63.

Johnson, S. M., & O'Connor, E. (2002). *The gay baby boom: The psychology of gay parenthood.* New York: New York University Press.

Johnson, T. C. (2000). Sexualized chil-dren and children who molest. *SIECUS Report, 29*(1), 35–39.

Johnstone, J., & Huws, R. (1997). Autoerotic asphyxia: A case report. *Journal of Sex and Marital Therapy, 23*(4), 326–332.

Jones, M. A., & Gabriel, M. A. (1999). Utilization of psychotherapy by lesbians, gay men, and bisexuals: Findings from a nationwide survey. *American Journal of Orthopsychiatry, 69*(2), 209–219.

Jones, R. K. (2006). Do U.S. family planning clinics encourage parent–child communication? Findings from an exploratory survey. *Perspectives on Sexual and Reproductive Health, 38*(3), 155–161.

Jones, R. K., & Boonstra, H. (2004). Confidential reproductive health services for minors: The potential impact of mandated parental involvement for contraception. *Perspectives on Sexual and Reproductive Health, 36*(5), 182–191.

Jones, R. K., Darroch, J. E., & Henshaw, S. K. (2002). Patterns in the socioeconomic characteristics of women obtaining abortions in 2000–2001. *Perspectives on Sexual and Reproductive Health, 34*(5), 226–235.

Jones, R. K., & Henshaw, S. K. (2002). Mifepristone for early medical abortion: Experiences in France, Great Britain and Sweden. *Perspectives on Sexual and Reproductive Health, 34*(3), 154–161.

Jones, R. K., Singh, S., & Purcell, A. (2005). Parent-child relations among minor females attending U.S. family planning clinics. *Perspectives on Sexual and Reproductive Health, 37*(4), 192–201.

Jonker-Pool, G., Van de Wiel, H. B. M., Hoekstra, H. J., Sleijfer, D. T., et al. (2001). Sexual functioning after treatment for testicular cancer: Review and meta-analysis of 36 empirical studies between 1975–2002. *Archives of Sexual Behavior, 30*(1), 55–73.

Jorgensen, C. (2000). *Christine Jorgensen: A personal autobiography.* San Francisco: Cleis Press.

Jossi, F. (2005). Sharp decline in teen pregnancy prompts researchers to ponder what works. *Contemporary Sexuality, 39*(9), 1, 4–6.

Joyce, T., Kaestner, R., & Colman, S. (2006). Changes in abortions and births and the Texas parental notification law. *New England Journal of Medicine, 354*(10), 1031–1038.

Juarez, F., & Martín, T. C. (2006). Safe sex versus safe love? Relationship context and condom use among male adolescents in the Favelas of Recife, Brazil. *Archives of Sexual Behavior, 35*(1), 25–35.

Julian, T. W., McKenry, P. C., Gavazzi, S. M., & Law, J. C. (1999). Test of family of origin structural models of male

verbal and physical aggression. *Journal of Family Issues, 20*(3), 397–423.

Jurgensen, M., Hampel, E., Hiort, O., & Thyen, U. (2006). "Any decision is better than none": Decision-making about sex of rearing for siblings with 17b-hydroxysteroid-dehydrogenase-3 deficiency. *Archives of Sexual Behavior, 35*(3), 359–371.

Kabakci, E., & Batur, S. (2003). Who benefits from cognitive behavioral therapy for vaginismus? *Journal of Sex and Marital Therapy, 29*(4), 277–288.

Kaeser, F., DiSalvo, C., & Moglia, R. (2000). Sexual behaviors of young children that occur in schools. *Journal of Sex Education and Therapy, 25*(4), 277–285.

Kaestle, C. E., et al. (2005). Young age at first sexual intercourse and sexually transmitted infections in adolescents and young adults. *American Journal of Epidemiology, 161*(8), 774–780.

Kahn, J. A., et al. (2002). Mediators of the association between age of first sexual intercourse and subsequent human papillomavirus infection. *Pediatrics, 109*(1), e5.

Kahn, R. H., et al. (2002). Screening for syphilis in arrestees: Usefulness for community-wide syphilis surveillance and control. *Sexually Transmitted Diseases, 29*(3), 150–156.

Kaiser, J. (2005). An earlier look at baby's genes. *Science, 309,* 1476–1478.

Kaiser Family Foundation. (2002). *Teens, sex, and TV: Survey snapshot.* Menlo Park, CA: KFF.

Kaiser Family Foundation and MTV. (2000). *Sex laws: Youth opinion on sexual health issues in the 2000 election.* Menlo Park, CA: Kaiser Family Foundation.

Kaiser Foundation. (2002a). *HIV/AIDS policy fact sheet.* Washington, DC: Henry J. Kaiser Family Foundation.

Kaiser Foundation. (2002b). *The sexual health of adolescents and young adults.* Washington, DC: Henry J. Kaiser Family Foundation.

Kalb, C. (1999, April 19). Hormones and the mind. *Newsweek,* 50.

Kalb, C. (2000, April 3). Still sexy after all these years. *Newsweek,* 74.

Kalb, C. (2001, August 13). Should you have your baby now? *Newsweek,* 40–50.

Kalb, C. (2003, February 3). Farewell to "Aunt Flo." *Newsweek,* 48.

Kalichman, S. C., Benotsch, E., Rompa, D., Gore-Felton, C., Austin, J., Luke,

W., DiFonzo, K., Buckles, J., Kyomugisha, F., & Simpson, D. (2001). Unwanted sexual experiences and sexual risks in gay and bisexual men: Associations among revictimization, substance abuse, and psychiatric symptoms. *Journal of Sex Research, 38*(1), 1–9.

Kalmuss, D. (2004). Nonvolitional sex and sexual health. *Archives of Sexual Behavior, 33*(3), 197–209.

Kaly, P. W., Heesacker, M., & Frost, H. M. (2002). Collegiate alcohol use and high risk sexual behavior: A literature review. *Journal of College Student Development, 43*(6), 838–850.

Kanas, N. (1999). Group therapy for sexually dysfunctional men—treatment without a pill! *International Journal of Group Psychotherapy, 49*(1), 147–149.

Kandyba, K., & Binik, Y. M. (2003). Hypnotherapy as a treatment for vulvar vestibulitis syndrome: A case report. *Journal of Sex and Marital Therapy, 29,* 237–242.

Kantrowitz, B. (2006, February 20). Sex and love: The new world. *Newsweek,* 51–60.

Kantrowitz, B., & Wingert, P. (1999, April 19). The science of a good marriage. *Newsweek,* 52–57.

Kaplan, E. (2004). With God on their side: How Christian fundamentalists trampled science, policy, and democracy in G. W. Bush's White House. *SIECUS Report, 32*(4), 4–8.

Kaplan, H. S. (1974). *The new sex therapy.* New York: Brunner/Mazel.

Kaplan, H. S. (1979). *Disorders of sexual desire and other new concepts and techniques in sex therapy.* New York: Brunner/Mazel.

Karasic, D., & Drescher, J. (2005). Introduction: Sexual and gender diagnoses of the diagnostic and statistical manual (DSM): A reevaluation. *Journal of Psychology and Human Sexuality, 17*(3/4), 1–5.

Kashiwase, H. (2002). Shotgun weddings a sign of the times in Japan. *Population Today, 30*(5), 1, 4.

Katz, E. (2003). *The selected papers of Margaret Sanger. Vol. 1: The woman rebel, 1900–1928.* Urbana, IL.: University of Illinois Press.

Kaufman, C. E., Clark, S., Manzini, N., & May, J. (2004). Communities, opportunities, and adolescents' sexual behavior in KwaZulu-Natal, South Africa. *Studies in Family Planning, 35*(4), 261–274.

Kauth, M. R. (2002). Much ado about homosexuality: Assumptions underlying current research on sexual orientation. *Journal of Psychology and Human Sexuality, 14*(1), 1–22.

Kauth, M. R. (2006a). Epilogue: Implications for conceptualizing human sexuality. *Journal of Psychology and Human Sexuality, 18*(4), 371–385.

Kauth, M. R. (2006b). The evolution of human sexuality: An introduction. *Journal of Psychology and Human Sexuality, 18*(2/3), 1–22.

Keefe, D. L. (2002). Sex hormones and neural mechanisms. *Archives of Sexual Behavior, 31*(5), 401–403.

Kees, N. L. (2005). Women's voices, women's lives: An introduction to the special issue on women and counseling. *Journal of Counseling and Development, 83,* 259–261.

Keller, S. N., & Brown, J. D. (2002). Media interventions to promote responsible sexual behavior. *Journal of Sex Research, 39*(1), 67–72.

Kelley, R. (2005, February, 21). Return of a silent killer. *Newsweek,* 62.

Kelly, B. C., & Muñoz-Laboy, M. A. (2005). Sexual place, spatial change, and the social reorganization of sexual culture. *Journal of Sex Research, 42*(4), 359–366.

Kelly, G. F. (2005). Re-visioning sexuality education: A challenge for the future. *American Journal of Sexuality Education, 1*(1), 5–21.

Kelly, M. P., Strassberg, D. S., & Turner, C. M. (2006). Behavioral assessment of couples' communication in female orgasmic disorder. *Journal of Sex and Marital Therapy, 32,* 81–95.

Kempner, M. E. (2003). True integration of prevention programs requires broad focus on sexual health. *SIECUS Report, 31*(3), 5–7.

Kempner, M. E. (2004). More than just say no: What some abstinence-only-until-marriage curricula teach young people about gender. *SIECUS Report, 32*(3), 2–4.

Kennedy, D. (2003). Stem cells: Still here, still waiting. *Science, 300,* 865.

Kenny, L., & Sternberg, J. (2003). Abstinence-only education in the courts. *SIECUS Report, 31*(6), 26–29.

Kerr, S. K., & Mathy, R. M. (2003). Introduction: The human ecology of lesbian and bisexual women's mental health. *Journal of Psychology & Human Sexuality, 15*(2/3), 1–9.

Kershaw, T. S., et al. (2003). Short and long term impact of adolescent pregnancy on postpartum contraceptive use: Implications for prevention

of repeat pregnancy. *Journal of Adolescent Health, 33*(5), 359–368.

Kertzner, R. M. (2002). The adult life course and homosexual identity in midlife gay men. *Annual Review of Sex Research, 12,* 75–92.

Khalife, S., Binik, Y. M., Cohen, D. R., & Amsel, R. (2000). Evaluation of clitoral blood flow by color Doppler ultrasonography. *Journal of Sex and Marital Therapy, 26,* 187–189.

Khattak, S., K-Moghtader, G., McMartin, K., Barrera, M., Kennedy, D., & Koren, G. (1999). Pregnancy outcome following gestational exposure to organic solvents: A prospective controlled study. *Journal of the American Medical Association, 281*(12), 1106–1109.

Kiersey, D., & Bates, M. (1984). *Please understand me: Character and temperament types.* Del Mar, CA: Prometheus-Nemesis Book Co.

Kihara, M. O., Kramer, J. S., Bain, D., Kihara, M., & Mandel, J. (2001). Knowledge of and attitudes toward the pill: Results of a national survey in Japan. *Family Planning Perspectives, 33* (3), 123–127.

Kimmel, M. S., & Mahler, M. (2003). Adolescent masculinity, homophobia, and violence. *American Behavioral Scientist, 46* (10), 1439–1458.

Kimura, D. (1992). Sex differences in the brain. *Scientific American, 26* (3), 119–125.

Kimura, D. (1999). *Sex and cognition.* Cambridge, MA: MIT Press.

King, D. (2003). Gender migration: A sociological analysis. *Sexualities, 6*(2), 173–194.

King, E. (2004). Review of *Talk of Love: How culture matters* by Ann Swidler. *Archives of Sexual Behavior, 33*(1), 76–77.

King, M., Green, J., Osborn, D., Arkell, J., Hetherton, J., & Pereira, E. (2005). Family size in white gay and heterosexual men. *Archives of Sexual Behavior, 34*(1), 117–122.

King, M-C., Marks, J. H., & Mandell, J. B. (2003). Breast and ovarian cancer risks due to inherited mutations in BRCA 1 and BRCA 2. *Science, 302,* 643–646.

Kingsberg, S. A. (2002). The impact of aging on sexual function in women and their partners. *Archives of Sexual Behavior, 31*(5), 431–437.

Kingsberg, S. A. (2005). The testosterone patch for women. *International Journal of Impotence Research, 17,* 465–466.

Kinnish, K. K., Strassberg, D. S., & Turner, C. W. (2005). Sex differences in the flexibility of sexual orientation: A multidimensional retrospective assessment. *Archives of Sexual Behavior, 34*(2), 173–183.

Kinsey, A. C., Pomeroy, W. B., & Martin, C. E. (1948). *Sexual behavior in the human male.* Philadelphia: W. B. Saunders Company.

Kinsey, A. C., Pomeroy, W. B., Martin, C. E., & Gebhard, P. H. (1953). *Sexual behavior in the human female.* Philadelphia: W. B. Saunders Company.

Kippax, S., & Smith, G. (2001). Anal intercourse and power in sex between men. *Sexualities, 4*(4), 413–434.

Kirby, D. (2002a). Effective approaches to reducing adolescent unprotected sex, pregnancy, and childbearing. *Journal of Sex Research, 39*(1), 51–57.

Kirby, D. (2002b). The impact of schools and school programs upon adolescent sexual behavior. *Journal of Sex Research, 39*(1), 27–33.

Kirshenbaum, S. B., Hirky, A. E., Correale, J., Goldstein, R. B., Johnson, M. O., Rotheram-Borus, J., & Ehrhardt, A. (2004). "Throwing the dice": Pregnancy decision-making among HIV-positive women in four U.S. cities. *Perspectives on Sexual and Reproductive Health, 36*(3), 106–113.

Klaf, F. S., & Brown, W. (1958). Necrophilia, brief review and case report. *Psychiatric Quarterly, 32,* 645–652.

Klamen, D. L., Grossman, L. S., & Kopacz, D. R. (1999). Medical student homophobia. *Journal of Homosexuality, 37*(1), 53–63.

Klein, F. (1990). The need to view sexual orientation as a multivariable dynamic process: A theoretical perspective. In D. P. McWhirter, S. A. Sanders, & J. M. Reinisch (Eds.), *Homosexuality/heterosexuality: Concepts of sexual orientation* (pp. 277–282). New York: Oxford University Press.

Klein, J. D., & Committee on Adolescence. (2005). Adolescent pregnancy: Current trends and issues. *Pediatrics, 116*(1), 281–286.

Klein, M. (2003). Sex addiction: A dangerous clinical concept. *SIECUS Report, 31*(5), 8–11.

Kleinplatz, P. J., & Moser, C. (2004). Towards clinical guidelines for working with BDSM clients. *Contemporary Sexuality, 38*(6), 1, 4.

Kleinplatz, P. J., & Moser, C. (2005). Politics versus science: An addendum and response to Drs. Spitzer and

Fink. *Journal of Psychology and Human Sexuality, 17*(3/4), 135–139.

Klotz, T., Mathers, M., Klotz, R., & Sommer, F. (2005). Why do patients with erectile dysfunction abandon effective therapy with sildenafil? *International Journal of Impotence Research, 17*(1), 2–4.

Klusmann, D. (2002). Sexual motivation and the duration of partnership. *Archives of Sexual Behavior, 31*(3), 275–287.

Knauft, B. M. (2004). What ever happened to ritualized homosexuality? Modern sexual subjects in Melanesia and elsewhere. *Annual Review of Sex Research, 14,* 137–158.

Knegtering, H., et al. (2006). A randomized open-label comparison of the impact of olanzapine versus risperidone on sexual functioning. *Journal of Sex and Marital Therapy, 32,* 315–326.

Koblin, B. A., et al. (2003). High-risk behaviors among men who have sex with men in 6 U.S. cities: Baseline data from the EXPLORE study. *American Journal of Public Health, 93*(6), 926–932.

Koch, P. B. (2006). Women's bodies as a "puzzle" for college men: Grounded theory research. *American Journal of Sexuality Education, 1*(3), 51–72.

Koch, P. B., Mansfield, P. K., Thurau, D., & Carey, M. (2005). "Feeling frumpy": The relationships between body image and sexual response changes in midlife women. *Journal of Sex Research, 42*(3), 215–223.

Koehler, J. D. (2002). Vaginismus: Diagnosis, etiology, and intervention. *Contemporary Sexuality, 36*(9), i–viii.

Kohlberg, L. (1981). *Essays on moral development.* San Francisco: Harper & Row.

Kohn, D. (2002). Working with out-of-school youth in Belize and Peru. *SIECUS Report, 30*(5), 16–18.

Koniak-Griffin, D., et al. (2003). Teen pregnancy, motherhood, and unprotected sexual activity. *Research in Nursing and Health, 26*(1), 4–19.

Kontula, O., & Haavio-Mannila, E. (2002). Masturbation in a generational perspective. *Journal of Psychology and Human Sexuality, 14*(2/3), 49–83.

Korber, B., Muldoon, M., Theiler, J., Gao, F., Gupta, R., Lapedes, A., et al. (2000). Timing the ancestor of the HIV-1 pandemic strains. *Science, 288,* 1789–1796.

Korenman, S., Kaestner, R., & Joyce, T. (2002). Consequences for infants of parental disagreement in pregnancy intention. *Perspectives on Sexual and Reproductive Health, 34*(4), 198–205.

Kornreich, J. L., Hearn, K. D., Rodriguez, G., & O'Sullivan, L. F. (2003). Sibling influence, gender roles, and the sexual socialization of urban early adolescent girls. *Journal of Sex Research, 40*(1), 101–110.

Koskimaki, J., et al. (2005). Are questions on both achieving and maintaining an erection needed to define erectile dysfunction? *International Journal of Impotence Research, 17,* 335–338.

Koukounas, E., & McCabe, M. P. (2001). Sexual and emotional variables influencing sexual response to erotica: A psychophysiological investigation. *Archives of Sexual Behavior, 30*(4), 393–408.

Krahè, B., Scheinberger-Olwig, R., & Bieneck, S. (2003). Men's reports of nonconsensual sexual interactions with women: Prevalence and impact. *Archives of Sexual Behavior, 32*(3), 165–175.

Krahè, B., Schütze, S., Fritsche, I., & Waizenhöfer, E. (2000). The prevalence of sexual aggression and victimization among homosexual men. *Journal of Sex Research, 37*(2), 142–150.

Krassas, N. R., Blauwkamp, J. M., & Wesselink, P. (2003). "Master your Johnson": Sexual rhetoric in *Maxim* and *Stuff* magazines. *Sexuality and Culture, 7*(3), 98–118.

Krueger, R. B., & Kaplan, M. S. (2001). Depot-leuprolide acetate for treatment of paraphilias: A report on twelve cases. *Archives of Sexual Behavior, 30*(4), 409–422.

Kuang, M., Mathy, R. M., Carol, H. M., & Nojima, K. (2003). The effects of sexual orientation, gender identity, and gender role on the mental health of women in Taiwan's *T-Po* lesbian community. *Journal of Psychology and Human Sexuality, 15*(4), 163–184.

Kuczynski, A. (1999, May 2). Women's magazines' feminist edge lost to sex. *Watertown* (NY) *Daily Times Sunday Weekly,* 9.

Kuefer, R., et al. (2005). Changing diagnostic and therapeutic concepts in high-flow priapism. *International Journal of Impotence Research, 17,* 109–113.

Kuile, M. M., & Weijenborg, P. M. (2006). A cognitive-behavioral group program for women with vulvar

vestibulitis sydrome (VVS): Factors associated with treatment success. *Journal of Sex and Marital Therapy, 32,* 199–213.

Kulczycki, A., Kim, D. J., Duerr, A., Jamieson, D. J., & Macaluso, M. (2004). The acceptability of the female and male condom: A randomized crossover trial. *Perspectives on Sexual and Reproductive Health, 36* (3), 114–119.

Kunkel, D., Cope, K. M., & Biely, E. (1999). Sexual messages on television: Comparing findings from three studies. *Journal of Sex Research, 36*(3), 230–236.

Kurth, A. E., et al. (2004). A comparison between audio computer-assisted self-interviews and clinician interviews for obtaining the sexual history. *Sexually Transmitted Diseases, 31* (12), 719–726.

LaBrie, J., Earleywine, M., Schiffman, J., Pedersen, E., & Marriot, C. (2005). Effects of alcohol, expectancies, and partner type on condom use in college males: Event-level analyses. *Journal of Sex Research, 42*(3), 259–266.

Lacey, J. V., Mink, P. J., Lubin, J. H., Sherman, M. E., Troisi, R., Hartge, P., Schatzkin, A., & Schairer, C. (2002). Menopausal hormone replacement therapy and risk of ovarian cancer. *Journal of the American Medical Association, 288*(3), 334–341.

Lacy, K. K. (2002). Mature sexuality: Patient realities and provider challenges. *SIECUS Report, 30*(2), 22–30.

Ladas, A. K. (1997). The G spot. *CliniScope, 3,* 1–4.

Ladas, A. K., Whipple, B., & Perry, J. (1983). *The G spot and other recent discoveries about human sexuality.* New York: Dell.

Laflin, M. T., Sommers, J. M., & Chibucos, T. R. (2005). Initial findings in a longitudinal study of the effectiveness of the *Sex Can Wait* sexual abstinence curriculum for grades 5-8. *American Journal of Sexuality Education, 1*(1), 103–117.

Lahelma, E., Palmu, T., & Gordon, T. (2000). Intersecting power relations in teachers' experiences of being sexualized or harassed by students. *Sexualities, 3*(4), 463–481.

Laland, K. N. (2003). The new interactionism. *Science, 300,* 1879–1880.

Lam, T. H., et al. (2004). Depressive symptoms among Hong Kong adolescents: Relation to atypical sexual feelings and behaviors, gender dissatisfaction, pubertal timing, and family and peer relationships. *Archives of Sexual Behavior, 33*(5), 487–496.

Lambert, T. A., Kahn, A. S., & Apple, K. J. (2003). Pluralistic ignorance and hooking up. *Journal of Sex Research, 40*(2), 129–133.

Lampman, C., Rolfe-Maloney, B., David, E. J., Yan, M., McDermott, N., Winters, S., Davis, J., & Lathrop, R. (2002). Messages about sex in the workplace: A content analysis of primetime television. *Sexuality and Culture, 6*(4), 3–21.

Landry, D. J., Darroch, J. E., Singh, S., & Higgins, J. (2003). Factors associated with the content of sex education in U.S. public secondary schools. *Perspectives on Sexual and Reproductive Health, 35*(6), 261–269.

Langdridge, D., & Butt, T. (2004). A hermeneutic phenomenological investigation of the construction of sadomasochistic identities. *Sexualities, 7*(1), 31–53.

Langstrom, N., Grann, M., & Lichtenstein, P. (2002). Genetic and environmental influences on problematic masturbatory behavior in children: A study of same-sex twins. *Archives of Sexual Behavior, 31*(4), 343–350.

Langstrom, N., & Hanson, R. K. (2006). High rates of sexual behavior in the general population: Correlates and predictors. *Archives of Sexual Behavior, 35*(1), 37–52.

Langstrom, N., & Seto, M. C. (2006). Exhibitionistic and voyeuristic behavior in a Swedish national population survery. *Archives of Sexual Behavior, 35,* 427–435.

Langstrom, N., & Zucker, K. J. (2005). Transvestic fetishism in the general population: Prevalence and correlates. *Journal of Sex & Marital Therapy, 31,* 87–95.

LaPera, G., Giannotti, C. F., Taggi, F., & Macchia, T. (2003). Prevalence of sexual disorders in those young males who later become drug abusers. *Journal of Sex and Marital Therapy, 29*(2), 149–156.

Larsson, I., & Svedin, C. (2002 June). Sexual experiences in childhood: Young adults' recollections. *Archives of Sexual Behavior, 31*(3), 263–273.

Laumann, E. O., Gagnon, J. H., Michael, R. T., & Michaels, S. (1994). *The social organization of sexuality.* Chicago: University of Chicago Press.

Laumann, E. O., Nicolosi, A., et al. (2006). Men treated with sildenafil for erectile dysfunction: Results.

Journal of General Internal Medicine, 21(10), 1069–1074.

Laumann, E. O., Paik, A., et al. (2006). A cross-national study of subjective sexual well-being among older women and men: Findings from the global study of sexual attitudes and behaviors. *Archives of Sexual Behavior, 35*(2), 143–159.

Laumann, E. O., et al. (2005). Sexual problems among women and men aged 40–80 y: Prevalence and correlates identified in the global study of sexual attitudes and behaviors. *International Journal of Impotence Research, 17,* 39–57.

Laumann, E. O., et al. (2006). A cross-national study of subjective sexual well-being among older women and men: Findings from the global study of sexual attitudes and behaviors. *Archives of Sexual Behavior, 35*(2), 145–161.

Lawler, A. (2006). Universities urged to improve hiring and advancement of women. *Science, 313,* 1712.

Lawrence, A. A. (2003). Factors associated with satisfaction or regret following male-to-female sex reassignment surgery. *Archives of Sexual Behavior, 32*(4), 299–315.

Lawrence, A. A. (2005). Sexuality before and after male-to-female sex reassignment surgery. *Archives of Sexual Behavior, 34*(2), 147–166.

Lawrence, A. A. (2006). Clinical and theoretical parallels between desire for limb amputation and gender identity disorder. *Archives of Sexual Behavior, 35*(3), 263–278.

Lawrence, A. A., Latty, E. M., Chivers, M. L., & Bailey, J. M. (2005). Measurement of sexual arousal in postoperative male-to-female transsexuals using vaginal photoplethysmography. *Archives of Sexual Behavior, 34*(2), 135–145.

Lawson, C. (1993). Mother–son sexual abuse: Rare or underreported? A critique of the research. *Child Abuse and Neglect, 17,* 261–269.

Lawson, D. M. (2003). Incidence, explanations, and treatment of partner violence. *Journal of Counseling and Development, 81,* 19–32.

Lawson, M. L., et al. (2003). Partner characteristics, intensity of the intercourse, and semen exposure during use of the female condom. *American Journal of Epidemiology, 157*(4), 282–288.

Layne, L. L. (1999). *Transformative motherhood: On giving and getting in a consumer culture.* New York: New York University Press.

Learman, L. A., et al. (2005). Abortion attitudes of pregnant women in prenatal care. *American Journal of Obstetrics and Gynecology, 192*(6), 1939–1947.

Lee, J. K., Jennings, J. M., & Ellen, J. M. (2003). Discordant sexual partnering: A study of high-risk adolescents in San Francisco. *Sexually Transmitted Diseases, 30*(3), 234–240.

Lefkowitz, E. S., Gillen, M. M., Shearer, C. L., & Boone, T. L. (2004). Religiosity, sexual behaviors, and sexual attitudes during emerging adulthood. *Journal of Sex Research, 41*(2), 150–159.

Lehman, C. D., et al. (2007). MRI evaluation of the contralateral breast in women with recently diagnosed breast cancer. *New England Journal of Medicine, 356*(12), 1295–1303.

Lehr, S. T., Demi, A. S., DiIorio, C., & Facteau, J. (2005). Predictors of father-son communication about sexuality. *Journal of Sex Research, 42*(2), 119–129.

Leibenluft, E. (1996). Sex is complex. *American Journal of Psychiatry, 153*(8), 969–972.

Leiblum, S. R., & Nathan, S. G. (2001). Persistent sexual arousal syndrome: A newly discovered pattern of female sexuality. *Journal of Sex and Marital Therapy, 27,* 365–380.

Leland, J. (1999a, February 22). Bad news in the bedroom. *Newsweek,* 47.

Leland, J. (1999b, September 20). More buck for the bang. *Time,* 61.

Lemoire, S. J., & Chen, C. P. (2005). Applying person-centered counseling to sexual minority adolescents. *Journal of Counseling and Development, 83,* 146–154.

L'Engle, K. L., Jackson, C., & Brown, J. D. (2006). Early adolescents' cognitive susceptibility to initiating sexual intercourse. *Perspectives on Sexual and Reproductive Health, 38*(2), 97–105.

Leonard, L. (2001). Interpreting female genital cutting: Moving beyond the impasse. *Annual Review of Sex Research, 11,* 158–190.

Leonard, L. M., & Follette, V. M. (2003). Sexual functioning in women reporting a history of child sexual abuse: Review of the empirical literature and clinical implications. *Annual Review of Sex Research, 13,* 346–388.

Lepowsky, M. (1994). *Fruit of the motherland: Gender in an egalitarian society.* New York: Columbia University Press.

Lev, A. I. (2005). Disordering gender identity: Gender identity disorder in the *DSM-IV-TR. Journal of Psychology and Human Sexuality, 17*(3/4), 35–69.

LeVay, S. (1996). *Queer science: The use and abuse of research into homosexuality.* Cambridge, MA: MIT Press.

Levesque, R. J. R. (2002). The roles and rules of law in sexual development. *Journal of Sex Research, 39*(1), 46–50.

Levin, R. J. (2002). The psychology of sexual arousal in the human female: A recreational and procreational synthesis. *Archives of Sexual Behavior, 31*(5), 405–411.

Levin, R. J. (2003). Do women gain anything from coitus apart from pregnancy? Changes in the human female genital tract activated by coitus. *Journal of Sex and Marital Therapy, 29,* 59–69.

Levin, R. J. (2004). An orgasm is . . . who defines what an orgasm is? *Sexual and Relationship Therapy, 19*(1), 101–107.

Levin-Epstein, J. (2005). To have and to hold: Congressional vows on marriage and sex. *SIECUS Report, 33*(1), 19–33.

Levine, J. (2002a). *Harmful to minors: The perils of protecting children from sex.* Minneapolis: University of Minnesota Press.

Levine, J. (2002b). Promoting pleasure: What's the problem? *SIECUS Report, 30*(4), 19–22.

Levine, S. B. (2002). Reexploring the concept of sexual desire. *Journal of Sex and Marital Therapy, 28,* 39–51.

Levine, S. B. (2003). The nature of sexual desire: A clinician's perspective. *Archives of Sexual Behavior, 32*(3), 279–285.

Levine, S. B. (2004). Commentary on Ribner's (2004) "Ejaculatory restrictions as a factor in the treatment of Haredi (ultra-orthodox) Jewish couples": How does therapy work? *Archives of Sexual Behavior, 33*(3), 309–310.

Levine, S. B. (2005). What is love anyway? *Journal of Sex and Marital Therapy, 31,* 143–151.

Levy-Lahad, E., & Plon, S. E. (2003). A risky business: Assessing breast cancer risk. *Science, 302,* 574–575.

Lew, M. (2004). Adult male survivors of sexual abuse: Sexual issues in treatment and recovery. *Contemporary Sexuality, 38*(11), i–vi.

Lewis, J., Maticka-Tyndale, E., Shaver, F., & Schramm, H. (2005). Managing risk and safety on the job: The experiences of Canadian sex workers.

Journal of Psychology and Human Sexuality, 17(1/2), 147–167.

Lewis, L. J., & Kertzner, R. M. (2003). Toward improved interpretation and theory building of African American male sexualities. *Journal of Sex Research, 40*(4), 383–395.

Li, R., et al. (2003). Prevalence of breastfeeding in the United States: The 2001 national immunization survey. *Pediatrics, 111*(5), 1198–1201.

Lieberman, L. D. (2006). Early predictors of sexual behavior: Implications for young adolescents and their parents. *Perspectives on Sexual and Reproductive Health, 38*(2), 112–114.

Lief, H. I. (2001). Boundary crossings: Sexual misconduct of clergy. *Journal of Sex Education and Therapy, 26,* 310–314.

Liehmann-Smith, J. (2001). Preteenage relationship with an older partner may lead to early first sex. *Family Planning Perspectives, 33*(3), 134.

Lindberg, L. D., Frost, J. J., Sten, C., & Dailard, C. (2006). The provision and funding of contraceptive services at publicly funded family planning agencies: 1995–2003. *Perspectives on Sexual and Reproductive Health, 38* (1), 37–45.

Lingiardi, V., Falanga, S., & D'Augelli, A. R. (2005). The evaluation of homophobia in an Italian sample. *Archives of Sexual Behavior, 34*(1), 81–93.

Lin-Liu, J. (2003, December 10). No sex, please, we're Taiwanese. *Chronicle of Higher Education,* A36–38.

Linz, D., Paul, B., & Yao, M. Z. (2006). Peep show establishments, police activity, public place, and time: A study of secondary effects in San Diego, California. *Journal of Sex Research, 43*(2), 182–193.

Lippa, R. A. (2001). Gender-related traits in transsexuals and nontranssexuals. *Archives of Sexual Behavior, 30*(6), 603–614.

Lippa, R. A. (2002a). *Gender, nature, and nurture.* Mahwah, NJ: Lawrence Erlbaum.

Lippa, R. A. (2002b). Gender-related traits of heterosexual and homosexual men and women. *Archives of Sexual Behavior, 31*(1), 83–98.

Lippa, R. A. (2003). Handedness, sexual orientation, and gender-related personality traits in men and women. *Archives of Sexual Behavior, 32*(2), 103–114.

Lipschitz, D. S., Winegar, R. K., Hartnick, E., Foote, B., & Southwick, S. M. (1999). Posttraumatic stress disorder in hospitalized adolescents: Psychi-

atric comorbidity and clinical correlates. *Journal of the American Academy of Child and Adolescent Psychiatry, 38*(4), 385–392.

Littner, M., Littner, L., & Shah, M. A. (2001). Sexuality issues for the disabled: Development of a United States policy. *SIECUS Report, 29*(3), 28–32.

Litzinger, S., & Gordon, K. C. (2005). Exploring relationships among communication, sexual satisfaction, and marital satisfaction. *Journal of Sex & Marital Therapy, 31,* 409–424.

Lloyd, E. A. (2005). *The case of the female orgasm: Bias in the science of evolution.* Cambridge, MA.: Harvard University Press.

Loeb, T. B., et al. (2003). Child sexual abuse: Associations with the sexual functioning of adolescents and adults. *Annual Review of Sex Research, 13,* 307–345.

Loehlin, J. C., & McFadden, D. (2003). Otoacoustic emissions, auditory evoked potentials, and traits related to sex and sexual orientation. *Archives of Sexual Behavior, 32*(2), 115–127.

Loewenson, P. R., Ireland, M., & Resnick, M. D. (2004). Primary and secondary sexual abstinence in high school students. *Journal of Adolescent Health, 34*(3), 209–215.

London, S. (2004). Current hormone therapy use linked to 30–100% rise in risk of breast cancer. *Perspectives on Sexual and Reproductive Health, 36* (1), 41–42.

Long, V. E. (2003). Contraceptive choices: New options in the U.S. market. *SIECUS Report, 31*(2), 13–18.

Lottes, I. L. (2002). Sexual health policies in other industrialized countries: Are there lessons for the United States? *Journal of Sex Research, 39*(1), 79–83.

Low, N., et al. (2006). Global control of sexually transmitted infections. *The Lancet, Early Online Publication* DOI:10.1016/S0140-6736(06)69482-8.

Luft, D. S. (2003). *Eros and inwardness in Vienna: Weininger, Musil, Doderer.* Chicago: University of Chicago Press.

Lykins, A. D., Janssen, E., & Graham, C. A. (2006). The relationship between negative mood and sexuality in heterosexual college women and men. *Journal of Sex Research, 43*(2), 136–143.

Macaluso, M., et al. (2003). Efficacy of the female condom as a barrier to semen during intercourse. *American Journal of Epidemiology, 157*(4), 289–297.

Maccoby, E. E. (1998). *The two sexes: Growing up apart, coming together.* Cambridge, MA: Harvard University Press.

MacCulloch, S. I., Gray, N. S., Phillips, H. K., Taylor, J., & MacCulloch, M. J. (2004). Birth order in sex-offending and aggressive men. *Archives of Sexual Behavior, 33*(5), 467–474.

Mack, K. A., & Lansky, A. (2003). HIV testing—United States, 2001. *Morbidity and Mortality Weekly Report, 52*(23), 540–545.

MacKay, A. P., Kiekle, B. A., Koonin, L. M., & Beattie, K. (2001). Tubal sterilization in the United States, 1994–1996. *Family Planning Perspectives, 33*(4), 161–165.

Maddock, J. W., & Larson, N. R. (1995). *Incestuous families: An ecological approach to understanding and treatment.* New York: W. W. Norton.

Mah, K., & Binik, Y. M. (2002). Do all orgasms feel alike? Evaluating a two-dimensional model of the orgasm experience across gender and sexual context. *Journal of Sex Research, 39*(2), 104–113.

Mah, K., & Binik, Y. M. (2005). Are orgasms in the mind or the body? Psychosocial versus physiological correlates of orgasmic pleasure and satisfaction. *Journal of Sex and Marital Therapy, 31,* 187–200.

Maher, J. E., Harvey, S. M., Bird, S. T., Stevens, V. J., & Beckman, L. J. (2004). Acceptability of the vaginal diaphragm among current users. *Perspectives on Sexual and Reproductive Health, 36*(2), 64–71.

Maisto, S. A., et al. (2004). The relationship between alcohol and individual differences variables on attitudes and behavioral skills relevant to sexual health among heterosexual young adult men. *Archives of Sexual Behavior, 33*(6), 571–584.

Major, B., Barr, L., Zubek, J., & Babey, S. H. (1999). Gender and self-esteem: A meta-analysis. In W. B. Swann & J. H. Langlois (Eds.), *Sexism and stereotypes in modern society: The gender science of Janet Taylor Spence* (pp. 223–253). Washington, DC: American Psychological Association.

Malakoff, D. (2003). New players, same debate in Congress. *Science, 299,* 799.

Malamuth, N. M., Addison, T., & Koss, M. (2001). Pornography and sexual aggression: Are there reliable effects and can we understand them? *Annual Review of Sex Research, 11,* 26–91.

Malcom, N. L. (2003). Constructing female athleticism: A study of girls' recreational softball. *American Behavioral Scientist, 46*(10), 1387–1404.

Maltz, W. (2003). Treating the sexual intimacy concerns of sexual abuse survivors. *Contemporary Sexuality, 37*(7), i–viii.

Manlove, J., Ryan, S., & Franzetta, K. (2004). Contraceptive use and consistency in U.S. teenagers' most recent sexual relationships. *Perspectives on Sexual and Reproductive Health, 36*(6), 265–275.

Marcell, A. V., Raine, T., & Eyre, S. L. (2003). Where does reproductive health fit into the lives of adolescent males? *Perspectives on Sexual and Reproductive Health, 35*(4), 180–186.

Marina, S. (1998). Human immunodeficiency virus type 1-serodiscordant couples can bear healthy children after undergoing intrauterine insemination. *Fertility and Sterility, 70*(1), 35–39.

Mark Clements Research. (1996). Sexual activity still flourishes after 65. *Contemporary Sexuality, 30*(4), 8.

Markels, A. (2003, October 13). A seismic shift in sex-case law. *U.S. News and World Report,* 45.

Marotta, S. A., & Asner, K. K. (1999). Group psychotherapy for women with a history of incest: The research base. *Journal of Counseling and Development, 77,* 315–322.

Marrazzo, J. M., Coffey, P., & Bingham, A. (2005). Sexual practices, risk perception and knowledge of sexually transmitted disease risk among lesbian and bisexual women. *Perspectives on Sexual and Reproductive Health, 37*(1), 6–12.

Marshall, E. (2002). Battle heats up over mammography benefits. *Science, 295,* 1624–1625.

Marshall, N. L. (2003). Introduction to special issue on social construction of gender. *American Behavioral Scientist, 46*(10), 1289–1295.

Marsiglio, W. (2003). Making males mindful of their sexual and procreative identities: Using self-narratives in field settings. *Perpsectives on Sexual and Reproductive Health, 35*(5), 229–233.

Marston, C., Meltzer, H., & Majeed, A. (2005). Impact on contraceptive practice of making emergency hormonal contraception available over the counter in Great Britain: Repeated cross sectional surveys. *British Medical Journal, 331* (7511), 271.

Martin, J. A., & Park, M. M. (1999). Trends in twin and triplet births: 1980–97. *National Vital Statistics, 46,* 24.

Martin, P. Y., & Collinson, D. L. (1999). Gender and sexuality in organizations. In M. M. Ferree (Ed.), *Revisioning gender* (pp.285–310). Thousand Oaks, CA: Sage.

Masters, W. H., & Johnson, V. E. (1966). *Human sexual response.* Boston: Little, Brown.

Masters, W. H., & Johnson, V. E. (1970). *Human sexual inadequacy.* Boston: Little, Brown.

Mathy, R. M. (2001). A nonclinical comparison of transgender identity and sexual orientation: A framework for multicultural competence. *Journal of Psychology and Human Sexuality, 13* (1), 31–54.

Mathy, R. M. (2002). Transgender identity and suicidality in a nonclinical sample: Sexual orientation, psychiatric history, and compulsive behaviors. *Journal of Psychology and Human Sexuality, 14*(4), 47–65.

Maticka-Tyndale, E., Herold, E. S., & Mewhinney, D. (1999). Casual sex on spring break: Intentions and behaviors of Canadian students. *Journal of Sex Research, 35*(3), 254–264.

Maticka-Tyndale, E., Herold, E. S., & Oppermann, M. (2003). Casual sex among Australian schoolies. *Journal of Sex Research, 40*(2), 158–169.

Maticka-Tyndale, E., Lewis, J., & Street, M. (2005). Making a place for escort work: A case study. *Journal of Sex Research, 42*(1), 46–53.

Mazur, T. (2005). Gender dysphoria and gender change in androgen insensitivity or micropenis. *Archives of Sexual Behavior, 34*(4), 411–421.

McCabe, M. P. (2001). Evaluation of a cognitive behavior therapy program for people with sexual dysfunction. *Journal of Sex and Marital Therapy, 27,* 259–271.

McCabe, M. P., McKern, S., McDonald, E., & Vowels, L. M. (2003). Changes over time in sexual and relationship functioning of people with multiple sclerosis. *Journal of Sex and Marital Therapy, 29*(4), 305–321.

McCabe, M. P., & Wauchope, M. (2005). Behavioral characteristics of men accused of rape: Evidence for different types of rapists. *Archives of Sexual Behavior, 34*(2), 241–253.

McCaffree, K. A. (1998). Who is a sexuality professional? *Journal of Sex Education and Therapy, 23*(1), 3–5.

McCarthy, B. W. (1999). The nonsexual marriage: Assessing viability and treatment options. *Journal of Sex and Marital Therapy, 25,* 227–236.

McCarthy, B. W. (2002). Sexual secrets, trauma, and dysfunction. *Journal of Sex and Marital Therapy, 28,* 353–359.

McCarthy, B. W., & Fucito, L. M. (2005). Integrating medication, realistic expectations, and therapeutic interventions in the treatment of male sexual dysfunction. *Journal of Sex and Marital Therapy, 31,* 319–328.

McCarthy, S. K., Telljohann, S. K., Coventry, B., & Price, J. (2005). Availability of services for emergency contraceptive pills at high school–based health centers. *Perspectives on Sexual and Reproductive Health, 37*(2), 70–77.

McCleary, R., & Meeker, J. W. (2006). Do peep shows "cause" crime? A response to Linz, Paul, and Yao. *Journal of Sex Research, 43*(2), 194–196.

McConaghy, N. (2005). Time to abandon the gay/heterosexual dichotomy? *Archives of Sexual Behavior, 34*(1), 1–2.

McFadden, D. (2002). Masculinization effects in the auditory system. *Archives of Sexual Behavior, 31* (1), 99–111.

McFarlane, M., Bull, S. S., & Reitmeijer, C. A. (2002). Young adults on the Internet: Risk behaviors for sexually transmitted diseases and HIV. *Journal of Adolescent Health, 31*(1), 11–16.

McGinn, D. (2004, October 4). Mating behavior 101. *Newsweek,* 44–46.

McIntyre, M. H. (2003). Digit ratios, childhood gender role behavior, and erotic role preferences of gay men [Letter]. *Archives of Sexual Behavior, 32*(6), 495–497.

McKee, A. (2005). The objectification of women in mainstream pornographic videos in Australia. *Journal of Sex Research, 42*(4), 277–290.

McKenna, K. E. (2000). Central nervous system pathways involved in the control of penile erection. *Annual Review of Sex Research, 9,* 157–183.

McKenna, K. Y. A., Green, A. S., & Smith, P. K. (2001). Demarginalizing the sexual self. *Journal of Sex Research, 38*(4), 302–311.

McKenna, W., Tiefer, L., & Schober, J. M. (2002). Reviews of *As nature made him. Archives of Sexual Behavior, 31*(3), 301–308.

M. D. Anderson Cancer Center (2006, December 14). *Decline in breast cancer cases likely linked to reduced use of hormone replacement.* News release.

Mead, M. (1930). *Growing up in New Guinea.* New York: New American Library.

Meana, M., & Nunnink, S. E. (2006). Gender differences in the content of cognitive distraction during sex. *Journal of Sex Research, 43*(1), 59–67.

Mehta, S. D., et al. (2003a). Generalizability of STD screening in urban emergency departments: Comparison of results from inner city and urban sites in Baltimore, Maryland. *Sexually Transmitted Diseases, 30*(2), 143–148.

Mehta, S. D., et al. (2003b). Gonorrhea reinfection in heterosexual STD clinic attendees: Longitudinal analysis of risks for first infection. *Sexually Transmitted Diseases, 79*(2), 124–128.

Melby, T. (2000). New study: Most medical schools provide less than 10 hours of sex education. *Contemporary Sexuality, 34*(8), 1, 4–5.

Melby, T. (2003). Facilitated sex: What happens when the disabled need help with sex? *Contemporary Sexuality, 37*(11), 1, 4–6.

Melby, T. (2004). Spotlight on a hidden crime. *Contemporary Sexuality, 38* (5), 1, 4–6.

Melby, T. (2005). With males in the mix, federal sex survey takes on greater importance. *Contemporary Sexuality, 39*(12), 1–6.

Melby, T. (2006a). America's sexual divide. *Contemporary Sexuality, 40*(12), 1, 4–7.

Melby, T. (2006b). As easy as ABC? *Contemporary Sexuality, 40* (6), 1–5.

Melby, T. (2006c). "The government is relentless." *Contemporary Sexuality, 40*(5), 1, 4–5.

Melby, T. (2006d). New generation, new worldview. *Contemporary Sexuality, 40*(10), 1–6.

Melendez, R. M., Hoffman, S., Exner, T., Leu, C. S., & Ehrhardt, A. A. (2003). Intimate partner violence and safer sex negotiation: Effects of a gender-specific intervention. *Archives of Sexual Behavior, 32*(6), 499–511.

Melnik, T., & Abdo, C. H. N. (2005). Psychogenic erectile dysfunction: Comparative study of three therapeutic approaches. *Journal of Sex and Marital Therapy, 31,* 243–255.

Melody, M. E., & Peterson, L. M. (1999). *Teaching America about sex: Marriage guides and sex manuals from the late Victorians to Dr. Ruth.* New York: New York University Press.

Mensch, B. S., Clark, W. H., & Anh, D. N. (2003). Adolescents in Vietnam: Looking beyond reproductive health. *Studies in Family Planning, 34*(4), 249–262.

Mensch, B. S., Ibrahim, B. L., Lee, S. M., & El-Gibaly, O. (2003). Gender-role attitudes among Egyptian adolescents. *Studies in Family Planning, 34*(1), 8–18.

Merikangas, K. R., & Risch, N. (2003). Genomic priorities and public health. *Science, 302,* 599–601.

Meston, C. M. (2000). The psychophysiological assessment of female sexual function. *Journal of Sex Education and Therapy, 25* (1), 6–16.

Meston, C. M. (2001). Receptivity and personal distress: Considerations for redefining female sexual dysfunction. *Journal of Sex and Marital Therapy, 27,* 179–182.

Meston, C. M. (2003). Validation of the female sexual dysfunction index (FSI) in women with female orgasmic disorder and in women with hypoactive sexual desire disorder. *Journal of Sex and Marital Therapy, 29,* 39–46.

Meston, C. M. (2004). The effects of hysterectomy on sexual arousal in women with a history of benign uterine fibroids. *Archives of Sexual Behavior, 33*(1), 31–42.

Meston, C. M., & Frohlich, P. F. (2003). Love at first fright: Partner salience moderates roller-coaster-induced excitation transfer. *Archives of Sexual Behavior, 32*(6), 537–544.

Meston, C. M., Heiman, J. R., & Trapnell, P. D. (1999). The relation between early abuse and adult sexuality. *Journal of Sex Research, 36*(4), 385–395.

Meston, C. M., Levin, R. J., Sipski, M. L., Hull, E. M., & Heiman, J. R. (2005). Women's orgasm. *Annual Review of Sex Research, 15,* 173–256.

Meston, C. M., & Worcel, M. (2002). The effects of yohimbine plus L-arginine glutamate on sexual arousal in postmenopausal women with sexual arousal disorder. *Archives of Sexual Behavior, 31*(4), 323–332.

Metz, M. E., & Epstein, N. (2002). Assessing the role of relationship conflict in sexual dysfunction. *Journal of Sex and Marital Therapy, 28,* 139–164.

Metz, M. E., & McCarthy, B. W. (2005). Erectile dysfunction: An integrative, biopsychosocial approach to evaluation, treatment, and relapse prevention. *Contemporary Sexuality, 39*(5), i–viii.

Metz, M. E., & Sawyer, S. P. (2004). Treating sexual dysfunction in sex offenders: A case example. *Journal of Sex and Marital Therapy, 30,* 185–197.

Meyer, I. H., Rossana, L., Ellis, J. M., & Bradford, J. (2002). A brief telephone interview to identify lesbian and bisexual women in random digit dialing sampling. *Journal of Sex Research, 39*(2), 139–144.

Meyer, M. D. E. (2005). Drawing the sexuality card: Teaching, researching, and living bisexuality. *Sexuality & Culture, 9*(1), 3–13.

Meyer, W., Bockting, W. O., Cohen-Kettenis, P., Coleman, E., et al. (2001). The Harry Benjamin International Gender Dysphoria Association's standards of care for gender identity disorders (sixth version). *Journal of Psychology and Human Sexuality, 13*(1), 1–30.

Meyer-Bahlburg, H. F. L., et al. (2004). Prenatal androgenization affects gender-related behavior but not gender identity in 5–12-year-old girls with congenital adrenal hyperplasia. *Archives of Sexual Behavior, 33*(2), 97–104.

Meyer-Bahlburg, H. F. L. (2005a). Gender identity outcome in female-raised 46,XY persons with penile agenesis, cloacal exstrophy of the bladder, or penile ablation. *Archives of Sexual Behavior, 34*(4), 423–438.

Meyer-Bahlburg, H. F. L. (2005b). Introduction: Gender dysphoria and gender change in persons with intersexuality. *Archives of Sexual Behavior, 34*(4), 371–373.

Meyerowitz, J. (2002). *How sex changed: A history of transsexuality in the United States.* Cambridge, MA: Harvard University Press.

Miccio-Fonseca, L. C. (2001). Somatic and mental symptoms of male sex offenders: A comparison among offenders, victims, and their families. *Journal of Psychology and Human Sexuality, 13*(3/4), 103–114.

Michael, R. T., Gagnon, J. H., Laumann, E. O., & Kolata, G. (1994). *Sex in America: A definitive study.* Boston: Little, Brown.

Miletski, H. (2001). Zoophilia—implications for therapy. *Journal of Sex Education and Therapy, 26*(2), 85–89.

Miletski, H. (2006). Introduction to bestiality and zoophilia. *Contemporary Sexuality, 40*(12), 8–13.

Milhausen, R. R., & Herold, E. S. (1999). Does the sexual double standard still exist? Perceptions of university women. *Journal of Sex Research, 36*(4), 361–368.

Milhausen, R. R., & Herold, E. S. (2001). Reconceptualizing the sexual double standard. *Journal of Psychology and Human Sexuality, 13*(2), 63–83.

Miller, B. C. (2002, February). Family influences on adolescent sexual and contraceptive behavior. *Journal of Sex Research, 39*(1), 22–26.

Miller, D. A., & Ellis, E. B. (2006). Pieces and parts. *American Journal on Sexuality Education, 1*(2), 67–73.

Miller, L., & Notter, K. M. (2001). Menstrual reduction with extended use of combination oral contraceptive pills: Randomized controlled trial. *Obstetrics and Gynecology, 98*(5), 771–778.

Miller, W. C., et al. (2005). The prevalence of trichomoniasis in young adults in the United States. *Sexually Transmitted Diseases, 32*(10), 593–598.

Millner, V. S., & Hanks, R. B. (2002). Induced abortion: An ethical conundrum for counselors. *Journal of Counseling and Development, 80,* 57–62.

Mills, E., & Rennie, S. (2006). HIV testing and individual rights. *Science, 314,* 417–418.

Mills, L. J., & Daniluk, J. C. (2002). Her body speaks: The experience of dance therapy for women survivors of child sexual abuse. *Journal of Counseling and Development, 80,* 77–84.

Min, K., Munarriz, R., Berman, J., Kim, N. N., et al. (2001). Hemodynamic evaluation of the female sexual response in an animal model. *Journal of Sex and Marital Therapy, 27*(5), 557–565.

Miner, M. H., & Coleman, E. (2001). Advances in sex offender treatment and challenges for the future. *Journal of Psychology and Human Sexuality, 13*(3/4), 5–24.

Minichiello, V., Marino, R., Browne, J., Jamieson, M., Peterson, K., Reuter, B., & Robinson, K. (2000). Commercial sex between men: A prospective diary-based study. *Journal of Sex Research, 37*(2),151–160.

Minnis, A. M., Shiboski, S. C., & Padian, N. S. (2003). Barrier contraceptive method acceptability and choice are not reliable indicators of use. *Sexually Transmitted Diseases, 30*(7), 556–561.

Mitchell, D., Angelone, D. J., Hirschman, R., Lilly, R. S., & Hall, G. C. N. (2002). Peer modeling and college men's sexually impositional behavior in the laboratory. *Journal of Sex Research, 39*(4), 326–333.

Modugno, F., et al. (2004). Oral contraceptive use, reproductive history, and risk of epithelial ovarian cancer in women with and without endometriosis. *American Journal of Obstetrics and Gynecology, 191*(3), 733–740.

Mohr, J. J. (2002). Heterosexual identity and the heterosexual therapist: Using identity as a framework for understanding sexual orientation issues in psychotherapy. *The Counseling Psychologist, 30,* 532–566.

Mohr, J. J., & Sedlacek, W. E. (2001). Perceived barriers to friendship with lesbians and gay men among university students. *Journal of College Student Development, 41*(1), 70–80.

Money, J. (2002). Amative criterion of homosexuality: Historical review of hormonal and cytogenetic syndromes. *Journal of Psychology and Human Sexuality, 14*(1), 23–36.

Money, J. (2003). History, causality, and sexology. *Journal of Sex Research, 40*(3), 237–239.

Monro, S., & Warren, L. (2004). Transgendering citizenship. *Sexualities, 7*(3), 345–362.

Montaldi, D. F. (2002). Understanding hypersexuality with an axis II model. *Journal of Psychology and Human Sexuality, 14*(4), 1–23.

Monto, M. A. (2001). Prostitution and fellatio. *Journal of Sex Research, 38*(2), 140–145.

Moore, K., & Smith, K. (2003). Policies needed to increase awareness of emergency contraception. *SIECUS Report, 31*(2), 9–12.

Moore, N. B., & Davidson, J. K. (2000). Communicating with new sex partners: College women and questions that make a difference. *Journal of Sex and Marital Therapy, 26,* 215–230.

Moore, T. M., Strauss, J. L., Herman, S., Donatucci, C. F. (2003). Erectile dysfunction in early, middle, and late adulthood: Symptom patterns and psychological correlates. *Journal of Sex and Marital Therapy, 29,* 381–399.

Moreau, C., Bajos, N., & Trussell, J. (2006). The impact of pharmacy access to emergency contraceptive pills in France. *Contraception, 73*(6), 602–608.

Morgan, C. A., & Grillon, C. (1999). Abnormal mismatch negativity in women with sexual assault–related posttraumatic stress disorder. *Biological Psychiatry, 45*(7), 827–832.

Morgan, T., & Cummings, A. L. (1999). Change experienced during group therapy by female survivors of childhood sexual abuse. *Journal of Consulting and Clinical Psychology, 67*(1), 28–36.

Morrison, C. S., et al. (2004). Hormonal contraceptive use, cervical ectopy, and the acquisition of cervical infections. *Sexually Transmitted Diseases, 31*(9), 561–567.

Morrison, T. G., & Whitehead, B. W. (2005). Strategies of stigma resistance among Canadian gay-identified sex workers. *Journal of Psychology and Human Sexuality, 17*(1/2), 169–179.

Morse, J. M., Swanson, J. M., & Kuzel, A. J. (Eds.). (2001). *The nature of qualitative evidence.* Thousand Oaks, CA: Sage.

Moser, C., & Kleinplatz, P. J. (2005). *DSM-IV-TR* and the paraphilias: An argument for removal. *Journal of Psychology and Human Sexuality, 17*(3/4), 91–109.

Mosher, D. L. (1986). Misinformation on pornography: A lobby disguised as an educational organization. *SIECUS Report, 14*(5), 7–10.

Muehlenhard, C. L. (2000). Categories and sexuality. *Journal of Sex Research, 37*(2), 101–107.

Muehlenhard, C. L., Peterson, Z. D., Karwoski, L., Bryan, T. S., & Lee, R. S. (2003). Gender and sexuality: An introduction. *Journal of Sex Research, 40*(1), 1–3.

Mulrine, A. (2003, September 29). Love.com. *U.S. News and World Report,* 52–58.

Munarriz, R., Talakoub, L., Kuohung, W., Gioia, M., et al. (2002). The prevalence of phimosis of the clitoris in women presenting to the sexual dysfunction clinic: Lack of correlation to disorders of desire, arousal and orgasm. *Journal of Sex and Marital Therapy, 28*(s), 181–185.

Murphy, D. A., et al. (2005). Longitudinal antiretroviral adherence among adolescents infected with human immunodeficiency virus. *Archives of Pediatrics and Adolescent Medicine, 159*(8), 764–770.

Muscarella, F. (2006). The evolution of male-male sexual behavior in

humans: The alliance theory. *Journal of Psychology and Human Sexuality, 18*(4), 275–311.

Mustanski, B. S. (2001). Getting wired: Exploiting the Internet for the collection of valid sexuality data. *Journal of Sex Research, 38*(4), 292–301.

Mustanski, B. S., Chivers, M. L., & Bailey, J. M. (2003). A critical review of recent biological research on human sexual orientation. *Annual Review of Sex Research, 13,* 89–140.

Mutchler, M. G., Ayala, G., Hebert, P., & Fernandez, R. (2004). Gay-boy talk: Discourse for stopping HIV infections among gay young men. *SIECUS Report, 32*(1), 31–34.

Myers, I. B., & McCaulley, M. H. (1985). *A guide to the development and use of the Myers-Briggs Type Indicator.* Palo Alto, CA: Consulting Psychologists Press.

Myers, J. E., Madathil, J., & Tingle, L. R. (2005). Marriage satisfaction and wellness in India and the United States: A preliminary comparison of arranged marriages and marriages of choice. *Journal of Counseling and Development, 83,* 183–190.

Najman, J. M., Dunne, M. P., & Boyle, F. M. (2007). Childhood sexual abuse and adult sexual dysfunction: Response to commentary by Rind and Tromovitch (2007). *Archives of Sexual Behavior, 36,* 107–109.

Najman, J. M., Dunne, M. P., Purdie, D. M., Boyle, F. M., & Coxeter, P. D. (2005). Sexual abuse in childhood and sexual dysfunction in adulthood: An Australian population-based study. *Archives of Sexual Behavior, 34*(5), 517–526.

Nangle, D. W., & Grover, R. L. (2001). Social behavior and condom use among males: A multidimensional assessment. *Journal of Sex Education and Therapy, 26*(2), 90–99.

Nannini, D. K., & Meyers, L. S. (2000). Jealousy in sexual and emotional infidelity: An alternative to the evolutionary explanation. *Journal of Sex Research, 37*(2), 117–122.

Nappi, R. E., Abbiati, I., Luisi, S., Ferdeghini, F., Polatti, F., & Genazzani, A. R. (2003). *Journal of Sex and Marital Therapy, 29,* 95–102.

Narod, S. A., et al. (2002). Oral contraceptives and the risk of breast cancer in BRCA1 and BRCA2 mutation carriers. *Journal of the National Cancer Institute, 94*(23), 1773–1779.

Natali, A., Mondaini, N., Lombardi, G., Del Popolo, G., & Rizzo, M.

(2005). Heavy smoking is an important risk factor for erectile dysfunction in young men. *International Journal of Impotence Research, 17,* 227–230.

National Center for Health Statistics. (2006). Advance Data from Vital and Health Statistics. *Sexual behavior and selected health measures: Men and women 15–44 years of age, United States, 2002.* Washington DC: National Center for Health Statistics.

National Council on Aging. (1998, September 29). Reporting on results of survey of senior citizens. Knight-Ridder Newspapers.

Neal, D. (2004, March 6). Help to become a retrosexual. *Watertown* (NY) *Daily Times,* B1,6.

Negy, C., & Eisenman, R. (2005). A comparison of African American and white college students' affective and attitudinal reactions to lesbian, gay, and bisexual individuals: An exploratory study. *Journal of Sex Research, 42*(4), 291–298.

Nelson, C. A., & Gottesman, I. I. (2005, February 25). A piece of a neuroscientist's mind. *Science,* 1204.

Ness, R. B., Hillier, S. L., & Richter, H. E. (2002). Douching in relation to bacterial vaginosis, lactobacilli, and facultative bacteria in the vagina. *Obstetrics and Gynecology, 100,* 765–772.

Neuman, M. G. (2002). *Emotional infidelity.* New York: Random House.

Niccolai, L. M., et al. (2004). New sex partner acquisition and sexually transmitted disease risk among adolescent females. *Journal of Adolescent Health, 34*(3), 216–223.

Niccolai, L. M., et al. (2005). Condom effectiveness for prevention of *Chlamydia trachomatis* infection. *Sexually Transmitted Infections, 81*(4), 323–325.

Nicholas, C. L. (2004). Gaydar: Eyegaze as identity recognition among gay men and lesbians. *Sexuality and Culture, 8*(1), 60–86.

Nobre, P. J., & Pinto-Gouveia, J. (2003). Sexual modes questionnaire: Measure to assess the interaction among cognitions, emotions, and sexual response. *Journal of Sex Research, 40*(4), 368–382.

Nobre, P. J., et al. (2004). Determinants of sexual arousal and the accuracy of its self-estimation in sexually functional males. *Journal of Sex Research, 41*(4), 363–371.

Nobre, P. J., & Pinto-Gouveia, J. (2006). Emotions during sexual activity:

Differences between sexually functional and dysfunctional men and women. *Archives of Sexual Behavior, 35,* 491–499.

Nobre, P. J., Pinto-Gouveia, J., & Gomes, F. A. (2006). Prevalence and comorbidity of sexual dysfunctions in a Portuguese clinical sample. *Journal of Sex and Marital Therapy, 32,* 173–182.

Noonan, D., & Springen, K. (2002, April 22). The prostate plan. *Newsweek,* 69–70.

Nordland, R., & Bartholet, J. (2001, March 19). The web's dark secret. *Newsweek,* 42–51.

Norman, C. (2004). A time for action. *Science, 304,* 1931.

O'Donnell, L., et al. (2005). Saving sex for later: An evaluation of a parent education intervention. *Perspectives on Sexual and Reproductive Health, 37*(4), 166–173.

Office of the Surgeon General. (2001). *Surgeon General's call to action to promote sexual health and responsible sexual behavior.* Washington DC: U.S. Government Printing Office.

Office on Violence Against Women. (2004). *A national protocol for sexual assault medical forensic examinations: Adults/adolescents.* Washington, DC: Department of Justice.

O'Hare, E. A., & O'Donohue, W. (1998). Sexual harassment: Identifying risk factors. *Archives of Sexual Behavior, 27*(6), 561–580.

Okami, P. (2004). True, new, and important. *Journal of Sex Research 41*(1), 2–4.

Okami, P., Olmstead, R., & Abramson, P. R. (1997). Sexual experiences in early childhood: 18-year longitudinal data from the UCLA family lifestyles project. *Journal of Sex Research, 34*(4), 339–347.

Okami, P., Olmstead, R., Abramson, P. R., & Pendleton, L. (1998). Early childhood exposure to parental nudity and scenes of parental sexuality ("primal scenes"): An 18-year longitudinal study of outcome. *Archives of Sexual Behavior, 27*(4), 361–384.

Okami, P., & Shackelford, T. K. (2002). Human sex differences in sexual psychology and behavior. *Annual Review of Sex Research, 12,* 186–241.

Oliver, B. E. (2005). Thoughts on combating pedophilia in non-offending adolescents. *Archives of Sexual Behavior, 34*(1), 3–5.

Olsen, F. (2001, February 16). 3% of female students are victims of rape or attempted rape. *Chronicle of Higher Education,* A49.

Olsen, G. W. (2004). The sodomitic lions of Granada. *Journal of the History of Sexuality, 13*(1), 1–25.

Olsson, S., & Moller, A. (2006). Regret after sex reassignment surgery in a male-to-female transsexual: A long-term follow-up. *Archives of Sexual Behavior, 35*(4), 501–506.

Oman, R. F., Vesely, S. K., & Aspy, C. B. (2005). Youth assets and sexual risk behavior: The importance of assets for youth residing in one-parent households. *Perspectives on Sexual and Reproductive Health, 37*(1), 25–31.

Ompad, D. C., et al. (2006). Predictors of early initiation of vaginal and oral sex among urban young adults in Baltimore, Maryland. *Archives of Sexual Behavior, 35*(1), 53–65.

Oncale, R. N., & King, B. M. (2001). Comparison of men's and women's attempts to dissuade sexual partners from the couple using condoms. *Archives of Sexual Behavior, 30*(4), 379–391.

Oosterhuis, H. (2001). *Stepchildren of nature: Krafft-Ebing, psychiatry, and the making of sexual identity.* Chicago: University of Chicago Press.

Ortiz, D. (2006). Review of *Otto Weininger: Sex, science, and self in imperial Vienna* by Chandak Sengoopta. *Archives of Sexual Behavior, 35*(3), 379–381.

Osborne, C., & Wise, T. N. (2002). Split gender identity: Problem or solution? Proposed parameters for addressing the gender dysphoric patient. *Journal of Sex and Marital Therapy, 28,* 165–173.

Ostovich, J. M., & Sabini, J. (2005). Timing of puberty and sexuality in men and women. *Archives of Sexual Behavior, 34*(2), 197–206.

O'Sullivan, L. F., & Allegeier, E. R. (1998). Feigning sexual desire: Consenting to unwanted sexual activity in heterosexual dating relationships. *Journal of Sex Research, 35*(3), 234–243.

Oswald, D. L., & Russell, B. L. (2006). Perceptions of sexual coercion in heterosexual dating relationships: The role of aggressor gender and tactics. *Journal of Sex Research, 43*(1), 87–95.

Oswalt, S. B., Cameron, K. A., & Koob, J. J. (2005). Sexual regret in college students. *Archives of Sexual Behavior, 34*(6), 663–669.

Ott, M. A., Millstein, S. G., Ofner, S., & Halpern-Felsher, B. L. (2006). Greater expectations: Adolescents' positive motivations for sex. *Perspectives on Sexual and Reproductive Health, 38*(2), 84–89.

Padma-Nathan, H., Brown, C., Fendl, J., Salem, S., Yeager, J., & Harning, R. (2003). Efficacy and safety of topical alprostadil cream for the treatment of female sexual arousal disorder (FSAD): A double-blind, multicenter, randomized, and placebo-controlled clinical trial. *Journal of Sex and Marital Therapy, 29,* 329–344.

Palmer, J. R., et al. (2003). Onset of natural menopause in African American women. *American Journal of Public Health, 93*(2), 299–306.

Pang, J. W., et al. (2002). Outcomes of planned home births in Washington state. *Obstetrics and Gynecology, 100*(2), 253–259.

Pardun, C. J., & Forde, K. R. (2003). Sex in the media: Do condom ads have a chance? *SIECUS Report, 31*(2), 22–23.

Parish, W. L., Das, A., & Laumann, E. O. (2006). Sexual harassment of women in urban China. *Archives of Sexual Behavior, 35,* 411–425.

Parish, W. L., Luo, Y., Stolzenberg, R., Laumann, E. O., Farrer, G., & Pan, S. (2007). Sexual practices and sexual satisfaction: A population based study of Chinese urban adults. *Archives of Sexual Behavior, 36,* 5–20.

Park, J. Y., Su, Y. Q., Ariga, M., Law, E., Jin, S. C., & Conti, M. (2004). EGF-like growth factors as mediators of LH action in the ovulatory follicle. *Science, 303,* 682–684.

Parker, B. A. (2004). Queer theory goes to college. *Journal of Sex Research, 41*(2), 221–223.

Parker, R., et al. (2005). Global transformations and intimate relations in the 21st century: Social science research on sexuality and the emergence of sexual health and sexual rights frameworks. *Annual Review of Sex Research, 15,* 362–398.

Parsons, J. T. (2005). Researching the world's oldest profession: Introduction. *Journal of Psychology and Human Sexuality, 17*(1/2), 1–3.

Pascoe, C. J. (2003). Multiple masculinities: Teenage boys talk about jocks and gender. *American Behavioral Scientist, 46*(10), 1423–1438.

Passie, T., et al. (2004). Acute hyperventilation syndromes induced by sexual intercourse: Evidence of a psychophysical mechanism to intensify sexual experience? *Archives of Sexual Behavior, 33*(6), 525–526.

Paul, M. E., et al. (2002). Early surgical abortion: Efficacy and safety. *American Journal of Obstetrics and Gynecology, 187*(2), 407–411.

Payne, K. A., et al. (2005). What is sexual pain? A critique of DSM's classification of dyspareunia and vaginismus. *Journal of Psychology and Human Sexuality, 17*(3/4), 141–154.

Pearson, Q. M. (2003). Breaking the silence in the counselor education classroom: A training seminar on counseling sexual minority clients. *Journal of Counseling and Development, 81,* 292–300.

Pedersen, W., Samuelsen, S. O., & Wichstrom, L. (2003). Intercourse debut age: Poor resources, problem behavior, or romantic appeal? A population-based longitudinal study. *Journal of Sex Research, 40*(4), 333–345.

Penfold, P. S. (1999). Why did you keep going for so long? Issues for survivors of long-term, sexually abusive "helping" relationships. *Journal of Sex Education and Therapy, 24,* 244–251.

Peplau, L. A., Spalding, L. R., Conley, T. D., & Veniegas, R. C. (2000). The development of sexual orientation in women. *Annual Review of Sex Research, 10,* 70–99.

Perez, R. M., DeBord, K. A., & Bieschke, K. J. (2000). *Handbook of counseling and psychotherapy with lesbian, gay and bisexual clients.* Washington, DC: American Psychological Association.

Perper, T., & Cornog, M. (2002). Eroticism for the masses: Japanese manga comics and their assimilation into the U.S. *Sexuality and Culture, 6*(1), 1–126.

Perry, B. L., & Wright, E. R. (2006). The sexual partnerships of people with serious mental illness. *Journal of Sex Research, 43*(2), 174–181.

Pertot, S. (2006). Sex therapy and the cultural construction of sexuality. *Contemporary Sexuality, 40*(4), 9–13.

Peterman, L. M., & Dixon, C. G. (2003). Domestic violence between same-sex partners: Implications for counseling. *Journal of Counseling and Development, 81,* 40–47.

Peters, V., et al. (2003). Missed opportunities for perinatal HIV prevention among HIV-exposed infants born 1996–2000, pediatric spectrum of HIV disease cohort. *Pediatrics, 111*(5), 1186–1191.

Pfaus, J. G. (2000). Revisiting the concept of sexual motivation. *Annual Review of Sex Research, 9,* 120–156.

Phelps, J., Albo, M., Dunn, K., & Joseph, A. (2001). Spinal cord injury and sexuality in married or partnered men: Activities, function, needs, and predictors of sexual adjustment. *Archives of Sexual Behavior, 30*(6), 591–602.

Philaretou, A. G. (2005). The sociocultural dimensions of sexual interactions. *Sexuality & Culture, 9*(3), 88–90.

Philipps, D. (2006, November 26). Studies take a look at science behind "gaydar". *Associated Press/Watertown Daily Times Sunday Weekly,* 9.

Philliber, S., Kaye, J. W., Herring, S., & West, E. (2002). Preventing pregnancy and improving health care access among teenagers: An evaluation of the children's aid society—Carrera program. *Perspectives on Sexual and Reproductive Health, 34*(5), 244–251.

Piaget, J. (1932). *The moral judgment of the child.* New York: Harcourt Brace.

Picardo, C. M., et al. (2003). Women's knowledge and sources of information on the risks and benefits of oral contraception. *Journal of the American Medical Women's Association, 58*(2), 112–116.

Pierce, A. P. (2000). The coital alignment technique (CAT): An overview of studies. *Journal of Sex and Marital Therapy, 26,* 257–268.

Pierre, R. E. (2004, January 11). Abstinence lessons going unheeded, five-year study finds. *Washington Post,* A2.

Pillsworth, E. G., Haselton, M. G., & Buss, D. M. (2004). Ovulatory shifts in female sexual desire. *Journal of Sex Research, 41*(1), 55–65.

Pinkerton, S. D., Bogart, L. M., Cecil, H., & Abramson, P. R. (2002). Factors associated with masturbation in a collegiate sample. *Journal of Psychology and Human Sexuality, 14*(2/3), 103–121.

Piot, P., Feachman, R. G., Jong-Wook, L., & Wolfensohn, J. D. (2004). A global response to AIDS: Lessons learned, next steps. *Science, 304,* 1909.

Pistole, C., & Arricale, F. (2003). Understanding attachment: Beliefs about conflict. *Journal of Counseling and Development, 81,* 318–328.

Pithers, W. D. (1999). Empathy: Definition, enhancement, and relevance to the treatment of sexual abusers. *Journal of Interpersonal Violence, 14*(3), 257–284.

Pitts, M., & Rahman, Q. (2001). Which behaviors constitute "having sex" among university students in the UK? *Archives of Sexual Behavior, 30*(2), 169–176.

Pitts, M. K., Smith, A. M. A., Grierson, J., O'Brien, M., & Misson, S. (2004). Who pays for sex and why? An analysis of social and motivational factors associated with male clients of sex workers. *Archives of Sexual Behavior, 33*(4), 353–358.

Plante, R. F. (2006). *Sexualities in context: A social perspective.* Boulder, CO: Westview Press.

Plaud, J. J., Gaither, G. A., Hegstad, H. J., Rowan, L., & Devitt, M. K. (1999). Volunteer bias in human psychophysiological sexual arousal research: To whom do our research results apply? *Journal of Sex Research, 36*(2), 171–179.

Plaud, J. J., Gaither, G. A., & Weller, L. A. (1998). Gender differences in the sexual rating of words. *Journal of Sex and Marital Therapy, 24,* 13–19.

Plugge-Foust, C., & Strickland, G. (2000). Homophobia, irrationality, and Christian ideology: Does a relationship exist? *Journal of Sex Education and Therapy, 25,* 240–244.

Ponholzer, A., Temml, C., Rauchenwald, M., & Madersbacher, S. (2006). Vascular risk factors and erectile dysfunction in a cohort of healthy men. *International Journal of Impotence Research, 18,* 489–493.

Poole, A. J., et al. (2006, December 1). Prevention of BRCA1-mediated mammary tumorigenesis in mice by a progesterone antagonist. *Science, 314,* 1467–1470.

Poole, H., Giles, D. C., & Moore, K. (2004). Researching sexuality and sexual issues: Implications for the researcher? *Sexual and Relationship Therapy, 19*(1), 79–86.

Pratt, M. W. (2003). Predicting adolescent moral reasoning from family climate: A longitudinal study. *Journal of Early Adolescence, 19,* 148–175.

Preves, S. E. (2003). *Intersex and identity: The contested self.* Newark, NJ: Rutgers University Press.

Prinstein, M. J., Meade, C. S., & Cohen, G. L. (2003). Adolescent oral sex, peer popularity, and perceptions of best friends' sexual behavior. *Journal of Pediatric Psychology, 28*(4), 243–249.

Pruitt, S. L., & Mullen, P. D. (2005). Contraception or abortion? Inaccurate descriptions of emergency contraception in newspaper articles. *Contraception, 71*(1), 14–21.

Pryke, S. (2001). The boy scouts and the 'girl question.' *Sexualities, 4*(2), 191–210.

Pukall, C. F. (2005). Vulvodynia: A hidden women's health issue. *SIECUS Report, 33*(3), 25–32.

Pukall, C. F., Binik, Y. M., & Khalife, S. (2004). A new instrument for pain assessment in vulvar vestibulitis syndrome. *Journal of Sex and Marital Therapy, 30,* 69–78.

Pulley, L., Klerman, L. V., Tang, H., & Baker, B. A. (2002). The extent of pregnancy mistiming and its association with maternal characteristics and behaviors and pregnancy outcomes. *Perspectives on Sexual and Reproductive Health, 34*(4), 206–211.

Purcell, D. W., Blanchard, R., & Zucker, K. J. (2000). Birth order in a contemporary sample of gay men. *Archives of Sexual Behavior, 29*(4), 349–356.

Purdon, C., & Holdaway, L. (2006). Nonerotic thoughts: Content and relation to sexual functioning and sexual satisfaction. *Journal of Sex Research, 43*(2), 154–162.

Quek, K. F., Loh, C. S., Low, W. Y., Razack, A. H., & Dublin, N. (2003). The male marital satisfaction following treatment for lower urinary tract symptoms. *Journal of Sex and Marital Therapy, 29*(2), 173–176.

Quindlen, A. (2003, January 13). Getting rid of the sex police. *Newsweek,* 72.

Race, K. (2001). The undetectable crisis: Changing technologies of risk. *Sexualities, 4*(2), 167–189.

Raghavan, R., Bogart, L. M., Elliott, M. N., Vestal, K. D., & Schuster, M. A. (2004). Sexual victimization among a national probability sample of adolescent women. *Perspectives on Sexual and Reproductive Health, 36*(6), 225–232.

Rahman, Q., & Hull, M. S. (2005). An empirical test of the kin selection hypothesis for male homosexuality. *Archives of Sexual Behavior, 34*(4), 461–467.

Rahman, Q., & Silber, K. (2000). Sexual orientation and the sleep-wake cycle: A preliminary investigation. *Archives of Sexual Behavior, 29*(2), 127–134.

Raina, R., et al. (2005). Early use of vacuum constriction device following radical prostatectomy facilitates early sexual activity and potentially earlier return of erectile dysfunction.

International Journal of Impotence Research, 18, 77–81.

Raine, T., Marcell, A. V., Rocca, C. H., & Harper, C. C. (2003). The other half of the equation: Serving young men in a young women's reproductive health clinic. *Perspectives on Sexual and Reproductive Health, 35*(5), 208–214.

Raine, T. R., et al. (2005). Direct access to emergency contraception through pharmacies and effect on unintended pregnancy and STIs: A randomized controlled trial. *Journal of the American Medical Association, 293*(1), 54–62.

Raj, A., Silverman, J. G., & Amaro, H. (2000). The relationship between sexual abuse and sexual risk among high school students. *Maternal and Child Health Journal, 4*(2), 125–134.

Rako, S., & Friebely, J. (2004). Pheromonal influences on sociosexual behavior in postmenopausal women. *Journal of Sex Research, 41*(4), 372–380.

Rana, R. K., et al. (2006). Sexual behavior and condom use among individuals with a history of symptomatic genital herpes. *Sexually Transmitted Infections, 82*(1), 69–74.

Randolph, M. E., & Mosack, K. E. (2006). Factors mediating the effects of childhood sexual abuse on risky sexual behavior among college women. *Journal of Psychology and Human Sexuality, 18*(1), 23–41.

Randolph, M. E., & Reddy, D. M. (2006). Sexual functioning in women with chronic pelvic pain: The impact of depression, support, and abuse. *Journal of Sex Research, 43*(1), 38–45.

Ranjit, N., Bankole, A., Darroch, J. E., & Singh, S. (2001). Contraceptive failure in the first two years of use: Differences across socioeconomic subgroups. *Family Planning Perspectives, 33*(1), 19–27.

Rasmussen, L. A. (1999). Factors related to recidivism among juvenile sexual offenders. *Sexual Abuse: Journal of Research and Treatment, 11*(1), 69–86.

Rathbone, J. (2001). *Anatomy of masochism.* Hingham, MA: Kluwer Academic Publishers.

Reavey, P., & Gough, B. (2000). Dis/locating blame: Survivors' constructions of self and sexual abuse. *Sexualities, 3*(3), 325–346.

Reback, C. J., Lombardi, E. L., Simon, P. A., & Frye, D. M. (2005). HIV seroprevalence and risk behaviors among

transgendered women who exchange sex in comparison with those who do not. *Journal of Psychology and Human Sexuality, 17*(1/2), 5–22.

Reddy, D. M., Fleming, R., & Swain, C. (2002). Effect of mandatory parental notification on adolescent girls' use of sexual health care services. *Journal of the American Medical Association, 288*(6), 710–714.

Redman, C. W., & Sargent, I. L. (2005). Latest advances in understanding preeclampsia. *Science, 308,* 1592–1594.

Reece, M., & Dodge, B. (2004). A study in sexual health applying the principles of community-based participatory research. *Archives of Sexual Behavior, 33*(3), 235–247.

Refaat, A., Dandash, K. F., El-Defrawi, M. H., & Eyada, M. (2001). Female genital mutilation and domestic violence among Egyptian women. *Journal of Sex and Marital Therapy, 27,* 593–598.

Rehman, J., Lazer, S., Benet, A. E., Schaefer, L. C., & Melman, A. (1999). The reported sex surgery satisfactions of 28 postoperative male-to-female transsexual patients. *Archives of Sexual Behavior, 281*(1), 71–89.

Reichert, T. (2003). Sex in advertising research: A review of content, effects, and functions of sexual information in consumer advertising. *Annual Review of Sex Research, 13,* 241–273.

Reichert, T., & Lambiase, J. (2003). How to get "kissably close": Examining how advertisers appeal to consumers' sexual needs and desires. *Sexuality and Culture, 3,* 120–136.

Reilly, J., Baker, G. A., Rhodes, J., & Salmon, P. (1999). The association of sexual and physical abuse with somatization: Characteristics of patients presenting with irritable bowel syndrome and non-epileptic attack disorder. *Psychological Medicine, 29*(2), 399–406.

Reinisch, J. M., & Sanders, S. A. (1992). Prenatal hormonal contributions to sex differences in human cognitive and personality development. In A. A. Gerall, H. Moltz, & I. L. Ward (Eds.), *Handbook of behavioral neurobiology: Vol. 11. Sexual differentiation* (pp. 221–243). New York: Plenum Press.

Reiss, I. L. (2002). *At the dawn of the sexual revolution.* Walnut Creek, CA: Altamira Press.

Reiss, M. (2000). In clinical trial, women using once-a-month injectable contraceptive avoid pregnancy and approve of method. *Family Planning Perspectives, 32* (2), 95–96.

Reissing, E. D., Binik, Y. M., Khalife, S., Cohen, D., & Amsel, R. (2004). Vaginal spasm, pain, and behavior: An empirical investigation of the diagnosis of vaginismus. *Archives of Sexual Behavior, 33*(1), 5–17.

Rellini, A. H., & Meston, C. M. (2007). Sexual desire and linguistic analysis: A comparison of sexually-abused and non-abused women. *Archives of Sexual Behavior, 36,* 67–77.

Remez, L. (2000). Oral sex among adolescents: Is it sex or is it abstinence? *Family Planning Perspectives, 32*(6), 298–304.

Rempel, J. K., & Baumgartner, B. (2003). The relationship between attitudes towards menstruation and sexual attitudes, desires, and behavior in women. *Archives of Sexual Behavior, 32*(2), 155–163.

Resnick, S. (2002). Sexual pleasure: The next frontier in the study of sexuality. *SIECUS Report, 30* (4), 6–11.

Rest, J. R., Narvaez, D., Thoma, S. J., & Bebeau, M. J. (2000). A neo-Kohlbergian approach to morality research. *Journal of Moral Education, 29*(4), 381–395.

Ribner, D. S. (2004). Ejaculatory restrictions as a factor in the treatment of Haredi (ultraorthodox) Jewish couples. *Archives of Sexual Behavior, 33*(3), 303–308.

Ribner, D. S., & Rosenbaum, T. Y. (2005). Evaluation and treatment of unconsummated marriages among Orthodox Jewish couples. *Journal of Sex and Marital Therapy, 31,* 341–353.

Richard, D. (2002). Tantra 101. *Contemporary Sexuality, 36*(11), 1, 4–7.

Richard, D. (2003). Rape in the ranks. *Contemporary Sexuality, 37*(7), 1, 4–6.

Richardson, D. (2000). Claiming citizenship? Sexuality, citizenship and lesbian/feminist theory. *Sexualities, 3* (2), 255–272.

Rickert, V. I., Sanghvi, R., & Wiemann, C. M. (2002). Is lack of sexual assertiveness among adolescent and young adult women a cause for concern? *Perspectives on Sexual and Reproductive Health, 34*(4), 178–183.

Rickert, V. I., et al. (2004). Rates and risk factors for sexual violence among an ethnically diverse sample of adolescents. *Archives of Pediatrics and Adolescent Medicine, 158*(12), 1132–1139.

Ricketts, S. A., Murray, E. K., & Schwalberg, R. (2005). Reducing low birthweight by resolving risks: Results from Colorado's prenatal plus program. *American Journal of Public Health, 95*(11), 1952–1957.

Ridley, C. A., et al. (2006). The ebb and flow of marital lust: A relational approach. *Journal of Sex Research, 43*(2), 144–153.

Ridley, M. (2003). *Genes, experience, and what makes us human.* New York: HarperCollins.

Riegel, D. L. (2004). Effects on boy-attracted pedosexual males of viewing boy erotica. *Archives of Sexual Behavior, 33*(4), 321–323.

Riegel, D. L. (2005). Pedophilia, pejoration, and prejudice: Inquiry by insinuation, argument by accusation. *Sexuality and Culture, 9*(1), 88–97.

Rieger, G., Chivers, M. L., & Bailey, J. M. (2005). Sexual arousal patterns of bisexual men. *Psychological Science, 16*(8), 579.

Riman, T., et al. (2002). Risk factors for invasive ovarian cancer: Results from a Swedish case-control study. *American Journal of Epidemiology, 156*(4), 363–373.

Rind, B. (2003). Adolescent sexual experiences with adults: Pathological or functional? *Journal of Psychology and Human Sexuality, 15*(1), 5–22.

Rind, B., & Tromovitch, P. (2007). National samples, sexual abuse in childhood, and adjustment in adulthood: A commentary on Najman, Dunne, Purdie, Boyle, and Coxeter. *Archives of Sexual Behavior, 36,* 101–106.

Rizzo, A., & Swisher, L. L. (2004). Comparing the Stewart-Sprinthall management survey and the Defining Issues Test-2 as measures of moral reasoning in public administration. *Journal of Public Administration Research and Theory, 14*(3), 335–348.

Robbins, A., & Wilner, A. (2004). *Conquering your quarterlife crisis: Advice from twentysomethings who have been there and survived.* New York: Perigee Books.

Robertson, A. A., et al. (2005). Predictors of infection with chlamydia or gonorrhea in incarcerated adolescents. *Sexually Transmitted Diseases, 32*(2), 115–122.

Robinson, J. D., & Parks, C. W. (2003). Lesbian and bisexual women's sexual fantasies, psychological adjustment, and close relationship functioning. *Journal of Psychology & Human Sexuality, 15*(4), 185–203.

Robinson, J. E., Birch, R. A., Foster, D. L., & Padmanabhan, V. (2002). Prenatal exposure of the ovine fetus to androgens sexually differentiates the steroid feedback mechanisms that control gonadotropin releasing hormone secretion and disrupts ovarian cycles. *Archives of Sexual Behavior, 31* (1), 35–41.

Rock, E. M., et al. (2005). A rose by any other name? Objective knowledge, perceived knowledge, and adolescent male condom use. *Pediatrics, 115*(3), 667–672.

Rofes, E. (2000). Bound and gagged: Sexual silences, gender conformity and the gay male teacher. *Sexualities, 3*(4), 439–462.

Rogers, L. (2001). *Sexing the brain.* New York: Columbia University Press.

Rollins, J. (2005, July). Breaking the silence, breaking the cycle. *Counseling Today,* 10–11.

Rosario, M., Schrimshaw, E. W., Hunter, J., & Braun, L. (2006). Sexual identity development among lesbian, gay, and bisexual youths: Consistency and change over time. *Journal of Sex Research, 43*(1), 46–58.

Roselli, C. E., Resko, J. A., & Stormshak, F. (2002). Hormonal influences on sexual partner preference in rams. *Archives of Sexual Behavior, 31*(1), 43–49.

Rosen, R. C. (2002). Sexual function assessment and the role of vasoactive drugs in female sexual dysfunction. *Archives of Sexual Behavior, 31*(5), 439–443.

Rosen, R. C., & Laumann, E. O. (2003). The prevalence of sexual problems in women: How valid are comparisons across studies? *Archives of Sexual Behavior, 32*(3), 209–211.

Rosen, R. C., & McKenna, K. E. (2003). PDE-5 inhibition and sexual response: Pharmacological mechanisms and clinical outcomes. *Annual Review of Sex Research, 13,* 36–88.

Rosen, R., et al. (2006). Psychological and interpersonal correlates in men with erectile dysfunction and their partners: A pilot study of treatment outcome with sildenafil. *Journal of Sex and Marital Therapy, 32,* 215–234.

Rosenberg, D. (2000, October 23). State of the union. *Newsweek,* 56–57.

Rosenberg, D. (2006, June 12). Politics of the altar. *Newsweek,* 34–35.

Rosenberg, K. P., Bleiberg, K. L., Koscis, J., & Gross, C. (2003). A survey of sexual side effects among severely mentally ill patients taking psychotropic medications: Impact on compliance. *Journal of Sex and Marital Therapy, 29*(4), 289–296.

Rosenberg, L. E., & Schechter, A. N. (2000). Gene therapist, heal thyself. *Science, 287,* 1751.

Rosengard, C., et al. (2004). Perceived STD risk, relationship, and health values in adolescents' delaying sexual intercourse with new partners. *Sexually Transmitted Infections, 80*(2), 130–137.

Ross, J., Godeau, E., Dias, S., Vignes, C., & Gross, L. (2004, Fall). Setting politics aside to collect cross-national data of sexual health of adolescents. *SIECUS Report, 32*(4), 28–34.

Ross, M. T., et al. (2005). The DNA sequence of the human X chromosome. *Nature, 434,* 325–337.

Ross, M. W. (2005). Typing, doing, and being: Sexuality and the Internet. *Journal of Sex Research, 42*(4), 342–352.

Ross, M. W., Daneback, K., Mansson, S., Tikkanen, R., & Cooper, A. (2003). Characteristics of men and women who complete or exit from an on-line Internet sexuality questionnaire: A study of instrument dropout biases. *Journal of Sex Research, 40*(4), 396–402.

Rowland, D. L., & Burnett, A. L. (2000). Pharmacotherapy in the treatment of male sexual dysfunction. *Journal of Sex Research, 37*(3), 226–243.

Rowland, D. L., Cooper, S. E., & Schneider, M. (2001). Defining premature ejaculation for experimental and clinical investigations. *Archives of Sexual Behavior, 30*(3), 235–253.

Rowland, D. L., Incrocci, L., & Slob, A. K. (2005). Aging and sexual response in the laboratory in patients with erectile dysfunction. *Journal of Sex and Marital Therapy, 31,* 399–407.

Rowland, D. L., & Tai, W. (2003). A review of plant-derived and herbal approaches to the treatment of sexual dysfunctions. *Journal of Sex and Marital Therapy, 29*(3), 185–205.

Rowland, D. L., Tai, W. L., & Slob, K. (2003). An exploration of emotional response to erotic stimulation in men with premature ejaculation: Effects of treatment with clomipramine. *Archives of Sexual Behavior, 32*(2), 145–153.

Rupp, L. J., & Taylor, V. (2003). *Drag queens at the 801 cabaret.* Chicago: University of Chicago Press.

Russell, S. T. (2001, April/May). LGBTQ youth are at risk in U.S. school envi-

ronment. *SIECUS Report, 29*(4), 19–21.

Russell, S. T., Lee, F. C. H., & the Latina/o Teen Pregnancy Prevention Workgroup. (2004). Practitioners' perspectives on effective practices for Hispanic teenage pregnancy prevention. *Perspectives on Sexual and Reproductive Health, 36*(4), 142–149.

Rust, P. C. R. (2003). Bisexuality: The state of the union. *Annual Review of Sex Research, 13,* 180–240.

Ryan, C., & Futterman, D. (2001). Social and developmental challenges for lesbian, gay, and bisexual youth. *SIECUS Report, 29*(4),5–18.

Sable, M. R., Schwartz, L. R., Kelly, P. J., Lisbon, E., & Hall, M. A. (2006). Using the theory of reasoned action to explain physician intention to prescribe emergency contraception. *Perspectives on Sexual and Reproductive Health, 38*(1), 20–27.

Sakalh-Ugurlu, N., & Glick, P. (2003). Ambivalent sexism and attitudes toward women who engage in premarital sex in Turkey. *Journal of Sex Research 40*(3), 296–302.

Saleh, F. (2005). A hypersexual paraphilic patient treated with leuprolide acetate: A single case report. *Journal of Sex and Marital Therapy, 31,* 433–444.

Salihu, H. M., et al. (2003). Childbearing beyond maternal age 50 and fetal outcomes in the United States. *Obstetrics and Gynecology, 102*(5), 1006–1014.

Samet, J. H., et al. (2003). Discontinuation from HIV medical care: Squandering treatment opportunities. *Journal of Health Care for the Poor and Underserved, 14*(2), 244–255.

Sanchez-Flores, H. (2004). Everything I do, a man does. *SIECUS Report, 32*(3), 17–20.

Sanders, G., Sjodin, M., & Chastelaine, M. (2002). On the elusive nature of sex differences in cognition: Hormonal influences contributing to within-sex variation. *Archives of Sexual Behavior, 31*(1), 145–152.

Sanders, G., & Wright, M. (1997). Sexual orientation differences in cerebral asymmetry and in the performance of sexually dimorphic cognitive and motor tasks. *Archives of Sexual Behavior, 26*(5), 463–480.

Sanders, J. S. (1978). Male and female vocabularies for communicating with a sexual partner. *Journal of Sex Education and Therapy, 4,* 15–19.

Sanders, S. A. (1999). Midlife sexuality: The need to integrate biological, psychological, and social perspectives. *SIECUS Report, 27*(3), 3–7.

Sanders, S. A., et al. (2003). Condom use errors and problems among young women who put condoms on their male partners. *Journal of the American Women's Medical Association, 58*(2), 95–98.

Sandfort, T. G., de Graff, R., & Bijl, R. V. (2003). Same-sex sexuality and quality of life: Findings from the Netherlands mental health survey and incidence study. *Archives of Sexual Behavior, 32*(1), 15–22.

Sandfort, T. G., & Keizer, M. (2002). Sexual problems in gay men: An overview of empirical research. *Annual Review of Sex Research, 11,* 93–120.

Sandfort, T. G. M. (2005). Sexual orientation and gender: Stereotypes and beyond. *Archives of Sexual Behavior, 34*(6), 595–611.

Santelli, J. S., Lindberg, L. D., Abma, J., McNeely, C. S., & Resnick, M. (2000, July/August). Adolescent sexual behavior: Estimates and trends from four nationally representative surveys. *Family Planning Perspectives, 32*(4), 156–194.

Santelli, J. S., Morrow, M., Anderson, J. E., & Lindberg, L. D. (2006). Contraceptive use and pregnancy risk among U.S. high school students, 1991–2003. *Perspectives on Sexual and Reproductive Health, 38*(2), 106–111.

Santelli, J. S., Rochat, R., Hatfield-Timajchy, K., et al. (2003). The measurement and meaning of unintended pregnancy. *Perspectives on Sexual and Reproductive Health, 35*(2), 94–100.

Santelli, J. S., et al. (2004). Initiation of sexual intercourse among middle school adolescents: The influence of psychosocial factors. *Journal of Adolescent Health, 34*(3), 200–208.

Santilla, P., Sandnabba, K., Alison, L., & Nordling, N. (2002). Investigating the underlying structure in sadomasochistically oriented behavior. *Archives of Sexual Behavior, 31*(2), 185–196.

Sapp, M., Farrell, W. C., Johnson, J. H., & Hitchcock, K. (1999). Attitudes toward rape among African American male and female college students. *Journal of Counseling and Development, 77,* 204–208.

Saunders, J. A. (2005). Adolescent pregnancy prevention programs: Theoretical models for effective program development. *American Journal of Sexuality Education, 1*(1), 63–84.

Savin-Williams, R. C. (2001). *Mom, Dad. I'm gay: How families negotiate coming out.* Washington, DC: American Psychological Association.

Savin-Williams, R. C. (2005). *The new gay teenager.* Cambridge, MA: Harvard University Press.

Savin-Williams, R. C., & Diamond, L. M. (2000). Sexual identity trajectories among sexual-minority youths: Gender comparisons. *Archives of Sexual Behavior, 29*(6), 607–627.

Savin-Williams, R. C., & Ream., G. L. (2006). Pubertal onset and sexual orientation in an adolescent national probability sample. *Archives of Sexual Behavior, 35*(3), 279–286.

Sax, L. (2002). How common is intersex? A response to Anne Fausto-Sterling. *Journal of Sex Research, 39*(3), 174–178.

Sbraga, T. P., & O'Donohue, W. (2001). Sexual harassment. *Annual Review of Sex Research, 11,* 258–285.

Schaalma, H. P., Abraham, C., Gillmore, M. R., & Kok, G. (2004). Sex education as health promotion: What does it take? *Archives of Sexual Behavior, 33*(3), 259–269.

Schackelford, T. K., Goetz, A. T., LaMunyon, C. W., Quintus, B. J., & Weekes-Schackelford, V. A. (2004). *Archives of Sexual Behavior, 33*(4), 405–412.

Schaffir, J. (2006). Hormonal contraception and sexual desire: A critial review. *Journal of Sex and Marital Therapy, 32,* 305–314.

Schairer, C., Lubin, J., Troisi, R., Sturgeon, S., Brinton, L., & Hoover, R. (2000). Menopausal estrogen and estrogen-progestin replacement therapy and breast cancer risk. *Journal of the American Medical Association, 283*(4), 485–491.

Scheper-Hughes, N., & Devine, J. (2003). Priestly celibacy and child sexual abuse. *Sexualities, 6*(1), 15–40.

Schieve, L. A., et al. (2002). Low and very low birth weight in infants conceived with use of assisted reproductive technology. *New England Journal of Medicine, 346*(10), 731–737.

Schindhelm, R. K., & Hospers, H. J. (2004). Sex with men before coming out: Relation to sexual activity and sexual risk-taking behavior. *Archives of Sexual Behavior, 33*(6), 585–591.

Schlesinger, A. (2001). We need to conquer student silence about sexual orientation. *SIECUS Report, 29*(4), 26–28.

Schmid, T. E., et al. (2007). The effects of male age on sperm DNA damage in healthy non-smokers. *Human Reproduction, 22*(1), 180–187.

Schmidt, G. (2002). The dilemma of the male pedophile. *Archives of Sexual Behavior, 31*(6), 473–477.

Schmiege, S., & Russo, N. F. (2005). Depression and unwanted first pregnancy: Longitudinal cohort study. *British Medical Journal, 331*(7528), 1303–1307.

Schneider, A. (2002). A possible link between stigmatization of sexual-erotic identities and sexual violence. *Sexuality and Culture, 6*(4), 23–43.

Schober, J. M., et al. (2005). Leuprolide acetate suppresses pedophilic urges and arousability. *Archives of Sexual Behavior, 34*(6), 691–705.

Schooler, D., Ward, L. M., Merriwether, A., & Caruthers, A. S. (2005). Cycles of shame: Menstrual shame, body shame, and sexual decision-making. *Journal of Sex Research, 42*(4), 324–334.

Schover, L. R., et al. (2004). Seeking help for erectile dysfunction after treatment for prostate cancer. *Archives of Sexual Behavior, 33*(5), 443–454.

Schrock, D. P., & Reid, L. L. (2006). Transsexuals' sexual stories. *Archives of Sexual Behavior, 35*(1), 75–86.

Schumm, W. R., Silliman, B., & Bell, D. B. (2000). Perceived premarital counseling outcomes among recently married army personnel. *Journal of Sex and Marital Therapy, 26,* 177–186.

Segal, N. L. (2003). X and Y, a wild pair. *Science, 301,* 599–600.

Seidman, S. N. (2006). Normative hypogonadism and depression: Does 'andropause' exist? *International Journal of Impotence Research, 18,* 415–422.

Seidman, S. N., & Roose, S. P. (2006). The sexual effects of testosterone replacement in depressed men: Randomized, placebo-controlled clinical trial. *Journal of Sex and Marital Therapy, 32,* 267–273.

Sellers, N., Satcher, J., & Comas, R. (1999). Children's occupational aspirations: Comparisons by gender, gender role identity, and socioeconomic status. *Professional School Counseling, 2*(4), 314–317.

Senn, C. Y., & Desmarais, S. (2001). Are our recruitment practices for sex studies working across gender? The effect of topic and gender of recruiter on participation rates of university men and women. *Journal of Sex Research, 38*(2), 97–101.

Seto, M. C. (2005). Pedophilia and sexual offenses against children. *Annual Review of Sex Research, 15,* 321–360.

Seto, M. C., Harris, G. T., Rice, M. E., & Barbaree, H. E. (2004). The screening scale for pedophilic interests predicts recidivism among adult sex offenders with child victims. *Archives of Sexual Behavior, 33*(5), 455–466.

Sevely, J. L. (1987). *Eve's secrets: A new theory of female sexuality.* New York: Random House.

Sgroi, S. M. (2000). Discovery, reporting, investigation, and prosecution of child sexual abuse. *SIECUS Report, 29*(1), 5–10.

Shaffer, D. R., & Augustine, M. L. (2002). Affective mediation of homophobic reactions to homosexual males. *Journal of Psychology and Human Sexuality, 14*(4), 67–85.

Shafii, T., et al. (2004). Is condom use habit forming? Condom use at sexual debut and subsequent condom use. *Sexually Transmitted Diseases, 31*(6), 366–372.

Shakib, S. (2003). Female basketball participation. *American Behavioral Scientist, 46*(10), 1405–1422.

Shaw, D. (2006). Sexual and reproductive health: Rights and responsibilities. *The Lancet, Early Online Publication.* DOI: 10.1016/S0140-6736(06)69487-7.

Shaw, J. (2001). When you're asked to speak about sex, intimacy, and Alzheimer's. *Journal of Sex Education and Therapy, 26*(2), 140–145.

Shepard, B. (2003). In search of a winning script: Moral panic vs. institutional denial. *Sexualities, 6*(1), 54–59.

Sherrow, G., Ruby, T., Brauerman, P. K., Bartle, N., Gibson, S., & Hock-Long, L. (2003). Man2man: A promising approach to addressing sexual and reproductive health needs of young men. *Perspective on Sexual and Reproductive Health, 35*(5), 215–219.

Shifren, J., & Ferrari, N. A. (2004, May 10). A better sex life. *Newsweek,* 86–87.

Shiri, R., et al. (2005). Relationship between smoking and erectile dysfunction. *International Journal of Impotence Research, 17*(2), 164–169.

Shiu-Ki, T. K. (2004). Queer at your own risk: Marginality, community and Hong Kong gay male bodies. *Sexualities, 7*(1), 5–30.

Shokrollahi, P., Mirmohamadi, M., Mehrabi, F., & Babaei, G. (1999). Prevalence of sexual dysfunction in women seeking services at family planning centers in Tehran. *Journal of Sex and Marital Therapy, 25,* 211–215.

Shotorbani, S., Zimmerman, F. J., Bell, J. F., Ward, D., & Assefi, N. (2004). Attitudes and intentions of future health care providers toward abortion provision. *Perspectives on Sexual and Reproductive Health, 36*(2), 58–63.

Sidley, G. (2003). Advocating for a condom availability program. *SIECUS Report, 31*(6), 25.

SIECUS (2003). *The truth about adolescent sexuality.* New York: Sex Information and Education Council of the U.S.

SIECUS (2004). Examples from the field: Culturally competent sexuality education programs. *SIECUS Report, 32*(1), 15–23.

Siegel, K., Karus, D., & Dean, L. (2004). Psychosocial characteristics of New York City HIV-infected women before and after advent of HAART. *American Journal of Public Health, 94*(7), 1127–1132.

Siegel, K., & Schrimshaw, E. W. (2003). Reasons for the adoption of celibacy among older men and women living with HIV/AIDS. *Journal of Sex Research, 40*(2), 189–200.

Siegel, K., Schrimshaw, E. W., & Lekas, H. M. (2006). Diminished sexual activity, interest, and feelings of attractiveness among HIV-infected women in two eras of the AIDS epidemic. *Archives of Sexual Behavior, 35,* 437–449.

Sierra, J. C., Ortega, V., & Zubeidat, I. (2006). Confirmatory factor analysis of a Spanish version of the sex fantasy questionnaire: Assessing gender differences. *Journal of Sex and Marital Therapy, 32,* 137–159.

Sieving, R. E., Eisenberg, M. E., Pettingell, S., & Skay, C. (2006). Friends' influence on adolescents' first sexual intercourse. *Perspectives on Sexual and Reproductive Health, 38*(1), 13–19.

Sigesmund, B. J. (2003, July 31). Boys r us. *Newsweek,* 52–53.

Signorella, M. L. (1999). Multidimensionality of gender schemas: Implications for the development of gender-related characteristics. In W. B. Swann & J. H. Langlois (Eds.), *Sexism and stereotypes in modern society: The gender science of Janet Taylor Spence* (pp. 107–126). Washington, DC: American Psychological Association.

Silber, S. J., et al. (2005). Ovarian transplantation between monozygotic twins discordant for premature ovarian failure. *New England Journal of Medicine, 353,* 58–63.

Silvestre, A. J., Faber, J. F., Shankle, M. D., & Kopelman, J. P. (2002). A model for involving youth in health planning: HIV prevention in Pennsylvania. *Perspectives on Sexual and Reproductive Health, 34* (2), 91–97.

Simon, W. (1999). Sexual conduct in retrospective perspective. *Sexualities, 2*(1), 126–133.

Simons, J. S., & Carey, M. P. (2001). Prevalence of sexual dysfunctions: Results from a decade of research. *Archives of Sexual Behavior, 30*(2), 177–219.

Singer, L. T., et al. (2002). Cognitive and motor outcomes of cocaine-exposed infants. *Journal of the American Medical Association, 287*(15), 1952–1960.

Singer, M. (2002). Childhood sexuality: An interpersonal-intrapsychic integration. *Contemporary Sexuality, 36* (11), i–viii.

Singh, D. (2004). Mating strategies of young women: Role of physical attractiveness. *Journal of Sex Research, 41*(1), 43–54.

Singh, S., Darroch, J. E., Frost, J. J., & the study team. (2001). Socioeconomic disadvantage and adolescent women's sexual and reproductive behavior: The case of five developed countries. *Family Planning Perspectives, 33* (6), 251–258.

Sipski, M. L. (2002). Central nervous system based neurologic female sexual dysfunction: Current status and future trends. *Archives of Sexual Behavior, 31*(5), 421–424.

Sipski, M. L., Rosen, R. C., Alexander, C. J., & Gómez-Marín, O. (2004). Sexual responsiveness in women with spinal cord injuries: Differential effects of anxiety-eliciting stimulation. *Archives of Sexual Behavior, 33*(3), 295–302.

Skaletsky, H., et al. (2003). The male-specific region of the human Y chromosome is a mosaic of discrete sequence classes. *Nature, 423,* 825–837.

Skegg, K., Nada-Raja, S., Paul, C., & Skegg, D. (2007). Body piercing, personality, and sexual behavior. *Archives of Sexual Behavior, 36,* 47–54.

Slade, J. W. (2001). *Pornography and sexual representation: A reference guide.* Westport, CT: Greenwood Press.

Slanger, T. E., Snow, R. C., & Okonofua, F. E. (2002). The impact of female genital cutting on first delivery in southwest Nigeria. *Studies in Family Planning, 33*(2), 173–184.

Slob, A. K., Berkel, A., & Bosch, J. J. (2000). Premature ejaculation treated by local penile anaesthesia in an uncontrolled clinical replication study. *Journal of Sex Research, 37*(3), 244–247.

Slob, A. K., Verhulst, A. C. M., Gijs, L., Maksimovic, P. A., & Bosch, J. J. (2002). Intracavernous injection during diagnostic screening for erectile dysfunction; Five-year experience with over 600 patients. *Journal of Sex and Marital Therapy, 28,* 61–70.

Sloss, C. M., & Harper, G. W. (2004). When street sex workers are mothers. *Archives of Sexual Behavior, 33*(4), 329–341.

Smalley, S. (2003, March 24). A new baby debate. *Newsweek,* 52.

Smallwood, G. H., Meador, M. L., Lenihan, J. P., et al. (2001). Efficacy and safety of a transdermal contraceptive system. *Obstetrics and Gynecology, 98,* 799–805.

Smallwood, S. (2003, December 5). Women take the lead in number of U.S. doctorates awarded, as total falls again. *Chronicle of Higher Education,* A26.

Smith, D. J. (2004). Premarital sex, procreation, and HIV risk in Nigeria. *Studies in Family Planning, 35*(4), 223–235.

Smith, E. J. (2002). Discussing sexuality fosters sexual health. *SIECUS Report, 30*(5), 7–12.

Smith, G. C. S., et al. (2002). Risk of perinatal death associated with labor after previous cesarean delivery in uncomplicated term pregnancies. *Journal of the American Medical Association, 287*(20), 2684–2690.

Smith, J. L. (1999). Boundary violations and subsequent treatment. *Journal of Sex Education and Therapy, 24*(4), 262–267.

Smith, J. S., et al. (2003). Cervical cancer and the use of hormonal contraceptives: a systematic review. *Lancet, 361*(9364), 1159–1167.

Smith, L. A. (2003). Partner influence on noncondom use: Gender and ethnic differences. *Journal of Sex Research, 40*(4), 346–350.

Smith, P. H., White, J. W., & Holland, L. J. (2003). A longitudinal perspective on dating violence among adolescent and college-age women. *American Journal of Public Health, 93*(7), 1104–1109.

Smith, Y. L. S., Cohen, L., & Cohen-Kettenis, P. T. (2002). Postoperative psychological functioning of adolescent transsexuals: A Rorschach study. *Archives of Sexual Behavior, 31*(3), 255–261.

Sobel, V., & Imperato-McGinley, J. (2004). Gender identity in XY intersexuality. *Child and Adolescent Psychiatric Clinics of North America, 13*, 609–622.

Sobo, E. J., & Bell, S. (2001). *Celibacy, culture, and society: The anthropology of sexual abstinence.* Madison, WI: University of Wisconsin Press.

Sommers, C. H. (2000). *The war against boys.* New York: Simon and Schuster.

Sonfield, A. (2002). Looking at men's sexual and reproductive health needs. *Guttmacher Report on Public Policy, 5*(2), 7–10.

Sorensen, R. (1973). *Adolescent sexuality in contemporary America.* New York: World.

South, S. J., Haynie, D. L., & Bose, S. (2005). Residential mobility and the onset of adolescent sexual activity. *Journal of Marriage and Family, 67* (2), 499–514.

Spencer, J. M., et al. (2002). Self-esteem as a predictor of initiation of coitus in early adolescents. *Pediatrics, 109* (4), 581–584.

Spiering, M., Everaerd, W., & Elzinga, B. (2002). Conscious processing of sexual information: Interference caused by sexual primes. *Archives of Sexual Behavior, 31*(2), 159–164.

Spiering, M., Everaerd, W., & Janssen, E. (2003). Priming the sexual system: Implicit versus explicit activation. *Journal of Sex Research, 40*(2), 134–145.

Spiering, M., Everaerd, W., & Laan, E. (2004). Conscious processing of sexual information: Mechanisms of appraisal. *Archives of Sexual Behavior, 33*(4), 369–380.

Spitalnick, J. S., & McNair, L. D. (2005). Couples therapy with gay and lesbian clients: An analysis of important clinical issues. *Journal of Sex and Marital Therapy, 31*, 43–56.

Spitzer, R. L. (2003). Can some gay men and lesbians change their sexual orientation? 200 participants reporting a change from homosexual to heterosexual orientation. *Archives of Sexual Behavior, 32*(5), 403–417.

Spitzer, R. L. (2005). Sexual and gender identity disorders: Discussion of questions for *DSM-V. Journal of Psychology and Human Sexuality, 17*(3/4), 111–116.

Sprecher, S. (1998). Social exchange theories and sexuality. *Journal of Sex Research, 35*(1), 32–43.

Sprecher, S. (2002). Sexual satisfaction in premarital relationships: Associations with satisfaction, love, commitment, and stability. *Journal of Sex Research, 39*(3), 190–196.

Springen, K. (2000, December 4). The right to choose. *Newsweek,* 73–74.

Springen, K., & Adler, J. (2003, June 16). Prostate cancer's difficult choices. *Newsweek,* 54–58.

Springer, C. A., & Lease, S. H. (2000). The impact of multiple AIDS-related bereavement in the gay male population. *Journal of Counseling and Development, 78*, 297–304.

Springer, K. (2000, Fall/Winter Special Issue). The circumcision decision. *Newsweek,* 50.

Stanwood, N. L., Garrett, J. M., & Konrad, T. R. (2002). Obstetrician-gynecologists and the intrauterine device: A survey of attitudes and practices. *Obstetrics and Gynecology, 99*(2), 275–280.

Stayton, W. R. (2002). A theology of sexual pleasure. *SIECUS Report, 30*(4), 27–29.

Steele, J. R. (1999). Teenage sexuality and media practice: Factoring in the influences of family, friends, and school. *Journal of Sex Research, 36* (4), 331–341.

Steffens, M. C., & Wagner, C. (2004). Attitudes toward lesbians, gay men, bisexual women, and bisexual men in Germany. *Journal of Sex Research, 41*(2), 137–149.

Steinauer, J. E. (2003). The effect of training on the provision of elective abortion: A survey of five residency programs. *American Journal of Obstetrics and Gynecology, 188*(5), 1161–1163.

Stephens, D. P., & Phillips, L. D. (2003). Freaks, gold diggers, divas, and dykes: The sociohistorical development of adolescent African American women's sexual scripts. *Sexuality and Culture, 7*(1), 3–49.

Stepp, L. S. (2003, January 19). The buddy system: Sex in high school and college: What's love got to do with it? *Washington Post.*

Stern, S. E., & Handel, A. D. (2001). Sexuality and mass media: The historical context of psychology's reaction to sexuality on the Internet. *Journal of Sex Research, 38*(4), 283–291.

Sternberg, R. J. (1986). A triangular theory of love. *Psychological Review, 93*, 119–135.

Sternberg, R. J. (1998). *Cupid's arrow: The course of love through time.* New Haven, CT: Yale University Press.

Stevens, R. A. (2004). Understanding gay identity development within the college environment. *Journal of College Student Development, 45*(2), 185–206.

Stewart, D. E. (2005). *Menopause: A mental health practitioner's guide.* Washington, DC: American Psychological Association.

Stewart, E., & Spencer, P. (2002). *The V book: A doctor's guide to complete vulvovaginal health.* New York: Bantam Books.

Stewart, P. (2004). Sexual encoding in eighteenth-century literature and art. *Sexuality and Culture, 8*(2), 3–23.

Stires, L. (1999). Two book reviews on pornography. *Archives of Sexual Behavior, 28*(1), 91–95.

Stockdale, J. (2003). Role model stories send integrated prevention messages to minority youth. *SIECUS Report, 31* (3), 8–10.

Stone, N., Hatherall, B., Ingham, R., & McEachran, J. (2006). Oral sex and condom use among young people in the United Kingdom. *Perspectives on Sexual and Reproductive Health, 38* (1), 6–12.

Stone, N., & Ingham, R. (2002). Factors affecting British teenagers' contraceptive use at first intercourse: The importance of partner communication. *Perspectives on Sexual and Reproductive Health, 34*(4), 191–197.

Stoner, B. P. (2003). Avoiding risky sex partners' risks vs. partners' self-reported risks. *Sexually Transmitted Infections, 79*(3), 197–201.

Strager, S. (2003). What men watch when they watch pornography. *Sexuality and Culture: An Interdisciplinary Quarterly, 7*(1), 50–61.

Strand, J., Wise, T. N., Fagan, P. J., & Schmidt, C. W. (2002). Erectile dysfunction and depression: Category or dimension? *Journal of Sex and Marital Therapy, 28*, 175–181.

Strassberg, D. S. (2003). A candle in the wind: Spitzer's study of reparative therapy. *Archives of Sexual Behavior, 32*(5), 451–452.

Strassberg, D. S., & Holty, S. (2003). An experimental study of women's Internet personal ads. *Archives of Sexual Behavior, 32*(3), 253–260.

Strassberg, D. S., & Lockerd, L. K. (1998). Force in women's sexual fantasies. *Archives of Sexual Behavior, 27*(4), 403–414. *Journal of Sex Research, 40*(1), 76–86.

Strong, D. A., Bancroft, J., Carnes, L. A., Davis, L. A., & Kennedy, J. (2005). The impact of sexual arousal on sexual risk-taking: A qualitative study. *Journal of Sex Research, 42* (3), 185–191.

Stroud, D. D. (1999). Familial support as perceived by adult victims of childhood sexual abuse. *Sexual Abuse: Journal of Research and Treatment, 11*(2), 159–175.

Struckman-Johnson, C., Struckman-Johnson, D., & Anderson, P. B. (2003). Tactics of sexual coercion: When men and women won't take no for an answer.

Stulhofer, A. (2006). How (un)important is penis size for women with heterosexual experience? *Archives of Sexual Behavior, 35*(1), 5–6.

Surratt, H. L., Kurtz, S. P., Weaver, J. C., & Inciardi, J. A. (2005). The connections of mental health problems, violent life experiences, and the social milieu of the "stroll" with the HIV risk behaviors of female street sex workers. *Journal of Psychology and Human Sexuality, 17* (1/2), 23–44.

Svedin, C. G., & Priebe, G. (2007). Selling sex in a population-based study of high school seniors in Sweden: Demographic and psychosocial correlates. *Archives of Sexual Behavior, 36,* 21–32.

Swindle, R. W., Cameron, A. E., Lockhart, D. C., & Rosen, R. C. (2004). The psychological and interpersonal relationship scales: Assessing psychological and relationship outcomes associated with erectile dysfunction and its treatment. *Archives of Sexual Behavior, 33*(1), 19–30.

Symonds, T., Boolell, M., & Quirk, F. (2005). Development of a questionnaire on sexual quality of life in women. *Journal of Sex and Marital Therapy, 31,* 385–397.

Symonds, T., Roblin, D., Hart, K., & Althof, S. (2003). How does premature ejaculation impact a man's life? *Journal of Sex and Marital Therapy, 29,* 361–370.

Tabachnick, J. (2000). Stop it now! challenges our thinking about sexual abuse. *SIECUS Report, 29*(1), 47–50.

Tambling, J. (2004). Review of *Shakespeare's Perfume: Sodomy and Sublimity in the Sonnets, Wilde,*

Freud, and Lacan by Richard Halpern. *Sexualities, 7*(1), 121–123.

Tanis, B. C., et al. (2001). Oral contraceptives and the risk of myocardial infarction. *New England Journal of Medicine, 345*(25), 1787–1793.

Tannen, D. (1990). *You just don't understand: Women and men in conversation.* New York: William Morrow.

Tannen, D. (1994). *Talking from 9 to 5.* New York: William Morrow.

Taveras, E. M., et al. (2003). Clinician support and psychosocial factors associated with breastfeeding discontinuation. *Pediatrics, 112*(1), 108–115.

Taverner, B. (2003). All together now: Combining pregnancy and STI prevention programs. *SIECUS Report, 31* (3), 14–17.

Taverner, W. J., & Brick, P. (2006). Unplanned pregnancy: Making a decision. *American Journal of Sexuality Education, 1*(3), 73–81.

Taylor, G. W., & Ussher, J. M. (2001). Making sense of S&M: A discourse analytic account. *Sexualities, 4*(3), 293–314.

Teachman, J. (2002). Premarital sex, premarital cohabitation, and the risk of subsequent marital dissolution among women. *Journal of Marriage and Family, 65*(2), 444–455.

Ten Reasons. (1994, Winter). Ten reasons to obtain consent for sex. *About Women on Campus, 2,* 1.

Tepper, M. S. (2001). Becoming sexually able: Education to help youth with disabilities. *SIECUS Report, 29*(3), 5–13.

Tepper, M. S., Whipple, B., Richards, E., & Komisaruk, B. R. (2001). Women with complete spinal cord injury: A phenomenological study of sexual experiences. *Journal of Sex and Marital Therapy, 27,* 615–623.

Terán, S., Walsh, C., & Irwin, K. L. (2001). Chlamydia infection in women: Bad news, good news, and next steps. *SIECUS Report, 30*(1), 17–23.

Thomas, G. (2006). Sex, politics, and money. *The Lancet, Early Online Publication,* DOI: 10-1016/S0140-6736(06)69488-9.

Thornhill, R., & Palmer, C. T. (2000). *A natural history of rape: Biological bases of sexual coercion.* Cambridge, MA: MIT Press.

Thukral, J. (2005). Behind closed doors: An analysis of indoor sex work in New York City. *SIECUS Report, 33*(2), 3–9.

Tiefer, L. (2001). The selling of "female sexual dysfunction." *Journal of Sex and Marital Therapy, 27,* 625–628.

Tiefer, L. (2002). Arriving at a "new view" of women's sexual problems: Background, theory, and activism. In L. Kaschak & L. Tiefer (Eds.), *A new view of women's sexual problems* (pp. 63–98). Binghamton, NY: Haworth Press.

Tiefer, L., Hall, M., & Tavris, C. (2002). Beyond dysfunction: A new view of women's sexual problems. *Journal of Sex and Marital Therapy, 28*(s), 225–232.

Timmerman, J. H. (2001). When religion is its own worst enemy: How therapists can help people shed hurtful notions that masquerade as good theology. *Journal of Sex Education and Therapy, 26*(4), 259–266.

Timreck, E. (2004). Placing gender at the heart of sexuality education. *SIECUS Report, 32*(3), 11–13.

Tolman, D. L. (2003). Improving women's sexual assertiveness [Letter]. *Perspectives on Sexual and Reproductive Health, 35*(1), 48.

Tolman, D. L., & Diamond, L. M. (2002). Desegregating sexuality research: Cultural and biological perspectives on gender and desire. *Annual Review of Sex Research, 12,* 33–74.

Tolman, D. L., Striepe, M. I., & Harmon, T. (2003). Gender matters: Constructing a model of adolescent sexual health. *Journal of Sex Research, 40* (1), 4–12.

Tomlinson, M. J., & Fassinger, R. E. (2003). Career development, lesbian identity development, and campus climate among lesbian college students. *Journal of College Student Development, 44*(6), 845–860.

Tone, A. (2000). *Devices and desires: A history of contraceptives in America.* Dawsonville, GA: Bridging the Gap Communications.

Touch, S. C., et al. (2002). Delayed childbearing and its impact on population rate changes in lower birth weight, multiple birth, and preterm delivery. *Pediatrics, 109*(3), 399–403.

Traeen, B., Holmen, K., & Stigum, H. (2007). Extradyadic sexual relationships in Norway. *Archives of Sexual Behavior, 36,* 55–65.

Traeen, B., Spitznogle, K., & Beverfjord, A. (2004). Attitudes and use of pornography in the Norwegian population 2002. *Journal of Sex Research, 41*(2), 193–200.

Traeen, B., Stigum, H., & Sorensen, D. (2002). Sexual diversity in urban Norwegians. *Journal of Sex Research, 39*(4), 249–258.

Trager, R. S. (2003). Raising new barriers against HIV infection. *Science, 299,* 39.

Traish, A. M., Kim, N., Min, K., Munarriz, R., & Goldstein, I. (2002). Androgens in female genital sexual arousal function: A biochemical perspective. *Journal of Sex and Marital Therapy, 28*(s), 233–244.

Traish, A. M., Kim, N., Munarriz, R., Moreland, R., & Goldstein, I. (2002). Biochemical and physiological mechanisms of female genital sexual arousal. *Archives of Sexual Behavior, 31*(5), 393–400.

Treas, J., & Giesen, D. (2000). Sexual infidelity among married and cohabiting Americans. *Journal of Marriage and the Family, 62,* 48–60.

Trends in sexual risk behaviors among high school students—United States, 1991–1997. (1998). *Morbidity and Mortality Weekly Reports, 47*(36), 749–752.

Trenholm, C., Devaney, B., Fortson, K., Quay, L., Wheeler, J., & Clark, M. (2007). *Impacts of four Title V, Section 510 abstinence education programs: Final Report.* Princeton, NJ.: Mathematica Policy Research Group.

Trudel, G. (2002). Sexuality and marital life: Results of a survey. *Journal of Sex and Marital Therapy, 28,* 229–249.

Tsu, R. C., et al. (2002). Telephone vs. face-to-face notification of HIV results in high-risk youth. *Journal of Adolescent Health, 30*(3), 154–160.

Tucker, J. B., & Keil, H. H. J. (2001). Can cultural beliefs cause a gender identity disorder? *Journal of Psychology and Human Sexuality, 13*(2), 21–30.

Tuomala, R. E., et al. (2002). Antiretroviral therapy during pregnancy and the risk of an adverse outcome. *New England Journal of Medicine, 346* (24), 1863–1870.

Turner, L., et al. (2003). Contraceptive efficacy of a depot progestin and androgen combination in men. *Journal of Clinical Endocrinology and Metabolism, 88* (10), 4659–4667.

Tyler, M. (2004). Managing between the sheets: Lifestyle magazines and the management of sexuality in everyday life. *Sexualities, 7*(1), 81–106.

Tyre, P., & McGinn, D. (2003, May 12). She works, he doesn't. *Newsweek,* 44–52.

UK Group on Transmitted HIV Drug Resistance. (2005). Time trends in primary resistance to HIV drugs in the United Kingdom: Multicentre observational study. *British Medical Journal, 331*(7529), 1368–1373.

UNAIDS. (2006). *UNAIDS report on the global AIDS epidemic 2006.* London: Author.

Utian, W. H., et al. (2005). A methodology study to validate a structured diagnostic method used to diagnose female sexual dysfunction and its subtypes in postmenopausal women. *Journal of Sex and Marital Therapy, 31,* 271–283.

Vaddiparti, K., et al. (2006). The effects of childhood trauma on sex trading in substance using women. *Archives of Sexual Behavior, 35,* 451–459.

Valappil, T., et al. (2005). Female condom and male condom failure among women at high risk of sexually transmitted disease. *Sexually Transmitted Diseases, 32*(1), 35–43.

Valiente, C. E., Belanger, C. J., & Estrada, A. U. (2002). Helpful and harmful expectations of premarital interventions. *Journal of Sex and Marital Therapy, 28,* 71–77.

Valle, R. F., Carignan, C. S., & Wright, T. C. (2001). Tissue response to the STOP micocoil transcervical permanent contraceptive device. *Fertility and Sterility, 76,* 974–980.

Van der Ploeg, I. (2002). *Prosthetic bodies: The construction of the fetus and the couple as patients in reproductive technologies.* Hingham, MA: Kluwer Academic Publishers.

Van der Poel, A., & Greeff, A. P. (2003). The influence of coronary bypass graft surgery on the marital relationship and family functioning of the patient. *Journal of Sex and Marital Therapy, 29,* 61–77.

Van Devanter, N., et al. (2002). Effect of an STD-HIV behavioral intervention on women's use of the female condom. *American Journal of Public Health, 92*(1), 109–115.

Vanwesenbeeck, I. (2002). Another decade of social scientific work on sex work: A review of research. 1990–2000. *Annual Review of Sex Research, 12,* 242–289.

Varga, C. A. (2003). How gender roles influence sexual and reproductive health among South African adolescents. *Studies in Family Planning, 34* (3), 160–172.

Vasey, P. L. (2006). Function and phylogeny: The evolution of same-sex sexual behavior in primates. *Journal of Psychology and Human Sexuality, 18*(2/3), 215–244.

Vassey, P. L. (2003). Same-sex sexual partner preference in hormonally and neurologically unmanipulated animals. *Annual Review of Sex Research, 13,* 141–179.

Vatten, I. J., & Skjaerven, R. (2003). Effects on pregnancy outcome of changing partner between first two births: Prospective population study. *British Medical Journal, 327*(7424), 1138–1141.

Vellani, F. (2006). Review of *Left Out. The Politics of Exclusion: Essays 1964–2002* by Martin Duberman. *Archives of Sexual Behavior, 35*(2), 235–236.

Verma, K. K., Khaitan, B. K., & Singh, O. P. (1998). The frequency of sexual dysfunctions in patients attending a sex therapy clinic in North India. *Archives of Sexual Behavior, 27*(3), 309–314.

Vilain, E. (2001). Genetics of sexual development. *Annual Review of Sex Research, 11,* 1–25.

Visser, R. O. de, Smith, A., Richters, J., & Rissel, C. E. (2007). Associations between religiosity and sexuality in a representative sample of Australian adults. *Archives of Sexual Behavior, 36,* 33–46.

Voegeli, T. A., & Effert, P. J. (2005). Pentaethylene-terephthalate (PET) bottles: A new device for autoerotic strangulation of the penis causing serious injury. *Archives of Sexual Behavior, 34*(4), 469–470.

Vogel, G. (2003). Scientists make sperm in a dish. *Science, 302,* 1875.

Vogel, G. (2004). Scientists take step toward therapeutic cloning. *Science, 303,* 937–939.

Vogel, G. (2006). Scientists derive line from single embryo cell. *Science, 313,* 10.

Von Hertzen, H., et al. (2002). Low dose mifepristone and two regimens of levonorgestrel for emergency contraception: A WHO multicentre randomised trial. *Lancet, 360*(9348), 1803–1810.

Wald, A., et al. (2005). The relationship between condom use and herpes simplex virus acquisition. *Annals of Internal Medicine, 143*(10), 707–713.

Walker, C. L., & Stewart, E. A. (2005). Uterine fibroids: The elephant in the room. *Science, 308,* 1589–1591.

Walker, J., Archer, J., & Davies, M. (2005). Effects of rape on men: A descriptive analysis. *Archives of Sexual Behavior, 34*(1), 69–80.

Wallen, K., & Zehr, J. L. (2004). Hormones and history: The evolution and development of primate female sexuality. *Journal of Sex Research, 41*(1), 101–112.

Walsh, F. (1996). *Sin and censorship: The Catholic Church and the motion picture industry.* New Haven: Yale University Press.

Walsh, T. L., Frezieres, R. G., Peacock, K., Nelson, V. A., & Bernstein, L. (2003). Evaluation of the efficacy of a nonlatex condom: Results from a randomized, controlled clinical trial. *Perspectives on Sexual and Reproductive Health, 35*(2), 79–86.

Walther, C. S., & Poston, D. L. (2004). Patterns of gay and lesbian partnering in the larger metropolitan areas of the United States. *Journal of Sex Research, 41*(2), 201–214.

Ward, L. M., & Rivadeneyra, R. (1999). Contributions of entertainment television to adolescents' sexual attitudes and expectations: The role of viewing amount versus viewer involvement. *Journal of Sex Research, 36*(3), 237–249.

Ward, R., Fidler, H., Lochyer, J. M., Basson, R. J., Elliott, R. J., & Toews, J. (2001). Physician outcomes following an intensive educational program on erectile dysfunction. *Journal of Sex Education and Therapy, 26*(4), 358–362.

Warkentin, K. M., Gray, R. E., & Wassersug, R. J. (2006). Restoration of satisfying sex for a castrated cancer patient with complete impotence: A case study. *Journal of Sex and Marital Therapy, 32,* 389–399.

Warner, L., et al. (2005). Application of the case-crossover design to reduce unmeasured confounding in studies of condom effectiveness. *American Journal of Epidemiology, 161*(8), 765–773.

Wassersug, R. J., Zelenietz, S. A., & Squire, G. F. (2004). New age eunuchs: Motivation and rationale for voluntary castration. *Archives of Sexual Behavior, 33*(5), 433–442.

Watkins, K. J., & Baldo, T. D. (2004). The infertility experience: Biopsychosocial effects and suggestions for counselors. *Journal of Counseling and Development, 82,* 394–402.

Watts, J. (2002). Japan opens dating agency to improve birth rate. *Lancet, 369*(9347), 1755.

Waugh, T. (1996). *Hard to imagine: Gay male eroticism in photography and film from their beginning to Stonewall.* New York: Columbia University Press.

Waugh, T. (2001). Homosociality in the classical American stag film: Off-screen, on-screen. *Sexualities, 4*(3), 275–291.

Weeden, J., & Sabini, J. (2007). Subjective and objective measures of attractiveness and their relation to sexual behavior and sexual attitudes in university students. *Archives of Sexual Behavior, 36,* 79–88.

Weeks, G. R., & Gambescia, N. (2002). *Hypoactive sexual desire: Integrating sex and marital therapy.* New York: W. W. Norton.

Weibley, S. (2001). New vaccines may give sexuality education advocates the shot they need. *SIECUS Report, 30*(1), 27.

Weinberg, M. S., Worth, H., & Williams, C. J. (2001). Men sex workers and other men who have sex with men: How do their HIV risks compare in New Zealand? *Archives of Sexual Behavior, 30*(3), 273–286.

Weinstock, H., Berman, S., & Cates, W. (2004). Sexually transmitted diseases among American youth: Incidence and prevalence estimates, 2000. *Perspectives on Sexual and Reproductive Health, 36*(1), 6–10.

Weiss, J. C. (2001). Treating vaginismus: Patient without partner. *Journal of Sex Education and Therapy, 26,* 28–33.

Weldin, M., et al. (2006). Expanding access to emergency contraception through state systems: The Washington state experience. *Perspectives on Sexual and Reproductive Health, 38* (4), 220–224.

Wellings, K., et al. (2006). Sexual behaviour in context: A global perspective. *The Lancet, Early Online Publication, DOI:* 10.1016/S0140-6736(06)69479-8.

Wertheimer, A. (2003). *Consent to sexual relations.* Cambridge, England: Cambridge University Press.

Wessel, J., & Buscher, U. (2002). Denial of pregnancy: Population-based study. *British Medical Journal, 324* (7335), 458.

Wessels, H., Lue, T. F., & McAninch, J. W. (1996). Penile length in the flaccid and erect states: Guidelines for penile augmentation. *Journal of Urology, 156,* 995–997.

West, D. J. (2001). Parental selection of children's sexual orientation: A commentary. *Archives of Sexual Behavior, 30*(4), 439–441.

Westhoff, C., Picardo, L., & Morrow, E. (2003). Quality of life following early medical or surgical abortion. *Contraception, 67*(1), 41–47.

Whipple, B., & Komisaruk, B. R. (2002). Brain (PET) responses to vaginal-cervical self-stimulation in women with complete spinal cord injury: Preliminary findings. *Journal of Sex and Marital Therapy, 28,* 79–86.

Whipple, B., Myers, B. T., & Komisaruk, B. R. (1998). Male multiple ejaculatory orgasms: A case study. *Journal of Sex Education and Therapy, 23*(2), 157–162.

Whitbeck, L. B., Chen, X., Hoyt, D. R., Tyler, K. A., & Johnson, K. D. (2004). Mental disorder, subsistence strategies, and victimization among gay, lesbian, and bisexual homeless and runaway adolescents. *Journal of Sex Research, 41*(4), 329–342.

Whitehead, N., & Lipscomb, L. (2003). Patterns of alcohol use before and during pregnancy and the risk of small-for-gestational-age birth. *American Journal of Epidemiology, 158*(7), 654–662.

Whitten, K. L., et al. (2003). The emotional experience of intercourse and sexually transmitted diseases. *Sexually Transmitted Diseases, 30*(4), 348–356.

Whittier, D. K., St. Lawrence, J., & Seeley S. (2005). Sexual risk behavior of men who have sex with men: Comparison of behavior at home and at a gay resort. *Archives of Sexual Behavior, 34*(1), 95–102.

Wickelgren, I. (2003). The great estrogen conundrum. *Science, 302,* 1136–1139.

Wickelgren, I. (2004). Resetting pregnancy's clock. *Science, 304,* 666–668.

Wiederman, M. W. (1998). The state of theory in sex therapy. *Journal of Sex Research, 35*(1), 88–99.

Wiederman, M. W. (1999). Volunteer bias in sexuality research using college student participants. *Journal of Sex Research, 36* (1), 59–66.

Wiederman, M. W., & Whitley, B. E. (2002). *Handbook for conducting research on human sexuality.* Mahwah, NJ: Lawrence Erlbaum Associates.

Wiesenfeld, H. C., et al. (2005). Knowledge about sexually transmitted diseases in women among primary care physicians. *Sexually Transmitted Diseases, 32*(11), 649–653.

Wilkes, P. T., et al. (2003). Risk factors for cesarean delivery at presentation of nulliparous patients in labor. *Obstetrics and Gynecology, 102*(6), 1352–1357.

Willard, H. F. (2003). Tales of the Y chromosome. *Nature, 423,* 810–813.

Williams, C. J., & Weinberg, M. S. (2003). Zoophilia in men: A study of sexual interest in animals. *Archives of Sexual Behavior, 32*(6), 523–535.

Williams, J. E., & Best, D. L. (1990). *Measuring sex stereotypes: A multination study.* Beverly Hills, CA: Sage.

Williams, S., & Payne, G. H. (2002). Perceptions of own sexual lies influenced by characteristics of liar, sex partner, and lie itself. *Journal of Sex and Marital Therapy, 28,* 257–267.

Williams, T. J., Pepitone, M. E., Christensen, S. E., Cooke, B. M., Huberman, A. D., Breedlove, N. J., Breedlove, T. J., Jordan, C. L., & Breedlove, S. M. (2000). Finger-length ratios and sexual orientation. *Nature, 404,* 455–456.

Willox, A. (2003). Branding Teena: (Mis)representations in the media. *Sexualities, 6*(3/4), 407–425.

Wilson, A. (2005). German dominatrices' choices of working names as reflections of self-constructed social identity. *Sexuality and Culture, 9*(2), 31–41.

Wilson, B. A., Holm, J. E., Bishop, K. L., & Borowiak, D. M. (2002). *Journal of Sex Research, 39*(4), 275–283.

Wilson, C. (2004). Fertility below replacement level. *Science, 304,* 207–208.

Wilson, R. (2004a, January 23). Women underrepresented in sciences at top research universities, study finds. *Chronicle of Higher Education,* A9.

Wilson, R. (2004b, June 4). Pitt's bitter battle over benefits. *Chronicle of Higher Education,* A8–10.

Wilson, R. J. (1999). Emotional congruence in sexual offenders against children. *Sexual Abuse: Journal of Research and Treatment, 11*(1), 33–48.

Winer, R. L., et al. (2003). Genital human papillomavirus infection: Incidence and risk factors in a cohort of female university students. *American Journal of Epidemiology, 157*(3), 218–226.

Wingood, G. M., et al. (2001). Dating violence and the sexual health of black adolescent females. *Pediatrics, 107*(5), e72.

Wingwood, G. M., & DiClemente, R. J. (2002). *Handbook of women's sexual and reproductive health.* Hingham, MA: Kluwer Academic Publishing.

Winter, A., & Daniluk, J. C. (2004). A gift from the heart: The experiences of women whose egg donations helped their sisters become mothers. *Journal of Counseling and Development, 82,* 483–495.

Witte, S. S., et al. (2006). Promoting female condom use to heterosexual couples: Findings from a randomized clinical trial. *Perspectives on Sexual and Reproductive Health, 38*(3), 148–154.

Wolfrandt, U., & Neumann, K. (2001). Depersonalization, self-esteem and body image in male-to-female transsexuals compared to male and female controls. *Archives of Sexual Behavior, 30*(3), 301–310.

Wolfthal, D. (1999). *Images of rape: The "heroic" tradition and its alternatives.* New York: Cambridge University Press.

Wolf-Wendel, L. E., Toma, J. D., & Morphew, C. C. (2001). How much difference is too much difference? Perceptions of gay men and lesbians in intercollegiate athletics. *Journal of College Student Development, 42*(5), 465–480.

Wong, C., & Tang, C. S. (2004). Sexual practices and psychosocial correlates of current condom use among Chinese gay men in Hong Kong. *Archives of Sexual Behavior, 33*(2), 159–167.

Wong, C. A., et al. (2005). The risk of cesarean delivery with neuraxial analgesia given early versus late in labor. *New England Journal of Medicine, 352,* 655–665.

Woods, G. L., White, K. L., Vanderwall, D. K., et al. (2003). A mule cloned from fetal cells by nuclear transfer. *Science, 301,* 1063.

Woody, J. D., Russel, R., D'Souza, H. J., & Woody, J. K. (2000). Adolescent non-coital sexual activity: Comparisons of virgins and non-virgins. *Journal of Sex Education and Therapy, 25*(4), 261–268.

World Health Organization. (2006, December 13). Statement on Kenyan and Ugandan trial findings regarding male circumcision and HIV. Press statement from WHO, UNFPA, and UNICEF.

Worthington, R. L., & Mohr, J. J. (2002). Theorizing heterosexual identity development. *The Counseling Psychologist, 30,* 491–495.

Worthington, R. L., Savoy, H. B., Dillon, F. R., & Vernaglia, E. R. (2002). Heterosexual identity development: A multidimensional model of individal and social identity. *The Counseling Psychologist, 30,* 496–531.

Wryobeck, J. M., & Wiederman, M. W. (1999). Sexual narcissism: Measurement and correlates among college men. *Journal of Sex and Marital Therapy, 25,* 321–331.

Wylie, K. R., & Davies-South, D. (2004). A study of treatment choices in men with erectile dysfunction and reduced androgen levels.

Wylie, K. R., Jones, R. H., & Walters, S. (2003). The potential benefit of vacuum devices augmenting psychosexual therapy for erectile dysfunction: A randomized controlled trial. *Journal of Sex and Marital Therapy, 29*(3), 227–236.

Wyrobek, A. J., et al. (2006). Advancing age has differential effects on DNA damage, chromatin integrity, gene mutations, and aneuploidies in sperm. *Proceedings of the National Academy of Sciences of the United States of America, 103*(25), 9601–9606.

Xantidis, L., & McCabe, M. P. (2000). Personality characteristics of male clients of female commercial sex workers in Australia. *Archives of Sexual Behavior, 29*(2), 165–176.

Xie, Y., & Shauman, K. A. (2003). *Women in science: Career processes and outcomes.* Cambridge, MA: Harvard University Press.

Yakushko, O., & Chronister, K. M. (2005). Immigrant women and counseling: The invisible others. *Journal of Counseling and Development, 83,* 292–298.

Yarber, W. L., Milhausen, R. R., Crosby, R. A., & Torabi, M. R. (2005). Public opinion about condoms for HIV and STD prevention: A midwestern state telephone survey. *Perspectives on Sexual and Reproductive Health, 37* (3), 148–154.

Yen, S., et al. (2003). Bacterial vaginosis in sexually experienced and non-sexually experienced young women entering the military. *Obstetrics and Gynecology, 102*(5), 927–933.

Yost, M. R., & Zurbriggen, E. L. (2006). Gender differences in the enactment of sociosexuality: An examination of implicit social motives, sexual fantasies, coercive sexual attitudes, and aggressive sexual behavior. *Journal of Sex Research, 43*(2), 163–173.

Youn, G. (2001). Perception of peer sexual activities in Korean adolescents. *Journal of Sex Research, 38*(4), 352–360.

Youn, G. (2006). Subjective sexual arousal in reponse to erotica: Effects of gender, guided fantasy, erotic stimulus, and duration of exposure. *Archives of Sexual Behavior, 35*(1), 87–97.

Zalewski, M., & Lloyd, M. (2003). Exceeding sex and gender? *Sexualities, 6*(3/4), 405–406.

Zamboni, B. D., & Crawford, I. (2002). Using masturbation in sex therapy: Relationships between masturbation, sexual desire, and sexual fantasy. *Journal of Psychology and Human Sexuality, 14*(2/3), 123–141.

Zelnik, M., & Kantner, J. F. (1980). Sexual activity, contraceptive use, and pregnancy among metropolitan-area teenagers, 1971–1979. *Family Planning Perspectives, 12,* 230–237.

Zerhouni, E. (2003). Stem cell programs. *Science, 300,* 911–912.

Zhu, B. P., et al. (1999). Effect of the interval between pregnancy on perinatal outcomes. *New England Journal of Medicine, 340*(8), 589–594.

Ziaei, S., et al. (2002). Comparative study and evaluation of side effects of low-dose contraceptive pills administered by the oral and vaginal route. *Contraception, 65*(5), 329–331.

Zimmer, C. (2001). Genetic trees reveal disease origins. *Science, 292,* 1090–1093.

Zimmer-Gembeck, M. J., Siebenbruner, J., & Collins, W. A. (2004). A prospective study of intraindividual and peer influences on adolescents' heterosexual romantic and sexual behavior. *Archives of Sexual Behavior, 33* (4), 381–394.

Zoll, R. (2003, September 14). Violating a vow. *Watertown Daily Times Sunday Weekly,* 6–7.

Zonana, H. V., & Norko, M. A. (1999). Sexual predators. *Psychiatric Clinics of North America, 22*(1), 109–127.

Zucker, K. J. (2000). Intersexuality and gender identity differentiation. *Annual Review of Sex Research, 9,* 1–69.

Zucker, K. J. (2002a). Associated features are irrelevant in deciding whether or not pedophilia is a mental disorder. *Archives of Sexual Behavior, 31*(6), 500–503.

Zucker, K. J. (2002b). Evaluation of sex- and gender-assignment decisions: A methodological and statistical note. *Journal of Sex and Marital Therapy, 28,* 269–274.

Zucker, K. J. (2003a). Global sexology. *Archives of Sexual Behavior, 32*(4), 297.

Zucker, K. J. (2003b). The politics and science of "reparative therapy." *Archives of Sexual Behavior, 32*(5), 399–402.

Zucker, K. J. (2005). Measurement of psychosexual differentiation. *Archives of Sexual Behavior, 34*(4), 375–388.

Zucker, K. J., & Blanchard, R. (2003). Birth order in the *fakafefine. Journal of Sex and Marital Therapy, 29*(4), 251–253.

Zucker, K. J., & Cantor, J. M. (2003). The numbers game: The impact factor and all that jazz. *Archives of Sexual Behavior, 32*(1), 3–5.

Zucker, K. J., & Cantor, J. M. (2006). The impact factor: The *Archives* breaks from the pack. *Archives of Sexual Behavior, 35*(1), 7–9.

Zucker, K. J., et al. (2004). Self-reported sexual arousability in women with congenital adrenal hyperplasia. *Journal of Sex and Marital Therapy, 30,* 343–355.

Zurbriggen, E. L., & Yost, M. R. (2004). Power, desire, and pleasure in sexual fantasies. *Journal of Sex Research, 41*(3), 288–300.

Zweig, J. M., Crickett, L. J., Sayer, A., & Vicary, J. R. (1999). A longitudinal examination of the consequences of sexual victimization for rural young adult women. *Journal of Sex Research, 36*(4), 396–409.

Credits

Photos

Part 1: p. 2 © Purestock/Punchstock; p. 4 Digital Vision/Getty Images; p. 5 © Tony Savino/The Image Works; p. 7 Sergei Grits/AP Images; p. 10 Pierre Ducharme/Reuters/Corbis; p. 16 Library of Congresss; p. 17 Reprinted by permission of the Kinsey Institute for Research in Sex Gender and Reproduction, Inc.; p. 18 Reprinted by permission of the Kinsey Institute for Research in Sex Gender and Reproduction, Inc., photo by William Dellenback; p. 19 Matthew Peyton/Getty Images; p. 20 Bettman/Corbis; p. 22 © Bruce Powell; p. 33 Dynamic Graphics / JupiterImages; p. 61 Ryan McVay/Getty Images; p. 76T Gary Hush/Tony Stone Images/Getty Images; p. 76B © liquidlibrary/PictureQuest; p. 80 Getty Images; p. 102 © Stockbyte/ Punchstock; p. 116 The McGraw-Hill Companies, Inc./Jill Braaten, photographer; p. 117 © Gabe Palmer/Corbis; p. 126 PhotoLink/Getty Images; p. 129 (left) © Edward Staper/ AP Images; p. 129 (right) © Chris Prevolosi/AP Images; p. 130 Library of Congress; p. 131 (top left) Bill Horsman/Stock Boston; p. 131 (top right) Photofest

Part 2: p. 138 Monica Lau/Getty Images; p. 140 © Photodisc/Getty Images; p. 142 Courtesy Nora Agbayani; p. 144 (left) © Elyse Lewin/Getty Images; p. 144 (right) © David J. Sams/Stock Boston; p. 147 © Lorcan/Getty Images; p. 148 © Hella Hammid/Photo Researchers Inc.; p. 154 Getty Images / SW Productions; p. 164 © Jeff Greenberg/The Image Works; p. 171 © Digital Vision/Getty Images; p. 173 © Peter Hvizdak / The Image Worksk; p. 179 © CO2/Getty Images; p. 185 Sean Murphy/Getty Images; p. 186 Stockbyte/Getty Images; p. 193 Stockbyte/Getty Images; p. 194 Eric Lessing/Art Resource; p. 195 Scala/Art Resource; p. 196 McGraw-Hill Companies, Inc./Gary He, photogra-pher; p. 199 Joel Gordon; p. 202 © Chapman/The Image Works; p. 208 The McGraw-Hill Companies, Inc./John Flournoy, photographer; p. 211 photosindia/Getty Images; p. 214 Creatas/JupiterImages; p. 216 © S. Rubin/The Image Works; p. 217 Mark Richards\PhotoEdit, Inc.; p. 221 Digital Vision/Getty Images; p. 226 Vincent Besnault/Getty Images; p. 228 Ryan McVay/Getty Images; p. 233 Getty Images; p.240 Philip Gould/Corbis; p. 245 Robert Koene/Getty Images

Part 3: p. 256 Rubberball/PictureQuest; p. 258 John Slater/Getty Images; p. 259 Don Fawcett/Science Source/Photo Researchers, Inc.; p. 260 Nick Koudis/Getty Images; p. 262 Petit Format/Photo Researchers, Inc.; p. 265 (top left) Lennart Nilsson, A Child Is Born; p. 265 (bottom left) Lennart Nilsson, Behold Man; p. 265 (top right) Lennart Nilsson, Behold Man; p. 265 (bottom right) Lennart Nilsson, A Child Is Born; p. 272 Studio/ Science Photo Library/Photo Researchers, Inc.; p. 278 Michael Newman/PhotoEdit; p. 279 Stockbyte/PunchStock; p. 284 Ruth Jenkinson/MIDIRS / Photo Researchers, Inc.; p. 286 David Austin/Woodfin Camp; p. 287 (left) David Austin/Woodfin Camp; p. 287 (right) David Austin/Woodfin Camp; p. 292 Royalty-Free/Corbis; p. 294 Bettmann/Corbis; p. 296 Spencer Grant/PhotoEdit ; p. 301 Joel Gordon; p. 308 SPL/Photo Researchers Inc.

Part 4: p. 328 The McGraw-Hill Companies, Inc./Andrew Resek, pho-tographer; p. 330 Jules Frazier / Getty Images; p. 338 Plush Studios/Getty Images; p. 357 Stockbyte/PunchStock; p. 358 © epa/Corbis; p. 360 The McGraw-Hill Companies, Inc./John Flournoy, photographer; p. 367 Royalty-Free/Corbis; p. 382 Laima Druskis/photographybynitya.com; p. 384 Kim Kulish; p. 385 Digital Vision/PunchStock; p. 389 PhotoAlto; p. 394 Joel Gordon; p. 397 Jaye Phillips/The Picture Cube/Index Stock; p. 397 (top) Photo courtesy of Dr. Daniel Greenwald; p. 397 (bot-tom) Photo courtesy of Dr. Daniel Greenwald; p. 399 Photo courtesy of Dr. Daniel Greenwald; p. 405 Jack Hollingsworth/Getty Images; p. 406 Joel Gordon; p. 415 Digital Vision; p. 416 Photo provided by The Kinsey Institute with permission granted by Akio Takamori. All rights reserved.; p. 417 Sipa Press/Art Resource; p. 418 (left) Scala/Art Resource ; p. 418 (right) Francis Li; p. 422 Courtesy Everett Collection; p. 426 Courtesy Everett Collection; p. 427 Billy E. Barnes/PhotoEdit

Part 5: p. 440 McGraw-Hill Companies, Inc./Gary He, photogra-pher; p. 442 Digital Vision/Getty Images; p. 444 JupiterImages; p. 447 Damian Dorarganes/AP Images; p. 455 Bill Aller/New York Times/Redux; p. 461 Bob Mahoney/The Image Works; p. 463 Picture Person Plus/The Image Works; p. 466 Courtesy Eymann Products; p. 478 Royalty-Free/Corbis; p. 487 Joe Miller/CDC; p. 488 (top left) Centers for Disease Control; p. 488 (bottom left) Centers for Disease Control; p. 488 (right) Centers for Disease Control; p. 489 Reproduction of "Chlamydia Is Not A Flower" poster has been granted with approval of Abbott Laboratories, Inc. All rights reserved.; p. 493 National Audio-Visual Center; p. 494 Dr. N. J. Flumara.; Dr. Gavin Hart/CDC; p. 495 National Audio-Visual Center; p. 496 (top) Dr. P. Marrazi/SPL/ Photo Researchers, Inc.; p. 496 (bottom) Dr. P. Marrazi/SPL/ Photo Researchers, Inc.; p. 497 National Audio-Visual Center; p. 503 Louis Dematteis/The Image Works; p. 505 Joel Gordon; p. 515 Digital Vision/PunchStock; p. 522 Stockbyte/PunchStock; p. 524 Hoby Finn/Getty Images; p. 530 McGraw-Hill Companies, Inc./Gary He, pho-tographer; p. 537 Michael Newman/PhotoEdit; p. 543 Ryan McVay/Getty Images

Index

National Health and Social Life
   Survey (NHSLS) *(continued)*
  on gay/lesbian/bisexual persons,
    380
  on group sex, 402
  HIV/AIDS, 51
  homosexual/bisexual percent-
    ages, 363*f*
  on incest, 470
  on intercourse, 349
  on male orgasm, 526
  on marital rape, 461
  on masturbation, 333, 344
  on oral sex, 340
  on orgasm, 516
  on rape of men by women, 462
  on sexual attitudes, 203,
    205–206
  on sexual disorders, 520
  on sexual fantasies, 401
  sexual orientation/behaviors,
    360–361, 379
  on sexual satisfaction, 345
  on STDs, 483
  vaginal intercourse and, 337,
    347
  on vibrators/dildos, 401
  on voyeurism, 408
  on X-rated movies, 400
National Institute of Mental Health,
  367
National Institutes of Health (NIH),
  277
National Longitudinal Study of
  Adolescent Health, 23, 457
National Longitudinal Survey of
  Youth, 324
National Opinion Research
  Center, at University of
  Chicago, 22
National Survey of Family
  Growth, 23
Native American cultures,
  intersexuality in, 104
Native Americans, 23
  menstrual cycle and, 53
natural childbirth, **285**
natural family planning/fertility
  awareness, **313**
nature *vs.* nurture, gender roles
  and, 105

NEA. *See* National Endowment for
  the Arts
necrophilia, **411,** 446
Negy, C., 206
Neisser, Albert, 486
Nelson, E. S., 105, 106, 227, 317
Nemeroff, C. J., 382
Ness, R. B., 39
Netherland, J., 158
Neumann, M. G., 246, 399
Neumark-Stainer, D., 152
New Republic, The, 20
New York City Board of Health,
  103
newborn, 286
  identification of, 287*f*
Newsweek, 13
Next Best Thing, The (film), 422
NHSLS. *See* National Health and
  Social Life Survey
Niccolai, L. M., 484, 508
Nicholas, C. L., 380
Nicolosi, A., 518
Nigeria, 21, 37
NIH. *See* National Institutes of
  Health
Nika, E., 446, 470
Nineteenth Amendment, 130
Nisita, C., 444
Nixon, Richard, 428
Nobre, P. J., 82, 84, 445, 517, 522,
  524, 531
Nojima, K., 365
nonspecific urethritis (NSU), **490,**
  490–491
Noonan, R. J., 73
Nordland, R., 428
Nordling, N., 408
Norko, M. A., 470
normal, **194**
normal asexuality, **522**
normalcy, 199
  definitions of, 198–199
  by expert opinion, 198
  moral, 199
  statistical, 198
normalization, **216**
Norman, C., 483
Norway
  extramarital sex in, 182
  pornography in, 428

Notter, K. M., 306
Nowell, A., 123
NSU. *See* nonspecific urethritis
nudity, 407
  in art, 416–418
  childhood sexuality and, 150
  dancing and, 435
Nunnink, S. E., 82
nymphomania, **392**

O

oblique model, of femininity/
  masculinity, 120
obscene telephone calls, 406, 446
obscenity, **416,** 432–433
OC, The (tv show), 426
O'Connor, E., 385
O'Donnell, L., 165
O'Donohue, W., 45, 447, 448
Office of the Surgeon General, 165
Office on Violence Against
  Women, 463
Ofner, S., 154
O'Hare, E. A., 448
Okami, P., 122, 148, 149, 150,
  175, 176, 390, 391, 393
Okonofua, F. E., 37
Oliver, B. E., 467
Olmstead, R., 148, 149
Olsen, F., 457
Olsson, S., 396, 399
Oman, R. F., 157
Ompad, D. C., 172
onanism, **337**
Oncale, R. N., 304
oocytes, **44**
oophorectomy, 45
Oosterhuis, H., 16
Oppermann, M., 159
opportunistic infection, **498**
oral contraceptives, 306–307
  combined, 306
  health risks of, 307
  noncontraceptive benefits of,
    307
  progestin-only, 306
oral sex, 172, 173, 196, 338,
  340–342
  in adolescents, 154–155